HANDBOOK OF
SOCIAL AND EMOTIONAL LEARNING

Handbook of Social and Emotional Learning

RESEARCH AND PRACTICE

Edited by

Joseph A. Durlak
Celene E. Domitrovich
Roger P. Weissberg
Thomas P. Gullotta

THE GUILFORD PRESS
New York London

A Division of Guilford Publications, Inc.
370 Seventh Avenue, Suite 1200, New York, NY 10001
www.guilford.com

Printed in the United States of America

This book is printed on acid-free paper.

Last digit is print number: 9 8 7 6 5 4 3 2 1

Library of Congress Cataloging-in-Publication Data

Handbook of social and emotional learning : research and practice / edited by Joseph A. Durlak, Celene E. Domitrovich, Roger P. Weissberg, Thomas P. Gullotta.
pages cm
Includes bibliographical references and index.
ISBN 978-1-4625-2015-2 (hardback)
1. Affective education—United States. 2. Social learning—United States.
I. Durlak, Joseph A.
LB1072.H37 2015
370.15′34—dc23

2014039363

About the Editors

Joseph A. Durlak, PhD, is Emeritus Professor of Psychology at Loyola University Chicago. He has been a member of the editorial boards of several professional publications, has written or coedited four books on prevention, and has a longstanding interest in the welfare of children and adolescents. Dr. Durlak's current work focuses on how to facilitate the implementation of evidence-based social and emotional learning and prevention programs in local communities and schools. He is a recipient of the Joseph E. Zins Award for Action Research in Social and Emotional Learning from the Collaborative for Academic, Social, and Emotional Learning (CASEL).

Celene E. Domitrovich, PhD, is Vice President of Research at CASEL and has academic affiliations with The University of Illinois at Chicago, The Pennsylvania State University, and Johns Hopkins University. Her research and publications focus on the development of social and emotional competence in children, the role of teachers in children's acquisition of these skills, and how these skills are related to success in school. Dr. Domitrovich is the developer of the Preschool PATHS Curriculum. She has served on the board of the Society for Prevention Research and is a recipient of the Joseph E. Zins Award for Action Research in Social and Emotional Learning from CASEL.

Roger P. Weissberg, PhD, is NoVo Foundation Endowed Chair in Social and Emotional Learning and Distinguished Professor of Psychology and Education at The University of Illinois at Chicago. He is also Chief Knowledge Officer of CASEL. Dr. Weissberg has authored numerous publications on preventive interventions with children. He has received awards including the Distinguished Contribution Award for Applications of Psychology to Education and Training from the American Psychological Association, the Distinguished Contribution to Theory and Research Award from the Society for Community Research and Action, and the Daring Dozen Award from the George Lucas Educational Foundation. He is an elected member of the National Academy of Education.

Thomas P. Gullotta, MA, MSW, is CEO of the Child & Family Agency of Southeastern Connecticut, Inc., and a member of the Departments of Psychology and Education at Eastern Connecticut State University. He is editor emeritus of the *Journal of Primary Prevention* and serves on the editorial boards of the *Journal of Early Adolescence*, *Journal of Adolescent Research*, and *Journal of Educational and Psychological Consultation*. Mr. Gullotta has published extensively on adolescents and primary prevention. He is a recipient of the Distinguished Contributions to Practice in Community Psychology Award from the Society for Community Research and Action, Division 27 of the American Psychological Association.

Contributors

J. Lawrence Aber, PhD, Department of Applied Psychology, Steinhardt School of Culture, Education, and Human Development, New York University, New York, New York

Anjali Alimchandani, MPP, Department of Applied Psychology, Steinhardt School of Culture, Education, and Human Development, New York University, New York, New York

George G. Bear, PhD, School of Education, University of Delaware, Newark, Delaware

Karen L. Bierman, PhD, Child Study Center, Department of Psychology, The Pennsylvania State University, University Park, Pennsylvania

Clancy Blair, PhD, Department of Applied Psychology, Steinhardt School of Culture, Education, and Human Development, New York University, New York, New York

Jessica C. Blank, PhD, Colonial School District, New Castle, Delaware

Marc A. Brackett, PhD, Yale Center for Emotional Intelligence, Yale University, New Haven, Connecticut

Jennifer Buffett, President and Co-Chair, NoVo Foundation, New York, New York

James P. Comer, MD, Child Study Center, Yale University School of Medicine, New Haven, Connecticut

Colleen S. Conley, PhD, Department of Psychology, Loyola University Chicago, Chicago, Illinois

Max Crowley, MS, Prevention Research Center, The Pennsylvania State University, University Park, Pennsylvania

Linda Darling-Hammond, EdD, Graduate School of Education, Stanford University, Stanford, California

Michael Davies, PhD, School of Education and Professional Studies, Griffith University, Mt. Gravatt, Queensland, Australia

Susanne A. Denham, PhD, Department of Psychology, George Mason University, Fairfax, Virginia

Celene E. Domitrovich, PhD, Collaborative for Academic, Social, and Emotional Learning, Chicago, Illinois; Prevention Research Center and Department of Human Development and Family Studies, College of Health and Human Development, The Pennsylvania State University, University Park, Pennsylvania

Joan Cole Duffell, Committee for Children, Seattle, Washington

Joseph A. Durlak, PhD, Department of Psychology, Loyola University Chicago, Chicago, Illinois

Linda A. Dusenbury, PhD, Collaborative for Academic, Social, and Emotional Learning, Chicago, Illinois

Nicole DuVal, MS, Youth-Nex, Curry School of Education, University of Virginia, Charlottesville, Virginia

Nicole A. Elbertson, Yale Center for Emotional Intelligence, Yale University, New Haven, Connecticut

Maurice J. Elias, PhD, Department of Psychology, Rutgers, The State University of New Jersey—Livingston Campus, Piscataway, New Jersey

Stephen N. Elliott, PhD, Sanford School of Social and Family Dynamics, Arizona State University, Tempe, Arizona

Abigail A. Fagan, PhD, Department of Sociology and Criminology and Law, University of Florida, Gainesville, Florida

Joseph Ferrito, PsyM, Graduate School of Applied and Professional Psychology, Rutgers, The State University of New Jersey, New Brunswick, New Jersey

Jennifer L. Frank, PhD, Department of Educational Psychology, Counseling, and Special Education, College of Education, The Pennsylvania State University, State College, Pennsylvania

Jennifer R. Frey, PhD, Department of Special Education and Disability Studies, Graduate School of Education and Human Development, George Washington University, Washington, DC

S. Andrew Garbacz, PhD, Department of Special Education and Clinical Sciences, University of Oregon, Eugene, Oregon

Mark Garibaldi, MA, American Institutes for Research, San Mateo, California

Daniel Goleman, PhD, Consortium for Research on Emotional Intelligence in Organizations, Rutgers, The State University of New Jersey, New Brunswick, New Jersey

Eric S. Gordon, MEd, Cleveland Metropolitan School District, Cleveland, Ohio

Paul Goren, PhD, Evanston/Skokie District 65, Evanston, Illinois

Mark T. Greenberg, PhD, Prevention Research Center, The Pennsylvania State University, University Park, Pennsylvania

Christina J. Groark, PhD, Office of Child Development, University of Pittsburgh, Pittsburgh, Pennsylvania

Nancy G. Guerra, EdD, Department of Psychological and Brain Sciences, University of Delaware, Newark, Delaware

Thomas P. Gullotta, MA, MSW, Child & Family Agency of Southeastern Connecticut, Inc.; Departments of Psychology and Education, Eastern Connecticut State University, Willimantic, Connecticut

Jennifer L. Hanson-Peterson, MA, Research and Policy Centre, Brotherhood of St. Laurence, Fitzroy, Victoria, Australia

Tucker B. Harding, EdD, Department of Mathematics, Science, and Technology in Education, Teachers College, Columbia University, New York, New York

Alexis Harris, PhD, Curry School of Education, University of Virginia, Charlottesville, Virginia

Bridget E. Hatfield, PhD, Program of Applied Developmental Psychology, Department of Psychology in Education, School of Education, University of Pittsburgh, Pittsburgh, Pennsylvania

J. David Hawkins, PhD, School of Social Work, University of Washington, Seattle, Washington

Michael L. Hecht, PhD, Department of Communication Arts and Sciences, The Pennsylvania State University, University Park, Pennsylvania

Allison A. Holzer, MAT, InspireCorps, WestHartford, Connecticut

Chris S. Hulleman, PhD, Center for the Advanced Study of Teaching and Learning, Curry School of Education, University of Virginia, Charlottesville, Virginia

Neil Humphrey, PhD, Manchester Institute of Education, University of Manchester, Manchester, United Kingdom

Shelley Hymel, PhD, Department of Educational and Counselling Psychology, and Special Education, University of British Columbia, Vancouver, British Columbia, Canada

Robert J. Jagers, PhD, School of Education, University of Michigan, Ann Arbor, Michigan

Patricia A. Jennings, PhD, Department of Curriculum, Instruction, and Special Education, Curry School of Education, University of Virginia, Charlottesville, Virginia

Damon Jones, PhD, Prevention Research Center, The Pennsylvania State University, University Park, Pennsylvania

Deirdre A. Katz, MEd, Prevention Research Center, The Pennsylvania State University, University Park, Pennsylvania

Kimberly Kendziora, PhD, American Institutes for Research, Washington, DC

Laura Cousino Klein, PhD, College of Health and Human Development, The Pennsylvania State University, University Park, Pennsylvania

Andrea Lamont, PhD, Department of Psychology, University of South Carolina, Columbia, South Carolina

Larry Leverett, EdD, Panasonic Foundation, Newark, New Jersey

Bonnie Mackintosh, MEd, Department of Human Development and Education, Harvard Graduate School of Education, Cambridge, Massachusetts

Claudia Madrazo, MA, La Vaca Independiente, Mexico City, Mexico

Sarah Mancoll, MS, Office for Policy and Communications, Society for Research in Child Development, Washington, DC

Sarah Mandell, BS, American Institute for Medical and Biological Engineering, Washington, DC

Amy Kathryn Mart, MEd, Department of Psychology, The University of Illinois at Chicago, and Office of Social and Emotional Learning, Chicago Public Schools, Chicago, Illinois

Robert J. Marzano, PhD, Marzano Research Laboratory, Centennial, Colorado

Clark McKown, PhD, Rush Neurobehavioral Center, Rush University Medical Center, Chicago, Illinois

Kathryn L. Modecki, PhD, School of Psychology, Murdoch University, Perth, Australia

Mojdeh Motamedi, MS, Child Study Center, Department of Psychology, The Pennsylvania State University, University Park, Pennsylvania

Jessica Zadrazil Newman, MA, Department of Psychology, The University of Illinois at Chicago, Chicago, Illinois

Emily Nichols, PhD, Department of Psychiatry, Boston's Children Hospital, Harvard University, Boston, Massachusetts

David Osher, PhD, American Institutes for Research, Washington, DC

Janet Patti, EdD, School of Education, Hunter College of The City University of New York, New York, New York

Olga Acosta Price, PhD, Center for Health and Health Care in School, George Washington University, Washington, DC

C. Cybele Raver, PhD, Department of Applied Psychology, Steinhardt School of Culture, Education, and Human Development, New York University, New York, New York

Sam Redding, EdD, Academic Development Institute, Lincoln, Illinois

Sara E. Rimm-Kaufman, PhD, Center for the Advanced Study of Teaching and Learning, Curry School of Education, University of Virginia, Charlottesville, Virginia

Susan E. Rivers, PhD, Yale Center for Emotional Intelligence, Yale University, New Haven, Connecticut

Sally Ruddy, PhD, American Institutes for Research, Washington, DC

Kimberly A. Schonert-Reichl, PhD, Department of Educational Psychology and Special Education, University of British Columbia, Vancouver, British Columbia, Canada

Peter Senge, PhD, MIT Sloan School of Management, Massachusetts Institute of Technology, Cambridge, Massachusetts

Valerie B. Shapiro, PhD, Department of Social Welfare, University of California, Berkeley, Berkeley, California

Susan M. Sheridan, PhD, Department of Educational Psychology, University of Nebraska–Lincoln, Lincoln, Nebraska

YoungJu Shin, PhD, Department of Communication Studies, Indiana University–Purdue University Indianapolis, Indianapolis, Indiana

Timothy P. Shriver, EdD, Chairman, Special Olympics, Washington, DC

Gary N. Siperstein, PhD, Center for Social Development and Education, John W. McCormack Graduate School of Policy and Global Studies, University of Massachusetts Boston, Boston, Massachusetts

Alexandra Skoog, MA, The New Teacher Project, Madison, Wisconsin

Cesalie Stepney, EdM, MS, Department of Psychology, Rutgers, The State University of New Jersey, New Brunswick, New Jersey

Robin S. Stern, PhD, Yale Center for Emotional Intelligence, Yale University, New Haven, Connecticut

Michelle S. Swanger-Gagné, PhD, Institute for the Family, Department of Psychiatry, University of Rochester Medical Center, Rochester, New York

Patrick H. Tolan, PhD, Youth-Nex, Curry School of Education, and Department of Psychiatry and Neurobehavioral Sciences, University of Virginia, Charlottesville, Virginia

Catalina Torrente, PhD, Yale Center for Emotional Intelligence, Yale University, New Haven, Connecticut

Herbert J. Walberg, PhD, Hoover Institution, Stanford University, Stanford, California; The University of Illinois at Chicago, Chicago, Illinois

Abraham Wandersman, PhD, Department of Psychology, University of South Carolina, Columbia, South Carolina

Shannon B. Wanless, PhD, Department of Psychology in Education, University of Pittsburgh, Pittsburgh, Pennsylvania

Roger P. Weissberg, PhD, Collaborative for Academic, Social, and Emotional Learning, and Department of Psychology, The University of Illinois at Chicago, Chicago, Illinois

Sara A. Whitcomb, PhD, Department of Student Development, University of Massachusetts Amherst, Amherst, Massachusetts

Andrew L. Wiley, PhD, School of Lifespan Development and Educational Sciences, Kent State University, Kent, Ohio

Ariel A. Williamson, MA, Department of Psychological and Brain Sciences, University of Delaware, Newark, Delaware

Amanda P. Williford, PhD, Center for the Advanced Study of Teaching and Learning, Curry School of Education, University of Virginia, Charlottesville, Virginia

Catherine Sanger Wolcott, MEd, Center for the Advanced Study of Teaching and Learning, Curry School of Education, University of Virginia, Charlottesville, Virginia

Annie Wright, PhD, Center on Research and Evaluation, Simmons School of Education and Human Development, Southern Methodist University, Dallas, Texas

Martha Zaslow, PhD, Office for Policy and Communications, Society for Research in Child Development, Washington, DC

FOREWORD

Social and Emotional Learning

Critical Skills for Building Healthy Schools

Linda Darling-Hammond

> [It has become possible] for a person 18 years of age to graduate from high school without ever having had to do a piece of work on which somebody else truly depended; without ever having cared for, or even held, a baby; without ever having looked after someone who was old, ill, or lonely; or without ever having comforted or assisted another human being who really needed help. . . . No society can long sustain itself unless its members have learned the sensitivities, motivations, and skills involved in assisting and caring for other human beings. (Bronfenbrenner, cited in Lantieri, 1999, p. 83)

I have no doubt that the survival of the human race depends at least as much on the cultivation of social and emotional intelligence as it does on the development of technical knowledge and skills. Most educators believe that the development of the whole child is an essential responsibility of schools, and this belief is what has motivated them to enter the profession.

However, U.S. education policies over more than a decade have focused primarily on labeling schools and students on the basis of standardized test results, creating a singular focus that has increasingly ignored the affective and social needs of children, as well as their engagement in active, empowering forms of learning. Time and attention to character development and emotional well-being have flagged in the era of punitive accountability.

The need to refocus American schools on the holistic development of children is profound. One national survey found, for example, that among 148,000 middle and high school students, well under half felt they had developed social competencies such as empathy, decision making, and conflict resolution skills. Only 29% indicated that their school provided a caring, encouraging environment. Other research has found that as many as 60% of students become chronically disengaged from school, and 30% of high school students engage in multiple high-risk behaviors such as substance abuse, sexual activity, violence, and attempted suicide (Durlak, Weissberg, Dymnicki, Taylor, & Schellinger, 2011).

Attending to students' psychological needs is as much a part of a quality education as ensuring that they have adequate resources, good instructional materials, and well-trained teachers. All young people—and particularly those who live in stressful contexts—need to be able to recognize and address their feelings, so that fear, hurt, and anxiety do not overwhelm them; to recognize and respect the feelings of others; to learn problem-solving and conflict resolution skills; to have the opportunity to contribute directly to the welfare of others; to understand that problems and challenges are part of the process of learning and living, so that they can persist in the face of difficulties; and to become "growth oriented" in their approach to life. Children and youth need to develop skills that enable self-regulation and dispositions that support self-efficacy and social contribution. To do this, they need to feel cared about and cared for, and to experience culturally responsive, engaging, and empowering learning opportunities in contexts that provide supportive relationships and community.

My colleagues and I have found in our research that when urban high school students experience these kinds of social and emotional learning opportunities in student-centered schools, they feel more positively about school and learning, achieve at higher levels, have greater aspirations, are more likely to graduate, and are more likely to succeed in college (Darling-Hammond, Ramos-Beban, Altimirano, & Hyler, in press; Friedlaender et al., 2014; Hamedani, Darling-Hammond, & Zheng, in press). As this *Handbook of Social and Emotional Learning* illustrates, these kinds of positive academic and life outcomes are found for children of all age groups in a wide range of settings by a growing body of research.

The Collaborative for Academic, Social, and Emotional Learning (CASEL) describes the skills associated with social–emotional learning as both "fundamental for life effectiveness" and "a framework for school improvement." The integration of individual development with organizational development offers a new pathway to progress. A key insight is that building developmentally supportive school organizations is perhaps the most effective way to develop psychologically healthy and productive young people and adults. This requires a comprehensive effort to design all aspects of school organizations—and enable professionals to work together—in support of strong relationships, active engagement in all aspects of learning, healthy identity development, and restorative approaches to discipline and community life. As Durlak and colleagues (2011) note, schools' efforts to support social and emotional learning (SEL) should involve both explicit instruction in the skills students need to become personally and socially aware and responsible and the construction of a safe, caring environment that acts as a respectful, prosocial community.

Fortunately, because of CASEL's efforts and those of many other educators and researchers, we have learned a great deal about what it takes to help students build and maintain social and emotional intelligence, and what it takes for schools to support this work. This *Handbook* is a testament to the extraordinary work that has been undertaken over the last two decades across a wide range of disciplines and in a variety of different settings to build a base of research, practice, and policy that supports more widespread and effective opportunities for SEL. The *Handbook* also outlines in great detail the work that lies ahead, serving as an invaluable resource to those who are committed to advancing this field and the human potential it enables.

As the contributors to this book show, there is a large body of scientific evidence demonstrating the positive outcomes of SEL and suggesting how these outcomes can be achieved. This scientific foundation challenges us to undertake a decidedly humanistic endeavor. In particular, this endeavor includes the humanization of school institutions that, as Max Weber described, were deliberately depersonalized in the early 20th century in order to function as more perfect bureaucracies—guided by rules and regulations that could avoid the need for individual considerations or feelings.

As Paulo Freire explained, humanization is "the process of becoming more fully human as social, historical, thinking, communicating, transformative, creative persons who participate in and with the world." Educators, he argued, must "listen to their students and build on their knowledge and experiences in order to engage in . . . personalized educational approaches that further the goals of humanization and transformation" (Freire, cited in Salazar, 2013, p. 126). Indeed, this is what we see in schools that successfully undertake the journey of becoming socially and emotionally educative.

We have reason to hope and trust that, as this work succeeds, transformations in human understandings and relationships will result. More intelligent and peaceful interactions leading to more creative solutions to the human condition on this planet are the most important outcomes of our collective experience. We can thank Joseph A. Durlak, Celene E. Domitrovich, Roger P. Weissberg, Thomas P. Gullotta, and all the contributors to this volume for advancing this critical mission.

References

Darling-Hammond, L., Ramos-Beban, N., Altimirano, R. P., & Hyler, M. (in press). *Be the change: The story of East Palo Alto Academy*. New York: Teachers College Press.

Durlak, J. A., Weissberg, R. P., Dymnicki, A. B., Taylor, R. D., & Schellinger, K. B. (2011). The impact of enhancing students' social and emotional learning: A meta-analysis of school-based universal interventions. *Child Development, 82*(1), 405–432.

Friedlaender, D., Burns, D., Lewis-Charp, H., Cook-Harvey, C. M., Zheng, X., & Darling-Hammond, L. (2014). *Student-centered schools: Closing the opportunity gap*. Stanford, CA: Stanford Center for Opportunity Policy in Education.

Hamedani, M. G., Darling-Hammond, L., & Zheng, X. (in press). *Learning from successful practice: Social emotional learning in three diverse urban high schools*. Stanford, CA: Stanford Center for Opportunity Policy in Education.

Lantieri, L. (1999). Hooked on altruism: Developing social responsibility in at-risk youth. *Journal of Emotional and Behavioral Problems, 8*(2), 83–87.

Salazar, M. (2013). A humanizing pedagogy: Reinventing the principles and practice of education as a journey toward liberation. *Review of Research in Education, 37*(1), 121–148.

INTRODUCTION

The Uncommon Core

Timothy P. Shriver and Jennifer Buffett

We wonder when all the talk about how to improve our schools will focus on the "real core" of education. We have had so many reform efforts, and we have focused on everything else but the real core—on the length of the day, the uniforms kids wear, the tests we take, the way we pay, whom to blame, whom to charter, how to discipline, what books to buy, what computers to use, what buildings to build. These all have a place in making it possible for children to learn. But none of these are the real core.

The real core of education is the relationship between the teacher and the student, and the extent to which that relationship nurtures the longing of the child to matter in the world, and the longing of the teacher to nurture and fulfill that desire. In so many ways, the whole science of child development and the best philosophy of education agree completely on the fundamental truth that learning is a relationship and that the success of education depends almost completely on the strength of the social and emotional dimensions of that relationship. The real core is just that: the social and emotional dimensions of the learning relationship.

Although we have been working on school reform for almost a half-century, if we are honest, we have not yet focused on the core. The social and emotional factors in learning are the core, but attention to them remains painfully uncommon in the debates about school reform.

We are happy to say that the gap between where we need to focus and where we currently are focusing is beginning to close, and this *Handbook* represents a significant step forward in trying to close it more quickly. Within these pages, many of the most prominent leaders in both the research and practice of social and emotional learning (SEL) present the most current findings about the best practices and their enormous promise. If there is one overriding conclusion to draw from all the contributions in this volume, then it is this: A dramatic improvement in both the academic and social–emotional outcomes for kids and teachers alike is within reach. The time is now for making the changes necessary to attain that longed-for outcome.

To the extent that we strengthen SEL, we increase the likelihood that students will learn to the best of their ability. After decades of practice, we know that social and emotional skills and values can indeed be taught. We know that when taught and modeled well by adults in schools, bonding increases, motivation to learn increases, problem behaviors decrease, and test scores go up. Careful attention to issues such as stress management, relationship skills, nonviolent problem solving, and learner-centered goal setting are critical. These issues can help students focus on "what" we want them to learn by helping teachers focus on "how" to connect, motivate, and inspire.

To the extent that we ignore SEL, we increase the likelihood that students will further disengage from learning, and that teachers will become increasingly frustrated by the ways in which the system makes it difficult for them to teach. In recent years, we have learned that large numbers of children do not believe that the academic content they are being asked to learn has any relevance to their lives. Similarly large numbers report not feeling safe in school and, of greatest concern, not feeling like anyone cares about them. We can and must face the reality that many of our children are resorting to alcohol and drugs, violence, and other risk-taking behavior because, from their point of view, these destructive choices make sense in the context of their increasing disengagement from the options that education offers.

More than five decades ago, a young minister saw his country at a similar juncture, one where problems that were once thought to be intractable were, on the contrary, close to being solvable. In the midst of great tension and violence, Dr. Martin Luther King, Jr., spoke to the nation of not only "valleys of despair" but also of the "fierce urgency of now." Despite conditions in the country that many thought hopeless, he offered an alternative message: Now is the time to act decisively to bend the arc of history toward justice.

In our own time, the ideals of education are falling prey not only to the grinding poverty and enormous economic pressures facing so many of our children and families but also to the perception that nothing works—that dropout and depression are inevitable, and that we should resign ourselves to expecting that many youth will be lonely, confused, and rudderless. Unlike Dr. King, we are too quickly resigned to solutions that we know cannot make a big difference because we are not sure a big difference can be made.

But as we know, Dr. King's reference to the "fierce urgency of now" was followed by his dream, and the dream changed everything. His was a dream of a more unified future, a dream that animated the nation and even the world to reach for what was bold but attainable—a future where all children and all men and women would be treated justly and be able to access fair opportunities to learn, earn, contribute, and lead fulfilling lives.

We believe that today is a time in need of a similar dream for education: a dream where all children love school; where all children meet teachers who understand them, believe in them, challenge them, and unlock them; and where the heart of learning is at the center of what is learned. We believe that today's dream, drawing on the best science and practice, must be a dream in which all children are told that they have within them a profound goodness and a noble purpose, that the purpose of education is to invite students to become engaged with great ideas and experiences that can in turn help them discover their own great ideas and purpose. We believe that education is first, and most importantly, about discovering one's place in the world, then seizing it. And we believe that we are on the verge of being able to teach in a way that allows all children to do just that.

This *Handbook* marks a turning point in the decades-old discussion about school reform. It invites all of us to allow the social and emotional longings of children to be recognized as the crucial force that they are. It invites all of us to focus on the ways in which those forces can be marshaled to create powerful relationships between students and teachers. And it invites all of us to focus on creating schools that use the best available science and practice to build those relationships and therefore create the most positive and highly motivated generation of citizens, workers, and family members we have ever seen.

Then and only then will we have addressed the core curriculum. Then and only then will this core go from being "uncommon" to being the common pathway for fulfilling our nation's dream of a more purpose-filled and meaningful education.

Acknowledgments

Almost 20 years ago, the Collaborative for Academic, Social, and Emotional Learning (CASEL) introduced the field of social and emotional learning (SEL) in *Promoting Social and Emotional Learning: Guidelines for Educators* (Elias et al., 1997). At that time, we wrote that we could "easily have an acknowledgment section reminiscent of the credits for a Cecil B. DeMille movie" (p. v). This *Handbook of Social and Emotional Learning: Research and Practice* could be considered, to use the movie phrase, a successful sequel! Actually, we have many more people to thank this time, including thousands of researchers, practitioners, policymakers, funders, child advocates, families, and students worldwide who have advanced SEL science, practice, and policies. Rather than write a very, very long acknowledgments section, we limit our focus to those individuals and organizations who literally made this book possible.

First, we want to thank all the contributors to the *Handbook*. There are close to 100 scholars who wrote excellent chapters, were responsive to feedback along the way, and met deadlines. We also want to thank Craig Thomas and his collaborators at The Guilford Press for their professionalism and support from the conceptualization of this volume through its publication.

We express our deep appreciation and a special "thank you" to Jessica Ramos, our editorial coordinator from the Child & Family Agency of Southeastern Connecticut, Inc. Jessica managed the process of reviewing multiple drafts from many authors masterfully, keeping our editorial team organized and focused on making progress. Her role in this *Handbook* was truly essential. We are also very thankful to Cynthia Coleman and Rawan Dissi from CASEL and The University of Illinois at Chicago, who effectively teamed with Jessica and supported the editors in carrying out this project.

Several extraordinary funders and thought-partners have been long-term supporters of CASEL, this *Handbook*, and the field of SEL in general, including Jennifer and Peter Buffett from the NoVo Foundation; Jennifer Hoos Rothberg, Itai Dinour, and Megan Schackleton from the Einhorn Family Charitable Trust; and Dinabandhu and Ila Sarley and Scott Kriens from the 1440 Foundation. We also appreciate the wisdom, guidance, and collaboration of the CASEL Board of Directors, several of whom contributed to the *Handbook*, including J. Lawrence Aber, Linda Darling-Hammond, Paul T. Goren, Mark T. Greenberg, and Timothy P. Shriver.

The *Handbook* complements a book series edited by Thomas P. Gullotta, Herbert

J. Walberg, and Roger P. Weissberg on *Issues in Children's and Families' Lives*. This series, which focuses attention on the pressing social problems facing children and their families today, is sponsored by Child & Family Agency of Southeastern Connecticut, one of the nation's leading family service agencies, and The University of Illinois at Chicago, a major research university that marshals scholarly resources to enhance quality of life in cities worldwide. For the *Handbook*, we must give additional credit and recognition to CASEL, the world's leading organization to foster evidence-based practice and policies to enhance the social, emotional, and academic competence of preschool to high school students.

We dedicate the *Handbook of Social and Emotional Learning* to two leaders in the SEL field whom we lost too early: Joseph E. Zins and Mary Utne O'Brien. To honor Joe's memory in 2007, CASEL established the Joseph E. Zins Award for Action Research in Social and Emotional Learning, which we present to innovative and impactful SEL scholars and scientists—several of whom contributed to this volume. To honor Mary's memory in 2011, CASEL established the Mary Utne O'Brien Award for Excellence in Expanding the Evidence-Based Practice of Social and Emotional Learning, which we present to courageous educators or policymakers who foster quality SEL programming for children and adolescents. We know that Joe and Mary would be as thrilled with the publication of a handbook that highlights the best SEL research and practice as we are.

Reference

Elias, M. J., Zins, J. E., Weissberg, R. P., Frey, K. S., Greenberg, M. T., Haynes, N. M., et al. (1997). *Promoting social and emotional learning: Guidelines for educators*. Alexandria, VA: Association for Supervision and Curriculum Development.

The editors wish to give special acknowledgment to the Child & Family Agency of Southeastern Connecticut, Inc., CASEL, and The University of Illinois at Chicago for their support.

Contents

PART III. Assessment

PART IV. Toward Widespread Practice and Policy

PART I

Foundations

CHAPTER 1

Social and Emotional Learning

Past, Present, and Future

Roger P. Weissberg, Joseph A. Durlak, Celene E. Domitrovich, and Thomas P. Gullotta

> SEL is currently the zeitgeist in education. It has captured the imagination of academics, policy-makers, and practitioners alike in recent years. To many, SEL is the "missing piece" in the quest to provide effective education for all children and young people.
>
> —NEIL HUMPHREY (2013, p. 1)

The time is right for the *Handbook of Social and Emotional Learning: Research and Practice*. The past 20 years have witnessed an explosion of interest in social and emotional learning (SEL). Research reviews have documented the value of SEL programs. Schools, families, and communities are partnering to promote the positive development and academic success of children and youth across the globe. Federal, state, and local policies have been established to foster the social, emotional, and academic growth of young people.

In terms of research, there are now more than 500 evaluations of the various types of SEL programs. The largest part of this literature involves universal school-based programs that span a range of educational levels, from preschool through higher education (Conley, Chapter 13, this volume; Durlak, Weissberg, Dymnicki, Taylor, & Schellinger, 2011; Sklad, Diekstra, De Ritter, & Ben, 2012). Although most evaluations have focused on school-based efforts, many programs extend beyond the school context, through parent training, in after-school programs, and in community-based organizations (Albright & Weissberg, 2010; Durlak, Weissberg, & Pachan, 2010). Although many SEL programs are universal in nature, in that they are intended for all youth, there have also been successful SEL efforts to target students who are experiencing different types of adjustment problems (Payton et al., 2008; in this volume, see Tolan, Nichols, & DuVal, Chapter 18; Wiley & Siperstein, Chapter 14).

In terms of practice, there are now SEL programs operating in thousands of schools across the United States and other countries around the world (Humphrey, 2013; Torrente, Alimchandani, & Aber, Chapter 37, this volume; Weare & Nind, 2011). Many teachers respond favorably to the possibility of providing SEL programming to their students, although they need administrative and policy support to do so effectively (Bridgeland, Bruce, & Hariharan, 2013; Merrell & Gueldner, 2010). Their efforts are enhanced when district and school leaders champion a vision, policies, professional learning communities, and supports for coordinated classroom, schoolwide, family, and community programming (Catalano,

Berglund, Ryan, Lonczak, & Hawkins, 2004; Elias, O'Brien, & Weissberg, 2006; Mart, Weissberg, & Kendziora, Chapter 32, this volume; Weissberg & Kumpfer, 2003).

In terms of policy, in 2004, Illinois became the first state to develop preschool to high school SEL learning standards that provide a framework and guidance for what students should know and be able to do in the domain of social–emotional competence. Currently, all 50 states have preschool social and emotional development standards, and many states and some countries (e.g., Singapore) have integrated SEL into their student academic learning standards (Dusenbury et al., Chapter 35, this volume). National policies can also provide funding and guidelines to implement evidence-based SEL programming through (1) legislative initiatives, such as the Academic, Social, and Emotional Learning Act (*www.govtrack.us/congress/bills/114/hr850*), and efforts to reauthorize the Elementary and Secondary Education Act; (2) Executive Branch initiatives aimed at enhancing SEL practice in educational and other key settings for children; and (3) science policy that addresses funding for SEL research and dissemination of findings (see, in this volume, Price, Chapter 8; Zaslow, Mackintosh, Mancoll, & Mandell, Chapter 36).

In summary, the achievements of the field have exceeded the expectations of those who introduced and defined SEL 20 years ago (Elias et al., 1997). However, there are many ways that SEL research, practice, and policy can be strengthened in the future.

Goals of the *Handbook*

Given these developments, the time is right for a comprehensive overview of the current SEL field and recommendations for the future. That is what the *Handbook* offers. More specifically, this *Handbook* has four major goals: (1) to offer critical, integrative, and up-to-date coverage of the state of SEL research, practice, and policy that can be used to develop and extend SEL efforts in school, community, and family settings; (2) to provide content relevant to those who wish to learn more about the research and practice literature regarding SEL, so that they may become more evidence-based in their approach; (3) to discuss critical unresolved issues affecting SEL related to theory and research, assessment, implementation, professional development, funding, and policy; and, finally, (4) to provide recommendations and guidelines to shape the future agenda for SEL research, practice, and policy.

Contents of This Chapter

In this chapter, we provide the reader with a rationale, definition, and conceptual framework for SEL. We highlight the need to coordinate SEL with kindred approaches that promote positive school climates and cultures, and enhance students' intrapersonal, interpersonal, and cognitive competence (e.g., Darling-Hammond, Friedlaender, & Snyder, 2014; National Research Council, 2012). Then we summarize some of the major research findings that clarify the evidence base for SEL programs. Numerous findings from implementation science have confirmed that a critical factor affecting outcomes of interventions is the quality of program implementation that is obtained. Some of the major issues related to quality implementation of SEL are also discussed in this section. As a portent of the remainder of this volume, we next discuss some critical research, practice, and policy issues that need to be resolved in order to drive the field of SEL forward in the most efficient and effective manner. We end the chapter with an overview of the contents of this volume.

SEL: Rationale, Definitions, and Frameworks

The Need for SEL

Families, educators, and community members seek to raise and educate children who are knowledgeable, responsible, caring, and socially competent—on their way to becoming positive family members and neighbors, contributing citizens, and productive workers. Although different terms are used, most agree about the core purposes of education. We want to ensure that all students attain mastery in all academic subjects and become culturally literate, intellectually reflective, and lifelong learners. We also want to teach young people to interact in socially skilled and respectful ways with their families, peers, and school staff and community members; to practice safe and healthy behaviors; and to develop work habits and dispositions for college, career, and life success (Dymnicki, Sambolt, & Kidron, 2013; Elias et al., 1997; Greenberg et al., 2003; Schaps & Weissberg, 2015).

There is broad agreement that today's schools must offer more than academic instruction to prepare students for life and work (National Research Council, 2012). The life conditions of children have changed dramatically during the last century (Weissberg & Greenberg, 1998; Weissberg, Walberg, O'Brien, & Kuster, 2003). Families face increased economic and social pressures. Children are exposed to an increasingly complex world through media and have unmediated access to information and social contacts through various technologies. In many communities, there is less support for and involvement in institutions that foster children's social–emotional development and character.

Today's educators face the major challenge of educating an increasingly multicultural and multilingual group of students from racially, ethnically, and economically diverse backgrounds. Teachers, student-support staff, and community agencies serve students with different abilities and motivation for engaging in learning, behaving positively, and performing academically. It has been estimated that 40 to 60% of U.S. high school students—across urban, suburban, and rural schools—are chronically disengaged (Klem & Connell, 2004). According to the 2013 Youth Risk Behavior Survey, large percentages of high school students engage in risky behaviors that jeopardize their futures (e.g., substance use, violence and bullying, unprotected sexual intercourse with multiple partners, and mental health difficulties). Furthermore, many students have social–emotional competence deficits that lower their academic performance and disrupt the educational experiences of their peers (Benson, 2006).

In response to these circumstances, schools have been inundated with well-intentioned prevention and youth development initiatives that address a variety of issues, including bullying, character, drugs, delinquency, family life, health education, sex education, truancy, and violence, to name a few (Elias et al., Chapter 3, this volume). Unfortunately, these efforts are typically introduced as short-term, piecemeal pilot programs that are not well integrated into the academic mission of schools. Furthermore, without strong leadership from district and school leaders, there is rarely effective staff development and support for quality implementation. When programs are insufficiently coordinated, monitored, evaluated, and improved over time, they are less beneficial to students and not likely to be sustained.

In 1994, a group of educators, researchers, and child advocates met at the Fetzer Institute to discuss effective, coordinated strategies to enhance students' social–emotional competence, academic performance, health, and citizenship, and to prevent and reduce health, mental health, and behavior problems. The Fetzer Group introduced the term "social and emotional learning" as a conceptual framework to promote the social, emotional, and academic competence of young people and to coordinate school–family–community programming to address those educational goals (Elias et al., 1997). Meeting attendees also launched the Collaborative for Academic, Social, and Emotional Learning (CASEL) as an organization with the mission to help establish evidence-based SEL as an essential part of preschool through high school education (see *www.casel.org*). For 21 years, CASEL has served as strategist, collaborator, convener, and supporter for individuals and organizations that prioritize promoting children's social–emotional development and academic performance. CASEL's mission is to help establish evidence-based SEL as an essential part of preschool through high school education (Weissberg & Cascarino, 2013). Its organizational goals are to advance the science of SEL, expand effective SEL practice, and improve federal and state policies that support broader implementation of evidence-based programming.

What Is SEL?

CASEL aspires to establish a unifying preschool through high school framework based on a coordinated set of evidence-based practices for enhancing the social–emotional–cognitive development and academic performance of all students (CASEL, in press; Meyers et al., in press; Zins, Weissberg, Wang, & Walberg, 2004). SEL programming involves implementing practices and policies that help children and adults acquire and apply the knowledge, skills, and attitudes that can enhance personal development, establish satisfying interpersonal relationships, and lead to effective and ethical work and productivity. These include the competencies to understand and manage emotions, set and achieve positive goals, feel and show caring and concern for others, establish and maintain positive relationships, and make responsible decisions (CASEL, 2012).

SEL involves fostering social and emotional competencies through explicit instruction and through student-centered learning approaches that help students engage in the learning process and develop analytical, communication, and collaborative skills (CASEL, 2012; Friedlaender et al., 2014). Through explicit instruction, social and emotional skills may be taught, modeled, practiced, and applied to diverse situations, so that young people and adults use them as part of their daily repertoires of behaviors. SEL programming also enhances students' social and emotional competence by establishing positive classroom/school cultures, climates, and conditions for learning that are safe, caring, cooperative, well managed, and participatory (Zins et al., 2004). Integrated systemic, schoolwide SEL programming takes place at the classroom and school levels, and through partnerships with families and community members (CASEL, in press; Meyers et al., in press). SEL includes universal programming for the entire student body and aligned early intervention and treatment supports for students at risk for or already experiencing social, emotional, and behavioral difficulties (Adelman & Taylor, 2006; in this volume, see Bear, Whitcomb, Elias, & Blank, Chapter 30, and Wiley & Siperstein, Chapter 14).

A Framework for Advancing Systemic SEL in Education Setting

A variety of frameworks for SEL have emerged to describe parameters of systemic SEL programming (Jennings & Greenberg, 2009; Jones & Bouffard, 2012; Meyers et al., in press; Zins et al., 2004). We present an updated framework in Figure 1.1 that highlights (1) five interrelated domains of cognitive, affective, and behavioral competencies that provide a foundation to navigate school and life successfully; (2) short- and long-term attitudinal and behavioral outcomes resulting from evidence-based SEL programming; (3) coordinated classroom, school, family, and community strategies that enhance children's social–emotional development and academic performance; and (4) district, state, and federal policies and supports that foster quality SEL implementation and better student outcomes.

CASEL's Five Competence Domains

SEL programming enhances students' capacity to integrate cognition, affect, and behavior to deal effectively daily tasks and challenges (Consortium on the School-Based Promotion of Social Competence, 1994). Like many kindred approaches, the CASEL domains include knowledge, skills, and attitudes that comprise intrapersonal, interpersonal, and cognitive competence (National Research Council, 2012). These include self-awareness, self-management, social awareness, relationship skills, and responsible decision making:

1. Competence in the *self-awareness* domain involves understanding one's emotions, personal goals, and values. This includes accurately assessing one's strengths and limitations, having positive mindsets, and possessing a well-grounded sense of self-efficacy and optimism. High levels of self-awareness require the ability to recognize how thoughts, feelings, and actions are interconnected.
2. Competence in the *self-management* domain requires skills and attitudes that facilitate the ability to regulate emotions and behaviors. This includes the ability to delay gratification, manage stress, control impulses, and persevere through challenges in order to achieve personal and educational goals.
3. Competence in the *social awareness* domain involves the ability to take the perspective of those with different backgrounds or cultures and to empathize and feel compassion. It also involves

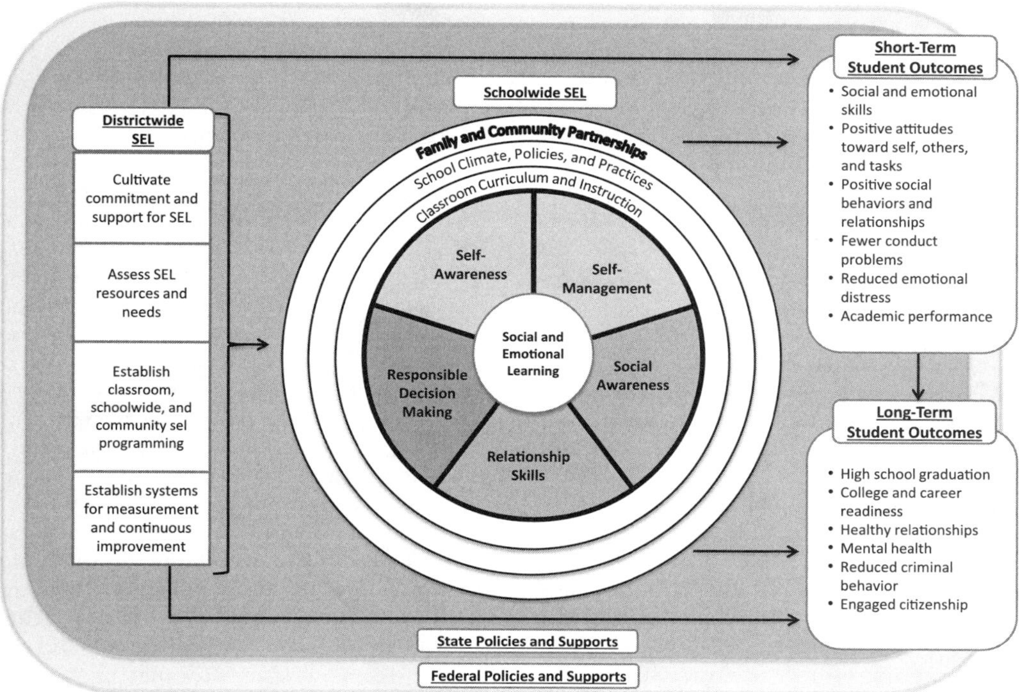

FIGURE 1.1. A conceptual model of SEL in educational settings.

understanding social norms for behavior and recognizing family, school, and community resources and supports.

4. *Relationship skills* provide children with the tools they need to establish and maintain healthy and rewarding relationships, and to act in accordance with social norms. Competence in this domain involves communicating clearly, listening actively, cooperating, resisting inappropriate social pressure, negotiating conflict constructively, and seeking help when it is needed.
5. Finally, *responsible decision making* is a competency domain that requires the knowledge, skills, and attitudes needed to make constructive choices about personal behavior and social interactions across diverse settings. Competence in this domain requires the ability to consider ethical standards, safety concerns, accurate behavioral norms for risky behaviors, to make realistic evaluation of consequences of various actions, and to take the health and well-being of self and others into consideration.

CASEL's inclusion of the word "learning" in the term "social and emotional learning" was purposeful and designed to reflect the fact that the acquisition of the skills and attitudes within the five competency domains is a process and schools are one of the primary places where this learning process takes place. Effective SEL approaches to promote social–emotional competencies often incorporate four elements represented by the acronym SAFE: (1) *Sequenced*: connected and coordinated set of activities to foster skills development; (2) *Active*: active forms of learning to help students master new skills; (3) *Focused*: a component that emphasizes developing personal and social skills; and (4) *Explicit*: targeting specific social and emotional skills (Durlak et al., 2010, 2011).

Short- and Long-Term Student Attitudinal and Behavioral Outcomes

Students are more successful in school and daily life when they (1) know themselves and can manage themselves, (2) take the perspectives of others and relate effectively with them, and (3) make sound choices about personal and social decisions. These social and emotional skills are one of several short-term student outcomes that SEL programs promote (depicted on the right side of Figure 1.1). Other benefits include (1) more positive attitudes toward oneself, others, and tasks including enhanced self-efficacy, confidence, persistence, empathy, connection and commitment to school, and sense of purpose; (2) more positive social behaviors and relationships with peers and adults; (3) reduced conduct problems and risk-taking behavior; (4) decreased emotional distress; and (5) improved test scores, grades, and attendance (Durlak et al., 2011; Farrington et al., 2012; Sklad et al., 2012). In the long run, greater social and emotional competence can increase the likelihood of high school graduation, readiness for postsecondary education, career success, positive family and work relationships, better mental health, reduced criminal behavior, and engaged citizenship (e.g., Hawkins, Kosterman, Catalano, Hill, & Abbott, 2008).

Systemic Schoolwide SEL Programming

Figure 1.1 highlights that students' social, emotional, and academic competencies are enhanced through coordinated classroom, school, family, and community strategies.

At the *classroom level*, SEL combines developmentally and culturally appropriate classroom instruction with ongoing formal and infused opportunities to build and reinforce students' social–emotional competence and positive behavior (in this volume, see Bierman & Motamedi, Chapter 9; Hecht & Shin, Chapter 4; Jagers et al., Chapter 11; Rimm-Kaufman & Hulleman, Chapter 10; Williamson, Modecki, & Guerra, Chapter 12). Promoting social and emotional development for all students in classrooms involves teaching and modeling social and emotional skills, providing opportunities for students to practice and hone those skills, and giving them an opportunity to apply these skills in various situations.

One of the most prevalent SEL approaches involves training teachers to deliver explicit lessons that teach social and emotional skills, then finding opportunities for students to reinforce their use throughout the day. Another curricular approach embeds SEL instruction into content areas such as English language arts, social studies, or math (Jones & Bouffard, 2012; Merrell & Gueldner, 2010; Yoder, 2013; Zins et al., 2004).

Teachers can also naturally foster skills in students through their interpersonal and student-centered instructional interactions throughout the school day. Adult–student interactions support SEL when they result in positive student–teacher relationships, enable teachers to model social–emotional competencies for students, and promote student engagement (Williford & Sanger Wolcott, Chapter 15, this volume). Teacher practices that provide students with emotional support and create opportunities for students' voice, autonomy, and mastery experiences promote student engagement in the educational process. These pedagogical approaches emphasize changing adult practices and the ways in which students interact with one another and their environment in an effort to promote student skills development.

At the *school level*, SEL strategies typically come in the form of policies, practices, or structures related to climate and student support services (Meyers et al., in press). Safe and positive school climates and cultures positively affect academic, behavioral, and mental health outcomes for students (Thapa, Cohen, Guffey, & Higgins-D'Alessandro, 2013). There are various schoolwide activities and policies that promote positive school environments, such as establishing a team to address the building climate and developing clear norms, values, and expectations for students and staff members. Fair and equitable discipline policies and bullying prevention practices that provide opportunities for students to resolve conflicts and repair damaged relationships while fostering relationship skills and responsible decision making are more likely to result in enduring skills and attitude change than purely behavioral methods that rely on reward or punishment to influence student behavior (Bear et al., Chapter 30, this volume). School leaders can organize activities that build positive relationships and a sense of community among students through structures such as regularly scheduled morning meetings or advisories that provide students with opportunities to connect with each other.

Educators' social–emotional competence and pedagogical skills influence classroom and school climate and culture, as well as the impact of SAFE SEL programming on student behavior. High-quality educator preparation and inservice professional learning related to SEL should include elements such as the theoretical knowledge and pedagogical strategies essential to teaching SEL, the development of teachers' and administrators' personal and social competencies, and ongoing supportive feedback from colleagues and administrators (in this volume, see Jennings & Frank, Chapter 28; Patti, Senge, Madrazo, & Stern, Chapter 29; Schonert-Reichl, Hanson-Peterson, & Hymel, Chapter 27; Williford & Sanger Wolcott, Chapter 15).

An important component of schoolwide SEL involves integration into multi-tiered systems of support. The services provided to students by professionals such as counselors, social workers, and psychologists should align with universal efforts in the classroom and building. Often through small-group work, student support professionals reinforce and supplement classroom-based instruction for students who need early intervention or more intensive treatment. When these individuals are familiar with the social and emotional content and instructional practices teachers are using in classrooms, they can incorporate them with their own work with students.

Family and community partnerships can strengthen the impact of school approaches extending learning into the home and neighborhood. Community members and organizations can support classroom and school efforts, especially by providing students with additional opportunities to refine and apply various SEL skills (Catalano et al., 2004). School–family–community relationships characterized by equality, shared goals, and meaningful roles for families and community partners enhance student SEL (in this volume, see Fagan, Hawkins, & Shapiro, Chapter 31; Garbacz, Swanger-Gagné, & Sheridan, Chapter 16).

After-school activities also provide opportunities for students to connect with supportive adults and peers (Gullotta, Chapter 17, this volume). They are a great venue to help youth develop and apply new skills and personal talents. Research has shown that after-school programs that devote time to student social and emotional development can significantly enhance student self-perceptions, bonding to school, positive social behaviors, school grades and achievement test scores, while reducing problem behaviors (Durlak et al., 2010).

It is evident from the contents of this book that there are many different settings or systems other than school in which SEL can be fostered in children and youth or the adults who support them. SEL begins in early childhood, so family and early childcare settings are important setting for SEL (Bierman & Motamedi, Chapter 9, this volume). At the other end of the education spectrum, higher education settings also have the potential to promote SEL in students (Conley, Chapter 13, this volume). Children and youth who engage in risky behavior often exhibit deficits in social and emotional skills, so systems that serve these populations (e.g., juvenile justice, mental health providers) are also potential settings for SEL.

District, State, and Federal Support

The left box in Figure 1.1 indicates that classroom and schoolwide SEL programming are most likely to be successfully implemented and sustained when they are aligned with district priorities and have the support of district administrators, school boards, and educator unions (Mart et al., Chapter 32, this volume). District leaders can champion policies, practices, and supports for systemic SEL programming by (1) partnering with stakeholders to cultivate commitment for SEL and fostering organizational supports and professional learning communities for SEL implementation; (2) auditing current district resources and needs, and building from effective programming that is already underway; (3) supporting coordinated classroom, schoolwide, and community SEL programming; and (4) establishing assessment systems for continuous improvement of practice (CASEL, in press; Mart et al., Chapter 32, this volume). CASEL is currently partnering with eight large urban districts (Anchorage, Austin, Chicago, Cleveland, Nashville, Oakland, Sacramento, and Washoe County [Nevada]) on preschool to high school systemwide SEL (CASEL, in press; Mart et al., Chapter 32, this volume; Wright, Lamont, Wandersman, Osher, & Gordon, Chapter 33, this volume). A third-party evaluation by the American Institutes for Research based on 3 years of implementation indicates that districts and schools have had considerable success in implementing evidence-based SEL programming and aligning SEL with other programs and diverse district priorities (Osher, Friedman, & Kendziora, 2014).

Federal and state policies and supports play critical roles in fostering evidence-based district, school, and classroom SEL programming (see Figure 1.1). One of the key ways that states can advance quality SEL programming is to establish SEL standards for students (Dusenbury et al., Chapter 35, this volume). Learning standards specify what students should know and be able to do as a result of educational instruction. Well-written and well-implemented standards communicate priorities to school staff members, families, and students. When they provide clear goals and developmental benchmarks, standards can help shape impactful educational planning, especially if those plans include implementation of evidence-based curricula, quality professional learning for educators, and assessment that helps teachers monitor students' progress toward goals. Illinois provides a groundbreaking model for freestanding preschool to high school SEL standards. Illinois students are expected to be working toward three SEL goals: (1) develop self-awareness and self-management skills to achieve school and life success; (2) use social awareness and interpersonal skills to establish and maintain positive relationships, and (3) demonstrate decision-making skills and responsible behaviors in personal, school, and community contexts (for a complete set of standards, benchmarks, and grade-level performance descriptors, see *www.isbe.net/ils/social_emotional/standards.htm*). Dusenbury and colleagues (Chapter 35, this volume) describe results from a 50-state scan of SEL standards and provide guidelines for the design of high-quality SEL standards that could be adopted across states, districts, and schools.

Over the past few years, SEL has gained significant traction in federal policy (Zaslow et al., Chapter 36, this volume). Members of Congress from both parties have introduced or support pending legislation that supports SEL. Also, the U.S. Department of Education has incorporated SEL in recent rounds of Race to the Top and Investing in Innovation competitive grants. Some legislative initiatives focus on universal SEL approaches, with the goal of promoting positive behaviors and reducing negative behaviors in all students. For example, recently, Congressman Tim Ryan introduced bipartisan legislation (H.R. 850: Academic, Social, and Emotional Learning Act of 2015) that provides training for teachers and principals in SEL programming. That Act defines SEL programming as

> Classroom instruction and schoolwide activities and initiatives that (a) integrate social and emotional learning with academic achievement; (b) provide systematic instruction whereby social and emotional skills are taught, modeled, practiced, and applied so that students use them as part of their daily behavior; (c) teach students to apply social and emotional skills to prevent specific problem behaviors such as substance use, violence, bullying, and school failure, and to promote positive behaviors in class, school, and community activities; and (d) establish safe and caring learning environments that foster student participation, engagement, and connection to learning and school. (*www.govtrack.us/congress/bills/114/hr850*)

Ideally, this language will be incorporated in the Elementary and Secondary Education Act and other policies the House and Senate adopt. Aligned federal, state, and district policies increase the likelihood that quality programming will be broadly implemented in schools and classrooms.

Systemic, Coordinated Education Is Vital

This framework shows that SEL programming occurs in a multilevel ecological system of contexts and relationships. A key challenge for SEL researchers, educators, policymakers, and funders involves synthesizing research from many disciplines, distilling the essentials from diverse programs and policies, and putting the pieces together in districtwide and schoolwide systemic SEL programming.

SEL inhabits a world of kindred educational approaches that aspire to promote children's social–emotional–cognitive competence and enhance the environmental conditions and contexts that influence their learning and development (Brown, Corrigan, & Higgins-D'Alessandro, 2012; Catalano et al., 2004; Elias et al., Chapter 3, this volume; Farrington et al., 2012; Gilman, Huebner, & Furlong; 2009; Goleman, 2005; National Research Council, 2012; Nucci, Narvaez, & Krettenauer, 2014; Wentzel & Wigfield, 2009). A sampling of approaches that address intrapersonal and interpersonal competence promotion includes character education, deeper learning, emotional intelligence, grit, habits of mind, health promotion, mindsets, noncognitive, project-based learning, prosocial education, positive behavior supports, positive youth development, school climate, student-centered learning, 21st-century skills, and whole-child education.

Unfortunately, most programs are introduced into schools as a succession of fragmented fads, isolated from other programs, and the school becomes a hodgepodge of prevention and youth development initiatives, with little direction, coordination, sustainability, or impact (Shriver & Weissberg, 1996). From the perspective of district and school educators, it is critical to establish infrastructures, strategies, and processes to integrate programming effectively to enhance students' social, emotional, and academic growth.

CASEL contends that the strongest benefit for children will come from looking for commonalities and coordinating programs in the context of systemic district and schoolwide programming (CASEL, in press; Elias et al., Chapter 3, this volume; Meyers et al., in press). Planned, ongoing, systematic SEL includes the following core features: (1) developing a shared vision for SEL that prioritizes the promotion of social, emotional, and academic learning for all students; (2) identifying existing strengths and supports for SEL and building from those strengths; (3) establishing central office and school infrastructures and resources that provide ongoing professional learning, including how to build SEL awareness, enhance adult social–emotional competence, and cultivate effective SEL instructional practices; (4) establishing SEL standards for students that guide a scope and sequence for SEL programming; (5) adopting and aligning evidence-based programs that will support social and emotional skills development in classrooms and throughout the school community; (6) integrating SEL and the development of classroom/school climate and culture into all school goals, priorities, initiatives, programs, and strategies; and (7) using a cycle of inquiry to improve SEL practice and student outcomes. Finally, assessments of consumer perspectives, program implementation, child outcomes, school and district resources, new state and federal policies, and scientific advances should continuously be reviewed to improve programs and aid decision making about their future course.

The SEL framework integrates powerfully with student-centered learning practices (Darling-Hammond et al., 2014; Friedlaender et al., 2014). In summary, SEL is strengths-based and offers developmentally informed guidance about the social, emotional, and academic competencies that educated students should master. It values students' thoughts, feelings, and voice, highlighting that students can contribute positively to their schools and communities. SEL involves personalization of the education process and engaging pedagogies and relevant curricula that offer opportunities for deeper learning and connection to the world beyond school. Creating a positive school culture and climate, and using authentic assessments that evaluate and inform teaching and learning, are core elements of quality SEL programming. It is critical that SEL coordinate with educational and child development movements that address these priorities.

Evidence for SEL Interventions

A body of correlational and longitudinal research indicates that social and emotional competencies are positively related to good adjustment outcomes and negatively related to a variety of problems (e.g., Heckman & Kautz, 2012; Moffitt et al., 2011). There is also evidence from a variety of reviews that SEL interventions produce positive attitudinal and behavioral effects. Instead of discussing the research evidence for specific programs (which is done in several chapters of this *Handbook*), we discuss the results of several influential publications that have brought SEL into prominence and summarize the research regarding its effectiveness as a school-based intervention.

The first of these was *Safe and Sound: An Educational Leader's Guide to Evidence-Based Social and Emotional Learning (SEL) Programs* (CASEL, 2003). This publication was the first comprehensive survey of existing school-based SEL programs that explained how SEL can be easily accommodated into (1) the academic mission of schools, (2) efforts to promote healthy behaviors and prevent high-risk behaviors, (3) comprehensive school reform, and (4) the creation of family and school partnerships. The 2003 guide provided educators with practical information on the procedural aspects and outcomes of various programs to help them in selecting the most appropriate programs for their particular setting. Safe and Sound became a popular source of information and was downloaded over 150,000 times from the CASEL website. CASEL recently published *2013 Guide: Effective Social and Emotional Learning Programs—Preschool and Elementary School Edition.* As the title indicates, it focuses on successful preschool and elementary programs (up through grade 5). The *2013 Guide* highlights 25 programs (seven at the preschool and 18 at the elementary level) that satisfied more rigorous research criteria than those used in the 2003 publication. A guide for the later school years will be released in 2015.

Zins and colleagues (2004) highlighted through detailed research examples how SEL programming promotes students' academic success. This book was particularly important in that its appearance coincided with national attention that focused on the often poor academic performance of many students in the United States. Contributions to the Zins and colleagues volume reinforced the notion that SEL is one possibility for improving students' academic development.

More recently, a large-scale meta-analysis of 213 studies involving over 270,000 students confirmed that SEL produces significant positive effects in six different aspects of adjustment (Durlak et al., 2011). These outcomes included improvements in academic performance, SEL skills, prosocial behaviors, and attitudes toward self and others (e.g., self-esteem, bonding to school), as well as reductions in conduct problems and emotional distress (e.g., anxiety, and depression). Furthermore, the magnitude of the effect sizes achieved in these areas (from 0.22 to 0.57 depending on the outcome) were comparable to or higher than those reported in meta-analyses of other well-established psychosocial interventions for youth. Overall, these findings indicated that SEL interventions should be considered an effective evidence-based approach for schoolchildren.

Several other findings that emerged from the Durlak and colleagues (2011) meta-analysis either supported the results of prior individual studies or spoke to important questions regarding the conduct of SEL programs. For instance, programs were effective regardless of their geographical setting (e.g., urban, suburban, or rural), or the ethnic composition of the student body. Teachers were more successful when conducting programs than were outside staff members who entered the school to administer programs. This indicated that SEL interventions can be incorporated into routine educational practice.

Furthermore, the quality of implementation varied across the reviewed programs and had an influential effect on outcomes. For example, student findings were compared for those participating in well-implemented versus poorly implemented programs. The former group of students' improvement in academic performance was *twice as high* as that of the latter group; and they showed *reductions* in emotional distress and levels of conduct problems that were *up to twice* the reduction shown by those in poorly implemented program. These results confirm other findings that the level of implementation obtained has an important bearing on program outcomes. In other words, we should not think of SEL programs as being effective; it is well-implemented SEL programs that are effective (Durlak, Chapter 26, this volume). It should be noted that a subsequent meta-analysis by an international group of researchers on a more select sample of universal, school-based SEL programs has replicated the positive effects on the six student outcome areas listed earlier (Sklad et al., 2012).

In summary, this brief overview of SEL research yields several important conclusions. Research findings have established that well-implemented SEL programs are an evidence-based approach that not only improves students' academic, behavioral, and personal adjustment but also prevents some important negative outcomes. SEL programs have been effective for preschool through high school students (and also for college students, see Conley, Chapter 13, this volume) across a range of locations and student populations, and can be effectively delivered by teachers provided that they receive sufficient training, consultation, and support (in this volume, see Jennings & Frank, Chapter 28; Patti et al., Chapter 29; Schonert-Reichl et al., Chapter 27; Williford & Sanger Wolcott, Chapter 15). In other words, SEL programming should be considered a viable option in any educational context for enhancing students' psychological, academic, and social functioning.

An Agenda for the Future of SEL

In this section, we suggest an agenda for future work in SEL that blends prior accomplishments and some of the suggestions and recommendations offered in various chapters of this *Handbook*. Space does not permit a comprehensive discussion of all relevant issues, so we focus our discussion around two central questions:

1. How can we improve the quality of evidence in support of SEL programs?
2. How can we scale-up evidence-based programs to reach as many students as possible?

Improving the Quality of SEL

Although many SEL programs have been successful, we need more research to identify the active ingredients and core components of successful programs. The theories and logic models behind most successful SEL programs focus on two important elements of interventions: (1) features of the environmental context (e.g., the classroom or school climate, teacher practices, the creation of family or community partnerships) and (2) the specific competencies that are targeted for interventions in one or more of the five SEL competence domains (Brackett, Elbertson, & Rivers, Chapter 2, this volume). It is essential to confirm which environmental features and which student competencies constitute the active ingredients of successful programs for different age groups. The active ingredients of interventions are what power the intervention and account for the obtained changes in participants. Although a few research groups have conducted mediational analyses to examine the active ingredients of their interventions (see Rimm-Kaufman & Hulleman, Chapter 10, this volume), the results are not always clear cut and require replication in multiple contexts.

Discovering the active ingredients of different SEL programs can go far in creating more effective and efficient interventions because this information provides guidance in terms of (1) which program aspects should be maintained as is, and which can be eliminated, reduced, or modified to suit different school situations, (2) which are the most important pieces of interventions that educators should learn to deliver and emphasize when conducting programs, and (3) what to measure in terms of program theory, implementation, and program outcomes.

Another important set of considerations focuses on the ethnic and cultural background of students (Hecht & Shin, Chapter 4, this volume). Although research has indicated that SEL interventions can be effective with diverse ethnic and cultural groups, we do not know how, or whether, modifications can make current programs more effective for different subgroups. We also can benefit from cross-cultural research studies. Some SEL programs developed in the United States have been successfully transported into other countries, but original SEL interventions are also present in other countries (Humphrey, 2013). Moreover, the educational systems of many countries around the world are conducive to promoting many SEL-related skills (Torrente et al., Chapter 37, this volume), and it is important to learn how different cultural and societal contexts influence program impact.

Scientific fields cannot progress very far in the absence of good measurement of critical constructs. Progress in SEL can be made in terms of both the breadth and types of assessment that are routinely conducted. In terms of breadth, it is important to investigate as many outcomes as possible in order to learn how different programs can help students. Reviews indicate that SEL interventions can increase students' self-confidence and self-esteem, improve their attitudes toward school and education, and increase their prosocial behaviors (e.g., cooperation and helpfulness with others), and their academic performance in terms of both grades and test scores. Interventions can also reduce problem behaviors such as aggression and levels of emotional distress (Durlak et al., 2011; Sklad et al., 2012). However, not every program can be expected to produce the same degree of change in each of these areas, and in many cases we have no information on how some programs affect participants in several of the previously described areas. Furthermore, as noted by Greenberg, Katz, and Klein (Chapter 6, this volume), it is also a good idea to assess key biomarkers of physical health because it is likely that some SEL interventions might obtain important effects in this area.

In terms of developing new types of assessments, it is critically important to have measures of the many different abilities that comprise the five SEL domains. Although a few tools are currently available (in this volume, see Denham, Chapter 19; Elliott, Frey, & Davies, Chapter 20; Marzano, Chapter 22; McKown, Chapter 21), the field needs to develop additional valid assessment strategies that encompass the full range of skills and attitudes. Assessment of multiple social–emotional competencies would help to determine which types of interventions would be most beneficial for which students, and for monitoring students' progress over time in order to make adjustment in the type or pacing of programming, and to judge how well an intervention promotes its targeted skills. Moreover, it would be very helpful if valid, easy-to-use assessment tools could be developed in the regular school context, that is, those that can be competently administered and interpreted by school staff members and do not require extensive time (in this volume, see Denham, Chapter 19; Redding & Walberg, Chapter 25).

Additional issues that need more research attention include how program duration relates to different outcomes, and, in general, the long-term impact of SEL programs. How long should a program be for students at different educational levels, and what initial skills sets would achieve positive effects across different outcome areas? Some researchers suggest that brief social psychological interventions that target students' thoughts, feelings, and beliefs can yield large gains in achievement and reduce achievement gaps years later (Yeager & Walton, 2011). Although it is logical to assume that longer programs produce better results, the data on this matter are not clear. Meta-analytic reviews have reported positive results at follow-up for student outcomes (Durlak et al., 2011; Sklad et al., 2012), but follow-up studies are in the minority. Given the need for cost-effective options, future research should clarify the differential impacts that short-term programs and multiyear interventions produce.

In the final analysis, we do not expect research to produce a short list of a few environmental conditions and skills that are universally effective in all situations. Rather, further research should be directed toward seeking answers to this question: What particular environmental conditions, combined with the promotion of which particular skill sets, are responsible for students at different educational levels and from different cultural backgrounds achieving which types of desirable outcomes in both the short and long term?

Going to Scale with Evidence-Based SEL Interventions

Promoting the widespread use of evidence-based approaches has become an important topic in fields such as medicine, education, and mental health treatment and prevention. Unfortunately, in each of these areas, there is a wide gap between research and practice in the sense that evidence-based programs may be applied far more broadly than they currently are. The same goes for SEL programs.

Several authors use the term "dissemination" to refer to the spread of evidence-based programs, but it is more helpful and thorough to employ Rogers's (2003) diffusion model, which has been very influential in helping us understand the processes by which an evidence-based program eventually becomes more widely used and accepted. According to Rogers, diffusion occurs as a result of five separate but related stages. The first stage of diffusion is "dissemination," which refers to communicating accurate and helpful information to potential users about the program. The second stage, "adoption," occurs when others decide to try out a program. The third stage is "implementation," which refers to conducting the program in a high-quality manner to provide a fair test of the program's ability to produce changes. The fourth stage, "evaluation," involves examining how well the new program achieved its intended goals. Finally, the fifth stage is "sustainability," which means that the program (if successful) now becomes a routine feature of the adopting organization's procedures. Each of these stages needs to be accomplished effectively to reach the final goal relating to widespread use, but problems often arise in the successful execution of each of these phases. For example, potential users may not receive or pay sufficient attention to useful information about new programs. They may choose to adopt the wrong (e.g., ill-fitting or ineffective) program for their setting, or fail to adopt a program that might be helpful. School staff may encounter serious difficulties or limitations in program implementation, or fail to evaluate the new program carefully to discern its true benefits. In some cases, new programs have not been sustained because of administrative, political, or financial reasons, even when evaluations have indicated their value in the new setting.

There are several ways to make progress by strengthening work in the different stages of program diffusion, and one common theme that runs across all of these potentially positive contributions is the value of collaboration with relevant stakeholders. Collaboration becomes important in the dissemination and adoption phase because of the potential value of asking educators what information would be most useful to them in terms of learning about SEL programs, deciding whether or not to adopt one for their school, and how they would most like to receive this information. Historically, experts have commonly thought they have the answers to important questions and have developed communications about scientific discoveries in ways they see fit. In terms of promoting SEL initiatives, it seems far better to ask educators what they need to know and respond accordingly. What information would help them to learn about the value of SEL programs and decide about using them? What concerns might they have about such programs? What is standing in the way of their school adopting programs and coordinating their use? Gathering such information systematically and across a diverse sample of educators would generate ideas about how to enhance work on the dissemination of information and program adoption.

Collaboration remains critically important in the next three stages of diffusion: implementation, evaluation, and sustainability (CASEL, in press; Meyers et al., in press). Durlak (Chapter 26, this volume) discusses these stages in more detail, but here it should be emphasized that quality implementation of SEL programs requires that professional development services be provided collaboratively by outside consultants and school professionals with SEL experience and expertise. Moreover, this needed training and technical assistance is best offered through a genuine collaboration, so that relevant stakeholders (e.g., educators, families, and students) have meaningful input into decisions about how the proposed program fits their needs and values, how it might have to be modified to achieve its ends, and how they will work together as a learning community to implement, evaluate, continuously improve, and sustain programming.

Collaboration is also critical with federal, state, and local policymakers, decision makers, and funders (in this volume, see Price, Chapter 8; Zaslow et al., Chapter 36). In addition to documenting that SEL benefits children, it is also important to make the economic case for SEL (Jones, Greenberg, & Crowley, Chapter 7, this volume). A recent study indicates that it is possible to apply benefit–cost analysis to SEL programming, and that these interventions offer high economic returns as economic investments (Belfield et al., 2014).

In summary, diverse stakeholders must work together to support the broader implementation of systemic, evidence-based SEL programming. These stakeholders include educators, family members, researchers, program developers, policymakers, funders, and advocates. Each has an important role to play in order to meld theory, research, practice, and policy together so that they work synergistically to achieve valued goals.

The Potential of Technology

Various technologies such as computers, websites, mobile applications, videoconferencing, and social media have the potential to increase the receptivity and wider use of SEL interventions (Stern, Harding, Holzer, & Elbertson, Chapter 34, this volume).We encourage others to evaluate how various technologies can best be used in the service of SEL. For example, websites can present and periodically update information on new SEL research, practice, and policies. Technology can also play a major role in training and coaching teachers through the use of virtual classroom realities, and interactive Web programs can be created to help teachers overcome the challenges related to effective program implementation (Stern et al., Chapter 34, this volume). Video conferencing can be an economical way to allow those conducting the same programs in different geographical areas to share their experiences and offer creative solutions to practical problems.

Technology also offers opportunities for real-time assessments related to the need for SEL skills, the course of program implementation, the monitoring of student progress over time, and end-of-program evaluations of desired outcomes. Readers can think of other innovative ways to use technological applications. The potential is vast; technology makes it possible (in practice, not just in theory) to reach large numbers of people instantly and simultaneously.

Overview of the Current Volume

This volume includes contributions by leading interdisciplinary researchers and practitioners who were carefully chosen in terms of their expertise in theory, research, practice, or policy. There are four main sections. In addition to this introductory chapter, Part I contains seven foundational chapters that cover issues related to theory and the relationship between SEL and matters such as diversity, neuroscience, physical health, and financing. Part II contains 10 chapters that focus on specific settings for SEL intervention (e.g., preschool through higher education, after-school activities, or justice-related institutions) or on particular aspects of SEL work (e.g., student–teacher relationships, school–family partnerships, or interventions for students with disabilities).

The chapters in Part II follow a standard format. Authors of each chapter provide an overview of theory and research relevant to their particular topic and categorize programs they review into three categories: What Works, What Is Promising, and What Does Not Work. These authors were asked to use the following general criteria for placing a program into one of these categories. "What Works" is defined as three or more successful trials of an intervention based on evaluations that are reasonably well controlled. "What Is Promising" refers to programs for which there are less than three successful trials. "What Does Not Work" is defined as evidence from evaluations that indicate an intervention has failed to achieve its intended impact. This last category refers to situations in which programs have been evaluated but have not achieved their intended goals. It does not refer to situations in which an SEL program has not been subjected to evaluation; in this case, data are missing to judge program impact. This three-category evaluative system is not perfect, but it does provide a consistent frame of reference across different research areas and a general snapshot of the evidence that exists to support different types of SEL programs. We feel such a perspective is very useful to potential consumers and to those who want a critical perspective on the impact of current programs in different areas.

Part III includes seven groundbreaking chapters on SEL assessment. Because what gets assessed gets addressed in education and the human services, it is critically important to establish SEL assessments that are scientifically sound, developmentally appropriate, feasible to administer and score, affordable, and actionable. Denham (Chapter 19, this volume) offers a developmental framework for preschool to high school SEL assessment and points out that tools can be used for screening, formative, interim, and summative functions. Currently, teacher, parent, and student self-report measures of social behaviors, attitudes, and perceptions of climate dominate the SEL assessment landscape. Although these approaches are informative, they have drawbacks due to issues such as social desirability and response bias.

A critical priority for SEL includes creating a battery of preschool to high school performance and observational assessment tools that evaluate the social–emotional skills of students and provide guidance on ways to improve them. Part III chapters on assessment include innovative perspectives on ways to assess and improve students' social competence and conditions for learning, performance assessments of students' social–emotional comprehension and skills, and formative assessment strategies to measure and enhance students' social–emotional competence. Other chapters focus on organizational readiness and practice assessments that can help school teams continuously assess current SEL practice, plan improvement, monitor implementation, and make adjustments to strengthen programming. Together, these chapters provide the next decade's road map for developing SEL assessments—a priority that many believe is the most important one for the field.

Finally, Part IV contains chapters on various topics such as professional development (for teachers, administrators, and student support personnel) and policy and dissemination issues (e.g., implementation, learning standards, SEL practices for schoolwide development efforts and attempts at school improvement, taking programs to scale, technology, federal policy, and international initiatives). We are pleased to have this volume include distinguished contributors whose comments at the beginning of this volume are contained in the form of a Foreword written by Linda Darling-Hammond and an Introduction by Timothy Shriver and Jennifer Buffett, and an Afterword at the end of the volume that includes commentaries by James Comer and Daniel Goleman.

Conclusion

In the 3-year journey leading to the publication of the *Handbook* intended for researchers, practitioners, program developers, and policymakers, our understanding of SEL has been shaped by the new developments in this exciting and promising area of helping young people and adults learn to live healthier lives. For all that has been accomplished, so much more remains unfinished. It is our hope that this volume inspires readers to engage in activities related to SEL research, practice, or policy, and challenges them to push the frontiers of knowledge beyond the boundaries that exist today.

Acknowledgments

We wish to express our appreciation for the many supporters of this *Handbook*, CASEL, and the SEL field. Funders and thought-partners include the S. D. Bechtel, Jr. Foundation, the Buena Vista Foundation, the Einhorn Family Charitable Trust, the 1440 Foundation, the Growald Family Fund, the Noyce Foundation, NoVo Foundation, the Robert Wood Johnson Foundation, the Spencer Foundation, the U.S. Department of Education, and the University of Illinois at Chicago. We also thank the talented contributors to the *Handbook* and the thousands of people and organizations who are collaborating to advance SEL research, practice, and policy.

References

Adelman, H., & Taylor, L. (2006). *The school leader's guide to student learning supports: New directions for addressing barriers to learning.* Thousand Oaks, CA: Corwin Press.

Albright, M. I., & Weissberg, R. P. (2010). School–family partnerships to promote social and emotional learning. In S. L. Christenson & A. L. Reschley (Eds.), *The handbook of school–family partnerships for promoting student competence* (pp. 246–265). New York: Routledge/Taylor & Francis Group.

Belfield, C., Bowden, B., Klapp, A., Levin, H., Shand, R., & Zander, S. (2014). *The economic value of social and emotional learning.* New York: Center for Benefit–Cost Studies in Education, Teachers College, Columbia University.

Benson, P. L. (2006). *All kids are our kids: What communities must do to raise responsible and caring children and adolescents.* San Francisco: Jossey-Bass.

Bridgeland, J., Bruce, M., & Hariharan, A. (2013). *The missing piece: A national survey on how social and emotional* learning *can empower children and transform schools.* Washington, DC: Civic Enterprises. Retrieved September 1, 2014, from *www.civicenterprises.net/medialibrary/docs/casel-report-low-res-final.pdf.*

Brown, P. H., Corrigan, M. W., & Higgins-D'Alessandro, A. (Eds.). (2012). *Handbook of prosocial education* (Vols. 1 & 2). New York: Rowman & Littlefield.

Collaborative for Academic, Social, and Emotional

Learning (CASEL). (2003). *Safe and sound: An educational leader's guide to evidence-based social and emotional learning (SEL) programs.* Chicago: Author.

Collaborative for Academic, Social, and Emotional Learning (CASEL). (2012). *2013 CASEL guide: Effective social and emotional learning programs—Preschool and elementary school edition.* Chicago: Author.

Collaborative for Academic, Social, and Emotional Learning (CASEL). (in press). *District guide to systemic social and emotional learning.* Chicago: Author.

Catalano, R. F., Berglund, M. L., Ryan, J. A. M., Lonczak, H. S., & Hawkins, J. D. (2004). Positive youth development in the United States: Research findings on evaluations of positive youth development programs. *Annals of the American Academy of Political and Social Science, 591*(1), 98–124.

Consortium on the School-based Promotion of Social Competence. (1994). The school-based promotion of social competence: Theory, research, practice, and policy. In R. J. Haggerty, N. Garmezy, M. Rutter, & L. R. Sherrod (Eds.), *Stress, risk, and resilience in children and adolescents: Processes, mechanisms, and interventions* (pp. 268–316). New York: Cambridge University Press.

Darling-Hammond, L., Friedlaender, D., & Snyder, J. (2014). *Student-centered schools: Policy supports for closing the opportunity gap.* Stanford, CA: Stanford Center for Opportunity Policy in Education.

Durlak, J. A., Weissberg, R. P., Dymnicki, A. B., Taylor, R. D., & Schellinger, K. B. (2011). The impact of enhancing students' social and emotional learning: A meta-analysis of school-based universal interventions. *Child Development, 82*, 405–432.

Durlak, J. A., Weissberg, R. P., & Pachan, M. (2010). A meta-analysis of after-school programs that seek to promote personal and social skills in children and adolescents. *American Journal of Community Psychology, 45*, 294–309.

Dymnicki, A., Sambolt, M., & Kidron, Y. (2013). *Improving college and career readiness by incorporating social and emotional learning.* Washington DC: American Institutes for Research College & Career Readiness and Success Center.

Elias, M. J., O'Brien, M. U., & Weissberg, R. P. (2006). Transformative leadership for social–emotional learning. *Principal Leadership, 7*(4), 10–13.

Elias, M. J., Zins, J. E., Weissberg, R. P., Frey, K. S., Greenberg, M. T., Haynes, N. M., et al. (1997). *Promoting social and emotional learning: Guidelines for educators.* Alexandria, VA: Association for Supervision and Curriculum Development.

Farrington, C. A., Roderick, M., Allensworth, E., Nagaoka, J., Keyes, T. S., Johnson, D. W., et al. (2012). *Teaching adolescents to become learners—the role of noncognitive factors in shaping school performance: A critical literature review.* Chicago: University of Chicago Consortium on Chicago School Research.

Friedlaender, D., Burns, D., Lewis-Charp, H., Cook-Harvey, C. M., Zheng, X., & Darling-Hammond, L. (2014). *Student-centered schools: Closing the opportunity gap.* Stanford, CA: Stanford Center for Opportunity Policy in Education.

Gilman, R., Huebner, E. S., & Furlong, M. J. (Eds.). (2009). *Handbook of positive psychology in schools.* New York: Routledge.

Goleman, D. (2005). *Emotional intelligence: Why it can matter more than IQ.* New York: Bantam Books.

Greenberg, M. T., Weissberg, R. P., O'Brien, M. U., Zins, J. E., Fredericks, L., Resnik, H., et al. (2003). Enhancing school-based prevention and youth development through coordinated social, emotional, and academic learning. *American Psychologist, 58*, 466–474.

Hawkins, J. D., Kosterman, R., Catalano, R. F., Hill, K. G., & Abbott, R. D. (2008). Effects of social development intervention in childhood 15 years later. *Archives of Pediatric Adolescent Medicine, 162*(12), 1133–1141.

Heckman, J. J., & Kautz, T. (2012). Hard evidence on soft skills. *Labor Economics, 19*, 451–464.

Humphrey, N. (2013). *Social and emotional learning: A critical appraisal.* Washington, DC: Sage.

Jennings, P. A., & Greenberg, M. T. (2009). The prosocial classroom: Teacher social and emotional competence in relation to student and classroom outcomes. *Review of Educational Research, 79*, 491–525.

Jones, S. M., & Bouffard, S. M. (2012). Social and emotional learning in schools: From programs to strategies. *Social Policy Report, 26*(4), 1–33.

Klem, A. M., & Connell, J. P. (2004). Relationships matter: Linking teacher support to student engagement and achievement. *Journal of School Health, 74*(7), 262–273.

Merrell, K. W., & Gueldner, B. A. (2010). *Social and emotional learning in the classroom: Promoting mental health and academic success.* New York: Guilford Press.

Meyers, D., Gil, L., Cross, R., Keister, S., Domitrovich, C. E., & Weissberg, R. P. (in press). *CASEL guide for schoolwide social and emotional learning.* Chicago: Collaborative for Academic, Social, and Emotional Learning.

Moffitt, T. E., Arseneault, L., Belsky, D., Dickson,

N., Hancox, R. J., Harrington, H., et al. (2011). A gradient of childhood self-control predicts health, wealth, and public safety. *Proceedings of the National Academy of Sciences, 108*(7), 2693–2698.

National Research Council. (2012). *Education for life and work: Developing transferable knowledge and skills in the 21st century* (Committee on Defining Deeper Learning and 21st Century Skills, J. W. Pellegrino & M. L. Hilton, Editors, Board on Testing and Assessment and Board on Science Education, Division of Behavioral and Social Sciences and Education). Washington, DC: National Academies Press.

Nucci, L., Narvaez, D., & Krettenauer, T. (2014). *Handbook of moral and character education* (2nd ed.). New York: Routledge.

Osher, D., Friedman, L. B., & Kendziora, K. (2014). *CASEL/NoVo Collaborating Districts Initiative: 2014 cross-district implementation summary.* Washington, DC: American Institutes for Research.

Payton, J., Weissberg, R. P., Durlak, J. A., Dymnicki, A. B., Taylor, R. D., Schellinger, K. B., et al. (2008). *The positive impact of social and emotional learning for kindergarten to eighth-grade students: Findings from three scientific reviews.* Chicago: Collaborative for Academic, Social, and Emotional Learning. Retrieved September 8, 2014, from *www.lpfch.org/sel/casel-fullreport.pdf.*

Rogers, E. M. (2003). *Diffusion of innovations* (5th ed.). New York: Free Press.

Schaps, E., & Weissberg, R. P. (2014). *Essential educational goals and practices.* Manuscript submitted for publication.

Shriver, T. P., & Weissberg, R. P. (1996, May 15). No new wars! *Education Week, 15*(34), 33, 37.

Sklad, M., Diekstra, R., De Ritter, M., & Ben, J. (2012). Effectiveness of school-based universal social, emotional, and behavioral programs: Do they enhance students' development in the area of skill, behavior, and adjustment? *Psychology in the Schools, 49*, 892–909.

Thapa, A., Cohen, J., Guffey, S., & Higgins-D'Alessandro, A. (2013). A review of school climate research. *Review of Educational Research, 83*(3), 357–385.

Weare, K., & Nind, M. (2011). Mental health promotion and problem prevention: What does the evidence say? *Health Promotion International, 26*, i29–i69.

Weissberg, R. P., & Cascarino, J. (2013). Academic + social–emotional learning = national priority. *Phi Delta Kappan, 95*(2), 8–13.

Weissberg, R. P., & Greenberg, M. T. (1998). School and community competence-enhancement and prevention programs. In W. Damon (Series Ed.) & I. E. Sigel & K. A. Renninger (Vol. Eds.), *Handbook of child psychology: Vol 4. Child psychology in practice* (5th ed., pp. 877–954). New York: Wiley.

Weissberg, R. P., & Kumpfer, K. (Eds.). (2003). Special issue: Prevention that works for children and youth. *American Psychologist, 58*, 425–490.

Weissberg, R. P., Walberg, H. J., O'Brien, M. U., & Kuster, C. B. (Eds.). (2003). *Long-term trends in the well-being of children and youth.* Washington, DC: Child Welfare League of America Press.

Wentzel, K. R., & Wigfield, A. (Eds.). (2009). *Handbook of motivation at school.* New York: Routledge.

Yeager, D. S., & Walton, G. M. (2011). Social-psychological interventions in education: They're not magic. *Review of Educational Research, 81*(2), 267–301.

Yoder, N. (2013) *Teaching the whole child: Instructional practices that support social and emotional learning in three teacher evaluation frameworks.* Washington, DC: American Institutes for Research Center on Great Teachers and Leaders.

Zins, J. E., Weissberg, R. P., Wang, M. C., & Walberg. H. J. (Eds.). (2004). *Building academic success on social and emotional learning: What does the research say?* New York: Teachers College Press.

CHAPTER 2

Applying Theory to the Development of Approaches to SEL

Marc A. Brackett, Nicole A. Elbertson, and Susan E. Rivers

When first introduced in the 1990s, the term "social and emotional learning" (SEL) represented an amalgamation of ideas from researchers, educators, and advocates with diverse interests in meeting the developmental, psychological, educational, and general health needs of children (Elias et al., 1997). SEL was used as a guiding mechanism for providing evidence-based programming in schools for students to acquire the skills necessary for attaining and maintaining well-being and success across the lifespan (Greenberg et al., 2003; Kress & Elias, 2006). SEL is defined now more specifically as "a process for helping children and even adults develop the fundamental skills for life effectiveness [including] . . . recognizing and managing . . . emotions, developing caring and concern for others, establishing positive relationships, making responsible decisions, and handling challenging situations constructively and ethically" (Collaborative for Academic, Social, and Emotional Learning [CASEL], 2013c). This definition, drawn from theories of social, emotional, and cognitive development, as well as behavior change, is intended to provide a framework to inform the design, implementation, and evaluation of approaches to SEL in schools; it also serves to guide principals and superintendents in selecting SEL initiatives for their schools (Payton et al., 2000).

The role of theory in designing approaches for developing social and emotional skills is important for researchers, program developers, and practitioners alike. Theory should inform how an approach is designed and implemented in ways that will lead to a specified set of outcomes. Evaluation of the effectiveness of different approaches to SEL and efforts to increase effectiveness are contingent upon a well-articulated theory about which specific components of an approach lead to outcomes. In this chapter, we describe the ways in which theory can be applied to guide SEL efforts from initial design through sustainability. To that end, we discuss the significance of theory to SEL strategy development and describe some of the primary theories informing established SEL approaches. We also provide suggestions for how to apply theory to creating programmatic content and devising implementation strategies. To facilitate understanding of the relevance of theory, we present the approach to SEL that we developed—RULER—and describe how theory informed its design, including its adaptations over time.

The Practicality of Theory

"Nothing is as practical as a good theory" (p. 129). This statement from Kurt Lewin

(1945) captures an idea that rings true today over a half a century later: Theory serves as a practical guide and starting point to many endeavors. A theory, as defined by the *Oxford English Dictionary*, is "a scheme or system of ideas or statements held as an explanation or account of a group of facts or phenomena; a hypothesis that has been confirmed or established by observation or experiment, and is propounded or accepted as accounting for the known facts; a statement of what are held to be the general laws, principles, or causes of something known or observed." In other words, a theory puts forth an explanation for why things are the way they are.

More precisely, social scientists, philosophers, and business professionals generally agree that there are four primary components to a theory: (1) definitions of terms and variables, (2) a domain or context to which the theory applies, (3) the identification of relationships among the terms or variables, and (4) specific predictions or factual claims (Reynolds, 1971; Wacker, 1998). A theory provides a narrative proposition about the causes underlying a phenomenon; as a proposition, it can be refuted or refined through observation and research. A theory facilitates more than just the observation and description of behavior; it enables the systematic dissection of observations and allows for more precise descriptions and explanations. A good theory incorporates all relevant ideas and empirical evidence about a phenomenon into a single, integrated statement of knowledge and thereby offers a process for both applying to practice what is known and building on that knowledge to develop a field (Popper, 1957).

In the context of SEL, the phenomenon in question is children and adults developing optimally for success in life. Thus, theories that guide SEL efforts need to identify and explain how different variables affect optimal human development. Approaches to SEL that are applied in schools need to specify which variables impact children's development—from what teachers teach and how they teach it, to how and what children learn, to how various environmental factors affect both teachers and children. SEL experts agree that theory is essential, declaring that, for an approach to be considered "high quality," it must be "based on sound theories of child development, learning, prevention science, and empirically validated practices" (Zins, Bloodworth, Weissberg, & Walberg, 2004, p. 10). Moreover, one criterion for evaluating the quality of SEL approaches is "clarity of rationale" behind program design, specifically that "program objectives and the methods for achieving them are based on a clearly articulated conceptual framework" (Payton et al., 2000, p. 181). As Lewin (1945) asserted, a "good" theory will provide clarity and structure—a road map. The road map that theory can provide for SEL approaches should be leveraged to guide design, implementation, and sustainment of efforts to enhance social and emotional skills in both children and adults.

Theory and SEL Strategies

There exists a unified vision for SEL, which is to promote the healthy development and success of children so they can grow to their fullest potential—socially, emotionally, academically, and eventually professionally (CASEL, 2013b). However, there are many ways to realize this vision. What makes each approach to SEL unique is the specific content it includes, how that content is presented, and how the presentation of content is sustained with quality within a school organization over time. SEL content and implementation strategies are two critical areas that theory can inform.

Content

One underlying premise of SEL is that emotions matter in the lives of children, and not having the skills to understand and manage emotions can be disruptive to optimal social and cognitive development. Without emotional skills, children may not be able to control their behavior, feel empathy for others, or focus on learning (Brackett, Rivers, & Salovey, 2011). Thus, theories that clarify the relationship between emotional skills and developmental outcomes need to guide programmatic design, as well as the implementation and sustainability of programs and strategies, so that targeted outcomes (i.e., optimal development) are realized. Theory, then, should inform the selection of specific skills that are to be developed as part of an SEL approach. A given theory would posit a set of skills as predictive of a set of targeted outcomes (e.g., optimal social and cognitive development) and by enhancing these skills, the SEL approach would be situated to achieve the intended results. Furthermore, theory that specifies developmental trajectories of those skills (e.g., effective emotion regulation strategies for 5-year-olds vs. teenagers) can inform how these skills might be best developed, including how to teach the skills across different developmental levels, and how many and what types of guided lessons or activities enhance those skills most effectively at various developmental levels (e.g., the content for and number of lessons on managing peer pressure will be different for second graders than for high school students).

Implementation Strategies

The effectiveness of an SEL approach is contingent on content that is both engaging and communicated in ways that resonate with the recipients, that is, that hold their interest and stimulate their involvement in learning the designated skills. The same information may be interpreted, absorbed, and applied differently and to a greater or lesser extent depending on how it is presented (McGuire, 1972). As we demonstrate in this chapter, theory can guide the focus and pace of instruction when training educators and when delivering content to students. Theory also can be referenced and leveraged when planning how best to ignite the interest of and present information to children, as well as to key stakeholders, opinion leaders, and those who will be implementing the program or strategies (i.e., teachers). For example, theories about child development provide guidance on how younger versus older children understand certain SEL concepts, and adult learning theories provide guidance on how adults acquire and remember information.

For the purposes of illustrating the role of theory in designing and implementing SEL efforts in schools, we present a case study with RULER, a CASEL SELect approach to SEL (CASEL, 2013a) developed at the Yale Center for Emotional Intelligence. In the next section, we provide a brief overview of RULER and the theories that have guided its development and implementation. Later in the chapter, we present a compilation of theories that inform more broadly the content and implementation of other well-established SEL efforts.

RULER: A Theoretically Based Approach to SEL

RULER is an approach to SEL that is designed to integrate the teaching of emotional skills into a whole school or district. With a general goal of creating a more emotionally intelligent society, we consulted emotional intelligence theory (Mayer & Salovey, 1997; Salovey & Mayer, 1990) as well as theories of emotional development (e.g., Denham, 1998; Saarni, 1999) in order to identify a set of skills that were related to child outcomes and could be developed through experience and practice. These theories and their supporting research showed that children and youth with more developed emotional skills have greater social competence, psychological well-being, and academic performance, and that those with less developed emotional skills are more likely to experience depression and anxiety, engage in more antisocial behaviors, abuse drugs and alcohol, participate in more destructive relationships, and have poor academic performance (e.g., Eisenberg, Fabes, Guthrie, & Reiser, 2000; Fine, Izard, Mostow, Trentacosta, & Ackerman, 2003; Halberstadt, Denham, & Dunsmore, 2001; Rivers et al., 2012). Accordingly, the original model underlying RULER specified that children will be more effective when they are able to Recognize, Understand, Label, Express, and Regulate emotions, hence the acronym, RULER (Brackett, Rivers, Maurer, Elbertson, & Kremenitzer, 2011; Maurer, Brackett, & Plain, 2004).

Early field tests of RULER, however, showed that children were not receiving sufficient instruction to develop these emotional skills. We found that whereas some educators were uncomfortable with the material, others felt unprepared or were unwilling to teach it, and even for those educators who were comfortable with RULER, teaching the skills was not enough. This led us to look beyond theories on emotional development and emotional intelligence. In doing so, it became clear that the context in which RULER instruction occurs was critical to integrate into the model. Accordingly, we adapted the RULER model to incorporate ecological systems theory, which specifies that myriad and interrelated aspects of settings (e.g., schools) influence student development, especially the adults in these settings (Bronfenbrenner & Morris, 1998). We modified the content and strategy for implementing RULER by integrating the teaching of emotional intelligence into the academic curriculum and provided opportunities for all adult stakeholders (e.g., school leaders, teachers, staff, and family members) to learn and then apply these skills in their daily interactions.

It also became clear when we watched teachers engaging with students about emotions that the climate in which the conversations occurred were impacting how openly children were discussing their feelings about a topic. Teachers who created healthy emotional climates for students—those who demonstrated warmth and respect toward their students, who were sensitive to their students' needs, who demonstrated a genuine interest in their students' ideas, who expressed the belief that these skills were teachable, and who were generally more positive and less cynical—led very different conversations about emotions than teachers who were just going through the motions of doing a lesson (see Garibaldi, Ruddy, Kendziora, & Osher, Chapter 23, this volume).

Two theories provided plausible explanations for what we observed in the field: self-determination theory and implicit theories of intelligence. Self-determination theory posits that key student outcomes (e.g., academic performance, well-being, and health) are contingent upon students' basic developmental needs for caring and supportive relationships being met, which includes students feeling that their opinions count and are respected (Deci & Ryan, 1985; Deci, Vallerand, Pelletier, & Ryan, 1991). When students' needs for competence, autonomy, and relatedness have been met, they are more self-motivated and psychologically healthy (Ryan & Deci, 2000). Implicit theories of intelligence refer to the mindset individuals have about their abilities, intellect, and talent, as either a "fixed" mindset (believing these qualities are stable and not malleable) or a "growth" mindset (believing these qualities are malleable and based on perseverance and experience; Dweck, 2000). Creating a climate that shapes a growth mindset, provides students with care and support, and also makes students feel empowered to learn and respected by adults and peers became another component of the RULER model (see also Catalano, Berglund, Ryan, Lonczak, & Hawkins, 2004; National Research Council & Institute of Medicine, 2002, 2004).

As we improved our theory about what content to incorporate into RULER and the most effective way to deliver it, our outcomes—including academic performance, relationship quality, and health and well-being—also improved, reinforcing the importance of using theory to guide our approach (Brackett, Rivers, Reyes, & Salovey, 2012; Reyes, Brackett, Rivers, White, & Salovey, 2012). In the next section, we present a framework for different theories that inform SEL efforts.

Theoretical Approaches for SEL

In this section we review some of the major categories of theories that can inform SEL content and implementation strategies. The categories include systems theories, learning theories, child development theories, information-processing theories, and behavior change theories.

Systems Theories

The environment or setting in which students and adults learn and teach is a critical variable impacting development. Thus, theories that both identify and explain how the environment impacts child outcomes must inform SEL practices. Accordingly, this review begins with systems theories, as the theories discussed in subsequent sections must be applied within the consideration of the system as a whole.

Systems theories, such as ecological systems theory, articulate that characteristics of the contexts in which children and adults spend their time contribute to outcomes (Bronfenbrenner & Morris, 1998; Tseng & Seidman, 2007). Taking into consideration how complex systems such as schools operate and influence student outcomes can guide decisions for fitting SEL into different levels of the school system. School administrators, teachers, and support staff have different roles and relationships to children and to each other. Furthermore, different norms govern behavior in each of these roles, and people in each of these roles wield differential power within the system. It follows then that SEL content and training strategies must address the norms, needs, and skills levels of each group of adults within the system. Examining and understanding the setting of a school—commonly referred to as the school's culture and climate (Hoy & Miskel, 2012)—is critical in order to design an SEL approach that addresses the many systems variables that can impact its quality of implementation and sustainability. If these variables are not considered and explicitly accounted for, then the approach's potential impact on child outcomes may be jeopardized (see Mart, Weissberg, & Kendziora, Chapter 32, this volume). The theories discussed in subsequent sections are relevant to developing and implementing SEL strategies for individuals within and across the school setting.

Learning Theories

Because most SEL initiatives share the same goal—to enhance social, emotional, and academic learning—learning theories should serve as a foundation to their design. In this section we discuss social learning theory and adult learning theory.

Social learning theory posits that social interactions, including role modeling, verbal instruction, and supervised feedback and support, influence the acquisition of new behavior (Bandura, Adams, & Beyer, 1977). The Raising Healthy Children program leverages various aspects of social learning theory by involving the parents of students, so that information, skills, and behaviors introduced through the program *in school* can be modeled, incentivized, and practiced *at home* (Catalano et al., 2003). In addition to parenting workshops on program components and special topics (e.g., how to support student success, family management skills), parents receive monthly newsletters and can receive in-home services if their child has behavior or academic problems.

Social learning theory is especially relevant for SEL program design because the success of any approach relies in large part on school administrators, teachers, and support staff. These adults are responsible for modeling emotional skills and positive social behaviors, as well as implementing and supporting programming (Elias, Zins, Graczyk, & Weissberg, 2003). One program that aligns with this theory is Cultivating Awareness and Resilience in Education (CARE), which addresses the skills of the adults involved in children's education by providing them with instruction on emotional skills, practice with mindfulness and stress reduction techniques, and exercises in listening and compassion (Jennings, 2011). CARE's training opportunities help educators to experience and understand the value of emotional skills, as well as the enhanced well-being and reduced stress that can result from developing these skills. These experiences make educators more likely to model the skills they want to see their students demonstrate, as well as create more positive climates in their classrooms and schools.

Adult learning theories can inform the specific training and instructional components for adults. These theories focus on how new information is presented and how instruction can be tailored to the unique characteristics of adult learners. Six principles have been identified as important for integrating into adult education: (1) clear articulation of the value of learning, (2) responsibility of adults for their own learning, (3) tying new information to past experiences and prior knowledge, (4) goal-oriented instruction with organized course objectives, (5) presentation of practical applications, and (6) respect from instructors who work with adult learners as partners (Knowles, Holton, & Swanson, 2011). Adult learning theory also can guide decisions about the focus and pace of instruction when training and coaching adult educators on SEL content and implementation protocols, so that learning can be optimized (Garet, Porter, Desimone, Birman, & Yoon, 2001). The developers of Responsive Classroom, for example, reference adult learning theory as a guide in determining the levels of professional development and support services they provide (Rimm-Kaufman & Sawyer, 2004). These services include introductory workshops, a 1-week initial training, onsite consulting services, customized follow-up workshops, as well as structured meetings to facilitate building teams within each school to sustain the program over time and ensure quality results.

Theories of Child Development

Because children are the primary focus of SEL efforts, theories of child development are useful in designing age- and culturally appropriate lessons that incorporate scenarios, language, and activities that match the cognitive, social, and emotional levels of children. Most approaches to SEL include lessons and materials that are tailored to the developmental level of specific age groups. Multiple offerings within an approach typically are based on grade or school level (elementary, middle, or high school). For example, Roots of Empathy offers distinct curricula for children in kindergarten, lower elementary, upper elementary, and middle school classrooms (Gordon, 2005). These grade-specific curricula are implemented in order to foster the continuous development of empathy and social problem-solving skills, among other skills, in children ages 5 to 14 years.

Theories of emotional development also are critical to understanding the level of emotional and social skills students typically possess at different ages, as well as the types of information and experiences students require in order to develop skills such as identifying, understanding, and managing their emotions. Some relevant theories include discrete emotion theory (Darwin, 1872/1965; Izard, 1991), the circumplex model of core affect (Russell, 1980), and functionalist approaches to emotions (Campos, Mumme, Kermoian, & Campos, 1994; Sroufe, 1995). The Promoting Alternative THinking Strategies (PATHS) also has its roots in theory on emotional development, specifically psychoanalytic developmental theory (Kusché & Greenberg, 1994). PATHS emphasizes the importance of attending to and leveraging emotions as opposed to repressing or stifling them. Among many skills, children receive age-appropriate instruction in identifying, labeling, expressing, and managing feelings, including understanding the differences between feelings and behavior.

Theories of Information Processing

Information-processing theories emerge from evidence showing that information may be perceived, acquired, retained, accessed, and used differently depending on how that information is presented (McGuire, 1972). Information-processing theories put forth approaches for optimizing short- and long-term memory and, in turn, enhancing retention and accessibility of new information (Goldman, 1997). By way of example, social information-processing theory provides a model of how children interpret social cues and make decisions based on their past experiences, as well as their goals for the situation, the outcomes they anticipate, and their self-efficacy (Crick & Dodge, 1994).

Several SEL approaches have turned to social information-processing theories to guide instruction on metacognitive problem solving. The elaboration likelihood model, for example, underscores the importance of making information salient to learners, rehearsing new information, categorizing it in meaningful ways, and associating it with visual images (Petty, Barden, & Wheeler, 2009; Petty & Cacioppo, 1986). Using picture or word cues, analogies, graphic organizers, acronyms, or slogans are examples of approaches grounded in this theoretical model. PATHS illustrates how information-processing theories can be applied in SEL practice with visual and word cues, information rehearsal, and presentation of SEL strategies within an age-appropriate story to contribute to retention (Kusché & Greenberg, 1994). Specifically, PATHS facilitates students in learning how to control their own behavior and solve problems effectively with a "Control Signals" poster. This poster resembles a three-colored traffic light, each color representing a different strategy in a few simple words: red for "Stop–Calm Down," yellow for "Go Slow–Think," and green for "Go–Try My Plan." Another strategy employed by PATHS, the "turtle technique," refers to a three-step method of calming down. The three steps are (1) stopping, (2) taking a breath, and (3) stating the problem and how one is feeling. The turtle technique is taught through a story about a wise turtle that teaches a young turtle the process. Students review and practice applying these strategies in various real-life and fictitious scenarios. The rich visualization helps children retain the steps of the technique.

Theories of Behavior Change

One major goal of SEL is to change behavior—both that of individuals (children *and* adults) and that of organizations, in terms of how schools operate. Many SEL initiatives function to create learning environments that develop the whole child, so that students have their social, emotional, and academic needs met. SEL programming also fosters behaviors among children and adults that facilitate learning (e.g., paying attention, using engaging instructional techniques), encourage prosocial actions (e.g., being cooperative and kind to others, expressing care and support), and enhance health and well-being (e.g., being physically active; making healthy choices related to food, alcohol, or safe sex). Theories of behavior change provide an essential repertoire of approaches to guide SEL at individual and organizational levels. By explaining what motivates and sustains behavior change, this set of theories can guide decisions about how SEL strategies are integrated into schools, including who delivers it and when, and where and how it is presented.

The social development model posits that children learn both prosocial and antisocial patterns of behavior from their social environments. It specifies that opportunities for involvement, skills, and reinforcements influence how children engage with their families and peers in and out of school and what types of attachments, commitments, and beliefs they form, as well as what types of choices they make (Catalano & Hawkins, 1996). Furthermore, the social development model suggests that social bonds between a child and a particular group, such as individuals at a school, encourage the child to act in accordance with the values, norms, and belief systems that are a part of that group. Raising Healthy Children, one SEL approach that is informed by this model, focuses on enhancing bonds to school as a means to reducing risky and antisocial behaviors and increasing positive development (Catalano et al., 2004).

Social cognitive theory asserts that behavior is determined by an individual's beliefs about the social and physical environment (Bandura, 1986). For example, if an individual believes that adopting a new behavior will lead to a desired outcome, then that person will be more likely to adopt a new behavior. Behavior change will be even more likely when the individual highly values that outcome. If, however, the individual lacks confidence in his or her ability to adopt that new behavior, then behavior change is less likely. The Too Good for Drugs and Violence programs (Mendez Foundation, 2000) leverage elements of social cognitive theory in their implementation strategies by correcting student misperceptions of others' behaviors (e.g., providing statistics on how many students their age actually abuse alcohol, which usually occurs at a much lower rate than many students assume), emphasizing the value of prosocial skills and behaviors, using role models, and focusing on skills for resisting pressures specific to the various social networks and physical environments in their lives.

Two other relevant social cognitive theories are the theory of planned behavior (Ajzen, 1988; Conner & Sparks, 2005) and its extension, the theory of reasoned action (Fishbein & Ajzen, 2010). These theories posit that changing intentions to engage in a behavior are essential for behavior change to occur, and that attitudes about the behavior, beliefs about one's ability to engage in the behavior (i.e., self-efficacy), as well as perceptions of social norms (e.g., is everyone doing it?) influence intentions to engage in the behavior. These theories can help developers of SEL approaches consider the beliefs held by individuals or groups about behaviors, then integrate into their program component mechanisms to modify belief systems so that they support behavior change. One example of this approach is Second Step, which provides teachers with tools to lead discussions and role-playing activities that focus on the value of considering perspectives of others who are different, challenges negative views of conflict by teaching that disagreement can be helpful as long as it is respectful, asks students to consider the role of the bystander in bullying, and debunks myths about substance abuse.

Taking into consideration how people and organizations progress toward behavior change in various stages of motivation, intention to change behavior, and behavioral engagement, is also important for effective SEL strategy development. The transtheoretical model of behavior, for example, examines the cognitive, emotional, and social processes that occur during the stages of behavior change (Prochaska & DiClemente, 1984; Prochaska, Redding, & Evers, 2008). Information on a person's or group's stage of behavior change, including the thoughts and attitudes the person or group holds, the feelings experienced, and the social supports in place can guide intervention efforts, so that communications and strategies are tailored accordingly. For instance, consider a school administrator who knows that one teacher in her school feels very comfortable with and excited about teaching social and emotional skills to students, that another thinks school is not the appropriate venue for SEL instruction, and that yet another questions whether or not there will be support and resources for the program to be effective. Knowing the teachers' status in terms of different stages of behavior change will help this administrator address these issues directly when attempting to get staff on board with an SEL implementation plan.

Another behavior change theory is the diffusion of innovation theory, which explains how innovations are accepted and adopted within settings and, accordingly, how innovations can be designed and integrated most effectively (Greenhalgh, Robert, MacFarlane, Bate, & Kyuriakidou, 2004; Rogers, 2003). Similar to the transtheoretical model, this theory assumes that the adoption of a new approach unfolds within a setting over time, and constituents within the environment are categorized by their stage in the adoption process (e.g., "early adopters," "late adopters"). This theory suggests flexibility in delaying or extending training and coaching over time, so that late adopters have the necessary supports when they eventually are ready to embrace programming (Atkins, Hoagwood, Kutash, & Seidman, 2010). Accordingly, leaders can be leveraged to enhance diffusion (e.g., a superintendent may decide to stagger a districtwide rollout based on buy-in of teachers in each school), assess quality of implementation (e.g., evaluations of implementation fidelity can acknowledge teacher characteristics and look at improvement of individual teachers over time), and identify program modifications that would encourage adoption (e.g., a principal may hold a staff meeting to discuss attitudes and barriers toward adopting a new SEL approach and modify implementation accordingly) (Atkins et al., 2008; Locock, Dopson, Chambers, & Gabbay, 2001). Accounting for how eager various stakeholders in a school are to adopt an SEL approach and being sensitive and supportive of those in various stages of adoption can make the program easier to implement and sustain.

Theory and the SEL Process: A Strategic Approach

In the previous section we reviewed theories that inform various approaches to SEL. The role of theory in guiding SEL programmatic content (e.g., what should be taught to whom) was reflected in the descriptions and examples of learning theories, child development theories, and information-processing theories. Behavior change theories, primarily, were described as guides for strategies of implementation (e.g., who delivers the approach and how is it delivered). Theory about how systems function undergirds the application of these theories and needs to be considered in designing both SEL programmatic content and its implementation.

Inarguably, the efficacy of an SEL initiative in achieving targeted goals and enhancing student behavior and performance depends in large part on the quality with which the program or strategy is implemented (Graczyk et al., 2000). Thus, monitoring the progress and impact of an SEL approach is essential. Formal and informal feedback should be collected from staff members, parents, students, and outside observers as the approach is being introduced and rolled out. This information can be used to assess and improve implementation fidelity, evaluate achievement of outcomes, guide modifications for improvement, and ultimately increase the likelihood that positive effects in students and school climates will be obtained and sustained (Domitrovich & Greenberg, 2000). Theory can help identify which variables are the most important to assess, how to assess them, and how to use such data to enhance programmatic content and strategies, implementation, and the achievement of targeted outcomes across diverse settings (e.g., in rural vs. urban schools; in general education vs. special education classrooms).

Program developers, as well as practitioners, can look to theories that support SEL to find the answers to their questions about designing, refining, implementing, and adapting effective SEL ventures. Table 2.1 includes a guide for this process.

Which Theory?

Our purpose in this chapter is to emphasize the importance of theory for designing successful SEL programming. We have described various theories that inform SEL efforts. Currently, no single theory is ascendant in the field of SEL or viewed as the "best." Two additional points are important: (1) one theory can be helpful for multiple aspects of SEL programming, and (2) multiple theories can be useful for the same program. For instance, different aspects of systems theory may help to determine which groups to target and outcomes upon which to focus; what content target populations need to receive in order to achieve these outcomes; how content should be delivered to maximize acquisition, retention, and application; and how to evaluate, modify, and sustain an SEL approach.

It is also possible to apply more than one theory in order to develop the most coherent and effective content and implementation strategy. Some theories may better provide information on *what* needs to be changed in order to promote student outcomes, and other theories may offer guidance on *how* to change it or *in what context* it can be changed. Still others may explain the best *ways to assess, modify*, and *sustain* an approach. Multiple theories can be merged to inform a single, cohesive SEL approach that includes its programmatic components and implementation strategies. Ultimately, the best approaches to SEL will combine multiple theories into a unique synergy to support each piece of programming from development to implementation, to evaluation to sustainment, so that the desired outcomes are achieved.

Conclusion and Future Directions

Our goals in this chapter are threefold: (1) to underline the importance of theory in the development of approaches to SEL, (2) to shed light on some of the various theories that inform current SEL approaches and have the potential to inform the future of SEL strategy development, and (3) to begin thinking about the types of questions that developers of SEL approaches should ask in order to determine how theory can inform each piece of program design. We described the essential role of theory in developing, implementing, evaluating, and sustaining an intervention.

By offering a process by which theory can be applied strategically to developing, implementing, evaluating, and sustaining SEL approaches, we hope to move the field of SEL forward. New strategies are being developed and applied every year across the globe. As novel approaches are created and implemented, the benefit of theory cannot be ignored. Ample time, thought, and resources must be devoted to examination of theoretical work to explain both how individuals and systems targeted by an approach to SEL function, and how the problems the program attempts to address can best be solved. The mission of the developer of any approach to SEL must be to identify the appropriate theories, understand how their insight can be applied to elements of program design, and determine how to transform abstract, theoretical ideas into specific, practical methods. A heightened focus on this agenda in the field of SEL could translate into larger strides toward a more socially and emotionally skilled society.

TABLE 2.1. Applying Theory to SEL Programming

Component of SEL process	Questions to ask
Programmatic content	*What are the goals of the SEL approach?* • What positive outcomes and problems are being targeted? • What beliefs, attitudes, and behaviors will the approach address? • What knowledge or skills will be taught by the approach? • What type of lessons, activities, messages, and other content will best deliver this information? *Who does the program target?* • Based on the targeted group's age, education, culture, race, socioeconomic status, or other variables, what can theory tell us about how this population learns and processes information? • Which theories will help us to understand this group's developmental capacities, concerns, values, and interests, and how these can be leveraged to achieve outcomes? *In what types of settings does the target population spend its time?* • What can theory tell us about how the targeted group's school, home, and community environments function? • How can theory guide us to know what content should be delivered in each setting to best achieve desired outcomes?
Implementation strategies	*Who are the key leaders who will make implementation decisions?* • How can theory help us to better understand how they learn and process information? • How can theory tell us about best practices for garnering and maintaining their support? • How will professional development and programming be implemented to reflect these best practices? *Who will promote the program and gain buy in from stakeholders?* • What can theory tell us about how we can leverage these opinion leaders? • How should professional development and program delivery be tailored to the characteristics and needs of stakeholders? *Who will implement the program?* • How do the program implementers usually process new information and acquire new skills? • How can this knowledge be translated into professional development strategies? • How can program implementation be customized to suit the needs and characteristics of program deliverers? *What characteristics of the school and home environments may promote or impede the successful implementation?* • How can theory help us to better understand how implementation protocols can be adapted to suit diverse school and home contexts?

References

Ajzen, I. (1988). *Attitudes, personality, and behavior.* Chicago: Dorsey Press.

Atkins, M. S., Frazier, S. L., Leathers, S. J., Graczyk, P. A., Talbott, E., Jakobsons, L., et al. (2008). Teacher key opinion leaders and mental health consultation in urban low-income schools. *Journal of Consulting and Clinical Psychology, 76*(5), 905–908.

Atkins, M. S., Hoagwood, K. E., Kutash, K., & Seidman, E. (2010). Toward the integration of education and mental health in schools. *Administration and Policy in Mental Health and Mental Health Services Research, 37*(1–2), 40–47.

Bandura, A. (1986). *Social foundations of thought and action: A social cognitive theory.* Englewood Cliffs, NJ: Prentice-Hall.

Bandura, A., Adams, N. E., & Beyer, J. (1977). Cognitive processes mediating behavioral change. *Journal of Personality and Social Psychology, 35*(3), 125–139.

Brackett, M. A., Rivers, S. E., Maurer, M., Elbertson, N. A., & Kremenitzer, J. P. (2011). Creating emotionally literate learning environments. In M. A. Brackett, J. P. Kremenitzer, M. Maurer, S. E. Rivers, N. A. Elberston, & M. D. Carpenter (Eds.), *Creating emotionally literate learning environments* (pp. 1–21). Port Chester, NY: National Professional Resources.

Brackett, M. A., Rivers, S. E., Reyes, M. R., & Salovey, P. (2012). Enhancing academic performance and social and emotional competence with the RULER Feeling Words Curriculum. *Learning and Individual Differences, 22*(2), 218–224.

Brackett, M. A., Rivers, S. E., & Salovey, P. (2011). Emotional intelligence: implications for personal, social, academic, and workplace success. *Social and Personality Psychology Compass, 5*(1), 88–103.

Bronfenbrenner, U., & Morris, P. A. (1998). The ecology of developmental processes. In R. M. Lerner (Ed.), *Handbook of child psychology: Vol. 1. Theoretical models of human development,* (5th ed., pp. 993–1028). New York: Wiley.

Campos, J. J., Mumme, D. L., Kermoian, R., & Campos, R. G. (1994). A functionalist perspective on the nature of emotion. *Monographs of the Society for Research in Child Development, 59*(2–3), 284–303.

Collaborative for Academic, Social, and Emotional Learning (CASEL). (2013a). Effective social and emotional learning programs. Retrieved July 26, 2013, from *http://casel.org/guide.*

Collaborative for Academic, Social, and Emotional Learning (CASEL). (2013b). Mission and vision. Retrieved July 26, 2013, from *http://casel.org/about-us/mission-vision.*

Collaborative for Academic, Social, and Emotional Learning (CASEL). (2013c). What is social and emotional learning (SEL)? Retrieved July 26, 2013, from *http://casel.org/why-it-matters/what-is-sel.*

Catalano, R. F., Berglund, L., Ryan, J. A. M., Lonczak, H. S., & Hawkins, J. D. (2004). Positive youth development in the United States: Research findings on evaluations of positive youth development programs. *Annals of the American Academy of Political and Social Science, 591*(1), 98–124.

Catalano, R. F., & Hawkins, J. D. (1996). The social development model. In J. D. Hawkins (Ed.), *Delinquency and crime* (pp. 149–197). New York: Cambridge University Press.

Catalano, R. F., Mazza, J. J., Harachi, T. W., Abbott, R. D., Haggarty, K. P., & Fleming, C. P. (2003). Raising healthy children through enhancing social development in elementary school: Results after 1.5 years. *Journal of School Psychology, 41*(2), 143–164.

Crick, N. R., & Dodge, K. A. (1994). A review and reformulation of social information-processing mechanisms in children's social adjustment. *Psychological Bulletin, 115,* 74–101.

Conner, M., & Sparks, P. (2005). The theory of planned behavior and health behaviors. In M. C. P. Norman (Ed.), *Predicting health behavior: Research and practice with social cognition models* (2nd ed., pp. 170–222). Maidenhead, UK: Open University Press.

Darwin, C. (1965). *The expression of the emotions in man and animals.* Chicago: University of Chicago Press. (Original work published 1872)

Deci, E. L., & Ryan, R. M. (1985). *Intrinsic motivation and self-determination in human behavior.* New York: Plenum Press.

Deci, E. L., Vallerand, R. J., Pelletier, L. G., & Ryan, R. M. (1991). Motivation and education: The self-determination perspective. *Educational Psychologist, 26*(3–4), 325–346.

Denham, S. A. (1998). *Emotional development in young children.* New York: Guilford Press.

Domitrovich, C. E., & Greenberg, M. T. (2000). The study of implementation: Current findings from effective programs that prevent mental disorders in school-aged children. *Journal of Educational and Psychological Consultation, 11*(2), 193–221.

Dweck, C. S. (2000). *Self-theories: Their role in motivation, personality, and development.* New York: Taylor & Francis.

Eisenberg, N., Fabes, R. A., Guthrie, I. K., & Reiser, M. (2000). Dispositional emotionality and regulation: Their role in predicting quality of social functioning. *Journal of Personality and Social Psychology, 78*(1), 136–157.

Elias, M. J., Zins, J. E., Graczyk, P. A., & Weissberg, R. P. (2003). Implementation, sustainability, and scaling up of social–emotional and academic innovations in public schools. *School Psychology Review, 32*(3), 303–319.

Elias, M. J., Zins, J. E., Weissberg, R. P., Frey, K. S., Greenberg, M. T., Haynes, N. M., et al. (1997). *Promoting social and emotional learning: Guidelines for educators.* Alexandria, VA: Association for Supervision and Curriculum Development.

Fine, S. E., Izard, C. E., Mostow, A. J., Trentacosta, C. J., & Ackerman, B. P. (2003). First grade emotion knowledge as a predictor of fifth grade self-reported internalizing behaviors in children from economically disadvantaged families. *Development and Psychopathology, 15*(2), 331–342.

Fishbein, M., & Ajzen, I. (2010). *Predicting and changing behavior: The reasoned action approach.* New York: Psychology Press.

Garet, M., Porter, A., Desimone, L., Birman, B., & Yoon, K. (2001). What makes professional development effective?: Analysis of a national sample of teachers. *American Education Research Journal, 38*, 915–945.

Goldman, S. R. (1997). Learning from text: Reflections on the past and suggestions for the future. *Discourse Processes, 23*(3), 357–398.

Gordon, M. (2005). *Roots of empathy: Changing the world child by child.* Toronto: Thomas Allen.

Graczyk, P. A., Weissberg, R. P., Payton, J. W., Elias, M. J., Greenberg, M. T., & Zins, J. E. (2000). Criteria for evaluating the quality of school-based social and emotional learning programs. In R. Bar-On & J. D. Parke (Eds.), *The handbook of emotional intelligence: Theory, development, assessment, and application at home, school and in the workplace* (pp. 391–410). San Francisco: Jossey-Bass.

Greenberg, M. T., Weissberg, R. P., O'Brien, M. U., Zins, J. E., Fredericks, L., Resnik, H., et al. (2003). Enhancing school-based prevention and youth development through coordinated social and emotional learning. *American Psychologist, 58*(6–7), 466–474.

Greenhalgh, M. T., Robert, G., MacFarlane, F., Bate, P., & Kyuriakidou, O. (2004). Diffusion of innovations in service organizations: Systematic review and recommendations. *Milbank Quarterly, 82*(4), 581–629.

Halberstadt, A. G., Denham, S. A., & Dunsmore, J. C. (2001). Affective social competence. *Social Development, 10*(1), 79–119.

Hoy, W., & Miskel, C. (2012). *Educational administration: Theory, research, and practice.* New York: McGraw-Hill Education.

Izard, C. E. (1991). *The psychology of emotions.* New York: Plenum Press.

Jennings, P. A. (2011). Promoting teachers' social and emotional competencies to support performance and reduce burnout. In A. Cohan & A. Honigsfeld (Eds.), *Breaking the mold of preservice and inservice teacher education: Innovative and successful practices for the 21st century* (pp. 133–143). Plymouth, UK: Rowman & Littlefield Education.

Knowles, M. S., Holton, E. F., & Swanson, R. A. (2011). *The adult learner: The definitive classic in adult education and human resource development.* Burlington, MA: Elsevier.

Kress, J. S., & Elias, M. J. (2006). Implementing school-based social and emotional learning programs: Navigating developmental crossroads. In I. Sigel & A. Renninger (Eds.), *Handbook of child psychology* (rev. ed., pp. 592–618). New York: Wiley.

Kusché, C. A., & Greenberg, M. T. (1994). The PATHS curriculum. Seattle, WA: Developmental Research and Programs.

Lewin, K. (1945). The research center for group dynamics at Massachusetts Institute of Technology. *Sociometry, 8*, 126–135.

Locock, L., Dopson, S., Chambers, D., & Gabbay, J. (2001). Understanding the role of opinion leaders in improving clinical effectiveness. *Social Science and Medicine, 53*(6), 745–757.

Maurer, M., Brackett, M. A., & Plain, F. (2004). *Emotional literacy in the middle school: A six-step program to promote social, emotional, and academic learning.* Port Chester, NY: National Professional Resources.

Mayer, J. D., & Salovey, P. (1997). What is emotional intelligence? In P. S. D. Sluyter (Ed.), *Emotional development and emotional intelligence: Educational implications* (pp. 3–31). New York: Basic Books.

McGuire, W. J. (1972). Attitude change: The information processing paradigm. In C. G. McClintock (Ed.), *Experimental social psychology* (pp. 118–138). New York: Holt, Rinehart & Winston.

Mendez Foundation. (2000). *Too good for drugs and violence in high school.* Tampa, FL: Author.

National Research Council & Institute of Medicine. (2002). *Community programs to promote youth development.* Washington, DC: National Academies Press.

National Research Council and Institute of Medicine. (2004). *Engaging schools: Fostering high school students' motivation to learn.* Washington, DC: National Academies Press.

Payton, J. W., Wardlaw, D. M., Graczyk, P. A., Bloodworth, M. R., Tompsett, C. J., & Weissberg, R. P. (2000). Social and emotional learning: A framework for promoting mental health and reducing risk behaviors in children and youth. *Journal of School Health, 70*(5), 179–185.

Petty, R. E., Barden, J., & Wheeler, S. C. (2009). The elaboration likelihood model of persuasion: Developing health promotions for sustained behavioral change. In R. J. DiClemente, R. A. Crosby, & M. Kegler (Eds.), *Emerging theories in health promotion practice and research* (2nd ed., pp. 185–214). San Francisco: Jossey-Bass.

Petty, R. E., & Cacioppo, J. T. (1986). The elaboration likelihood model of persuasion. In L. Berkowitz (Ed.). *Advances in experimental social psychology* (Vol. 19, pp. 123–205). New York: Academic Press.

Popper, K. R. (1957). Philosophy of science: A personal report. In C. A. Mace (Ed.), *British philosophy in mid-century* (pp. 155–189). London: Allen & Unwin.

Prochaska, J. O., & DiClemente, C. C. (1984). *The transtheoretical approach: Crossing traditional boundaries of change.* Homewood, IL: Dorsey Press.

Prochaska, J. O., Redding, C. A., & Evers, K. E. (2008). The transtheoretical model and stages of chance. In K. Glanz, B. Rimer, & K. Viswanath (Eds.), *Health behavior and health education: Theory, research and practice* (4th ed., pp. 97–121). San Francisco: Jossey-Bass.

Reyes, M. R., Brackett, M. A., Rivers, S. E., White, M., & Salovey, P. (2012). Classroom emotional climate, student engagement, and academic achievement. *Journal of Educational Psychology, 104*(3), 700–712.

Reynolds, P. D. (1971). *A primer in theory construction.* New York: Macmillan.

Rimm-Kaufman, S. E., & Sawyer, B. E. (2004). Primary-grade teachers' self-efficacy beliefs, attitudes toward teaching, and discipline and teaching practice priorities in relation to the "responsive classroom" approach. *Elementary School Journal, 104*(4), 321–330.

Rivers, S. E., Brackett, M. A., Reyes, M. R., Mayer, J. D., Caruso, D. R., & Salovey, P. (2012). Measuring emotional intelligence in early adolescence with the MSCEIT-YV: Psychometric properties and relationship with academic performance and psychosocial functioning. *Journal of Psychoeducational Assessment, 30*(4), 344–366.

Rogers, E. M. (2003). *Diffusion of innovations* (5th ed.). New York: Free Press.

Russell, J. A. (1980). A circumplex model of affect. *Journal of Personality and Social Psychology, 39*(6), 1161–1178.

Ryan, R. M., & Deci, E. L. (2000). Self-determination theory and the facilitation of instrinsic motivation, social development, and well-being. *Americal Psychologist, 55*, 68–78.

Saarni, C. (1999). *The development of emotional competence.* New York: Guilford Press.

Salovey, P., & Mayer, J. D. (1990). Emotional intelligence. *Imagination, Cognition and Personality, 9*(3), 185–211.

Sroufe, L. A. (1995). *Emotional development.* New York: Cambridge University Press.

Tseng, V., & Seidman, E. (2007). A systems framework for understanding social settings. *American Journal of Community Psychology, 39*(3–4), 217–228.

Wacker, J. G. (1998). A definition of theory: research guidelines for different theory-building research methods in operations management. *Journal of Operations Management, 16*(4), 361–385.

Zins, J. E., Bloodworth, M. R., Weissberg, R. P., & Walberg, H. J. (2004). The scientific base linking social and emotional learning to school success. In J. E. Zins, R. P. Weissberg, M. C. Wang, & H. J. Walberg (Eds.), *Building academic success on social and emotional learning: What does the research say?* (pp. 3–22). New York: Teachers College Press.

CHAPTER 3

Integrating SEL with Related Prevention and Youth Development Approaches

Maurice J. Elias, Larry Leverett, Joan Cole Duffell, Neil Humphrey, Cesalie Stepney, and Joseph Ferrito

> Successful schools ensure that all students master reading, writing, math, and science. They also foster a good understanding of history, literature, arts, foreign languages, and diverse cultures. However, most educators, parents, students, and the public support a broader educational agenda that also involves enhancing students' social–emotional competence, character, health, and civic engagement . . . In addition to producing students who are culturally literate, intellectually reflective, and committed to lifelong learning, high-quality education should teach young people to interact in socially skilled and respectful ways; to practice positive, safe, and healthy behaviors; to contribute ethically and responsibly to their peer group, family, school, and community; and to possess basic competencies, work habits, and values as a foundation for meaningful employment and engaged citizenship.
>
> —GREENBERG ET AL. (2003, pp. 466–467)

Every school in the United States, and indeed, every school in the world, addresses the social–emotional and character development of the students who pass through its doors. Indeed, it is impossible to bring adults and children together for long periods of time over multiple weeks, months, and years and not influence children's competencies and the kind of persons they will become when putting those competencies to use.

These processes, for many years, have been informal and haphazard. Figure 3.1 shows two images. The top one illustrates the kind of schoolhouse that is most prevalent, filled with evidence-based social and emotional learning (SEL) and character development, prevention, service learning, and related programs that are disconnected and uncoordinated. When presented to educators, this schoolhouse strikes many as similar to the schools in which they work, and they resonate with the negative effects of fragmentation on staff morale and student engagement and learning (Elias, 2009). The bottom image illustrates a schoolhouse in which various SEL and related efforts are comprehensive and coordinated, and linked to academics, parents, and community involvement, including after-school programming. In such schools, students understand that they need academic and SEL competencies to accomplish valued goals; to contribute to the greater good, as well as their own good; and to strive to be persons of sound character and health. Correspondingly, the educators in those schools understand that for students to build their SEL competencies, it is necessary for what happens within a school to be not only coordinated but also synergistically connected to efforts in other schools in the district and the efforts of parents, after-school program providers, and com-

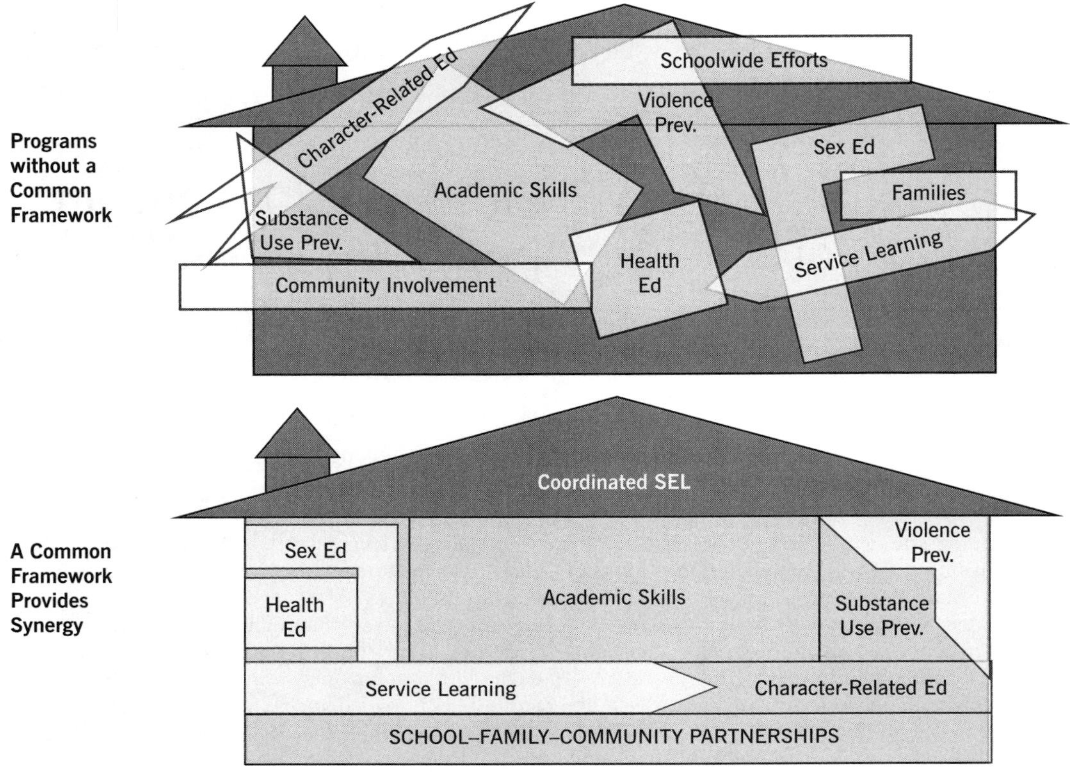

FIGURE 3.1. Coordinated SEL and related approaches: The jumbled and synergized schoolhouses.

munity support resources. Other chapters in this volume focus on coordinating SEL policies and practices at the district level (Mart, Weissberg, & Kendziora, Chapter 32, this volume) and linking to parents and the community (Garbacz, Swanger-Gagné, & Sheridan, Chapter 16, this volume). Here, the focus is on coordination within schools, a necessary first step toward more systemic efforts.

The cornerstone of SEL efforts is the delivery of essential skills and competencies to students, without which children are at a distinct disadvantage when navigating classrooms, school, workplace, civic, and even family settings. Some children are fortunate enough to go through experiences with parents and other loved ones, educators, and communities that afford them the opportunity to have these competencies nurtured and refined. However, it is evident that too many children do not have these experiences, or at least do not have them consistently, and as a result, struggle academically and socially, and find themselves on a path toward problem behaviors and academic underachievement relative to their abilities.

The skills students need have been elaborated elsewhere, but in summary, they are represented by these domains (Collaborative for Academic, Social, and Emotional Learning [CASEL], 2013):

- *Self-awareness*: especially recognition and labeling of one's feelings and accurately assessing one's strengths and limitations.
- *Self-management*: including emotion regulation, delaying gratification, managing stress, motivating oneself, and setting and working toward achieving goals.
- *Social awareness*: involving the ability to empathize and take others' perspectives, and recognize and mobilize diverse and available supports.

- *Relationship skills*: among which are clear communication, accurate listening, cooperation, nonviolent and constructive conflict resolution, and knowing when and how to be a good team player and a leader.
- *Responsible decision making*: defined as making ethical choices based on consideration of feelings, goals, alternatives and outcomes, and planning and enacting solutions with potential obstacles anticipated.

In the nearly two decades since these skills were articulated (Elias et al., 1997), much has been learned about the ecological context within which SEL skills are developed and internalized, perhaps best characterized as a "maelstrom of many competing forces" (Elias, Kranzler, Parker, Kash, & Weissberg, 2014). Hence, the presentation of SEL skills in programs may be seen, at best, as a necessary but not sufficient condition for skills acquisition. Incorporating these skills into a framework that becomes part of children's identities requires coordination of emotion, cognition, and behavior, over time. For skills to become part of children's regular social performance, they need to be learned, supported, and valued in a range of contexts. When schools function successfully as one of those contexts, they tend to share five main characteristics (Elias et al., 1997, 2014):

1. A school climate that articulates specific themes, character elements, or values, such as respect, responsibility, fairness, and honesty, and conveys an overall sense of purpose for attending school.
2. Explicit instruction and practice in skills for participatory competence.
3. Developmentally appropriate instruction in ways to promote health and prevent specific problems.
4. Services and systems that enhance students' coping skills and provide social support for handling transitions, crises, and conflicts.
5. Widespread, systematic opportunities for positive contributory service.

Embedded within item 4 is the way in which so-called Tier 1, 2, and 3 interventions must be coordinated within schools as part of comprehensive SEL. These tiers can be viewed respectively as representing universal interventions given to all students, interventions given to students showing early signs of difficulty or failure to acquire the skills being taught in universal interventions, and those provide for students with significant behavioral–emotional difficulties. Synergy is created in the schoolhouse when the same focal skills from the universal programs are also the focus of Tier 2 and 3 interventions. This runs counter to the standard practice of keeping these levels, and often the implementing personnel and systems, separate. The Social Decision Making/Social Problem Solving (SDM/SPS) program provides examples of how this can work well (Elias & Bruene, 2005). All students in a school (grades K–8) get the SDM/SPS curriculum; those having difficulty are provided with supplemental modules included in the curriculum or use a computer-based tutorial program, Ripple Effects, modified to be in alignment with the SDM/SPS curriculum. Students involved in special education or anticipatory guidance for transitions, crises, and conflicts are provided with SDM/SPS-based skills-building activities, including an SDM laboratory, pedagogically adjusted for their context (Elias, 2004; Elias & Bruene, 2005).

As reviewed elsewhere (e.g., Rimm-Kaufman & Hulleman, Chapter 10, this volume), there is extensive research showing a positive and powerful impact of well-implemented, skills-focused, pedagogically sound SEL programs. Among the areas of impact are improved social and emotional skills, more positive attitudes toward self and others, improved social behavior, reduced conduct and emotional difficulties, and meaningfully higher levels of academic performance (Durlak, Weissberg, Dymnicki, Taylor, & Schellinger, 2011). This is complemented by evidence that schools with the characteristics noted earlier create the most hospitable contexts for student growth and learning (Berkowitz, 2011; Berman, Chang, & Barnes, 2012; Leverett, 2008; Lickona & Davidson, 2005; Pasi, 2001; Reeves, 2009).

Despite the impressive evidence for the kinds of schools in which children thrive academically and socially, there is not broad consensus about the need to change our education system in this direction. Even among those who do agree about this goal, there are differences in how to go about it. The stakes are truly high: Education has emerged as a lead institution in preparing learners to achieve success in a world that requires them to know more, solve complex problems working with others, manage diversity, resolve conflict, and maintain a sense of efficacy needed for setting and achieving personal goals and wellness (Cowen, 1994; Elias et al., 1997). Because of social inequities, as well as the challenges of a globalized society characterized by a rapid pace of change, there are no U.S. school districts that can justifiably ignore the urgency for all students to be equipped with the skills, knowledge, and disposition necessary to negotiate the many challenges related to productive living in the 21st century. The answer is not to prepare students for a life of tests but rather to prepare them for the tests of life. For this to happen, schoolhouses cannot afford to be jumbled, and they must meet the challenge of preparing students with the full array of skills and perspectives needed for college and career success, and a life of contribution and caring. SEL is an essential aspect of this.

As the number of schools and districts concerned with academic success of all learners steadily increases, there will be growing recognition of SEL's essential role. Therefore, as districts and schools embrace SEL as a core component of the mission to prepare learners to succeed academically and socially, the technology for sustained implementation of schoolwide SEL must also scale up. This scaling up inevitably requires a coordinated effort, so that students, and educators, are not beset with a jumble of well-meaning but fragmented programs, and school can become places where, in James Comer's words, all children can "catch" character and SEL from those around them in ways that become integral to their lives. We use the word "all" intentionally because, unlike experimental studies in which hypotheses can be "proven" despite many participants not conforming to the predicted pattern, schools in practice need all students to thrive. "All" means *all.*

This chapter provides guidance to those seeking to understand and navigate the long road of creating the synergized schoolhouse shown in the bottom part of Figure 3.1. Other chapters in this volume provide information to consider the district-level context, parent and community involvement, and specific elements within the schoolhouse. Our focus is:

1. What are important considerations in bringing SEL into schools with other SEL or related programs directed toward similar goals, such as Positive Youth Development, so that coherent schoolwide integration can take place?
2. What are the challenges and pitfalls that will be faced by virtually everyone seeking to bring coordinated SEL into their schools, and what is the best guidance available for understanding and addressing these challenges? Included in this are the areas, such as urban education, in which future progress will be of greatest importance for those interested in advancing the field of SEL and creating positive school cultures and climates for learning.

Seven Activities to Guide Coordinated School-Level SEL Implementation with Sustainability

We begin with the process of unjumbling the jumbled schoolhouse in Figure 3.1. In our view, which is based on a synthesis of literature and our collective experience of over a century of implementation in thousands of schools across literally all parts of the world, moving from the jumbled schoolhouse to the synergized schoolhouse requires a series of seven interrelated activities best organized within 8-week planning cycles that will most likely require 3 years to bring to fruition, depending on the starting point. There is no blueprint for the order in which these activities should be carried out, which is why the seventh of these activities—learning from others—is so important. Factors such as the history and present status of SEL-related programming, staff knowledge of SEL, school climate, sociodemographic factors, leadership style and history, and current mandates and priorities, as well as the school's capacities, will determine the timing and sequencing of these activities.

Activity 1: Develop a school infrastructure that can integrate and support SEL

and positive school culture and climate development, and ongoing implementation into all aspects of school goals, priorities, programs, strategies, and initiatives. Some entity—a committee, work group, or team—must have responsibility for the long-term implementation of SEL-related approaches and for unjumbling the schoolhouse. This entity itself must grow in effectiveness and needs time and support to learn how to work and to problem-solve, to obtain administrative support, and to achieve and celebrate success. For this to happen, distributed leadership is essential, but with clear responsibilities to avoid fragmentation and ensure accountability. Consolidating infrastructures is also helpful. One school with which we worked put its SEL, discipline, morale, and antibullying committees under an encompassing umbrella of a School Culture and Climate Committee. Finally, we have found it helpful for such teams not to overreach (especially early in their formation), and instead use planning cycles that identify one primary goal and an action plan to accomplish it, in successive 8-week periods of time, to structure activities, keep efforts focused, and promote accountability.

Activity 2: Assess your schoolhouse. Education exists in an environment too often characterized by adding new programs and initiatives without explicit articulation with what already exists. This additive approach results in increased pressure and competition for time, resources, and focus within a school. Teachers and other educators experience frustration from the "flavor of the day" changes that are seldom integrated into an array of coordinated efforts to achieve instructional aims. Ultimately, there should be harmony across the five characteristics of effective schools noted earlier, with SEL as the integrative glue.

Assessing the schoolhouse requires careful examination of all SEL-related efforts taking place in a school, such as those involving culture and climate, character, antibullying, prevention, discipline, classroom management, positive behavioral interventions and supports (PBIS), or even multiple SEL programs. Also included are the approaches being used at Tiers 1, 2, and 3 of intervention. Consider also the expected/mandated behaviors of school professionals and their accountability systems. Examine informal routines, including those in the playground, cafeteria, hallways, and on buses. The goal is to examine how SEL skills and values are, and can better be, integrated across various schoolwide programs, procedures, policies, and routines. We have found it helpful to organize these by grade level, look at how transitions are articulated, and look for gaps, discontinuities, or inconsistencies. The SEL leadership committee plays a lead role in identifying ways to resolve discontinuities and harmonize discrepancies, even if this means making some modifications in existing structured, evidence-based programs. This is a multiyear task, and local factors will determine whether is it best to begin comprehensively within one or more grade levels, or schoolwide in a particular area (e.g., SEL programming or disciplinary procedures). Tools to assist in the process are available (Devaney, O'Brien, Resnik, Keister, & Weissberg, 2006), and it can be helpful to compare with CASEL's scope and sequence chart of SEL activities across grade levels (Elias et al., 1997, Appendix C) and comprehensive frameworks that have resulted from such an assessment process (e.g., Anchorage School District, 2013) in orienting one's efforts.

Activity 3: Assess your school's culture and climate. There are a variety of tools that can be used for assessing a school's culture and climate, from the perspective of students, staff, and/or parents. These can include surveys, walk-throughs, focus groups, and analysis of artifacts. Reports generated from culture and climate assessment can be shared with school leaders, staff members, and student leaders and priorities can be set for addressing school needs. Data should be presented by gender and ethnicity, as well as by grade level within the school and staff position, so that differential perceptions of the school culture and climate can be uncovered.

Activity 4: Articulate shared values, themes, and essential life habits. Schools must stand for something. Skills unaligned with values (or, as some schools prefer to call them, "themes" or "essential life habits") risk developing skills that may be used for antisocial ends. Examples of values that schools emphasize include responsibility, integrity, service, justice, respect, leadership, exploration, and organization. Often, schools have mottos or mission statements that are not enacted as part of the life of the school. In our experience, articulating schoolwide focal values and bringing them into alignment so that students are learning them within and across grade levels plays an essential role in reducing fragmentation and increasing the likelihood that students will become inspired. One conceptualization of this is the need to complement moral character with performance character, that is, the competencies to live according to cherished ideals (Lickona & Davidson, 2005). Shared values also become points of access for parents and community stakeholders.

When done properly, this is far more than slogans or posters on walls, or brief lessons covering core values. The field of Character Education has had a long and sustained focus on the school as the level of implementation. The Character Education Partnership (2013b) designates what it refers to as "National Schools of Character (NSOCs)," based on these schools' adhering to its 11 principles of character education. Among these principles is a clear set of values and empirical evidence that these values are carried through in all aspects of school organization, structure, social and academic programming, and relationships. Schools take multiple years to achieve this status, and they are not awarded without a site visit, complementing an extensive self-study with documentation. The site visitors are not only verifying the specific claims made by the schools but they are also looking for the pervasive sense of coherence within them, based on the themes–values–essential life habits that characterize those schools. Notably, in recent years, schools implementing SEL programs have been recognized as NSOCs but only in cases where the SEL programs were in all grade levels, and the language and focus of the SEL program was adopted schoolwide, including integration into academics and classroom routines and the discipline system.

Because Activity 4 has been less emphasized in the SEL world, we provide an example from Berkowitz (2011), drawing largely from his extensive work over two decades as the director of the Leadership Academy in Character Education (LACE), which has functioned for two decades to train, support, and network educational leaders seeking to bring SEL-related approaches into their school culture. In Berkowitz's analysis of many case examples, success requires a set of core beliefs and linked actions. These core beliefs (or values), noted below, can be accompanied by a variety of actions driven directed toward creating a school culture and skills focus that exemplifies them:

- The best way to make a more just and caring world is to make more just and caring people.
- The mandate of schools is fundamentally and broadly developmental and cannot be limited to the intellectual and academic; it must encompass the moral and civic development of students.
- For schools to optimally impact the development of student character (both moral and civic), they must be moral and democratic institutions, and this requires leaders who understand, prioritize, and have the leadership competencies to nurture such institutional growth.
- Schools must intentionally and relentlessly promote healthy relationships among all school community members, foster internalization of social and moral values through encouraging adults to model the kind of persons they wish students to become, and use pedagogical and organizational strategies so that all school community members are partners in the school.

Activity 5: Unify problem-solving strategies and other skills to be imparted. Programs vary in the specific skills they wish to emphasize, but often these differences are not fundamental. For example, students are taught many different steps to take for problem solving, decision making, self-awareness and self-management strategies, conflict resolution, and so forth, within SEL and related programs as well as across subject areas within grade levels, and then across grade levels (e.g., ICPS, Promoting Alternative Thinking Strategies [PATHS] Stoplight model, FIG TESPN [Feelings; Identification of the issue; Guiding oneself to a goal; Thinking of possibilities; Envisioning end results for each option; Selecting the best solution; Planning the procedure; and Noticing what happened]; cf. Elias et al., 1997). When presented to children without coherent articulation, the impact is likely to be more confusing than illuminating, with the learning less likely to find its way into children's minds, hearts, and actions. This leads to students' uncertainty as to how to solve real-life problems, especially when they are under stress. Also, many times these steps are simply presented to students but not actually taught and practiced with continued, reinforced use. Bringing these various steps and processes into alignment allows students to learn a common method within grade levels and build the likelihood of continuity or coordination across grade levels. This is no less true for any of the SEL skills domains—the language of self-regulation, emotional awareness, and the like, should be examined and a common vernacular used for SEL-related concepts and lessons. This may require modification of one or more existing, intact, evidence-based program. But the goal is to create a culture of caring, citizenship, and success and language is a key part of defining culture. Only when students are given consistent and ongoing opportunities to practice the skills can they become internalized and used when most needed in real-life peer and classroom situations and when students are faced with ethical/moral dilemmas.

Activity 6: Improve faculty readiness to teach SEL. Time must be taken to show how teaching or using SEL-related approaches aligns with responsibilities and expectations that faculty already have. This only happens when there is a deep understanding of the theory and literature and pedagogy of SEL. There cannot be rote implementation of a manual. The need for adaptation is constant in education, and the key to sustainability is the capacity to bring SEL into whatever standards, rubrics, and mandates come along. Hence, for successful SEL readiness, more time might be spent on conceptual understanding than on "training," since competent educators and school support staff should have the basic skills set to implement SEL approaches well if they are clearly and fully understood. At the time of this writing, schools were being asked to implement codes of student conduct and other antibullying-related procedures, the Common Core Curriculum Standards, and new teacher evaluation frameworks. SEL not only needs to be aligned and integrated with each of these, but their successful implementation also ultimately depends on SEL (Elias, 2014). Part of the infrastructure should include a regular review of how the actual language of the SEL approaches being used in the school become part of the code of conduct, discipline system, and classroom management, so that students literally hear the same words often. There are clear examples of school and district-level alignment of SEL with academic mandates even in the high-pressure context of low-achieving, disadvantaged urban schools (Elias & Leverett, 2011); core content standards emphasize problem solving, decision making, and critical thinking, all part of SEL, across content areas. Hargreaves (2009) believes that sustainability is generated by an inspiring vision and a strong sense of staff investment in and responsibility for maintaining the focus, elements, and pedagogy of an intervention despite contextual changes, with students as true partners in creating and maintaining change. This is why deep understanding of SEL is required on the part of teachers, and, ultimately, why is must become part of the preparation of all educators. Darling-Hammond (2009, p. 63) concurs: "There are no policies that can improve schools if the people in them are not armed with the knowledge and skills they need." In practice, this understanding will radiate outward from those who are part of core SEL infrastructure groups to those who quickly grasp the benefits of SEL in their professional activities and student success, to those who see their colleagues being more effective.

Activity 7: Connect to those who are walking the walk. The difficulties that any school or district encounters in implementation will have been confronted and overcome by many other schools farther along down the road of SEL. While compilations of these obstacles and solutions exist (Elias, 2010; Elias et al., 1997), the greatest success comes from direct consultative mentoring (Kress & Elias, 2013). National organizations that might have locally available resources, or the capacity to triage to local resources, include CASEL and the National Association of School Psychologists. Other excellent sources of support can be the central headquarters of SEL programs such as Committee for Children, Lions Quest International, Northeast Foundation for Children, Open Circle, SDM/SPS, and PATHS (cf. CASEL, 2003, 2012). The NSOC and State Schools of Character networks administered by the Character Education Partnership (*www.character.org/schools-of-character*) are particularly sensitive to schoolwide implementation issues, and those implementing these approaches locally can become allies even if their own setting is not implementing an identical approach.

As noted earlier, the seven activities presented earlier represent an analysis and summation of many implementation efforts presented by the authors, colleagues, and the literature, over a range of contexts that literally spans the globe. The SEL world is not lacking for models of change (Berman et al., 2012; CASEL, 2003, 2012; Devaney et al., 2006; Domitrovich et al., 2010; Novick, Kress, & Elias, 2002; Pasi, 2001; Schaps, Battistich, & Solomon, 2004; Vetter, 2008). Readers will no doubt see omissions among our seven activities, or have their own view of priorities and ordering. Regardless of specifics, successful change efforts follow Reeves (2009, p. 243): "Complex organizations that create meaningful change in a short period of time are not weighed down by voluminous strategic plans; they have absolute clarity about a few things that have to be done." Hence, we recommend more integrative and selective, rather than expansive, models.

The empirical literature to date in SEL has focused more on the impact of programs than on the integration of SEL within the fabric of schools. In what may be the largest naturalistic study of the effectiveness of SEL-related programs, Gager and Elias (1997) found that even evidence-based and acclaimed programs were as likely to be on the failure side of the ledger as on the success side, results that were replicated in a sustainability study of many of those same programs (Elias, 2010). Yet this does not reflect the effectiveness of the programs per se but reflects more an underemphasis of focusing on the schoolwide culture and on implementation and supports, key factors in determining whether or not programs are likely to achieve their goals. For SEL, the challenge is that curricula often have complex structures that ultimately must be integrated with a school's broader efforts to enhance children's positive social, moral, civic, and academic development and prevent problem behaviors (CASEL, 2012; Elias et al., 1997). Yet there is no question that SEL skills must be imparted to students in systematic and explicit ways, and this requires some form of curriculum structure, whether explicit or implicit.

So it is not surprising that the most common feature encountered in attempts to unjumble and synergize the processes implied in Figure 3.1 is the presence of preexisting, or different, SEL-related approaches or programs. As implied earlier, coordinating with preexisting programs is not a simple technical matter, as outlined in Activity 5, though that certainly must happen correctly. It is also a matter of understanding existing program philosophies, infrastructures, inroads into existing routines, and connections to consultants and other outside resources (Devaney et al., 2006; Mart et al., Chapter 32, this volume). In providing an example of alignment considerations, we chose positive youth development, a substantial model with a tradition at least as long as that of SEL.

Integrating SEL with Related Programs: A Positive Youth Development Example

In the course of determining the nature and extent of fragmented SEL-related programming in one's schoolhouse, it is possible to uncover other significant efforts to improve school-wide culture and climate. One approach, highly akin to SEL, is positive youth development (PYD). Programs created from a PYD perspective typically seek to foster positive life skills and to enhance resiliency by consistently offering an environment where youth's strengths are emphasized in program design, implementation, and adaptation. Therefore, much can be learned about the challenges of creating the synergized schoolhouse by looking at the literature and experience of PYD. As we will see, this approach is distinctive in that it has had a strong after-school and community presence, and issues of its integration are particularly instructive.

Because PYD is more an approach than it is a specific program, it is especially important to grasp the underlying elements likely to be present in its efficacious implementation. "Five Cs" are frequently referred to in the PYD literature and include competence, confidence, (positive social) connection, character, and caring (or compassion) (Eccles & Gootman, 2002; Roth & Brooks-Gunn, 2003). Lerner (2004) added that when all Five Cs are present in a setting, a sixth C, contribution to self, family, community, and civil society, emerges. Much of this was presaged in early PYD work (Brendtro, Brokenleg, & Van Bockern, 1990).

In a review of PYD programs, Catalano, Berglund, Ryan, Lonczak, and Hawkins (2004) identified 161 PYD program evaluation studies. Of those that had strong empirical designs and provided detailed study methodology, they found 25 programs that demonstrated significant effects on youth behavior, including improvements in interpersonal skills, academic achievement, and quality of peer and adult relationships, and reductions in alcohol and drug use, violence and aggression, school misbehavior and truancy, and high-risk sexual behavior. Utilizing a list of 15 youth development and SEL skills and attitude constructs, the authors set out to categorize the focus areas of successful programs. The constructs of competence, self-efficacy, and prosocial norms were addressed in all 25 of the efficacious programs, and they also addressed at least two and often as many as five other competencies (Catalano et al., 2004; Greenberg et al., 2003).

Despite the clear consonance of PYD and related approaches, and SEL, an important difference is the emphasis on skills. CASEL's (2012) most recent guidelines on the implementation of SEL in preschools and elementary schools, along with the earlier *Safe and Sound* guide (2003), review a number of SEL programs that have been found to be successful in improving student outcomes. They cannot be said to address uniformly all five of the CASEL skills domains, and this is also true of effective PYD programs. Similarly, effective SEL programs join PYD and related programs in having a broader focus than skills training, but not a clearly distinguishable alternative structure. As the *2013 CASEL Guide* provides a framework for SEL efforts, the 5 Cs perform a similar function for PYD efforts (and the 11 Principles for Character Education, etc.). The process of harmonization requires decision making about skills, language, integration into academics and school routines and structures, all tiers of intervention levels, and prioritizing core values and generating clear messaging statements. This happens through a representative group of educators, some knowledgeable about SEL, others about PYD (or whatever programs already exist in the school), making some pragmatic decisions that must be treated as "pilots"—works in progress requiring adjustment as needed. If the preexisting program has not penetrated the school culture fully, it does not make the task of doing so with SEL easier; one must uncover why that integration did not occur and grapple with staff expectations that programs are discrete entities that are supposed to transmit their benefits to students through lessons that children hear, grasp, internalize, and act upon.

PYD in After-School Programs

One area in the synergistic schoolhouse where SEL continuity is valued is after-school programming (Durlak & Weissberg, 2013). This is an area in which PYD is generally more developed than formal SEL programs (Snyder & Flay, 2012). After-school programs (ASPs) provide an opportunity to emphasize SEL skills, especially when implementation is spotty during the school day due to pressure on teachers and administrators to focus on academic curriculum and test preparation. ASPs can provide a safe and structured environment for children, potentially filling a need to have organized activities for children outside of school hours (Durlak, Mahoney, Bohnert, & Parente, 2010).

The most efficacious after-school PYD programs feature a high degree of youth engagement, providing physical and psychological safety, supportive relationships with adults and peers, a sense of efficacy, skills-building opportunities, and integration of school, family, and community efforts (National Research Council, 2002; Roth &

Brooks-Gunn, 2003; Yohalem & Wilson-Ahlstrom, 2010). This has two important implications for SEL efforts. First, for at least some students and sometimes many, the school is not the place where they experience engagement, safety, supportive relationships, and efficacy. Therefore, even when skills-building opportunities are available, students may not benefit from them. Indeed, this has been found within the PYD field as well: Otherwise effective programming has less or no impact within after-school centers that have a troubled culture and climate (Hirsch, Deutsch, & DuBois, 2011). Nevertheless, ASPs may provide an essential opportunity for some students to learn SEL skills.

The second implications follows from research suggesting that in order to work to their greatest potential, ASPs should be integrated with school efforts (Durlak et al., 2010; Greenberg et al., 2003). SEL-related programs that are held after school should aim to complement what is taught during the school day; therefore, after-school program staff members (if they are not school staff) should be in communication with school administrators and teachers to use a common vocabulary and emphasize similar concepts. This makes it more likely that skills taught will generalize into community contexts and reduce the fragmentation experienced by students regarding what skills they should be learning. Overall, then, the PYD example shows the need to consider not only the presence of programs already in the system and the need to ally skills-building elements but also to understand how existing programs map into the ecology of the school and the community, and how to ensure the SEL initiative being brought in both creates synergy and recognizes and strategically addresses limitations in the existing implementation structure.

Problems, Pitfalls, and Defining the Next Frontiers for SEL

Leaders in SEL and related fields share a burning desire to see all children in the world develop the skills they need to make healthy, ethical choices, solve problems peacefully, regulate their emotions appropriately, work collaboratively, and achieve academically. But many questions arise: What should SEL look like in contexts that are very, very different from those in which SEL programs were first developed and evaluated? What should SEL "integration" look like when brought into very different education systems, schoolhouses, and teaching practice? How will current SEL approaches fit in contexts where extended families and village members play disparate roles in children's upbringing? Which aspects of existing SEL fields are portable into entirely new settings and cultures—and which are not? Does the growing proliferation of mobile technology offer new possibilities for delivering teaching and learning tools? All these questions ensure the evolution of entirely new ways of thinking about what a quality, effective, sustainable SEL intervention might look like. Yet how diverse elements come together in schools with existing histories, strengths, and constraints represents a process that is unlikely to change dramatically in the foreseeable future. Thus, we identify below some of the areas that occur to us as challenges containing pitfalls, obstacles, and opportunities simultaneously. All have been surmounted somewhere; few have been surmounted in most schools. The latter must be reversed if scaling up of high-quality, coordinated SEL is to characterize schools in the United States and worldwide.

SEL's Role in Achievement of Rigorous Academic Standards

At the time of this writing, the tenor of educational policy and major reform strategies continues to have the impact of narrowing the curriculum to focus on curriculum content evaluated by performance on high-stakes accountability tests. This serves to create a perception that there is a competition for time, and the time devoted to SEL is time "taken away" from academics. Unfortunately, this argument is most prevalent in schools that serve poor children in highly stressed urban environments. So a significant obstacle to comprehensive SEL is the lack of deep understanding of the well-documented connections between SEL and academic performance (see Durlak et al., 2011). The latest school reform in the United States, the Common Core Curriculum Standards adopted by 47 states, requires students to master social–emotional competencies such as the CASEL 5 (Elias, 2014). Pressure to persist in tasks and assessments high in cognitive demand and rigor is almost certain to trigger emotions that could result in frustration, anger, and lack of self-efficacy needed for continuous engagement. This is especially true of disadvantaged learners and students with histories of academic failure. Whether for the purpose of college or careers, students require skills to enable them to carry out cooperative work, make sound decisions related to peer pressure, persist in tasks, communicate effectively, and regulate their strong emotions. The need to make the case explicitly and repeatedly for the connection between school and life success and emotional wellness is part of effective SEL implementation despite the convincing empirical, case study, and practice-based evidence available and its common-sense appeal to SEL adherents (Zins, Bloodworth, Weissberg, & Walberg, 2004).

The Challenges of Urban Contexts

Urban schools are disproportionally challenged by conditions of poverty, competing priorities, student histories of failure, educator turnover, and a culture in which there is significant pessimism about the ability of learners and adults to be successful in an environment of rigorous standards and assessment (Rothstein, 2004). Issues of race/ethnicity make these challenges even more formidable. In our experience, beyond harmonizing the variety of SEL-related approaches in schools, those working in urban schools must pay particular attention to Activities 1 and 4. A strong infrastructure and committed cadre is essential, and there must be clarity about core values, including the mindset that success is possible for all (Leverett, 2008). Beyond the school level, the greater needs make synergy and district-level coordination even more essential (Mart et al., Chapter 32, this volume).

Context Challenges of Systemic Implementation

Fitting SEL initiatives into an already packed school day is a common challenge to schools, whether urban, suburban, or rural. Adaptations range from relatively minor adjustment to major changes in the way school activities and classroom instruction are organized. Those seeking to bring in SEL will have to analyze how structures, processes, systems, rituals, and routines will have to be changed to reduce resistance associated with adding another mandated intrusion on long-standing commitments to organizational routines and resources (Mart et al., Chapter 32, this volume). Careful assessments of culture, climate, curriculum, instructional delivery, and capacity-building activities are necessary to increase chances of achieving sustainable SEL initiatives and activities. An analysis of relationships, programs, resource allocations, and work processes should precede efforts to infuse SEL into ongoing activities and program delivery systems in schools and communities. There is no formula or set of procedures to guide this analysis, and failure to engage in adequate organizational assessment of the current context will likely threaten the system's ability to garner the support and commitment necessary to navigate the fragmentation and complexity that practitioners face in their work in classrooms and schools.

Furthermore, schoolwide SEL initiatives should be responsive to the demographics of the student and community population to increase relevance of strategies and activities to the culture, values, and customs. Many combinations of demographics often must be accommodated, requiring a sensitive approach to identifying which SEL approaches are most appropriate and what adaptations are needed.

Communications, Relationships, and Leadership within Schools

Too often, communications are one way and relationships are superficial, creating obstacles that militate against integrating SEL into the work of schools, thereby providing few opportunities for collaboration among school leaders who are responsible for the successful implementation of a coherent, aligned approach to SEL. Attention is needed to provide ongoing interactions and experiences for school leaders (principals, department heads, instructional coaches, child study team consultants, teacher leaders, program coordinators, etc.) to work together to build a shared sense of purpose, knowledge, role clarity, and reinforcement of expectations. A common, deep understanding of the SEL approach being implemented is essential for sustainability (Elias, 2010).

Additionally, leadership must be evident at all levels of school structure to implement high-quality SEL initiatives in school districts (Leverett, 2008). This is not the current situation in most schools. For comprehensive SEL to thrive, there must be an explicit commitment to intended durability of SEL as a "high-leverage" commitment that extends beyond the tenure of a principal or other school leaders. Hence, there is a need to root it in the core values–purpose–mission of a school. The possibility of attaining and sustaining the desired SEL visions, goals, and outcomes increases when the infrastructure has leadership that is spread across the school or district horizontally and vertically, and when people in the organization share the zeal and commitment to make meaningful change happen (Leverett, 2008; Vetter, 2008). From this launching point, leadership can arrange professional development and training, and engagement of parents, students, teachers, administrators, educational support staff and community resources in ways coordinated with the school's SEL approach, thereby accelerating student competencies that contribute to academic performance in emotionally healthy and physically safe living environments in which students will flourish.

Particularly in urban and highly diverse contexts, the roots of leadership must be deeply embedded into the soil of every facet of the school. This should include representatives of instructional and noninstructional staff members, school social workers, psychologists, nurses, coaches, security personnel, parents, and community and business leaders. Significant student leadership and engagement is also essential; ultimately, the school belongs to the students, and their voices must join all others in pursuit of a safe, civil school that is dedicated to fostering learning and making positive contributions in a setting not beset by harassment, intimidation, and bullying (Berman & McCarthy, 2006; Pasi, 2001).

Accountability

Assessment is a common challenge for schools implementing SEL programs. Each must develop indicators that meaningfully define what success looks like and collect, analyze, and use data to inform improvement of efforts at all stages of the implementation process. The adage "Don't let perfection be the enemy of the good" applies to the development of assessment strategies. The Culture of Excellence and Ethics approach advocates using "good enough" rubrics, reflecting the reality that when assessment tools do not exist in validated ways tailored to the context of application within particular schools, there is value to even a rough set of first-generation assessment tools and processes that can be revised, supplemented, or replaced as data and information gathering needs become better defined and techniques developed (Davidson, Khmelkov, & Baker, 2011). Forums are needed for sharing a variety of practice-based approaches to formative assessment of SEL. Schools also need ways to gauge the extent to which SEL outcomes are being achieved. Current work suggests that the report card process may be a feasible vehicle for assessing students' social–emotional and character development (Elias, Ferrito, & Moceri, 2014), and that tools also exist for the systematic and ongoing assessment of school culture and climate (Cohen & Elias, 2011).

External Support from Experts in the SEL Field

The careful selection of external consultants with extensive experience in school implementation is vital to the overall implementation plan (Kress & Elias, 2013; Leverett, 2008). From the beginning, it should be understood that the job of the external consultant is to work toward gradual release of responsibility to result in a much-reduced but ongoing role as the school develops its capacity to sustain SEL implementation. Sustainability is more likely when the consultant has a district-level role, or at least is able to share expertise across multiple schools. Track record in building internal capacity should be a major consideration in the selection of the external consultant.

Some factors to consider in the selection of the external expert are (1) development of an explicit statement of work defining the consultant's role, authority, deliverables, and limitations ; (2) frequent interaction with the consultant to ensure alignment of work to the statement of work; (3) strategy formulation for working directly with school and, where possible, district leadership; (4) on-the-scene involvement with school-level SEL leaders, SEL coordinating teams, school-based SEL coordinators, department chairs, school improvement teams, professional learning communities, project directors, teacher leaders, principals, school improvement teams, or school-based SEL coordinating teams; (5) advisement, coaching, and delivery of professional development for school staff; and (6) support and assistance to engage community service internships with graduate or undergraduate students from nearby colleges or universities, parent groups, community volunteers, high school students involved in service learning, community-based organizations and other local assets that can build the resolve to develop and sustain a long-term commitment to advancing the effectiveness of a systemwide implementation approach. Maintaining a relationship with an expert consultant and/or joining with a consortium of implementing schools is also important to provide ongoing, practice-based troubleshooting of problems and the infusion of refreshing ideas from outside one's immediate practice context (Kress & Elias, 2013).

External Factors That Influence School Implementation Success

Individual schools exist within a larger ecological context, and what happens in that context influences the effectiveness, and shape, of a school's SEL efforts. Most pragmatically, schools must be concerned with the skills and mindsets with which students enter their buildings; hence, elementary schools must be concerned about preschool education and parenting. Middle and high schools must be concerned with what sending schools are doing. This bridges to the topic of district-level coordination, which is beyond the focus of this chapter but is addressed fully by Mart and colleagues (Chapter 32, this volume). How districts balance maintaining fidelity to a systemwide set of core values, vision, mission goals, strategic directions, theory of action, and student performance expectations with defining the level of flexibility and adaptation at the school level to accommodate particularized needs, interests, resources, and constraints has clear implications for individual schools. Districts may select one or two evidence-based SEL programs to be deployed systemwide or have a broader portfolio of choices of evidenced-based SEL programs. In either situation, systems of support and integrated organizational infrastructure must be established to allow schools to implement successfully.

The Importance of a Global Perspective

It is beyond the scope of this chapter to provide an authoritative statement about whether and how SEL is integrated into education on a global scale. Perhaps the only generalization we can make is to say that recent years have seen a significant upsurge in interest in SEL across the world (e.g., European Network for Social and Emotional Competence, 2013) and that readers should seek to determine the current situation at the time of their reading rather than our time of writing. As Torrente, Alimchandani, and Aber (Chapter 37, this volume) show, there is great variety in how SEL is thought about and practiced, and there is much that we can learn from these differences.

With regard to the schoolwide adoption of comprehensive SEL, some international examples are especially instructive. In England, Social and Emotional Aspects of Learning (SEAL) was a National Strategy launched by the Labour government in the primary (elementary) school sector in 2005 and the secondary (high) school sector in 2007. By 2010, SEAL was in use in almost all primary schools and most secondary schools across the country (Humphrey, Lendrum, & Wigelsworth, 2010).

SEAL broadly comprises four main components: (1) use of a whole-school approach to create a positive school climate and ethos, (2) direct teaching of social and emotional skills in whole-class contexts, (3) use of teaching and learning approaches that support the learning of such skills, and (4) continuing professional development for school staff (Humphrey et al., 2010). It includes both universal and targeted/indicated materials. Implementation of SEAL was designed to be flexible rather than prescriptive, with schools encouraged to explore different approaches to implementation that supported identified school improvement priorities rather than following a single model. This "bottom-up" approach was welcomed by schools, but it proved extremely challenging for many; without a clear road map, staff championing SEAL found it difficult to gain traction (Humphrey et al., 2010).

What happened subsequently reflects what has happened in a number of other countries, that is, a return to a more program-focused approach, such as PATHS or Second Step (Holsen, Smith, & Frey, 2008; Humphrey, 2013). The situation in Scandinavia is particularly instructive. Those seeking to improve skills tend to adopt evidence-based programs; those looking for whole-school models related to bullying prevention and discipline bring in approaches such as those of Olweus and PBIS (Kimber, Sandell, & Bremberg, 2008; Ogden, Sørlie, Arnesen, & Wilhelm, 2012; Salmivalli, Kärnä, & Poskiparta, 2011). To put a positive spin on this, the success stories of international efforts to integrate SEL programs with other SEL-related efforts in schools are likely to contain important lessons that will transfer to U.S. efforts, and vice versa, thus placing a premium on greater international sharing of implementation experiences. Unfortunately, there are ultimately no shortcuts. Schools must address their culture and climate, explicitly teach skills, support students at all levels of competence/need based on their skills model, provide systemic and district-level coordination so as to create continuity and synergy across grade levels and schools, and involve parents and the wider community.

One excellent example is KidsMatter, the Australian government's main SEL-related initiative for primary schools. KidsMatter's (*www.kidsmatter.edu.au*) four components speak to the integration of elements in the jumbled schoolhouse: (1) *a positive school community* focuses on developing the school ethos and environment such that it promotes mental health, respectful relationships, and a sense of belonging among students and staff; (2) *SEL for students* provides an effective SEL curriculum for all children and allows them opportunities to practice and transfer their skills; (3) *working with parents and caregivers* promotes collaboration between schools and parents/caregivers, provides support for parents in relation to their children's mental health, and helps to develop parent and caregiver support networks; and (4) *helping children experiencing mental health difficulties* addresses the need to coordinate Tier 1, 2, and 3 interventions by expanding schools' understanding of mental health difficulties, improving help seeking, and developing appropriate interventions. Materials and resources (e.g., guidance documents, information sheets) are provided to support each of these strands, in addition to professional development/training opportunities for school staff (Slee et al., 2009).

KidsMatter provides a balance between flexibility and rigidity. So for each component, all schools are provided with the same basic materials and resources; all schools get a guide to over 70 available interventions, with information covering the areas of focus, evidence base, theoretical framework, structure, and other factors to enable them to make informed choices that suit their local context and needs. They also can access professional development and consultative support. For example, a KidsMatter school might choose to implement Steps to Respect to fulfill the positive school community component, the SDM/SPS program as their SEL curriculum, the Positive Parenting Program (Triple P) to support the parental strand, and the FRIENDS for Life intervention to provide targeted support for children experiencing difficulties (Slee et al., 2009). (A similar effort, MindMatters [*www.mindmatters.edu.au*], operates at the secondary level.)

A repository of well-explicated case studies of all of these implementation examples, of the kind maintained by the Character Education Partnership for its NSOC program (2013a), would be of tremendous value for both researchers and practitioners. Such a repository, organized to ensure discussion of the seven implementation activities noted earlier, as well as other contextual parameters known to influence implementation outcomes, would allow for a better inductive understanding of the configural ways in which comprehensive SEL does and does not find its way into schools sustainably. The specific details of how diverse program elements are woven together are too often missing from research reports, journal articles, shorter accounts, and the most generally accessible forms of media. Indeed, much has been learned from similar case study approaches that would not have been derived from more nomothetic means (Elias et al., 1997).

Concluding Thoughts

Implementing SEL schoolwide is not a task for those who thrive on order, sequential and logical processes, or predictability. It is a never-ending configural task that requires constant alignment to changing conditions. It will be rare indeed when the seven activities essential for unjumbling a schoolhouse will unfold in the same way, lead to the same processes, and follow the same path to success in different schools. The process of schoolwide implementation has been likened to an ocean voyage or a jazz concert, or any number of related analogies (Dalton, Elias, & Wandersman, 2007; Elias, Bruene-Butler, Blum, & Schuyler, 2000). The destination is clear, the course is set, but only by successfully adapting to conditions, with a boat that is fundamentally sound and a competent crew and cooperative passengers, can the destination be reached. But September rolls around and the journey begins again, never to replicate what happened earlier. This has implications for how we train and support educational leaders, select and orient school board members, and prepare school support professionals and consultants.

As of this writing, the field of SEL and related approaches is evolving and holds considerable promise for transforming educational practice into a humanizing experience for all those who pass through, work in, support, visit, and relate to our schools. Progress must be made in many areas, beyond those covered in this chapter, and doing so is a developmental imperative for youth across cultures and contexts. Yet emerging research pointing to SEL's positive effects on behavior and academic outcomes elevates its importance as foundational to a quality education. This represents a sea change from SEL as a nonessential "add on" whose success depended on whether school leaders had the time, money, or inclination to focus on it. The future challenge is not "if" but rather "how."

References

Anchorage School District. (2013). ASD | CIS | Social & Emotional Learning (SEL). Retrieved April 1, 2013, from *www.asdk12.org/depts/SEL.*

Berkowitz, M. W. (2011). Leading schools of character. In A. M. Blankstein & P. D. Houston (Eds.), *Leadership for social justice and democracy in our schools* (pp. 93–121). Thousand Oaks, CA: Corwin Press.

Berman, S., Chang, F., & Barnes, J. (2012). The district superintendent's role in supporting prosocial education. In P. M. Brown, M. Corrigan, & A. Higgins-D'Allesandro (Eds.), *Handbook of prosocial education* (Vol. 2, pp. 691–707). New York: Rowman & Littlefield.

Berman, S., & McCarthy, M. H. (2006). The connection between character, service, and social–emotional learning. In M. J. Elias & H. A. Arnold (Eds.), *The educator's guide to emotional intelligence and academic achievement* (pp. 46–57). Thousand Oaks, CA: Corwin Press.

Brendtro, L. K., Brokenleg, M., & Van Bockern, N. (1990). *Reclaiming youth at risk: Our hope for the future.* Bloomington, IN: National Educational Service.

Catalano, R. F., Berglund, M. L., Ryan, J. A. M., Lonczak, H. S., & Hawkins, J. D. (2004). Positive youth development in the United States: Research findings on evaluations of positive youth development programs. *Annals of the American Academy of Political and Social Science, 591*(1), 98–124.

Character Education Partnership. (2013a). CEP. Retrieved April 1, 2013, from *www.character.org.*

Character Education Partnership. (2013b). Schools of Character | CEP. Retrieved April 1, 2013, from *www.character.org/schools-of-character.*

Cohen, J., & Elias, M. J. (2011). *School climate: Building safe, supportive, and engaging classrooms and schools.* Port Chester, NY: National Professional Resources.

Collaborative for Academic Social and Emotional Learning (CASEL). (2003). *Safe and sound: An educational leader's guide to evidence-based social and emotional learning (SEL) programs.* Chicago: Author.

Collaborative for Academic, Social, and Emotional Learning (CASEL). (2012). *2013 CASEL guide: Effective social and emotional learning programs—Preschool and elementary school edition.* Chicago: Author.

Collaborative for Academic, Social, and Emotional Learning (CASEL). (2013). CASEL | Success in school: Skills for life. Retrieved April 1, 2013, from *www.casel.org.*

Cowen, E. L. (1994). The enhancement of psychological wellness: Challenges and opportunities. *American Journal of Community Psychology, 22*(2), 149–179.

Dalton, J., Elias, M. J., & Wandersman, A. (2007).

Community psychology: Linking individuals and communities (2nd ed.). Belmont, CA: Wadsworth.

Darling-Hammond, L. (2009). Teaching and the change wars: The professionalism hypothesis. In A. Hargreaves & M. Fullan (Eds.), *Change wars* (pp. 45–70). Bloomington, IN: Solution Tree.

Davidson, M., Khmelkov, V., & Baker, K. (2011). Sustainability and enduring impact: Shaping an international culture of excellence and ethics. *Journal of Character and Leadership Integration, 2*(1), 35–51.

Devaney, E., O'Brien, M. U., Resnik, H., Keister, S., & Weissberg, R. P. (2006). *Sustainable schoolwide social and emotional learning: Implementation guide and toolkit.* Chicago: Collaborative for Academic, Social, and Emotional Learning (CASEL).

Domitrovich, C. E., Bradshaw, C. P., Greenberg, M. T., Embry, D., Poduska, J. M., & Ialongo, N. S. (2010). Integrated models of school-based prevention: Logic and theory. *Psychology in the Schools, 47*(1), 71–88.

Durlak, J. A., Mahoney, J. L., Bohnert, A. M., & Parente, M. E. (2010). Developing and improving after-school programs to enhance youth's personal growth and adjustment: A special issue of AJCP. *American Journal of Community Psychology, 45*(3–4), 285–293.

Durlak, J. A., & Weissberg, R. P. (2013). Afterschool programs that follow evidence-based practices to promote social and emotional development are effective. In T. K. Peterson (Ed.), *Expanding minds and opportunities: Leveraging the power of afterschool and summer learning for student success* (pp. 194–198). Washington, DC: Collaborative Communications Group.

Durlak, J. A., Weissberg, R. P., Dymnicki, A. B., Taylor, R. D., & Schellinger, K. B. (2011). The impact of enhancing students' social and emotional learning: A meta-analysis of school-based universal interventions. *Child Development, 82*(1), 474–501.

Eccles, J. S., & Gootman, J. A. (2002). *Beyond the front stoop: Community programs to promote youth development*: Washington, DC: National Academies Press.

Elias, M. J. (2004). The connection between social–emotional learning and learning disabilities: Implications for intervention. *Learning Disability Quarterly, 27*(1), 53–63.

Elias, M. J. (2009). Social–emotional and character development and academics as a dual focus of educational policy. *Education Policy, 23*(6), 831–846.

Elias, M. J. (2010). Sustainability of social–emotional learning and related programs: Lessons from a field study. *International Journal of Emotional Education, 2*(1), 17–33.

Elias, M. J. (2014). Let's put caring in the Common Core: Promoting social–emotional competence is the first step toward mastery. *NJEA Review, 87*(6), 10–13.

Elias, M. J., & Bruene, L. (2005). *Social Decision Making/Social Problem Solving for elementary and middle school students.* Champaign, IL: Research Press.

Elias, M. J., Bruene-Butler, L., Blum, L., & Schuyler, T. (2000). Voices from the field: Identifying and overcoming roadblocks to carrying out programs in social and emotional learning/emotional intelligence. *Journal of Educational and Psychological Consultation, 11*(2), 253–272.

Elias, M. J., Ferrito, J. J., & Moceri, D. C. (2014). *The other side of the report card: A guide to modifying report card comments to include social–emotional learning and character development.* New Brunswick, NJ: Rutgers Social–Emotional Learning Lab.

Elias, M. J., Kranzler, A., Parker, S. J., Kash, V. M., & Weissberg, R. P. (2014). The complementary perspectives of social and emotional learning, moral education, and character education. In L. Nucci, T. Krettenauer, & D. Narvaez (Eds.), *Handbook of moral and character education* (2nd ed., pp. 272–289). New York: Routledge.

Elias, M. J., & Leverett, L. (2011). Consultation to urban schools for improvements in academics and behavior: No alibis. No excuses. No exceptions. *Journal of Educational and Psychological Consultation, 21*(1), 28–45.

Elias, M. J., Zins, J. E., Weissberg, R. P., Frey, K. S., Greenberg, M. T., Haynes, N. M., et al. (1997). *Promoting social and emotional learning: Guidelines for educators.* Alexandria, VA: Association for Supervision and Curriculum Development.

European Network for Social and Emotional Competence. (2013). ENSEC. Retrieved April 1, 2013, from *http://enseceurope.org.*

Gager, P. J., & Elias, M. J. (1997). Implementing prevention programs in high-risk environments: Application of the resiliency paradigm. *American Journal of Orthopsychiatry, 67*(3), 363–373.

Greenberg, M. T., Weissberg, R. P., O'Brien, M. U., Zins, J. E., Fredericks, L., Resnik, H., et al. (2003). Enhancing school-based prevention and youth development through coordinated social, emotional, and academic learning. *American Psychologist, 58*(6–7), 466–474.

Hargreaves, A. (2009). The fourth way of change. In A. Hargreaves & M. Fullan (Eds.), *Change wars* (pp. 11–43). Bloomington, IN: Solution Tree.

Hirsch, B., Deutsch, N., & DuBois, D. (2011). *After-school centers and youth development: Case studies of success and failure.* New York: Cambridge University Press.

Holsen, I., Smith, B. H., & Frey, K. S. (2008). Outcomes of the social competence program Second Step in Norwegian elementary schools. *School Psychology International, 29*(1), 71–88.

Humphrey, N. (2013). *Social and emotional learning: A critical appraisal.* London: Sage.

Humphrey, N., Lendrum, A., & Wigelsworth, M. (2010). *Secondary social and emotional aspects of learning (SEAL): National evaluation.* Nottingham, UK: DFE Publications.

Kimber, B., Sandell, R., & Bremberg, S. (2008). Social and emotional training in Swedish classrooms for the promotion of mental health: Results from an effectiveness study in Sweden. *Health Promotion International, 23*(2), 134–143.

Kress, J. S., & Elias, M. J. (2013). Consultation to support sustainability of Social and Emotional Learning initiatives in schools. *Consulting Psychology Journal: Practice and Research, 65*(2), 149–163.

Lerner, R. M. (2004). *Liberty: Thriving and civic engagement among American youth.* Thousand Oaks, CA: Sage.

Leverett, L. (2008). Pursuit of sustainibility. In A. M. Blankstein, P. D. Houston, & R. W. Cole (Eds.), *Sustaining professional learning communities* (pp. 121–142). Thousand Oaks, CA: Corwin Press.

Lickona, T., & Davidson, M. (2005). *Smart and good high schools: Integrating excellence and ethics for success in school, work, and beyond.* Courtland, NY: Center for the 4th and 5th Rs (Respect and Responsibility).

National Research Council. (2002). *Community programs to promote youth development.* Washington, DC: National Academy Press.

Novick, B., Kress, J. S., & Elias, M. J. (2002). *Building learning communities with character: How to integrate academic, social, and emotional learning.* Alexandria, VA: Association for Supervision and Curriculum Development.

Ogden, T., Sørlie, M.-A., Arnesen, A., & Wilhelm, M. H. (2012). The PALS School-Wide Positive Behaviour Support Model in Norwegian primary schools—Implementation and evaluation. *International Perspectives on Inclusive Education, 2*, 39–55.

Pasi, R. (2001). *Higher expectations: Promoting social emotional learning and academic achievement in your school.* New York: Teachers College Press.

Reeves, D. B. (2009). *Leading change in your school: How to conquer myths, build commitment, and get results.* Alexandria, VA: Association for Supervision and Curriculum Development.

Roth, J. L., & Brooks-Gunn, J. (2003). What exactly is a youth development program?: Answers from research and practice. *Applied Developmental Science, 7*(2), 94–111.

Rothstein, R. (2004). *Class and schools: Using social, economic, and educational reform to close the black–white achievement gap.* Washington, DC: Economic Policy Institute.

Salmivalli, C., Kärnä, A., & Poskiparta, E. (2011). Counteracting bullying in Finland: The KiVa program and its effects on different forms of being bullied. *International Journal of Behavioral Development, 35*(5), 405–411.

Schaps, E., Battistich, V., & Solomon, D. (2004). Community in school as key to student growth: Findings from the Child Development Project. In J. E. Zins, R. P. Weissberg, M. C. Wang, & H. J. Walberg (Eds.), *Building academic success on social and emotional learning: What does the research say?* (pp. 189–208). New York: Teachers College Press.

Slee, P., Lawson, M., Russell, A., Askell-Williams, H., Dix, K., Owens, L., et al. (2009). *Kidsmatter primary evaluation final report.* Flinders, Australia: Flinders University.

Snyder, F. J., & Flay, B. R. (2012). Positive youth development. In P. M. Brown, M. Corrigan, & A. Higgins-D'Allesandro (Eds.), *Handbook of prosocial education* (Vol. 2, pp. 415–443). New York: Rowman & Littlefield.

Vetter, J. B. (2008). A leadership team approach to sustaining social and emotional learning. In A. M. Blankstein, P. D. Houston, & R. W. Cole (Eds.), *Sustaining professional learning communities* (pp. 97–120). Thousand Oaks, CA: Corwin Press.

Yohalem, N., & Wilson-Ahlstrom, A. (2010). Inside the black box: Assessing and improving quality in youth programs. *American Journal of Community Psychology, 45*(3), 350–357.

Zins, J. E., Bloodworth, M. R., Weissberg, R. P., & Walberg, H. J. (2004). The scientific base linking social and emotional learning to school success. In J. E. Zins, R. P. Weissberg, M. C. Wang, & H. J. Walberg (Eds.), *Building academic success on social and emotional learning: What does the research say?* (pp. 3–22). New York: Teachers College Press.

CHAPTER 4

Culture and Social and Emotional Competencies

Michael L. Hecht and YoungJu Shin

Social and emotional learning (SEL), like all learning, occurs within a cultural context (Bronfenbrenner & Morris, 2006). From the more obvious cultural learning through enculturation of members born into the culture and acculturation of members who immigrate to the less obvious cultural learning involving family, school, and region, culture exerts its influence through an often nebulous nexus of intersecting processes. One might even argue that culture defines SEL, although as this chapter indicates, the evidence for this is not definitive. Even less clear is whether these skills are universal across all cultures. The situation is complicated because culture is often an ill-defined construct. Thus, we start with culture, the presumed basis for social and emotional competencies, before discussing cultural influences on SEL.

Underlying most modern approaches is the assumption that culture is more of a lens than a clear analytical category; that is, these approaches consider culture as a frame of reference guiding thought and behavior rather than reduce it to a category such as race or ethnicity. For example, a culture that values individualism provides a lens that may be more conducive to intrapersonal skills than to interpersonal skills. As a result, an individualistic conceptualization of culture can lead researchers and practitioners to focus on the behaviors of individuals, but it can miss the social structures that produce these practices. On the other hand, a culture that values collectivism is more likely to focus on the value of social relationship development than on intrapersonal skills. Consequently, a collectivistic conceptualization of culture can guide researchers to concentrate on the importance of social interactions and practices.

Procedural requirements of granting agencies that categorize participants according to discrete racial or ethnic groups assume homogeneity within these groups and ignore the heterogeneity within groups that is often as great as the variability across groups (Mann et al., 1998). Overgeneralization is one potentially negative outcome of this practice, and a more dangerous result is stereotyping. Moreover, the practice may mask the true contribution of culture. Thus, much is to be gained from richer, more complex conceptualizations of culture. In this chapter we present a perspective that emphasizes a variety of approaches to understanding culture, then attempt to explain how these approaches are related to social and emotional competencies. We start with the basic question—what is culture?—before moving to the relationship between culture and these competencies. We conclude the chapter with a discussion of guidelines, recommendations, and challenges for future research. We do not intend an exhaustive review of SEL and culture; rather a conceptual overview of their relationship with appropriate exemplars.

Ways of Conceptualizing Culture

In 2006, Baldwin, Faulkner, Hecht, and Lindsley (2006) propose a framework for defining culture that identifies three themes that are most relevant to the current discussion: (1) culture as product, (2) culture as function, and (3) culture as process.

First, culture as structure refers to culture as comprising patterns or regularities. These may consist of patterns in "a way of life," cognition, individual or collective behavioral systems, language and discourse, relational systems, and/or social organization. For example, definitions of culture as a belief or value system fall into this category, as do those focusing on norms, religions, political systems, or social networks. Social cognitive approaches can be considered structural in that they identify cultural scripts and schemas, while those taking a more symbolic approach to culture are concerned with language structures, including shared talk, symbols and meanings, as well as cultural network structures.

Second, culture as function refers to its utilitarian aspect or as a means to an end; that is, culture establishes valued outcomes and defines the means to accomplish them. For example, culture defines the importance of relationships and how they can be established. Arguments about the definition of marriage in the United States revolve around the ways in which the mainstream culture defines this institution and how families are constituted. Prioritizing educational outcomes, as was done in the recent educational reform movement in the United States, is a functional approach to educational cultures that is achieved by defining what it means to become an educated person. A culture's definitions of health and being healthy provide examples by specifying what healthy behaviors accomplish (e.g., defining ideal weight targets or cholesterol levels). For example, the U.S. Department of Health and Human Services launched Healthy People 2020 in an effort to increase public awareness of what it takes to be healthy, how to eliminate health disparities, and how to promote quality of life. Cultures tell us what it means to be healthy and to have a healthy lifestyle.

Finally, the third tradition conceptualizes culture as a process, or a series or sequence of actions. Whereas structures are entities and functions are outcomes, process-oriented definitions of culture are concerned with actions that change over time. For example, in contrast to the functional approach stressing outcomes, process approaches are concerned about the actions or developmental processes themselves. For example, process approaches are concerned with healthy lifestyles, whereas functional approaches focus on achieving healthy outcomes. So a process approach would focus on a person's diet (or food purchases and preparation) and how it might be adjusted in an ongoing fashion, whereas the functional approach would focus on weight gain or loss, or cholesterol levels. The structure, function, and outcome definitions of culture overlap and are often used in concert. For example, a structural approach would focus on how obesity is defined. The functional approach would be concerned with desired healthy weight and obesity levels, while the process approach would examine how weight is gained or lost. Researchers will recognize simple causal models (structure → process → outcome/function) in the merger of the three approaches.

Culture and Social and Emotional Competencies

In the following sections we examine the relationships among structural, functional, and process elements of culture and the five social and emotional competency domains of *self-awareness* (i.e., accurately recognizing one's own thoughts and emotions, as well as their effects on behaviors), *self-management* (i.e., regulating one's thoughts, emotions, and behaviors), *social awareness* (i.e., taking the perspective of and empathizing with others), *relationship skills* (i.e., ability to establish and maintain healthy relationships), and *responsible decision making* (i.e., making responsible and constructive choices) as they are defined by Collaborative for Academic, Social and Emotional Learning (CASEL; 2012). Previous research shows that there are cultural influences on social and emotional competencies that include variables such as immigrant arrival, race, class, language, generation, gender, or cultural expectations, and so forth (Chen, 2009). These influences appear to encompass how competencies are defined and developed, as well as their relative importance in various cultures.

Cultural Structures and Social and Emotional Competencies

As explained previously, cultural structures are perceived as patterns or regularities. Cultures differ in their constructions in many ways, none more basic than how the self is defined, which influences all five of the CASEL competencies and is therefore discussed first. It is important whether a culture considers the self as an individualistic or collectivist construct. Most, if not all, cultures have both individualistic and collectivist elements in their notions of self; the differences lie in their relative emphasis and/or the situations and relationships for which they are relevant (Kim, Triandis, Kagitçibasi, Choi, & Yoon, 1994).

Cultures that primarily value individualism tend to see the self as being fundamentally about personhood, with individual goals, initiatives, achievements, and rights. Independence is valued above interdependence. In contrast, cultures that primarily value collectivism tend to be organized around groups or communities, and behaviors that advance the group are valued. Unity, connectivity, working with others, and selflessness are valued, and interdependence and cooperation are normative. Competencies such as self-awareness and self-management are more highly salient in more individualistic cultures, whereas social awareness and relationship skills are more highly salient in more collectivist cultures. For example, when the individual is the focus, accurately recognizing and regulating one's own thoughts, emotions, and behaviors is stressed. In more collectivist cultures, taking the perspective of and getting along with others is stressed. Moreover, these cultural differences would also influence how these competencies are developed and whether they are taught through one-on-one tutorials or in groups. We turn next to factors influencing each of the social and emotional competencies.

Self-Awareness

Cultural structures influence self-awareness in many ways. As indicated earlier, more individualistic cultures consider self-awareness to be focused on a person's emotions, thoughts, and influences. However, for those immersed in more collectivist cultures, this process involves a broader perspective that includes significant others and the context. This manifests itself in a number of ways. For example, one study suggests that these cultural orientations result in different experiences of the body (Maister & Tsakiris, 2014). In Western societies, body image tends to coalesce around an individual's physical attributes, whereas in East Asian societies, it tends to be linked to external appearance, with social aspects of self-identity such as getting along with others. In addition, people in individualistic cultures are more aware of emotions and dispositions as causes of behavior, whereas in collectivist cultures they are more likely to attribute behavior to situational structures such as norms and roles (Suh, Diener, Oishi, & Triandis, 1998). Suh and colleagues (1998) argue that in more individualistic cultures the self is seen as an "autonomous, self-sufficient entity that is essentially independent from its surrounding interpersonal context" (p. 482) and "internal attributes, such as attitudes, emotions, preferences, and beliefs, become the diagnostic markers of one's identity" (p. 483). Similarly, youth in the more collectivist Danish culture provide fewer private and more public and collective self-descriptions than members of less collectivist Spanish and Mexican cultures. Other studies show that individualistic and collectivist cultural structures differentiate between children's attention to internal, personal self-image and a more integrated more communal awareness of self. For example, within the more collectivist culture of Iceland, many Icelandic youth found questions such as "What are you like?" too strange to answer, but they were able to describe other people (Hart & Fegley, 1997). Cultural orientation also influences the stability of self-awareness (English & Chen, 2007). Asian Americans tend to be less consistent in their self-descriptions across contexts than do European Americans. However, Asian American self-descriptions tend to remain consistent over time *within* context, demonstrating that the contextualization of self-awareness is more collectivistic.

Self-Management

Cultural structures such as beliefs, rules, and expectations play an important role in self-management. In a study of 23 countries, Matsumoto, Yoo, and Nakawa (2008) found that cultural beliefs influence overall emotion regulation. Cultures that emphasize a longer-term perspective and social order are more likely to inhibit emotional expression, whereas those that place a higher value on individuals are more likely to express them.

Display rules guide emotional expressions and differ by culture (Matsumoto, 1991). Whereas loud, positive expressions of emotion may be expected at an Irish wake, funerals in some other cultures are expected to be more somber (Rosenblatt, 1993). Something as simple as eye contact also is rule governed. If one neglects to make eye contact with a person while conversing in mainstream U.S. culture, for example, one may be thought to lack self-confidence, whereas a person who makes eye contact is thought to be confident and bold (Scudder, 2012).

As can be seen from the discussion of displays rules, cultures differ widely in terms of people's expectations and norms about self-expression. It should not be surprising, then, that people in various cultures differ in their reactions to expressiveness. For example, assertiveness may actually mean different things in different cultures (Pacquiao, 2000). People in Malaysian, U.S., and Filipino cultures are more likely to speak up clearly when they disagree than are people in Japanese culture.

Social Awareness

In contrast to self-awareness and self-management, social awareness shifts the emphasis to connections between and among people. In general, cultural awareness is a foundation of communication, and it involves the cognitive ability to stand back from ourselves and become aware of our cultural values, beliefs, and perceptions, as well as those of others around us. Why do people do things in that way? How do people see the world? Why do people react in that particular way? This is structural because it requires a cognitive system to evaluate or judge. Cultural awareness becomes particularly critical when we have to interact with people from other cultures. For example, on Friday at the beginning of Sabbath, an Orthodox Jewish man would not shake hands with a woman other than his wife (Noble, Rom, Newsome-Wicks, Engelhardt, & Woloski-Wruble, 2009). This rule structure can be quite unfamiliar to people who do not understand its cultural basis.

As may be apparent from the previous discussion, collectivist cultures are more integrated and operate more on consensus of norms, with disapprobation toward individuals who deviate from shared norms. Individual behavior is judged by others, not by the individual, and individuals seek approbation from others. Thus, social awareness is very highly valued in these cultures. Other studies point to differences in "face saving" or the practice of interaction that allows people to feel proud of themselves. In Eastern cultures, rules exist to guide interactions toward face saving, which is less valued in Western cultures (Tse, Lee, Vertinsky, & Wehrung, 1988).

Finally, social structures also may play a role in social awareness. Less powerful people, for example, actually tend to have stronger perspective-taking competencies because they must accommodate more powerful people (Gregory & Webster, 1996). Power also plays a role in eye contact and other nonverbal behaviors (Guerrero & Hecht, 2008).

Relationship Skills

There are a number of structural differences in relationship skills. These may occur in something as subtle as eye contact, which regulates conversations in every culture, although often in different ways. In the United States, most cultural groups consider eye contact a sign of interest in the other, whereas avoidance expresses a lack of interest (Kalbfleisch, 2009). However, among many Native Americans in the United States, direct eye contact when addressing a higher status other can be interpreted as rude or disrespectful (Kalbfleisch, 2009). In contrast, in the Middle East, direct eye contact is much less common and considered less appropriate. Middle Eastern cultures, largely Muslim, have strict rules regarding eye contact between the sexes; these rules are connected to religious laws about appropriateness (Simpson & Carter, 2008). Only a brief moment of eye contact, if any, would be permitted between a man and a woman. A third set of eye contact rules can be found in Asia, Latin America, and Africa, where extended eye contact can be taken as an affront or a challenge of authority (Zhang, 2006). It is often considered more polite to have only sporadic or brief eye contact, especially between people of different social registers (e.g., a student and teacher).

Responsible Decision Making

Structural factors also affect the choices people make. Although people in all cultures are likely to value decisions that fulfill individual needs and promote community norms, standards, and outcomes (Mann et al., 1998), those in individualistic cultures tend to value more highly the decisions that promote individual needs, whereas those in collectivist cultures value those that promote group outcomes. Similarly, Triandis (1995) argues that collectivists are socialized toward responsibility taking. Personal or individual competence is stressed more by Western students, who tend to be individualistic, whereas those in Eastern or collectivist cultures are more likely to see decision making as a shared activity and defer to group opinions (Mann et al., 1998). Suh and colleagues (1998) reported that Westerners typically form judgments based on internal assessments and inner feelings criteria valued in individualistic cultures. Thus, there appear to be cultural differences in responsible decision making both in terms of who makes decisions (self or group) and the criteria for judging decisions.

Structural differences also may exist in other aspects of responsible decision making. Some cultures have very strict rules for who may interact with whom (e.g., the caste system in India; restrictions on gender interactions among fundamentalist Muslims) that affect who may make decisions (Singh, 2012). Normative practices for respectful interaction also vary (Hofstede, 1986). The Quaker meeting practice of sitting in silence while waiting for the next participant and the Native American decision-making practice of passing of the stick to regulate turns are both examples of responsible decision-making practices that vary based on cultural structures.

Cultural Functions and Social and Emotional Competencies

We turn next to an examination of social and emotional competencies as cultural functions, focusing on families because they are one of the primary means by which acculturation and enculturation occur. While socialization itself is a cultural process and families are cultural structures, in this section we consider what is achieved, or the outcomes of socialization.

Self-Awareness

Families, especially parents, are the primary socialization agent and exert significant influence on how children perceive themselves and identify who they are (Socha, 2009). On the one hand, in more individualistic cultures (e.g., the United States), parents typically teach their children the value of independence and equality, which places more emphasis on the self. Parents in more collectivistic cultures, on the other hand, are more likely to socialize their children with the notion of pursuing harmony with others and being respectful to others higher in the social hierarchy (Guilamo-Ramos et al., 2007). These cultural values shape children's perceptions of who they are in relation to others. For example, happiness in one culture may be attained by one's self-confidence, whereas in another culture it is gained through a sense of one's belonging and through others' happiness.

Self-Management

Each culture establishes display rules that determine effective self-management. The rules guide behavior by establishing rubrics for determining effective and appropriate emotional expression through social structures regarding which emotions should be expressed in a situation and how they should be expressed. Rule-following behavior maximizes interpersonal effectiveness and is one of the self-management methods children learn and practice as they grow older. This is accomplished by parents, teachers, and other adults who normalize display of rules during interaction with children (Socha, 2009).

One of the cultural differences in display rules concerns the range of emotions that can be acceptably expressed in any situation (Leersnyder, Boiger, & Mesquita, 2013). People are expected to manage emotions, so that they stay within that specified range. If they conform to the rules, their behavior is likely to be judged appropriate. There are other consequences of conforming to or violating these cultural expression rules. For example, individuals whose own emotion regulation patterns match their culture's norms tend to report lower levels of depression and higher levels of satisfaction in relationships than those who displays do not match their cultural norms (Matsumoto et al., 2008).

Social Awareness

Culture also defines what is socially appropriate in interpersonal relationships, and families reinforce the consistent values that profoundly shape children's social awareness. For example, humbleness toward others is more likely to be socially desirable and acceptable in collectivistic cultures than in the individualistic culture that values self-confidence and assertiveness in relationships (Kim, 2003). Sacrifice for family or close friends is another example that may enable different interpretations. In more individualistic cultures, sacrifice for others is perceived less desirable than it is in more collectivistic cultures in which sacrifice for loved ones is more likely to be perceived as an honorable opportunity to make others happy and is interchangeable with love.

Relationship Skills

One way children learn socially and culturally appropriate communication skills is by observing family members. Prior to institutional education, parents teach children to speak the native language and how to use nonverbal cues in a social manner (e.g., through eye contact, body gesture, touch, or personal distance). In Korean culture, for example, children are taught to use formal language with older persons or those in a higher social position (e.g., teacher, doctor). This requires recognition of the social hierarchy (social awareness), as well as relational skills. If they violate this social norm, parents are blamed for their failure in "home discipline" (Shin & Koh, 2005). The cultural value of respect for older people creates implications for verbal and nonverbal communication skills in Korean society, and an individual's violation of such expectation may lead to blame falling on the parents or family. In other cultures, there is less pressure on distinguishing and recognizing the power distance between individuals based on social hierarchy. This requires more equality in social norms and communicative practices. In general, children's misbehavior or misconduct significantly influences parents' and family's reputation in collectivist cultures.

Responsible Decision Making

The process of decision making varies greatly by family culture. Culture plays a major role in determining who holds power in the family and who makes a final decision. In more collectivistic cultures, the parent has predominant power over children's decision making. Children are socially taught that they need to be obedient to parents and follow parents' decision (Oak & Martin, 2000). By contrast, children in more individualist cultures are strongly encouraged to make their own decisions based on their individual needs rather than on their parents' or family's needs.

Cultural Processes and Social and Emotional Competencies

Cultural as process is the final approach. Culture as process examines development and enactments of the competencies. For example, are there cultural differences in how a culture's individuals express emotion, deal with conflict, or work with others? We have already discussed display rules for emotions. The process approach is more about how these rules are enacted than about the structural properties as rules or the outcomes of rule following.

Self-Awareness

The structural distinction between individualism and collectivism discussed earlier in the chapter is central to cultural processes of self-awareness. Individualistic cultures tend to emphasize an independent person's awareness of emotions and behaviors, whereas collectivist cultures conceptualize feelings and behaviors as interdependent within the group. Collectivist interpretations of the self also take into account the context more broadly, while individualists tend to be more aware of self as separate from the situation. This influences the attributions people make about the role of the self in social interaction. People who are highly interdependent and collectivist tend to attribute negative events to external causes rather than to individuals, whereas those who are less independent and individualistic attribute them to the individuals involved (Maister & Tsakiris, 2014).

Self-Management

Cultures also differ in the process of self-management. For example, too much self-expression or assertiveness tends to be discouraged in Japanese culture because of its possible negative effects on harmonious relationships among members of a group. Malaysian, U.S., and Filipino people are more likely to speak up clearly when they disagree than those in Japanese culture (Nakanishi, 1986). In Japanese culture there is a tendency to avoid bringing up different ideas and, instead, individuals feign understanding even when the meaning of the person with whom they are conversing is not clear.

These management processes can be complex. Regulation takes place at the individual, relational, and contextual levels, with culture playing a role at all levels (Leersnyder et al., 2013). Students, for example, tend to regulate their behavior in school through cognitive processes. At the relational level, parents may participate in "coregulation" when they highlight or reinforce certain experiences that are culturally important. Immigrants tend to recognize the extremes of regulation (e.g., when they are expected to be silent) and adopt these patterns. Furthermore, those in individualistic cultures are likely to adopt a "promotion focus," putting themselves in situations where they are likely to succeed in order to achieve high self-esteem. Conversely, those in collectivist cultures are more likely to adopt a "prevention focus," actively avoiding situations perceived as having a high risk of failure in order to avoid shame.

Social Awareness

The individualistic–collectivist distinction also applies to the processes involved in social awareness. People in individualistic cultures tend to describe emotional situations from their own perspective, whereas individuals in collective cultures tend to describe emotional situations from the perspective of those around them (Leersnyder et al., 2013). In other words, collectivism encourages social awareness. In addition, people are more likely to be credited with their own successes in individualistic cultures rather than having it ascribed to chance or to those around them, as in collectivist orientations. The belief that one can control one's situation also is very individualistic, whereas individuals in collectivist cultures tend to think that they are not necessarily in control of their own situation. Parenting styles enforce these ideas (focusing on one's own feelings or the feelings of others) along with social regulation and environment.

Paying close attention to nonverbal feedback and subtle situational cues, competent communicators can move from the general to the specific and/or from the opaque to the transparent with mastery (Nakanishi, 1986). Some evidence suggests that these processes result in greater perspective taking in collectivist cultures than in more individualistic ones. Cohen and Gunz (2002) report that people from more collectivist cultures tend to recall salient events as an outsider or observer would, whereas those from more individualistic cultures describe the event from their own, personal perspective. Interestingly, language can trigger one orientation or another in bicultural individuals. Bicultural Chinese describe themselves more individualistically in English than they do in Chinese (Ross, Xun, & Wilson, 2002).

Relationship Skills

The cultural process literature on relationship skills is broad, especially in terms of communication competencies. However, a number of key, culturally based processes are required in order to establish and maintain competently healthy relationships. We focus on how respect and consideration for other's feelings are managed to illustrate this approach.

For many Koreans, respect is communicated via formality (especially in introductions), using the correct or family name rather than one's given name, unless it is a close friend and/or informal setting. One the one hand, this practice also involves acknowledging age and status so as to treat elders with deference (Miller & Mackenzie, 2009). On the other hand, for many Americans, respect is communicated in initial interactions by treating others as equals and expressing sincere pleasure in making a new acquaintance. There also are differences within cultures. For example, within overall U.S. culture, African American culture often privileges "involvement politeness" (i.e., laughter, animation), whereas Korean Americans often use "restraint politeness" (i.e., silence, terse verbal response) (Bailey, 1998). As a result, Korean storeowners in lower-socioeconomic-status African American neighborhoods may be perceived as unfriendly and racist, while their African American customers are seen as selfish and ill-mannered.

A second area in which cultural processes influence relationship skills involves consideration for other people's feelings. For example, both Japanese and Malaysians are prone to consider other people's feelings by keeping their opinions to themselves to avoid seeming overly forward and/or as hurting other people's feelings (Nakanishi, 1986). In Eastern cultures, rules exist to guide interactions toward "face saving," the practice of allowing others to avoid embarrassment, while in Western cultures, this is less highly valued (Tse et al., 1988).

Overall, people from collectivistic cultures usually avoid conflicts because the "mutual face" or the face of the group is the top concern (Ting-Toomey, 2005). For example, members of the Utku Inuit culture tend to structure their interactions to avoid confrontation at all costs (Leersnyder et al., 2013).

These distinctions also are present when we examine how personal and private information is disclosed to others. For example, whereas Americans tend to judge the degree to which speakers are open based on the amount of information disclosure, Japanese are less likely to rely on specific information to judge openness. Overall, there tend to be higher levels of interrogation and self-disclosure among Americans than Japanese (Gudykunst & Nishida, 1984). In fact, people in Japanese and Chinese cultures may view higher levels of disclosure as less competent compared to the way openness is seen in U.S. culture (Nakanishi, 1986).

Responsible Decision Making

As in other areas, individualistic and collectivist cultures tend to enact different decision-making processes. For example, individuals with higher levels of individualism (e.g., Americans, Germans) tend to be more rational in their decision-making processing, while those with higher levels of collectivism (e.g., Ghana) tend to be more dependent and less likely to betray the interests of members of more central in-groups in favor of less central in-groups (Lefebvre & Franke, 2013). In Germany, autonomy in decision-making is likely to be emphasized (Blank, 2011).

Cultures even differ with regard to whom to include in the decision-making process. The involvement of other parties (besides patients, doctors, and patients' families) in medical decision making is common in some Asian, African, and Native American cultures (Yates & Alattar, 2009). Those other parties include people with religious responsibilities, such as Shamans, or nonreligious traditional or alternative healers. For example, Eastern cultures view illness as a shared family affair, and this differs from the view in Western cultures (Blank, 2011). Research also indicates that it is common practice in Asian cultures, such as India and Taiwan, for physicians not to disclose the complete truth of the illness, especially to a patient with terminal cancer, because it is considered the family's responsibility to tell the truth (Chattopadhyay & Simon, 2008). As noted, cultures are not monolithic. Within

U.S. society, seriously ill older Latinos are likely to favor more family-centered decisions and limited patient autonomy than other groups (Blank, 2011).

Guidelines and Recommendations for Research and Practice

Although this chapter makes clear that culture plays a role in social and emotional competencies, two important questions remain unanswered: (1) whether the competencies are universal, and (2) how interventions should deal with cultural variation.

Universality of Social and Emotional Competencies

On the one hand, it is hard to argue with the statement that all humans have emotions and somehow learn to manage them to one degree or another. In principle, the competencies that allow consideration of another's mental state (i.e., social awareness) are so important for social action that humans must develop them in some form to function in any culture. The evidence regarding social cognitive development also supports the idea that social awareness and perspective taking can be universal. Young children confound their private knowledge with the knowledge of others, failing to understand that others can have false beliefs. Only after age 4 do children typically distinguish their knowledge from that of other people. This developmental trajectory appears to be the same across countries and cultures. For instance, Sabbagh, Xu, Carlson, Moses, and Lee (2006) found that Chinese and American children are the same age when they develop the social awareness that other people can have false beliefs. The development of the mind does not seem to depend on schooling or literacy. Even children in an isolated, preliterate, hunter–gatherer culture show the same trajectory for the appreciation of the other's mind through perspective taking as do U.S. children (Avis & Harris, 1991). So people's endowed ability for perspective taking, a key element of the social awareness competency of SEL, seems universal.

What is less clear, however, is whether this particular set of competencies is equally relevant across cultures (e.g., are different sets of competencies needed in various cultures?), or whether the same set of competencies exists but differs in structures, processes, and functions. Future research is needed to address this issue.

On the other hand, we argue that there is considerable cultural variation in the expression of social and emotional competencies. For example, previously discussed research demonstrates cultural differences in emotional display rules (i.e., when it is acceptable to express certain emotions). There do not appear to be cultural differences in the ways human brains develop, suggesting that functions such as emotion regulation and decision making that require a level of brain functionality may be universal developmental issues (Steinberg, 2007). As a result, we believe that the competencies have universal utility even if they are often defined (structured), expressed (processed), and achieved (functional) differently across cultures. Research also is needed to confirm this thesis.

Universality of Research Guidelines and Recommendations

Issues surrounding the universality of social and emotional competencies both as a set as well as each individually invite further research (Gonzales, Lau, Murry, Piña, & Barrera, 2013). Our analysis organized the literature around the five competencies. In a sense, we "imposed" this structure on the research findings without empirically testing how well the model fit. To our knowledge, no typological methodology (e.g., factor analysis, latent profile analysis) has been utilized to confirm whether the grouping into five competencies is maintained cross-culturally. In addition, many cultural researchers would recommend a culture-centric or emic approach to examining the question of universality (Singer, Dressler, George, & the NIH [National Institutes of Health] Expert Panel on Defining and Operationalizing Culture for Health Research, 2013). This means starting with a culture and seeing whether the five competencies emerge out of research conducted from within the specific culture's various processes, structures, and functions. One might almost conceptualize a "meta-emic" approach in which simultaneous and independent examinations of basic developmental competencies are conducted within a number of different cultures, spanning the developed and developing worlds, as well as various religions and other cultural signifiers. At the "meta" level, one could examine whether the resulting frameworks could then be mapped onto the social and emotional competencies. What is clear is that the SEL framework itself provides insight into development across cultures and, conversely, culture provides insight into SEL.

Specifically, we recommend the following basic research priorities:

1. Determine whether (or the degree to which) each of the five social and emotional competency domains is relevant cross-culturally.
2. Determine whether (or the degree to which) the five social and emotional competencies are valid cross-culturally as a set.
3. Have papers specify their conceptual definition and operationalization of culture.

SEL Interventions

We turn next to consideration of SEL interventions. There has been much discussion in the prevention implementation literature about the need for cultural adaptation, although no consensus has emerged about the overall advantages of targeted or tailored interventions over universal intervention. Nor do we know much about what aspects of the intervention (e.g., content or delivery) should be adapted for maximal impact (Colby et al., 2013). Instead, we know that under some conditions, whereas adapted interventions appear to have advantages, there appear to be universal interventions that maintain their effectiveness across groups. The problem in drawing overall conclusions about the comparative advantages of adapted interventions is that not all adaptations are equal. Poorly executed adaptations that fail to produce effects do not mean that adaptation itself is ineffective. Absent a metric for evaluating adaptation, a tool that has yet to emerge but is needed, it is difficult to assess these comparative advantages of one approach or the other.

Conversely, a universal program that is effective across groups does not mean a culturally adapted version might not produce stronger outcomes. The fact that, for example, multisystemic therapy has been found effective among various ethnic and racial minorities (Henggeler & Schaeffer, 2010) does not mean a culturally appropriate version would not improve outcomes for some groups.

Thus, there is enough evidence to argue that, under some circumstances, well-executed adaptations are effective (for reviews, see Colby et al., 2013; Gonzales et al., 2013) and this may have important implications for SEL interventions. The first question, then, is when is it appropriate to adapt? Barrera and Castro (2006) suggest that an adaptation is justified when (1) it is likely to impact recruitment, retention, or participation; (2) there are unique risk or resilience factors underlying the intervention that function differently across cultural groups; (3) there are culturally unique symptoms of a common disorder; and (4) a universal intervention has proven ineffective for a particular cultural group. Comparing the cost-effectiveness of universal versus adapted interventions is another consideration.

Furthermore, Sanders (2012) argues that community members should be consulted regarding possible adaptations. This is the premise behind many of the arguments for community-based participatory research. Although potential participants are experts in some areas (e.g., providing information about recruitment, evaluation of intervention activities or look, learning/teaching styles), it is not at all clear to us that nonexperts are positioned to make determinations about issues such as strategies for adaptation. Clearly, community members are valuable partners in development and implementation of prevention interventions and can participate in some decisions about what to adapt and how to adapt it. However, we believe that roles need to be assigned with an understanding of knowledge and skills, a process that might be called *community engagement*. Unfortunately, like much about cultural adaptation, these processes have yet to be clearly articulated.

A final issue concerns message targeting. *Targeting* is a common communication and marketing strategy that involves developing and delivering messages to specific groups. However, in prevention, it is not clear what we would do with information that a certain intervention works more effectively with a segment of the population (e.g., females) in situations in which messages cannot be effectively delivered to one subgroup rather than the entire group. School-based interventions provide an example of a situation in which it is probably impractical to expect that males and females will participate separately in drug prevention curricula even if a certain curriculum is more effective for one group or the other. As a result, we have argued for a multicultural approach under circumstances such as these. Multiculturalism involves incorporation of cultural elements from as many segments of the audience as feasible. One way this can be accomplished is by presenting a variety of cultural narratives. Evaluation research of one drug prevention program, Keepin' it REAL, suggests that the strategy of cultural grounding (Hecht & Krieger, 2006), which produces a multicultural curriculum incorporating the cultures of a variety of groups, is at least as effective and in many cases is more effective overall than one targeting a specific cultural group (Hecht, Graham, & Elek, 2006). For example, in this research, a multicultural intervention that included elements of Mexican American, African American, and European American cultures (e.g., communication styles, values, and beliefs) was at least as effective in reducing substance use among the entire audience as a program that incorporated only Mexican American cultural features. However, this example does not prove the rule, and more research is needed that directly tests multiculturalism.

Resnicow, Soler, Braithwaite, Ahluwalia, and Butler (2000) argued that there are two important distinctions to be made about adaptations. Surface adaptations occur when curricular design includes observable but more superficial characteristics (e.g., people, places, language, food, and clothing). Deeper adaptations involve the inclusion of underlying structures such as cultural values and meanings. A more specific and elaborate taxonomy was proposed by Kreuter, Lukwago, Bucholtz, Clark, and Sanders-Thompson (2003). As with surface adaptations, they define peripheral adaptation to refer to how the curriculum is "packaged" to give the appearance of cultural appropriateness (e.g., colors, images, fonts, pictures). Using images of African Americans on the cover of a curriculum would be an example of peripheral adaptation. Interventions can be adapted by providing health information relevant to a particular group, an approach called an "evidential strategy," or by adapting the curriculum into a new language using a linguistic strategy. Next are constituent-involving strategies that use community members in program design. Finally, sociocultural strategies are seen as similar to Resnicow and colleagues' conception of "deep structure" and involve integrating cultural values and characteristics of the intended audience.

Within the cultural sensitivity literature, Hecht and Krieger (2006) articulated a position characterized as the principle of cultural grounding. Although the adaptation literature focuses on the role of culture, much of the literature is concerned with how to transport a curriculum to a new culture through what Resnicow and colleagues (2000) would label "surface adaptations" and Kreuter and colleagues (2003) would call "peripheral strategies." These types of adaptions refer to the cultural adaptation of evidence-based interventions. Complementing the cultural adaptation and sensitivity literature, and emerging out of similar theoretical and conceptual roots, the principle of cultural grounding is a prevention philosophy derived from communication competence and narrative theories, as well as multiculturalism. The central theoretical construct of this approach, "grounding," emphasizes deriving prevention messages from the culture, with cultural group members as active participants in message design and production. It also invokes core values, narratives, and communication styles as central features of deep structure. This theoretical move is a "difference of degree" because those ascribing to related sensitivity and adaptation approaches also enlist cultural group members and incorporate their insights.

Finally, there is the issue of cultural adaptation of SEL-based interventions. In general, universal school-based interventions are the norm among SEL programs, although some have been culturally adapted. The PATHS (Providing Alterative THinking Strategies) program, for example, is being implemented on four continents and has been adopted for both rural and urban U.S. cultures. Greenberg (personal communication, February 14, 2014), one of the primary authors of the PATHS curriculum, describes the adaptation process involving language translation, use of familiar analogies, and changing certain text to reflect cultural norms. The process involved utilizing community-based participatory practices but, in essence, tended to make surface changes with the core curriculum remaining fairly constant. Gonzales and colleagues (2013) noted that much of the work on SEL adaptation has been oriented in a manner that does not engage deeper questions about the core competencies.

Intervention Recommendation and Guidelines

As yet there does not exist a widely accepted typology of adaptation methods or a means for evaluating the quality of these efforts. Without such a system, it is impossible to address conclusively whether, when, or how SEL interventions should be adapted. If we assume that some adaptation is inevitable (Colby et al., 2013), then the question becomes whether changes involve cultural adaptation (or some other type) and what are the outcomes of the changes (Miller-Day et al., 2013). Finally, the role of the participant in prevention interventions is almost unexamined. Questions of participants' cognitive processing and interpretations of messages, as well as the social proliferation of spread of messages through interaction (Larkey & Hecht, 2010), remain to be considered as part of the adaptation process.

Specifically we recommend the following:

1. Develop a metric for evaluating the nature and quality of adaptation.
2. Develop a theory and metric for assessing when adaptation is needed.
3. Conduct comparative research between adapted and universal SEL interventions.
4. Clarify the role of community members in adaptation processes.
5. Conduct formative research to identify salient cultural dimensions. Both quantitative and qualitative methods can be used here.
6. Conduct more research on issues affecting implementation and sustainability.

Potential Problems and Pitfalls

It has not been our intention to resolve or even address all relevant issues; rather we have attempted to bring a richer perspective on culture to bear on the study of social and emotional competencies. At the same time, certain problems and pitfalls must be acknowledged. First, and perhaps foremost, is the ecological fallacy (Piantadosi, Byar, & Green, 1988) of assigning cultural values to the individual. Although there may be a tendency for social and emotional competencies to be processed one way in culture *A* and a different way in culture *B*, all individuals in each culture will not match the cultural norm. In fact, this match or cultural consonance is of great significance for health and health outcomes. For example, individuals whose own emotional patterns best match their cultures tend to report lower levels of depression and higher levels of satisfaction in relationships (Leersnyder et al., 2013). Our own work on identity suggests that cultures differ somewhat in the social processes involved in drug offers (e.g., how they are offered, by whom, where, and how individuals respond to them; Marsiglia, Kulis, Hecht, & Sills, 2004), and that there also are differences based on geography within the same culture (Pettigrew, Miller-Day, Krieger, & Hecht, 2012). At the same time, this work suggests that there is a common core of strategies youth use to resist pressures from peers to use substances and also similar social processes at work in resisting sexual pressure among adolescent Latinas (Norris, Hughes, Hecht, Peragallo, & Nickerson, 2013). Thus, it is important not to assume cultural uniformity when conducting research. Cultures are heterogeneous, and there may be more variance within groups than between them. Instead some measure of cultural identification or adherence should be included to allow the within-group variation to be recognized and its potential influence on outcomes to be assessed.

Specifically, the construct of culture provides the following challenges:

1. Do not assume that the findings from one cultural group generalize to others without direct testing.
2. Do not assume that findings for the

entire culture apply to all subgroups or to individuals. Utilizing a measure such as cultural congruence or identity will provide insight into within- group variance that avoids overgeneralization and stereotyping.

Conclusions

We hope our discussion of culture and social and emotional competencies provides insight into the complexities involved. Culture is not a simple categorical variable (i.e., white/black/Latino) but rather a lens for understanding the processes, structures, and functions that characterize membership in groups. The application of this construct to SEL will challenge researchers and practitioners but, at the same time, produce richer theory and practice.

References

Avis, J., & Harris, P. L. (1991). Belief–desire reasoning among Baka children: Evidence for a universal conception of mind. *Child Development, 62*(3), 460–467.

Bailey, R. G. (1998). *Ecoregions of North America* (No. 1548). Washington, DC: U.S. Department of Agriculture, Forest Service.

Baldwin, J. R., Faulkner, S. L., Hecht, M. L., & Lindsley, S. L. (Eds.). (2006). *Redefining culture: Perspectives across the disciplines.* Mahwah, NJ: Erlbaum.

Barrera, M., & Castro, F. G. (2006). A heuristic framework for the cultural adaptation of interventions. *Clinical Psychology: Science and Practice, 13*(4), 311–316.

Blank, R. H. (2011). End-of-life decision making across cultures. *Journal of Law, Medicine, and Ethics, 39*(2), 201–214.

Bronfenbrenner, U., & Morris, P. A. (2006). The bioecological model of human development. In W. Damon & R. M. Lerner (Eds.), *Handbook of child psychology: Vol. 1. Theoretical models of human development* (6th ed., pp. 793–828). Hoboken, NJ: Wiley.

Chattopadhyay, S., & Simon, A. (2008). East meets West: Cross-cultural perspective in end-of-life decision making from Indian and German viewpoints. *Medicine, Health Care and Philosophy, 11*(2), 165–174.

Chen, S. F. (2009). Performance prediction for exponential language models. In *Proceedings of Human Language Technologies: The 2009 Annual Conference of the North American Chapter of the Association for Computational Linguistics* (pp. 450–458). Stroudsburg, PA: Association for Computational Linguistics.

Cohen, D., & Gunz, A. (2002). As seen by the other: Perspectives on the self in the memories and emotional perceptions of Easterners and Westerners. *Psychological Science, 13*(1), 55–59.

Colby, M., Hecht, M. L., Miller-Day, M., Krieger, J. R., Syverstsen, A. K., Graham, J. W., et al. (2013). Adapting school-based substance use prevention curriculum through cultural grounding: An exemplar of adaptation processes for rural schools. *American Journal of Community Psychology, 51,* 190–205.

Collaborative for Academic, Social, and Emotional Learning (CASEL). (2012). What is social and emotional learning? Retrieved February 16, 2014, from *www.casel.org/social-and-emotional-learning.*

English, T., & Chen, S. (2007). Culture and self-concept stability: Consistence across and within contexts among Asian Americans and European Americans. *Journal of Personality and Social Psychology, 93*(3), 478–490.

Gonzales, N. A., Lau, A. S., Murry, V. M., Piña, A. A., & Barrera, M., Jr. (2013). Culturally adapted preventive interventions for children and adolescents. Retrieved March 15, 2014, from *www.prevention.psu.edu/events/documents/gonzalesetal.culturaladaptationchapter.pdf.*

Gregory, S. W., & Webster, S. (1996). A nonverbal signal in voices of interview partners effectively predicts communication accommodation and social status perceptions. *Journal of Personality and Social Psychology, 70*(6), 1231–1240.

Gudykunst, W. B., & Nishida, T. (1984). Individual and cultural influences on uncertainty reduction. *Communication Monographs, 51*(1), 23–36.

Guerrero, L. K., & Hecht, M. L. (2008). Power and persuasion. In L. K. Guerrero & M. L. Hecht (Eds.), *The nonverbal communication reader: Classical and contemporary perspectives* (3rd ed., pp. 448–449). Prospect Heights, IL: Waveland.

Guilamo-Ramos, V., Dittus, P., Jaccard, J., Johansson, M., Bouris, A., & Acosta, N. (2007). Parenting practices among Dominican and Puerto Rican mothers. *Social Work, 52*(1), 17–30.

Hart, D., & Fegley, S. (1997). Children's self-awareness and self-understanding in cultural context. In U. Neisser & D. A. Jopling (Eds.), *The conceptual self in context: Culture, experience, self-understanding* (pp. 128–153). New York: Cambridge University Press.

Hecht, M. L., Graham, J. W., & Elek, E. (2006). The Drug Resistance Strategies Intervention:

Program effects on substance use. *Health Communication, 20*(3), 267–276.

Hecht, M. L., & Krieger, J. K. (2006). The principle of cultural grounding in school-based substance use prevention: The Drug Resistance Strategies Project. *Journal of Language and Social Psychology, 25*(3), 301–319.

Henggeler, S. W., & Schaeffer, C. M. (2010). Treating serious emotional and behavioural problems using multisystemic therapy. *Australian and New Zealand Journal of Family Therapy, 31*(2), 149–164.

Hofstede, G. (1986). Cultural differences in teaching and learning. *International Journal of Intercultural Relations, 10*(3), 301–320.

Kalbfleisch, P. J. (2009). Effective health communication in native populations in North America. *Journal of Language and Social Psychology, 28*(2), 158–173.

Kim, S. H. (2003). Korean cultural codes and communication. *International Area Studies Review, 6*(1), 93–114.

Kim, U., Triandis, H. C., Kagitçibasi, C., Choi, S. C., & Yoon, G. (Eds.). (1994). *Individualism and collectivism: Theory, method, and applications.* Thousand Oaks, CA: Sage.

Kreuter, M. W., Lukwago, S. N., Bucholtz, R. D., Clark, E. M., & Sanders-Thompson, V. (2003). Achieving cultural appropriateness in health promotion programs: Targeted and tailored approaches. *Health Education and Behavior, 30*(2), 133–146.

Larkey, L., & Hecht, M. L. (2010). A model of effects of narrative as culture-centric health promotion. *Journal of Health Communication, 15*(2), 114–135.

Leersnyder, J. D., Boiger, M., & Mesquita, B. (2013). Cultural regulation of emotion: Individual, relational, and structural sources. *Frontiers in Psychology, 4*(55), 1–11.

Lefebvre, R., & Franke, V. (2013). Culture matters: Individualism vs. collectivism in conflict decision-making. *Societies, 3*(1), 128–146.

Maister, L., & Tsakiris, M. (2014). My face, my heart: Cultural differences in integrated bodily self-awareness. *Cognitive Neuroscience, 5*(1), 10–16.

Mann, L., Radford, M., Burnett, P., Ford, S., Bond, M., Leung, K., et al. (1998). Cross-cultural differences in self-reported decision-making style and confidence. *International Journal of Psychology, 33*(5), 325–335.

Marsiglia, F. F., Kulis, S., Hecht, M. L., & Sills, S. (2004). Ethnicity and ethnic identity as predictors of drug norms and drug use among preadolescents in the Southwest. *Substance Use and Misuse, 39*(7), 1061–1094.

Matsumoto, D. (1991). Cultural influences on facial expressions of emotion. *Southern Journal of Communication, 56*(2), 128–137.

Matsumoto, D., Yoo, S. H., & Nakawa, S. (2008). Culture, emotion regulation, and adjustment. *Journal of Personality and Social Psychology, 94*(6), 925–937.

Miller, J., & Mackenzie, L. (2009). The seventh sense: Understanding cultural differences. In *Squadron officer college expeditionary leadership coursebook.* Montgomery, AL: Air University.

Miller-Day, M., Pettigrew, J., Hecht, M. L., Shin, Y., Graham, J., & Krieger, J. (2013). How prevention curricula are taught under real-world conditions: Types of and reasons for teacher curriculum adaptations. *Health Education, 113*(4), 324–344.

Nakanishi, M. (1986). Perceptions of self-disclosure in initial interaction: A Japanese sample. *Human Communication Research, 13*(2), 167–190.

Noble, A., Rom, M., Newsome-Wicks, M., Engelhardt, K., & Woloski-Wruble, A. (2009). Jewish laws, customs, and practice in labor, delivery, and postpartum care. *Journal of Transcultural Nursing, 20*(3), 323–333.

Norris, A. E., Hughes, C., Hecht, M. L., Peragallo, N. P., & Nickerson, D. (2013). A randomized trial of a peer resistance skill building game for Hispanic early adolescent girls: Impact and feasibility of DRAMA-RAMA. *Nursing Research, 62*(1), 25–35.

Oak, S., & Martin, V. (2000). *American/Korean contrast: Patterns and expectations in the U.S. and Korea.* Elizabeth, NJ: Hollym.

Pacquiao, D. F. (2000). Impression management: An alternative to assertiveness in intercultural communication. *Journal of Transcultural Nursing, 11*(1), 5–6.

Pettigrew, J., Miller-Day, M., Krieger, J., & Hecht, M. (2012). The rural context of illicit substance offers: A study of Appalachian rural adolescents. *Journal of Adolescent Research, 27*(4), 523–550.

Piantadosi, S., Byar, D. P., & Green, S. B. (1988). The ecological fallacy. *American Journal of Epidemiology, 127*(5), 893–904.

Resnicow, K., Soler, R., Braithwaite, R. L., Ahluwalia, J. S., & Butler, J. (2000). Cultural sensitivity in substance use prevention. *Journal of Community Psychology, 28,* 271–290.

Rosenblatt, P. C. (1993). Cross-cultural variation in the experience, expression, and understanding of grief. In D. P. Irish, K. F. Lundquist, & V. J. Nelsen (Eds.), *Ethnic variations in dying, death, and grief: Diversity in universality* (pp. 13–19). Philadelphia: Taylor & Francis.

Ross, M., Xun, W. E., & Wilson, A. E. (2002). Language and the bicultural self. *Personality and Social Psychology Bulletin, 28*(8), 1040–1050.

Sabbagh, M. A., Xu, F., Carlson, S. M., Moses, L. J., & Lee, K. (2006). The development of executive functioning and theory of mind a comparison of Chinese and U.S. preschoolers. *Psychological Science, 17*(1), 74–81.

Sanders, M. R. (2012). Development, evaluation, and multinational dissemination of the Triple P-Positive Parenting program. *Annual Review of Clinical Psychology, 8,* 345–379.

Scudder, R. (2012, January 20). Eye contact: What does it communicate in various cultures? Retrieved October 23, 2013, from *www.brighthubeducation.com/social-studies-help/9626-learning-about-eye-contact-in-other-cultures.*

Shin, S., & Koh, M. S. (2005). Korean education in cultural context. *Essays in Education, 14,* 1–10.

Simpson, J. L., & Carter, K. (2008). Muslim women's experiences with health care providers in a rural area of the United States. *Journal of Transcultural Nursing, 19*(1), 16–23.

Singer, M. K., Dressler, W., George, S., and the NIH Expert Panel on Defining and Operationalizing Culture for Health Research. (2103). *Transforming the use of culture in health research.* Bethesda, MD: Office of Behavioral and Social Science Research.

Singh, N. (2012). Insight of Caste System in India: Its reflection in 21th century. *International Indexed and Referred Research Journal, 39,* 9–11.

Socha, T. J. (2009). Family as agency of potential: Toward a positive ontology of applied family communication theory and research. In L. R. Frey & K. N. Cissna (Eds.), *Routledge handbook of applied communication research* (pp. 309–330). New York: Routledge.

Steinberg, L. (2007). Risk taking in adolescence new perspectives from brain and behavioral science. *Current Directions in Psychological Science, 16*(2), 55–59.

Suh, E., Diener, E., Oishi, S., & Triandis, H. C. (1998). The shifting basis of life satisfaction judgments across cultures: Emotions versus norms. *Journal of Personality and Social Psychology, 74*(2), 482–493.

Ting-Toomey, S. (2005). The matrix of face: An updated face-negotiation theory. In W. B. Gudykunst (Ed.), *Theorizing about intercultural communication,* (pp. 71–92). Thousand Oaks, CA: Sage.

Triandis, H. C. (1995). *Individualism and collectivism.* Boulder, CO: Westview Press.

Tse, D. K., Lee, K., Vertinsky, I., & Wehrung, D. A. (1988). Does culture matter?: A cross-cultural study of executives' choice, decisiveness and risk adjustment in international marketing. *Journal of Marketing, 52*(4), 181–195.

Yates, J. F., & Alattar, L. (2009). Cultural issues. In M. W. Kattan (Ed.), *Encyclopedia of medical decision making* (pp. 247–252). Thousand Oaks, CA: Sage.

Zhang, L. (2006). Communication in academic libraries: An East Asian perspective. *Reference Services Review, 34*(1), 164–176.

CHAPTER 5

The Neuroscience of SEL

Clancy Blair and C. Cybele Raver

According to the Collaborative for Academic, Social, and Emotional Learning (CASEL; 2014), social and emotional learning (SEL) includes "recognizing and managing our emotions, developing caring and concern for others, establishing positive relationships, making responsible decisions, and handling challenging situations constructively and ethically. These are the skills that allow individuals to calm themselves when angry, make friends, resolve conflicts respectfully, and make ethical and safe choices." These skills are summarized by CASEL in five domains of competency that are the target of SEL programming: self-awareness, self-management, social awareness, relationship skills, and responsible decision making.

The topic of research in our laboratory, self-regulation, touches on all five domains of competency listed by CASEL but is most clearly associated with the domains of self-management, self-awareness, and responsible decision making. In this chapter, we present a psychobiological model of the development of self-regulation and apply findings from the literatures that support this model to an examination of the theory and practice of SEL. Effective self-regulation in many ways underlies and facilitates the thoughts, feelings, emotional states, and behaviors that are characteristic of SEL and enables individuals to engage in and to learn from beneficial interactions with others. In particular, in our research, we are interested in the mechanisms, ranging from the biological to the sociocultural, through which SEL programming affects competencies across the five domains identified by CASEL and thereby benefits children's academic and life outcomes. In this chapter, we consider the neurobiology of self-regulation in light of the well-documented empirical finding that provision of SEL programming to children, particularly children growing up in the context of poverty, benefits academic achievement as well as social–emotional well-being. A recent meta-analysis of 213 school-based, universal SEL programs involving 270,034 children has documented significant social–emotional and academic gains resulting from SEL programs evaluated using randomized designs (Durlak, Weissberg, Dymnicki, Taylor, & Schellinger, 2011). Given the strength of this evidence in support of SEL, it is important to address the theoretical and neuroscientific basis for the expectation that SEL programming will benefit children academically. To this end, we directly address the question of how programming that enhances children's social and emotional well-being may be related to changes in the developing brain and can be expected to affect academic outcomes meaningfully.

Self-regulation and self-regulated learning are manifestly important for academic achievement. Whether defined in terms of aspects of temperament and personality, such as emotionality and effortful control, self-efficacy beliefs and perceptions of the self, or the ability to control attention volitionally and engage working memory, inhibitory control, and attention shifting skills referred to jointly as "executive functions," self-regulation has been shown robustly to predict academic achievement over and above other child characteristics, such as intelligence (Blair & Razza, 2007; Elliott & Dweck, 1988; McClelland et al., 2007). In our research, we are interested in how self-regulation processes at multiple levels, from the neural to the behavioral to the social, are integrated and interrelated developmentally. To this end, we define "self-regulation" as a biobehavioral system in which attention and emotional responses to stimulation are organized, through volitional and nonvolitional means, to facilitate the reflective, goal-directed cognitive processes and strategies referred to as executive functions and to a temperament type, referred to as effortful control, that is characterized by the effective regulation of emotion, attention, perseverance, and determination in the face of challenge (Blair, 2002, 2010; Blair & Ursache, 2011). From this definition, and the theory and research we describe below, we demonstrate that SEL is integral to effective academic learning.

A Neurobiological Theory of Self-Regulation

In our theoretical model, self-regulation is understood to be the integration of neural, physiological, emotional, cognitive, and behavioral responses to stimulation that are hierarchically organized and reciprocally integrated. By this, we mean that self-regulation (or self-management, self-awareness, and responsible decision making, in the parlance of CASEL) is the product of a neurobiological system characterized by interactions across multiple levels of analysis and for which change in any one aspect of the system may have recursive effects on all others. An overarching result of neuroscience research early in the 21st century concerns the interconnected nature of the brain (Castellanos & Proal, 2012), and integration of biology and experience (Meaney, 2001). Although a large and impressive body of research and theorizing about the brain has demonstrated the role that its various areas play in a given cognitive or emotional function or ability, an equally large and impressive theoretical and empirical effort has demonstrated the importance of connectivity between brain areas: both the structural connections, that is, the actual nerve fibers that connect one area of the brain to another, and the functionval connections between brain areas, or the way in which activity in one brain area precedes, follows, or occurs simultaneously with activity in another brain area (Fox & Raichle, 2007). As such, it is increasingly clear that in order to understand best the way in which the brain is related to human behavior it is necessary to understand the brain as a system, one that is malleable and open to the effects of experience over time.

Of paramount importance is the understanding that many of the brain's connections *are shaped over time by experience* (Fox, Levitt, & Nelson, 2010). The general picture is one of the brain as a big, interconnected system in which different brain areas have distinct and specialized jobs, but that in order to complete those jobs, it is necessary that brain areas communicate with one another. In this way, the developing brain can be likened to the development of a finely tuned and highly trained orchestra, in which each musician comes to play his or her own role in ways that crescendo, or build off of other players' performances in ways that are precisely timed, highly synchronous, and carefully coordinated. Extending this analogy, the types of compositions that this orchestra plays as its predominant themes throughout its lifespan can be seen as a manifestation of the strength of connections among brain areas that are built over time by experience.

In Figure 5.1, we present a theoretical model of self-regulation that is consistent with this holistic connectionist experiential approach to brain development. The model extends the connectionist approach to examine ways in which multiple contributing components of self-regulation influence neural activity and developing con-

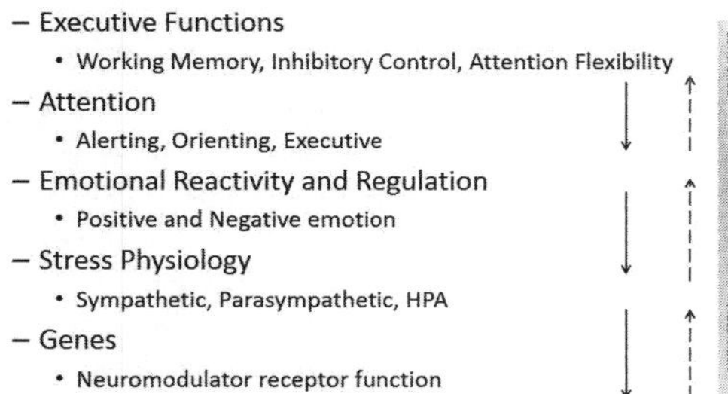

The Architecture of Self-Regulation
– Executive Functions
• Working Memory, Inhibitory Control, Attention Flexibility
– Attention
• Alerting, Orienting, Executive
– Emotional Reactivity and Regulation
• Positive and Negative emotion
– Stress Physiology
• Sympathetic, Parasympathetic, HPA
– Genes
• Neuromodulator receptor function
Controlled
Automatic

FIGURE 5.1. Architecture of self-regulation.

nectivity in the brain. These influences are arrayed along a continuum from the more overtly conscious and volitional to the more overtly nonconscious and automatic. These components include, at a minimum, aspects of cognition, notably attention and executive function, emotion, temperament, stress physiology, and genetic background, that combine to make up what can be referred to as the psychobiological architecture or architectonics of self-regulation.

Although common sense would seem to indicate that for self-regulation to occur, the individual must be consciously aware and engaging in some effort to regulate behavior, the conscious control of behavior is at best only half of the story. This is because self-regulation is characterized both by nonconscious, automatic "bottom-up" influences on behavior and conscious, effortful "top-down" influences. Such "dual-process" models are a mainstay of psychological research (Evans, 2008) and make reference to general rapid, automatic, implicit, reactive, or otherwise preconscious processing of information in relation to slower, effortful, explicit, and reflective conscious processing of information. While such models are perhaps most famously known under the guise of psychodynamic theory, that theory is only one example of a dual-process model, albeit one with specific assumptions about the origin of nonconscious influences on conscious behavior. There are, however, many examples of dual-process models of self-regulation, or what are known as cybernetic or self-adjusting systems. Self-regulation of the individual, as depicted in Figure 5.1, can be seen as a self-adjusting system (Luu & Tucker, 2004). These influences, from the genetic to the behavioral level, work in concert to establish and to maintain, and when needed, to alter, a given self-regulation set point in response to current and expected conditions. Importantly, the model is one in which perturbations to the system occurring at any level, from the neural and physiological to the social and cultural, can lead to the establishment of a new set point and alter systems at higher and lower levels in order to maintain the equilibrium of that new set point. Accordingly, questions about the development and malleability of self-regulation can be addressed by examining multiple levels of analysis and recursive effects throughout the system from changes occurring at a given level.

Genetics

The most fundamental level of bottom-up influence in the neurobiological model of self-regulation is genetic—that is, genes that code for variants of neural receptors for chemicals that modulate neural activity throughout the brain, most specifically for present purposes in the brain areas that underlie the executive functions, namely prefrontal cortex (PFC) and associated cortical and subcortical circuitry. Variation in these genes, whether in single-nucleotide polymorphisms or in repeating polymorphisms known as tandem repeats, is associated with variation in the sensitivity of neurons in PFC and related brain areas to specific neural chemicals and hormones, including most prominently dopamine, serotonin, norepinephrine, and cortisol. For example, individuals with a specific version of the catechol-O-methyltransferase (*COMT*) gene, in which one of the essential amino acids, valine, is substituted for another, methionine, more rapidly catabolize dopamine and therefore have a shorter time course during which dopamine is present and influencing neural activity in various brain areas (Tunbridge, Harrison, & Weinberger, 2006). Similarly, individuals with what is known as the 7-repeat version of the gene that codes for the dopamine D4 receptor appear to have a variant of this type of receptor for dopamine in PFC that work less efficiently. As well, individuals with one or two copies of the short form of one of the allele for the serotonin transporter gene do not process serotonin as quickly and efficiently as those who have the long form of the allele.

The extent to which any of these gene variants is associated with a given psychological outcome, however, is presumed to be dependent on the context in which development is occurring; that is, for some individuals in certain situations, decreased dopamine sensitivity or increased serotonin turnover may be a good thing, but in other situations, the opposite may be the case. In other words, an individual who may be less sensitive to the activity of dopamine in PFC due to genetic variation may be more tolerant of high and even chaotic levels of stimulation and find such stimulation to be acceptably arousing, whereas an individual characterized by greater sensitivity to dopamine would find the same level of stimulation to be excessive and overarousing. Indeed, such a scenario is consistent with an increasingly growing research literature suggesting that a given personality type (high emotionality) and genetic background (high sensitivity to dopamine) is associated with a higher risk for poor physical and mental health outcomes in risky, chaotic environments. Interestingly, this same personality type and genetic background is associated with the likelihood of the best physical and mental health outcomes in advantaged, less chaotic environments (Belsky & Pluess, 2009). The implication that this plasticity in response to environmental influence, and the idea that such plasticity might be environmentally driven, has important implications for understanding the effectiveness of SEL and for whom and in which context SEL programming might be most effective. Within this scenario, the expectation is that effective SEL programming enables a child to maintain an optimal level of arousal to support attention and engagement: down-regulating physiology when arousal is too high, and up-regulating physiology in situations in which arousal is too low.

Stress Hormones

The potential beneficial effects of SEL programming on arousal levels are best seen in the ways in which variation among individuals at the genetic level of the theoretical model of self-regulation in Figure 5.1 influences variation at successive levels. Genetic variation in sensitivity to hormones that act as neuromodulators will be associated with variation among individuals in the physiological response to stimulation and resulting levels of stress hormones. This physiological response is indicated by activity in the hypothalamic–pituitary–adrenal (HPA) axis and levels of the glucocorticoid hormone cortisol, and by activity in the sympathetic and parasympathetic branches of the autonomic nervous system, as indicated by heart rate indices and levels of catecholamines such as norepinephrine, detectable in saliva through the enzyme alpha-amylase. In turn, variation in circulating levels of cortisol and norepinephrine is associated with variation in neural activity in brain regions that underlie reactivity and regulation of emotion and attention in response to stimulation. Notably, the functional form of this relation between stress hormones and behavioral reactivity and regulation to stimulation is the familiar inverted U-shaped curve of the Yerkes–Dodson principle presented in Figure 5.2 (Arnsten, 2009; Tunbridge et al., 2006). At moderate levels, hormones increase neural activity in areas of the brain (PFC) associated with the effective control of attention and regulation of emotion that are hallmarks of SEL and that in our theory facilitate executive function abilities. At very low or very high hormone levels, however, activity in the neural substrates of the regulation of emotion and attention is reduced. Indeed, at very high levels, activity is reduced in brain areas that regulate attention and emotion, and increased in brain areas that underlie reactive emotional, attentional, and motoric responses to stimulation and automatic forms of learning and memory, such as fear conditioning (Arnsten, 2009; Champagne et al., 2008). That is, at high levels of emotional and stress arousal, learning of associations and the formation of episodic memory is facilitated and hard to extinguish, as in the phenomenon of flashbulb memories (e.g., September 11, 2001; the *Challenger* disaster). In contrast, complex learning and task performance of the type associated with executive functions is facilitated at moderate levels of emotional and stress arousal, such as in the way that being slightly anxious before a big test or important meeting can help to focus effort and attention.

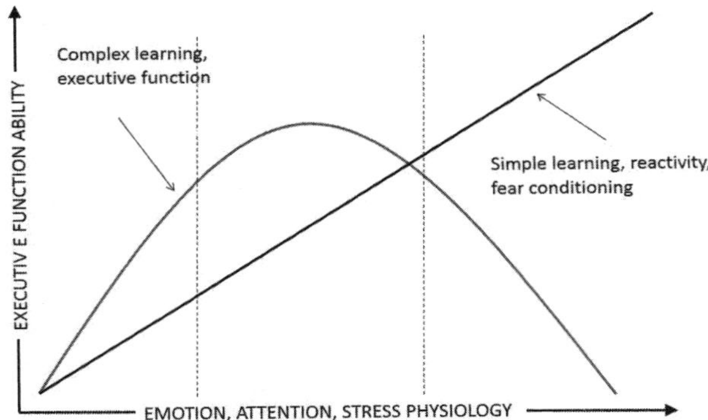

FIGURE 5.2. The Yerkes–Dodson principle and simple and complex forms of learning.

The mechanism of the inverted U-shaped relation between arousal, as indicated by hormone levels and self-regulation, relates not only to gene variants, such as *COMT* (described earlier), but also to variation in types of neural receptors for these hormones and their distribution throughout the brain. In PFC, described earlier as the brain's volitional control center, receptors with a high sensitivity to or affinity for catecholamines (dopamine and norepinephrine) and glucocorticoids (cortisol in humans) tend to predominate. As a result, moderate increases result in increased occupation of a specific type of neural receptor that promotes neural activity in areas of PFC associated with the active and volitional regulation of attention and emotion (Ramos & Arnsten, 2007). At increases beyond a moderate level, however, this type of receptor becomes saturated, and receptors with a lower affinity become active. These receptors predominate in subcortical and posterior brain regions that are associated with reactive and automatic rather than reflective and controlled responses to stimulation. In this way, levels of stress hormones influence the neural activity in response to stimulation.

Developmentally, neurochemical activity occurring in response to experience, for present purposes effective SEL programming, is understood to influence the pattern of connections between brain areas, leading the individual toward a more reactive or more reflective behavioral profile, or phenotype, in response to stimulation. A general principle in brain development is "cells that fire together, wire together." As such, experientially induced neural activity can be understood to shape the relative strength of developing connections between brain areas in ways that lead to differences in cognitive and emotional profiles of self-regulation; that is, experience acting in concert with individual differences in genetic background and neural receptor balance is actively shaping the brain in ways that have implications for understanding self-regulation development and the ways in which SEL programming can be understood to affect not only behavior but also the development of the underlying neurobiology that supports self-regulation.

We describe the shaping of behavior and underlying neurobiology as an instance of the experiential canalization of development. In this instance, what is being shaped by the combined action of biology and experience is the pattern and strength of neural connections between the brain's limbic structures, amygdala, hippocampus, and ventromedial cortex, areas associated with rapid processing of information and emotional responses to stimulation, and areas of PFC, dorsolateral and inferior frontal, that support executive functions. Shaping of connections among these areas is understood to produce a general pattern of behavior that is more reflective and prototypically well regulated when connections are weighted to PFC control over limbic structures, and more reactive when connections are weighted to limbic input to PFC.

Important for SEL programming designed to counter the effects of poverty and early psychosocial disadvantage, a growing research literature demonstrates that poverty is associated with physiological changes in children that can have both short- and long-term consequences for mental and physical health and well-being (Blair, Granger, et al., 2011; Evans, 2003; Hanson et al., 2010; Miller et al., 2009). These studies in humans increasingly demonstrate what has been clearly shown in animal models, namely that stressful early experience alters neural functioning and connectivity within and between the limbic structures and areas of PFC that are important for regulating the stress response and emotion, and for coordinating thought and action in the control of behavior through executive functions (Holmes & Wellman, 2009).

Implications of the Neurobiological Model of Development for SEL

The neurobiological model of self-regulation development offers a novel way to understand the relation between experience and development, one that highlights the way in which SEL programming might be seen to assist children in regulating physiological arousal in response to stimulation in ways that benefit thinking skills and regulation of attention and emotion that are essential for success in school environments. Generally speaking, the type of model we are describing has been used to understand differences between individuals in terms of temperament, or what has been described as trait-based biobehavioral dispositions to approach or avoid new people, places, and things (Kochanska, Murray, & Harlan, 2000; Rothbart & Ahadi, 1994). But this theoretical model has also been extensively expanded to understand processes of self-regulation in multiple aspects of psychological functioning and behavior that aid in understanding individual development and individual differences in emotional and social competence, over time and across diverse and changing contexts.

The Importance of Early Experience

Given a relatively straightforward general theoretical model of self-regulation, what are its implications for children's well-being and for programs to promote SEL in children at risk for behavior problems? Developmentally, one key implication has to do with the importance of early relationships and effects of very early experience with caregivers on the regulation of stress hormones, most clearly seen, as noted earlier, in animal models (e.g., Meaney, 2001). Importantly, findings from animal models align well with recent reports, our own and others, in humans that lower levels of supportive and responsive maternal care is associated with infants' altered physiological reactivity (Blair, Raver, et al., 2011; Hane & Fox, 2006). For this reason, our attention is sharpened to focus on the key role that caregiving relationships may play in shaping self-regulation development, and how these caregiving relationships may be disrupted in conditions of high adversity. Effective early caregiving comprises multiple factors, including high levels of warmth and positive regard as, well as direction of information and attention, and scaffolding. Definitions of high-quality care for children emphasize active structuring of experience and the scaffolding of children's behavior, such as when caregivers are emotionally supportive and contingently responsive when children are frightened, sad or upset, and when caregivers actively play and encourage children's agency, creating opportunities for children to accomplish small tasks such as stacking blocks, instead of simply completing the game or task for the child without encouragement or restricting the child's actions and attempts to do so. These types of behaviors benefit children's cognitive and emotional development with effects that are discernible at the neural and physiological level. They also illustrate the clearly interlocking nature of biology and experience.

A focus on parenting as the appropriate structuring of experience helps to illustrate the idea that moderate exposure to novelty is beneficial for development. This central point naturally extends to the educational context of preschool and the early elementary grades. For example, findings of "stress inoculation" studies with rodents and nonhuman primates suggest that controlled exposure to stress promotes regulation of the stress physiology (Parker, Buckmaster, Schatzberg, & Lyons, 2004). In keeping with the Yerkes–Dodson principle, described earlier, theory and data clearly highlight the ways that a well-regulated, moderate stress hormone increase is beneficial to self-regulation: Moderate levels of stress under supportive and controlled conditions enhance rather than inhibit development of the ability to regulate stress and emotion and support prototypically optimal cognitive and behavioral development. The notion of scaffolded learning and of appropriate moderate levels of stimulation and challenge are key components of effective pedagogy. Currently there are no data of which we are aware that have specifically addressed the idea that such educational environments might in part be effective because they are optimally arousing for children. We suspect that some of the benefits of more cognitively challenging preschool early literacy interventions may accrue through this mechanism, whereby young children are not only given access to richer linguistic environments but also are expected to be more cognitively active, attentive participants in activities such as book reading (see, e.g., Wasik, Bond, & Hindman, 2006). In many ways, the idea of an optimally arousing educational environment forms the basis for one approach to the broadly construed area known as "educational neuroscience" (Blair, 2010; McCandliss, 2010). Of immediate concern for SEL and social and educational policy directed at positive youth development is the idea that children in households where caregiving quality is jeopardized by environmental stressors such as poverty, and may be harsh or threatening (e.g., where parenting may be on the lower and more insensitive end of a continuum of adequate caregiving) experience a type of care that has clear negative physiological and neural consequences for self-regulation development (Blair et al., 2008; Blair, Granger, et al., 2011). It is for those children at greatest environmental risk that SEL is hypothesized to be most effective (see Blair & Raver, 2012; Bryck & Fisher, 2012).

Person-by-Environment Interaction

It is important to note that theory and data do not suggest a deterministic relation between experience and psychological development. Findings suggest a range of outcomes because the development of children's own early temperamental proneness to sensitivity or reactivity to the environment may moderate their subsequent neurobiological responses to the quality of care they receive from their family members and from teachers in school. Recall the key role played by genes at the "bottom" of the bottom-up process of self-regulation outlined earlier. Genes involved in the regulation of stress physiology, such as the *FKBP5* gene, which modulates glucocorticoid receptor functioning, have recently been found to serve as strong candidates in moderating the role between chronic exposure to traumatic levels of lower-quality care and later disruptions in emotional and cognitive regulation (Zimmermann et al., 2011). In this way, not all children are affected to the same extent by very similar environmental stressors; rather, their trajectories may be substantially deflected by the interaction of biological and environmental forces.

New findings from the study of children's hormonal responses to chronic exposure to threatening caregiving conditions (e.g., interparental conflict and violence) illustrate the complexity of the processes under study. For children witnessing and exposed to high levels of violence between parents in the household, an increased level of cortisol was found only for those who had been rated as initially highly temperamentally reactive in infancy; for children with temperamental profiles of greater surgency and lower reactivity, however, over time, no such relation between interparental aggression and changes in child cortisol were found (Davies, Sturge-Apple, & Cicchetti, 2011). Children's disrupted HPA axis functioning, in turn, was clearly predictive of both internalizing and attention-deficit/hyperactivity disorder (ADHD) symptoms, indicating ways that the quality of early care, when mediated through neurophysiological pathways, is predictive of difficulties in regulating emotion, inhibitory control, and attention at later time points (Davies et al., 2011).

Experiential Canalization of Development by SEL

Attention to self-regulation within the context of the home environment and classroom has clear implications for attempts to promote academic outcomes and psychosocial well-being for children in poverty. The experiential canalization model of self-regulation development suggests that one way in which poverty "gets under the skin" to influence life outcomes is through the effects of physical and psychosocial stressors on the behavior of teachers and caregivers thereby on child stress physiology. Consequently, efforts to alter the behavior of teachers and caregivers, and thereby the environment, have recursive effects on children's self-regulation profiles. Several ongoing programs of research are examining the potential effects of the environment of poverty on neurobiological development in children.

Findings from the Family Life Project

In our own research with a population-based longitudinal sample known as the Family Life Project (FLP), we found that children growing up in poverty, relative to somewhat more advantaged peers, had higher resting levels of the steroid hormone cortisol, as measured in saliva between 7 and 24 months of age, and that observed parenting behavior largely mediated the effects of poverty on cortisol levels in children (Blair et al., 2008; Blair, Granger, et al., 2011). Children whose primary caregivers (in almost all cases, the mother) exhibited a higher level of sensitive scaffolding of children's behavior, which means that they provide structured support for their children to accomplish a goal, had offspring who were initially more reactive to an emotionally arousing task at age 7 months but by age 15 months exhibited lower levels of cortisol overall, indicating lower levels of stress and increased ability to respond to stress when needed. We also found in this sample that the high level of maternal scaffolding of children's behavior was associated with a higher level of executive function in children at age 3 years (Blair, Granger, et al., 2011). Notably, this relation was both direct, through the effect of maternal behavior on child executive function, and indirect, through the effect of maternal scaffolding on child cortisol levels. Here, consistent with the neurobiological model of self-regulation development described earlier, we found that experiences during the child's first 2 years influenced levels of stress hormones and thereby self-regulation development. Furthermore, following the sample to age 4 years, we found that *turbulence* in the household, defined as "two or more adult entrances or exits from the family" was associated with children's higher levels of resting cortisol between ages 7 and 48 months. The typical pattern for resting cortisol levels adjusted for time of day of data collection (as opposed to diurnal change) is a general decline from infancy through early childhood; however, for children in more turbulent households, this was not the case (Blair, Raver, et al., 2011). As well, we have also examined the extent to which cortisol levels in children may be dependent on other aspects of stress physiology. We found that children exhibiting higher levels of a marker of norepinephrine levels, salivary alpha-amylase, and lower levels of cortisol between ages 7 and 24 months had the highest levels of executive function at age 4 years (Berry, Blair, Willoughby, & Granger, 2012), indicating a more optimal stress profile in children, one that is conducive to the regulation of attention and emotion.

At the behavioral level, we have examined the regulation of emotion in infancy and early childhood in our sample and the possibility that emotional reactivity accompanied by emotion regulation is associated with higher levels of self-regulation at school entry, as indicated by executive function. In this analysis, we examined data on child emotional reactivity and regulation in response to emotionally arousing tasks at age 15 months. We found that children who reacted strongly to the tasks but exhibited high levels of regulatory behavior in response to the arousal, such as avoidance or self-soothing, typical emotion regulation responses in toddlers, had higher levels of executive function 2.5 years later, at age 48 months. In contrast, children exhibiting high levels of reactivity but no or low levels of regulation of reactivity at 15 months had the lowest levels of executive function at 48 months (Ursache, Blair, Stifter, & Voegtline, 2012). Furthermore, consistent with the idea of experiential shaping of self-regulation, we found that children exhibiting a profile of high reactivity accompanied by a high level of regulation were more likely than other children in the sample to have mothers who had exhibited high levels of scaffolding behavior when the children were infants. Additionally, similar to the findings for the analysis of emotional reactivity and regulation, we also examined the chronicity of poverty in the sample between ages 7 and 48 months, and found that a greater number of "spells" in poverty (defined as income adjusted for family size, or income-to-need ratio), was associated with lower levels of executive function in children (Raver et al., 2013). We found, however, consistent with the neurobiological model of self-regulation development, that this effect for length of time in poverty on children's executive function was greatest for children with high levels of negative emotional reactivity. In contrast, when in more advantaged environments, these more emotionally reactive children benefited the most from experience, demonstrating the highest level of executive functioning at age 4 years.

Promoting SEL by Countering the Effects of Early Disadvantage

Although a growing number of studies provides evidence of the shaping of child self-regulation outcomes by early experience, considerable research confirms the possibility of the amelioration of early disadvantage, and point to natural extensions of these findings to educational contexts generally and to SEL programming specifically. These models demonstrate a need for ongoing experimental research designed to address questions about ways in which poverty may influence child development through linked processes of caregiving and stress physiology (Blair & Raver, 2012). Several noteworthy early intervention programs of the 1970s and 1980s have demonstrated long-term benefits to program recipients. Findings from the Perry, the Abecedarian, and the Chicago Parent–Child programs indicate increased school completion, reduced special education placements, increased college attendance and, in some of the programs, increased employment and earnings, and reduced rates of arrest and incarceration (Reynolds & Temple, 2008). Although intervention effects in these programs were initially interpreted in terms of IQ gains, fading of these gains over time accompanied by sustained impacts on life outcomes such as higher educational attainment and reduced incarceration rates suggests that a self-regulation mechanism was likely at work (Knudsen, Heckman, Cameron, & Shonkoff, 2006). In addition, nonexperimental longitudinal findings from the Dunedin Multidisciplinary Health Study, following children from infancy through adulthood, provide additional evidence for self-regulation as one plausible pathway for those benefits. In that analysis, poor self-regulation, as measured by a composite of assessments between ages 3 and 11 years, was meaningfully related to a range of negative adult outcomes such as lower earnings, substance abuse, and problem gambling (Moffitt et al., 2011; Slutske, Moffitt, Poulton, & Caspi, 2012).

Recent evidence from intervention studies of preschool and school-age children, using randomized controlled trial (RCT) designs, indicates clear short-term benefits for children's self-regulation and cognitive outcomes and persuasively supports these hypothesized pathways. For example, the Tools of the Mind curriculum (Bodrova & Leong, 2007) focuses specifically on promoting the development of executive function as a means to increase student learning and engagement (Diamond, Barnett, Thomas, & Munro, 2007). Using an RCT design, children assigned to the Tools of the Mind curriculum performed significantly better than did children assigned to a control group on more challenging direct assessments of executive function; treatment-assigned children were also rated by teachers as showing significantly lower levels of behavior problems (Diamond et al., 2007). Findings from the Chicago School Readiness Project (CRSP), a multicomponent, classroom-based intervention targeting children's self-regulation, led to clear reductions in children's emotional and behavioral difficulty, as indicated by fewer internalizing (or sad and withdrawn) and fewer externalizing (acting out and aggressive behavior problems) behaviors, as rated by teachers, from the fall to the spring of the Head Start year (Raver et al., 2009). Findings suggested that the CSRP improved low-income children's executive function skills (as indexed by assessors' ratings of children's attentional and impulse control, as well as direct assessments), with concomitant benefits for children's preacademic skills (Raver et al., 2011). Importantly, the effect sizes of this intervention were substantial, ranging from 0.34 to 0.63, and these findings were partially replicated in additional randomized trials (Morris, Millenky, Raver, & Jones, 2013). Additional studies suggest the benefits of curricula and teaching practices that focus on self-regulation for children facing economic disadvantage. For example, preschool-age children receiving the comprehensive preschool REDI (or Research-Based, Developmentally Informed) intervention were found to demonstrate stronger levels of self-regulation on a direct assessment of attention and impulsivity at posttest than did low-income preschoolers in the control group (Bierman, Nix, Greenberg, Blair, & Domitrovich, 2008).

Among school-age children, similar findings have emerged from rigorous intervention studies implemented in classroom contexts. For example, the 4Rs intervention (implemented in 18 elementary schools with over 1,000 children) targets children's effective modulation of negative emotions and their ability to respond prosocially to peers in emotionally charged situations, including episodes of conflict and social rejection (Brown et al., 2010; Jones, Brown, & Aber, 2011). After 2 years of involvement in the 4Rs (Reading, Writing, Respect, and Resolution) intervention, children demonstrated greater improvements in a number of social–emotional domains relative to their counterparts in the control group. Those benefits included improvements in the treatment group's greater ability to interpret correctly the emotions and intentions of others, to manage their own feelings of sadness and anxiety, and to focus attention in a classroom context. Importantly, benefits of the intervention extended to academic domains, such as improved reading scores for those children identified earlier in their educational trajectories as at highest educational and behavioral risk. This finding of differential benefit from intervention for children at initially greatest risk are aligned with the groundbreaking work completed by the Conduct Problems Prevention Research Group (whose work was entitled the Fast Track Project) in the 1990s. In that large-scale, multisite prevention trial, findings revealed substantial benefit to children's ability to regulate emotions and behavior (as indexed by measures of aggression, hyperactivity, and disruption), with largest impact on aggression found for children at highest risk of aggression at baseline (Conduct Problems Prevention Research Group, 2010). These findings are in keeping with our earlier discussion of "sensitivity to context." It highlights ways that teachers and educational policy leaders can tailor their provision of classroom-based support to meet the needs of different groups of children, with the possibility that those children who may be perceived as "difficult to work with" may benefit most from SEL services in school contexts.

One important question is the extent to which intervention is successful in not only improving children's self-regulation at the behavioral level but also ameliorating the neurobiological processes that underlie those behavioral competencies. Recent findings from a comprehensive home- and school-based intervention suggest that regulatory support provided by the important adults in children's lives not only reduces children's behavioral risk but also has significant impact on hormonal indicators of reactivity to stress, such as lower cortisol (Brotman et al., 2011). Those treatment-induced hormonal changes have in turn been clearly linked empirically to children's subsequent decreased risk of a range of negative behavioral and health risks, such as aggression and obesity (Brotman et al., 2012; O'Neal et al., 2010). These findings highlight the ways that targeting self-regulation at the behavioral level may yield clear benefit at the neurophysiological level, supporting the theoretical supposition that children's self-regulation is environmentally modifiable, with the quality of adults' care and support playing a key role in its canalization (see Blair & Raver, 2012, for further discussion).

Programs designed to alter parental behavior for families in poverty or caring for children from high-risk backgrounds also demonstrate significant benefits. Results from prior parenting interventions strongly suggest the beneficial effect of such intervention on stress levels in children and on self-regulation development (Dozier & Peloso, 2006). Specifically, Dozier's Attachment and Biobehavioral Catch-Up (ABC) intervention is based on theoretical principles aligned with the neurobiological model of self-regulation development: More secure relationships with caregivers can help children who have been exposed to high levels of environmental risk to develop improved physiological and behavioral regulation. It targets three specific issues: helping caregivers learn to reinterpret children's dysregulated behaviors as signals that elicit care, override their own psychological barriers that interfere with providing nurturing care, and provide an environment that helps children develop regulatory capabilities.

In an evaluation with high-risk children in foster care, the ABC intervention has been shown substantially to increase foster parents' provision of sensitive, responsive care to children who may have developed more emotionally negative and behaviorally reactive profiles as a result of multiple foster home placements and prolonged exposures to poverty-related stressors. Positive program effects were observed for children's cortisol levels, indicating that the program enhances children's ability to regulate physiology. An additional sample of children who were not in the foster care system was also included as a comparison group. Intervention comprised 10 individually administered sessions that took place at approximately weekly intervals. Children of caregivers receiving the ABC intervention demonstrated lower cortisol levels, in terms of both morning to evening slopes 1-month postintervention (Dozier & Peloso, 2006) and in response to a stressful situation administered in a laboratory setting (Dozier, Peloso, Lewis, Laurenceau, & Levine, 2008), than did children in the control condition. In addition, for children in the intervention condition, cortisol levels did not differ from those of less disadvantaged children who had never been in foster care. Sessions took place in families' homes and followed procedures outlined in a structured training manual. All families completed all sessions, which were videotaped, allowing for assessments of program fidelity. The format, duration, and frequency of the sessions were kept as similar as possible across the two interventions. To date, the efficacy of this intervention model has only been tested with high-risk samples of children and families in the foster care system. The three principles on which the intervention is based, however, are highly applicable to families facing multiple poverty-related hazards, more generally (M. Dozier, personal communication, June 18, 2011), and are highly similar to those found in other parenting programs.

For example, evaluation of the Playing and Learning Strategies (PALS) program with low-income families found positive program impacts on maternal behavior and attention-related child outcomes for low-income families with low and very low birthweight infants (Landry, Smith, & Swank, 2006; Landry, Smith, Swank, & Guttentag, 2008). Across 10, 1.5-hour sessions, home visitors worked with intervention group mothers to develop their abilities to respond contingently and warmly to their infants' needs, maintain and redirect infant attention, and verbally scaffold and encourage positive behaviors. The control group received home visits, with general support (e.g., developmental screening, pamphlets on development). Across multiple measures of maternal sensitivity and responsivity, mothers receiving the PALS intervention showed greater gains in positive caregiving behaviors across the intervention period compared to mothers in the control group. Most importantly for our purposes, infants in the PALS intervention group showed more effective goal-directed behavior during free-play tasks, as well as more positive behavior during interactions with a novel adult.

Similar parenting interventions have shown notable impacts on self-regulation-related outcomes. In their intervention with mothers of 1- to 3-year-old children at high risk for externalizing problems (i.e., highly overactive, aggressive), Van Zeijl and colleagues (2006) similarly adopted a coaching-based approach to improve maternal sensitivity and build child-discipline strategies particular to highly externalizing children. Intervention families received six 1.5-hour sessions in which coaches used video of the mother–child interactions as a tool to scaffold more effective parenting strategies. Control families received six phone calls, in which general child development issues were discussed. Compared to control mothers, those who received the intervention showed more positive discipline strategies and had children who showed larger decreases in their parent-rated overactive behaviors over time.

Problems and Pitfalls

Taken together, a clear indication is emerging that changing children's caregiving experiences during infancy, toddlerhood, and early schooling can have positive impacts on children's physiological responses to stress, with implications for emerging self-regulation skills that are central to school readiness and early academic ability. In particular, adult–child interactions marked by consistent and accurate perceptions, and contingent and appropriate responses to infant behaviors, may lead to dyadic regulatory processes between adult and infants that set the stage for reductions in the impact of poverty on infant stress physiology and developing self-regulation. There are clear parallels between the implications of the literature on parenting and preschool experience for children's self-regulation development and those for K–8 or K–12 schooling. Few studies, however, have specifically addressed the topic of self-regulation development in the elementary or secondary grades. As well, although there is increasing interest in adolescence as a period of increased sensitivity to experiential influence on brain development (Blakemore & Choudhury, 2006), no studies of which we are aware have examined the effects of SEL types of programming on the neurobiology of self-regulation in adolescents. We look forward to the findings that will undoubtedly emerge from this growing area of prevention science research.

There are several challenges that will be encountered in the attempt to extend the neurobiological model of self-regulation development to the context of SEL programming, not only to adolescents but also to children of all ages, from infancy through early adulthood. These include a variety of broad issues. One issue concerns the methodological difficulty of studying brain activity in response to experience in ways that are ecologically valid and allow for relatively strong inferences about the effects of experience on the developing brain. By and large, most studies attempting to link brain structure and function to experience are correlational, and as such provide relatively weak inference about the causal relation of experience to brain function. Optimally, studies of SEL programming and other educational interventions using RCT designs will begin to incorporate brain imaging and psychophysiological methods, including structural and functional magnetic resonance imaging (MRI) and electroencephalography, as well as measures of stress physiology obtained through saliva samples to measure stress hormone levels and electrocardiographic data. Having this information as outcome data in experiments examining SEL curricula would greatly strengthen inference about the neurobiological basis for expectations regarding the effectiveness of these programs. Barring experimental data, longitudinal data that include measurement of the environment and children's home and school experiences, and simultaneous measures of brain activity and stress physiology, at multiple time points can allow one to leverage information on change to gain stronger inferences about the relation of experience to neurobiological data. Such longitudinal data can be analyzed using residual change, fixed effects, and growth model analyses that allow for stronger inferences about the relation of experience to neurobiology by determining the extent to which change in experience, controlling for baseline levels of experience, relates to later change in neurobiological constructs of interest. Such "change on change" statistical models are widely used to increase confidence in conclusions based on nonexperimental data across a wide variety of social science disciplines (Allison, 1990; McArdle, 2009). Incorporation of neurobiological measures in these designs could provide for the type of interdisciplinary collaboration between neuroscience and social science that is needed to sustained progress in both.

Related to the issue of the need for increased methodological strength in the study of the association between educational experience and the development of the neurobiology that underlies self-regulation and SEL is the problem of perceptions that the collection of biological information is invasive and an inherent threat to research participants' confidentiality. In all of our studies in which we collect biological information, we routinely encounter some resistance to our efforts to obtain these data. This comes in many forms, ranging from opinions of school administrators that parents will be put off by this request to general concerns from parents and teachers about the amount and type of information that we will be able to obtain, particularly from saliva samples. Concerns about confidentiality and the ethics of data collection, biological information included, must be taken very seriously. By and large, participants are assured by informed consent procedures that clearly detail what will be collected and why, for how long samples will be kept, and what information specifically will be extracted. Although these assurances are important, they can in no way counter the threat of selection if certain segments of the targeted participant group select themselves out of the research process due to concerns about biological data collection. Such a threat of selection can lead to unintended bias in findings and limit generalizabilty of research results. Although it is difficult to estimate the extent to which this may cause a problem in all data collection with biological samples, evaluations of educational interventions included, it is a legitimate concern that is best addressed by providing clear information that can work to change public perceptions about the meaning of biological data.

In keeping with the foregoing, a third challenge concerns the need for clear and meaningful translation of findings from neuroscience in ways that can remove some of the mystique that surrounds data on brain function or stress hormones. There is a justifiable fascination with information about the brain and about stress physiology that in many ways has benefited research in neuroscience and in public perceptions of science generally. One aspect of this fascination, however, is the perception that biological information is somehow more valid or real than behavioral and psychological data. This misperception of what biological data represent feeds into the idea that these data make research participants more vulnerable to breaches of confidentiality. With the possible exception of genetic data in some instances, however, this is simply not the case. It is becoming increasingly clear, even with genetics, that biological information on its own provides little that is ultimately revealing of the individual that can realistically lead to prejudicial treatment in terms of health care, job qualifications, or any other relevant aspect of the individual's well-being. What is needed is increased understanding of the potential for malleability in all aspects of the person's biological makeup, from changes associated with neural plasticity in response to experience to changes in physiology occurring over time in response to variation in stress in one's life, to variation in gene expression occurring at different points through the lifespan as a function of experience and behavior.

Guidelines and Recommendations

As illustrated in the examples provided earlier, multiple studies (across both experimental and correlational designs) suggest that the impact of ecological context and high-quality caregiving on child neurobiological functioning can be powerful and sustained. Long-term benefits to meaningful life outcomes associated with high-quality early education and care for children in poverty provide the rationale for ongoing comprehensive and methodologically sound investigation of mechanisms through which such program effects occurred. Interrelated areas of inquiry concern questions about the specific content of the programs and, particularly for present purposes, about key aspects of psychobiological development that might have been impacted by children's experiences in the programs. Essential questions remain concerning the specific psychological and neurobiological mechanisms underlying program impacts on long-term improvements in recipients' lives. It is vitally important for investigators to be able to carry out longer-term follow-up studies of randomized trials combining both psychobiological and behavioral outcomes, in order to be able to answer those key questions of mechanism.

To anticipate potential problems, it is important to be prepared, ahead of time, for the level of planning, coordination, and effort required. Multiple intervention studies now successfully include physiological assays (e.g., the collection of hair, urine, and saliva) in their data collection efforts (e.g., Administration for Children and Families, 2014; Dozier et al., 2008), with clear guidelines for ways to communicate with agencies, teachers, home visitors, and families about the importance of studying brain development and health. Future research will benefit from these vanguard efforts to integrate neuroscience and learning, but only when we accurately estimate the cost of conducting that research and build in the resources to maximize our chances of success in implementing those plans.

References

Administration for Children and Families. (2014, June 19). Early Head Start University Partnership Grants: Buffering children from toxic stress, 2011–2016. Retrieved July 15, 2014, from *www.acf.hhs.gov/programs/opre/research/project/early-head-start-university-partnership-grants-buffering-children-from.*

Allison, P. D. (1990). Change scores as dependent variables in regression analysis. *Sociological Methodology, 20,* 93–114.

Arnsten, A. F. T. (2009). Stress signaling pathways that impair prefrontal cortex structure and function. *Nature Reviews Neuroscience, 10*(6), 410–422.

Belsky, J., & Pluess, M. (2009). Beyond diathesis stress: Differential susceptibility to environmental influences. *Psychological Bulletin, 135*(6), 885–908.

Berry, D., Blair, C., Willoughby, M., & Granger, D. A. (2012). Salivary alpha-amylase and cortisol in infancy and toddlerhood: Direct and indirect relations with executive functioning and academic ability in childhood. *Psychoneuroendocrinology, 37*(10), 1700–1711.

Bierman, K. L., Nix, R. L., Greenberg, M. T., Blair, C., & Domitrovich, C. E. (2008). Executive functions and school readiness intervention: Impact, moderation, and mediation in the head start REDI program. *Development and Psychopathology, 20*(3), 821–843.

Blair, C. (2002). School readiness: Integrating cognition and emotion in a neurobiological conceptualization of child functioning at school entry. *American Psychologist, 57,* 111–127.

Blair, C. (2010). Stress and the development of self-regulation in context. *Child Development Perspectives, 4*(3), 181–188.

Blair, C., Granger, D. A., Kivlighan, K. T., Mills-Koonce, R., Willoughby, M., Greenberg, M. T., et al. (2008). Maternal and child contributions to cortisol response to emotional arousal in young children from low-income, rural communities. *Developmental Psychology, 44*(4), 1095–1109.

Blair, C., Granger, D. A., Willoughby, M., Mills-Koonce, R., Cox, M., Greenberg, M. T., et al. (2011). Salivary cortisol mediates effects of poverty and parenting on executive functions in early childhood. *Child Development, 82*(6), 1970–1984.

Blair, C., & Raver, C. C. (2012). Child development in the context of adversity: Experiential canalization of brain and behavior. *American Psychologist, 67*(4), 309–318.

Blair, C., Raver, C. C., Granger, D., Mills-Koonce, R., & Hibel, L., & the FLP Investigators (2011). Allostasis and allostatic load in the context of poverty in early childhood. *Development and Psychopathology, 23,* 845–857.

Blair, C., & Razza, R. P. (2007). Relating effortful control, executive function, and false-belief understanding to emerging math and literacy ability in kindergarten. *Child Development, 78,* 647–663.

Blair, C., & Ursache, A. (2011). A bidirectional model of executive functions and self-regulation. In K. D. Vohs & R. F. Baumeister (Eds.), *Handbook of self-regulation: Research, theory, and applications* (2nd ed., pp. 300–320). New York: Guilford Press.

Blakemore, S. J., & Choudhury, S. (2006). Development of the adolescent brain: implications for executive function and social cognition. *Journal of Child Psychology and Psychiatry, 47,* 296–312.

Bodrova, E., & Leong, D. J. (2007). Play and early literacy: A Vygotskian approach. In K. A. Roskos & J. F. Christie (Eds.), *Play and literacy in early childhood: Research from multiple perspectives* (2nd ed., pp. 185–200). Mahwah, NJ: Erlbaum.

Brotman, L. M., Calzada, E., Huang, K. Y., Kingston, S., Dawson-McClure, S., Kamboukos, D., et al. (2011). Promoting effective parenting practices and preventing child behavior problems in school among ethnically diverse families from underserved, urban communities. *Child Development, 82*(1), 258–276.

Brotman, L. M., Dawson-McClure, S., Huang, K. Y., Theise, R., Kamboukos, D., Wang, J., et al. (2012). Early childhood family intervention and long-term obesity prevention among high-risk minority youth. *Pediatrics, 129*(3), e621–e628.

Brown, J. L., Jones, S. M., LaRusso, M. D., & Aber, J. L. (2010). Improving classroom quality: Teacher influences and experimental impacts of the 4Rs Program. *Journal of Educational Psychology, 102*(1), 153–167.

Bryck, R. L., & Fisher, P. A. (2012). Training the brain: Practical applications of neural plasticity from the intersection of cognitive neuroscience, developmental psychology, and prevention science. *American Psychologist, 67,* 87–100.

Castellanos, F. X., & Proal, E. (2012). Large-scale brain systems in ADHD: Beyond the prefrontal–striatal model. *Trends in Cognitive Sciences, 16,* 17–26.

Champagne, D. L., Bagot, R. C., van Hasselt, F., Ramakers, G., Meaney, M. J., de Kloet, E. R., et al. (2008). Maternal care and hippocampal plasticity: Evidence for experience-dependent structural plasticity, altered synaptic functioning, and differential responsiveness to glucocorticoids and stress. *Journal of Neuroscience, 28*(23), 6037–6045.

Collaborative for Academic, Social, and Emotional Learning (CASEL). (2014, June 19). CASEL: Success in school. Skills for life. Retrieved July 14, 2014, from *http://casel.org.*

Conduct Problems Prevention Research Group. (2010). The effects of a multi-year universal social–emotional learning program: The role of student and school characteristics. *Journal of Consulting and Clinical Psychology, 78,* 156–168.

Davies, P. T., Sturge-Apple, M. L., & Cicchetti, D. (2011). Interparental aggression and children's adrenocortical reactivity: Testing an evolutionary model of allostatic load. *Development and Psychopathology, 23*(3), 801–814.

Diamond, A., Barnett, W. S., Thomas, J., & Munro, S. (2007). Preschool program improves cognitive control. *Science, 318,* 1387–1388.

Dozier, M., & Peloso, E. (2006). The role of early stressors in child health and mental health outcomes. *Archives of Pediatrics and Adolescent Medicine, 160*(12), 1300–1301.

Dozier, M., Peloso, E., Lewis, E., Laurenceau, J. P., & Levine, S. (2008). Effects of an attachment-based intervention on the cortisol production of infants and toddlers in foster care. *Development and Psychopathology, 20*(3), 845–859.

Durlak, J. A., Weissberg, R. P., Dymnicki, A. B., Taylor, R. D., & Schellinger, K. B. (2011). The impact of enhancing students' social and emotional learning: A meta-analysis of school-based universal interventions. *Child Development, 82,* 405–432.

Elliott, E. S., & Dweck, C. S. (1988). Goals: An approach to motivation and achievement. *Journal of Personality and Social Psychology, 54*(1), 5–12.

Evans, G. W. (2003). A multimethodological analysis of cumulative risk and allostatic load among rural children. *Developmental Psychology, 39*(5), 924–933.

Evans, J. S. B. (2008). Dual-processing accounts of reasoning, judgment, and social cognition. *Annual Review of Psychology, 59,* 255–278.

Fox, M. D., & Raichle, M. E. (2007). Spontaneous fluctuations in brain activity observed with functional magnetic resonance imaging. *Nature Reviews Neuroscience, 8*(9), 700–711.

Fox, S. E., Levitt, P., & Nelson, C. A. (2010). How the timing and quality of early experiences influence the development of brain architecture. *Child Development, 81*(1), 28–40.

Hane, A. A., & Fox, N. A. (2006). Ordinary variations in maternal caregiving influence human infants' stress reactivity. *Psychological Science, 17*(6), 550–556.

Hanson, J. L., Chung, M. K., Avants, B. B., Shirtcliff, E. A., Gee, J. C., Davidson, R. J., et al. (2010). Early stress is associated with alterations in the orbitofrontal cortex: A tensor-based morphometry investigation of brain structure and behavioral risk. *Journal of Neuroscience, 30*(22), 7466–7472.

Holmes, A., & Wellman, C. L. (2009). Stress-induced prefrontal reorganization and executive dysfunction in rodents. *Neuroscience and Biobehavioral Reviews, 33*(6), 773–783.

Jones, S. M., Brown, J. L., & Aber, J. L. (2011). Two-year impacts of a universal school-based social–emotional and literacy intervention: An experiment in translational developmental research. *Child Development, 82*(2), 533–554.

Knudsen, E. I., Heckman, J. J., Cameron, J. L., & Shonkoff, J. P. (2006). Economic, neurobiological, and behavioral perspectives on building America's future workforce. *Proceedings of the National Academy of Sciences, 103*(27), 10155–10162.

Kochanska, G., Murray, K. T., & Harlan, E. T. (2000). Effortful control in early childhood: Continuity and change, antecedents, and implications for social development. *Developmental Psychology, 36*(2), 220–232.

Landry, S. H., Smith, K. E., & Swank, P. R. (2006). Responsive parenting: Establishing early foundations for social, communication, and independent problem-solving skills. *Developmental Psychology, 42*(4), 627–642.

Landry, S. H., Smith, K. E., Swank, P. R., & Guttentag, C. (2008). A responsive parenting intervention: The optimal timing across early childhood for impacting maternal behaviors and child outcomes. *Developmental Psychology, 44*(5), 1335–1353.

Luu, P., & Tucker, D. M. (2004). Self-regulation by the medial prefrontal cortex: Limbic representation of motive set points. In M. Beauregard (Ed.), *Consciousness, emotional self-regulation, and the brain* (pp. 123–162). Amsterdam, The Netherlands: Benjamins.

McArdle, J. J. (2009). Latent variable modeling of differences and changes with longitudinal data. *Annual Review of Psychology, 60,* 577–605.

McCandliss, B. D. (2010). Educational neuroscience: The early years. *Proceedings of the National Academy of Sciences, 107*(18), 8049–8050.

McClelland, M. M., Cameron, C. E., Connor, C. M., Farris, C. L., Jewkes, A. M., & Morrison,

F. J. (2007). Links between behavioral regulation and preschoolers' literacy, vocabulary, and math skills. *Developmental Psychology, 43*(4), 947–959.

Meaney, M. J. (2001). Maternal care, gene expression, and the transmission of individual differences in stress reactivity across generations. *Annual Review of Neuroscience, 24,* 1161–1192.

Miller, G. E., Chen, E., Fok, A. K., Walker, H., Lim, A., Nicholls, E. F., et al. (2009). Low early-life social class leaves a biological residue manifested by decreased glucocorticoid and increased proinflammatory signaling. *Proceedings of the National Academy of Sciences, 106*(34), 14716–14721.

Moffitt, T. E., Arseneault, L., Belsky, D., Dickson, N., Hancox, R. J., Harrington, H. L., et al. (2011). A gradient of childhood self-control predicts health, wealth, and public safety. *Proceedings of the National Academy of Sciences, 108*(7), 2693–2698.

Morris, P., Millenky, M., Raver, C. C., & Jones, S. M. (2013). Does a preschool social and emotional learning intervention pay off for classroom instruction and children's behavior and academic skills?: Evidence from the Foundations of Learning Project. *Early Education and Development, 24*(7), 1020–1042.

O'Neal, C. R., Brotman, L. M., Huang, K.-Y., Gouley, K. K., Kamboukos, D., Calzada, E. J., et al. (2010). Understanding relations among early family environment, cortisol response, and child aggression via a prevention experiment. *Child Development, 81,* 290–305.

Parker, K. J., Buckmaster, C. L., Schatzberg, A. F., & Lyons, D. M. (2004). Prospective investigation of stress inoculation in young monkeys. *Archives of General Psychiatry, 61*(9), 933–941.

Ramos, B. P., & Arnsten, A. F. T. (2007). Adrenergic pharmacology and cognition: Focus on the prefrontal cortex. *Pharmacology and Therapeutics, 113*(3), 523–536.

Raver, C. C., Blair, C., Willoughby, M. W., & the FLP Investigators. (2013). Poverty as a predictor of 4-year-olds' executive function: New perspectives on models of differential susceptibility. *Developmental Psychology, 49,* 292–304.

Raver, C. C., Jones, S. M., Li-Grining, C., Zhai, F., Bub, K., & Pressler, E. (2011). CSRP's impact on low-income preschoolers' preacademic skills: Self-regulation as a mediating mechanism. *Child Development, 82*(1), 362–378.

Raver, C. C., Jones, S. M., Li-Grining, C., Zhai, F., Metzger, M. W., & Solomon, B. (2009). Targeting children's behavior problems in preschool classrooms: A cluster-randomized controlled trial. *Journal of Consulting and Clinical Psychology, 77*(2), 302–316.

Reynolds, A. J., & Temple, J. A. (2008). Cost-effective early childhood development programs from preschool to third grade. *Annual Review of Clinical Psychology, 4,* 109–139.

Rothbart, M. K., & Ahadi, S. A. (1994). Temperament and the development of personality. *Journal of Abnormal Psychology, 103*(1), 55–66.

Slutske, W. S., Moffitt, T. E., Poulton, R., & Caspi, A. (2012). Undercontrolled temperament at age 3 predicts disordered gambling at age 32: A longitudinal study of a complete birth cohort. *Psychological Science, 23*(5), 510–516.

Tunbridge, E. M., Harrison, P. J., & Weinberger, D. R. (2006). Catechol-O-methyltransferase, cognition, and psychosis: Val158Met and beyond. *Biological Psychiatry, 60,* 141–151.

Ursache, A., Blair, C., Stifter, C., & Voegtline, K. (2012). Emotional reactivity and regulation in infancy interact to predict executive functioning in early childhood. *Developmental Psychology, 49,* 127–137.

Van Zeijl, J., Mesman, J., Van IJzendoorn, M. H., Bakermans-Kranenburg, M. J., Juffer, F., Stolk, M. N., et al. (2006). Attachment-based intervention for enhancing sensitive discipline in mothers of 1- to 3-year-old children at risk for externalizing behavior problems: A randomized controlled trial. *Journal of Consulting and Clinical Psychology, 74*(6), 994–1005.

Wasik, B. A., Bond, M. A., & Hindman, A. (2006). The effects of a language and literacy intervention on Head Start children and teachers. *Journal of Educational Psychology, 98,* 63–74.

Zimmermann, P., Brückl, T., Nocon, A., Pfister, H., Binder, E. B., Uhr, M., et al. (2011). Interaction of *FKBP5* gene variants and adverse life events in predicting depression onset: Results from a 10-year prospective community study. *American Journal of Psychiatry, 168*(10), 1107–1116.

CHAPTER 6

The Potential Effects of SEL on Biomarkers and Health Outcomes

A Promissory Note

Mark T. Greenberg, Deirdre A. Katz, and Laura Cousino Klein

One of the most exciting set of findings that has emerged in child development research in the past decades is the effect of developmental environments on children's short- and long-term physical and mental health (Biglan, Flay, Embry, & Sandler, 2012). It is now clear that children's early and ongoing interactions with their environments impact a variety of biological systems—immune, cardiovascular, endocrine, and brain (Blair et al., 2011; Hertzman & Boyce, 2010; Shonkoff, 2012; Shonkoff, Boyce, & McEwen, 2009). The emerging field of epigenetics has shown that exposure to certain environmental contexts can change whether and how genes are expressed (Meaney et al., 1996). Environments that are chronically stressful lead to physiological changes that place children at risk for long-term health and mental health consequences. Early childhood trauma, abuse, and neglect have been associated with health issues in adulthood such as chronic cardiovascular disease, alcoholism, decreased immune function, and mental health issues (Gunnar & Fisher, 2006; Shonkoff et al., 2009). Furthermore, poverty can have negative effects on children's emotional well-being because it affects caregiver responsivity, child characteristics, and resources. In contrast, nurturing environments that minimize biologically and psychologically toxic events and promote self-regulation and psychological flexibility can reduce mental and emotional disorders (Biglan et al., 2012).

Research on the effects of environmental stress on the child's social, physical, and cognitive development is a rapidly growing topic of research. Furthermore, a child's ability to regulate his or her emotions and behavior, as well as the quality of the family and classroom environment, will influence how he or she perceives and manages a variety of environmental stressors (Grant et al., 2011). Social and emotional learning (SEL) interventions seek to develop children's resilience by facilitating five key domains of skills: self-awareness, social awareness, responsible decision making, self-management, and relationship management (Durlak, Weissberg, Domitrovich, & Gullotta, Chapter 1, this volume). SEL interventions may influence these outcomes both through skill-based curriculum models as well as creating supportive environments that foster these skills (Collaborative for Academic, Social, and Emotional Learning [CASEL], 2013). As illustrated throughout this handbook, SEL interventions have a variety of positive proximal and distal outcomes for student's social functioning and academic performance (see Bear, Whitcomb, Elias, & Blank, Chapter 30, this volume; Bierman & Motamdi, Chapter 9, this volume; Rimm-Kaufman & Hulleman, Chapter 10, this volume).

Assessing outcomes from SEL interventions is challenging because of diverse settings, populations, and measurement issues (see Denham, Chapter 19, this volume). Most universal interventions are commonly evaluated by observer reports (teachers, parents), student self-reports, or assessment of SEL or academic skills. However, proximal and distal physical health outcomes have rarely been assessed in SEL evaluations to date. Given the review below of the relations between social–emotional functioning and health, we believe that assessment of short- and long-term health processes and outcomes offers an unexplored dimension of potential SEL impacts.

Current research and theory create a logical basis on which to hypothesize that building social and emotional competencies could positively influence short- and long-term health outcomes. As indicated in Figure 6.1, an individual's biological characteristics and lifetime experiences shape his or her biobehavioral stress response systems (i.e., proximal physiological indicators of health status). Short-term physiological indicators of health such as elevated levels of stress hormones and blood pressure precede physical illness and longer-term health outcomes. A 2000 report by the Institute of Medicine (IOM) found substantial evidence of diverse psychosocial influences (e.g., family or peer interactions) on morbidity and mortality in adulthood (Smedley & Syme, 2000). The report concluded that the physiological systems associated with the response to stress are especially potent contributors to illness. The report also suggested that factors such as the inability to cope effectively with stress or regulate one's emotions transcend particular diseases, and may be considered generic risk factors related to numerous disease processes by the manner in which they influence physiological response systems.

We propose that SEL interventions that develop children's social and emotional skills, especially their self-regulatory capacity, have impacts both on short-term markers of biobehavioral health and long-term health outcomes (see Blair & Raver, Chapter 5, this volume). This is because the five SEL domains can play a key role in determining both children's exposure to life stress and their ability to regulate responses to stressors. This hypothesis is based on two streams

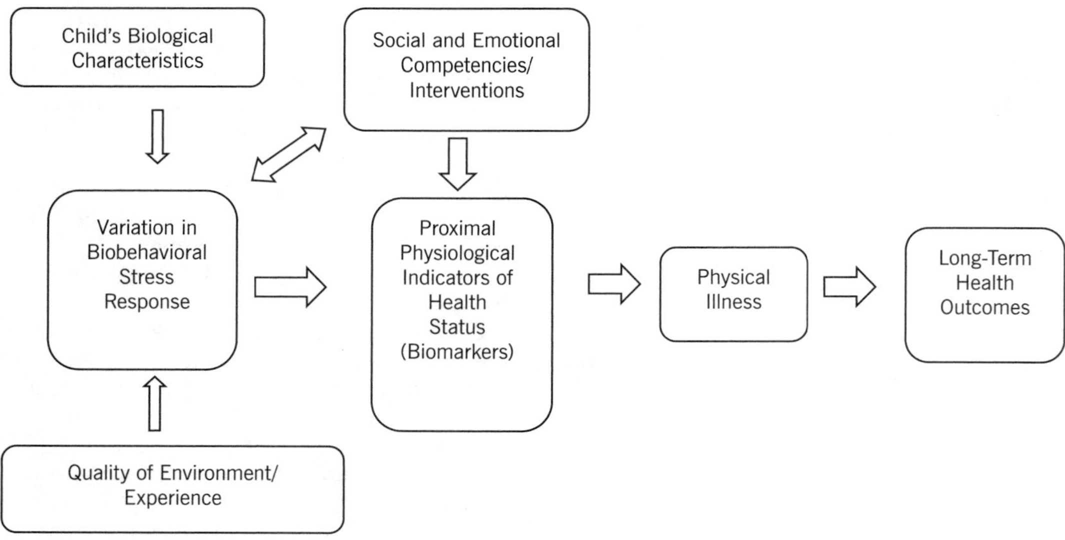

FIGURE 6.1. A conceptual model of the potential role of social and emotional competencies in the mediation of long-term health outcomes.

of research: (1) research linking environments and cumulative stressors to children's biobehavioral systems and long-term mental and physical health, and (2) the findings on the effects of SEL interventions. Thus, we propose the following question: *How can the development of social and emotional competencies contribute to positive long-term health outcomes?* Here, we address the unexplored potential of SEL programs to impact short- and, possibly, long-term health outcomes. We first review research on stress and health, then connect these findings by considering the potential effects of SEL interventions.

The Effects of Stress on Biomarkers and Health

Our biobehavioral stress response system develops as a result of complex interactions between individual biology and environmental influences (Gottlieb, 2007). Researchers posit that early experience can affect a person's long-term health in two ways: by accumulation of damage over time, or by biological embedding during sensitive periods (Hertzman & Boyce, 2010). Physiological damage that accumulates over time can result from both psychological and physical stress (i.e., allostatic load; McEwen & Stellar, 1993). Exposure to heightened stress during developmentally sensitive periods may permanently alter physiological processes and, ultimately, long-term health functioning. For example, chronically poor emotion regulation evidenced by both depressive affect and/or high hostility have long been implicated in cardiovascular disease (Williams, 2001). Boyce and Ellis (2005) proposed a conditional adaptation model in which heighted biological responsivity indicates a sensitivity to context mediated by the brain. One example is that highly reactive children have greater morbidity when raised in adverse environments, but lower morbidity rates when raised in supportive, low-stress families. This leads to individual differences in behavior and adaptive patterns of responsivity.

The effects of stress on the physiological system are often measured by biomarkers which are indicators of underlying physiological mechanisms that can indicate either normative or disease-causing processes (Baum & Grunberg, 1997). For example, an estrogen increase in women is a biomarker of ovulation, whereas elevated resting blood pressure is a biomarker of risk for cardiovascular disease. Biomarkers have the potential to provide additional insight into biological mechanisms associated with positive behavioral change that is achieved by preventive interventions, including the study of the effects of SEL. There are a variety of biomarkers available to index how stress exposure affects the body. These health status biomarkers are becoming of interest to prevention researchers because of their potential to improve treatment efficacy in intervention studies, as well as inform program design and implementation strategies (Beauchaine, Neuhaus, Brenner, & Gatzke-Kopp, 2008). Below we present information on both broad physiological systems and exemplar noninvasive biomarkers of health that may be useful in social and emotional intervention research for measuring and predicting health outcomes.

Physiological Systems Activated by Stress

The stress response is a biological process that prepares us to encounter challenges (Lupien, McEwen, Gunnar, & Heim, 2009). Exposure to stressors triggers a cascade of coordinated biobehavioral responses designed to increase survival of the organism. Although multiple biobehavioral systems are activated during stress, for the scope of this chapter, we focus on three primary physiological systems: the autonomic nervous system (ANS), the immune systems, and the cardiovascular response. Here we discuss exemplar biomarkers associated with each system that can be measured in the laboratory or the school context. It is important to note that there are numerous biomarkers associated with each of these physiological systems. Thus, rather than an exhaustive review of biomarkers, we provide examples commonly used in biobehavioral research that, we hypothesize, may be associated with social–emotional competencies. Understanding the origin of these biomarkers may be useful for understanding how social and emotional interventions may influence them.

We focus primarily on salivary biomarkers because they are noninvasive and relatively easy to collect. Table 6.1 summarizes the biological functions and health outcomes associated with these proximal physiological indicators of health status.

The Autonomic Nervous System

The perception of stress triggers a cascade of coordinated biobehavioral responses. The autonomic nervous system (ANS), stimulates the sympathetic-adrenal-medullary (SAM) axis and the hypothalamic–pituitary–adrenal (HPA) axis in response to stress.

The SAM Axis and Salivary Alpha-Amylase

The sympathetic branch of the ANS, the SNS, is fast-responding and involved in initiating the "fight or flight" response, which results in the release of epinephrine (EPI) and norepinephrine (NE). Norepinephrine slows digestion and dilates pupils, whereas epinephrine increases glucose release, heart rate, and blood pressure. These physiological responses enable the organism to fight or flee from the stressor.

Salivary alpha-amylase (sAA) is a purported marker of this system. SAA exhibits diurnal patterns with sharp decrease in concentration soon after waking and a gradual increase over the day (Granger, Kivlighan, El-Seikh, Gordis, & Stroud, 2007; Nater & Rohleder, 2009). The frequency and length of SAM activation increases as stressors become chronic, and prolonged activation can result in tissue damage (Piazza, Almeida, Dmitrieva, & Klein, 2010). Chronic stressors may have long-term effects on the SAM axis. Recent studies have found relationships between sAA release and affective

TABLE 6.1. Some Proximal Physiological Indicators of Health Status That May Be Useful in Social and Emotional Intervention Research

Biomarker	System	Definition	Function	Association with health
Cortisol	HPA	Corticosteroid released from the adrenal cortex	Involved in neuroendocrine response to stress; increases energy production, reduces inflammation, communicates with immune system, supports fight-or-flight response.	Consistently high levels associated with coronary heart disease, depression and anxiety.
sAA	SAM	Salivary enzyme	Digestion of carbohydrates and starch.	Deficient levels related to poor oral health.
CRP	Immune	Biomarker of systemic inflammation	Enhances the disposal of foreign or damaged cells in the inflammatory response.	Elevated levels associated with increased risk of cardiovascular disease.
BP	Cardiovascular	Pressure exerted by circulating blood on blood vessel walls. Systolic (SBP): peak BP; Diastolic (DBP); minimum pressure	Indicator of cardiovascular health.	Elevated SBP and/or DBP can indicate hypertension and cardiovascular disease.

Note. HPA, hypothlamic–pituitary–adrenal; sAA, salivary alpha-amylase; SAM, sympathetic adrenomedullary; CRP, C-reactive protein; BP, blood pressure. Based on Piazza, Almeida, Dmitrieva, and Klein (2010).

behavior. For example, 9-year-old girls who had experienced peer victimization exhibited high task frustration in conjunction with high sAA reactivity over the course of a laboratory stressor. In the same study, children of both sexes who reported victimization showed higher levels of aggression and anticipatory sAA activation while waiting for a laboratory-based social challenge than did children not reporting victimization (Rudolph, Troop-Gordon, & Granger, 2010). In another laboratory study with 2-year-olds, children with high basal levels of sAA showed more positive affect and approach behavior during emotion-eliciting tasks (Fortunato, Dribin, Granger, & Buss, 2008). Both studies suggest that sAA activation may reflect sensitivity to context, but neither provides definitive conclusions about patterns of sAA release with respect to affective behavior. SAA research is relatively new compared to other biomarkers reviewed here, yet the data suggest clear links between sAA reactivity and affective responding, making sAA a novel biomarker that should be further explored in SEL intervention studies.

The HPA Axis and Cortisol

The ANS also activates the HPA axis in response to a stressor, which results in the release of cortisol from the adrenal cortex. The HPA axis responds more slowly to stressors and takes longer to return to baseline because it works through the release of glucocorticoids, which take some time to produce (Gunnar & Quevedo, 2007). Cortisol draws glucose out of cells, providing energy to face a threat. Increased cortisol also helps increase oxygen intake and blood flow, reduce inflammation, and enhance immune responses to stress. Short-term increases in cortisol reflect normal physiological responses to challenge.

Salivary cortisol is a primary biomarker for psychological stress and a reliable indicator of emotional well-being (Juster et al., 2011; Steptoe & Wardle, 2005). The release of cortisol leads to physiological adaptation under most circumstances but can be detrimental if overproduced or dysregulated. Consistent exposure to stress can produce either chronically elevated levels of cortisol or very low levels that can negatively impact long-term health, including cardiovascular function (McEwen & Stellar, 1993; Shonkoff et al., 2009) immune function, reproduction, growth and cognition (Danese & McEwen, 2012; Juster et al., 2011). Although this biological system functions similarly in most people, its activation varies significantly between individuals.

Healthy newborns exhibit a highly reactive HPA response to stressors. In young children, greater cortisol reactivity is associated with being identified as having a fearful temperament (Talge, Donzella, & Gunnar, 2008). Research indicates a powerful environmental influence on cortisol activation. Preexisting vulnerability to elevated cortisol may be due to a combination of genetics or early experience that can lead to abnormal brain development and mental health disorders when cortisol levels are consistently elevated (Gunnar & Fisher, 2006). The quality of care (e.g., sensitivity and responsivity of maternal care) that infants receive can influence the development of this stress response, as does the cumulative stress of poverty. Toddlers with negative emotional temperaments are most likely to exhibit elevations in cortisol under conditions of less optimal care (Gunnar & Donzella, 2002). Thus, when children have a secure attachment with their caregiver, it may buffer the effect of fearful temperament on cortisol activation. This sensitivity of the HPA axis to social regulation persists into later childhood and extends to friendships. Studies show that bullying is associated with altered HPA axis activity, with bullied children showing blunted cortisol reactivity (Knack, Jensen-Campbell, & Baum, 2011; Rudolph et al., 2010).

There is some suggestion that cortisol levels and sAA levels have a reciprocal relationship with one another, in that the former declines throughout the day, whereas sAA levels increase (Nater, Rohleder, Schlotz, Ehlert, & Kirschbaum, 2007). Using a multisystem approach to understanding the influence of biomarkers, Family Life Project researchers found that asymmetrical diurnal cortisol (biomarker of HPA axis activity and sAA, a biomarker of SAM axis activity) profiles in infancy were predictive of optimal developmental outcomes in terms of executive function and academic abilities in prekindergarten (Berry, Blair, Willoughby,

& Granger, 2012). Another study of preschoolers indicated that cortisol and sAA were related to different aspects of behavioral regulation (Lisonbee, Pendry, Mize, & Gwynn, 2010). Children with greater increases in sAA following a challenge task were less able to delay gratification. Those with greater cortisol elevations had lower performance on a slow-down motor task.

The Immune System and C-Reactive Protein

The role of the human inflammatory response is to recruit immune cells to repair injury and fight off pathogens. In the acute phase of an infection, the synthesis of C-reactive protein (CRP) is stimulated, reaching a peak 48 hours after activation. Elevated CRP levels can indicate infection or inflammation. CRP is a biomarker of immune status that can also be measured in saliva or blood; elevated CRP levels are a known risk factor for cardiovascular disease (Ridker, 2003). Elevated CRP levels are believed to be a part of the cascade of biological responses to chronic stress and have been found in adults and children with a variety of diseases (McEwen & Stellar, 1993). Childhood CRP levels positively correlate with cardiovascular disease risk factors, which predict poor adult outcomes (Juonala et al., 2006). Adults who experienced maltreatment as children and become depressed have significantly higher CRP than those with no experience with maltreatment (Danese et al., 2008) Children living in neighborhoods with high levels of crime or poverty also have elevated CRP levels compared to children from other neighborhoods (Broyles et al., 2012). It should be noted that CRP is only one of a variety of immune markers that have been related to both mental and physical health. Other measures quantify the number and/or percentage of various white blood cells in peripheral blood (helper T cells, cytotoxic/suppressor T cells, B cells, natural killer cells, monocytes), or of immunoglobulins in blood (primarily IgG, IgM, IgA) or saliva (secretory IgA) (Granger, Granger, & Granger, 2006; Kiecolt-Glaser & Glaser, 1997). Although some of these biomarkers may also have value in SEL research, as most are collected using blood, they are less likely to be used in universal intervention trials.

The Cardiovascular System and Blood Pressure

Blood pressure (BP) is a measurement of the force against artery walls as the heart pumps blood through the body. High blood pressure, also known as hypertension, is a common cause of heart disease, strokes, and heart attacks. It is commonly known that high blood pressure levels in adults are associated with future development of cardiovascular disease and mortality (Smedley & Syme, 2000).

Longitudinal studies show that BP levels in childhood predict higher adult cardiovascular risk (Dekkers, Snieder, Van den Oord, & Treiber, 2002). Exposure to psychosocial stress contributes to the development of hypertension (Sparrenberger et al., 2009). Identifying mechanisms responsible for increased BP in childhood, as well as ways to reduce BP, could improve prevention of hypertension. A recent study indicated a significant reduction in the ambulatory BP of adolescents who were at high risk for heart disease after a breathing awareness meditation intervention (Gregoski, Barnes, Tingen, Harshfield, & Treiber, 2011). This finding indicates that BP is sensitive to contextual interventions. Although there are no available data on universal interventions for children or youth, it is possible that interventions such as relaxation training, yoga, or other mindfulness-based approaches also may impact blood pressure.

Allostatic Load

Rather than rely on only a single assessment of physiological status, multiple assessments of the effects of chronic stress can be indexed using the concept of allostatic load. *Allostasis* is a process of constant balancing of multiple physiological systems in response to environmental changes and individual needs (Bauer, Quas, & Boyce, 2002). Thus, allostatic load is an aggregate measure of biomarkers that can falter as a function of stress hormone imbalances (Seeman, McEwen, Rowe, & Singer, 2001). The allostatic load model suggests that greater cumulative stress burden can influence stress-responsive physiology and lead to a variety of health issues. Furthermore, although we presented the physiological systems earlier as "separate," they are part of a larger system that manages neurogenic inflammation. Allostatic load measures dysregulated patterns of stress response *across* systems rather than alterations only in an individual system. Allostatic load may be a useful index for predicting physiological pathology and a broad measure of the effects on interventions in dampening this load.

The measurement of allostatic load involves use of an index with four primary mediators (e.g., hormones and inflammatory cytokines) and six secondary outcomes (e.g., blood pressure and cholesterol) for predicting longer-term health outcomes (Seeman et al., 2001). Indices are measured simultaneously and an overall allostatic load index is calculated by adding together the number of biomarkers that reach specific cutoffs (upper or lower quartiles, depending on whether the biomarker is unhealthy at lower or higher levels). Increased allostatic load has been linked to tertiary outcomes such as cardiovascular disease, depression, and cognitive impairments in adulthood (Juster et al., 2011). It is hypothesized that, from infancy, there are cascading relationships between environmental factors and genetic predispositions that lead to large and growing individual differences in susceptibility to stress (McEwen & Stellar, 1993). Although the allostatic load model has been primarily applied to adults, there is increased interest in applying it to children to measure the broad impact of stress on physiological systems (Bush, Obradović, Adler, & Boyce, 2011; Johnson, Bruce, Tarullo, & Gunnar, 2011). However, there are numerous challenges in applying this model to children (Ganzel, Morris, & Wethington, 2010). There are developmental changes in children's stress-mediating systems; thus, the long-term consequences of allostatic load might vary depending on the developmental timing of stressors and the duration of overactivation of the stress-mediating systems. The result is that it is unclear whether the same biomarkers (e.g. cholesterol) used to assess allostatic load in adults are useful indicators in children. These issues encourage caution when applying the model to children and indicate the need for further research on the interpretation of this higher-order construct for children.

Stress, Physical Illness, and SEL Skills in Children

The relationship between stress and illness has long been of interest. Thousands of years ago, Greek physicians noted that people who were depressed were more likely to develop cancer than those who were not. Research has well established that negative emotions, coping styles, and management of stress are predictive of a variety of adult diseases and morbidity. Furthermore, much of this relationship among emotion, coping, stress, and disease is mediated by changes in physiological systems previously discussed, including immune function and the HPA axis (Kiecolt-Glaser, McGuire, Robles, & Glaser, 2002). Despite long-observed interest in the subject in adults (Cohen & Williamson, 1991), empirical evidence for the stress–illness relationship in children is relatively new. However, numerous studies show that children get sick more often when they are under emotional stress (Berntsson & Köhler, 2001; Torsheim & Wold, 2001). Chen and colleagues (2006) documented that children with asthma who experienced higher levels of chronic home-life stress had greater asthma symptoms, even after they controlled for a variety of medical and demographic characteristics. In two related studies with preschoolers, Boyce and colleagues (1995) found that family stress was associated with increased child illness, but only among those children who showed heighted stress reactivity in a laboratory-based challenge task. Illnesses such as colds, skin conditions, and psychosomatic disorders, as well as anxiety and depression, are often believed to be triggered by stressors.

One set of childhood illnesses that has received substantial attention for the stress–illness connection falls under the rubric of *somatization*, which is the expression of psychological disturbance in physical symptoms. Examples of somatic disorders in children include psychogenic asthma, headaches, chest pain, peptic ulcers, and recurrent abdominal pain (RAP). RAP is characterized by repeated episodes of pain in the absence of identifiable organic etiology. Studies have shown that compared to healthy children, children with RAP have higher levels of anxiety, depression, and other somatization symptoms (e.g., Wasserman, Whittington, & Rivara, 1988). Children with RAP have both mothers who show higher rates of anger and hostility and higher rates of family problems (Liakopoulou-Kairis et al., 2002). At a broader level, multiple studies have demonstrated that dysfunctional patterns of family interaction and parental psychopathology are linked to a broad range of health problems associated with increased utilization of pediatric health services (Woodward et al., 1988). Pediatricians and psychiatrists typically recommend treating the symptoms of somatic disorders with drugs (e.g., antacids for ulcers) as well as psychological therapies to help children to express and regulate feelings such as worry, separation anxiety, and sadness (Garralda, 1999). Thus, teaching SEL skills might be considered a broad stress management prevention strategy to improve the host's capacity to resist disease and improve health.

Self-Regulatory Abilities as a Link from SEL to Health Outcomes

With the mounting evidence that early experiences influence our biological systems and may have lasting effects on our physiological functioning, many researchers are calling for policy to address childhood stress (Shonkoff et al., 2009). Because research shows that the child's biological system is sensitive to negative contexts, it is worth considering whether individual biology may be sensitive to positive experiences as well (Ryff & Singer, 1998).

Social and Emotional Competencies: The Importance of Self-Regulation

Social and emotional competencies (SECs) include a person's ability to recognize and regulate emotions, show concern for others, maintain positive relationships, and make responsible decisions (for more details, see Durlak et al., Chapter 1, this volume). Among the five SEL domains, self-awareness, self-management, and problem-solving may be particularly relevant for health outcomes because they are central to the broader construct of self-regulation. As further elaborated by Blair and Raver (Chapter 5, this volume), self-regulation is a set of skills that is linked to the biobehavioral system and supports effective regulation of one's emotions and attention in order to advance goal-directed behavior in a particular context (Blair, 2002; Blair & Raver, 2012). Blair suggests a neurobiologically based model of self-regulation, in which self-regulation comprises interdependent bottom-up and top-down components. The bottom-up components are the automatic processes of stress, emotional arousal, and attention. The top-down components are generally referred to as executive functions (EFs), which include working memory, inhibitory control, and flexible sharing of attentional focus (Blair & Raver, 2012). These systems work bidirectionally, influencing and being influenced by one another. Thus, self-regulation involves both inhibitory control, the ability to suppress disruptive emotions, *and* the promotion of positive emotions. As elaborated by Blair and Raver (Chapter 5, this volume), optimal self-regulation involves a balance between emotional arousal and inhibitory control.

Importantly, the systems that regulate emotional arousal and EFs mature at different rates over the lifespan. The bottom-up processes of the limbic system emerge in infancy, with much of a child's regulation skills indicative of top-down processes, whereas frontal lobe activity emerges in preschool-age children and continues into early adulthood (Gogtay et al., 2004). Research indicates the importance of experience in early childhood in shaping self-regulation development, which is associated with many long-term outcomes (Boyce & Ellis, 2005; Lupien, King, Meaney, & McEwen, 2001). In the Dunedin Study of development that longitudinally followed 1,000 children from birth to age 32, findings indicated that early self-regulation predicted a range of long-term outcomes, including physical health, substance dependence, personal finances, and criminal activity (Moffitt et al., 2011). Another study showed that toddlers with low self-regulation skills at age 2 were more likely to be obese at age 5 (Graziano, Calkins & Keane, 2010).

Interpersonal problem-solving skills are also a central part of many SEL interventions and can have significant long-term effects in children's lives. For instance, more mature social problem-solving skills moderate the effects of maltreatment on behavioral outcomes in childhood (Dodge, Pettit, Bates, & Valente, 1995). Problem-solving skills also moderated the association between exposure to violence and psychological distress in a study of adolescents (LeBlanc, Self-Brown, Shepard, & Kelley, 2011). Problem-solving skills, as well as self-regulatory processes, impact both social and biological measures of wellness.

Much of the overlap in what is taught in SEL programs usually involves all or most of the five SEL skills domains. We hypothesize that skills learned through SEL interventions can function as protective factors that may bolster both physical and mental resilience. Although a meta-analysis of 213 studies on the effects of different SEL curricula showed the effective development of SEL skills such as emotional awareness, self-control, conflict-resolution strategies, and interpersonal problem-solving skills, as well as improvements in behavior and academic skills, there was no information on the programs' impact on either short- or long-term physical health outcomes (Durlak, Weissberg, Dymnicki, Taylor, & Schellinger, 2011).

As SEL interventions have gained widespread support, the overwhelming majority of outcome measures have focused only on student academic achievement, or on mental, emotional, or behavioral outcomes. We argue here that findings from developmental psychobiological studies give rise to the logic that teaching children self-regulation skills may also build their biological resilience, preventing the long-term negative effects of stress. Yet, at the current time, we are not aware of any published, peer-reviewed studies of universal SEL intervention studies that have assessed biological markers of stress or, more broadly, allostatic load.

When children develop more effective social and emotional skills, they are changing the way they respond to stress and may be creating new patterns of neurocircuitry, or physiological patterns of response that may have lasting positive effects on how they adapt to their environment and cope with stress. This is currently an unexplored area of research with regard to universal SEL interventions. *Teaching children self-regulation skills may change the way they interact with their environment, and this could have a lasting effect on these biological substrates and functions.* For example, when a person has well-developed SECs, he or she is better able to manage stressful situations and the accompanying negative affective states (anger, frustration, anxiety, or sadness) and more successfully cope with challenging events. We hypothesize that by regularly coping successfully with stressful circumstances and down-regulating their physiological system (lowering heart rate or reducing cortisol activation), children with high SECs would be less likely to develop risky short-term physiological indicators that are prodromal to long-term health outcomes. For example, decreased chronic activation of the HPA reduces the amount of cortisol in the system, which may help to attenuate negative health outcomes (Gunnar & Fisher, 2006). Furthermore, increased emotional regulation could lead to decreased blood pressure and activation of CRP, thus reducing risk for cardiovascular disease (e.g., Danese et al., 2008).

Because some SEL interventions specifically support the development of self-regulation by focusing on emotional and behavioral regulation, teaching self-awareness, self-control, and problem-solving skills, these may be good prospects for examining biomarkers and health outcomes. In addition, some SEL interventions have examined their effects on EFs, which play a role in self-regulation and may affect stress-related biomarkers (Diamond & Lee, 2011). For example, studies of the Providing Alternative Thinking Strategies (PATHS) curriculum have shown effects on EF, as well as self-regulatory abilities, both in preschool and in grades 2–4 (Bierman, Nix, Greenberg, Blair, & Domitrovich, 2008; Riggs, Greenberg, Kusché, & Pentz, 2006). In two other experimental evaluations of prekindergarten school readiness curricula, Tools of the Mind (Diamond, Barnett, Thomas, & Munro, 2007) and the Chicago School Readiness Project (Raver et al., 2011) effects on both EFs and self-regulatory skills have been demonstrated.

Although many SEL interventions focus on regulatory processes, the logic models of numerous SEL interventions are often missing the necessary links to the study of biobehavioral markers and physiological functions. We argue that current SEL models would be substantially enriched by acknowledging the potential effects of interventions on biomarkers and other physical health outcomes. Furthermore, research documenting program impact on physical functioning and health outcomes could also lead to analyses indicating substantially increased economic benefits resulting from various SEL interventions (Jones, Greenberg, & Crowley, Chapter 7, this volume).

Biomarkers in Intervention Research

Although there are no published studies to date on the use of biomarkers in universal classroom-based SEL programs in schools, intervention studies that include biomarkers with already identified populations are on the rise. Rappolt-Schlichtmann and colleagues' (2009) study used cortisol measures to assess effects of a small-group intervention in a childcare setting. Results showed that quality childcare, characterized by participation in small pull-out groups with low teacher–student ratios and positive teacher–student relationships, reduced cortisol levels for children from difficult home environments compared to those children who remained in typical childcare environments. Fisher and Stoolmiller (2008) demonstrated that an intervention with foster parents to reduce their own stress in responding to problem behaviors was associated with reduced stress hormones in their foster children.

An area of SEL research that may be of particular importance is interventions that focus specifically on coping with stress, including those focused on nurturing mindfulness. In adult populations, mindfulness meditation practice has been shown to cultivate empathy (Singer & Lamm, 2009), focus attention and cognitive regulation (Jha, Krompinger, & Baime, 2007) and inhibit emotionally charged but irrelevant information (Ortner, Kilner, & Zelazo, 2007). In addition, adult studies have demonstrated its efficacy for improving chronic pain, rheumatoid arthritis, fibromyalgia, anxiety, and depression (Arias, Steinberg, Banga, & Trestman, 2006). Moreover, studies with adults show positive effects on both biomarkers and health status (Davidson et al., 2003; Rosenkranz et al., 2013). A sample of African American youth with high blood pressure showed significant decreases in blood pressure after a 3-month school intervention of breathing awareness meditation (Gregoski et al., 2011). In a randomized trial of mindful yoga with inner-city minority children (grades 4 and 5), reductions were found in ruminative and intrusive thought and regulation of emotional arousal (Mendelson et al., 2010).

Measurement of Biomarkers

With the growing popularity of physiological measurements in behavioral intervention studies, it is important for researchers to be knowledgeable about the limitations and challenges in using physiological measurements (Dennis, Buss, & Hastings, 2012). Noninvasive biomarker measurement techniques are improving rapidly, and many biomarkers including sAA, cortisol, and CRP can now be assayed from saliva, making sample collection relatively easy (Buxton, Klein, Williams, & McDade, 2013; Granger, Kivlighan, El-Sheikh, et al., 2007). Salivary samples can be collected by participants in a variety of settings, reducing the need for laboratory visits and increasing collection in the field. Additionally, saliva contains many biomarkers, which allows for multivariate analyses without multiple samples.

Yet there are at least three cautions in the use of biomarkers. First, the biomarkers discussed here can be affected by several factors, including how the sample is collected (e.g., passive drool vs. cotton swab to collect saliva; automated BP monitoring vs. manual BP determination). These measurement factors must be carefully considered in order to use them with validity (e.g., Buxton et al., 2013). Thus, scientists interested in integrating biomarkers into their research should work closely with the laboratory that will conduct salivary assays to determine the appropriate saliva collection procedures required for accurate biomarker assessment (e.g., Granger, Kivlighan, Fortunato, et al., 2007). Second, examining only one of these biomarker or systems may ignore the dynamic, interdependent nature of human biology and may not fully explain the effects of SEL interventions. Biobehavioral research is moving away from assessing only a single system and favoring incorporation of multiple biomarkers from multiple physiological systems, as discussed earlier. Third and last, even though the use of biomarkers in intervention studies is becoming more popular, it is important to consider the research question and determine whether biomarkers are necessary to answer the research question being asked.

Although there is a paucity of studies, intervention science is beginning to adopt models and methods from developmental biology and use biobehavioral measures to examine how interventions may effect physiology or neurocognitive function (Bradshaw, Goldweber, Fishbein, & Greenberg, 2012). Riggs and Greenberg (2004) delineated three ways in which such measures might have utility. First, such measures could be direct outcomes of intervention. Second, these measures might be conceptualized as moderators, therefore clarifying for whom the interventions are most effective. Studies may reveal characteristics that make some participants more or less responsive to different intervention, allowing prevention scientists to target specific populations with interventions catering to their needs. Third, such measures might reflect important meditational processes by identifying the pathways by which intervention leads to both shorter- and longer-term change.

Though biomarker collection and analysis is improving, there are a variety of challenges in measuring physiological indicators of health. First, participant compliance to sample collection protocol can pose problems. Because a researcher is not required to be present when participants collect their own saliva, participant compliance to protocol is an issue and can impact the sample's integrity. Researchers have to create clear parameters in an attempt to control participant sample collection (Granger, Kivlighan, El-Sheikh, et al., 2007).

Timing is a consistent challenge for biobehavioral data collection. Timing and eating practices prior to collecting a sample can also greatly affect outcomes. The time of day and month samples are collected also can influence results. Biomarkers that show diurnal patterns such as sAA and cortisol require careful tracking of saliva collection times (Buxton et al., 2013). Pubertal and menstrual cycle timing can also affect hormone measures. Researchers can control for this by examining estradiol and testosterone levels in assays, though assay of these hormones requires that the salivary collection must be passive drool (Shirtcliff, Granger, Schwartz, & Curran, 2001). In addition, physiological systems change with development, and changes may affect the interpretation of physiological data (Fox, Kirwan, & Reeb-Sutherland, 2012).

Last, studies that use biomarkers might face decreased participation because of a lack of understanding about biological measures, as well as the complexity of sample collection and handling. Researchers need to provide clear rationales for study measures and clarity on how the data will be used in order to decrease participant concerns. Limited participation is especially of concern with children in school contexts in which the parents may withhold consent because they do not understand the research study and worry about having their children give biological samples for analysis. This said, an extensive literature indicates that salivary biomarkers can be successfully obtained from children (Berry et al., 2012).

Although the value of the concept of allostatic load has not yet been proven in child studies, future studies that juxtapose physiological reactivity and behavior should investigate *patterns* of physiological responses among multiple concurrent systems rather than only focusing on individual response systems (Bauer et al., 2002). As biological systems interact with one another, our understanding of their joint contributions should shed further light on their influence on observed behaviors. Last, SEL researchers should carefully consider the measurement of both short-term and longer-term health outcomes whenever possible. If SEL interventions have the potential to affect a child's long-term physical health, such documentation could have substantial effects on both education and health policies.

Conclusions: A Promissory Note

To investigate further whether SEL skills have a positive effect on both biomarkers and longer term health outcomes, research will need specific components. First, when appropriate, logic models for the effects of intervention will need to adopt explicit frameworks that incorporate hypothesized biobehavioral and health outcomes. Second, careful selection and measurement of biomarkers that are sensitive to the developmental model of the intervention is required. This will entail truly transdisciplinary collaborations in which prevention scientists, physiologists, pediatric researchers, and educators work together to develop and test increasingly well-elaborated theoretical and assessment models. This line of transdisciplinary research may lead to the creation of new programs that are more effective in influencing health outcomes. Because the field of developmental psychophysiology of child health is itself a young field of study, in some cases further basic research may be necessary in order to develop fully clear logic models for SEL interventions. Intervention trials may create the opportunity to increase the pace of breakthroughs in this basic work and could answer fundamental questions (e.g., "Are there particular periods in which different physiological systems are more vulnerable to change?").

The potential to demonstrate both short- and long-term health outcomes from skills acquired in SEL interventions is exciting. Such findings could increase understanding and interest in the benefits of SEL on the part of policymakers, educators, and the public. Knowledge of short- and long-term health outcomes of SEL skills could help to legitimize SEL further in schools and demonstrate long-term cost savings. It is time to begin an extensive set of interdisciplinary studies both to understand further the potential benefits of SEL interventions and deepen our understanding of the connections between emotional health, physical health, and well-being.

Acknowledgments

This work was supported by Grant No. R305B090007 from the Institute of Education Sciences. The views expressed in this chapter are ours and do not represent the granting agency.

References

Arias, A. J., Steinberg, K., Banga, A., & Trestman, R. L. (2006). Systematic review of the efficacy of meditation techniques as treatments for medical illness. *Journal of Alternative and Complementary Medicine, 12*, 817–832.

Bauer, A. M., Quas, J. A., & Boyce, W. T. (2002). Associations between physiological reactivity and children's behavior: Advantages of a multisystem approach. *Journal of Developmental and Behavioral Pediatrics, 23*(2), 102–113.

Baum, A., & Grunberg, N. (1997). Measurement of stress hormones. In S. Cohen, R. C. Kessler, & L. U. Gordon (Eds.), *Measuring stress: A guide for health and social scientists* (pp. 745–774). New York: Oxford University Press.

Beauchaine, T. P., Neuhaus, E., Brenner, S. L., & Gatzke-Kopp, L. (2008). Ten good reasons to consider biological processes in prevention and intervention research. *Development and Psychopathology, 20*(3), 745–774.

Berntsson, L. T., & Köhler, L. (2001). Long-term illness and psychosomatic complaints in children aged 2–17 years in the five Nordic countries: Comparison between 1984 and 1996. *European Journal of Public Health, 11*(1), 35–42.

Berry, D., Blair, C., Willoughby, M., & Granger, D. A. (2012). Salivary alpha-amylase and cortisol in infancy and toddlerhood: Direct and indirect relations with executive functioning and academic ability in childhood. *Psychoneuroendocrinology, 37*(10), 1700–1711.

Bierman, K. L., Nix, R. L., Greenberg, M. T., Blair, C., & Domitrovich, C. E. (2008). Executive functions and school readiness intervention: Impact, moderation, and mediation in the Head Start REDI Program. *Development and Psychopathology, 20*, 821–844.

Biglan, A., Flay, B. R., Embry, D. D., & Sandler, I. N. (2012). The critical role of nurturing environments for promoting human well-being. *American Psychologist, 67*(4), 257–271.

Blair, C. (2002). School readiness: Integrating cognition and emotion in a neurobiological conceptualization of children's functioning at school entry. *American Psychologist, 57*(2), 111–127.

Blair, C., Granger, D. A., Willoughby, M., Mills-Koonce, R., Cox, M., Greenberg, M. T., et al. (2011). Salivary cortisol mediates effects of poverty and parenting on executive functions in early childhood. *Child Development, 82*(6), 1970–1984.

Blair, C., & Raver, C. C. (2012). Individual development and evolution: Experiential canalization of self-regulation. *Developmental Psychology, 48*(3), 647–657.

Boyce, W. T., Chesney, M., Alkon, A., Tschann, J. M., Adams, S., Chesterman, B., et al. (1995). Psychobiologic reactivity to stress and childhood respiratory illnesses: Results of two prospective studies. *Psychosomatic Medicine, 57*(5), 411–422.

Boyce, W. T., & Ellis, B. J. (2005). Biological sensitivity to context: I. An evolutionary–developmental theory of the origins and functions of stress reactivity. *Development and Psychopathology, 17,* 271–301.

Bradshaw, C. P., Goldweber, A., Fishbein, D., & Greenberg, M. T. (2012). Infusing developmental neuroscience into school-based preventive interventions: Implications and future directions. *Journal of Adolescent Health, 51*(Suppl. 2), S41–S47.

Broyles, S. T., Staiano, A. E., Drazba, K. T., Gupta, A. K., Sothern, M., & Katzmarzyk, P. T. (2012). Elevated C-reactive protein in children from risky neighborhoods: Evidence for a stress pathway linking neighborhoods and inflammation in children. *PloS ONE, 7*(9), 1–8.

Bush, N. R., Obradović, J., Adler, N., & Boyce, W. T. (2011). Kindergarten stressors and cumulative adrenocortical activation: The "first straws" of allostatic load? *Development and Psychopathology, 23,* 1089–1106.

Buxton, O. M., Klein, L. C., Williams, S., & McDade, T. (2013). Biomarkers in work and family research. In J. Grzywacz & E. Demerouti (Eds.), *New frontiers in work and family research.* (pp. 170–190). East Sussex, UK: Taylor & Francis Group.

Chen, E., Hanson, M. D., Paterson, L. Q., Griffin, M. J., Walker, H. A., & Miller, G. E. (2006). Socioeconomic status and inflammatory processes in childhood asthma: The role of psychological stress. *Journal of Allergy and Clinical Immunology, 117*(5), 1014–1020.

Cohen, S., & Williamson, G. M. (1991). Stress and infectious disease in humans. *Psychological Bulletin, 109,* 5–24.

Collaborative for Academic, Social, and Emotional Learning (CASEL). (2013). Effective social and emotional learning programs: Preschool and elementary school edition. Retrieved June 14, 2012, from *http://casel.org/guide.*

Danese, A., Moffitt, T. E., Pariante, C. M., Ambler, A., Poulton, R., & Caspi, A. (2008). Elevated inflammation levels in depressed adults with a history of childhood maltreatment. *Archives of General Psychiatry, 65*(4), 409–415.

Danese, A., & McEwen, B. S. (2012). Adverse childhood experiences, allostasis, allostatic load, and age-related disease. *Physiology and Behavior, 106*(1), 29–39.

Davidson, R. J., Kabat-Zinn, J., Schumacher, J., Rosenkranz, M., Muller, D., Santorelli, S. F., et al. (2003). Alterations in brain and immune function produced by mindfulness meditation. *Psychosomatic Medicine, 65*(4), 564–570.

Dekkers, J. C., Snieder, H., Van den Oord, E. J. C. G., & Treiber, F. A. (2002). Moderators of blood pressure development from childhood to adulthood: A 10-year longitudinal study. *Journal of Pediatrics, 141*(6), 770–779.

Dennis, T. A., Buss, K. A., & Hastings, P. D. (2012). Introduction to the monograph: physiological measures of emotion from a developmental perspective: State of the science. *Monographs of the Society for Research in Child Development, 77*(2), 1–5.

Diamond, A., Barnett, W. S., Thomas, J., & Munro, S. (2007). Preschool program improves cognitive control. *Science, 318,* 1387–1388.

Diamond, A., & Lee, K. (2011). Interventions shown to aid executive function development in children 4 to 12 years old. *Science, 333,* 959–964.

Dodge, K. A., Pettit, G. S., Bates, J. E., & Valente, E. (1995). Social information-processing patterns partially mediate the effect of early physical abuse on later conduct problems. *Journal of Abnormal Psychology, 104*(4), 632–643.

Durlak, J. A., Weissberg, R. P., Dymnicki, A. B., Taylor, R. D., & Schellinger, K. B. (2011). The impact of enhancing students' social and emotional learning: a meta-analysis of school-based universal interventions. *Child Development, 82*(1), 405–432.

Fisher, P. A., & Stoolmiller, M. (2008). Intervention effects on foster parent stress: Associations with child cortisol levels. *Development and Psychopathology, 20*(3), 1003–1021.

Fortunato, C. K., Dribin, A. E., Granger, D. A., & Buss, K. A. (2008). Salivary alpha-amylase and cortisol in toddlers: Differential relations to affective behavior. *Developmental Psychobiology, 50*(8), 807–818.

Fox, N. A., Kirwan, M., & Reeb-Sutherland, B. (2012). Measuring the physiology of emotion and emotion regulation—timing is everything. *Monographs of the Society for Research in Child Development, 77*(2), 98–108.

Ganzel, B. L., Morris, P. A., & Wethington, E. (2010). Allostasis and the human brain: Integrating models of stress from the social and life sciences. *Psychological Review, 117*(1), 134–174.

Garralda, M. E. (1999). Practitioner review: assessment and management of somatization in childhood and adolescence: A practical perspective. *Journal of Child Psychology and Psychiatry, 40*(8), 1159–1167.

Gogtay, N., Giedd, J. N., Lusk, L., Hayashi, K. M., Greenstein, D., Vaituzis, A. C., et al. (2004). Dynamic mapping of human cortical development during childhood through early adulthood. *Proceedings of the National Academy of Sciences, 101*(21), 8174–8179.

Gottlieb, G. (2007). Probabilistic epigenesis. *Developmental Science, 10*(1), 1–11.

Granger, D. A., Granger, G., & Granger, S. (2006). Immunology and developmental psychopathology. In D. Cicchetti & D. J. Cohen (Eds.), *Developmental psychopathology* (Vol. 2, pp. 677–709). Hoboken, NJ: Wiley.

Granger, D. A., Kivlighan, K. T., El-Sheikh, M., Gordis, E. B., & Stroud, L. R. (2007). Salivary α-amylase in biobehavioral research: Recent developments and applications. *Annals of the New York Academy of Sciences, 1098*(1), 122–144.

Granger, D. A., Kivlighan, K. T., Fortunato, C., Harmon, A. G., Hibel, L. C., Schwartz, E. B., et al. (2007). Integration of salivary biomarkers into developmental and behaviorally-oriented research: Problems and solutions for collecting specimens. *Physiology and Behavior, 92*(4), 583–590.

Grant, K. E., McMahon, S. D., Duffy, S. N., Taylor, J. J., Compas, B. E., & Contrada, R. J. (2011). Stressor and mental health problems in childhood and adolescence. In A. Baum (Ed.), *The handbook of stress science: Biology, psychology, and health* (pp. 359–372). New York: Springer.

Graziano, P. A., Calkins, S. D., & Keane, S. P. (2010). Toddler self-regulation skills predict risk for pediatric obesity. *International Journal of Obesity, 34*, 633–641.

Gregoski, M. J., Barnes, V. A., Tingen, M. S., Harshfield, G. A., & Treiber, F. A. (2011). Breathing awareness meditation and lifeskills training programs influence upon ambulatory blood pressure and sodium excretion among African American adolescents. *Journal of Adolescent Health, 48*(1), 59–64.

Gunnar, M. R., & Donzella, B. (2002). Social regulation of the cortisol levels in early human development. *Psychoneuroendocrinology, 27*(1–2), 199–220.

Gunnar, M. R., & Fisher, P. A. (2006). Bringing basic research on early experience and stress neurobiology to bear on preventive interventions for neglected and maltreated children. *Development and Psychopathology, 18*, 651–677.

Gunnar, M., & Quevedo, K. (2007). The neurobiology of stress and development. *Annual Review of Psychology, 58*, 145–173.

Hertzman, C., & Boyce, T. (2010). How experience gets under the skin to create gradients in developmental health. *Annual Review of Public Health, 31*, 329–347.

Jha, A., Krompinger, J., & Baime, M. (2007). Mindfulness training modifies subsystems of attention. *Cognitive, Affective, and Behavioral Neuroscience, 7*(2), 109–119.

Johnson, A. E., Bruce, J., Tarullo, A. R., & Gunnar, M. R. (2011). Growth delay as an index of allostatic load in young children: Predictions to disinhibited social approach and diurnal cortisol activity [Special issue]. *Development and Psychopathology, 23*(3), 859–871.

Juonala, M., Viikari, J. S. A., Rönnemaa, T., Taittonen, L., Marniemi, J., & Raitakari, O. T. (2006). Childhood C-reactive protein in predicting CRP and carotid intima-media thickness in adulthood. *Arteriosclerosis, Thrombosis, and Vascular Biology, 26*(8), 1883–1888.

Juster, R. P., Bizik, G., Picard, M., Arsenault-Lapierre, G., Sindi, S., Trepanier, L., et al. (2011). A transdisciplinary perspective of chronic stress in relation to psychopathology throughout life span development [Special issue]. *Development and Psychopathology, 23*(3), 725–776.

Kiecolt-Glaser, J., & Glaser, R. (1997). Measurement of immune response. In S. Cohen, R. C. Kessler, & L. U. Gordon (Eds.), *Measuring stress: A guide for health and social scientists* (pp. 213–229). New York: Oxford University Press.

Kiecolt-Glaser, J. K., McGuire, L., Robles, T. F., & Glaser, R. (2002). Emotions, morbidity, and mortality: New perspectives from psychoneuroimmunology. *Annual Review of Psychology, 53*, 83–107.

Knack, J. M., Jensen-Campbell, L. A., & Baum, A. (2011). Worse than sticks and stones?: Bullying is associated with altered HPA axis functioning and poorer health. *Brain and Cognition, 77*(2), 183–190.

LeBlanc, M., Self-Brown, S., Shepard, D., & Kelley, M. L. (2011). Buffering the effects of violence: Communication and problem-solving skills as protective factors for adolescents exposed to violence. *Journal of Community Psychology, 39*(3), 353–367.

Liakopoulou-Kairis, M., Alifieraki, T., Protagora, D., Korpa, T., Kondyli, K., Dimosthenous, E., et al. (2002). Recurrent abdominal pain and headache. *European Child and Adolescent Psychiatry, 11*(3), 115–122.

Lisonbee, J. A., Pendry, P., Mize, J., & Gwynn, E. P. (2010). Hypothalamic–pituitary–adrenal and sympathetic nervous system activity and children's behavioral regulation. *Mind, Brain, and Education, 4*(4), 171–181.

Lupien, S. J., King, S., Meaney, M. J., & McEwen, B. S. (2001). Can poverty get under your skin?:

Basal cortisol levels and cognitive function in children from low and high socioeconomic status. *Development and Psychopathology, 13*(3), 653–676.

Lupien, S. J., McEwen, B. S., Gunnar, M. R., & Heim, C. (2009). Effects of stress throughout the lifespan on the brain, behaviour and cognition. *Nature Reviews Neuroscience, 10*, 434–445.

McEwen, B. S., & Stellar, E. (1993). Stress and the individual: Mechanisms leading to disease. *Archives of Internal Medicine, 153*(18), 2093–2101.

Meaney, M. J., Diorio, J., Francis, D., Widdowson, J., LaPlante, P., Caldji, C., et al. (1996). Early environmental regulation of forebrain glucocorticoid receptor gene expression: Implications for adrenocortical responses to stress. *Developmental Neuroscience, 18*(1–2), 49–72.

Mendelson, T., Greenberg, M., Dariotis, J., Gould, L., Rhoades, B., & Leaf, P. (2010). Feasibility and preliminary outcomes of a school-based mindfulness intervention for urban youth. *Journal of Abnormal Child Psychology, 38*(7), 985–994.

Moffitt, T. E., Arseneault, L., Belsky, D., Dickson, N., Hancox, R. J., Harrington, H., et al. (2011). A gradient of childhood self-control predicts health, wealth, and public safety. *Proceedings of the National Academy of Sciences, 108*(7), 2693–2698.

Nater, U. M., & Rohleder, N. (2009). Salivary alpha-amylase as a non-invasive biomarker for the sympathetic nervous system: Current state of research. *Psychoneuroendocrinology, 34*(4), 486–496.

Nater, U. M., Rohleder, N., Schlotz, W., Ehlert, U., & Kirschbaum, C. (2007). Determinants of the diurnal course of salivary alpha-amylase. *Psychoneuroendocrinology, 32*(4), 392–401.

Ortner, C. M., Kilner, S., & Zelazo, P. (2007). Mindfulness meditation and reduced emotional interference on a cognitive task. *Motivation and Emotion, 31*(4), 271–283.

Piazza, J. R., Almeida, D. M., Dmitrieva, N. O., & Klein, L. C. (2010). Frontiers in the use of biomarkers of health in research on stress and aging. *Journals of Gerontology B: Psychological Sciences and Social Sciences, 65*(5), 513–525.

Rappolt-Schlichtmann, G., Willett, J. B., Ayoub, C. C., Lindsley, R., Hulette, A. C., & Fischer, K. W. (2009). Poverty, relationship conflict, and the regulation of cortisol in small and large group contexts at child care. *Mind, Brain, and Education, 3*(3), 131–142.

Raver, C. C., Jones, S. M., Li-Grining, C., Zhai, F., Bub, K., & Pressler, E. (2011). CSRP's impact on low-income preschoolers' preacademic skills: Self-regulation as a mediating mechanism. *Child Development, 82*(1), 362–378.

Ridker, P. M. (2003). Clinical application of C-reactive protein for cardiovascular disease detection and prevention. *Circulation, 107*(3), 363–369.

Riggs, N. R., & Greenberg, M. T. (2004). The role of neurocognitive models in prevention research. In D. Fishbein (Ed.), *The science, treatment, and prevention of antisocial behaviors: Application to the criminal justice system: Evidence-based practice* (Vol. 2, pp. 249–262). Kingston, NJ: Civic Research Institute.

Riggs, N. R., Greenberg, M. T., Kusché, C. A., & Pentz, M. A. (2006). The mediational role of neurocognition in the behavioral outcomes of a social-emotional prevention program in elementary school students: Effects of the PATHS Curriculum. *Prevention Science, 7*, 91–102.

Rosenkranz, M. A., Davidson, R. J., MacCoon, D. G., Sheridan, J. F., Kalin, N. H., & Lutz, A. (2013). A comparison of mindfulness-based stress reduction and an active control in modulation of neurogenic inflammation. *Brain, Behavior, and Immunity, 27*(1), 174–184.

Rudolph, K. D., Troop-Gordon, W., & Granger, D. A. (2010). Peer victimization and aggression: Moderation by individual differences in salivary cortisol and alpha-amylase. *Journal of Abnormal Child Psychology, 38*(6), 843–856.

Ryff, C. D., & Singer, B. S. (1998). The contours of positive human health. *Psychological Inquiry, 9*, 1–28.

Seeman, T. E., McEwen, B. S., Rowe, J. W., & Singer, B. H. (2001). Allostatic load as a marker of cumulative biological risk: MacArthur studies of successful aging. *Proceedings of the National Academy of Sciences, 98*, 4770–4775.

Shirtcliff, E. A., Granger, D. A., Schwartz, E., & Curran, M. J. (2001). Use of salivary biomarkers in biobehavioral research: Cotton-based sample collection methods can interfere with salivary immunoassay results. *Psychoneuroendocrinology, 26*(2), 165–173.

Shonkoff, J. P. (2012). Leveraging the biology of adversity to address the roots of disparities in health and development. *Proceedings of the National Academy of Sciences, 109*(Suppl. 2), 17302–17307.

Shonkoff, J. P., Boyce, W. T., & McEwen, B. S. (2009). Neuroscience, molecular biology, and the childhood roots of health disparities: Building a new framework for health promotion and disease prevention. *Journal of the American Medical Association, 301*(21), 2252–2259.

Singer, T., & Lamm, C. (2009). The social neuroscience of empathy. *Annals of the New York Academy of Sciences, 1156*, 81–96.

Smedley, B. D., & Syme, S. L. (2000). *Promoting health: Intervention strategies from social and behavioral research.* Washington, DC: National Academy Press.

Sparrenberger, F., Cichelero, F. T., Ascoli, A. M., Fonseca, F. P., Weiss, G., Berwanger, O., et al. (2009). Does psychosocial stress cause hypertension?: A systematic review of observational studies. *Journal of Human Hypertension, 23*(1), 12–19.

Steptoe, A., & Wardle, J. (2005). Positive affect and biological function in everyday life. *Neurobiology of Aging, 26*(1), 108–112.

Talge, N. M., Donzella, B., & Gunnar, M. R. (2008). Fearful temperament and stress reactivity among preschool-aged children. *Infant and Child Development, 17*(4), 427–445.

Torsheim, T., & Wold, B. (2001). School-related stress, school support, and somatic complaints: A general population study. *Journal of Adolescent Research, 16*(3), 293–303.

Wasserman, A. L., Whittington, P. F., & Rivara, F. P. (1988). Psychogenic basis for abdominal pain in children and adolescents. *Journal of the American Academy of Child and Adolescent Psychiatry, 27*(2), 179–184.

Williams, R. B. (2001). Hostility: Effects on health and the potential for successful behavioral approaches to prevention and treatment. In A. Baum, T. A. Revenson, & J. E. Singer (Eds.), *Handbook of health psychology* (pp. 661–668). Hillsdale, NJ: Erlbaum.

Woodward, C. A., Boyle, M. H., Offord, D. R., Cadman, D. T., Links, P. S., Munroe-Blum, H., et al. (1988). Ontario child health study: Patterns of ambulatory medical care utilization and their correlates. *Pediatrics, 82*(3), 425–434.

CHAPTER 7

The Economic Case for SEL

Damon Jones, Mark T. Greenberg, and Max Crowley

Scientific study of social and emotional learning (SEL) has grown dramatically over the past few decades. In most modern technological societies, citizens and policymakers are concerned about the extent to which today's children and youth experience suboptimal academic achievement, high rates of early substance use, and intolerable exposure to violence. Failure to graduate from high school, early drug use, and delinquency are all costly outcomes that reduce individual and community well-being and have high financial burden (Cohen & Piquero, 2009; Levin, 2009). Because of their central roles in society and youth development, schools are the primary setting in which many initial concerns arise, and also a context in which they can be effectively remediated. Schools remain a primary setting in which children first learn to negotiate complex social relations with peers and have the opportunity to build the essential skills that will allow them to be productive members of society. Because of their central role, schools not only focus on traditional core subjects, but they also support children's development into effectively functioning constructive and contributing citizens. In our global, competitive society, schools play an important role in attempting to ensure that all students learn how to interact with others from diverse backgrounds in socially and emotionally skilled ways, practice healthy behaviors, and behave responsibly and respectfully (Greenberg et al., 2003).

The potential benefits of improved behavior and well-being of school-age children are both direct and long term. Improved behavior leads to a healthier classroom atmosphere and reduced interruptions, and supports effective instruction that influences academic achievement. Broader and longer-term benefits also accrue from improvements in social relations with others and reductions in delinquency, antisocial behavior, school dropout, academic failure, and mental health problems. Building protective factors to promote mental health can in turn reduce the likelihood of future health problems and poor adult outcomes (Greenberg, Domitrovich, & Bumbarger, 2001; Weissberg, Kumpfer, & Seligman, 2003).

The Need for Economic Evaluation

As discussed in other chapters of this handbook, universal SEL programs can be effective in reducing problems, promoting competence and improving school success. Yet, in spite of this evidence, SEL is marginalized in educational decision making by most educators and policymakers. We believe that one missing component in the analysis of social and emotional education is high-quality evaluation that will provide evidence of the potential economic benefit of implementing SEL models in schools. It is quite clear that policymakers, as well as educators, place considerable value on economic evaluation in their decisions about educational decision making (Greenstone, Harris, Li, Looney, & Patashnik, 2012). In addition to information on the potential cost savings of SEL programs, budget administrators require clear information on the immediate and longer-term costs of effectively implementing new programs. Given these needs, we have three major goals in this chapter: (1) to introduce SEL researchers and practitioners to the field of economic evaluation, (2) to review what is currently known about potential economic costs and benefits of SEL programs, and (3) to provide guidance on how to conduct sound economic evaluations. In pursuing these goals, we first discuss the importance of universal intervention programs in studying the economic case for SEL. Second, we provide description of the steps involved in conducting an economic evaluation of programs (using a hypothetical example of how an SEL researcher could plan an economic assessment of an effective program). Finally, we discuss the needed research to move this field forward, and some of the uncertainty and complexity surrounding economic analysis.

Why Focus on Universal SEL Interventions?

Although there are numerous types of school-based interventions, such as improved classroom management and school disciplinary models (Greenberg, 2010), the economic impact of universal SEL school programs remain largely unexplored. These interventions teach skills that build all students' competence to engage in positive peer and adult relations, to develop self-regulation, and to cultivate healthy values and norms to resist engagement in deviant or dangerous behavior. SEL programs attempt to improve competence in five domains: self-awareness, social awareness, responsible decision making, self-management, and relationship management (see Durlak, Weissberg, Domtrovich, & Gullotta, Chapter 1, this volume). This focus on broad competence building differs from more narrow programs that seek to alter a specific behavior and obtain a discrete goal or indicated interventions that target students at most risk. From an economic perspective, these broad SEL efforts can be seen as aiding individuals in human capital accumulation (Becker, 2009; Heckman, 2000). Human capital is generally seen as the competencies required for an individual to perform labor and produce economic value. Thus, while some programs seek to reduce a specific outcome (e.g., delinquency) that may lead to future cost savings (e.g., lower incarceration rates), we hypothesize that the wider breadth of SEL may result in larger gains in human capital that lead to multiple benefits in several areas, including greater productivity (e.g., long-term employment, taxable earnings, good health) and societal benefits (e.g., less crime, less need for government services), in addition to the primary personal and social outcomes experienced by students.

There are a number of very desirable features of universal SEL programs that provide part of the rationale for economic evaluation. First, universal programs help youth learn adaptive coping strategies across an array of experiences and settings. Second, because universal SEL programs are positive, proactive, and provided independent of risk status, their potential for stigmatizing participants is minimized. Third, when SEL programs are conducted in schools, students are "captive populations"; this reduces recruitment costs and helps to keep attrition rates low. Finally, as all children participate, they have the capacity to cultivate positive attitudes, norms, and behaviors throughout broad social networks (Gest, Osgood, Feinberg, Bierman, & Moody, 2011).

Another advantage of universal models that target fundamental risk and protective factors and intervene early in development is the potential for a single preventive intervention to reduce or prevent multiple problems. A growing body of research indicates that many poor outcomes, such as psychopathology, substance abuse, delinquency, and school failure, have overlapping associated risk factors and a significant degree of comorbidity (Greenberg et al., 2001). Because of their focus on risk reduction and health promotion, universal preventive interventions often produce reductions in multiple problem areas (Spoth, Trudeau, Guyll, & Shin, 2012). Positive program effects on multiple outcomes increase the likelihood for a return on investment from the intervention, especially given that universal programs can be low cost (i.e., average cost per child).

A final advantage is that universal school models serve all children, as compared to programs that only target specific children (i.e., selective and indicated approaches). Durlak (1995) pointed out that if only 8% of well-adjusted children will go on to have serious adjustment problems as adults (as opposed to 30% of clinically dysfunctional children who might be targeted), these children will still represent 50% of the population of maladjusted adults, based on real numbers. This follows Rose's (1981) maxim that *a large number of people exposed to a low risk is likely to produce more cases than a small number of people exposed to a high risk*. It may then be beneficial to provide universal preventive interventions despite the relatively low prevalence rates of certain childhood disorders. Moreover, when dealing with common and costly disorders such as depression or conduct disorder, there may be more justification for preventive efforts that are universal (Merry & Spence, 2007).

What Is the Current Evidence for the Effectiveness of School-Based Prevention?

The past two decades have brought clear progress and a stronger empirical understanding to the fields of school-based prevention and the broader field of SEL (Greenberg et al., 2003). There are now a considerable number of evidence-based classroom and family-based curricula that have been shown to reduce adverse mental health symptoms, substance use, and associated risk factors. Reviews and meta-analyses of the prevention of substance abuse (Gottfredson & Wilson, 2003; Lochman & van den Steenhoven, 2002), violence and anti-social behavior (Fagan & Catalano, 2013; Wilson, Lipsey, & Derzon, 2003), poor mental health (Greenberg et al., 2001; Hoagwood et al., 2007), and positive youth development (Catalano, Berglund, Ryan, Lonczak, & Hawkins, 2004) have shown that both universal and targeted prevention programs can substantially reduce the rate of problem behaviors and symptoms, as well as build protective factors that reduce further risk in child and adolescent populations. A recent meta-analysis examined the effectiveness of universal school-based SEL interventions on a variety of outcomes (Durlak, Weissberg, Dymnicki, Taylor, & Schellinger, 2011). This review indicated that interventions have a substantial impact on a variety of outcomes, including aggression and disruption, social and emotional competence, school bonding, prosocial norms, disciplinary referrals, emotional distress, and academic achievement.

Do Universal SEL Programs Lead to Economic Gains?

Although SEL programs have shown numerous behavioral, social–emotional, cognitive, and academic outcomes, there has been almost no analysis of the economic costs and benefits of such programs. Although this may seem surprising, there are number of important factors that contribute to the lack of studies. First, most rigorous evaluations of SEL programs (e.g., randomized clinical trials) are conducted when participants are in either the preschool or elementary school years. As most monetized outcomes (wages, payment of taxes, use of public services and benefit programs) do not occur until adulthood, there usually exists a long period of time between occurrence of the intervention and most observable economic benefits from an effective elementary school SEL program. Most program evaluations have not included long-term longitudinal follow-up into adolescence or early adulthood. This is in contrast to specialized early childhood programs for low-income children (targeted intervention) for which numerous outcomes have been reported in adulthood. Landmark economic studies showing the economic return from investment in targeted early childhood interventions include the Perry Preschool Program (Belfield, Nores, Barnett, & Schweinhart, 2006), the Abecedarian program (Barnett & Masse, 2007), and the Chicago Child–Parent Centers (Reynolds, Temple, White, Ou, & Robertson, 2011). For SEL programs it is much easier to monetize outcomes for programs conducted during middle or high school that produce direct effects on things such as use of special education services, dropout, juvenile arrests, or immediate drug use.

Second, most SEL program outcomes focus on linear changes in outcome measures such as a reductions in behavioral problems or increases in social problem-solving skills, rather than changes on dichotomous outcomes such as meeting criteria for a diagnosis. Unfortunately, a 0.30 effect size reduction in aggression or a 0.20 effect size increase in learning outcomes in third grade are not as readily linked to monetized current or future outcomes ("shadow prices" of such effects must be determined, as further discussed below). Third, as universal programs are delivered to all students, there has been little focus on outcome measurement that may only impact a very small percentage of the school population but may still be very important for economic analysis. For example, if an SEL program leads to a 5% reduction in the number of children receiving certain disciplinary or mental health care, then this could have substantial economic effects given the high costs associated with extreme cases. However, such outcomes are usually not measured in evaluations of universal SEL models. Economic analysis also requires careful measurement of program resources, and such cost analyses have rarely been undertaken for SEL programs (Crowley, Jones, Greenberg, Feinberg, & Spoth, 2012). Finally, the background of SEL researchers does not typically include experience in methods for conducting economic evaluation or understanding its importance. Thus, in most cases, no plans are made for an economic analysis as part of the program evaluation, or for carefully measuring program resources–costs. This lack of attention to economic issues among SEL researchers is one reason why few have been conducted aside from those done separately by economic experts using secondary data. Nevertheless, a few available studies demonstrate promising results. For example, the Seattle Social Development Project—a program directed toward improving child social and emotional functioning across elementary school into early middle school—was found to have an effect on outcomes extending into young adulthood, covering areas of mental and emotional health, as well as reduced crime and substance use. Economic evaluation estimated a return on investment that exceeded $2,500 per participant linked to program impact on outcomes such as increased likelihood to graduate from high school, lower rates of K–12 grade retention, lower rates of initiation of sexual activity, and less criminal activity among intervention group participants (Lee et al., 2012). The Life Skills Project provides another example of the potential for economic benefit from a school-based universal program. This low-cost intervention (roughly $34 per participant) delivered by teachers in classroom settings across 3 years in middle school addresses risks for substance use in adolescence, with components that teach students self-management skills, social skills, and information regarding the dangers of substance abuse. The most recent assessment of this program estimated a return on investment of almost $1,300 per participant, representing over $37 returned (to participants and society) per dollar invested. These results were based on program effects on substance misuse (including tobacco, alcohol, and illicit drugs) and associated criminal activity (Lee et al., 2012).

Other studies have provided examples of the economic returns that may be expected from universal programs. For instance, a 2008 report from the Substance Abuse and Mental Health Services Administration Center for Substance Abuse Prevention (SAMHSA) summarized the economic benefits of effective programs targeting substance use and misuse (which teach numerous SEL skills), noting that across programs a large-scale investment in school-based prevention would produce an $18 return per dollar invested and save state and local governments an estimated $1.3 billion (Miller & Hendrie, 2009). This report emphasized the relevance of substance use outcomes to societal costs, including the associated increased criminal activity, need for health services, and future loss of productivity. Although these studies demonstrate how universal programs that teach SEL skills can have an economic impact, it must be noted that estimates are largely based on program effects for more readily monetized outcomes. As discussed, an obstacle in determining the economic value of SEL is the lack of such monetizable measures for many SEL programs, especially for younger children. Because of this, an increased focus on the economic value of social–emotional competence and SEL at early ages is needed.

The Economic Impact of "Noncognitive" Factors

Schools are now faced with many competing demands, and educational leaders face difficult choices about priorities (Berends, Bodilly, & Kirby, 2002). Especially in the United States, educational leaders and policymakers have for the past two decades been singularly focused on student academic performance. Although a potential benefit of the No Child Left Behind Act is the promotion of academic excellence and equity, its main outcome has been an obsessive focus on high-stakes testing, a narrowing of the curriculum, and a loss of the "whole child" in education. A consequence of No Child Left Behind has been a marginalization of most prevention efforts that have not shown strong impact on educational outcomes, especially on achievement test scores (Ravitch & Cortese, 2009). Critics caution that without attending to students' social and emotional needs, many of these actions may be ineffective at best and harmful at worst, especially for economically disadvantaged groups (Meier, 2004).

However, the tide or dialectic now seems to be turning. As recent studies on the relation of educational achievement to adult outcomes have shown, early achievement accounts for a relatively small portion of the effect on either adult wages or monetized use of health services, social services, and criminal justice costs (Almlund, Duckworth, Heckman, & Kautz, 2011; Levin, 2012). With the leading work of Heckman and colleagues, who conceptualize a developmental approach to child well-being—termed the "technology of cognitive and noncognitive skills formation" (e.g., Cunha & Heckman, 2008)—there is convincing evidence that factors other than academic test scores explain much of the variance in adult wages, health utilization, and other public costs, including early morbidity. These factors have been labeled as "noncognitive" given they involve outcomes other than measured achievement/test scores (Farrington et al., 2012). In truth, this characterization is a misnomer because these abilities must be based on cognitive processes such as attention and executive functions, social and emotional competencies (e.g., self-control and persistence), and the effective use of learning strategies. Importantly, social and emotional competencies are one component of this larger set of noncognitive skills that account for the variability between people in most economic costs of adulthood. Furthermore, while poverty is a distant explanation for adult morbidity, these noncognitive factors appear to mediate these outcomes, and at least partially explain how the effects of poverty are transmitted in technological societies (Conti & Heckman, 2012). We return to this issue in our discussion of future work at the end of the chapter.

The second converging factor of change is the advent of the Common Core Curriculum in U.S. schools. The introduction of the Common Core Curriculum in most states will create a sea change in educational curriculum and instruction, if effectively implemented, because the Common Core Curriculum focuses on the underlying skills that are believed to be most important for adult vocational and economic success, and less single-mindedly focus on short-term impacts on achievement tests (McTighe & Wiggins, 2012). A central part of the Common Core Curriculum is a recognition of the need to build "21st century skills" as a central component of education; these skills focus on problem solving and reflective thinking, and the ability to communicate effectively to others and to work effectively in groups to solve problems (Pellegrino & Hilton, 2012). As such, it places many of the skills included as SEL competencies as central to educational goals and pedagogy.

The confluence of the recent economic study focusing on the importance of noncognitive skills and the rapid development and broad acceptance of the Common Core Curriculum have the potential to move the field of SEL further toward the center of leading educational thought and action. It should be noted that there are many concerns about how well the Common Core Curriculum will be implemented and whether it will truly value SEL competencies. Thus, it becomes even more important to understand what curricular models, at what ages, and with which children are most likely to yield academic and social, as well as economic, outcomes. In addition, policymakers have become more interested in getting the most "bang for the buck," and this will call for comparative effectiveness research of SEL programs, just as similar work is being done in the field of evidence-based medicine and health care economics (Bloom, 2004; Brent, 2004). To consider these issues further, we now turn our attention toward how one would incorporate economic evaluation into the assessment of effective SEL interventions.

Evaluating the Economic Impact of SEL: A Case Study

The use of economic evaluation can provide key information on the value of SEL programs, as well as levels of efficiency in program delivery. Careful planning of this process is crucial given the many facets of the evaluation. The remainder of the chapter focuses on economic evaluation as it pertains to SEL programs. It is important to emphasize from the outset that an economic evaluation is only one component of a full research endeavor and cannot replace either qualitative or quantitative analyses of program effects, especially those that are not economically relevant. For a broader and deeper introduction to economic evaluation, readers can consult sources that provide full overviews of economic evaluation (e.g., Gold, Siegel, Russell, & Weinstein, 1996; Haddix, Teutsch, & Corso, 2003; Levin & McEwan, 2000). These sources include more detail on key methodological aspects of economic evaluation not presented here, such as the necessary adjustments to monetary estimates based on time (namely due to inflation and discounting of dollars invested). To guide our presentation, we present an illustrative example of how an SEL researcher could plan an economic evaluation of an effective intervention within a school setting. This case example is hypothetical and used to demonstrate the decisions one would encounter and the steps one would accomplish in such an economic analysis.

Project Details

A researcher who has conducted a pilot study of a middle school SEL curriculum has found promising effects. The curriculum was taught two times a week in the context of sixth- and seventh-grade language arts and social studies, and combines some specific skills training (emotional understanding and communication, peer communication and resistance skills, identity development, and interpersonal problem solving) with the use of literature (both novels and nonfiction) and journal writing to embed and extend the understanding and use of these skills into other curricular areas. In the previous pilot randomized control trial, she found the following effects: Teachers in language arts and social studies reported fewer classroom disruptions and more student engagement; students reported significantly greater engagement and enjoyment of these classes, and greater attachment to school. Students also reported significantly less positive attitudes toward cigarette and drug use and lower rates of initiation. Finally, school records showed a 15% reduction in office-reported bullying and a 5% reduction in school suspensions. She now wants to move to a larger study that will compare the effects of the program in 12 intervention and 12 control middle schools that would involve approximately 100 teachers and 2,200 students. The researcher has developed a logic model of the program in which the learning of these SEL skills leads to short-term outcomes of greater engagement and attention in the classroom, greater bonding to school, more positive peer relations, understanding/self-efficacy in managing difficult emotions, and navigating interpersonal conflicts in more effective ways. These effects lead in the longer run to better grades, lower initiation of early alcohol, tobacco, and drug use, and lower rates of delinquency. Below are recommended steps for how the investigator could add an economic component to the evaluation. Table 7.1 provides more detail on appropriate measurement for the hypothetical program.

Step 1: Choosing the Type of Economic Analysis

A key decision is what type of economic analysis (or analyses) will be employed in the study. We consider two primary approaches here: benefit–cost analysis and cost-effectiveness analysis. If the primary goal is to determine the dollar benefit resulting

TABLE 7.1. Possible Measurement Domains and Outcomes for Economic Evaluation of a Hypothetical Middle School SEL Intervention

Program costs			
Direct costs	*Staff time*	*Opportunity costs*	*Evaluation costs*
• Program materials/ curriculum • Training wages and material • Administrative/project director costs • Ongoing consultation/team meetings	• For training • For administrative tasks • For consultation	• Space/facilities value • Teacher/staff time • Extra family time • Student time	(Any costs going toward assessing program effects; should be identified but excluded from program costs)

Program economic benefits (by recipient): possible short-term proximal effects				
On students	*On teachers*	*On host school*	*On family*	*On society*
• Improved academic performance • Lower rates of grade retention • Lower rates of special education placement • Less problem behavior[a] • Higher class engagement[a] • Increased positive attitudes/motivation[a] • Fewer bullying victims[a] • Increased school bonding[a] • Fewer office referrals/ suspensions • Lower rates of substance use/later initiation	• Job satisfaction[a] • Student relationships[a] • Lower stress[a] • Better mastery/self-efficacy[a] • Less time needed for class disruptions[a]	• Improved climate[a] • Improved reputation[a]	• Improved family relationships[a]	• Reduced use of mental health services • Fewer police contacts/ court costs • Less crime/ delinquency

Program economic benefits (by recipient): possible long-term distal effects		
On students	*On family*	*On society*
• Higher educational attainment • Employment success • Quality of life[a]	• Quality of life[a] • Family relationships[a]	• Reduced need for public (financial) assistance • Increased tax contributions • Lower health/mental health costs • Fewer health consequences

[a] Nonmonetized outcome.

from program participation, the researcher will undertake a *benefit–cost analysis*. This analysis compares the total costs required to implement the program with the current *and* future monetary benefits that are attributed to program participation. For the latter, the dollar amounts may comprise some costs that are directly measured as current study outcomes for participants (e.g., through follow-up assessment) and others that are projected from program outcomes that are not directly monetized (e.g., the estimated increase in lifetime earnings due to increased rates of high school graduation). Such projections involve the use of *shadow prices*—valuation of program benefits that are not tangibly measurable in dollar amounts—that are key to performing benefit–cost analysis in the behavioral sciences. This process is not unique to evaluation of interventions for children. For example, the economic benefits of interventions for heart disease are not fully based on medical costs associated with heart attacks or strokes. Because cholesterol levels (which are not valued) are directly linked to future heart attack and morbidity, one can examine the effects of exercise, diet, or drug therapy on cholesterol in economic evaluation given a shadow price for changes in cholesterol levels (e.g., Oster & Epstein, 1986).

By comparing estimated dollar amounts of both costs and benefits, a straightforward calculation can determine the program's economic cost or savings, such as net benefit (total program monetary benefits minus program costs) and benefit–cost ratio (BCR; ratio of benefits to costs, or an estimate of the return per dollar spent). Although these two values will similarly indicate whether the program is cost-effective, their magnitude will be influenced by program characteristics. A low-cost program such as a school-based universal program could produce a large return-on-investment number, even if the overall monetized benefits are relatively low as well. For example, if a program cost is $50 and the valued benefit is $550 (per person), the net benefit is $500. This will yield a BCR of 11 return for each dollar spent ($550 divided by $50). In contrast, if a very expensive program costs $20,000 and yields total benefits of $23,000 (per person), the net benefit would be much larger than the prior example. However, the BCR of 2.3 is much smaller. Either figure may be informative depending on the policy analysis and the needs of the population of interest. Regardless, if the net benefit of the program is positive or BCR exceeds 1, the program is determined to be cost-effective in addition to being effective in general.

Naturally, dollar benefits resulting from program participation are estimated from the measures that can be directly or indirectly monetized, such as outcomes associated with crime, employment, use of health/mental health services, public assistance, and early childbearing. Monetary benefits can also involve dollars *saved* by the program if, for instance, the intervention reduces the need for public expenditures among participants (e.g., reducing the likelihood to commit crimes, decreased resources needed for repeating a grade in school). Or a program may lead to dollars *generated* among participants through something like increased employment success over time. In this case, the program leads to increased earnings for participants, as well as increased tax revenue for the public. Of course, a successful program may instigate substantial initial costs that would not have otherwise occurred while providing a larger economic benefit in the future. For instance, an educational intervention that leads to fewer students dropping out of school will require increased funds for continuing students; or a program that effectively motivates participants to seek necessary mental health services for a condition will require therapy or pharmaceutical costs. Nevertheless, the improved health or educational gains *in the long run* will lead to economic gains (e.g., better employment prospects, improved health) that exceed these initial additional expenses.

Of course, an analysis strictly based on monetized outcomes will not embody the full impact of the program, especially when key study outcomes are not easily valued and/or participants are very young (as is often the case with SEL interventions). An alternative economic assessment involves a *cost-effectiveness analysis*, where the cost to achieve (nonmonetized) program effects is determined. This approach allows researchers to study the efficiency of the program in another way and may be useful for assessing outcomes that are *valued* by participants or society even if not explicitly represented in dollar amounts (Haddix et al., 2003). For example, such a study might focus on the costs to reduce depression in children in their early teens through an effective school program. We return to this approach below. For the middle school program, we assume a benefit–cost approach is selected, which is appropriate given the outcomes affected by the program that can be monetized.

Step 2: Choosing a Perspective for Analyses

The decision for the most appropriate *perspective* for analysis is a fundamental first step in economic evaluation. In simplest terms, the economic perspective reflects whose viewpoint is most relevant to the study. The selected perspective establishes the framework for the study and ultimately determines what to include in the analysis.

In particular, it can determine how costs of the program are represented, as well as what current or future economic benefits should be included. For preventive intervention programs, one typically adopts a *societal* perspective in which overall costs and resources necessary to implement a program are considered versus the program economic benefits realized by society as a whole. In terms of program costs/resources this would include what everyone (i.e., taxpayers, participants, and other funders) would have to provide in order to deliver the program. Similarly, in terms of benefits, the societal perspective would take into consideration the economic impact and benefits experienced by everyone (e.g., participants, funders, and nonparticipants). In general, the societal perspective is all-inclusive, reflecting the costs and gains to anyone affected directly or indirectly by the program. For the middle school program, the societal perspective is most appropriate given the program effects on various outcomes relevant to participants and nonparticipants (e.g., substance abuse, class disruption). In addition, delivery of the program depends on contributions and resources across multiple inputs that should be recognized and may not involve dollar amounts (including costs for materials, teacher time, and allocated space within the school), as discussed in the next section. It is often important to consider the implications that choice of perspective will have on overall results. For instance, some studies employ a participant perspective in which only costs and benefits to the participants are considered. Such a perspective is not as appropriate for this example, so we refer the reader to the sources cited earlier for more coverage of alternative perspectives in economic analysis.

Related to the choice of perspective, the evaluator should have some sense of the *scope* of economic impact. Specifically, what is the expected reach of program effects in an economic sense across time and across people? Such decisions will influence what measures are included for economic evaluation (discussed below), as well as how much economic models should involve projections of effects. The process of representing time in an economic evaluation can vary widely across studies. For example, the evaluator may consider economic impact only within the time frame of the program, or across some portion of the study participants' lifetimes. The former is analytically simpler but may shortchange the economic impact. The decision for the analytic time frame could be based on how strong and sustained study effects are expected to be in general. The evaluator should also consider reach of program effects beyond those participating. For instance, if effects are strong enough to have a positive influence on other family members or others close to the subject (e.g., teachers), it could be worthwhile to assess economic impact more broadly (see Step 4 below). The analysis should consider the program reach to those unrelated to the participants as well. For instance, if the program reduces criminal activity among participants, this should reduce costs to (avoided) crime victims who are nonparticipants (reduced health care costs, reduced pain and suffering, etc.). With an effective intervention, it is easy to see how the impact can extend past the individuals who received the program. The challenge is identifying where and how extensive this reach is, especially given that most evaluations focus mostly on participants.

In our middle school program example, it would make sense to develop models to estimate longer-term effects given previously detected effects (e.g., longer-term effects on substance use outcomes). It will be important to estimate how these effects may translate into economic benefits over time. The age to project to may be subjective, and ideally would be based on prior research. We assume in this case that the evaluator will represent economic impact through middle adulthood (say, age 45)—an age when effects from a strong program may still be detectable and economic benefits are not completely diminished by devaluing of investment over time. Based on prior findings for this program, we do not expect to find program effects extending to other nonparticipants (e.g., siblings or teachers), although possible measures for nonparticipants are listed in Table 7.1 because they are theoretically worth considering.

Step 3: Assessing the Costs and Resources Necessary to Implement the Program

Regardless of the type of economic analysis chosen (Step 1), the evaluation process should begin with plans to assess thoroughly the costs and resources necessary to implement the intervention. The information provided through this step alone provides key data for interventionists, such as how resources will vary by function and over time, as well as how cost efficiency for program delivery may be improved. For economic analysis, careful and accurate procedures for attaining cost estimates will be crucial in leading to valid conclusions.

Because our example involves the societal perspective, it is necessary to consider all the resources required to implement the program successfully—direct expenses, as well as less tangible costs. Tracking costs through standard budgets and accounting of resources is only part of the process. The process should include not only the basic expenditures, such as purchasing the SEL curriculum and training teachers, but also recognizes all resources required to establish and deliver the program. The analysis should consider what is required for the intervention, and also how it affects the systems within which it operates. For instance, if teachers or administrators donate their time outside of school in order to launch a new SEL effort, this activity should make up part of the program's cost. Such changes in how individuals behave and allocate their time may result in a cost to some other activity (e.g., leisure time, classroom planning time). These shifts in resources involve what economists consider to be *opportunity* costs (i.e., what is given up by allocating resources to one program compared to the next best option; Foster, Dodge, & Jones, 2003; Karoly, 2010). There are a variety of resources that can assist evaluators in developing a cost inventory and conducting a full cost analysis of intervention programs (e.g., Drummond, Sculpher, & Torrance, 2005; Haddix et al., 2003; Yates, 1996). Accurate determination of the costs—as well as understanding how these costs will typically vary across implementations—will set the course for sound overall estimates of economic impact. Failing to capture the entire cost of the program could not only lead to underfunding for future program implementations but also result in an inaccurate estimate of its economic impact.

With this in mind, the researcher should develop an inventory of all the resources required to successfully implement the program. This will likely be broken down broadly into personnel and nonpersonnel categories but should include every program input necessary for implementation. The evaluator will then need to estimate the cost of each of these inputs. Some of these costs can easily be monetized (e.g., curricula), whereas others may be more difficult (e.g., teacher volunteer time). For those less tangible resource inputs, the researcher may need to consider strategies to impute costs (e.g., using the market value of teacher's work time to value volunteer time). Categorization of costs over time will help the evaluator and future researchers understand the systemic needs of the intervention. For instance, it will be useful to track periodic costs (e.g., training costs) or costs that vary depending on the number of children being served. Any costs necessary for continued program development should also be distinguished. Costs necessary for research or evaluative purposes should also be identified but excluded from total program costs (i.e., identifying them will ensure that they are excluded). Table 7.1 also presents a potential set of program cost categories that fit this case study.

Step 4: Determining the Necessary Outcome Measures for Economic Evaluation

With the procedures in place to measure program costs effectively, the researcher must next decide the best strategy for investigating how program effects will translate into economic gains. With the chosen analytic perspective, this should include assessing economic benefits in both the short and long term. This primarily involves determining which outcomes affected by the intervention result in a monetized economic impact (i.e., outcomes that can be measured in or viably translated into dollar amounts). Given the logic model of this middle school program, the following domains would be most relevant: students' educational attainment, educational/systemic needs (special education services, grade retention, school disciplinary needs), early substance initiation/misuse, risky sexual behavior, and use of health and mental health services. The researcher should make sure to include measures that cover these domains, including those in which program effects were detected in pilot research (detailed earlier). For example, it would be important to measure the amount of cigarette use among participants, as well as the age when they started using. Collection of school records is also important, including counts of the number of office referrals, suspensions, and use of special services. From these outcomes one could then estimate the amount of school resources that might be saved or avoided due to the program. The evaluator should measure educational achievement through test measures and grades to estimate the likelihood for outcomes that can be more readily linked to economic gains, namely, high school graduation and college attendance. Other measures may be added primarily for the sake of the economic evaluation, such as use of mental health services and delinquency/police contact outside of school.

The choice of measures also is influenced by the scope of the anticipated program effects (as discussed earlier). If possible, measurement plans would include follow-up data collection that would enable observation of the longer-term program impact beyond middle school (see Table 7.1). Because the program had an effect on student behavior, the evaluator may want to follow subjects long enough to assess effects on school disciplinary services and overall educational achievement through high school. Extending measurement into young adulthood would enable collection of important data such as longer-term substance abuse, health services use, and involvement in the criminal justice system.

As noted earlier, valuation of measured outcomes may rely on shadow prices. For instance, substance misuse may be monetized in terms of lost productivity, necessary health costs, and/or likelihood to commit a crime and related court costs. Other domains should also be considered as future or indirectly affected outcomes: employment, criminal justice/arrest, public assistance, early childbearing, and child abuse/neglect. Projection of these indirect program benefits, while not yet observable in the middle school program evaluation, can be based on changes in measured outcomes either during the program or in follow-up assessment. As noted, improvement on either observed or projected outcomes translate into dollars generated by participants (e.g., higher educational attainment translates into future earnings for participant and subsequent tax revenue for society) or saved (e.g., reduced delinquency translates into lower likelihood for arrests and therefore lower costs to process crimes). Net benefits may be realized when an effective program has a measurable impact in *any one* of these categories as long as total economic gains exceed program costs. Table 7.1 presents a potential list of both shorter- and longer-term measures that might be assessed in our example. These include measures that are theoretically worth considering, although some may be determined unnecessary given expected program effects. Note that certain outcomes (marked by [a]) may be relevant in terms of some contingent value, but not readily monetized for the sake of a benefit–cost analysis. Such outcomes may be more useful for a cost-effectiveness analysis (discussed below).

Consideration of program reach (discussed earlier) is also important for determining what should be measured, especially if a societal perspective is chosen. As noted earlier, based on prior findings, the evaluator in this example would not be concerned with measuring program impact on other family members. However, if the intervention leads to effects that could feasibly extend to peers and families, the measure of siblings' outcomes would be advisable. For example, reductions in drug and alcohol use in an older sibling may influence lower usage by younger siblings. An effective SEL program in a school may not only improve child outcomes but also reduce teacher stress, which in turn would affect the teacher's health, number of days needed for teacher substitutes, health care utilization, or teacher turnover (Jennings & Greenberg, 2009). In summary, for determining necessary measures, it is appropriate in an economic analysis to consider changes not only in the program participant but also in those with whom that person interacts. The evaluator should consider all possible measurement domains (which are represented in Table 7.1), then decide what measures should be included based on the program's logic model and prior evidence for where program effects have occurred.

Step 5: Representing Analytic Uncertainty

Uncertainty in estimates related to a range of factors in both program costs and outcomes can be represented through use of a *sensitivity analysis* (i.e., how sensitive estimates are considering various facets of the model). This is a crucial part of the economic evaluation, allowing one to represent uncertainty in final estimates that acknowledge the many analytic assumptions involved in achieving point estimates. Specifically, the sensitivity analysis produces a range of feasible estimates given anticipated variation in study parameters (e.g., program implementation characteristics, per-unit costs used for valuation of benefits); this variation in inputs could represent expected differences across regions or contexts in which the program could occur (Johns, Baltussen, & Hutubessy, 2003). In general, the complexity of these analyses can vary based on the assumptions being made within the analysis (Levin & McEwan, 2000). Evaluations in which few assumptions about program cost or future benefits are made would be relatively simple. In the context of SEL programs that intervene early and may see benefits across the lifespan, more complex sensitivity analyses that consider numerous assumptions are more appropriate. These approaches could employ probabilistic methods (e.g., bootstrapping or Monte Carlo techniques) for handling uncertainty due to the numerous assumptions that may vary across setting and time (Claxton et al., 2005). Overall, well-thought-out sensitivity analyses lead to more informative evaluation results and can educate decision makers about the *likelihood* that programs will see a positive return on investment as opposed to relying on single estimates. For further coverage of sensitivity analysis, we refer the researcher to the resources cited earlier.

In our example, the evaluator can assess what parameters in the benefit–cost analysis may be most likely to vary based on uncertainty or expected variation across implementations of the program itself. For instance, she could incorporate a range of costs for certain key ingredients of the program (ranging from low to high), such as the expected costs of intervention materials. For valuation of outcomes, she could consider a range of monetized unit effects, such as for long-term cost of cigarette use (i.e., based on different cost of illness studies). Given the various program resources and outcomes involved in the full benefit–cost analysis, many ranges of costs could be integrated into the analysis. By assessing what key inputs of the model could vary on both sides of the benefit–cost equation, the researcher can effectively characterize the expected deviation from the bottom-line estimate for the middle school program.

Considering the Value of Nonmonetized Outcomes

In the previous example, we chose a benefit–cost analysis approach for our economic evaluation. However, this approach is limited for many SEL programs in which the full impact of the program cannot be easily captured in terms of outcomes that can be monetized. An alternative economic assessment involves a *cost-effectiveness analysis (CEA)*, in which the cost to achieve (nonmonetized) program effects is determined (Haddix et al., 2003; Levin & McEwan, 2000). This method allows researchers to study the efficiency of the program in another way and may be useful for assessing outcomes that are *valued* by participants and/or society even if not explicitly represented in dollar amounts. To do this, a CEA often involves calculating an *incremental cost-effectiveness ratio (ICER)*, which is the ratio of program costs to the effect on an outcome of interest (which can be represented by an effect size or difference between intervention and control groups on a key study outcome). For example, the middle school researcher could calculate an ICER to represent the incremental costs to prevent one case of bullying from occurring to be $1,000, determined from dividing the program costs by the program effect size on bullying (other approaches that avoid the ratio metric include regression-based methods; e.g., Hoch & Smith, 2006). ICERs can be particularly useful in comparing different interventions to determine which program is the most cost-effective for achieving the same effect. For example, one program's ICER might be $600 per bullying incident compared to another program's ICER of $1,000. Comparisons of ICERs could be useful for policymakers and administrators in deciding how to achieve the most results given a fixed cost. Comparisons can also be used *within* a program if, for instance, there are multiple components used to achieve an effect (Foster, Olchowski, & Webster-Stratton, 2007). That is, cost-effectiveness analysis could enable comparison of intervention components to determine best use of resources (e.g., comparing internet delivery, internet and face-to-face combinations, the added value of apps for both teachers and students).

An alternative cost-effectiveness approach can involve an assessment of more global/holistic improvement that may be associated with an intervention (Hoch & Smith, 2006; Levin & McEwan, 2000). This can be represented through a metric such as quality-adjusted life years (QALY), determined through separate measurement that assesses recent emotional states such as stress and happiness (or through a composite index for quality of life). A focus on quality of life could be suitable for assessing something like improvement in SEL given the relevance to various facets of personality, cognition, and behavior. For more detail on CEA methods, as well as the advantages and disadvantages of such approaches, we refer the reader to the economic evaluation resources cited previously. For the sake of our hypothetical program, certain measures represented in Table 7.1 could be more appropriate to a CEA approach for the middle school program (such as those marked with [a]).

Current Issues and Challenges in Economic Analysis of SEL Programs

The previous example highlights how one would plan an economic evaluation for a specific SEL program. By attending to all relevant costs and benefits, one can execute a rigorous and comprehensive economic evaluation of an SEL intervention. As noted, we refer the reader to cited resources for more detailed information on carrying out economic evaluation, especially regarding more complicated aspects of the analysis. We finish this chapter by considering more global issues surrounding the quality of studies, as well as how future research may further the economic case for SEL.

Improving Current and Future Economic Evaluation

In order to make the best case for the economic value of SEL programs, it will be important for future research to have high quality and comparability across studies. The more that the key steps discussed earlier are omitted or handled in widely different ways across evaluations, the less likely results can be collectively considered. Among economic evaluations of early childhood interventions, substantial differences have been noted in the outcomes selected to be monetized, the age of follow-up data available, the degree of projections involved, and whether participant time is valued for opportunity costs (among other things). For example, a collective assessment of various benefit–cost studies of early childhood interventions differed on whether or not they included valuation of intangible crime benefits (e.g., benefits to crime victims; Karoly, 2010). A key difference such as this impedes the ability to compare results to seek consensus. The inconsistency in methodology and procedures across studies makes interpretation and generalizability of results more complicated for policymaking. Indeed, improving and standardizing benefit–cost analysis methodology is identified by the Benefit–Cost Analysis Center (University of Washington's Evans School of Public Affairs) as a primary challenge in the broad field of economic assessment (Beatty, 2009).

Consistent methodology across various studies may be a challenge given the different backgrounds and training of researchers. Collaborations with economists, or at least researchers with experience in economic evaluation, would help to increase consistency across studies. Having such expertise will enable better planning for measurement of economically relevant outcomes, as well as more consistent use of procedures for evaluating program resources. Having this expert guidance at the beginning of the study will help to ensure that future results are not limited by inadequate measurement for targeted outcomes or for assessing program costs/resources.

There also are logistical limitations affecting the ability to include appropriate procedures and measurement plans. As noted earlier, measurement for the sake of economic evaluation should be as complete and extensive as possible; ideally it would involve longer-term tracking of subjects and assessment of multiple outcomes within adolescence or young adult periods (i.e., when more economically relevant outcomes are measurable). Although follow-up tracking of subjects is useful, there are many unknowns, such as whether extended research funding will be secured, whether key evaluation personnel will still be available, and whether enough participants are tracked over time to enable representative results. Regardless, from the outset, studies can put in place the necessary measures and procedures to facilitate continued tracking if project resources continue. For instance, the study design may include plans to incorporate a periodic assessment of a random subsample into adulthood. In this way, modern analytic techniques such as planned missing data designs can be useful for approximating results from the full original sample (Graham, Taylor, Olchowski, & Cumsille, 2006).

Strategies to increase consistency and inclusion of appropriate measurement across studies could be supported through professional organizations and meetings of leading SEL researchers. For instance, guidelines could be established that direct how program evaluators initiate analytic plans and measurement for economic evaluation. This could involve generating lists of recommended measures for economic evaluation. In addition, it may be that certain programs would provide a better focus for economic evaluation, and an organized effort could be made toward economic assessment only on studies that have been shown to be the most effective. Studies such as Durlak and colleagues' (2011) meta-analysis shed light on the collective effectiveness of SEL programs for improving outcomes on a large scale. In this review, the authors demonstrate how SAFE (sequenced, active, focused, and explicit) programs—those that followed four recommended practices for better quality in intervention programs—had higher likelihood for positive impact on SEL outcomes. This type of designation could guide plans regarding where to direct evaluation of economic impact.

Although improving the consistency and quality of studies is critical, understanding the potential benefits also will rely on research that illuminates the links between SEL outcomes and future adult and economic success. Currently, an economic evaluation of a program directed toward younger children will likely be conservative given the incomplete understanding of the nature and degree to which important SEL skills observed at young ages are linked to future adult outcomes that can be monetized (e.g., employment and educational attainment). For our hypothetical example, we chose a middle school universal SEL program because it more readily accommodated an economic assessment. An economic evaluation of a program for younger children is harder to carry out given the lack of economically relevant outcomes for those ages and the shortage of well-established empirical links between early developmental and adult outcomes. As noted, many monetary benefits depend on shadow prices for observed program effects and projection of costs into the future (e.g., early school success predicts the likelihood to obtain a college degree, which can predict future earnings). Because many such connections have not yet been established, projection models are likely to underestimate benefits. Accurate shadow prices for elementary school outcomes would go a long way toward improving benefit–cost analyses for SEL programs.

In general, future research on the economic benefits of early learning and intervention should incorporate more complicated representation of improvement in the developmental course for children. As we noted in our opening text, recent research has focused on the importance of effective interventions occurring early enough to achieve long-term economic improvement. Conti and Heckman (2012) discuss this in terms of "child well-being," advocating that a core set of capabilities covering cognition, personality, and biology should be an area of focus in regard to their influence on future adult economic status and health. In the presence of socioeconomic disadvantage, early intervention to alter trajectories may be vital to increasing the likelihood of well-being before later problems occur. The concept of starting early is counterintuitive from an economic standpoint, where the general rule is that the gap between program delivery (investment of resources) and achievement of economic impact should be as short as possible. Yet program effectiveness may be vastly increased by reaching subjects at developmentally sensitive ages at which important changes in self-regulatory abilities and social–emotional competence could more than make up for any monetary discounting that occurs due to the time between investing in early intervention and an economic benefit realized years later (Conti & Heckman, 2012). The ability to influence a child positively at an appropriate early stage may improve the developmental cascades that shape future outcomes. Where trajectories are altered toward more positive pathways at an early age, the result could be accumulated positive outcomes and reduced likelihood for subsequent, multiple, negative developmental outcomes/exposures (Bornstein, Hahn, & Haynes, 2010; Dodge, Greenberg, & Malone, 2008).

Despite current studies focusing on the importance of noncognitive factors, the links between SEL outcomes and cost outcomes are still unclear. Economic studies still rely largely on outcomes that are monetized. As studies illuminate the connection between early social–emotional skills and adult outcomes, we will be better equipped to link program impact of improved SEL skills to long-term economic gains on more types of outcomes. Additionally, if studies can place value on outcomes observed at young ages, there would be less need to rely on long-term follow-up data. Better understanding of these associations will also provide researchers with information on the most useful outcome measures for program evaluation, even when subjects are young. Some progress in this area is occurring, as evidenced by multistudy benefit–cost assessments that incorporate program effects on outcomes such as child aggression and depression (Aos et al., 2011). Still, substantial work is necessary to link changes in early academic, behavioral, and social–emotional improvements to later monetized outcomes.

Conclusion

The value of prevention when it comes to general health is usually unquestioned; a goal for SEL researchers might be to frame effective prevention programs in the same light, as necessary on a large scale for the sake of public budgets, as well as both personal and societal well-being. We see substantial benefits in the economic value of SEL. Hundreds of billions of dollars in public money are required each year to address societal problems associated with crime, substance abuse, and poor physical and mental health in general (e.g., Insel, 2008; McCollister, French, & Fang, 2010; Rehm et al., 2009). The vast funds necessary for addressing such problems once they become entrenched greatly exceed the resources directed toward preventive efforts whose short- and long-term benefits could improve lives and avoid large public and personal costs. Increasing the quality and volume of economic evaluations of evidence-based SEL programs is a necessary step in convincing policymakers and the public to support more broadly children's social and emotional development toward improving our public health.

References

Almlund, M., Duckworth, A. L., Heckman, J. J., & Kautz, T. D. (2011). Personality psychology and economics. In E. A. Hanushek, S. Machin, & L. Woessmann (Eds.), *Handbook of the economics of education* (Vol. 4B, pp. 1–181). Amsterdam, The Netherlands: Elsevier.

Aos, S., Lee, S., Drake, E., Pennucci, A., Klima, T., Miller, M., et al. (2011). *Return on investment: Evidence-based options to improve statewide outcomes.* Olympia: Washington State Institute for Public Policy.

Barnett, W. S., & Masse, L. N. (2007). Comparative benefit–cost analysis of the Abecedarian program and its policy implications. *Economics of Education Review, 26*(1), 113–125.

Beatty, A. (2009). *Strengthening benefit–cost analysis for early childhood interventions: Workshop summary.* Washington, DC: National Academy Press.

Becker, G. S. (2009). *Human capital: A theoretical and empirical analysis, with special reference to education.* Chicago: University of Chicago Press.

Belfield, C. R., Nores, M., Barnett, S., & Schweinhart, L. (2006). The High/Scope Perry Preschool Program cost–benefit analysis using data from the age-40 follow-up. *Journal of Human Resources, 41*(1), 162–190.

Berends, M., Bodilly, S. J., & Kirby, S. N. (2002). *Facing the challenges of whole-school reform: New American Schools after a decade.* Santa Monica, CA: RAND Corporation.

Bloom, B. S. (2004). Use of formal benefit/cost evaluations in health system decision making. *American Journal of Managed Care, 10*(5), 329–335.

Bornstein, M. H., Hahn, C.-S., & Haynes, O. M. (2010). Social competence, externalizing, and internalizing behavioral adjustment from early childhood through early adolescence: Developmental cascades. *Development and Psychopathology, 22*(4), 717–735.

Brent, R. J. (2004). *Cost–benefit analysis and health care evaluations.* Northhampton, MA: Edward Elgar.

Catalano, R. F., Berglund, M. L., Ryan, J. A. M., Lonczak, H. S., & Hawkins, J. D. (2004). Positive youth development in the United States: Research findings on evaluations of positive youth development programs. *Annals of the American Academy of Political and Social Science, 591*(1), 98–124.

Claxton, K., Sculpher, M., McCabe, C., Briggs, A., Akehurst, R., Buxton, M., et al. (2005). Probabilistic sensitivity analysis for NICE technology assessment: Not an optional extra. *Health Economics, 14*(4), 339–347.

Cohen, M. A., & Piquero, A. R. (2009). New evidence on the monetary value of saving a high risk youth. *Journal of Quantitative Criminology, 25*(1), 25–49.

Conti, G., & Heckman, J. J. (2012). *The economics of child well-being* (NBER Working Paper Series No. 18466). Cambridge, MA: National Bureau of Economic Research. Retrieved November 15, 2012, from *www.nber.org/papers/w18466.*

Crowley, D. M., Jones, D. E., Greenberg, M. T., Feinberg, M. E., & Spoth, R. L. (2012). Resource consumption of a diffusion model for prevention programs: The PROSPER Delivery System. *Journal of Adolescent Health, 50*(3), 256–263.

Cunha, F., & Heckman, J. J. (2008). Formulating, identifying and estimating the technology of cognitive and noncognitive skill formation. *Journal of Human Resources, 43*(4), 738–782.

Dodge, K. A., Greenberg, M. T., & Malone, P. S. (2008). Testing an idealized dynamic cascade model of the development of serious violence in adolescence. *Child Development, 79*(6), 1907–1927.

Drummond, M., Sculpher, M. J., & Torrance, G. (2005). *Methods for the economic evaluation of health care programs* (3rd ed). Oxford, UK: Oxford University Press.

Durlak, J. A. (1995). *School-based prevention programs for children and adolescents.* Newbury Park, CA: Sage.

Durlak, J. A., Weissberg, R. P., Dymnicki, A. B., Taylor, R. D., & Schellinger, K. B. (2011). The impact of enhancing students' social and emotional learning: A meta-analysis of school-based universal interventions. *Child Development, 82*(1), 405–432.

Fagan, A. A., & Catalano, R. F. (2013). What works in youth violence prevention: A review of the literature. *Research on Social Work Practice, 23*(2), 141–156.

Farrington, C., Roderick, M., Allensworth, E., Nagaoka, J., Keyes, T., Johnson, D., et al. (2012). *Teaching adolescents to become learners: The role of noncognitive factors in shaping school performance: A critical literature review.* Chicago: University of Chicago Consortium on Chicago School Research.

Foster, E. M., Dodge, K. A., & Jones, D. E. (2003). Issues in the economic evaluation of prevention programs. *Applied Developmental Science, 7*(2), 76–86.

Foster, E. M., Olchowski, A. E., & Webster-Stratton, C. H. (2007). Is stacking intervention components cost-effective?: An analysis of the Incredible Years Program. *Journal of the American Academy of Child and Adolescent Psychiatry, 46*(11), 1414–1424.

Gest, S. D., Osgood, D. W., Feinberg, M. E., Bierman, K. L., & Moody, J. (2011). Strengthening prevention program theories and evaluations: Contributions from social network analysis. *Prevention Science, 12*(4), 349–360.

Gold, M. R., Siegel, J. E., Russell, L. B., & Weinstein, M. C. (1996). *Cost-effectiveness in health and medicine.* Oxford, UK: Oxford University Press.

Gottfredson, D. C., & Wilson, D. B. (2003). Characteristics of effective school-based substance abuse prevention. *Prevention Science, 4*(1), 27–38.

Graham, J. W., Taylor, B. J., Olchowski, A. E., & Cumsille, P. E. (2006). Planned missing data designs in psychological research. *Psychological Methods, 11*(4), 323–343.

Greenberg, M. T. (2010). School-based prevention: Current status and future challenges. *Effective Education, 2*(1), 27–52.

Greenberg, M. T., Domitrovich, C., & Bumbarger, B. (2001). The prevention of mental disorders in school-aged children: Current state of the field. *Prevention and Treatment, 4,* Article 1. Retrieved July 1, 2012, from *http://psycnet.apa.org/journals/pre/4/1/1a.pdf.*

Greenberg, M. T., Weissberg, R. P., O'Brien, M. U., Zins, J. E., Fredericks, L., Resnik, H., et al. (2003). Enhancing school-based prevention and youth development through coordinated social, emotional, and academic learning. *American Psychologist, 58*(6–7), 466–474.

Greenstone, M., Harris, M., Li, K., Looney, A., & Patashnik, J. (2012). *A dozen economic facts about K–12 education.* Washington, DC: Hamilton Project, The Brookings Institution. Retrieved December 22, 2012, from *www.hamiltonproject.org/papers/a_dozen_economic_facts_about_k-12_education.*

Haddix, A. C., Teutsch, S. M., & Corso, P. S. (Eds.). (2003). *Prevention effectiveness: A guide to decision analysis and economic evaluation* (2nd ed.). Oxford, UK: Oxford University Press.

Heckman, J. J. (2000). Policies to foster human capital. *Research in Economics, 54*(1), 3–56.

Hoagwood, K. E., Olin, S. S., Kerker, B. D., Kratochwill, T. R., Crowe, M., & Saka, N. (2007). Empirically based school interventions targeted at academic and mental health functioning. *Journal of Emotional and Behavioral Disorders, 15*(2), 66–92.

Hoch, J. S., & Smith, M. W. (2006). A guide to economic evaluation: Methods for cost-effectiveness analysis of person-level data. *Journal of Traumatic Stress, 19*(6), 787–797.

Insel, T. (2008). Assessing the economic costs of serious mental illness. *American Journal of Psychiatry, 165*(6), 663–665.

Jennings, P. A., & Greenberg, M. T. (2009). The prosocial classroom: Teacher social and emotional competence in relation to student and classroom outcomes. *Review of Educational Research, 79*(1), 491–525.

Johns, B., Baltussen, R., & Hutubessy, R. (2003). Programme costs in the economic evaluation of health interventions. *Cost Effectiveness and Resource Allocation, 1*(1), 1. Retrieved November 15, 2012, from *www.resource-allocation.com/content/1/1/1.*

Karoly, L. A. (2010). *Principles and standards for benefit–cost analysis of early childhood interventions* (Unpublished working paper). Arlington, VA: RAND Corporation.

Lee, S., Aos, S., Drake, E., Pennucci, A., Miller, M., & Anderson, L. (2012). *Return on investment: Evidence-based options to improve statewide outcomes* (Vol. 4). Olympia: Washington State Institute for Public Policy.

Levin, H. M. (2009). The economic payoff to investing in educational justice. *Educational Researcher, 38*(1), 5–20.

Levin, H. M. (2012, February). More than just test scores. *Prospects*, pp. 1–16.

Levin, H. M., & McEwan, P. J. (2000). *Cost-effectiveness analysis: Methods and applications* (Vol. 4). Thousand Oaks, CA: Sage.

Lochman, J. E., & van den Steenhoven, A. (2002). Family-based approaches to substance abuse prevention. *Journal of Primary Prevention, 23*(1), 49–114.

McCollister, K. E., French, M. T., & Fang, H. (2010). The cost of crime to society: New crime-specific estimates for policy and program evaluation. *Drug and Alcohol Dependence, 108*(1), 98–109.

McTighe, J., & Wiggins, G. (2012). *Unpacking the Common Core Standards using the UbD framework* [DVD]. Alexandria, VA: Association for Supervision and Currciulum Development.

Meier, D. (2004). *Many children left behind: How the No Child Left Behind Act is damaging our children and our schools.* Boston: Beacon Press.

Merry, S. N., & Spence, S. H. (2007). Attempting to prevent depression in youth: A systematic review of the evidence. *Early Intervention in Psychiatry, 1*(2), 128–137.

Miller, T., & Hendrie, D. (2009). *Substance abuse prevention dollars and cents: A cost–benefit analysis* (DHHS Pub. No. (SMA) 07-4298). Rockville, MD: Center for Substance Abuse Prevention, Substance Abuse and Mental Health Services Administration.

Oster, G., & Epstein, A. M. (1986). Primary prevention and coronary heart disease: The economic benefits of lowering serum cholesterol. *American Journal of Public Health, 76*(6), 647–656.

Pellegrino, J. W., & Hilton, M. L. (Eds.). (2012). *Education for life and work: Developing transferable knowledge and skills in the 21st century* (A report of the National Research Council). Washington, DC: National Academies Press.

Ravitch, D., & Cortese, A. (2009). Why we're behind: What top nations teach their students but we don't. *Education Digest: Essential Readings Condensed for Quick Review, 75*(1), 35–38.

Rehm, J., Mathers, C., Popova, S., Thavornchароensap, M., Teerawattananon, Y., & Patra, J. (2009). Global burden of disease and injury and economic cost attributable to alcohol use and alcohol-use disorders. *Lancet, 373*, 2223–2233.

Reynolds, A. J., Temple, J. A., White, B. A. B., Ou, S. R., & Robertson, D. L. (2011). Age 26 cost–benefit analysis of the Child–Parent Center Early Education Program. *Child Development, 82*(1), 379–404.

Rose, G. (1981). Strategy of prevention: Lessons from cardiovascular disease. *British Medical Journal (Clinical Research Edition), 282*, 1847–1851.

Spoth, R. L., Trudeau, L. S., Guyll, M., & Shin, C. (2012). Benefits of universal intervention effects on a youth protective shield 10 years after baseline. *Journal of Adolescent Health, 50*(4), 414–417.

Weissberg, R. P., Kumpfer, K. L., & Seligman, M. E. (2003). Prevention that works for children and youth: An introduction. *American Psychologist, 58*(6–7), 425–432.

Wilson, S. J., Lipsey, M. W., & Derzon, J. H. (2003). The effects of school-based intervention programs on aggressive behavior: A meta-analysis. *Journal of Consulting and Clinical Psychology, 71*(1), 136–149.

Yates, B. T. (1996). *Analyzing costs, procedures, processes, and outcomes in human services: An introduction.* Thousand Oaks, CA: Sage.

CHAPTER 8

Financing and Funding for SEL Initiatives

Olga Acosta Price

> Having clarity about how a nonprofit will fund its mission is as important as having clarity about how it will deliver its programmatic impact. Almost every nonprofit has two jobs, each with its own set of external stakeholders. One job is to identify beneficiaries and make a difference for them with programs. But beneficiaries rarely pay the tab—or at least not all of it. Hence the second job: cultivating a distinct set of funders. Building and scaling sustainable financial support is as complicated and important as figuring out the programmatic dimensions.
>
> —KIM, PERREAULT, AND FOSTER (2011, p. 4)

A growing body of evidence calls attention to the importance of fostering social and emotional learning (SEL) throughout a child's school years in order to support healthy lifelong development and successful academic engagement. Systematic empirical reviews demonstrate the positive impact of universal prevention programs on various health and education outcomes (Durlak, Weissberg, Dymnicki, Taylor, & Schellinger, 2011; Sklad, Diekstra, De Ritter, Ben, & Gravesteijn, 2012; Weare & Nind, 2011). Supporters of SEL programs and practices point to the evidence base for SEL interventions and argue that improving fidelity of implementation and increasing understanding of environmental factors that support SEL programs will contribute to their long-term sustainability. Yet these factors are not sufficient. An explicit plan for financing these strategies is often either missing or insufficient for program planning and implementation. Most would agree that SEL initiatives require an approach that recognizes the funding sources and financing strategies likely to secure programmatic and systemic advances.

A discussion of financing strategies and funding sources must take into consideration the status of national and state economies. Education programs and institutions have been particularly hard hit given the current fiscal crisis (Committee for Education Funding, 2013; Oliff, Mai, & Leachman, 2012). Reductions in federal spending, as well as state and local budget cuts, suggest that new public dollars to implement or expand SEL programs are unlikely for several years to come.[1] For this reason, actions that maximize existing program efficiencies while maintaining positive outcomes will dominate discussions, even as demands for specialized instruction and services increase.

In order to determine the likelihood of program continuity, a comprehensive sustainability strategy for any child-focused program must take into account additional factors, such as the depth of commitment from influential leaders, the opportunities for growth, the impact of the political environment, the existence of supportive policies, and the strength of advocacy pathways already in place to promote children's issues. Child health and education system improvements are not necessarily dependent on the availability of funding, but, inevitably, where and how money is spent will become a significant measure of success and community commitment. My purpose in this chapter is to identify funding streams available to support SEL activities and to outline financing strategies that may be helpful for the future. Examples of the variety of public and private funding sources that have been used to advance the SEL agenda are described.

The Big Picture: What Impacts Sustainability?

A number of factors influence the availability of funding for any initiative, but unique challenges emerge when considering the best ways to sustain health initiatives that take place in educational settings. First, schools and health systems operate in different policy environments and therefore have different goals, targets, and institutional structures, and work under different political pressures. Stated most simply, by Constitutional allocation of powers, states and their communities have primary responsibility for elementary and secondary schooling. It then follows that K–12 education funding reflects the predominant role of state and local governments. According to the U.S. Department of Education, over 90% of funding for K–12 education comes from nonfederal sources (Johnson, Zhou, & Nakamoto, 2011), most of which comes from state and local government. In contrast, health spending is dominated by private payers (60%), and among public funders, the federal government is the main contributor. Thus, whereas educators tend to look to their states and communities for financial support, health professionals may focus primarily on the federal government.

Second, the way SEL is conceptualized and the language used to characterize its activities has implications for what gets funded. Therefore, the types of funding opportunities and the most promising fund-raising targets are associated with the definition of SEL. Depending on whether we categorize these programs and approaches as social skills training, positive youth development, bullying prevention, civic and character education, conflict resolution, or school climate initiatives will influence the funding options available.

Third, the successful implementation of prevention programs, such as SEL, requires careful consideration of related costs. Staff time, the purchase of curricula, materials and supplies, and consultant fees are typical, but often are not the only expenses (see Jones, Greenberg & Crowley, Chapter 7, this volume). Advocates suggest that a coordinated approach to SEL in schools includes certain key components, such as learning standards, evidence-based programs, support for teacher professional development, and assessment processes to track student progress (Kendziora, Weissberg, Ji, & Dusenbury, 2011). The costs associated with each of these components are not yet well understood, but they will ultimately determine the longevity of an SEL approach.

Funding SEL Programs: Public and Private Agencies at the Local, State, and Federal Levels

Financial support for SEL programs in K–12 schools may draw on multiple sources. Because these programs are commonly classroom-based and universal in their target population, some school districts have identified line items within their budgets to support this work. SEL programs may also be viewed as mental health-promoting initiatives, allowing public spending for health or mental health programs to be a source of support. And, finally, because private foundations have historically supported pilot projects and multisite demonstration programs in child development, these sources may offer time-limited funding for SEL initiatives. The primary message is that early SEL adopters have found support at the local, state, and national levels, with funding coming from both public and private agencies.

Local Support for SEL Programs and Practices

Local government funding often comes from a line item in the general fund revenues (typically unrestricted funds that policymakers can earmark for specific programs and services), as an appropriation through an agency budget, or dedicated revenues (e.g., revenues from taxes on alcohol, tobacco, property, or through lottery or gaming revenue). School-connected programs and services depend on all these types of local support, especially for long-term success. In particular, K–12 education relies heavily on local revenues. On average, local communities contribute approximately 44% to the education budget[2] (Johnson et al., 2011), with these dollars drawn mostly from local property taxes. Local elected officials and government agency staff then determine the mechanisms by which these public revenues are distributed.

In education, where decision-making authority is more localized than in other systems, district school boards and district superintendents often make the decisions about the school district's budget, as well as endorsing strategies that promise to improve students' academic performance. In the instance in which a school board is well informed about the links between health and academic achievement, members would have the authority to enact SEL-friendly policies and to allocate resources in directions consistent with those policies. Toward that end, collaborative relationships among key stakeholders (i.e., providers, child-serving agencies, educators, and advocates) are an effective foundation for influencing policymakers about the best ways to use limited community resources to yield maximum benefit.

County Block Grant Program Used to Support SEL Implementation

The Preventive Health and Health Services (PHHS) block grant (Centers for Disease Control and Prevention, 2013b), authorized in 1981, allows state public health authorities the flexibility to address their most pressing public health needs through prevention and health promotion programs. A portion of these funds distributed to local public health departments is used to leverage existing funds to support community-based initiatives. Although chronic disease prevention is typically the focus of primary block grant expenditures, activities related to SEL have also received support from this source. For example, in 2009 the Health Department of Barron County, Wisconsin, adopted a strategy to reduce the prevalence of underage drinking by partnering with local schools and implementing two evidence-based substance abuse curricula with strong SEL components (Project Northland and Class Action; CDC, n.d.).

Local Tax Levy to Support Educational Programming

In Lyndhurst, Ohio, where over 85% of the school district budget depends on local tax dollars, voters passed an extension for a levy on residential properties that would generate about $4.5 million dollars a year to support *educational programming* over the next 3 years (Support SEL Schools, n.d.). Energetic community-based advocacy promoting the benefits of SEL interventions led to the successful passage of the levy.

Another Local Levy Supports SEL

In Seattle, Washington, which passed the city's first Families and Education Levy in 1990, city government officials have used this local revenue source to invest in student academic performance and health outcomes (Seattle Department of Neighborhoods, Office of Education, n.d.). The levy, renewed in 2011 and estimated at $230 million (an increase of over $100 million more than dedicated 2004 levels of funding) is to be spent over the next 7 years, with the aim to improve academic achievement by funding comprehensive approaches that include the provision of "social, emotional, and behavioral" support (Families and Education Levy Advisory Committee, 2011, pp. 3, 17–18). Reports from the city's Office of Education indicate that city officials have maintained a strong focus on addressing the academic needs, as well as the social and emotional challenges, of students through this long-term financial investment (City of Seattle Office of Education, 2013).

A Public Agency/Nonprofit Health Partnership Supports SEL

The Boston Public Health Commission is coordinating a 2-year project with Boston public schools and Partners HealthCare, the nonprofit hospital system that invested $1 million to fund the collaborative project. The purpose of the project is to help students manage their emotions and cultivate healthy relationships. Together, these partners are implementing Open Circle, an evidence-based SEL program in 23 Boston public schools. The initiative will build on professional development training for the 750 teachers, teaching assistants, and administrators who implement the program (Wellesley Centers for Women, 2012).

State Support for SEL Programs and Practices

The largest portion of funding for public elementary and secondary schools, approximately 47%, comes from state dollars (Johnson et al., 2011). Although generally there is variability in state revenue sources across the 50 states, state education funding is generated by a combination of income taxes, corporate taxes, sales taxes, and fees. In states that do not collect income taxes, there is often greater reliance on local revenues. Regardless of the revenue source, however, each state has its own formula for financing K–12 education. Typically, the state board of education is authorized to set educational priorities for the state and to establish policies that govern how state resources will be used. Furthermore, state boards of education are responsible to help develop the state education budget, provide oversight to the state education agency, and create rules and regulations for the administration of state-funded programs. Several states elect their board members, while others have a combination of elected and appointed members. However, in the most common scenario for establishing a state board of education, members are appointed by the governor and confirmed by the state legislature (National Association of State Boards of Education, 2013). Knowing this information is helpful in planning for sustainability as it helps to understand to whom members of the state board of education are accountable. Furthermore, identifying members of the board can help target advocacy efforts by influencing individuals with budgeting authority to support SEL programming.

An Example of State-Supported SEL Activities: California

In 2004, California voters passed a proposition to charge a 1% income tax on high-income residents of the state to support the Mental Health Services Act (California Department of Mental Health, 2004). This legislation allows the California Department of Mental Health to support county mental health programs and also requires that roughly 20% of the funds be dedicated to implement prevention and early intervention activities. One approved prevention-oriented statewide project, the Student Mental Health Initiative (California Department of Mental Health, 2007), makes funding available to local *selected education entities* to promote mental health among students and to train educational staff on effective prevention and wellness activities.

An Example of State-Supported SEL Activities: Illinois

Also in 2004, the Illinois State Board of Education (ISBE), essentially the state education agency, helped Illinois become the first state to pass comprehensive K–12 SEL learning standards (see Dusenbury et al., Chapter 35, this volume). The Illinois Children's Mental Health Partnership and Voices for Illinois Children, a statewide advocacy organization, secured a $3 million appropriation from the General Assembly to implement a number of school-based strategies. Of the total, $1 million was to be used to conduct professional development of the SEL standards. Among other things, this funding facilitated the development of infrastructure to provide SEL training for Illinois schools (Gordon, Ji, Mulhall, Shaw, & Weissberg, 2011).

An Example of State-Supported SEL Activities: New York

The 2006 Children's Mental Health Act of New York State authorized the development of a statewide plan, *The Children's Plan: Improving the Social and Emotional Well Being of New York's Children and Their Families* (New York State Office of Mental Health, 2008), which recommended a number of state-supported strategies that are now being implemented. For example, the Promise Zones for Urban Education initiative, supported by delinquency prevention funding from the New York State Division of Criminal Justice Services, is being piloted in three cities. The initiative strengthens collaboration among local school districts and child-serving agencies to "alter school culture and climate in ways that foster individual social and emotional competencies, school attendance and achievement" (Council on Children and Families, 2010, p. 3). Furthermore, the call for greater coordination and communication has led to the creation of online interactive technology to share the latest statewide developments in the program, as well as a social marketing campaign to promote the importance of children's social and emotional well-being (Council on Children and Families, 2013).

Federal Funding for SEL Programs and Practices

Established under the Patient Protection and Affordable Care Act (ACA), the National Prevention Strategy aims to coordinate federal prevention initiatives by engaging national, state, and local partners in a multilayered, multifaceted partnership (National Prevention Council, 2011). The strategic plan identifies *mental and emotional well-being* as one of seven key national priorities and promotes positive social and emotional skills throughout the document. Although the promise of a coordinated prevention strategy at the federal level is encouraging, the benefit of this approach to driving policymaking or funding has yet to be demonstrated.

Currently, despite incremental improvements in communication and planning over the past decade, the distribution of federal dollars for prevention programs remains disjointed and underfunded. Prevention programs offered in schools have traditionally relied on numerous federal sources of support for their initial development and implementation, although research indicates that programs that rely heavily on government funding have less stability than those with less federal support (Miller, 2008). Therefore, financing plans that take advantage of federal dollars to launch or advance social programs, while also taking into account the precarious nature of these funding streams, have greater utility and value. (Refer to Appendices 8.1 and 8.2 for additional information about the federal budgeting process and federal block grant programs.)

Federal Education Funding

Over the past 50 years, the role of the federal government in K–12 public education has been to ensure equal educational access and to provide resources for those students who need additional supports. The Elementary and Secondary School Act (ESEA) of 1965, as amended, determines the allocation of federal funding for state education agencies (SEAs) and local school districts (also called local education agencies, LEAs) through the U.S. Department of Education's discretionary programs. The President and the Secretary of Education may propose changes to the statute that reflect the administration's policy priorities and the educational improvement strategies. For their part, schools and school districts often see ESEA funding as a vehicle for addressing issues that may be barriers to learning. District and state officials have had to consider increasingly creative ways to maximize use of ESEA-driven funding (Cascarino, 2000; Stark Rentner & Acosta Price, 2014).

Among the ESEA provisions that direct federal dollars to SEAs, LEAs, and even directly to school buildings, Title I is the largest discretionary grant program targeting elementary and secondary schools and is received by more than half of all public schools.[3] For schools with more than 40% of their student population exceeding federal poverty levels, administrators have the option to use Title I dollars to implement programs to enhance performance of the entire school population (i.e., universal prevention programs; U.S. Department of Education, 2011). Additionally, the Title II provision of ESEA supports activities related to teacher quality, teacher retention, and teacher preparation, and has typically been used for districtwide professional development activities. Districts that adopt strategies to improve school climate and strengthen social and emotional competencies through teaching strategies are particularly interested in Title II funding. For example, Austin Independent School District leaders have begun implementing SEL programs across schools in their district and have used Title II dollars to fund this effort (Raven, 2013). Table 8.1 details some ESEA provisions and specific programs funded in 2013 that hold promise for supporting SEL activities.

TABLE 8.1. Potential Sources of Support for SEL Activities Funded through ESEA

Provision	Name	Purpose	Proposed FY 2013 programs ($)
Title I, Part A	Improving basic programs operated by local educational agencies	Allocates funding to school districts with a high percentage of students in poverty with the primary goal to provide additional services and academic supports to them.	School turnaround grants ($533.6 million)
Title I, Part H	School dropout prevention	Supports dropout prevention activities and the identification of children at risk, and provides services to keep them in school.	Promise Neighborhoods ($100 million)
Title II	Preparing, training, and recruiting high quality teachers and principals	Supports the implementation of activities related to teacher quality, teacher retention, and teacher preparation.	Effective teaching and learning for a well-rounded education ($90 million)
Title IV, Part A	Safe and drug-free schools and communities	Supports programs to prevent violence in and around schools, prevent the use of drugs and foster a safe learning environment that supports academic achievement.	Successful, safe, and healthy students ($195.9 million)
Title IV, Part B	21st-century community learning centers	Provide opportunities for academic enrichment and additional services such as drug and violence prevention programs, counseling programs, and character development programs.	21st-century community learning centers ($1.2 billion)
Title V, Part A	Innovative programs	Provides formula grants to schools to implement promising educational reform and school improvement programs, to meet educational needs of at-risk youth, and to implement professional development activities.	Race to the Top ($850 million)
Title V, Part D	Fund for the improvement of education	Supports nationally significant programs to improve quality of education through systemic education reform, research, development, or evaluation activities designed to improve student academic achievement and parent and community involvement.	Fund for the improvement of education ($36.3 million)

Note. ESEA (Elementary and Secondary Education Act) is also referred to as the No Child Left Behind (NCLB) Act of 2001, the last amendment of ESEA. Based on U.S. Department of Education (2010, 2012, 2013).

Examples of Federal Education Funding to Promote SEL. In 2008, the Kansas Department of Education received a 4-year Partnerships in Character Education grant from the U.S. Department of Education. Focused on high schools, this award developed, implemented, and evaluated a nationally recognized character education curriculum. The federal discretionary funding helped establish the state's Social, Emotional, and Character Development (SECD) learning standards as voluntary standards that include principles of both SEL and character development (Kansas State Department of Education, n.d.). Although the federal character education grant program is no longer available, the Kansas Department of Education received a Safe and Supportive Schools (S3) grant allowing them to continue promotion of SECD standards in instructional practices and teacher professional development. The State Department of Education in Tennessee, another recipient of the S3, has used these federal funds to facilitate positive school climate and improve conditions for learning. The department formed a Center for School Climate that coordinates training and technical assistance to Tennessee schools (Tennessee Department of Education, n.d.).

Federal Mental Health Funding

The Substance Abuse and Mental Health Services Administration (SAMHSA), a division within the U.S. Department of Health and Human Services (USDHHS), has a long history of supporting community-based and school-connected initiatives that promote public mental health. SAMHSA's youth-related initiatives have emphasized the need for system coordination and integrated policies but have typically targeted those with more severe behavioral health conditions. Within the last several years, discretionary funding for preventive interventions from SAMHSA's Center for Mental Health Services has focused primarily on suicide prevention activities and stigma reduction campaigns. However, a few recent organizational shifts may facilitate support for additional mental health-promoting activities, such as those that strengthen SEL competencies. These include the expansion of SAMHSA's block grant program and the development of a state mental health prevention initiative called Project LAUNCH (Linking Actions for Unmet Needs in Children's Health). Guidance on the use of SAMHSA's two state block grants, the Substance Abuse Prevention and Treatment Block Grant (SABG) and the community Mental Health Block Grant (MHBG), explicitly encourages use of these funds for "primary prevention: universal, selective, and indicated prevention activities and services for persons not identified as needing treatment" (USDHHS, SAMHSA, 2013, p. 7). In addition, Project LAUNCH enables states to conduct evidence-based prevention interventions that will "promote the wellness of young children from birth to 8 years by addressing the physical, social, emotional, cognitive and behavioral aspects of their development" and minimize risk factors that may lead to substance abuse and mental illness (USDHHS, SAMHSA, 2012, p. 5).

Examples of Federal Mental and Public Health Funding to Promote SEL. Another source of prevention funding from the health sector became available through the Patient Protection and Affordable Care Act of 2010. Passage of this landmark legislation signaled an unprecedented federal commitment to promoting health and wellness, and preventing chronic diseases through the establishment of the Prevention and Public Health Fund (also called the Prevention Fund) (USDHHS, 2013). Although the Prevention Fund budget has been substantially trimmed during its initial 3 years, it remains a resource to provide communities with funding to invest in effective prevention efforts, including initiatives aimed at addressing health disparities and improving access to behavioral health services.

Community Transformation Grants (CTG), one major initiative funded by dollars from the Prevention Fund and administered by the CDC, are awarded to state public health agencies and local health departments. Although seemingly focused on adults and on early interventions to prevent mental illness, a number of recent awardees have identified the promotion of *social and emotional wellness* as an overarching goal in their applications, including the state health departments in Illinois, Massachusetts, and West Virginia, and the county health departments of Douglas County (Nebraska), Los Angeles (California), and Philadelphia (Pennsylvania) (CDC, 2013a). The value of partnering with schools and focusing on child health was explicit in the award to LiveWell Greenville in South Carolina, whose local superintendent was quoted as saying, "We all know the importance of good health to the academic performance of our students and to the well-being of our employees" (*The Travelers Rest Tribune*, 2012).

Federal Sources of Funding for Early Childhood Initiatives

More peripheral sources of funding may be available to sustain SEL programs offered in K–12 schools, such as Title V funding (USDHHS/Health Resources and Services Administration, n.d.). Strengthening social and emotional competencies in young children (i.e., ages 0–5 years) and promoting their readiness to learn has been a fundamental aspect of early childhood initiatives. Agencies and organizations that implement early childhood programs are familiar with the value of social and emotional skills because they are integrated into the fabric of what early care providers do, from early instruction and social skills building to professional development activities; however, these benefits have not been well connected to the broader K–12 education system. Some researchers have recently described the potential benefits, as well as the pitfalls, of strengthening the connection between early childhood education and K–12 schooling (Halpern, 2013). Although the focus of this chapter is on financing for SEL programs for school-age populations, it is important to recognize that public and private funders supporting early childhood care and education have also developed methods to leverage limited dollars in order to advance these initiatives and reach the greatest number of vulnerable children (Flynn & Hayes, 2003). Tools and detailed information on financing of early childhood initiatives are accessible for those interested in sustaining SEL activities that are linked with institutions serving very young children and their families (Lind et al., 2009).

A Caution about Discretionary Funding

Many school districts have previously supported the implementation of SEL activities from discretionary grant programs administered by a number of federal agencies, including the U.S. Department of Education. Discretionary grant programs, by their nature, are subject to swift changes in policy direction when new leadership is elected. One such example is the Department of Education's Successful, Safe, and Healthy Schools program, a new initiative proposed for fiscal year 2013, which authorized funds to create safe and health-promoting environments that facilitate improved teaching and learning by consolidating (and essentially eliminating) a number of grant programs that were instrumental in the expansion of SEL interventions across schools and districts (e.g., the Elementary and Secondary School Counseling, Mental Health Integration in Schools, and Safe and Drug-Free Schools and Communities programs; U.S. Department of Education, 2013). This move to allow states and localities greater flexibility and control over spending may result in significantly more instructional programs being funded in lieu of nonacademic support services. SEL advocates may therefore feel increased pressure to convince state and local decision makers that investing in universal prevention programs is a smart use of limited education dollars.

Foundations

Foundations have played an important role in developing innovative education and health initiatives. These philanthropies provide a flexible pool of resources that can be directed toward infrastructure development, operating expenses, piloting new initiatives, or scaling up promising ones. Whereas some foundations sustain established community cultural and charitable institutions, such as the local symphony or local United Way, other foundations are organizing institutions dedicated to new purposes, such as Andrew Carnegie's libraries, the Gates Foundation's restructured high schools, or the Robert Wood Johnson Foundation's school-based health centers.

Legally, a *foundation* is a nonprofit entity or a charitable trust, incorporated with the chief purpose of making grants to unrelated organizations, institutions, or individuals. There are generally two types of foundations: private foundations and public charities, both of which may target funding to national, state, regional (involving areas within a state or across several states), or local levels. Foundation giving has been increasing steadily in the United States over the past several decades, reaching $46 billion in 2011 (Lawrence, 2012), with more than 40% of funding in 2010 dedicated to programmatic activities (Foundation Center, Foundation Giving Trends, 2012).

Private Foundations

Private foundations are typically created with support from a primary donor (i.e., an individual, family, or corporation) and often award grants to support desired charitable activities. These foundations make up the majority of grant-making institutions in the United States, with an estimated 85,000 private foundations engaged in grant making in 2010 (National Center for Charitable Statistics, 2010).

Public Charities

Public charities are nonprofit organizations that rely primarily on financial support from the general public but may also receive grants from individuals, governments, and private foundations. Although some public charities engage in grant-making activities, most provide a direct service or charitable activity. *Community foundations* are nonprofit entities that grant money to public charities but are actually considered public charities themselves. There are more than 700 community foundations in the United States. Although large in number, they represented only 9% of total foundation giving in 2010 (Foundation Center, 2012). Similar to a nonprofit charity, community foundations seek support for themselves from the general public, but like private foundations, they also provide grants, most often to address the needs of the community or region in which they are located.

An Example of Foundation Support for SEL: National Foundations. A number of independent foundations have invested in developing SEL-related projects with the intent of making national impact. The NoVo Foundation, based in New York City, has committed to building the evidence base for SEL and advocating for SEL as integral to national education reform. One initiative piloted by NoVo supports eight school districts that are integrating SEL programs and practices districtwide (Collaborative for Academic, Social, and Emotional Learning [CASEL], 2013). The Robert Wood Johnson Foundation (RWJF) is complementing this Collaborating District Initiative (CDI) by supporting a study of factors contributing to long-term sustainability of SEL programs. In an effort to reach millions of students, NoVo and RWJF have also joined with other private funders to support the development of a K–5 academic curriculum that integrates SEL concepts and strategies into core academic materials (W. Yallowitz, personal communication, July 31, 2013).

An Example of Foundation Support for SEL: Regional Foundations. Additional foundations are supporting universal prevention programming within individual states or regions of the country. The Hogg Foundation, for example, funds services, research, policy development, and education related to mental health issues throughout Texas (Hogg Foundation for Mental Health, 2012a). In 2012 the Hogg Foundation awarded multiyear grants to eight Houston-based organizations to offer prevention, early identification, and treatment services in schools and community settings (Hogg Foundation for Mental Health, 2012b). In Ohio, the Health Foundation of Greater Cincinnati (recently renamed Interact For Health) serves 20 counties in neighboring areas, as well as communities in Kentucky and Indiana. The foundation also has supported a 4-year implementation of universal prevention programs in elementary schools in those communities (K. Keller, personal communication, March 7, 2012).

An Example of Foundation Support for SEL: Local Foundations. Public charities, entities that are more likely to support local initiatives, have also begun to direct their attention to the benefits associated with SEL. The Women's Initiative of United Way, part of the United Way of Greater Toledo, has supported the implementation of SEL programs for students through a partnership with the Toledo Public Schools and Toledo Federation of Teachers (United Way of Greater Toledo, 2012). The initiative, which aims to promote a caring school environment and build students' social and emotional competencies, has been implemented in six public schools and has trained 115 Toledo public school teachers in an evidence-based SEL program called Responsive Classroom.

Braided or Blended Funding

Strategies to ensure sustainability of programs and initiatives often require an integration of services and resources, and therefore involve multiple systems or organizations to succeed long-term. These coordinated or collaborative strategies help reduce duplication of services and ease the administrative burden associated with managing multiple grants. *Blended funding*, one such strategy, refers to a process whereby funding from different sources is pooled together in order to maximize impact. Alternatively, braided funding is achieved when funds that may have distinct but complimentary purposes are woven together to support a specific activity, but reporting and accountability to each funder remain separate.

An Example of Blended Funding for SEL

One of the most widespread federal discretionary grant programs to promote mental health was the Safe Schools/Healthy Students (SS/HS) initiative. More than a decade since its initial implementation, this landmark initiative pooled federal funding from the U.S. Departments of Health and Human Services, Education, and Justice to support comprehensive violence prevention activities conducted by more than 350 community-based partnerships (including local schools). The strong conceptual link between this national initiative and the key components of SEL made SS/HS an effective vehicle for introducing SEL to hundreds of communities nationwide (National Center for Mental Health Promotion and Youth Violence Prevention and CASEL, 2008). Although funding has decreased incrementally and the fate of this initiative is in question, results demonstrate that better system coordination across the continuum of care has led to improvements in student health and academic outcomes (SS/HS, 2013).

An Example of Braided Funding for SEL

In 2011, the Washington State legislature authorized funding for the Washington Kindergarten Inventory of Developing Skills (WaKIDS) initiative, a readiness assessment to determine whether young children, as well as their schools and communities, have the necessary skills to ensure success in school. WaKIDS includes a comprehensive assessment of a child's social and emotional development. It is jointly supported by a Race to the Top/Early Learning Challenge (RTT-ELC) grant, appropriations from the Washington State legislature, as well as by private funders, including the Bill and Melinda Gates Foundation (Dorn & Hyde, 2011).

Guidance Informed by Lessons Learned

The communities cited throughout this chapter have successfully leveraged partnerships and implemented innovative funding strategies after having overcome a series of trials and tribulations. Several important lessons are shared below that can facilitate or hinder successful fund-raising efforts, including guidelines, recommendations, potential pitfalls, and guiding questions.

Guidelines and Recommendations

- *Relationships matter.* Not only *what* you know but also *who* you know makes a difference. Who are the power brokers and decision makers for eligible funding streams? Program planners and administrators must get to know these individuals and help make the connection between what is important to them and the known benefits of prevention programs.
- *Partnerships matter.* In light of national and state budget deficits, stand-alone programs, no matter how effective, are not likely to survive. Partnerships, especially with organizations that bring complemen-

tary expertise, remain critical for program sustainability. Programs also need to be meaningfully linked to broader social initiatives to maximize their staying power.

• *United fronts matter.* Groups of individuals that speak with one collective voice are difficult to ignore or to silence and can therefore be quite influential. With policy moving to offer increased control for states and districts over spending, advocacy for desired prevention programs and comprehensive school reforms must be well coordinated, communicated, and executed.

Potential Problems and Pitfalls

• *Adopt a flexible frame but have a frame.* To take advantage of current funding opportunities, programs may need to use a conceptual frame that is specific enough to mobilize supporters but broad enough to capture the trend of the moment. Describing how a universal prevention program can address a number of issues over time may allow programs to ride numerous political waves successfully. However, being too flexible may convey a lack of focus or authenticity.

• *More is not always better, and this goes for funding, too.* If a program is established within an institutional setting (i.e., a government agency or university), then it is more likely to have the necessary infrastructure to acquire and manage a diverse funding portfolio. On the other hand, nonprofit or community-based organizations usually have limited administrative resources and must therefore discern the best funding options to help advance their cause without sacrificing the resources needed to obtain the desired results.

Guiding Questions

Securing funding for SEL or any other initiative requires an assessment of the fit between a particular funding source and an organization's priorities and strengths. Funders generally have greater confidence in applicants who not only demonstrate an alignment between their expertise and the funding objective but also have strong internal systems in place (i.e., fiscal management, communications, data collection, and evaluation) and demonstrate a clear vision and mission, as well as effective partnerships outside of the organization. These elements are essential preconditions for organizations creating viable long-term funding strategies, developing a corresponding business plan, attracting the right partners, identifying the most reliable funding sources, and ultimately *delivering [their] programmatic impact.* Appendix 8.3 contains several questions to keep in mind that should help organizations in their quest for funding.

Conclusion

Leaders need to avoid the pitfall of chasing dollars opportunistically. Rather, you need to build and maintain a diverse portfolio of funds that are aligned with the specific strategies, activities and capacities you want to sustain. A strategic financing approach is a framework for identifying the fiscal needs of your initiative over time, and designing and implementing financing strategies to meet those needs.

—LIND ET AL. (2009, p. 7)

Effective interventions such as SEL programs need more than strong scientific evidence to flourish; they need money and political support to establish and maintain them. Realizing the full potential of programs and interventions that promote positive social and emotional skills development requires keen understanding of the resources available to sustain and expand SEL initiatives, as well as knowledge about how to achieve a balance between raising funds and managing continued funding. Investigations of the nonprofit sector suggest that organizations with more than two funders, ironically, tend to be less profitable and successful than those with one or two major funders. This is often due to the greater demands placed on nonprofits that must manage additional funders, requiring greater organizational complexity and ultimately driving up internal costs (Miller, 2008). This chapter provides an overview of funding sources typically available at local, state, and national levels, and offers some guidance on possible pathways to long-term sustainability. The essential point is that those looking to fund SEL initiatives must be inventive, cognizant of the particularities of their specific locale, ready to take advantage of the opportunities that present themselves, and realistic about both their organizational capacity and the benefits and limitations associated with any funding source.

Notes

1. The recession took a serious toll on school financing across the country and led to a one-time infusion of federal funding for schools. The American Recovery and Reinvestment Act (ARRA), signed in 2009, provided more than $100 billion in education aid to offset devastating budget cuts. A number of education reform efforts were initiated, such as Race to the Top and Promise Neighborhoods, but these *stimulus* funds were intended to provide temporary relief and avert an economic depression, not to serve as long-term solutions.

2. Revenue for public elementary and secondary schools is reported for fiscal year 2009, as opposed to fiscal year 2010. Short-term funding directed to schools as a result of ARRA resulted in an inflated estimate of federal revenues contributing to education budgets.

3. The U.S. Department of Education has recently begun to accept waivers to requirements set by No Child Left Behind. This waiver, sought by a majority of the states, would allow state education agencies flexibility in their use of federal education funds with the promise that accountability measures would remain intact. A number of states have received a waiver that would allow them to use Title I funds (20% of their Title I, Part A grant awards) to support interventions of various kinds in high-poverty schools. Both Tennessee and Alaska, for example, have successfully applied for waivers that will allow their state education agencies to dedicate some of their Title I, Part A funds to improving school climate and addressing the social, emotional, and health needs of students in high-poverty schools.

References

California Department of Mental Health. (2004). Mental Health Services Act. Retrieved October 1, 2013, from *www.dmh.ca.gov/prop_63/mhsa/docs/mhsaafterab100.pdf.*

California Department of Mental Health. (2007). Mental Health Services Act: Prevention and Early Intervention (PEI). Retrieved October 1, 2013, from *www.dmh.ca.gov/dmhdocs/docs/notices08/08-25_enclosure1.pdf.*

Cascarino, J. (2000). *Many programs, one investment: Combining federal funds to support comprehensive school reform.* Arlington, VA: New American Schools.

Centers for Disease Control and Prevention (CDC). (2013a). Community transformation grants (CTG). Retrieved November 11, 2013, from *www.cdc.gov/communitytransformation/funds/programs.htm.*

Centers for Disease Control and Prevention (CDC). (2013b). Preventive health and health services block grant. Retrieved November 11, 2013, from *www.cdc.gov/phhsblockgrant.*

Centers for Disease Control and Prevention (CDC). (n.d.). Preventive health and health services block grant: Wisconsin. Retrieved October 1, 2013, from *www.cdc.gov/phhsblockgrant/states/pdfs/wisconsin.pdf.*

City of Seattle Office of Education. (2013). 2004 Families and Education levy seven-year summary and 2011–12 school year annual report. Retrieved October 1, 2013, from *www.seattle.gov/neighborhoods/education/documents/annualreport_final.pdf.*

Collaborative for Academic, Social, and Emotional Learning (CASEL). (2013). Collaborating districts. Retrieved November 11, 2013, from *www.casel.org/collaborating-districts.*

Committee for Education Funding. (2013). The budget response, fiscal year 2013. Retrieved October 1, 2013, from *http://cef.org/wp-content/uploads/2011/04/budget-response-fy-13-1-page-view.pdf.*

Council on Children and Families. (2010). The New York State Children's Plan update. Retrieved October 1, 2013, from *http://ccf.ny.gov/childplan/cpresources/2010childrensplanupdate.pdf.*

Council on Children and Families. (2013). Engage. Retrieved November 11, 2013, from *http://ccf.ny.gov/engage/index.cfm.*

Dorn, R.; & Hyde, E. M. (2011). The Washington Kindergarten Inventory of Developing Skills (WaKIDS) pilot: A report to the Washington State legislature. Retrieved October 1, 2013, from *www.k12.wa.us/wakids/about/default.aspx.*

Durlak, J. A., Weissberg, R. P., Dymnicki, A. B., Taylor, R. D., & Schellinger, K. B. (2011). The impact of enhancing students' social and emotional learning: A meta-analysis of school-based universal interventions. *Child Development, 82,* 405–432.

Families and Education Levy Advisory Committee. (2011). Recommendations of the 2011 Families and Education Levy Advisory Committee. Retrieved October 1, 2013, from *www.seattle.gov/neighborhoods/education/documents/ltr_2011levylacfinalrecommendations.pdf.*

Flynn, M., & Hayes, C. D. (2003, January). *Blend-*

ing and braiding funds to support early care and education initiatives. Washington, DC: Finance Project. Retrieved October 1, 2013, from *www.financeproject.org/publications/fpblendingfunds1_24.pdf.*

Foundation Center. (2012). *Aggregate fiscal data by foundation type, 2010.* New York: Author. Retrieved October 1, 2013, from *http://foundationcenter.org/findfunders/statistics.*

Foundation Center, Foundation Giving Trends. (2012). *Types of support awarded by foundations, circa 2010.* New York: Author. Retrieved October 1, 2013, from *http://foundationcenter.org/findfunders/statistics.*

Gordon, R., Ji, P., Mulhall, P., Shaw, B., & Weissberg, R. P. (2011). *Social and emotional learning for Illinois students: Policy, practice, and progress* (The Illinois Report 2011). Champaign: Institute of Government and Public Affairs, University of Illinois.

Halpern, R. (2013). Tying early childhood education more closely to schooling: Promise, perils and practical problems. *Teachers College Record, 115,* 1–28.

Hogg Foundation for Mental Health. (2012a). A guide to understanding mental health systems and services in Texas. Retrieved October 1, 2013, from *http://hoggblogdotcom.files.wordpress.com/2013/01/hoggmentalhealthguide.pdf.*

Hogg Foundation for Mental Health. (2012b). Hogg Foundation awards $2 million in grants to benefit mental health services for Houston-area children. Retrieved November 11, 2013, from *www.hogg.utexas.edu/detail/265/.html.*

Johnson, F., Zhou, L., & Nakamoto, N. (2011). Revenues and expenditures for public elementary and secondary education: School year 2008–2009 (fiscal year 2009) (NCES 2011-329). Retrieved October 1, 2013, from *http://nces.ed.gov/pubs2011/2011329.pdf.*

Kansas State Department of Education. (n.d.). Partnership in character education program grant progress report. Retrieved October 1, 2013, from *www.ksde.org/portals/30/partnership%20in%20character%20education%20progress%20reportweb.pdf.*

Kendziora, K., Weissberg, R. P., Ji, P., & Dusenbury, L. A. (2011). *Strategies for social and emotional learning: Preschool and elementary grade student learning standards and assessment.* Newton, MA: National Center for Mental Health Promotion and Youth Violence Prevention, Education Development Center.

Kim, P., Perreault, G., & Foster, W. (2011, August). Finding your funding model: A practical approach to nonprofit sustainability. Retrieved October 1, 2013, from *www.bridgespan.org/publications-and-tools/funding-strategy/finding-your-funding-model-a-practical-approach-to.aspx#.uspr_ej8tbw.*

Lawrence, S. (2012, June). Foundation growth and giving estimates. New York: Foundation Center. Retrieved October 1, 2013, from *http://foundationcenter.org.*

Lind, C., Crocker, J., Stewart, N., Torrico, N., Bhat, S., & Schmid, W. (2009, May). *Finding funding: Supporting making connections core result that children are healthy and prepared to succeed in school.* Washington, DC: Finance Project. Retrieved October 1, 2013, from *www.financeproject.org/publications/findingfundingsupportingmakingconnections.pdf.*

Miller, C. (2008). Truth or consequences: The implications of financial decisions. Retrieved October 1, 2013, from *www.nonprofitquarterly.org/management/20281-truth-or-consequences-the-implications-of-financial-decisions.html.*

National Association of State Boards of Education. (2013). State education governance. Retrieved November 11, 2013, from *www.nasbe.org/wp-content/uploads/state-education-governance-2013-state-by-state-matrix.pdf.*

National Center for Charitable Statistics. (2010). Number of private foundations in the United States, 2010. Retrieved October 1, 2013, from *http://nccsdataweb.urban.org/pubapps/profiledrilldown.php?state=us&rpt=pf.*

National Center for Mental Health Promotion and Youth Violence Prevention and CASEL. (2008). Social and emotional learning and student benefits: Research implications for the SS/HS core elements. Retrieved October 1, 2013, from *www.promoteprevent.org/content/social-and-emotional-learning-and-student-benefits-research-implications-sshs-core-elements.*

National Prevention Council. (2011). National prevention strategy. Retrieved October 1, 2013, from *www.surgeongeneral.gov/initiatives/prevention/strategy.*

New York State Office of Mental Health. (2008). The children's plan: Improving the social and emotional well being of New York's children and their families. Retrieved October 1, 2013, from *http://ccf.ny.gov/childplan/cpresources/childrens_plan.pdf.*

Oliff, P., Mai, C., & Leachman, M. (2012). New school year brings more cuts in state funding for schools. Retrieved October 1, 2013, from *www.cbpp.org/cms/?fa=view&id=3825.*

Raven, S. (2013). *CASEL collaborating districts initiative implementation grant: Year 1 interim report.* Austin, TX: Austin Independent School District.

Safe Schools/Healthy Students (SS/HS). (2013). Safe

Schools/Healthy Students National Evaluation. Retrieved November 11, 2013, from *www.sshs.samhsa.gov/community/evaluation.aspx.*

Seattle Department of Neighborhoods, Office of Education. (n.d.). 2011 Families and Education Levy overview. Retrieved October 1, 2013, from *www.seattle.gov/neighborhoods/education/overview.htm.*

Sklad, M., Diekstra, R., De Ritter, M., Ben, J., & Gravesteijn, C. (2012). Effectiveness of school-based universal social, emotional, and behavioral programs: Do they enhance students' development in the area of skill, behavior, and adjustment? *Psychology in the Schools, 49*(9), 892–909.

Stark Renter, D., & Acosta Price, O. (2014, May). *A guide to federal education programs that can fund K–12 universal prevention and social and emotional learning activities.* Washington, DC: Center for Health and Health Care in Schools. Retrieved November 23, 2014, from *www.healthinschools.org/en/School-Based-Mental-Health/Funding-Guide-for-SEL.aspx.*

Support SEL Schools. (n.d.). Support SEL schools. Retrieved November 11, 2013, from *www.supportselschools.com/levyinformation.aspx.*

Tennessee Department of Education. (n.d.). School climate. Retrieved November 11, 2013, from *www.tennessee.gov/education/safe_schls/climate/index.shtml.*

The Travelers Rest Tribune. (2012, October 7). LiveWell Greenville awarded $1.95 million to help create healthier communities in Greenville County. Retrieved on October 1, 2013, from *www.trtribune.com/index.php?option=com_content&view=article&id=5346.*

United Way of Greater Toledo. (2012). History/women's initiative. Retrieved November 11, 2013, from *www.unitedwaytoledo.org/womensinitiative/history.*

U.S. Department of Education. (2010). Elementary and secondary education. Retrieved November 5, 2013, from *www2.ed.gov/policy/elsec/leg/esea02/index.html.*

U.S. Department of Education. (2011). Improving basic programs operated by local education agencies (Title I, Part A). Retrieved November 11, 2013, from *www2.ed.gov/programs/titleiparta/index.html.*

U.S. Department of Education. (2012). Fiscal year 2013 budget, summary and background information. Retrieved on November 5, 2013, from *www2.ed.gov/about/overview/budget/budget13/summary/13summary.pdf.*

U.S. Department of Health and Human Services (USDHHS). (2013). Prevention and public health fund. Retrieved November 11, 2013, from *www.hhs.gov/open/recordsandreports/prevention.*

U.S. Department of Health and Human Services, Health Resources and Services Administration. (n.d.). Title V maternal and child health services block grant program. Retrieved November 11, 2013, from *http://mchb.hrsa.gov/programs/titlevgrants.*

U.S. Department of Health and Human Services, Substance Abuse and Mental Health Services Administration (SAMHSA). (2012). Cooperative agreements for linking actions for unmet needs in children's health (RFA No. SM-12-009). Retrieved October 1, 2013, from *www.samhsa.gov/grants/2012/sm-12-009.pdf.*

U.S. Department of Health and Human Services, Substance Abuse and Mental Health Services Administration (SAMHSA). (2013). FY 2014-2015 block grant application. Retrieved on October 1, 2013 from *www.samhsa.gov/grants/blockgrant/doc2/bg-application.pdf.*

Weare, K., & Nind, M. (2011). Mental health promotion and problem prevention in schools: What does the evidence say? *Health Promotion International, 26*(Suppl. 1), i29–i69.

Wellesley Centers for Women. (2012). $1M investment to implement Open Circle in 23 Boston public schools. Retrieved October 1, 2013, from *www.wcwonline.org/2013/1m-investment-to-implement-open-circle-in-23-boston-public-schools.*

APPENDIX 8.1. The Basics of Federal Funding

In principle, federal spending requires authorizing language (i.e., legislation) that permits appropriation of funding and eventual budget approval by the Senate and House of Representatives. Although authorizations are typically for 5 to 10 years, the federal budget must be approved annually by the House and Senate. The federal budget outlines federal expenditures (e.g., entitlement programs such as Medicaid or Title I, as well as defense and nondefense appropriations, such as highway construction, environmental protection, and federal judiciary), and federal revenues from individual income taxes, payroll taxes, corporate taxes, and the borrowing of money through the sale of bonds. The President triggers the process by laying out his priorities for federal programs in a budget request that is submitted to Congress. Congress then debates and negotiates general spending (appropriations) and revenue amounts until a budget can be passed and funds authorized and then dispensed by the federal agencies.

The executive branch of the federal government is responsible for federal appropriations, such as discretionary or appropriated programs that make up approximately one-third of all federal spending, and create either categorical or block grants in order to distribute this funding. Categorical grants specify how the money can be spent and are distributed either on a formula basis to states, usually according to population size or population in poverty, or on a project basis, also known as "discretionary grants." Congress annually appropriates an overall fixed level of funding for each discretionary grant program; eligible applicants (i.e., state authority, local education agency, nonprofit organization, private entity) compete for this funding and awards are made based on merit.

On the other hand, block grants, originally established with the passage of the Omnibus Budget Reconciliation Act of 1981 as part of the Social Security Act of 1935, are lump sums that allow maximum flexibility in their use through a broad range of eligible activities by giving more discretion to recipients to identify problems and design programs to address those problems. Federal block grants are directed by a federal agency and awarded to the appropriate state agency, such as state education, public health, or mental health agencies, which administers the funds to local governments using granting guidelines set by the state (see Appendix 8.2 for a list of federal block grants). State authorities often submit an application to the designated federal agency, where a number of requirements must be met, including state planning and reporting, stakeholder input into the use of funds, and sometimes state monetary match (i.e., a proportion of state and/or local funds that must be set aside to support the activities outlined in the application). As with many discretionary grants programs, block grant amounts are often determined by statutory formulas and are linked to population characteristics or demographics, such as rates of poverty or illness.

APPENDIX 8.2. Federal Block Grants Associated with Children's Social and Emotional Health

Block grant program name	U.S. federal agency	State/local recipient	Purpose	FY 2012 amount (est.)	Proposed for FY 2013
Child Care and Development Block Grant (CCDBG)	Department of Health and Human Services/ Administration for Children and Families	States, territories, tribes, and tribal organizations	Helps low-income families gain access to quality, affordable childcare and after-school programs.	$2,278,000,000	Increase
Community Development Block Grant (CDBG)	Department of Housing and Urban Development	Larger cities and urban counties	Provides resources to address community development needs.	$3,408,000	Decrease
Community Services Block Grant (CSBG)	Department of Health and Human Services/ Administration for Children and Families	State human service agencies or Community Action Agency—local	Alleviates the causes and conditions of poverty by providing effective services in communities.	$666,673,000	Decrease
Maternal and Child Health Block Grant (MCHBG)	Department of Health and Human Services/HRSA	State Health Department and local health departments	Improves the health of all mothers and children.	$639,000,000	Increase
Mental Health Services Block Grant (MHBG)[a]	Department of Health and Human Services/SAMHSA	State and local mental health authorities	Improves public mental health service systems.	$439,000,000	Same
Preventive Health and Health Services Block Grant (PHHS)	Centers for Disease Control and Prevention (CDC)	State and local public health authorities (and tribes and territories)	Tailors prevention and health promotion programs to particular public health needs.	$80,000,000	Eliminated
Social Services Block Grant (SSBG)	Department of Health and Human Services/ Administration for Children and Families	State human service agencies (including territories)	Supports programs that help communities maintain economic self-sufficiency and reduce dependency on social services.	$1,700,000,000	Decrease
Substance Abuse Prevention and Treatment Block Grant (SABG)[a]	Department of Health and Human Services/SAMHSA	State and local substance abuse prevention agencies (include territories)	Enables states to provide substance abuse treatment and prevention services.	$1,456,000	Decrease

[a]The FY 2014–2015 SAMHSA block grant application allows states to submit a combined application for mental health and substance abuse services as well as a biannual versus an annual plan. Based on U.S. Department of Health and Human Services, SAMHSA (2013).

APPENDIX 8.3. Questions to Facilitate Access to Available Funding Sources

Organizations hoping to acquire long-term funding need to ask a number of targeted questions that will help them navigate an increasingly complex funding terrain. Questions about funding needs and internal capacity, about who makes or influences funding decisions, and about how to access specific funding streams effectively will facilitate discussions of the most appropriate strategies for sustaining prevention programs. Examples include the following:

Questions about Funding Needs

- What type of funding is best suited for our organization and to achieve our mission/mandate?
  - When is this funding most essential (i.e., for initial launch, short-term adoption, or long-term integration or our program)?
- How many different funding streams are we able to manage given our capacity and our goals?
  - How do funding time tables match with our organization's projected growth or development?
- What are we seeking to finance (i.e., research/evaluation, program implementation, training, collaboration, system development)?
  - What will be accomplished with this support (i.e., individual education-related outcomes, health-related outcomes, system-related outcomes, a combination)?
- Do we have the right mix of skills and/or collaborators to accomplish these goals?

Questions about Decision Makers

- What are the priorities for children's health and education in my state?
  - Who are the legislators who have sponsored a pro-children agenda?
  - Who are the influential child advocacy organizations that help set the state or local agenda?
- What are major funding sources that support children in this region or state, and where does this funding come from (e.g., federal, state, local, private funders)?
  - Who are the gatekeepers for this funding source?
  - Is accessing this funding source politically feasible and who are the potential competitors?
- Is there an interagency, cross-system entity that is authorized to examine and help address the needs of children and youth in this state (i.e., a Children's Cabinet or Council)?
  - Do they have any funding authority?
- Who is on the state board of education, and what vision have they set for education in the state?
  - Is the state board accountable to an electorate or to the governor?
- Who is elected to the local school board and what issues seem prominent to their agenda?
  - How would someone share information about the benefits of health-promoting programs offered in schools with a board member?
- What local revenue streams support K–12 education?
  - What individuals or committees have oversight or determine funding priorities for local dollars?

Questions about Accessing Funding Streams

- Is my organization, coalition, or program eligible to apply for the identified funds?
  - If not, what adjustments can be made in order to meet eligibility requirements?
- What block grant program(s) has my state or county applied for and/or received?
  - What are the goals of the application/plan?
  - What state agency is accountable for reporting on that block grant, and who is the state contact?
- Is there a required advisory group or planning committee that determines how block grant funds can be used?
  - Who sits on that advisory group and how does one gain entry into the group?
  - What is the mechanism for offering public comment, suggestions, information, or feedback to the advisory group?
  - How are final decisions made and are certain people, organizations, or types of information (i.e., data vs. personal testimony) more/less influential in that process?
- What are some examples of successful blending or braiding of public and private funding?
  - How much flexibility is associated with this identified pot of money?
  - Are there specific reporting and accounting requirements outlined by this funder?
- What foundations actively award grants in my city/county, region, or state?
  - Do any of my organization's staff, board members, or partners have a relationship with any program officer or senior staff person at this foundation?

- How does the project we propose fit with the foundation's mission?
  - With what portfolio or strategic area of the foundation does this proposed activity align?
  - What other similar organization or program has this foundation funded in the past?
  - For how long? For how much?

Related Online Resources

Bridgespan
www.bridgespan.org

Fundsnet Services
www.fundsnetservices.com/showcats/91/foundation-directory.html

Foundation Center:
http://foundationcenter.org

Finance Project
www.financeproject.org

School Grants
www.schoolgrants.org

PART II

Evidence-Based Programming

CHAPTER 9

SEL Programs for Preschool Children

Karen L. Bierman and Mojdeh Motamedi

Over the past half century, the culture of childhood has changed dramatically, such that early educational experiences play an increasingly important role in children's lives. Whereas preschool was once a part-time experience primarily for middle-class children, now a majority (69%) of 4- and 5-year-olds in the United States are enrolled in center-based early childhood programs, and 45 of the 50 United States offer state-funded prekindergarten programs (U.S. Department of Education, 2007). Developmental research, combined with the accountability pressures of the No Child Left Behind Act of 2001, have focused attention on the importance of early learning for later school success (Blair, 2002). Most schools now initiate formal reading and math instruction in kindergarten, and expect that children will enter kindergarten ready for focused academic learning.

Yet many children enter school underprepared for these demands. Children growing up in poverty are particularly likely to show delays in the social–emotional and self-regulation skills needed for school success, due in part to heightened stress exposure and low levels of early learning support (McClelland, Acock, & Morrison, 2006). An increasing proportion of American children risk school readiness delays, as the changing demographics of the United States have resulted in an increasing proportion of preschool children growing up in poverty (25%) or in low income families (50%) (National Center for Children in Poverty, 2011).

These societal changes and educational expectations amplify the pressures on preschool programs to promote the acquisition of the core social–emotional skills that foster readiness to learn, including the capacity to function effectively in a group context, get along with other children, follow classroom rules and routines, focus attention, and enjoy goal-oriented learning (McClelland et al., 2006; Zaslow, Tout, Halle, Vick, & Lavelle, 2010). These social–emotional skills predict positive school adjustment over time, enhancing learning engagement, reducing discipline problems, increasing high school graduation rates, and even promoting future employment and adult health (Denham & Burton, 2003). Correspondingly, interest in social–emotional learning (SEL) programs for preschool children has increased in recent years, accompanied by a growing research base on effective programs and practices. This chapter provides a brief review of the history of preschool SEL programs, describes the unique developmental needs of preschool children and their impact on the design and content of SEL programs, and reviews the evidence base for preschool SEL programs.

Definitions and Scope of Preschool SEL Programs

The use of systematic school-based programming to promote children's social–emotional skill development first gained momentum in the 1970s and has sustained the steady interest of educational practitioners and researchers since then (Greenberg, 2006). Initially termed "primary prevention" and later reconceptualized as a "universal" prevention approach, the basic idea is that well-designed curriculum components and teaching practices can promote positive child development by teaching social–emotional skills, thereby enhancing student well-being, improving school attainment, and preventing later mental health difficulties. In high-risk settings, these competencies might also promote resilience, reducing child risk for later risky behaviors (e.g., substance use, antisocial activity) or emotional distress (Elias et al., 1997).

A considerable evidence base now exists to support the efficacy of SEL programs used in elementary school and at higher grade levels. In 2011, Durlak, Weissberg, Dymnicki, Taylor, and Shellinger (2011) conducted a meta-analysis of SEL studies, examining 213 school-based, universal SEL programs involving kindergarten through high school students. Positive effects were documented on social and emotional skills, attitudes, behavior, and academics, including an overall 11% gain in achievement associated with the use of evidence-based SEL programs. This important review validated the critical role of evidence-based SEL programming in educational practice and led the authors to recommend its widespread adoption (Durlak et al., 2011).

The positive impact of SEL programming for grade-school students has increased interest in the potential of developing and evaluating similar programming for preschool children. However, the downward extension of SEL programming into the preschool years requires careful consideration of the unique developmental characteristics of preschool children and preschool contexts. For example, SEL programs for grade school children often target multiple skills domains associated with healthy social–emotional functioning, including self-awareness, self-management, social awareness, relationship skills, and responsible decision making (Durlak et al., 2011; Elias et al., 1997). During the preschool years, children are just beginning to develop many of the cognitive structures and skills that provide a foundation for social- and self-awareness, such as perspective taking and reasoning; hence, the skills targeted by SEL programs for preschoolers need to address the more basic foundational skills that support later social–emotional development. In addition, grade school SEL programs generally attain their goals by providing systematic instruction in social–emotional skills, emphasizing the promotion of self-control, as well as creating a positive climate that fosters feelings of security and supports the practice of the targeted social–emotional and self-regulation skills (Greenberg, 2006). In preschool children, the neural structures that facilitate self-control are just emerging; therefore, relative to older children, preschool children are less able to "sit, listen, and learn," and they are much more dependent on external supports and adult management in order to regulate their emotions and behaviors. Hence, relative to instructions and lessons, adult support and positive classroom management play a particularly central role in promoting social–emotional competencies.

Finally, the implementation issues in SEL program delivery require particular attention in the preschool context. Preschool teachers are much less likely to have college degrees than elementary school teachers, and many do not have even a 2-year Child Development Associate degree (Zaslow et al., 2010). Hence, the curriculum materials and professional development supports used to foster high-quality program delivery need to take into account the lower level of formal education and training that characterize the preschool teaching force, relative to elementary school teachers. In the next section we discuss progressions in social–emotional and self-regulatory skills development during the preschool years, and the implications for the selection of SEL skill targets, program goals, and program design, before we describe the existing evidence base on preschool SEL effectiveness.

Preschool Social–Emotional Development and Implications for SEL Program Design

Normatively, the preschool years represent a critical time period for the development of basic social–emotional skills that provide the foundation for later social–emotional competence (Denham & Burton, 2003). Between ages 3 and 6, most children make the remarkable transition from impulsive and self-focused toddlers to responsible, rule-abiding, and socially integrated elementary school students. During this period of rapid development, dramatic transformations occur in children's social skills and social reasoning, their emotional understanding and emotion regulation, and their self-awareness and self-control. Developmental increases in children's capacities for mental representation and language create new opportunities for them to gather and organize information about their own and others' emotions, intentions, social roles, and social expectations, thereby expanding their capacity to benefit from SEL instruction and adult supports (Bierman, 1988).

Social–behavioral skills are an important facet of preschool SEL and support the first friendships that typically emerge during these years. Children's social interaction skills typically progress from parallel play at age 3 (e.g., side-by-side play, imitating each other) to extended collaborative social play by ages 5–6, as they learn how to share, cooperate, take turns, and inhibit aggressive and intrusive behavior (Bierman & Erath, 2006). Through play, preschoolers extend their knowledge about social roles and expectations, and practice communication, emotion regulation, and social problem-solving skills, thereby benefiting emotionally and cognitively. In the domain of emotional understanding, preschoolers begin by making rudimentary distinctions (happy vs. sad/mad by age 3) and acquire more nuanced distinctions (sad vs. scared vs. mad) reliably by age 7 (Bierman, 1988). Whereas 3-year-olds focus on basic cues and therefore make simple emotional assessments (e.g., all children are happy at a birthday party), by kindergarten (age 5), most children consider multiple cues and make more sophisticated assessments (e.g., the frowning children are unhappy at the party) (Bierman, 1988).

Underlying and supporting the preschool child's developing ability for more sensitive social interaction and more sophisticated emotional understanding are developmental advances in key areas of language and executive function skills (Blair, 2002; Greenberg, 2006). The prefrontal cortex grows rapidly between the ages of 3-6, accompanied by improvements in core areas of executive function, including working memory, inhibitory control, and attention set-shifting. These executive function skills improve the child's ability to anticipate and plan social interactions, to inhibit reactive impulses, and engage in more flexible social problem-solving. Children begin to recognize cause-and-effect patterns in social interaction and become more able to take more responsibility for setting goals and managing their own behavior.

The implication of this developmental research is that SEL programs might have unique developmental leverage when implemented during the preschool years (Feil et al., 2009). That is, SEL programming focuses on normative areas of development that grow rapidly between ages 3 and 6, at a time when children are dependent on and generally highly responsive to adult input and support. In addition, SEL programming during the preschool years has the potential to reduce the risk for the negative cascade of academic, behavioral, and peer failures that is often initiated when children enter school with underdeveloped social and self-regulation skills (Bierman, 2004). Yet, at the same time, preschool SEL programming must take into account the rudimentary nature of children's emerging social–emotional and self-regulation skills, and recognize that children are still heavily reliant on external supports provided by parents and teachers to control their behavior and regulate their social and emotional experiences (Bernier, Carlson, & Whipple, 2010).

Given the developmental characteristics of young children, preschool SEL programs need to be structured and focused in ways that differ from elementary school SEL programs. Contentwise, salient SEL skills for preschoolers include basic friendship and play skills, emotional understanding, intentional self-control, and basic social problem solving. In terms of structure, instructional strategies to teach skills concepts need to be brief, engaging, experiential, and concrete. Opportunities to practice skills need to be plentiful, so that young children experience repeated, adult-supported opportunities to use and refine their skills performance, with feedback and positive consequences. Preschool children may also need explicit support to develop the vocabulary, oral language, social perception, and reasoning skills that provide a foundation for more mature social–emotional understanding and functioning.

Theoretical Foundations and Intervention Approaches in Preschool SEL Programs

SEL programs have their theoretical roots in approaches that emerged initially as treatment strategies and were then transported into community and classroom settings and adapted to serve as primary prevention strategies to promote competencies, resilience, and general well-being. Prior to the first classroom-based SEL programs in the 1970s, treatment strategies to promote positive behavior in young children relied primarily on behavior management and instrumental conditioning models. For example, a number of studies documented that preschool teachers could reduce aggression and increase positive student behavior by differentially reinforcing desired behaviors (using contingent praise, attention, or concrete reinforcements) and by implementing consequences to decrease problem behaviors (e.g., by using a time-out or a response-cost, so that children lost points or privileges if they engaged in disallowed behaviors) (see Bierman, 2004, for a review). These behavioral management strategies proved effective at improving classroom behaviors and remain a core feature of some SEL programs, such as the Incredible Years program (Webster-Stratton, Reid, & Hammond, 2001). However, during the subsequent decades, additional, overlapping mechanisms of change began to inform the design of SEL programs, including an emphasis on social cognitive variables (in social learning theory and social information-processing models), emotional variables (in differential emotion and attachment theories), and self-regulation (featuring executive function skills), as follows.

A Focus on Social Cognitions

Social Learning Theory

Social learning theory expanded behavioral intervention models by positing that children learn social behavior by observing others, imitating, and responding to instruction and verbal feedback. Accordingly, social skills coaching programs used the following steps: (1) Teach the target skill concept using a combination of modeling, instruction, and discussion; (2) provide opportunities for behavioral rehearsal, practicing the skill with peer partners; (3) provide feedback on skills performance to foster refinement; and (4) program for generalization, by including cues and reinforcements to encourage children to use the skill in naturalistic social contexts (Bierman, 2004). Reflecting their social learning theory roots, most SEL programs designed for young children include lessons in which teachers use modeling stories, puppets, and pictures to illustrate target skills concepts and explain, demonstrate, and discuss the target skills. Lessons also typically include practice activities (role plays, cooperative activities) that allow children to practice the skills. Finally, teachers provide support to help children generalize the use of the skills in their everyday interactions in the classroom.

Social Information-Processing Models

Also reflecting an emphasis on the cognitive processes that influence social behavior, social information-processing models emerged in the 1980s and continue to inform preschool SEL programs. These models focus on the covert thinking processes that link social perceptions (encoding and interpreting social cues), social goals, and social problem solving (generating alternative behavioral solutions to a problem, considering their likely consequences, and selecting a solution)—particularly in situations of social provocation or conflict. A core hypothesis is that deficits, delays, or distortions in social information-processing skills lead to inadequate or biased social interpretations and inadequate or biased response generation, which places children at risk for problematic social behavior. One of the earliest SEL programs developed for preschool children, *I Can Problem Solve* (Shure, 1992; Shure & Spivack, 1982), focused centrally on improving children's abilities to assess and interpret social problem scenarios and to generate multiple solutions. Similarly, as described in more detail below, training in social problem-solving skills appears as a core component of several preschool SEL programs, based on the hypothesis that children's abilities to accurately identify social problems, set prosocial goals, generate and evaluate multiple potential responses, and select prosocial options provide a core foundation for adaptive social behavior.

A Focus on Emotions

More recent developmental research has emphasized emotional and motivational processes that influence social–emotional functioning and the role that stress exposure, emotional reactivity, and emotion regulation play in social–emotional development and adaptation. Several theoretical models have influenced the inclusion of emotional and motivational factors in preschool SEL programs, including differential emotions theory (Izard, 2002), attachment theory (Denham & Burton, 2003), and developmental models of self-regulatory processes (Bierman, Nix, Greenberg, Blair & Domitrovich, 2008; Greenberg, 2006).

Differential Emotions Theory

Differential emotional theory posits that emotional experiences involve a dynamic interaction between neurobiological arousal, cognitive inference, and verbal labeling processes (Izard, 2002). Within this framework, socialization experiences enhance social–emotional competence when they increase children's capacities to recognize the internal and external cues associated with differentiated emotions and promote their abilities to talk about their feelings. Hence, several preschool SEL programs focus lessons on identifying and labeling emotions. In addition, learning to regulate emotional arousal is a critical social–emotional skill, which is highly dependent on the development of connections between emotional arousal and linguistic and cognitive control systems (Izard, 2002). Many preschool SEL programs include lessons designed to enhance emotion regulation by strengthening these connections. For example, the "turtle technique" teaches children how to use language intentionally to regulate strong feelings and direct themselves in appropriate behavioral responding (Robin, Schneider, & Dolnick, 1976). In the original application of this technique, disruptive children were instructed to withdraw into an imaginary shell and tell themselves to relax when they felt that they were about to become disruptive. The goal was to calm down to prepare for a problem-solving discussion. Although initially conceptualized as a cognitive-behavioral intervention (e.g., self-instruction to guide alternative responding), since then, theorists have suggested that the "turtle technique" may enhance emotion regulation capacity by building stronger connections between developing neurocognitive control structures (language and executive function skills) and the emotional arousal system (Greenberg, 2006; Izard, 2002).

Attachment Models and the Teacher–Student Relationship

Many preschool SEL programs also place a central emphasis on promoting positive teacher–student relationships that, theoretically, play a central role in the development of children's self-regulatory capacities. Attachment theory posits that young children are inherently motivated to form attachments with caregiving adults; when these relationships are reliable, warm, and caring, they foster a sense of well-being in children, which promotes feelings of security (reduced anxiety and stress) and enhances children's capacity to initiate social interactions and effectively manage affective arousal (anger or distress) (Denham & Burton, 2003). Through such relationships, children also learn empathy and become more aware and caring toward others. In addition, a general tenet of most SEL programs is that social–emotional development is facilitated when teachers provide a safe and caring learning environment, characterized by positive management skills and low levels of aggressive–disruptive behavior (Denham & Burton, 2003).

A Focus on Self-Regulation

Most recently, SEL programs for preschool children have focused on promoting self-regulation. Conceptually, promoting emotional knowledge, social interaction skills, and social problem-solving skills should all enhance the capacity of the preschool child to inhibit aggressive and intrusive behaviors, and become more sensitive and responsive to social feedback from teachers and peers (Bierman, 2004). However, recent research in the area of developmental neuroscience has increased interest in developing preschool language and executive function skills as mechanisms associated with the improved capacity to regulate emotional arousal and strategically control and shift attention, thereby enhancing social competence and learning engagement in school (Blair, 2002; Greenberg, 2006). Correspondingly, theoretical models increasingly focus on the way experiences that promote the development of executive functions and self-regulation can be built into preschool SEL interventions (Bierman & Torres, in press; Ursache, Blair, & Raver, 2012). Only recently have researchers begun to include executive function measures routinely as SEL program outcomes, so empirical evidence regarding "what works" to enhance them during preschool is just beginning to accumulate. Prevailing models suggest that several different intervention strategies might enhance executive function skills development, including those that promote a positive and well-ordered classroom climate, those that enhance children's emotional understanding and emotion management, and those that emphasize problem-solving skills and sociodramatic play (Ursache et al., 2012).

Specific Interventions that Promote Social–Emotional School Readiness

In general, preschool SEL programs are characterized by multifaceted conceptual frameworks, as described in the previous section, but they vary in the degree of emphasis placed on social–behavioral, cognitive, emotional, and self-regulatory skills and processes. Each program attempts, to some degree, to promote adaptive social cognitions, to foster children's emotional understanding and empathy, and to support the development of self-regulation skills. Similarly, each program emphasizes the critical role that supportive and responsive adults play in fostering social–emotional growth. In this way, the programs overlap and reflect an integration of ideas drawn from different conceptual foundations. Yet the programs are also distinct in terms of the specific "logic models" that inform the organization and *relative* emphasis of the intervention, and guide the selection and design of intervention activities. Examples of effective programs that reflect different logic models are reviewed in the following sections. First, we describe programs that work. In this category, we place programs with evidence of effectiveness based on at least two randomized trials, including an independent evaluation conducted by researchers other than the developers and measures that extend beyond ratings provided by the teachers who implemented the program. Then, we describe programs that are promising. In this category, we place programs with evidence of effectiveness based on a randomized trial by the developers. We consider these programs promising because they have a solid theoretical foundation, well-developed curriculum guides and implementation procedures, and empirical evidence of efficacy. However, in each case, the evidence base remains limited to a single randomized trial. Within each category, we distinguish between intervention approaches that are implicit rather than explicit in terms of the SEL focus. Programs that rely primarily on changing the quality of teacher–student interactions, modifying classroom management strategies, and/or introducing new ways of structuring peer interactions have an *implicit* focus on SEL because these programs expect gains in social–emotional skills to occur as a function of improved classroom processes. In contrast, programs that place a central emphasis on an SEL curriculum, with target skills and instructional practices designed to teach those skills, represent an *explicit* approach to coaching in SEL skills.

Programs that Work

The development and evaluation of SEL programs for preschool children is relatively new, and many of the existing empirical trials were published within the past decade. At this point in time, only two programs have evidence of effectiveness in multiple, rigorous randomized trials, including at least one trial undertaken by independent researchers.

Incredible Years Teacher Training Program

The Incredible Years (IY) series, which includes distinct programs for parents, teachers, and children, originally was developed as treatment components for children ages 4–8 diagnosed with oppositional defiant or conduct disorder. These programs are heavily rooted in social learning theory and designed to address the risk and protective factors associated with the development of antisocial behavior (Webster-Stratton & Herman, 2010). In this chapter, we focus only on the more recent applications of IY as a universal school-based intervention for preschool children, using the teacher training and child SEL curriculum.

The *Incredible Years Teacher Training Program* takes an *implicit* approach to SEL designed to help teachers improve their positive classroom management skills and thereby promote child prosocial behavior and aggression control (Webster-Stratton & Herman, 2010). The approach is systematic, targeting five teaching skills: (1) using specific, contingent attention and praise to support positive behavior; (2) using incentives to motivate learning effort; (3) structuring the classroom effectively to prevent behavior problems; (4) using nonpunitive consequences to decrease inappropriate behavior; and (5) strengthening positive teacher–student relationships. The intervention involves monthly workshops for teachers, during which certified trainers present skills concepts, review modeling videotapes, moderate group discussions, review practice assignments, and provide consultation in program implementation.

Two studies have evaluated the IY teacher training program as a universal preschool prevention strategy. In the first, 34 Head Start classrooms in low-income, ethnically mixed areas were randomly assigned to receive the intervention (which included IY teacher training plus IY parent training) or to serve as a "usual practice" control group (Webster-Stratton et al., 2001). All parents were invited to attend 12 weekly training groups, 2.5 hours each, co-led by Head Start family service workers and research team members. Outcome measures included composites of observations and teacher (or parent) ratings. In the intervention classrooms, relative to "usual practice" control classrooms, teachers exhibited significantly more positive and fewer negative behaviors, and children exhibited significantly lower rates of problem behavior. Positive parent–teacher involvement increased significantly at the end of Head Start, then declined significantly below the control group in kindergarten (Webster-Stratton et al., 2001). In a second study, the IY Teacher Training Program was implemented in Head Start as part of the Chicago School Readiness Project (Raver et al., 2008). In this project, 18 Head Start centers (35 classrooms; 94 teachers) were randomly assigned to the intervention condition or to a "usual practice" control group. The intervention included the IY Teacher Training Program, delivered in five 1-day workshops spread over the course of the year. Mental health consultants made weekly visits to intervention classrooms, met with teachers to enhance their classroom management skills and provide emotional support, and developed individualized management plans for highly disruptive children. When observed at the end of the year, relative to teachers in the control group, intervention teachers exhibited higher levels of positive climate, teacher sensitivity, and positive behavior management (Raver et al., 2008). Observers also documented lower levels of child aggressive–disruptive behavior, and tests revealed greater growth in vocabulary, letter knowledge, math, and attention control among children in the intervention classrooms compared to those in the control classrooms (Raver et al., 2009, 2011). The investigators postulate that improvements in teacher classroom management skills led to increases in instructional time and child learning engagement, thereby promoting gains in academic as well as social–emotional skills. These studies suggest that the IY Teacher Training Program, which is designed to improve children's SEL *implicitly* via the provision of more positive behavioral support and improved teacher–student interactions, is effective in improving child social–emotional behavior. It is worth noting, however, that neither of these studies evaluated the IY Teacher Training Program used alone (the first study also included the IY Parent Training Program, and the second included mental health consultant services).

More recently, the IY child-focused SEL curriculum, the *Dinosaur School Social Skills and Problem-Solving Program* (Dinosaur School), has been adapted for use as a prevention curriculum providing *explicit* instruction in social–emotional skills. This program element adds explicit SEL lessons to the IY intervention approach. Originally, Dinosaur School was developed as a social skills training program for small groups of children with conduct disorders. Central to Dinosaur School are modeling DVDs that illustrate positive classroom behaviors, problem-solving strategies, social skills, feelings literacy, and self-regulation skills. One study revealed that the combination of the Dinosaur School and the IY Teacher Training program promoted more positive classroom management strategies (relative to a "usual practice" control group), and produced higher levels of social–emotional competence, better social problem-solving skills, and fewer conduct problems among students (Webster-Stratton, Reid, & Stoolmiller, 2008). However, this trial also included older children (kindergarten and first-grade classrooms), as well as prekindergarten classrooms, and used research staff to lead classroom lessons with the teachers. Hence, future research is needed to determine whether Dinosaur School is effective specifically in preschool classrooms when delivered by preschool teachers.

Preschool PATHS (Promoting Alternative Thinking Strategies)

Developed during the 1990s, the *Preschool PATHS Curriculum* (Domitrovich, Greenberg, Cortes, & Kusche, 1999) was designed as a developmentally appropriate downward extension of the elementary school version of the PATHS Curriculum (see Rimm-Kaufman & Hulleman, Chapter 10, this volume). Preschool PATHS focuses on basic social–emotional skills in four domains: (1) friendship skills and prosocial behaviors (e.g., helping, sharing, taking turns); (2) emotional knowledge (e.g., recognizing and labeling core feelings); (3) self-control (e.g., using the "turtle technique"); and (4) social problem solving. A particular goal is to improve the capacity of young children to use language effectively to support emotion regulation, inhibitory control, and social problem solving. There are 33 brief (15- to 20-minute) lessons with stories, pictures, and puppets that provide skills instruction, designed for use during circle time, one to two times per week. In addition, teachers are trained in interaction strategies to help children generalize their skills performance throughout the day, including emotion coaching (e.g., using feeling words, helping children notice their own and others' feelings), reminding children to use the turtle technique when excited or upset, and using problem-solving dialogue to help children manage frustration and resolve conflicts.

Preschool PATHS has been evaluated in three randomized trials. In the first study, 20 Head Start classrooms were randomized to the intervention (Preschool PATHS) or a "usual practice" control group; 287 children were followed for 1 year, with skills assessed at the start and at the end of the year. At posttest, children in Preschool PATHS classrooms, relative to the control classrooms, showed significantly greater gains in emotion knowledge and emotion recognition skills, and more improvement on teacher and parent ratings of social competence, but no differences in aggression (Domitrovich, Cortes, & Greenberg, 2007). In the second study, children in 44 Head Start classrooms were randomly assigned to receive the Head Start Research-Based, Developmentally Informed (REDI) program, which included the Preschool PATHS Curriculum along with a literacy intervention, or to "usual practice" Head Start. Four-year-old children were assessed at the start and at the end of the year. In addition to positive effects on vocabulary and emergent literacy skills that were targeted by the literacy intervention, children in the intervention condition showed significantly higher levels of emotional understanding, social problem-solving skills, and observed learning engagement than children in the control classrooms, as well as significantly lower levels of teacher-rated aggression. Additional, marginally significant effects for the intervention included higher teacher-rated and teacher-observed social competence, improved executive function task performance, and lower parent-rated aggression and attention problems (Bierman, Domitrovich, et al., 2008; Bierman, Nix, Greenberg, Blair, & Domitrovich, 2008). One year later, follow-up assessments collected after these children had transitioned into kindergarten revealed sustained effects for the intervention on measures of learning engagement, social competence, reduced aggressive–disruptive behavior, and for the subgroup attending schools characterized by low achievement, reduced attention problems (Bierman et al., 2014). These positive social–emotional effects likely reflect the impact of Preschool PATHS, although it is possible that the added literacy intervention components amplified the effects of SEL (e.g., see Nix, Bierman, Domitrovich, & Gill, 2013).

In a third study, Preschool PATHS was combined with a Web-based professional development program, MyTeachingPartner (MTP; Hamre, Pianta, Mashburn, & Downer, 2012). In this study, 233 prekindergarten teachers from school districts throughout the state were randomly assigned to one of three conditions: (1) PATHS-High, which included the Preschool PATHS curriculum, access to Web-based videos, and the MTP consultancy; (2) PATHS-Low, which included the Preschool PATHS curriculum and access to Web-based videos but not the MTP consultancy; and (3) "usual practice" control, which did not include PATHS or the MTP resources or consultancy. As described in more detail later in this chapter, the MTP consultancy provided teachers with individualized coaching. Teachers videotaped themselves in their classrooms, reviewed their videotapes with their online coach, and received feedback and suggestions designed to help them improve their classroom organization, instructional management, and emotional support. Implementation measures revealed that PATHS lessons were implemented at the same frequency (on average, once per week) and with the same quality (average of 7.9 on a 10-point scale) in both the High and Low conditions. Analyses of the results revealed that relative to the "usual practice" control group, children in both of these Preschool PATHS conditions showed significantly greater improvements in teacher-rated social competencies (frustration tolerance, assertiveness skills, task orientation, social skills), but no differences on behavior problems. In general, teachers in the PATHS-High condition utilized the Web-based resources more frequently than did teachers in the PATHS-Low condition, and teachers who conducted more PATHS lessons and spent more time using the MTP Web-based resources also reported greater increases in children's social competence, suggesting that both the curriculum and the Web-based resources facilitated positive student outcomes.

Promising Programs

Tools of the Mind

The *Tools of the Mind* program (Tools; Bodrova & Leong, 2007) approaches the promotion of social–emotional skills using *implicit* strategies. Tools is based on Vygotsky's model, in which self-regulation develops in the context of social interactions, particularly pretend sociodramatic play (Bodrova & Leong, 2007). Tools includes a daily 50-minute, make-believe play session, during which teachers support and enhance sustained and complex sociodramatic play, emphasizing planning skills, character development, and interpersonal negotiation skills in the context of that play. In addition, the program includes games that involve the practice of self-regulation (controlling the speed of movement, remembering directions over time). The program also pairs children into dyads for many learning activities, in order to provide opportunities for more active engagement.

In the first randomized controlled trial to evaluate Tools, a sample of 210, 3- and 4-year-old preschoolers (primarily Latino [93%]) were assigned to classrooms in which teachers used Tools or a curriculum developed by the school district (Barnett et al., 2008). At the end of the year, observers documented the significant impact of Tools on the specific teaching practices targeted by the program, including classroom structure and use of time, the use of scaffolding techniques by teachers in their interactions with children, and the quality of the literacy environment and instruction (Barnett et al., 2008). However, no effects were observed on a more general measure of the quality of student–teacher interaction. At the end of the year, children in the intervention classrooms were rated by teachers as having fewer behavior problems relative to children in the control group, and they also showed gains on a vocabulary test, but not on tests of emergent literacy or math skills (Barnett et al., 2008).

One year after the Barnett and colleagues (2008) evaluation, Diamond, Barnett, Thomas, and Munro (2007) followed up the children in the original sample (who were still in prekindergarten) and administered executive functioning tests. One school was dropped from this second study because the whole school had adopted Tools, and six new classes were added that had not participated in the original study. In this evaluation, children in the Tools classrooms outperformed those in the control classrooms on tests of executive function skills (Diamond et al., 2007). However, given the changes in the study sample, and the lack of pretests to show equivalence in the intervention and control samples, these findings should be considered preliminary. Since then, two additional randomized trials have evaluated Tools. In one, Tools was compared with "usual practice" preschool in six school districts and produced no significant effects on child literacy, math, or executive function skills, or on teacher ratings of child social and behavioral competence (Wilson & Farran, 2012). In the other randomized trial, Clements, Sarama, Unlu, and Layzer (2012) compared "usual practice" preschool with two intervention conditions: one that included a preschool mathematics curriculum (Building Blocks), and the other that paired Building Blocks with a modified version of Tools. No group differences emerged for one executive function task (pencil tapping). Children in the Building Blocks condition outperformed those in the control group on two other tasks (Head–Toes–Knees–Shoulders and backward digit span), but children in the Building Blocks plus Tools condition did no better than the "usual practice" control group on these tasks. Implementation challenges and/or adaptations made to the Tools program may have reduced program impact in these latter two trials, but at this point, evidence for its impact on social–emotional school readiness and self-regulation skills requires further documentation. It is worth noting that relative to other preschool SEL programs, Tools is more complex and may be more difficult for preschool teachers to master. Hence, it is possible that teachers require more than 1 year to implement this intervention approach as intended, and that randomized controlled trials that evaluate impact after the first year of teacher implementation underestimate program effects.

Whereas Tools takes an *implicit* approach to SEL, each of the promising programs described next in this section include *explicit* lessons on the targeted social–emotional skills, along with professional development supports designed to help teachers provide a positive classroom environment that supports SEL.

I Can Problem Solve

The *I Can Problem Solve* program [ICPS] was one of the first explicit SEL programs developed for preschool children (Shure, 1992; Shure & Spivack, 1982). The logic model for this intervention emphasizes the importance of developing the covert thinking skills that allow children to respond thoughtfully and flexibly to a variety of social problems. The overall goal of the program is to improve children's ability to navigate social challenges, by improving their capacity to flexibly generate solutions to challenging interpersonal situations, and anticipate the consequences of different behavioral choices. The ICPS curriculum includes 46 short (20- to 30-minute) lessons. It starts with instruction in the basic cognitive skills that provide a foundation for problem solving, including concepts such as "same–different" and "if–then," and the ability to identify basic emotions (happy, angry, and sad). Next, it presents a series of interpersonal problem situations that children discuss by identifying multiple solutions, then considering the consequences of different solutions. Teacher demonstration and puppet play are used to illustrate the training concepts, and whenever possible, the problem-solving methods are applied to actual classroom problems.

In a randomized trial of the program involving 113 African American, inner-city children (ages 4–5 years), the children in intervention classrooms improved relative to children in "usual practice" classrooms on measures of alternative and consequential thinking, as well as teacher ratings of frustration tolerance, impulsivity, and task engagement. Improvements were maintained at follow-up 1 year later, when children were rated by new teachers, blind to experimental condition (Shure & Spivack, 1982).

Al's Pals: Kids Making Healthy Choices

Al's Pals is a comprehensive SEL program for preschool, kindergarten, and first-grade children (Lynch, Geller, & Schmidt, 2004), designed to promote social–emotional competence and build the coping skills and resilience of young children growing up in impoverished, high-risk environments. It is informed by social learning theory and includes activities designed to coach children in the acquisition of communication skills, emotional expression, positive social interaction, self-control, anger management, and social problem-solving skills. In addition, the program is designed to inspire hope in children who are growing up in highly disadvantaged urban settings and exposed to community violence, and to teach them "survival skills," such as monitoring the environment for safety and making healthy choices regarding substance use. The program is designed for implementation by classroom teachers, who present two brief (15- to 20-minute) lessons per week over a 23-week period. The manual provides scripts for each session, additional notes, and activity guides for teachers. A 2-day introductory workshop is designed to promote a positive classroom climate and support for skills generalization. Professional development topics in this teacher workshop include active listening, nonjudgmental responding to children's disclosure of sensitive topics, and techniques to guide children in problem solving and healthy decision making.

Al's Pals was developed and refined through a series of quasi-experimental studies (Lynch et al., 2004). One randomized controlled trial has been undertaken with 33 Head Start classrooms (17 intervention, 16 "usual practice" control). A total of 399 children of mixed ethnicity participated. Teacher ratings of child behavior revealed significantly higher mean levels of social skills and lower mean levels of problem behaviors (internalizing and externalizing problems combined) for children in the intervention group compared with the control group (Lynch et al., 2004). *Al's Pals* also produced nonsignificant trends favoring the intervention group on teacher ratings of positive coping and "distract/avoid" methods of coping but had no effect on negative coping behaviors (venting and aggression), cooperation skills, or interaction skills. Although the results of this study were positive and several other quasi-experimental studies also show promising effects (as reviewed in Lynch et al., 2004), the findings are limited by the reliance on teacher ratings as the only measure of program impact. Because teachers implemented the program, their ratings of change in child skills and behavior may be subject to bias. Hence, additional rigorous, randomized comparisons are needed, using multi-informant measures to confirm the program's impact.

Other Programs That Use Explicit SEL

Small pilot studies suggest that additional SEL programs may have benefits for preschool children. However, none of these programs has yet been tested with preschool children in the context of a large, rigorous, randomized controlled trial. These include the Second Step Program, preschool level (McMahon, Washburn, Felix, Yakin, & Childrey, 2000), the Emotions-Based Prevention Program (Izard et al., 2008), and the Strong Start PreK program, preschool level (Gunter, Caldarella, Korth, & Young, 2012), all of which share some common core concepts with the previously mentioned programs.

Programs That Do Not Work

There are no programs that fit this category because of a lack of evidence; that is, multiple evaluations have not been conducted on specific programs to document that they do not achieve their intended impact.

Critical Issues in Preschool SEL Programming

Professional Development Support

As noted earlier, the provision of sufficient professional development support to enable preschool teachers to implement SEL programs with high fidelity is a critical issue affecting program impact on children. In contrast to elementary school teachers, many preschool teachers do not have 4-year college degrees, and some have only a high school degree (Zaslow et al., 2010). Preschool teachers vary substantially in the amount of on-the-job training and supervision they receive, and few receive any systematic training in how to support social–emotional development and enhance children's self-regulation skills in the preschool context. Even when SEL programs provide a detailed manual for program delivery, professional development support is necessary to foster optimal implementation. In addition, professional development support is needed to promote emotionally supportive teaching practices and the use of positive classroom management strategies that support the generalization of SEL skills. Most evidence-based SEL programs use a combination of workshop training and onsite coaching to foster high-fidelity implementation and positive teaching practices. Research is needed to identify the most effective and efficient strategies for providing this professional development support.

A particular challenge is how to scale-up coaching models for preschool teachers, in order to increase the accessibility of professional development support for teachers using SEL programs. One promising strategy involves the use of technology to improve the accessibility of high-quality coaching. For example, Pianta, Mashburn, Downer, Hamre, and Justice (2008) developed a Web-based platform, MyTeachingPartner (MTP), to deliver professional development support. As noted earlier, a first study of MTP involved coaching prekindergarten teachers in the implementation of Preschool PATHS, comparing two levels of support—the provision of Web-based models with (or without) additional online coaching and consultation. The findings from this randomized trial suggested that the online coaching in combination with the access to Web resources facilitated more positive gains in teaching practices than the provision of a workshop alone (Pianta et al., 2008). Additional research is needed in this important area.

Involving Parents

Another issue that is particularly important during the preschool years is the involvement of parents because children's social–emotional development is so heavily dependent on the quality of parent–child relationships during early childhood (Bernier et al., 2010). In addition, many preschool programs are only half-day, potentially limiting the impact of an SEL program delivered only in the school context. Preschool PATHS and Al's Pals both include information sheets and suggestions for parent–child activities that are sent home regularly during the school year to increase synchronous home and school support for children's SEL. In addition, a few studies have examined the utility of offering more intensive parent training interventions as universal supports to help parents get positively involved with their child's school, to reduce the use of punitive discipline practices, and to increase the use of positive management strategies at home. A few randomized trials suggest that these universal programs can improve parenting practices, but engaging parents is difficult, and thus far, the impact on child behavior is typically small.

For example, two randomized studies have offered the IY Parent Training Program to the parents of children attending Head Start, to extend and complement a classroom SEL program. In the first of these, Webster-Stratton and colleagues (2001) evaluated a combined intervention approach (IY teacher training plus IY parent training) in a randomized trial involving 14 Head Start centers. In that study, only 50% of the eligible parent population enrolled in the study and remained at Head Start through the end-of-year posttest. Of those, 63% of the parents assigned to the intervention group attended at least one of the parent intervention sessions, and the average parent level of attendance was only 5.73 of the 12 parenting sessions. At posttreatment, parents in the intervention condition demonstrated significantly lower levels of negative parenting and higher levels of positive parenting than parents in the control condition; however, child problem behavior at home decreased significantly only for a subset of children with elevated problems at pretreatment assessments. In a second study, Project STAR (Kaminski, Stormshak, Good, & Goodman, 2002), 14 Head Start centers were randomly assigned to three conditions, including a classroom SEL program, a combined intervention (classroom SEL lessons and the IY parent training program), or a "usual practice" control group. The parenting program also included home visits the following year, when children were in kindergarten. In this study, even though free transportation and childcare was provided, only 36% of the families assigned to the parent training condition attended more than four parent group sessions. The intervention produced significant improvements (relative to the control group) in caregiver involvement and school bonding, as well as child social competence. (However, child competence was also improved with the SEL classroom program alone.)

A third study that warrants mention here used a randomized controlled design to evaluate the impact of a universal parenting and child-focused program (ParentCorps) offered to the children and parents attending public prekindergarten in four elementary schools (compared to four "usual practice" schools) (Brotman-Miller et al., 2011). Covering a similar set of parenting skills as the IY program, the ParentCorps parenting program was adapted culturally to meet the needs of immigrant parents, and administered at schools during early evening hours, along with a parallel program for children. Only 30% of the prekindergartners' parents enrolled in the study. Of those who enrolled, 70% of the eligible parents attended at least one session, and average attendance was only 5.93 of 13 sessions. At postintervention assessments, significant improvements were evident on measures of parenting practices and on teacher ratings of child behavior problems in school.

Taken together, these studies suggest that interventions designed to support the parents of preschool children can improve the parenting practices associated with positive child social–emotional development and, in some cases, also promote positive changes in child social–emotional competence. However, these studies also illustrate the significant challenge of engaging parents of preschool children in universal parenting programs, particularly low-income parents who often have multiple stressors. Even with substantial efforts to reduce the barriers to engagement, the studies noted earlier were typically able to recruit only 30–50% of the eligible parent sample into their study, and of those who signed up, the average rate of participation was fewer than half of the parenting sessions. These findings raise questions about the cost-effectiveness of universal parent groups as a strategy for promoting SEL in preschool children, and call for additional research regarding approaches that might have equivalent impact but place less burden on parents.

Summary

From a developmental perspective, the preschool years represent a unique period of leverage for SEL programming (Feil et al., 2009), when effective interventions may reduce the school readiness gap associated with socioeconomic disadvantage and provide children with skills that promote resilience and success at school entry. The efficacy trials reviewed in this chapter demonstrate the potential of evidence-based SEL programs to promote positive social behavior, emotional understanding, and self-regulation skills, and to reduce off-task and aggressive behaviors during the preschool years. Effective SEL interventions for preschool children share some common features but vary in the degree to which they target behavioral, cognitive, and/or emotional skills. Each of the effective models described here included efforts to alter the preschool classroom context systematically in order to provide more support for social–emotional skills development; however, they varied in the degree to which they included explicit lessons or relied primarily on changes in teaching quality and classroom organization to promote change. At this point in time, the two preschool SEL programs with the strongest evidence of efficacy are each supported by at least two randomized trials, including one conducted by independent investigators rather than the program developers—the *Incredible Years Teacher Training Program*, which emphasizes positive classroom management skills with an implicit focus on social–emotional skills, and the *Preschool PATHS Curriculum*, which includes explicit lessons teaching social–emotional skills. Comparative studies have not yet been completed to determine whether one approach is more effective than another. In addition, longitudinal studies are needed to determine whether one approach promotes greater resilience in the years following preschool, when children move into elementary school. It is possible that a more explicit emphasis on the development of emotional understanding, self-control, and social problem-solving skills (as in PATHS) provides a stronger foundation for coping with the demands of elementary school than a program that focuses primarily on effective external control during preschool (as in IY) because the explicit instruction approach may more effectively promote children's internal capacities to monitor and cope with social challenges. However, no study has yet compared the long-term value of an explicit SEL curriculum in preschool with an effective classroom management program.

More research is also needed to determine whether, and under what conditions, preschool SEL programs can promote children's later academic outcomes. Some studies reviewed here showed "crossover" impact, with the social–emotional intervention promoting vocabulary (Barnett et al., 2008) or emergent literacy and math skills (Raver et al., 2011), and one study found direct evidence of synergistic gains when both social–emotional and language/emergent literacy skills were targeted together in preschool (Nix et al., 2013).

Finally, additional research is needed to identify optimal professional development models for supporting high-fidelity implementation of preschool SEL programs, as well as to determine the cost–benefit value of including parents with varying levels of intensity in universal programs designed to enhance the social emotional competencies of preschool children.

References

Barnett, W. S., Jung, K., Yarosz, D., Thomas, J., Hornbeck, A., Stechuk, R., et al. (2008). Educational effects of the Tools of the Mind curriculum: A randomized trial. *Early Childhood Research Quarterly, 23*(3), 299–313.

Bernier, A., Carlson, S. M., & Whipple, N. (2010). From external regulation to self-regulation: Early parenting precursors of young children's executive functioning. *Child Development, 81*, 326–339.

Bierman, K. L. (1988). The clinical implications of children's conceptions of social relationships. In S. Shirk (Ed.), *Cognitive development and child psychotherapy* (pp. 247–272). New York: Plenum Press.

Bierman, K. L. (2004). *Peer rejection: Developmental processes and intervention strategies.* New York: Guilford Press.

Bierman, K. L., Domitrovich, C. E., Nix, R. L., Gest, S. D., Welsh, J. A., Greenberg, M. T., et al. (2008). Promoting academic and social–emotional school readiness: The Head Start REDI program. *Child Development, 79,* 1802–1817.

Bierman, K. L., & Erath, S. A. (2006). Promoting social competence in early childhood: Classroom curricula and social skills coaching programs. In K. McCartney & D. Phillips (Eds.), *Blackwell handbook on early childhood development* (pp. 595–615). Malden, MA: Blackwell.

Bierman, K. L., Nix, R. L., Greenberg, M. T., Blair, C., & Domitrovich, C. E. (2008). Executive functions and school readiness intervention: Impact, moderation, and mediation in the Head Start REDI Program. *Development and Psychopathology, 20,* 821–843.

Bierman, K. L., Nix, R. L., Heinrichs, B.S., Domitrovich, C. E., Gest, S. D., Welsh, J. A., et al. (2014). Effects of Head Start REDI on children's outcomes one year later in different kindergarten contexts. *Child Development, 85*(1), 140–159.

Bierman, K. L., & Torres, M. (in press). Promoting the development of executive functions through early education and prevention programs. In J. A. Griffin, L. S. Freund, & P. McCardle (Eds.), *Executive function in preschool age children: Integrating measurement, neurodevelopment and translational research.* Washington, DC: American Psychological Association.

Blair, C. (2002). School readiness: Integrating cognition and emotion in a neurobiological conceptualization of child functioning at school entry. *American Psychologist, 57,* 111–127.

Bodrova, E., & Leong, D. J. (2007). *Tools of the Mind: The Vygotskian approach to early childhood education* (2nd ed.). Upper Saddle River, NJ: Prentice-Hall.

Brotman-Miller, L., Calzada, E., Huang, K., Kingston, S., Dawson-McClure, S., Kamboukos, D., et al. (2011). Promoting effective parenting practices and preventing child behavior problems in school among ethnically diverse families from underserved, urban communities. *Child Development, 82*, 258–276.

Clements, D. H., Sarama, J., Unlu, F., & Layzer, C. (2012, March 8). *The efficacy of an Intervention synthesizing scaffolding designed to promote self regulation with an early mathematics curriculum: Effects on executive function.* Paper presented at the annual meeting of the Society for Research in Educational Effectiveness, Washington, DC.

Denham, S. A., & Burton, R. (2003). *Social and emotional prevention and intervention programming for preschoolers*. New York: Kluwer Academic/Plenum Press.

Diamond, A., Barnett, W. S., Thomas, J., & Munro, S. (2007). Preschool program improves cognitive control. *Science, 318*, 1387–1388.

Domitrovich, C. E., Cortes, R., & Greenberg, M. T. (2007). Improving young children's social and emotional competence: A randomized trial of the preschool PATHS curriculum. *Journal of Primary Prevention, 28*, 67–91.

Domitrovich, C. E., Greenberg, M. T., Cortes, R., & Kusche, C. (1999). *Manual for the Preschool PATHS Curriculum*. University Park: Pennsylvania State University.

Durlak, J. A., Weissberg, R. P., Dymnicki, A. B., Taylor, R. D., & Shellinger, K. B. (2011). The impact of enhancing students' social and emotional learning: A meta-analysis of school-based universal interventions. *Child Development, 82*, 405–432.

Elias, M. J., Zins, J. E., Weissberg, R. P., Frey, K. S., Greenberg, M. T., Haynes, N. M., et al. (1997). *Promoting social and emotional learning: Guidelines for educators*. Alexandria, VA: Association for Supervision and Curriculum Development.

Feil, E. G., Walker, H., Severson, H., Golly, A., Seeley, J. R., & Small, J. W. (2009). Using positive behavior support procedures in Head Start classrooms to improve school readiness: A group training and behavioral coaching model. *NHSA Dialog: A Research to Practice Journal for the Early Childhood Field, 12*, 88–103.

Greenberg, M. T. (2006). Promoting resilience in children and youth: Preventive interventions and their interface with neuroscience. *Annals of the New York Academy of Science, 1094*, 139–150.

Gunter, L., Caldarella, P., Korth, B. B., & Young, K. R. (2012). Promoting social and emotional learning in preschool students: A study of Strong Start Pre-K. *Early Childhood Education Journal, 40*, 151–159.

Hamre, B. K., Pianta, R. C., Mashburn, A. J., & Downer, J. (2012). Promoting young children's social competence through the Preschool PATHS Curriculum and MyTeachingPartner professional development resources. *Early Education and Development, 23*, 809–832.

Izard, C. E. (2002). Translating emotion theory and research into preventive interventions. *Psychological Bulletin, 128*, 796–824.

Izard, C., King, K. A., Trentacosta, C. J., Morgan, J. K., Laurenceau, J., Krauthamer-Ewing, .S., et al. (2008). Accelerating the development of emotion competence in Head Start children: Effects on adaptive and maladaptive behavior. *Development and Psychopathology, 20*, 369–397.

Kaminski, R. A., Stormshak, E. A., Good, R. H., & Goodman, M. R. (2002). Prevention of substance abuse with rural Head Start children and families: Results of Project STAR. *Psychology of Addictive Behaviors, 16*, 511–526.

Lynch, K. B., Geller, S. R., & Schmidt, M. G. (2004). Multi-year evaluation of the effectiveness of a resilience-based prevention program for young children. *Journal of Primary Prevention, 24*, 335–353.

McClelland, M. M., Acock, A. C., & Morrison, F. J. (2006). The impact of kindergarten learning-related skills on academic trajectories at the end of elementary school. *Early Childhood Research Quarterly, 21*, 471–490.

McMahon, S. D., Washburn, J., Felix, E. D., Yakin, J., & Childrey, G. (2000). Violence prevention: Program effects on urban preschool and kindergarten children. *Applied and Preventive Psychology, 9*, 271–281.

National Center for Children in Poverty. (2011). Basic facts about low-income children, 2009. Retrieved December 21, 2012, from *http://nccp.org/publications/pub_975.html.*

Nix, R. L., Bierman, K. L., Domitrovich, C. E., & Gill, S. (2013). Promoting preschool social–emotional skills with the Head Start REDI Program enhances academic and behavioral outcomes in kindergarten. *Early Education and Development, 24*, 1000–1019.

Pianta, R. C., Mashburn, A. J., Downer, J. T., Hamre, B. K., & Justice, L. M. (2008). Effects of web-mediated professional development resources on teacher–child interactions in pre-kindergarten classrooms. *Early Childhood Research Quarterly, 23*, 431–451.

Raver, C. C., Jones, S. M., Li-Grining, C. P., Metzger, M., Smallwood, K., & Sardin, L. (2008). Improving preschool classroom processes: Preliminary findings from a randomized trial implemented in Head Start settings. *Early Childhood Research Quarterly, 23*, 10–26.

Raver, C. C., Jones, S. M., Li-Grining, C., Zhai, F., Bub, K., & Pressler, E. (2011). CSRP's impact on low-income preschoolers' preacademic skills: Self-regulation as a mediating mechanism. *Child Development, 82*, 362–378.

Raver, C. C., Jones, S. M., Li-Grining, C., Zhai, F., Metzger, M. W., & Solomon, B. (2009). Targeting children's behavior problems in preschool classrooms: A cluster-randomized controlled trial. *Journal of Consulting and Clinical Psychology, 77*, 302–316.

Robin, A., Schneider, M., & Dolnick, M. (1976). The turtle technique: An extended case study of self-control in the classroom. *Psychology in the Schools, 13*, 449–452.

Shure, M. B. (1992). *I Can Problem Solve: An interpersonal cognitive problem-solving program: Kindergarten and primary grades*. Champaign, IL: Research Press.

Shure, M. B., & Spivack, G. (1982). Interpersonal problem-solving in young children: A cognitive approach to prevention. *American Journal of Community Psychology, 10*, 341–355.

Ursache, A., Blair, C., & Raver, C. C. (2012). The promotion of self-regulation as a means of enhancing school readiness and early achievement in children at risk for school failure. *Child Development Perspectives, 6*, 122–128.

U.S. Department of Education. (2007). Enrollment in early childhood education programs. Retrieved December 21, 2012, from *http://nces.ed.gov/pubs2007/2007064.pdf*.

Webster-Stratton, C., & Herman, K. (2010). Disseminating Incredible Years series early-intervention programs: Integrating and sustaining services between home and school. *Psychology in the Schools, 47*, 36–54.

Webster-Stratton, C., Reid, M. J., & Hammond, M. (2001). Preventing conduct problems, promoting social competence: A parent and teacher training partnership in Head Start. *Journal of Clinical Child and Adolescent Psychology, 30*, 283–302.

Webster-Stratton, C., Reid, M. J., & Stoolmiller, M. (2008). Preventing conduct problems and improving school readiness: Evaluation of the Incredible Years teacher and child training programs in high-risk schools. *Journal of Child Psychology and Psychiatry, 49*, 471–488.

Wilson, S. J., & Farran, D. C. (2012, March 8). *Experimental evaluation of the Tools of the Mind Preschool Curriculum*. Paper presented at the annual meeting of the Society for Research in Educational Effectiveness, Washington, DC.

Zaslow, M., Tout, K., Halle, T., Vick, J., & Lavelle, B. (2010). Towards the identification of features of effective professional development for early childhood educators: A review of the literature (Report prepared for the U.S. Department of Education). Retrieved December 21, 2012, from *http://ed.gov/rschstat/eval/professional-development/literature-review.pdf*.

CHAPTER 10

SEL in Elementary School Settings

Identifying Mechanisms That Matter

Sara E. Rimm-Kaufman and Chris S. Hulleman

The Collaborative for Academic, Social, and Emotional Learning (CASEL; 2013) defines social and emotional learning as "a process for helping children and even adults develop the fundamental skills for life effectiveness." SEL skills consist of "recognizing and managing our emotions, developing caring and concern for others, establishing positive relationships, making responsible decisions, and handling challenging situations constructively and ethically" (CASEL, 2013). There has been tremendous growth in the past several decades in the presence of interventions designed to teach elementary students SEL skills and the establishment of the evidential basis for these interventions (Durlak, Weissberg, Dymnicki, Taylor, & Schellinger, 2011). Elementary school SEL interventions have been viewed as levers to produce school improvement. This reality is exemplified in the way that SEL has been integrated into state learning standards (Dusenbury, Zadrazil, Mart, & Weissberg, 2011) and supported in the proposed federal Academic, Social, and Emotional Learning Act of 2013 (2013).

New resources that review elementary school SEL interventions have become available in the last several years. The *2013 CASEL Guide* categorized and described preschool- and elementary-level SEL programs based on program design, effectiveness, and supports for implementation. A recent meta-analysis synthesized research on SEL interventions and their efficacy in producing behavioral and academic gains (Durlak et al., 2011). The What Works Clearinghouse catalogues the quality of evidence for SEL interventions (U.S. Department of Education, 2014). Although these resources describe program design, composition, and effectiveness, they do not examine the key mechanisms in SEL interventions that are intended to impact student outcomes. Adopting an SEL intervention translates into shifts in teachers' and students' day-to-day behaviors and experiences in the classroom. This chapter builds on prior work by looking inside classrooms to consider student and teacher mechanisms responsible for program effects. We call these shifts in teachers and students the *mechanisms that matter.*

In particular, we consider how various SEL interventions change what teachers do and how students spend their time. We describe how specific SEL interventions emphasize some student skills versus others.

Definitions and Scope

We begin by introducing a set of terms to describe SEL interventions. All SEL interventions ascribe to a "theory of change"; that is, SEL interventions are designed as a set of program elements and/or steps that can be described in conceptual terms and give insight into the process of change (Knowlton & Phillips, 2008). The theory of change helps identify "intervention core components," defined as the key aspects of the intervention that contain the intervention active ingredients intended to produce changes in students' social, emotional, and/or academic skills (Hulleman, Rimm-Kaufman, & Abry, 2013). Intervention core components are created and/or selected by the intervention developer because, in theory, they change what occurs in the classroom to improve student outcomes. Explicit instructions in social skills or regular use of a mixed-age buddy activity are examples of intervention core components.

The theory of change helps differentiate between proximal and distal outcomes expected to result from using the intervention in the classroom. *Proximal outcomes* are immediate, close-at-hand results of the intervention; in essence, the first signs in a classroom that an intervention is creating a change. For instance, when a teacher begins using an SEL intervention, she may see evidence of more prosocial conversation among peers in her classroom or improved attentional skills among several students. *Distal outcomes* occur as distant, long-term results of an intervention. When a teacher implements a SEL intervention, he may be supporting a set of interpersonal skills that may not be immediately apparent but may lead to improved social skills and long-term gains in students' ability to relate, show empathy toward, and communicate with other people inside and outside of school. Proximal outcomes of an intervention can be viewed as important outcomes unto themselves because they signal potential efficacy of the intervention. Furthermore, proximal outcomes can *mediate* or bring about the effects of the intervention to the distal outcome—yet another way in which they substantiate the theory of change.

Initiating use of an SEL program sets in motion a process that unfolds over time. In theory, intervention core components become agents of change that bring about proximal outcomes. In turn, those proximal outcomes become agents of change that lead to distal outcomes. If intervention core components are used properly in the classroom and are truly effective, then the mechanisms underlying the process of change—intervention core components and proximal outcomes—represent what we call the mechanisms that matter in SEL. *Mechanisms that matter* are typically described in broad or specific terms by the developers of interventions, and in essence, reflect the theories or beliefs about how an SEL intervention is designed to improve students' social and academic performance. Focusing on the mechanisms that matter provides a unique vantage point for understanding SEL. This approach enables us to zoom in to consider what occurs inside classrooms in the presence of SEL interventions and to illustrate variety among the many existing approaches to improving SEL.

Describing mechanisms that matter also poses a significant challenge. Most research on SEL interventions examines the efficacy of multicomponent SEL interventions in which many intervention core components are combined into a single intervention and used in the classroom. There is too little work that isolates each intervention core component within any single intervention and tests it rigorously, so that we know which components are potent and which are extraneous for enhancing student outcomes. Therefore, based on the current state of research, we can describe which interventions have substantial versus less evidence for their efficacy in improving social and emotional outcomes. However, in relation to the various intervention core components and how they produce changes within classrooms, we mostly talk about *presumed* mechanisms that matter, not actual demonstrated evidence of the effects of those mechanisms.

Our purpose in this chapter is to review selected literature on elementary school

SEL. We describe SEL theory in a way that emphasizes mechanisms that matter and present a brief overview of SEL strategies used in elementary school classrooms. Next, we select 10 SEL interventions and categorize them into those that work (based on three or more studies of the intervention) and those that seem promising (but have fewer than three studies of their efficacy). For each intervention, we summarize existing research on the efficacy of the intervention on distal outcomes. In addition, we describe the presumed mechanisms that matter based on intervention websites and published work. After describing what works and what is promising in elementary SEL, we provide a brief description of what does not work. Finally, we close with a summary and implications for research and practice.

Theories

The SEL conceptual framework we use is grounded in theory and research in educational and developmental science. We draw from work by Zins, Bloodworth, Weissberg, and Wahlberg (2004), CASEL (2012), and Jennings and Greenberg (2009), and integrate other frameworks (Jones & Bouffard, 2012) to describe how school-based SEL interventions are designed to improve students' social and academic performance. The conceptual framework shown in Figure 10.1 depicts how effective use of SEL intervention core components in classrooms sets new classroom experiences into motion. Some intervention core components involve explicit instruction in SEL skills described by a curriculum. This type of component involves teachers' enactment of lessons on SEL topics (e.g., how to label emotions, how to resolve conflict with a peer) or explicit modeling of a desired behavior (e.g., how to take turns with a peer, how to stand in line). Alternatively, intervention core components can be integrated into the academic curricula. For example, teachers may incorporate SEL skills development into literature lessons by reading and discussing an age-appropriate book and having students' connect the experience to their own lives and decision making in social situations. Intervention core components can also be embedded in SEL classroom teaching practices. Such practices refer to the way that teachers interact with students to facilitate student learning in social and emotional skills. For example, SEL classroom teaching practices may include facilitation of a group activity that offers students opportunities to practice social and emotional skills, and teacher language that implicitly supports students' motivation or autonomy (CASEL, 2012).

In theory, *effective use of SEL intervention core components leads to improved proximal outcomes: the classroom social environment and students' skills in the*

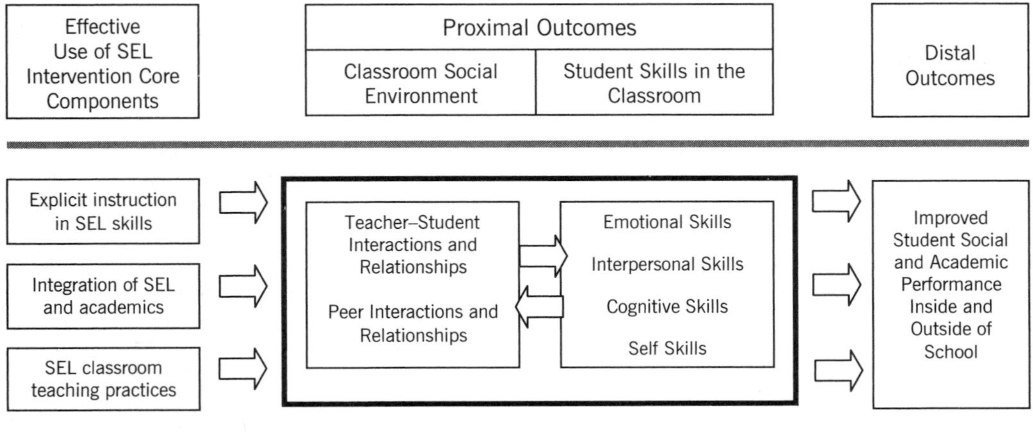

FIGURE 10.1. Conceptual framework describing the contribution of SEL interventions to proximal and distal outcomes.

classroom. Improved quality of the classroom social environment may be evident in the way that teachers show greater awareness of and emotional responsiveness to students or via teachers' enhanced approach to classroom management (Jennings & Greenberg, 2009). Better quality of classroom social environments may mean that students are more cooperative and prosocial toward one another. Whether the improvements stem from teacher and/or student interactions, students who experience better quality classroom social environments are likely to be exposed to more frequent opportunities to learn and practice SEL skills.

SEL intervention core components are designed to improve students' SEL skills, which include emotional, interpersonal, cognitive, and/or self skills. *Emotional skills* include the ability to recognize, understand, label, express, and regulate emotions. *Interpersonal skills* include communication, prosocial, and relationship development skills. *Cognitive skills* involve the management of attention, planning of future actions, and inhibition of short-term response for a long-term goal (Jones & Bouffard, 2012). *Self skills* are students' attitudes and perceptions about themselves as learners and the school context, including students' sense of self as a learner, feelings of bonding toward school, and motivation to learn (Skinner, Kindermann, Connell, & Wellborn, 2009).

SEL theory describes various possible mechanisms for how classroom social environments and student SEL skills interact. Use of intervention core components may operate directly by improving students' SEL skills or indirectly by enhancing the social climate of the classroom, thus exposing students to more positive social environments, then improving students' SEL skills. Regardless of mechanism, a core idea in SEL theory is that SEL skills become important child assets with positive consequences for development because these skills provide students with internal resources needed to take advantage of social and academic opportunities offered in the classroom. In this way (and perhaps via other mechanisms), *enhanced classroom social environments and students' improved skills interact to improve distal outcomes, social and academic performance, both inside and outside of school.*

The conceptual framework implies a direction of influence (i.e., use of SEL intervention core components leads to proximal, then distal outcomes). Although beyond the scope of this chapter, it is safe to assume the presence of bidirectional influences in this model (Skinner et al., 2009). For instance, as students in a classroom develop emotional, interpersonal, cognitive skills and self skills, they may raise the level of discourse surrounding instruction in SEL skills and cause teachers to elevate use of SEL classroom teaching practices to a higher level of sophistication (e.g., from basic peer social skills to conflict resolution skills).

Overview of Strategies

A wide variety of approaches for improving SEL are available to educators. Intervention core components vary in the way that they are delivered (e.g., explicit lessons, integration with academic content, change in teaching practices; CASEL, 2012). Some SEL interventions place primacy on the development of some skills over others, whereas many target multiple skills domains. Despite the variability, there are common themes among SEL interventions. All SEL interventions ascribe to a theory of change and can be described in relation to presumed mechanisms that matter. Virtually all SEL interventions recognize that developing skills in one domain (e.g., emotional) have implications for students' skills in another (e.g., interpersonal). For instance, competent emotional skills enable students to perceive their friends' emotional cues and manage their own feelings of frustration in ways that do not interfere with friendship (Downer, Sabol, & Hamre, 2010). Students' development of cognitive regulation skills improves their ability to engage in classroom activities available to them, which in turn, improves their sense of self and attitude toward learning (Liew, 2012).

Below, we describe 10 SEL interventions that are administered by teachers inside elementary school classrooms. These 10 interventions were selected to illustrate variety of presumed mechanisms that matter. (See the *2013 CASEL Guide* [2012] for a more thorough listing of SEL approaches.) Some of the selected interventions have additional family components, school components, or reach into the middle school years—topics covered elsewhere in this volume.

What Works

There are five interventions with three or more studies demonstrating intervention efficacy: Caring School Community (CSC), Promoting Alternative Thinking Strategies (PATHS), Positive Action (PA), the Responsive Classroom (RC) approach, and Second Step. We describe existing research on use of the intervention and distal outcomes for each. Then, we described the presumed (or actual) mechanisms that matter by describing intervention core components and proximal outcomes.

Caring School Community

CSC is designed to create caring classroom and school communities, such that students experience increased connection and bonding toward school. The program targets interpersonal and self skills, especially enhanced relationships among peers and between teachers and students, and increased connection to school. Several studies provide evidence for the efficacy of CSC. Findings from a randomized controlled trial point to the efficacy of the approach for increasing students' sense of connection to school and engagement in learning, as well as improved interpersonal skills (altruistic behavior). Research shows that students' perception of an increased sense of community in the school relates to a rise in interpersonal skills (prosocial behaviors) and self skills (academic motivation and engagement), as well social and achievement outcomes (Solomon, Battistich, Watson, Schaps, & Lewis, 2000). Finding from a recent quasi-experimental study of third through fifth graders reflect the efficacy of CSC for improving self skills (i.e., feelings of autonomy and influence in the classroom, students' perception of classroom supportiveness) (Chang & Munoz, 2006). Turning attention to distal outcomes, students experiencing CSC showed some improved achievement and behavioral outcomes (Battistich, Schaps, & Wilson, 2004), particularly when schools implemented the intervention as intended (Battistich, Solomon, Kim, Watson, & Schaps, 1995; Chang & Munoz, 2006).

Returning to the SEL conceptual model, intervention core components emphasize integration of SEL and academics, and SEL classroom teaching practices with some curricular components. The intervention core components include Class Meetings, Cross-Age Buddy Activities, Homeside Activities, and Schoolwide Community-Building Activities matched to students' developmental level. The Class Meetings provide opportunities for teachers and students to establish classroom norms, engage in social problem solving (e.g., how to respond to teasing and social exclusion), build teams, and reflect on the classroom as a community. The Cross-Age Buddy Activities pair older students with younger students as they work on meaningful academic tasks together. The buddy experience requires the older student to prepare, engage in the buddy activity, then reflect. The program has family and schoolwide components as well. Homeside Activities involve initiating an activity at school that students take home and use to elicit conversation with their family members. Schoolwide Community-Building Activities are designed to create collaboration among students, families, and the out-of-school community. These intervention core components are designed to create a more caring classroom and school environment, and they comprise the mechanisms that matter in CSC. Based on program theory, these mechanisms that matter develop students' connection toward school, thus improving students' motivation, social skills, behavior, and achievement (Developmental Studies Center, 2013).

Promoting Alternative Thinking Strategies

PATHS (2013) is a curriculum-based intervention designed to enhance students' self-regulation, understanding of emotions, self-esteem, social relationships, and social problem solving. Various randomized controlled trials demonstrate links between PATHS and proximal outcomes pertaining to three developmental domains: emotional, interpersonal, and cognitive. Exposure to PATHS has been linked to improved emotional skills (i.e., emotion recognition, emotional coping) in young children from poor families, as well as elementary school–age students with hearing impairments (Conduct Problems Prevention Research Group [CPPRG], 1999; Greenberg & Kusché, 1998). PATHS has been linked to improved interpersonal skills, including enhanced social problem solving and increased positive peer interaction (CPPRG, 1999), as well as decreased aggression and fewer problems with acceptance of authority (CPPRG, 2010). Furthermore, PATHS has been associated with enhanced cognitive skills (e.g., cognitive concentration, inhibitory control, verbal fluency; Greenberg, 2006, 2010). Work describing PATHS and distal outcomes (social and academic performance) suggests efficacy. One randomized controlled trial showed that 3 years of PATHS exposure to be linked to less disruptive behavior and aggression (CPPRG, 2010). A randomized controlled trial of PATHS among students with special needs (in grades 1–3) found that 1 year of PATHS exposure decreased externalizing behaviors and mitigated growth trends in internalizing symptoms as reported by teachers 2 years after the intervention (Kam, Greenberg, & Kusché, 2004).

Inside the classroom, the PATHS intervention core components take the form of explicit instruction in SEL skills and SEL classroom teaching practices that promote application of those skills (CPPRG, 2010). The PATHS curriculum includes age-appropriate units that teach students to recognize and label emotional cues, differentiate between feelings and behaviors, create and sustain friendships, show good manners, take turns, share, and reconcile challenging friendship issues (CPPRG, 2010). PATHS targets a very broad set of SEL goals. The presumed mechanisms that matter are the lessons (involving explicit instruction, behavioral modeling, discussion, stories, and videos) and the teachers' extension of those lessons as "teachable moments" throughout the school day (PATHS, 2013).

Positive Action

PA is designed around the premise that self-concept plays a critical role in students' behavior. The intervention is designed to create "a cycle of reinforcement in which positive thoughts lead to positive behaviors that generate positive feelings about self, which, in turn, lead to more positive thoughts and behaviors" (Washburn et al., 2011, p. 315). The numerous quasi-experimental and experimental PA studies show a consistent pattern of positive results. Pertaining to proximal outcomes are results from three experimental PA studies that followed children longitudinally for 3–4 years between the ages of 6 and 11. Developmental trends in the total sample showed declines in self skills (self-control, being honest to oneself, working toward continual improvement). However, the declines were smaller in PA than in comparison schools (Washburn et al., 2011). Studies also show the efficacy of PA on distal outcomes. Fifth-grade students who received PA earlier in elementary schools showed less substance use and sexual activity (Beets et al., 2009); less violent and bullying behavior (Li et al., 2011); and improved reading and math achievement (Flay, Allred, & Ordway, 2001).

Inside the classroom, intervention core components are enacted through explicit instruction in SEL skills on topics including self-concept; positive action in relation to one's body; responsible management of social interactions, emotional responses, and relationships; honesty to self and others; and self-improvement (goal setting, persistence) (PA, 2013). In addition, intervention core components are embedded in SEL teaching practices between teachers and students and among students via small-group activities including games, skills practice, and role-play activities (Beets et al., 2009). The program involves schoolwide changes and community and family involvement components to support classroom components. Together, the teacher-led lessons and their accompanying activities and materials comprise the presumed mechanisms that matter. Based on program theory, these mechanisms that matter enhance self skills so that students will learn and internalize healthy decision making that will set into motion a positive recursive process leading to a broad range of SEL skills and positive outcomes (PA, 2013).

The Responsive Classroom Approach

The RC approach targets improvement of the classroom social environment by enhancing teachers' capacity to create a caring community, use proactive approaches to classroom management, and develop student autonomy and engagement in learning. Two quasi-experimental and one randomized controlled trial have been conducted on the RC approach. Research linking the RC approach to proximal outcomes suggests that RC practices foster students' assertiveness and prosocial skills (Elliott, 1999; Rimm-Kaufman & Chiu, 2007) and contributes to students' positive views of their classroom environment (i.e., liking for school, learning, teachers, and peers) (Brock, Nishida, Chiong, Grimm, & Rimm-Kaufman, 2008). Studies from a randomized controlled trial show links between training in the *RC* approach and improved teacher-child interactions. Training in the *RC* approach predicted more inquiry-based mathematics practices compared to teachers at control schools (Ottmar, Rimm-Kaufman, Berry, & Larsen, 2013). Teachers who implemented more *RC* practices showed higher quality teacher–child interactions (Abry, Rimm-Kaufman, Larsen, & Brewer, 2013) and closer relationships with their students (Baroody, Rimm-Kaufman, Larsen, & Curby, 2014). Research has linked the RC approach to the distal outcome of achievement. Findings from two studies show gains in math and reading achievement after 2–3 years' exposure to RC practices (Rimm-Kaufman, Fan, Chiu, & You, 2007; Rimm-Kaufman et al., 2014).

Looking inside the classroom, RC emphasizes strategies that integrate SEL and academics via 10 teaching practices that focus on improving students' interpersonal, cognitive, and self skills. The teaching practices constitute intervention core components and guide the structure of interactions between teachers and students. As examples of the 10 teaching practices, teachers use daily Morning Meeting to integrate SEL and academics, establish a sense of community, learn and practice social skills, and create a spark for academic and social learning. Teachers use Academic Choice as means to adopt a structured approach to offering students choice and autonomy in academic activities and Interactive Modeling to teach expected social behaviors and self-regulatory skills. The presumed mechanisms that matter are the RC practices and their intended changes in the quality of teachers' interactions with students and students' interactions with each other. Based on program theory, these mechanisms that matter shift the classroom social environment; create opportunities to teach, model, and practice SEL skills; and lead to social and academic gains (Northeast Foundation for Children, 2011).

Second Step

Second Step is designed to improve emotional, interpersonal, and cognitive skills of students in grades K–8. Second Step offers a set curriculum involving lessons and activities designed to help each student in the classroom learn and practice a broad range of SEL skills (Committee for Children, 2013). There have been several research studies of Second Step. A randomized controlled trial of grades 2–5 showed increased interpersonal skills (increased prosocial goals, decreased aggression, improved social behavior) as a consequence of receiving the intervention. Furthermore, exposure to the intervention related to improved cooperation, an interpersonal skill that is crucial for group learning; this finding was present for girls but not boys (Frey, Nolen, Edstrom, & Hirschstein, 2005). Research in Norway suggests improved social competence for fifth- and sixth-grade students, as well as decreased externalizing among sixth-grade boys (Holsen, Smith, & Frey, 2008). Results from a randomized controlled trial in Germany indicated that children in Second Step showed improved social behavior, less anxiety, and less internalizing behavior compared to control students in grades K–3 (Schick & Cierpka, 2005).

Inside the classroom, the intervention core components are delivered to students via explicit instruction in SEL skills. The presumed mechanisms that matter are prepared scripts and lessons, stories with discussion, practice activities to reinforce new skills, and selected books—all of which are organized around a single topic each week. Topics include solving social problems (e.g., staying calm, following a set of problem solving steps, describing the problem without assigning blame) and skills for learning (e.g., how to focus attention, listen, be assertive, and use self-talk to manage one's attention). Second Step also has a home-based component. Based on program theory, Second Step teaches students a broad range of skills (empathy, management of emotions, problem solving, conflict resolution, skills for learning) that enable them to take full advantage of the classroom learning environment (Committee for Children, 2013).

These five interventions—CSC, PATHS, PA, RC, and Second Step—have distinct intervention core components and mechanisms that matter. Consider the primary approach to implementation: CSC and RC approaches emphasize use of SEL classroom teaching practices and do not have a set of sequenced, established lessons for explicit instruction in SEL. In contrast, PATHS, PA, and Second Step offer a specific curriculum and sequenced lessons to be enacted in the classroom. Yet another distinction among these interventions is the ways in which they are designed to modify the classroom social environment versus targeting student skills directly. CSC and RC place more emphasis on building teacher capacity and creating changes to the classroom social environment (teacher–student interactions, peer relationships), with the premise that modifications of students' social environment will result in improvement in students' SEL skills. In contrast, PATHS, PA, and Second Step place greater emphasis on improving individual students' skills, with the idea that students will then apply these skills in the classroom and in life. These five interventions also differ in the extent to which they concentrate on a narrow band of SEL skills (with the goal that students will use those skills to improve other SEL skills) versus focusing on a full range of SEL skills. For instance, CSC emphasizes interpersonal and self skills with the premise that bonding toward school will enhance other SEL schools and distal outcomes. PA targets self skills first, with the notion that once those self skills are developed, they will translate into a broader range of SEL skills. In contrast, PATH, Second Step, and RC target a broad range of skills. The five interventions have existed for a decade or more and each has three or more studies demonstrating intervention efficacy. Now, we turn our attention to newer and/or less well-researched interventions that look promising.

What Is Promising

We selected five promising SEL interventions that represent notable variation in presumed mechanisms that matter in SEL: Tribes Learning Communities, RULER, MindUp, Resolving Conflict Creatively, and 4Rs (Reading, Writing, Respect, and Resolution). Again, the interventions selected are illustrative, not exhaustive.

Tribes Learning Communities

Tribes Learning Communities (Tribes) is designed to enhance students' sense of community inside and outside of school, with the goal of reducing aggression, disruptive behavior, and violence. The most distinctive intervention core component is that teachers organize students into small working groups that last for the full academic year. The one randomized controlled trial of Tribes focused on students in grades 1–4 and examined proximal and distal effects. There was some suggestion that Tribes students showed more sharing and increased engagement compared to the comparison group after 1 year of exposure (Hanson, Izu, Petrosino, Delong-Cotty, & Zheng, 2011). Tribes tended to benefit boys but be unfavorable for girls. Among boys exposed to Tribes, teachers noted higher affective and intrapersonal skills, and parents reported more intrapersonal skills and less rule breaking at home. In contrast, girls exposed to Tribes unexpectedly showed a decrease in language and math student test scores. Findings differed for younger (grades 1 and 2) and older (grades 3 and 4) students. In grades 1 and 2, Tribes enhanced intrapersonal and interpersonal skills for girls but not boys. In grades 3 and 4, Tribes improved intrapersonal and interpersonal skills for boys but not girls (Hanson et al., 2011).

Tribes integrates a set of collaborative activities into the existing curriculum. One intervention core component involves facilitation of small-group projects that engage students in meaningful work. Teachers use SEL classroom teaching practices to teach and reinforce collaborative skills; to foster students' appreciation, respect, high expectations for each other, and a positive emotional climate in the classroom (Tribes Learning Community, 2014). The presumed mechanisms that matter are the long-lasting work groups designed to give students practice and experience with relationships skills and the teachers' efforts to support collaboration skills. Based on program theory, these mechanisms that matter enhance student skills and knowledge in ways that foster individual resiliency in the classroom and other contexts (Hanson et al., 2011).

RULER

Very few SEL interventions have been designed to primarily target emotional skills as proximal outcomes toward the distal goal of improvement in social and/or academic skills. The RULER Feeling Words Curriculum (RULER, 2013) is one such intervention; it involves explicit instruction in a set of emotional skills described by the developer as "RULER" skills (i.e., Recognizing, Understanding, Labeling, Expressing, and Regulating emotions) in order to enhance emotional literacy. To date, one quasi-experimental and one randomized controlled trial have been conducted. Existing research suggests that the intervention boosts proximal outcomes (specifically, students' emotion and interpersonal skills, and the classroom social environment) and distal outcomes (report card grades). One quasi-experimental study of fifth and sixth graders showed improved emotional skills (RULER skills), interpersonal skills (social competence), and grades after receiving the intervention (Brackett, Rivers, Reyes, & Salovey, 2010). A follow-up randomized controlled trial among sixth graders showed that when teachers received high-quality training in the intervention and students received sufficient dosage, students were more likely to show improved emotional skills (students' understanding and regulation of emotion) and social problem-solving skills (Reyes, Brackett, Rivers, Elbertson, & Salovey, 2012). Classrooms using RULER have had more positive, emotionally supportive social environments than have counterparts using business-as-usual approaches (Rivers, Brackett, Reyes, Elbertson, & Salovey, 2013).

RULER intervention core components involve explicit instruction in SEL skills in lessons that teach students to recognize emotions in themselves and others, understand causes and consequences of emotional states, label emotions using a range of words introduced in lessons, regulate their own emotions, and express emotions in socially appropriate ways. Thus, the presumed mechanisms that matter are the teacher-administered lessons, opportunities to practice emotion vocabulary in ways that integrate with language arts instruction, and the positive social interactions and emotional climate in the classroom (Brackett et al., 2010; Rivers et al., 2013). RULER implementation leads with a schoolwide effort, followed by introduction of the RULER in the classroom.

MindUP

The MindUP intervention approach is unique because of its integration of mediation-oriented practices into classroom life. One quasi-experimental study of MindUP in fourth through seventh graders showed increased optimism and positive impact on self-concept among the fourth graders. Teachers' ratings of students indicated greater attentiveness, concentration, emotion regulation, and emotional and social competence among students in the intervention group compared to those in a control condition (Schonert-Reichl & Lawlor, 2010).

The MindUP intervention core components involve explicit instruction in SEL in the form of teacher lessons in mindfulness and teaching practices to extend those lessons as teachers lead students in mindfulness exercises (based on scripts) three times a day for about 3 minutes each time (Schonert-Reichl & Lawlor, 2010). Thus, the presumed mechanisms that matter are the mindfulness lessons and exercises designed to focus students on breathing and help them increase awareness of the present moment. Based on program theory, the mechanisms that matter enhance emotional skills (management of negative emotions), cognitive skills (strengthened executive function skills, including attention), and self skills (awareness of self and others), with the implication that development of these skills will enhance social and academic performance (MindUP, 2013; Schonert-Reichl & Lawlor, 2010).

Resolving Conflict Creatively

Perhaps the most common SEL interventions are those designed to promote students' interpersonal skills by improving prosocial skills and reducing student aggression.

The Resolving Conflict Creatively Program (RCCP) stands out because it is designed to attenuate a set of negative developmental processes that often emerge as children progress from early to late childhood. RCCP is a curriculum that comprises interactive lessons to teach students conflict resolution techniques and skills to improve social interactions, cooperation, and feelings of safety in classrooms and schools (Educators for Social Responsibility [ESR], 2014). A randomized controlled trial of RCCP examined students (ages 6–12) for a 2-year period to assess program efficacy. Results showed the efficacy of the program in relation to slowing the growth of certain negative processes that tend to develop over middle childhood. That is, over a 2-year period, children in the intervention group showed lower levels of hostile attributions overall than the comparison group, and decreases in hostile attribution and aggressive approaches to problem solving. Among students in the intervention group, those exposed to more lessons showed increases in prosocial behavior and decreases in aggressive behavior over 2 years of intervention (Aber, Pedersen, Brown, Jones, & Gershoff, 2003).

Within the classroom, the intervention core components are integrated into a curriculum to teach caring, positive approaches for handling conflict, active listening, reducing prejudice, managing anger and frustration, developing cooperative relationships, showing empathy, and other topics. RCCP includes peer mediation and administrator, family, and school staff training components as well. The interactive instructions that correspond to the curriculum constitute the mechanisms that matter. Program theory links the mechanisms that matter to student interpersonal and self skills, and, in turn, distal outcomes, including success in school and reduced violence and violence-related behavior (ESR, 2014).

4Rs

The 4Rs (Reading, Writing, Respect, and Resolution) is a promising intervention that integrates SEL into students' language arts curriculum. The 4Rs is designed to enhance social cognition based on the notion that the interpretation of social cues and beliefs about aggression and interpersonal negotiation strategies underlie the more complicated skills implicated in intergroup understanding and conflict resolution (Morningside Center, 2012). The one randomized controlled trial on 4Rs studied students for 2 years (grades 3 and 4). Work examining 4Rs and proximal outcomes (classroom social environment) showed that third-grade teachers trained to integrate language arts learning with SEL learning had improved the quality of classroom interactions (i.e., instructional and emotional support), after researchers accounted for teachers' social and emotional functioning (Brown, Jones, LaRusso, & Aber, 2010). Students at both control and intervention schools showed increased hostile attribution bias and aggressive interpersonal negotiations strategies from the beginning of third grade to the end of fourth grade. However, students in the intervention schools showed slower rates of growth in both of these constructs compared to students in control schools (Jones, Brown, & Aber, 2011). Furthermore, intervention students with high aggression who entered the study reported fewer aggressive fantasies, such as having thoughts emerge in their minds about hurting, hitting, or fighting with someone (Jones, Brown, Hoglund, & Aber, 2010).

As enacted in the classroom, 4Rs intervention core components are embedded in a sequence of literacy lessons and SEL teaching practices to extend those lessons. One intervention core component is a Read-Aloud of a book relevant to an SEL theme. Another intervention core component is Book Talk, which comprises conversation, role playing, and writing opportunities that help students understand the theme and connect it to their own experiences. 4Rs has a family component as well. The 4Rs program stands out from other classroom-based interventions in that the presumed mechanisms that matter are integrated into curricular features of the classroom, and the intent is for students to learn SEL skills through academically meaningful experiences. Program theory and research suggests these mechanisms improve the quality of interactions in the classroom (Brown et al., 2010) and lead to distal outcomes (Jones et al., 2010, 2011).

These five interventions—Tribes, RULER, MindUP, RCCP, and 4Rs—show remarkable variety in their presumed mechanisms that matter. RULER, RCCP, and MindUP embed their intervention core components into curricula and explicit instruction in SEL. Even in the presence of that commonality, each targets a distinct SEL skill as primary: RULER emphasizes emotional skills, RCCP targets interpersonal skills, and MindUP focuses on cognitive skills. Both Tribes and RCCP target interpersonal skills; however, the presumed mechanism that matters in Tribes pertains to the classroom social environment, whereas RCCP views teaching student skills and techniques as primary. 4Rs is distinct among these five SEL interventions because of the way in which SEL learning is integrated with books, materials, and academic content. The five interventions share a common quality: They are school-based SEL interventions that look promising but require further research.

What Does Not Work

Looking inside the classroom provides a unique perspective on what does not work in elementary school SEL. Specific conditions need to be present for evidenced-based SEL interventions to translate into mechanisms that matter in the classroom. In this chapter, evidence of efficacy rests on the assumption that teachers implement intervention core components in ways that are consistent with program theory and the developer's intent. It is important to question this assumption. Thus, we describe three prominent factors that prevent SEL from being implemented successfully in elementary schools: (1) Interventions tend to be adopted but not fully used; (2) interventions are often adapted in ways that cause the intervention core components to lose their integrity; and (3) intervention efforts are often initiated in early childhood and not sustained over the course of students' development. Below, we describe each barrier to effective SEL programming and describe current work that casts light on the challenges that these barriers pose.

SEL interventions do not work if they are adopted but not fully utilized in the classroom (Webster-Stratton & Herman, 2010). The efficacy of SEL practices hinges on high fidelity of implementation, which means using the intervention core components as intended and designed (O'Donnell, 2008). In practice, this means that making the decision to adopt an intervention and training teachers in school-based interventions are only the initial steps toward actual production of the mechanisms that matter in the classroom. Theory and research provide several insights into conditions that contribute to high fidelity of implementation.

Teacher receptivity, high-quality teacher training, ongoing consultation and supportive coaching, administrative support and system-level alignment with the intervention represent a few of the provisions needed to ensure high-fidelity implementation (Fixsen, Blasé, Naoom, & Wallace, 2009). Teachers who feel more efficacious and less burned out adopt new SEL practices more readily than their counterparts who feel less efficacious and more burned out (Ransford, Greenberg, Domitrovich, Small, & Jacobson, 2009). Teachers are more likely to implement SEL interventions in the presence of administrative support and high-quality coaching experiences (Ransford et al., 2009; Wanless, Patton, Rimm-Kaufman, & Deutsch, 2013). Despite strong theory and new research, identification of conditions conducive to SEL implementation is far from straightforward. One recent study assessing teachers' comfort, commitment, and culture in relation to SEL showed that teachers who were more comfortable with and committed to SEL showed more openness to SEL programming (in this case, RULER). However, there was no empirical link among culture, comfort, and commitment to SEL early in the year and later implementation of RULER practices (Brackett, Reyes, Rivers, Elbertson, & Salovey, 2011). Further work is needed to identify and conduct rigorous tests of factors that contribute to full implementation of SEL interventions.

SEL interventions do not work if they are adapted to the point that they lose their potency. Many SEL interventions are packaged programs or approaches that teachers learn through manuals, trainings, and coaching experiences. However, as teachers apply SEL intervention core components to their classrooms, they may adapt the components to match the culturally specific, developmental, and individual needs of children, their own teaching style, as well as other features of their classroom and schools. Teachers face a delicate balance between implementing interventions with fidelity and adapting interventions to meet local circumstances, a topic that has been discussed elsewhere (Datnow & Stringfield, 2000; Hulleman et al., 2013; O'Donnell, 2008).

Managing problems related to adaptation requires empirically based identification of which intervention core components are more or less effective, then communication about the rationale and key ingredients behind those intervention core components to the teachers or other practitioners implementing and adapting the intervention. To start, very few interventions have the research base to differentiate between the more versus less effective intervention core components (Abry, Hulleman, & Rimm-Kaufman, in press). Thus, there is a need for rigorous research that identifies "evidence-based kernels" (Embry & Biglan, 2008, p. 75), defined as the specific practices that teachers use with their students that are critical to the success of the intervention. In addition to investigation, all interventions need to give clear explanations for *why* practices matter. SEL interventions need to be taught in such a way that teachers understand the purpose of each intervention core component, the psychological explanation supporting it, and the parameters for acceptable adaptation. Even in the absence of empirical data about which intervention core components are more effective than others, the quality of SEL practice can be improved by helping teachers understand the theory behind the practices that they use, so that they are more effective at deciding whether their adaptations are appropriate or whether they would diminish intervention efficacy.

Students may not retain SEL skills if they receive SEL interventions in early childhood without age-appropriate follow-up support. A review of the literature reveals that more SEL interventions are available for earlier grades (PreK–2) compared to the later grades (3–6). This imbalance is problematic. Developmental research shows normative declines in students' feelings about school, social competence, and aspects of self-control as they progress from the elementary into the middle school years. Declines may be partially attenuated by the presence of SEL interventions (Jones et al., 2011; Washburn et al., 2011) but, still, the declines exist at the exact time that school bonding and application of SEL skills to social and academic situations becomes important for long-term success. Strategic approaches to practice can address this issue. Some SEL interventions are designed around the fact that students in the upper elementary grades have different SEL skills and developmental needs than do students in earlier grades. Districts can lay out a plan for the development of students' SEL skills that begins in preschool years and extends through the high school years. Some promising social psychological interventions tap into self skills at pivotal moments in development, resulting in effective attributions or feelings of school belonging that have long-lasting influence on students over time, even without the presence of ongoing intervention (Yaeger & Walton, 2011).

Summary

Several consistent themes emerge in relation to elementary school-based SEL, although these interventions vary greatly in their approach and differ in the presumed mechanisms that matter. All point to the critical importance of learning and practicing SEL skills in the elementary school years for future growth and development. Obtaining SEL skills provides children with personal resources and relationship skills that enable them to benefit from and emotionally connect to positive classroom environments that contribute to further SEL and academic growth. Thus, either explicitly or implicitly, a guiding premise of most SEL programs is that they will set into a motion a positive recursive developmental process. Teaching children SEL skills enables them to utilize more fully the social and academic resources available to them. By teaching SEL skills to a classroom of students and facilitating their use of those skills in academic learning, teachers can improve students' access to the various growth opportunities available in the classroom.

Clear recommendations follow from looking *inside* classrooms. Researchers need to provide better road maps for decision making. A shift in focus is needed to understand what intervention core components are essential to its efficacy. Teachers working with children need opportunities to learn about SEL in ways that explain *why* and *how* an intervention works and *what* constitutes acceptable and unacceptable adaptations. SEL needs more replication trials, more research conducted across a variety of samples and ages, and, in particular, research that differentiates mechanisms that matter from less important intervention components. School practitioners, intervention developers, and researchers need to collaborate to construct continuous improvement practices to support practitioners' sustained use of high-quality SEL practices.

Looking *inside* classrooms provides insights into the future. Consider the effect that the accountability movement and standardized testing has placed on what occurs inside classrooms in schools in the United States. Establishing a metric of academic performance has modified day-to-day classroom experiences to focus on particular academic content and specific academic goals in elementary school classrooms. Consider the usefulness of a comparable national metric to assess students' social and emotional competencies. How would day-to-day classroom experiences differ if teachers were held accountable for students' emotional and social development? How would classroom social environments be different? What SEL skills would students exhibit regularly in their classrooms? Envisioning answers to these questions provides insight into how elementary school classrooms would change if national educational goals included SEL objectives designed to prepare students for school, work, and life ahead.

References

Aber, J. L., Pedersen, S., Brown, J. L., Jones, S. M., & Gershoff, E. T. (2003). *Changing children's trajectories of development: Two-year evidence for the effectiveness of a school-based approach to violence prevention.* New York: National Center for Children in Poverty.

Abry, T., Hulleman, C. S., & Rimm-Kaufman, S. E. (in press). Using indices of fidelity to intervention core components to identify program active ingredients. *American Journal of Evaluation.*

Abry, T., Rimm-Kaufman, S. E., Larsen, R. A., & Brewer, A. J. (2013). The influence of fidelity of implementation on teacher–student interaction quality in the context of a randomized controlled trial of the *Responsive Classroom* approach. *Journal of School Psychology, 51*, 437–453.

Academic, Social, and Emotional Learning Act. (2011). H. R. 2437. Retrieved January 16, 2014, from *www.govtrack.us/congress/bills/113/hr1875.*

Baroody, A. E., Rimm-Kaufman, S. E., Larsen, R. A., & Curby, T. W. (2014). The link between *Responsive Classroom* training and student–teacher relationship quality in the fifth grade: A study of fidelity of implementation. *School Psychology Review, 43*(1), 69–85.

Battistich, V., Schaps, E., & Wilson, N. (2004). Effects of an elementary school intervention on students' "connectedness" to school and social adjustment during middle school. *Journal of Primary Prevention, 24*(3), 243–262.

Battistich, V., Solomon, D., Kim, D., Watson, M., & Schaps, E. (1995). Schools as communities, poverty levels of student populations, and students' attitudes, motives, and performance: A multilevel analysis. *American Educational Research Journal, 32*(3), 627–658.

Beets, M. W., Flay, B. R., Vuchinich, S., Snyder, F. J., Acock, A., Li, K.-K., et al. (2009). Use of a social and character development program to prevent substance use, violent behaviors, and sexual activity among elementary-school students in Hawaii. *American Journal of Public Health, 99*(8), 1438–1445.

Brackett, M. A., Reyes, M. R., Rivers, S. E., Elbertson, N. A., & Salovey, P. (2011). Assessing teachers' beliefs about social and emotional learning. *Journal of Psychoeducational Assessment, 30*(3), 219–236.

Brackett, M. A., Rivers, S. E., Reyes, M. R., & Salovey, P. (2010). Enhancing academic performance and social and emotional competence with the RULER Feeling Words Curriculum. *Learning and Individual Differences, 22*(2), 218–224.

Brock, L. L., Nishida, T. K., Chiong, C., Grimm, K. J., & Rimm-Kaufman, S. E. (2008). Children's perceptions of the classroom environment and social and academic performance: A longitudinal analysis of the contribution of the responsive classroom approach. *Journal of School Psychology, 46*(2), 129–149.

Brown, J. L., Jones, S. M., LaRusso, M. D., & Aber, J. L. (2010). Improving classroom quality: Teacher influences and experimental impacts of the 4Rs program. *Journal of Educational Psychology, 102*(1), 153–167.

Chang, F., & Munoz, M. A. (2006). School personnel educating the whole child: Impact of character education on teachers' self-assessment and student development. *Journal of Personnel Evaluation in Education, 19*, 35–49.

Collaborative for Academic, Social, and Emotional

Learning [CASEL]. (2012). *The 2013 CASEL guide: Effective social and emotional learning programs—Preschool and elementary school edition*. Chicago: Author.

Collaborative for Academic, Social, and Emotional Learning [CASEL]. (2013). What is social and emotional learning? Retrieved July 20, 2013, from *www.casel.org/social-and-emotional-learning.*

Committee for Children. (2013). Second Step: Social Skills for Early Childhood—Grade 8. Retrieved December 22, 2013, from *www.cfchildren.org/second-step.aspx.*

Conduct Problems Prevention Research Group (CPPRG). (1999). Initial impact of the Fast Track prevention trial for conduct problems: I. The high risk sample. *Journal of Consulting and Clinical Psychology, 67*(5), 631–647.

Conduct Problems Prevention Research Group (CPPRG). (2010). The effects of a multiyear universal social–emotional learning program: The role of student and school characteristics. *Journal of Consulting and Clinical Psychology, 78*(2), 156–168.

Datnow, A., & Stringfield, S. (2000). Working together for reliable school reform. *Journal of Education for Students Placed at Risk, 5*(1–2), 183–204.

Developmental Studies Center. (2013). Caring School Community. Retrieved December 22, 2013, from *www.devstu.org/caring-school-community.*

Downer, J., Sabol, T. J., & Hamre, B. (2010). Teacher–child interactions in the classroom: Toward a theory of within-and cross-domain links to children's developmental outcomes. *Early Education and Development, 21*(5), 699–723.

Durlak, J. A., Weissberg, R. P., Dymnicki, A. B., Taylor, R. D., & Schellinger, K. B. (2011). The impact of enhancing students' social and emotional learning: A meta-analysis of school-based universal interventions. *Child Development, 82*(1), 405–432.

Dusenbury, L., Zadrazil, J., Mart, A., & Weissberg, R. (2011). State learning standards to advance social and emotional learning: The state scan of social and emotional learning standards, preschool through high school. Retrieved June 6, 2012, from *http://casel.org/wp-content/uploads/forum-brief-on-the-state-scan-5-10-2011.pdf.*

Educators for Social Responsibility. (2014). Resolving Conflict Creatively Program. Retrieved January 8, 2014, from *http://esrnational.org/professional-services/early-childhood-elementary-and-after-school-services/resolving-conflict-creatively-program.*

Elliott, S. (1999). A multi-year evaluation of the *Responsive Classroom* Approach: Its effectiveness and acceptability in promoting social and academic competence. Retrieved June 14, 2006, from *www.responsiveclassroom.org/pdf_files/final_report.pdf.*

Embry, D. D., & Biglan, A. (2008). Evidence-based kernels: Fundamental units of behavioral influence. *Clinical Child and Family Psychology Review, 11*(3), 75–113.

Fixsen, D. L., Blasé, K. A., Naoom, S. F., & Wallace, F. (2009). Core implementation components. *Research on Social Work Practice, 19*, 531–540.

Flay, B. R., Allred, C. G., & Ordway, N. (2001). Effects of the Positive Action program on achievement and discipline: Two matched-control comparisons. *Prevention Science, 2*(2), 71–89.

Frey, K. S., Nolen, S. B., Edstrom, L. V. S., & Hirschstein, M. K. (2005). Effects of a school-based social–emotional competence program: Linking children's goals, attributions, and behavior. *Applied Developmental Psychology, 26*, 171–200.

Greenberg, M. T. (2006). Promoting resilience in children and youth: Preventive interventions and their interface with neuroscience. *Annual New York Academy of Sciences, 1094*, 139–150.

Greenberg, M. T. (2010). School-based prevention: Current status and future challenges. *Effective Education, 2*(1), 27–52.

Greenberg, M. T., & Kusché, C. A. (1998). Preventive interventions for school-age deaf children: The PATHS curriculum. *Journal of Deaf Studies and Deaf Education, 3*(1), 49–63.

Hanson, T., Izu, J. A., Petrosino, A., Delong-Cotty, B., & Zheng, H. (2011). *A randomized experimental evaluation of the Tribes learning communities prevention program*. Washington, DC: WestEd.

Holsen, I., Smith, B. H., & Frey, K. S. (2008). Outcomes of the social competence program second step in Norwegian elementary schools. *School Psychology International, 29*, 71–91.

Hulleman, C. S., Rimm-Kaufman, S. E., & Abry, T. A. (2013). Whole–part–whole: Construct validity, measurement, and analytical issues for fidelity assessment in education research. In T. G. Halle, A. J. Metz, & I. Martinez-Beck (Eds.), *Applying implementation science in early childhood programs and systems* (pp. 65–93). Baltimore: Brookes.

Jennings, P. A., & Greenberg, M. T. (2009). The prosocial classroom: Teacher social and emotional competence in relation to student and classroom outcomes. *Review of Educational Research, 79*, 491–525.

Jones, S. M., & Bouffard, S. M. (2012). Social and emotional learning in schools: From programs to strategies. *Social Policy Report, 26*(4), 1–22.

Jones, S. M., Brown, J. L., & Aber, L. (2011). Two-year impacts of a universal school-based social–emotional and literacy intervention: An experiment in translational developmental research. *Child Development, 82*(2), 533–554.

Jones, S. M., Brown, J. L., Hoglund, W. L. G., & Aber, J. L. (2010). A school-randomized clinical trial of an integrated social–emotional learning and literacy intervention: Impacts after 1 school year. *Journal of Consulting and Clinical Psychology, 78*(6), 829–842.

Kam, C.-M., Greenberg, M. T., & Kusché, C. A. (2004). Sustained effects of the PATHS curriculum on the social and psychological adjustment of children in special education. *Journal of Emotional and Behavioral Disorders, 12*, 66–78.

Knowlton, L. W., & Phillips, C. C. (2008). *The logic model guidebook: Better strategies for great result.* Los Angeles: Sage.

Li, K.-K., Washburn, I., DuBois, D. L., Vuchinich, S., Ji, P., Brechling, V., et al. (2011). Effects of the positive action programme on problem behaviours in elementary school students: A matched-pair randomised control trial in Chicago. *Psychology and Health, 26*(2), 187–204.

Liew, J. (2012). Effortful control, executive functions, and education: Bringing self-regulatory and social–emotional competencies to the table. *Child Development Perspectives, 6*(2), 105–111.

MindUP. (2013). MindUP. Retrieved January 8, 2014, from *www.thehawnfoundation.org/mindup.*

Morningside Center. (2012). The 4Rs program. Retrieved January 8, 2014, from *www.morningsidecenter.org/node/36.*

Northeast Foundation for Children. (2011). The *Responsive Classroom* approach. Retrieved January 4, 2011, from *www.responsiveclassroom.org.*

O'Donnell, C. L. (2008). Defining, conceptualizing, and measuring fidelity of implementation and its relationship to outcomes in K–12 curriculum intervention research. *Review of Educational Research, 78*(1), 33–84.

Ottmar, E. R., Rimm-Kaufman, S. E., Berry, R. Q., & Larsen, R. A. A. (2013). Results from a randomized controlled trial: Does the *Responsive Classroom* approach impact the use of standards-based mathematics teaching practices? *Elementary School Journal, 113*(3), 434–457.

PATHS. (2013). How the PATHS program works. Retrieved January 8, 2014, from *www.channing-bete.com/prevention-programs/paths/overview.html.*

Positive Action. (2013). Positive Action. Retrieved December 22, 2013, from *www.positiveaction.net.*

Ransford, C. R., Greenberg, M. T., Domitrovich, C. E., Small, M., & Jacobson, L. (2009). The role of teachers' psychological experiences and perceptions of curriculum supports on the implementation of a social and emotional learning curriculum. *School Psychology Review, 38*(4), 510–532.

Reyes, M. R., Brackett, M. A., Rivers, S. E., Elbertson, N. A., & Salovey, P. (2012). The interaction effects of program training, dosage, and implementation quality on targeted student outcomes for the RULER approach to social and emotional learning. *School Psychology Review, 41*(1), 82–99.

Rimm-Kaufman, S. E., & Chiu, Y. I. (2007). Promoting social and academic competence in the classroom: An intervention study examining the contribution of the *Responsive Classroom* approach. *Psychology in the Schools, 44*(4), 397–413.

Rimm-Kaufman, S. E., Fan, X., Chiu, Y. J., & You, W. (2007). The contribution of the responsive classroom approach on children's academic achievement: Results from a three year longitudinal study. *Journal of School Psychology, 45*(4), 401–421.

Rimm-Kaufman, S. E., Larsen, R., Curby, T., Baroody, A., Merritt, E., Abry, T., et al. (2014). Efficacy of the Responsive Classroom Approach: Results from a three year, longitudinal randomized controlled trial. *American Educational Research Journal, 51*(3), 567–603.

Rivers, S. E., Brackett, M. A., Reyes, M. R., Elbertson, N. A., & Salovey, P. (2013). Improving the social and emotional climate of classrooms: A clustered randomized controlled trial testing the RULER approach. *Prevention Science, 14*(1), 77–87.

RULER. (2013). Emotions matter. Retrieved December 22, 2013, from *www.ei.yale/edu/ruler.*

Schick, A., & Cierpka, M. (2005). Faustlos: Evaluation of a curriculum to prevent violence in elementary schools. *Applied and Preventive Psychology, 11*, 157–165.

Schonert-Reichl, K. A., & Lawlor, M. S. (2010). The effects of a mindfulness-based education program on pre- and early adolescents' well-being and social and emotional competence. *Mindfulness, 1*(3), 137–151.

Skinner, E. A., Kindermann, T. A., Connell, J. P., & Wellborn, J. G. (2009). Engagement and disaffection as organizational constructs in the dynamics of motivational development. In K. R. Wentzel

& A. Wigfield (Eds.), *Handbook of motivation at school* (pp. 223–245). New York: Routledge.

Solomon, D., Battistich, V., Watson, M., Schaps, E., & Lewis, C. (2000). A six-district study of educational change: Direct and mediated effects of the child development project. *Social Psychology of Education, 4*(1), 3–51.

Tribes Learning Community. (2014). Tribes Learning Community. Retrieved January 8, 2014, from *www.tribes.com.*

U.S. Department of Education. (2013). What Works Clearinghouse. Retrieved June 1, 2013, from *http://ies.ed.gov/ncee/wwc.*

Wanless, S. B., Patton, C. L., Rimm-Kaufman, S. E., & Deutsch, N. L. (2013). Setting-level influences on implementation of the responsive classroom approach. *Prevention Science, 14*(1), 40–51.

Washburn, I. J., Acock, A., Vuchinich, S., Snyder, F., Li, K., Ji, P., et al. (2011). Effects of a social–emotional and character development program on the trajectory of behaviors associated with social–emotional and character development: Findings from three randomized trials. *Prevention Science, 12*(3), 314–323.

Webster-Stratton, C., & Herman, K. C. (2010). Disseminating Incredible Years series early-intervention programs: Integrating and sustaining services between school and home. *Psychology in the Schools, 47*(1), 36–54.

Yaeger, D. S., & Walton, G. M. (2011). Social-psychological interventions in education: They're not magic. *Review of Educational Research, 81*, 267–301.

Zins, J. E., Bloodworth, M. R., Weissberg, R. P., & Walberg, H. J. (Eds.). (2004). *The scientific base linking social and emotional learning to school success.* New York: Teachers College Press, Columbia University.

CHAPTER 11

A Review of Classroom-Based SEL Programs at the Middle School Level

Robert J. Jagers, Alexis Harris, and Alexandra Skoog

In this chapter, we review classroom-based social and emotional learning (SEL) programs for middle school students. These programs are intended for early adolescents, roughly 10–14 years of age and primarily in grades 6–8. Young people in this developmental period undergo considerable physical and cognitive maturation and are striving to demonstrate greater competence, achieve increased autonomy, and cultivate mutually beneficial relationships with others (e.g., Ryan & Deci, 2000). However, the middle school context and the increased social pressures associated with early adolescence can make it a difficult developmental period. This is especially true for youth of color from underresourced communities (Balfanz, Herzog, & MacIver, 2007; Eccles & Roeser, 2011).

Scholarship on SEL for elementary and secondary school students proposes that social–emotional competencies represent important developmental outcomes that can also enhance students' abilities to participate constructively in classroom settings and thereby support learning and academic achievement (Fleming et al., 2005). Importantly, a recent meta-analysis evaluating school-based interventions substantiates that SEL programs can promote adjustment in various ways in terms of more positive self-perceptions, social behaviors, prosocial attitudes, and academic performance, and decreases in conduct problems and emotional distress (Durlak, Weissberg, Dymnicki, Taylor, & Schellinger 2011). Much of the work in the area of SEL has focused on prekindergarten and elementary schoolchildren. There remains a need to identify SEL programs and practices that support the optimal development of youth during secondary school, particularly in the context of the unique challenges of the middle grades. This chapter examines the available evidence on programs promoting social–emotional competence for youth at the middle school level.

Definitions and Scope

Some basic research has shown that social and emotional competencies of middle school students significantly predict concurrent and prospective grade point average and achievement test scores (Fleming et al., 2005; Wentzel, 1993). This pattern of relationships is consistent with the development of academically successful, socially competent young people. However, other studies suggest that middle school can be a time of declining prosocial attitudes and prosocial behaviors (Carlo, Crockett, Randall, & Roesch, 2007; Jackson & Tisak, 2001), and academic motivation (Eccles & Roeser, 2011) and that there are various competence and risk profiles and trajectories among early adolescents (Zimmerman, Phelps, & Lerner, 2008). Risk factors such as school discipline problems, school disengagement, and academic underachievement can make youth vulnerable to engaging in problems behaviors such as fighting/violence, substance use (alcohol, tobacco, and other drugs [ATOD]) and unsafe sexual behaviors (e.g., early initiation and unprotected sex). Recent research suggests that these problem behaviors are less prevalent today than in the past two decades (Mulye et al., 2009). However, fighting/bullying, experimentation with cigarettes and marijuana, and unsafe sexual behaviors remain significant concerns among present-day youth, especially youth of color and those from low-resourced settings (Centers for Disease Control and Prevention, 2012). As such, the middle school years represent a prime time to promote social and emotional competencies not only to advance students' school performance but also to prevent some possible deterioration that might occur during this time period for some students.

It has been argued that the structure and relational context of middle-grades classrooms is often mismatched with adolescents' developmental needs, failing to facilitate the close relationships they strive for and to take advantage of their growing cognitive, social, and emotional competencies (Eccles & Roeser, 2011). Universal classroom-based SEL programs represent strategies to align the classroom content and context better with youth developmental needs. They can create space in the school day for applied learning of critical life skills relevant to the daily challenges that youth face, while also providing a safe and supportive interactional context to practice these skills with peers and nonfamilial adults. Such opportunities create classroom and school contexts that are more facilitative of positive adolescent developmental outcomes in the middle school years and beyond.

Core SEL Theories

Consistent with other chapters in this volume, our thinking about SEL programs is grounded in the Collaborative for Academic, Social, and Emotional Learning (CASEL; 2012) framework, which is anchored by five SEL competency domains that include skills considered essential to healthy development across the lifespan: *self-awareness, self-management, social awareness, relationship skills*, and *responsible decision making*. Several developmental frameworks have informed our understanding of youth social–emotional development. Consistent with the CASEL framework for SEL, a recent conceptualization of adolescent social–emotional competence developed by Guerra and Bradshaw (2008) integrates research in positive development and risk prevention. In their model, the five identified core social and emotional competencies reflect "what it means to be a healthy youth" (p. 4), and they include positive sense of self (e.g., self-awareness, agency, self-esteem), self-control (e.g., regulation and management of cognitions, emotional and behavior), decision making (e.g., making sound choices that minimize missteps and lead to positive outcomes), a moral system of beliefs (e.g., moral reasoning, perspective taking, and empathy), and prosocial connectedness (e.g., belonging; engagement and bonding in family, school, and community contexts). These core competencies are predictive of both positive development and risk prevention. They are reflective of the core elements of many empirically supported frameworks, models, and theories, such as positive youth development (Zimmerman et al., 2008), youth sociopolitical development (Watts & Flanagan, 2007), developmental theories of competence and resilience (Luthar, Cicchetti, & Becker, 2000; Masten, Burt, & Coatsworth, 2006), the social development model (Catalano & Hawkins, 1996; Catalano, Hawkins, & Smith, 2001), and the prosocial classroom model (Jennings & Greenberg, 2009). In this volume, Brackett, Elbertson, and Rivers (Chapter 2) provide a more complete treatment of prominent theories relevant to SEL.

Current Research

Given the importance of social–emotional competence promotion for middle school-age youth, in this review we attempt to identify and distinguish among middle school SEL programs that work, show promise, or do not work. At the middle school level, many relevant programs come from a prevention perspective and emphasize the prevention of substance use, violence, or other problem behaviors. We include such prevention-oriented programs under the umbrella of SEL when their core strategies involve promotion of competence or positive relationships within the environment. We define "programs that work" as those programs that have three or more successful randomized controlled or quasi-experimental trials of the intervention program. Successful trials are those that produce significant impacts in the expected direction on the targeted behavior(s). Programs with multiple outcomes were included if expected effects were found for a majority of the specified outcomes. Programs were classified as "promising" if they had fewer than three successful trials but yielded expected patterns of results in either evaluation or preliminary studies. Most of the programs reviewed were classified as promising. "Programs that do not work" are defined as programs that have been evaluated in at least three trials and do not achieve their intended impacts across the studies.

We attended to several aspects of the programs we reviewed, including their delivery and evaluation. One of the central dimensions is program characteristics, including whether the program focuses on explicit skills instruction and/or classroom structures and processes that promote development of social and emotional competence. The preponderance of reviewed studies focused on teaching youth explicit skills that would improve student behaviors. There was fairly little attention to teacher instructional practices.

The number and type of lessons used in the SEL skill instruction programs are also reported on in this review. In a recent meta-analysis, Durlak and colleagues (2011) concluded that SEL programs that use sequenced lessons, employ active learning opportunities, and focus on and are explicit about targeted skills tend to yield greater student outcomes. We also considered whether implementation was done by project staff or classroom teachers, and whether data on implementation quality was reported and/or incorporated into analyses of program effects. We found that although curricula varied in the number of lessons offered, most studies described curricula with the key features identified by Durlak and colleagues. Many programs in this review were implemented by health educators or prevention specialists. Most researchers commented on implementation quality, but there were relatively few efforts to discern whether implementation quality influenced reported program effects.

In addition, we were interested in the degree to which researchers sought to take the important step of testing mechanisms of action for intervention effects. This is consistent with examining the theories and conceptual frameworks that highlight the role of social–emotional competencies as mediators of intervention effects on problem behaviors (e.g., Guerra & Bradshaw, 2008) and academic achievement (Durlak et al., 2011). Relatively few studies we reviewed attempted such analyses.

Finally, we considered differential intervention effects for subgroups of participants (e.g., as a function of gender or risk status). Several of the reviewed studies probed whether the intervention impacted outcomes differently depending on the risk status of participants at baseline assessment.

Overview of Search Strategies

This review focuses primarily on research studies published in peer-reviewed journals. Dissertation studies were not included. Relevant studies were first identified through computer searches of PsycINFO, Education Resources Information Center (ERIC), and Google Scholar. Search terms included "social–emotional competence," "social–emotional learning programs," "social skills programs," "character education programs," and "risk prevention programs" (conflict resolution, bullying, substance use, unsafe sex, and violence). All terms were conditioned by early adolescence, middle school, or junior high school in order to keep the search maximally relevant. In addition, we searched the National Registry of Evidence-Based Programs and Practices (NREPP) provided through the Substance Abuse and Mental Health Services Administration (SAMHSA; *www.nrepp.samhsa.gov*) and the Institute of Education Science (IES; *whatworks.ed.gov*) What Works Clearinghouse for middle school character education programs.

Detailed abstracts were first reviewed to determine whether the studies were quantitative and included a control group design of a universal SEL intervention at the middle or junior high school level. Universal programs are made available to all youth, regardless of risk status. We opted to exclude studies of programs developed for youth at high risk (selected) or with identified social, emotional, or behavioral problems (targeted). A substantial portion of the available literature was considered in this review. However, the volume of the relevant literature and space limitations resulted in decisions about what programs to feature in this chapter. As such, we consider this an informed, but not exhaustive, review of middle school SEL programs.

Programs That Work

We found only two programs that met the criteria of having been examined in the context of at least three successful experimental studies. Table 11.1 outlines key findings for these programs.

Life Skills Training Program

Life Skills Training (LST) is primarily a substance use prevention program that emphasizes drug resistance skills in the context of promoting students' competence in personal and social skills related to self-management, healthy relationships, and responsible decision making. General skills taught include decision making, problem solving, goal setting, coping with anxiety and frustration, assertiveness, communication, and identifying and interpreting media influences. Specific drug resistance competence is addressed through knowledge, attitudes, and normative expectations about ATOD, as well as the promotion of resistance skills. The curriculum materials also include optional modules on violence prevention (Botvin & Griffin, 2004).

LST is designed to be taught by classroom teachers in middle schools (typically in health classes), with 15 core sessions in the first year and 15 booster sessions to be implemented over the following two years. Teaching methods emphasize cognitive-behavioral skills training and include didactic instruction, discussions, classroom demonstrations, experiential learning, feedback, and behavioral homework assignments.

A number of large randomized controlled trials and quasi-experimental studies document the expected effects of LST on youth outcomes (see Botvin & Griffin, 2004, for review). For example, students exposed to LST had lower ATOD use and higher resistance self-efficacy skills than controls at posttest and at 1-year follow-up, lower binge drinking at 1- and 2-year follow-ups, and improved normative expectations for substance use at posttest and both follow-

TABLE 11.1. Programs That Work

Program	Settings and populations	Design notes	Summary of significant outcomes
Life Skills Training	Diverse sixth and seventh graders	Multiple RCTs	Increased refusal skills and decreased substance use, fighting, delinquency, anxiety, risky driving and sexual behaviors; improved assertiveness, locus of control, decision making, and problem solving.
Responding in Peaceful and Positive Ways	Diverse sixth and seventh graders	Multiple QE trials with randomization	Decreased substance use, aggression and violent behavior, delinquent behavior, school code violations and knowledge and attitudes related to violence, increased peer support for nonviolence, decreased peer pressure to use drugs, physical aggression, substance use, and life satisfaction.

Note. RCTs, randomized controlled trials; QE, quasi-experimental.

ups (Botvin, Griffin, Diaz, & Ifill-Williams, 2001a, 2001b). Also, compared to controls, seventh-grade students receiving the LST program had less ATOD use, and fewer driving violations and points on their licenses at a 12th-grade follow-up (Botvin, 2000; Botvin, Baker, Dusenbury, Botvin, & Diaz, 1995) and less HIV risk behavior at age 24 years (Griffin, Botvin, & Nichols, 2004, 2006). Spoth, Clair, Shin, and Redmond (2006; Spoth, Randall, Trudeau, Shin, & Redmond, 2008) replicated the impact of LST on substance use and found that, compared to students in the control group, seventh-grade student participants in LST reported significantly lower rates of alcohol, tobacco, marijuana, and methamphetamine use at the 12th-grade follow-up.

In addition, LST has been associated with positive impacts on students' social–emotional competencies. Impacts on outcomes related to self-management and social skills vary across studies but have included assertiveness, locus of control, decision making, and problem solving (see Botvin & Griffin, 2004, for a review).

Botvin and colleagues have attended to implementation quality across these various trials, using trained staff to monitor implementation in selected classrooms. They report that implementation fidelity (e.g., completeness of lessons) and dosage (number of lessons) by teachers vary widely (Botvin & Griffin, 2004). These are important considerations; for example, Botvin, Griffin, and Nichols (2006) found significant differences in intervention effects on violence and delinquency outcomes based on whether students received more or less than half of the LST intervention.

Responding in Peaceful and Positive Ways

Responding in Peaceful and Positive Ways (RIPP) is a violence prevention curriculum that was originally developed for urban, African American middle school youth (Farrell, Meyer, & White, 2001), but it has also demonstrated efficacy in diverse rural middle schools (Farrell, Valois, & Meyer, 2002; Farrell, Valois, Meyer, & Tidwell, 2003). RIPP includes curricula for sixth, seventh, and eighth grades, but the eighth-grade curriculum was not evaluated in any of the four quasi-experimental trials of the program's efficacy. RIPP can be integrated into the academic curricula of social studies, health, and science, but it is designed to be taught by a trained prevention specialist and implemented in conjunction with a schoolwide peer mediation program. RIPP uses experiential and didactic activities to affect knowledge, attitudes, and schoolwide norms related to nonviolence and positive risk taking, and to promote skills for problem solving and conflict resolution.

The RIPP intervention targets violence prevention and conflict resolution at each grade level, but the foci of the curricula shift as students' progress through sixth to eighth grades, in an attempt to meet the unique developmental needs of students. In sixth grade, the program addresses sixth graders' increased experience of autonomy by emphasizing the recognition and avoidance of risks for violence in the environment. In response to seventh graders' increasing perspective-taking abilities and time spent with peers, the focus shifts more heavily to managing interpersonal conflict, especially in friendships. Finally, the eighth-grade curriculum emphasizes preparing students for the transition to high school.

Research evidence supports the efficacy of RIPP for preventing violence and other problem behaviors among students in urban and rural middle schools. Evaluation studies have demonstrated intervention impacts on knowledge and attitudes about violence, conflict-resolution strategies, and self-reported violent behavior (Farrell et al., 2001, 2002; Farrell, Meyer, Sullivan, & Kung, 2003; Farrell, Valois, et al., 2003). In addition to self-reported behavior, evaluators have examined school record data and demonstrated intervention effects on school disciplinary code violations for violent offenses and in-school suspensions. In some cases, impacts differed by gender or by pretest levels of aggressive/delinquent behavior (Farrell, Meyer, et al., 2003; Farrell et al., 2001). For example, students with the higher baseline problem behaviors were most likely to benefit from RIPP, and reductions in suspensions were sustained at 12-month follow-up for boys but not girls. Furthermore, in one evaluation, RIPP improved students' life satisfaction outcomes relative to controls (Farrell, Valois, et al., 2003). Although substance use is not an outcome specifically targeted by the program, it has been consistently measured in evaluations. Impacts on self-reported drug use and pressure to use drugs have been mixed, with most studies reporting no significant intervention effects in this area.

Promising Programs

The majority of programs reviewed in this chapter are classified as promising programs. These programs have some evidence, usually in a controlled study, of expected effects. Key findings for these programs appear in Table 11.2.

Aban Aya Youth Project

Aban Aya Youth Project (AAYP) is a multicomponent (classroom, family, and community) program designed to prevent the onset and growth of violence, substance use, and unsafe sexual behaviors among African American middle school students. AAYP is grounded in African American cultural val-

TABLE 11.2. Promising Programs

Program	Settings and population	Design notes	Significant outcomes
Aban Aya Youth Project	Low-income African American fifth through eighth graders	RCT	Increased empathy and violence reduction; significant decreases in the growth of violence, provoking behaviors, delinquency, substance use, and unsafe sex for boys
All Stars (and All Stars Plus)	Predominately white sixth and seventh graders	2 QE studies	Increased goal setting, school bonding, and perceived parental attention, commitments, ideals, reduced violence, sexual activity, substance use, beliefs about lifestyle incongruence of substance use
Facing History and Ourselves	Predominantly white urban and suburban eighth graders	QE	Increased social competence, reduced racist attitudes
Keepin' It Real	Predominately urban Latino seventh graders	RCT	Decreased substance use, norms, attitudes, and improved resistance strategies
Lions Quest	Diverse seventh graders	RCT	Decreased lifetime marijuana use; recent marijuana use; binge drinking for baseline drinkers
MindUP	Diverse fourth and seventh graders (Canada)	QE	Improved teacher-rated attention/concentration and social–emotional competence; mixed results for general self-concept
Olweus	Diverse sixth through eighth graders	1 QE, 1 noncontrolled evaluation	Decreased bullying, victimization, and isolation for boys and white students; increased empathy and support for bullied peers
TimeWise	Predominantly white rural seventh graders	QE	Positive leisure participation and leisure time use, planning and decision making, initiative, and motivation

Note. RCT, randomized controlled trial; QE, quasi-experimental.

ues such as unity, self-determination, and collective responsibility (Flay et al., 2004).

The Aban Aya Social Development Curriculum (AA-SDC) is a classroom curriculum that includes 16–21 lessons across grades 5–8 that may be integrated with social studies curricula. The SDC promotes social–emotional development (e.g., communication, stress and anger management, decision making, problem solving and conflict resolution, and social networking) and a sense of self and purpose (e.g., empathy, future planning, and personal strengths), while also targeting attitudes, beliefs, and perceived peer and family norms and pressures that can prompt problem behaviors such as violence, delinquency, substance use, and unsafe sex. Program activities emphasize culturally relevant teaching methods and incorporate African American history and literature. The Aban Aya School and Community Intervention (AA-SCI) condition targets the school climate and parenting practices through school, family, and community task force activities.

In a randomized trial of AAYP, the interventions produced reductions in the growth of violent behavior, substance use, unsafe sex, provoking behavior, and school misbehavior over time for boys (Flay et al., 2004). Evidence suggests that the program effects for both substance use and violence were mediated by increases in negative personal attitudes and beliefs, and decreases in estimates of peer norms and pressures supporting these behaviors (Liu, Flay, & the Aban Aya Investigators, 2009; Ngwe, Liu, Flay, Segawa, & the Aban Aya Investigators, 2004). Furthermore, the violence reduction effect of AAYP was due in part to the program's positive impact on the growth of students' empathy (Jagers, Morgan-Lopez, Howard, Browne, & Flay, 2007). In addition, compared to controls, the AA-SCI condition reduces violent behavior among students who joined the program after its inception (Jagers, Morgan-Lopez, & Flay, 2009).

All Stars

All Stars is a character education and problem behavior prevention program that aims to slow the onset of adolescent risky behaviors, particularly substance use and sexual activity, by reducing students' motivations to engage in such behaviors. Like many other prevention-oriented programs, All Stars Core targets students' normative expectations about substance use. In addition, the All Stars Core approach includes the promotion of bonding to the school community, beliefs around the incongruence of risky behaviors with students' valued lifestyles, and personal commitments to avoid risk behaviors. The All Stars Plus curriculum is an extension of the Core curriculum that promotes competency in decision making, goal setting, and peer pressure resistance skills.

All Stars Core and Plus curricula are designed to be taught in middle schools in health class or in shorter sessions in advisory periods, and may also include one-on-one meetings between teachers and students and homework activities to be completed with parents. The curricula are interactive and include discussions, role plays, games, and other activities.

Based on two quasi-experimental[1] trials in which All Stars was implemented by classroom or health teachers, there is evidence to support the impact of All Stars on its social–emotional mediators, including commitments, beliefs about lifestyle incongruence, school bonding, and decision making, and mixed evidence of its impact on normative beliefs. Prevention effects on substance use were also evident for the All Stars Core and Plus curricula (Hansen & Dusenbury, 2004; Harrington, Giles, Hoyle, Feeney, & Yungbluth, 2001; McNeal, Hansen, Harrington, & Giles, 2004). Although All Stars is quite promising when implemented by classroom teachers, there is evidence that it is not effective when implemented by outside specialists or in the context of after-school programs (Gottfredson, Cross, Wilson, Rorie & Connell, 2010; Harrington et al., 2001; McNeal et al., 2004).

Facing History and Ourselves

Facing History and Ourselves (FHAO) is a character education program integrated into regular social studies and language arts instruction, and it employs historical examples of conflict, injustice, and discrimination to teach tolerance, social skills, and civic responsibility. The program also targets teaching practices and classroom climate. Although it has been evaluated in multiple trials, including one effectiveness trial, to date only one trial that included middle school students has been published in a peer-reviewed journal.

A quasi-experimental trial (pre–post, nonrandomized controls) involving predominantly white urban and suburban eighth-grade classrooms demonstrated significant impacts on students psychosocial competence and racist attitudes, as well as marginal effects on students' fighting behavior, but not on civic awareness or moral reasoning (Schultz, Barr, & Selman, 2001). More recently, a randomized effectiveness trial was conducted in low-income, urban, middle school classrooms (seventh and eighth grades). This study is not yet published, but the investigators report promising results in the areas of students' social–emotional functioning, self-reported prosocial behavior and conduct problems, civic attitudes, and perceptions of school and classroom climate (Domitrovich et al., 2014).

Keepin' It Real

Keepin' It Real (KIR), a middle school substance use prevention skills-training program, targets the SEL area of responsible decision making (Hecht et al., 2003). KIR features a 10-lesson curriculum that uses videos to help teachers to highlight narrative and performance elements of the program. The KIR curriculum materials are grounded in youth, ethnic, and gender cultures to strengthen its relevance to middle school students. For example, the Mexican American and African American versions of KIR were constructed from cultural narratives and literature on cultural values endorsed within each culturally distinct group. These insights informed the content of core program elements of communication competence, narrative-based knowledge, social norms and motivations, social learning of life skills, decision making and risk assessment, and drug resistance strategies used in each version. A multicultural version combined content from each of these culture-specific curricula.

In a test of the three versions of the program, observations of teachers revealed that most were appropriately implementing the program materials. Compared to controls, students exposed to KIR had more favorable outcomes in terms of attitudes, use of resistance strategies, and self-reported substance use, especially use of alcohol and marijuana (Hecht et al., 2003; Hecht, Graham, & Elek, 2006). The Multicultural version was most broadly effective, but the Mexican American version also had significant impacts. Although the original seventh-grade version of the program demonstrated these promising outcomes, a modified version of the program that was later tested in a trial with fifth and seventh graders did not demonstrate any positive impacts on student behavior (Elek, Wagstaff, & Hecht, 2010).

Lions Quest

Lions Quest Skills for Adolescence (SFA) is a comprehensive social–emotional skills program addressing all five SEL domains, including a module specifically focused on the prevention of ATOD use. The developers have created multiple implementation models for middle schools that span from 1 to 3 years. SFA uses interactive lessons to promote skills such as emotion management, self-concept, personal responsibility, communication and assertiveness, decision making, and resistance skills. Additional modules include bullying prevention and service learning.

An effectiveness trial has demonstrated the substance use prevention impact of Lions Quest SFA. Compared to the control condition, substance use (marijuana and alcohol) was significantly lowered in schools participating in a version of SFA that featured eight required lessons related to preventing drug use (Eisen, Zellman, & Murray, 2003). Students' self-efficacy for resisting substance use was also positively impacted in Lions Quest SFA schools. Lions Quest SFA includes a comprehensive set of lessons promoting adolescents' social–emotional skills but, unfortunately, the extent of students' gains in skills such as emotion management and communication has not been evaluated.

MindUP

Schonert-Reichl and Lawlor (2010) conducted a quasi-experimental study of the MindUP (MU) program. Mindfulness is defined as "bringing one's complete attention to the present experience on a moment to moment basis with a non-judgmental stance" (Schonert-Reichl & Lawlor, 2010, p. 143). A 10-lesson curriculum is used by classroom teachers to help students accomplish four key program goals: quieting the mind, developing mindful attention, managing negative thoughts and feelings, and acknowledging self and others. Lessons are intended to be delivered for 40–50 minutes, once a week, over a 3-month period. Classroom teachers receive a 1-day training and biweekly consultation from the program developers. Although the curriculum includes detailed scripts, the training employs interactive discussions of achieving classroom implementation using lecture, readings, videos, and role play.

In their initial study, Schonert-Reichl and Lawlor (2010) compared a relatively small number of MU and control classrooms of preadolescents (grades 4 and 5) and early adolescents (grades 6 and 7) in terms of possible changes in optimism, self-concept, and social-emotional competencies. Monitoring of implementation fidelity revealed that teachers delivered a high percentage of the specified mindfulness exercises each week (72–100%). Results indicated that, compared to students in the control classrooms, students in the MU classrooms reported greater optimism at posttest. In addition, classroom teachers indicated that MU students were more attentive, displayed more emotional regulation, were more socially and emotionally competent than students in control classrooms. Among younger participants, those in the MU condition were found to have improved self-concept levels, whereas there was a decrease in self-concept among controls. In contrast, early adolescents in the intervention condition reported a decrease in self-concept, while those in the control condition were found to have increased self-concept.

Olweus Bullying Prevention Program

The Olweus Bullying Prevention Program (OBPP) was originally designed to reduce existing bullying, to prevent the onset of new bullying problems, and generally to improve adult–student and student–student relations in Norwegian elementary, middle, and high schools (Olweus, 1993). The program is based on adults acting as role models and authority figures, showing warmth toward and interest in students, and using consistent nonaggressive consequences to address student's rule violations.

OBPP uses several program components to impact at the level of the community, school, classroom, and the individual. A Bullying Prevention Coordinating Committee comprised of school administrators, teachers, and other school staff, parents, and several community members serves to organize the deployment of OBPP. This group is trained by a certified OBPP trainer and develops plans for implementing the program in the school. After establishing rules about bullying within the school community, weekly classroom meetings are held to discuss and role-play ways to deal with direct or indirect bullying exposure and related issues. Staff discussion groups are used to support fidelity of implementation through conversations about bullying and the OBPP.

Initial evaluation studies in Norway revealed reduced levels of perceived and experienced bullying victimization and bullying of others (Olweus & Limber, 2010). Despite the popularity of OBPP, relatively few evaluation studies have been conducted in U.S. schools. Among these, Limber, Nation, Tracy, Melton, and Flerx (2004) reported on a 2-year pre–post design study in which participating students reported a decrease in bullying of others in Year 1, but that dissipated in Year 2. Similarly, boys reported decreases in both being bullied and feeling isolated in Year 1 that were not obtained in Year 2 when implementation support was minimized. Similar nonsignificant trends were found for girls. Contrary to expectation, there were decreases in reported bystander intervention into bullying and bullying incidents being reported to parents. The authors attribute these two findings to reduced frequency of bullying incidents.

Bauer, Lozano, and Rivara (2007) conducted a controlled trial of OBPP with middle school students. Compared to controls, sixth-grade students in the intervention condition felt more empathy for a bullied peer. Overall, students across all grades in the intervention schools were more likely to perceive other students as helping peers experiencing bullying. However, only white students in their sample reported significant reductions in relational and physical victimization when compared to controls. There were no such effects for students from other racial/ethnic backgrounds.

TimeWise

TimeWise, a leisure education program that aims to promote positive developmental trajectories of leisure time use and to prevent substance and other problem behaviors (Caldwell, Baldwin, Walls, & Smith, 2004), addresses the SEL areas of self-awareness, self-management, and responsible decision making by specifically targeting positive leisure awareness and participation, motivation, well-being, and other competencies related to leisure time use. The TimeWise program is a good fit for implementation within middle school health and physical education curricula and involves six topics, covered over 12 days, plus additional optional topics.

A quasi-experimental trial evaluating TimeWise showed significant intervention effects in motivation, well-being, and leisure-related competencies, such as planning and decision making, ability to restructure, and initiative. In addition, TimeWise was associated with increased awareness, interest, and participation in positive leisure activities (Caldwell et al., 2004). The developers of TimeWise are currently evaluating HealthWise, a modification of the TimeWise program for eighth- and ninth-grade students, with expanded content targeting the management of anxiety and emotions, and the prevention of substance use and risky sexual behaviors. Although HealthWise has only been implemented in South Africa, there is evidence that it is a promising approach to impacting leisure motivation and preventing risky behaviors such as substance use and sexual risk taking (Caldwell, Patrick, & Smith, 2010; Caldwell et al., 2008; Smith et al., 2008).

Programs That Do Not Work

No programs in the available literature that were evaluated in three trials did not yield expected findings across studies.

Future Directions

This review points to a number of programs and practices that reduce risk and have the potential to promote desirable social–emotional competencies at the middle school level. It also is evident that considerable work is needed in order to test adequately and effectively disseminate SEL to middle school youth.

Very few middle school SEL programs have been subjected to multiple evaluation trials, and even fewer of these are randomized controlled trials. Some efforts to replicate programs have not generated expected findings (Komro et al., 2010; St. Pierre, Osgood, Mincemoyer, Kaltreider, & Kauh, 2005). In addition, the majority of the findings highlighted in this review provide evidence of prevention and/or reductions in problem behaviors. This is important at the middle school level because many problem behaviors first emerge during this developmental period. However, there are numerous ways in which future work on middle school SEL can be improved.

For example, more research is needed into program effects on the growth and promotion of social–emotional competencies in middle school youth. Many prevention-oriented programs target social–emotional competencies as hypothesized mediators of impacts on problem behaviors. Unfortunately, few studies have tested the proposed mediating effects of SEL skills on problem behaviors. Moreover, social–emotional competencies in and of themselves represent important developmental outcomes. Youth civic engagement outcomes warrant particular attention in this regard. Follow-up data are desirable in order to understand the long-term program impacts and additional supports required for optimal youth development. In addition, there is a need to understand better the ways in which gender, socioeconomic status, race, and cultural background of participating youth influence program effectiveness. This includes explicit attention to how these issues are addressed in program theory, content, delivery, and evaluation.

Future work in this area also needs to consider the characteristics of the program implementer. Programs have varied in terms of whether project staff or classroom teachers delivered the program. Full integration and sustainability of a classroom program requires classroom teachers to act as implementers if the program is going to become part of everyday school practice. A few of the classroom-focused skills-development programs (All Stars and KIR) have begun to consider the importance of teacher's pedagogic practices in program delivery (Giles et al., 2008; Harthun, Drapeau, Dustman, & Marsiglia, 2008). Attention to teachers should include investigation of setting-level supports (Wanless, Patton, Rimm-Kaufman, & Deutsch, 2013), their social–emotional competencies, typical teaching practices, and motivation as correlates of the quality of implementation of SEL programs and eventual impact on their students (Jennings & Greenberg, 2009; Kwame-Ross, Crawford, & Klug, 2011).

Finally, we limited this review to classroom-based SEL programs. However, there are a number of effective family- and community-based SEL programs for middle school students that warrant attention by researchers and practitioners concerned with this age group, particularly if they are linked to school-based efforts (see Garbacz, Swanger-Gagné, & Sheridan, Chapter 16, this volume). Programs that include school, family, and community components can create continuity in the lived experiences of youth from diverse backgrounds. Research designs that allow for the testing of separate and interactive effects of school, family, and community can shed light on essential features that maximize the academic, social, and emotional growth of early adolescent youth, especially those from underresourced backgrounds.

Note

1. All Stars Core has been subjected to an independent evaluation with a randomized experimental design. In this study, however, the condition in which teachers implemented the curriculum was not randomized, and the randomized condition in which specialists taught did not effectively impact most mediators or any of the problem behavior outcomes. For these reasons, we consider the evidence from this trial supporting the efficacy of All Stars when implemented by teachers to be quasi-experimental.

References

Balfanz, R., Herzog, L., & MacIver, D. J. (2007). Preventing student disengagement and keeping students on the graduation path in urban middle-grades schools: Early identification and effective interventions. *Educational Psychologist, 42*, 223–235.

Bauer, N., Lozano, P., & Rivara, F. P. (2007). The effectiveness of the Olweus Bullying Prevention Program in public middle schools: A controlled trial. *Journal of Adolescent Health, 40*, 266–274.

Botvin, G. J. (2000). Preventing drug abuse in schools: Social and competence enhancement approaches targeting individual-level etiologic factors. *Addictive Behaviors, 25*, 887–897.

Botvin, G. J., Baker, E., Dusenbury, L., Botvin, E. M., & Diaz, T. (1995). Long-term follow-up results of a randomized drug abuse prevention trial in a white middle-class population. *Journal of the American Medical Association, 273*(14), 1106–1112.

Botvin, G. J., & Griffin, K. W. (2004). Life skills training: Empirical findings and future directions. *Journal of Primary Prevention, 25*(2), 211–232.

Botvin, G. J., Griffin, K. W., Diaz, T., & Ifill-Williams, M. (2001a). Drug abuse prevention among minority adolescents: Posttest and one-year follow-up of a school-based preventive intervention. *Prevention Science, 2*(1), 1–13.

Botvin, G. J., Griffin, K. W., Diaz, T., & Ifill-Williams, M. (2001b). Preventing binge drinking during early adolescence: One- and two-year follow-up of a school-based preventive intervention. *Psychology of Addictive Behaviors, 15*(4), 360–365.

Botvin, G. J., Griffin, K. W., & Nichols, T. R. (2006). Preventing youth violence and delinquency through a universal school-based prevention approach. *Prevention Science, 7*, 403–408.

Caldwell, L. L., Baldwin, C. K., Walls, T., & Smith, E. (2004). Preliminary effects of a leisure education program to promote healthy use of free time among middle school students. *Journal of Leisure Research, 36*, 310–335.

Caldwell, L., Patrick, M., & Smith, E. (2010). Influencing adolescent leisure motivation: Intervention effects of HealthWise South Africa. *Journal of Leisure Research, 42*, 203–220.

Caldwell, L., Younker, A., Wegner, L., Patrick, M. E., Vergnani, T., Smith, E. A., et al. (2008). Understanding leisure-related program effects by using process data in the HealthWise South Africa project. *Journal of Park and Recreation Administration, 26*(2), 146–162.

Carlo, G., Crockett, L. J., Randall, B. A., &

Roesch, S. C. (2007). Parent and peer correlates of prosocial development in rural adolescents: A longitudinal study. *Journal of Research on Adolescence, 17,* 301–324.

Catalano, R. F., & Hawkins, J. D. (1996). The social development model. In J. D. Hawkins (Ed.), *Delinquency and crime: Current theories* (pp. 149–197). New York: Cambridge University Press.

Catalano, R. F., Hawkins, J. D., & Smith, B. H. (2001). Delinquent behavior. *Pediatrics in Review, 23*(11), 387–392.

Collaborative for Academic, Social, and Emotional Learning (CASEL). (2012). *Effective social and emotional learning programs: Preschool and elementary school edition.* Chicago: Author.

Centers for Disease Control and Prevention. (2012). Youth Risk Behavior Surveillance—United States, 2011. *Morbidity and Mortality Weekly Report Surveillance Summaries, 61,* 1–168.

Domitrovich, C. E., Harris, A. R., Syvertsen, A. K., Cleveland, M., Moore, J. E., Jacobson, L., et al. (2014). *The effects of Facing History and Ourselves on classroom climate and middle school students' attitudes and behaviors.* Manuscript in preparation.

Durlak, J. A., Weissberg, R. P., Dymnicki, A. B., Taylor, R. D., & Schellinger, K. B. (2011). The impact of enhancing students' social and emotional learning: A meta-analysis of school-based universal interventions. *Child Development, 82*(1), 405–432.

Eccles, J. S., & Roeser, R. W. (2011). School as developmental context during adolescence. *Journal of Research on Adolescence, 21*(1), 225–241.

Eisen, M., Zellman, G. L., & Murray, D. M. (2003). Evaluating the Lions-Quest "Skills for Adolescence" drug education program: Second-year behavior outcomes. *Addictive Behaviors, 28,* 883–897.

Elek, E., Wagstaff, D. A., & Hecht, M. L. (2010). Effects of the 5th and 7th grade enhanced versions of the *Keepin' It REAL* substance use prevention curriculum. *Journal of Drug Education, 40*(1), 61–79.

Farrell, A., Meyer, A., Sullivan, T., & Kung, E. (2003). Evaluation of the Responding in Peaceful and Positive Ways (RIPP) seventh grade violence prevention curriculum. *Journal of Child and Family Studies, 12*(1), 101–120.

Farrell, A. D., Meyer, A. L., & White, K. S. (2001). Evaluation of Responding in Peaceful and Positive Ways (RIPP): A school-based prevention program for reducing violence among urban adolescents. *Journal of Clinical Child Psychology, 30*(4), 451–463.

Farrell, A., Valois, R., & Meyer, A. (2002). Evaluation of the RIPP-6 violence prevention program at a rural middle school. *American Journal of Health Education, 33,* 167–172.

Farrell, A. D., Valois, R. F., Meyer, A. L., & Tidwell, R. P. (2003). Impact of the RIPP violence prevention program on rural middle school students. *Journal of Primary Prevention, 24*(2), 143–167.

Flay, B. R., Graumlich, S., Segawa, E., Burns, J. L., Holliday, M. Y., & the Aban Aya Investigators. (2004). Effects of two prevention programs on high-risk behaviors among African American youth. *Archives of Pediatric and Adolescent Medicine, 158,* 377–384.

Fleming, C. B., Haggerty, K. P., Catalano, R. F., Harachi, T. W., Mazza, J. J., & Gruman, D. H. (2005). Do social and behavioral characteristics targeted by preventive interventions predict standardized test scores and grades? *Journal of School Health, 75,* 342–349.

Giles, S. M., Jackson-Newsom, J., Pankratz, M. M., Ringwalt, C. L., Hansen, W. B., & Dusenbury, L. (2008). Measuring quality of delivery in a substance use prevention program. *Journal of Primary Prevention, 28*(6), 489–501.

Gottfredson, D. C., Cross, A., Wilson, D., Rorie, M., & Connell, N. (2010). An experimental evaluation of the All Stars prevention curriculum in a community after school setting. *Prevention Science, 11*(2), 142–154.

Griffin, K. W., Botvin, G. J., & Nichols, T. R. (2004). Long-term follow-up effects of a school-based drug abuse prevention program on adolescent risky driving. *Prevention Science, 5*(3), 207–212.

Griffin, K. W., Botvin, G. J., & Nichols, T. R. (2006). Effects of a school-based drug abuse prevention program for adolescents on HIV risk behavior in young adulthood. *Prevention Science, 7*(1), 103–112.

Guerra, N. G., & Bradshaw, C. (2008). Linking prevention of problem behaviors and positive youth development: Core competencies for positive youth development. *New Directions in Child and Adolescent Development, 122,* 1–17.

Hansen, W., & Dusenbury, L. (2004). All Stars Plus: A competence and motivation enhancement approach to prevention. *Health Education, 104*(6), 371–381.

Harrington, N. G., Giles, S. M., Hoyle, R. H., Feeney, G. J., & Yungbluth, S. C. (2001). Evaluation of the All Stars problem behavior prevention program: Effects on mediator and outcome variables for middle school students. *Health Education and Behavior, 28,* 533–546.

Harthun, M. L., Drapeau, A. E., Dustman, P. A., & Marsiglia, F. F. (2008). Implementing a prevention curriculum: An effective researcher–teacher partnership. *Education and Urban Society, 34*, 353–364.

Hecht, M. L., Graham, J. W., & Elek, E. (2006). The drug resistance strategies intervention: Program effects on substance use. *Health Communication, 20*(3), 267–276.

Hecht, M. L., Marsiglia, F. F., Elek, E., Wagstaff, D. A, Kulis, S., Dustman, P., et al. (2003). Culturally grounded substance use prevention: An evaluation of the Keepin' It R.E.A.L. curriculum. *Prevention Science, 4*(4), 233–248.

Jackson, M., & Tisak, M. S. (2001). Is prosocial behaviour a good thing?: Developmental changes in children's evaluations of helping, sharing, cooperating and comforting. *British Journal of Developmental Psychology, 19*, 349–367.

Jagers, R. J., Morgan-Lopez, A. A., & Flay, B. R. (2009). The impact of age and type of intervention on youth violent behaviors. *Journal of Primary Prevention, 30*(6), 642–658.

Jagers, R. J., Morgan-Lopez, A. A., Howard, T., Browne, D. C., & Flay, B. R. (2007). Mediators of the development and prevention of violent behavior. *Prevention Science, 8*(3), 171–179.

Jennings, P. A., & Greenberg, M. T. (2009). The prosocial classroom: Teacher social and emotional competence in relation to student and classroom outcomes. *Review of Educaional Research, 79*(1), 491–525.

Komro, K. A., Perry, C. L., Veblen-Mortenson, S., Farbakhsh, K., Toomey, T. L., Stigler, M. H., et al. (2010). Outcomes from a randomized controlled trial of a multi-component alcohol use preventive intervention for urban youth: Project Northland Chicago. *Addiction, 103*, 606–618.

Kwame-Ross, T., Crawford, L., & Klug, E. (2011). Developmental designs: A description of the approach and implementation in schools. *Middle Grades Research Journal, 6*(3), 145–162.

Limber, S. P., Nation, M., Tracy, A. J., Melton, G. B., & Flerx, V. (2004). Implementation of the Olweus Bullying Prevention programme in the Southern United States. In P. K. Smith, D. Pepler, & K. Rigby (Eds.), *Bullying in schools: How successful can intervention be?* (pp. 55–79). Cambridge, UK: Cambridge University Press.

Liu, L. C., Flay, B. R., & the Aban Aya Investigators. (2009). Evaluating mediation in longitudinal multivariate data: Mediation effects for the Aban Aya Youth Project Drug Prevention Program. *Prevention Science, 10*, 197–207.

Luthar, S. S., Cicchetti, D., & Becker, B. (2000). The construct of resilience: A critical evaluation and guidelines for future work. *Child Development, 71*(3), 543–562.

Masten, A. S., Burt, K., & Coatsworth, J. D. (2006). Competence and psychopathology. In D. Cicchetti & D. Cohen (Eds.), *Developmental psychopathology, Vol 3. Risk, disorder and psychopathology* (2nd ed., pp. 696–738). New York: Wiley.

McNeal, R. B., Hansen, W. B., Harrington, N. G., & Giles, S. M. (2004). How All Stars works: An examination of program effects on mediating variables. *Health Education and Behavior, 31*, 165–178.

Mulye, T. P., Park, M. J., Nelson, C. D., Adams, S. H., Irwin, C. E., & Brindis, C. D. (2009). Trends in adolescent and young adult health in the United States. *Journal of Adolescent Health, 45*, 8–24.

Ngwe, J. E., Liu, L. C., Flay, B. R., Segawa, E., & the Aban Aya Investigators. (2004). Violence prevention among African American adolescent males. *American Journal of Health Behavior, 28*(Suppl. 1), S24–S37.

Olweus, D. (1993). *Bullying at school: What we know and what we can do.* Oxford, UK: Blackwell.

Olweus, D., & Limber, S. P. (2010). The Olweus Bullying Prevention Program: Implementation and evaluation over two decades. In S. R. Jimerson, S. M. Swearer, & D. L. Espelage (Eds.), *The handbook of school bullying: An international perspective* (pp. 377–402). New York: Routledge.

Ryan, R., & Deci, E. (2000). The darker and brighter sides of human existence: Basic psychological needs as a unifying concept. *Psychological Inquiry, 11*, 319–338.

Schonert-Reichl, K. A., & Lawlor, M. S. (2010). The effects of a mindfulness-based education program on pre- and early adolescents' well-being and social and emotional competence. *Mindfulness, 1*, 137–151.

Schultz, L. H., Barr, D. J., & Selman, R. L. (2001). The value of a developmental approach to evaluating character development programmes: An outcome study of Facing History and Ourselves. *Journal of Moral Education, 30*(1), 3–27.

Smith, E. A., Palen, L., Caldwell, L. L., Flisher, A. J., Graham, J. W., Mathews, C., et al. (2008). Substance use and sexual risk prevention in Cape Town, South Africa: An evaluation of the HealthWise program. *Prevention Science, 9*(4), 311–321.

Spoth, R. L., Clair, S., Shin, C., & Redmond, C. (2006). Long-term effects of universal preventive interventions on methamphetamine use among adolescents. *Archives of Pediatrics and Adolescent Medicine, 160*(9), 876–882.

Spoth, R. L., Randall, G. K., Trudeau, L., Shin, C., & Redmond, C. (2008). Substance use outcomes

5½ years past baseline for partnership-based, family-school preventive interventions. *Drug and Alcohol Dependence, 96*(1–2), 57–68.

St. Pierre, T. L., Osgood, D. W., Mincemoyer, C. C., Kaltreider, D. L., & Kauh T. J. (2005). Results of an independent evaluation of Project ALERT delivered in schools by Cooperative Extension. *Prevention Science, 6*(4), 305–317.

Wanless, S. B., Patton, C. L., Rimm-Kaufman, S. E., & Deutsch, N. L. (2013). Setting-level influences on implementation of the Responsive Classroom approach. *Prevention Science, 14*(1), 40–51.

Watts, R. J., & Flanagan, C. (2007). Pushing the envelope on youth civic engagement: A developmental and liberation psychology. *Journal of Community Psychology, 35*, 779–792.

Wentzel, K. R. (1993). Social and academic goals at school: Motivation and achievement in early adolescence. *Journal of Early Adolescence, 13*, 4–20.

Zimmerman, S. M., Phelps, E., & Lerner, R. M. (2008). Positive and negative developmental trajectories in U.S. adolescents: Where the positive youth development perspective meets the deficit model. *Research in Human Development, 5*(3), 153–165.

CHAPTER 12

SEL Programs in High School

Ariel A. Williamson, Kathryn L. Modecki, and Nancy G. Guerra

Adolescence is a time of personal and social development that requires a sophisticated repertoire of social–emotional skills for healthy adjustment. Teenagers often face considerable difficulties negotiating the biological, cognitive, and physiological changes associated with puberty (Yurgelun-Todd, 2007). For example, as advances in neuroscience have shown, there is a marked shift toward reward seeking, while self-regulation skills struggle to keep pace (Steinberg, 2008). As adolescents increasingly interact with peers, they must simultaneously contend with peer pressure. Teenagers also must navigate the vicissitudes of identity development and the search for purpose and meaning as they transition into adulthood (Erikson, 1968, 1993). These developmental and contextual shifts challenge positive youth development and increase normative risk for problem behaviors such as violence, sexual risk taking, substance use, and school dropout (Guerra & Bradshaw, 2008; Steinberg, Vandell, & Bornstein, 2011).

On the other hand, the increasing maturation of emotional and cognitive abilities provides a solid foundation for building social and emotional learning (SEL) skills. Indeed, many of the capacities that develop or become more complex during adolescence are aligned with the five social and emotional competency domains identified by the Collaborative for Academic, Social, and Emotional Learning (CASEL; 2012), which are *self-awareness, self-management, social awareness, relationship skills*, and *responsible decision-making*. These skills are malleable and are logical targets for intervention due to the theoretical relevance of these competencies to positive youth development, resilience, and risk prevention.

For example, programs that target *self-awareness* may be especially efficacious during adolescence, when youth experience demonstrable gains in abstract thought and other cognitive capacities and are increasingly motivated to establish their identities and set goals for the future (Steinberg et al., 2011). Programs that facilitate *self-management* skills are also highly germane to adolescents, for whom a biologically driven reward imbalance leads to deficits in self-regulation (Casey, Jones, & Hare, 2008; Steinberg, 2008). Furthermore, compared to earlier developmental periods, adolescence is a time of improved social cognition and more sophisticated perspective-taking skills (Steinberg et al., 2011). These developmental challenges likely impact the *social awareness* competency domain. Adolescents' increased focus on peer contexts also suggests that programs that improve *relationship skills* may be useful for negotiating peer pressure and conflicts that are especially endemic to this developmental stage, and help them connect in a positive and productive fashion to peers (Dodge, Dishion, & Lansford, 2006). Finally, adolescents are confronted with real-world decisions that impact their life course, and *responsible decision-making* represents a critical developmental task. As such, it is particularly important that interventions focus on improving these capacities during adolescence.

Given the clear links between the skills within the five competency domains defined by CASEL and adolescent adjustment, it is surprising that few school-based SEL programs have been designed for or evaluated with high school students. Indeed, there are a small number of middle school SEL programs and very few evidence-based SEL programs for high school youth. This relative neglect of high school programs is regrettable because adolescents have cognitive capacities that younger children do not, making attempts to improve SEL skills especially appropriate during the teenage years. In fact, findings from various reviews suggest that SEL programs are effective with adolescents, and can mitigate problem behavior and bolster positive outcomes such as positive youth development (PYD), social adjustment, school participation, and academic achievement (e.g., Catalano, Berglund, Ryan, Lonczak, & Hawkins, 2002; Durlak, Weissberg, Dymnicki, Taylor, & Schellinger, 2011; Wilson & Lipsey, 2007). Moreover, SEL skills are germane to all of the major theoretical models of prevention and promotion in adolescence. Thus, middle school and high school represent salient developmental periods for SEL programs that have been somewhat overlooked but remain highly promising contexts for future research.

Definitions and Scope

In this chapter, SEL refers to school-based intervention or prevention programming, including universal, selected, and indicated programs that target one or more of the five CASEL competency domains. The degree to which programs targeted one or more SEL domain was determined by a review of program descriptions, stated goals, and measured outcomes. Although CASEL will only designate a program as "SELect" if it targets the promotion of skills in all five domains, high school SEL programs vary considerably in terms of which domains are targeted, and typically promote SEL skills development while also targeting other outcomes. For instance, because schools are often concerned with preventing youth problems, and because deficits in SEL skills contribute to the development of poor adolescent outcomes, many programs that target SEL skills development also focus on the prevention of one or more problem behaviors (e.g., youth violence). SEL can also be embedded in programs that focus on health promotion, positive development, and/or academic achievement.

We focus this review on SEL programs conducted with students in high school, which is defined as grades 9–12 in the United States. We were not able to include a "What Works" section of programs evaluated in at least three trials and found to have positive effects because there were no programs that met this requirement. Rather, we emphasized "What Is Promising," defined as examples of potentially promising programs with two or fewer successful trials, or programs that are theoretically applicable to high schools. There are a number of high school SEL programs available on developer or other websites; however, the majority of these programs have not been empirically evaluated and as such are not included in this chapter. The "What Does Not Work" section refers to programs or techniques that have not obtained their intended outcomes for high school youth. We also highlight future directions for SEL program research in high school contexts.

Theoretical Links between SEL and Adolescent Outcomes

Many important theoretical models of PYD and risk reduction link SEL with positive outcomes during adolescence. To contextualize our focus on youth problem behavior, we briefly review prevalence data for common risk behaviors that concern high school personnel, policymakers, and parents. We then discuss four popular approaches to understanding risk behavior and PYD, all of which either explicitly or implicitly target

SEL as a key mechanism. These approaches include resilience, risk and prevention, asset building, and life skills.

Prevalence of Adolescent Problem Behavior

Data from nationally representative surveys of adolescent behavior have consistently demonstrated that many high school youth engage in some form of problem behavior, such as violence, risky sexual behavior, substance use, or school dropout or failure. A recent U.S. survey conducted by the Centers for Disease Control and Prevention (CDC) with students in grades 9 through 12 indicates that engagement in such problem behaviors remains highly prevalent, particularly among older adolescents. For example, in the 30 days prior to the survey, 16.6% of youth reported carrying a weapon to school (gun, knife, or club), 32.8% reported having been in a physical fight, and 20.1% reported experiencing bullying on school grounds (Eaton et al., 2012). Indeed, for youth between ages 15 and 19, the first leading cause of death is unintentional injury, followed by assault (homicide) and suicide (Heron, 2012).

In the area of sexual risk taking, although 84% of youth reported being educated about HIV or AIDS at school, 12.9% of those who endorsed being sexually active (33.7% of the sample) used no method of contraception or protection from sexually transmitted diseases (STDs) during their most recent sexual intercourse, and 15.3% reported having had intercourse with four or more partners in their lifetime (Eaton et al., 2012). Approximately 22.1% of sexually active youth also reported using drugs or alcohol prior to their most recent sexual encounter (Eaton et al., 2012). Alcohol, marijuana, and cigarettes are still the most widely used substances by high school students (Johnston, O'Malley, Bachman, & Schulenberg, 2012). For instance, 70% of youth reported they had tried alcohol, with 21.9% of students reporting binge drinking (five or more drinks in a row, within a few hours) and 38.7% reported having had at least one drink in the 30 days prior to the survey (Eaton et al., 2012). School dropout also is an important concern for high schools. The dropout rate in 2010 was 7.4% for all youth, with substantially higher dropout rates for Latino (15.1%) and Native American/Alaska Native (12.4%) youth (U.S. Department of Education, National Center for Education Statistics, 2012).

Models of Risk and Youth Development

Many different approaches or theoretical frameworks have been used to study and to prevent youth problems or promote healthy development. The most influential frameworks all emphasize SEL skills as their principal focus or integrate these skills more peripherally.

Resilience

Resilience refers to a set of *protective processes* that buffer some individuals from the effects of adverse experiences. Given the difficulty of effecting economic and political change at the societal level, a focus on resilience provides key insights into how youth overcome a range of obstacles. Grounded in public health, one of the earliest and most widely cited studies of resilience was conducted by Emily Werner (Werner & Smith, 1982). She followed a cohort of extremely poor Hawaiian children who were likely to have alcoholic or mentally ill parents and few economic opportunities. Although approximately two-thirds of these children grew up to have a range of chronic problems, one-third of them did not, and were somehow able to overcome adversity, a key feature of resilience. One distinguishing feature of resilient youth was their possession of social and emotional skills, including strong coping abilities and high levels of autonomy, self-efficacy, and self-esteem (Werner, 1997).

Subsequent researchers have added to this literature by examining children who do well despite experiencing a range of difficulties, including the Great Depression, the U.S. farm crisis, and being a refugee with little economic support (Masten, 2007). Many individual and contextual characteristics have been associated with resilience across studies. In this work, the concept of resilience has been applied to different types of adjustment in the face of personal, family, school, and community adversity, including competence under stress, recovery from trauma, or doing better than expected given risk status. For instance, research has shown that competencies such as personal discipline and work habits distinguish academically resilient youth from other high-risk youth who perform poorly or drop out of school (Finn & Rock, 1997).

Among the individual competencies that characterize resilience, many are also consistent with SEL: self-esteem, self-efficacy, problem-solving skills, and self-control (Masten & Obradović, 2006). Also similar to SEL, the resilience literature confirms the need to promote a range of skills that improve youth outcomes, as opposed to a selective focus on isolated competencies (e.g., Luthar, 1995; Luthar & Zigler, 1992).

Risk Prevention

Interest in risk prevention for youth emerged from epidemiological research. As such, risk-focused models seek to identify discrete *risk factors* that *increase* the likelihood of a specific, negative outcome in the future. They also highlight the role of *protective factors* that *reduce* the likelihood of subsequent negative outcomes in the presence of risk. Many risk and protective factors relate to the presence or absence of SEL skills. For example, low psychosocial functioning and poor social problem-solving skills have been shown to increase risk for aggression and delinquency (Modecki, 2009). On the other hand, good self-regulation skills are protective against a number of problem behaviors (Guerra & Bradshaw, 2008). By building social and emotional competencies, interventions also serve to mitigate risks.

Youth Asset Building

Models that highlight resilience and risk direct attention to overcoming adversity and adjustment problems. In contrast, youth asset building focuses on promoting strengths for all youth, framing their mission as "all youth thrive" rather than preventing problems per se. A common slogan is "problem-free is not prepared" (Pittman, 1991), suggesting that all youth, not just those who experience adversity, can benefit from asset building. Previous studies substantiate the conviction that SEL assets lead to better developmental outcomes, such as decreased substance use and violence, and increased academic performance, leadership, and helping behaviors (Scales, Benson, Leffert, & Blyth, 2000). Such developmental assets are also predictive of academic success across White middle class and ethnic minority urban adolescents (Scales, Foster, Mannes, Horst, & Rutherford, 2005).

To a certain extent, asset-building approaches have followed the path of a social movement reacting against programs designed to fix "at-risk" youth. A popular framework in the U.S. and internationally is the Search Institute's Developmental Asset Profile. The Institute's 40 assets capture a range of characteristics that represent broad components of "external" and "internal" assets. Many of the internal assets reflect the skills within the five CASEL competency domains (e.g., a positive sense of self; decision-making skills). However, although the Search Institute's asset framework provides general guidance for a range of desired SEL and other skills, more detail and empirical support for each construct are needed to maximize its utility as a guide for programming.

Life Skills

Similar to the asset-building models, a life skills framework emphasizes the personal skills youth need to thrive. These skills can be framed narrowly, based on key skills for success in school and work. These typically include work and study habits, planning, goal setting, accessing and using community resources, money management, computer literacy, and relationship skills. With some exceptions (e.g., computer literacy), these skills are not addressed in most school curricula, yet they are essential for success during adulthood. Life skills can be framed broadly to include a wide range of psychological, practical, and SEL skills linked to broad well-being. For example, the World Health Organization (WHO; 2003) defines life skills as

> abilities for adaptive and positive behaviour that enable individuals to deal effectively with the demands and challenges of everyday life. In particular, life skills are a group of psychosocial competencies and interpersonal skills that help people make informed decisions, solve problems, think critically and creatively, communicate effectively, build healthy rela-

> tionships, empathise with others, and cope with and manage their lives in a healthy and productive manner. (p. 3)

In summary, many contemporary frameworks directly or indirectly emphasize SEL skills as important targets of healthy adolescent development. SEL skills are broadly associated with resilience, risk prevention, and the development of interpersonal assets and life skills. Thus, inclusion of SEL skills is critical for programs promoting healthy development for all adolescents.

Current Research and Overview of Strategies

Most interventions designed to prevent youth problems or promote adjustment have been grounded in one of the frameworks described earlier. Regardless of the specific framework, these programs typically include components that either explicitly or implicitly promote SEL. Despite the theoretical role of SEL skills as a mediating mechanism in most models of adolescent behavior change, few programs have empirically tested this link. Thus, it remains unclear whether SEL skills are a mechanism of behavioral change within effective interventions. At the same time, to understand the broad impact of these programs, a number of meta-analyses and reviews have been conducted on a wide range of programs across multiple frameworks. In general, studies and reviews including preventive programs for bullying, youth development, and universal SEL have shown that K–12 school-based programs have positive effects on youth (e.g., Catalano et al., 2002; Durlak et al., 2011; Farrington & Totfi, 2009; Wilson & Lipsey, 2007).

For example, in a meta-analysis of 213 SEL programs for elementary, middle, and high school youth by Durlak and colleagues (2011), beneficial program effects were found across age groups in social and emotional skills, attitudes, behavior, and academic achievement. However, as Durlak and colleagues noted, SEL programs have been studied in high schools less often than in other settings; evaluations of high school programs made up only 13% of the studies included in their meta-analysis. Similarly, in a meta-analysis, Wilson and Lipsey (2007) also found that school-based programs were effective in reducing disruptive behavior, but only 20% of studies in the meta-analysis included youth older than age 14. Other reviews of school-based programs have also noted limited interventions available for high school youth (e.g., Guerra & Leidy, 2008), or diminished intervention effects with increasing age of program participants (Smith, 2010).

Although there *are* published studies of high school intervention programs with positive effects included in meta-analyses and review papers, these studies rarely are replicated, leaving few high school-specific or high school-tested programs that have been evaluated more than once. The lack of replicated high school intervention programs has led to a paucity of evidence-based SEL programming for this age group. By *evidence-based*, we mean programs that could be designated under the "What Works" category, which have three or more successful evaluations, according to the guidelines for this chapter and similar to other reviews of evidence-based treatments for youth (e.g., Eyberg, Nelson, & Boggs, 2008). Although meta-analytic reviews have proven useful in determining which broad program and student characteristics are associated with stronger intervention effects across program packages and theoretical orientations (Wilson & Lipsey, 2007), there remains a need to demonstrate which specific SEL programs for high school students are effective across multiple studies. Likewise, studies are needed to identify and measure mechanisms of change within effective programs, so that those aspects of SEL that are particularly successful in mediating program outcomes can be identified.

What Works: Promising Approaches

Given the lack of SEL programs for high school youth that have shown positive effects in three or more research trials, we cannot provide a review of "What Works." However, it is important to note that the lack of evidence-based programs does not mean that nothing "can work." At this juncture, we can only highlight promising approaches to promoting SEL that are feasible to implement in high schools and that have some initial evidence of effectiveness.

To begin with, implementing high school SEL programs presents unique challenges. The most common approach to promotion of SEL has been through structured lessons provided during the regular school day. This is relatively easy in elementary schools, where students remain in a single classroom, although it still can prove difficult when programs compete with academic instructional time. In most high schools, however, students move from class to class, with few venues for integrating stand-alone SEL programs. School personnel also are faced with increasing adolescent risk behaviors and may look for more targeted prevention programs.

Consequently, intervention programs often are directed at preventing negative outcomes such as school dropout, high-risk sexual behavior, and violence. The focus of these programs is primarily on changing behavior, and few studies measure SEL outcomes, even when these skills are addressed in lessons and activities. Some prevention programs target schoolwide changes in policies and practices, whereas other programs provide individual lessons in classrooms or small groups. A separate set of programs relevant for SEL addresses health promotion and wellness, usually in health classes or wellness centers, although these programs sometimes are tied to risk prevention. Another type of program emphasizes learning about diversity, ethics, and social responsibility, which is related to but not the same as SEL. Other programs target SEL directly, although evidence of effectiveness is limited to single studies using quasi-experimental designs.

In the absence of evidence that meet criteria for "What Works," we provide examples of different types of programs that are potentially promising (Table 12.1), either because they build on evidence-based programs for younger children or have some initial empirical support. It is our hope that this approach will provide a basis for future empirical studies with high school youth, and promote interest in additional program development and validation at the high school level.

Positive Behavioral Interventions and Supports

Although not an SEL program, positive behavioral intervention and supports (PBIS; *www.pbis.org*) provide contingencies for positive student and school staff behavior in all grades K–12 as a method to increase school safety, promote a positive school climate, reduce problem behavior, and improve academic performance (Sugai & Horner, 2002). This focus on positive behaviors may encompass SEL skills such as self- and social awareness, self-management skills, and relationship skills. A detailed description of PBIS and its potential integration with SEL is provided elsewhere in this volume (Bear, Whitcomb, Elias, & Blank, Chapter 30, this volume). Briefly, PBIS operates in a multi-tiered framework, in which programming is directed at whole-school (universal), classroom, small-group (selected), and individual (indicated) levels (Waasdorp, Bradshaw, & Leaf, 2012). Students are exposed to schoolwide discipline policies that include clear, positively phrased school rules and behavioral expectations (e.g., "be ready to learn"; Sugai & Horner, 2002; Waasdorp et al., 2012).

It would be useful to evaluate the impact of this type of comprehensive school-wide strategy on SEL skills, particularly if SEL programming is built into the focused selected and indicated programs, as well as to determine whether changes in SEL skills might mediate behavioral gains. Randomized controlled trials (RCTs) and other studies of PBIS at the elementary and middle school levels have shown positive results, including reductions in school bullying and discipline procedures and improvements in school climate (e.g., Bradshaw, Mitchell, & Leaf, 2010; Waasdorp, Bradshaw, & Leaf, 2012). PBIS has been evaluated less frequently at the high school level (Flannery, Sugai, & Anderson, 2009), although a randomized controlled trial (RCT) of PBIS in public high schools is being conducted by the Center for the Prevention of Youth Violence at the Johns Hopkins School of Public Health (C. P. Bradshaw, personal communication, August 14, 2012).

Too Good for Drugs and Violence High School

Too Good for Drugs and Violence High School (TGFD&V; see *www.mendezfoundation.org/toogood/high*) is a universal (whole-school) prevention strategy that aims to reduce school violence and drug use by changing norms related to these behaviors and building SEL strengths in areas such as decision making, conflict resolution, emotion regulation, stress management, and interpersonal relationships. Lessons also include information about the consequences of substance use and involvement in violent behavior. The high school program contains 14 lessons that can be implemented by teachers, 12 lessons that can be incorporated into subject-specific areas by grade level, staff and parent education materials, and community-based intervention strategies. Student lessons include interactive role plays and cooperative learning activities to facilitate student engagement, skills building, and skills generalization.

A pilot, quasi-experimental study with 241 students in 11 Florida high schools demonstrated that following classroom-based program implementation by trained TGFD&V instructors, intervention students' intentions to use substances and engage in violence decreased, and their self-efficacy, decision-making, and peer resistance skills increased relative to the control group (Bacon, 2001b). Another study (Bacon, 2001a, as cited by the What Works Clearinghouse, 2006) evaluated the program in a pretest–posttest RCT with 303 students in five Florida high schools. Program participants showed increased SEL competencies and peer resistance skills, although no significant effects were found relative to drug use, violence, or decision making. Taken together, the studies of TGFD&V are promising because both have been evaluated with high school populations and show some effects on SEL competencies and other outcomes.

Teenage Health Teaching Modules

The Teenage Health Teaching Modules (THTM; *www.thtm.org*) have been evaluated in two studies, one that was published and included high school youth (Errecart et al., 1991), and another that included middle school students (Slaby, Wilson-Brewer, & DeVos, 1994, as cited by CASEL, 2003). The THTM, which is meant for delivery as a student health curriculum, originally contained 16 modules for students in middle and high school, each of which targeted the skills of self-assessment, communication, decision making, health advocacy, and healthy self-management (Ross, Gold, Lavin, Errecart, & Nelson, 1991). These modules align with the five CASEL competency domains of self-awareness, self-management, relationship skills, and responsible decision making. Each module also includes lessons that cover a variety of adolescent health concerns, such as youth violence, sexual behavior, and substance use.

One published quasi-experimental, pretest–posttest evaluation of the THTM by Errecart and colleagues (1991) involved 4,806 middle school students and high school seniors. Students in the intervention condition (n = 2,530) were nested in schools that had either already adopted the THTM ("naturalistic" schools) or were trained to use the THTM ("experimental" schools; Ross et al., 1991). Different modules were used in the middle schools and high schools, with high school students exposed to the modules focused on healthy eating, stress management, and future planning, among others (Ross et al., 1991). Study findings revealed that following exposure to the THTM, high school seniors showed reductions in cigarette smoking, illegal drug use, and eating fried foods, and increases in general health knowledge relative to the control condition (Errecart et al., 1991). Impacts on SEL were not assessed, and it would be important to examine whether behavioral changes actually were associated with changes in SEL skills.

Facing History and Ourselves

Facing History and Ourselves (FHAO; *www.facing.org*) is an example of how teaching SEL competencies can be integrated with academics in high school. FHAO promotes civic engagement and social responsibility through the teaching of history lessons that are infused with critical thinking, moral development, and other skills-building activities (Barr et al., 2014; Barr & Facing History and Ourselves [FHAO], 2010; Schultz, Barr, & Selman, 2001). Targeted student outcomes include social and ethical awareness, civic learning, and historical understanding (Barr et al., 2014). FHAO also aims to improve teacher self-efficacy, professional satisfaction, and engagement. According to a recent report, FHAO is cur-

TABLE 12.1. Examples of Promising Intervention Program Approaches for High School Youth and Links to the Five CASEL Skills

Program	Links to CASEL	Sources	Sample	Design	Selected results
PBIS	Self-management Self-awareness Relationship skills	Bohanon et al. (2006)	*N* = 1 high school	Pretest–posttest; no control case study	Decreased school-level discipline referrals
		Muscott et al. (2008)	*N* = 28 schools, four of which were high schools	Longitudinal; no control case study	Decreased detention referrals
		Simonsen et al. (2012)	*N* = 428 schools, 17 of which were high schools	Longitudinal; no control case study	Increased achievement; decreased office referrals and suspensions
TGFD&V	Self-management Self-awareness Decision making	Bacon (2001a)	*N* = 201 students in grades 9–12	Quasi-experimental; pretest–posttest	Decreased intention to use substances or engage in violence; increased self-efficacy, decision-making, and peer resistance skills
		Bacon (2001b)	*N* = 303 students in grades 9–12	RCT; pretest–posttest	Increased emotional competence, social skills, and peer resistance
THTM	Self-management Self-awareness Decision making Relationship skills	Errecart et al. (1991)	*N* = 4,806 middle school and high school students	Quasi-experimental; pretest–posttest	Decreased cigarette smoking, use of drugs, and consumption of fried foods; increased health knowledge
		Slaby et al. (1994)	*N* = 237 students in grades 7 and 8	Pretest–posttest; no control	Increased positive teacher-rated behavior; marginally improved social skills

Check & Connect	Relationship skills	Sinclair et al. (1998)	*N* = 94 students in grade 9	RCT, pretest–posttest	Increased school engagement and credits
		Sinclair et al. (2005)	*N* = 144 students in grade 9	RCT; pretest–posttest	Decreased dropout; increased attendance and school completion
FHAO	Social awareness	Barr et al. (2014)	*N* = 1,371 students in grades 9 and 10	RCT; pretest–posttest with 1-year follow-up	Increased history knowledge and civic learning
		Schultz et al. (2001)	*N* = 346 students in grade 8	Quasi-experimental; pretest–posttest	Increased relationship maturity; decreased fighting
CLP	Self-awareness Decision making Relationship skills	Eichas et al. (2010)	*N* = 178 students in alternative high school	Quasi-experimental; pretest–posttest	Increased positive identity and personal expressiveness
PLC	Self-management Self-awareness Decision making Relationship skills Social awareness	Williamson et al. (2013)	*N* = 27 students in alternative high school	Pilot pretest–posttest; no control	Decreased verbal and physical aggression propensity, increased sense of self, moral beliefs, and decision making

Note. RCT, randomized controlled trial; PBIS, Positive Behavior Intervention Supports; TGFD&V, Too Good for Drugs and Violence; THTM, Teenage Heath Teaching Modules; FHAO, Facing History and Ourselves; CLP, Changing Lives Program; PLC, Positive Life Changes. Selected outcomes are presented. Some programs described in the chapter text are not pictured.

rently being used by 2,900 trained educators and delivered to approximately 1.9 million students (Barr & FHAO, 2010). FHAO is typically delivered by classroom teachers during semester-long units and varies according to individual teachers. A core program resource uses historical lessons about the Holocaust to motivate discussions about identity development and intergroup relations, which are supplemented by related student self-reflection and journal-writing activities, as well as films and guest speakers (Barr et al., 2014; Schultz et al., 2001).

Although FHAO is an extremely popular program, most program evaluations are unpublished and not available for review. However, Barr and colleagues (2014) recently published findings of an RCT (wait-list control) of the curriculum in a sample of 1,371 ninth- and 10th grade students (n = 612 intervention participants) and 113 teachers (n = 53 intervention teachers), in 60 high schools. Although only half of the intervention teachers implemented the full FHAO curriculum, there were several positive intervention effects on student- and teacher-reported outcomes. Study findings showed that FHAO students had higher self-reported levels of overall historical understanding and aspects of civic learning, including political tolerance, civic efficacy, and positive perceptions of the classroom climate and of opportunities for civic engagement (Barr et al., 2014). No statistically significant results were found on student measures of social and ethical awareness. Barr and colleagues also found positive effects on teacher self-efficacy domains, among other positive teacher-related outcomes. Again, SEL outcomes were not specifically measured, although constructs such as tolerance for others' political views and civic efficacy can map on to the five CASEL competencies (e.g., social awareness).

Check & Connect

Check & Connect (*checkandconnect.umn.edu*) targets students at risk for school dropout (Sinclair, Christenson, & Thurlow, 2005). Check & Connect promotes youth engagement with school through *check* and *connect* components. These include the continued assessment of student engagement indicators, such as attendance, grades, and disciplinary referrals (the *check* component) and the provision educational intervention by program staff members, called monitors, who routinely meet with students on their caseload to provide individualized intervention based on student needs (the *connect* component). Monitors also provide a context for relationship and problem-solving skills building, which align with the five CASEL competency domains, as well as academic motivation.

The two published RCTs of Check & Connect with adolescents at risk for school dropout provide preliminary support for positive effects on school attendance, school completion, and reduced dropout. One study found positive effects when a sample of students received the intervention in middle school grades 7 and 8 and were subsequently randomized to the intervention or a no-intervention control in grade 9, with students who received the program in grade 9 showing better school attendance and progress toward graduation (Sinclair, Christenson, Evelo, & Hurley, 1998). A second study of the program implemented in grade 9 similarly showed better school attendance and progress, as well as reduced dropout (Sinclair et al., 2005). Again, specific SEL outcomes were not addressed directly, although part of the program focuses on relationship and problem-solving skills. Teacher ratings using a broad social competence measure in one study (Sinclair et al., 1998) showed improved academic competence and reduced behavior problems in students who received the intervention. An RCT in a high school currently is under way (C. P. Bradshaw, personal communication, August 14, 2012).

Changing Lives Program

The Changing Lives Program (CLP; *http://w3.fiu.edu/ydp/about_clp.htm*) is an intervention program for at-risk adolescents that operates from a "participatory transformative" approach (Eichas et al., 2010), and aims to empower adolescents to positively change their sense of self and identity. This intervention focus is aligned with the SEL skill of self-awareness and is framed in a developmentally relevant manner emphasizing identity exploration and commitment. Adolescents in the program are active participants in the intervention, and are asked to identify problems in their lives and methods to resolve these problems, a strategy that is consistent with the promotion of the CASEL relationship and decision-making skills. The intervention is typically implemented in groups and can run from 8 to 12 weeks during the school semester.

Eichas and colleagues (2010) evaluated the CLP with 178 adolescents (*n* = 61 controls) ages 14–18 attending an alternative school. The intervention was part of the school's counseling program, with groups led by graduate-level group facilitators. Results showed that CLP participants increased in their positive identity, with changes in informational identity style mediating increases in this outcome. Eichas and colleagues also found evidence that increases in positive identity mediated decreases in internalizing problems that were not directly targeted by CLP. Gender moderated the direct effects of CLP participation on internalizing behavior, with only females showing reductions in this outcome. Ethnicity moderated the effects of one program mediator, identity resolution, such that Hispanic youth in CLP showed improvements in this regard, whereas African American participants did not. CLP offers promising directions for future research, especially given the lack of research on change mechanisms in SEL and other interventions.

Positive Life Changes

Positive Life Changes (PLC; *www.researchpress.com/books/656/positive-life-changes*) is a competency-based, social cognitive program designed to reduce adolescent problem behaviors through the promotion of five core competencies: self-esteem, self-control, decision-making skills, prosocial connectedness, and moral beliefs. These competencies have been linked to PYD (Guerra & Bradshaw, 2008) and map directly on to the five CASEL competency skills domains. PLC was designed specifically for older, at-risk adolescents in the juvenile justice system or in alternative and public school settings. School staff can implement the program in small groups or classrooms. PLC consists of 30 lessons, divided evenly into three workbooks, which are included to increase ease of program implementation and flexibility (i.e., lessons may be assigned as homework).

Although PLC has not yet been examined in a study that includes a control group, it is currently used in several juvenile justice centers, and was recently evaluated in a pretest–posttest no-control pilot study with 27 alternative school youth in grades 9–12 (Williamson, Dierkhising, & Guerra, 2013). PLC was implemented in four groups over a 6-week period, with half of the program lessons (15) assigned for homework. Analyses revealed increases in participants' self-esteem, decision-making skills, and moral beliefs, and reductions in their propensity for physical and verbal aggression. PLC is a promising program for future research, particularly due to its focus on at-risk adolescents and its flexible format.

Positive Psychology for Youth Program

The Positive Psychology for Youth Program is a high school version of the Penn Resiliency Program (*www.ppc.sas.upenn.edu/prpsum.htm*), a school-based intervention designed to promote well-being and prevent depression among youth ages 10–14 (Brunwasser, Gillham, & Kim, 2009; Seligman, Ernst, Gillham, Reivich, & Linkins, 2009). This intervention is a cognitive-behavioral program that teaches optimism, coping strategies, and problem solving to promote resilience and help youth identify and increase their interpersonal strengths (Seligman et al., 2009). The program is delivered in 20–25 classroom-based 80-minute sessions and comprises discussions, activities, homework, and journal entries (Seligman et al., 2009). Specific examples of the program exercises are described in detail by Seligman and colleagues (2009).

PRP been widely evaluated with elementary and middle school youth in school or community settings (Brunwasser et al., 2009). A meta-analysis including 17 experimental studies, mostly with middle school youth, showed that PRP was associated with reductions in depressive symptoms, which were maintained for at least 12 months (Brunwasser et al., 2009). One large-scale randomized trial of PRP that has been conducted to date with high school-age youth included 347 ninth-grade students in public high school language arts classes (Seligman et al., 2009). Full program effects have yet to be published, although this work is currently in progress (J. Gillham, personal communication, September 20, 2012).

What Does Not Work

Publication bias against null effects makes it difficult to characterize ineffective SEL-type programs. Authors, policymakers, and journals are reluctant to publish evidence of what does not work—either with no effects or even with negative (iatrogenic) effects. It also may be that a given program was (1) useful or necessary but not sufficient; (2) sufficient but poorly implemented; or (3) poorly designed for the target audience. It also is important to understand more fully how challenges faced by adolescents are linked to SEL skills development. As noted earlier, adolescence is characterized by vulnerabilities in several SEL-related competency domains, and these liabilities require developmentally salient tactics to elicit positive change. It may not be enough to adapt programs for elementary or middle school youth without considering the changing context of adolescence and the important characteristics of high schools.

Indeed, a number of SEL-relevant programs seem to be less potent for older than for younger adolescents (i.e., substance use prevention programs [see Perry et al., 2002]; bullying programs [see Smith, 2010]). Moreover, some programs that are not effective with adolescents actually run counter to current conceptualizations of decision making during the teenage years. As an example, the Drug Abuse Resistance Education (D.A.R.E.) program emphasizes two SEL skills: peer pressure resistance (relationship skills) and decision making (Birkeland, Murphy-Graham, & Weiss, 2005). However, the program's main strategy is to alarm or "scare" youth by emphasizing an array of negative consequences. This strategy may be appropriate for younger children who are motivated to follow rules. However, this focus is inconsistent with adolescent decision research (Modecki, 2009). As a general rule, adolescents do not underestimate the risks associated with substance use and other problem behaviors but are motivated by increased reward seeking (e.g., Steinberg, 2008). The need to shift the focus of skills-building interventions to align with adolescent developmental advances is consistent with the literature on rehabilitation programs such as *Scared Straight* that use only scare tactics (i.e., taking youth to visit jails) and have been shown to be ineffective or even harmful with youth (Petrosino, Turpin-Petrosino, Hollis-Peel, & Lavenberg, 2013; Sherman et al., 1999). Overall, both age-related differences in effectiveness and a lack of effectiveness with adolescents call attention to a noticeable gap in current SEL programming for adolescents. Adolescents would likely benefit from enhancement of developmentally relevant program features that serve to integrate their unique social–emotional circumstances and age-related liabilities with SEL skills-development.

Summary and Future Directions

Although a number of stand-alone SEL program evaluation studies with positive findings for high school youth is included in meta-analyses or reviews of bullying, PYD, and SEL interventions, few programs effects have been replicated more than once, and no programs have been shown to be effective in three or more studies. Compared to the range of SEL interventions available for middle or elementary school youth (see CASEL, 2012; Jagers, Harris, & Skoog, Chapter 11, this volume; Rimm-Kaufman & Hulleman, Chapter 10, this volume), there is a pressing need for continued development and research on high school SEL programs. There are some positive high school evaluations of programs discussed in this chapter, and several others are under way. For example, C. P. Bradshaw (personal communication, August 14, 2012) is conducting a large-scale RCT of several programs for high school students, including PBIS and Check & Connect.

Extending to high school youth the middle school programs that have been shown to be effective during early adolescence is one approach to improving evidence-based programming in this setting. Indeed, there is a growing evidence base for SEL programming in middle schools (see Jagers et al., Chapter 11, this volume). However, a central issue is whether the topics covered in middle school SEL programs and methods of implementation are relevant for older adolescents in high school settings. As Smith (2010) has noted, there are a number of organizational challenges associated with the high school setting, including changes in academic goals, teacher–student relationships, peer contexts, and school and class size. Any extension of middle school programs into high school settings will require a careful consideration of the organizational and program implementation challenges associated with this context, as well as the risk and developmental characteristics of older adolescents (reviewed earlier).

An important missing link in the literature that is particularly relevant for adolescents is the increasing role and/or potential to leverage technology to foster SEL skills. A recent survey of adolescent technology usage found that 93% of teens have a computer or home access to one, and 78% of teens have a cell phone, with 37% of all teens using smartphones (Madden, Lenhart, Duggan, Cortesi, & Gasser, 2013). Programs should ideally be developed to support adolescent SEL competencies using mobile applications ("Apps") or computerized programs that can reduce barriers to program success. Computerized modules could be developed for discrete SEL skills, and students could use an online assessment protocol to identify skills components they need to improve. Using Apps, youth could work only on relevant skills (e.g., self-control; decision making) at times and locations of their choosing. Apps could be specially designed to integrate SEL into adolescent's daily experiences. Underwood, Rosen, More, Ehrenreich, and Gentsch (2012) have used smartphones to code adolescents' e-mail and text messages as a method to further understand social networks. Specific to intervention programming, Khanna and Kendall (2010) adapted the evidence-based child anxiety treatment, Coping Cat, into a computer-assisted format, Camp Cope-A-Lot, which they found to be as effective in reducing anxiety as the standard program.

Another approach can build on comprehensive K–12 education initiatives, such as the Hewlett Foundation Deeper Learning Program (see *www.hewlett.org/deeper-learning*), which aims to improve students' academic and social skills through better instructional practices. Students are taught to master five interconnected skills: core academic content, critical thinking, problem solving, working collaboratively, and learning how to monitor and direct one's own learning (self-directed learning). The initiative plans to assess 15% of students nationwide on these "deeper learning" skills and projects that 80% of U.S. students will benefit from this program by 2025. Initial support focuses on middle schools, high schools, and community colleges, with teachers receiving additional training and support. Several of the skills targeted in this deeper learning project overlap with the skills included in the five CASEL competency domains. Other examples of this type of collaborative and comprehensive effort are the Hewlett Foundation Envision Schools (see *www.envisionschools.org*), which specially prepare students for college admission.

It may also be possible to enhance many of the extracurricular offerings in which high school students engage as tools to promote SEL (Fredricks & Eccles, 2006). For instance, playing sports or being in school clubs can provide a foundation for improving all five of the CASEL skills. Some evidence also suggests that involvement in certain extracurricular activities may be especially beneficial for youth who are at risk due to early pubertal timing (e.g., Modecki, Barber, & Eccles, 2014), or low socioeconomic status (e.g., Blomfield & Barber, 2011). However, greater understanding of the specific practices that contribute to these outcomes (Eccles, Barber, Stone, & Hunt, 2003) or potentially blunt them (Mays & Thompson 2009) is required.

In summary, although the need for SEL programming in high schools is clear, little is known about "What Works" to promote SEL competencies and reduce risk in high school students using specific intervention packages. However, given data from meta-analytic inquiries and reviews of SEL programs, as well as stand-alone studies of high school interventions described here and elsewhere, we know that high school SEL programming *can* work. What the field now needs is a body of evidence to support replicable and generalizable SEL interventions that are appropriate for diverse high school students and contexts. Such evidence will ideally test the mechanism by which SEL affects outcomes because it is essential that researchers identify SEL processes that account for program results.

References

Bacon, T. P. (2001a). *Evaluation of the Too Good for Drugs and Violence—High School prevention program* (Report). Tallahassee: Florida Department of Education, Department of Safe and Drug-Tree Schools.

Bacon, T. P. (2001b). Impact on high school students' behaviors and protective factors: A pilot study of the Too Good for Drugs and Violence prevention program. *Florida Education Research Council, Inc. Research Bulletin, 32*(3–4), 1–40. Retrieved September 5, 2012, from *www.mendezfoundation.org/toogood/high.*

Barr, D. J., Boulay, B., Selman, R. L., McCormick, R., Lowenstein, E., Gamse, B. C., et al. (2014). A randomized controlled trial of professional development for interdisciplinary civic education: Impacts on humanities teachers and their students. *Teachers College Record, 117*(4). Retrieved May 13, 2014, from *www.tcrecord.org.*

Barr, D. J., & Facing History and Ourselves [FHAO]. (2010). Continuing a tradition of research on the foundations of democratic education: The National Professional Development and Evaluation Project. Retrieved September 5, 2012, from *www.facinghistory.org.*

Birkeland, S., Murphy-Graham, E., & Weiss, C. (2005). Good reasons for ignoring good evaluation: The case of the drug abuse resistance education (D.A.R.E.) program. *Evaluation and Program Planning, 28*, 247–256.

Blomfield, C. J., & Barber, B. L. (2011). Developmental experiences during extracurricular activities and Australian adolescents' self-concept: Particularly important for youth from disadvantaged schools. *Journal of Youth and Adolescence, 40*, 582–594.

Bohanon, H., Flenning, P., Carney, K. L., Minnis-Kim, M. J, Anderson-Harriss, S., Moroz, K. B., et al. (2006). Schoolwide application of Positive Behavior Support in an urban high school: A case study. *Journal of Positive Behavior Interventions, 8*, 131–145.

Bradshaw, C. P., Mitchell, M. M., & Leaf, P. J. (2010). Examining the effects of schoolwide positive behavioral interventions and supports on student outcomes: Results from a randomized controlled effectiveness trial in elementary schools. *Journal of Positive Behavior Interventions, 12*, 133–148.

Brunwasser, S. M., Gillham, J. E., & Kim, E. S. (2009). A meta-analytic review of the Penn Resiliency Program's effect on depressive symptoms. *Journal of Consulting and Clinical Psychology, 77*, 1042–1054.

Casey, B. J., Jones, R. M., & Hare, T. A. (2008). The adolescent brain. *Annals of the New York Academy of Sciences, 1124*, 111–124.

Catalano, R. F., Berglund, M. L., Ryan, J. A. M., Lonczak, H. S., & Hawkins, J. D. (2002). Positive youth development in the United States: Research findings on evaluations of positive youth development programs. *Prevention and Treatment, 5*, Article 15.

Collaborative for Academic, Social, and Emotional Learning [CASEL]. (2003). Program descriptions: A companion to Safe and Sound, an educational leader's guide to evidence- based social and emotional learning programs. Retrieved September 5, 2012, from *http://casel.org/in-schools/selecting-programs/additional-resources-for-safe-and-sound.*

Collaborative for Academic, Social, and Emotional Learning [CASEL]. (2012). *2013 CASEL guide: Effective social and emotional learning programs—Preschool and elementary school edition.* Chicago: Author.

Dodge, K. A., Dishion, T. J., & Lansford, J. E. (2006). The problem of deviant peer influences in intervention programs. In K. A. Dodge, T. J. Dishion, & J. E. Lansford (Eds.), *Deviant peer influences in programs for youth: Problems and solutions* (pp. 3–13). New York: Guilford Press.

Durlak, J. A., Weissberg, R. P., Dymnicki, A. D., Taylor, R. D., & Schellinger, K. B. (2011). The impact of enhancing students' social and emotional learning: A meta-analysis of school-based universal interventions. *Child Development, 82*, 405–432.

Eaton, D. K., Kann, L., Kinchen, S., Shanklin, S., Flint, K. H., Hawkins, J., et al. (2012). Youth Risk Behavior Surveillance—United States, 2011. *Surveillance Summaries, 61*(4), 1–162. Retrieved September 5, 2012, from *www.cdc.gov/healthyyouth/yrbs/index.htm.*

Eccles, J. S., Barber, B. L., Stone, M., & Hunt, J. (2003). Extracurricular activities and adolescent development. *Journal of Social Issues, 59*, 865–889.

Eichas, K., Albrecht, R. E., Garcia, A. J., Ritchie, R. A., Varela, A., & Garcia, A., et al. (2010). Mediators of positive youth development intervention change: Promoting change in positive and problem outcomes? *Child Youth Care Forum, 39*, 211–237.

Erikson, E. H. (1968). *Identity: Youth and crisis.* New York: Norton.

Erikson, E. H. (1993). *Childhood and society* [Reissue]. New York: Norton.

Errecart, M. T., Walberg, H. J., Ross, J. G., Gold, R. S., Fiedler, J. L., & Kolbe, L. J. (1991). Effectiveness of Teenage Health Teaching Modules. *Journal of School Health, 61*, 26–30.

Eyberg, S. M., Nelson, M. M., & Boggs, S. R.

(2008). Evidence-based psychosocial treatment for children and adolescents with disruptive behavior. *Journal of Clinical Child and Adolescent Psychology, 37*, 215–237.

Farrington, D. P., & Totfi, M. M. (2009). School-based programs to reduce bullying and victimization. *Campbell Systematic Reviews, 6*. Retrieved September 5, 2012, from *www.campbellcollaboration.org/lib/download/718*.

Finn, J. D., & Rock, D. A. (1997). Academic success among students at risk for school failure. *Journal of Applied Psychology, 82*, 221–234.

Flannery, K. B., Sugai, G., & Anderson, C. M. (2009). School-wide positive behavior support in high school: Early lessons learned. *Journal of Positive Behavior Interventions, 11*, 177–185.

Fredricks, J. A., & Eccles, J. S. (2006). Is extracurricular participation associated with beneficial outcomes?: Concurrent and longitudinal relations. *Developmental Psychology, 42*, 698–713.

Guerra, N. G., & Bradshaw, C. P. (2008). Linking the prevention of problem behaviors and positive youth development: Core competencies for positive youth development. *New Directions for Child and Adolescent Development, 122*, 1–17.

Guerra, N. G., & Leidy, M. S. (2008). Lessons learned: Recent advances in understanding and preventing childhood aggression. In R. V. Kalil (Ed.), *Advances in child development and behavior* (Vol. 36, pp. 287–330). Boston: Elsevier.

Heron, M. (2012). Deaths: Leading causes for 2008. *National Vital Statistics Report, 60*(6), 1–94. Retrieved September 5, 2012, from *www.cdc.gov/nchs/data/nvsr/nvsr60/nvsr60_06.pdf*.

Johnston, L. D., O'Malley, P. M., Bachman, J. G., & Schulenberg, J. E. (2012). *Monitoring the Future national results on adolescent drug use*. Ann Arbor: Institute for Social Research, University of Michigan. Retrieved September 5, 2012, from *www.monitoringthefuture.org*.

Khanna, M. S., & Kendall, P. C. (2010). Computer-assisted cognitive behavioral therapy for child anxiety: Results of a randomized trial. *Journal of Consulting and Clinical Psychology, 78*, 737–745.

Luthar, S. S. (1995). Social competence in the school setting: prospective cross-domain associations among inner-city teens. *Child Development, 66*, 416–429.

Luthar, S. S., & Zigler, E. (1992). Intelligence and social competence among high-risk adolescents. *Development and Psychopathology, 4*, 287–299.

Madden, M., Lenhart, A., Duggan, M., Cortesi, S., & Gasser, U. (2012). *Teens and technology 2013*. Washington, DC: Pew Research Center, Internet and American Life Project. Retrieved September 5, 2012, from *http://pewinternet.org/~/media//files/reports/2013/pip_teensandtechnology2013.pdf*.

Masten, A. S. (2007). Resilience in developing systems: Progress and promise as the fourth wave rises. *Development and Psychopathology, 19*, 921–930.

Masten, A. S., & Obradović, J. (2006). Competence and resilience in development. *Annals of the New York Academy of Sciences, 1094*, 13–27.

Mays, D., & Thompson, N. J. (2009). Alcohol-related risk behaviors and sports participation among adolescents: An analysis of 2005 Youth Risk Behavior Survey data. *Journal of Adolescent Health, 44*, 87–89.

Modecki, K. L. (2009). "It's a rush": Psychosocial content of antisocial decision making. *Law and Human Behavior, 33*, 183–193.

Modecki, K. L., Barber, B. L., & Eccles, J. S. (2014). Binge drinking trajectories across adolescence: Extra-curricular activities are protective for youth with early pubertal development. *Journal of Adolescent Health, 54*, 61–66.

Muscott, H. S., Mann, E. L., & LeBrun, M. R. (2008). Positive behavioral interventions and supports in New Hampshire: Effects of large-scale implementation of school wide positive behavior support on student discipline and academic achievement. *Journal of Positive Behavior Interventions, 10*, 190–205.

Perry, C. L., Williams, C. L., Komro, K. A., Veblen-Mortenson, S., Stigler, M. H., Munson, K., et al. (2002). Project Northland: Long-term outcomes of community action to reduce adolescent alcohol use. *Health Education Research, 17*, 117–132.

Petrosino, A., Turpin-Petrosino, C., Hollis-Peel, M. E., & Lavenberg, J. G. (2013). Scared Straight and other juvenile awareness programs for preventing juvenile delinquency: A systematic review. *Campbell Systematic Reviews, 5*. Retrieved October 6, 2014, from *www.campbellcollaboration.org/lib/project/3*.

Pittman, K. J. (1991). *Promoting youth development: Strengthening the role of youth serving and community organizations*. Washington, DC: Academy for Educational Development.

Ross, J. G., Gold, R. S., Lavin, A. T., Errecart, M. T., & Nelson, G. D. (1991). Design of the Teenage Health Teaching Modules evaluation. *Journal of School Health, 61*, 21–25.

Scales, P. C., Benson, P. L., Leffert, N., & Blyth, D. (2000). Contribution of development assets to the prediction of thriving among adolescents. *Applied Development Science, 2*(1), 27–46.

Scales, P. C., Foster, K., Mannes, M., Horst, M., & Rutherford, A. (2005). School–business partnerships, developmental assets, and positive outcomes among urban high school students:

A mixed-methods study. *Urban Education, 40*, 144–189.

Schultz, L. H., Barr, D. J., & Selman, R. L. (2001). The value of a developmental approach to evaluating character development programmes: An outcome study of Facing History and Ourselves. *Journal of Moral Education, 30*, 3–27.

Seligman, M. E. P., Ernst, R. M., Gillham, J., Reivich, K., & Linkins, M. (2009). Positive education: Positive psychology and classroom interventions. *Oxford Review of Education, 35*, 293–311.

Sherman, L. W., Gottfredson, D. C., MacKenzie, D. L., Eck, J., Reuter, P., & Bushway, S. D. (1999). *Preventing crime: What works, what doesn't, what's promising.* New York: Russell Sage Foundation.

Simonsen, B., Eber, L., Black, A. C., Sugai, G., Lewandowski, H., Sims, B., et al. (2012). Illinois statewide positive behavioral interventions and supports: Evolution and impact on student outcomes across the years. *Journal of Positive Behavior Interventions, 14*, 5–16.

Sinclair, M. F., Christenson, S. L., Evelo, D. L., & Hurley, C. M. (1998). Dropout prevention for youth with disabilities: Efficacy of a sustained school engagement procedure. *Exceptional Children, 65*, 7–21.

Sinclair, M. F., Christenson, S. L., & Thurlow, M. L. (2005). Promoting school completion of urban secondary youth with emotional or behavioral disabilities. *Exceptional Children, 71*, 465–482.

Slaby, R. G., Wilson-Brewer, R., & DeVos, E. (1994). *Aggressors, victims and bystanders: An assessment-based middle school violence prevention curriculum.* Newton, MA: Education Development Center.

Smith, P. K. (2010). Bullying in primary and secondary schools: Psychological and organizational comparisons. In S. R. Jimerson, S. M. Swearer, & D. L. Espelage (Eds.), *Handbook of bullying in schools: An international perspective* (pp. 137–150). New York: Routledge.

Steinberg, L. (2008). A social neuroscience perspective on adolescent risk-taking. *Developmental Review, 28*, 78–106.

Steinberg, L., Vandell, D. L., & Bornstein, M. H. (2011). *Development: Infancy through adolescence.* Belmont, CA: Wadsworth, Cengage Learning.

Sugai, G., & Horner, R. (2002). The evolution of discipline practices: School-wide positive behavior supports. *Child and Family Behavior Therapy, 24*, 23–50.

Underwood, M. K., Rosen, L. H., More, D., Ehrenreich, S. E., & Gentsch, J. K. (2012). The BlackBerry Project: Capturing the content of adolescents' text messaging. *Developmental Psychology, 48*, 295–302.

U.S. Department of Education, National Center for Education Statistics. (2012). The Condition of Education 2012 (NCES 2012-045). Retrieved from *nces.ed.gov/fastfacts/display.asp?id=16.*

Waasdorp, T. E., Bradshaw, C. P., & Leaf, P. J. (2012). The impact of school-wide positive behavioral interventions and supports on bullying and peer rejection: A randomized controlled effectiveness trial. *Archives of Pediatrics and Adolescent Medicine, 166*, 149–156.

Werner, E. E. (1997). Vulnerable but invincible: High-risk children from birth to adulthood. *Acta Paediatrica, 86*, 103–105.

Werner, E. E., & Smith, R. S. (1982). *Vulnerable but invincible: A longitudinal study of resilient children and youth.* New York: McGraw-Hill.

What Works Clearinghouse. (2006). *Too Good for Drugs and Violence—High School.* Washington, DC: U.S. Department of Education. Retrieved September 5, 2012, from *http://ies.ed.gov/ncee/wwc/interventionreport.aspx?sid=516.*

Williamson, A. A., Dierkhising, C. B., & Guerra, N. G. (2013). Brief report: Piloting the Positive Life Changes (PLC) program for at-risk adolescents. *Journal of Adolescence, 36*, 623–628.

Wilson, S. J., & Lipsey, M. W. (2007). School-based interventions for aggressive and disruptive behavior: Update of a meta-analysis. *American Journal of Preventative Medicine, 33*, S130–S143.

World Health Organization (WHO). (2003). *Skills-based education including life skills: An important component of a child-friendly health-promoting school.* Geneva, Switzerland: Author. Retrieved September 5, 2012, from *www.who.int/school_youth_health/media/en/sch_skills4health_03.pdf.*

Yurgelun-Todd, D. (2007). Emotional and cognitive changes during adolescence. *Current Opinion in Neurobiology, 17*, 251–257.

CHAPTER 13

SEL in Higher Education

Colleen S. Conley

For nearly 20 years, researchers and practitioners of social and emotional learning (SEL) have aimed to determine the best practices available for intra- and interpersonal skills enhancement, problem prevention, health promotion, and positive development (Collaborative for Academic, Social, and Emotional Learning [CASEL], 2012; Elias et al., 1997). Specifically, SEL scholars have identified the value of building five core competencies—self-awareness, self-management, responsible decision making, social awareness, and relationship skills—and have worked to promote these strengths through school-based programming (CASEL, 2003, 2012). Because these domains and competencies are relevant for the entire lifespan, SEL is not inherently tied to any particular educational context or developmental period. To date, however, the theoretical and empirical literature on SEL has focused primarily on preschool through secondary school students, and guidelines for SEL practices routinely mention goals and applications for these student populations (CASEL, 2003; Greenberg et al., 2003; Zins, Weissberg, Wang, & Walberg, 2004). In contrast, the SEL framework has not yet been applied to higher education populations and settings. Certainly, SEL education is of prime importance for children in that it can chart a positive developmental trajectory during an early, formative period of life. Yet the need for SEL does not end in high school. The case can easily be made that the mission of higher education institutions, similar to those of primary and secondary schools, "is to educate students to be knowledgeable, responsible, socially skilled, healthy, caring, and contributing citizens" (Greenberg et al., 2003, p. 466; also see Seal, Naumann, Scott, & Royce-Davies, 2010). Likewise, similar to the research on the academic benefits of SEL for youth (Zins, Bloodworth, Weissberg, & Walberg, 2004), research in higher education populations demonstrates that social and emotional adjustment is associated with positive academic outcomes, including academic performance and retention (Gloria & Ho, 2003). Furthermore, social and emotional skills are associated with benefits extending beyond academic contexts and outcomes, such as success in work, positive interpersonal relationships, and better mental health and overall well-being (Bar-On, Handley, & Fund, 2006; Jordan & Ashkanasy, 2006; Lopes, Salovey, Coté, & Beers, 2005; Mayer, Salovey, & Caruso, 2004). Thus, the value of SEL is vital in higher education.

There is a growing literature on mental health promotion and prevention for higher education students, and many of these programs focus on social and emotional outcomes (for reviews, see Conley, Durlak, & Dickson, 2013; Conley, Durlak, & Kirsch, in press). Although these programs have not yet been conceptualized within an SEL framework, they share many of the same elements and target similar aspects of social and emotional learning as SEL programs for youth. This chapter reviews this literature in the context of SEL and offers suggestions for future research and practice addressing SEL in higher education.

Theoretical and Empirical Background: Expanding SEL to Higher Education

Decades of theoretical work document the higher education years as a formative developmental period (e.g., Astin, 1984; Evans, Forney, Guido, Patton, & Renn, 2009) and note the various social, emotional, and academic challenges that place substantial strain on students' mental health and adjustment (Howard, Schiraldi, Pineda, & Campanella, 2006; McDonald, Pritchard, & Landrum, 2006). Higher education settings typically present students with less structure, more demands, new roles, and increased pressures, contributing to their struggles with stress, distress, and adjustment difficulties. Indeed, a substantial body of research on higher education students documents that stress, maladjustment, and mental health problems are high among this population, compared to developmental and clinical norms (Stallman, 2010; Stewart-Brown et al., 2000).

The social and emotional skills that are most relevant to higher education students are those that can promote their personal and interpersonal awareness and competence, and therefore help them navigate new and challenging academic, social, and emotional terrain. Promoting these competencies, in turn, is likely to curb problems or maladjustment in emotional and social domains. Thus, SEL competencies are valuable both as aspects of positive adjustment and for their ability to forestall related aspects of negative adjustment. The following list, adapted from CASEL (2003, p. 5; 2012, p. 9), applies the five core SEL competencies to higher education populations:

- *Self-awareness*: Accurately recognizing one's thoughts and emotions, and their influence on behaviors; accurately assessing one's strengths and limitations; possessing a well-grounded sense of self-esteem, self-efficacy, self-confidence, perceived control, and optimism.
- *Self-management*: Effectively regulating one's thoughts, emotions, and behaviors; managing stress; savoring emotional well-being; successfully engaging in skills such as coping, problem solving, mindfulness, relaxation, and positive and productive thinking.
- *Social awareness*: Identifying appropriate social resources and supports; displaying accurate perspective taking, respect for others, and empathy.
- *Relationship skills*: Establishing and maintaining healthy relationships; seeking and providing help when needed; communicating effectively; negotiating conflict constructively; solving interpersonal problems.
- *Responsible decision making*: Making constructive, responsible, and ethical choices that promote self and other well-being; effectively managing goals, time, and tasks.

In higher education settings, the structure and support of predetermined school schedules, parental monitoring, and family routines typically give way, shifting from externally to internally focused responsibility, which in turn emphasizes the need for students' continual use of skills such as self-awareness, self-management, and responsible decision making. Socially, the transition to higher education often involves forging new relationships with roommates, an entirely new peer group, and a faculty and staff who serve *in loco parentis*. Thus, higher education students also experience a heightened need for social awareness and relationship skills. Indeed, research has demonstrated that social and emotional competencies in these five SEL domains are critical to higher education students' development, adjustment, and success. For example, students with positive self-awareness and self-perceptions appear to adapt most successfully in higher education contexts (e.g., Ramos-Sanchez & Nichols, 2007). Similarly, self-management skills have beneficial effects for students' personal and emotional adjustment, as well as their academic and cognitive performance (e.g., Deckro et al., 2002; Palmer & Roger, 2009; Parker, Duffy, Wood, Bond, & Hogan, 2005). In contrast, poor self-management can lead to symptoms of emotional distress, such as depression, anxiety, and stress, which are consistently noted among the most prevalent and challenging adjustment problems facing higher education students (Adlaf, Gliksman, Demers, & Newton-Taylor, 2001; American College Health Association, 2011; Bayram & Bilgel, 2008), and can have detrimental effects on academic functioning and retention (Pritchard & Wilson, 2003). Furthermore, because social skills, social support, and social stress are key elements of adjustment in higher education (Gerdes & Mallinckrodt, 1994), *social awareness* and *relationship skills* are essential for successful navigation in this context (Hefner & Eisenberg, 2009; Tao, Dong, Pratt, Hunsberger, & Pancer, 2000). Finally, research in higher education settings demonstrates the importance of *responsible decision making*, with regard to both curricular (e.g., academic goals and study skills; Robbins et al., 2004) and extracurricular (e.g., substance use; Wolaver, 2002) behaviors. In summary, helping students to develop strengths and assets that promote their social and emotional well-being seems to be just as worthwhile an investment in higher education as it is in earlier educational contexts.

Scope of This Chapter

This chapter reviews published and unpublished evaluations of 113 SEL-related prevention and promotion programs that were conducted in higher education settings (i.e., 2- or 4-year colleges and universities, trade and vocational schools, and graduate and professional programs such as medical school or law school). (A complete list of all programs reviewed in this chapter, categorized by program type and success status, is available from the author.) In particular, this chapter focuses on universal prevention or promotion programs rather than those targeted at students with established or early-identified problems. Furthermore, this review focuses on programs that assessed one or more the following SEL outcomes—emotional distress, self-perceptions, social–emotional skills, and relationships with others—as these are the most commonly assessed social and emotional outcomes in higher education that map onto similar research on younger students (e.g., Catalano, Berglund, Ryan, Lonczak, & Hawkins, 2004; Greenberg, Domitrovich, & Bumbarger, 2001). Finally, although several interventions for higher education students are geared toward reducing substance use, sexual assault, body dissatisfaction, and eating disorders (for reviews, see Anderson & Whiston, 2005; Carey, Scott-Sheldon, Carey, & DeMartini, 2007; Yager & O'Dea, 2008), this review focuses on programs that target higher education students' *general* social and emotional well-being.

Conley and colleagues (2013) reviewed a similar body of research to assess the methodology and impact of higher education interventions on various social and emotional, as well as academic and health-related, outcomes. This chapter reconceptualizes this body of research within an SEL framework, using a slightly different study sample, and focuses specifically on the social and emotional outcomes achieved by these interventions. Furthermore, this chapter summarizes the impact of these programs in a different way, as described below.

Current Research: Overview of Strategies

Methodological Issues

The programs reviewed here were evaluated in designs that include a control group and involved quantitative assessment of outcomes that fell into one or more of the following categories: emotional distress, social and emotional skills, self-perceptions, and relationships with others. Another inclusion criterion for this review was that the program needed to continue for more than one session, outside of suggested home practice.

Intervention Types

Because the research on promoting social and emotional competencies in higher education has not yet been organized within an SEL framework or promoted as a focus for systematic programming or policy (in contrast to that for younger populations;

CASEL, 2012), these interventions tend not to be as organized, structured, or uniform as the model SEL programs for youth. CASEL (2012) has identified several "SELect" programs for preschool and elementary students that address all five of the CASEL competencies and provide multiple opportunities to practice and develop skills, both within the program and in real-life situations, over multiple years. In contrast, the social and mental health promotion programs for higher education populations typically address some, but not all, of the SEL core competencies and are usually brief (i.e., lasting only a few weeks and rarely extending beyond one semester).

Despite the lack of systematic organization in the research promoting social and emotional competencies in higher education, there are some common categories that emerge from these interventions. *Psychoeducational* programs are interventions that primarily provide didactic information to participants on topics such as stress, coping, and ways to relax. The didactic content of these programs varies, but they are unified by their assumption that providing information, rather than building skills, will improve students' adjustment. Among the *skills-oriented programs* are the five main categories described below. Although the terminology used to describe these interventions differs from the typical terminology in SEL programming for youth, the practical elements and intended outcomes of these programs are quite similar. To illustrate the connections between youth SEL programs and higher education promotion programs, the social and emotional skills most commonly emphasized in each program category are noted in Table 13.1 on pages 202–203 and are briefly described here:

- *Cognitive-behavioral* interventions tend to emphasize self-awareness and self-management skills such as monitoring and modifying cognitions in order to change emotional and behavioral reactions. They also frequently employ techniques to enhance social awareness, relationship skills, and responsible decision making.
- *Meditation* interventions encompass a variety of meditation techniques intended to enhance self-awareness and self-management skills.
- *Mindfulness* interventions primarily target self-awareness and self-management skills, with some focus also on social awareness and relationship skills, by training the mind to function in a mode of moment-to-moment awareness, acceptance, nonjudgment, and compassion.
- *Relaxation* interventions target self-awareness and self-management strategies designed to teach students how to relax, such as progressive muscle relaxation, breathing techniques, or guided imagery.
- *Social skills* interventions focus primarily on social awareness and relationship competencies, with the aim of improving skills such as assertiveness, communication, and conflict management.

One notable finding from the SEL literature on younger populations is that skills-oriented preventive programs tend to have much greater success than psychoeducational or purely didactic programs (Durlak, 1997; Durlak, Schellinger, Weissberg, Dymnicki, & Taylor, 2011; Greenberg et al., 2001). The literature suggests this is a function of these programs, including multiple opportunities for participants to practice and then apply the skills they are learning effectively (Gresham, 1995). In the mental health promotion and prevention research on higher education populations, interventions with such supervised skills practice were found to be seven times more likely to yield significant outcomes compared to psychoeducational-only programs, and five times more likely to yield significant outcomes compared to other skills-oriented interventions that did not include supervised practice (Conley et al., 2013). SEL researchers and theorists also have noted the importance of skills practice, both within an intervention program and in their applications to real-life situations, to allow for skills development over time (CASEL, 2012). Following these recommendations and existing evidence, this chapter separately reviews skills-building interventions that incorporate supervised skills practice.

Outcomes Evaluated

As noted earlier, this review focuses on four main social and emotional outcome areas. *Emotional distress* outcomes predominantly include depression, anxiety, or stress, as well as general psychological distress or well-being. *Social and emotional skills* outcomes include different types of cognitive, affective, and social skills, such as effective coping techniques, mindfulness, rational beliefs, emotional awareness and management, relaxation strategies, assertiveness, and other communication skills. *Self-perception* outcomes primarily include self-esteem and self-efficacy, and also some assessments of self-compassion, sense of control or agency, optimism, and resilience. *Interpersonal relationship* outcomes include assessments of relationship quality and satisfaction, social support and adjustment, and patterns of conflict and communication with others.

Review of Research Findings

Given the large body of research it reviews, this chapter utilizes a high criterion for success, in order to yield a selective subset of interventions from which to make recommendations for future research and practice. Specifically, a *successful trial* is one in which intervention participants, compared to controls, evidenced statistically significant benefits ($p \leq .05$) on *at least half* of the study's assessed outcomes in social and emotional domains. An *unsuccessful trial* is one in which *less than half* of these assessed outcomes demonstrate benefits.

Given the large amount of research on higher education students, this review only considers interventions that have been evaluated in at least three trials, and applies more stringent criteria than might be used for populations and interventions in which fewer trials are available. Following the same initial method as the other chapters in this book's section on *Evidence-Based Programming, what works* includes interventions that have had at least three successful trials in promoting social and emotional learning. However, because of the large number of studies on higher education students, an additional criterion was added, based on the percentage of successful trials that were obtained by the different types of interventions. To be included in the category of *Programs that Work*, more than 66% of the trials for that intervention category had to be successful (i.e., achieve significance on at least half of the social and emotional outcomes). In other words, for programs that work, the odds had to be at least two to one that successful trails were achieved by that intervention category. The *What Is Promising* category included interventions with successful trials occurring between 33 and 66% of the time. The *What Does Not Work* category included interventions in which less than 33% of trials involving social and emotional outcomes were successful. In other words, among all the trials of that particular type of intervention, the odds were at least two to one *against* the program achieving a successful trial. Based on previous research findings with youth (Durlak, 1997) and higher education populations (Conley et al., 2013, in press), this review separates interventions with supervised skills practice from those without this important element.

What Works: Mindfulness

To date, only one intervention category for higher education students meets the stringent criteria for *what works*. The evidence is clear that mindfulness interventions with supervised skills practice work as a primary prevention and promotion strategy for enhancing social and emotional adjustment in higher education students. Notably, seven of the nine reviewed mindfulness interventions (78%) were successful trials that at postintervention yielded improvements in emotional distress, self-perceptions, and/or social–emotional skills (none of these studies assessed interpersonal relationships; Astin, 1997; Hoffmann Gurka, 2005; Oman, Shapiro, Thoresen, Plante, & Flinders, 2008; Rosenzweig, Reibel, Greeson, Brainard, & Hojat, 2003; Sears & Kraus, 2009; Shapiro, Brown, & Biegel, 2007; Shapiro, Oman, Thoresen, Plante, & Flinders, 2008; Shapiro, Schwartz, & Bonner, 1998). Notably, one of the trials without positive results at postintervention did demonstrate later success at the 4-month follow-up, with program participants evidencing gains over controls in both depression and stress (Leggett, 2010). The other unsuccessful trial demonstrated significant pre–post effects (with medium to large effect sizes; *d* ranged from 0.52 to 2.63) for all assessed outcomes in the intervention group, but none of the out-

TABLE 13.1. Skills Commonly Targeted in Higher Education Interventions in Relation to Core SEL Competency Domains

General type of intervention	SEL competency domains				
	Self-awareness	Self-management	Social awareness	Relationship skills	Responsible decision making
Cognitive-behavioral	• Recognizing triggers of stress and distress • Identifying automatic thoughts • Identifying positive self-statements • Scheduling pleasant events • Self-affirmations	• Stress management, reduction, inoculation • Cognitive modification or restructuring: challenging distortions; generating counterarguments to negative self-statements; increasing positive self-talk • Coping skills training • Relaxation (see Relaxation, below)	• Using social support to reduce stress and enhance well-being	• Social skills (see Social Skills, below)	• Taking steps to reduce stress • Modifying maladaptive behavior • Goal setting; time management
Meditation	• Focusing attention on a single item (e.g., one's breath; a sound, object, or body part; the passing of one's thoughts)	• Passively disregarding distracting thoughts or sensations, gently returning the mind to the original object or thought • Relaxation exercises, including breathing and body scan	• *Generally not covered*	• *Generally not covered*	• *Generally not covered*
Mindfulness	• Awareness of sensory experiences, somatic sensations, thoughts, feelings, and behaviors	• Mindfulness (bringing attention to the present moment, nonjudgmentally) • Mindful approaches to everyday	• Other-directed "loving-kindness":	• Mindfulness in relationships (e.g., mindful listening, empathy)	• *Generally not covered*

	• Self-acceptance (accepting "whatever arises") • Self-directed "lovingkindness" (compassion, friendliness, joy, peacefulness)	practices and experiences such as work, school, stress, pain, suffering • Patience, letting go, slowing down, detachment • Relaxation; stress reduction	friendliness, compassion, joy, peacefulness		
Relaxation	• Awareness of bodily sensations related to stress and relaxation	• Breathing techniques (e.g., slow, deep breathing) • Bodily relaxation (progressive muscle relaxation, autogenic training, cue-controlled relaxation) • Mental relaxation (e.g., guided imagery)	• *Generally not covered*	• *Generally not covered*	• *Generally not covered*
Social skills	• Recognizing filters that impair good communication	• Effectively dealing with filters to improve communication	• Recognizing risk factors for relationship dysfunction and distress • Listening with understanding	• Communication • Assertiveness • Relationship problem solving • Conflict management and resolution • Enhancing positive aspects of relationships	• *Generally not covered*

Note. Terms in the table are drawn directly from the authors of the intervention studies. Individual programs within each intervention category vary in the specific skills they emphasize and do not always encompass every skill listed here. Some items that overlap into multiple areas of SEL competency domains are listed in the most central area.

comes in the control group; yet likely due to small sample sizes (10 intervention and six control participants) the between-group differences posttreatment did not reach statistical significance (Lynch, Gander, Kohls, Kudielka, & Walach, 2011).

The success of mindfulness interventions for improving SEL in higher education students seems attributable both to content and structural elements. As listed in Table 13.1, these interventions typically cultivate skills in self-awareness (including awareness of sensory and somatic experiences, thoughts, emotions, and behaviors; self-acceptance; self-compassion), self-management (including mindfulness, patience, relaxation, and stress management), social awareness (e.g., compassion toward others), and relationship skills (including mindfulness in relationships, mindful listening, and empathy). Furthermore, these interventions generally aim to cultivate mindfulness in a broad way, through skills and practices, as well as motivation and attitudes (e.g., Oman et al., 2008; Shapiro et al., 2008). Typically, mindfulness interventions call on participants to apply their newly learned skills to multiple aspects of their everyday lives (e.g., encouraging mindfulness in relationships, at school, and at work; taking a mindful approach to eating; engaging in mindful approaches to stress). Given their emphasis on incorporating a broad array of SEL-related competencies into daily life, it is not surprising that mindfulness programs yield benefits for emotional distress (including depression, anxiety, stress, general emotional wellness, affect, and mood), social–emotional skills (including higher levels of mindfulness, rational beliefs, empathy, and forgiveness, and lower levels of rumination), and self-perceptions (including heightened self-compassion, sense of control, and hope).

Beyond the content of these interventions, several structural elements are notable as well. These mindfulness interventions are manualized, using session protocols based either on Kabat-Zinn's (1982, 1990) mindfulness-based stress reduction or Easwaran's (1978, 1991) Eight-Point Program. A typical mindfulness session includes a *didactic element* with formal instruction of a mindfulness meditation or practice (e.g., sitting meditation, passage meditation, breath awareness, body scan, mindful movement, loving-kindness meditation, mindful stretching, or hatha yoga), as well as an *experiential element* that involves practicing the skills in session, and encouraging students to practice outside of session as well (typically with provided audio recordings and practice logs). The success of mindfulness programs is impressive given their brevity. Interventions ranged from 3 to 10 weekly sessions, lasting 1–3 hours each, yielding an average of approximately 30 hours total intervention time.

What Is Promising

Three intervention categories meet criteria as *promising*. Although further research is needed, cognitive-behavioral, relaxation, and social skills interventions show some promise in improving social and emotional outcomes in higher education students.

Cognitive-Behavioral Interventions

Cognitive-behavioral interventions with supervised skills practice satisfy the *what is promising* criteria for promoting social and emotional benefits in higher education students. Among the 30 reviewed interventions, 18 (60%) meet the criteria for a successful trial. Cognitive-behavioral interventions are somewhat variable in their methods, but they typically follow a manualized protocol or structured framework (e.g., Beck, Emery, & Greenberg, 1985; Burns, 1999; Ellis, 2001; Meichenbaum, 1985). As listed in Table 13.1, these interventions promote skills in the self-awareness and self-management categories, such as recognizing triggers of stress and distress, identifying automatic thoughts and self-statements, modifying or restructuring cognitions, improving coping skills, relaxing, and managing or reducing stress. Some cognitive-behavioral interventions for higher education students also address social awareness and relationship skills (e.g., using social support to enhance personal well-being, and improving social skills) and responsible decision making (e.g., taking steps to reduce stress, modifying maladaptive behaviors, setting goals and improving time management, and making healthy lifestyle choices).

An illustrative example of a successful cognitive-behavioral intervention, designed to reduce stress and distress in college students, was reported by Deckro and colleagues (2002). This 6-week, skills-based intervention emphasized many of the social and emotional learning competencies noted in Table 13.1, particularly in the categories of self-awareness (including awareness of thoughts, bodily sensations, and their connection), self-management (including challenging cognitive distortions, relaxation, stress management, coping), and responsible decision making (including goal setting). This intervention was manualized (both trainers and students had manuals to guide their practice), and each session included a mix of the following elements: (1) lecture, discussion, and demonstration of new material, (2) review of weekly skills practice, and (3) supervised practice of the targeted skills. Facilitators encouraged skills practice outside of session, providing students with a manual and guided audio files for completing the exercises, sending weekly e-mail reminders about skills practice, and asking students to complete daily logs of practice. Ultimately, the skills were intended to be integrated into students' lives on a regular basis.

Across the 18 identified successful cognitive-behavioral interventions, several areas of social and emotional outcomes have yielded significant benefits, in the categories of emotional distress (including depression, suicidality, anxiety, stress, negative vs. positive affect, general psychological distress, emotional well-being), self-perceptions (including self-esteem, self-concept of academic ability, self-actualization, optimism), social and emotional skills (including coping, positive thinking styles, emotional awareness and management, relaxation, stress management, trust), and interpersonal relationships (including social awareness, communication patterns, conflict resolution). Despite this success, it is important to note that 12 of the 30 cognitive-behavioral interventions failed to meet the criteria for a successful trial. Future research should aim to clarify what makes some of these interventions successful and others not.

Relaxation Interventions

This review identified 12 relaxation interventions with supervised skills practice, and six (50%) were successful. The successful interventions utilized a variety of relaxation methods, including autogenic training (Kanji, White, & Ernst, 2006), progressive muscle relaxation (Lyons & Lufkin, 1967), biofeedback (Ratanasiripong, Ratanasiripong, & Kathalae, 2012; Turner, 1991), relaxing breathing exercises (Baker, 2012), or a combination of such methods (Charlesworth, Murphy, & Beutler, 1981). As reported by Kanji and colleagues (2006), autogenic training included six standard exercises focused on (1) muscular relaxation, (2) feeling warm, (3), calming cardiac activity, (4) slowed respiration, (5) warmth in the abdominal region, and (6) coolness in the head. Progressive muscle relaxation entails tensing then relaxing a series of muscle groups, noting the feelings of warmth, heaviness, and relaxation. The biofeedback interventions trained students to monitor and modulate their basic physiological responses to stress, such as their heart rate, muscle tension, or skin temperature. As noted in Table 13.1, these and related relaxation techniques primarily target self-awareness and self-management, specifically by raising awareness of bodily sensations related to stress and relaxation, and by inducing bodily and mental relaxation. Accordingly, these relaxation interventions focused on assessing emotional distress outcomes (e.g., anxiety, stress, tension), and the three successful trials found relaxation to have a significant impact on physiological indicators of stress (including blood pressure, pulse, and an electromyographical measure of tension) and on self-reports of anxiety and stress.

Although these six successful trials are promising, this review also identified six unsuccessful trials. Further research is needed to account for the mixed success of relaxation programs in higher education settings.

Social Skills Interventions

Out of five social skills interventions with supervised skills practice, two (40%) were successful (Braithwaite & Fincham, 2007; Waldo, 1982). Although they were similar in their focus on enhancing social skills through behavioral interventions (see Table 13.1), their specific methods differed sufficiently to warrant describing both interventions here. Waldo (1982) administered a relationship skills workshop designed to enhance positive communication between roommates, including "listening with understanding and offering honest self-disclosure during difficult interpersonal situations" (p. 5). Through a combination of lectures, demonstrations, readings, written reports, and, most notably, "structured experiences designed to foster a supportive interpersonal environment" (p. 5), the intervention provided opportunities to develop competence in "values clarification, communication and conflict resolution" (p. 5). Compared to controls, intervention participants showed significantly enhanced levels of positive communication with roommates postintervention.

Braithwaite and Fincham (2007) administered ePREP, a computer-based intervention based on the Prevention and Relationship Enhancement Program (Markman, Stanley, & Blumberg, 2001), an empirically validated approach to improving romantic relationship quality. Through self-paced content delivered in slide format, participants learned about communication and conflict-management techniques, and interpersonal problem-solving skills. An important aspect of supervised skills practice, participants took quizzes to ensure mastery of the material. After completing the intervention, participants received a printed copy of the material, as well as weekly reminder e-mails to prompt and assess their implementation of the targeted skills. Following the intervention, participants evidenced benefits in six out of 10 outcomes across the SEL domains of emotional distress (i.e., lower levels of depression, anxiety, and negative affect, but not higher levels of positive affect), social and emotional skills (higher levels of trust), and interpersonal relationships (lower levels of psychological aggression and physical assault during conflict, but not higher levels of negotiation during conflict, and no significant differences in relationship satisfaction or in constructive communication patterns). Of note, the authors replicated the ePREP intervention twice more (Braithwaite & Fincham, 2009, 2011) but found weaker support in these replications. The 2009 trial utilized latent growth curve modeling to determine benefits over time, including both postintervention (8 weeks) and follow-up (10 months). These models yielded only one (of seven) significant group effect (intervention vs. control) on social and emotional outcomes: specifically, the intervention seemed to impact anxiety but not depression, constructive communication, relationship satisfaction, or the three conflict resolution skills noted earlier. However, the authors point out strong effect sizes (range 0.36 to 2.69) in seven of the 10 outcomes at the 10-month follow-up assessment. Furthermore, the 2011 trial found some support for enhancing social and emotional outcomes in women only (in four of 10 outcomes assessed) or in men only (in two of 10 outcomes assessed). Although further research is needed to sort out the mixed pattern of findings, the ePREP intervention does seem to offer promise for enhancing social and emotional competencies in higher education populations.

What Does Not Work

Three intervention categories meet criteria as *what does not work*, as empirical evaluations to date have demonstrated them to be ineffective in the majority (67% or more) of evaluated trials. As detailed below, the evidence appears to argue against the social and emotional benefits of (1) meditation interventions, (2) interventions that emphasize skills but do not contain supervised practice of these skills, and (3) psychoeducational interventions that focus on didactics rather than skills.

Meditation

This review identified six meditation interventions with supervised skills practice, but only one of these (17%) was successful (i.e., produced benefits in half or more of the assessed social and emotional outcomes—in this one case, for perceived stress, state and trait anxiety; Baker, 2012). Meditation practices, such as transcendental or concentration meditation, aim to focus participants' attention on a single item (e.g., a sound, object, or body part; one's breath, or the passing of one's thoughts) and passively disregard other distracting thoughts or sensations, gently refocusing the mind on the intended object or thought (see Winzelberg & Luskin, 1999). These practices are theorized to improve stress management via physiological effects (e.g., reducing arousal and inducing relaxation). Although there is some evidence that meditation has beneficial effects for reducing arousal and anxiety in adults and in some medical patients (for reviews, see Eppley, Abrams, & Shear, 1989; Smith, 1975), the existing research on the social and emotional benefits in higher education populations does not sufficiently document that it is an effective technique for improving social and emotional outcomes. Specifically, the preponderance of studies reviewed here found a lack of significant impact, or mixed findings at best, for several examined SEL benefits, including reducing emotional distress (anxiety, stress, general distress vs. well-being), enhancing self-perceptions (e.g., self-efficacy), and improving social and emotional skills (e.g., coping) (Fulton, 1990; Kindlon, 1983; Moss, 2003; Winzelberg & Luskin, 1999; Zuroff & Schwarz, 1978).

Interventions without Supervised Skills Practice

This review identified 23 skills-oriented programs without supervised practice, but only five (22%) were successful (Abel, 2005; Epstein, Sloan, & Marx, 2005; Grassi, Preziosa, Villani, & Riva, 2007; Heaman, 1995; Winterdyk et al., 2008). Furthermore, among the 18 unsuccessful programs, 13 failed to obtain significant effects on *any* social and emotional outcomes. Given that these interventions are nearly four times more likely to be unsuccessful rather than successful, interventions that do not incorporate supervised skills practice do not appear to work, or even be promising, for promoting social and emotional adjustment in higher education populations. No distinguishing features emerged to set apart the five successful programs, compared to the 18 unsuccessful ones, in terms of intervention type or programmatic features (e.g., sample, design, format, length of exposure, delivery format). Thus, although these programs as a whole include an important element of focusing on skills, their lack of supervised practice over multiple sessions seems to limit their ability to yield social and emotional benefits.

Psychoeducational Interventions

Of the 28 psychoeducational (didactic, not skills-oriented) interventions identified for this review, only four (14%) meet criteria for being successful (Jones, 2004; MacLeod, Coates, & Hetherton, 2008; Mattanah et al., 2010; Walker & Frazier, 1993). In other words, psychoeducational interventions are six times more likely to be unsuccessful as successful. Additionally, of the 24 unsuccessful trials, 17 demonstrated no significant benefits on any of their assessed social and emotional outcomes. Thus, psychoeducational interventions do not appear to realize the intended impact of achieving social and emotional benefits in higher education populations. It is not surprising that, on the whole, programs that do not focus on skills development tend not to yield successful social and emotional outcomes because this same finding has appeared in interventions for both higher education students (Conley et al., 2013) and younger populations (Durlak, 1997; Durlak et al., 2011; Greenberg et al., 2001).

Summary and Recommendations for Future Research and Practice

Although the concept of social and emotional learning has not previously been applied to higher education settings, there are many mental health promotion and prevention programs that can be considered successful or promising in enhancing social and emotional development in higher education students, extending findings for primary and secondary school students (in this volume, see Jagers, Harris, & Skoog, Chapter 11; Rimm-Kaufman & Hulleman, Chapter 10; Williamson, Modecki, & Guerra, Chapter 12). As with the literature on SEL for youth, not all programs in higher education are equally effective. Among skills-oriented programs with supervised practice, one intervention type—mindfulness—emerges as clearly effective, and three others—cognitive-behavioral, relaxation, and social skills interventions—show promise. A fifth category, meditation programs, appears to be ineffective for improving social and emotional adjustment in higher education settings.

Cutting across the topical focus of programs, two categories of interventions appear not to work for enhancing social and emotional learning in higher education students. Skills-oriented programs without a supervised practice component do not effectively improve social and emotional adjustment. Furthermore, psychoeducational programs that do not emphasize skills but instead focus on didactic information are unsuccessful in producing social and emotional benefits in nearly all cases. In summary, just as with SEL programs for school-age youth (Botvin, 2000; Durlak et al., 2011; Lösel & Beelmann, 2003), supervised skills practice appears to be one central component for successfully promoting social and emotional development in higher education students.

Although the current findings are encouraging, it is important to note that this review evaluated effectiveness immediately following the intervention period. Only about one-third of the programs included in this review assessed outcomes at a follow-up period, and these were usually of short duration. Thus, further research is needed to evaluate the long-term impact of SEL programs in higher education. Beyond the demonstrated importance of supervised skills practice, further research is needed to examine the active components and mechanisms accounting for the success of some programs but not others. For example, mediation analyses can clarify whether gains in different SEL skills are responsible for program outcomes. Research also is needed to *compare* different types of SEL interventions in higher education to determine their relative impact for different types of students and delivery formats. For example, first-year orientation programs are common on college campuses, but little research has investigated their potential impact on social and emotional functioning, and the research that does exist rarely includes the important element of supervised skills practice.

To date, programs that promote social and emotional competencies in higher education tend to be researcher-initiated, relatively brief interventions that are disconnected from the institutions' curricula, staff, and goals. An important next step for SEL in higher education is to extend promising research findings into everyday practice by integrating successful SEL interventions into higher education institutions and curricula programmatically. Following important implementation guidelines from SEL researchers and practitioners, this would include being (1) institution-initiated and designed to meet the specific needs of that institution; (2) coordinated within the institution's existing curricula and programming in an ongoing, systematic way; (3) supported by school administrators and leadership, and performed in collaboration with key institutional staff; and, finally, (4) carefully monitored and evaluated over time to enhance program improvement and sustainability (CASEL, 2012; Greenberg et al., 2003; Zins, Bloodworth, et al., 2004; Zins & Elias, 2006).

To take initial steps toward implementing best practices, higher education personnel must first agree on the value and role of social and emotional, as well as academic, learning. Administrators can draw on many of the existing structural features in higher education settings that lend themselves to systematic SEL programming in order to establish mechanisms for implementing and supporting institutionwide SEL initiatives. A critical element in this process is to coordinate "systems of support" (Zins & Elias, 2006, p. 2) to develop SEL goals for the institution, and to implement and monitor suitable programs to meet these goals. Key players in higher education include student representatives, institutional administrators, and frontline staff from across the university community, including student development, counseling and health centers, and academic departments with related interests such as psychology and health education. The tools and platforms for delivering successful programs should include both curricular and cocurricular offerings. This review identified several successful programs that were offered as elective classes, and these seemed to be successful in attracting students. Developing courses that promote SEL within the *core* (not just elective) curriculum, such as through required first-year seminars, would reach more students and provide SEL benefits on a broader scale. Incorporating SEL into co-curricular offerings, such as new-student orientation and residence hall programming, also would expose more students to skills that will help them manage the challenges of navigating the higher education environment.

This review of SEL interventions suggests the value of systematically integrating SEL into higher education settings. Working together, SEL researchers and higher education practitioners can coordinate institutions' goals and existing programs with evidence-based SEL interventions such as those reviewed here. Ultimately, these efforts can promote social and emotional learning in this important developmental period and context.

Acknowledgments

Special thanks to Joseph Durlak, Daniel Dickson, Alexandra Kirsch, Alison Stoner, and my team of fabulous research assistants for their contributions to this chapter.

References

Abel, H. S. (2005). *The evaluation of a stress management program for graduate students.* Unpublished doctoral dissertation, Texas A&M University, Corpus Christi, TX. Retrieved from ProQuest Dissertations and Theses (*www.proquest.com*).

Adlaf, E. M., Gliksman, L., Demers, A., & Newton-Taylor, B. (2001). The prevalence of elevated psychological distress among Canadian undergraduates: Findings from the 1998 Canadian campus survey. *Journal of American College Health, 50*(2), 67–72.

American College Health Association. (2011). *American College Health Association–National College Health Assessment II: Reference Group Data Report Spring 2011.* Hanover, MD: Author.

Anderson, L. A., & Whiston, S. C. (2005). Sexual assault education programs: A meta-analytic examination of their effectiveness. *Psychology of Women Quarterly, 29*(4), 374–388.

Astin, A. J. (1997). Stress reduction through mindfulness meditation: Effects on psychological symptomatology, sense of control, and spiritual experiences. *Psychotherapy and Psychosomatics, 66*(2), 97–106.

Astin, A. W. (1984). Student involvement: A developmental theory for higher education. *Journal of College Student Personnel, 25*(4), 297–308.

Baker, N. C. (2012). *Does daily meditation or coherent breathing influence perceived stress, stress effects, anxiety, or holistic wellness in college freshmen and sophomores?* Unpublished doctoral dissertation, Boston College. Retrieved from ProQuest Dissertations and Theses (*www.proquest.com*).

Bar-On, R., Handley, R., & Fund, S. (2006). The impact of emotional intelligence on performance. In V. U. Druskat, F. Sala, & G. Mount (Eds.), *Linking emotional intelligence and performance at work* (pp. 3–19). Mahwah, NJ: Erlbaum.

Bayram, N., & Bilgel, N. (2008). The prevalence and socio-demographic correlations of depression, anxiety and stress among a group of university students. *Social Psychiatry and Psychiatric Epidemiology, 43*(8), 667–672.

Beck, A. T., Emery, G., & Greenberg, R. L. (1985). *Anxiety disorders and phobias: A cognitive perspective.* New York: Basic Books.

Botvin, G. J. (2000). Preventing drug abuse in schools: Social and competence enhancement approaches targeting individual-level etiologic factors. *Addictive Behaviors, 25*(6), 887–897.

Braithwaite, S. R., & Fincham, F. D. (2007). ePREP: Computer based prevention of relationship dysfunction, depression, and anxiety. *Journal of Social and Clinical Psychology, 26*(5), 609–622.

Braithwaite, S. R., & Fincham, F. D. (2009). A randomized clinical trial of a computer based preventive intervention: Replication and extension of ePREP. *Journal of Family Psychology, 23*(1), 32–38.

Braithwaite, S. R., & Fincham, F. D. (2011). Computer-based dissemination: A randomized clinical trial of ePREP using the actor partner interdependence model. *Behaviour Research and Therapy, 49*(2), 126–131.

Burns, D. D. (1999). *Feeling good: The new mood therapy.* New York: Avon Books.

Carey, K. B., Scott-Sheldon, L. A., Carey, M. P., & DeMartini, K. S. (2007). Individual-level interventions to reduce college student drinking: A meta-analytic review. *Addictive Behaviors, 32*(11), 2469–2494.

Catalano, R. F., Berglund, M. L., Ryan, J. A. M., Lonczak, H. S., & Hawkins, J. D. (2004). Positive youth development in the United States: Research findings on evaluations of positive youth development programs. *Prevention and Treatment, 5*(1), 98–124.

Charlesworth, E. A., Murphy, S., & Beutler, L. E. (1981). Stress management skill for nursing students. *Journal of Clinical Psychology, 37*(2), 284–290.

Collaborative for Academic, Social, and Emotional Learning (CASEL). (2003). *Safe and sound: An educational leader's guide to evidence-based social and emotional learning (SEL) programs.* Chicago: Author.

Collaborative for Academic, Social, and Emotional Learning (CASEL). (2012). *2013 CASEL guide: Effective social and emotional learning programs—Preschool and elementary school edition*. Chicago: Author.

Conley, C. S., Durlak, J. A., & Dickson, D. A. (2013). An evaluative review of outcome research on universal mental health promotion and prevention programs for higher education students. *Journal of American College Health, 61*(5), 286–301.

Conley, C. S., Durlak, J. A., & Kirsch, A. C. (in press). A meta-analysis of universal mental health prevention programs for higher education students. *Prevention Science*.

Deckro, G. R., Ballinger, K. M., Hoyt, M., Wilcher, M., Dusek, J., Myers, P., et al. (2002). The evaluation of a mind/body intervention to reduce psychological distress and perceived stress in college students. *Journal of American College Health, 50*(6), 281–287.

Durlak, J. A. (1997). *Successful prevention programs for children and adolescents*. New York: Plenum Press.

Durlak, J. A., Schellinger, K. B., Weissberg, R. P., Dymnicki, A. B., & Taylor, R. D. (2011). The impact of enhancing students' social and emotional learning: A meta-analysis of school-based universal interventions. *Child Development, 82*(1), 405–432.

Easwaran, E. (1978). *Meditation: Commonsense directions for an uncommon life*. Petaluma, CA: Nilgiri Press.

Easwaran, E. (1991). *Meditation: A simple eight-point program for translating spiritual ideals into daily life* (2nd ed.). Tomales, CA: Nilgiri Press.

Elias, M. J., Zins, J. E., Weissberg, R. P., Frey, K. S., Greenberg, M. T., Haynes, N. M., et al. (1997). In J. O'Neil, J. Houtz, J. A. Jones, & K. Peck (Eds.), *Promoting social and emotional learning: Guidelines for educators*. Alexandria, VA: Association for Supervision and Curriculum Development.

Ellis, A. (2001). *Overcoming destructive beliefs, feelings, and behaviors: New directions for rational emotive behavior therapy*. Amherst, NY: Prometheus Books.

Eppley, K. R., Abrams, A. I., & Shear, J. (1989). Differential effects of relaxation techniques on trait anxiety: A meta-analysis. *Journal of Clinical Psychology, 45*(6), 957–974.

Epstein, E. M., Sloan, D. M., & Marx, B. P. (2005). Getting to the heart of the matter: Written disclosure, gender, and heart rate. *Psychosomatic Medicine, 67*, 413–419.

Evans, N. J., Forney, D. S., Guido, F. M., Patton, L. D., & Renn, K. A. (2009). *Student development in college theory, research, and practice*. San Francisco: Wiley.

Fulton, M. A. (1990). *The effects of relaxation training and meditation on stress, anxiety, and subjective experience in college students*. Unpublished doctoral dissertation, Lehigh University, Bethlehem, PA. Retrieved from ProQuest Dissertations and Theses (*www.proquest.com*).

Gerdes, H., & Mallinckrodt, B. (1994). Emotional, social, and academic adjustment of college students: A longitudinal study of retention. *Journal of Counseling and Development, 72*(3), 281–288.

Gloria, A., & Ho, T. (2003). Environmental, social, and psychological experiences of Asian American undergraduates: Examining issues of academic persistence. *Journal of Counseling and Development, 81*, 93–105.

Grassi, A., Preziosa, A., Villani, D., & Riva, G. (2007). A relaxing journey: The use of mobile phones for well-being improvement. *Annual Review of CyberTherapy and Telemedicine, 5*, 123–131.

Greenberg, M. T., Domitrovich, C., & Bumbarger, B. (2001). The prevention of mental disorders in school-aged children: Current state of the field. *Prevention and Treatment, 4*(1), 1–62.

Greenberg, M. T., Weissberg, R. P., O'Brien, M. U., Zins, J. E., Fredericks, L., Resnik, H., et al. (2003). Enhancing school-based prevention and youth development through coordinated social, emotional, and academic learning. *American Psychologist, 58*(6/7), 466–474.

Gresham, F. M. (1995). Best practices in social skills training. In A. Thomas & J. Grimes (Eds.), *Best practices in school psychology* (Vol. 3, pp. 1021–1030). Washington, DC: National Association of School Psychologists.

Heaman, D. (1995). The quieting response (QR): A modality for reduction in psychophysiologic stress in nursing students. *Journal of Nursing Education, 34*(1), 5–10.

Hefner, J. L., & Eisenberg, D. (2009). Social support and mental health among college students. *American Journal of Orthopsychiatry, 79*(4), 491–499.

Hoffmann Gurka, A. C. (2005). *Mindfulness meditation for college students: A study of its utility and promotion of its practice post treatment*. Unpublished doctoral dissertation, Marquette University, Milwaukee, WI. Retrieved from ProQuest Dissertations and Theses (*www.proquest.com*).

Howard, D. E., Schiraldi, G., Pineda, A., & Campanella, R. (2006). Stress and mental health among college students: Overview and promising prevention intervention. In M. V. Landow (Ed.),

Stress and mental health of college students (pp. 91–123). New York: Nova Science.

Jones, L. V. (2004). Enhancing psychosocial competence among black women in college. *Social Work, 49*(1), 75–84.

Jordan, P. J., & Ashkanasy, N. M. (2006). Emotional intelligence, emotional self-awareness, and team effectiveness. In V. U. Druskat, F. Sala, & G. Mount (Eds.), *Linking emotional intelligence and performance at work* (pp. 145–163). Mahwah, NJ: Erlbaum.

Kabat-Zinn, J. (1982). An outpatient program in behavioral medicine for chronic pain patients based on the practice of mindfulness meditation: Theoretical considerations and preliminary results. *General Hospital Psychiatry General Hospital Psychiatry, 4*(1), 33–47.

Kabat-Zinn, J. (1990). *Full catastrophe living: Using the wisdom of your body and mind to face stress, pain, and illness.* New York: Delacorte Press.

Kanji, N., White, A., & Ernst, E. (2006). Autogenic training to reduce anxiety in nursing students: Randomized controlled trial. *Journal of Advanced Nursing, 53*, 729–735.

Kindlon, D. J. (1983). Comparison of use of meditation and rest in treatment of test anxiety. *Psychological Reports, 53*(3), 931–938.

Leggett, D. K. (2010). *Effectiveness of a brief stress reduction intervention for nursing students in reducing physiological stress indcators and improving well-being and mental health.* Unpublished doctoral dissertation, University of Utah, Salt Lake City. Retrieved from ProQuest Dissertations and Theses (*www.proquest.com*).

Lopes, P. N., Salovey, P., Coté, S., & Beers, M. (2005). Emotion regulation abilities and the quality of social interaction. *Emotion, 5*(1), 113–118.

Lösel, F., & Beelmann, A. (2003). Effects of child skills training in preventing antisocial behavior: A systematic review of randomized evaluations. *Annals of the American Academy of Political and Social Science, 587*(1), 84–109.

Lynch, S., Gander, M., Kohls, N., Kudielka, B., & Walach, H. (2011). Mindfulness-based coping with university life: A non-randomized wait-list controlled pilot evaluation. *Stress and Health, 27*, 365–375.

Lyons, M. D., & Lufkin, B. (1967). Evaluation of tension control courses for college women. *Research Quarterly of the American Association for Health, Physical Education, and Recreation, 38*(4), 663–670.

MacLeod, A. K., Coates, E., & Hetherton, J. (2008). Increasing well-being through teaching goal-setting and planning skills: Results of a brief intervention. *Journal of Happiness Studies, 9*, 185–196.

Markman, H., Stanley, S., & Blumberg, S. L. (2001). *Fighting for your marriage: Positive steps for preventing divorce and preserving a lasting love.* San Francisco: Jossey-Bass.

Mattanah, J. F., Ayers, J. F., Brand, B. L., Brooks, L. J., Quimby, J. L., & McNary, S. W. (2010). A social support intervention to ease the college transition: Exploring main effects and moderators. *Journal of College Student Development, 51*(1), 93–108.

Mayer, J. D., Salovey, P., & Caruso, D. R. (2004). Emotional intelligence: Theory, findings, and implications. *Psychological Inquiry, 15*(3), 197–215.

McDonald, T. W., Pritchard, M. E., & Landrum, R. E. (2006). Facilitating preventative mental health interventions for college students: Institutional and individual strategies. In M. V. Landow (Ed.), *Stress and mental health of college students* (pp. 225–241). New York: Nova Science.

Meichenbaum, D. (1985). *Stress inoculation training.* New York: Pergamon Press.

Moss, S. B. (2003). *The effects of cognitive behavior therapy, meditation, and yoga on self-ratings of stress and psychological functioning in college students.* Unpublished doctoral dissertation, University of Southern Mississippi, Hattiesburg, MS. Retrieved from ProQuest Dissertations and Theses (*www.proquest.com*).

Oman, D., Shapiro, S. L., Thoresen, C. E., Plante, T. G., & Flinders, T. (2008). Meditation lowers stress and supports forgiveness among college students: A randomized controlled trial. *Journal of American College Health, 56*(5), 569–578.

Palmer, A., & Roger, S. (2009). Mindfulness, stress, and coping among university students. *Canadian Journal of Counseling, 43*(3), 198–212.

Parker, J. D. A., Duffy, M. J., Wood, L. M., Bond, B. J., & Hogan, M. J. (2005). Academic achievement and emotional intelligence: Predicting the successful transition from high school to university. *Journal of the First-Year Experience, 17*(1), 67–78.

Pritchard, M. E., & Wilson, G. S. (2003). Using emotional and social factors to predict student success. *Journal of College Student Development, 44*(1), 18–28.

Ramos-Sanchez, L., & Nichols, L. (2007). Self-efficacy of first-generation and non-first-generation college students: The relationship with academic performance and college adjustment. *Journal of College Counseling, 10*(1), 6–18.

Ratanasiripong, P., Ratanasiripong, N., & Kathalae, D. (2012). Biofeedback intervention for stress and anxiety among nursing students: A randomized controlled trial. *ISRN Nursing, 2012*, Article 827972.

Robbins, S. B., Lauver, K., Le, H., Davis, D., Langley, R., & Carlstrom, A. (2004). Do psychosocial and study skill factors predict college outcomes?: A meta-analysis. *Psychological Bulletin, 130*(2), 261–288.

Rosenzweig, S., Reibel, D. K., Greeson, J. M., Brainard, G. C., & Hojat, M. (2003). Mindfulness-based stress reduction lowers psychological distress in medical students. *Teaching and Learning in Medicine, 15*(2), 88–92.

Seal, C. R., Naumann, S. E., Scott, A. N., & Royce-Davies, J. (2010). Social emotional development: A new model of student learning in higher education. *Research in Higher Education Journal, 10*, 1–13.

Sears, S. R., & Kraus, S. (2009). I think therefore I om: Cognitive distortions and coping style as mediators for the effects of mindfulness meditation on anxiety, positive and negative affect, and hope. *Journal of Clinical Psychology, 65*(6), 561–573.

Shapiro, S. L., Brown, K. W., & Biegel, G. M. (2007). Teaching self-care to caregivers: Effects of mindfulness-based stress reduction on the mental health of therapists in training. *Training and Education in Professional Psychology, 1*(2), 105–115.

Shapiro, S. L., Oman, D., Thoresen, C. E., Plante, T. G., & Flinders, T. (2008). Cultivating mindfulness: Effects on well-being. *Journal of Clinical Psychology, 64*(7), 840–862.

Shapiro, S. L., Schwartz, G. E., & Bonner, G. (1998). Effects of mindfulness-based stress reduction on medical and premedical students. *Journal of Behavioral Medicine, 21*, 581–599.

Smith, J. C. (1975). Meditation as psychotherapy: A review of the literature. *Psychological Bulletin, 82*(4), 558–564.

Stallman, H. M. (2010). Psychological distress in university students: A comparison with general population data. *Australian Psychologist, 45*(4), 249–257.

Stewart-Brown, S., Evans, J., Patterson, J., Petersib, S., Doll, H., Balding, J., et al. (2000). The health of students in institutes of higher education: An important and neglected public health problem? *Journal of Public Health Medicine, 22*(4), 492–499.

Tao, S., Dong, Q., Pratt, M. W., Hunsberger, B., & Pancer, S. M. (2000). Social support: Relations to coping and adjustment during the transition to university in the People's Republic of China. *Journal of Adolescent Research, 15*(1), 123–144.

Turner, J. T. (1991). *The effect of a biofeedback and stress management course on college student anxiety and academic performance.* Unpublished doctoral dissertation, University of Northern Colorado, Greeley.

Waldo, M. (1982, August). *Relationship skills workshops in university residence halls: A preventive intervention.* Paper presented at the annual convention of the American Psychological Association, Washington, DC.

Walker, R., & Frazier, A. (1993). The effect of a stress management educational program on the knowledge, attitude, behavior, and stress level of college students. *Wellness Perspectives, 10*(1), 52–60.

Winterdyk, J., Ray, H., Lafave, L., Flessati, S., Huston, M., Danelesko, E., et al. (2008). The evaluation of four mind/body intervention strategies to reduce perceived stress among college students. *College Quarterly, 11*(1), 1–10.

Winzelberg, A. J., & Luskin, F. M. (1999). The effect of a meditation training in stress levels in secondary school teachers. *Stress Medicine, 15*(2), 69–77.

Wolaver, A. M. (2002). Effects of heavy drinking in college on study effort, grade point average, and major choice. *Contemporary Economic Policy, 20*(4), 415–428.

Yager, Z., & O'Dea, J. A. (2008). Prevention programs for body image and eating disorders on university campuses: A review of large, controlled interventions. *Health Promotion International, 23*(2), 173–189.

Zins, J. E., Bloodworth, M. R., Weissberg, R. P., & Walberg, H. J. (2004). The scientific base linking social and emotional learning to school success. In J. E. Zins, R. P. Weissberg, M. C. Wang, & H. J. Walberg (Eds.), *Building academic success on social and emotional learning: What does the research say* (pp. 3–39). New York: Teachers College Press.

Zins, J. E., & Elias, M. J. (2006). Social and emotional learning. In G. G. Bear, K. M. Minke, & National Association of School Psychologists (Eds.), *Children's needs III: Development, prevention, and intervention* (pp. 1–14). Bethesda, MD: National Association of School Psychologists.

Zins, J. E., Weissberg, R. P., Wang, M. C., & Walberg, H. J. (2004). *Building academic success on social and emotional learning: What does the research say?* New York: Teachers College Press.

Zuroff, D. C., & Schwarz, J. C. (1978). Effects of transcendental meditation and muscle relaxation on trait anxiety, maladjustment, locus of control, and drug use. *Journal of Consulting and Clinical Psychology, 46*, 264–271.

CHAPTER 14

SEL for Students with High-Incidence Disabilities

Andrew L. Wiley and Gary N. Siperstein

Success in school and in life depends to a large extent on acquiring and making good use of the knowledge and skills associated with social and emotional competence (Zins & Elias, 2007). *Social competence* is the ability to initiate and sustain positive relationships and to accomplish a wide range of social tasks (e.g., initiating a conversation, dealing with teasing, playing games, expressing disagreement). *Emotional competence* is the ability to understand and appropriately regulate emotions. The recognition that social and emotional competence, academic achievement, and postschool success are inextricably intertwined has led to a growing interdisciplinary effort to promote social and emotional learning (SEL) in children and youth (Elias et al., 1997). For nearly two decades, the SEL field has focused on developing and researching programs designed to improve the social–emotional functioning of all students in schools (Greenberg et al., 2003). SEL programs use a variety of research-based methods to target five key social and emotional competencies—self-awareness, self-management, social awareness, relationship skills, and responsible decision making (Osher, Bear, Sprague, & Doyle, 2010).

Of course, the term *all students* includes students with disabilities. Just over 10% of all students in American public schools receive special education services for an identified disability. In the effort to improve the social–emotional functioning of *all* students, students with disabilities represent a special case for two important reasons. First, students with disabilities are, on average, more likely than their nondisabled peers to exhibit significant deficits in social and emotional competence. The difficulties that many students with disabilities experience with acquiring and using interpersonal skills (i.e., those related to interacting with others) and intrapersonal skills (i.e., those related to coping with their own thoughts and feelings) place these students at high risk for negative outcomes in multiple areas of functioning (i.e., psychosocial, academic, vocational) (Caprara, Barbaranelli, Pastorelli, Bandura, & Zimbardo, 2000; Parker & Asher, 1987). Consequently, students with disabilities may be especially in need of interventions that promote social and emotional competence. Second, and conversely, the impairments that students with disabilities may exhibit in other domains (e.g., cognition, academic achievement, language) may make it less likely that they will benefit from SEL interventions designed for students without disabilities. In other words, students with disabilities may need social–emotional interventions that are specially designed to address their unique learning needs.

Our purpose in this chapter is to present critical issues and current knowledge related to improving the social and emotional competence of students with disabilities. In the special education literature, interventions designed to increase the social competence of students with disabilities are collectively referred to as *social skills training* (SST; Gresham, Robichaux, York, & O'Leary, 2012). One specific issue that we examine in this chapter is the potential benefits and challenges of combining or coordinating research and practice in the field of SEL with research and practice focusing specifically on SST for students with disabilities. To set the stage for understanding the ways that SEL and SST might work together to improve the social and emotional competence of students with disabilities, we must first describe some basic similarities and differences between SEL and SST.

Comparing and contrasting SEL and SST may seem fairly straightforward, but the similarities and differences between these two areas of research and practice can be subtle and somewhat confusing. For example, an obvious similarity is that SEL and SST both focus on student outcomes related to social competence. However, there are some differences between the two approaches in terms of which aspects of social competence are emphasized and targeted. SEL primarily targets the underlying cognitive and emotional processes associated with social competence (Zins & Elias, 2007), while SST tends to focus on changing overt, observable behaviors that enable social success (Gresham et al., 2012). This distinction is not perfect—many SEL programs include observable behaviors as intervention targets, and many SST interventions have cognitive and other "nonbehavioral" components. Nonetheless, it is correct to say that in terms of *outcomes and methods* that are emphasized, SEL is more strongly rooted in cognitive, emotional, and relational approaches (Osher et al., 2010), while SST is more explicitly based on the principles and technologies of behavioral analysis (Gresham, 2010).

Another obvious difference between SEL and SST is the *populations* that the two approaches target: SEL focuses more on students without disabilities, while SST focuses more on students with disabilities. Although this is generally true, there is more overlap in the populations included in SEL and SST research than might be immediately apparent. It is accurate to say that the SST literature encompasses more research focusing on students with disabilities receiving special education services than the SEL literature, although some SEL studies have also focused specifically on this population (e.g., Kam, Greenberg, & Kusché, 2004). However, as we discuss in more detail later, not all students with disabilities are formally identified by schools for special education services, and both SEL and SST researchers have focused, to varying degrees, on these unidentified at-risk students who display social and emotional problems but do not receive special education services. Despite these overlaps, it is fair to say that compared to SEL, SST focuses more on students with disabilities and those at risk for disabilities.

Perhaps the most helpful similarity between SEL and SST is the emphasis of both on *multitiered approaches* to school-based intervention (Gresham, 2010; Zins & Elias, 2007). A multitiered approach involves the simultaneous implementation of schoolwide programs targeting all students (Tier 1 universal interventions), more intensive interventions targeting groups of students at risk for significant social problems (Tier 2 selected interventions), and the most intensive interventions for individuals who already have significant social problems (Tier 3 intensive interventions) (Sugai & Horner, 2009).These tiered interventions are typically "nested" within each other, such that some students receive more intensive interventions (Tier 2 or Tier 3) *in addition to* (rather than separate from) universal (Tier 1) supports. For students with identified disabilities, intensive individualized interventions are typically delivered through special education. Although special education services can be delivered through a variety of placement options (e.g., resource rooms, special classrooms, special schools), most students with disabilities receive the majority of their instruction in general education classrooms.

By far, most of the interventions in the SST literature are Tier 2 group interventions and, to a much lesser extent, Tier 3 individualized interventions (Gresham, 2010). In contrast, most of the SEL research focuses on Tier 1 universal programs designed to address social and emotional learning at the schoolwide level. Again, this distinction is not perfect: Some SEL research focuses Tier 2 interventions targeting students at risk for significant social and emotional problems (Payton et al., 2008), and a substantial body of research in special education has been devoted to Tier 1 schoolwide systems of positive behavioral interventions and support (SWPBIS; Sugai & Horner, 2009). Keeping in mind this overlap in "tiers" between SEL and SST, as well as the other similarities and differences in outcomes and populations that we discussed previously, we choose in this chapter to use the term "SEL" to refer primarily to Tier 1 schoolwide programs that emphasize cognitive, affective, and connectedness approaches to enhancing the social competence of all students (Osher et al., 2010), and the term "SST" to refer primarily to intensive Tier 2 interventions designed to enhance the social competence of students with disabilities, including students with disabilities who have not been identified for special education (Gresham et al., 2012).

The central message of this chapter is that the effort to promote the social and emotional competence of all students *must include students with disabilities*. Including students with disabilities in school-based reforms aimed at social and emotional learning requires a clear understanding of lessons learned from decades of SST research in special education and related fields. A persistent and unfortunate reality in education reform is that many reforms ignore or fail to consider the unique needs of students with disabilities, or the role that special education should play in accomplishing the objectives of these reforms (Kauffman & Hallahan, 2005). It does not have to be this way. We believe that the current push for school-based SEL programs presents a tremendous opportunity for collaboration between SEL and SST to identify and implement evidence-based practices that can achieve the best possible social and emotional learning outcomes for students with disabilities.

The first step, then, in achieving the purpose of this chapter is to understand *who* we are talking about when we talk about students with disabilities. In the next section, we present authoritative definitions for some of the most common disabilities and briefly relate these definitions to relevant social and emotional characteristics.

Definition and Scope of Students with High-Incidence Disabilities

The federal law that regulates the provision of special education in U.S. schools is the Individuals with Disabilities Education Act (IDEA), which provides authoritative definitions for 13 different disability categories. Contrary to some popular perceptions, the most prevalent disabilities are *mild* disabilities. Disabilities that are considered to be mild are learning disabilities (LD), emotional and behavioral disorders (EBD), and mild intellectual disabilities (MID). Unfortunately, the term "mild disability" can be misleading. Mild disabilities are "mild" only relative to more severe disabilities. In fact, the impairments associated with "mild" disabilities can be very disabling, as evidenced by the substantial academic and social problems experienced by students with these disabilities (Sabornie, Cullinan, Osborne, & Brock, 2005). Because mild disabilities (LD, EBD, MID) occur at a *relatively* high frequency, they are known as *high-incidence* disabilities (as opposed to *low-incidence* disabilities—such as multiple disabilities, physical disabilities, sensory disabilities—that are less prevalent).

In this chapter, we focus on high-incidence disabilities for two reasons. First, among students with disabilities, students with high-incidence disabilities are the most likely to be taught in general education classrooms, and almost all school professionals and other service providers will work frequently with these students. We also focus on students with high-incidence disabilities because the SST research base for these students is broader and more thoroughly developed than the SST research base for students with low-incidence disabilities. There is no question that students with low-incidence disabilities need interventions and supports to enhance their social and emotional learning, and the reader who works with these students is encouraged to make use of the research that has been conducted thus far in this area. However, in this chapter we overview what we know about teaching social skills and SEL for students with high-incidence disabilities. Before we present definitions and prevalence data for LD, EBD, and MID, we mention three challenges associated with defining disabilities that must be kept in mind. The first is recognizing that students with disabilities do not fit neatly into clearly defined disability categories. In reality, there is a degree of overlap across disability groups in academic, social, and psychological characteristics. This overlap is partly attributable to the nature of the disabilities themselves. It is also partly attributable to idiosyncrasies in the way that schools identify students for special education. For example, there is evidence to suggest that schools sometimes "bend the rules" and identify students with MID as LD to avoid the stigma of the MID label. Consequently, some students labeled LD by schools exhibit academic and cognitive profiles that are more consistent with definitions of MID (MacMillan & Siperstein, 2002).

A second challenge is recognizing the substantial heterogeneity that exists *within* disability categories. Students within each disability category vary widely in the nature and extent of their impairments in academic, social, or emotional functioning. Thus, it is impossible to talk about the "typical" student with LD, EBD, or MID. This variability within disability categories is a critical consideration in both research and practice.

Finally, it is important to understand that not all students with disabilities are formally identified for special education services. Some students with disabilities do not need special education to succeed in school. However, some students with disabilities are not identified or served despite clear indications of need. Underidentification is especially pronounced for students with EBD (Kauffman, Mock, & Simpson, 2007). Problems with the federal definition of EBD may contribute to underidentification, along with other factors (Wiley & Siperstein, 2011). In SST research, students who exhibit the characteristics of EBD but are not identified are referred to as *at risk* for EBD, or simply *at risk*.

Learning Disabilities

The disability category with the highest prevalence is LD. Just over 5% of students ages 6–17 (more than 2.5 million students) are served under the LD category, accounting for nearly half of all students identified for special education (U.S. Department of Education, Office of Special Education Programs, 2011). A critical defining feature of LD is *unexpected underachievement* in one or more specific areas of academic functioning (e.g., reading, writing, language, math; Kavale, 2002). Underachievement in LD is unexpected because the student demonstrates average to above average ability to learn, yet fails to do so. The learning problems experienced by students with LD appear to be related to central nervous dysfunction, which is caused by biological, genetic, and/or environmental factors (Hallahan, Kauffman, & Pullen, 2011). The federal definition of LD that guides eligibility for special education is as follows:

> GENERAL—The term "learning disability" means a disorder in one or more of the basic psychological processes involved in understanding or in using language, spoken or written, that may manifest itself in the imperfect ability to listen, think, speak, read, write, spell, or do mathematical calculations.
>
> DISORDERS INCLUDED: "Learning disability" includes conditions such as perceptual disabilities, brain injury, minimal brain dysfunction, dyslexia, and developmental aphasia. (Individuals with Disabilities Education Improvement Act, 2004).

LD and Social–Emotional Functioning

Although the key defining feature of LD is unexpected underachievement in specific academic areas, it is clear that students with LD are also far more likely than their nondisabled peers to exhibit significant deficits in their social–emotional functioning, with estimates ranging up to 75% of students with LD experiencing major social problems (Kavale & Forness, 1996). Social problems include poorly developed interpersonal skills and higher risk for social rejection (Bryan, Burstein, & Ergul, 2004).

Multiple explanations for the social–emotional problems of students with LD have been offered. There is evidence to suggest that the difficulties with language and communication that are often associated with LD also negatively impact social–

emotional functioning (e.g., Vallance, Cummings, & Humphries, 1998). Deficits in social–emotional functioning may be related to inadequate learning of effective problem-solving strategies (Tur-Kaspa & Bryan, 1995) or co-occurring psychiatric disorders (Forness, Kavale, & Bauman, 1998). Some research indicates that social isolation may arise as a "side effect" of academic problems (e.g., Siperstein & Bak, 1989) and low self-esteem due to school failure (e.g., Vogel & Forness, 1992). Whereas exact etiologies may be difficult to determine, there is no question that students with LD need effective interventions that improve their social–emotional functioning and related outcomes.

Emotional and Behavioral Disorders

Just under 1% of students ages 6–17 (0.87%, or almost 430,000 students) are served in the special education category of *emotional disturbance*, the special education category designated for students with EBD (U.S. Department of Education, Office of Special Education Programs, 2011). Defining EBD is not easy. Most definitions include emotions and behavior that differ significantly from an appropriate comparison group, are more than a temporary response to unusual circumstances, and interfere with functioning in one or more domains (academic, interpersonal, vocational). The federal definition of "emotional disturbance" for special education purposes is as follows:

> The term means a condition exhibiting one or more of the following characteristics over a long period of time and to a marked extent, which adversely affects educational performance: a) an inability to learn that cannot be explained by intellectual, sensory, or health factors; b) an inability to build or maintain satisfactory relationships with peers or teachers; c) inappropriate types of behavior or feelings under normal circumstances; d) a general pervasive mood of unhappiness or depression; or, e) a tendency to develop physical symptoms or fears associated with personal or school problems. (Individuals with Disabilities Education Improvement Act [IDEIA], 2004)

The definition explicitly excludes students who are "socially maladjusted," unless it is determined that they are also emotionally disturbed. Confusion surrounding the social maladjustment exclusion clause and other vague and ambiguous terms in the definition may, in part, explain why students with EBD are vastly underserved in special education (Kauffman, Mock, & Simpson, 2007; Wiley & Siperstein, 2011).

EBD and Social–Emotional Functioning

Unlike LD, *impairment in social–emotional functioning* is central to the federal definition for EBD. The social problems that students with EBD experience are directly linked to the patterns of problem behavior that these students display (Walker, Ramsay, & Gresham, 2004). Researchers generally focus on two broad dimensions of problem behavior (externalizing or internalizing) that negatively impact the social–emotional functioning of students with EBD. *Externalizing behavior* refers to problem behaviors that are directed outward toward the environment and other people—for example, aggression, disruption, destroying property, stealing, and so on. *Internalizing behavior* refers to problem behavior (and related negative emotions) that are directed inward—for example, depression, anxiety, and social withdrawal. Students with EBD may display either externalizing behavior or internalizing behavior to different degrees, but most display both (comorbidity) to at least some extent (Hallahan et al., 2011).

The pronounced social–emotional problems displayed by students with EBD appear to develop through multiple pathways that include individual factors (e.g., temperament, neurological dysfunction, genetics) and environmental factors (e.g., family, community, school, peers) (Walker et al., 2004). Although the federal definition does not specifically mention academic deficits, it is important to recognize that most students with EBD exhibit significant learning problems.

Similar to LD, there is no question that students with EBD need interventions designed to promote social and emotional competence. At a minimum, students with EBD need targeted Tier 2 SST interventions, and most will need Tier 3 individualized interventions. Again, many students identified as EBD spend at least part of their school day in general education settings, so any intensive interventions that these students receive should be *in addition to* their participation in Tier 1 schoolwide SEL programs.

Mild Intellectual Disabilities

Almost 1% of students ages 6–17 (0.9%, or just over 440,000) are served in special education under the category of *mental retardation*, the category designated for students with mild, moderate, and severe *intellectual disabilities* (ID). To be identified as ID, a student must exhibit both subaverage intelligence and impairment in adaptive behavior. Currently, most schools and professional organizations define *subaverage intelligence* as two standard deviations or more below the mean. On an IQ test with a mean of 100, this is a score of 70 or below. Most students with ID (80–90%) fall in the *mild* range of ID, which is an IQ of 55–70. Remember that a significant number of students with mild ID may be misidentified as LD; thus, the students who are actually served under the ID category may be skewed toward those students who have more moderate to severe ID. Although a significant proportion of students identified as ID spend more than half of their school day in general education settings, most receive instruction primarily in separate special education classrooms. The federal definition for ID specifically states:

> "Intellectual disability" means significantly subaverage general intellectual functioning, existing concurrently with deficits in adaptive behavior and manifested during the developmental period, that adversely affects a child's educational performance.

MID and Social–Emotional Functioning

Impairments in adaptive behavior are usually defined as deficits in *practical intelligence* (the ability to complete everyday tasks) and *social intelligence* (the ability to understand and interpret social situations and social interactions; Greenspan, 2006). Thus, deficits in social competence are a key defining feature of ID and MID (Siperstein & Leffert, 1997). For students with MID, the consequences of deficits in social and emotional functioning are similar to some of those experienced by students with LD and those with EBD (e.g., poor social interaction skills, social isolation, higher levels of problem behavior; Hallahan et al., 2011).

Clear but often subtle deficits in social cognition may be part of the "essence" of MID, in the sense that the social impairments displayed by this population may be primarily due to difficulties understanding and responding to the complexities of the social environment (Greenspan, 2006). Leffert and Siperstein (2002) synthesized research on the social skills of individuals with MID in relation to five social cognitive processes outlined in social information-processing theory—perception and interpretation of social cues, goal consideration, strategy formulation, and the selection and evaluation of social strategies (Crick & Dodge, 1994). For example, students with MID may mistakenly attribute hostile intentions to benign behavior, leading to an inappropriate (hostile or aggressive) response (Leffert & Siperstein, 1996). These findings suggest that Tier 2 SST interventions for students with MID may need to incorporate direct efforts to remediate social cognitive deficits. For students with MID who participate in general education, Tier 1 SEL interventions must be adapted to address the social and emotional characteristics associated with this disability.

In this section, we have presented definitions for three high-incidence disability categories—LD, EBD, and MID. Each of these disabilities is associated with varying degrees of impairment in social–emotional functioning. Similarities and differences in the nature of social–emotional impairments for each of these disabilities may have important implications for intervention. We turn next to conceptual models in SST research that we believe have direct implications for school-based interventions for students with disabilities.

SST Conceptual Models

Although SST research and practice may have their deepest roots in behaviorism, they also have at least some roots in other well-established theories of human development and learning, including social learning theory, cognitive-behavioral theory, and social information processing. Within these theoretical frameworks, SST researchers have developed several conceptual models that can be used to guide school-based interventions for students with disabilities. The first conceptual model distinguishes between *acquisition* deficits and *performance* deficits in social–emotional functioning. The second conceptual model is the *competing problem behavior* model and the related idea of *replacement behavior training* in SST.

A vital conceptual distinction that has been made in SST intervention research is between acquisition deficits and performance deficits. An *acquisition deficit* in social skills means that a student does not know how to perform a social skill, or how to use the skill fluently when it is needed (Gresham, 2010). Gresham refers to this type of deficit as a "can't-do" problem because the student "cannot perform a given social skill even under the most optimal conditions of motivation" (p. 342). A *performance deficit*, on the other hand, occurs when the student knows how to perform the skill but does not adequately do so. A performance deficit is a "won't-do" problem; the student knows what to do but does not do it.

This distinction is critical because different types of interventions are needed for acquisition deficits ("can't-do" problems) and performance deficits ("won't-do" problems). When students do not know what a skill is or how to perform it fluently (acquisition deficits), the skill must be explicitly and actively taught with direct instructional techniques. These techniques include modeling (showing how to perform the skill), behavioral rehearsal (practicing the skill), coaching (providing feedback on performance of the skill), and social problem solving (helping the student think about when and how to apply the skill in various situations; Gresham et al., 2012).

For students with *performance* deficits—those who already know the relevant skills but do not use them at adequate levels—direct social skills instruction will miss the mark. Teaching students what they already know is unlikely to result in positive outcomes. This point is critical because many Tier 1 SEL programs and Tier 2 SST programs devote considerable time and resources to a practice (directly teaching social skills or social knowledge) that may be ineffective for students with performance deficits. Students with performance deficits require a whole set of different interventions, including antecedent interventions to prompt the use of the social skills (e.g., cueing, precorrection, peer-mediated strategies), and manipulation of consequences (e.g., praise, performance feedback, points, contracts, activity rewards, home notes) (Gresham, 2010). Programs designed to promote social competence must do more than just teach students the "what" of skilled social interaction—they must actively and deliberately create classroom and school environments that prompt, reinforce, and maintain desirable social behavior (Sugai & Horner, 2009).

Another critical consideration for SST intervention is the impact of problem behaviors on the social functioning of students with high-incidence disabilities. In addition to social skills deficits (i.e., the failure to display skilled social behavior), students with LD, EBD, and MID may display problem behavior *excesses* (i.e., high levels of problem behaviors that interfere with social interaction). *Competing problem behaviors* can "compete" with social skills in the sense that, from the student's perspective, inappropriate behavior may be more effective or efficient than appropriate behavior (social skills) in obtaining social outcomes that the student likes (peer or teacher attention, desired objects and activities, being left alone, etc.) (Maag, 2005).

Thus, when implementing SST interventions for students with high-incidence disabilities, it may be necessary to carefully assess the function, or purpose, that competing problem behaviors serve for the student and to teach the student specific *replacement* behaviors (social skills) that he or she can use to achieve *the same purpose* or obtain similar types and levels of reinforcement (Maag, 2005). Additionally, the student's environment may need to be "engineered" so that social skills actually do work better to obtain reinforcement than competing problem behaviors. Arranging social environments that support appropriate behavior and discourage problem behavior is one area in which Tier 1 SEL programs and Tier 2 SST interventions may be integrated or coordinated to maximize the effectiveness of both—we discuss this further when we discuss the effectiveness of SST interventions below. Whether or not the specific function or purpose of competing problem behaviors is assessed and addressed, Tier 1 SEL programs and Tier 2 SST interventions will almost always need to include, in addition to remediation of acquisition and/or performance deficits, components designed to *decrease competing problem behaviors*. This might involve various differential reinforcement procedures, the judicious use of mild, nonviolent aversive consequences, teaching cognitive coping skills or anger control, or other forms of self-monitoring or problem-solving instruction (Gresham, 2010).

Successful coordination of Tier 1 SEL programs with Tier 2 and Tier 3 SST interventions will require careful attention to the conceptual models we have discussed here. It will also require an understanding of the research that has been conducted to date on interventions to improve the social functioning of students with high-incidence disabilities. We summarize this research in the next section.

The Effectiveness of SST for Students with High-Incidence Disabilities

To summarize current knowledge about the effectiveness of SST for students with high-incidence disabilities, we first present a very brief summary of important findings from several published research reviews that have synthesized decades of SST intervention research.

Next, we sort existing SST programs or curricula into three categories—what works, what is promising, and what does not work. To sort SST programs into these three categories, we looked at the number of "successful trials" for each program. We defined a "successful trial" as a well-designed randomized or quasi-experimental group study demonstrating a clearly positive impact on the social competence of students with or at-risk for high-incidence disabilities. SST programs with three or more successful trials were categorized as *what works*. SST programs with fewer than three successful trials and/or with mixed evidence of effectiveness were categorized as *what is promising*. Finally, SST programs with three or well-designed group studies with no positive impact (or a negative impact) on the social competence of students with high-incidence disabilities were categorized as *what does not work*. Note that in the sections identifying what works, what is promising, and what does not work, we focused only on Tier 2 SST programs or curricula (as opposed to Tier 3 individualized interventions) evaluated using group designs (as opposed to single-subject designs).

Reviews and Syntheses of SST Research

The large body of SST research has been extensively reviewed in dozens of narrative and quantitative research syntheses (e.g., Cook et al., 2008; Forness & Kavale, 1996; Gresham, 2010; Gresham et al., 2012; Gresham, Sugai, & Horner, 2001; Maag, 2006; Quinn, Kavale, Mathur, Rutherford, & Forness, 1999; Sukhodolsky & Butter, 2006). The picture that has emerged regarding the efficacy of Tier 2 SST interventions for students with high-incidence disabilities can best be described as both promising and unclear.

For example, Gresham and colleagues (2012) determined that approximately 65% of the students with high-incidence disabilities who received SST interventions made significant gains in social competence compared to 35% of students with high-incidence disabilities who did not receive SST. However, much smaller effects were found in meta-analyses of SST for students with EBD (Quinn et al., 1999) and LD (Forness & Kavale, 1996), and inconsistent effects were found in a narrative review of SST interventions for students with ID (Sukhodolsky & Butter, 2006). Thus, the true efficacy of current SST interventions for students with high-incidence disabilities remains a matter of some uncertainty (Leffert & Siperstein, 2003).

Although there is general disagreement about the overall effectiveness of SST, there is some clarity about what types of SST techniques are more effective than others. It appears that the most effective SST interventions for students with disabilities involve a combination of modeling, coaching, practice, feedback, and the other methods derived from applied behavioral analysis. The research support for cognitive or cognitive-behavioral approaches (social problem solving, self-instruction) is weaker, especially when examining the effects on actual social behavior in naturalistic settings (Gresham et al., 2012). The reviews of SST research also clearly show that poor or inconsistent generalization of student gains is a persistent problem in Tier 2 SST interventions for students with high-incidence disabilities (Gresham, 2010). That is, students with disabilities may show some improvement in the training situation or on the particular measure used to examine the impact of the intervention or curriculum, but these gains are frequently short-lived and/or they do not translate into improved behavior in the "real-life" settings where they are needed (Gresham, 2010; Gresham et al., 2001; Maag, 2006).

In addition, the competencies that are targeted by Tier 1 SEL programs (self-awareness, self-discipline, self-management) may be associated, if they are learned, with longer lasting improvements in social, emotional, and behavioral functioning (Osher et al., 2010). The logical assumption is that students who are self-controlled are more likely to maintain social competence over time and across settings than students who are controlled by external consequences. A critical point, however, is that many, if not most, students with disabilities—especially those who exhibit competing problem behaviors—may not be able to learn self-control, particularly in the initial stages, without behavioral interventions that include the skillful application of external consequences such as positive reinforcement (Epstein, Atkins, Cullinan, Kutash, & Weaver, 2008). The social cognitive focus of SEL programs may also be a good fit for students with MID because, as we discussed previously, many of their interpersonal problems may be related to social cognitive deficits. Future cooperative research efforts between SEL and SST should seek to identify the most effective ways to help students with disabilities achieve the competencies targeted by SEL programs (see, e.g., Kam et al., 2004).

Overall, although much has been learned from these reviews of research on SST interventions for students with high-incidence disabilities, some key questions remain, and caution is warranted (Leffert & Siperstein, 2003). Most importantly, because SST often encompasses an eclectic set of practices, it is difficult to discern from the research which practices are most effective or most critical for achieving short- and long-term gains in social competence.

Next, we apply our criteria for what works, what is promising, and what does not work to see whether a clearer picture emerges regarding effective Tier 2 SST programs for students with high-incidence disabilities. Again, we sorted Tier 2 SST programs into three categories—what works (three or more well-designed group studies with clear evidence of effectiveness); what is promising (fewer than three well-designed group studies and/or mixed evidence of effectiveness); what does not work (three or more well-designed group studies with no evidence of positive effects and/or evidence of negative effects).

What Works

No Tier 2 SST programs met our criteria for "what works"—three or more well-designed randomized or quasi-experimental group studies with clear, unambiguous evidence of effectiveness.

What Is Promising

Four specific Tier 2 SST intervention programs for students with disabilities (*Coping Power, Early Risers, First Step to Success, Incredible Years*) met our criteria for "what is promising." All four of these programs target students with EBD or at risk for EBD. Because none of these programs was designed or tested for students with LD or MID, it is not known whether they would be effective for these students. However, considering the overlap in disability categories we explained previously, it is possible that some aspects of these programs could benefit at least some students identified as LD or MID.

Note that one Tier 2 program (a modified version of the *Promoting Alternative Thinking Strategies* [PATHS] curriculum) was evaluated for 133 special education students attending seven elementary schools (Kam et al., 2004), including students with LD, MID, and EBD. PATHS did not meet our criteria for "what is promising." Whereas PATHS was effective in reducing externalizing and internalizing behavior, it was not effective in improving social competence and it had only marginal positive effects on social problem solving. Similar results were obtained for at-risk kindergartners (n = 891) who received PATHS as a Tier 1 intervention and *Families and Schools Together* (FAST Track) as a Tier 2 intervention (Conduct Problems Prevention Research Group, 2002). In contrast, PATHS is recognized as a program that works for elementary school students when applied as a universal intervention (see Rimm-Kaufman & Hulleman, Chapter 10, this volume).

Coping Power

Coping Power is a Tier 2 program designed to teach students at-risk for EBD the social and emotional skills necessary for successful transition to middle school. The program includes child and parent components, and it comprises 34, 50-minute group sessions (and periodic individual sessions) delivered over 15–18 months. The parent component includes training in effective behavior management strategies (communicating expectations, praise, dealing with stress, and communication) that support the child component. The child group sessions in Coping Power are conducted by trained school staff (mostly counselors) in school settings. These sessions focus on goal setting, emotional awareness, using self-statements to cope with negative feelings and situations, relaxation techniques, study skills, and refusal skills. The parent training comprises 16 group sessions, intermittent visits to the home, and individual communication and support. Parent sessions focus on setting behavior management goals, establishing rules, giving directions effectively, rewarding appropriate behavior, using negative consequences effectively, and establishing weekly family meetings. To promote generalization of skills to natural settings, school staff make brief, regularly scheduled contacts with individual children in the classroom (Lochman, Boxmeyer, Powell, Roth, & Windle, 2006; Lochman et al., 2009; Lochman & Wells, 2004).

The effectiveness of *Coping Power* has been evaluated in three high quality randomized group studies (Lochman et al., 2006, 2009; Lochman & Wells, 2004) and one quasi-experimental group study (Lochman & Wells, 2002). Across these four studies, 895 students at risk for EBD in fourth to sixth grade participated. Coping Power has significant positive effects on the externalizing behavior of participants; that is, this program is effective in reducing negative behaviors such as disruption, aggression, noncompliance, and delinquency, as measured by teacher, parent, and child ratings (Lochman et al., 2006, 2009; Lochman & Wells, 2004). Follow-up data 1 year after intervention showed that improvements were maintained on three out of five outcome measures, including teacher ratings of problem behavior. The Coping Power program also has *potentially* positive effects on social competence, based on statistically significant differences between treatment and control or comparison groups on teacher ratings of social competence (Lochman et al., 2009; Lochman & Wells, 2002). Thus, Coping Power is a promising SST intervention because it can reduce the externalizing behavior that often interferes or competes with social skills and social competence, and because it may improve the social competence of fourth- to sixth-grade students at risk for EBD.

The Coping Power program may be especially well suited to augmenting and complementing schoolwide Tier 1 SEL programs because the many of the cognitive-behavioral interventions and student outcomes targeted by Coping Power align well with the key program components and competencies targeted by many Tier 1 SEL programs. The key competencies targeted by SEL programming typically include self-awareness (e.g., identification of emotions and strengths), social awareness (e.g., empathy, perspective taking), responsible decision making (e.g., reflective problem solving), self-management (e.g., goal setting, dealing with stress), and relationship skills (Zins & Elias, 2007). As we noted previously, reviews of SST research suggest that cognitive or cognitive-behavioral interventions (like some included in Coping Power and in Tier 1 SEL programs) have been generally less effective for students with disabilities than more behavioral approaches (Gresham et al., 2012). However, Coping Power incorporates both cognitive *and* behavioral approaches, particularly in the parent training component. The inclusion of explicit behavior management strategies may at least partly account for the positive impact of Coping Power on externalizing behavior.

Early Risers

This multiyear program includes child, school, and parent components. The program is coordinated by a *family advocate*, who must have an undergraduate degree in an appropriate field and experience working with children. The Child Skills component focuses on developing skills related to emotional and behavioral self-control, improving peer relationships and interactions, and improving academic performance. The Child School Support component includes individualized plans targeting difficulties experienced by the student in the classroom. The Parent Skills component involves weekly family meetings that focus on developing effective parenting skills, and positive parent–child relationships and home–school connections.

The effectiveness of *Early Risers* has been evaluated in two randomized group studies (August, Hektner, Egan, Realmuto, & Bloomquist, 2002; August, Lee, Bloomquist, Realmuto, & Hektner, 2003). Early Risers targets elementary school-age students at-risk for EBD (aggressive and disruptive behavior). In the two studies, 389 students at risk for EBD in kindergarten through second grade participated. Early Risers was found to have potentially positive effects on social outcomes and academic performance, but no discernible effects on externalizing or internalizing behavior. The extent of this evidence is considered to be medium to large. Early Risers is a promising SST intervention because it may improve the social skills of early elementary school students at-risk for EBD. However, follow-up analyses indicated that student gains were not maintained 1 year after implementation (August, Lee, Bloomquist, Realmuto, & Hektner, 2004). Again, it is possible that a multi-tiered approach that combines the Early Risers Tier 2 SST interventions with schoolwide Tier 1 SEL programs could lead to more durable improvements in the social competence of students at risk for EBD.

Incredible Years

The *Incredible Years* program is designed to teach social–emotional skills to students at risk for EBD (oppositional and defiant) up to the age of 12 (mostly preschool through early elementary grades). The program is delivered in 20- to 30-minute lessons that focus on managing anger, solving problems, getting along with friends, and emotional awareness. The lessons are presented by classroom teachers to target children and/or the entire class, two to three times a week. Target students also participate in a clinical program (18–20 weekly small-group sessions, 2 hours each). A parent training component focuses on positive discipline, supporting child learning and growth, and home–school connections. There are also two teacher training components, one for classroom management, the other for teachers who will teach the lessons in their classrooms.

One randomized group study (Webster-Stratton, Reid, & Hammond, 2004) examined the effectiveness of the Incredible Years program for students with disabilities. The randomized study included 51 4- to 8-year-old children with oppositional defiant disorder. The evidence suggests that the Incredible Years program has potentially positive effects on externalizing behavior (based on parent ratings of Child Conduct Problems) and potentially positive effects on social outcomes (based on ratings of Social Competence with Peers) (Webster-Stratton et al., 2004). Most of the treatment gains were maintained at 1-year follow-up, with the exception of conduct problems in the classroom (Webster-Stratton et al., 2004). With its emphasis on social problem solving and emotional awareness, the Incredible Years program aligns well with the competencies targeted by Tier 1 SEL programs (Zins & Elias, 2007).

First Step to Success

First Step to Success is designed for young students at-risk for EBD who exhibit aggressive or antisocial behavior patterns. A trained behavior coach works with each student, as well as his or her teacher, parent, and classroom peers. The program takes 50–60 hours over 3 months. First Step to Success includes screening, school intervention, and parent support. The screening procedure is used to identify students at the highest risk for EBD as candidates for the program. The school component (Contingencies for Learning Academic and Social Skills [CLASS]) involves school-based interventions designed to increase prosocial behavior and reduce problem behavior. The behavior coach trains the teacher to implement school interventions using modeling and feedback. The target student is taught appropriate behaviors to replace inappropriate ones, and classroom peers are trained to reinforce and support the appropriate behaviors. The three phases of the CLASS component (coach, teacher, maintenance) takes 30 days to complete. The parent training component (HomeBase) is coordinated with the school component. Parents are trained to promote various child competencies, including problem solving, making friends, being cooperative, and communicating with others.

Two randomized group studies (Walker et al., 1998, 2009) and one quasi-experimental group study (Nelson et al., 2009) examined the effectiveness of First Step to Success. A total of 416 first- through third-grade students at risk for EBD participated in these studies. First Step to Success is effective in reducing externalizing behavior in young students at risk for EBD. The program had significant positive effects on externalizing behavior, as measured by teacher and parent ratings on several different problem behavior scales (Nelson et al., 2009; Walker et al., 1998, 2009). The program also had potentially positive effects on internalizing behavior (social withdrawal; Walker et al., 1998). First Step to Success had positive (Nelson et al., 2009) or potentially positive (Walker et al., 2009) effects on social outcomes, as measured by teacher and parent ratings of social skills and adaptive behavior. Finally, a potentially positive effect was found for academic competence, as measured by teacher ratings (Walker et al., 2009).

Like the other promising Tier 2 SST programs, First Step to Success could work well within a multi-tiered intervention framework. Indeed, in one study (Nelson et al., 2009), First Step to Success was implemented as the second tier (secondary prevention) of a three-tier schoolwide model. However, we note that of the four promising Tier 2 SST interventions we have identified, *First Step to Success* is arguably the most "behavioral," with relatively less direct emphasis on underlying cognitive and emotional aspects of social competence. Thus, First Step to Success may not "fit" as well with schoolwide Tier 1 SEL programs that focus primarily on the knowledge, thoughts, and feelings of students, with less of a direct focus on behavior. We suggest that, in this instance particularly, it is Tier 1 SEL programs that may need to be redesigned to fit with First Step to Success, rather than the other way around. We say this because a large body of research indicates that explicit schoolwide positive behavioral interventions and supports (teaching, prompting, and reinforcing appropriate behavior) may be critical to achieving schoolwide goals related to the social success of all students, especially if "all students" includes at-risk students and students with disabilities (Osher et al., 2010; Sugai & Horner, 2009). Thus, SEL researchers should examine ways to incorporate more explicit behavioral components (like those used in First Step to Success) within Tier 1 SEL programs, just as SST researchers should examine ways to merge or coordinate Tier 2 SST interventions with Tier 1 SEL programs. We believe that future research should build on findings from both SEL research and SST research for students with disabilities, and that doing so will lead to better social and emotional outcomes for all students in our schools.

What Does Not Work

No Tier 2 SST programs met our criteria for "what does not work"—SST programs or curricula evaluated by three or more well-designed group studies with no positive effects and/or negative effects on the social competence of students with disabilities.

Comments on Promising Tier 2 SST Programs

There is much that is encouraging about the promising Tier 2 SST programs we have identified in this chapter. It is encouraging that programs with positive and potentially positive effects on the social outcomes and problem behavior of students at risk for EBD have been identified. These reports and these programs give us direction in identifying ways to improve the social and emotional competence of students with and at risk for EBD.

Several specific observations about these promising SST programs should be noted. First, these programs typically involved multiple components (e.g., teacher training, parent training, small group, individualized supports), multiple settings (school, home, clinic), and multiple intervention agents (specially trained interventionists, teachers, parents, peers, child). Therefore, it is safe to say that each of these four programs was both intensive and comprehensive in a way that many SST interventions (and all Tier 1 SEL programs) are not. The critical lesson here is that achieving positive outcomes for students with and at risk for EBD requires multiple highly intensive interventions carefully coordinated and maintained across settings and interventionists.

Note that even with this high level of intensity, the outcomes of these SST interventions were not always positive or long-lasting. An important question for future research is whether evidence-based Tier 2 SST interventions might be more effective when integrated with a high-quality, evidence-based Tier 1 SEL and/or SWPBIS program. As we have suggested repeatedly in this chapter, future research investigating the potential combined (or synergistic) effects of SST and SEL must build on prior research in both of these areas. Researchers must consider ways in which effective Tier 2 SST interventions might be strengthened by incorporating elements of SEL. Equally important is developing Tier 1 schoolwide SEL programs that, when combined with more intensive Tier 2 or Tier 3 SST interventions, help to address the unique social and emotional learning needs of students with disabilities.

Also, the lack of adequately researched Tier 2 SST interventions for students with LD and MID is disappointing. We look forward to future high-quality intervention studies that include students with LD and students with MID as participants. Although there are similarities in the characteristics of students with high-incidence disabilities (LD, EBD, MID), there are also differences that may impact the effectiveness of SST interventions.

Summary and Recommendations: SEL for Students with Disabilities

In closing, we would like to highlight some "big ideas" that we believe could emerge from current initiatives that focus on promoting the social and emotional competence of *all* students. First, there is the profound but often overlooked idea that "all students" truly means *all students*, including students with disabilities. In terms of identifying and implementing effective school-based practices, this means not assuming that what works for the average student will work for students with disabilities. Many students with disabilities will need social–emotional interventions that are *special*, in terms of their intensity, their methods, their focus, who implements them, and how they are delivered. Second, there is the idea that SEL and SST do not have to work separately or in parallel, that Tier 1 SEL interventions and Tier 2 SST interventions could have strong *combined* effects for students with disabilities. The third "big idea" is that reform efforts and policy initiatives focusing on SEL ought to be seen as integral to, rather than separate from, other reforms and initiatives that directly impact students with disabilities. In particular, multi-tiered interventions to promote positive peer interactions should be viewed as an essential part of increasing the social inclusion of students with disabilities in school.

When we consider what has been learned about improving the social and emotional competence of students with disabilities, one option is to view the glass as half-empty. Consistently effective, clearly defined, evidence-based practices continue to elude us. Too many students with disabilities continue to experience significant social problems, as well as the negative short- and long-term developmental and educational outcomes associated with these problems (Walker et al., 2004). The complexities and challenges of SST research persist, including those related to how to measure outcomes, how to maintain treatment gains across time and settings, and how interventions and programs should take into consideration the substantial heterogeneity of students with disabilities, both between and within disability categories.

The other possibility is to view the glass as half-full. Although much work remains to be done, we have learned a great deal about the nature of the social skills deficits exhibited by students with high-incidence disabilities, and we have begun to identify promising school-based interventions for students with EBD that could substantially better the odds of greater social and academic success for these students (Gresham et al., 2012). The rapid growth of SEL as a field and as an initiative for comprehensive reforms in K–12 education presents an especially exciting opportunity to collaborate across disciplines in order to identify and implement the most effective interventions possible for all students, including students with disabilities.

Interdisciplinary collaboration requires researchers and practitioners in both SEL and SST to heed the lessons learned in both fields. We suggest that practitioners who implement SEL programs should pay particular attention to the following lessons learned through research in SST and special education. First and foremost, it is clear that achieving positive social outcomes for at least some students with disabilities (i.e., students with EBD) requires intensive, sustained, and carefully coordinated interventions and supports. Second, although disability categories can tell us some things about the social–emotional characteristics and needs of the students who fall within them, the substantial heterogeneity within these categories means that researchers and practitioners must always be careful to consider individual differences when implementing SST or SEL for students with high-incidence disabilities. Especially important is assessing the extent to which a student with a disability displays an acquisition deficit (does not know how or when to use a social skill, or does not know how to use it fluently) or a performance deficit (knows how to use a social skill but is not motivated to use it). Specific social cognitive deficits should also be identified and addressed. Selection of interventions must be based on the type of skills deficit the student exhibits, and the intensity of the intervention must match the intensity of the student's social skills deficits. Relatedly, SEL and SST interventions must incorporate effective strategies for reducing *competing problem behaviors*. A major focus of these strategies should be determining the purpose or function that these problem behaviors serve for the student and teaching *replacement behaviors* that serve the same or a similar purpose (Gresham et al., 2012).

The differences between SEL and SST in their epistemological and empirical roots (Osher et al., 2010) should not dissuade either discipline from exploring the full range of intervention approaches (cognitive, relational, behavioral) that could lead to better short- and long-term social and emotional learning outcomes for students with disabilities. We are hopeful that the occurrence of greater collaboration between SEL and SST will accelerate progress toward meeting the significant social and emotional learning needs of students with disabilities.

References

August, G. J., Hektner, J. M., Egan, E. A., Realmuto, G. M., & Bloomquist, M. L. (2002). The Early Risers longitudinal prevention trial: Examination of 3-year outcomes in aggressive children with intent-to-treat and as-intended analyses. *Psychology of Addictive Behaviors, 16*, S27–S39.

August, G. J., Lee, S. S., Bloomquist, M. L., Realmuto, G. M., & Hektner, J. M. (2003). Dissemination of an evidence-based prevention innovation for aggressive children in culturally diverse, urban neighborhoods: The Early Risers effectiveness study. *Prevention Science, 4*, 271–286.

August, G. J., Lee, S. S., Bloomquist, M. L., Realmuto, G. M., & Hektner, J. M. (2004). Maintenance effects of an evidence-based prevention intervention for aggressive children living in culturally diverse urban neighborhoods: The Early Risers effectiveness study. *Journal of Emotional and Behavioral Disorders, 12*, 194–205.

Bryan, T., Burstein, K., & Ergul, C. (2004). The social–emotional side of learning disabilities: A science-based presentation of the state of the art. *Learning Disability Quarterly, 27*, 45–51.

Caprara, G. V., Barbaranelli, C., Pastorelli, C., Bandura, A., & Zimbardo, P. G. (2000). Prosocial foundations of children's academic achievement. *Psychological Science, 11*, 302–306.

Conduct Problems Prevention Research Group. (2002). Evaluation of the first 3 years of the Fast Track prevention trial with children at high risk for adolescent conduct problems. *Journal of Abnormal Child Psychology, 30*, 19–35.

Cook, C. R., Gresham, F. M., Kern, L., Barreras, R. B., Thornton, S., & Crews, S. D. (2008). Social skills training for secondary students with emotional and/or behavioral disorders: A review and analysis of the meta-analytic literature. *Journal of Emotional and Behavioral Disorders, 16*, 131–144.

Crick, N. R., & Dodge, K. A. (1994). A review and reformulation of social information-processing mechanisms in children's social adjustment. *Psychological Bulletin, 115*, 74–101.

Elias, M. J., Zins, J. E., Weissberg, R. P., Frey,

K. S., Greenberg, M. T., Haynes, N. M., et al. (1997). *Promoting social and emotional learning: Guidelines for educators.* Alexandria, VA: Association for Supervision and Curriculum Development.

Epstein, M., Atkins, M., Cullinan, D., Kutash, K., & Weaver, R. (2008). *Reducing behavior problems in the elementary school classroom: A practice guide* (NCEE No. 2008-012). Washington, DC: National Center for Education Evaluation and Regional Assistance, Institute of Education Sciences, U.S. Department of Education.

Forness, S. R., & Kavale, K. A. (1996). Treating social skill deficits in children with learning disabilities: A meta-analysis of the research. *Learning Disability Quarterly, 19*, 2–13.

Forness, S. R., Kavale, K. A., & Bauman, S. S. (1998). The psychiatric comorbidity hypothesis revisited. *Learning Disability Quarterly, 21*, 203–206.

Greenberg, M. T., Weissberg, R. P., O'Brien, M. U., Zins, J. E., Fredericks, L. R., Resnik, H., et al. (2003). Enhancing school-based prevention and youth development through coordinated social, emotional, and academic learning. *American Psychologist, 58*, 466–474.

Greenspan, S. (2006). Mental retardation in the real world: Why the AAMR definition is not there yet. In H. N. Switsky & S. Greenspan (Eds.), *What is mental retardation?: Ideas for an evolving disability in the 21st century* (rev. ed., pp. 165–183). Washington, DC: American Association on Mental Retardation.

Gresham, F. M. (2010). Evidence-based social skills interventions: Empirical foundations for instructional approaches. In M. Shinn & H. Walker (Eds.), *Interventions for achievement and behavior problems in a three-tier model including RTI* (pp. 337–362). Bethesda, MD: National Association of School Psychologists.

Gresham, F. M., Robichaux, N., York, H., & O'Leary, K. (2012). Issues related to identifying and implementing evidence-based social skills interventions for students with high incidence disabilities. In B. G. Cook, M. Tankersley, & T. J. Landrum (Eds.), *Advances in learning and behavioral disabilities* (Vol. 25, pp. 23–45). Bingley, UK: Emerald Publishing Group.

Gresham, F. M., Sugai, G., & Horner, R. H. (2001). Interpreting outcomes of social skills training for students with high-incidence disabilities. *Exceptional Children, 67*, 331–344.

Hallahan, D. P., Kauffman, J. M., & Pullen, P. C. (2011). *Exceptional learners* (12th ed.). Upper Saddle River, NJ: Pearson.

Individuals with Disabilities Education Improvement Act. (2004). Public Law 108-446.

Kam, C., Greenberg, M. T., & Kusché, C. A. (2004). Sustained effects of the PATHS curriculum on the social and psychological adjustment of children in special education. *Journal of Emotional and Behavioral Disorders, 12*, 66–78.

Kauffman, J. M., & Hallahan, D. P. (2005). *Special education: What it is and why we need it.* Boston: Allyn & Bacon.

Kauffman, J. M., Mock, D. R., & Simpson, R. L. (2007). Problems related to underservice of students with emotional or behavioral disorders. *Behavioral Disorders, 33*, 43–57.

Kavale, K. A. (2002). Discrepancy models in the identification of learning disability. In R. Bradley, L. Danielson, & D. P. Hallahan (Eds.), *Identification of learning disabilities: Research to practice* (pp. 369–426). Mahwah, NJ: Erlbaum.

Kavale, K. A., & Forness, S. R. (1996). Social skill deficits and learning disabilities: A meta-analysis. *Journal of Learning Disabilities, 29*(3), 226–237.

Leffert, J. S., & Siperstein, G. N. (1996). Assessment of social cognitive processes in children with mental retardation. *American Journal on Mental Retardation, 100*, 441–455.

Leffert, J. S., & Siperstein, G. N. (2002). Social cognition: A key to understanding adaptive behavior in individuals with mild mental retardation. *International Review of Research in Mental Retardation, 25*, 135–181.

Leffert, J. S., & Siperstein, G. N. (2003). *Social skills instruction for students with learning disabilities* (Current Practice Alert Series). Reston, VA: Council for Exceptional Children.

Lochman, J. E., Boxmeyer, C., Powell, N., Qu, L., Wells, K., & Windle, M. (2009). Dissemination of the Coping Power Program: Importance of intensity of counselor training. *Journal of Consulting and Clinical Psychology, 77*, 397–409.

Lochman, J. E., Boxmeyer, C., Powell, N., Roth, D. L., & Windle, M. (2006). Masked intervention effects: Analytic methods for addressing low dosage of intervention. *New Directions for Evaluation, 2006*, 19–32.

Lochman, J. E., & Wells, K. C. (2002). The Coping Power Program at middle school transition: Universal and indicated prevention effects. *Psychology of Addictive Behaviors, 16*, S40–S54.

Lochman, J. E., & Wells, K. C. (2004). The Coping Power Program for preadolescent aggressive boys and their parents: Outcome effects at the 1-year follow-up. *Journal of Consulting and Clinical Psychology, 72*, 571–578.

Maag, J. W. (2005). Social skills training for youth with emotional and behavioral disorders: Problems, conclusions, and suggestions. *Exceptionality, 13*, 155–172.

Maag, J. W. (2006). Social skills training for students with emotional and behavioral disorders:

A review of reviews. *Behavioral Disorders, 32*, 5–17.

MacMillan, D. L., & Siperstein, G. N. (2002). Learning disabilities as operationalized by the schools. In R. Bradley, L. Danielson, & D. P. Hallahan (Eds.), *Identification of learning disabilities: Research to practice* (pp. 287–233). Mahwah, NJ: Erlbaum.

Nelson, J. R., Hurley, K. D., Synhorst, L., Epstein, M. H., Stage, S., & Buckley, J. (2009). The child outcomes of a behavior model. *Exceptional Children, 76*, 7–30.

Osher, D., Bear, G. G., Sprague, J. R., & Doyle, W. (2010). How can we improve school discipline? *Educational Researcher, 39*, 48–58.

Parker, J. G., & Asher, S. R. (1987). Peer relations and later personal adjustment: Are low-accepted children at risk? *Psychological Bulletin, 102*, 357–389.

Payton, J., Weissberg, R. P., Durlak, J. A., Dymnicki, A. B., Taylor, R. D., Schellinger, K. B., et al. (2008). *The positive impact of social and emotional learning for kindergarten to eighth grade students: Findings from three scientific reviews*. Chicago: Collaborative for Academic, Social, and Emotional Learning.

Quinn, M. M., Kavale, K. A., Mathur, S. R., Rutherford, R. B., & Forness, S. R. (1999). A meta-analysis of social skill interventions for students with emotional or behavioral disorders. *Journal of Emotional and Behavioral Disorders, 7*, 54–64.

Sabornie, E. J., Cullinan, D., Osborne, S. S., & Brock, L. B. (2005). Intellectual, academic, and behavioral functioning of students with high-incidence disabilities: A cross-categorical meta-analysis. *Exceptional Children, 72*, 47–63.

Siperstein, G. N., & Bak, J. J. (1989). Social relationships of adolescents with moderate mental retardation. *Mental Retardation, 27*, 5–10.

Siperstein, G. N., & Leffert, J. S. (1997). Comparison of socially accepted and rejected children with mental retardation. *American Journal on Mental Retardation, 101*, 339–351.

Sugai, G., & Horner, R. H. (2009). Responsiveness-to-intervention and school-wide positive behavior supports: Integration of multi-tiered system approaches. *Exceptionality, 17*, 223–237.

Sukhodolsky, D. G., & Butter, E. (2006). Social skills training for children with intellectual disabilities. In J. W. Jacobsen & J. A. Mulick (Eds.), *Handbook of mental retardation and developmental disabilities* (pp. 601–617). New York: Kluwer Academic.

Tur-Kaspa, H., & Bryan, T. (1995). Teachers' ratings of the social competence and school adjustment of students with LD in elementary and junior high school. *Journal of Learning Disabilities, 28*, 44–52.

U.S. Department of Education, Office of Special Education Programs. (2011). *Annual report to Congress on the implementation of the Individuals with Disabilities Education Act, selected years, 1979 through 2006*. Washington, DC: Author.

Vallance, D. D., Cummings, R. L., & Humphries, T. (1998). Mediators of the risk for problem behavior in children with language learning disabilities. *Journal of Learning Disabilities, 31*, 160–171.

Vogel, S. A., & Forness, S. R. (1992). Social functioning in adults with learning disabilities. *School Psychology Review, 21*, 375–386.

Walker, H. M., Kavanagh, K., Stiller, B., Golly, A., Severson, H. H., & Feil, E. G. (1998). First Step to Success: An early intervention approach for preventing school antisocial behavior. *Journal of Emotional and Behavioral Disorders, 6*, 66–80.

Walker, H. M., Ramsey, E., & Gresham, F. (2004). *Antisocial behavior in school: Evidence-based practices* (2nd ed.). Belmont, CA: Wadsworth/Thomson Learning.

Walker, H. M., Seeley, J. R., Small, J., Severson, H. H., Graham, B. A., Feil, E. G., et al. (2009). A randomized controlled trial of the First Step to Success early intervention: Demonstration of program efficacy in a diverse, urban school district. *Journal of Emotional and Behavioral Disorders, 17*, 197–212.

Webster-Stratton, C., Reid, M. J., & Hammond, M. (2004). Treating children with early-onset conduct problems: Intervention outcomes for parent, child, and teacher training. *Journal of Clinical Child and Adolescent Psychology, 33*, 105–124.

Wiley, A. L., & Siperstein, G. N. (2011). Seeing red, feeling blue: The impact of state political leaning on state identification rates for emotional disturbance. *Behavioral Disorders, 36*, 195–207.

Zins, J. E., & Elias, M. J. (2007). Social and emotional learning: Promoting the development of all students. *Journal of Educational and Psychological Consultation, 17*, 233–255.

CHAPTER 15

SEL and Student–Teacher Relationships

Amanda P. Williford and Catherine Sanger Wolcott

Children's relationships with adults are critical for healthy development from infancy through adolescence. These relationships are first formed within the family but quickly extend to the school setting. This transition often occurs in preschool, but it can take place as early as the infant and toddler years. Within schools, teachers are responsible for helping children learn a variety of interpersonal and academic skills. Students are taught to communicate with others, persist in challenging assignments, comply with classroom norms, and find the motivation to achieve. From preschool through the secondary grades, teachers' shared emotional engagement, sensitivity and responsiveness, support of children's autonomy, and levels of conflict predict a host of children's social–emotional and academic outcomes. When there are high-quality teacher–student relationships, students use their teacher as a resource to solve problems, actively engage in learning activities, and better navigate the demands of school.

Our goal in this chapter is to provide a review of the evidenced-based programs that can be used in schools to promote children's social and emotional learning (SEL) by improving the teacher–student relationship. We begin with an overview that defines teacher–student relationships and summarizes the major theories used to understand their development and importance. We then briefly describe the current research base on teacher–student relationships as it relates to SEL. In another section we provide a summary of programs that work to enhance the teacher–student relationship. These interventions are diverse and extend from preschool to the secondary grades and vary in their scope of implementation. Finally, we end with a summary of remaining questions.

Definitions and Scope

The quality of relationships that students form with their teachers has been repeatedly linked with students' academic and social–emotional outcomes (Hamre & Pianta, 2001). High quality teacher–student relationships are most often characterized by high levels of warmth, sensitivity, and emotional connection and low levels of dependency, negativity, and conflict (Pianta, 1999; Spilt, Koomen, Thijs, & Van der Leij, 2012). Teachers and children interact with each other in reciprocal exchanges that continuously provide information to each participant. For example, a teacher may notice and respond to a student's cue that he or she is having trouble with an assignment, as evidenced by the student repeatedly writing and erasing an answer. Or, a teacher may notice that a child and a peer are struggling to work on a group assignment. The teacher acknowledges this challenge (e.g., "You two are working hard to figure this out") and provides a scaffold (e.g., "I'm here if you need me to weigh in on something . . ."). This provides the support the student needs to sustain task engagement, learn the material, or resolve a conflict.

In the next section, we provide an overview of several key theories than have informed how teacher–student relationships are defined and understood; these theories have been used to guide the design of programs focused on enhancing the teacher–student relationship.

Theories

Attachment Theory

Attachment theory, which initially described the parent–child relationship, has also been widely used to explain the importance of interactions between teachers and young students. This framework emphasizes that parental warmth and sensitivity are critical to the development of a secure parent–child attachment. This secure attachment ultimately allows young children to explore novel environments and appropriately cope with distress (Ainsworth, Bell, & Stayton, 1974). Similarly, a warm and supportive teacher–student attachment is theorized to provide the child the emotional security necessary to engage in learning activities needed to develop the full range of academic, behavioral, and social–emotional skills (Pianta, 1999). Relational interactions between a teacher and student become integrated into an internal working model, or schema, of the relationship that creates expectations and guides subsequent perceptions for both the teacher and the child (Pianta, 1999). The quality of information conveyed—specifically, how it is exchanged (e.g., tone of voice, posture and proximity, timing of behavior, and levels of reciprocity)—is just as important as what is said or done within the dyad. When the quality of teacher–student interactions is high, it promotes a student's feeling of attachment and security toward the teacher. This, in turn, allows a student to engage more fully in school activities that support his or her school adjustment. When teachers are able to establish an emotional connection and match levels of support to students' abilities, they are more effective in addressing young students' problems and concerns. This responsiveness optimizes students' ability to use the classroom environment to learn and develop.

Self-Determination Theory

For children in upper elementary and secondary school grades, self-determination theory (Deci & Ryan, 1985) has often been used to describe the importance of teacher–student relationships. According to this theory, children are motivated to engage in school because of their psychological needs for relatedness (developing secure connections with others), competence (understanding how to attain a particular outcome effectively), and autonomy (self-initiation of one's actions). Teachers help students meet these needs when their relationships are warm, responsive, and provide support for independence, thereby increasing students' desire to engage in learning activities and maximize performance in school (Roorda, Koomen, Spilt, & Oort, 2011).

Developmental Systems Theory

Developmental systems theory (i.e., the developmental–ecological model) has also been used as an organizing framework and places the formation of teacher–student relationships within a larger environmental and multilevel system (Bronfenbrenner & Morris, 1998). This theory emphasizes that children's development occurs within a context of dynamic, bidirectional influences ranging from more proximal to more distal (e.g., from individual → family, teacher, peer → neighborhood, school). At the proximal level, the teacher–student relationship comprises moment-to-moment behavioral exchanges between the student and the teacher that are bidirectional and transactional. These interactions are influenced by characteristics of the teachers and the students themselves, such as their gender, age, and temperament or personality. The teacher–student relationship is also influenced by the characteristics of the classroom, such as how much time the teacher spends with individual children, the number of students and adults in the classroom, and how the classroom is organized and structured. At a more distal level, the overall climate of the school can also influence teacher–student relationships (e.g., the principal of a school may encourage teachers to spend extra time with struggling students across grade levels). Again, these interactions are bidirectional. For example, the sensitive and responsive interactions shared between members of a particular teacher–student dyad may generalize to the larger classroom as the teacher engages in more responsive interactions with other students in the classroom, and/or the student may enlist the help of peers more often at school.

Current Research

More than a decade of well-controlled research provides compelling evidence that teacher–student relationships foster children's school engagement and academic skills, and serve as a protective factor for children with problem behaviors (for reviews, see Sabol & Pianta, 2012; Roorda et al., 2011). Roorda and colleagues (2011) conducted a meta-analysis to examine the associations between teacher–student relationships and children's school engagement spanning preschool through high school. They found medium associations between teacher–student relationships and children's engagement (average r = .34–.39). They also noted small associations between teacher–student relationships and academic achievement (average r = .16). Other researchers have found that the positive associations between high-quality teacher–student relationships and children's academic and behavioral adjustment hold both concurrently and in longitudinal examinations (e.g., Maldonado-Carreño & Votruba-Drzal, 2011). Conversely, teacher–student relationships characterized by high negativity, disagreement, and/or conflict are associated with lower levels of school adjustment (Birch & Ladd, 1997). In fact, a high-quality teacher–student relationship can be especially protective for children who display behavior problems because these children tend to enter into conflictual relationships with their teachers, and a positive relationship with a teacher can help prevent coercive teacher–student interaction cycles, thereby decreasing children's externalizing behavior and increasing their achievement (Doumen et al., 2008). In summary, results from a large body of research indicate that students' supportive relationships with their teachers promote positive long-term developmental outcomes, including improved academic outcomes and reduced problem behavior.

Although changing the teacher–child relationship has been shown to impact long-term academic and behavioral outcomes, less experimental work has explicitly measured how teacher–student interventions impact children's development of SEL skills. In many cases, these links are implied. For example, much of the literature on the teacher–student relationship focuses on reducing problem behavior (Sabol & Pianta, 2012). A potential mechanism for this reduction might be a corresponding increase in social–emotional skills such as self-management. However, if self-management is not explicitly measured while testing interventions targeting the teacher–student relationship, then decreases in children's problem behavior cannot be attributed to improvements in social–emotional skills per se. Similarly, improved classroom engagement likely relies on children's ability to make responsible decisions and better manage relationships in the classroom, but, again, there is no empirical evidence to suggest that this social–emotional skill is the mechanism for change. In most cases, the specific links between strengthening the teacher–child relationship, social–emotional skills, and improved student outcomes are not explicitly explored. Consequently, we discuss outcomes and constructs as they are defined and operationalized in the research, and we describe more proximal links to specific social–emotional skills where applicable.

The previously discussed research suggests that targeting the teacher–student relationship holds particular promise as a strategy to prevent negative outcomes for students at higher risk. Early intervention may deflect children from poor school adjustment, particularly those children who are at risk socially and academically. In the next section we review evidence-based programs that focus on improving this important relationship.

Overview of Intervention Strategies

This section describes interventions that focus on the teacher–student relationship as a mechanism for improving children's outcomes that are either explicitly or implicitly related to children's social–emotional development. The review includes programs that impact both teacher and student outcomes. Each program had to describe specifically how enhancing the teacher–student relationship contributes to students' proximal social–emotional outcomes, or in most cases, their long-term developmental outcomes, including academic achievement and reduced behavior problems. In cases in which this link is not explicit in the research, we discuss the way that interventions may have affected children's social–emotional skills. The reviewed interventions are quite diverse. For example, some programs target teacher knowledge and practice through coursework, and others engage the teacher–student dyad in purposefully structured interaction sessions. Interventions also vary in their focus on the teacher–student relationship as the primary mechanism for change. Some are grounded solely in improving the quality of this important relationship, although most interventions are multicomponent, addressing various processes such as parenting skills or teacher instruction. Because of the diversity among interventions, we discuss strategies not only in the order of their effectiveness but also by their degree of focus on the teacher–student relationship. For interventions that focus on multiple systems, some of which fall outside the scope of the teacher–student relationship, our summary is centered on the components that specifically target the teacher–student relationship and its associated social–emotional and developmental outcomes. Table 15.1 presents details on the interventions described in this review and includes the authors of the study, the age range of students, the focus of the intervention (e.g., schoolwide or within the teacher–student dyad), and the positive outcomes associated with the program.

What Works

Our criteria for interventions that work demonstrate three or more successful trials with positive outcomes for students, teachers, or both groups of participants. All three trials must have included a research design with a control or comparison group, thereby supporting the conclusion that the intervention is what led to changes in teacher or child outcomes. Thus, case study or time series designs would not qualify as successful trials in this category. Importantly, some interventions targeted multiple processes in addition to the teacher–student relationship. For these studies, if the teacher–student relationship was emphasized as a major component of the trial and corresponding effects resulted, then the intervention was considered successful—even if the teacher–student component of the intervention could not be isolated as the mechanism specifically tied to this change.

The Incredible Years Training Programs: Teacher Classroom Management Program

The Incredible Years (Webster-Stratton, Reid, & Hammond, 2001) is an effective multicomponent intervention. The program is designed for children ages 4–8 in preschool and elementary school, and includes a parent training program, a child training program, a teacher training program, and a social–emotional curriculum called Dinosaur School. The teacher training program focuses on improving teachers' classroom management by using five techniques: (1) building positive relationships with students, (2) praising and encouraging students, (3) using incentives, (4) preventing behavior problems, and (5) decreasing inappropriate behaviors. These components of the program are extensive and range from 4 full days of training (28 hours in total) to 6 full days of training, once per month (36 hours in total) (Webster-Stratton, Reid, & Hammond, 2004). During these trainings, teachers learn classroom management strategies as a group and watch videos of teacher–student interactions, which serve to spark discussion around topics taught in sessions (Webster-Stratton et al., 2001).

The Teacher Classroom Management program begins by focusing on the importance of teacher–student relationships (Webster-Stratton et al., 2004). These sessions emphasize that building a positive relationship with challenging children fosters student motivation, improves cooperation, and increases children's learning. Strategies for

TABLE 15.1. Summary of Reviewed Interventions that Improve Children's School Adjustment via an Improved Student–Teacher Relationship

Intervention	Authors[a]	Type	Grades	Focus	Student–teacher outcomes
Incredible Years: Teacher Training	Webster-Stratton et al. (2001)	Universal	PreK–elementary	Classroom	Improved positive teacher behaviors; reduced student disruptive behavior
Chicago School Readiness Project	Raver et al. (2008)	Targeted/ universal	PreK	Individual classroom	Increased teacher sensitivity; increased children's self-regulation; reduced child behavior problems
MyTeachingPartner	Hamre & Pianta (2005)	Universal	PreK–secondary	Classroom	Increased teacher sensitivity; increased student regulation; improved student academic outcomes
Banking Time	Driscoll & Pianta (2010)	Targeted	PreK	Teacher–student dyad	Increased teacher competence; increased teacher reported closeness with students; decreased student behavior problems
Relationship-Focused Reflection	Spilt et al. (2012)	Targeted	K	Teacher–student dyad	Increased teacher sensitivity; reduced conflict for high-efficacy teachers
Teacher–Child Interaction Training	McIntosh et al. (2000)	Targeted/ universal	PreK	Teacher–student dyad	Improved teacher use of praise; decreased student disruptive behavior
Child Development Project/Caring School Community	Solomon et al. (2000)	Universal	Elementary	Classroom/schoolwide	Increased student prosocial and interpersonal concerns; increased motivation and academic achievement
Responsive Classroom Approach	Rimm-Kaufman et al. (2007)	Universal	PreK–middle	Classroom/schoolwide	Increased student pro-social behavior; improved math and reading achievement
First Things First	Connell & Klem (2006)	Universal	Secondary middle	Schoolwide	Improved student test scores; increased attendance and graduation rates; reduced dropout rates
Career Academies	Kemple & Snipes (2000)	Universal	High school	Schoolwide	Improved student engagement and academic performance; reduced drop-out rates; improved completion rates

[a]Citation provided from original trial.

this portion of the program include encouraging teachers to become more familiar with their students, which can be done by asking children about their hobbies outside of school or expressing interest in their lives. Teachers are also encouraged to spend individual time with students and attend to their interests and accomplishments. This can be achieved by sending home "happygrams"; having children in the classroom applaud each other's accomplishments; and encouraging an atmosphere of care, warmth, and trust. Teachers are invited to share thoughts and feelings with their students, support collaboration, and promote positive self-talk. Positive teacher–student interactions are further promoted through behavior-based techniques including consistent praise, selective attention to children's positive behaviors, and the use of incentives for desired child behaviors.

The Incredible Years curriculum and training has repeatedly improved outcomes for both teachers and students. In a randomized controlled trial that used both parent and teacher training components, the program improved teachers' classroom management, increased teachers' reports of children's social competence, reduced teachers' reports of conduct problems, and improved children's observed behavior at school (Webster-Stratton et al., 2001). In another trial that involved parent training, teacher training, and individual child therapy, observed disruptive behavior at home decreased, and the teacher training component led to improvements in teachers' positive classroom management (Webster-Stratton et al., 2004). More recently, the Incredible Years teacher training program and Dinosaur School curriculum were implemented together, and the program reduced child conduct problems, improved school readiness, and enhanced social–emotional skills (Webster-Stratton, Reid, & Stoolmiller, 2008). These results suggest that the Incredible Years teacher training program, in combination with Dinosaur School, child training, and parent training components, is effective in changing teachers' behavior management skills, reducing children's disruptive behavior, improving school readiness, and developing students' social–emotional skills.

Although the Incredible Years program effectively changes teacher behaviors and improves classroom-level teacher–student interactions, this relationship is not the only targeted area for change. Still, positive behavior management is an integral piece of the intervention, and warm relationships are believed to contribute to classroom climate and lay the foundation for effective discipline. Importantly, the design of studies examining the effectiveness of the Incredible Years program makes it difficult to determine whether changes in the teacher–student relationship are specifically responsible for positive outcomes. Ultimately, however, the Incredible Years program highlights that teacher practices, such as forming positive relationships in order to facilitate effective behavior management, are a critical part of improving students' regulation and school readiness.

Chicago School Readiness Program

Recently, the Incredible Years teacher training program has been adapted for use within an early-childhood, multicomponent, teacher consultation model (Raver et al., 2008, 2009). Evidence suggests that these extensions may improve the quality of teachers' practice and children's behavioral and emotional outcomes. The Chicago School Readiness Program (CSRP) is an example of an effective, school-based, multicomponent treatment that combines the use of several evidence-based programs delivered largely through mental health consultation (Raver et al., 2009). The project targeted children in preschool Head Start classrooms and was intended to improve the emotional and behavioral regulation of students living in poverty. Mental health consultants (MHCs) helped teachers form positive relationships with their students through classroom management and engagement techniques. The intervention occurred across an entire school year and comprised four components: (1) teacher training, (2) coaching focused on strategy implementation, (3) mental health consultation for teacher stress reduction, and (4) mental health consultation for challenging students.

Each part of the intervention occurred during four discrete phases. The first part of the intervention was based on the Incredible Years program (Webster-Stratton et al., 2004), which specifically targets teachers' effective classroom management. The second component of the intervention involved teachers and consultants working together to implement strategies learned in the training. This coaching was a collaborative process between teachers and consultants, and included goal creation, observation of teacher–student interactions, sharing feedback, and engaging in problem solving. The third component of the intervention focused on teachers' stress reduction and personalized discussions between consultants and teachers around ways to cope with difficult situations. The last piece of the intervention, child mental health consultation, occurred during the final 10 weeks of the program. At this time, consultants provided individual and group therapy to children identified as evidencing high levels of behavior problems.

The results from the initial trial of CSRP indicated that the program increased positive teacher practices and reduced children's behavior problems (Raver et al., 2008). Teachers in the intervention condition showed increases in teacher sensitivity and were more likely to demonstrate improved behavior management skills relative to controls (Raver et al., 2008). The intervention was also effective in improving student behaviors; students in treatment sites showed significant reductions in behavior problems according to both teacher report and classroom behavioral observations (Raver et al., 2009). These results suggest that the intervention effectively changed classroom dynamics and simultaneously improved children's behavioral outcomes. Furthermore, because the control condition included a teacher aide to equalize the presence of consultants in treatment classrooms, results cannot be attributed to an extra adult in the classroom. CSRP has been replicated in two larger trials (now known as the Foundations of Learning Project) that also evidenced increases in positive child outcomes (Morris, Millenky, Raver, & Jones, 2013). In both trials, participation in the intervention resulted in teachers providing more effective classroom management, in children displaying fewer problem behaviors and improved cognitive regulation skills (i.e., attention, working memory, inhibitory control), and in increased classroom task engagement. Interestingly, although these studies showed that the intervention reduced negative behaviors, there were no significant gains in positive relational outcomes, such as positive social behavior. While authors noted that these components were not explicitly targeted by the intervention, these results highlight that reductions in problem behavior do not necessarily imply a simultaneous increase in prosocial behaviors. Still, results from the CSRP suggest that targeting teacher skills can improve children's ability to manage their behavior more effectively, as evidenced by increases in their inhibitory control. Unfortunately, these studies are limited by the inability to disentangle the various components that may have been most effective in changing children's outcomes. However, the consultation model as a whole appears to be an effective way to improve certain social–emotional skills of preschoolers exposed to risk factors associated with poverty.

My Teaching Partner

MyTeachingPartner (MTP) is a Web-mediated, individualized coaching model focused on improving teacher–student interactions (Pianta, Mashburn, Downer, Hamre, & Justice, 2008). It is based on the hypothesis that teacher–student interactions directly contribute to children's achievement through increased engagement, motivation, and on-task behavior (Hamre & Pianta, 2005). The program uses the Classroom Assessment Scoring System (CLASS; Pianta, LaParo, & Hamre, 2008) as the basis for observing and analyzing video and giving feedback on teacher practice. The CLASS organizes teacher–student interactions into three broad domains: emotional support, classroom organization, and instructional support. MTP coaching emphasizes that teachers benefit from extensive opportunities to (1) observe videotaped high-quality teacher–student interactions, (2) identify effective interactive responses to students' cues, and (3) receive ongoing individualized feedback and problem-solving analysis of the teacher's own interactions with students. The MTP coach and teacher go through five steps together: (1) The teacher videotapes interactions with students in the classroom (e.g., a math lesson, circle time, or small-group instruction); (2) the coach edits the video and prepares written prompts that focus on particular dimensions of the CLASS (e.g., support for student autonomy) to facilitate the teacher's self-analysis skills; (3) the teacher views the video and responds; (4) the teacher and coach conference by phone; and (5) the two mutually construct an action plan for the teacher to change how he or she interacts with students. This MTP coaching cycle is spread over 2 weeks and repeats continually for approximately 12 cycles across the academic year. Teachers and coaches interface primarily through an online portal that includes a video library of over 200 video clips that illustrate effective teacher–student interactions, allowing teachers to observe high-quality interactions in other classrooms. These MTP elements focus on helping teachers become better observers of their own practice and understand how their actions in the classroom affect children's behaviors, so as to increase opportunities for children to engage effectively in the classroom.

The impact of MTP has been examined in three trials to date. In the first preschool trial, MTP coaching was combined with implementation of a language and literacy and social-motional curriculum (Pianta, Mashburn, et al., 2008). In this trial, teachers who engaged in MTP coaching showed more positive growth in teacher–student interactions as measured by gains in CLASS scores during the school year. These effects were greater in classrooms where more children came from impoverished backgrounds (Pianta, Mashburn, et al., 2008). MTP coaching significantly increased students' literacy, receptive vocabulary, task orientation, and assertiveness (Hamre et al., 2012; Mashburn, Downer, Hamre, Justice, & Pianta, 2010). In a recent trial, preschool teachers displayed higher quality instructional support in their interactions with children than teachers in control classrooms. Similarly, compared to students whose teachers did not receive coaching, students whose teachers received coaching showed more positive engagement (Downer et al., 2014). Although there were no main treatment effects on children's readiness indicators during the coaching year, in the postintervention year, teachers who had participated in MTP had, on average, students with higher levels of inhibitory control, both in direct assessments and teacher report (Pianta et al., in press). MTP has also been tested in secondary schools, and results showed that students of teachers participating in the intervention saw significant academic gains in the year following intervention (Allen, Pianta, Gregory, Mikami, & Lun, 2011). Collectively, these results suggest that improving teacher–student interactions at the classroom level by using targeted professional development and consultation show promise in improving children's academic and social–emotional outcomes.

What Is Promising

In this review, "promising" interventions are those defined as having fewer than three successful trials, or more than three trials with a design that did not employ a control group. As in the "What Works" category, "promising" interventions could have impacted either teacher or student outcomes. However, if teacher outcomes were targeted, they must have been clearly linked to positive student social–emotional learning in previous literature.

Banking Time

Banking Time is a dyadic intervention intended to improve a teacher's relationship to a specific student with whom the teacher has had trouble connecting (Driscoll & Pianta, 2010). This may be because the child is displaying disruptive behaviors in the classroom or is socially reticent. Or, because the teacher, for any number of reasons, tends to rarely engage with a particular student. The intervention is called Banking Time because when a teacher invests in his or her relationship with the child, the relationship can become a resource in the classroom for both the student and the teacher during times of challenge (e.g., when the child is engaged in a difficult learning activity or having trouble navigating the classroom peer network). The hypothesized mechanism for change is strengthening the teacher–child bond, which helps children develop important social–emotional skills such as better communication, emotion awareness, effective help-seeking behavior, and improved self-management skills. These skills can be used in the classroom with adults and peers to improve school success in both social–

emotional and academic areas. In Banking Time sessions, teachers engage in brief, 10- 15-minute, one-on-one interactions that convey messages of support for exploration, sensitivity, predictability, and encouragement. These sessions occur when the teacher is available to provide individualized attention, which may be when the rest of the class is having recess, working independently, or participating in an activity with a teacher's assistant. The child leads each Banking Time session by choosing materials and guiding play and interactions. Specifically, the teacher is instructed to refrain from asking questions, giving commands, or teaching a lesson. Instead, the teacher observes the student's behavior, describes the student's actions, labels the student's positive and negative emotions, and emphasizes positive themes within the relationship. The teachers carefully observes the student's behaviors, words, and feelings, as well as monitoring his or her own thoughts and feelings during the interaction in order to allow the student to take initiative. This process also serves to help the teacher get to know the child better. The teacher describes what the student is doing by narrating the child's actions or through imitation (e.g., if the child draws a picture, the teacher could describe what the child is drawing or draw a similar picture) to show that he or she is attending to the student and supporting what the student is doing. The teacher labels the student's positive and negative emotions in order to emphasize acceptance of the student's feelings. Finally, the teacher chooses a specific relational theme in order to convey a message to the student about the importance of his or her connection to the student during the session. For example, if the student has low self-confidence when working on new learning activities, the teacher may choose a theme of "you do things well." These techniques are intended to enhance both the teacher's and the child's responsiveness to each other. This in turn creates a relational resource between the teacher and the child that can be used while interacting in the larger classroom setting.

At present, the links between Banking Time and teacher and child outcomes have been examined in samples of preschool teachers and children. Two studies show that the implementation of Banking Time is associated with increases in teachers' perceptions of closeness with students. In one study, information about Banking Time was made available to teachers who were participating in a Web-based teacher professional development intervention (Driscoll, Wang, Mashburn, & Pianta, 2011). Teachers could choose to implement the techniques in their classroom in an effort to improve teacher–student relationships. Researchers found that over the course of the year, teachers who engaged in Banking Time had closer relationships with these students, as measured by teacher report, than did teachers and students who did not utilize the Banking Time strategies. Although this study did not randomly assign students to the intervention, the trial suggested that Banking Time could be helpful in changing teacher perceptions of closeness with students. In a second study that randomly assigned teachers in two different sites to Banking Time or a control condition, researchers once again found that teachers participating in Banking Time reported increased closeness in their relationships with children (Driscoll & Pianta, 2010). Furthermore, teacher reports of classroom behavior revealed that students participating in the intervention had increased frustration tolerance and classroom task orientation, and decreased levels of conduct problems.

These trials suggest that Banking Time is a promising intervention for improving teacher perceptions of their relationships with disruptive preschool children and improving children's self-management skills (e.g., increased frustration tolerance). Although the pilot study showed no effects for observed classroom behavior, site differences and a limited sample size may have interfered with the detection of these differences (Driscoll & Pianta, 2010). Importantly, because a warm teacher–student relationship is related to positive student outcomes, changing this relationship may help to improve children's school readiness and decrease levels of disruptive behavior (Driscoll & Pianta, 2010). A large, federally funded randomized controlled trial of Banking Time is currently under way (Williford, 2010). This study is examining whether teachers' implementation of Banking Time with 3- and 4- year-old children at risk for a disruptive behavior disorder can improve children's behavioral and emotional outcomes. This study uses classroom observations, direct assessment, and informant report (teachers', parents' and children's) to assess the teacher–student relationship and children's behavioral and emotional outcomes. This study also includes a time-controlled comparison group (teachers who take the same amount of individual time with children but are free to choose how to spend that time) in addition to a business-as-usual comparison group. Accordingly, this study should begin disentangling the ingredients necessary for enhancing the teacher–student relationship. Furthermore, because the study assesses outcomes such as teacher-rated social competence and children's observed relationships with teachers and peers, results will also clarify how improving the teacher–student relationship may lead to gains in social–emotional skills.

Relationship Focused Reflection Program

Building off the work that emphasizes the importance of teacher perceptions and young children's development, the Relationship-Focused Reflection Program (RFRP; Spilt, Koomen, Thijs, & Van der Leij, 2012) asks kindergarten teachers to examine directly their relationship to disruptive children in their classroom. The intervention comprises two 45- to 60-minute sessions with a consultant. In the first session, the teacher's perceptions of his or her relationship with a difficult child are elicited using the Teacher Relationship Interview (TRI; Pianta, 1999), which assesses the teacher's representation of relationships with students by having the teacher talk about his or her students, then measure the emotions that are expressed. To facilitate this sharing of information with the consultant, the teacher is encouraged to narrate and reflect on positive and negative experiences with a challenging student. In the second session, the consultant and the teacher watch videotapes of interactions filmed in the classroom. The consultant explains a profile of strengths and weaknesses gathered from both observational and interview data. The profile is then linked to the teacher's initial reflections that were elicited in the first interview. Following these discussions, the teacher and the consultant identify areas for improvement. The same process is repeated with a second difficult child in the classroom.

In a study with 32 teachers and 64 kindergarten children randomly assigned to either the RFRP condition or another intervention focused on interpersonal skills, researchers observed that teacher sensitivity increased in the RFRP condition classrooms. They also observed decreases in teacher–child conflict for the RFRP teachers who rated themselves as having high levels of efficacy (Spilt et al., 2012). There were no overall improvements in observed child behavior (Spilt et al., 2012). This pattern of results highlights that some aspects of the teacher–student relationship, such as conflict, are differentially affected, based on teacher characteristics such as efficacy. The study also suggests that teachers' cognitive understanding of their relationship to students may be a critical ingredient in changing teacher–student interactions. Although this study indicated that targeting the teacher–child relationship led to improvements in teachers' social and emotional competence (i.e., increased sensitivity), future work is needed to examine the ways in which these changes may in turn affect children's social–emotional skills as well.

Teacher–Child Interaction Training

Another intervention targeting preschool children and their teachers is teacher–child interaction training (TCIT; Lyon et al., 2009), which seeks to improve teachers' relationships with students by increasing positive interactions and using effective discipline. TCIT has been tested in the classroom setting across studies that have used case study designs (McIntosh, Rizza, & Bliss, 2000), multiple time series designs (Lyon et al., 2009), and experimental designs (Tiano & McNeil, 2006). The TCIT intervention comprises nine group sessions that train teachers on two different topics: child-directed interaction (CDI) and teacher-directed interaction (TDI). CDI skills are taught in the first four sessions, TDI skills are taught in the subsequent four sessions, and the final session is dedicated to a graduation ceremony. Each training lasts 1.5 hours and occurs once a week for 9 weeks. In addition to these group sessions, teachers receive weekly *in vivo* coaching up to three times per week for 20 minutes. Initially, coaching focuses on interactions with a few children and gradually expands to address situations at the classroom level.

CDI focuses on teachers' use of PRIDE skills—Praise, Reflections, Imitations, Descriptions of behavior, and Enthusiasm—to enhance positive interactions between teachers and students. Praise contributes to warm interactions and increases good behavior; Reflections demonstrate that the teacher understands the child; Imitations of student behavior promote cooperation within the teacher–student dyad; Descriptions of the child's behavior allow the teacher to communicate interest; and Enthusiasm allows the teacher to keep the child engaged in the task at hand. These techniques increase warmth within the relationship and help teachers connect to children in new ways while increasing children's autonomy and control.

TDI, on the other hand, focuses on prevention and management of challenging behaviors through the use of positive attention, effective commands, natural consequences, and time-out. In teaching these classroom management skills, the intention of the program is to help teachers reduce levels of problem behaviors, and prevent coercive and negative discipline. The first session focuses on using attention on good behavior to increase desired student actions. The second session shifts to use of effective commands, which helps children understand classroom expectations. The third session focuses on "Sit and Watch" planning, which is similar to sending a child to "Time-Out." The final TDI session reviews all skills and allows teachers to problem-solve situations that they find to be particularly difficult.

Results from a multiple baseline investigation of TCIT involving four classrooms and 78 preschool children from a low-income, ethnic/minority sample showed that teachers increased their use of positive strategies in the classroom (Lyon et al., 2009). These results were consistent with a previous study in seven Head Start classrooms, which indicated that compared to teachers in control classrooms, teachers using TCIT used more labeled praise (Tiano & McNeil, 2006). Combined, these results suggest that TCIT is effective in meaningfully changing teacher behaviors to promote positive teacher–student interactions in the classroom. Specifically, positive attention increased after training, suggesting that TCIT has the potential to increase warmth in teacher–student relationships, while simultaneously decreasing potentially damaging interaction patterns that put children at risk for negative outcomes (Lyon et al., 2009; Tiano & McNeil, 2006). By improving teacher practices, the intervention may improve children's developmental outcomes, specifically, the reduction of children's behavior problems. However, because SEL outcomes were not measured and there were no significant effects for student outcomes in the experimental study (Tiano & McNeil, 2006), it is unclear whether changes in teachers' behaviors are tied to corresponding increases in children's SEL. Future work should examine and measure the extent to which students' social–emotional skills may improve as a result of TCIT by testing the intervention in a larger, more representative sample of children.

The Child Development Project/Caring School Communities

The Child Development Project, now known as *Caring School Community* (CSC), was initially implemented in 24 elementary schools across the country (Solomon, Battistich, Watson, & Lewis, 2000). The program is founded on the belief that schools play an important role in fulfilling the social and personal needs of students. For the school to meet these needs, students must (1) experience caring and supportive relationships with one another, and with teachers and adults in the school; (2) have opportunities to participate in decision making relative to their own learning and behavior; and (3) find opportunities for success in their social and academic lives. To foster these relationships, teachers and students generate norms for their classroom with the intention of encouraging responsible behavior through commitment to the community. By emphasizing high-quality interpersonal relationships as part of this community, the program is intended to increase students' investment in their academic and social progress. In addition to focusing on the quality of adult–child interactions, the program uses developmental discipline, cooperative learning, literature-based reading instruction, and family involvement. Results from trials implementing the CSC program suggest that the intervention leads to increases in students' academic motivation and achievement, gains in interpersonal concerns, improved conflict management skills, more cooperative learning, and increases in prosocial behavior (Solomon et al., 2000). Furthermore, student reports of whether a CSC was developed during the intervention mediated almost all student outcomes (Solomon et al., 2000). Although the focus on positive and supportive teacher–student relationships cannot be directly tied to these social–emotional outcomes, this work suggests that developing responsive relationships with adults is an important component of creating a school environment that fosters positive SEL outcomes.

Responsive Classroom Approach

Another intervention that targets classroom and school climate through the teacher–student relationship is the Responsive Classroom (RC) approach (Rimm-Kaufman, Fan, Chiu, & You, 2007). Similar to the CSC, the RC approach emphasizes the important role of school and classroom climate. It puts equal emphasis on teaching social–emotional goals and academics. The program stresses that children learn best when they are safe, challenged, and excited to learn. To create this type of academic environment, teachers are encouraged to know and understand children individually, developmentally, and culturally. Through this knowledge, teachers are able to encourage all children. Results from quasi-experimental studies showed that the use of RC practices after 1 year were associated with improved reading achievement, greater closeness among teachers and children, increased student prosocial behaviors and assertiveness, and decreased student fearfulness (Rimm-Kaufman et al., 2007). Students also showed significant gains in math and reading tests, and 3 years of implementation resulted in greater gains than use of the program for either 1 or 2 years. These improvements indicate that implementing the intervention led to increases in prosocial behaviors and improvements in student academic performance.

First Things First (FTF) and Career Academies

Like CSC and the RC approach, First Things First (FTF) and career academies address the teacher–student relationship, although they do so in the context of school reform (Quint, 2006). It is important to note that although FTF and career academies have been shown to improve long-term developmental outcomes, such as improved academic performance, investigations have not explicitly tested whether students' social–emotional skills are improved through these interventions. However, because both programs target social–emotional processes such as improving relationships and encouraging students to think about their interests and career goals (possibly related to self-awareness or responsible decision making), the programs are described below. FTF is an intervention that includes three core components: small learning communities, a family advocate system, and instructional improvement efforts (Quint, Bloom, Black, & Stephens, 2005). These small learning communities enhance students' school experience by creating consistency in adult–child relationships. FTF allows students to remain with teachers for longer periods during the day and for multiple years of schooling. This strategy is hypothesized to increase persistence and self-confidence by providing students the opportunity to form meaningful and consistent relationships during their high school career. In Kansas City, where the program was implemented in middle and high schools, students in FTF schools showed significant gains in attendance and graduation, reduced dropout rates, and improvement on the Kansas State Reading and Math tests (Quint et al., 2005). Importantly, other districts that subsequently adopted the program did not see the same consistent pattern of results, suggesting that challenges exist when scaling-up this type of program (Quint et al., 2005).

Similar to FTF, career academies (Kemple & Snipes, 2000) are based on the principles of small learning communities. Career academies are small schools within schools that create a personalized and supportive learning environment for students and teachers. They combine academic and career-related coursework in an effort to increase high school students' engagement and academic performance. Like FTF, students remain with teachers for long periods of time across multiple years. Career academies have existed for many years, and recent evaluations suggest that they contribute to positive outcomes. They have been found to (1) increase the level of interpersonal support students experience during high school, (2) reduce dropout rates, (3) improve attendance and academic course taking for students most at risk, (4) increase the likelihood of graduating on time for students least at risk, and (5) increase engagement in career awareness activities (Kemple & Snipes, 2000). Although these outcomes are not explicitly linked to SEL, it may be that a focus on improving relationships while increasing student engagement is linked to SEL (e.g., responsible decision making and self-awareness). Thus, although career academies are effective in improving students' long-term developmental outcomes, particularly when the program increases levels of interpersonal support between teachers and students (Kemple & Snipes, 2000), the extent to which social–emotional gains may facilitate these improved outcomes has not been explicitly tested.

What Does Not Work

In our examination, we did not find any programs that were carefully evaluated and found not to have worked.

Summary

In this chapter, we have provided an introduction to the underlying theories and current research on teacher–student relationships. Our review of the evidenced-based programs is intended to enhance the quality of teacher–student interactions and to show that strengthening the bond between teachers and students is linked with greater student social–emotional and academic learning. Still, much remains to be learned about the impact of teacher–student relationships on students' SEL. In particular, the mechanisms by which this relationship impacts student outcomes are still not well understood. As our review clearly indicates, the effect of teacher–student relationships has focused on short- and long-term developmental outcomes (often the reduction of problem behavior), and not on the more proximal and mediational outcomes of SEL. Still, observational studies have shown the links between teacher–student relationships and SEL skills. Future research should examine how a sensitive and supportive teacher–student relationship may improve students' relationship management, self-awareness, and decision-making skills.

In addition, many of the programs described in this chapter focus on improving the quality of teacher–student interactions within the context of a more comprehensive program. As a result, for some interventions, we do not know whether the enhanced teacher–student relationship, another aspect of the program, or the combination of strategies is responsible for children's improved SEL. Future research that "unpacks" these comprehensive programs will help to determine whether certain components are critical for improving the teacher–student relationship and children's social–emotional adjustment. We also note that most successful teacher–student relationship interventions have been conducted with younger students (preschool- and early elementary school–age children), and more work is needed to test the impacts of these programs in middle and high school. Additionally, our review has summarized programs that vary in implementation, from universal and schoolwide to targeted and dyadic. More research is necessary to help decision makers choose which programs are best for their school community. Finally, the evidence summarized in this chapter is taken from relatively small studies; thus, effectiveness trials that implement interventions under routine, everyday practice are needed to determine whether related effects can be maintained when these interventions are taken to scale.

Acknowledgments

This chapter was supported in part by a grant awarded to Dr. Amanda P. Williford and colleagues and to Dr. Robert Pianta and colleagues by the Institute of Education Sciences, U.S. Department of Education, through Grant Nos.

R324A100215 and R305B040049, respectively, to the University of Virginia. The opinions expressed are those of the authors and do not represent views of the U.S. Department of Education.

References

Ainsworth, M. D., Bell, S. M., & Stayton, D. J. (1974). Infant–mother attachment and social development: Socialization as a product of reciprocal responsiveness to signals. In M. Richards (Ed.), *The integration of a child into a social world* (pp. 9–135). London: Cambridge University Press.

Allen, J. P., Pianta, R. C., Gregory, A., Mikami, A. Y., & Lun, J. (2011). An interaction-based approach to enhancing secondary school instruction and student achievement. *Science 333*, 1034–1047.

Birch, S. H., & Ladd, G. W. (1997). The teacher–child relationship and children's early school adjustment. *Journal of School Psychology, 35*, 61–79.

Bronfenbrenner, U., & Morris, P. A. (1998). The ecology of developmental processes. In W. Damon & R. M. Lerner (Eds.), *Handbook of child psychology: Vol. 1. Theoretical models of human development* (5th ed., pp. 993–1023). New York: Wiley.

Connell, J. P., & Klem, A. M. (2006). First Things First: A framework for successful secondary school reform. *New Directions in Youth Development, 111*, 53–66.

Deci, E. L., & Ryan, R. M. (1985). *Intrinsic motivation and self-determination in human behavior.* New York: Plenum Press.

Doumen, S., Verschueren, K., Buyse, E., Germeijs, V., Luyckx, K., & Soenens, B. (2008). Reciprocal relations between teacher–child conflict and aggressive behavior in kindergarten: A three-wave longitudinal study. *Journal of Clinical Child and Adolescent Psychology, 37*(3), 588–599.

Downer, J. T., Pianta, R. C., Burchinal, M., Field, S., Hamre, B. K., Locasale-Crouch, J. L., et al. (2014). *Coaching and coursework focused on teacher–child interactions during language/literacy instruction: Effects on teacher beliefs, knowledge, skills, and practice.* Manuscript submitted for publication.

Driscoll, K. C., & Pianta, R. C. (2010). Early education and development of Banking Time in Head Start: Early efficacy of an intervention designed to promote supportive teacher–child relationships. *Early Education and Development, 21*(1), 37–41.

Driscoll, K. C., Wang, L., Mashburn, A. J., & Pianta, R. C. (2011). Fostering supportive teacher–child relationships: Intervention implementation in a state-funded preschool program. *Early Education and Development, 22*(4), 593–619.

Hamre, B. K., & Pianta, R. C. (2001). Early teacher–child relationships and the trajectory of children's school outcomes through eighth grade. *Child Development, 72*(2), 625–638.

Hamre, B. K., & Pianta, R. C. (2005). Can instructional and emotional support in the first grade classroom make a difference for children at risk of school failure? *Child Development, 76*(5), 949–967.

Hamre, B. K., Pianta, R. C., Burchinal, M., Field, S., LoCasale-Crouch, J., Downer, J. T., et al. (2012). A course on effective teacher–child interactions: Effects on teacher beliefs, knowledge, and observed practice. *American Educational Research Journal, 49*(1), 88–123.

Kemple, J., & Snipes, J. (2000). Career academies impacts on students' engagement and performance in high school. Washington, DC: Manpower Demonstration Research Corporation.

Lyon, A. R., Gershenson, R. A, Farahmand, F. K., Thaxter, P. J., Behling, S., & Budd, K. S. (2009). Effectiveness of Teacher–Child Interaction Training (TCIT) in a preschool setting. *Behavior Modification, 33*(6), 855–884.

Maldonado-Carreño, C., & Votruba-Drzal, E. (2011). Teacher–child relationships and the development of academic and behavioral skills during elementary school: A within- and between-child analysis. *Child Development, 82*(2), 601–616.

Mashburn, A. J., Downer, J. T., Hamre, B. K., Justice, L. M., & Pianta, R. C. (2010). Consultation for teachers and children's language and literacy development during pre-kindergarten. *Applied Developmental Science, 14*(4), 179–196.

McIntosh, D., Rizza, M., & Bliss, L. (2000). Implementing empirically supported interventions: Teacher–child interaction therapy. *Psychology in the Schools, 37*(5), 453–462.

Morris, P., Millenky, M., Raver, C. C., & Jones, S. (2013) Does a preschool social–emotional intervention pay off for classroom instruction and children's behavior and academic skills?: Evidence from the Foundations of Learning Project. *Early Education and Development, 24*(7), 1020–1042.

Pianta, R. C. (1999). *Enhancing relationships between children and teachers.* Washington, DC: American Psychological Association.

Pianta, R. C., Burchinal, M., Hamre, B. K., Downer, J. T., LoCasale-Crouch, J., Williford, A., et al. (2014). *Early childhood professional development: Coaching and coursework effects on indicators of children's school readiness.* Manuscript submitted for publication.

Pianta, R. C., LaParo, K., & Hamre, B. K. (2008). *Classroom Assessment Scoring System (CLASS).* Baltimore: Brookes.

Pianta, R. C., Mashburn, A. J., Downer, J. T., Hamre, B. K., & Justice, L. (2008). Effects of web-mediated professional development resources on teacher–child interactions in pre-kindergarten classrooms. *Early Childhood Research Quarterly, 23*(4), 431–451.

Quint, J. (2006). *Meeting five critical challenges of high school reform lessons from research on three reform models.* Washington, DC: Manpower Demonstration Research Corporation.

Quint, J., Bloom, H. S., Black, A. R., & Stephens, L. (2005). *The challenge of scaling up educational reform.* Washington, DC: Manpower Demonstration Research Corporation.

Raver, C. C., Jones, S. M., Li-Grining, C. P., Metzger, M., Smallwood, K., & Sardin, L. (2008). Improving preschool classroom processes: Preliminary findings from a randomized trial implemented in head start settings. *Early Childhood Research Quarterly, 63*(3), 253–255.

Raver, C. C., Jones, S. M., Li-Grining, C., Zhai, F., Metzger, M. W., & Solomon, B. (2009). Targeting children's behavior problems in preschool classrooms: A cluster-randomized controlled trial. *Journal of Consulting and Clinical Ppsychology, 77*(2), 302–316.

Rimm-Kaufman, S. E., Fan, X., Chiu, Y. J., & You, W. (2007). The contribution of the Responsive Classroom Approach on children's academic achievement: Results from a three year longitudinal study. *Journal of School Psychology, 45*(4), 401–421.

Roorda, D. L., Koomen, H. M., Spilt, J. L., & Oort, F. J. (2011). The influence of affective teacher–student relationships on students' school engagement and achievement: A meta-analytic approach. *Review of Educational Research, 81*(4), 493–529.

Sabol, T. J., & Pianta, R. C. (2012). Recent trends in research on teacher–child relationships. *Attachment and Human Development, 14*(3), 213–231.

Solomon, D., Battistich, V., Watson, M., & Lewis, C. (2000). A six-district study of educational change: Direct and mediated effects of the Child Development Project. *School Psychology of Education, 4*(1), 3–51.

Spilt, J. L., Koomen, H. M., Thijs, J. T., & Van der Leij, A. (2012). Supporting teachers' relationships with disruptive children: The potential of relationship focused reflection. *Attachment and Human Development, 14*(3), 305–318.

Tiano, J. D., & McNeil, C. B. (2006). Training head start teachers in behavior management using parent–child interaction therapy: A preliminary investigation. *Journal of Early and Intensive Behavioral Intervention, 3*(2), 220–233.

Webster-Stratton, C., Reid, M. J., & Hammond, M. (2001). Preventing conduct problems, promoting social competence: A parent and teacher training partnership in head start. *Journal of Clinical Child Psychology, 30*(3), 283–302.

Webster-Stratton, C., Reid, M. J., & Hammond, M. (2004). Treating children with early-onset conduct problems: Intervention outcomes for parent, child, and teacher training, *Journal of Clinical and Adolescent Psychology, 33*(1), 105–124.

Webster-Stratton, C., Reid, M., & Stoolmiller, M. (2008). Preventing conduct problems and improving school readiness: Evaluation of the Incredible Years Teacher and Child Training Programs in high-risk schools. *Journal of Child Psychology and Psychiatry, 49*(5), 471–488.

Williford, A. P. (2010). Examining the efficacy of Banking Time: A teacher–child early intervention to improve children's emotional and behavioral development (Institute of Education Sciences, NCSER, IES Award No. R324A100215). Retrieved January 26, 2014, from *http://ies.ed.gov/funding/grantsearch/details.asp?id=994.*

CHAPTER 16

The Role of School–Family Partnership Programs for Promoting Student SEL

S. Andrew Garbacz, Michelle S. Swanger-Gagné, and Susan M. Sheridan

Social and emotional learning (SEL) programs foster children's academic success and lifelong learning by improving social and emotional skills, attitudes, behavior, and academic performance (Durlak, Weissberg, Dymnicki, Taylor, & Schellinger, 2011; Zins, Bloodworth, Weissberg, & Walberg, 2004). An SEL approach to intervention promotes a set of interrelated competencies in children and youth around self-awareness, self-management (e.g., self-regulation), social awareness (e.g., perspective taking), relationship skills (e.g., cooperating), and/or responsible decision making through direct instruction and by creating an environment that supports the development of these competencies (Collaborative for Academic, Social, and Emotional Learning [CASEL], 2012). Individual competencies are the short-term goals of SEL programs, whereas increasing positive social behavior, reducing disruptive behavior and emotional distress, and improving academic performance (CASEL, 2012) are the longer term goals of most programs.

Children spend the majority of their time under parent supervision (Walberg, 1984), which positions parents as key teachers for their children. National policy has highlighted the important role parents have in children's development by advocating for parents as full educational partners (No Child Left Behind Act, 2001) and decision makers in educational programming (U.S. Department of Education, Office of Planning, Evaluation and Policy Development, 2010). Including families in systematic efforts to promote SEL addresses the multiple systemic influences in a child's life (Bronfenbrenner, 1977) and allows for learning and reinforcement to occur across contexts (Albright & Weissberg, 2010). Furthermore, Henderson and Mapp (2002) report "consistent, positive, and convincing" (p. 7) evidence supporting the family's role in children's school achievement and life success. Numerous studies have found positive associations between family educational involvement and several of the same outcomes targeted by SEL programs, including student academic performance (Fan & Chen, 2001; Power et al., 2012) and behavior (Sheridan et al., 2012) in elementary school and high school (Jeynes, 2012). Families promote SEL competencies through modeling and employing specific parenting practices. Examples of effective parenting strategies include supporting appropriate behavior, setting limits, building relationships, and monitoring (Dishion & Stormshak, 2007). The use of these parenting practices is linked with decreases in youth behavior problems (Dishion et al., 2008) and increases in social and emotional skills, including self-management (Stormshak, Fosco, & Dishion, 2010).

SEL programs typically emphasize universal, schoolwide, multiyear efforts to develop student skills (CASEL, 2012). However, coordinated selected or indicated efforts are often also required when students do not respond to the schoolwide universal approaches (Zins & Elias, 2006). Indeed, efforts to support all students in developing skills and competencies, and enhancing procedures to identify and assist students demonstrating greater need (Gutkin, 2012) through selected and indicated procedures are necessary. A multi-tiered approach to service delivery in schools (Biglan, 1995; Horner et al., 2009; Metzler, Biglan, Rusby, & Sprague, 2001) structures services in ways that (1) prevent the occurrence of problem behavior by building student skills to support appropriate behavior (i.e., universal), (2) target those at risk for developing severe problems (i.e., selected), and (3) intervene for students who require intensive forms and levels of support (i.e., indicated). Across all tiers, parallel promotion of skills and planning for generalization of proximal SEL competencies may be most effective through the active engagement of families and educators in mutual goal setting, collaborative planning, and coordinated implementation.

Our purpose in this chapter is to review SEL programs across the tiers of service delivery from preschool through high school that involve families and to identify those that include elements of school–family partnership (SFP), which is a specific educational approach to working with families. Before describing our review process and inclusion criteria, we define the main components of SFP, provide the theoretical and empirical basis for the approach, and highlight the ways that it is aligned with the SEL approach to school-based interventions.

Definitions and Scope

Many different terms have been used to describe the quality and ways in which schools and families work together to promote student outcomes, but the focus of this chapter is SFP. To place this work in context, we review key terms from the research literature and explain how they relate to our conceptualization of the most effective ways that families and schools should work together. "Family involvement" is a term that is routinely used when describing families' educationally oriented behaviors that occur in either home or school settings (Fantuzzo, Tighe, & Childs, 2000). These include reading to a child, helping with homework, or volunteering in the classroom or at the school. In addition, "family involvement" refers to communications shared by families and educators (e.g., via phone calls or e-mails; Fantuzzo et al., 2000).

Family members and school personnel inevitably develop relationships as they interact with one another over time (Pianta & Walsh, 1996), but research suggests that the quality of these relationships varies (Clarke, Sheridan, & Woods, 2010). For example, families and educators often discuss student learning objectives during parent–teacher conferences. However, if teachers dictate these objectives without asking parents for their perspective or involving them in decision making, it is unlikely parents and teachers will develop a positive relationship or act in ways that enhance student performance (Adams & Christenson, 1998). Similarly, if parents lack efficacy in terms of their abilities to help their children, they may be less likely to be involved in their children's education (Hoover-Dempsey, Bassler, & Brissie, 1992). Thus, both the nature of the interactions and the quality of the relationship that evolves from them are important ingredients in considering how schools and families can work most effectively together. Furthermore, to facilitate healthy working relationships with families, school structures and programs should be equally accessible for all families (Mapp & Hong, 2010).

Moving beyond family involvement, the term "school–family partnership" (SFP) characterizes a relationship that includes meaningful communication and active participation of both families and educators, which leads to genuine collaboration between both parties (Epstein, 1995; Sheridan, Rispoli, & Holmes, 2013). The term "partnership" implies that the work is shared. Many programs designed to promote SFPs use a combination of partnership-centered components to produce positive student outcomes, although researchers have yet to determine which features are most critical to this particular approach.

We propose a multicomponent SFP framework based on theory (Bronfenbrenner, 1977) and empirical literature (Jeynes, 2012; Sheridan et al., 2012). The five main components are as follows:

1. The roles of educators and family members reflect their shared responsibility for promoting child and youth development.
2. The program clearly specifies that family members and educators are to engage in shared or joint work.
3. The nature of interactions between educators and family members is collaborative and focuses on enhancing student outcomes.
4. Both home and school contexts are targeted in intervention activities.
5. There is open communication that allows for a multidirectional flow of information (Christenson, 1995; Epstein, 1995; Fantuzzo et al., 2000; Sheridan, Rispoli et al., 2013).

In SFPs, families and educators share responsibility for educating children, and decisions regarding children are made in a joint fashion (Epstein, 1995). Furthermore, the roles and responsibilities of each party are identified and reflect a partnership orientation in educating children. The nature of school–family work is collaborative, and the focus is on helping students achieve positive social and emotional, behavioral, and academic outcomes (Christenson, 1995). For example, families and schools may work together to construct a plan that encourages a child to develop self-management skills. To maximize benefits for children, partnership efforts include planning for success across settings. There are important partnership activities that occur in homes and at schools (Albright & Weissberg, 2010; Fantuzzo et al., 2000). Finally, communication is a key ingredient in partnership activities (Christenson & Sheridan, 2001). Within SFPs, communication is clear and inclusive, and allows for a message to originate from either a parent or educator (i.e., communication should be multidirectional; Sheridan, Rispoli, et al., 2013).

Theories

The theoretical foundations for SFPs and SEL are complementary. Both SFPs and SEL are based on ecological systems and social support theories. In addition, social learning theory specifies the unique roles of families and other key individuals in a child's development of SEL competencies and outcomes. We briefly review these theoretical approaches and link them to SFPs and proximal SEL competencies and distal SEL outcomes.

Bronfenbrenner (1977) articulated a theory that emphasizes the influence of nested ecological systems on a child's development. Specifically, children are thought to develop and reside in the context of many environmental microsystems (e.g., homes, neighborhoods, after-school programs). A child's experiences in one setting (i.e., microsystem) may affect behavior in another setting. For example, a child may learn that he or she can receive teacher attention at school by correctly answering a question during a class discussion and may expect parent attention at home when engaging in a similar behavior. Essential SEL skills permeate across systems and settings, including home and school (Jones & Bouffard, 2012). Thus, efforts to integrate families and school personnel in SEL activities are important (Zins et al., 2004). The term "mesosystem" refers to the connections among microsystems (e.g., home, school) that affect development. In fact, it is within the mesosystem that SFPs occur (Reschly & Christenson, 2012). Ecological theory suggests that children may encounter difficulties when there are disconnects within the mesosystem, or between parents and educators (Bronfenbrenner, 1979).

Social support theory (Boyce, 1985) specifies supportive networks that exist within families; however, the concept of social support is easily translated to schools in which school personnel support children's development of SEL and appropriate social behavior. The family system (Boyce, 1985) and school climate provide proximal social support to children. According to an ecological systems view of child development, systems that influence children (e.g., microsystems of school and home) are dynamic and cannot be fully understood without also capturing the influence of other systems (e.g., neighborhoods, schools). It is important to identify the function of different systems and their roles in conceptualizing child development, yet as Sameroff (2009) indicates, development occurs as a set of transactions whereby developmental changes and settings are "interdependent and change as a function of their mutual influence on one another" (p. 7). Indeed, a child's performance (e.g., development of SEL, appropriate social behavior) is only considered in terms of a broader range of systemic factors that support it (Gutkin, 2012). In fact, parents can have a substantial influence on a child's development of skills from an early age.

Social learning theory suggests children can learn skills and behaviors from others (e.g., parents, other children; Bandura, 1969). Because children and youth spend the majority of their time under parental supervision, many behaviors observed by children are those of their immediate family. Whether a child performs observed behaviors relates to a complex set of ecological and transactional issues (e.g., parent and child interactions; Patterson 1982). Indeed, the developmental literature has for years suggested the important role parents have their child's development (Moore & Patterson, 2009). That literature suggests that parents have considerable knowledge about their child's development and are in an important position to partner with educational stakeholders to promote child and youth success.

Overview of Strategies

SFP programs target SEL in different ways. Some are designed to promote a proximal SEL competency (e.g., self-management), whereas others attempt to change a distal SEL outcome (e.g., social behavior). In the review of programs that follows, certain intervention effects are highlighted in terms of the specific SEL competencies and outcomes identified in the *2013 CASEL Guide* (CASEL, 2012).

Current Review of Research

A targeted review of relevant literature was conducted to identify successful SEL programs that incorporate families and might also contain components of SFP (Albright & Weissberg, 2010; CASEL, 2012; Christenson & Carlson, 2005; Cox, 2005; Durlak et al., 2011). We identified 11 programs that use SFP components and focus on proximal SEL competencies and/or distal SEL outcomes. We coded the 11 programs on the five aforementioned components of SFP. Review procedures included assigning quantitative ratings (0 = *not met*, 1 = *partially met*, 2 = *fully met*) to each of the five SFP components. A rating of *not met* indicated that no mention of that component was provided. A rating of *partially met* indicated that some (i.e., ≥ 1), but not all, aspects of that component were included. A rating of *fully met* indicated that all aspects of that component were included. From the 11 coded programs, six were determined to align closely with the majority of SFP components. Table 16.1 includes the 11 reviewed programs and their alignment with SFP components; in this chapter, we discuss only the six programs that demonstrated high alignment with SFP components.

After rating each of the SFP components, we evaluated the empirical evidence that exists for each of the six programs to determine their fit within the following categories: What Works, What Is Promising, and What Does Not Work. To be included in the What Works category, the program needed to demonstrate three or more successful trials on proximal SEL competencies and/or distal SEL outcomes. A successful "trial" could include studies that used a randomized controlled design, a single-case experimental design, and/or a quasi-experimental design without major design problems. For a program to be included in the What Is Promising category, it needed to demonstrate one or more of the following on proximal SEL competencies and/or distal SEL outcomes: less than three successful trials; mixed trial results; or in the absence of research, appeared promising based on a combination of theory and research. The What Does Not Work category indicated that an evaluation of an intervention failed to reach its intended impact. In addition, we assessed the tier of support (e.g., universal) addressed by the program. Finally, we provide a brief synopsis of future research suggestions for programs based on methodological and statistical issues as appropriate. Table 16.2

TABLE 16.1. SEL Programs, School–Family Partnership Criteria, and Ratings

	School–family partnership criteria					
SEL programs	A	B	C	D	E	Total
Conjoint Behavioral Consultation	2	2	2	2	2	10
Parent–Teacher Action Research Teams	2	1	2	2	2	9
Family Check-Up	1	1	2	2	1	7
Caring School Community	1	0	1	2	2	6
Incredible Years Training Series	1	1	2	2	0	6
Second Step	1	1	1	2	1	6
Seattle Social Development Project	1	1	1	1	0	4
Project Achieve	0	0	1	2	0	3
Reach Out to Schools: Social Competency Program/Open Circle	0	0	1	1	1	3
Responsive Classroom	0	0	1	1	1	3
I Can Problem-Solve	0	0	1	1	0	2

Note. Quantitative ratings of coding criteria for each program are presented. Programs were rated on a Likert-type scale (0 = *not met*, 1 = *partially met*, 2 = *fully met*). Coding criteria considered five school–family partnership components include A: roles of educators and family members reflect their shared responsibility for promoting child and youth development, B: the program clearly specifies that family members and educators are to engage in shared or joint work , C: the nature of interactions between educators and family members is collaborative and focused on enhancing student outcomes, D: both home and school contexts are targeted in intervention activities, and E: there is open communication allowing for multidirectional flow of information.

includes each of the six programs and provides an overview of the program (e.g., tier of support targeted, intervention strategies).

What Works

Caring School Community

Caring School Community (CSC) is a modified version of the Child Development Project. CSC is a universal elementary school program whose aim is that schools become caring communities of learners (Battistich, Schaps, Watson, & Solomon, 1996). A caring community is established by creating supportive relationships, collaborating with students and parents, and developing a common purpose and commitment to core values (Battistich et al., 1996). According to theory, outcomes are maximized by warm and supportive relationships, commitments to core values, collaboration, accessible and engaging curricula, student engagement, and a constructivist approach to teaching and learning (Battistich et al., 1996). This approach is believed to fulfill students' basic needs, facilitate bonding to the school community, and encourage intellectual and sociomoral development (Battistich et al., 1996).

CSC includes the following core elements of the Child Development Project: class meeting lessons, cross-age peer-pairing programs, activities at home, and schoolwide community programs (U.S. Department of Education, Institute of Education Sciences, What Works Clearinghouse, 2007). Class meeting lessons use norms and rules developed collaboratively by students and teachers to frame social and interpersonal skills-building activities (Solomon, Battistich, Watson, Schaps, & Lewis, 2000). Activities focused on the home aim to connect family

TABLE 16.2. Core Features of SEL Programs That Closely Align with SFP Components

	Tier of support	Primary research designs	Intervention strategies	Representative competencies and outcomes
What works				
Conjoint Behavioral Consultation	Selected or indicated	RCT, single-case experimental, quasi-experimental	Partnership-centered behavioral consultation	Positive social behavior, relationship skills
Family Check-Up	Selected or indicated with some universal	RCTs	Ecological family-centered assessment and feedback	Fewer conduct problems, self-management
Caring School Community	Universal	RCT, quasi-experimental	Multicomponent, schoolwide modules	Academic success, positive social behavior, social awareness
Incredible Years	Universal, selected, or indicated	RCTs	Structured group training for parents, teachers, and children	Positive social behavior, responsible decision making
Second Step	Universal	RCTs, quasi-experimental	Structured group training for children	Positive social behavior fewer conduct problems, social awareness
What is promising				
Parent–Teacher Action Research Teams	Selected or indicated	Quasi-experimental	Collaborative consultation with parents and teachers	Positive social behavior, relationship skills

Note. RCT, randomized controlled trial.

members to the school community by engaging in discussions with children about topics such as family history and values (Solomon et al., 2000). After children learn about their family background, they can share it in the classroom, thereby building home–school connections (Battistich et al., 1996). Schoolwide programs are designed to build a sense of community among stakeholders (e.g., parents, teachers) through participation on projects and other activities (Solomon et al., 2000). Finally, there is a program component that connects younger and older students to foster helping relationships. CSC includes many members of the school community, and engages them in activities across settings to foster a sense of community and to support students' development of skills, competencies, and supportive relationships.

Evidence for CSC has been established through a randomized controlled trial and quasi-experimental designed studies. CSC is identified as a CASEL SELect program (CASEL, 2012). Evaluations of CSC have found positive effects for behavior and social adjustment (Battistich, 2003), student attitudes and values (Solomon et al., 2000), and academic performance (Battistich, Schaps, & Wilson, 2004). However, other reviews have noted a lack of significant changes on many student variables (Cox, 2005). In addition, findings indicate that CSC produces positive effects to the extent that it is implemented as designed (Solomon et al., 2000).

In the many core activities of CSC, some elements of an SFP framework are present, but many features are missing. CSC does not identify that educators and families are engaging in shared or jointly defined work. Rather, CSC targets the home and school settings, and engages parents in a variety of activities aimed at enhancing outcomes for students. Thus, the home and school settings are targeted, but families are not involved in joint program decision making. In addition, some home–school communication methods are used with homework, but the procedures do not fully allow for multidirectional communication to occur. For example, the home-based activities allow students and parents to engage in discussions that are later shared with the class (Battistich et al., 1996). Beyond family engagement in homes with students, CSC invites parents to be involved with teachers and students in school community projects (Battistich et al., 1996). Parents may also serve on a coordinating team with teachers to plan family–school activities (Solomon et al., 2000). In summary, CSC offers multiple roles for parents' involvement in their children's learning at home and school. However, the way these activities are framed is not entirely consistent with a partnership orientation.

Further research on CSC is needed to disentangle the influence of moderating and mediating variables, and to better understand mechanisms for effects. Regarding CSC's school–family framework, it may be useful for the program to move from a parent participation and involvement perspective to one that more fully embodies a partnership orientation. This might be accomplished by partnering with families on implementation of core features, and encouraging school personnel to communicate to parents that the program represents a shared effort among key individuals in their child's life. In addition, building communication mechanisms that allow for multidirectional communication would be helpful to foster collaboration among educators and parents.

Conjoint Behavioral Consultation

Conjoint behavioral consultation (CBC) is typically conceptualized as a selected or indicated approach that uses an indirect service delivery model focused on enhancing student outcomes (e.g., relationship skills, social behavior) through collaborative problem solving (Sheridan & Kratochwill, 2008). CBC is based on principles of behavioral consultation, and grounded in behavioral and ecological theory (Bronfenbrenner, 1977), and family-centeredness (Dunst, Trivette, & Hamby, 2007). Hence, CBC is focused on creating positive connections among key individuals in a student's life to maximize outcomes (Sheridan, Rispoli, et al., 2013). Implementation of CBC occurs through a series of stages, including meetings and between-session activities over approximately 8 weeks (Sheridan et al., 2012). A CBC consultant guides CBC meetings with a student's teacher and parent/caregiver. He or she has expertise in behavioral problem solving and evidence-based interventions, and facilitates partnership-centered meetings to determine how to best meet students' needs and plan for future success (Sheridan et al., 2012).

The CBC process begins by establishing agreement about target concerns/behaviors and setting observable and quantifiable goals, and proceeds through implementing evidence- and function-based appropriate behavior support plans across settings, to evaluating progress toward goals. These primary foci are addressed across four stages, all of which are implemented conjointly: needs identification, needs analysis and plan development, plan implementation, and plan evaluation (Sheridan & Kratochwill, 2008). CBC includes structured meetings, but the model is designed to be a dynamic process that includes a series of interactions and between-meeting activities (e.g., brief check-ins with a teacher).

Evidence in support of CBC exists from published studies for a variety of presenting concerns (e.g., social skills, social behavior, homework completion) across settings. Specifically, positive findings for CBC are supported from single case experimental design studies (e.g., Colton & Sheridan, 1998), quasi-experimental studies (e.g., Sheridan, Eagle, Cowan, & Mickelson, 2001), and randomized controlled trials (Sheridan et al., 2012; Sheridan, Ryoo, Garbacz, Kunz, & Chumney, 2013). In addition to direct effects on student outcomes (e.g., social skills, adaptive skills), Sheridan and colleagues (2012) found that strengthening relationships among parents and teachers was partially responsible for CBC's effect on student outcomes. Furthermore, Guli (2005) found CBC to be among the few family-school and parent consultation models that has documented evidence for intervening with school-related concerns.

CBC is well aligned with a partnership-centered framework. CBC explicitly indicates that families and educators share responsibility for enhancing student outcomes by developing mutual goals, implementing interventions, and evaluating progress. This focus on shared decision making and mutual goal setting is communicated to all parties when CBC is initiated. In addition to educator and family active engagement in problem solving, behavior support plans are implemented at home and school to build sustainable systems of support across settings, and to enhance environmental consistency (Crosnoe, Leventhal, Wirth, Pierce, & Pianta, 2010). Finally, CBC advocates and builds multidirectional communication networks wherein information sharing can be initiated from any source and be shared with any participant.

Empirical findings demonstrating CBC's ability to promote proximal SEL competencies and distal SEL outcomes are promising; however, important future directions in CBC research are important to consider. Specifically, preliminary CBC findings are beginning to uncover contributing mechanisms (e.g., the teacher–parent relationship) for CBC's positive effects. More work is needed to replicate these findings, as are studies that intentionally assess the moderating or mediating role of partnership-centered variables (e.g., multidirectional communication, shared responsibility, and joint decision making).

Family Check-Up with School Intervention

The Family Check-Up (FCU; Dishion, Nelson, & Kavanagh, 2003; Dishion & Stormshak, 2007) is part of a multi-tier intervention model (i.e., the ecological approach to family intervention and treatment [EcoFIT]; Stormshak & Dishion, 2009). The universal tier includes a family resource room within schools that is designed to facilitate family engagement with a variety of materials (e.g., books, videos) and services (e.g., consultation) supporting positive parenting (Stormshak, Connell, & Dishion, 2009). At the selected/indicated tier, the FCU is an assessment process that helps families connect with resources that can lead to interventions at home and/or school. The FCU aims are to reduce child problem behavior, improve student skills and family interactions, and increase family-school relationships. Thus, the FCU includes universal and selected/indicated procedures that produce favorable outcomes associated with proximal SEL competences and distal SEL outcomes. An ecological theoretical orientation guides the implementation of the FCU (Dishion & Stormshak, 2007).

The FCU intervention includes three phases: (1) an intake interview, (2) an ecological assessment, and (3) a feedback/motivation session, each of which is guided by a parent consultant and conducted collaboratively with families. During the intake interview, the consultant builds rapport with the family and completes a general and unique needs assessment to understand services that are most appropriate. The ecological assessment involves a home visit whereby family interactions and adjustments are directly observed. Children's adjustment across settings, such as school and home, is assessed. In the third phase, the family is provided feedback about family strengths, practices, and behaviors. During this phase, families are connected to services and resources. Last, parents choose to continue with recommendations that may include services such as brief interventions, family therapy, or school-based programs.

Empirical evidence for the FCU is strong. In a series of trials that have tested the efficacy of the FCU (e.g., Dishion et al., 2003; Dishion & Stormshak, 2007), findings indicate that the FCU effectively increased positive parenting; decreased family conflict; and reduced child behavior problems, deviant peer affiliation, and substance use (Dishion et al., 2008; Van Ryzin, Stormshak, & Dishion, 2012). Participation in the FCU is also linked with improved youth self-management (i.e., self-regulation), school engagement, and attendance (Stormshak et al., 2009, 2010).

When the FCU is conducted such that a family and school intervention are implemented together, multiple SFP elements are met, especially when the intervention focuses on goals within each setting. For example, providing the FCU provided within a school setting focuses on family involvement in education, parenting practices, and school engagement (Stormshak et al., 2010). This model (i.e., the FCU school-based intervention) addresses goals in both home and school settings, may involve families and educators, and aims to meet a shared goal of student success. To enhance alignment with a partnership framework, the FCU might focus on shared goals and responsibilities among educators and families.

The FCU lends itself well to becoming a partnership model because it has a strong foundation in family-centered services and ecological theory. The current form of the FCU focuses on family assessment, motivation, and resources. Home and school settings are both targeted in the intervention phase in some, but not all, cases. Thus, the FCU might be expanded to routinely involve a school intervention component, such as a form of family–school communication or homework coaching. An alternative structure, a "Family–School Check-Up", might expand the FCU's reach and increase its alignment with a partnership-centered framework. For example, in a "Family–School Check-Up", the consultant could complete a family check-up and a school check-up either in a joint fashion or separately to assess needs, motivations, and resources of each setting, then combine both settings in the intervention phase and associated meetings. In the joint setting intervention phase, parents and educators can develop interventions to emphasize shared decision making, jointly defined goals and responsibilities, and environmental consistency.

Incredible Years Training Years Series

The Incredible Years® Training Series (2014; Webster-Stratton, 1981) is a multicomponent program that uses a structured group training approach to build family behavioral parenting skills, teacher behavior management skills, and children's social competence. The ultimate goal of the Incredible Years Series is to prevent and reduce conduct problems in children through the use of a systems approach. The Incredible Years Training Series may be implemented at the universal, selected, or indicated tiers of support, is aligned with many SFP criteria, and promotes SEL competencies and outcomes (Menting, Orobio de Castro, & Matthys, 2013; Menting, Orobio de Castro, Wijngaards-de Meiji, & Matthys, 2014; Webster-Stratton, Reid, & Beauchaine, 2011). The series includes parent and teacher modules, and a classroom-based or small-group curriculum that teachers or therapists use to provide explicit SEL skills instruction. Children are taught self-management, social awareness, relationship skills, and decision-making or problem-solving skills. The modules can be implemented separately or as a combined package.

The parenting module includes multiple programs. Information is presented within a developmental framework for families with children from birth to age 12 (Webster-Stratton, 2000) through the use of videotaped modeling to promote observational learning and, most recently, in-home coaching (Webster-Stratton & Reid, 2014). The parenting programs range from recommendations for building a child's academic readiness to those that enhance the parenting skills of parents of elementary school–age children. Participants also learn how to set up the home and school environments to build children's social and emotional skills. The BASIC parent training program includes programs for preschool- and elementary school–age children that focus on teaching parents basic parenting skills such as praising their child, playing with their child, implementing limit-setting procedures, and supporting academic learning in the home (The Incredible Years, 2014). The ADVANCE parent training program focuses on parenting and academically oriented skills such as training parents to problem-solve with teachers and develop behavior support plans for children (Webster-Stratton, Reid, et al., 2011).

In addition to a focus on the family system, the Incredible Years Training Series provides training to teachers about evidence-based classroom strategies. For example, strategies promote proactive and developmentally appropriate teaching; behavior management; teacher–child relationships; and child emotional regulation, social competence, and problem-solving. Emphasis is also placed on recommendations to teachers about collaborating with families, specifically, collaborative problem solving, positive communication with parents, and coordinating behavior plans with parents (Webster-Stratton, Reinke, Herman, & Newcomer, 2011).

The child training aspect of the Incredible Years Training Series, or the Dina Dinosaur Social Emotional Skills and Problem-Solving Curriculum focuses on building children's social and emotional skills and reducing disruptive behaviors (The Incredible Years, 2014; Webster-Stratton & Herman, 2010). Social skills, emotional regulation skills, and skills for how to be successful at school are also reviewed. These same social and emotional skills are discussed in the parent and teacher training programs to build consistency within the series and promote generalization of skills across settings.

The Incredible Years Series has been researched extensively and is recognized as a model program by various organizations (e.g., CASEL, 2012). Multiple randomized controlled trials (e.g., Webster-Stratton, Reinke, et al., 2011) have indicated that the general child, teacher, and parent training programs are associated with children's improved social and emotional outcomes; replication studies continue to demonstrate positive child social and emotional outcomes (The Incredible Years, 2014; Webster-Stratton & Herman, 2010) for children with various diagnoses (e.g., attention-deficit/hyperactivity disorder; Webster Stratton, Reid, et al., 2011; Webster-Stratton & Reid, 2014). Findings from a recent meta-analytic review indicated that the Incredible Years Series is effective in decreasing disruptive behavior and increasing adaptive behavior (Menting et al., 2013). Results from other studies reveal an increase in positive teacher classroom management skills, child–peer interactions and engagement in school, and improved child problem-solving skills (Webster-Stratton & Herman, 2010; Webster-Stratton, Reid, & Hammond, 2004). No specific randomized controlled trial has investigated the effectiveness of the training programs, with or without supplemental training on family–school collaboration.

When programs are implemented as a package or series, the intervention involves many elements of a SFP framework. Specifically, the series encourages family involvement, although it does not proactively plan for facilitating school–family partnerships. For example, if the series were to be provided to educators and caregivers, target the home and school settings, and focus participants' efforts on the shared goal of children's success, then it would more fully embody a partnership-centered orientation. The training series emphasizes a partnership orientation through a focus on family–educator collaboration about the ways in which parties can work together to support student academic performance (e.g., team problem solving; Webster-Stratton & Herman, 2010). Mutual roles, responsibilities, and goals are identified; however, student goals are not individualized to each child, teacher, or caregiver. School–family partnerships can be strengthened within the Incredible Years Training Series if families and educators of the same children are involved in the programs simultaneously. For example, a joint family and school training session would allow for opportunities to set specific shared goals, make joint decisions, and develop multidirectional communication methods.

Future research on the Incredible Years Training Series may aim to enhance program alignment with a partnership framework, and examine empirical findings and pathways to outcomes for specific family–school variables. For example, it is important to identify mechanisms through which child outcomes occur when parents and teachers participate in the programs simultaneously. Specifically, it may be useful to examine outcomes of the family–school collaboration training sessions when accounting for the influence of environmental consistency to support educationally relevant activities. Finally, integration of multidirectional communication methods to support shared responsibility for child outcomes through frequent communication among stakeholders allows each party the opportunity to share and respond to concerns.

Second Step

Second Step is a universal, classroom-based intervention whose aim is to improve social and emotional skills of PreK to eighth-grade children (Committee for Children, 1991). The program is often conducted as a universal prevention program aimed at preventing behavior problems and building social competencies, and the latter target also indicates its relevance as a SEL program. The core program component is direct classroom instruction to develop children's skills, such as empathy, emotion regulation, friendships, and problem solving; however, a strategy that connects home and school is also included. School professionals (in most cases, classroom teachers) complete a workshop and provide the instruction. During these workshops, one social and emotional theme is targeted each week (e.g., social problem solving). In addition, a new small- or large-group activity is conducted to provide structured opportunities to practice and reinforce the skill. Based on a cognitive problem-solving and social learning model, activities such as modeling, observing, and practicing are used as primary teaching methods. At the end of the week, an activity is sent home to provide an opportunity for children to teach their parents the skills and to practice at home. Some schools also choose to provide parenting sessions in which parents to learn about social and emotional skills.

An expanded version of the Second Step program involves teacher and schoolwide training in the social and emotional skills the children are learning (Frey, Hirschstein, & Guzzo, 2000). In addition, parent training is available through the *A Family Guide to Second Step* (Committee for Children, 1995) which includes instructional videos that review vocabulary and concepts covered during classroom-based sessions with students. Both teacher and parent training can be implemented in various ways. One method includes a 1-day workshop for parents or teachers. In other cases, the videotaped modules may be sent home. Ideally, the skills associated with each module would be reviewed, modeled and practiced in six separate parent group sessions.

Two randomized trials and multiple quasi-experimental studies of Second Step have resulted in positive child outcomes such as increased positive social behavior, increased social competence, and reduced conduct problems (Beland, 1992; Grossman et al., 1997; McMahon, Washburn, Felix, Yakin, & Childrey, 2000). Second Step also met the criteria for a CASEL SELect program (CASEL, 2012).

When the Second Step program's child classroom training component is combined with the teacher and parent training components, it includes many elements of a SFP framework. For example, providing similar training to parents and educators about ways to build social and emotional skills promotes environmental consistency and generalization. The combined parent and teacher training programs in Second Step target home and school settings and provide opportunities to create shared goals. The primary aim of these strategies is to enhance outcomes for students across settings.

There are a few primary ways that Second Step could be modified to increase its alignment with a SFP framework. For example, more collaboration among parents and educators that focuses on jointly defined goals and priorities would be beneficial. The activity that connects home is an important school–home communication method, but it could be expanded to include deliberate procedures to encourage multidirectional communication. In this way, congruent strategies for practicing and reinforcing skills at home or at school can be shared with each party. In addition, if offered, joint parent and teacher training sessions could align parent and educator procedures, and promote environmental consistency. Future research might investigate the impact of a combined school–home format of the Second Step program on child social and emotional learning.

What Is Promising

As stated earlier, a program is considered promising if it demonstrated one or more of the following on proximal SEL competencies and/or distal SEL outcomes: less than three successful trials; mixed trial results; or, in the absence of research, it appears promising, based on a combination of theory and research. A successful "trial" included studies that used a randomized controlled design, a single-case experimental design, and/or a quasi-experimental design without major design problems.

Parent–Teacher Action Research Teams plus Social Skills Instruction

Parent–Teacher Action Research (PTAR) teams provide a framework to bring parents and teachers together as equal partners to identify goals and action plans for students having some behavioral difficulties (McConaughy, Kay, & Fitzgerald, 1998). Thus, the main tier of support is at the selected/indicated level. The Achieving, Behaving, Caring (ABC) project evaluated PTAR teams for elementary school students at risk for developing behavior concerns. All identified students were assigned to PTAR teams or a comparison group; students in both groups received whole-class social skills instruction. Thus, the ABC project evaluated the effect of PTAR teams plus social skills instruction on decreasing behavioral problems and promoting students' social skills in the treatment group compared to the sample that only received social skills instruction.

PTAR teams included the child's general education teacher, the child's parent(s), a parent liaison, and a facilitator. PTAR team meetings begin by identifying child strengths and mutual parent–teacher goals. Goals can focus on academic, social, or behavioral targets that are evaluated through observable indicators (McConaughy et al., 1998). The PTAR team engages in an action research cycle that includes collecting and analyzing data, developing a plan of action, and evaluating progress.

Evidence in support of PTAR teams is primarily through the ABC project. Immediate posttest findings revealed statistically significant decreases in parent- and teacher-reported behavior concerns and increases in parent-reported prosocial behavior for students whose parents participated in PTAR (McConaughy, Kay, & Fitzgerald, 1999) compared to students who received only classroom-based social skills training. Outcomes at the end of 2 years of participation were even more favorable (McConaughy, Kay, & Fitzgerald, 2000). For example, children whose parents participated in PTAR teams showed reductions in problem behavior and increases in behavioral competencies, cooperation, and self-control (McConaughy et al., 2000).

PTAR teams epitomize many components of a SFP framework: PTAR teams identify parents and educators as equal partners in enhancing outcomes for students. This guiding principle is manifested by creation of mutual parent–teacher goals and taking steps to remove the power differential that may exist between school personnel and families (McConaughy et al., 1998). Collaboration on PTAR teams focuses on enhancing outcomes for students through a positive, strengths-based approach. The home and school settings are targeted by the creation of observable goals for student performance in both settings (McConaughy et al., 1998). Finally, multidirectional communication is encouraged through a set of rules about PTAR team interactions. One rule indicates that parents are to speak first. In addition, the back-and-forth nature of PTAR team meetings is consistent with multidirectional communication strategies.

Although promising findings currently exist, there are important directions for future research. Primary empirical support for PTAR teams is from the ABC project. Thus, trials investigating the efficacy of PTAR teams should be conducted by additional investigators. Based on procedural details of PTAR teams in published articles, it may be possible to communicate more explicitly to parents their equal role in decision making and goal setting. Finally, PTAR teams plus social skills instruction have been compared to a group of students that received social skills instruction. Future studies should attempt to examine PTAR teams without social skills instruction.

What Does Not Work

Our review did not identify any programs that failed to achieve a statistically significant impact on at least one outcome. However, there are three limitations to general approaches to school–family work that merit attention. First, the efforts of many schools to engage families often reach only a small fraction of families. It is important for schools to identify systemic factors that stand in the way of partnering parents in a school community (Mapp & Hong, 2010). Second, it is important to consider the SEL competencies and outcomes of interest when determining prevention and intervention activities. Specifically, identifying the SFP program that has demonstrated positive effects on target variables of primary interest may be helpful. For example, if a teacher would like to decrease a middle school student's conduct problems and increase self-management, the FCU may be useful to consider. Third, our review identified both programs that are implemented as universal, schoolwide efforts and when students or families demonstrate a need for additional targeted support. Identifying the tier of support most relevant for each school community based in part on existing policies facilitates implementation of complementary procedures with a shared mission.

Next Steps for an SFP Framework

Our SFP framework based on five components of partnership-centered practice was built on theoretical and empirical work about family–school relationships. The empirical investigations that have included the framework's key components (e.g., Sheridan et al., 2012) have implemented partnership-centered practices as part of an intervention package. Thus, it will be helpful for future research to assess the relative contribution of the SFP components included in this framework. For example, the following questions should be addressed: Which of the five components are more or most important for proximal SEL competencies and distal outcomes? For whom and under what conditions are certain components most important? Answering these and related questions will empirically link SFP components with specific student competencies and outcomes.

Summary

Programs that target SEL foster students' lifelong learning (Zins et al., 2004) by targeting interrelated skills and competencies (e.g., social awareness; CASEL, 2012). Empirical evidence suggests SFPs enhance outcomes for children (e.g., Henderson & Mapp, 2002). However, many SEL programs do not explicitly engage families in partnership-centered activities. Our focus in this chapter has been to review programs that target proximal SEL competencies and distal SEL outcomes, and actively include families. Specifically, our review evaluated a program's alignment with an SFP framework.

Variation across programs exists with regard to (1) their alignment with a SFP framework, (2) the tier of support, and (3) the SEL competencies and outcomes targeted. For example, CSC engages parents and children in universal activities at home and provides opportunities for families and educators to participate jointly in activities; CBC and PTAR are selected or targeted programs that identify parents and educators as jointly responsible co-equals in planning for children's success. All programs included in this review are uniquely positioned to promote positive SEL outcomes for students through meaningful family engagement.

Substantial empirical evidence supports the use of many of the programs identified in this review, but empirical support for programs that include components of SFPs can be strengthened through more randomized trials and evaluating causal mechanisms and pathways through which positive findings occur. Although research is needed that disentangles the relative contribution of each component in the SFP framework, many programs could be more aligned with an SFP framework. For example, CSC could be expanded so that families are involved as co-equals in programmatic decision making. In summary, SFP and SEL programs are uniquely positioned to benefit children. Building partnerships among the key individuals in a child's life (e.g., parents, teachers) can foster environmental congruence and stability that promote critical prosocial skills necessary for lifelong success.

References

Adams, K. S., & Christenson, S. L. (1998). Differences in parent and teacher trust levels: Implications for creating collaborative family–school relationships. *Special Services in the Schools, 14*, 1–22.

Albright, M. I., & Weissberg, R. P. (2010). School–family partnerships to promote social and emotional learning. In S. L. Christenson & A. L. Reschly (Eds.), *Handbook of school–family partnerships* (pp. 246–265). New York: Taylor & Francis/Routledge.

Bandura, A. (1969). Social learning of moral judgments. *Journal or Personality and Social Psychology, 11*, 173–199.

Battistich, V. (2003). Effects of a school-based program to enhance prosocial development on children's peer relations and social adjustment. *Journal of Research in Character Education, 1*, 1–17.

Battistich, V., Schaps, E., Watson, M., & Solomon,

D. (1996). Prevention effects of the child development project: Early findings from an ongoing multisite demonstration trial. *Journal of Adolescent Research, 11*, 12–35.

Battistich, V., Schaps, E., & Wilson, N. (2004). Effects of an elementary school intervention on students' "connectedness" to school and social adjustment during middle school. *Journal of Primary Prevention, 24*, 434–262.

Beland, K. (1992). *Second Step: A Violence Prevention Curriculum for Grades 1–5* (Revised). Seattle, WA: Committee for Children.

Biglan, A. (1995). Translating what we know about the context of antisocial behavior into a lower prevalence of such behavior. *Journal of Applied Behavior Analysis, 28*, 479–492.

Boyce, W. T. (1985). Social support, family relations, and children. In S. Cohen & S. L. Syme (Eds.), *Social support and health* (pp. 151–173). Orlando, FL: Academic Press.

Bronfenbrenner, U. (1977). Toward an experimental ecology of human development. *American Psychologist, 32*, 513–531.

Bronfenbrenner, U. (1979). Contexts of child rearing. *American Psychologist, 34*, 844–850.

Christenson, S. L. (1995). Families and schools: What is the role of the school psychologist? *School Psychology Quarterly, 10*, 118–132.

Christenson, S. L., & Carlson, C. (2005). Evidence-based parent and family interventions in school psychology: State of scientifically based practice. *School Psychology Quarterly, 20*, 525–528.

Christenson, S. L., & Sheridan, S. M. (2001). *Schools and families: Creating essential connections for learning.* New York: Guilford Press.

Clarke, B. L., Sheridan, S. M., & Woods, K. E. (2010). Elements of healthy family–school relationships. In S. L. Christenson & A. L. Reschly (Eds.), *Handbook of school–family partnerships* (pp. 61–79). New York: Taylor & Francis/Routledge.

Collaborative for Academic, Social, and Emotional Learning (CASEL). (2012). *2013 CASEL guide: Effective social and emotional learning programs—Preschool and elementary school edition.* Chicago: Author.

Colton, D. L., & Sheridan, S. M. (1998). Conjoint behavioral consultation and social skills training: Enhancing the play behaviors of boys with attention deficit hyperactivity disorder. *Journal of Educational and Psychological Consultation, 9*, 3–28.

Committee for Children. (1991). *Second Step: A Violence Prevention Curriculum: Preschool–Kindergarten.* Seattle, WA: Author.

Committee for Children. (1995). *A family guide to Second Step.* Seattle, WA: Author.

Cox, D. D. (2005). Evidence-based interventions using home-school collaboration. *School Psychology Quarterly, 20*, 473–497.

Crosnoe, R., Leventhal, T., Wirth, R. J., Pierce, K. M., & Pianta, R. C. (2010). Family socioeconomic status and consistent environmental stimulation in early childhood. *Child Development, 81*, 972–987.

Dishion, T. J., Nelson, S. E., & Kavanagh, K. (2003). The family check-up with high-risk young adolescents: Preventing early-onset substance use by parent monitoring. *Behavior Therapy, 34*, 553–571.

Dishion, T. J., Shaw, D., Connell, A., Gardner, F., Weaver, C., & Wilson, M. (2008). The Family Check-Up with high-risk indigent families: Preventing problem behavior by increasing parents' positive behavior support in early childhood. *Child Development, 79*, 1395–1414.

Dishion, T. J., & Stormshak, E. (2007). *Intervening in children's lives: An ecological, family-centered approach to mental health care.* Washington, DC: American Psychological Association.

Dunst, C. J., Trivette, C. M., & Hamby, D. W. (2007). Meta-analysis of family-centered helpgiving practices research. *Mental Retardation and Developmental Disabilities Research Reviews, 13*, 370–378.

Durlak, J. A., Weissberg, R. P., Dymnicki, A. B., Taylor, R. D., & Schellinger, K. B. (2011). The impact of enhancing students' docial and emotional learning: A meta-analysis of school-based universal interventions. *Child Development, 82*, 405–432.

Epstein, J. L. (1995). School/family/community partnerships: Caring for the children we share. *Phi Delta Kappan, 76*, 701–712.

Fan, X., & Chen, M. (2001). Parental involvement and students' academic achievement: A meta-analysis. *Educational Psychology Review, 13*, 1–22.

Fantuzzo, J., Tighe, E., & Childs, S. (2000). Family Involvement Questionnaire: A multivariate assessment of family participation in early childhood education. *Journal of Educational Psychology, 9*, 367–376.

Frey, K., Hirschstein, M., & Guzzo, B. (2000). Preventing aggression by promoting social competence. *Journal of Emotional and Behavioral Disorders, 8*, 102–113.

Grossman, D. C., Neckerman, H. J., Koepsell, T. D., Liu, P. Y., Asher, K. N., Beland, K., et al. (1997). Effectiveness of a violence prevention curriculum among children in elementary school. *Journal of the American Medical Association, 277*, 1605–1611.

Guli, L. A. (2005). Evidence-based parent consultation with school-related outcomes. *School Psychology Quarterly, 20*, 455–472.

Gutkin, T. B. (2012). Ecological psychology: Replacing the medical model paradigm for school-based psychological and psychoeducational services. *Journal of Educational and Psychological Consultation, 22*, 1–20.

Henderson, A. T., & Mapp, K. L. (2002). *A new wave of evidence; The impact of school, family, and community connections on students achievement.* Austin, TX: National Center of Family and Community Connections with Schools: Southwest Educational Development Laboratory.

Hoover-Dempsey, K. V., Bassler, O. C., & Brissie, J. S. (1992). Explorations in parent–school relations. *Journal of Educational Research, 85*, 287–294.

Horner, R. H., Sugai, G., Smolkowski, K., Eber, L., Nakasato, J., Todd, A. W., et al. (2009). A randomized, wait-list controlled effectiveness trial assessing school-wide positive behavior support in elementary schools. *Journal of Positive Behavior Interventions, 11*, 133–144.

Jeynes, W. (2012). A meta-analysis of the efficacy of different types of parental involvement programs for urban students. *Urban Education, 47*, 706–742.

Jones, S. M., & Bouffard, S. M. (2012). Social and emotional learning in schools. *Social Policy Report, 26*(4), 1–22.

Mapp, K. L., & Hong, S. (2010). Debunking the myth of the hard-to-reach parent. In. S. L. Christenson & A. L. Reschly (Eds.), *Handbook of school–family partnerships* (pp. 345–361). New York: Routledge.

McConaughy, S. H., Kay, P. J., & Fitzgerald, M. (1998). Preventing SED through parent–teacher action research and social skills instruction: First-year outcomes. *Journal of Emotional and Behavioral Disorders, 6*, 81–93.

McConaughy, S. H., Kay, P. J., & Fitzgerald, M. (1999). The Achieving, Behaving, Caring project for preventing ED: Two-year outcomes. *Journal of Emotional and Behavioral Disorders, 7*, 224–239.

McConaughy, S. H., Kay, P. J., & Fitzgerald, M. (2000). How long is long enough?: Outcomes for a school-based prevention program. *Exceptional Children, 67*, 21–34.

McMahon, S., Washburn, J., Felix, E., Yakin, J., & Childrey, G. (2000). Violence prevention: Program effects on urban preschool and kindergarten children. *Applied and Preventive Psychology, 9*, 271–281.

Menting, A. T. A., Orobio de Castro, B., & Matthys, W. (2013). Effectiveness of the incredible years parent training to modify disruptive and prosocial child behavior: A meta-analytic review. *Clinical Psychology Review, 33*, 901–913.

Menting, A. T. A., Orobio de Castro, B., Wijngaards-de Meiji, D. N. V., & Matthys, W. (2014). A trial of parent training for mothers being released from incarceration and their children. *Journal of Clinical Child and Adolescent Psychology, 43*, 381–396.

Metzler, C. W., Biglan, A., Rusby, J. C., & Sprague, J. R. (2001). Evaluation of a comprehensive behavior management program to improve school-wide positive behavior support. *Education and Treatment of Children, 24*, 448–479.

Moore, K. J., & Patterson, G. R. (2009). Parent training. In W. O'Donohue & J. E. Fisher (Eds.), *General principles and empirically supported techniques of cognitive behavior therapy* (pp. 481–487). Hoboken, NJ: Wiley.

No Child Left Behind Act of 2001, 20 U.S.C. § 6319 (2008).

Patterson, G. R. (1982). *A social learning approach: Vol. 3. Coercive family process.* Eugene, OR: Castalia.

Pianta, R. C., & Walsh, D. J. (1996). *High-risk children in schools: Constructing sustaining relationships.* New York: Routledge.

Power, T. J., Mautone, J. A., Soffer, S. L., Clarke, A. T., Marshall, S. A., Sharman, J., et al. (2012). A family–school intervention for children with ADHD: Results of a randomized clinical trial. *Journal of Consulting and Clinical Psychology, 80*, 611–623.

Reschly, A. L., & Christenson, S. L. (2012). Moving from "context matters" to engaged partnerships with families. *Journal of Educational and Psychological Consultation, 22*, 62–78.

Sameroff, A. (2009). The transactional model. In. A. Sameroff (Ed.), *The transactional model of development: How children and contexts shape each other* (pp. 3–21). Washington, DC: American Psychological Association

Sheridan, S. M., Bovaird, J. A., Glover, T. A., Garbacz, S. A., Witte, A., & Kwon, K. (2012). A randomized trial examining the effects of conjoint behavioral consultation and the mediating role of the parent–teacher relationship. *School Psychology Review, 41*, 23–46.

Sheridan, S. M., Eagle, J. W., Cowan, R. J., & Mickelson, W. (2001). The effects of conjoint behavioral consultation results of a 4-year investigation. *Journal of School Psychology, 39*, 361–385.

Sheridan, S. M., & Kratochwill, T. R. (2008). *Conjoint behavioral consultation: Promoting family–school connections and intervention* (2nd ed.). New York: Springer.

Sheridan, S. M., Rispoli, K., & Holmes, S. (2013). Treatment integrity in conjoint behavioral consultation: Active ingredients and potential pathways of influence. In L. Sanetti & T. Kratochwill (Eds.), *Treatment integrity: A foundation for evidence-based practice in applied psychology* (pp. 255–278). Washington, DC: American Psychological Association.

Sheridan, S. M., Ryoo, J. H., Garbacz, S. A., Kunz, G. M., & Chumney, F. L. (2013). The efficacy of conjoint behavioral consultation on parents and children in the home setting: Results of a randomized controlled trial. *Journal of School Psychology, 51*, 717–733.

Solomon, D., Battistich, V., Watson, M., Schaps, E., & Lewis, C. (2000). A six-district study of educational change: Direct and mediated effects of the child development project. *Social Psychology of Education, 4*, 3–51.

Stormshak, E. A., Connell, A., & Dishion, T. J. (2009). An adaptive approach to family-centered intervention in schools: Linking intervention engagement to academic outcomes in middle and high school. *Prevention Science, 10*, 221–235.

Stormshak, E. A., & Dishion, T. J. (2009). A school-based, family-centered intervention to prevent substance use: The Family Check-Up. *American Journal of Drug and Alcohol Abuse, 35*, 227–232.

Stormshak, E. A., Fosco, G. M., & Dishion, T. J. (2010). Implementing interventions with families in schools to increase youth school engagement. The Family Check-Up model. *School Mental Health, 2*, 82–92.

The Incredible Years®. (2014). Incredible Years Programs. Retrieved July 1, 2014, from *www.incredibleyears.com*.

U.S. Department of Education, Institute of Education Sciences, What Works Clearinghouse (2007, April). Caring School Community™ (formerly, the Child Development Project). Retrieved July 1, 2014, from *http://whatworks.ed.gov*.

U.S. Department of Education, Office of Planning, Evaluation and Policy Development. (2010). *A blueprint for reform: The reauthorization of The Elementary And Secondary Education Act*. Washington, DC: Author.

Van Ryzin, M. J., Stormshak, E. A., & Dishion, T. J. (2012). Family and peer predictors of substance use from early adolescence to early adulthood: An 11-year prospective analysis. *Addictive Behaviors, 37*, 1314–1324.

Walberg, H. (1984). Families as partners in educational productivity. *Phi Delta Kappan, 65*, 397–400.

Webster-Stratton, C. H. (1981). Modification of mothers behaviors and attitudes through videotape modeling group discussion program. *Behavior Therapy, 12*, 634–642.

Webster-Stratton, C. H. (2000). *How to promote social and academic competence in young children*. London: Sage.

Webster-Stratton, C. H., & Herman, K. C. (2010). Disseminating incredible years series early-intervention programs: Integrating and sustaining services between school and home. *Psychology in the Schools, 47*, 36–54.

Webster-Stratton, C. H., & Reid, M. J. (2014). Tailoring The Incredible Years parent, teacher, and child interventions for young children with ADHD. In J. K. Ghuman & H. S. Ghuman (Eds.), *ADHD in preschool children: Assessment and treatment* (pp.113–131). New York: Oxford University Press.

Webster-Stratton, C. H., Reid, M. J., & Beauchaine, T. (2011). Combining parent and child training for young children with ADHD. *Journal of Clinical and Adolescent Psychology, 40*, 191–203.

Webster-Stratton, C. H., Reid, M. J., & Hammond, M. (2004). Treating children with early-onset conduct problems: Intervention outcomes for parent, child, and teacher training. *Journal of Clinical Child and Adolescent Psychology, 33*, 105–124.

Webster-Stratton, C. H., Reinke, W. M., Herman, K. C., & Newcomer, L. L. (2011). The Incredible Years teacher classroom management training: The methods and principles that support fidelity of training delivery. *School Psychology Review, 40*, 509–529.

Zins, J. E., Bloodworth, M. R., Weissberg, R. P., & Walberg, H. J. (2004). The scientific base linking social and emotional learning to school success. In J. Zins, R. Weissberg, M. Wang, & H. Walberg (Eds.), *Building academic success on social and emotional learning: What does the research say?* (pp. 3–22). New York: Teachers College Press.

Zins, J. E., & Elias, M. J. (2006). Social and emotional learning. In G. Bear & K. Minke (Eds.), *Children's needs III: Development, prevention, and intervention* (pp.1–13). Washington, DC: National Association of School Psychologists.

CHAPTER 17

After-School Programming and SEL

Thomas P. Gullotta

Times were that mothers stayed at home, children went to neighborhood schools, and every child was keenly aware that the slightest indiscretion would be promptly reported to a parent by a neighbor. Now, revisionist historians have qualified each of the foregoing remarks, but the facts are that in 1890, women comprised 17.2% of the labor force. This grew such that 28.8% of the labor force was female in 1950, 42.6% in 1980 (Waite, 1981, p. 2) and 47% in 2010 (U.S. Department of Labor, 2011). Importantly, in 2010, over 64% of working women had children under the age of 17 (Bureau of Labor Statistics, 2013, p. 21). Walking to a neighborhood school has declined as communities have responded to equality of education issues that require busing, regionalization has gained momentum, and small schools have been deemed cost-inefficient. Last, the suburban lifestyle of large lot isolation, the transience found in many urban communities, and the decline of individuals working near where they resided has made knowing one's neighbor an increasingly uncommon occurrence.

In support of the old adage that "idle hands are the devil's playground," young people are at the greatest risk for engaging in delinquent behavior and other nefarious behaviors such as substance misuse and sexual experimentation between the work week hours of 2:00 P.M. to 6:00 P.M., which just so happens to coincide with many parents' work schedules (Cohen, Farley, Taylor, Martin, & Schuster, 2002; Gottfredson, Gerstenblith, Soule, Womer, & Lu, 2004, p. 255).

Even if the young person is not tempted to wander from the path of righteousness, many latch-key youth find themselves with television or computer games as their companion until a parent arrives home. It is doubtful that either Fred Rogers or *Reading Rainbow* is being watched, or that Google is being employed for homework purposes.

As with childcare, recreation, and other youth programs, the origins of after-school programming can be traced to the Progressive era at the turn of the century. In part driven by the arrival of southern Europeans (mostly Italians), urban missionaries (think YMCA/YWCA), settlement houses (Hull House and the B. P. Learned Mission) and individual reformers, there was launched a multitude of activities to enrich both the body and soul of the young people attracted to their doors (Gullotta, Adams, & Markstrom, 2000).

From its tenement roots, the concept of constructively occupying young people's time has spread across much of America. Programming can be as simple as offering a somewhat supervised space for undertaking homework and playing board games as one awaits a parent, to intentionally planned activities that are intended to improve a child's literacy and develop his or her social and emotional skills. This chapter reviews the literature primarily with an eye toward identifying programs that nourish both mind and soul. Some examples of practices (e.g., curricula) are also examined.

Definitions and Scope

The term "after-school programs" refers to activities held both after the school day and when school is not in session, such as on holidays and vacations.

Social and emotional learning (SEL) involves

> the processes of developing social and emotional competencies. . . . It is based on the understanding that the best learning emerges in the context of supportive relationships that make learning challenging, engaging, and meaningful; social and emotional skills are critical to being a good student, citizen, and worker; and many different risky behaviors (e.g., drug use, violence, bullying, and dropout) can be prevented or reduced when multi-year, integrated efforts develop students' social and emotional skills. This is best done through effective classroom instruction, student engagement in positive activities in and out of the classroom, and broad parent and community involvement in program planning, implementation, and evaluation. (Collaborative for Academic, Social, and Emotional Learning [CASEL], 2013)

What are these social and emotional competencies? They include self-awareness, self-management, social awareness, relationship skills, and responsible decision making (*www.casel.org*). In this chapter, we examine the scant literature on the programs that incorporate SEL curricula into after-school efforts to nourish the development of SEL skills in young people. The section "What Works" offers examples of SEL curricula that with minor, if any, modifications can be incorporated into an after-school setting.

Theories

There are a multitude of theoretical perspectives that have been offered as paradigms for encouraging the growth and development of SEL. These borrow from areas such as neuroscience (Blair & Raver, Chapter 5, this volume; Greenberg, Katz, & Klein, Chapter 6, this volume), social learning (Bandura, 1986), child development (Piaget & Inhelder, 2000), intellectual development (Gardner, 1983) and ecological theory (Durlak, Mahoney, Bohnert, & Parente, 2010).

In this vast forest of theoretical richness, the program developer can become lost. Fortunately, signposts exist to assist the traveler. Here are some of the most important ones that repeatedly occur in the chapters of this handbook. Learning evolves over time through repeated experience. Learning entails observation and modeling. Relationships matter in what lessons are actually learned. Active, moving, and doing learning is preferable to passive, sitting, hearing-only activities. Activities, or exercises, if you prefer, should be developmentally appropriate and at the same time novel enough to stimulate the imagination. Most importantly, and emphasized in this chapter, the culture of the host program must be safe, ordered, and foster both motivation and engagement in learning. Teachable moments must be continually created to increase the possibilities of generalizing newly learned skills. The specialized curricula that fill the *Handbook of Social and Emotional Learning*, no matter how effective in the laboratory, will fail if the host does not provide a setting in which new learning can take root.

Current Research

Over the past three decades, out-of-school programming has attracted the interest of many funders. In turn, these funders, wishing to spend their dollars wisely, have asked the academic community to explore this programming area. This has resulted in the publication of numerous articles and a special issue of the *American Journal of Community Psychology*. This literature suggests three prominent conclusions and two reservations about commonly held assumptions.

First, there are a variety of program models. Some are structured; others are not. Some are offered privately, others are offered in schools and municipal settings such as youth service bureaus, and still others are offered in nonprofit settings such as churches, settlement houses, or buildings specifically intended for these activities (e.g., Boys and Girls Clubs). There is no single program model. Second, effective programs that offer SEL opportunities possess four characteristics that form the acronym SAFE. The *S* represents sequenced, meaning the program develops the intended skills in a planned and intentional manner. The *A* represents active, meaning the activities used to teach the skills entail movement, participation, manipulation, and practice. *F* represents focused, which means that sufficient time is devoted to the activities that are intended at least in part to develop a young person's social and emotional skills. Last, the *E* stands for explicit, which means that the intervention is aimed at developing a specific skill, such as responsible decision making or social awareness (Durlak, Weissberg, & Pachan, 2010).

Third, in keeping with previous studies on the effective implementation of prevention programming (Gullotta, Bloom, Gullotta, & Messina, 2009), successful programs employ qualified educated staff that have strong positive relationships with program participants who enjoy coming to the program. Staff members are well versed in the elements of the curriculum or curricula being used, and they have longevity with the agency using the program (Cross, Gottfredson, Wilson, Rorie, & Connell, 2010). In a world where the delivery of programming is increasingly drawn from a manual, Larson and Walker (2010) express the need for staff to individualize responses to the situations that arise in novel circumstances, recognizing that *every* circumstance involving a group of youth is novel. They speak to the need for staff to develop these leadership abilities. Some address this skills set by suggesting a mentoring approach, whereas Gullotta and his colleagues (2009) urge a more directive "coaching" methodology.

Interestingly, two largely subscribed to assumptions are being questioned in the out-of-school literature. The first is the value of school-related academic work in after-school settings. For example, Riggs and Greenberg (2004) caution that an overemphasis on homework or supplemental academic work may forgo a program's ability to engage in positive youth development activities. Kohn (2006) goes further in his analysis of the research on the value of homework to conclude that it is a worthless activity.

The second questionable assumption is the matter of "dosage," which refers to the amount of exposure to a program that a participant receives. In many implementation studies of prevention and treatment, those receiving the full program dosage did better than those who did not. In the after-school literature, this is not always the case (Hirsch, Mekinda, & Stawicki, 2010; Larson & Walker, 2010; Roth, Malone, & Brooks-Gunn, 2010; Shernoff, 2010). What these authors are detecting is the importance of overall program quality and its effect on the delivery of a particular element (or curriculum) of the program. To illustrate, imagine many of the evidence-based practices in this handbook as a flavorful sauce adorning a fish entrée. Now atop a freshly caught and properly prepared fish, this sauce can add subtle flavors and enhance the eating experience enormously. However, no sauce can save an entrée whose flesh has begun to decay and whose odor is overwhelmingly sickening. Simply put, no evidence-based curriculum will work if the host setting stinks like a rotten fish! This analogy leads us to the heart of this chapter and a search for programs embracing the SAFE principles and staffing characteristics described earlier.

What Works

Given that our primary interest is in the program that hosts curricula that are intended to promote SEL, it is regrettable to report that no host program met the standard of three successful trials. That said, we can identify specific school-based curricula that appear to be suitable for an after-school setting with little, if any, alteration.

All Stars Prevention Curriculum

The All Stars curriculum is a universal preventive intervention that has shown success with delaying first use of substance and other problematic behaviors in middle school students between ages 11 and 14. All Stars seeks to develop positive ideals, encourage accepted norms, develop individual resistance skills, increase the bonding of youth with their community, and strengthen parental communication and monitoring. It accomplishes these objectives by using interactive group activities, games and art projects, individual sessions with participating youth, a parent component, and a graduation event. The intervention lasts for 27 weeks and is provided twice each week for 45 minutes. Prior to the delivery of the program, staff are involved in 3 days of curriculum training. The program has developed two additional curricula that can be used to extend this intervention for up to 3 years (Hansen & Dusenbury, 2004; McNeal, Hansen, Harrington, & Giles, 2004).

Promoting Alternative Thinking Strategies

Promoting Alternative Thinking Strategies (PATHS) is a universal preventive curriculum developed for an elementary school population (K–6). It is intended to promote several SEL competencies, including self-control, emotional understanding, problem solving, and positive self-esteem. It accomplishes this by teaching explicit skills throughout the school year and across the elementary school experience. Children learn to recognize and label emotions, create and sustain friendships, share, take turns, and show proper manners. The scripted classroom program on average is taught twice a week for approximately 30 minutes. Staff members then use teachable moments to reinforce learning between sessions. Research suggests the usefulness of this program in reducing behavioral problems and increasing social problem-solving skills (Conduct Problems Prevention Research Group, 1992; Greenberg, Kusché, Cook, & Quamma, 1995).

Life Skills Training

Life Skills Training is a universal preventive curriculum designed for youth in grades K–12. Initially designed as substance abuse prevention program, it has evolved over the years to promote personal self-management and general social skills. Examples of these skills are enhancement of self-esteem and adaptive coping strategies, friendship formation and conversation abilities, and enabling youth to be assertive in situations in which following the group may be harmful. As with the other, previously described evidence-based effective initiatives, these skills are best taught using a cognitive-behavioral approach that involves the delivery of information, role playing, feedback, and reinforcement. With repeated practice in and outside the educational setting, skills habituate (Botvin & Griffin, in press).

What Is Promising

Four specifically designed after-school programs for promoting aspects of SEL warrant further evaluation because of their promising features.

The B. P. Learned Mission

The first is the B. P. Learned Mission (Gullotta et al., 2009). Established in 1859 in the red-light district of New London to "rescue" city youth from the temptations of sin found in a whaling port, the B. P. Learned Mission is open today to low-income, inner-city youth between ages 7 and 18. With an approximate enrollment of 65 youth, the racial/ethnic makeup of the program is 40% African American, 50% Latino, and 10% European American. Most youth enroll in the Mission in the first grade and remain until the fifth grade. The program's expectation is that enrolled youth will attend the program regularly when school is not in session. Daily attendance rates exceed 95% (Monday through Friday, school holidays, and vacations). In recent years, the opening of a counselor-in-training (CIT) component has resulted in a growing number of fifth-grade graduates remaining involved with the Mission into their high school years.

The Mission's stated purpose is to promote prosocial behavior and academic achievement for those youth who attend. The program's theoretical foundation is built on social learning theory, Piaget's cognitive-developmental theory, and Gardner's multiple intelligence theory. The Mission uses a wide range of intentional teaching activities, such as theater, sports, dance, cooking, and crafts, to achieve its goal. Although competiveness is discouraged, group success is celebrated. Staff members are employed full-time and are trained in and expected to embrace the prosocial curriculum developed at the Mission. The curriculum that was developed and evaluated with a multiyear grant from the Salmon Foundation reflects the core SEL competencies of self-awareness, self-management, responsible decision making, social awareness, and relationship skills (CASEL, 2013). Staff members work closely with the schools that the children attend and have daily contact with their parents or guardians.

Findings in a small pilot study, undertaken in 2008, revealed that in comparison to a matched sample of youth attending the same school, Mission youth showed significant improvement ($p < .05$) in their reading ability, development of work habits, and respect for others. Three other variables (self-control, cooperation, and kindness) approached but did not reach significance. In another small pilot study in 2010, report cards were examined against a matched sample, and significant differences for respect and self-control were evident for program youth ($p < .05$), with other variables (cooperation, and kindness) approaching but not reaching significance. In a third small pilot study, mastery test scores for the year 2012 were examined. Young people attending the Mission outperformed their classroom peers, their school average, the district average, other school districts grouped with New London, and, in many cases, the state average. At the time this study was undertaken, the school district was under the guidance of a state-assigned professional to treat poor academic performance.

After-School Program for Latino Youth

The second program (Riggs, Bohnert, Guzman, & Davidson, 2010) does not require youth to attend daily but was set up so that youth might drop in. Operated by a community agency that predominantly serves the Latino community, the out-of-school program operates on a year-round basis. Programming includes homework help, sports activities, computer access, and exploration of one's culture. An expressed goal of the program is the enhancement of young peoples' skills and self-worth. Cultural programming is offered by trained staff through organized and informal interactions with youth.

Findings from the pilot study suggest that those youth who more frequently attended the program thought more highly of the program. A positive significant relationship was reported between attendance, value of the program, and increases in self-worth and positive feelings about education.

WINGS

WINGS originated in Charleston, South Carolina for an elementary school-age population attending poorly performing schools in low socioeconomic status (SES) neighborhoods. The program begins at the close of the school day with a snack and extends to 6 P.M. on weekdays. WINGS requires that enrolled children attend the program on a regular basis and excludes youth who cannot meet that requirement.

The WINGS curriculum also encompasses the five core SEL competencies of self-awareness, self-management, responsible decision making, social awareness, and relationship skills (CASEL, 2013). Like the Mission, WINGS emphasizes the importance of equipping staff with the necessary skills to undertake and adhere to its curriculum that is built on social learning theory. The curriculum is structured around six activities that occur during the week. A unique feature of the program is the development of a software program that tracks a young person's SEL growth across time.

Findings from pilot studies suggest that youth who attended the WINGS program were more likely to graduate high school. Report card data suggest that youth still enrolled in the program do better academically and socially than nonattending peers (Abry, Brock, & Rimm-Kaufman, 2013).

AfterZone

The last program deserving replication is AfterZone. Developed for Providence, Rhode Island middle school students in grades 6–8, AfterZone operates three sessions, 4 days a week, for 2½ hours each day across the school year. Its operating model provides core training and support to member organizations and is built on developmentally appropriate activities that promote improvement in academic outcomes. Unlike other programs discussed in this section, AfterZone does not directly offer programming. Rather, it has enlisted existing sister agencies that already provide services to these youth and seeks to improve that programming effort (Kauh, 2011).

Initial AfterZone research is hampered by the inability to determine the quality of programs participating in the initiative and in the quasi-experimental and qualitative methods employed by the evaluation team. Still, the authors report data suggestive of the value of this type of effort. For example, for students who regularly attended the program their school attendance improved, and for a subset of these youth, math performance improved. Noteworthy is the clear statement from the authors that dosage mattered in achieving these outcomes. The evaluation design did not permit the determination of fidelity to the program. That said, the critical self-examination of the program by its evaluators offers the opportunity to improve perceived areas of weakness in the model (Kotloff & Korom-Djakovic, 2010). Given the difficulty of programming that captures the interest of middle school youth and the reality that a variety of different programs exist, an attempt to steer students gently in a direction that would increase school attendance and academic improvement, and promote SEL deserves additional attention.

What Does Not Work

Although the study of after-school programming is in its infancy, certain reoccurring results offer guidance on how *not* to operate an after-school program. These findings are as follows: Do not employ poorly qualified staff; do not operate a program that experiences high staff turnover; and do not create a program in which child–staff relationships are negative. Furthermore, it seems doubtful that SEL can be promoted in after-school programs that offer only supervision (babysitting), do not require regular attendance, and do not hold staff accountable for nonadherence to the program's curriculum.

Closing

There has been significant growth in after-school programming in recent years. While a number of effective evidence-based, free-standing curricula have been used in these settings, sometimes successfully, the fundamental structure has received little attention.

To improve the quality of after-school programming requires not only adequate funding but also the development of core standards for operation. These standards should encompass basic criteria such as staff qualifications, minimum program operating hours, and curriculum. It is this last area that needs researchers' attention. My colleagues and I neither seek nor suggest a "one size fits all" curriculum mentality. Indeed, given the increasing diversity and complexity of the U.S. population, such an approach would fail. Still, embracing the theoretical frameworks of learning, developmental, and multiple intelligence theories, researchers can develop frameworks for engaging youth of different ages, genders, and SES backgrounds. For example, how can a program attract and maintain the active involvement of inner-city male youth from the seventh to the 12th grade? Furthermore, in this call for action, I am not suggesting that researchers develop new programs. Rather, I am encouraging them to identify existing programs in their community and to partner with those programs in their evaluation and possible modification or reinvention as needed. I cannot imagine a better departmental agenda for a school of community psychology or school work than this.

References

Abry, T. D. S., Brock, L. L., & Rimm-Kaufman, S. E. (2013). *A preliminary report of the contribution of the WINGS after-school program to students' social development and classroom behavior.* Unpublished manuscript.

Bandura, A. (1986). *Social foundations of thought and action: A social cognitive theory.* Upper Saddle River, NJ: Prentice-Hall.

Botvin, G. J., & Griffin, K. W. (in press). Life skills in adolescence. In T. P. Gullotta & M. Bloom (Eds.), *The encyclopedia of primary prevention and health promotion* (2nd ed.). New York: Springer.

Bureau of Labor Statistics. (2013, March 26). *Women in the labor force: Report 1040*. Washington, DC: U.S. Government Printing Office.

Cohen, D. A., Farley, T. A., Taylor, S. N., Martin, D. H., & Schuster, M. A. (2002). When and where do youths have sex?: The potential role of adult supervision. *Pediatrics, 110*(6), e66.

Collaborative for Academic, Social, and Emotional Learning (CASEL). (2013). What is SEL? Retrieved December 28, 2013, from *http://casel.org/why-it-matters/what-is-sel*.

Conduct Problems Prevention Research Group. (1992). A developmental and clinical model for the prevention of conduct disorders: The FAST Track program. *Development and Psychopathology, 4*, 509–527.

Cross, A. B., Gottfredson, D. C., Wilson, D. M., Rorie, M., & Connell, N. (2010). Implementation quality and positive experiences in afterschool programs. *American Journal of Community Psychology, 45*, 370–380.

Durlak, J. A., Mahoney, J. L., Bohnert, A. M., & Parente, M. E. (2010). Developing and improving after-school programs to enhance youth's personal growth and adjustment: A special issue of AJCP. *American Journal of Community Psychology, 45*, 285–293.

Durlak, J. A., Weissberg, R., & Pachan, M. (2010). A meta-analysis of after-school programs that seek to promote personal and social skills in children and adolescents. *American Journal of Community Psychology, 45*, 294–309.

Gardner, H. (1983). *Frames of mind*. New York: Basic Books.

Gottfredson, D. C., Gerstenblith, S. S., Soule, D. A., Womer, S. C., & Lu, S. (2004). Do after school programs reduce delinquency? *Prevention Science, 5*(4), 253–266.

Greenberg, M. T., Kusché, C. A., Cook, E. T., & Quamma, J. P. (1995). Promoting emotional competence in school-aged children: The PATHS curriculum. *Development and Psychopathology, 7*, 117.

Gullotta, T. P., Adams, G. R., & Markstrom, C. A. (2000). *The adolescent experience*. New York: Academic Press.

Gullotta, T. P., Bloom, M., Gullotta, C. F., & Messina, J. C. (2009). *A blueprint for promoting academic and social competence in after school programs*. New York: Springer.

Hansen, W. B., & Dusenbury, L. (2004). All Stars Plus: A competence and motivation enhancement approach to prevention. *Health Education, 104*, 371–381.

Hirsch, B. J., Mekinda, M. A., & Stawicki, J. (2010). More than attendance: The importance of after-school program quality. *American Journal of Community Psychology, 45*, 447–452.

Kauh, T. J. (2011). AfterZone: Outcomes for youth participating in Providence's citywide afterschool system. Retrieved December 21, 2013, from *www.ppv.org*.

Kotloff, L. J., & Korom-Djakovic, D. (2010). AfterZones: Creating a citywide system to support and sustain high-quality after-school programs. Retrieved December 21, 2013, from *www.ppv.org*.

Kohn, A. (2006). Abusing research: The study of homework and other examples. *Phi Delta Kappan, 87*, 8–22.

Larson, R. W., & Walker, K. C. (2010). Dilemmas of practice: Challenge to program quality encountered by youth program leaders. *American Journal of Community Psychology, 45*, 338–349.

McNeal, R. B., Hansen, W. B., Harrington, N. G., & Giles, S. M. (2004). How All Stars works: An examination of program effects on mediating variables. *Health Education and Behavior, 31*, 165–178.

Piaget, J., & Inhelder, B. (2000). *The psychology of the child*. New York: Basic Books.

Riggs, N., Bohnert, A. M., Guzman, M. D., & Davidson, D. (2010). Examining the potential of community-based after school programming for Latino youth. *American Journal of Community Psychology, 45*, 417–429.

Riggs, N., & Greenberg, M. T. (2004). After school youth development programs: A developmental–ecological model of current research. *Clinical Child and Family Psychology Review, 7*, 177–190.

Roth, J. L., Malone, L. M., & Brooks-Gunn, J. (2010). Does the amount of participation in afterschool programs relate to developmental outcomes?: A review of the literature source. *American Journal of Community Psychology, 45*, 430–444.

Shernoff, D. (2010). Engagement in after-school programs as a predictor of social competence and academic performance. *American Journal of Community Psychology, 45*, 325–337.

U.S. Department of Labor. (2011). Employment and earnings. Retrieved December 2, 2013, from *www.bls.gov/opub/ee/empearn201101.pdf*.

Waite, L. J. (1981). *Women at work*. Santa Monica, CA: RAND Corporation.

CHAPTER 18

SEL Programs for Juvenile Justice Settings and Populations

Patrick H. Tolan, Emily Nichols, and Nicole DuVal

This chapter summarizes current knowledge about effective programs for social and emotional learning (SEL) in relation to juvenile justice and delinquency. It is a new idea to link concepts that are endemic to SEL to youth crime/delinquency. However, from the inception of the juvenile court, a core assumption has been that much of delinquency can be traced to problems in social and emotional functioning (Shaw & McKay, 1942). In fact, the legal term "delinquency" is used to differentiate youth crime from adult crime based on the assumption that youth are still forming personality and that a major cause of juvenile crime is a disturbance in emotional development and sense of social responsibility. The focus, then, is on social and emotional development rather than crime as a willful act committed by a mature person (Tolan & Titus, 2009). A concordant implication is that social and emotional functioning should be the focus of intervention to prevent or curtail delinquency and to redirect what might otherwise be a trajectory toward adult criminality (Tolan, 2002). Thus, while there has been considerable cognizance of the social and emotional developmental factors that may help explain delinquency and many delinquency interventions target what might be termed SEL skills, this chapter is the first to explicitly link SEL as formally conceptualized in this handbook to juvenile justice settings. Also, while there has been cognizance of social and emotional development issues in understanding and intervening regarding delinquency, in practice, particularly over the past 30 years, such concerns have been overshadowed by emphasis on legal procedures and penalizing perpetrators (Elliott & Tolan, 1999; Tolan & Titus, 2009).

Currently, there are no substantial SEL-based efforts that are specific to juvenile justice settings, nor has the SEL framework had meaningful incorporation into juvenile justice policy or practice. Instead it is necessary and more useful to consider intervention efforts for delinquents that focus on psychopathology or social and emotional skills and behavior. Similarly,programs that have been offered are typically included on listings of SEL programs that have effects on delinquency or its predecessors and closely related outcomes (e.g., aggression, violence). Fortunately, the systematic and sound evaluation of the field of delinquency intervention and programs indicates valid evidence of substantial evaluations of effects. Given this state of affairs, this chapter identifies empirically supported prevention (universal, selective, and indicated) and developmental support programs intended to affect delinquency risk, its close proxies, or its predecessors (e.g., aggression or conduct disorder), and to examine the potential value of SEL in these settings (Collaborative for Social, Academic, and Emotional Learning [CASEL], 2003). We summarize SEL-related programs with delinquents as the population of interest and also programs that focus on social and emotional processes among the SEL skills with demonstrated effects on delinquency and closely related behavioral outcomes. These two types of programs are examined from a perspective of SEL processes that might account for some of those effects.

Identifying Evidence-Based Programs: Blueprints Standards for Program Inclusion

As in other areas, a survey of the interventions in use and even of those evaluated in regard to the intersection of SEL and delinquency reveal that only a small proportion has sound enough evaluation studies for inclusion in systematic program reviews or meta-analyses of promising features (Advisory Board of Blueprints for Violence Prevention, 2011). One principle of importance, particularly regarding summary reviews of programs, is that for confidence to be accorded to the review, it is important that consistency of application of criteria occur for all considered programs (Tolan, 2013). Considering the value of building from existing efforts and that even the most studied relevant programs have very few sound evaluations, we relied on the Blueprints for Healthy Youth Development effort to identify programs for inclusion in this review (Center for the Study and Prevention of Violence [CSPV], 2013). This 20-year effort has been based on clear and specific requirements for design and for determining valid effects. The criteria are applied to render designation of programs into categories corresponding to this volume's distinction of "Promising" and "What Works" (models). The Blueprints criterion for being considered of adequate methodological strength to evaluate results is either a randomized trial or two strong quasi-experimental evaluations with significant positive impact on an outcome (not simply a predictor of outcome) for the Promising category. To be considered a model program, evidence must come from at least one randomized trial and a separate replication (that can be quasi-experimental) with consistent results across trials, with at least one of these demonstrating sustained effects 12 months after the intervention ends. Model programs are considered ready to be used, whereas promising programs are considered to have solid evidence of effects but lack replication or proof of sustained effects.

Inclusion of Programs in This Review

For this chapter, we considered only Blueprints model and promising programs that (1) had demonstrated effects on aggression, violence, or delinquency, or (2) selected at-risk youth based on being at risk for or showing violence, aggression, delinquency, or juvenile justice involvement. We used definitions of SEL provided by CASEL (2003) to characterize likely components from programs not explicitly using an SEL framework. As such, we considered a program to include a "self-management" component if it in any way (1) appeared to teach students to handle emotions, so that they facilitate rather than interfere with the task at hand; (2) appeared to be conscientious and delay gratification to pursue goals; or (3) appeared to persevere in the face of setbacks and frustrations. Program elements or outcomes aimed at students' ability to know what they are feeling in the moment, to have a realistic assessment of their own abilities and a well-grounded sense of self-confidence were labeled as "self-awareness." Program elements and outcomes labeled as "social awareness" were those aimed at students' understanding of what others are feeling, their ability to take others' perspectives or to appreciate and interact positively with diverse groups. We labeled program outcomes and components as "relationship skills" if they concerned the effective handling of emotions in relationships, the establishment and maintenance of healthy and rewarding relationships, resistance to inappropriate social pressure, negotiation of solutions to conflict, and help seeking. Elements and outcomes labeled "responsible decision making" were aimed at youth decisions based on an accurate consideration of relevant factors and likely consequences of alternative courses of action, respect for others, and ability to take responsibility for one's decisions.

Organization of the Review

We organized this review of programs into three groups: What Works (Blueprints model programs), What Is Promising (Blueprints Promising programs), and What Does Not Work (sound evidence of no effect or negative effects). Within each of these categories, we differentiate the following: (1) programs that included only SEL-specific components (SEL Specific), (2) multicomponent programs that included one or more SEL components (Multicomponent), (3) programs that included skills that were not SEL-specific but overlapped with SEL theory (SEL-Overlapping), and (4) programs that did not include SEL components but resulted in the development of SEL skills (SEL Outcomes).

Overview of Programs

The Blueprint model and Promising programs that met criteria for inclusion are summarized in Table 18.1. For each program we list SEL components present in the program and those measured as an outcome. We also note the age range and risk level of the participants (universal, at-risk for delinquency, juvenile justice involved), the justice-related behaviors that were targeted, and effects on those behaviors. As can be seen in Table 18.1, seven programs were designed for adolescents (ages 13–18), three for preadolescents (ages 9–12), and seven for children (ages 4–12). Most programs for preadolescents and children were skills-based manualized programs, with preadolescent programming often focusing on developing relationships with peers, family members, and school staff. None were based on juvenile justice settings. There was a mix of universal (whole population), selective (at-risk population inclusion), and indicated (youth showing early signs of delinquency proclivity) for children and preadolescents. Most programs for adolescents were family interventions, such as family therapy, and were selective or indicated prevention for youth involved with the justice system. Because it is usual practice not to involve youth in the juvenile justice system before adolescence, it is not surprising that there is correspondence between a justice-system-involved focus and adolescent inclusion. Only three of the Blueprint model programs were designed for youth involved in the juvenile justice system. Nine of the programs are designed for youth and adolescents at risk for engaging in criminal behaviors or already involved in it, while 10 programs are to be implemented as a universal program.

SEL-Related Components in Reviewed Programs

The extent to which reviewed programs can be mapped onto the CASEL-based SEL framework varies. One reason is that most of these programs were developed, implemented, and tested for efficacy before the emergence of the SEL framework and naming of the basic skill constructs. In fact, several of the programs included in this review represent work that was part of the basis for that framework (e.g., Providing Alternative Thinking Strategies [PATHS]; Kam, Greenberg, & Kusché, 2004). When mapped onto the SEL framework, we find that, typically, these programs target one or two SEL outcomes or processes. The most common SEL skills focus was on some aspect of relationship skills development (14 of the programs). Responsible decision making was emphasized in nine of the programs, while self-management and social awareness training were each included in eight different programs. Five of the programs had a component that emphasized enhancing self-awareness. Four of the programs emphasized multiple SEL skills. For example, Life Skills Training includes improving relationship skills, and increasing both social and self-awareness (Botvin, Griffin, & Nichols, 2006). Twelve programs reported significant improvements in SEL-related outcomes. Most commonly, effects were found for relationship skills, with social awareness also frequently affected. Only two programs from the list showed significant outcome effects for each of the other SEL skills (decision making, self-management, or self-awareness).

TABLE 18.1. Blueprints Programs with SEL Components and Outcomes

				SEL processes[b]					SEL outcomes[b]				
Program	Age	Risk level[a]	Justice-related outcomes	SM	SeA	RD	RS	SA	SM	SA	RD	RS	SoA
Big Brothers Big Sisters of America	6–18	Selective	Drug use and aggressive behavior						×			×	
Functional Family Therapy	11–18	Indicated	Recidivism			×	×					×	×
2Life Skills Training	13–17	Universal	Aggression, fighting, and delinquency	×		×	×	×					
Multidimensional Treatment Foster Care	13–17	Selective	Antisocial behaviors, symptoms of conduct disorder, arrests and days incarcerated				×					×	
Promoting Alternative Thinking Strategies	6–12	Universal	Aggression scores	×	×	×	×	×	×	×		×	×
The Incredible Years	2–10	Selective		×		×	×	×			×	×	×
Behavioral Monitoring and Reinforcement	Grades 7–9	Selective					×	×					
FAST Track	Grades K–6	Selective	Aggressive behavior	×	×	×	×		×	×		×	

Good Behavior Game	Grades K–1	Universal	Peer and teacher reports of aggression	×								×	
Guiding Good Choices	9–14	Universal	Delinquency				×	×				×	
I Can Problem Solve	PreK–K	Universal			×		×		×		×		
Perry Preschool Project	4–5	Selective	Delinquency and crime rates			×	×					×	
Seattle Social Development Project	Grades 1–6	At Risk, universal	Externalizing behaviors, aggression			×	×					×	
Raising Healthy Children Program	Grades 1–2	Universal	Alcohol and marijuana use				×	×				×	×
Steps to Respect	Grades 3–5	Universal	Bullying		×		×	×			×	×	
Strengthening Families Program	6–12	Universal	Delinquency and aggression	×	×	×	×	×				×	
Linking the Interests of Families and Teachers	6–12	Universal	Aggression	×		×	×	×				×	

[a]Universal (whole population), selective (at-risk selection), or indicated (early intervention).
[b]SM, self-management; SeA, self-awareness; RD, responsible decision making; RS, relationship skills; SoA, social awareness.

What Works

SEL-Specific Programs

PATHS is an example of a model program that corresponds in design and emphasis to the SEL framework. It includes all five SEL components—self-management, self-awareness, responsible decision making, relationship skills, and social awareness—in its curriculum, with the aim of fostering social and emotional competence in its preschool-age students, and subsequently reducing delinquent or aggressive behavior (Domitrovich, Cortes, & Greenberg, 2007). It also is a rare example, perhaps a prototype, of a program that integrates these skills systematically for an intended overall effect. The PATHS curriculum includes a unit on self-control; a unit on feelings, which teaches children how to recognize their own emotions; lessons on responsible decision making; a unit on relationship skills; and lessons on social awareness, which teach children how their behavior can affect others (Conduct Problems Prevention Research Group, 1999; Domitrovich et al., 2007; Kam et al., 2004). Children who participated in PATHS showed greater self-control, better understanding of their own emotions, better relationship skills, especially in terms of nonconfrontational conflict resolution, and a greater ability to recognize feelings in other people than did children who did not receive the PATHS intervention (Domitrovich et al., 2007; Kam et al., 2004). PATHS children also showed reduced aggression and reduced rate of growth in internalizing and externalizing behaviors compared to children who did not receive the PATHS intervention (Conduct Problems Prevention Research Group, 1999; Kam et al., 2004). Participation in PATHS not only fosters social and emotional competence in preschool children but also reduces the risk of aggressive behavior, potentially decreasing risk for later delinquency. There is also the suggestion (at least as part of a comprehensive effort such as Fast Track, which included PATHS with family and other interventions) that high-risk youth with conduct disorders had lower rates of criminal behavior (Conduct Problems Prevention Research Group, 2011).

SEL in Multicomponent Programs

Many Blueprints model programs directly incorporate SEL components as one aspect of a multicomponent program with other emphases, such as family functioning and parenting, or improving academic skills. The Incredible Years Program, designed for use with preschool- and elementary-age children at risk for and/or presenting with conduct problems, combines SEL components with other family- and school-related efforts. Child-focused training delivered as part of The Incredible Years includes lessons in self-management (specifically, using self-talk to calm oneself down), problem solving, social skills and coping with teasing, and learning to identify feelings of other children (Webster-Stratton, Reid, & Hammond, 2004). In addition, the program offers parent training, which targets parenting skills, such as how to play with children, helping children learn, and effective limit setting. The program also includes components designed to promote effective interpersonal skills between parents, including communication skills, anger management, and problem solving. Academic performance is targeted by parent- and teacher-focused program elements. In the parent-focused programming, emphasis is placed on encouraging parental involvement in school by setting up predictable homework routines and building collaborative relationships with teachers. The teacher-focused series promotes effective classroom management—lessons include the effective use of teacher attention, using praise and encouragement, incentives for difficult behavior problems, proactive teaching strategies, and building positive relationships with students.

SEL-Overlapping Programs

Three of the Blueprint model programs particularly designed for youth involved in the justice system include nonspecified SEL components and intervention targets. These programs also demonstrate robust effects and substantial cost benefits (Aos, Lieb, Mayfield, Miller, & Pennucci, 2004). Multisystemic therapy, functional family therapy, and multidimensional treatment foster care are all intended for youth already involved in the juvenile justice system, each intervening at different levels of justice involvement (Tolan & Titus, 2009). For each program, emphasis is centered on family processes as the key to reducing risk. Although each intervention can be seen as potentially improving self-awareness and relationship skills, and may lead to self-management and responsive decision making through changes in family interactions, none self-describe or can be readily characterized as SEL programs. Each has some individual SEL skills promotion, often within family sessions and family interactions, but these are more typically viewed as shifts in communication and family management than in child change specifically. However, each program has demonstrated effects on SEL skills or synonymous child characteristics. These SEL skills have been linked to a reduction in problem behaviors, although more tenuously they show predictive relations with probability of subsequent criminal involvement (Tolan & Titus, 2009).

Multisystemic therapy (MST) is an intensive, wraparound treatment for juvenile offenders (ages 12–17) who are at high risk for out-of-home placement and typically have substantial prior involvement in juvenile justice. This treatment targets the ecology (family, school, and community) of violent and repeat juvenile offenders to reduce antisocial behaviors (Henggeler, Mihalic, Rone, Thomas, & Timmons-Mitchell, 1998). Several strategies are designed to change the family management of the child, and the relation between the family and other systems (e.g., school, peers, and juvenile justice). The shift in dynamics and influence toward more considerate, appropriate, and self-controlled behaviors have similarities to several SEL skills. Although there is no direct language suggesting the intervention is informed by an SEL framework or measured outcome of SEL skills, such as increased relationship skills or social awareness, SEL development may well be occurring through the various interventions being implemented as the descriptions of the intervention processes overlap some with SEL framework.

Functional family therapy (FFT) is a short-term (eight to 30 one-hour sessions) intervention that targets a range of problem youth, from those at risk for delinquency to those demonstrating serious symptoms of conduct disorder and recidivism (Alexander et al., 1998). The goal of FFT is to reduce risk factors such as behavioral problems, hopelessness, and poor parenting skills, and to promote protective factors such as family alliance, supportive communication, and positive parenting. This is accomplished through three distinct phases: (1) engagement and motivation of the adolescent and family members, (2) behavior change, and (3) generalization of learned skills. There are overlaps between the skills taught through FFT and SEL, specifically, relationship skills such as communication and conflict resolution. Outcomes of trial evaluations include improvements in family functioning, involvement, positive parenting and communication, reduction in recidivism, and out-of-home placements (Alexander et al., 1998). The role of youth relationship skills improvement and reduced delinquency risk has not been empirically demonstrated in part because of limitations in teasing apart the meditational role of multiple change strategies occurring within session activities (MacKinnon, Fairchild, & Fritz, 2007).

Multidimensional treatment foster care (MTFC) is an intensive, wraparound service for adolescents as an alternative to institutional, residential, and group care placement (Chamberlain & Reid, 1997). The foster children are at risk for such placement due to delinquent behavior and aggression. The intervention places the children for 6–9 months with specially trained foster parents, who implement a structured individualized treatment plan that follows a behavioral parent training approach combined with extra casework and support for the family. Thus, each child is under the supervision of a clinical case manager, in addition to receiving individual and in home–family therapy. As with MST and FFT, the effort is multicomponent and any SEL characteristics have a family process emphasis. Child effects are seen as the result of change in family parenting practices and extension of these principles to other settings. Clearly, child self-control is implied as an outcome of the approach, and it appears that relationships skills and perhaps self-awareness would also be intended mediators of the outcomes. Evaluations show that the intervention results in a reduction in arrests, days incarcerated, and problem behaviors (Chamberlain & Reid, 1997). However, evaluations to date have not tested any effects on processes that would correspond to the SEL framework.

Given these three programs' intended focus and substantial evidence of benefits for those at risk and involved in delinquency, an important question arises: Would SEL-focused efforts be a good fit to reduce delinquency of those most at risk, particularly once involvement is started, or can the effects on the family and that system's relation to others be traced through effects on SEL processes? If family interventions show their effects by changing family communication, consistency, quality of parenting practices, and improved organization for problem solving, these changes may set conditions for improvement in SEL. Alternatively, it may be that the mechanisms of import are not SEL, at least for those adolescents already involved with juvenile justice, but are related to conditions that evoke and support problem behavior, such as poor family functioning. Mapping these relations seems to be a key area for more study. In addition, it may be useful to see how augmenting these approaches with efforts that do intend to directly affect SEL through family intervention fare. Might they be as effective or might such augmentation improve outcomes? Because there are no SEL-specific family interventions, the creation and examination of such interventions may be an important contribution to understanding SEL's potential in encouraging healthy development in juvenile justice settings and populations. This seems like a critical area for further research.

A different type of SEL-overlapping programming is exemplified by the mentoring program of Big Brothers and Big Sisters of America (Grossman & Tierney, 1998). Mentoring, typically a relatively unstructured, relationship-based effort, has demonstrated effects as an approach for reducing delinquency risk (Tolan, Henry, Schoeny, Lovegrove, & Nichols, in press). In this instance, whether SEL processes are at work is difficult to discern because much of the intervention is not carefully detailed or proscribed and little research has been conducted to test formally how different features of mentoring might mediate important developmental processes and behavioral outcomes (MacKinnon et al., 2007; Tolan et al., in press). In particular, there is a need for mapping processes through a framework of theorized effects (e.g., SEL promotion) to illuminate why and how mentoring influences obtained any benefits. It may well be that SEL processes are engendered through adult interest, companionship, and informal advising, and doing so can account for delinquency prevention and other benefits. Efforts such as mentoring may demonstrate that SEL can be promoted indirectly or incidentally in an informal intervention. Along with studies of interventions with additional program components, such as those in the Midwestern Prevention Project (MPP), such efforts could expand our understanding of the role SEL plays in reducing delinquency.

As these examples illustrate, in some SEL-overlapping programs, the overlap is through conceptualization of the risk and protective processes based in other developmentally influential systems (e.g., family) in ways that are congruent with either subsequent SEL effects for the individual child or what might be considered SEL processes of the larger system (e.g., family). In other cases, the interventions have not been analyzed conceptually or empirically from an SEL framework (e.g., mentoring) but seem likely to be promoting skills that fall within the SEL framework. Certainly, research to explicate how SEL processes/skills look at the family, peer group, school, and neighborhood unit level, as well as efforts to review and if possible recode intervention effects from an SEL approach, would aid in this understanding (Catalano et al., 2003).

Still other initiatives identify additional resources and emphasize the value of consistent support of prosocial engagement and norms that undercut delinquency and related behavior (Pentz, Mihalic, & Grotpeter, 1998). These programs raise the question of how embedding SEL programming into a multipronged effort might affect delinquency and delinquents. For example, the MPP (Pentz et al., 1998) employs a system of well-coordinated, communitywide strategies, including mass media programming, community organization and training, and local policy initiatives to promote norms against substance use and encourage use of social skills thought to lessen risk due to peer pressure. Embedding SEL components into a program that also directly engages community-based resources may be catalyzing other programs' potential for greater impact. Certainly, it would be valuable to see whether SEL processes mediate the skills training or the norm influences of MPP. More generally, the program design and its similarity in some areas of content and focus to SEL suggest that better understanding of juvenile delinquency and related problem prevention as an SEL-based effort should include consideration of different system processes that might promote or reinforce SEL and/or how SEL training effects might depend on embedding in other forms of intervention.

Programs with SEL Outcomes

The previously described model programs resulted in significant improvements in delinquency, aggression, or violence. Many programs also empirically demonstrated effects on social and emotional skills and evidenced SEL programming. For example, self-monitoring was an enhanced and explicit focus of the PATHS project (Kam et al., 2004) while youth self-awareness was an effect but not an explicit focus of the Big Brothers and Big Sisters program (Turner & Scherman, 1996). Similarly, the evaluation of PATHS shows increased self-awareness (Kam et al., 2004). Responsible decision making was increased through the Incredible Years program. Relationship skills and social awareness were impacted by all of the model programs except the Life Skills Training program.

Because most of these effects have been discussed in great detail in previous sections, we focus on only one program to describe the processes of impact on SEL skills. Participation in the Incredible Years program resulted in better problem-solving skills by parents and increased warmth and more positive interactions between the parents and children (based on measured observations). In addition, improved prosocial behavior rates were noted in the children, with reductions in conduct problems at home and at school (Webster-Stratton et al., 2004). The suggested chain of effects is to improve parental behavior management, which increases opportunity for children to improve SEL skills, and this translates to less behavior problems. As this example illustrates, and the number of programs with effects on SEL skills supports, there would be great value in measuring and evaluating meditational processes of avenues to effects on SEL skills and how these relate to outcomes such as reduced behavior problems, aggression, and later lower rates of delinquency.

What Is Promising

The Blueprints organization has identified many (approximately 40) programs that meet criteria for the designation of Promising, with a subset demonstrating significant reductions in delinquency and related outcomes and/or effects on SEL skills for populations at risk for delinquency. All of these programs are listed in Table 18.1, and we have selected a few of those to describe as examples.

SEL-Specific Programs

The Seattle Social Development Project and it derivation, Raising Healthy Children, and the Good Behavior Game are examples of programs that focus on one or two specific aspects of SEL. The Good Behavior Game is an elementary school-based prevention program that focuses on the self-regulation aspect of SEL; specifically, the program uses group contingency strategies to help inculcate in children the skills for self-control, with the goal of reducing aggressive behavior and improving school learning. Children who participated in the Good Behavior Game were less likely to have aggressive behavior when reassessed at outcome and at follow-up points throughout elementary school and high school, showing a slower rate of growth for aggressive and disruptive behaviors than did children who did not participate in the Good Behavior Game. They also showed lower rates of antisocial personality (Kellam et al., 2008). Because antisocial personality is a psychiatric diagnosis that corresponds well with criminal activity, this suggests that the game, and the self-control gained from participating in it, might reduce later criminal involvement.

The Seattle Social Development Project/ Raising Healthy Children program focuses on the social awareness and relationship skills components of SEL. Both versions of the program are school-based prevention programs for elementary school-age children that aim to reduce delinquency and alcohol and drug use by targeting risk and protective factors at an early age. These programs utilize a combination of teacher training, parent education, and child social skills training (O'Donnell, Hawkins, Catalano, Abbott, & Day, 1995). Specifically, the Seattle Social Development Project/Raising Healthy Children program concentrates on teaching children the skills for interacting appropriately with other people, and includes lessons on relationship skills, social awareness, conflict negotiation and resolution, and refusal skills (Catalano et al., 2003; O'Donnell et al., 1995). Participation in the programs leads not only to more prosocial behavior but also a decrease in delinquent behavior. For example, those children who participated in the Seattle Social Development Project/Raising Healthy Children program, compared to controls, showed increased communication and attachment to family, cooperation with peers, and ability to understand others' feelings (Catalano et al., 2003; Hawkins et al., 1992). Participants also showed less externalizing, aggressive, and self-destructive behaviors, and a greater decline in the frequency of alcohol and marijuana use than those who did not participate in the programs (Brown, Catalano, Fleming, Haggerty, & Abbott, 2005). Notably, The Good Behavior Game and the Seattle Social Development Project/Raising Healthy Children program target different SEL skills, yet both show long-term effects that are relevant to the juvenile justice system. This may indicate that multiple aspects of SEL can help reduce involvement in juvenile delinquency.

SEL in Multicomponent Programs

Fast Track, a promising multicomponent program that is an intensive intervention for children with early-onset conduct problems, is implemented from first grade through high school; however, the intervention has only been evaluated through sixth grade (Conduct Problems Prevention Research Group, 2004). The components of the program delivered to children specifically target SEL elements, including lessons teaching self-control, emotional understanding and communication, the development of relationship skills with friends and parents, as well as responsible decision making (Conduct Problems Prevention Research Group, 1999, 2004). In part, this is because Fast Track incorporates the PATHS program. Like PATHS, Fast Track aims to improve students' decision-making skills by teaching them how to identify problems, generate responses to those problems, and evaluate those responses. In addition to directly addressing SEL issues, the program incorporates other components to augment this individual effort. First, provided parent training is aimed at improving children's academic performance, as well as parents' communication with the school, control of anger, and use of effective discipline. Home visits target parents' feelings of efficacy, empowerment, problem-solving skills, and parenting skills. Furthermore, Fast Track provides academic tutoring three times per week to improve children's reading skills. This selective intervention that focuses on at-risk youth suggest that SEL elements, perhaps when included with family relationship and skills training, may help to reduce likelihood of eventual delinquency in youth with early, serious aggression.

SEL-Overlapping Programs

While a few promising programs have elements and emphases that clearly correspond to SEL as conceptualized by CASEL (2003), others are better characterized as either touching on areas of functioning or development that seem similar to but not the same as SEL. As previously mentioned, in many cases, this may represent a different conceptualization by the program developer of the processes at work, while in other cases it may be that the conceptualization predates formal articulation of the SEL model. For example, the Perry Preschool Project emphasizes self-control as one of the capabilities of children thought to be promoted by the programming, but it did not seem to have a skills-building or training orientation. It is hard to estimate how frequently and to what degree programs like this might be rated as having SEL activity if one were to observe them in action, and how many would seem to have SEL targets but not such activities.

SEL Outcomes

All of the promising programs from the Blueprints projects had demonstrated gains in developing healthy relationship skills through their interventions, although not all of them impacted both SEL skills and problem behavior. Fast Track has been found to be effective in improving both SEL-related skills and problem behavior. Participation in Fast Track resulted in improved self-management (specifically, improved emotion coping), improved emotion recognition, and better relationship skills (specifically, better social problem-solving skills and more positive peer interactions) (Conduct Problems Prevention Research Group, 1999, 2004). Fast Track program involvement has been found also to relate to reductions in aggressive, disruptive, and oppositional behavior at school.

Like the model programs, some Promising programs among the Blueprint efforts emphasize SEL effects, not due to SEL training of the child, but through change in developmentally influencing systems that then affect the child. Others seem not to target direct effect on the child through these systems, but instead to create developmental environments in which SEL skills are reinforced and can flourish. For example, Steps to Respect focuses on organization of the school to reduce bullying (Frey et al., 2005). As part of this emphasis, there is more attention to self-control, social awareness, and responsible decision making, although these are not direct emphases of the program and the program is not designed to affect these SEL processes specifically. Instead, there is design of rules, norm promotion, and personal responsibility that would make such skills more likely, more valued, and more functional. Similarly, Linking Interests of Families and Teachers (LIFT; Reid, Eddy, Fetrow, & Stoolmiller, 1999) emphasizes home–school communication and parent–teacher cooperation for behavioral reinforcement of on-task and nonaggressive problem solving. This improved communication and multisystem behavior management approach also is thought to improve opportunities for use of SEL skills as a product of the school–home relationship change and the resulting environment conditions.

These interventions, with indirect or setting condition targets rather than promotion of specific skills, raise an important issue for further consideration of SEL with juvenile justice populations and settings. That is, how much SEL programs are meant to be skills inculcation that children take with them as habits to other settings, and how much the impact is through environments that support such skills and increase reliance on them. This is a question of transfer versus differential utility as the process through which SEL skills are seen as having an effect on delinquency and related behaviors. While not just applicable to the juvenile justice population and settings, this focus does highlight the value of research that explicates the processes at the individual and setting levels (Tseng & Seidman, 2007).

What Does Not Work

There is a long list of SEL-oriented and SEL-affecting programs that have not had adequate quality or extent of evaluation to permit judgment of effects. There are also many efforts with some evidence that might be judged positive, some with mixed results, others with some evaluation that does not show significant effects, and a few with what might suggest negative effects. Those are not reviewed here because the evidence is not sufficient to determine placement in such categories. Two programs have been intended to prevent delinquency and involvement in the juvenile justice system, and have elements that are related to SEL and have demonstrated negative effects (exposure relates to increased risk for delinquency).

Scared Straight aims to inform at-risk youth of the negative consequences of a life of crime by allowing those youth to visit prisons and be exposed to inmates' experience in prison. Inmates tell youth about the negative aspects of prison life, sharing "prison horror stories" in an attempt to dissuade youth from misunderstanding what one consequence of crime is like. Inmates also talk about the poor choices that ultimately led them to prison (Buckner & Chesney-Lind, 1983; Klenowski, Bell, & Dodson, 2010). This type of program generally emphasizes confrontation to shock youth into increased self-awareness and divert them away from delinquency. Multiple, well-evaluated experiments with

Scared Straight have shown that exposure increases likelihood of subsequent arrest. Notably, participants do report greater self-awareness (Buckner & Chesney-Lind, 1983; Klenowski et al., 2010). Whether Scared Straight utilizes an incorrect understanding of SEL skills development (e.g., confrontation) or the relation of the skills change to the outcome is different for this compared to other SEL programs is not known. However, the negative behavioral effects are replicated and seem substantial.

D.A.R.E. (Drug Abuse Resistance Education), a program created in 1983 in Los Angeles, has become a national, school-based approach to reducing drug use and violence. The original program was modified in reaction to evaluations demonstrating no effects in general and negative effects for some populations (Ringwalt et al., 1994). Modifications included a focus on violence prevention and incorporation of more skills practice and elements thought to be important in other effective programs (Sloboda et al., 2009). Notably, these changes align the program with SEL principles. The D.A.R.E. core curriculum's 17 lessons, usually offered once a week for 45–60 minutes to middle school students, focus on teaching the ill effects of drug use and the skills needed to recognize and resist social pressures to use drugs or violence. Sessions are taught by police officers trained to teach D.A.R.E. in school classrooms. Lessons included in the program emphasize self-esteem, decision making, and interpersonal communications skills, all of which are SEL skills. Well-designed and controlled studies have shown consistently small negative effects on substance use or intent to use, particularly for youth from middle- or upper-middle-class suburban communities, with negative effects demonstrated more for non-Hispanic white students than other ethnicities. A meta-analysis by Ennett, Tobler, Ringwalt, and Flewelling (1994) evaluating the effectiveness of D.A.R.E. reported that it had a nonsignificant and negligible reductive effect on substance use—the effect size was only 0.06. Interestingly, however, the meta-analysis by Ennett and colleagues did indicate that participation was significantly associated with improved social skills (d = 0.19). A more recent randomized evaluation of D.A.R.E., revised to incorporate more SEL components (Sloboda et al., 2009), found that students who participated had higher rates of binge drinking and other outcomes of problem behavior compared to students in a control group. No significant effects on SEL skills or closely related constructs were noted.

While D.A.R.E. fits well within an SEL approach and Scared Straight fits less well, both have well-evaluated evidence of negative effects for at least some exposed individuals. It seems important to consider how SEL principles or practices might be effectively transmitted and trained, and how the opposite can occur. There have been numerous discussions about each program and the reasons for these findings, but there has been scant demonstration of mediation through specific processes. Thus, it is unclear how the problematic impact of these programs relates to the SEL emphasis—whether it is a mischaracterization of what SEL training is, the method of delivery, or the context for the delivery. Understanding how these features may contribute to effects, positive or negative, is another important area for investigation.

Future Directions for SEL Programming in Juvenile Justice Settings

As previously noted, there is not a conceptualized SEL approach to those involved in the juvenile justice system. This means there is not a current, empirically supported intervention that is designed specifically to promote SEL within justice settings or one that is based on the conception that SEL skills will reduce the probability of delinquency. What we offer in this review is the current state of the prevention field related to the nexus of SEL and delinquency, which may suggest some aspects of such a framework and promising areas for immediate further research.

By applying the SEL framework to a set of programs that possesses sufficient evidence to be considered empirically supported, we were able to identify efforts that have SEL components and demonstrate positive effects for preventing engagement in delinquency. We have also identified programs that affected SEL processes, but did not directly focus on these as part of the intervention design. In some cases, such as MST, FFT, and multidimensional family therapy, programs are offered as part of juvenile justice system interventions, specifically as diversion programs. Also, several programs that focus on SEL skills have impact on aggression, behavior problems, violence, and/or delinquency. Additional programs that focus on developmentally influencing processes and systems that correspond to or are theoretically well linked to SEL have demonstrated effectiveness. Thus, the pattern suggests that SEL efforts might be important in preventing delinquency. What is uncertain is how effective, compared to other approaches, SEL efforts are, or whether those effects found in other systems would occur in juvenile justice settings. Thus, it can be said that programs with an SEL focus have shown important and promising effects on reducing the involvement in delinquency and/or its proxies, such as aggression.

Any interpretation about the value of SEL for those involved with the juvenile justice system, about what aspects of programs are critical, and how implementation might be promoted must be heavily qualified as preliminary and inferentially based. For example, there is need for a formulation of how specific SEL skills might relate to delinquency risk (or protection against such risk), as well as affect outcomes for youth involved with the juvenile justice system. Such formulation is needed to evaluate existing programs that measures SEL processes (as mediators of behavioral effects and as proximal outcomes affecting long-term functioning). SEL formulation might also suggest additional programs that may be effective for delinquency prevention. Furthermore, there is need to consider and to articulate how SEL processes occur in relationships within families and classrooms, and to to interpret effects of current programs and design additional, potentially valuable efforts. Additional research would be helpful that advances understanding of behavior- and setting-focused prevention that promotes SEL skills, and how these are similar or different than methods meant to train such skills directly (e.g., programs meant to affect the SEL atmosphere and mores within a school vs. those that use classrooms to train students in specific skills). With these considerations, programs might be designed or modified to work through affecting these SEL processes, permitting more confident evaluation of whether SEL-affecting programs are important for reducing delinquency and delinquency risk. Also, such a framework might permit clarification about which SEL skills are important or advantageous emphases in such programs.

In addition, our review of programs suggests that some SEL components have had relatively little consideration in juvenile justice settings or for those at risk for juvenile crime. This does not mean such programs do not exist, just that they have not demonstrated effects using evaluation designs that are adequate enough to permit sound inference of potential benefits. For example, there has been little work with justice system-involved youth that attempts to teach specific skills related to self-management and self-awareness. These skills might be crucial before, during, and after a youth's incarceration because impulsivity has been well documented as a mediator for delinquent behaviors (White et al., 1994) and skills such as improved self-management and awareness may help adolescents better manage their impulsive behaviors and responses. Responsible decision-making skills, such as those taught in the Guiding Good Choices program, might also be important, and if taught to adolescents at risk for or involved in the juvenile justice system might have substantial benefit.

One concern about advancing SEL in juvenile justice contexts is the limited interest in the emotional or social development of youth within the juvenile justice settings. The continued emphasis on establishing criminal responsibility and related punishment-oriented dispositions has eclipsed almost all of the interest in relating problems in development to early susceptibility and involvement with crime that was historically central to formation of the juvenile justice system (Tolan & Titus, 2009). In addition, SEL has focused primarily on educational settings, both in terms of conceptualization and in application. As such, there has not been any substantial consideration of explicit SEL programming with respect to juvenile justice settings, policies, and practices, and the pertinent characteristics of youth served in this system.

It may be that seeking to infuse SEL in the juvenile justice system is not the preferable goal, not because SEL emphasis would not be helpful, but because the juvenile justice system is ill-suited for adequate valuing of such programs. It may be that such programs are not as effective if based within such institutions as they are when part of community efforts (Tolan & Titus, 2009). Perhaps, as the programs identified here emphasize, the goal should be to utilize SEL as a protective and preventive focus within school and other settings of typical development to decrease the number of youth entering and being encumbered by juvenile justice settings and programs.

References

Advisory Board of Blueprints for Violence Prevention. (2011). [Peer commentary on "Replication in prevention science" by J. C. Valentine, A. Biglan, R. F. Boruch, F. G. Castro, L. M. Collins, B. R. Flay, et al.]. *Prevention Science, 12*(2), 121–122.

Alexander, J., Barton, C., Gordon, D., Grotpeter, J., Hansson, K., Harrison, R., et al. (1998). *Blueprints for Violence Prevention: Book Three. Functional Family Therapy*. Boulder, CO: Center for the Study and Prevention of Violence.

Aos, S., Lieb, R., Mayfield, J., Miller, M., & Pennucci, A. (2004). *Benefits and costs of prevention and early intervention programs for youth: Technical appendix* (Document No. 04-07-3901). Olympia: Washington State Institute for Public Policy.

Botvin, G. J., Griffin, K. W., & Nichols, T. R. (2006). Preventing youth violence and delinquency through a universal school-based prevention approach. *Prevention Science, 7,* 403–408.

Brown, E. C., Catalano, R. F., Fleming, C. B., Haggerty, K. P., & Abbott, R. D. (2005). Adolescent substance use outcomes in the Raising Healthy Children project: A two-part latent growth curve analysis. *Journal of Consulting and Clinical Psychology, 73,* 699–710.

Buckner, J. C., & Chesney-Lind, M. (1983). Dramatic cures for juvenile crime: An evaluation of a prisoner-run delinquency prevention program. *Criminal Justice and Behavior, 10,* 227–247.

Catalano, R. F., Mazza, J. J., Harachi, T. W., Abbott, R. D., Haggerty, K. P., & Fleming, C. B. (2003). Raising healthy children through enhancing social development in elementary school: Results after 1.5 years. *Journal of School Psychology, 41*(2), 143–164.

Center for the Study and Prevention of Violence (CSPV). (2013). Blueprints for healthy youth development. Retrieved April 1, 2013, from *www.blueprintsprograms.com.*

Chamberlain, P., & Reid, J. B. (1997). Comparison of two community alternatives to incarceration for chronic juvenile offenders. *Journal of Consulting and Clinical Psychology, 66*(4), 624–633.

Collaborative for Academic, Social, and Emotional Learning (CASEL). (2003). *Safe and sound: An educator's guide to evidence based social and emotional learning programs.* Chicago: Author.

Conduct Problems Prevention Research Group. (1999). Initial impact of the Fast Track prevention trial for conduct problems: II. Classroom effects. *Journal of Consulting and Clinical Psychology, 67,* 648–657.

Conduct Problems Prevention Research Group. (2004). The effects of the Fast Track program on serious problem outcomes at the end of elementary school. *Journal of Clinical Child and Adolescent Psychology, 33,* 650–661.

Conduct Problems Prevention Research Group. (2011). The effects of the Fast Track preventive intervention on the development of conduct disorder across childhood. *Child Development, 82*(1), 331–345.

Domitrovich, C. E., Cortes, R. C., & Greenberg, M. T. (2007). Improving young children's social and emotional competence: A randomized trial of the Preschool "PATHS" curriculum. *Journal of Primary Prevention, 28,* 67–91.

Elliott, D., & Tolan, P. H. (1999). Youth violence prevention, intervention, and social policy: An overview. In D. Flannery & R. Hoff (Eds.), *Youth violence: Prevention, intervention, and social policy* (pp. 3–46). Washington, DC: American Psychiatric Association.

Ennett, S. T., Tobler, N. S., Ringwalt, C. L., & Flewelling, R. L. (1994). How effective is drug abuse resistance education?: A meta-analysis of project DARE outcome evaluations. *American Journal of Public Health, 84,* 1394–1401.

Frey, K. S., Hirchstein, J. L., Snell, J. L., Van Schoiack Edstrom, L., MacKenzie, E. P., & Broderick, C. J. (2005). Reducing playground bullying and supporting beliefs: An experimental trial of the Steps to Respect program. *Developmental Psychology, 41,* 479–491.

Grossman, J. B., & Tierney, J. P. (1998). Does mentoring work?: An impact study of the Big Brothers Big Sisters program. *Evaluation Review, 22,* 403–426.

Hawkins, J. D., Catalano, R. F., Morrison, D. M., O'Donnell, J., Abbott, R. D., & Day, L. E. (1992). The Seattle Social Development Project: Effects of the first four years on protective factors and problem behaviors. In J. McCord & R.

E. Tremblay (Eds.), *Preventing antisocial behavior: Interventions from birth through adolescence* (pp. 139–161). New York: Guilford Press.

Henggeler, S. W., Mihalic, S. F., Rone, L., Thomas, C., & Timmons-Mitchell, J. (1998). *Multisystemic therapy: Blueprints for violence prevention, Book Six*. Boulder: Center for the Study and Prevention of Violence, Institute of Behavioral Science, University of Colorado.

Kam, C. M., Greenberg, M. T., & Kusché, C. A. (2004). Sustained effects of the PATHS curriculum on the social and psychological adjustment of children in special education. *Journal of Emotion and Behavioral Disorders, 12*(2), 66–78.

Kellam, S. G., Brown, C. H., Poduska, J., Ialongo, N., Wang, W., & Wilcox, H. C. (2008). Effects of a universal classroom behavior management program in first and second grades on young adult behavioral, psychiatric, and social outcomes. *Drug and Alcohol Dependencies, 95*(Suppl. 1), S5–S28.

Klenowski, P. M., Bell, K. J., & Dodson, K. D. (2010). An empirical evaluation of juvenile awareness programs in the United States: Can juveniles be "scared straight"? *Journal of Offender Rehabilitation, 49*, 254–272.

MacKinnon, D. P., Fairchild, A. J., & Fritz, M. S. (2007). Mediation analysis. *Annual Review of Psychology, 58*, 593–614.

O'Donnell, J., Hawkins, J. D., Catalano, R. F., Abbott, R. D., & Day, L. E. (1995). Preventing school failure, drug use, and delinquency among low-income children: Long-term intervention in elementary schools. *American Journal of Orthopsychiatry, 65*(1), 87–100.

Pentz, M. A., Mihalic, S. F., & Grotpeter, J. K. (1998). *Blueprints for violence prevention, Book One: The Midwestern Prevention Project*. Boulder, CO: Center for the Study and Prevention of Violence.

Reid, J. B., Eddy, J. M., Fetrow, R. A., & Stoolmiller, M. (1999). Description and immediate impacts of a preventive intervention for conduct problems. *American Journal of Community Psychology, 27*, 483–517.

Ringwalt, C. L., Greene, J. M., Ennett, S. T., Iachan, R., Clayton, R. R., & Leukefeld, C. G. (1994). *Past and future direction of the D.A.R.E. program: An evaluation review*. Research Triangle Park, NC: Research Triangle Institute.

Shaw, C. R., & McKay, H. D. (1942). *Juvenile delinquency and urban areas*. Chicago: University of Chicago Press.

Sloboda, Z., Stephens, R. C., Stephens, P. C., Grey, S. F., Teasdale, B., Hawthorne, R. D., et al. (2009). The Adolescent Substance Abuse Prevention Study: A randomized field trial of a universal substance abuse prevention program. *Drug and Alcohol Dependence, 102*(1–3), 1–10.

Tolan, P. H. (2002). Crime prevention: Focus on youth. In J. Q. Wilson & J. Petersilia (Eds.), *Crime: Public policies for crime control* (pp. 109–128). Oakland, CA: ICS Press.

Tolan, P. H. (2013). Making and using lists of empirically tested programs: Value for violence interventions for progress and impact. In *Evidence for violence prevention across the lifespan and around the world: A workshop of the Forum on Global Violence Prevention*. Washington, DC: Institute of Medicine/National Academy of Sciences.

Tolan, P. H., Henry, D., Schoeny, M., Lovegrove, P., & Nichols, E. (in press). Mentoring programs to affect delinquency and associated outcomes of youth at risk: A comprehensive meta-analytic review. *Journal of Experimental Criminology*.

Tolan, P. H., & Titus, J. A. (2009). Therapeutic jurisprudence in juvenile justice. In B. L. Bottoms, C. J. Najdowski, & G. S. Goodman (Eds.), *Children as victims, witnesses, and offenders: Psychological science and the law* (pp. 313–333). New York: Guilford Press.

Tseng, V., & Seidman, E. (2007). A systems framework for understanding social settings. *American Journal of Community Psychology, 39*, 217–228.

Turner, S., & Scherman, A. (1996). Big brothers: Impact on little brothers' self-concepts and behaviors. *Adolescence, 31*, 874–882.

Webster-Stratton, C., Reid, M. J., & Hammond, M. (2004). Treating children with early-onset conduct problems: Intervention outcomes for parent, child, and teacher training. *Journal of Clinical Child and Adolescent Psychology, 30*, 283–302.

White, J., Moffitt, T., Caspi, A., Bartusch, D. J., Needles, D. J., & Stouthamer-Loeber, M. (1994). Measuring impulsivity and examining its relationship to delinquency. *Journal of Abnormal Psychology, 103*(2), 192–205.

PART III

Assessment

CHAPTER 19

Assessment of SEL in Educational Contexts

Susanne A. Denham

Children's and adolescents' social and emotional learning (SEL) has become an important topic because of its conceptual and empirical links with children's academic readiness and success, school adjustment, social relations, personal well-being and mental health, ultimate workplace performance, and general adaptive resilience in the face of stressful circumstances (e.g., Brackett, Rivers, & Salovey, 2011; Raver & Knitzer, 2002). In particular, this chapter focuses on assessing those dimensions of SEL that enable children and adolescents to be successful in an essential context: *their schools*. Among the numerous salutary effects of SEL, I highlight ways in which SEL supports school adjustment and both academic readiness and success, and the most effective ways to assess SEL competencies.

As Zins, Bloodworth, Weissberg, and Walberg (2007, p. 191) have noted, "Schools are social places, and learning is a social process." Students learn alongside and in collaboration with teachers and peers, and must be able to utilize their emotions to facilitate learning; children with SEL competencies participate more in the classroom, have more positive attitudes about and involvement with school, are more accepted by classmates, and are given more instruction and positive feedback by teachers. Without SEL competencies, young children are more likely to dislike school and perform poorly on academic tasks, and later experience grade retention and dropout (Raver & Knitzer, 2002).

Given these crucial outcomes, the focus of this chapter is on recommendations concerning appropriate educational assessments of various SEL competencies, keeping the different developmental tasks of each age and the nature of each SEL competency in mind. Assessment is an integral, indispensable part of an educational system that includes (1) clear goals and benchmarks (i.e., standards) for children's SEL progress; (2) evidence-based curricula and instruction, along with support for teachers to implement such programming, so that such standards may be met (Durlak, Weissberg, Dymnicki, Taylor, & Schellinger, 2011); and (3) universal and targeted screening and progress monitoring (formative, interim, and summative).

Figure 19.1 shows my thinking on the relations among the elements in this system: (a) developmental tasks are the substrate upon which SEL competencies are demonstrated and developed; (b) standards are (or should be) created that correspond to these important SEL competencies; (c) standards inform assessment, and vice versa; (d) both standards and assessment are useful in that they lead to instruction (which often leads to the need for further, regular assessment and

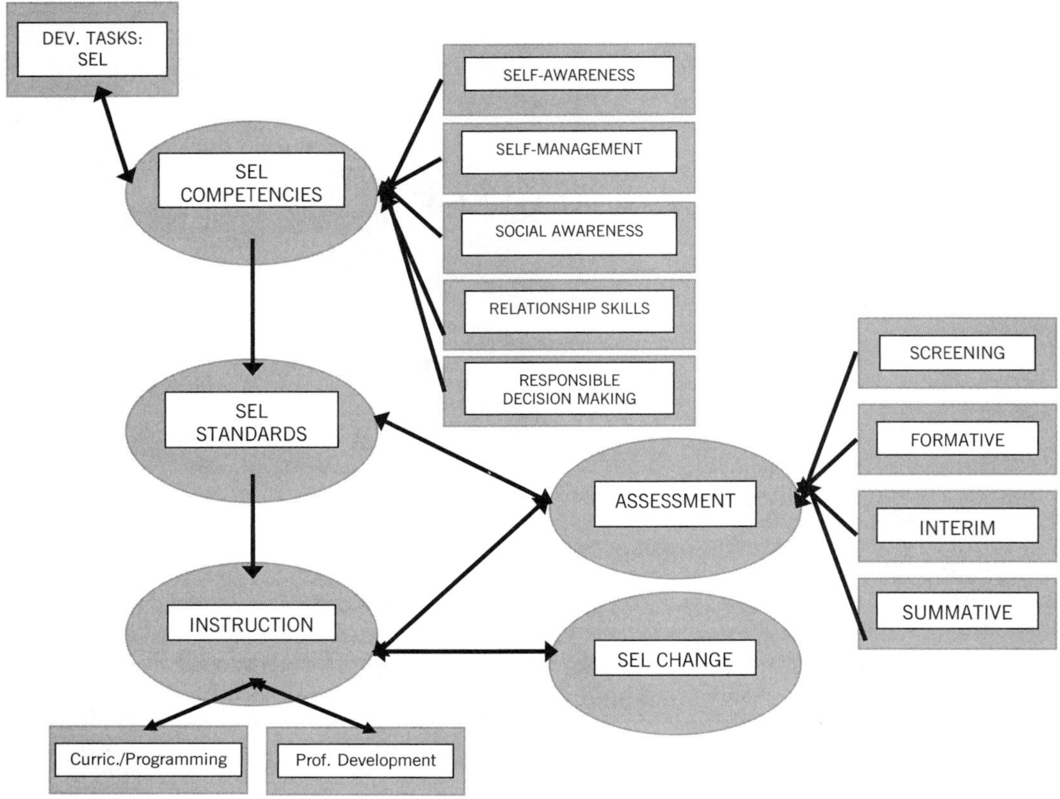

FIGURE 19.1. Interrelated system of SEL skills development in educational settings.

revised standards, and is supported by both professional development and curriculum); and finally, (e) change in SEL skills is the end point toward which we strive.

Given the structure set forth in Figure 19.1, I review evidence for the developmental tasks of SEL and their relation to academic success. I also show how SEL assessment must flow from educational standards in the area, as well as describe SEL-specific assessment criteria and several useful SEL assessment tools for use in academic settings. Finally, I offer some conclusions about where we stand as a field in this area and what our targets should be.

Developmental Task Contexts for SEL Competencies

SEL competencies must be viewed in terms of key tasks faced by children at each age range from early childhood to adolescence. Assessment tools should acknowledge, at least implicitly, these shifts in developmental focus. During the early childhood years, SEL competencies are organized around the social developmental tasks of positive engagement with the social and nonsocial environment, as well as management of emotional arousal within social interaction, and remaining connected with adults while successfully moving into the world of peers. These developmental tasks, can be difficult to navigate: To perform both play and preacademic activities successfully, young children are often required to sit still or wait, attend, follow directions, approach group play, and get along with others.

SEL tasks then change radically for children entering middle childhood. As children become aware of a wider social network, key SEL developmental tasks are transformed into ways to navigate the sometimes treacherous waters of peer inclusion, acceptance, and friendship. Managing how and when to show emotion becomes crucial, as does knowing with whom to share emotion-laden experiences and ideas.

Adolescents are expected to form more intimate relationships with both opposite- and same-gender peers; successfully negotiate a larger peer group and other challenges in the transition to middle and high school; come to understand the perspectives of others more clearly than ever before; achieve emotional independence from parents and other adults, while retaining attachment relationships with them; establish clear gender identity and body acceptance; prepare for tasks of adulthood, such as occupation, marriage, and family life; and establish a personal value or ethical system and achieve socially responsible behavior. In the academic realm, older children and adolescents are required to become much more independent in their engagement with ever more complex coursework, and to consider how their achievement is moving them toward independence. Across ages, these developmental tasks serve as important benchmarks against which to evaluate a child's SEL success and its relation with school adjustment and academic success; it is within these developmental tasks that all the components of SEL are operative.

Key SEL Competencies

Five core SEL competencies have been identified; as they change throughout development, they support successful negotiation of the developmental tasks just reviewed: self-awareness, self-management, social awareness, relationship/social skills, and responsible decision making (Payton et al., 2000; Zins et al., 2007). All components of SEL are likely interrelated; because of this overlap, the delineations made here between SEL competencies are solely my own. Furthermore, all the following assertions about these competencies' relation with positive outcomes are evidence-based; although space precludes exhaustive citations, interested readers can refer to Denham, Brown, and Domitrovich (2010) or contact me.

Self-awareness includes the ability to assess personal feelings, interests, values and strengths accurately. This aspect of SEL also includes identifying and labeling one's feelings. Even preschoolers have a well-defined, relatively stable sense of self (e.g., whether they are becoming adept with numbers and letters), and these aspects of self-awareness have been shown to relate to achievement. Children in the early years of schooling continue to develop a sense of their academic capability, and evaluations of self-perceived academic competence are positively correlated with seeking out experiences in, and performing well at, academic tasks. In summary, a child's or adolescent's perceived self-competence, as well as self-esteem or self-efficacy, may lay the groundwork for future academic motivation and accomplishments.

Self-management includes the ability to handle one's emotions, attention, and behavior in productive ways—especially in terms of being aware of feelings, monitoring them, expressing them appropriately, and modifying them when necessary, so that they aid rather than impede the ways in which the child is able to cope with varying situations. Such self-management is related to children's school adjustment and academic achievement. Specifically, children and adolescents who have difficulties dealing with negative emotions may not have the personal resources to focus on learning, whereas those who can maintain a positive emotional tone might be able to remain positively engaged with, and successful, at classroom tasks.

Social awareness includes the ability to take others' perspectives, understand their feelings, and empathize with them, appreciating others' similarities and differences. Children's constant attempts to understand their own and others' behaviors and emotions convey crucial interpersonal information that can guide interaction. Inability to interpret emotions can make the classroom a confusing, overwhelming place. More and more, contemporaneous and longitudinal links are found between both school adjustment and academic success, and young children's emotion knowledge (i.e., accurate identification of expressions, situations, and causes of emotions; emotion knowledge has also been shown to be negatively related to adolescents' behavior problems).

The goal of *relationship skills* is to promote positive and effective exchanges with others and, ultimately, relationships that last over time. Numerous skills are crucial, including making positive overtures to play with others; initiating and maintaining conversations; cooperating; and developing friendship skills, including asserting oneself, resolving conflict, and addressing others' needs through negotiation. Numerous researchers have found that the social skills constituting this component of SEL are related to academic success (e.g., sometimes even when contributions of earlier achievement were accounted for).

Responsible decision making becomes important as everyday social interactions of preschoolers increase in frequency and complexity. Children must learn to analyze social situations, identify problems, set prosocial goals, and determine effective ways to solve differences that arise within their peer group. As children age and their SEL-related developmental tasks become more complex, responsible decision making increasingly includes making ethical decisions, complying with classroom rules, resisting peer pressure, and controlling disruptive behavior reflect such responsibility. Elements of young children's social problem solving are linked to their school adjustment, as well as academic functioning. Older children's social problem-solving skills are related to their grade point average, often with important covariates controlled. Choosing a prosocial response when facing adversity appears to assist in academic success.

Addressing SEL Needs of Children and Adolescents

SEL is therefore integral to key developmental tasks from preschool through adolescence and is often related to children's success in the school context. Research reviewed here suggests that when asked how to increase children's performance across academic domains and overall well-being, instead of automatically turning to literacy or numeracy, educators and parents should ask the questions: *What can we do to foster their SEL? What are our children's social–emotional competencies?* To meet children's SEL needs, we must decide what constitutes optimal development in self-awareness, self-management, social awareness, relationship skills, and responsible decision making, and how can we determine children's competency in each area.

Goals and Benchmarks: Standards

Standards, as statements about "what students should know and be able to do as a result of educational instruction" (Dusenbury, Zadrazil, & Mart, 2011, p. 3; see also Dusenbury et al., Chapter 35, this volume) reflect key stakeholders' decisions about optimal development. Standards are therefore the foundation through which states and other local education agencies determine educational goals, select evidence-based methods and support teachers' high-quality instruction to meet these goals, and monitor student progress toward the goals via assessment (as in the pivotal placement of standards in Figure 19.1).

Because SEL is so important, standards in this area are as crucial as those in any other area (and, I would argue, possibly *more important*). However, in the national arena, standards for SEL are few and unclear. Specifically, the Common Core State Standards (Common Core State Standards Initiative, 2010a, 2010b; National Research Council (NRC; 2012) are being adopted by 45 states as of this writing. They include some attempt at SEL-related skills within interpersonal and intrapersonal domains: The "interpersonal domain" includes two clusters of competencies—teamwork and collaboration, and leadership; the "intrapersonal domain" includes three clusters of competencies—intellectual openness, work ethic/conscientiousness, and positive self-evaluation.

Although it is true that the interpersonal domain addresses competencies such as responsibility, conflict resolution, communication, and collaboration, and the intrapersonal domain includes flexibility, initiative, appreciation of diversity, and metacognition, these do not translate into or parallel SEL as described here. In fact, the NRC (2012) acknowledges that cognitive competencies have been addressed more extensively than have interpersonal and intrapersonal ones, which have been covered more unevenly.

Moreover, inter- and intrapersonal standards are not covered in the assessment tools being developed to evaluate attainment of benchmarks in the Common Core standards (Partnership for Assessment of Readiness for College and Career [PARCC], n.d.; Smarter Balance Assessment Consortium, n.d.). In its report, the NRC (2012) asserts that for SEL competencies (i.e., what is termed "intrapersonal" and "interpersonal" domains, in which the NRC considers conscientiousness and antisocial behavior to be the best predictors of academic outcomes), we still need research to develop and use appropriate SEL assessment tools.

So Common Core State Standards do not sufficiently or clearly address SEL needs, either in terms of standards or assessment. Where does this leave the search for SEL assessment tools? To unite SEL standards, assessment, and instruction as in Figure 19.1, one must search out exemplars of SEL standards that as clearly as possible cover the five SEL domains. To that end, Dusenbury and colleagues (Chapter 35, this volume) have described states' SEL standards. They have reported that the prekindergarten age level has the most well-developed, widely disseminated SEL standards in 49 states, with states often referencing benchmarks from Head Start and/or the National Association for the Education of Young Children. As for SEL standards for older children (K–12), there have been three different approaches: (1) free-standing, comprehensive social and emotional learning standards; (2) free-standing standards focusing on one or more dimensions of social and emotional learning; and (3) integration of goals and benchmarks related to SEL within learning standards for other domains (Dusenbury et al., 2011).

Free-standing SEL standards are ideal because they lift up and clarify key SEL competencies; not all states, and certainly not Common Core as it currently stands, have such focus. Several states have, however, adopted excellent free-standing SEL standards (although not always across grade levels). The Illinois model is a good example of K–12 free-standing SEL standards (Illinois State Board of Education, 2006), each SEL standard for early and late elementary, middle school, and early or late high school is organized around three goals that take in all the aspects of SEL that are enumerated here:

Goal 1 is to develop self-awareness and self-management skills to achieve school and life success.
Goal 2 is to use social awareness and interpersonal (i.e., relationship) skills to establish and maintain positive relationships.
Goal 3 is to demonstrate decision-making skills and responsible behaviors in personal, school, and community contexts.

Each goal is accompanied by at least three standards.

The very existence of SEL standards such as those in Illinois is encouraging. Clearly, these standards closely follow the current conception of SEL and could guide both assessment and instruction, along with promoting the synergistic relations between the two, as put forth in Figure 19.1. When SEL standards are in place, it becomes more necessary to develop and/or adopt SEL assessment tools. Before detailing the criteria by which we can evaluate such assessments for use in educational settings for information gathering and decision making within schools, it is necessary to describe the functions that SEL assessment could (and should) take in the classroom. We need SEL assessment, but exactly when and how do we plan to use it?

Functions of SEL Assessment

In educational settings, we can use SEL assessment tools for screening, formative, interim, and summative functions. *Screening* allows for implementation of a three-tiered model of instruction—from universally providing SEL instruction to all children to targeted interventions for those at risk, to individualized work for those presenting persistent challenges; screening cutoffs can demarcate targeted and at-risk children whose educational needs may differ from those of children not at risk.

Formative assessment can be seen as assessment *for* learning, minute-by-minute, that is integrated into instruction (NRC, 2012). Such assessment makes learning goals clear to students because it is linked directly to the current unit of instruction. Classroom teachers use such assessment to identify gaps in children's skills, so that they can work together with pupils to improve student SEL. Furthermore, the tasks presented in formative assessment may vary from one student to another, depending on the student's current SEL competencies. In short, formative assessment is used to monitor students' progress, and to involve students and give them feedback (Perie, Marion, & Gong, 2009). Recent meta-analytic findings on the use of formative assessment in non-SEL content areas indicate that its use is associated with positive student outcomes, especially when teachers are given professional development in its use, and when it is delivered via computer-based systems (Kingston & Nash, 2011).

Formative assessment can be more a criterion-referenced endeavor (with results interpretable in terms of a defined set of learning tasks, e.g., standards), than a norm-referenced one (i.e., with results interpretable in terms of an individual's relative standing in some known group). Given that some writers assert that formative assessment need not be limited by certain requirements of interim and summative assessments (e.g., psychometric reliability), it may be that teachers can use actual SEL standards for formative assessment. Alternatively, some of the assessment tools I describe here may also be useful for formative assessment.

Interim assessment has some characteristics of formative assessment (e.g., it may possibly be used for instructional purposes) and some characteristics of summative assessment (e.g., it is often used for evaluative and predictive purposes). As part of its hybrid nature, it is often administered by teachers; a crucial identifying characteristic is that, unlike formative assessment, interim assessment is summarized at the classroom, school, or district level (Perie et al., 2009); it is performed less frequently than formative assessment, but often mid-year or more often, so that results can be used during an academic year.

Non-SEL interim assessments have often been based on standards-based benchmarks (thereby allowing for alignment of curriculum, instruction, and professional development; Bulkley, Oláh, & Blanc, 2010), and serve three functions. First, educators can use the results of interim assessment to tailor instruction and curriculum to meet overall classroom needs. Second, interim assessments can provide information about whether classrooms of students are meeting specific goals, so that at a school- or systemwide level, educators can make standardized programmatic level adjustments to improve instruction and, ultimately, student performance. Third, interim assessment can predict each student's likelihood of meeting criteria on summative assessment, and therefore inform decisions at both the classroom level and beyond.

Theoretically, then, interim assessment should influence practice at the classroom, school, and district levels. Some argue, however, that in practice, interim assessment often requires generating, storing, and reporting test score data that remain disconnected from instruction (Burch, 2010). The important step of *doing something* with the assessment data unfortunately can too easily be obviated (Halverson, 2010); even when teachers do use these data, they may unintentionally focus on teaching to the test. Most importantly, these issues have not yet been systematically addressed with SEL assessment.

Finally, *summative assessment* is assessment *of* learning, and currently, along with interim assessment, is often associated with high-stakes accountability assessment. Summative assessments are often given one time at the end of the semester or school year to evaluate students' performance against a defined set of content standards. These assessments are typically given statewide (but could be more narrow, as in districtwide, or more broad, as in national administration), and are usually used as part of an accountability program or to otherwise inform policy. They could also be teacher-administered end-of-unit or end-of-semester tests that are used solely for student evaluation, or used as measures of pre/post change in response to programming.

Given these functions of assessment and attendant concerns, I now describe the criteria by which we should choose high-quality SEL assessment for potential usability for each function. Thus, criteria for "best-bet" measures are now outlined, followed by choices of assessment tools and commentary on how to plan effective SEL assessment in schools.

Criteria for SEL Assessment Tools

We know that some states—but not yet, at least fully and coherently, the Common Core State Standards—are acknowledging the importance of SEL competencies and assessment. In order to support these states as fully as possible in the current climate of accountability and to move the field forward, we need to determine whether there are adequate extant SEL assessment tools. Using quality assessment tools helps to ensure that we make better decisions about how to facilitate children's SEL functioning. Denham, Wyatt, Bassett, Echeverria, and Knox (2009) and Kendziora, Weissberg, and Dusenbury (2011) have enumerated criteria for SEL assessment tools specifically for educational usage (most, if not all, would hold for other domains of assessment and for research usage). Several are paramount.

First, because any assessment starts with adequate documentation for the user, to choose an assessment tool, one must be able to judge its content as appropriate, before one is able to move on to more technical and pragmatic concerns. Hence, SEL assessment tools should have a manual that contains a description of the measure, the SEL constructs assessed, and assignment of items to scales; it is helpful, furthermore, if a more detailed behavioral definition is given for each item; very few SEL assessments include rubrics such as this. The manual should also make it clear whether and how the measure is useful for multiple purposes (screening, formative, etc.). More and more assessment tools are making these possible uses clear, but this area of concern is far from systematized and still requires much planning from users. Specifically for SEL purposes, documentation should make clear that the assessment is developmentally appropriate. Families of measures that cut across age periods are desirable; several "best-bet" measures have different forms for different age levels. I would add that clear delineation of *all* the specific SEL competencies within the model presented here, with sufficient numbers of items per skill to be useful for formative assessment, is very desirable. Furthermore, the presence of a screening tool parallel to the assessment tool can be very useful.

Second, qualities of the actual assessment tool must be considered. Psychometric properties must be excellent; assessment tools should have at least adequate reliability and validity in all their forms, and as far as possible should be fair, unbiased, and generalizable across ages and demographic groups. All measures cited in this chapter meet psychometric requirements, but information on generalizability is sometimes less complete. For example, norms and psychometric data for measures are needed for diverse samples representing U.S. demographics, with cultural sensitivity regarding the norms for various SEL behaviors in different cultures. Native language and dialect must be considered when selecting and using self- or parent reports. However, *most* assessment tools, SEL or academic, fall short of adequately meeting at least some of these diversity needs.

Third, we must think about utility; it is helpful for assessments to have benchmarks or external anchors, such as norms and/or standards, to assist in meaningful interpretations of scores and their change over time, so that assessment tools are useful in tracking the results of instruction and programming. Also in terms of utility, such tools should be administrable within a reasonable time frame (e.g., 10–20 minutes). The acceptability of administration time in part depends on whether all children in a school or classroom, or only select children, are assessed. Finally, where possible and for most uses, electronic administration and scoring are desired because they are faster and less expensive than paper-based administration and hand scoring. All of these criteria regarding utility are reflected in cost: Costs of assessment tools in terms of completion time, skills and equipment required, test forms, and/or scoring must be reasonable.

Fourth, where possible, multiple informants of the same dimension's measurement are recommended, given that behavior is often rater- and context-specific, and to ward off problems of bias; in the case of school-based SEL assessment, aggregating information from multiple sources (e.g., a subset of teachers, school personnel, mental health professionals, parents, and/or, students themselves) could be especially powerful.

Tools for Assessing SEL in Educational Settings

A number of assessment tools have been developed and evaluated as useful for determining the ways in which SEL competencies promote various positive outcomes from the preschool period through adolescence. Many of these instruments have been included in compendia, such as those of Denham, Hamre, and Ji (2010), Denham and colleagues (2009), Haggerty, Elgin, and Woolley (2011), Ringwalt (2008), and Sosna and Mastergeorge (2005); recent reviews also exist (e.g., Crowe, Beauchamp, Catroppa, & Anderson, 2011; Humphrey et al., 2011). In general, the compendia are targeted at either research (e.g., Denham et al., 2009; Denham, Hamre, et al., 2010) or applied settings (e.g., Haggerty et al., 2011; Ringwalt, 2008; Sosna & Mastergeorge, 2005), and cover ages from infancy (e.g., Ringwalt, 2008) to adulthood (Denham et al., 2009). The reviewers have searched for SEL measures, usually for research purposes, across a broad range of criteria and have listed them for their colleagues' benefit. Usually (but not universally) both compendia and reviews categorize measures by the developmental domains covered, intended uses, age ranges, details of administration, scoring and interpretation, length of time the measure's completion requires, and diversity issues. These materials form an important adjunct to this chapter.

What is obvious from these compendia and reviews is that SEL competencies have been measured via a wide variety of mechanisms, including informant ratings, direct assessment, observation, and structured or unstructured interviews (Denham, Hamre, et al., 2010). For assessing many SEL competencies, direct assessment and observation can be invaluable (Denham, 2006). In many applied cases, however, feasibility is an overriding issue: The time required for direct assessments, observations, and interviews, as well as resources required for training, establishing observer/coder reliability, and coding or scoring, make these tools most practical for research usage (but see McKown, Chapter 21, this volume, who makes the point that at the level of services for at-risk or targeted children, such assessment tools are not only feasible but also quite useful).

We await the development of practical, usable, feasible, and theory-based direct and observational assessment tools. At this point in time, rating systems are likely to be more feasible, and when carefully crafted to meet as many of the previously referenced criteria as possible, are appropriate for educational settings (as well as useful for research purposes); therefore, multi-informant rating scales are reviewed in this chapter.

Specific SEL Assessment Tools

Along with Kendziora and colleagues (2011), and after study of the compendia and reviews cited, I have chosen to describe several assessment tools that fulfill many of the criteria already set forward. The tools are exemplary of quality SEL assessment for educational settings (i.e., the list may not be considered exhaustive), and include the Devereux Scales, Social–Emotional Assets and Resilience Scales, Behavioral and Emotional Rating Scale, Second Edition, and Social Skills Information System Rating Scales. Table 19.1 shows, for each measure, the appropriate age level, informant(s), core SEL competencies addressed, and qualities such as generalizability, utility, and types available (e.g., screening, summative). Table 19.1 can be used to begin the choice of measures, with more details indicated in the following sections.

Devereux Early Childhood Assessment, Second Edition

For PreK evaluations, the Devereux Early Childhood Assessment, Second Edition (DECA) is a nationally normed assessment that evaluates within-child protective factors associated with resiliency in preschool children (LeBuffe & Naglieri, 1999a). The assessment checklist can be completed by both parents and teachers, in either English or Spanish, and evaluates the presence of 27 positive behaviors common in preschool children (along with 10 problem behaviors, which are not a focus here but potentially may be important in certain situations). Scales include Attachment, Initiative, and Self-Regulation (important in their own right, but not aligning excellently with the SEL model put forward here). DECA-C is a Clinical version, also completed by a par-

TABLE 19.1. Summary Information on SEL Assessment Tools Described in This Chapter

	When and by whom		Core SEL competencies addressed					Qualities of assessment tool			Utility			Types of assessment available			
Assessment tool	Grade	Informant	Self-awareness	Self-management	Social awareness	Relationship skills	Responsible Decision Making	Adequacy of manual [a]	Psychometric qualities	Generalizability/ diversity issues[b]	Cost[c]	Time required	Electronic administration	Screener	Formative	Interim	Summative
BERS-2	K–12	T, P	✓	✓	✓	✓		✓	✓	✓	$198	10 min		✓	~[d]		~[d]
P-BERS	K	T, P		✓		✓		✓	✓	~	$109	10 min		✓	?	?	?
DECA	Preschool	T, P		✓		✓		✓	✓	✓	$200[e]	10 min	✓[f]		?	✓	✓
DESSA	K– 8	T, P	✓	✓	✓	✓	✓	✓	✓	✓	$116	10 min	✓	✓	✓	✓	✓
SEARS	K–12	T, P, C, A	✓	✓	✓	✓		✓	✓	~	$15–$305	15–20 min	Scoring only	✓	✓	✓	✓
SSIS-RS	Preschool–high school	T, P, C, A		✓	✓	✓	✓	✓	✓	✓	$261–$342	10– 25 min	Scoring only	~	✓	✓	✓

Note. DECA, Devereux Early Childhood Assessment; DESSA, Devereux Student Strengths Assessment; BERS, Behavioral and Emotional Rating Scale, 2nd edition; P-BERS, Behavioral and Emotional Rating Scale, Preschool Version; SEARS, Social–Emotional Assets and Resilience Scale; SSIS, Social Skills Improvement System Rating Scales; K, kindergarten; T, teacher; P, parent; C, child; A, adolescent. ✓, quality present; ~, quality partially present based on available information; ?, unknown as of this writing.

[a]Rubric/item-by-item descriptions not available for any measure, except partially for the DESSA.

[b]Partial presence of generalizability due to nationally representative norms and/or Spanish form for parents, but other information lacking.

[c]Costs depend on whether multiple informant versions are purchased, for example; publishers should be contacted.

[d]Potential for use in instruction and program evaluation for groups and individuals.

[e]DECA-C price = $126 for use by mental health professionals.

[f]e-DECA license for both DECA and DESSA = $250/year.

ent or teacher, that allows for examination of a broadband Behavioral Concerns Scale and four problem behavior subscales; it also includes a guide that connects results to targeted intervention strategies (LeBuffe & Naglieri, 1999b). Recent investigations of the DECA show (1) reliability and moderate agreement for both the English and Spanish versions for teachers and parents of impoverished, ethnically diverse preschoolers and (2) good reliability and factor structure similar to that of the norming sample (Jaberg, Dixon, & Weis, 2009; Ogg, Brinkman, Dedrick, & Carlson, 2010; but see Oades-Sese, Kaliski, & Weiss, 2010). The DECA-C, furthermore, is not prone to either false positives or false negatives.

Both scales fall within the desired 10- to 20-minute time frame for assessment, and Web-based administration, scoring, and interpretation is available. Because the DECA and DECA-C include norming information (i.e., standard scores and percentile ranks), they can be used for interim and summative assessment. The authors assert that these measures could conceivably also be used as formative assessment for progress monitoring and individualized planning; in the second edition, the ability to perform individualized item analyses has been added to support such usage. Furthermore, comparisons of raters and pretest–posttest comparisons are possible with electronic scoring. The measures can also be used in research and to evaluate SEL programming. However, lack of alignment with the current SEL model is a concern.

Devereux Student Strengths Assessment

The Devereux Student Strengths Assessment (DESSA; LeBuffe, Shapiro, & Naglieri, 2009) and four-item accompanying screener, the DESSA-Mini (Naglieri, LeBuffe, & Shapiro, 2011) are behavior rating scales for elementary school-age children (K–8), completed by parents and/or teachers. The DESSA measures child strengths that map very directly onto the SEL skills described here. Specifically, it provides ratings on 72 items across eight scales, including Optimistic Thinking, Self-Management, Goal-Directed Behavior, Self-Awareness, Social Awareness, Personal Responsibility, Decision Making, and Relationship Skills. A social–emotional composite score is also included, which is based on a combination of the eight scales. Web-based administration, scoring, and interpretation are available.

Recent independent investigations indicate evidence of convergent and divergent validity for the main measure, as well as reliability, lack of false positives and negatives, and predictive power of the DESSA-Mini (Nickerson & Fishman, 2009). The DESSA requires 15 minutes, and the DESSA-Mini is touted as a 1-minute screener.

Given its level of comprehensiveness and focus on child strengths, and its fit with other criteria listed here, the DESSA provides useful information for intervention planning and can also be applied to create classroom profiles that can be used for subsequent prevention strategies; scores can also be used for ongoing progress monitoring. Thus, this measure could conceivably be used for interim and formative functions, as well as summative functions, because of its standardization. High school students cannot be rated, but for children and early adolescents, this measure appears very promising.

Social–Emotional Assets and Resilience Scale

The Social–Emotional Assets and Resilience Scale (SEARS) includes a screener, as well as 52- to 54-item Teacher (SEARS-T) Parent (SEARS-P), Child (SEARS-C) and Adolescent (SEARS-A) versions, and examines SEL from a conceptual framework that is close, but not identical, to that sketched here: responsibility, social competence, empathy, and self-regulation. K–12 children can be rated; both the SEARS-T and SEARS-P (Merrell, Cohn, & Tom, 2011; Merrell, Felver-Gant, & Tom, 2011) have demonstrated reliability, validity based on convergent methods, expected subgroup differences (e.g., gender), and robust factor structure (although responsibility and self-regulation are grouped together for the SEARS-P).

The SEARS screener also shows promising reliability (internal consistency and test–retest reliability) and concurrent validity, along with differentiation of groups of children receiving or not receiving special education (Nese, Doerner, Kaye, Romer, & Merrell, 2011). This family of measures does not conform completely to the current SEL model, but it captures several SEL components and conforms to time requirements (i.e., taking 15-20 minutes), and a scoring program, as well as a Spanish version for parents, is available.

Given its level of comprehensiveness and focus on child strengths, the SEARS measures (although somewhat less conforming to the SEL model than the DESSA) provide useful information for intervention planning and can also be applied to create student profiles that can be used for ongoing progress monitoring and subsequent prevention strategies; Score Reports, Progress-Monitoring Reports, and Integrated Score Reports are available for both long and short forms. Thus, like the DESSA, this measure could conceivably be used for interim and formative functions, as well as summative functions, because of its standardization. The publisher notes that the screener is practical for repeated assessment (i.e., formative/interim progress monitoring) or class- or schoolwide screening of students, and the authors assert that program evaluation and research functions can be met by the measure as well.

Social Skills Improvement System Rating Scales

The Social Skills Improvement System Rating Scales (SSIS-RS; Gresham & Elliott, 2008) is a set of rating scales designed to assess children's social behavior and assist in the implementation of interventions, which is part of the whole system. The measure is an updating of the widely used and positively evaluated Social Skills Rating Scales (Gresham & Elliott, 1990; see also Elliott, Frey, & Davies, Chapter 20, this volume); improvements include updated norms, four additional subscales for a broader conceptualization of social–emotional development, greater overlap across forms, validity scales, improved psychometric properties, Spanish versions of forms, and direct links to intervention (Crosby, 2011; Frey, Elliott, & Gresham, 2011; Gresham, Elliott, Vance, & Cook, 2011). The system includes rating scales for teachers and parents covering the PreK to 18 years age range, and self-report versions for students at the grade school level and beyond. Scales cover Social Skills and Academic Competence, as well as Problem Behaviors (SSIS; Gresham & Elliott, 2008).

All versions include cooperation, assertion, and self-control subscales, and the parent version also includes responsibility and empathy scales. Thus, the measure accesses four of five areas of SEL noted here: self-management, social awareness, responsible decision making, and relationship skills. Although the measure falls within the 10- to 25-minute time window for completion, there is no screener. There is an option for computer scoring. Because the SSIS-RS includes norming information (i.e., standard scores and percentile ranks), it can be used for interim and summative assessment. Given that it includes frequency and importance ratings of each item, it could conceivably also be used for formative assessment.

Behavioral and Emotional Rating Scale

The Behavioral and Emotional Rating Scale (BERS-2; Benner, Beaudoin, Mooney, Uhing, & Pierce, 2008; Buckley, Ryser, Reid, & Epstein, 2006; Drevon, 2011; Epstein, Mooney, Ryser, & Pierce, 2004) and the Preschool BERS (P-BERS; Epstein, Synhorst, Cress, & Allen, 2009; Griffith et al., 2010), are strength-based SEL instruments. Both show robust, replicable factor structures, as well as reliability and validity (i.e., both convergent and subgroup difference validity for Teacher, Parent, and Youth self-report versions; the publisher notes that school psychologists, as well as children's mental health, juvenile justice, and social service workers may also complete the BERS-2). A Spanish version is available for parent completion.

The BERS-2 and P-BERS versions' fit with the SEL model espoused here is less than perfect, but there are enough points of intersection to make the measures potentially useful. Their factors are Emotional Regulation, School Readiness, Social Confidence, and Family Involvement for the P-BERS, and Interpersonal Strengths, Family Involvement, Intrapersonal Strengths, School Functioning, and Affective Strengths for the BERS-2 Parent and Youth versions (the Youth version also includes a Career Strength scale). The measure takes about

10 minutes to complete. Gonzalez, Ryser, Epstein, and Shwery (2006) have found support for use of the BERS-2 with Latino parents. In terms of any difficulties, Drevon (2011) considers the item sample (42) for the P-BERS too limited for use in formative assessment for instruction and fine-tuning interventions, and expressed concern that the measure still lacks (as of that writing) parent norms. However, the publisher suggests that the BERS-2 can be used for screening and summative/outcome reasons.

Conclusions

It should be clear by now that SEL assessment is a complex matter that requires actions from a number of simultaneous directions, by a number of constituents, and that to some extent it lags behind current assessment methods in other domains. Along with Kendziora and colleagues (2011), I can make several recommendations that, I hope, identify clear action steps for SEL measurement by professionals and educators. First and foremost, it is imperative that schools, school systems, and states evaluate the system depicted in Figure 19.1 from the standpoint of SEL, and determine the specific, defined needs and functions of *their usage* of SEL assessment (after creating free-standing standards, I hope). Presumably, the goal of SEL assessment is to elucidate students' SEL strengths and weaknesses, and assist in making data-informed decisions that help to facilitate children's SEL, thereby fostering broad, long-term positive outcomes. The means by which these outcomes can take place is via planning assessment-based classroom instruction and broader SEL programming. These goals, as illustrated in Figure 19.1, are really the only reason to undertake the process of SEL assessment, which requires personal and economic resources from everyone concerned, from the students, to the teachers, to administrators (Kendziora et al., 2011).

Users also need to distinguish among screening, formative, interim, and summative assessment based on their specific needs. For example, Naglieri and colleagues (2011) have argued that screeners can be sensitive enough to use for formative progress monitoring, but others (e.g., Drevon, 2011) assert that any assessment needs sufficient items to inform instruction in the moment. Similarly, in examining the boundaries of formative/interim usage, users and assessment professionals need to decide whether a given assessment is really able to perform the dual functions of predicting future outcomes (e.g., interim assessment) while simultaneously and microanalytically contributing to teachers' understanding of what to do day-by-day with a classroom or particular child (formative assessment). This may be no mean task; it is not always easy to discriminate between formative and interim assessment in any case (Perie et al., 2009).

In fact, the differences among formative, interim, and summative assessment may in part reside more in the minds of theoreticians than in practice, in terms of the information derived (Bulkley et al., 2010). In theory, any technology that enables educators at school, district, and/or state levels to store data and generate multiple reports for multiple audiences allows them not only to gather data from students but also to analyze it in ways that serve the different purposes. Thus, developers and users of SEL assessments should work together to ascertain the uses to which specific tools are to be used, and the ability of any single assessment to perform multiple assessment functions. Clearly the field needs to resolve these issues—even if these resolutions are somewhat parochial—surrounding how any SEL assessment is best used.

After such functional decisions are made, the strengths and limitations of individual assessment tools must be recognized, and choices must be made within states, school systems, and schools as to which tool or tools to use. I have illustrated what I and others consider to be useful SEL assessment tools for educational settings, but each set of stakeholders must evaluate tools to use given their own specific needs. Moreover, it should be reiterated that, with McKown (Chapter 21, this volume) and others, I believe that creation of theory-based, direct assessment and observation tools that are psychometrically sound, feasible to administer, and lead to coherent action by educators constitutes a crucial challenge and goal for our field. Knowledge of specific children's performance of specific SEL competencies, *in context*, could be instrumental in creating educational action plans for them. Moreover, some argue that rating systems are prone to subjectivity (Kyllonen, 2012).

However, given the current state of affairs in the assessment of SEL competencies, and the parameters set up earlier in this chapter (e.g., that at this point in time multi-informant rating systems are most feasible), how can the rather daunting task of assessment selection be accomplished? One method is by returning to the criteria enumerated earlier following Denham and colleagues (2009) and Kendziora and colleagues (2011), and creating a system to check, in detail, that these criteria are met as best as possible. In that vein, Li, Marion, Perie, and Gong (2010) developed a potentially useful evaluation method that can help state- and district-level decision makers evaluate any interim assessment system, but their perspective seems applicable to all types of assessment. Thus, the steps in this evaluation tool require description; they include (1) *examination of any assessment tool's purpose and use;* (2) *test development and documentation at the item-, test-, and multiple-test levels*; (3) *administration and inclusion*; and (4) *utility*.

In concert with the recommendations already made here, their instrument first includes *examination of any assessment tool's purpose and use*; it is crucial that users articulate the mechanisms and processes by which SEL assessment will foster positive student outcomes, as well as the target population they intend to assess, and to ensure that any assessment tool was developed with those students in mind.

Li and colleagues (2010) next consider *test development and documentation at the item-, test-, and multiple-test levels.* Items should be examined to ensure that they map onto the needed content area; tests should be scrutinized to determine mapping to standards (or subdomains of SEL, where standards are not present), number of items per standard, psychometric adequacy, as well as scoring and interpretation. Multiple test-level criteria refer to considering how often to administer an assessment, a decision that is tied intimately to its purpose and also to characteristics of both the tool itself and the instruction/programming to which it contributes (e.g., How are its multiple administrations tied to the sequence of curricular instruction? How have test developers taken potential heterotypical development into account?).

Next, Li and colleagues (2010) address *administration and inclusion:* To what degree are assessment tools appropriate for children with special needs, and when used as self- or parent reports, what considerations are made for English as a second language? Their next category of evaluation is test scores and reports. For example, it is important to use appropriate types of scores for varying uses; criterion-referenced scores, such as attainment of standards, might be appropriate for formative assessment, with norm-referenced scores more useful for interim and summative assessment. Score reports are also very important: Both individual and aggregated reports should be available to various stakeholders and provide information aligned with test purposes. The assessment tools reviewed here are all working toward this last goal; the more information that teachers and other stakeholders (e.g., parents, principals) can get from each tool, the better—and the assessment report is the perfect means to impart such information.

As already noted, *test utility* is also important and forms the next aspect of Li and colleagues' (2010) means of evaluating assessment tools. Any SEL assessment must fit with curriculum, instructional supports for students, and professional development for teachers, which suggests that the task for stakeholders is far more complex than merely picking SEL assessment; on the contrary, planning must include the entire system depicted in Figure 19.1. As Halverson (2010) noted, similar to Li and colleagues' call for a theory of action for assessment, educators must be able to translate results of SEL assessments into usable information, decisions, and instructional action. Potential utility should be evaluated *prior to* implementation, with actual utility determined *after* implementation in an ongoing, dynamic manner. Finally, practicality and logistics, including but not limited to flexibility of administration, ease of installation and maintenance of an assessment system, ease of use for all informants, and degree of technical support, are considerations for school and district leaders. Adequate resources and training for teachers and others are crucial, so that assessment is fair and is used constructively. For example, assessors should be given training on the meaning of each item according to the manual, and on how to judge waypoints on each rating scale; such steps are very rarely taken.

The application of these criteria is a vital step. Li and colleagues (2010) gave examples in their article of uses for each of these criteria, often by accessing documentation from assessment publishers, and included in their article customizable tables for each step of evaluating the criteria, which can be utilized by end users of assessment tools. In these tables they also include subcriteria and narrative descriptions of evaluation of each main criterion. Such a tool could be very useful in evaluating SEL assessments. I would recommend that users and assessment professionals come together to make decisions about what SEL assessment tool to use in any specific state, city, or other local education agency, by choosing several (potentially from those suggested here) and going through Li and colleagues' advantageous process to evaluate them.

In short, much work needs to be done—from the very acknowledgment of the importance of SEL to the creation of standards and better assessment tools, to the connections with assessment and instruction, and professional development for teachers in both SEL instruction and assessment. Although these efforts are likely to be difficult, the rewards promise to be well worth it.

References

Benner, G. J., Beaudoin, K., Mooney, P., Uhing, B. M., & Pierce, C. D. (2008). Convergent validity with the BERS-2 Teacher Rating Scale and the Achenbach Teacher's Report Form: A replication and extension. *Journal of Child and Family Studies, 17,* 427–436.

Brackett, M. A., Rivers, S. E., & Salovey, P. (2011). Emotional intelligence: Implications for personal, social, academic, and workplace success. *Social and Personality Psychology Compass, 5,* 88–103.

Buckley, J. A., Ryser, G., Reid, R., & Epstein, M. H. (2006). Confirmatory factor analysis of the Behavioral and Emotional Rating Scale–2 (BERS-2) Parent and Youth Rating Scales. *Journal of Child and Family Studies, 15,* 27–37.

Bulkley, K. E., Oláh, L. N., & Blanc, S. (2010). Introduction to the special issue on benchmarks for success: Interim assessments as a strategy for educational improvement. *Peabody Journal of Education, 85,* 115–124.

Burch, P. (2010). The bigger picture: Institutional perspectives on interim assessment technologies. *Peabody Journal of Education, 85,* 147–162.

Common Core State Standards Initiative. (2010a). *The standards: English language arts standards.* Washington, DC: National Governors Association and Council of Chief State School Officers. Retrieved from *www.corestandards.org/the-standards/english-language-arts-standards.*

Common Core State Standards Initiative. (2010b). *The standards: Mathematics standards.* Washington, DC: National Governors Association and Council of Chief State School Officers. Retrieved December 28, 2012, from *www.corestandards.org/assets/ccssi_math%20standards.pdf.*

Crosby, J. W. (2011). Test review: In F. M. Gresham & S. N. Elliott (Eds.), Social Skills Improvement System Rating Scales. *Journal of Psychoeducational Assessment, 29,* 292–296.

Crowe, L. M., Beauchamp, M. H., Catroppa, C., & Anderson, V. (2011). Social function assessment tools for children and adolescents: A systematic review from 1988 to 2010. *Clinical Psychology Review, 31,* 767–785.

Denham, S. A. (2006). Social–emotional competence as support for school readiness: What is it and how do we assess it? [Special issue]. *Early Education and Development: Measurement of School Readiness, 17,* 57–89.

Denham, S. A., & Brown, C. A., & Domitrovich, C. E. (2010). "Plays nice with others": Social–emotional learning and academic success [Special issue]. *Early Education and Development, 21,* 652–680.

Denham, S., Hamre, B. K., & Ji, P. (2010). *Compendium of social–emotional learning and associated assessment measures.* Chicago: Collaborative for Academic, Social, and Emotional Learning. Retrieved December 28, 2013, from *http://casel.org/publications/compendium-of-sel-assessment-tools.*

Denham, S. A., Wyatt, T. M., Bassett, H. H., Echeverria, D., & Knox, S. S. (2009). Assessing social–emotional development in children from a longitudinal perspective. *Journal of Epidemiology and Community Health, 63*(Suppl. 1), I37–I52.

Drevon, D. D. (2011). Test review. *Journal of Psychoeducational Assessment, 29,* 84–88.

Durlak, J. A., Weissberg, R. P., Dymnicki, A. B., Taylor, R. D., & Schellinger, K. B. (2011). The impact of enhancing students' social and emotional learning: A meta-analysis of school-based universal interventions. *Child Development, 82,* 405–432.

Dusenbury, L., Zadrazil, J., & Mart, A. (2011). *State learning standards to advance social and emotional learning: The state scan of social and emotional learning standards, preschool through high school.* Chicago: Collaborative for Academic, Social, and Emotional Learning.

Epstein, M. H., Mooney, P., Ryser, G., & Pierce, C. D. (2004). Validity and reliability of the Behavioral and Emotional Rating Scale (2nd Edition): Youth Rating Scale. *Research on Social Work Practice, 14*, 358–367.

Epstein, M. H., Synhorst, L. L., Cress, C. J., & Allen, E. A. (2009). Development and standardization of a test to measure the emotional and behavioral strengths of preschool children. *Journal of Emotional and Behavioral Disorders, 17*, 29–37.

Frey, J. R., Elliott, S. N., & Gresham, F. M. (2011). Preschoolers' social skills: Advances in assessment for intervention using social behavior ratings. *School Mental Health, 3*, 179–190.

Gonzalez, J. E., Ryser, G. R., Epstein, M. H., & Shwery, C. S. (2006). The Behavioral and Emotional Rating Scale–Second Edition: Parent Rating Scale (BERS-II PRS): A Hispanic cross-cultural reliability study. *Assessment for Effective Intervention, 31*, 33–43.

Gresham, F. M., & Elliott, S. N. (1990). *Social Skills Rating System.* Minneapolis, MN: NCS Pearson.

Gresham, F. M., & Elliott, S. N. (2008). *Social Skills Improvement System Rating Scales manual.* Minneapolis, MN: NCS Pearson.

Gresham, F. M., Elliott, S. N., Vance, M. J., & Cook, C. R. (2011). Comparability of the Social Skills Rating System to the Social Skills Improvement System: Content and psychometric comparisons across elementary and secondary age levels. *School Psychology Quarterly, 26*, 27–44.

Griffith, A. K., Hurley, K. D., Trout, A. L., Synhorst, L., Epstein, M. H., & Allen, E. (2010). Assessing the strengths of young children at risk: Examining use of the Preschool Behavioral and Emotional Rating Scale with a Head Start population. *Journal of Early Intervention, 32*, 274–285.

Haggerty, K., Elgin, J., & Woolley, A. (2011). Social–emotional learning and school climate assessment measures for middle school youth (Report commissioned by the Raikes Foundation). Seattle: Social Development Research Group, University of Washington. Retrieved January 30, 2012, from *https://audition.prevention.org/resources/documents/seltools.pdf.*

Halverson, R. (2010). School formative feedback systems. *Peabody Journal of Education, 85*, 130–146.

Humphrey, N., Kalambouka, A., Wigelsworth, M., Lendrum, A., Deighton, J., & Wolpert, M. (2011). Measures of social and emotional skills for children and young people: A systematic review. *Educational and Psychological Measurement, 71*, 617–637.

Illinois State Board of Education. (2006). *Social emotional learning standards: Goals 1, 2, and 3.* Chicago: Author.

Jaberg, P. E., Dixon, D. J., & Weis, G. M. (2009). Replication evidence in support of the psychometric properties of the Devereux Early Childhood Assessment. *Canadian Journal of School Psychology, 24*, 158–166.

Kendziora, K., Weissberg, R. P., & Dusenbury, L. (2011). *Strategies for social and emotional learning: Preschool and elementary grade student learning standards and assessment.* Newtown, MA: National Center for Mental Health Promotion and Youth Violence Prevention, Education Development Center.

Kingston, N., & Nash, B. (2011). Formative assessment: A meta-analysis and a call for research. *Educational Measurement: Issues and Practice, 30*, 28–37.

Kyllonen, P. C. (2012, May). Measurement of 21st century skills within the Common Core State Standards. *Proceedings in Invitational Research Symposium on Technology Enhanced Assessments* (pp. 7–8). Princeton, NJ: Educational Testing Services.

LeBuffe, P. A., & Naglieri, J. A. (1999a). *The Devereux Early Childhood Assessment (for children ages 2 to 5 years).* Lewisville, NC: Kaplan Press.

LeBuffe, P. A., & Naglieri, J. A. (1999b). *The Devereux Early Childhood Assessment Clinical Form.* Lewisville, NC: Kaplan Press.

LeBuffe, P. A., Shapiro, V. B., & Naglieri, J. A. (2009). *The Devereux Student Strengths Assessment (DESSA).* Lewisville, NC: Kaplan Press.

Li, Y., Marion, S., Perie, M., & Gong, B. (2010). An approach for evaluating the technical quality of interim assessments. *Peabody Journal of Education, 85*, 163–185.

Merrell, K. W., Cohn, B. P., & Tom, K. M. (2011). Development and validation of a teacher report measure for assessing social–emotional strengths of children and adolescents. *School Psychology Review, 40*, 226–241.

Merrell, K. W., Felver-Gant, J. C., & Tom, K. M. (2011). Development and validation of a parent report measure for assessing social–emotional competencies of children and adolescents. *Journal of Child and Family Studies, 20*, 529–540.

Naglieri, J. A., LeBuffe, P., & Shapiro, V. B. (2011). Universal screening for social–emotional competencies: A study of the reliability and validity of the DESSA-Mini. *Psychology in the Schools, 48,* 660–671.

National Research Council (NRC). (2012). *Education for life and work: Developing transferable knowledge and skills in the 21st century.* Washington, DC: National Academies Press.

Nese, R., Doerner, E., Kaye, N., Romer, N., & Merrell, K. (2011). The utility of brief behavior rating scales: A discussion of the SEARS Short-Form Assessment System. Retrieved December 28, 2012, from *http://psycnet.apa.org/psycextra/523462012-003.*

Nickerson, A. B., & Fishman, C. (2009). Convergent and divergent validity of the Devereux Student Strengths Assessment. *School Psychology Quarterly, 2,* 48–59.

Oades-Sese, G. V., Kaliski, P. K., & Weiss, K. (2010). Factor structure of the Devereux Early Childhood Assessment Clinical Form in low-income Hispanic American bilingual preschool children. *Journal of Psychoeducational Assessment, 28,* 357–372.

Ogg, J. A., Brinkman, T. M., Dedrick, R. F., & Carlson, J. S. (2010). Factor structure and invariance across gender of the Devereux Early Childhood Assessment protective factor scale. *School Psychology Quarterly, 25,* 107–118.

Partnership for Assessment of Readiness for College and Career (PARCC). (n.d.). The PARCC Assessment. Retrieved December 28, 2012, from *www.parcconline.org/parcc-assessment-design.*

Payton, J. W., Wardlaw, D. M., Graczyk, P. A., Bloodworth, M. R., Tompsett, C. J., & Weissberg, R. P. (2000). Social and emotional learning: A framework for promoting mental health and reducing risk behavior in children and youth. *Journal of School Health, 70,* 179–186.

Perie, M., Marion, S., & Gong, B. (2009). Moving toward a comprehensive assessment system: A framework for considering interim assessments. *Educational Measurement: Issues and Practice, 28*(3), 5–13.

Raver, C. C., & Knitzer, J. (2002). *Ready to enter: What research tells policymakers about strategies to promote social and emotional school readiness among three- and four-year-olds.* Chicago: Harris School of Public Policy Studies, University of Chicago. Retrieved December 5, 2004, from *http://ideas.repec.org/p/har/wpaper/0205.html.*

Ringwalt, S. (2008). *Developmental screening and assessment instruments with an emphasis on social and emotional development for young children ages birth through five.* Chapel Hill: University of North Carolina, FPG Child Development Institute, National Early Childhood Technical Assistance Center.

Smarter Balance Assessment Consortium. (n.d.). Retrieved December 28, 2012, from *www.smarterbalanced.org.*

Sosna, T., & Mastergeorge, A. (2005). *Compendium of screening tools for early childhood social–emotional development.* Sacramento: California Institute for Mental Health. Retrieved from *www.cimh.org.*

Zins, J. E., Bloodworth, M. R., Weissberg, R. P., & Walberg, H. J. (2007). The scientific base linking social and emotional learning to school success. *Journal of Educational and Psychological Consultation, 17,* 191–210.

CHAPTER 20

Systems for Assessing and Improving Students' Social Skills to Achieve Academic Competence

Stephen N. Elliott, Jennifer R. Frey, and Michael Davies

Social skills matter, particularly in the educational lives of children and youth. They are neither part of the Common Core State Standards (CCSS; National Governors Association Center for Best Practices, Council of Chief State School Officers, 2010) nor a graduation requirement, but without them, learning suffers, school is less satisfying, and many students fail to graduate. Social skills matter because they facilitate the development of mutually supportive relationships with others and enable academic skills and positive emotional growth (e.g., Capara, Barbaranelli, Pastorelli, Bandura, & Zimbardo, 2000).

In this chapter, we examine social skills and suggest that learning social skills is a subset of social and emotional learning (SEL). Then we take a close look at social skills that matter most before examining social skills assessment methods and intervention approaches in use today.

Fundamental Concepts of Social Skills

Definition of Social Skills

SEL has been defined as the process of acquiring core competencies to recognize and manage emotions, set and achieve positive goals, appreciate the perspectives of others, establish and maintain positive relationships, make responsible decisions, and handle interpersonal situations constructively (Elias et al., 1997). Although no specific definitional comparison of SEL and social skills was found in the literature, it seems apparent that learning social skills is a subset of SEL (Davies & Cooper, 2013). In their recent meta-analysis of school-based universal interventions and their impact on enhancing students' SEL, Durlak, Weissberg, Dymnicki, Taylor, and Schellinger (2011) indicated that SEL covers a broad conceptualization of core "cognitive, affective, and behavioral competencies" that include "self-awareness, self-management, social awareness, relationship skills, and responsible decision-making" (p. 406). Numerous definitions of social skills exist; however, nearly all of them describe a set of behaviors that facilitates the initiation and maintenance of positive social relationships, contributes to peer acceptance, allows individuals to cope with and adapt to the demands of the social environment, and results in satisfactory school adjustment (Gresham, 2002). These skills are clearly embedded within SEL core competencies.

Social skills have two key dimensions. First, social skills consist of both verbal and nonverbal behaviors. Second, behaviors are often situation-specific. Collectively, these two dimensions stress the interactive, context-specific nature of social skills.

Another useful way of thinking about social skills is based on the concept of social validity (Wolf, 1978). From this perspective, *social skills* can be defined as social behaviors occurring in specific situations that result in important social outcomes for children and youth (Gresham, 1981b). Socially important outcomes are those that social agents (peers, teachers, and parents) consider important, adaptive, and functional within specific settings. In other words, socially important outcomes are those that make a difference in individuals' adaptation to both societal expectations and the behavioral demands of specific environments in which they function. Thus, for the purposes of this chapter, *social skills* are defined as socially acceptable, learned behaviors that enable an individual to interact effectively with others and to avoid or escape unacceptable behaviors that result in negative social interactions with others (Gresham & Elliott, 1984, 1990, 2008).

Key Categories of Social Skills

Based on reviews of the social skills intervention literature and factor-analytic research for purposes of scale development, Gresham and Elliott (1990) characterized social skills as a multidimensional construct that comprises cooperation, assertion, responsibility, empathy, and self-control behaviors. Over the past decade, with the increase in assessment and intervention research for students with autism spectrum disorders, two additional dimensions of social skills—communication and engagement—have become prevalent. Thus, today we believe there are seven fundamental and functional response classes of social skills that can be reliably assessed and targeted for intervention: *communication, cooperation, assertion, responsibility, engagement, empathy,* and *self-control.* These seven social skills response classes align very well with the developmental outcomes—self-awareness, self-management, social awareness, relationship management skills, and responsible decision making—valued in the framework provided by the Collaborative for Academic, Social, and Emotional Learning (CASEL).

The Importance of Social Skills in the Development of Children and School Outcomes

Teachers at the elementary and secondary school levels classify several social behaviors as critical for students' classroom success. These include following directions, paying attention to instructions, controlling temper with both adults and peers, and managing conflict (Hersh & Walker, 1983; Lane, Givner, & Pierson, 2004; Lane, Stanton-Chapman, Jamison, & Phillips, 2007). At the preschool level, teachers have identified several specific social behaviors that are necessary for successful classroom experiences: following directions and classroom rules, controlling temper in conflict situations with adults and peers, and interacting well with other children (Frey, Elliott, & Kaiser, 2014; Lane et al., 2007).

Parents' importance ratings of preschoolers' social skills also have been examined. Lane and colleagues (2007) used the Social Skills Rating Scale (SSRS; Gresham & Elliott, 1990) to document parents' and teachers' perceptions of what social skills are critical for functioning at home and school, respectively. Lane and colleagues suggested that if preschool parents and teachers have similar social behavior expectations, then children may have fewer behavioral adjustments when entering school, but if parents and teachers have different behavioral expectations, then preschool children may experience greater challenges when making the transition to school and succeeding in the classroom. In an investigation of parents' and teachers' ratings of the importance of social skills for preschoolers using the Social Skills Improvement System Rating Scales (SSIS-RS), Frey and colleagues (2014) found that both parents and teachers rated four behaviors as critical or important for preschoolers' academic success and development: (1) follows directions, (2) is well behaved when unsupervised, (3) interacts well with other children, and (4) takes responsibility for his or her own actions. In addition, both parents and teachers rated cooperation and responsibility as the two most important domains overall. Next, parents rated communication skills as essential, and teachers rated self-control skills as necessary for success in their classrooms. For parents, the domain with the lowest importance ratings was engagement, and for teachers, the domain with the lowest importance ratings was empathy. Differences in parents' and teachers' importance ratings of social behaviors may be attributed to the context and settings in which parents and teachers interact with children.

Researchers for decades have also documented that some of the most socially important outcomes for children and youth include peer acceptance (Bierman, 2004; Newcomb, Bukowski, & Pattee, 1993; Parker & Asher, 1987) and teacher and parent acceptance (Gresham, 2002; Gresham & Elliott, 1990). In a classic review of research, Parker and Asher (1987) found that children who had difficulties managing relationships with peers often demonstrated patterns of antisocial and/or aggressive behavior and had histories of school norm violations. Without effective interventions, these behavior patterns were likely to persist and potentially to escalate into other forms of maladaptive behavior (Walker, Ramsay, & Gresham, 2004). Researchers also have documented a predictive relationship between children's social behaviors and their long-term academic achievement (Caprara et al., 2000; DiPerna & Elliott, 2002; DiPerna, Volpe, & Elliott, 2002; Malecki & Elliott, 2002; Wentzel, 1993).

The concept of academic enablers evolved from the work of researchers who explored the relationship between students' nonacademic behaviors (e.g., social skills and motivation) and their academic achievement (Gresham & Elliott, 1990; Wentzel, 1993). In a longitudinal study with 500 students, Caprara and colleagues (2000) found that social skills of third graders, as assessed by teachers, were slightly better predictors of eighth-grade academic achievement than third-grade achievement test results. Even stronger findings were reported by Malecki and Elliott (2002), who found that social skills correlated approximately .70 with end-of-year academic achievement as measured by high-stakes tests. Therefore, it appears that social skills are vitally important academic enablers for children in schools.

Social Skills Strengths and Weaknesses

Like any skills, whether social, cognitive, or physical, social skills develop through stages, from nonexistent, emerging, and proficient, to accomplished. At any given point in a child's development, some of his or her social skills will be relatively strong or prevalent and others will be relatively weak or infrequently used. An important conceptual feature of social skills weaknesses that has direct implications for the design and delivery of social skills intervention programs is the distinction between social skills *acquisition deficits* and social skills *performance deficits* (Gresham, 1981a, 1981b; Gresham & Elliott, 2008). This distinction is important because different intervention approaches in remediating social skills deficits are required, and different settings (e.g., general education classroom vs. pull-out groups) are indicated for different tiers of intervention (universal, selected, or targeted/intensive).

Acquisition deficits result from the absence of knowledge about how to perform a given social skill, an inability to enact fluently a sequence of social behaviors, or difficulty knowing which social skill is appropriate in specific situations (Gresham, 1981a, 2002). According to this conceptualization, acquisition deficits can result from deficits in social cognitive abilities, difficulties in integrating fluent response patterns, or deficits in appropriate discrimination of social situations. Acquisition deficits can be characterized as "can't do" problems because the child cannot perform a given social skill even under optimal conditions of motivation.

Performance deficits can be conceptualized as the failure to perform a given social skill at acceptable levels, even though the child knows how to perform the social skill (Gresham, 1981a). That is, performance deficits refer to skills a child has in his or her repertoire but does not consistently perform. Performance deficits are due to motivational or performance difficulties rather than challenges in learning the skill.

Another important component in the conceptualization of social skills deficits is the concept of *competing or interfering problem behaviors* (Gresham & Elliott, 1990). Competing problem behaviors fall into two broad categories: (1) externalizing behavior patterns, which include behaviors such as noncompliance, aggression, or coercion, or (2) internalizing behavior patterns, such as social withdrawal, anxiety, or depression. These externalizing or internalizing behaviors often compete with or block the acquisition or performance of a given social skill.

Base Rates for Social Skills Deficits

Base rate information is important in assessment because one cannot know how unusual or typical a phenomenon is without first knowing its normal rate in the population. Gresham, Elliott, and Kettler (2010) conducted an empirical study to establish the base rates of social skills acquisition/performance deficits, social skills strengths, and problem behaviors. Specifically, they empirically determined the base rates of social skills acquisition and performance deficits, social skills strengths, and problem behaviors, using a nationally representative sample of children and adolescent ages 3–18 years. Using the national standardization sample (*N* = 4,550 children) of the SSIS-RS across three informants (teacher, parent, and student) and across three broad age groupings (3–5 years, 6–12 years, and 13–18 years), base rates were computed. Results showed that the base rates for social skills acquisition deficits and problem behaviors are extremely low in the general population. Base rates for social skills performance deficits and social skills strengths were considerably higher with students in the age 6–12 group, who reported fewer performance deficits and social skills strengths than older children (13–18 years), teachers, and parents across all three age groups.

As suggested by the base rates research with the SSIS-RS standardization sample, social skills performance deficits, rather than social skills acquisition deficits, are the form of difficulty likely to confront interventionists. That is, many children can perform desired social behaviors, but they may need support in knowing in which contexts the behaviors should be performed or additional motivation to perform these behaviors. Once such deficits are reliably identified, an intervention from an array of evidence-based methods can be implemented to reduce or eliminate social skill deficits. Of course, when co-occurring problem behaviors are competing with performance of the desired behavior, the intervention is more complicated, but again, an array of interventions is available to reduce such competing behaviors.

Assessment of Social Skills

Several methods exist for assessing children's social skills, including direct observations, interviews, role plays, and rating scales. Over the past two decades, however, the most frequently used method for assessing social skills has been rating scales (Crowe, Beauchamp, Catroppa, & Anderson, 2011; Humphrey et al., 2011). There are a number of reasons for this rating scale preference. First, rating scales are relatively efficient tools for representing summary characterizations of individuals' observations of other people or their own behavior. As noted by Elliott and Busse (2004), rating scales are imperfect "mirrors" for reflecting images of individuals' social, emotional, and personal functioning; yet, in many cases, the information reflected by a well-constructed rating scale can be very useful. There are, however, many investigators and practitioners who believe that direct observation is the "gold standard" for assessing social behavior.

Based on research like that of Doll and Elliott (1994), the term "gold standard" takes on added meaning. That is, observations can be expensive in terms of time if the aim is to achieve a highly representative sampling of the targeted behaviors. For example, in a study of preschoolers, Doll and Elliott addressed the issue of how much observational data are enough to predict accurately children's typical frequency of social skills and problem behaviors in their classroom. Specifically, they used a correlational research design to examine the number of 30-minute classroom observations it takes to gain an accurate and representative sample of a preschool child's social behavior. Twenty-four children were observed using a partial-interval sampling procedure. Observations were conducted over 6 weeks, and each child was observed and videotaped for nine 30-minute periods in his or her classroom through one-way mirrors during free-play periods. Doll and Elliott compared early observation sessions to later sessions using correlations and kappa coefficients. Results from these comparisons indicated that neither two nor three observation sessions were sufficient, from a reliability perspective, to describe a consistent pattern of social behavior. After five observations, six out of eight behaviors correlated highly (r = .80) with the total observation record. From these data, the authors concluded that at least five 30-minute observation sessions across several weeks would adequately represent students' social skills. Doll and Elliott also found that the *type* of behavior accounted for the variation in predictability of behaviors. Some behaviors, such as directed play or physical aggression, occurred much more consistently than others. A less consistent social behavior, such as sharing, often depended more on context or setting events than did other behaviors and was therefore difficult to predict even with seven or eight observations. The authors concluded that "depending upon the behaviors of interest for a particular child, observational records might need to be quite lengthy before a sufficiently consistent description of child behavior can be recorded" (p. 234).

Behavior rating scales and inventories are versatile assessment tools and are the most common methods for quantifying teacher and parent judgments (Elliott & Busse, 2004; Merrell, 2003). Rating scales can be used repeatedly, across settings, and by numerous sources (i.e., teachers, parents, therapists, children themselves) to provide multiple indicators of a wide range of behavior. Well-designed behavior rating scales essentially are raters' summary characterizations of recent observations and experiences with children or youth. Of course, rating scales have limitations and must be used as part of a more comprehensive database to increase the likelihood that their resulting scores are reliable and valid.

Practical and Technical Issues that Influence Use of Rating Scales

Behavior rating scales appear to be more than an aggregation of a series of structured direct observations. The rater often is a "participant" in the environment where the target child behaves, and the behavior to be rated is often a more comprehensive collection of skills than that typically operationalized via a direct observation system. Rating scales offer an efficient means for collecting data to create a relatively comprehensive picture of functioning. Although some behaviorists will argue that rating scales are not the "gold standard" for assessing youth and children's social skills, they provide one component of a sound multiple-measure, multiple-source assessment. For many practitioners, with limited time and the need to sample a range of social behaviors, rating scales are a critical component of their assessment for intervention work.

Researchers have identified several potential issues with rating scales that influence their use. These include the degree of agreement among informants, the use of self-reports, and the validity of rating results in comparison to direct observations.

Multiple Informants

Typically, informants are teachers, parents, and children themselves. Some behavior rating scales are for teachers only; others are for parents only or children only; and still others utilize all three informants. Some informants are in a better position to rate certain behaviors, based on the context(s) in which the behaviors are likely to occur. For instance, teachers are in a better position to rate attention span, classroom behaviors, social interactions in school settings, and the like. Parents are likely to be more knowledgeable about behaviors such as sibling interactions, mealtime behaviors, and so forth.

The best practice in using behavior rating scales is to employ multiple informants to rate the same child's behavior to provide a more complete view of a child's behavior across situations and settings. Of course, researchers have repeatedly found that multiple informants often agree only moderately at best (Achenbach, McConaughy, & Howell, 1987; Gresham, Elliott, Cook, Vance, & Kettler, 2010; Ruffalo & Elliott, 1997). Despite moderate to low cross-informant agreement, using multiple informants allows one to discern which behaviors tend to occur across a variety of situations and which ones appear to be situation-specific. This information can be of use in classification decisions, as well as intervention planning.

Self-Report Assessments

Self-report assessments require individuals to provide standardized information about themselves, such as thoughts, feelings, and physical experiences. They allow researchers and practitioners to gain information about an individual's own perceptions, which can "provide 'red flags' that may be indicative of general social or emotional distress," and in some cases, they can isolate specific areas of concern in which additional assessment is needed (Merrell, 2003, p. 180). Self-report information can be used in screening and can aid in making diagnoses and formulating interventions. Kazdin (1986) recommended the use of self-reports in the assessment of children's internalizing symptoms, and several researchers have documented the utility of children assessing their own anxiety levels. A number of concerns, however, about the use of self-report measures have been noted. First, self-report measures require individuals to provide information about their own perceptions, which are relatively subjective (McConaughy & Ritter, 1995), are retrospective in nature (Kratochwill & Shapiro, 2000), and are often setting specific (Kazdin, 1979). Second, self-report measures of behavior also need to be developmentally appropriate for their intended population, and users must consider respondents' cognitive, language, and reading abilities. These factors may play a significant role in determining whether responses are valid. Third, another set of factors that influences the validity of respondents' completion of a self-report scale is commonly referred to as "response bias factors," and includes faking, acquiescence, or social desirability (Merrell, 2003). Despite criticism or concerns about them, self-report measures play a role in research and the comprehensive assessment and treatment of students with social–emotional difficulties. Well-designed multidimensional scales that include self-report measures, such as the SSIS-RS, include methods for detecting faking or likely response bias.

Validity of Rating Scales with Direct Observation

As with any assessment instrument, the scores from a rating scale need to have evidence for their valid use. Given that behavior rating scales are intended to be indirect observational measures, it is logical that an important part of the validation effort for a rating scale is to compare its results with those from direct observations of the same target child. This logic is especially true within a behavioral model of assessment, wherein direct observation is considered the "gold standard" with which all other assessments should be compared. Few authors of behavior rating scales, however, report information about the relationships between ratings and observations. This may surprise readers, but most direct observation systems and behavior rating scales differ in several significant ways that result in only a modest comparability of results. A key difference is that behaviors targeted for direct observation are often far more molecular or discrete than those operationalized by items on a rating scale. Another difference is that the results from a direct observation of behavior are rarely aggregated across response classes or subscales as they are on most behavior rating scales. In addition, behavior assessed via direct observation is often limited to one or two discrete skills, whereas a rating scale commonly gathers information on 50 or 60 behaviors or skills. These differences in coverage and scoring reduce the comparability of the results of direct and indirect observational assessments and decrease concurrent validity estimates.

As noted by Doll and Elliott (1994), the research data are limited regarding how much observational data one should collect to gain a representative sample of children's social behavior, whereas with most behavior rating scales a rater is expected to summarize his or her observations over a period of 1 or 2 months. To ensure representativeness, an observational procedure should acquire a sufficiently large sample of behavior, but it can only be estimated how often the periods of observation should occur and how long they should last (Doll & Elliott, 1994; Johnston & Pennypacker, 1980). It is considered best practice to use a multisource, multimethod approach in the assessment of children's social–emotional behavior. One must recognize, however, that variance exists in all assessments. Common sources of variance stem from different methods, informants, settings, and times. Given this variance, consider two fundamental measurement principles: (1) Error exists in all measures, and (2) tests are samples of behavior.

The reaction to these fundamental measurement principles has been to use multiple sources and multiple methods to reduce error and gain more representative samples, despite the chance that there may not be high agreement among the methods or sources. For example, Achenbach and colleagues (1987), in a meta-analysis of 119 studies that examined agreement among informants' ratings of children's behavior, found that the mean correlations among all types of informants were statistically significant, yet moderate in magnitude. Similar informants (e.g., pairs of teachers, pairs of mental health workers) had the highest correlations (mean r = .64 and .54, respectively). Informants with different roles (e.g., teacher/parent pairs) had lower but still significant, correlations, with the highest occurring between teacher and observer pairs (mean r = .42). Mean agreement between pairs of observers was r = .57.

Though different informants using the same assessment method can have significant levels of agreement, it is another issue to conclude different assessment methods share consistency. Elliott, Gresham, Freeman, and McCloskey (1988) found that teachers' and observers' ratings on the Social Skills Rating Scale–Teacher Version (SSRS-T; Gresham & Elliott, 1990) and observers' observations correlated moderately with observed behaviors. Likewise, Merrell (1993) found correlations between the Child Behavior Checklist–Direct Observation Form (CBC-DOF; Achenbach & Edelbrock, 1986) and the School Social Behavior Scale (SSBS; Merrell, 1993) were weak to moderate between teachers and observers for problem behavior scores (r = –.06 to –.39) and moderate for on-task ratings (r = .26 to –.52).

Frequently Used Behavior Rating Scales

Recently, there have been two major reviews of measures of social and emotional skills for children and youth (i.e., Crowe et al., 2011; Humphrey et al., 2011). Both teams of researchers conducted a comprehensive search of the research literature for measures used in empirical investigations of youth and children's social behavior. The Humphrey team identified 189 measures, whereas the Crowe team, using a more restrictive set of search criteria, identified 86 measures, all of which were also identified by Humphrey and colleagues. Of these measures, Humphrey and his colleagues (2011) selected 12 measures based on the criterion "used in four or more articles [reporting research] in peer-reviewed academic journals" (p. 625). They further indicated that only three of the measures had been used in 10 or more research articles. These were the Diagnostic Analysis of Nonverbal Accuracy (DANVA), Scale of Competence and Behavior Evaluation (SCBE), and the SSRS/SSIS-RS. The Crowe team (2011) identified the SSRS/SSIS-RS as the measure with the most citations of any published measure—1,300 during the period 1988–2010. We summarize these 12 measures, along with key technical dimensions, in Table 20.1, then focus on the SSRS/SSIS because of its status in the research literature.

The SSRS (Gresham & Elliott, 1990) is the predecessor of the SSIS (Gresham & Elliott, 2008). Both the SSRS and the SSIS are sold today because there continues to be a research demand for the SSRS, and it takes about 10 minutes less time to complete. The SSRS is a broad-based, multirater assessment of students' social behavior that examines teacher–student relations, peer interactions, and academic performance. The SSRS and SSIS-RS are the only social skills rating scales that yield information from three key rating sources: teachers, parents, and students. These assessments solicit information from these three sources for students in grades 3–12 and from parents and teachers for children from preschool through second grade. The two instruments also have three forms reflecting three developmental age ranges: preschool (ages 3–5 years), elementary (grades K–6), and secondary (grades 7–12). The SSRS and SSIS-RS focus on a comprehensive assessment of social skills. In addition, they also measure problem behaviors that often compete with the acquisition and/or performance of socially skilled behaviors. Additionally, the teacher version of these rating scales includes a measure of academic competence because poor social skills, competing problem behaviors, and poor academic performance often co-occur.

TABLE 20.1. Characteristics of 12 Social–Emotional Measures

Measure	Age (years)	Versions	Test length	Completion time (minutes)	Scales and subscales	Response scales	Other languages
Assessment of Children's Emotion Skills (Schultz, Izard, & Bear, 2004)	4–8	Child	56	10–25	Emotional attribution accuracy, anger attribution tendencies, happiness attribution tendencies, sadness attribution tendencies	Multiple choice 1–5	
Bar-On Emotional Quotient Inventory: Youth Version (Bar-On & Parker, 2008)	7–18	Child	60, 30 (short form)	20–25, 15–15 (short form)	Total emotional intelligence, interpersonal, intrapersonal, adaptability, stress management, general mood, positive impression, inconsistency index	Likert 1–4	Pedi (South Africa)
Child Assertive Behaviour Scale (Michelson & Wood, 1982)	8–12	Child, parent, teacher	27	10–15	Total assertiveness, passivity, and aggressiveness	Multiple choice 1–5	Spanish, Dutch
Child Rating Scale (Hightower et al., 1987)	5–13	Child, parent, teacher	24, 38 (teacher), 18 (parent)	10–20	Rule compliance/acting out, anxiety/withdrawal, interpersonal social skills, self-confidence (child); acting out, shy–anxious, learning, frustration tolerance, assertive social skills, task orientation, peer sociability (teacher); acting out, frustration tolerance, shy-anxious and peer sociability (parent)	Likert 1–3	
Diagnostic Analysis of Nonverbal Accuracy Scale (Nowicki & Duke, 1994)	4–adult	Child	16–32	30	Interpretation of child and adult faces, paralanguage and posture	Multiple choice 1–4	
Differential Emotions Scale (Izard, Dougherty, Bloxom, & Kotsch, 1974)	7–adult	Child	36	10–15	Positive emotionality (interest, joy, surprise), negative emotionality (shyness, sadness, anger, disgust, contempt, self-hostility, fear, guilt, and shame)	Likert 1–5	

Emotion Regulation Checklist (Shields & Cicchetti, 1997)	6–12	Parent, teacher	24	10	Negativity, emotional regulation	Likert 1–4	
Matson Evaluation of Social Skills with Youngsters (Matson, Rotatori, & Helsel, 1983)	4–18	Child, teacher	64 (teacher), 62 (child)	10–25	Appropriate social skills, inappropriate assertiveness, impulsiveness, overconfident behavior, jealousy	Likert 1–5	Japanese, Spanish, Turkish, Chinese, Dutch, Portuguese
Preschool and Kindergarten Behaviour Scales–2 (Merrell, 1996)	3–6	Teacher, parent	76	12	Social cooperation, social interaction, social independence, externalizing problems and internalizing problems	Likert 1–4	Spanish
Prosocial Tendencies Measure—Revised (Carlo, Hausmann, Christiansen, & Randall, 2003)	11–18	Child	25	30	Public, anonymous, dire, emotional, compliant and altruistic prosocial behavior	Likert 1–5	
Competence and Behavior Evaluation Scale (LaFreniere & Dumas, 1996)	2.5–6.5	Teacher, parent	80, 30 (short form)	15	Depressive–joyful, anxious–secure, angry–tolerant, isolated–integrated, aggressive–calm, egotistical–prosocial, oppositional–cooperative, dependent–autonomous, and four summary scales: social competence, externalizing problems, internalizing problems, and general adaptation	Likert 1–6	French Canadian, Spanish, Japanese, Russian, Chinese, Portuguese, Italian, Austrian-German
Social Skills Improvement System (Gresham & Elliott, 1990)	3–18	Child, parent, teacher	79 (parent), 75 (child), 83 (teacher)	10–25	Social skills (communication, cooperation, assertion, responsibility, empathy, engagement, self-control), competing problem behaviors (externalizing, bullying, hyperactivity/ inattention, internalizing, autism spectrum), and academic competence (reading achievement, math achievement, motivation to learn)	Likert 1–4	Spanish

Note. Based on Humphrey et al. (2011, Table 4, pp. 626–628).

The SSIS-RS has a number of advantages over its predecessor, including (1) updated national norms; (2) four additional subscales (Communication, Engagement, Bullying, and Autism Spectrum); (3) greater overlap in topics covered across raters, improved psychometric properties, and validity scales; (4) Spanish versions of parent and student forms; (5) scoring and reporting software; and (6) a direct link from item scores to the skills-focused interventions part of the overall SSIS program. All forms of the SSIS-RS include common social skills across seven subdomains: Communication, Cooperation, Assertion, Responsibility, Empathy, Engagement, and Self-Control. Each item on the SSIS-RS is rated on a 4-point frequency scale (0 = *Never*, 1 = *Seldom*, 2 = *Often*, and 3 = *Almost Always*) based on the rater's perception of the frequency of the behavior. In addition, all SSIS-RS forms (except the Student Elementary Form) use a 3-point importance rating (0 = *Not Important*, 1 = *Important*, 2 = *Critical*) as a means of identifying deficits requiring immediate intervention.

The teacher and parent SSIS forms include problem behaviors from the following five subdomains: Externalizing, Bullying, Hyperactivity/Inattention, Internalizing, and Autism Spectrum. The teacher form includes an Academic Competence scale measuring student performance in reading and math, student motivation, parental support, and general cognitive functioning. Scores on the main scales (Total Social Skills, Total Problem Behaviors, and Total Academic Competence) are expressed as standard scores (M = 100, SD = 15).

The SSIS-RS was normed on a nationwide representative sample totaling 4,700 children and adolescents ages 3–18 years, assessed in 115 sites in 36 states. Each age group sample was designed to have equal numbers of males and females and to match the U.S. population with regard to race/ethnicity, socioeconomic status (SES), and geographic region.

The SSIS-RS has strong psychometric properties in terms of internal consistency and test–retest reliability estimates. Median scale reliabilities of the Social Skills and Problem Behavior scales are in the .90's for every age group on each form. Test–retest indices for Total Social Skills were .82 for the Teacher Form, .84 for the Parent Form, and .81 for the Student Form. Median subscale stability indices for the Social Skills subscales were in the .80's across Teacher, Parent, and Student Forms and in the .80's for the Problem Behavior subscales across all raters. The stability estimate for the Academic Competence scale was .92.

An examination of the SSIS subscales and items reveals that it measures almost all the components of CASEL's SEL model. Specifically, Self-Awareness, as defined by CASEL, is analogous to self-control items on the SSIS-RS; Self-Management, as defined by CASEL, is virtually synonymous with the Self-Control Scale on the SSIS-RS; Social Awareness in the CASEL model is well represented by items from both the Empathy and Engagement Scales on the SSIS-RS; Relationship Management Skills, as defined by the CASEL model, is a broad construct and is measured by items on the SSIS-RS's Communication, Cooperation, and Assertion scales; and finally, CASEL's Responsible Decision Making construct is very similar to Responsibility items on the SSIS-RS.

Intervening to Improve Social Skills

Effective and individualized interventions to improve children's social skills must be based on valid assessments and sound implementation procedures with evidence-based methods. In the remainder of this chapter, we focus on key aspects of social skills interventions.

Fundamental Components and Procedures

Effective methods for teaching social skills include modeling correct behavior, eliciting an imitative response, providing corrective feedback and reinforcement, and arranging opportunities to practice the new skills. In a recent meta-analysis of school-based social skills interventions for preschoolers, Frey and Kaiser (2012) found that in studies with positive, statistically significant effect sizes, children learned social skills by observing adult models, practicing the target skill, receiving immediate feedback, and discussing their experiences after practicing the target skill. Elliott and Gresham (2007), as part of the SSIS intervention components, also reviewed the social skills intervention literature and existing social skills intervention programs across all ages and identified six components of effective social skills programs: *Tell, Show, Do, Practice, Monitor Progress*, and *Generalize*. In the *Tell* component, a teacher or interventionist establishes a learning objective for a social skill he or she wants to teach, introduces and defines the skill, discusses why the skill is important, and specifies how to perform the behavior. In the *Show* component, the teacher or interventionist models the behavior and provides both examples and nonexamples of the target skill. The teacher or interventionist may construct a role-play situation with the students to further demonstrate the skill. In the *Do* component, the teacher or interventionist asks students to define the skill, discuss why the skill is important, and state the steps required to accomplish the skill. Then students practice the skill through role playing. Students provide feedback to the students using the skill in the role plays. In the *Practice* component, the teacher or interventionist has students complete activities in which they can practice the skill with a classmate. The teacher or interventionist prompts use of the desired social skill, when necessary, and positively reinforces students when they exhibit the desired social skill. To *Monitor Progress*, the teacher or interventionist asks students to reflect on their use of the target social behavior and to complete a self-evaluation of their skills performance. Finally, the *Generalize* component requires teachers or interventionists to ask students to use the skill outside of classroom with support of a parent or sibling. Use of these six program components should result in students learning social skills, performing these desired behaviors more frequently and consistently, and continuing to perform the behaviors after completion of the intervention program (Elliott, Frey, & DiPerna, 2012).

Training Teachers to Deliver Social Skills Training

The success of social skills intervention programs in schools relies on teachers' confidence "in their abilities to implement a program and have the skills and resources to deliver the program as designed" (Buchanan Gueldner, Tran, & Merrell, 2009, p. 190). Training teachers to deliver social skills that align and compete with problem behaviors is important for teacher confidence and program success. Davies and Cooper (2013) strongly recommended that teachers need training (Voegler-Lee & Kupersmidt, 2010), regular support, and constructive feedback on their performance (CASEL, 2002) to implemented social skills training effectively.

Four central components of teacher training provide a framework to promote social skills and emotional development to support appropriate behavior and prevent challenging behaviors in children (Fox, Dunlap, Hemmeter, Joseph, & Strain, 2003). These components include building positive relationships with children, families, and colleagues; designing supportive and engaging environments to promote positive behaviors; teaching social and emotional skills; and developing individualized interventions for children with the most challenging behaviors.

Research on the Efficacy of Social Skills Interventions

Numerous reviews and meta-analyses have investigated the effectiveness of social skills interventions. Most reviews have focused on social skills interventions for school-age children across all grades (Ang & Hughes, 2002; Beelmann, Pfingsten, & Losel, 1994; Durlak, Weissberg, & Pachan, 2010; Erwin, 1994; Hanson, 1988; Losel & Beelmann, 2003; Pellegrini & Urbain, 1985; Schneider, 1992) or specifically for preschool (Frey & Kaiser, 2012; Kennedy, 2010; Vaughn et al., 2003), elementary (Goldston, 2000), or secondary (Alwell & Cobb, 2009) students. Reviews and meta-analyses of social skills interventions also have been conducted with a focus on specific populations of students with disabilities, such as autism spectrum disorders (Bellini, Peters, Benner, & Hopf, 2007; Buettel, 2007; Wang, Cui, & Parrila, 2011; Wang & Spillane, 2009), emotional and behavioral disorders (Cook et al., 2008; Quinn, Kavale, Mathur, Rutherford, & Forness, 1999), and learning disabilities (e.g., Forness & Kavale, 1996). Across reviews, social skills interventions generally have been found effective in increasing the social skills of children and adolescents, with and without disabilities, but authors of these reviews consistently have noted significant variability in findings across studies. Moderator analyses have suggested there are differences in intervention effectiveness across populations and interventionists. For example, in a recent meta-analysis examining whether preschoolers who received school-based social skills intervention performed better on social skills measures after intervention compared to preschoolers who did not receive the intervention (Frey & Kaiser, 2012), significant differences were observed for children with disabilities, children classified as at risk due to poverty-related risk factors, and children without disabilities. Specifically, the greatest intervention effects were observed in studies including children with disabilities, followed by experimental studies of children without disabilities. The effect sizes for intervention studies including children classified as at risk were not statistically significant, and the overall effect size across this subgroup of studies was 0.05. In addition, significant differences in effect sizes were observed for interventions implemented by researchers versus teachers. Interventions implemented by researchers were associated with a 0.8 standard deviation increase in posttreatment social skills outcome measures for children in the treatment group compared to children in the comparison group, whereas interventions implemented by teachers were associated with only a 0.17 standard deviation increase in posttreatment outcomes.

With relatively low dosages of intervention, children with and without disabilities can acquire or increase performance of prosocial behaviors through participation in social skills interventions. However, based on the variability across studies and recommendations provided by reviews and meta-analyses of social skills interventions, several factors influencing the effectiveness of social skills interventions must be considered. First, the selection of skills to target in the intervention should be based on assessment results, observations, and cultural and developmental expectations, and the skills must be socially valid for the population targeted in the intervention. Second, training and support provided to teachers implementing social skills intervention programs should be preplanned and utilize evidence-based professional development and coaching practices. Third, intervention implementation should be monitored (i.e., measure treatment fidelity). Variability in results across studies could be related to insufficient training or support for teachers and interventionists and/or intervention programs not being implemented as designed.

Using the reporting standards for group design studies (Gersten et al., 2005), Frey and Kaiser (2012) evaluated the methodological quality of the studies included in their meta-analysis. They found that most studies provided little information about the selection of behaviors to address in the social skills interventions, background information for the teachers and interventionists, intervention training procedures (and follow-up support) for teachers implementing the interventions, social validity of the intervention, and procedural fidelity or treatment integrity data. Future research on the effectiveness of social skills interventions is needed and should measure and report treatment integrity or procedural fidelity, characteristics of the interventionists across conditions, and social validity (Frey & Kaiser, 2012). These factors should be considered when interpreting the outcomes of social skills interventions.

An Integrated System for Assessing and Improving Social Skills

Throughout this chapter we have referred to parts of the SSIS assessment to intervention system as an example of a comprehensive set of tools that allow educators to increase the prosocial behavior of preschoolers through young adults. We have primarily provided descriptions of the family of SSIS rating scales and the intervention methods. These intervention methods, along with the target behaviors assessed by the rating scales, are part of two intervention manuals: the SSIS Classwide Intervention Program (CIP; Elliott & Gresham, 2007) that focuses on the top 10 social skills identified by teachers and designed for an entire class of students and the SSIS Intervention Guide (IG; Elliott & Gresham, 2008) that focuses on students who are nonresponsive to the CIP or who have serious co-occurring problem behaviors that interfere with the production of desired social skills.

Assessment data, from either the SSIS Performance Screening Guide (SSIS-PSG;

Elliott & Gresham, 2007) or the SSIS-RS, drive decisions about target behaviors for intervention. As illustrated in Figure 20.1, the collection of SSIS tools is organized to create an evidence-based multi-tiered assessment to intervention model.

Application of the SSIS System in an Australian School

Schoolwide SEL programming can foster whole-school community-building activities and family connectedness as part of a broad supportive culture. Schools, however, that serve a disproportional number of families with low SES often have a large number of students with low levels of SEL, and therefore provide more of a challenge. In these settings, the efficacy of SEL is inherently linked to reducing inappropriate problem behaviors. Studies have shown that many children who live in situations of poverty, family dysfunction, abuse, and neglect are more at risk of developing behavioral, social, academic, and mental health issues (Doll & Lyon, 1998, cited in Buchanan et al., 2009). These children are also more likely to have language and learning difficulties that make access to the learning environment more problematic. Incidents of trauma and other stressful events also tend to be more frequent in low SES communities (Hatch & Dohrenwend, 2007, cited in January, Casey, & Paulson, 2011). Schools with students who have multiple risk factors may require multiple intervention responses to mediate effective learning.

Bundamba State School (BSS), a low-SES school in southeastern Queensland, has a population of 649 students. While the results of the 2011 national achievement tests indicate that 45% of Year 3 students in Australia achieved results within the top two bands of reading, only 16.2% of Year 3 students at BSS achieved the same standard. School data also show up to 45% of students consistently being identified for extra support in reading. In addition, 33% of preparatory students were referred for speech and language support and developmental delays. As a key initiative of a 4-year National Partnership Plan, the school community in 2011 agreed to target SEL along with behavior and learning as key focus areas in an effort to provide a schoolwide approach to support the mental health and academic learning of students (see Davies & Cooper, 2013).

The school fosters a whole-school commitment to universal practices that promote student resilience and well-being, and build teacher capacity in an attempt to ensure sustainability in programs and interventions. Schoolwide positive behavior support (SWPBS) was the first strategy introduced in 2007 as a system-based approach to managing behavior. While some improvement was evident, the need for specific intervention to improve social skills was identified. It was considered strategic to provide social skills training to students over four grade levels from the Preparatory (or Kindergarten) year to Year 3 and to maintain a training intervention program over a 4-year period. The school leadership committed to providing resources, materials, and teacher training to maintain the delivery and integrity of the program. After considerable research, the school guidance officer identified the SSIS as an SEL program based on best practice and sustainability that would dovetail and complement current school universal services. The SSIS provided a multi-tiered model of universal assessment and intervention that enabled efficient and effective classwide interventions. Moreover, the assessment components of the SSIS were considered culturally valid, since they had recently been successfully applied in Australian schools (Kettler, Elliott, Davies, & Griffin, 2012). All teaching staff members initially attended an information session on current research and best practice around SEL, its relationship to both academic performance and behavior problems, an overview of the SSIS, and an outline of the project. Teachers were challenged not only to consider the importance of teaching literacy and numeracy as part of improving academic outcomes but also to realize that developing social and emotional competencies was key to promoting resilience and broadening the social, emotional, and behavioral repertoires of all students.

At BSS, all class teachers teaching Preparatory to Year 3 ($N = 15$) used the SSIS-PSG to evaluate all students in their class against five levels of criteria, then applied the SSIS-RS with those students with low Prosocial behaviors (Levels 1 and 2) to identify social skills for targeting and training. Of the 372

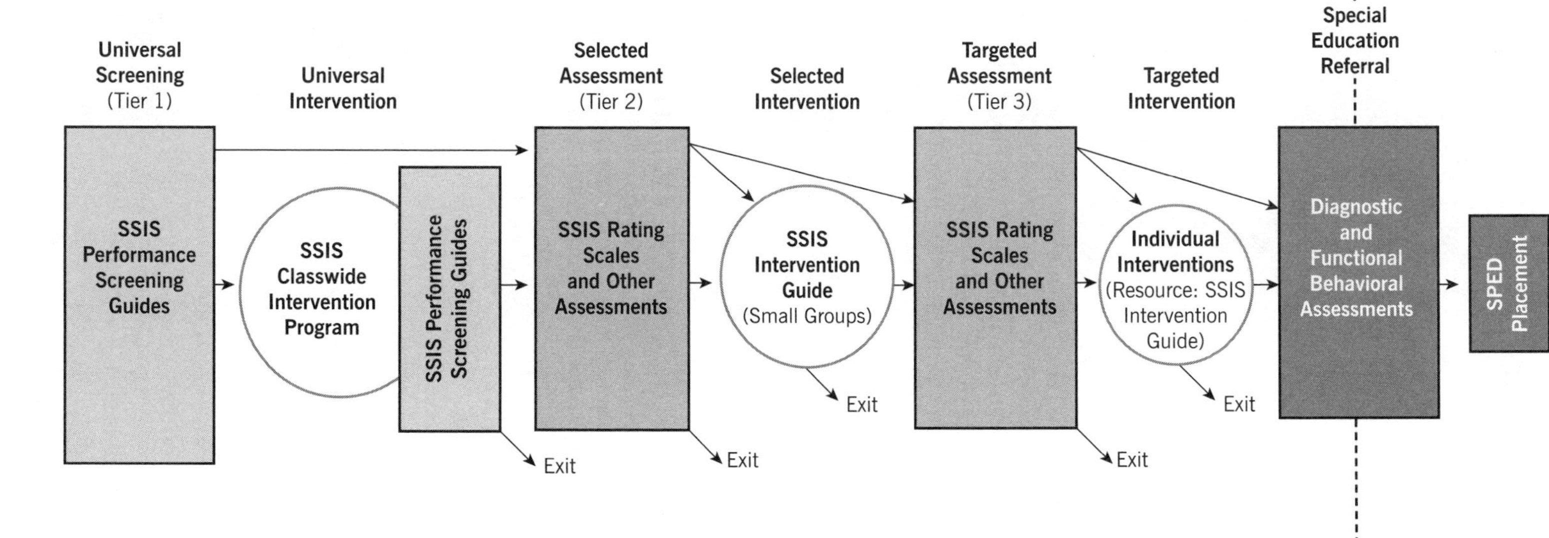

FIGURE 20.1. SSIS multi-tiered assessment and intervention model. Adapted by permission. All rights reserved. "SSIS" is a trademark, in the United States and other countries, of Pearson Education, Inc., or its affiliates.

students involved in the first year of the program, almost 16% were indigenous, over 15% had English as a second language, and almost 5% had a disability. When evaluated on Prosocial Behavior, almost 11% were judged to be at Level 1 and more than 21% at Level 2, so almost one-third of students were subsequently assessed using the SSIS-RS Teacher Form. The social skills acquisition deficits identified by application of the SSIS-RS that were most common among these students in their class were then specifically taught by the class teacher to the whole class, while the other 10 social skills were also more generally covered by the class. Normally the SSIS-RS drives individual interventions, but it was used in this project to target the more common skills deficits and drive interventions to the whole class.

Preliminary data from Year 1 of a 4-year project indicated that teacher ratings of all students on all four components of the PSG (Reading, Math, Motivation to Learn, and Prosocial Behavior) increased significantly after training. Moreover, students with low Prosocial Behavior ($N = 81$) who were evaluated on the SSIS-RS significantly improved on ratings of social skills and academic competence, while problem behavior ratings were significantly lower. These results are all in the intended direction and very promising.

Teachers' ($n = 14$) reflections on the use of the SSIS were also surveyed and documented (Davies & Cooper, 2013). All teachers believed that social skills enhanced academic outcomes and should be taught by classroom teachers, and all teachers were highly motivated to implement social skills training in their classrooms. They were generally satisfied with their current knowledge, skills, and ability to implement the SSIS-CIP in their classroom. After teaching social skills for several months, teachers were very satisfied with the SSIS-CIP as an intervention program, and reported that it met the SAFE (sequenced, active, focused, and explicit) criteria (see Durlak et al., 2011), in that the program is sequenced with connected and coordinated activities, with active and engaging lessons, is focused on at least one social skills component, and targets specific social skills by identifying explicit goals. However, in this challenging setting, with almost one-third of students with social skills deficits, teachers commented that whereas students who function well socially enjoy the program, those students who need social skills often do not respond to the standard SSIS student worksheet that targets a social skill, or do not sit long enough to listen, then comment on how boring it is. Inappropriate behavior was identified by many teacher respondents as a barrier to getting through the content.

The BSS teachers recognized that students with social skills deficits had great difficulty engaging with learning, and unless these students improved their social skills through direct instruction, they would fail to engage and learn academic skills. As such, it would seem to be imperative that students in these challenging settings must be provided with social skills training as early as possible or in conjunction with academic programming if the learning and development goals of these students are to be achieved. The BSS social skills project, although not progressing exactly as planned, is continuing with the guidance of sound assessment data and an effective structure for delivering social skills training to many children.

Conclusions

Socially competent students are happier, healthier, and more engaged in learning. In many cases, social skills are critical components that enable positive development of key behaviors that facilitate students' growth socially, emotionally, and academically. Students who have proficient social skills stay connected with others and are aware of important nuances of others' behaviors and attitudes toward them. When students fail to develop appropriate social skills, there are a number of reliable and valid tools for assessing these skills and identifying skills in need of improvement. The methods for improving these identified skills have also been well researched and have resulted in a number of viable intervention programs that vary by age and theoretical orientation. In the end, intervention programs are more alike than different. They all emphasize students' learning by observing others who exhibit desired behaviors, by discussing how these behaviors can be used to help advance constructive relationships, and, finally, by practicing these behaviors with others in multiple situations and locations.

The SSIS was featured throughout the chapter to illustrate a comprehensive and systematic approach to understanding and improving socially valid social skills such as communication, cooperation, engagement, and self-control. This system clearly emphasizes many social skills that are included within the CASEL Framework for Social–Emotional Learning.

More research is always welcome, and more class time for teaching social skills is needed, but at this point in time, the means for impacting the social skills development of thousands of students exists. Making such improvement a priority with teachers and parents is driven by the realization that social skills matter, because they foster relationships with peers, parents, and teachers, and facilitate many of conditions that make learning at school successful. Thus, social skills are socially and academic important every day in the lives of schoolchildren.

References

Achenbach, T., & Edelbrock, C. (1986). *Manual for the Teacher's Report Form and Teacher Version of the Child Behavior Profile.* Burlington: University of Vermont, Department of Psychiatry.

Achenbach, T., McConaughy, S., & Howell, C. (1987). Child/adolescent behavioral and emotional problems: Implications of cross-informant correlations for situational specificity. *Psychological Bulletin, 101*, 213–232.

Alwell, M., & Cobb, B. (2009). Social and communicative interventions and transition outcomes for youth with disabilities: A systematic review. *Career Development for Exceptional Individuals, 32*(2), 94–107.

Ang, R. P., & Hughes, J. N. (2002). Differential benefits of skills training with antisocial youth based on group composition: A meta-analytic investigation. *School Psychology Review, 31*, 164–185.

Bar-On, R., & Parker, J. D. A., (2008). *Emotional Quotient Inventory: Youth Version.* North Tonawanda, NY: Multi-Health Systems.

Beelmann, A., Pfingsten, U., & Lösel, F. (1994). Effects of training social competence in children: A meta-analysis of recent evaluation studies. *Journal of Clinical Child Psychology, 23*, 260–271.

Bellini, S., Peters, J. K., Benner, L., & Hopf, A. (2007). A meta-analysis of school-based social skills interventions for children with autism spectrum disorders. *Remedial and Special Education, 28*, 153–162.

Bierman, K. L. (2004). *Peer rejection: Developmental processes and intervention strategies.* New York: Guilford Press.

Buchanan, R., Gueldner, B. A., Tran, O. K., & Merrell, K. W. (2009). Social and emotional learning in classrooms: A survey of teachers' knowledge, perceptions and practices. *Journal of Applied School Psychology, 25*(2) 187–203.

Buettel, M. P. (2007). Research-based social–emotional interventions for Asperger syndrome: A meta-analysis. *Dissertation Abstracts International: Humanities and Social Sciences, 68*(7-A), 2823–2845.

Caprara, G. V., Barbaranelli, C., Pastorelli, C., Bandura, A., & Zimbardo, P. G. (2000). Prosocial foundations of children's academic achievement. *Psychological Science, 11*(4), 302–306.

Carlo, G., Hausmann, A., Christiansen, S., & Randall, B. (2003). Sociocognitive and behavioral correlates of a measure of prosocial tendencies for adolescents. *Journal of Early Adolescence, 231*, 107–134.

Collaborative for Academic, Social, and Emotional Learning (CASEL). (2002). *Guidelines for effective social and emotional learning: Quality programs for school and life success.* Retrieved August 20, 2012, from *www.casel.org/ publications.*

Cook, C. R., Gresham, F. M., Kern, L., Barreras, R. B., Thornton, S., & Crews, S. D. (2008). Social skills training for secondary students with emotional and/or behavioral disorders: A review and analysis of the meta-analytic literature. *Journal of Emotional and Behavioral Disorders, 16*, 131–144.

Crowe, L. M., Beauchamp, M. H., Catroppa, C., & Anderson, V. (2011). Social function assessment tools for children and adolescents: A systematic review from 1988 to 2010. *Clinical Psychology Review, 31*, 767–785.

Davies, M., & Cooper, G. (2013). Training teachers to target and develop social skills as an academic enabler. In B. Knight & R. Van Der Zwan (Eds.), *Teaching innovations supporting student outcomes in the 21st century* (pp. 45–55). Taragindi, Australia: Oxford Global Press.

DiPerna, J. C., & Elliott, S. N. (2002). Promoting academic enablers to improve student achievement. *School Psychology Review, 31*(3), 293–298.

DiPerna, J. C., Volpe, R., & Elliott, S. N. (2002). A model of academic enablers and elementary reading/language arts achievement. *School Psychology Review, 31*(3), 298–312.

Doll, E., & Elliott, S. N. (1994). Consistency of observations of preschoolers' social behavior. *Journal of Early Intervention, 18*(2), 227–238.

Durlak, J. A., Weissberg, R. P., Dymnicki, A. B., Taylor, R. D., & Schellinger, K. B. (2011). The impact of enhancing students' social and emotional learning: A meta-analysis of school based universal interventions. *Child Development, 82*(1), 405–432.

Durlak, J. A., Weissberg, R. P., & Pachan, M. (2010). A meta-analysis of after-school programs that seek to promote personal and social skills in children and adolescents. *American Journal of Community Psychology, 45*, 294–309.

Elias, M. J., Zins, J. E., Weissberg, R. P., Frey, K. S., Greenberg, M. T., Haynes, N. M., et al. (1997). *Promoting social and emotional learning: Guidelines for educators*. Alexandria, VA: Association for Supervision and Curriculum Development.

Elliott, S. N., & Busse, R. T. (2004). Assessment and evaluation of students' behavior and intervention outcomes: The utility of rating scale methods. In R. B. Rutherford, M. M. Quinn, & S. R. Mathur (Eds.), *Handbook of research in behavioral disorders* (pp. 123–142). New York: Guilford Press.

Elliott, S. N., Frey, J. R., & DiPerna, J. C. (2012). Promoting social skills: Enabling academic and interpersonal successes. In S. E. Brock & S. R. Jimerson (Eds.), *Best practices in school crisis prevention and intervention II* (pp. 55–78). Bethesda, MD: National Association of School Psychologists.

Elliott, S. N., & Gresham, F. M. (2007). *SSIS Classwide Intervention Program teacher's guide*. Minneapolis, MN: Pearson Assessments.

Elliott, S. N., & Gresham, F. M. (2008). *Social Skills Improvement System Intervention Guide* manual. Minneapolis, MN: Pearson Assessments.

Elliott, S. N., Gresham, F. M., Freeman, T., & McCloskey, G. (1988). Teachers' and observers' ratings of children's social skills: Validation of the Social Skills Rating Scale. *Journal of Psychoeducational Assessment, 6*, 152–161.

Erwin, G. (1994). Effectiveness of social skills training with children: A meta-analytic study. *Counseling Psychology Quarterly, 7*(3), 305–315.

Forness, S. R., & Kavale, K. A. (1996). Treating social skills deficits in children with learning disabilities: A meta-analysis of the research. *Learning Disability Quarterly, 19*, 2–13.

Fox, L., Dunlap, G., Hemmeter, M. L., Joseph, G. E., & Strain, P. S. (2003). The teaching pyramid: A model for supporting social competence and preventing challenging behavior in young children. *Young Children, 58*(4), 48–52.

Frey, J. R., Elliott, S. N., & Kaiser, A. P. (2014). Social skills intervention planning for preschoolers: Using the SSiS-Rating Scales to identify target behaviors valued by parents and teachers. *Assessment for Effective Intervention, 39*(3), 182–192.

Frey, J. R., & Kaiser, A. P. (2012). *Effects of school-based social skills interventions on the social behaviors of preschoolers: A meta-analysis*. Nashville, TN: Vanderbilt University.

Gersten, R., Fuchs, L. S., Compton, D., Coyne, M., Greenwood, C., & Innocenti, M. S. (2005). Quality indicators for group experimental and quasi-experimental research in special education. *Exceptional Children, 71*, 149–164.

Goldston, D. (2000). A meta-analysis of social skills literature: Elementary children. *Dissertation Abstract International: The Sciences and Engineering, 61*(6-B), 3276.

Gresham, F. M. (1981a). Assessment of children's social skills. *Journal of School Psychology, 19*, 120–134.

Gresham, F. M. (1981b). Social skills training with handicapped children: A review. *Review of Educational Research, 51*, 139–176.

Gresham, F. M. (2002). Teaching social skills to high-risk children and youth: Preventive and remedial approaches. In M. Shinn, H. Walker, & G. Stoner (Eds.), *Interventions for academic and behavior problems: II. Preventive and remedial approaches* (pp. 403–432). Bethesda, MD: National Association of School Psychologists.

Gresham, F. M., & Elliott, S. N. (1984). Assessment and classification of children's social skills: A review of methods and issues. *School Psychology Review, 13*, 292–301.

Gresham, F. M., & Elliott, S. N. (1990). *Social Skills Rating System*. Circle Pines, MN: American Guidance Service.

Gresham, F. M., & Elliott, S. N. (2008). *Social Skills Improvement System-Rating Scales*. Minneapolis, MN: Pearson Assessments.

Gresham, F. M., Elliott, S. N., Cook, C. R., Vance, M. J., & Kettler, R. J. (2010). Cross-informant agreement for social and problem behavior ratings: An investigation of the Social Skills Improvement System Rating Scales. *Psychological Assessment, 22*(1), 157–166.

Gresham, F. M., Elliott, S. N., & Kettler, R. J. (2010). Base rates of social skills acquisition/performance deficits, strengths, and problem behaviors: An analysis of the Social Skills Improvement System-Rating Scales. *Psychological Assessment, 22*(4), 809–815.

Hanson, R. E. (1988). Social skill training: A critical meta-analytic review. *Dissertation Abstracts International, 50*(4-A), 903–909.

Hersh, R., & Walker, H. M. (1983). Great expectations: Making schools effective for all students. *Policy Studies Review, 2*, 47–188.

Hightower, A. D., Cowen, E. L., Spinell, A. P., Lotyczewski, B. S., Guare, J. C., Rohrbeck, C. A., et al. (1987). The Child Rating Scale: The development and psychometric refinement of a socioemotional self-rating scale for young school children. *School Psychology Review, 16*, 239–255.

Humphrey, N., Kalambouka, A., Wigelsworth, M., Lendrum, A., Deighton, J., & Wolpert, M. (2011). Measures of social and emotional skills for children and young people: A systematic review. *Educational and Psychological Measurement, 71*(4), 617–637.

Izard, C. E., Dougherty, F. E., Bloxom, B. M., & Kotsch, N. E. (1974). *The Differential Emotions Scale: A method of measuring the subjective experience of discrete emotions.* Nashville, TN: Department of Psychology, Vanderbilt University.

January, A. M., Casey, R. J., & Paulson, D. P. (2011). A meta-analysis of classroom-wide interventions to build social skills: Do they work? *School Psychology Review, 40*(2), 242–256.

Johnston, J. M., & Pennypacker, H. S. (1980). *Strategies and tactics of human behavioral research.* Hillsdale, NJ: Erlbaum.

Kazdin, A. E. (1979). Situational specificity: The two-edged sword of behavioral assessment. *Behavioral Assessment, 1*, 57–75.

Kazdin, A. E. (1986). Comparative outcome studies of psychotherapy: Methodological issues and strategies. *Journal of Consulting and Clinical Psychology, 54*, 95–105.

Kennedy, A. (2010). A meta-analysis of interventions to improve social competence in early childhood. *Dissertation Abstracts International Section A: Humanities and Social Sciences, 71*(6-A), 1899–1924.

Kettler, R., Elliott, S. N., Davies, M. D., & Griffin, P. (2012). Testing a multi-stage screening system: Predicting performance on Australia's national achievement test using teachers' ratings of academic and social behaviors. *School Psychology International, 33*(1), 93–111.

Kratochwill, T. R., & Shapiro, E. S. (2000). Conceptual foundations of behavioral assessment in schools. In E. S. Shapiro & T. R. Kratochwill (Eds.), *Behavioral assessment in the schools* (2nd ed., pp. 3–15). New York: Guilford Press.

LaFreniere, P. J., & Dumas, J. E. (1996). Social competence and behavior evaluation in children aged three to six: The Short Form (SCBE-30). *Psychological Assessment, 8*(4), 369–377.

Lane, K. L., Givner, C. C., & Pierson, M. R. (2004). Teacher expectations of student behavior: Social skills necessary for success in elementary school classrooms. *Journal of Special Education, 38*, 104–110.

Lane, K. L., Stanton-Chapman, T., Jamison, K. R., & Phillips, A. (2007). Teacher and parent expectations of preschoolers' behavior: Social skills necessary for success. *Topics in Early Childhood Special Education, 27*, 86–97.

Losel, F., & Beelmann, A. (2003). Effects of child skills training in preventing antisocial behavior: A systematic review of randomized evaluations. *Annals of the American Academy of Political and Social Science, 587*, 84–109.

Malecki, C. K., & Elliott, S. N. (2002). Children's social behaviors as predictors of academic achievement: A longitudinal analysis. *School Psychology Quarterly, 17*(1), 1–23.

Matson, J. L., Rotatori, A. F., & Helsel, W. J. (1983). Development of a rating scale to measure social skills in children: The Matson Evaluation of Social Skills with Youngsters (MESSY). *Behavior Research and Therapy, 21*, 335–340.

McConaughy, S. H., & Ritter, D. R. (1995). Multidimensional assessment of emotional or behavioral disorders. In A. Thomas & J. Grimes (Eds.), *Best practices in school psychology III* (pp. 865–877). Washington, DC: National Association of School Psychologists.

Merrell, K. W. (1993). Using behavior rating scales to assess social skills and antisocial behavior in school settings: Development of the school social behavior scales. *School Psychology Review, 22*, 115–133.

Merrell, K. W. (1996). Social-emotional problems in early childhood: New directions in conceptualization, assessment, and treatment. *Education and Treatment of Children, 19*, 458–473

Merrell, K. W. (2003). *Behavioral, social, and emotional assessment of children and adolescents* (2nd ed.). Mahwah, NJ: Erlbaum.

Michelson, L., & Wood, R. (1982). Development and psychometric properties of the Children's Assertive Behavior Scale. *Journal of Behavioral Assessment, 4*(1), 3–13.

National Governors Association Center for Best Practices, Council of Chief State School Officers. (2010). *Common Core State Standards.* Washington, DC: Author.

Newcomb, A., Bukowski, W., & Pattee, L. (1993). Children's peer relations: A meta-analytic review of popular, rejected, neglected, controversial, and average sociometric status. *Psychological Bulletin, 113*, 99–128.

Nowicki, S., & Duke, M. P. (1994). Individual differences in the nonverbal communication of affect: The Diagnostic Analysis of Nonverbal Accuracy Scale. *Journal of Nonverbal Behavior, 18*(1), 9–35.

Parker, J. G., & Asher, S. R. (1987). Peer relations and later personal adjustment: Are low-accepted children at risk? *Psychological Bulletin, 102*, 357–389.

Pellegrini, D. A., & Urbain, E. S. (1985). An evaluation of interpersonal cognitive problem solving training with children. *Journal of Child Psychology and Psychiatry, 26*, 17–41.

Quinn, M. M., Kavale, K. A., Mathur, S. R., Rutherford, R. B., & Forness, S. R. (1999). A meta-analysis of social skill interventions for students with emotional or behavioral disorders. *Journal of Emotional and Behavioral Disorders, 7*, 54–64.

Ruffalo, S. L., & Elliott, S. N. (1997). Unraveling the situational specificity argument: An examination of cross-informant agreements among raters of children's social behavior. *School Psychology Review, 26*(3), 488–500.

Schneider, B. H. (1992). Didactic methods for enhancing children's peer relations: A quantitative review. *Clinical Psychology Review, 12*, 363–382.

Schultz, D., Izard, C. E., & Bear, G. A (2004). Children's emotion processing: Relations to emotionality and aggression. *Development and Psychopathology, 16*, 371–387.

Shields, A., & Cicchetti, D. (1997). Emotion regulation among school-age children: The development and validation of a new criterion Q-sort scale. *Developmental Psychology, 33*, 906–916.

Vaughn, S., Kim, A., Morris Sloan, C. V., Hughes, M. T., Elbaum, E., & Sridhar, D. (2003). Social skills interventions for young children with disabilities: A synthesis of group design studies. *Remedial and Special Education, 24*, 2–15.

Voegler-Lee, M. E., & Kupersmidt, J. B. (2010). Intervening in childhood social development. In P. K. Smith & C. H. Hart (Eds.), *Wiley-Blackwell handbook of childhood social development* (2nd ed., pp. 605–625). Hoboken, NJ: Wiley-Blackwell.

Walker, H. M., Ramsay, E., & Gresham, F. M. (2004). *Antisocial behavior in school: Evidence-based practices.* Belmont, CA: Wadsworth/Thomson Learning.

Wang, S., Cui, Y., & Parrila, R. (2011). Examining the effectiveness of peer-mediated and video-modeling social skills interventions for children with autism spectrum disorders: A meta-analysis in single-case research using HLM. *Research in Autism Spectrum Disorders, 5*, 562–569.

Wang, P., & Spillane, A. (2009). Evidence-based social skills interventions for children with autism: A meta-analysis. *Education and Training in Developmental Disabilities, 44*, 318–342.

Wentzel, K. R. (1993). Does being good make the grade?: Social behavior and academic competence in middle school. *Journal of Educational Psychology, 85*, 357–364.

Wolf, M. M. (1978). Social validity: The case for subjective measurement or how applied behavior analysis is finding its heart. *Journal of Applied Behavior Analysis, 11*, 203–214.

CHAPTER 21

Challenges and Opportunities in the Direct Assessment of Children's Social and Emotional Comprehension

Clark McKown

As the pages of this volume make clear, social and emotional learning (SEL) includes a constellation of mental, emotional, and behavioral processes that play a critical role in the lives of children and adults. According to the Collaborative for Academic, Social, and Emotional Learning (CASEL; *www.casel.org*), SEL encompasses a variety of important skills, including (1) *self-awareness* of feelings, strengths, and challenges; (2) *social awareness*, defined as understanding the feelings and perspectives of others (3) *relationship skills*, including the ability to form positive relationships and manage interpersonal conflict; (4) *responsible decision making*, including making positive choices about personal and social behavior; and (5) *self-management*, defined as the ability to manage one's emotions to achieve a goal (Elias et al., 1997).

One critical issue for researchers and practitioners alike is how to measure these important dimensions of SEL. There have been several promising developments in the assessment of SEL, described in this chapter and elsewhere in this handbook by Denham (Chapter 19 and Elliot, Frey, and Davies (Chapter 20). However, a great deal remains to be accomplished before usable, feasible, and scientifically sound instruments are available and are suitable for mass administration. The lack of such tools greatly limits the extent to which the impact of SEL initiatives can be known, and the extent to which children's acquisition and use of SEL skills can be systematically and periodically monitored. Furthermore, without rigorous and robust SEL assessment systems, the meaning and impact of state and national SEL standards will be difficult to evaluate.

This chapter is for researchers and practitioners interested in the assessment of children's SEL. Its purpose is to (1) describe the policy and practice context in which SEL assessment is embedded, (2) review the state of the art in SEL assessment practices, (3) discuss the promise and future directions of direct assessment for ascertaining children's SEL, and (4) outline challenges in SEL assessment and the implications for educational practice. This will be followed by recommendations regarding the kinds of SEL assessments that are needed and examples of innovative tools that foreshadow future developments in SEL assessment.

The Growth of SEL Programs and Policies

Theory and research have clarified what SEL is, how to cultivate it, and what its impact is on youth development. For example, we have learned that well-developed SEL is associated with positive development, as indicated by, for example, higher quality peer relationships (Dodge & Price, 1994; Nowicki & Duke, 1994), and better academic outcomes (DiPerna, Volpe, & Elliott, 2005; Wentzel, 1993). In addition, over the past three decades, a variety of school-based intervention models have been developed and evaluated. The weight of evidence suggests that such programs enhance children's SEL (Durlak, Weissberg, Dymnicki, Taylor, & Schellinger, 2011). We have also learned that when children participate in well-implemented, evidence-based SEL programs, they do better on a range of outcome domains (Durlak et al., 2011).

The increasing recognition that SEL matters has led to significant developments in educational policy and programs. Thus far, many states have adopted K–12 educational standards that either include significant SEL components or, in the case of Illinois, include free-standing SEL standards (see Dusenbury et al., Chapter 35, in this volume). Furthermore, at least two federal bills have been introduced that contain provisions for advancing children's SEL. These developments reflect a broadening consensus that SEL matters. Indeed, the increasing state and federal emphasis on SEL reflects a shift from establishing evidence that SEL matters to the development of policies and resources to enhance SEL among schoolchildren.

A growing number of strategies are available to help educators meet state SEL standards. In particular, a large number of effective school-based SEL programs have been developed. Although the emphases of these SEL programs vary, all are designed to promote one or more dimensions of SEL among elementary and secondary students. Rigorous field trials have demonstrated the efficacy of many of these interventions. The existence of programs with demonstrated efficacy gives greater confidence that state and federal policies can be met through the wise adoption of evidence-based curricula that have a broad and lasting benefit to students and the systems that serve them. Just as it is important to measure and monitor children's academic progress, it is important to know what SEL skills children bring to the school, and how they are progressing in response to programs designed to enhance SEL skills. However, there are fewer tools available to assess children's SEL. The lack of SEL assessment tools poses an obstacle to the advancement of the field.

The State of the Art in SEL Assessment

The Purposes of Assessment

There are many purposes to which assessment of any construct, including SEL, can be applied. Assessment may be used to measure environments or individuals, to measure processes (formative assessment) or outcomes (summative assessment), to measure teacher practices or student behaviors, to assess programs, to identify children with emerging or frank problems, to diagnose individual children, or to monitor response to intervention. While I recognize the critical importance of all of these assessment goals to the SEL movement and to strengthening schools and children, this chapter focuses on the direct assessment of individual children's SEL, and in particular, their ability to encode, interpret, and reason about social–emotional information, referred to in this chapter as "social–emotional comprehension." The main reasons for such a focus are that (1) social–emotional comprehension is associated with child outcomes, (2) SEL programs and standards focus on the development of social–emotional comprehension, and (3) few, if any, usable, feasible instruments for the mass assessment of social–emotional comprehension exist.

Guiding Theory

Just as theory has guided intervention development and policy, theory should guide the development of targeted, meaningful, scientifically sound, and practical assessments. The theory of SEL that guides all the chapters of this volume is particularly important, both because it integrates a number of strands and, perhaps more importantly, because it can serve as the basis of state standards that should and, I hope, will drive school-based SEL assessment and programming. That theory of SEL encompasses a very broad swath of human social and emotional propensities. For my purposes in this chapter, a more narrowly tailored theory of SEL, consistent with the broad model used in this volume, is used.

A number of relevant influential models of SEL may provide focused guidance for the development and use of assessments and interventions. Examples of relevant and useful frameworks include the affective social competence model established by Halberstadt, Denham, and Dunsmore (2001), the social information-processing model established by Crick and Dodge (1996), the emotional intelligence model of Salovey and colleagues (Mayer & Salovey, 1997; Mayer, Salovey, & Caruso, 2004; Salovey & Mayer, 1990), the SEL framework of Lipton and Nowicki (2009), and the social neuroscience model of Adolphs (2003). For additional information about SEL-related theories, see Brackett, Elbertson, and Rivers (Chapter 2, this volume).

These models vary in their emphasis about what social–emotional phenomena are important, how those phenomena operate, and how they are related to various life outcomes. However, they share some important guiding themes that will help researchers and practitioners alike as they seek to conceptualize SEL and evaluate SEL assessment and intervention practices.

First, adopting the terminology of Lipton and Nowicki (2009), all of the theories previously mentioned acknowledge that SEL involves *comprehension* of social–emotional information, which includes encoding, interpreting, and reasoning about social–emotional information. All of the theories also acknowledge that SEL involves the *execution* of goal-directed behaviors in interpersonal contexts. All of the theories mentioned acknowledge that comprehension and execution are intimately related. Finally, these theories reflect the reality that effective social–emotional functioning reflects students' skills at both comprehension and execution, and some children may have the former skills but not the latter. Bearing in mind the distinction between social–emotional comprehension and execution, the different classes of assessment, which I next review briefly, are each suited better to assessing some aspects of SEL than others.

Classes of Assessment

A variety of methods are available to assess children's social–emotional repertoires. Behavior rating scales and behavioral observation systems share a focus on behavior, or social–emotional *execution.* These systems are well suited to measuring the presence or absence of behaviors that either facilitate or interfere with positive social relationships. For example, the Social Skills Improvement System (SSIS) rating scales (Gresham & Elliott, 1990, 2009) includes parent-, teacher-, and self-report assessments of the frequency with which a child engages in socially skilled behaviors such as cooperativeness and assertiveness (Elliott et al., Chapter 20, this volume). It also includes scales that assess the presence of aggression, hyperactivity, and other problem behaviors. Behavioral observation is also well suited to capturing the frequency and intensity of socially facilitating and interfering behavior (Reynolds & Kamphaus, 2004). Similarly, peers can assess the presence of socially positive and interfering behavior (McKown, Gumbiner, & Johnson, 2011). Self-report questionnaires can be useful for ascertaining a child's view of his or her social–emotional characteristics (Harter, 1982; Kovacs, 2011; Measelle, Ablow, Cowan, & Cowan, 1998).

There are advantages and disadvantages of each kind of assessment. Behavior rating scales and peer nominations require raters to assess of the frequency with which the target child displays certain behaviors or characteristics *in general.* As a result, these methods provide little or no information about the contexts in which the behaviors take place. They may be better at capturing infrequent but high-impact behaviors, such as extreme aggression, that might not occur during direct observation. Peer nominations can yield an important additional perspective on children's behavior and has many of the strengths and weaknesses of behavior rating scales. Behavioral observation that provides an assessment of behavior in naturalistic contexts can be informative. However, obtaining reliable observational scores requires observation across settings and occasions, which is often prohibitively time and resource intensive. In addition, observations may not fully capture important child behaviors that are not displayed during the observation periods. Self-report measures are irreplaceable sources of information about children's views of themselves. Often, however, they are not feasible with young children, and depending on what is measured, social desirability response bias or lack of insight can compromise their validity.

A comprehensive list of the strengths and weaknesses of these assessment methods is beyond the scope of this chapter. The interested reader is directed to other works (Denham, Ji, & Hamre, 2010; Gresham, 2011; Humphrey et al., 2011; Merrell, 2009; Wigelsworth, Humphrey, Kalambouka, & Lendrum, 2010). What is important is that these assessment methods reflect the main available tools for anyone wanting to assess children's social–emotional *execution*.

Several important conclusions can be drawn about these assessment methods and their potential to guide and inform the SEL movement. First, they are useful tools that play an important role in assessing children's SEL. Second, there are some dimensions of SEL that are not currently, but should be, measured by new or refined measures of this type. For example, "relationship skills", a key feature of the CASEL model of SEL, are only obliquely measured by existing assessments. Third, some dimensions of SEL that are not yet measured by existing instruments require different assessment approaches for valid measurement.

In particular, teacher rating scales, behavioral observation, peer nominations, and child self-report are better suited to assessing social–emotional *execution* than social–emotional *comprehension*. This is illustrated through analogy with academic assessment. Teacher ratings, behavioral observation, peer nomination, and child self-report can provide a useful general estimate of academic competence. However, academic skills are probably more reliably and validly measured through "direct assessment", or assessments that require children to demonstrate their mastery by solving problems of varied difficulty (Begeny, Krouse, Brown, & Mann, 2011; Kilday, Kinzie, Mashburn, & Whittaker, 2012). Similarly, observers, peers, and children themselves may provide a rough estimate of a child's social–emotional comprehension (e.g., SSIS: Gresham & Elliott, 2009; Emory Dyssemia Index [EDI]: Love, Nowicki, & Duke, 1994). However, social–emotional comprehension, like reading, involves the activation and deployment of invisible mental processes. Accordingly, social–emotional comprehension would be better measured with direct assessments that require children to demonstrate their mastery of social–emotional skills by solving social–emotional problems of varied difficulty.

Direct Assessment of SEL

There are some measures that directly assess children's social–emotional comprehension. These tools assess a subset of the constructs of interest to SEL researchers and practitioners. What follows is a review of selected SEL direct assessments, organized by the dimension of SEL that is assessed. This review includes illustrative examples of direct assessment practices and is not intended as an exhaustive compendium. Furthermore, many of the assessments described next establish the feasibility of scientifically sound direct assessments *in concept*, although they engender significant obstacles to wide use in applied settings, including difficulty in administering, scoring, and interpreting the results from assessments, and requiring more time than is typically available (McKown, Allen, Russo-Ponsaran, & Johnson, 2013). Table 21.1 provides a summary of the assessments reviewed in this chapter. Readers interested in a more comprehensive compendium of assessment options are directed elsewhere (Denham et al., 2010; Gresham, 2011; Humphrey et al., 2011; Merrell, 2009; Wigelsworth et al., 2010).

Self-Awareness

No direct assessments of children's awareness of their social–emotional strengths, challenges, and emotions have been developed. Self-awareness is a complex construct to measure because, by definition, it requires some form of self-reflection and self-report, and this can be inaccurate or clouded by social desirability response bias or limited insight. Nevertheless, models of direct assess-

TABLE 21.1. Direct Assessments of Various Dimensions of Social–Emotional Learning

Construct	Related constructs	Direct assessments	Assessment development need
Self-awareness of feelings, strengths, and challenges	Self-concept, self-esteem, self-efficacy, self-image accuracy	Berkeley puppet interview (Measelle et al., 1998); self-concept scale (Harter, 1982)	Definitional clarity about what constitutes healthy self-awareness at different ages Usable, feasible, and scalable assessments for a wide age range
Social awareness, or the ability to understand others' feelings	Nonverbal accuracy	DANVA (Nowicki & Duke, 1994); Denham scales (Denham, 1986)	Scalable assessments
Social awareness, or the understanding of others' perspectives	Theory of mind, social perspective-taking	Experimental measures of theory of mind (Happé, 1994)	Usable, feasible, and scalable assessments for a wide age range
Relationship skills, or the ability to form positive relationships	Social skills, friendship quality	None	Definitional clarity about what constitutes relationship skills Usable, feasible, scalable, and scientifically sound assessments corresponding to construct definition
Relationship skills, or the ability to deal effectively with conflict	Conflict resolution, social problem solving, social information processing	SIP-AP (Kupersmidt et al., 2011); TOPS (Bowers et al., 2005); SLDT (Bowers et al., 2008)	Scalable assessments to characterize dimensions of individual children's SEL skills related to conflict resolution.
Relationship skills, such as the ability to work in teams	Social skills	None	Usable, feasible, validated, and scalable assessments to accurately characterize dimensions of individual children's SEL skills related to teamwork
Responsible decision making, including making ethical constructive choices about personal and social behavior	Social conventional and moral development, social problem solving	SIP-AP (Kupersmidt et al., 2011); TOPS (Bowers et al., 2005); SLDT (Bowers et al., 2008)	Definitional clarity about responsible decision making at different ages Scalable assessments
Self-management, the ability to manage emotions and behaviors to achieve a goal	Self-regulation, emotion regulation	PSRA in preschool (Smith-Donald et al., 2007); nothing in elementary school and beyond	Definitional clarity about what constitutes self-management Usable, feasible, scalable, and scientifically sound direct assessments

Note. DANVA, Diagnostic Analysis of Nonverbal Accuracy; SIP-AP, Social Information Processing Application; TOPS, Test of Problem Solving; PSRA, Preschool Self-Regulation Assessment.

ment have been developed for constructs related to self-awareness that may prove instructive for future assessment development efforts. Harter (1982) developed a reliable and valid 28-item self-report questionnaire to assess perceived self-competence. The Harter Scale is appropriate for children ages 9 and older. For younger children, Measelle and colleagues (1998) developed the Berkeley Puppet Interview (BPI) to measure young children's self-concepts. For the BPI, children interact with and are "interviewed" by two puppets. For each item, the puppets make paired and opposite statements about themselves, then ask the child which puppet the child is more like. The BPI includes scales measuring perceived academic competence, achievement motivation, social competence, peer acceptance, internalizing symptoms, and externalizing symptoms. Consistent with the CASEL model of SEL, some of the BPI scales pertain to the general idea of being aware of one's strengths and needs. Measelle and colleagues found that young children have a multidimensional self-concept, and could reliably report their self-concepts, with internal consistency reliabilities ranging from .62 to .78. In addition, the BPI exhibits evidence of criterion-related validity, with performance on the BPI correlated with a variety of criterion measures in theoretically consistent ways. The BPI takes about 45 minutes to administer, which likely limits its usefulness for practitioners.

Recognizing Emotions in Others

Some direct SEL assessments measure children's ability to recognize what others are feeling from nonverbal behaviors such as facial expressions, tone of voice, or posture. Assessments that measure emotion recognition skills have arisen from varied theoretical traditions, including affective social competence (Halberstadt et al., 2001), nonverbal communications (Nowicki & Duke, 1994), and social information-processing theory (Crick & Dodge, 1996). Here, I review four assessments that can be used to measure emotion recognition skills in preschoolers through adolescents. All are individually administered assessments and most require a trained test administrator to work individually with a child to complete the assessment. For all but one assessment reviewed below, administrators must hand-score the assessments and convert raw scores to more interpretable metrics.

For assessing emotion knowledge in preschool-age children, Denham (1986) created the Affect Knowledge Test (AKT). For the AKT, children are tested individually by a trained administrator, who uses puppets with removable faces displaying different emotions to evaluate children's knowledge of basic emotions and the situations that evoke them. Internal consistency and test–retest reliabilities for the AKT range from .60 to .85 (Denham et al., 2010). Furthermore, the AKT exhibits criterion-related validity, with a body of research demonstrating that performance on the AKT is associated with peer and teacher report of social competence (Denham et al., 2003) and other concurrent and later indicators of adjustment (Cutting & Dunn, 1999; Denham et al., 2002; Dunn & Herrera, 1997). The AKT takes about 10 minutes to administer.

Similarly, the Child and Adolescent Recognition of Emotion (CARE) is an emotion recognition task with five subtests, three of which assess facial emotion recognition and two of which assess emotional posture recognition (Innovation Research and Training, 2008). CARE is a computer-administered assessment with automated score reporting that was developed for children ages 4–6. The facial emotion recognition tasks use Facial Action Coding System (FACS; Ekman, Friesen, & Hager, 2002) coded photographs of children. CARE demonstrates evidence of criterion-related validity, with performance on the CARE associated with other direct assessments of facial emotion recognition and teacher report of positive social behavior of 4-year-olds (Warren-Khot et al., 2012). The CARE takes about 30 minutes to administer.

The NEPSY-II (developmental NEuroPSYchological assessment) Affect Recognition (AR) test involves three facial emotion recognition tasks (Korkman, Kirk, & Kemp, 2007). For all three tasks, children view photographs of other children. First, children view pairs of faces and indicate whether the children in the paired photographs feel the same. Next, children view a set of photographs and select, from among several, the two children who are feeling the same. Finally, children view a target face and select one of several other faces whose emotional expression is the same as the target face. AR provides an overall score intended to reflect a respondent's ability to read facial expressions. The NEPSY-II was normed on a nationally representative sample of 1,200 children ages 3–16 in the United States. AR demonstrates internal consistency reliabilities (Cronbach's alpha) between .64 and .88, and test–retest reliabilities (r_{12}) between .46 and .66 depending on child age (Korkman et al., 2007). Performance on AR is associated with expected outcome measures such as the Comprehension subtest of the Wechsler scales and diagnostic status (Korkman et al., 2007). NEPSY-II AR takes about 10 minutes to administer.

Another direct assessment that is suitable for measuring emotion recognition in school-age through adult individuals is the Diagnostic Assessment of Nonverbal Accuracy (DANVA; Nowicki & Duke, 1994). The DANVA measures children's recognition of emotions from facial expressions, posture, and tone of voice. A large number of studies have demonstrated that the DANVA scores exhibits good internal consistency reliability, ranging from .68 to .88, and good test–retest reliability, ranging from .70 to .86 (Nowicki & Duke, 1994). The DANVA also demonstrates good criterion-related validity, with children's performance on the DANVA associated with conceptually related indicators of adjustment, including peer acceptance and academic outcomes (Nowicki & Duke, 1994). Provisional norms have been developed for the DANVA for children ages 6 and up, but those norms are based on a compilation of nonrepresentative samples from existing research (Nowicki & Duke, 1994; Nowicki & Mitchell, 1998). Each subtest of the DANVA takes 5–10 minutes to administer.

Recognizing Others' Perspectives

Another critical dimension of SEL involves taking the perspectives of others. Research on social perspective taking (Selman, 1980) and theory of mind (Flavell, 1999) broadly describe "perspective taking" as the ability to infer another person's mental state, including another person's beliefs, desires, opinions, and intentions. A large variety of clever experimental tasks have been developed to assess children's ability to infer the contents of others' minds. For example, a classic "false-belief" task from the theory-of-mind tradition involves showing a child a box of candy and asking what is inside the box. Most children indicate that candy is in the box. The experimenter then reveals that the box actually contains something unexpected, such as pencils. The pencils are replaced in the box and the child is asked, "If someone walked into the room and had never seen the box, what would they think is in it?" To know that a naive observer would think the box contained candy requires that the child understand that what he or she believes to be true and what another person believes to be true are different, and to infer the other person's false belief.

Most efforts to measure false beliefs have been developed to understand the typical course of cognitive development. For example, researchers have long been interested in when children normatively develop an understanding of what minds are, and what others are thinking (Gopnik & Meltzoff, 1997; Selman, 1980). Other work on perspective taking and theory of mind has focused on understanding the consequences of impaired social perspective-taking abilities. For example, in the 1990s, researchers established clearly that children with autism, a disorder characterized by serious social impairment, perform more poorly than their typically developing peers on theory-of-mind tasks (Baron-Cohen, 1995; Happé, 1994). This insight strengthened the conclusion that social perspective taking is an important foundation for the capacity to develop social relationships.

Experimental measures have been well scaled (Wellman & Liu, 2004). However, few theory-of-mind assessments have been sufficiently validated to interpret an individual child's assessment performance. One exception is the Theory of Mind subtest of the NEPSY-II (NEPSY-II ToM; Korkman et al., 2007). I described the normative sample of the NEPSY-II in the earlier discussion of the NEPSY-II AR. NEPSY-II ToM includes 15 core items that assess false-belief understanding and related constructs, such as nonliteral language and idioms. ToM yields a single score designed to reflect children's understanding of others' beliefs and intentions. The reported internal consistency of NEPSY-II ToM ranges from .76 to .84, depending on age, and the reported test–retest reliability is .77 (Korkman et al., 2007). Performance on NEPSY-II ToM is associated with expected outcomes, including language disorder status, and teacher report of school readiness and social awareness. NEPSY-II ToM takes 10–15 minutes to administer.

Making Responsible Decisions and Relationship Skills

No theory, empirical research, or measurement approach maps neatly onto the concept of "responsible decision making" or "relationship skills." To the extent that responsible decision making and relationship skills both involve the ability to understand and solve complex real-world social problems, there are bodies of scholarship, with associated measurement strategies, that can be used to assess decision-making processes. One prominent theoretical and empirical basis for the measurement of decision-making processes is the social information-processing approach described by Crick and Dodge (1996). In their model, when confronted with social situations, children engage in a series of cognitive processes to make sense of that information and evaluate and select a response. These processes include defining the problem, formulating a social goal, considering a range of response options, and selecting the optimal response option.

Direct assessments have been developed based on this model. Most have been created as vignette-based interviews in which children are told about hypothetical social problems, then asked questions to ascertain their social problem-solving style. Many of these assessments are suitable for interpretation at a group level of aggregation but are not sufficiently reliable to diagnose an individual child's strengths and needs. Three direct assessments have been standardized and are adequate for use to assess individual students. One is a Web-delivered assessment called the Social Information Processing Application (SIP-AP; Kupersmidt et al., 2011), which measures children's understanding of and ability to solve hypothetical social problems. The SIP-AP was developed to measure social information processing and is based on the Crick and Dodge (1996) model. The SIP-AP includes eight video vignettes shot from a first-person perspective and depicts situations involving ambiguous provocation toward the protagonist in variety of situations.

Standard administration of the SIP-AP includes all eight vignettes; after each vignette, children are asked to answer 16 questions using a 5-point response scale. Questions are designed to assess problem encoding, cue interpretation, emotional response, social goals, and response access. The vignettes and questions that are asked can be customized, and additional questions can be created. In a study that included 244 boys who completed the SIP-AP, Kupersmidt and colleagues (2011) reported scale internal consistency reliabilities between .83 and .94 for all but one scale. The factor structure of the items was consistent with SIP theory. In addition, performance on the SIP-AP was associated with expected criterion measures: Hostile attributions, retribution goals, and aggressive response evaluation and selection were associated with parent and teacher report of antisocial behavior. The SIP-AP was normed with a sample of 269 boys ages 8–12. The standard version of the SIP-AP takes about 30 minutes to administer.

Two additional assessments, originating from the field of speech and language pathology, have many of the characteristics of a social decision-making assessment. One, the Test of Problem Solving, Elementary Form, Third Edition (TOPS-3; Bowers, Huisingh, & LoGuidice, 2005, p. 9), is described in the test manual as assessing "how children use language skills to reason and think their way through everyday situations." Although the design, content, and format of this assessment do not correspond precisely to the Crick and Dodge (1996) model, it nevertheless appears on its face to assess children's higher-order reasoning about a variety of complex real-world social situations. For the Elementary Form of the TOPS-3, children look at 18 photographs of a person or people engaged in everyday activities. For each situation, children are asked questions assessing their ability to make inferences about the situation, to reason about the sequence of events depicted, to infer counterfactuals (negative questions), to generate appropriate solutions to problems, to predict events, and to provide reasons about the origins of the situation depicted. Average internal consistency reliabilities for the scales range from .56 to .69. Test–retest reliability for the scales ranges from .62 to .70 and is .84 for the overall scale. Children with language disorders score significantly lower than typical controls at each 1-year age band from 6 to 13. The TOPS-3 was normed on a nationally representative sample of U.S. schoolchildren between ages 6 and 13. The TOPS-3 takes approximately 35 minutes to administer.

The Social Language Development Test (SLDT), developed by the authors of the TOPS-3 (Bowers et al., 2008), assesses "social language skills, including nonverbal communication, for elementary students ages 6:0 through 11:11" (p. 12). The SLDT assesses higher-order problem solving about social information in a way that corresponds more closely than the TOPS to the Crick and Dodge (1996) model of social information processing. One subtest, called Interpersonal Negotiations, includes 12 hypothetical vignettes involving conflict and negotiation. Children are asked three questions. One question assesses problem encoding by asking children to state the problem. An additional question in Interpersonal Negotiations assesses solution generation.

Another subtest, called Making Inferences, assesses cue interpretation. For this task, children view photographs of people in a variety of situations and are asked to say what the person is thinking. Two additional subtests do not correspond neatly to the Crick and Dodge (1996) model. Multiple Interpretations assesses children's ability to describe more than one underlying cause to a social situation. The Supporting Peers subtest assesses the things that a child can say to be supportive to peers in a variety of stressful situations. Internal consistency reliability for the SLDT ranges from .65 to .93, and test–retest reliability ranged from .45 to .79. At most ages and for most subtests and a composite score, typically developing children performed better on the SLDT than their peers with language disorders. The SLDT was normed on a nationally representative sample of 1,100 children ages 6–11. The SLDT takes about 45 minutes to administer.

Pragmatic Judgment

Although language skills are not typically emphasized as a core dimension of SEL as discussed in this handbook, there are aspects of language and its assessment that, for conceptual and practical reasons, are important to consider. From a conceptual point of view, the field of pragmatics is a subfield of linguistics that deals with the ways speakers and listeners infer the meaning of language from not only its surface content but also contextual cues, prior understanding, and social conventions. Pragmatic judgment in its concrete form involves being able to infer a speaker's social intentions and knowing what to say, and how to say it, in a variety of social contexts to achieve social goals. From a practical point of view, pragmatic language is critical to social success. In our research, performance on tests of pragmatic judgment are consistently associated with children's socially competent behavior (McKown, 2007; McKown, Gumbiner, Russo, & Lipton, 2011; McKown et al., 2013).

Several individually administered tests of pragmatic judgment have been published. The Comprehensive Assessment of Spoken Language (CASL; Carrow-Woolfolk, 1999) includes a subtest that focuses on pragmatic judgment and includes 60 items in which children judge the appropriateness of social language in a variety of social contexts or produce social language in response to hypothetical social situations. Internal consistency reliability ranges from .77 to .92, and test–retest reliability ranges from .65 to .83, depending on age (Carrow-Woolfook, 1999). In terms of validity evidence, typically developing children perform better than language- but not speech-impaired children (Carrow-Woolfolk, 1999). In addition, better performance on this test is associated with parent and teacher reports of socially competent behavior (McKown, 2007; McKown et al., 2011). The CASL was normed on a nationally representative sample of 1,700 in 1-year age bands from ages 3 to 11 and 2-year age bands from ages 12 to 21. The CASL Pragmatic Judgment subtest takes 10–15 minutes to administer.

The Test of Pragmatic Language, Second Edition (TOPL-2; Phelps-Terasaki & Phelps-Gunn, 2007) is a 39-item assessment of children's communicative competence, which is defined by the authors as "the use of the social rules of language to convey or interpret intentions that are contextually appropriate" (p. 1). The assessment, which is individually administered, is designed for youth ages 6–18. The examiner shows the examinee illustrations and for each asks a question that gets at the examinee's pragmatic skills. Reported internal consistency reliability ranges from .82 to .93 (average .91) and reported test–rest reliability ranges from .94 to .99. Performance on the TOPL-2 is highly correlated with performance on other language assessments. Typically developing children score significantly better than children with language disorders or learning disabilities (Phelps-Terasaki & Phelps-Gunn, 2007). The TOPL-2 was normed on a nationally representative sample of 1,136 children ages 6–18. Administration time is 60–90 minutes.

Self-Management

Self-management is defined as the ability to manage one's thoughts, emotions, and behavior to achieve a goal. For preschool-age children, Raver and colleagues developed the Preschool Self-Regulation Assessment (PSRA; Smith-Donald, Raver, Hayes, & Richardson, 2007), a naturalistic direct measure that assesses children's regulation of emotion, attention, and impulses. For the PSRA, children complete a series of tasks requiring regulation, and their behavior is scored as they complete the task. For example, for one subtest, Snack Delay, children are instructed to wait until the examiner gives a signal before they eat a candy under a clear cup. Their ability to wait is scored as an indicator of impulse control. PSRA internal consistency and interrater reliabilities consistently exceed .80. Factor structure and concurrent associations with other measures suggest that the PSRA is a valid assessment of self-regulation. (Smith-Donald et al., 2007). Total time to administer the PSRA is 35–45 minutes. Direct assessments of self-regulation with analogous construct coverage for children in elementary school and beyond have not been well developed.

For older children, the self-report Grit Scale and other self-report instruments (Duckworth, 2011) have been developed to measure varied dimensions of self-control. In addition, the Mayer–Salovey–Caruso Emotional Intelligence Test: Youth Version (MSCEIT:YV) assesses several aspects of emotion understanding and regulation. The MSCEIT:YV is a direct assessment in which youth ages 10–17 solve emotional problems that measure the ability to accurately perceive, use, emotion, and manage emotions, which are the four dimensions of emotion intelligence in the Mayer–Salovey–Caruso model of emotional intelligence. The MSCEIT-YV is well suited to assessing the emotion management dimension of self-management. For the adult MSCEIT, split-half reliabilities range from .79 to .83 (Mayer et al., 2004). In addition, performance on the MSCEIT is positively associated with adaptive outcomes such as enthusiasm and social relatedness, and negatively associated with maladaptive outcomes, including physical altercations and tobacco use. For the MSCEIT:YV, internal consistency reliability ranged from .70 to .85. In addition, the better children performed on the MSCEIT:YV, the higher teachers rated their social skills and the lower teachers rated their externalizing behavior (Rivers, Brackett, & Salovey, 2008).

Combining Direct SEL Assessments

Many of the assessments reviewed previously measure one dimension of social–emotional comprehension and leave other dimensions unmeasured. In most cases, this is because the assessment arose from a particular theoretical or empirical tradition and was designed to advance the cause of measurement within that tradition. State standards and applied practice, however, are broader in their focus, demanding that practitioners attend to multiple dimensions of social–emotional learning. This raises the question of whether theoretically and empirically coherent social–emotional assessments that measure across multiple dimensions of social–emotional comprehension can be developed, and whether they provide incremental validity over more narrowly tailored measurement approaches.

The work of my colleagues and myself suggests that the answer is yes. In one study that examined chart data from a clinic sample, McKown (2007) found that several direct SEL comprehension assessments were associated with parent and teacher report of social behavior. In addition, when controlling for age, sex, and IQ, performance on the pragmatic judgment subtest of the CASL and on the TOPS were each significantly associated with parent and teacher report of social behavior on the Behavioral Assessment System for Children (BASC; Reynolds & Kamphaus, 2004). In a second study, McKown and colleagues (2009), examining a general education sample and a clinic-referred sample, found that direct SEL assessments measuring nonverbal accuracy, mental state inference skills, pragmatic judgment, and social problem solving exhibited a theoretically coherent three-factor structure, and that a composite SEL factor was strongly associated with a third-party report of children's socially competent behavior. That composite SEL factor was more strongly associated with social behavior than any of the single factors alone, suggesting that measuring across domains is more informative than measuring within a single, more narrowly tailored domain. Extending that work, McKown and colleagues (2013), examining typically developing and clinic-referred children, found that assessments of social–emotional comprehension demonstrated a three-factor solution, that those factor scores were highly reliable, that the factor scores demonstrated convergent and discriminant validity, and that children demonstrated theoretically expected age and diagnostic differences in performance on the assessments.

Challenges and Implications for Educational Practice

The assessments reviewed previously are among a small number of tools designed to measure children's social–emotional comprehension directly through children's performance on social–emotional tasks. They are also among the few direct assessments with demonstrated reliability, validity, and normative data. As discussed previously, many direct SEL assessments demonstrate consistency of measurement across items and time, and validity, as judged by coherent factor structures and theoretically expected relationships with age, diagnostic status, and other criterion measures. There are, however, limitations to existing measurement strategies, particularly for practitioners interested in the mass assessment of children's social–emotional comprehension. Because of proliferating SEL standards and the accompanying need to monitor children's skill against those standards, this is a significant challenge for the field.

Existing assessments are designed for and best suited to individual assessment in the context of a clinical evaluation. Those assessment strategies are generally not suitable for universal application, either for screening or regular measurement of SEL. Multiple barriers prevent existing direct SEL assessments from being well suited to universal assessment. All but one of the assessments reviewed in this chapter are individually administered, and most require significant training to ensure standardized administration. For most of the assessments, scoring and interpretation requires further work and specialized knowledge. Furthermore, each of the assessments reviewed in this chapter takes a significant amount of time to administer.

One of the reasons it is possible to administer standardized achievement tests is that the barriers to mass administration, scoring, interpretation, and application are low. In contrast, existing direct SEL assessments are not suitable for mass administration, and the practical barriers to their use are often prohibitive. What is needed in the future are practical, usable, feasible, scientifically sound assessments that are suitable for mass administration. With support from the Institute of Education Sciences, my colleagues and I are developing such a system for K–3 children. Until that system, or something like it, is developed, in practice, existing direct SEL assessments can best be deployed to assess children identified with social–emotional difficulties. Understanding the patterns of social–emotional strength and need of socially impaired children can help educators develop well-informed case formulations and corresponding educational plans to remedy social impairment and increase children's ability to participate successfully in school life.

Another significant challenge is the lack of direct assessment strategies that use a unified theory of SEL to guide the measurement of SEL comprehension. Existing direct assessments generally measure one dimension of social–emotional comprehension, such as recognition of emotions in others. No single assessment battery broadly samples across all potentially critical dimensions of social–emotional comprehension. Standardization samples and procedures vary widely. For example, DANVA norms are bootstrapped from a large number of empirical studies (Nowicki & Duke, 1994). The SIP-AP has norms for boys between ages 8 and 12, and is designed to assess social cognitive correlates of aggression (Kupersmidt et al., 2011). As a result, to measure a child's social–emotional comprehension, practitioners must administer many different assessments that have been normed on different samples with different goals, without knowing how those scores are related, limiting the value and interpretability of the results.

Guidelines and Recommendations

What is clear from this review is that the direct assessment of social–emotional comprehension is possible. Indeed, technically sound direct assessments of many dimensions of SEL have been developed. Although the assessments reviewed previously originate from a variety of different theories and vary in their construct coverage, there is significant overlap between what they assess and the SEL standards that are proliferating at the state level. We know that these assessments can provide useful and actionable information. Although further study across multiple age ranges is still needed, completed research suggests that performance on these assessments is associated with social–emotional execution, and social acceptance and other life outcomes (e.g., McKown et al., 2009). Deficits identified by any of these assessment approaches may point to the need for intervention in the area in which the deficit is identified. Several considerations may guide researchers and practitioners interested in the use of direct assessment. It is important to note that these guidelines apply to the use of existing SEL assessments, which are better suited to clinical assessment than to universal assessment.

- *Guideline 1: Use direct assessment for indicated cases.* Although there have been promising advances in the direct assessment of social–emotional comprehension, what is readily apparent from this review is that the vast majority of assessments were designed for individual administration by a trained clinician or researcher. As a result, there are no technically feasible delivery mechanisms for mass administration. These assessments are all well suited to addressing basic and applied research questions. Perhaps the best current clinical and educational application of existing direct assessments is as a means to understand the social–emotional strengths and needs of children referred for assessment because of a concern about their academic, social, or emotional functioning.

- *Guideline 2: Adopt, adapt, or develop a theory of SEL.* This is a particularly exciting moment in the field of SEL, with state standards and evidence-based practices coming to the fore. A consensus appears to be emerging from state standards and advocacy organizations about what SEL is and what it is not. In addition, the scholarly literature includes vigorous inquiry into social–emotional processes that often overlap the emerging applied definition. However, models of SEL in the scientific and applied arenas are not the same. As a result, there is not yet universal agreement about the definitions and dimensions of SEL. For researchers and practitioners alike, it will be critical to have a coherent mental model of what constitutes the relevant dimensions of SEL, either by adopting an existing framework, adapting it, or developing and evaluating a new hybrid model. I am not advocating a crazy quilt of theories of SEL. Rather, I recommend that all researchers and practitioners develop and articulate an evidence-informed point of view about what dimensions of social–emotional comprehension and execution are important, and how they shape functional outcomes. Developing a theory is no mere thought exercise. Armed with a mental model of what things are important and how they work, researchers and practitioners can select assessments that correspond to those constructs and develop theoretically coherent, practical, and useful information to achieve their measurement goals.

- *Guideline 3: Let educators inform assessment.* If theory is a critical foundation of good assessment practice, then so is the practical wisdom of educators. In particular, the wise assessment researcher and practitioner will pay close attention to what teachers do, the instructional issues they care about, what they need to be successful, and the challenges they face every day. If teachers view an assessment as irrelevant or unresponsive to their needs, even the most elegant data will not benefit them or their students. If, on the other hand, an assessment solves a real-world problem that teachers care about, assessment data have great potential to benefit teachers and their students. With the ultimate goal of developing and deploying assessments that will be used constructively to inform practice decisions, assessment researchers and practitioners would do well to understand teachers, who are ultimately the ones who will use or ignore academic, social, and emotional assessment information.

- *Guideline 4: Assess neither too broadly nor too narrowly.* Depending on the researcher's or the practitioner's theory of SEL, it will be important to sample the dimensions of SEL broadly enough to obtain a complete picture. At the same time, this should not require assessing everything under the sun. For example, if one adopted an emotional intelligence framework, it might be sufficient to assess perception, use, understanding, and management of emotions. If one adapted a social information-processing model, it might be enough to administer a vignette-based social problem-solving measure. Even at this relatively early stage in the development of direct SEL assessments, there are many more assessments than there is time to administer them. Let theory guide, and neither over- nor undersample the theoretically relevant dimensions of SEL.

- *Guideline 5: Develop a flexible assessment battery, loosely held.* As a researcher's or practitioner's theory of SEL comes into clear focus, and the domains that need assessing become clearer, the universe of relevant assessment tools will also declare itself. It may be useful for a researcher or practitioner to develop a battery of direct SEL assessments that fulfills the goal of sampling the relevant dimensions of SEL that can be flexibly applied in research and clinical assessment contexts. The second part of this recommendation is to hold on to the battery loosely. It seems likely that, over time, new assessments will be developed, and it will behoove anyone interested in the direct assessment of SEL to scan the assessment landscape regularly for new instruments that reflect an improvement over past practices. When that happens, researchers and practitioners should be ready to let go of an instrument that no longer reflects the state of the art.

- *Guideline 6: Use direct assessment in conjunction with other methods.* In the context of research and clinical and educational assessment, it is most often true that multimethod, multirater assessment is preferred over monomethod, monorater assessment. Nowhere is this more feasible than in the arena of child assessment. In addition to direct assessment of social–emotional comprehension, direct assessment of a huge array of mental and behavioral processes is available, as are a large number of excellent teacher and parent behavior rating scales (see Denham et al., 2010). The kind and content of assessment administered should be driven by the questions that a researcher or practitioner seeks to answer. Although it is conceivable that these questions would be narrowly tailored, to assess well, it will rarely suffice to administer direct SEL assessments alone. For researchers, to understand complex social phenomena will require varied assessment approaches to triangulate data. For clinicians and educators, to understand contributors to social impairment requires the measurement of social–emotional comprehension (e.g., assessed through direct assessment), social execution (e.g., measured through teacher report), and socially interfering behaviors (e.g., measured through direct observation).

- *Guideline 7. Know the psychometric limits of direct assessments.* As in any area of assessment, the reliability and validity of direct SEL assessments vary. The confidence with which an individual child's score can be interpreted and the meaning that can be ascribed to that score depends on the reliability of the samples of behavior on which that score was derived, and the construct validity of the assessment. Unlike the area of cognitive or academic testing, in which the reliability and validity of assessments, and the attendant meaning of the scores derived from tests in these domains, are well established, the psychometric properties of direct assessments of social–emotional comprehension are more varied. The burden therefore rests more heavily on researchers and practitioners alike to know what can and cannot be concluded from a child's performance on a direct assessment.

A Vision: Assessments that Yield Data Readily Translated into Action

Despite technical challenges, direct assessment that can be deployed for universal screening and assessment should play a growing and important role in advancing SEL practices in schools, and in guiding administrators, teachers, and other professionals as they seek to understand the social–emotional repertoires of their students. The assessments described previously demonstrate that it is possible to develop scientifically sound instruments that reliably and validly measure varied dimensions of social–emotional comprehension. What is needed is a suite of instruments that is easy for researchers and educators to use, easily scalable, time- and cost-efficient, and that provide reliable and valid information. This system should be capable of screening, monitoring, and evaluating the development of SEL skills for all children. Developmentally appropriate assessments should be consistent with theory and empirical evidence about what SEL dimensions are most important at what ages. Furthermore, because direct SEL assessments are better-suited to measuring social–emotional comprehension than social–emotional execution, it will be important to develop complementary SEL assessment tools, such as teacher rating forms and observation systems that assess how children act with peers and adults.

This is an exciting time in the field of SEL. Over the past three decades, the field has taken huge strides toward developing policies and practices that stand to benefit entire generations of children. Although assessment practices lag behind policy and practice, promising and scientifically sound direct assessments of social–emotional comprehension have been developed. Currently, these assessment tools are best suited to research and the clinical assessment of children who struggle socially. For the SEL movement to continue to progress, and to benefit children and the systems that serve them, it will be critical to develop usable, feasible, and scientifically sound systems for the universal assessment of children's SEL.

Acknowledgments

Work on this chapter was supported by the Institute of Education Sciences through Grant No. R305A110143 to Rush University Medical Center. The opinions expressed are those of the authors and do not represent views of the Institute or the U.S. Department of Education.

References

Adolphs, R. (2003). Cognitive neuroscience of human social behaviour. *Nature Reviews Neuroscience, 4*, 165–178.

Baron-Cohen, S. (1995). *Mindblindness: An essay on autism and theory of mind*. Boston: MIT Press.

Begeny, J. C., Krouse, H. E., Brown, K. G., & Mann, C. M. (2011). Teacher judgments of students' reading abilities across a continuum of rating methods and achievement methods. *School Psychology Review, 41*, 23–38.

Bowers, L., Huisingh, R., & LoGuidice, C. (2005). *Test of Problem Solving, Elementary Version* (3rd ed.). East Moline, IL: LinguiSytems.

Bowers, L., Huisingh, R., & LoGuidice, C. (2008). *Social Language Development Test Elementary*. East Moline, IL: LinguiSystems.

Carrow-Woolfolk, E. (1999). *Comprehensive assessment of spoken language manual*. Circle Pines, MN: American Guidance Service.

Crick, N. R., & Dodge, K. A. (1996). Social information-processing mechanisms on reactive and proactive aggression. *Child Development, 67*(3), 993–1002.

Cutting, A. L., & Dunn, J. (1999). Theory of mind, emotion understanding, language, and family background: Individual differences and interrelations. *Child Development, 70*, 853–865.

Denham, S. (1986). Social cognition, pro-social behavior, and emotion in preschoolers—Contextual validation. *Child Development, 57*, 194–201.

Denham, S. A., Blair, K. A., DeMulder, E., Levitas, J., Sawyer, K., Auerbach-Major, S., et al. (2003). Preschool emotional competence: Pathway to social competence? *Child Development, 74*, 238–256.

Denham, S. A., Caverly, S., Schmidt, M., Blair, K., DeMulder, E., Caal, S., et al. (2002). Preschool understanding of emotions: Contributions to classroom anger and aggression. *Journal of Child Psychology and Psychiatry and Allied Disciplines, 43*, 901–916.

Denham, S. A., Ji, P., & Hamre, B. (2010). *Compendium of preschool through elementary school social–emotional learning and associated assessment measures.* Chicago: Collaborative for Academic, Social, and Emotional Learning.

DiPerna, J. C., Volpe, R. J., & Elliott, S. N. (2005). A model of academic enablers and mathematics achievement in the elementary grades. *Journal of School Psychology, 43*, 379–392.

Dodge, K. A., & Price, J. M. (1994). On the relation between social information processing and socially competent behavior in early school-aged children. *Child Development, 65*, 1385–1897.

Duckworth, A. (2011). A meta-analysis of the convergent validity of self-control measures. *Journal of Research in Personality, 45*, 259–268.

Dunn, J., & Herrera, C. (1997). Conflict resolution with friends, siblings, and mothers: A developmental perspective. *Aggressive Behavior, 23*, 343–357.

Durlak, J. A., Weissberg, R. P., Dymnicki, A. B., Taylor, R. D., & Schellinger, K. B. (2011). The impact of enhancing students' social and emotional learning: A meta-analysis of school-based universal interventions. *Child Development, 82*(1), 405–432.

Ekman, P., Friesen, W. V., & Hager, J. C. (2002). *Facial action coding system.* Salt Lake City, UT: A Human Face.

Elias, M. J., Zins, J. E., Weissberg, R. P., Frey, K. S., Greenberg, M. T., Haynes, N. M., et al. (1997). *Promoting social and emotional learning: Guidelines for educators.* Alexandria, VA: Association for Supervision and Curriculum Development.

Flavell, J. H. (1999). Cognitive development: Children's knowledge about the mind. *Annual Review of Psychology, 50*, 21–45.

Gopnik, A., & Meltzoff, A. N. (1997). *Words, thoughts, and theories.* Cambridge, MA: MIT Press.

Gresham, F. M. (2011). Social behavioral assessment and intervention: Observations and impressions. *School Psychology Review, 40*, 275–283.

Gresham, F. M., & Elliott, S. N. (1990). *Social Skills Rating System manual.* Circle Pines, MN: American Guidance Service.

Gresham, F. M., & Elliott, S. N. (2009). *Social Skills Improvement System manual.* Minneapolis, MN: Pearson.

Halberstadt, A. G., Denham, S. A., & Dunsmore, J. C. (2001). Affective social competence. *Social Development, 10*, 79–119.

Happé, F. (1994). An advanced test of theory of mind: Understanding of story characters' thoughts and feeling by able autistic, mentally handicapped, and normal children and adults. *Journal of Autism and Developmental Disorders, 24*(2), 129–154.

Harter, S. (1982). The perceived self-competence scale for children. *Child Development, 53*, 87–97.

Humphrey, N., Kalambouka, A., Wigelsworth, M., Lendrum, A., Deighton, J., & Wolpert, M. (2011). Measures of social and emotional skills for children and young people: A systematic review. *Educational and Psychological Measurement, 71*, 617–637.

Innovation Research and Training. (2008). *Child and Adolescent Recognition of Emotion (CARE)* [Computer software]. Durham, NC: Author.

Kilday, C. R., Kinzie, M. B., Mashburn, A. J., & Whittaker, J. V. (2012). Accuracy of teacher judgments of preschoolers' math skills. *Journal of Psychoeducational Assessment, 30*(2), 148–159.

Korkman, M., Kirk, U., & Kemp, S. (2007). *NEPSY–Second Edition (NEPSY-II).* San Antonio, TX: Pearson Assessment.

Kovacs, M. (2011). *Children's Depression Inventory 2.* San Antonio, TX: Pearson Assessment.

Kupersmidt, J. B., Stelter, R., & Dodge, K. A. (2011). Development and validation of the social information processing application: A web-based measure of social information processing patterns in elementary school-age boys. *Psychological Assessment, 23*(4), 834–847.

Lipton, M., & Nowicki, S. (2009). The social emotional learning framework (SELF): A guide for understanding brain-based social emotional learning impairments. *Journal of Developmental Processes, 4*(2), 99–115.

Love, E. B., Nowicki, S., & Duke, M. P. (1994). The Emory Dyssemia Index—a brief screening instrument for the identification of nonverbal language deficits in elementary school children. *Journal of Psychology, 128*, 703–705.

Mayer, J. D., & Salovey, P. (1997). What is emotional intelligence? In P. Salovey & D. Sluyter (Eds.), *Emotional development and emotional intelligence: Implications for educators* (pp. 3–31). New York: Basic Books.

Mayer, J. D., Salovey, P., & Caruso, D. R. (2004). Emotional intelligence: Theory, findings, and implications. *Psychological Inquiry, 15*, 197–215.

McKown, C. (2007). Concurrent validity and clinical usefulness of several tests of social–emotional cognition. *Journal of Clinical Child and Adolescent Psychology, 36*, 29–41.

McKown, C., Allen, A. A., Russo-Ponsaran, N. M., & Johnson, J. K. (2013). Direct assessment of children's social–emotional comprehension. *Psychological Assessment, 25*, 1154–1166.

McKown, C., Gumbiner, L. M., & Johnson, J. (2011). Diagnostic efficiency of several methods of identifying socially rejected children and effect of participation rate on classification accuracy, *Journal of School Psychology, 49*, 573–595.

McKown, C., Gumbiner, L. M., Russo, N. M., & Lipton, M. (2009). Social–emotional learning skill, self-regulation, and social competence in typically developing and clinic-referred children. *Journal of Clinical Child and Adolescent Psychology, 38*(6), 858–871.

Measelle, J. R., Ablow, J. C., Cowan, P. A., & Cowan, C. P. (1998). Assessing young children's views of their academic, social, and emotional lives: An evaluation of the self-perception scales of the Berkeley Puppet Interview. *Child Development, 69*, 1556–1576.

Merrell, K. W. (2009). *Behavioral, social, and emotional assessment of children and adolescents* (3rd ed.). New York: Routledge.

Nowicki, S., & Duke, M. P. (1994). Individual differences in the nonverbal communication of affect: The Diagnostic Analysis Of Nonverbal Accuracy Scale. *Journal of Nonverbal Behavior, 18*(1), 9–35.

Nowicki, S., & Mitchell, J. (1998). Accuracy in identifying affect in child and adult faces and voices and social competence in preschool children. *Genetic Social and General Psychology Monographs, 124*, 39–59.

Phelps-Terasaki, D., & Phelps-Gunn, T. (2007). *Test of Pragmatic Language 2*. East Moline, IL: LinguiSystems.

Reynolds, C. R., & Kamphaus, R. (2004). *Behavioral Assessment System for Children 2*. San Antonio, TX: Pearson Assessment.

Rivers, S. E., Brackett, M. A., & Salovey, P. (2008). Measuring emotional intelligence as a mental ability in adults and children. In G. J. Boyle, G. Matthews, & D. H. Saklofske (Eds.), *The SAGE handbook of personality theory and assessment* (Vol. 2, pp. 440–462). Los Angeles: Sage.

Salovey, P., & Mayer, J. D. (1990). Emotional intelligence. *Imagination, Cognition, and Personality, 9*, 185–211.

Selman, R. (1980). *The growth of interpersonal understanding: Developmental and clinical analysis*. New York: Academic Press.

Smith-Donald, R., Raver, C. C., Hayes, T., & Richardson, B. (2007). Preliminary construct and concurrent validity of the Preschool Self Regulation Assessment (PSRA) for field-based research. *Early Childhood Research Quarterly, 22*, 173–187.

Warren-Khot, H. K., Parker, A., Mathis, E. T., McKown, C., Allen, A., & Kupersmidt, J. (2012, February). *Preliminary validity of a web-based measure of preschoolers emotion identification.* Poster presented at the annual meeting of the National Association of School Psychologists, Philadelphia, PA.

Wellman, H., & Liu, D. (2004). Scaling theory of mind tasks. *Child Development, 75*, 523–541.

Wentzel, K. R. (1993). Does being good make the grade?: Social behavior and academic competence in middle school. *Journal of Educational Psychology, 85*(2), 357–364.

Wigelsworth, M., Humphrey, N., Kalambouka, A., & Lendrum, A. (2010). A review of key issues in the measurement of children's social and emotional skills. *Educational Psychology in Practice, 26*, 173–186.

CHAPTER 22

Using Formative Assessment with SEL Skills

Robert J. Marzano

Certainly, formative assessment has been established as one of the mainstay classroom strategies for enhancing student learning. It is interesting to note that the term "formative" was borrowed and adapted from the field of evaluation; the genesis of formative assessment, then, is not from the world of assessment. The distinction between formative and summative evaluation was first popularized by Michael Scriven (1967) as part of an American Educational Research Association monograph in 1967. There, Scriven made a distinction between those programs that are being formulated versus those programs that have evolved to their final state. He explained that the evaluation process takes on different characteristics during the development of a project than it does when the project is completed—hence, the terms "formative" and "summative" evaluation.

According to Popham (2008), Benjamin Bloom tried in 1969 to transplant the formative–summative evaluation distinction into assessment, but "few educators were interested in investigating this idea further because it seemed to possess few practical implications for the day-to-day world of schooling" (p. 4). It is fair to say that Bloom's dream has been realized, in that formative assessment is now part of the vernacular of most, if not all, K–12 teachers in the United States.

The Research on Formative Assessment

Formative assessment owes its current popularity to a publication in 1998, in which Black and Wiliam provided a synthesis of the research on the topic. Black and Wiliam summarized the findings from more than 250 studies on classroom assessment. Their overall conclusion was that formative assessment is potentially one of the most powerful tools that a classroom educator can use to enhance student learning. An often-cited quote from their study follows:

> The research reported here shows conclusively that formative assessment does improve learning. The gains in achievement appear to be quite considerable, and as noted earlier among the largest ever reported for educational interventions. As an illustration of just how big gains are, an effect size of 0.7, if it could be achieved on a nationwide scale would be equivalent to raising the mathematic attainment score of an "average" country like England, New Zealand, or the United States into the "top five" after the Pacific Rim countries

of Singapore, Korea, Japan, and Hong Kong. (Black & Wiliam, 1998, p. 61)

Based on such conclusions, formative assessment was embraced by teachers and administrators alike. For over a decade it has been unquestioned in its utility and often named as essential to effective classroom practice. For example, by mid-2011, the study had been cited over 2,700 times (Kingston & Nash, 2011). Shepard (2009) noted that "since that time, virtually no scholarly or popular treatment of formative assessment can begin without acknowledging Black and Wiliam's compelling research synthesis demonstrating the power of formative assessment to raise student achievement" (p. 32).

Problems with Early Interpretations of Formative Assessment Research

While formative assessment has been widely accepted due to early interpretations of the research, particularly as articulated by Black and Wiliam (1998), more recently these interpretations have been challenged. Kingston and Nash (2011, p. 29) explained that other researchers have concluded that Black and Wiliam's original synthesis did not support the claims made in their report: "In summary, critiques of the Black and Wiliam review conclude that the studies used to support their claim with respect to effect sizes associated with formative assessment do not actually support such a conclusion."

In an attempt to verify the original conclusions about formative assessment, Kingston and Nash (2011) conducted their own meta-analytic review. They examined more than 300 studies that appeared to address the efficacy of formative assessment in grades K–12: "Many of the studies had severely flawed research designs yielding uninterruptable results. Only 13 of the studies provided sufficient information to calculate relevant effect sizes" (p. 28). Their final conclusion was that the average effect size for formative assessment was much smaller than originally reported. A total of 42 independent effect sizes were available. The median observed effect size was 0.25. Using a random effects model, a weighted effect size of 0.20 was calculated (p. 28).

Although the Kingston and Nash (2011) analysis is not nearly as well known as the 1998 review by Black and Wiliam, it still casts a shadow of doubt on the original enthusiasm about formative assessment.

A reasonable question a practitioner might ask is why the discrepant results? The answer can be found in the study by Kingston and Nash (2011), who noted that the manifestations of formative assessment were so varied from study to study as not to constitute a single construct. In some studies, "formative" assessment was defined as the types of questions that teachers ask of students and the feedback provided to students regarding their answers. In other studies, "formative" assessment was defined as specific types of tests administered in a specific sequence and designed in specific ways, and so on.

So What Does the Social and Emotional Learning Practitioner Do?

Social and emotional learning (SEL) practitioners teach students to acquire and effectively apply the knowledge, skills, and attitudes to understand and manage emotions, set and achieve positive goals, feel and show empathy for others, establish and maintain positive relationships, and make responsible decisions (Elias et al., 1997; Zins, Weissberg, Wang, & Walberg, 2004). The Collaborative for Academic, Social, and Emotional Learning (CASEL; 2013) has identified five interrelated clusters of intrapersonal and interpersonal competencies that provide a foundation for being a good student, citizen, and worker: (1) self-awareness—accurately recognizing one's emotions and thoughts, and their influence on behavior; (2) self-management—regulating thoughts, emotions, and behaviors in different situations and being able to set and achieve personal and academic goals; (3) social awareness—taking the perspective of and empathizing with others from diverse backgrounds; (4) relationship skills—establishing and maintaining constructive relationships with diverse individuals and groups; and (5) responsible decision making—making ethical and respectful choices about personal behavior and social interactions.

SEL practitioners can help develop competencies in every type of school and in students of every background through systematically teaching, modeling, and facilitating students' application of these competencies in daily life, and establishing caring and highly engaging classroom and schoolwide learning environments. More than two decades of research document that well-designed, effectively implemented SEL programs enhance students' social and emotional skills, self-esteem, bonding to school, classroom behavior and academic achievement; and reduce disruptive classroom behavior, aggression, bullying, and substance use (Durlak et al., 2011; Greenberg et al., 2003; Sklad, Dieskstra, De Ritter, Ben, & Gravesteijn, 2012; Zins et al., 2004).

Given these positive findings, another reasonable question a practitioner might ask is, what am I supposed to do regarding formative assessment and SEL? If a practitioner's answer to this question were that formative assessment should not be used, then he or she would be making a strategic mistake. The equivocal findings to date for formative assessment are not because it is an ineffective strategy. Rather the equivocal findings are a function of the broad and varied descriptions of formative assessment in the research literature. That is, as discussed in the literature, the term "formative assessment" refers to a great many strategies, some of which are quite disparate in their foci. When one narrows the focus of formative assessment, some rather clear guidance can be found. Again Kingston and Nash (2011) provide some direction. Specifically, they cite the research on feedback as directive if one wishes to identify the critical characteristics of formative assessment. In particular, they highlighted the meta-analytic work of Hattie and Timperley (2007).

The research on feedback is a logical place to begin, since feedback has always been associated with effective formative assessment. For example, Wiliam and Leahy (2007, p. 31, original emphasis) described formative assessment in the following way:

> The qualifier *formative* will refer not to an assessment or even to the purpose of an assessment, but rather to the function it actually serves. An assessment is formative to the extent that information from the assessment is fed back within the system and actually used to improve the performance of the system in some way (i.e., that the assessment *forms* the direction of improvement).

Similarly, Heritage (2008, p. 2) explained that "the purpose of formative assessment is to provide feedback to teachers and students during the course of learning about the gap between students' current and desired performance so that action can be taken to close the gap."

In their study, Hattie and Timperley (2007) included a dozen meta-analyses that incorporated the findings from 196 studies and almost 7,000 effect sizes on feedback. Based on this synthesis, the authors developed a model for effective feedback that focuses on learning goals. As Kingston and Nash (2011, p. 29) explained, "Using these findings, Hattie and Timperley (2007) developed a model for effective feedback that incorporates learning goals, progress toward those and steps needed to make better progress toward those goals." While effective feedback is not synonymous with effective formative assessment, the research on feedback does provide the foundation for developing a clear and focused approach to one manifestation of formative assessment—a manifestation that focuses on establishing clear learning goals, tracking student progress toward those goals, and helping students identify the next steps they might take to attain those goals.

This chapter lays out a model of formative assessment that fits these characteristics and details how it can be used with SEL skills. Specifically, this chapter describes a model of formative assessment that focuses on providing (1) explicit learning goals regarding SEL skills, (2) progress toward those goals, and (3) guidance in the steps needed to progress toward those goals. To design such a system, one must begin with an understanding of the nature of human knowledge and how knowledge can be organized into learning progressions. As Heritage (2008, p. 2) explained, to provide effective feedback to students in the context of formative assessment,

> teachers need to have in mind a continuum of how learning develops in any particular knowledge domain so that they are able to locate students' current learning status and decide on pedagogical action to move students' learning forward. Learning progressions that clearly articulate a progression of learning in a domain can provide the big picture of what is to be learned, support instructional planning,

and act as a touchstone for formative assessment.

The Nature of Knowledge

To understand learning progressions it is useful to begin with a consideration of the nature of human knowledge. Of course, there are many ways to describe the nature of knowledge. The one used here is based on the distinction between declarative and procedural knowledge which is a common way to partition knowledge in taxonomies of learning (see Anderson & Krathwohl, 2001). Declarative knowledge is informational. For example, the following are examples of declarative knowledge that are common to K–12 academic subject areas: knowing the letters of the alphabet, understanding the sequence of events leading up to Napoleon's removal from power in France, understanding the concept of buoyancy, and so on. Procedural knowledge is "actionable" in the sense that it is characterized by a series of steps one might take or strategies one might use to accomplish a specific goal. The following are examples of procedural knowledge that are common to K–12 academic subject areas: being able to balance an equation in algebra, being able to read a bar graph, being able to write a brief persuasive essay.

The declarative–procedural distinction provides a useful way to think about SEL standards. In recent years, there have been advances in designing preschool–grade 12 SEL standards (see Dusenbury et al., Chapter 35, this volume). Illinois has been a leader in establishing PreK–12 standards structured around three learning goals: (1) development of self-awareness and self-management skills to achieve school and life success; (2) use of social awareness and interpersonal skills to establish and maintain positive relationships; and (3) demonstration of decision-making skills and responsible behaviors in personal, school, and community contexts (Gordon, Ji, Mulhall, Shaw, & Weissberg, 2011). Recently, my colleagues and I collaborated with CASEL, the Illinois State Board of Education, and a broadly representative team of Illinois educators to develop formative assessment of SEL from kindergarten through high school for 10 SEL standards (copies of these assessment strategies can be requested from Roger Weissberg at *rpw@uic.edu*). To illustrate the application of the declarative–procedural distinction, consider a standard from the Illinois State Board of Education: "2A.5a. Demonstrate how to express understanding of those who hold different opinions." This standard is intended for high school students and is component of the "social awareness and interpersonal skills" goal within the state framework (Illinois State Board of Education, 2013).

At its core, the standard appears to be procedural in nature, in that expressing an understanding of those who hold different opinions is actionable—to satisfy this standard, the student must execute specific strategies, such as the following:

- Acknowledge that there is a difference of opinion.
- Make a conscious decision to assume that the individual with whom you disagree is operating in good faith.
- Actively listen to what the other person is saying and try to understand his or her reasons for having that opinion.
- When making a point that is counter to the opinion of the other person, focus on the logic of your point.
- Make sure that during your discussion you do not say anything that is negative about the person.

In addition to these strategies, the standard can be thought of has having some declarative components, such as the following:

- Understanding the characteristics of an opinion.
- Understanding one's own opinions on a topic.
- Understanding the indicators that two people have different opinions on a specific topic.
- Understanding one's typical emotional response when interacting with someone who holds an opposite opinion.
- Understanding that strong emotions can cloud one's thinking.

Finding a mix of declarative and procedural knowledge is quite common in skills learning. Declarative knowledge is considered a formal part of the process. Learning a skill (technically referred to as a "procedure") typically involves three stages. Fitts (1964) referred to the first as the *cognitive stage*. Here the learner understands the steps or strategies in the procedure and is able to verbalize them (i.e., describe them if asked). According to Anderson (1983), at this stage, it is common to observe verbal mediation during which the learner rehearses the information necessary to execute the skill. The second stage is referred to as the *associative stage*. Here the learner's performance in the skill is smoothed out. Errors in the initial understanding of the skill are corrected. Important elements that were not included in the initial understanding of the procedure are added, and some elements that were part of the learner's original understanding of the procedure are adapted to meet specific needs and preferences of the learner. During this stage, the need for verbal rehearsal is extinguished. During the third stage, the *autonomous stage*, the skill is refined. By the end of this stage, the learner can execute the steps of the procedure with little conscious effort. This allows the learner to consider other metacognitive elements that might be associated with the procedure, such as making adaptations due to extenuating circumstances.

The "Will" Component in SEL Standards

One thing that differentiates SEL skills from more traditional subject-matter skills is that they contain a "will" component (Blumenfeld & Marx, 1997; McCombs & Marzano, 1990; Montaivo & Torres, 2004). By definition, the "will" component associated with any procedure involves the self-system.

The self-system is generally considered to be the architect of human volition (Harter, 1982; Markus & Ruvolo, 1989). McCombs and Marzano (1990, p. 66) described the self-system in the following way: "The self as agent, as the basis of will and volition can be thought of, in part, as a generative structure that is goal directed. . . .it . . . consciously or unconsciously defines who we are, what we think, and what we do." Boekaerts (2009, p. 110) included principles in the structure of the self-system:

> It is generally accepted that a small set of higher order goals, or principles, should be placed at the apex of a hierarchical goal network. This set of basic principles contributes to a person's sense of Self because the principles represent the person's basic values and the traits that he or she considers ideal. As such, higher order goals provide general organization and orientation to a person's life and optimize meaning making processes. Marzano and Marzano (2010, pp. 347–348) further delineated the role of principles in the self-system. They explained that "basic operating principles" are superordinate to goals: These principles are very general, and therefore, they influence a great deal of human behavior. For example, a basic operating principle one teacher might hold is "all students can reach high levels of achievement if a teacher knows how to unlock their potential." Any time this teacher interacts with a student, this principle will elicit certain types of behavior from him or her—regardless of the students' past achievement. On the other hand, if a teacher has a basic operating principle that "students' academic success is determined by their home environment," then he or she will exhibit other types of behavior as a result of this principle.

As they relate to SEL skills, basic operating principles (also known as "beliefs") most probably control whether students actually decide to use a skill in real-life situations. If use of a particular skill is consistent with one or more of the student's basic operating principles, the student will typically choose to use the SEL skill in his or her day-to-day life. If not, the student will typically choose not to use the SEL skill outside the classroom.

Learning Progressions for SEL Skills

This discussion of the nature of knowledge and its specific application to SEL skills allows for an ordering of the knowledge specific to an SEL skill into a learning progression. As mentioned previously, learning progressions are central to the effective execution of formative assessment (Heritage, 2008). The generic form for an SEL progression is outlined in Figure 22.1.

The declarative knowledge associate with an SEL skill is at the lowest level of the learning progression. This makes sense given the first stage (the cognitive stage) of learning a

Higher
Making conscious decisions to use the skill in appropriate situations: • Understanding one's basic operating principles in terms of their influencing one's behavior • Making necessary changes in one's basic operating principles to increase the probability of using a specific SEL skill
Being able to execute the steps or strategies associated with an SEL skill without error and with some fluency: • Becoming fluent in the execution of the skill • Shaping the steps or strategies through practice
Understanding the declarative knowledge important to an SEL skill and being able to perform a rough approximation of the skill: • Knowing the steps or strategies that compose the skill • Knowing factual information important to the skill • Knowing important vocabulary relative to the skill
Lower

FIGURE 22.1. Generic form for SEL progressions.

skill—that at which the learner knows about the skill, understands some basic terms associated with the skill, and can perform a rough approximation of it when prompted.

At the next level of the learning progression, the student is actually practicing the skill with the intent of developing fluency. These practice sessions are most probably structured and guided by the teacher. This, of course, is consistent with the associative stage of learning a new skill.

At the highest level of an SEL progression, the student recognizes that use of an SEL skill is consistent or not consistent with his or her basic operating principles (i.e., beliefs). If he or she recognizes that the skill is not being employed in situations where it can be of personal use, the student examines his or her beliefs and makes adaptations, if necessary, to increase the real-world use of the skill.

The progression depicted in Figure 22.1 can be turned into a rather rudimentary rubric or scale that allows for the tracking of a student's progress and nicely fits the criteria for formative assessment suggested by the research on feedback. That is, it provides a clear goal—in this case, the ability to execute the SEL skill at the top level. It allows students to track their progress over time. Additionally, it provides guidance as to the next steps that must be taken by students. For example, if a student understands the declarative knowledge appropriate to the SEL skill, the next step would be to begin practicing and shaping the skill.

Developing a Scale for Formative Assessments and SEL Skills

In a series of works, Marzano (2006, 2009, 2010) has described a generic rubric or proficiency scale that can be used to render learning progressions such as that in Figure 22.1 more amenable to formative assessment. That scale is depicted in Figure 22.2.

The left-hand side of Figure 22.2 depicts the generic form of the scale; the right-hand side depicts its translation to the specific SEL skill of expressing understanding of those who hold different opinions. Score values 2.0, 3.0, and 4.0 simply contain the three levels of the SEL progression shown in Figure 22.1. However, it also contains some half-point scores. A score of 3.5 indicates competence regarding the content at score value 2.0 and 3.0, and partial success at score 4.0 content. For example, the student makes attempts to understand the beliefs (i.e., basic operating principles) that stop him or her from using the skill in real-life situations but does so only partially or with some significant errors. A score of 2.5 indicates success with score 2.0 content and partial success with the score 3.0 content.

Also note that the scale contains whole point values for scores 1.0 and 0.0. However, these score values do not contain new content relative to the SEL skill. Rather, the score value of 1.0 indicates that the student cannot perform at the score 2.0 or 3.0 levels independently but can do so at least partially with help. A score of 0.0 means that even with help the student cannot perform any of the score 2.0 or 3.0 content. Finally, the half-point score of 0.5 means that with help the student can successfully perform some of the 2.0 content.

Score	Generic Form of SEL Proficiency Scales	Specific Example for an SEL Skill
4.0	Making conscious decisions to use the skill in appropriate situations: • Understanding one's basic operating principles in terms of their influencing one's behavior • Making necessary changes in one's basic operating principles to increase the probability of using a specific SEL skill	Making conscious decisions to use the skill of expressing understanding of those who hold different opinions: • Understanding the beliefs the student might have that stops him or her from expressing understanding of those who hold different opinions • Making revisions in beliefs that hinder the student from expressing understanding of those who hold different opinions
3.5	In addition to score 3.0 performance, partial success at score 4.0	In addition to score 3.0 performance, partial success at score 4.0
3.0	Being able to execute the steps or strategies associated with an SEL skills without error and with some fluency: • Becoming fluent in the execution of the skill • Shaping the steps or strategies through practice	Expressing understanding of those who hold different opinions in real-life situations without significant error and with some fluency using strategies like the following: • Acknowledging that there is a difference of opinions • Making a conscious decision to assume that the individual with whom you disagree is operating in good faith • Actively listen to what the other person is saying and try to understand his or her reasons for having that opinion • When making a point that is counter to the opinion of the other person, focusing on the logic of your point • Making sure that during your discussion you do not say anything that is negative about the person
2.5	No major errors regarding score 2.0 content, and partial success at score 3.0 content	No major errors regarding score 2.0 content, and partial success at score 3.0 content
2.0	Understanding the declarative knowledge important to an SE skill and being able to perform a rough approximation of the skill: • Knowing the steps or strategies that comprise the skill	Being able to perform a rough approximation of the skill of expressing understanding of those who hold different opinions, and being able to explain or describe:

	• Knowing factual information important to the skill • Knowing important vocabulary relative to the skill	• The fact that the SE skill commonly involves steps such as the following: o Acknowledging that there is a difference of opinion o Making a conscious decision to assume the individual with whom you disagree is operating in good faith\ o Actively listening to what the other person is saying and trying to understand his or her reasons for having that opinion o When making a point that is counter to the opinion of the other person, focusing on the logic of your point o Making sure that during your discussion you do not say anything negative about the person • Factual information about the skill, such as the following: o The characteristics of an opinion o The student's own opinion on specific topics o Behaviors that indicate a difference of opinion between two people o The student's typical emotional response when someone disagrees with him or her o The ways strong emotion can influence one's thinking • The meaning of basic terms such as *opinion, disagreement, conflict, confrontation*, and *respect*
1.5	Partial success at score 2.0 content, but major errors or omissions regarding score 3.0 content	Partial success at score 2.0 content, but major errors or omissions regarding score 3.0 content
1.0	With help partial success at score 2.0 content, and score 3.0 content	With help partial success at score 2.0 content, and score 3.0 content
0.5	With help partial success at score 2.0 content but not at score 3.0 content	With help partial success at score 2.0 content but not at score 3.0 content
0.0	Even with help, no success	Even with help, no success

FIGURE 22.2. Marzano Scale adapted for SEL skills.

Different Types of Assessments

If proficiency scales like those depicted in the right-hand side of Figure 22.2 are used with SEL skills, the assessment options available to gather information from students can be greatly expanded. In fact, proficiency scales allow for a number of types of classroom assessments that go well beyond the traditional paper–pencil test. In particular, three types of assessments are easily employed when proficiency scales are in place: probing discussions, unobtrusive assessments, and student-generated assessments.

Probing Discussions

When using a probing discussion, a teacher meets with an individual student and asks him or her questions about the SEL skill, making sure to address the score 2.0 content, the score 3.0 content, and the score 4.0 content. In this scenario, the teacher has the flexibility to continue asking questions of a student until he or she is reasonably confident about the student's level of proficiency. At the end of the discussion, the teacher makes a determination as to the student's level of performance using the proficiency scale. For example, if the teacher determines that the student has demonstrated adequate understanding of the simpler content (i.e., score 2.0 content) and demonstrated partial understanding of the score 3.0 content, the student is assigned a score of 2.5. If the teacher determines that the student can respond accurately to very little independently, but with some cueing and prompting can demonstrate partial understanding of the score 2.0 content and the score 3.0 content, the student is assigned a score of 1.0, and so on.

Unobtrusive Assessments

When an unobtrusive assessment is used, a particular student might not even be aware that he or she has been assessed. For example, assume that a teacher observes one student interacting with another student regarding a topic about which they disagree. The teacher notices that the first student is trying to use strategies specific to the skill of expressing understanding of those who hold different opinions, which indicates score 3.0 behavior on the part of the student. However, the student is making some errors or omissions in the execution of those strategies. The teacher would assign a score of 2.5 for that student at that particular at point in time.

Student-Generated Assessments

Student-generated assessments are perhaps the most powerful form of assessment that can be made available to students when proficiency scales are used. In such situations, the student approaches the teacher and proposes what he or she will do to exhibit a specific level of performance on the proficiency scale. For example, a student who is currently at the score 3.0 level relative to the proficiency scale in Figure 22.2 for the skill of expressing understanding of those who hold different opinions might propose that he or she will describe the specific beliefs he or she had to adjust to begin using the skill in situations where the student previously had not done so. As evidence that he or she now operates at the score 4.0 level, the student might make that presentation in a video recording that is given to the teacher.

Setting Goals and Monitoring Progress

Armed with proficiency scales like those depicted in Figure 22.2 for the specific SEL skills a teacher is addressing in class and the variety of types of assessments that can be used to determine each student's current status on a particular skill, a teacher can satisfy the criteria for effective feedback suggested by the Hattie and Timperley (2007) meta-analysis. Specific goals can be set for each student regarding his or her progress on a specific skill. For example, one student might set a goal of reaching score 4.0 status on the skill of expressing understanding of those who hold different opinions by the end of the semester, while another student might set a goal of reaching score 3.0 status by the end of the semester. Additionally, students should know what they have to do to reach their desired status by consulting the proficiency scales. The student who sets score 4.0 status as a goal knows that he or she must examine his or her beliefs that might be impeding use of the skill in specific situation. The student who sets score 3.0 as a goal knows that he or she must practice the strategies associated with the skill to a level of fluency.

Finally, the scales can be used to demonstrate progress over time. The student who starts the semester at a score of 0.5 for a specific SEL skill might keep track of his or her status each week. Scores might be graphed over time. In this way, the student could see his or her progress up through the half-point and full-point scores. Such tracking would provide many opportunities to celebrate growth and whole-score milestones along with way.

Grading

If SEL skills are explicitly taught and used in PreK–12 classrooms, teachers will eventually have to address the issue of translating formative assessment scores to grades. They would do this by using the final summative score for SEL skills at the end of a grading period. For example, assume that teacher addressed three SEL skills during a semester, and that students tracked their progress on these skills in graphic form. At the end of the semester, a summative score would be assigned for each SEL skill that represented each student's final status—the skills level the student had reached by the semester's end. These three summative scores could be combined using a weighted or unweighted average. The average of these summative scores could be translated into traditional grades using a scheme such as the following:

3.51 to 4.00 = A
3.00 to 3.50 = A–
2.84 to 2.99 = B+
2.60 to 2.83 = B
2.50 to 2.66 = B–
2.34 to 2.49 = C+
2.17 to 2.33 = C
2.00 to 2.16 = C–
1.84 to 1.99 = D+
1.67 to 1.83 = D
1.50 to 1.66 = D–
0.00 to 1.49 = F

In this system, an average score across the three skills of 3.51 to 4.0 translates into an A. An average score of 2.17 to 2.33 translates to a letter grade of C, and so on.

In addition to the overall grade, parents and students can see how much the student has progressed relative to each SEL skill. By examining the proficiency scales themselves, parents and students can ascertain the student's strengths and most pressing needs. Options for combining scores other than computing the average are also possible (Marzano, 2010).

A Continuous Improvement Approach

Perhaps the biggest advantage to using proficiency scales for formative assessment is that they allow students to update their scores continuously on specific topics. This means that as the school year progresses, students are allowed to raise scores from previous grading periods. To illustrate, assume that three SEL skills have been addressed in the first semester. We saw earlier how summative scores on these skills can be translated into an overall grade. Now assume that four more skills are addressed in the second semester. Again, at the end of the grading period, these scores can be translated into an overall grade. However, if students are allowed continuously to update their scores, during the second semester they would be encouraged to raise their scores on the three skills from the first semester. Of course, this means that the second semester's overall grade would be based on the four skills addressed during the second semester and the three skills addressed during the first semester. Such a system allows students to improve continuously on their levels of proficiency for specific SEL skills, and receive recognition and credit for their efforts.

Guidelines and Recommendations

To implement the suggestions presented in this chapter, a teacher must begin by unpacking SEL standards with an eye toward identifying the explicit or implicit skill. Next, the teacher translates the skill into a learning progression like that depicted in the right-hand side of Figure 22.2.

Scales should be presented to students and translated into "student-friendly" language. This is best done by asking students to work in small groups and translate the score 2.0, 3.0, and 4.0 content into familiar language and examples that students readily understand.

The student-friendly scales can be used initially as the basis for instruction. The declarative knowledge inherent in score 2.0 content should be exemplified and discussed. Students should have ample opportunity to practice the steps and strategies inherent in score 3.0 content. Practice activities should begin using highly structured and teacher-directed scenarios, but then progress over time to more open-ended opportunities for students to use the steps or strategies associated with the SEL skill. Finally, for score 4.0 content, students can record their insights about beliefs they have that inhibit their use of SEL skills in a journal that is shared only with the teacher. This allows students to be candid about their self-discovery and interact privately with the teacher through the journals.

Having students track their progress on specific SEL skills using charts or bar graphs is a very powerful and motivational tool. Each level of advancement on the proficiency scale is an opportunity for positive interaction between teacher and student. Advancement on the scale should always be acknowledged and celebrated.

Finally, the more that student-generated assessments are used to demonstrate competence at different levels of the scale, the better. These assessments put students in charge of their own success and afford them control over how they will demonstrate competence. By definition, such deliberations make students think deeply about a particular SEL skill.

Potential Problems and Pitfalls

A common tendency when trying to teach and assess SEL skills is that they are treated at a surface level. Stated differently, some teachers might have a tendency not to address SEL skills at the requisite level of rigor to produce increases in students' self-awareness and social awareness and changes in their behavior. The use of proficiency scales and the various types of assessments that can be employed help safeguard against this tendency, but it is still a pitfall that should be consciously addressed.

Mastering an SEL skill represents one of the more significant challenges students face in their PreK–12 careers, in no small part due to the attention that must be paid to the self-system and students' beliefs about themselves, their peers, and the world around them. This cannot be done in a cavalier manner. Before asking students to examine their beliefs, teachers should spend a great deal of time providing students with information about the self-system and its hierarchical structure of goals and basic operating principles. Students should have a firm grounding in the fact that their behavior is greatly influenced by their beliefs and goals. More importantly, they should have a firm grounding in the fact that regardless of the beliefs they currently hold, they have the power to change in them in ways that enhance their own lives and the lives of those with whom they come into contact.

Perhaps this is the ultimate goal of teaching and assessing SEL skills—providing students with an understanding of why humans make decisions, and the power of making decisions that are based on well-reasoned beliefs as opposed to beliefs they have inherited from their past or their immediate surroundings.

References

Anderson, J. R. (1983). *The architecture of cognition*. Cambridge, MA: Harvard University Press.

Anderson, L. W., & Krathwohl, D. R. (Eds.). (2001). *A taxonomy for learning, teaching, and assessing: A revision of Bloom's taxonomy of educational objectives*. New York: Longman.

Black, P., & Wiliam, D. (1998). Assessment and classroom learning. *Assessment in Education, 1*, 7–75.

Bloom, B. S. (1969). Some theoretical issues relating to educational evaluation. In R. W. Taylor (Ed.), *Educational evaluation: New roles, new means: The 68th yearbook of the National Society for the Study of Education, Part II* (pp. 26–50). Chicago: University of Chicago Press.

Blumenfeld, P. C., & Marx, R. W. (1997). Motivation and cognition. In H. J. Walberg & G. D. Haertel (Eds.), *Psychology and educational practice* (pp. 79–106). Berkeley, CA: McCutchan.

Boekaerts, M. (2009). Goal-directed behavior in the classroom. In K. R. Wentzel & A. Wigfield (Eds.), *Handbook of motivation at school* (pp. 105–122). New York: Routledge.

Collaborative for Academic, Social, and Emotional Learning. (2013). *2013 CASEL Guide: Effective social and emotional learning programs–Preschool and elementary school edition.* Chicago: Author.

Durlak, J. A., Weissberg, R. P., Dymnicki, A. B., Taylor, R. D., & Schellinger, K. (2011). The impact of enhancing students' social and emotional learning: A meta-analysis of school-based universal interventions. *Child Development, 82*, 405–432.

Elias, M. J., Zins, J. E., Weissberg, R. P., Frey, K. S., Greenberg, M. T., Haynes, N. M., et al. (1997). *Promoting social and emotional learning: Guidelines for educators.* Alexandria, VA: Association for Supervision and Curriculum Development.

Fitts, P. M. (1964). Perceptual-motor skill learning. In A. W. Melton (Ed.), *Categories of human learning* (pp. 107–131). New York: Wiley.

Gordon, R., Ji, P., Mulhall, P., Shaw, B., & Weissberg, R. P. (2011). Social and emotional learning for Illinois students: Policy, practice, and progress. In *The Illinois Report 2011* (pp. 68–83). Urbana: Institute of Government and Public Affairs, University of Illinois.

Greenberg, M. T., Weissberg, R. P., O'Brien, M. U., Zins, J. E., Fredericks, L., Resnik, H., et al. (2003). Enhancing school-based prevention and youth development through coordinated social, emotional, and academic learning. *American Psychologist, 58*, 466–474.

Harter, S. (1982). The perceived competence scale for children. *Child Development, 53*, 218–235.

Hattie, J., & Timperley, H. (2007). The power of feedback. *Review of Educational Research, 77*, 91–112.

Heritage, M. (2008). *Learning progressions: Supporting instruction and formative assessment.* Washington, DC: Council of Chief State School Officers.

Illinois State Board of Education. (2013). *Social/emotional learning (SEL).* Springfield, IL: Author. Retrieved January 12, 2013, from *www.isbe.state.il.us/ils/social_emotional/standards.htm on.*

Kingston, N., & Nash, B. (2011). Formative assessment: A meta-analysis and a call for research. *Educational Measurement: Issues and Practice, 30*(4), 28–37.

Markus, H., & Ruvolo, A. (1989), Possible selves: Personalized representations of goals. In L. A. Pervin (Ed.), *Goal concepts in personality and social psychology* (pp. 211–241). Hillsdale, NJ: Erlbaum.

Marzano, R. J. (2006). *Classroom assessment and grading that work.* Alexandria, VA: Association for Supervision and Curriculum Development.

Marzano, R. J. (2009). *Designing and teaching learning goals and objectives.* Bloomington, IN: Marzano Research Laboratory.

Marzano, R. J. (2010). *Formative assessment and standards-based grading.* Bloomington, IN: Marzano Research Laboratory.

Marzano, R. J., & Marzano, J. S. (2010). The inner game of teaching. In. R. J. Marzano (Ed.), *On excellence in teaching* (pp. 345–367). Bloomington, IN: Solution Tree Press.

McCombs, B. J., & Marzano, R. J. (1990). Putting the self in self-regulated learning: The self as agent in integrating will and skill. *Educational Psychologist, 25*, 51–69.

Montaivo, F. T., & Torres, M. C. G. (2004) Self-regulated learning: Current and future directions. *Electronic Journal of Research in Educational Psychology, 2*(1), 1–34.

Popham, W. J. (2008). *Transformative assessment.* Alexandria, VA: Association for Supervision and Curriculum Development.

Scriven, M. (1967). The methodology of evaluation. In R. F. Stake (Ed.), *Curriculum evaluation: American Educational Research Association monograph series on evaluation* (No. 1, pp. 39–83). Chicago: Rand McNally.

Shepard, L. A. (2009). Commentary: Evaluating the validity of formative and interim assessment. *Educational Measurement: Issues and Practice, 28*(3), 32–37.

Sklad, M., Diekstra, R., De Ritter, M., Ben, J., & Gravesteijn, C. (2012). Effectiveness of school-based universal social, emotional, and behavioral programs: Do they enhance students' development in the area of skill, behavior, and adjustment? *Psychology in the Schools, 49*(9), 892–909.

Wiliam, D., & Leahy, S. (2007). A theoretical foundation for formative assessment. In J. H. McMillan (Ed.), *Formative classroom assessment* (pp. 29–42). New York: Teachers College Press.

Zins, J. E., Weissberg, R. P., Wang, M. C., & Walberg, H. J. (Eds.). (2004). *Building academic success on social and emotional learning: What does the research say?* New York: Teachers College Press.

CHAPTER 23

Assessment of Climate and Conditions for Learning

Mark Garibaldi, Sally Ruddy, Kimberly Kendziora, and David Osher

School climate is a complex and important construct (Van Houtte, 2005), and researchers and practitioners have assessed many of its aspects (Cohen, McCabe, Michelli, & Pickeral, 2009; Zullig, Koopman, Patton, & Ubbes, 2010). For instance, the range of these constructs includes but is not limited to *school structure and organization* (e.g., school rules, class size, collaboration among departments, disciplinary polices and protocols), *culture* (e.g., beliefs, norms, and values), *relationships* (e.g., interactions between and among adults and students; trust among members of the school community), *student and adult behaviors* (e.g., bullying, intimidation, or sarcasm; engagement, safety), or the effects of others' competencies (e.g., quality of teachers, and social and emotional skills (e.g., communication, empathy, and conflict resolution) (O'Malley, Ritchey, Renshaw, & Furlong, 2011; Stamler, Scheer, & Cohen, 2009).

School climate is important not only because context matters but also because climate is linked with students' academic performance, social development, and later life outcomes (for a review, see Thapa, Cohen, Guffey, & Higgins-D'Alessandro, 2013). The National Longitudinal Study of Adolescent Health examined protective factors for adolescent health and well-being in grades 7–12 and found that school connectedness—one aspect of school climate—was the strongest protective factor in terms of decreasing substance use, school absenteeism, early sexual initiation, violence, and the risk of unintentional injury (Blum, 2005; Resnick et al., 1997). There are also policy-related reasons for schools to examine school climate. Since 2011, the U.S. Department of Education has granted to 43 states waivers from the some of the core tenets of the No Child Left Behind Act, including the provision that 100% of tested students be proficient in reading and mathematics by 2014. Many of the new teacher evaluation and school accountability systems being developed by states as part of their waiver requirements include concepts related to positive school climate. In this chapter, we describe three prominent models that represent policy or practice and research-based frameworks for defining and assessing school climate. Then, we identify and describe core elements of school climate. In Appendix 23.1, we provide an abbreviated sample from a list of federally vetted instruments that may be used to measure school climate. Finally, we provide guidelines and recommendations for selecting school climate surveys, and discuss applications of these models and the use of school climate data.

Three Prominent Models of School Climate

Conditions for Learning

In August 2005, staff from the American Institutes of Research (AIR) gathered with national experts and Chicago Public Schools staff to develop a consensus on (1) the most important factors that schools should address if the goal is to improve student attendance, achievement, graduation rates, and postsecondary success, and (2) actionable indicators of these factors, which we call the social and emotional "conditions for learning", which are those aspects of school climate that are most proximal to the process of teaching and learning in schools. These conditions, in interaction with student and teacher academic and social and emotional competencies, affect motivation, engagement, and achievement (Fredricks, Blumenfeld, & Paris, 2004; McNeely, Nonnemaker, & Blum, 2002; Osher, Dwyer, & Jimerson, 2005; Osher & Kendziora, 2010; Ryan & Patrick, 2001; Thuen & Bru, 2009). The conditions and examples of their impact on learning include perceptions of the following:

- *Physical and emotional safety*, including fair treatment and freedom from harassment, which affects the willingness to attend school and the level of stress that students feel in school, which in turn can affect attention, memory, and willingness to take academic risks.
- *Support*, through which students feel cared about and motivated to engage in schoolwork, are connected to peers, and feel like they belong in their school.
- *Challenge*, including high expectations from both students and teachers at school, the rigor and relevance of the curriculum, and personal motivation to succeed.
- *Peer social and emotional climate*, which includes cultural competence, responsibility, persistence, cooperative teamwork, and contribution to school and community.

National School Climate Council

In 2007, the National School Climate Center and the Education Commission of the States formed the National School Climate Council. The Council concluded that school climate may be broadly defined and assessed as "patterns of people's experiences of school life (that) reflect norms, goals, values, interpersonal relationships, teaching, learning and leadership practices, and organizational structures" (Cohen et al., 2009, p. 2). Represented by four broad areas of school or individual characteristics, school climate is understood to comprise the following:

- *Safety*, which encompasses students' experience of social and physical security and well-being.
- *Institutional Environment*, which refers to the school supports, supplies, and resources that bolster order and learning by countering impedances (e.g., crowding, inadequate facilities, and institutional morale) affecting teaching, learning, and safety.
- *Interpersonal Relationships*, which are characterized by tolerance, respective for diversity, trust, and communication in student–student and student–teacher relationships.
- *Teaching and Learning*, which highlights individualized support with constructive feedback, opportunities for risk taking, and an integrated curriculum that promotes social and emotional skills, healthy development, safety, relationships, and academic achievement.

This framework accounts for school and individual characteristics, and posits that capturing the interaction of these two characteristics is essential for understanding how school-based experiences and social and emotional competencies contribute to school climate.

Safe and Supportive Schools

In 2009, a team of leading climate scholars, policymakers, and stakeholders were brought together by the U.S. Department of Education's Office of Safe and Healthy Students to draft a proposed model for measuring school climate. After extensive listening sessions and consultation with researchers and practitioners, the team developed a comprehensive model that incorporates many aspects of climate under three broad pillars (Harper, 2010; see Figure 23.1). This model is the framework for a national effort to promote the efficient, actionable measurement of conditions for learning in schools nationwide, and the productive use of those data to create safe, supportive, and successful schools that have strong conditions for learning.

Surveys based on and related to this model have been developed and used by 11 state grantees in the federal Safe and Supportive Schools Program. The components in the Safe and Supportive Schools model include the following:

- *Engagement* refers to (1) the quality of relationships within and between students, teachers, and parents; (2) the level of family, staff, and student participation and involvement in school activity; and (3) connectedness between school and the broader community.
- *Safety* highlights the physical and emotional security of the school setting and school-related activities as perceived, experienced, and created by students, staff, and communities.
- *Environment* includes (1) the physical and mental health supports offered to students, (2) the physical plant of the school, (3) the academic environment, and (4) the fairness and adequacy of disciplinary procedures.

Core Elements in School Climate Across Frameworks

Regardless of the lens through which one examines climate and the performance of individuals in schools, what is evident is that characteristics of students, adults, and schools as organizational systems all interact to influence student outcomes. Supportive school climates include contextual elements that contribute to a caring, supportive, and encouraging environment among students and staff. In the following sections, we discuss elements of school climate—*physical conditions, safety, challenge, support*, and *engagement*—that are common across the three frameworks and how these elements relate to student outcomes.

Physical Conditions

Research indicates that the physical environment of schools can significantly influence students' ability to learn efficiently (Doan & Jablonski, 2012; National School Boards Association, 1996). Three salient elements of a school building that influence student outcomes are order, quality, and physical space. Student misbehavior that often emerges in conditions of disrepair may not only disrupt the classroom and interfere with instructional time (Dinkes, Kemp, & Baum, 2009) but may also have a broader effect on teachers' professionalism and students' distractions and anxiety (Browers & Tomic, 2000; Hastings & Bham, 2003). The physical condition of a school building (e.g.,

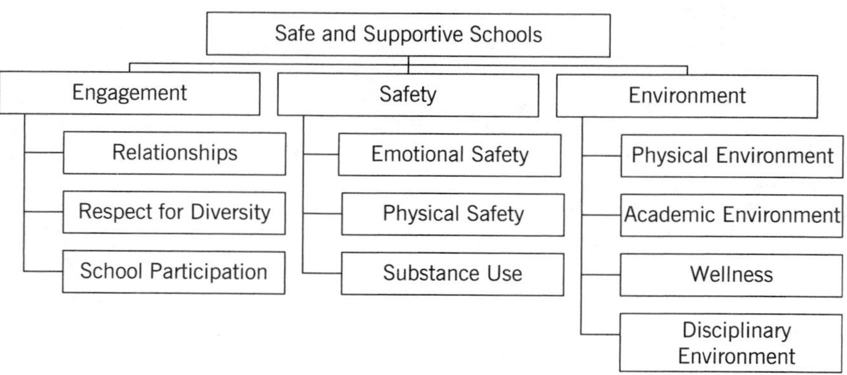

FIGURE 23.1. The three main components of climate in the safe and supportive schools model (Harper, 2010).

unclean floors and walls, unrepaired ceilings, broken furniture and fixtures, chipped paint) has also been linked to student misbehavior, teacher satisfaction, and academic achievement (Bullock, 2007; Earthman, 2004; O'Sullivan, 2006; Schneider, 2002). For instance, in a longitudinal study of high school sophomores, 66% of students identified at least one improper building condition (Planty & DeVoe, 2005). In addition, the lowest achieving students (based on standardized tests) were more often found to attend schools with vandalism, disrepair, and uncleanliness.

Safety

Safety is a fundamental requirement for all schools (Dwyer & Osher, 2000). Schools can expose students to risk factors that compromise learning and academic performance, and are associated with antisocial and delinquent behaviors (Casebeer, 2012; Glew, Fan, Katon, Rivara, & Kernic, 2005). In a national survey on school crime and safety, 74% of public schools recorded that one or more violent crimes (e.g., assault, rape, robbery) had taken place at school in the 2009–2010 school year (Robers, Zhang, & Truman, 2012). In addition to physical attacks, verbal aggression is also prevalent; 28% of students ages 12–18 in the United States were bullied at school over the course of a school year (Robers et al., 2012).

Challenge

Schools may be safe and orderly, but students are ideally positioned for academic success when teachers have high academic and behavioral expectations, particularly for students who are at risk for dropping out (Catalano, Haggerty, Oesterle, Flemings, & Hawkins, 2004; J. Lee, 2012; V. E. Lee, Smith, Perry, & Smylie, 1999). By "challenge", we refer to high expectations, student investment in and motivation to engage in schoolwork, and relevant, rigorous academic content. However, when teachers press students with higher expectations without adequate support, student learning and academic performance suffer (V. Lee & Smith, 1999). High academic expectations should always be accompanied by appropriate student support.

Support

Researchers have demonstrated the important role of teacher support in positive student outcomes (Brewster & Bowen, 2004; Muller, 2001; Wentzel, 1997, 2002). Establishing effective methods of student support involves ensuring that the significant adults in students' lives work collaboratively to encourage, support, and nurture them. Traditional perspectives about the effect of *teacher quality* (in terms of teacher certification or academic degrees) on student outcomes reveal only a modest contribution (Ballou & Podgursky, 2000; Darling-Hammond, 2000; Darling-Hammond & Youngs, 2002; Goldhaber & Brewer, 1999). More recent conceptualizations focus on *teacher effectiveness*, which combines high-quality instruction with supportiveness, responsiveness, and caring. Teachers who display these skills are more able to encourage a range of positive student outcomes (Brewster & Bowen, 2004; Lee & Burkam, 2003; Lee & Smith, 1999). In addition, teachers who do not demonstrate these skills experience greater stress and burnout (Tsouloupas, Carson, Matthews, Grawitch, & Barber, 2010).

Related to these competencies are the relationships and sense of caring forged by effective teachers who contribute to students' learning and well-being (Hamre & Pianta, 2005; Wentzel & Wigfield, 1998). This type of student support involves providing fair and equitable treatment, asking students if they need help, making class interesting, making sure that students understand the content taught in class, and directly communicating about students' academic progress (Spier, Garibaldi, & Osher, 2011; Wentzel, 1997, 2002).

Engagement

Student engagement is a key element of school climate, with a large body of research linking it to academic achievement. Student engagement has affective, cognitive, and behavioral components, overlapping substantially with the concepts of "school connectedness", "school bonding", and "belonging." Engagement is linked to attendance and, in turn, to academic performance and dropout rates (Croninger & Lee,

2001; Goodenow, 1993; Willingham, Pollack, & Lewis, 2002). Although incentives and school policies to encourage attendance can influence student engagement, research suggests that enhancing curricula and pedagogy to be relevant and meaningful to students significantly affects engagement and, ultimately, positive student outcomes (Ryan & Deci, 2000; Yazzie-Mintz, 2010).

Measuring School Climate

Both theoretical frameworks and empirical research have demonstrated robust associations between students' experience of physical conditions, safety, challenge, support, and engagement at school, and their academic, social, and emotional outcomes. Climate matters, and one of the most important steps school leaders can take to begin to address the climate in their buildings is to measure it. Axioms about measurement abound (e.g., "What gets assessed gets addressed"; "You don't get what you expect, you get what you inspect"; "What's measured matters"), but the value of having some indicators that show how students (and potentially staff and families) perceive their schools cannot be understated. Accurate measurement is the foundation of understanding needs, identifying targets for improvement, and monitoring progress over time. In this section, we review measures of school climate.

Recommendations and Guidelines for Selecting Measures

Multiple factors need to be considered when choosing a school climate survey. For example, selection of measures should be based on their appropriateness for the respondent group (students, school staff, families, and/or school administrators) and, for students, appropriateness to the grade level. Other considerations (e.g., ease of use, format, and length of administration; cost; provisions for reporting and interpreting results; and programmatic planning needs of the school, district, or state) also need to be addressed when choosing a school climate survey.

In selecting measures, users should consider the technical and practical potential of a survey, as well as how it aligns with school improvement efforts. Instruments should be both technically and practically viable to ensure the usefulness of school climate data. *Technically viable* instruments should be conceptually and psychometrically sound: They should be reliable and possess concurrent, construct, and face validity. School climate scales should correlate with one another and capture the multiple dimensions of school climate. When adopting or creating a *practically viable* instrument for school climate, it is important to address the item structure (e.g., incidence data, yes–no items, ordinal items, or nominal items), length of the survey or scales, and ease with which the data can be scored, reported, and acted upon.

Items and scales should ideally generate data that empower users by providing information that is meaningful (e.g., that raises awareness and sense of responsibility to improve/maintain school climate), that yields insights about areas of improvement, and that outlines actionable steps for making those improvements. This can be facilitated by disaggregating data in order to understand how subgroups experience school climate. Perhaps the best example of linking school climate measurement to school improvement is the systematic, decades-long effort by the Consortium on Chicago School Research (CCSR) to measure multiple aspects of school functioning (including climate, as rated by students, teachers, and school administrators) in Chicago Public Schools (Bryk, Sebring, Allensworth, Luppescu, & Easton, 2010). Years of research have identified five aspects of school functioning that are most strongly predictive of school improvement: (1) ambitious instruction, (2) effective leaders, (3) collaborative teachers, (4) involved families, and (5) supportive environment. CCSR has built an online, interactive dashboard (*http://cps.5-essentials.org/2013*) that allows educators to explore school-level results. Use of both color and graphics in the score reports allows users quickly to identify areas of strength or need.

A helpful resource for those considering the use of existing measures has been developed by the Office of Safe and Healthy Students (OSHS), part of the U.S. Department of Education's National Center on Safe Supportive Learning Environments

(NCSSLE). The NCSSLE website includes a compendium of 17 student, family, and staff school climate surveys, along with a description of each survey, its constructs, intended respondents, key source reports, and information about obtaining the survey instruments. Details about all 17 can be found on the NCSSLE website (*http://safesupportivelearning.ed.gov*). A few examples of these surveys are presented in Appendix 23.1. All 17 surveys were nominated in an open call to the field, reviewed by technical staff, and vetted by OSHS as valid and reliable.

Among the surveys in the compendium are those that have been vetted for students as young as second grade, such as AIR's Conditions for Learning Survey; that include a suite of surveys for multiple respondents, such as those in the CAL-SCHLS (California School Climate, Health, and Learning Survey) data system; focus on community risk and protective factors, such as the Communities That Care Youth Survey; and are relatively brief, such as the Perceived School Experiences Scale, which includes 14 items that measure three indicators.

Special Considerations for Family Voice

Active involvement of families in schools is a strong indicator of school health because family engagement can help students learn, advance the school's mission, and strengthen community connections and resources (Bryk, Sebring, Allensworth, Luppescu, & Easton, 2010). Measuring family perceptions of school climate through surveys can be particularly challenging, however. Students, teachers, and administrators, who spend all day at school, can use this time during the school day to complete surveys, but parents generally must be reached outside the school building. School districts cannot always maintain current contact information for parents who do not have stable living situations. Both family members who have had bad experiences with schools and disengaged families may be reluctant to respond, raising the risk of response bias. In addition, family members may require more language options than students, and the choice of paper, Web, mobile, or phone survey modes all influence the information yielded in ways that may create bias in the results (Feil et al., 2007; Gribble & Haupt, 2005; Van de Kerckhove, Montaquila, Carver, & Brick, 2009). Because of the many challenges in surveying families, typical response rates for district-sponsored surveys are generally around 25–30% (Nathanson, McCormick, Kemple, & Sypek, 2013), which is too low to ensure that the survey results are representative of all families. Reaching families may require innovative strategies that are family-driven and culturally competent, and that leverage community organizations, including family organizations and the faith community.

The Future of School Climate Assessment

In January 2013, as part of an initiative to make schools safer, President Obama announced that his administration would develop a school climate survey that would provide "reliable data to help schools implement policies to improve climate" (The White House, 2013, p. 13). To fulfill this commitment, the U.S. Department of Education's National Center for Education Statistics has launched an effort to develop, test, benchmark, then make freely available a set of national school climate survey instruments. The work is being carried out by the American Institutes for Research and Sanametrix. The set will include measures to assess school climate (using the Safe and Supportive Schools framework of engagement, safety, and environment) from the perspectives of middle and high school students, teachers and staff, principals, and family members. These instruments will be built on an online platform that will allow schools and districts the flexibility to administer the surveys independently and receive immediate results. These results will provide school personnel with a basis for understanding and improving the educational climate for their students and the ability to compare their results to both national benchmarks and the results of other schools and districts.

The National School Climate Survey will begin field testing in the spring of 2015, and the collection of nationally representative benchmark data is scheduled for the spring of 2016. If work proceeds according to plan, schools and districts could have free access to reliable and valid set of instruments for understanding their school climate and comparing it to others' in time for the 2016–2017 school year. Some schools and districts that have a history of measuring school climate using existing instruments (e.g., Chicago, Cleveland, New York City, Anchorage, states that had Safe and Supportive school grants, and the many California districts that use the California Healthy Kids Survey) may stay with their current measures, so that they do not lose the capacity to follow trends over time. For the many other states, districts, and schools that have not committed to a particular set of instruments, the availability of a national school climate survey may come as a tremendous boon and greatly expand knowledge about both school climate and efforts to build safe and nurturing climates in schools.

Potential Problems and Pitfalls

Developing a system in a school, district, or state in which school climate or conditions for learning data are systematically collected, scored, reported, and used is a challenging process. In this section, we describe some major challenges and share ideas about what might be done to address them.

Relying Solely on School Office Referral, Suspension, or Expulsion Data

Although it may be advantageous to use existing district data to validate findings from a student, staff, or family survey, discipline data, although widely available, are not necessarily the best indicators of school safety or climate (Furlong, Morrison, Cornell, & Skiba, 2004). Such data are strongly influenced by idiosyncratic school policies and practices relative to reporting and categorizing student behavior, which may not be done systematically and are not standardized across schools or districts. In addition, data on suspensions and expulsions may be better indicators of school discipline policies than of actual student misbehavior. The information schools need to act upon to improve climate and conditions for learning must come from the students and/or staff themselves (and, potentially, families and community members). Surveys are an efficient way to gather this information, but they present their own challenges.

Problems in Survey Development, Administration, Analysis, and Reporting

There are many examples of the use of bad surveys in schools. These surveys do not do a good job of measuring what they are intended to measure. The instruments are not subjected to analysis for statistical soundness and their results sit unused in binders in central offices. NCSSLE has archived a 2011 series of webinars related to the process of collecting and using data on school climate and conditions for learning, and has offered a wealth of practical advice (the webinars are archived at *http://safesupportivelearning.ed.gov*). Among the strategies to overcome these challenges is to begin with a clear vision of what one wants to know, then select or develop items/scales accordingly. Using items from established surveys (with permission where needed) can jump-start development and support soundness and usefulness; items that are newly written or are to be given to a new population should be tested using "think-aloud" interviews (also known as "cognitive laboratories"). Pilot testing surveys with a small sample allows both the items and the administration procedures to be refined before a large-scale administration is attempted. It is useful to keep surveys short to promote better attention and completion. Involve stakeholders in publicizing and promoting participation in the survey. Confirm the reliability and validity of the data before they are reported, and report caveats as necessary. Even with high response rates (targets are generally 80% for student or staff surveys), analyze results to ensure that they are adequately representative of the population of interest. Share findings with stakeholders (including respondents) as quickly as is feasible, with a focus on the recommended actions emerging from the results.

Not Developing a Clear Vision for the Kinds of Climate or Desired Conditions for Learning

For too many schools, measuring school climate is something done to comply with district mandates, and not part of their own improvement process. The National School Climate Council (2007) has pointed out that quality or improvement standards for school climate, which could potentially link schools' data with improvement plans and technical assistance, are rare. The development of a vision for what a school or district wants to realize in terms of its conditions for learning, and the operationalization of that vision in terms of concrete indicators, can help schools begin to succeed.

Conclusion

School climate for learning can be validly measured and effectively used to monitor progress and continuous improvement. For instance, in partnership with AIR, Alaska has been measuring school climate (and connectedness) among students, teachers, and families for nearly a decade. Similarly, Cleveland began using school climate data for monitoring, planning, and accountability in 2008, and has now expanded it to charter schools.

To continue improving school climate, Osher and Kendziora (2010) have highlighted three major barriers to overcome and broad recommendations to improve aspects of school climate that contribute to positive social, emotional, and academic learning. First, it is essential to show the importance of social and emotional elements in education that can be assessed via climate surveys. However, more supporting evidence is still needed, so districts and states need to develop the capacity to assess and monitor the climate and social and emotional conditions for learning while the evidence is still accumulating. Second, there are often limited financial resources to conduct school climate assessments. In response, stakeholders need to be made aware of the importance of school climate and conditions for learning. Third, climate surveys should be used in conjunction with the academic and social–emotional programming in schools, so that both can be monitored over time. For example, a positive school climate can enhance a program's impact or be improved as a result of it, whereas strong negative features of school climate can undermine a program's effectiveness. States or districts should provide schools and communities with effective tools, strategies, and supports to improve the conditions for learning.

It is an act of courage on the part of administrators, teachers, and staff to collect and review data that tell the truth about the perceptions of the learning environment held by students and school staff, then use those truths to inform decisions about how to improve the school environment. The basic process in using survey data is to understand the facts, share the facts, then act on the facts—but measurement must come first.

References

Anderson-Butcher, D., Amorose, A., Iachini, A., & Ball, A. (2011). The development of the Perceived Schools Experiences Scale. *Research on Social Work Practice, 22(2)*, 186–194.

Ballou, D., & Podgursky, M. (2000). Reforming teacher preparation and licensing: What is the evidence? *Teachers College Record, 102*, 5–27.

Blum, R. W. (2005). *School connectedness: Improving the lives of students*. Baltimore: Johns Hopkins Bloomberg School of Public Health.

Brewster, A., & Bowen, G. (2004). Teacher support and the school engagement of Latino middle and high school students at risk of school failure. *Child and Adolescent Social Work Journal, 21*, 47–67.

Browers, A., & Tomic, W. (2000). A longitudinal study of teacher burnout and perceived self-efficacy in classroom management. *Teaching and Teacher Education, 16*, 249–253.

Bryk, A. S., Sebring, P. B., Allensworth, E., Luppescu, S., & Easton, J. Q. (2010). *Organizing schools for improvement: Lessons from Chicago*. Chicago: University of Chicago Press.

Bullock, C. C. (2007). *The relationship between school building conditions and student achievement at the middle school level in the Commonwealth of Virginia*. Unpublished doctoral dissertation, Virginia Polytechnic Institute, Blacksburg, VA.

Casebeer, C. M. (2012). School bullying: Why quick fixes do not prevent school failure. *Preventing School Failure, 56*(3), 165–171.

Catalano, R. F., Haggerty, K. P., Oesterle, S., Fleming, C. B., & Hawkins, J. D. (2004). The importance of bonding to school for healthy development: Findings from the Social Development Research Group. *Journal of School Health, 74*, 252–261.

Cohen, J., McCabe, E. M., Michelli, N. M., & Pickeral, T. (2009). School climate: Research, policy, teacher education and practice. *Teachers College Record, 111*, 180–213.

Croninger, R. G., & Lee, V. E. (2001). Social capital and dropping out of high school: Benefits to at-risk students of teachers' support and guidance. *Teachers College Record, 103*(4), 548–581.

Darling-Hammond, L. (2000). Reforming teacher preparation and licensing: Debating the evidence. *Teachers College Record, 102*, 28–56.

Darling-Hammond, L., & Youngs, P. (2002). Defining "highly qualified teachers": What does "scientifically-based research" actually tell us? *Educational Researcher, 31*, 13–25.

Dinkes, R., Kemp, J., & Baum, K. (2009). *Indicators of school crime and safety: 2009* (NCES 2010-012/NCJ 228478). Washington, DC: National Center for Education Statistics and Bureau of Justice Statistics.

Doan, K., & Jablonski, B. (2012). In their own words, urban students make suggestions for improving the appearance of their schools. *Urban Review: Issues and Ideas in Public Education, 44*, 649–663.

Dwyer, K., & Osher, D. (2000). *Safeguarding our children: An action guide*. Washington, DC: U.S. Departments of Education and Justice, American Institutes for Research.

Earthman, G. I. (2004). *Prioritization of 31 criteria for school building adequacy*. Baltimore: American Civil Liberties Union Foundation of Maryland.

Feil, E. G., Severson, H., Taylor, T. K., Boles, S., Albert, D. A., & Blair, J. (2007). An innovative, effective and cost effective survey method using a survey-check response format. *Prevention Science, 8*(2), 133–140.

Fredricks, J. A., Blumenfeld, P. C., & Paris, A. H. (2004). School engagement: Potential of the concept, state of the evidence. *Review of Educational Research, 74*, 5–109.

Furlong, M. J., Morrison, G. M., Cornell, D. G., & Skiba, R. (2004). Methodological and measurement issues in school violence research: Moving beyond the social problem era. *Journal of School Violence, 3*(2/3), 5–12.

Glew, G., Fan, M., Katon, W., Rivara, F. P., & Kernic, M. A. (2005). Bullying, psychosocial adjustment, and academic performance in elementary school. *Archives of Pediatric and Adolescent Medicine, 159*, 1026–1031.

Goldhaber, D., & Brewer, D. (1999). Teacher licensing and student achievement. In M. Kanstoroom & C. E. Finn, Jr. (Eds.), *Better teachers, better schools* (pp. 83–102). Washington, DC: Fordham Foundation.

Goodenow, C. (1993). The psychological sense of school membership among adolescents: Scale development and educational correlates. *Psychology in the Schools, 30*, 79–90.

Gribble, R. K., & Haupt, C. (2005). Quantitative and qualitative differences between handout and mailed patient satisfaction surveys. *Medical Care, 43*(3), 276–281.

Hamre, B. K., & Pianta, R. C. (2005). Can instructional and emotional support in the first-grade classroom make a difference for children at risk of school failure? *Child Development, 76*, 949–967.

Harper, K. (2010, December). *Measuring school climate*. Paper presented to the Safe and Supportive Schools Grantee Meeting, Washington, DC.

Hastings, R. P., & Bham, M. S. (2003). The relationship between student behaviour patterns and teacher burnout. *School Psychology International, 24*, 115–127.

Khmelkov, V. T. (2010). *Culture of Excellence and Ethics Assessment, Student and Faculty Survey: Reliability, validity and other psychometric data, high school sample* [PowerPoint presentation]. Manlius, NY: Institute for Excellence and Ethics. Retrieved January 10, 2014, from *http://excellenceandethics.org*.

Lee, J. (2012). The effects of the teacher–student relationship and academic press on student engagement and academic performance. *International Journal of Educational Research, 53*, 330–340.

Lee, V. E., & Burkam, D. T. (2003). Dropping out of high school: The role of school organization and structure. *American Educational Research Journal, 2*, 353–393.

Lee, V., & Smith, J. (1999). Social support and achievement for young adolescents in Chicago: The role of school academic press. *American Educational Research Journal, 36*, 907–945.

Lee, V. E., Smith, J. B., Perry, T. E., & Smylie, M. A. (1999). *Social support, academic press, and student achievement: A view from the middle grades in Chicago*. Chicago: Chicago Annenberg Challenge.

McNeely, C. A., Nonnemaker, J. M., & Blum, R. W. (2002). Promoting school connectedness: Evidence from the National Longitudinal Study of Adolescent Health. *Journal of School Health, 72*, 138–146.

Muller, C. (2001). The role of caring in the teacher–student relationship for at-risk students. *Sociological Inquiry, 71*(2), 241–255.

Nathanson, L., McCormick, M., Kemple, J. J., & Sypek, L. (2013). *Strengthening assessments of school climate: Lessons from the NYC School Survey*. New York: Research Alliance for New York City Schools. Retrieved January 5, 2014, from *http://steinhardt.nyu.edu/research_alliance/publications*.

National School Boards Association. (1996). *Learning by design: A school leader's guide to architectural services*. Alexandria, VA: Author.

National School Climate Council. (2007). *The school climate challenge: Narrowing the gap between school climate research and school climate policy, practice guidelines and teacher education policy*. New York: Author.

O'Malley, M., Ritchey, K., Renshaw, T., & Furlong, M. J. (2011). Gauging the system: Trends in school climate measurement and intervention. In S. R. Jimerson, A. B. Nickerson, M. J. Mayer, & M. J. Furlong (Eds.), *Handbook of school violence and school safety: International research and practice* (2nd ed., pp. 317–329). New York: Routledge.

Osher, D., Dwyer, K., & Jimerson, S. (2005). Foundations of school violence and safety. In S. R. Jimerson & M. J. Furlong (Eds.), *Handbook of school violence and school safety* (pp. 51–71). Mahwah, NJ: Erlbaum.

Osher, D., & Kendziora, K. (2010). Building conditions for learning and healthy adolescent development: Strategic approaches. In B. Doll, W. Pfohl, & J. Yoon (Eds.), *Handbook of youth prevention science* (pp. 121–140). New York: Routledge.

Osher, D., Kendziora, K., & Chinen, M. (2008). *Student connection research: Final Narrative Report to the Spencer Foundation*. Washington, DC: American Institutes for Research.

O'Sullivan, S. (2006). *A study of the relationship between building condition and student academic achievement in Pennsylvania's high schools*. Unpublished doctoral dissertation, Virginia Polytechnic Institute and State University, Blacksburg, VA.

Planty, M., & DeVoe, J. F. (2005). *An examination of the condition of school facilities attended by 10th grade students in 2002* (NCES 2006-302). Washington, DC: U.S. Department of Education.

Resnick, M. D., Bearman, P. S., Blum, R. W., Bauman, K. E., Harris, K. M., Jones, J., et al. (1997). Protecting adolescents from harm: Findings from the National Longitudinal Study on Adolescent Health. *Journal of the American Medical Association, 278*, 823–832.

Robers, S., Zhang, J., & Truman, J. (2012). *Indicators of school crime and safety: 2011* (NCES 2012-002/NCJ 236021). Washington, DC: National Center for Education Statistics, U.S. Department of Education and Bureau of Justice Statistics, Office of Justice Programs, U.S. Department of Justice.

Ryan, R., & Deci, E. (2000). Self–determination theory and the facilitation of intrinsic motivation, social development, and well–being. *American Psychologist, 55*, 68–78.

Ryan, A. M., & Patrick, H. (2001). The classroom social environment and changes in adolescents' motivation and engagement during middle school. *American Educational Research Journal, 38*, 437–460.

Schneider, M. (2002). *Do school facilities affect academic outcomes?* Washington, DC: National Clearinghouse for Educational Facilities.

Spier, E., Garibaldi, M. L., & Osher, D. (2011). *Alaska school climate and connectedness focus groups: 2011 results*. Washington, DC: American Institutes for Research.

Stamler, J. K., Scheer, D. C., & Cohen, J. (2009). *Assessing school climate for school improvement: Development, validation and implications of the Student School Climate Survey*. New York: National School Climate Center.

Thapa, A., Cohen, J., Guffey, S., & Higgins-D'Alessandro, A. (2013). A review of school climate research. *Review of Educational Research, 83*, 357–385.

The White House. (2013, January 16). Now is the time: The President's plan to protect our children and our families by reducing gun violence. Retrieved January 17, 2014, from *www.whitehouse.gov/sites/default/files/docs/wh_now_is_the_time_full.pdf*.

Thuen, E., & Bru, E. (2009). Are changes in students' perceptions of the learning environment related to changes in emotional and behavioral problems? *School Psychology International, 30*(2), 115–136.

Tsouloupas, C. N., Carson, R. L., Matthews, R., Grawitch, M. J., & Barber, L. K. (2010). Examining teachers' emotional regulation strategies as mediators between student disruptive behavior and teacher burnout. *Educational Psychology, 30*(2), 173–189.

Van de Kerckhove, W., Montaquila, J. M., Carver, P. R., & Brick, J. M. (2009). *An evaluation of bias in the 2007 National Household Education Surveys Program: Results from a special data collection effort* (NCES 2009-029). Washington, DC: National Center for Education Statistics.

Van Houtte, M. (2005). Climate or culture?: A plea for conceptual clarity in school effectiveness research. *School Effectiveness and School Improvement, 16*(1), 71–89.

Wentzel, K. R. (1997). Student motivation in middle school: The role of perceived pedagogical caring. *Journal of Educational Psychology, 89*, 411–419.

Wentzel, K. R. (2002). Are effective teachers like good parents?: Interpersonal predictors of school adjustment in early adolescence. *Child Development, 73*, 287–301.

Wentzel, K. R., & Wigfield, A. (1998). Academic and social motivational influences on students' academic performance. *Educational Psychology Review, 10*, 155–175.

Willingham, W. W., Pollack, J. M., & Lewis, C. (2002). Grades and test scores: Accounting for observed differences. *Journal of Educational Measurement, 39*, 1–37.

Yazzie-Mintz, E. (2010). *Charting the path from engagement to achievement: A report on the 2009 High School Survey of Student Engagement.* Bloomington, IN: Center for Evaluation and Education Policy.

Zullig, K. J., Koopman, T. M., Patton, J. M., & Ubbes, V. A. (2010). School climate: Historical review, instrument development, and school assessment. *Journal of Psychoeducational Assessment, 28*, 139–152.

APPENDIX 23.1. Examples of School Climate Surveys

A complete list of the 17 school climate surveys vetted by the OSHS is available at *http://safesupportivelearning.ed.gov*. Here, we present three surveys that are publicly available. Although a new National School Climate Survey will be freely available to districts and schools starting in 2016–2017, some educators may wish to begin measuring climate sooner, perhaps as part of safe schools, discipline reform, or educator evaluation initiatives. Users such as these may want to consider the following instruments, or any included in the online compendium.

American Institutes for Research Conditions for Learning Survey

- **Description.** *Number of items:* grades 2–4, 23; grades 5–8, 53; grades 9–12, 56. *Administration:* paper or online, school-based. Grades 2–4, 3-point response option; grades 5–12, 4-point Likert scales; 4-point frequency response option.
- **Constructs.** Safe and Respectful Climate; High Expectations; Student Support; Social and Emotional Learning.
- **Respondents.** Students (grades 2–4, 5–8, 9–12).
- **Reliability.** *Range of Cronbach's alphas:* grades 2–4, α = .54–.71; grades 5–8, α = .74–.80; grades 9–12, α = .77–.83.
- **Key report.** Osher, D., Kendziora, K., & Chinen, M. (2008). *Student connection research: Final Narrative Report to the Spencer Foundation.* Washington, DC: American Institutes for Research.
- **Survey instruments.** There is no charge for using this survey. Contact David Osher at *dosher@air.org* for additional information.

Culture of Excellence and Ethics Assessment

- **Description.** *Number of items:* Student survey, 105; faculty/staff survey, 134; parent survey, 70. *Administration:* student, paper, school-based; faculty/staff, paper and online; parent, paper; 5-point Likert scales.
- **Constructs.** *Students:* Competencies: Excellence (Version 4.2 only); Competencies: Ethics (Version 4.2 only); School Culture: Excellence; School Culture: Ethics; Faculty Practices: Excellence; Faculty Practices: Ethics, Student Safety, Faculty Support for and Engagement of Students. *Faculty/staff:* Competencies: Excellence (Version 4.2 only); Competencies: Ethics (Version 4.2 only); School Culture: Excellence; School Culture: Ethics; Faculty Practices: Excellence; Faculty Practices: Ethics, Student Safety, Faculty Support for and Engagement of Students, Leadership Practices, Faculty Beliefs and Behaviors, Home–School Communication and Support. *Parents:* Perception of School Culture, School Engaging with Parents, Parents Engaging with School, Learning at Home/Promoting Excellence, Parenting/Promoting Ethics.
- **Respondents.** Students (middle and high school grades), faculty/staff, parents.
- **Reliability.** Range of Cronbach's alphas: student (high school) α = .85–.91; faculty/staff, α = .84–.93; parent, α = .45–.91.
- **Key report.** Khmelkov, V. T. (2010). *Culture of excellence and ethics assessment, student and faculty survey: Reliability, validity and other psychometric data, high school sample.* [PowerPoint presentation]. Manlius, NY: Institute for Excellence and Ethics. Available at *excellenceandethics.org*.
- **Survey instruments.** These survey instruments may be used free of charge, subject to the conditions of the User Agreement, and can be found at *excellenceandethics.com*. Contact Vlad Khmelkov at *vkhmelkov@excellenceandethics.com* for additional information.

Perceived School Experiences Scale

- **Description.** *Number of items:* 14; *Administration:* paper, school based; 5-point Likert scales.
- **Constructs.** Academic Motivation, Academic Press, School Connectedness.
- **Respondents.** Students (grades 7–12).
- **Reliability.** Range of Cronbach's alpha: α = .88–.90.
- **Key report.** Anderson-Butcher, D., Amorose, A., Iachini, A., & Ball, A. (2011). The development of the Perceived Schools Experiences Scale. *Research on Social Work Practice*, 22(2), 186–194.
- **Survey instruments.** There is no charge for using this survey. Contact Dawn Anderson-Butcher at *anderson-butcher.1@osu.edu* for additional information.

CHAPTER 24

Assessing Organizational Readiness

Shannon B. Wanless, Christina J. Groark, and Bridget E. Hatfield

Organizations that serve children are often settings for delivering social and emotional learning (SEL) interventions. SEL interventions vary in their scope and method of delivery but generally aim to develop skills such as self-awareness, self-management, social awareness, building relationships, and responsible decision making (Collaborative for Academic, Social, and Emotional Learning [CASEL], 2012; Zins, Bloodworth, Weissberg, & Walberg, 2004). A broad range of organizations may be interested in helping children to develop these social–emotional competencies because having these skills may facilitate children's success in the organization. For example, schools may be interested in promoting social–emotional competence because these skills help children attain academic competence. Residential care facilities may support children's social–emotional competence to increase their ability to manage their disability. Orphanages may support children's social–emotional development as a means of building resilience and the ability to attach to a future adopted caregiver. Sports teams may be interested in developing players' social–emotional competence as a means of improving children's teamwork and athletic performance. Fortunately, some organizations provide direct service providers with SEL training so they can support children's social–emotional development. Even when training for direct service providers is high in quality, however, it does not always translate into effective practices (Hemmeter & Conroy, 2012). There are many contextual characteristics of organizations and of individuals within organizations that relate to whether SEL intervention practices will be delivered effectively (Domitrovich et al., 2008). Since high-quality use of SEL intervention practices relates to improved child outcomes, understanding contextual characteristics that may improve use of SEL practices is an important first step for many types of organizations serving children.

Implementation Quality

The quality and quantity of delivery of SEL intervention practices often varies substantially (Weisz, Sandler, Durlak, & Anton, 2005). Previous research has established, however, that when the critical components of an SEL intervention are delivered with high quality and the intended frequency (dosage), children have better outcomes (Durlak & DuPre, 2008). Critical components are the key aspects of an intervention that must be present for the program to be considered "in use" in a setting (Century, Rudnick, & Freeman, 2010). Without these aspects in place, there would be no reason to expect the intervention to have an effect on child outcomes. Moreover, implementing critical components is not sufficient. These critical components must be implemented carefully and be of sufficient duration to elicit a change in child outcomes. The presence of critical SEL intervention components with sufficient quality and quantity indicates that the intervention is being used with high fidelity of implementation.

Implementation quality, however, is broader than the concept of fidelity of implementation. In addition to delivering the intervention practices in the way the intervention designers intended (fidelity of implementation), implementation quality also involves being able to adapt the practices to the context in ways that improve the efficacy of the practices (positive adaptation) and genuinely embody the main messages of the intervention, so that those messages seep into unscripted moments (generalization) (Domitrovich, Gest, Jones, Gill, & DeRousie, 2010). In the majority of research, "implementation quality" has been described as being synonymous with "fidelity of implementation." Although delivering intervention practices as they were designed is a central component of implementation quality, we extend this definition and suggest that although fidelity of implementation may indicate one important piece of implementation quality, it may not provide the full picture of what strong implementation entails. Deep understanding of, and commitment to, the aims of the intervention may help implementers go beyond enacting certain activities as they were designed, to effectively integrating SEL strategies throughout the day and the context (Jones & Bouffard, 2012). This type of context-specific integration, in addition to implementing the intervention's critical components with quality and the intended frequency (fidelity of implementation), represents a comprehensive definition of high implementation quality. Finally, we suggest that implementation quality is on a continuum (low to high), and that any organization using an SEL intervention should aim for high implementation quality.

Predictors of Implementation Quality

Implementation quality is largely a result of the training and ongoing support provided for use of a SEL intervention. Examples include initial training for the direct service providers, intervention coaches, or trainers who work with implementers on an ongoing basis, and sufficient resources and support to allow direct service providers to focus their time and energy on using the new intervention practices. Intervention designers are encouraged to articulate the conditions that are necessary for successful support of each SEL intervention (Wandersman et al., 2008). Although optimal levels of support for high implementation quality are often not provided, they have been linked to improved implementation quality and are a necessary part of an overall approach to ensuring that SEL interventions are used effectively (Kretlow & Bartholomew, 2010).

Predictors of implementation quality are at work, however, before initial intervention training begins. These preexisting characteristics reflect an organization's readiness to implement a new SEL intervention successfully. Organizational readiness, in other words, reflects the initial overall capacity of the organization to learn and use new practices (see Figure 24.1). Specifically, aspects of the organization and of the individuals within the organization comprise the organization's "readiness" to implement the SEL intervention practices. Unfortunately, in practice, time is rarely taken to consider whether organizations are ready to implement a new SEL intervention. Examining aspects of the organization and the individuals in the organization to determine readiness before SEL training begins is worth the time and effort, largely because this process may offer insight into potential challenges to implementation quality.

One main reason we argue for greater attention to organizational readiness is that it presents an opportunity to be proactive in raising implementation quality and therefore SEL intervention effectiveness. By understanding an organization's readiness to implement an SEL intervention before training begins, it may be possible to tailor the intervention training to respond to the specific strengths and challenges of the orga-

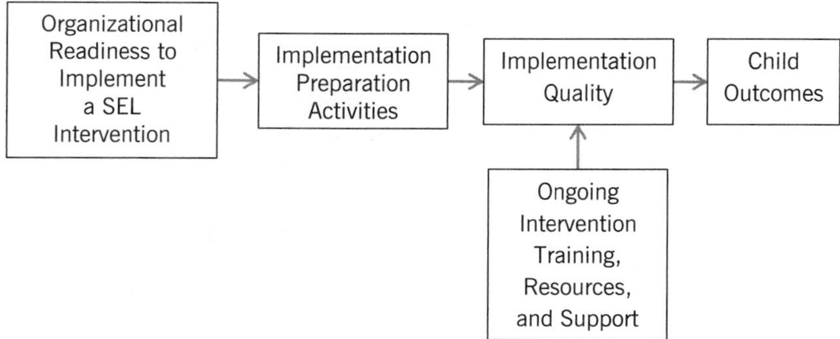

FIGURE 24.1. Conceptual model of the process of moving from building organizational readiness to shifting child outcomes.

nization (Peterson & Baker, 2011). Specifically, the intervention trainer may determine whether an organization (1) needs to build more capacity before moving forward with the SEL intervention training; (2) is generally ready but may need some specific types of support during training; or (3) is ready for the standard training in the SEL intervention and will likely be successful. By taking this proactive approach to supporting implementation quality, it may be possible to prevent implementation problems before they occur, and ultimately, to achieve higher SEL outcomes for children.

Based on the importance of understanding organizational readiness to improve SEL implementation quality, the goals of this chapter are to (1) provide a rationale for the importance of focusing on understanding an organization before SEL intervention training begins; (2) summarize some of the key contextual readiness characteristics associated with SEL intervention implementation quality; (3) identify some issues in measurement of organizational readiness; and (4) share lessons from the field, including practical suggestions for assessing whether an organization is ready to use SEL intervention practices effectively.

Understanding the Organization *before* SEL Intervention Preparation Begins

The process of implementing an SEL intervention ideally begins with a phase of preparing to implement (implementation preparation activities), then leads to the actual implementation of new practices (implementation quality). One of the first researchers to acknowledge the preparation stage was Lewin (1947), who termed it "unfreezing" and described this stage's purpose as cultivating motivation to change practices. In line with this aim, contemporary implementation models have included implementation preparation activities such as getting a leader's initial commitment to the intervention, creating a steering committee of key stakeholders (leaders, direct service providers, families), and developing a shared vision of the importance of SEL for children (Devaney, O'Brien, Resnik, Keister, & Weissberg, 2006). Sometimes these tasks are described as part of a "planning" or "preadoption" or "exploratory" stage (CASEL, 2006; Fixsen, Naoom, Blase, Friedman, & Wallace, 2005; Greenberg, Domitrovich, Graczyk, & Zins, 2005). Most recently, researchers have synthesized best practices regarding the process of implementation into the quality implementation framework (QIF), which includes 14 steps (Meyers, Durlak, & Wandersman, 2012). In the QIF, Steps 5–10 echo critical preparation activities described earlier, such as obtaining buy-in to the intervention, creating implementation teams, and developing an implementation plan. These capacity-building activities are extremely important in preparing for successful implementation and may require more or less attention depending on certain characteristics of the organization and the individuals within the organization. To know where to begin with implementation preparation activities and on which efforts to focus, it is necessary to understand existing readiness characteristics of the organization that will be implementing the SEL intervention.

Although some implementation efforts ascertain organizational readiness during the implementation preparation stage, we have encountered situations in the field that necessitate having an understanding of the organization's readiness before preparation activities begin. Preparation activities, such as creating a committee of stakeholders and developing a vision for SEL, require time and initial investment from the organization and the interventionists. We describe three example scenarios that required decision makers (funders, superintendents, researchers) to understand the organization's degree of readiness, so they may decide whether to begin engaging with the organization in implementation preparation activities. First, when applying for funding of SEL intervention training, funders may require evidence that the organization has the capacity to implement the program successfully. Second, superintendents or heads of multisite organizations may be interested in an SEL intervention but only have funding to begin implementation in some sites. In this case, knowing the overall readiness of an organization to implement a new intervention would help to determine the most effective sites in which to invest the limited funding. Third, researchers studying the efficacy of a particular SEL intervention need to determine which organizations are most likely to translate training into high implementation quality effectively. In each of these cases, it is not practical to engage organizations in implementation preparation activities before they have been selected to participate, based on their readiness. By developing an assessment of organizational readiness that can be given before implementation preparation activities begin, decision makers can use this information to make informed decisions about which organizations to begin working with.

In the 14 QIF steps to quality implementation, the steps that occur prior to Steps 5–10 describe precursors to preparation activities that elucidate the organization's readiness (Meyers et al., 2012). Specifically, the authors outline assessment strategies for getting to know the organization. These assessment strategies target "initial considerations regarding the host setting" (p. 468). In other words, by assessing organizational readiness, we can determine how and whether to proceed with preparation activities, intervention training, and actual use of the SEL intervention practices. In this chapter, we focus on this process of getting to know the organization and refer to it as assessing the organization's "readiness."

Readiness Characteristics

In this section, we describe some of the key aspects of an organization, and the individuals within the organization, that comprise its readiness. We focus our attention on readiness characteristics supported empirically by previous research, and supplement these with a few key characteristics that stand out from our experiences working with organizations.

Organizations: Setting, History, and Climate

Working Relationships and Policies in the Community

An organization's readiness to implement an SEL intervention may be reflected by its formal and informal connections with other organizations in the community (Anderson-Butcher et al., 2010). Formal relationships may arise from being a member of a larger community organization (i.e., a preschool being an active member of the local chapter of the National Association for the Education of Young Children) or from engaging in regular, structured opportunities to network with other organizations (i.e., a Head Start center monthly meeting with other Head Start centers funded via the same grantee). Informal relationships are less structured but may surface when organization leaders know each other personally, or when there is overlap in the organizations' missions or clientele. As examples, a foster care agency's relationship with the local domestic violence shelter or an orphanage's relationship with the local children's hospital may facilitate added supports that indicate higher levels of readiness. In research on community coalitions supporting the use of evidence-based practices, coalitions with a history of strong relationships with other community organizations provided stronger implementation support (Brown, Feinberg, & Greenberg, 2010). Benefits of relationships with external organizations may include added social capital, financial support, and in-kind resources. If an organization shows weak relationships with other organizations, trainers should pay special attention to the intentional development of these connections to improve implementation quality.

Being in a state, county, or district that emphasizes the importance of SEL in policies and funding decisions may also indicate organizational readiness to implement an SEL intervention. There is variability in the degree to which communities and school systems focus on the importance of SEL. As evidence of this variability, preliminary findings from CASEL's analysis of state SEL standards for schools suggest that comprehensive SEL standards are much more thoroughly articulated in preschools than in the K–12 system (Kendziora, Weissberg, Ji, & Dusenbury, 2011). Specifically, for preschools, 49 states and the District of Columbia had SEL-related learning standards. For the K–12 system, however, only one state (Illinois) had developed comprehensive SEL learning standards. Schools that are fortunate enough to be in communities with well-articulated SEL standards for the state's K–12 system may have access to SEL resources, such as training, books, and materials, that may be shared across the system (for examples of domain-specific community support in the context of a language and literacy intervention, see Zukoski & Luluquisen, 2006). Moreover, organizations in communities that prioritize SEL may have more SEL-specific grant-funding opportunities from local foundations or state government agencies. To assess the extent to which SEL is prioritized by the organization's community, it may be useful to examine recent local policies directly, review overview documents such as the SEL State Scan (*http://casel.org/policy-advocacy/sel-in-your-state*), or talk with local policy experts. Although it may be difficult to change the policy context in the short term, it is important to get to know local conditions, so that training can be responsive to them. If there are policies that prioritize a domain, such as STEM (science, technology, engineering, and mathematics), over SEL, for example, trainers can be prepared to think about how to integrate the SEL intervention goals and activities with the STEM-focused goals and activities that are being supported.

History and Climate of an Organization

Every organization has a history of experiences, a unique culture, and a set of beliefs that shape the way it will respond to a new SEL intervention (Kress & Elias, 2006). One particularly salient aspect of an organization's history is whether it has recently tried to implement other new programs targeting either SEL or another domain. In general, if prior implementations were successful and the prior programs were well received by leaders and direct service providers, the organization will be more receptive to taking on another intervention. If the organization had a negative experience with an intervention, this facet of the organization's history could be a barrier to future implementation efforts that should be addressed directly if the organization begins another implementation process. For example, talking with participants about their perceptions of the barriers to implementation quality they faced in the past, and about ways to address these barriers during the current implementation process, may help to distinguish this intervention effort as different from the past.

An organization also has its own unique climate that contributes to its readiness to implement. In fact, in a recent study, implementation levels were more highly similar within organizations compared to between organizations (Baker, Kupersmidt, Voegler-Lee, Arnold, & Willoughby, 2010). This finding suggests there are unique characteristics about organizations that are meaningful for understanding readiness. In fact, in studies of organizational social climates, the more positive and less stressful/resistant the climates, the more optimal child outcomes were (Williams & Glisson, 2014). As another example, an overall climate of work-related stress and burnout has been associated with lower implementation quality and lower client engagement in the intervention, particularly when subsequent relationships with intervention trainers or coaches were not strong (Ball, 2011; Landrum, Knight, &

Flynn, 2012; Ransford, Greenberg, Domitrovich, Small, & Jacobson, 2009). It is noteworthy, however, that when trainers are aware of this readiness detractor from the start, they can tailor SEL intervention training to compensate for it. For example, they may also try to alleviate the stress in the organization by including stress management as part of their intervention training (Jennings & Greenberg, 2009; Raver et al., 2011). A related aspect of an organization's climate is the amount of social support (Hall & Hord, 2001). In previous research in elementary and middle schools, teachers with strong social support, including opportunities for open communication and interaction with other implementers, achieved higher implementation quality than their peers (Kallestad & Olweus, 2003; Leithwood & Jantzi, 1990). Building collaborative relationships with other implementing organizations may strengthen this readiness characteristic.

In addition, pervasive beliefs about the needs of the population the organization serves (e.g., students), are also an important organizational readiness factor. Previous research indicated organizations that perceived their students to have high mental health needs showed more readiness to implement a related intervention (Ball, 2011). This relation was also seen among middle school teachers who believed their school needed a bullying intervention, then implemented a program with high quality (Kallestad & Olweus, 2003). One way to help an organization to develop beliefs about the need for an SEL intervention is to collect and review data about the SEL strengths and challenges of children served by the organization (Kendziora et al., 2011). This aspect of a needs assessment is an important implementation preparatory activity for any organization but needs to be particularly emphasized if the organization's beliefs about its clientele's social–emotional competence does not initially indicate readiness.

In some cases, the organizational readiness characteristics presented are amenable to change during training. In other cases, change may be more difficult. In either case, knowledge of the organization's readiness status can provide invaluable insight that may inform next steps. Although none of these characteristics should be seen as a requirement to proceeding with implementation, an organization without strengths in many of these areas may need to consider whether or not to move forward immediately with the SEL intervention.

Leaders and Direct Service Providers within Organizations

In addition to organizational factors, individuals' characteristics are also associated with an organization's readiness for implementation and therefore impact the success of an intervention. This section describes the readiness characteristics of individuals who work in organizations, including the organization leader and direct service providers.

Leader Relationships and Commitment

Leaders within an organization often set the tone for the climate and beliefs of the organization. Particularly related to readiness, a leader's relationships with the direct-service providers and their commitment to the intervention topic (SEL) may play a role in the organization's readiness. In fact, leaders' (e.g., principals) supportive relationships with direct service providers (e.g., teachers) have been associated with intervention implementation quality in previous research (Ackerman, 2008; Leithwood & Jantzi, 1990). Supportive relationships may include providing encouragement, genuine praise, and public recognition of the direct service providers' efforts. Taking these steps to build supportive relationships may make the direct service providers feel more comfortable taking risks when trying unfamiliar intervention practices and may set the stage for providing constructive criticism when needed.

Beyond supportive relationships with direct service providers, a strong commitment to the importance of SEL may be the most essential leader characteristic for successful implementation of SEL interventions. Genuine commitment to SEL may be so powerful because it translates into supporting SEL efforts in staff selection, professional development, and the organization's overall vision. Direct service providers are able to recognize when their leaders are committed to implement an intervention for funding or political reasons, rather than based on a genuine commitment to the importance of SEL (Mancini et al., 2009; Wanless, Patton, Rimm-Kaufman, & Deutsch, 2013). Moreover, the leader needs to be committed not only to SEL in general but also to the particular SEL intervention chosen (Kam, Greenberg, & Walls, 2003). Some suggest that the first step in ensuring successful SEL implementation is getting the leader to "champion" the intervention (CASEL, 2006; Greenberg et al., 2005). In fact, some SEL interventions require buy-in from the leader before training can begin. This approach may be justified given the significant influence of leader buy-in on implementation quality (Kam et al., 2003; Wanless et al., 2013). A site leader's buy-in to a particular intervention may be difficult to assess, however, before implementation preparation activities begin. Specifically, if an external funder, superintendent, or executive director is trying to determine which sites show the highest readiness levels before introducing the site leaders to the specifics of the SEL intervention, it may be impossible to know whether the site leader is specifically bought into the new program. A leader's general commitment to SEL, however, may be a precursor to an intervention-specific buy-in, which can be assessed as a readiness characteristic.

Direct Service Providers' Social–Emotional Competence, Self-Efficacy, Mental Health, and Openness to Change

Implementing intervention practices that support SEL development often places particularly high demands on the implementer's own social–emotional competence (Jennings & Greenberg, 2009). For example, many SEL interventions ask that the implementer notice and recognize children's emotions and help children develop vocabulary for talking about the emotions they are feeling. Some direct service providers, however, may struggle with these tasks, relying on preconceived notions of how the child must be feeling in a certain situation rather that attentively observing and listening to the child in that moment. Developing this level of responsivity takes practice and demands that the implementer commit to cultivating this social–emotional competence within him- or herself. Moreover, the direct service provider's social–emotional competence, such as his or her ability to regulate negative emotions and executive functioning skills, is particularly important when discussing SEL interventions. Some universities, such as the University of Pittsburgh, University of British Columbia, and San Jose State University, are making formal efforts to incorporate social–emotional competence development into their teacher preparation programs. Individuals implementing SEL interventions need to be good role models of the social–emotional competencies they are trying to develop in children (Jennings & Greenberg, 2009). Consequently, a teacher who has trouble regulating his or her own negative affect is less likely to attend to children who are behaving positively (Raver, Blair, & Li-Grining, 2012), to take the child's perspective, and to respond positively during negative interactions (Swartz & McElwain, 2012). Advances in neuroscience research suggest that in many cases these individuals are not able to retrieve an alternative (perhaps more positive) way of interacting without intentional skills development (Arnsten & Li, 2005). When the aim of an intervention is to change these automatic responses in order to promote more positive, relationship-based strategies, individuals are forced to "rewire" the automatic response, which may be challenging (Raver et al., 2012). Prior to implementation of an SEL intervention, there should be careful attention to assessing the social–emotional competence of direct service providers and, when necessary, support to develop positive, regulated skills. In summary, although implementing many types of interventions requires commitment and skills building, SEL interventions in particular may require the development of highly personalized skills that are challenging to learn and only recently have begun to be discussed explicitly in teacher preparation programs.

High self-efficacy, mental health, and openness to change may also increase the likelihood that direct service providers will implement intervention practices successfully. Specifically, self-efficacy largely determines the intensity of effort given to a task, and it may translate to more targeted investment and delivery of the intervention, even when the intervention strategies may be difficult to use (Han & Weiss, 2005). In addition, particularly salient for the successful implementation of an SEL intervention is the personal well-being of the direct service provider. Teacher-reported anxiety and anger were related to lower involvement in a recent study of a teacher-based intervention (Hatfield et al., 2012). This readiness characteristic, however, may be malleable during training, as seen in research on SEL interventions that incorporate mental health consultants for direct service providers into their training. In one example, for direct service providers with more depressive symptoms, the intervention's provision of a mental health consultant meant that fewer sessions needed to be devoted to training to promote empathy and develop positive relationships in the classroom (Li-Grining et al., 2010). Finally, openness to change has been related to higher implementation quality and may translate into engagement in SEL intervention training (Lieber et al., 2009). Like many readiness characteristics, intentional efforts to promote self-efficacy, mental health, and openness to change may be effective and should be undertaken for direct service providers who struggle with these aspects of readiness.

Overall, we have reviewed some of the key readiness characteristics from multiple organizational levels that reflect existing empirical research and the authors' practical experiences. This list of readiness characteristics is likely incomplete, however, and we hope research will continue in this area. For example, few studies have examined the relation between children's characteristics (psychological, sociodemographic) and implementation quality. In fact, in conversations with trainers, we have heard that child characteristics do not influence implementation. Yet, at the same time, direct service providers often express their skepticism about an SEL intervention by saying, "Not with *my* students", as if they are unable to implement this program because of particular characteristics of the children they serve. This difference between trainer and teacher report may be a result of their different perspectives, or a result of nuances across child characteristics. Certainly, trainer ratings and teacher ratings of implementation-related variables have not always aligned in the past (Wanless et al., 2013). Perhaps measures of each would relate differently to future implementation. In summary, one reason for these and other gaps in our readiness knowledge may be that there are some limitations to existing organizational readiness assessments.

Assessing Organizational Readiness

Organizational readiness assessments measure the degree to which an organization is ready to begin implementing a new SEL intervention. Assessing readiness, however, is not as simple as administering a scale and tallying the item scores. Existing assessments have different strengths, and we suggest consideration of two main issues when choosing an assessment, or combination of assessments, that is right for each situation. First, in this chapter we have suggested that readiness includes organizational characteristics and individual characteristics. As such, we recommend assessing readiness across both of these levels. Second, readiness assessments vary in terms of their psychometric properties. Using multiple raters to triangulate findings may be one way to deal with this challenge. For a review of a wide range of existing readiness assessments, see a meta-analysis from the health services field by Weiner, Amick, and Lee (2008). Unfortunately, none of the existing assessments is designed specifically to address readiness for SEL interventions.

Before describing each of these issues in more detail, it is important to reiterate our working definition of "readiness." In this chapter, we describe readiness as an organization's general capacity to take on a new intervention and implement it with high quality. Some organizational readiness assessments take this approach and focus on general readiness characteristics such as those described in the previous section. Other readiness assessments, however, take the perspective of an organization that considers trying a new intervention, and focus on assessing the organization's progress in executing implementation preparation activities necessary for that specific intervention, such as building an SEL intervention steering committee. The latter assessments are a useful road map for organizations that are driving their own engagement with a new SEL intervention. We acknowledge that these may have greater specificity than general readiness assessments that can be used before an organization begins implementation preparation activities. Regardless of this limitation, we encourage dialogue about the use of general readiness assessments because they may be useful in many cases. For example, an external entity such as a funder, researcher, or umbrella organization supervisor (i.e., superintendent) may be interested in assessing which organizations are ready to be approached about implementing a new SEL intervention. In such cases, the focus is on the organization's general readiness, before any implementation preparation activities have begun. Readiness assessments at this stage require a general assessment. We suggest that the degree of specificity that is lost by using general readiness assessments is worth the loss, so that decision makers (funders, superintendents, researchers) may have a sense of which organizations to invest in, before investment in implementation preparation activities has begun. Below we describe issues with rating this type of general capacity readiness and provide examples of existing assessments that fit this purpose.

Assessing a Comprehensive Set of Readiness Characteristics

Existing measures of "organizational readiness for change" have been created for organizations, including clinics, social service agencies, schools, and hospitals. These assessments vary in their conceptualization of readiness. For example, some of these assessments focus on characteristics of organizational leaders, others focus on characteristics of direct service providers, and still others assess characteristics across multiple levels. For example, the Stage of Change Scale for Early Education and Care 2.0 is a measure that solely assesses a direct service provider's readiness for change (Montes, Peterson, & Reynolds Weber, 2011). This assessment has seven items that intend to capture the individual's intention to make a change, awareness of the need for change, interest in learning new information, self-efficacy, belief in one's ability to overcome obstacles, perceived social support, and view of self as a professional. Although the prompts mention childcare, the items are fairly general and seem easily adaptable to other types of direct service providers. The intervention coach or mentor completes this measure to inform his or her approach to the next steps in the training process. Although this measure captures some important aspects of readiness, it does not assess leader or organizational characteristics. In fact, none of the existing measures fully tap all of the readiness characteristics we described in this chapter. Therefore, combining existing measures to assess a broad range of readiness characteristics may produce the most robust and practically useful assessment of readiness.

Although we direct readers to a meta-analysis by Weiner and colleagues (2008) for a review of existing measures, we describe one of those measures here: the Texas Christian University (TCU) Organizational Readiness for Change–4 Domain (TCU ORC-D4; Lehman, Greener, Rowan-Szal, & Flynn, 2012). We choose to describe this particular measure because it has items that tap multiple levels of readiness (organization, leader, direct service provider), is focused on general readiness and not implementation preparation activities, and is accessible to users. Although the measure is not designed specifically for readiness to implement SEL interventions, efforts have been made in the past to translate items to work with various organizations and interventions. For example, the measure has been adapted to work for criminal justice organizations and social agencies.

The TCU ORC-D4 is meant to assess the organization's motivation for change, adequacy of resources, staff attributes, and organizational climate. Many of the items overlap with the readiness characteristics described in this chapter. Specifically, at the organization level, there are items about history of implementation experiences (training utilization), work-related stress and burnout, and social support (cohesion). For leaders, there are items about supportive leadership style (director leadership). For direct service providers, there are items about self-efficacy and openness to change (adaptability).

We recommend assessing some remaining characteristics for readiness to implement SEL interventions (working relationships with other organizations, local SEL policies, beliefs about child SEL needs, leader commitment to SEL, direct service providers' social–emotional competence and mental health) that are not measured by the TCU ORC-D4. Supplementing existing readiness measures to address these remaining readiness characteristics would deal with this issue. For example, organizations' relationships with other groups have been assessed in previous research with interview questions (e.g., Sharp, 2001); local policies can be determined by researching public records; and overall perception of child social–emotional needs has been assessed through direct service provider questionnaires (Ball, 2011). For leaders, CASEL's Sustainable Schoolwide Social– Emotional Learning Toolkit provides a self-reflection tool for organization leaders to assess about their commitment to SEL (see Tool 6, p. 67, in Devaney et al., 2006). Finally, scales are available to assess direct service providers' social–emotional competence (Mayer–Salovey–Caruso Emotional Intelligence Test: Mayer, Salovey, & Caruso, 2002) and mental health (Center for Epidemiologic Studies Depression Scale [CES-D]: Radloff, 1977; Positive and Negative Affect Schedule [PANAS]: Watson, Clark, & Tellegen, 1988). In summary, combining existing readiness measures with additional scales may increase the validity of readiness data.

Using Multiple Raters

Multiple raters are needed to obtain the most valid information. Many readiness assessments rely on individual report. This approach may capture aspects of implementation that are difficult to observe,but in some cases has been found to produce less valid scores than ratings by an observer (Durlak, 2010; Dusenbury, Brannigan, Falco, & Hansen, 2003). It may make sense to obtain individual reports from many perspectives (e.g., from leaders, direct service providers, community partners). Whenever possible, however, previous research suggests, getting an external rater who is familiar with the organization to rate readiness may be optimal. External raters may be previous intervention coaches, community partners, or consultants who visit the organization regularly but are engaged in other organizations as well.

In summary, although previous research supports the predictive validity of some individual readiness constructs, more formal assessments of organizational readiness rarely have strong empirical evidence of relations with implementation quality (Weiner et al., 2008). Despite this limitation, we caution funders, stakeholders, and interventionists to assess organizational readiness to gain information to help them serve organizations that are trying to implement a new SEL intervention. At this point, we encourage researchers to continue to work on measurement development in this area, and suggest that they supplement existing measures with individual scales of relevant readiness characteristics or with assessments by multiple raters to increase the validity of readiness data. In other words, we *always* recommend assessing organizational readiness, and suggest triangulating measures and assessment approaches to strengthen the quality of readiness information.

Lessons from the Field

Gaining an understanding of an organization's readiness to embark on the process of implementing an SEL intervention offers insights about whether the organization should move forward with the intervention training, and if so, how that training can be tailored to be most effective. Assessing organizational readiness, however, may raise questions:

1. How should readiness be assessed?
2. How do results indicate where an organization falls on the readiness continuum?
3. How should readiness results be shared with the organization?

We present these potential problems and pitfalls below and follow with guidelines and recommendations that may support readiness assessment in the field. Unfortunately, there are many unanswered questions about the definition of readiness, the most effective way to assess it, and how to interpret readiness scores. More research is needed, but in the meantime, we provide guidelines based on best practices. Incorporating these guidelines into future SEL intervention studies would allow further analyses linking readiness and ensuing implementation quality.

Potential Problems and Pitfalls

Assessing Readiness

Although there are readiness assessments, many existing readiness assessments are not designed for organizations serving children directly, and we have limited evidence of their psychometric properties and rely heavily of self-report. In almost all cases, for example, it is likely that readiness assessments do not address all aspects of readiness. Eventually, we need research to determine which dimensions of readiness are most relevant for predicting future implementation quality. Assessing a broad range of readiness characteristics of organizations and of the individuals within the organizations, will provide the most complete understanding of an organization's readiness to begin training on a new SEL intervention. In addition, finding an external rater to assess the organization's readiness may be challenging and add an additional cost. If there are no researchers associated with the implementation process, and no intervention trainers working with the organization yet, it may not be clear who would be a qualified external assessor. Getting leader and direct service provider perspectives of organizational readiness offers useful information but not the whole picture. It is important to be aware of these psychometric concerns; however, they should not be mistaken for roadblocks to moving forward with readiness assessment.

Another potential pitfall to measuring readiness is that no matter what measures are used, assessing readiness requires some time and money, which are often in short supply. Financial concerns arise with almost any initiative and, we hope, will be less relevant in the future as organizations, interventionists, and funders understand the negative implications of skipping a readiness assessment. Lack of time, however, may be particularly challenging. Sometimes organizations decide to begin a new SEL intervention and hire interventionists with the expectation that they will begin training right away. In some cases, the interventionist is asked to train direct service providers as soon as possible to meet a district mandate, professional development requirement, or grant deadline. Similarly, funders often expect researchers who receive grants to study use of an SEL intervention to begin training providers immediately. When those grants have time-limited schedules, researchers are also forced to decide whether to postpone training to comprehensively measure readiness, or to begin training right away so that there is more time near the end of the grant period to see intervention effects. We hope that by highlighting the importance of assessing readiness, externally imposed time lines may start to shift accordingly.

In summary, these potential measurement problems may lead to a lack of confidence in the readiness assessment process. Each of these issues, however, can be addressed over time by continued research and education on this crucial aspect of the implementation process. In the short term, creative and comprehensive measurement strategies are needed. We describe these recommendations below in further detail. For now, we emphasize that the aim of a readiness assessment is to get to know the strengths of an organization and the challenges it faces before implementation problems arise. Even imperfect attempts at measuring readiness will lead to a more thoughtful approach to training and supporting SEL intervention implementation than no attempt at all. We strongly advocate always assessing readiness despite measurement challenges. Any readiness information that is gleaned can only strengthen the trainer's knowledge of the context and stimulate conversations about how to move forward.

Deciding Where the Organization Falls on the Readiness Continuum

Once organizational readiness has been assessed, there are few examples of how to turn that assessment data into a clear articulation of how ready the organization is for SEL intervention implementation. To a certain extent, however, the ambiguity of readiness scores reflects the nature of readiness. Multiple organizational and individual characteristics comprise readiness, and expecting that a certain number of characteristics equates readiness, regardless of their composition, is not reasonable. We have described many aspects of readiness, but it is not necessary to assume that all readiness indicators must be met to begin working with an organization. For example, we have seen organizations that are working in isolation but have managed to develop relationships with other implementing organizations over time. Even though this readiness characteristic (interorganizational relationships) was not present before training, it could be cultivated. Further research is needed to determine whether certain readiness factors must be present for high implementation quality to be attainable. Moreover, are certain combinations of readiness characteristics more beneficial than others? The answers to these questions are not yet known, and as such, many readiness assessments explicitly state that cutoff scores should not be used to make readiness decisions (National Implementation Research Network, 2012). We take this opportunity to reiterate the potential problem of using organizational readiness scores for high-stakes decision making before these assessments have evidence of strong predictive validity. Without empirical evidence of a stronger link between readiness assessments and later implementation quality, readiness assessments may be best used to generate meaningful discussion that will help to determine whether to proceed with implementation, and if so, how to individualize SEL training.

Although there is research yet to be done to determine the most valid way to do this, it remains indisputable that readiness assessment data are useful. Discussion among SEL intervention stakeholders that is not driven by readiness assessment results risks bias, unintentionally weighting some readiness characteristics over others, and having a narrow conceptualization of readiness. For instance, in some cases, organizations may initiate contact with funders or interventionists and express strong and genuine interest in implementing SEL intervention. This enthusiasm, or buy-in, may appear to indicate readiness, but it may not convey the whole picture. We have seen examples of leaders who were very enthusiastic about the SEL intervention but had unrealistic expectations about the resources needed to implement it, and inflated views of their direct service providers' general skills level. These leaders' zeal overshadowed other areas of concern. Given that no readiness assessment was conducted, the complete training for the direct service providers was not provided because their needs in understanding the intervention were masked by the enthusiasm of the leaders. Without this knowledge from a readiness assessment, implementation quality was low, direct service providers became discouraged, and back pedaling in training was necessary. In summary, although leader buy-in is a critical aspect of readiness and is often evident without a readiness assessment, no single readiness characteristic should be taken as a sign that an assessment is not needed. A thorough assessment, including multiple perspectives, may not produce an exact readiness score, but it might generate a discussion that reveals this issue.

Sharing Readiness Results with the Organization

The readiness stage can be a time of relationship building among funders, organizations, direct service providers, interventionists, and, in some cases, researchers. It may feel uncomfortable during this time to suggest the need to ascertain the strengths and challenges of an organization if it is a new collaborator. Moreover, telling organization personnel that the organization does not seem ready for the proposed intervention, and needs to spend time building capacity building before considering implementation of an SEL intervention, may seem even more daunting. These concerns are warranted but can be dealt with delicately, without sacrificing frank conversations that will ultimately strengthen implementation efforts.

Guidelines and Recommendations

The following recommendations should help when confronted with the previously discussed problems and pitfalls.

Assessing Readiness

Researchers continue to refine organizational readiness measures, but in the meantime, we need a strategy for effectively assessing organizational readiness. We suggest choosing a few different assessments, so that their strengths may compensate for other assessments' weaknesses. A few examples of how this approach may be beneficial follow. First, looking for consistent patterns of readiness across more than one measure engenders more confidence in an organization's readiness scores. For example, finding two measures that suggest there is low stress in the organizational climate leads to greater assurance that this is actually the case. Second, although self-reports from leaders or direct service providers are generally easier and less expensive to obtain than external reports, supplementing self-reports with a few selected external ratings may strengthen readiness scores. If it seems difficult to find an external rater, look to some staff members who work peripherally with the organization but are also associated with other organizations (e.g., a mental health consultant who works with many schools, or a professional development trainer who works from time to time with the organization when inservice training is needed). They may know the organization well enough to provide not only valid ratings but also an outside perspective that is unbiased by organizational politics.

Third, we have outlined readiness characteristics at the organizational and individual levels. Unfortunately, most assessments only address one level or the other. Intentionally choosing assessments that target organizational and individual aspects of readiness will give the most complete picture of organizational readiness. Finally, conducting a proper readiness assessment takes time and money. Although time and money are often hard to come by, they have the potential to impact many aspects of implementation, so they need to be considered part of the cost of the entire implementation process. The readiness assessment is the first step in this process and should not be shortchanged.

By assessing multiple levels of readiness, and by taking the opportunity to obtain many perspectives, it is possible to gain a more complete understanding of readiness. A thorough approach makes sense when considering the purposes of the readiness data. On one hand, the data may be used to decide whether to move forward with an SEL intervention or spend time building capacity. Readiness scores can also provide rich data for a training or intervention coach, driving the individualization process. Overall, collecting data from the leader, direct service providers, key stakeholders, and a knowledgeable external rater may provide the rich array of information needed to triangulate the organization's actual readiness level.

Interpreting Readiness Assessment Results

To weigh the amount of time and effort it will require to address readiness characteristics that are not yet developed helps to determine whether to work on them during SEL intervention training or focus solely on building these capacities before SEL intervention training begins. Organizational readiness parallels to a child's readiness for formal schooling. *School readiness* refers to a child having a certain level of social, emotional, cognitive, and physical skills. Readiness is often assessed by teachers and staff during the preschool years to determine whether children are ready for kindergarten. However, there are some cases in which the child may not be "ready" to move to formal schooling. Parents and teachers use information from the school readiness assessment to determine how best to individualize teaching so that the child can either continue to kindergarten with added support or spend another year building skills. Instead of using one school readiness score to make a decision about a child's advancement to kindergarten, multiple strands of data from multiple perspectives are taken into account to inform next steps. This procedure is largely congruent with understanding where an organization is on the readiness continuum for implementing an SEL intervention. The main aim of assessing organizational readiness for implementation is to make an informed decision about next steps, not to produce an exact score that directly translates into a decision without further deliberation.

We propose a decision tree for using organizational readiness data to inform SEL intervention training decisions. Begin the process by determining the degree to which readiness characteristics are present. Next, focus on the readiness characteristics that are not present at sufficient levels, and ask two key questions. For each readiness characteristic that needs further attention, how much time and other resources will it take to build the organization's capacity in each of these areas? Furthermore, looking across all of the readiness characteristics that are areas of concern, do there seem to be too many that demand a lot of time and resources to address realistically in the upcoming year or two during SEL intervention training?

Although many readiness characteristics can be developed or compensated for during implementation, addressing too many areas of concern can be overwhelming. If readiness assessors and stakeholders decide that too many readiness characteristics are not in place, it may make the most sense to postpone the SEL intervention and focus exclusively on building readiness. This decision should weigh the degree to which readiness characteristics are not in place, the difficulty in developing them, and the number of readiness challenges that are competing for capacity-building resources. For example, if the organization's direct service providers have low self-efficacy around SEL practices, and low initial social–emotional competence, trainers may be able to focus intentionally on these issues during training and overcome both challenges.

If the organization needs to spend time building readiness before initiating SEL intervention training, the length of time to focus on capacity building may vary from organization to organization. After capacity building occurs, the focus turns to determining how to move forward with the SEL implementation process. Specifically, it is unlikely that any organization is strong in all readiness characteristics, and attuning the implementation process to build on readiness strengths and speak directly to less developed readiness characteristics may yield the highest implementation quality. Adaptations to the training process (approved by the intervention designers) may be made to facilitate high implementation quality. For example, the case mentioned earlier included an organization with direct service providers who had low self-efficacy and low social–emotional competence. An intervention trainer who is aware of these issues may decide to do more role playing during training, highlighting small wins to increase a sense of efficacy. Also, it may be necessary to conduct additional training on skills building before translating these skills into professional practices. In summary, being thoughtful about developing approved training adaptations for implementation preparation activities, intervention training, and ongoing implementation support may lead to the most optimal SEL intervention outcomes.

Sharing Readiness Assessment Results

It may be uncomfortable to suggest the need for a readiness assessment. However, this is best described as part of the implementation process and a necessary diagnostic step. The readiness assessment findings should be balanced with strengths and needs of the organization. If the conversation is positive and needs are dealt with delicately, the potentially uncomfortable discussion of weaknesses can build the assessor's relationship with the organization, and ultimately increase implementation quality. For example, the conversation may begin with a description of the strengths of the organization and proceed with the selection of a few key areas to address. To ensure that these potentially difficult but essential conversations take place, we recommend that interventionists require readiness assessments before working with an organization, and that funders require readiness assessments before funding an organization to implement an SEL intervention.

Conclusion

In this chapter, we have proposed that organizational readiness includes a broad array of characteristics, and that assessing readiness is an essential step before beginning an SEL program. Specifically, assessing readiness offers initial insight into the likelihood that an organization will use an SEL intervention with high implementation quality. After conducting a readiness assessment based on multiple perspectives, a trainer can clearly see the strengths and challenges of the organization and address them directly. Although further research is needed to develop organizational readiness assessments, the act of assessing, with one or a combination of available tools, will lead to higher implementation quality and more positive outcomes for the children served.

References

Ackerman, D. J. (2008). Coaching as part of a pilot quality rating scale initiative: Challenges to—and supports for—the change-making process. *Early Childhood Research and Practice, 10*(2).

Retrieved April 14, 2014, from *http://ecrp.uiuc.edu/v10n2/ackerman.html.*

Anderson-Butcher, D., Lawson, H. A., Iachini, A., Bean, G., Flaspohler, P. D., & Zullig, K. (2010). Capacity-related innovations resulting from the implementation of a community collaboration model for school improvement. *Journal of Educational and Psychological Consultation, 20*(4), 257–287.

Arnsten, A. F. T., & Li, B. M. (2005). Neurobiology of executive functions: Catecholamine influences on prefrontal cortical functions. *Biological Psychiatry, 57*(11), 1377–1384.

Baker, C. N., Kupersmidt, J. B., Voegler-Lee, M. E., Arnold, D. H., & Willoughby, M. T. (2010). Predicting teacher participation in a classroom-based, integrated preventive intervention for preschoolers. *Early Childhood Research Quarterly, 25*(3), 270–283.

Ball, A. (2011). Educator readiness to adopt expanded school mental health: Findings and implications for cross-systems approaches. *Advances in School Mental Health Promotion, 4*(2), 39–50.

Brown, L. D., Feinberg, M. E., & Greenberg, M. T. (2010). Determinants of community coalition ability to support evidence-based programs. *Prevention Science, 11*(3), 287–297.

Century, J., Rudnick, M., & Freeman, C. (2010). A framework for measuring fidelity of implementation: A foundation for shared language and accumulation of knowledge. *American Journal of Evaluation, 31*(2), 199–218.

Collaborative for Academic, Social, and Emotional Learning (CASEL). (2006). CASEL practice rubric for schoolwide SEL implementation. Retrieved April 1, 2013, from *http://casel.org/wp-content/uploads/2011/04/rubric.pdf.*

Collaborative for Academic, Social, and Emotional Learning (CASEL). (2012). What is SEL? Retrieved May 7, 2012, from *http://casel.org/why-it-matters/what-is-sel.*

Devaney, E., O'Brien, M. U., Resnik, H., Keister, S., & Weissberg, R. P. (2006). *Sustainable schoolwide social and emotional learning (SEL).* Chicago: Collaborative for Academic, Social, and Emotional Learning, University of Illinois.

Domitrovich, C. E., Bradshaw, C. P., Poduska, J. M., Hoagwood, K., Buckley, J. A., Olin, S., et al. (2008). Maximizing the implementation quality of evidence-based preventive interventions in schools: A conceptual framework. *Advances in School Mental Health Promotion, 1*(3), 6–28.

Domitrovich, C. E., Gest, S. D., Jones, D., Gill, S., & DeRousie, R. M. S. (2010). Implementation quality: Lessons learned in the context of the Head Start REDI trial. *Early Childhood Research Quarterly, 25*(3), 284–298.

Durlak, J. A. (2010). The importance of doing well in whatever you do: A commentary on the special section, "Implementation research in early childhood education." *Early Childhood Research Quarterly, 25*(3), 348–357.

Durlak, J. A., & DuPre, E. P. (2008). Implementation matters: A review of research on the influence of implementation on program outcomes and the factors affecting implementation. *American Journal of Community Psychology, 41*(3–4), 327–350.

Dusenbury, L., Brannigan, R., Falco, M., & Hansen, W. B. (2003). A review of research on fidelity of implementation: Implications for drug abuse prevention in school settings. *Health Education Research, 18*(2), 237–256.

Fixsen, D. L., Naoom, S. F., Blase, K., Friedman, R. M., & Wallace, F. (2005). *Implementation research: A synthesis of the literature.* Tampa: University of South Florida, Louis de la Parte Florida Mental Health Institute, National Implementation Research Network.

Greenberg, M. T., Domitrovich, C. E., Graczyk, P. A., & Zins, J. E. (2005). *The study of implementation in school-based preventive interventions: Theory, research, and practice* (Vol. 3). Rockville, MD: Center for Mental Health Services, Substance Abuse and Mental Health Services Administration.

Hall, G. E., & Hord, S. M. (2001). *Implementing change: Patterns, principles, and potholes.* Needham Heights, MA: Allyn & Bacon.

Han, S. S., & Weiss, B. (2005). Sustainability of teacher implementation of school-based mental health programs. *Journal of Abnormal Child Psychology, 33*(6), 665–679.

Hatfield, B., Hamre, B. K., Locasale-Crouch, J., Pianta, R., Downer, J. T., Williford, A., et al. (2012, March 9). *Teacher characteristics influence involvement in a course and a consultancy focused on effective teacher–child interactions.* Paper presented at the annual meeting of the Society for Research on Educational Effectiveness, Washington, DC.

Hemmeter, M. L., & Conroy, M. A. (2012). Supporting the social competence of young children with challenging behavior in the context fo the Teaching Pyramid Model: Research-based practices and implementation in early childhood settings. In R. C. Pianta (Ed.), *Handbook of early childhood education* (pp. 416–434). New York: Guilford Press.

Jennings, P. A., & Greenberg, M. T. (2009). The prosocial classroom: Teacher social and emotional competence in relation to student and classroom outcomes. *Review of Educational Research, 79*(1), 491–525.

Jones, S. M., & Bouffard, S. M. (2012). Social and

emotional learning in schools: From programs to strategies. *Social Policy Report* (Vol. 26). Ann Arbor, MI: Society for Research in Child Development. Retrieved April 14, 2014, from *www.srcd.org/sites/default/files/documents/spr_264_final_2.pdf.*

Kallestad, J. H., & Olweus, D. (2003). Predicting teachers' and schools' implementation of the Olweus Bullying Prevention Program: A multilevel study. *Prevention and Treatment, 6*(1), 1–29.

Kam, C.-M., Greenberg, M. T., & Walls, C. T. (2003). Examining the role of implementation quality in school-based prevention using the PATHS curriculum. *Prevention Science, 4*(1), 55–63.

Kendziora, K., Weissberg, R. P., Ji, P., & Dusenbury, L. (2011). *Strategies for social and emotional learning: Preschool and elementary grade student learning standards and assessment.* Newton, MA: National Center for Mental Health Promotion and Youth Violence Prevention, Education Development Center, Inc.

Kress, J. S., & Elias, M. J. (2006). School based social and emotional learning programs. In K. A. Renninger & I. E. Sigel (Eds.), *Handbook of child psychology* (6th ed., Vol. 4, pp. 592–618). Hoboken, NJ: Wiley.

Kretlow, A. G., & Bartholomew, C. C. (2010). Using coaching to improve the fidelity of evidence-based practices: A review of studies. *Teacher Education and Special Education, 33*(4), 279–299.

Landrum, B., Knight, D. K., & Flynn, P. M. (2012). The impact of organizational stress and burnout on client engagement. *Journal of Substance Abuse Treatment, 42*(2), 222–230.

Lehman, W. E. K., Greener, J. M., Rowan-Szal, G. A., & Flynn, P. M. (2012). Organizational readiness for change in correctional and community substance abuse programs. *Journal of Offender Rehabilitation, 51*(1–2), 96–114.

Leithwood, K., & Jantzi, D. (1990). Transformational leadership: How principals can help reform school cultures. *School Effectiveness and School Improvement, 1*(4), 249–280.

Lewin, K. (1947). Frontiers in group dynamics. *Human Relations, 1*(1), 5–41.

Lieber, J., Butera, G., Hanson, M., Palmer, S., Horn, E., Czaja, C., et al. (2009). Factors that influence the implementation of a new preschool curriculum: Implications for professional development. *Early Education and Development, 20*(3), 456–481.

Li-Grining, C., Raver, C. C., Champion, K., Sardin, L., Metzger, M., & Jones, S. M. (2010). Understanding and improving classroom emotional climate and behavior management in the "real world": The role of Head Start teachers' psychosocial stressors. *Early Education and Development, 21*, 65–94.

Mancini, A. D., Moser, L. L., Whitlet, R., McHugo, G. J., Bond, G. R., Finnerty, M. T., et al. (2009). Assertive community treatment: Facilitators and barriers to implementation in routine mental health settings. *Psychiatric Services, 60*, 189–195.

Mayer, J., Salovey, P., & Caruso, D. (2002). *The Mayer–Salovey–Caruso Emotional Intelligence Test (MSCEIT).* Toronto: Multi-Health Systems.

Meyers, D. C., Durlak, J. A., & Wandersman, A. (2012). The quality implementation framework: A synthesis of critical steps in the implementation process. *American Journal of Community Psychology, 50*, 462–480.

Montes, G., Peterson, S. M., & Reynolds Weber, M. (2011). Reliability and validity of the Stage of Change scale for Early Education and Care 2.0: Mentor/Coach form. Rochester, NY: University of Rochester, Children's Institute.

National Implementation Research Network. (2012). *Intervention Assessment Tool: A discussion tool for assessing and selecting evidence-based programs and practices.* Chapel Hill, NC: Author.

Peterson, S. M., & Baker, A. C. (2011). Readiness to change in communities, organizations, and individuals. In J. A. Sutterby (Ed.), *The early childhood educator professional development grant: Research and practice* (Vol. 15, pp. 33–60). Boston: Emerald.

Radloff, L. S. (1977). The CES-D scale: A self report depression scale for research in the general population. *Applied Psychological Measurement, 1*, 385–401.

Ransford, C. R., Greenberg, M. T., Domitrovich, C. E., Small, M., & Jacobson, L. (2009). The role of teachers' psychological experiences and perceptions of curriculum supports on the implementation of a social and emotional learning curriculum. *School Psychology Review, 38*(4), 510–532.

Raver, C. C., Blair, C., & Li-Grining, C. P. (2012). Extending models of emotion self-regulation to classroom settings: Implications for professional development. In C. Howes, B. K. Hamre, & R. C. Pianta (Eds.), *Effective early childhood professional development: Improving teacher practice and child outcomes* (pp. 113–130). Baltimore: Brookes.

Raver, C. C., Jones, S. M., Li-Grining, C., Zhai, F., Bub, K., & Pressler, E. (2011). CSRP's impact on low income preschoolers' preacademic skills: Self regulation as a mediating mechanism. *Child Development, 82*(1), 362–378.

Sharp, J. S. (2001). Locating the community field: A study of interorganizational network structure and capacity for community action. *Rural Sociology, 66*(3), 403–424.

Swartz, R. A., & McElwain, N. L. (2012). Preservice teachers' emotion-related regulation and cognition: Associations with teachers' responses to children's emotions in early childhood classrooms. *Early Education and Development, 23*, 202–226.

Wandersman, A., Duffy, J., Flaspohler, P. D., Noonan, R., Lubell, K., Stillman, L., et al. (2008). Bridging the gap between prevention research and practice: The interactive systems framework for dissemination and implementation. *American Journal of Community Psychology, 41*(3), 171–181.

Wanless, S. B., Patton, C. L., Rimm-Kaufman, S. E., & Deutsch, N. L. (2013). Setting-level influences on the implementation of the *Responsive Classroom* approach. *Prevention Science, 14*, 40–51.

Watson, D., Clark, L. A., & Tellegen, A. (1988). Development and validation of brief measures of positive and negative affect: The PANAS. *Journal of Personality and Social Psychology, 54*, 1063–1070.

Weiner, B. J., Amick, H., & Lee, S. Y. D. (2008). Review: Conceptualization and measurement of organizational readiness for change. *Medical Care Research and Review, 65*(4), 379–436.

Weisz, J. R., Sandler, I. N., Durlak, J. A., & Anton, B. S. (2005). Promoting and protecting youth mental health through evidence-based prevention and treatment. *American Psychologist, 60*(6), 628–648.

Williams, N. J., & Glisson, C. (2014). Testing a theory of organizational culture, climate and youth outcomes in child welfare systems: A United States national study. *Child Abuse and Neglect, 38*(4), 757–767.

Zins, J., Bloodworth, M. R., Weissberg, R., & Walberg, H. (2004). The scientific base linking social and emotional learning and school success. In J. Zins, R. Weissberg, M. C. Wang, & H. Walberg (Eds.), *Building academic success on social and emotional learning* (pp. 3–22). New York: Teachers College, Columbia University.

Zukoski, A. P., & Luluquisen, E. M. (2006). Building community support for early literacy. In S. E. Rosenkoetter & J. Knapp-Philo (Eds.), *Learning to read the world: Language and literacy in the first three years* (pp. 429–454). Washington, DC: Zero to Three Press.

CHAPTER 25

Indicators of Effective SEL Practice

Sam Redding and Herbert J. Walberg

Over the past 30 years, despite substantial increases in school funding, the National Assessment of Educational Progress has shown scant improvement in student learning. "Distance is dead" is the new mantra, and American workers now compete not only among themselves but also with better-educated people in other countries. This competitive disadvantage has led to increasing worries about our country's future and the need for research on how achievement and other school outcomes may best be attained. This chapter examines the intersection of research that demonstrates the contribution of social and emotional learning (SEL) to academic learning and a school improvement methodology that recognizes that outcomes are improved by careful attention to specific and interrelated professional practices.

Thanks to the work of Durlak, Weissberg, Dymnicki, Taylor, and Schellinger (2011), it can be said on the basis of considerable research that SEL is an important end in its own right, and that it contributes significantly to better student achievement and other school outcomes. Our purpose in this chapter is to describe the operationalization of SEL practices in schools through meticulous attention to specific indicators of effective SEL practice within the context of a comprehensive school improvement system. We first describe the indicator-based, Internet-facilitated school improvement system, Indistar, which is currently used in more than 6,000 schools in 21 states, before describing SEL practices and indicators that comport with the Indistar approach.

Indistar is a Internet-facilitated system (see *www.indistar.org*) that guides a school-based Leadership Team in implementing effective practices, as demonstrated by an array of indicators. Indistar was developed by the Academic Development Institute (ADI), with partial support from the U. S. Department of Education to ADI's Center on Innovation and Improvement (CII), a national content center. Sam Redding served as the center's Director and Herb Walberg as its Chief Scientific Officer from 2005 to 2012. Indistar's methodology and underlying research are derived from Walberg's edited *Handbook on Restructuring and Substantial School Improvement* (2007) and Redding's *The Mega System: Deciding, Learning, Connecting* (2006). These works, and the research base initially informing Indistar, gave little attention to SEL. In 2011, Redding and Walberg turned to their colleagues at the Collaborative for Academic, Social, and Emotional Learning (CASEL) for help in producing specific indicators for effective SEL practice.

Definitions and Scope

As used in the foundational books for Indistar (Redding, 2006; Walberg, 2007), the term "indicator" is a binary expression of the presence or absence of a specific element of an effective practice. By "binary", this means that the indicator is not measured across a range or continuum of markers but is either present or absent. An "indicator" of effective practice is a concrete, behavioral expression of a professional practice that is demonstrated by research to contribute to student learning. (The sums of multiple indicators, however, can be standardized, and used to summarize a school's strengths and weaknesses and their changes during periods of intervention.) An indicator is expressed in plain language, so that a school team can answer with certainty whether or not it is routinely practiced in the school and, if not, can plan for its full implementation. As previously mentioned, we describe in this chapter the general system of indicators of effective practice as now included in Indistar and concentrate on the SEL indicators that have more recently been developed (see Appendix 25.1).

The Internet-facilitated Indistar system guides a school Leadership Team in making an informed assessment of the current level of implementation of very specific indicators of effective practice. Emphasis is placed on universal and routinized execution of multiple indicators of effective practices. The assessment is informed by links from the indicators to *Wise Ways* briefs of the underlying research and examples of implementation. Furthermore, Internet-accessible tutorials, *Indicators in Action*, provide video demonstration of the indicators by school leaders, teacher teams, teachers, and parent leaders. The video demonstrations are explained by a narrator and in video interviews with the personnel included in the demonstrations. Facilitator guides and workbooks accompany the modules for use in professional development.

The Indistar system links the school, district, and state, so that coaches provided by the district or state can review the work of the school team and comment on it. Reports are submitted electronically to the state, replacing the paper plans previously used by the states. Because the system utilizes a continuous improvement process, the plans span annual reporting dates and remain in effect until evidence of full implementation of the indicators is provided by the team. Over time, the cycle is repeated to ensure that practices have remained in consistent application.

Theory Base for School Improvement Guided by Specific Indicators

Though Indistar can be employed to improve all sorts of schools, it was initially a response to the unprecedented No Child Left Behind (NCLB) legislation (2001) that requires schools to prepare annual improvement plans and to enable schools that do not make adequate yearly progress for 5 consecutive years to develop plans for restructuring in the fifth year. Failing again in the sixth year requires reopening the school as a public charter school; replacing all or most of the school staff, which may include the principal; contracting with an outside group that has a demonstrated record of effectiveness to operate the school; turning the operation of the school over to a state agency; or engaging in another form of restructuring that makes fundamental reforms.

In 2011, the U. S. Department of Education provided flexibility for states in implementing the NCLB legislation and at the same time strengthened its focus on the lowest-achieving schools. More recently, Indistar can and is being used in states given waivers to depart from previous NCLB requirements to take greater responsibility for school improvement. Nearly all U.S. schools, moreover, can be improved; so Indistar is useful for the whole range.

Unfortunately, when NCLB was introduced, little theory and research were available to guide substantial improvement efforts. Some research, little of it meeting high standards of rigor such as randomized field trials or control-group comparisons, was available on "turnarounds" in organizations, even in industrial firms and corporations. But restructuring (and later, turnaround intervention) was proceeding, and an effort was made, given the national crisis, to assemble the best available theory and evidence to provide guidance in the effort to improve U.S. education, particularly continually failing schools. The publication of *Turning Around Chronically Low-Performing Schools* (Herman et al., 2008) by the Institute of Education Sciences was an early attempt to establish a theory base for school turnarounds.

Because states, districts, and schools were struggling to find reliable strategies for raising the performance of low-achieving schools, ADI's CII commissioned outstanding authorities on various aspects of school improvement to write modules that could be used by educators, and these were assembled in the book mentioned previously (Walberg, 2007). In 2008, Division H of the American Educational Research Association gave this book an "outstanding publication of the year" award. Although the book focused on restructuring and substantial school improvement, for schools with histories of low performance, many of its tenets have wider application and are, in fact, used in Indistar for district and school improvement in general.

The *Handbook* formed the basis of six improvement domains, effective practices, and specific indicators. The introduction of the book made clear that the chapters drew on social science theory and educators' insights, as well as the limited research available. Sponsored by the CII, however, a subsequent book, *Improving Student Learning: Action Principles for Families, Schools, Districts, and States* (Walberg, 2011) drew on much more extensive and rigorous research on improving schools in general rather than turnaround schools alone. The book has a section on SEL theory, central ideas, and related indicators, though less extensively than in this volume.

The use of specific indicators of effective practice to guide and assess school improvement processes is derived from performance management methodology, which emphasizes evidence-based procedures that achieve results, as exemplified by Ebener, Hunter, Imm, and Wandersman (2007). Indistar, then, weds the research on substantial school improvement with the performance management methodology of specific indicators of effective practice.

The effective practices and indicators, derived from the *Handbook on Restructuring and Substantial School Improvement* (Walberg, 2007), first populating Indistar and adopted by states for their school improvement, did not include SEL practices or indicators. The SEL practices and indicators later developed with CASEL may be adopted by a state to supplement the school improvement indicators or used by a district or school for the specific purpose of improving SEL.

Indicators of Effective Practice in SEL

Given the earlier description of the Indistar system and its theory base, this section summarizes the research on SEL, which led to the SEL indicators. (A complete specification of the SEL indicators may be found in Appendix 25.1.) Though dozens of resource references may be cited, the most useful are Cefai (2008), CASEL (2003), CASEL and the University of Illinois at Chicago (UIC) Research Group (2011), Dwyer, Osher, and Warger (1998), Epstein (2009), Haggerty, Elgin, and Woolley, (2011), Larson (2005), Marzano (2003), Marzano and Pickering (2003), McPartland (1994), National Center on Safe Supportive Learning Environments (2014), Redding, Murphy, and Sheley (2011), Social Development Research Group (2011), Stiggins (2001), Walberg (2011), Zins, Weissberg, Wang, and Walberg (2004)—many of which have extensive additional references to research and practice publications. For the best single collection of SEL references and resources, see CASEL's website (*www.casel.org*).

Appendix 25.1 lists effective SEL school practices and indicators. The domain of Social and Emotional Learning at the school level is divided into four categories of effective practice—Leadership, Professional Development, Teaching and Learning, and Learning Environment—and each effective practice is further defined through multiple indicators of the practice. These categories are arranged roughly in order of priority, although a school Leadership Team is given the latitude to approach them in the order it sees fit. Including indicators for effective practice relative to SEL along with indicators for other aspects of school improvement ensures that SEL receives its due attention and also acknowledges that SEL is a driver for school improvement.

Leadership

Effective Practice

The principal and Leadership Team promote, plan, and evaluate SEL

Indicators of Effective Practice.

The six indicators for Leadership (see Appendix 25.1) provide greater specificity for the practice of the principal and Leadership Team. While providing greater specificity with concrete statements, the indicators also leave open the specific path chosen by the Leadership Team in achieving objectives derived from indicators not currently met. In this manner, the Leadership Team becomes engaged in reviewing research relative to the indicators, considering options, creating and executing its plan, analyzing data to determine effectiveness, and making adjustments in course.

For example, a Leadership Team may determine that the indicator—"The principal regularly monitors implementation of evidence-based social–emotional programs"—is not currently being met. It then describes the current situation, explaining that the school has instituted an evidence-based program but that the principal does not have in place a means for monitoring its implementation. In planning to implement the objective fully (the indicator now stated in future tense), the Leadership Team determines an appropriate monitoring protocol for the principal to utilize. Thus, the Leadership Team, for each indicator, constructs its own course of action to meet the objective. The Wise Ways research briefs and related resources may provide ideas, but the Leadership Team is responsible for choosing its best course in meeting the objective. The final test is that when the Leadership Team determines that the objective is met, it must provide evidence of how it knows the objective is met.

Students' social and emotional development, as well as their academic growth, have come to be seen as an essential school responsibility (Bencivenga & Elias, 2003). The leadership activities of the principal and the Leadership Team are critical in elevating the importance of SEL in the school and in successfully implementing evidence-based programs and practices. A study of six inner-city schools found that compared to schools with low principal support, schools with high levels of principal support were more than twice as likely to see improvements in students social and emotional competence, aggressive behavior, and behavioral regulation as when implementing a delinquency prevention program, even when implementation quality was high in both groups (Kam, Greenberg, & Walls, 2003). The principal is responsible for providing a clear focus for what the school is trying to accomplish and making sure every aspect of the culture supports the achievement of those goals.

Leaders can use a variety of data sources to determine the effectiveness of the school's efforts to promote SEL. These assessments include program evaluations, appraisals of individual (and aggregate) student social and emotional competencies, and measures of school climate. The Raikes Foundation commissioned the Social Development Research Group (2011) at the University of Washington to review and identify reliable, valid, and usable schoolwide assessments to measure the social and emotional well-being of middle school students. The group chose 10 assessments that met the review criteria. Other useful information in the report includes aligning CASEL's five social–emotional competencies with the type of rating checklists or scales. The assessment tools are listed with explanations of purpose and constructs. This is useful information because no single assessment tool will meet the needs of all schools.

The tools to assess social and emotional competencies are broad and include multiple frameworks, such as youth risk and protective factors and youth developmental assets. Some of these tools have adopted CASEL's five core competency domains as an organizing structure. The intention of the Raikes report was to provide schools with a manageable list of assessment measures appropriate for large student populations over time. As a result of choosing the most appropriate assessment tool, schools are able to plan action steps to improve students' social and emotional competencies and have a positive impact on student outcomes.

Professional Development

Effective Practice

The school provides professional development for staff on evidence-based approaches to promote SEL.

Indicators of Effective Practice

The two indicators for Professional Development (see Appendix 25.1) provide guidance for the school's planning and delivery of professional development for teachers and other staff. Professional development is critical for success in evidence-based programs because it helps to ensure high-quality implementation. Research has increasingly indicated that the success of educational programs often depends on the quality of implementation, and implementation requires both initial training of staff and continuous coaching. Attention to quality of implementation became focused in the 1970s, with the publication of a RAND report that analyzed federal programs supporting educational innovation. Berman and McLaughlin (1978) provide many references to research, and the edited book by Zins and colleagues (2004) describes many applications of SEL programs.

Quality of implementation has been discussed in terms of different dimensions: (1) adherence, which refers to following program methods and delivering the program completely as outlined in the manual; (2) adaptation, which refers to modifications to the methods or content of a program, often to meet local needs (e.g., to make the program more appropriate developmentally or culturally); (3) dosage, which refers to giving students sufficient time and exposure in the program; and (4) interactivity, which refers to how students are actively engaged in the program (Dusenbury, Brannigan, Falco, & Hansen, 2003). Each of these concepts has been examined in empirical studies, although studies to date have tended to focus on one or two dimensions of implementation and have not typically addressed all dimensions.

Studies that have assessed quality of implementation find that high-quality implementation is seldom achieved in practice. Ringwalt and his colleagues (2003) found that only about 15% of experienced teachers follow curriculum guides "very closely." Teachers they interviewed said that they frequently adapted the curriculum, especially to meet the needs of the populations they served. Ringwalt and colleagues found that adherence improved when teachers received training and professional development. These findings underscore the importance of professional development. In such studies, fidelity of implementation has been associated with improved outcomes on a number of variables, including SEL (Durlak et al., 2011). Research has demonstrated that professional development (including formal training) is key to program success. When programs provide professional development, including initial trainings and ongoing support and coaching, quality of implementation is enhanced, and student outcomes are improved (see Berman & McLaughlin, 1978, and references therein).

Teaching and Learning

Effective Practice

Teachers and teacher teams plan, implement, and assess student mastery of SEL objectives.

Indicators of Effective Practice

The 10 indicators for Teaching and Learning (see Appendix 25.1) cover the processes through which the instructional staff members establish SEL objectives, develop instructional plans including the objectives, deliver the instruction, and assess student mastery of the objectives. The indicators ensure alignment of the taught curriculum with standards (where available) and with the formative assessments used to determine student mastery of social and emotional objectives. The indicators also stress an individualized or differentiated approach that adapts the learning activities to the demonstrated readiness and needs of each student. Included in the indicators are classroom management procedures that encourage and reinforce social and emotional competencies.

Standards tend to be taken more seriously when they are connected to assessment. Together, standards and assessment, in turn, are likely to create demand and opportunities for professional development. Finally, where standards are taken seriously, they become the plan or blueprint for instruction, shaping and influencing what happens in the classroom.

When standards for SEL were introduced in Illinois, schools responded by developing plans, selecting evidence-based programs, and seeking out high-quality professional development in SEL for teachers. CASEL's work on evidence-based practices for SEL (e.g., CASEL, 2003) provided guidance for schools. Connecting formative assessments to standards is important, and after the state of Illinois developed SEL standards, Robert Marzano collaborated with CASEL to develop formative assessments that align with the benchmarks for these standards. Schools that were implementing the SEL standards participated in the writing of the formative assessment and have had an opportunity to pilot-test the assessment in their schools at different grade levels. To support schools in identifying good assessment tools, CASEL works with a group of experts to select the best tools available to monitor student progress in social and emotional development. This group reviews the formative assessment tools developed by Marzano Research Associates and CASEL, and decides how to best implement them in schools. For background research, see Berman and McLaughlin (1978) for many references to research and the edited book by Zins and colleagues (2004).

In the development of units of instruction, it is important for teachers to address the holistic needs of students, applying an objectives-based approach to SEL, as well as academic learning. Teachers must consider students' prior knowledge, learning experiences, and technical skills, as well as their questions and academic areas of interest, in order to promote academic and intellectual engagement. Teachers must also consider the stage of students' social and emotional development, and the unique impact of learning particular subjects or domains of study.

Integral to supporting students' growth in various academic subjects, teachers must also consider students' "readiness" for particular concepts and ideas based on their emotional maturity. Teachers should foster a collaborative, active learning process that engages students intellectually and promotes their analytical and logical thinking and inquiry in addition to mere acquisition of facts/information.

Student academic and intellectual growth is organically connected to the development of social and emotional competencies. This includes the students' age-related stage of social and emotional development, self-concept and self-worth, self-regulation and self-direction, peer and teacher–student relations, emotional lives and family–community challenges, racial/ethnic identities, and related personal and sociocultural factors.

The social and emotional development of students is integral to their engagement in the learning process. Teachers must understand and respect each student's unique qualities and differences, and tap into the student's emotional investment in areas of inquiry. The teaching–learning process, including instruction and classroom management, is premised upon educational experiences that are grounded in healthy classroom relationships that have meaning in students' lives, support intellectual curiosity, and provide personal fulfillment through collaborative learning experiences. This is not to diminish the importance of explicit instruction, including the direct teaching of knowledge and skill related to social and emotional competencies.

Learning Environment

Effective Practice

The entire school community supports SEL through communication, education, and association of its members.

Indicators of Effective Practice

The eight indicators for Learning Environment (see Appendix 25.1) expand the scope of SEL beyond the classroom to include the broader school community that comprises students, their families, teachers, administrators, school staff, and volunteers. This broader learning environment is sometimes referred to as the "school culture" or "school climate."

Having a school vision for a learning environment that is emotionally safe and conducive to learning is the focus that keeps the work targeted. A clear vision keeps schools from making decisions that are inconsistent with what has been identified as necessary for an optimum learning environment. Of course, a school vision and many other elements of effective school operations found in the SEL indicators are appropriate for school improvement in general. But adding the specificity of SEL to this set of indicators ensures that SEL is not neglected.

One aspect of the operationalization of the vision is establishing rules and procedures with appropriate consequences for violations, and establishing a program that teaches self-discipline and responsibility to all students. While this is critically important, other aspects of the school environment are also important to school achievement. Four of these aspects are (1) a physical environment that is welcoming and conducive to learning; (2) a social environment that promotes communication and interaction; (3) an affective environment that promotes a sense of belonging and self-esteem; and (4) an academic environment that promotes learning and self-fulfillment. These broader factors promote collaboration, positive relationships, and a sense of community that have a positive impact on student learning.

"School culture" refers to the quality and character of school life and reflects norms, goals, values, interpersonal relationships, teaching, learning, leadership practices, and organizational structures. In a positive learning environment, all members of the school community are respected, engaged, and work together to develop, live, and contribute to a shared school vision. This includes the families of students, as well as the students and the school staff. Berman and McLaughlin (1978) and Walberg (2007, 2011) provide many references to research, and the edited book by Zins and colleagues (2004) provides examples applied to school life and culture.

Culture, a natural by-product of people working in close proximity, can be a positive or negative influence on a school's effectiveness. Fostering a school culture that indirectly affects student achievement is a strong theme in the literature on principal leadership. Researchers find that the principal's direct interaction with students in or out of the classroom may be motivating, inspiring, instructive, or otherwise influential, but it is limited in scope. Most of the influence is indirect or mediated through teachers and others. The following characterize schools with constructive cultures (see Zins et al., 2004).

- Promoting cohesion among staff members
- Promoting a sense of well-being among staff members
- Developing an understanding of purpose among staff members
- Developing a shared vision of what the school could be like

To illustrate, principals exercise their responsibility for culture when they take time at faculty meetings to point out and praise examples of teachers working together and when they extend discussion with faculty members regarding the underlying purpose and mission of the school. Likewise, faculty meetings and professional development activities reiterate the SEL objectives for the school as a whole, as well as for specific grade levels, subjects, and individual students.

Collegiality is characterized by authentic, professional behaviors, including openly sharing failures and mistakes, demonstrating respect for each other, and constructively analyzing and criticizing practices and procedures. Though collegiality is sometimes interpreted as involving mere social interactions and explicit friendships among teachers, true collegiality means discussing professional issues, and giving and seeking advice about them. This is often referred to as a "culture of candor." An environment that nurtures trust and in which personnel are confident of each other's competence engenders a culture of candor.

Turning to relations among teachers and students, discipline must fit within school district policies because districts set broad goals, assign authority, and set in place controls that make school management possible. Within such a framework, a well-written, effective discipline policy should be a requirement of every school. A specific recommended strategy is to formulate a well-designed, rigorously enforced code of conduct to encourage behaviorally skilled, physically nonaggressive students. Special training may be necessary for repeated misbehavior, particularly chronic fighting. Even within the frameworks for discipline and expected behavior established by the district and school, each teacher should engage students in formulating and adhering to rules and procedures specific to that classroom. Expected behaviors are defined, taught, reinforced, and rewarded.

More positively, senses of belonging, participation, and strong identification with the school are signs of student engagement and illustrate social and emotional factors necessary for academic learning (Domitrovich et al., 2008; Durlak & DuPre, 2008; Fixsen, Naoom, Blasé, Friedman, & Wallace, 2005; Meyers, Durlak, & Wandersman, 2012; Zins et al., 2004). Student engagement requires psychological connections within the academic environment (e.g., positive adult–student and peer relationships).

McPartland (1994) suggests four broad intervention components to enhance student engagement: (1) providing opportunities for success in schoolwork; (2) creating a caring school and supportive environment; (3) communicating the relevance of education to future endeavors; and (4) helping students with personal problems within the school environment. The following factors positively influence engagement in learning:

1. *School policies and practice.* School practices and policies such as tracking, retention, suspension, and rigid rule structures negatively affect student engagement, whereas policies and practices such as smaller schools (or schools within schools), opportunities for creativity as student choice, and highlighting the relevance of curricula to personal life goals enhance levels of engagement.

2. *Schools with caring classroom environments.* Evidence indicates that schools with committed faculty, positive teacher–student relationships, and orderly, warm, caring, supportive environments are associated with greater academic success. In addition, teaching practices that foster student autonomy, student participation, and a feeling of competence are also critical (McPartland, 1994; Walberg, 2007, 2011).

3. *Relationships between students.* Students who are more socially integrated have a greater sense of belonging than those with less peer acceptance.

4. *Family support and involvement.* Students who perceive greater parental support (i.e., discussion about school, appropriate monitoring of homework) and greater academic resources in the home have greater success in school (McPartland, 1994; Redding et al., 2011).

Students who feel that the teacher cares about them and their learning are more likely to do their best. Additionally, physically well-maintained and comfortable classrooms with attractive displays of student work, in which rigorous and relevant learning takes place, is an essential condition for learning.

Because climate has an impact on student motivation and achievement, it is important to have a way to assess the classroom and school climate. Some common approaches to measuring a student's connection to school include attendance data and behavioral and perceptual surveys. When students feel connected to school, there is an increase in student engagement and a reduction in negative behaviors. Reviewing the data around discipline, behavior, perception, and attendance for specific students, and as a whole school, is one way to measure the impact of the learning environment. The Safe and Supportive Schools website includes a *School Climate Survey Compendium*, published in May 2011 (see *http://safesupportiveschools.ed.gov/index.php?id=01*).

A caring community of learners occurs when students feel valued and believe that they are contributing, influential members of the classroom. Students have psychological needs for belonging, autonomy, and competence. Students are motivated to learn when their needs are met in a caring school environment. The Raikes Foundation report, previously described, and the CASEL website list options of school climate surveys.

The assessment system should also include a way to measure perception of the climate from the viewpoint of students, staff, and parents. Teaching and learning social–emotional skills are more effective when the classroom and school climate is safe, caring, participatory, and well structured. Another way to express the importance of the learning climate is to use the phrase "caring community of learners" (Zins et al., 2004), which refers to the prevalence of positive relationships, norms, and values within a school.

Finally, SEL assessment should be integrated with other, already existing data in the schools, such as demographic data, attendance data, discipline/behavioral data, and student academic data. Understanding how to use data to promote improved student academic and behavior outcomes is an essential part of a comprehensive assessment system.

How the Process Works

Responsibilities and Procedural Steps

In assessing the current level of implementation of an indicator of effective professional practice in the district or school, the goal is not simply to check off an item but to acquire a deeper understanding of the practice and achieve a high degree of consistent application of it. To provide evidence of full implementation, the Leadership Team must ask and answer several questions:

1. What is the straightforward, literal meaning and intent of the indicator?
2. How would or do we know the extent to which the indicator is implemented?
3. What data must be analyzed to determine the level of implementation?
4. What instruments can be used or must be created to gather the data?
5. Who will make the information available?
6. How can it best be obtained?
7. What does the information say now, and what will we strive for in the future?

By placing on the Leadership Team the responsibility for determining the necessary data sources, gathering the data, and analyzing the data, the Leadership Team becomes engaged in "deep practice" not only to provide the information but also to obtain greater understanding and skill, and to drive the district or school's improvement. Although many schools are capable of candidly and effectively using this system to guide their improvement, Indistar includes coaching features (see below) that enable a state or district coach to review the team's work, offer comments, and maintain a dialogue with the team.

The planning and progress-monitoring steps in Indistar require the same amount of Leadership Team engagement as the assessment step. The plan is specific to the indicator of effective practice, now expressed as an objective. The team first determines "what it will look like" when the objective is met. The plan makes sense within the context of the district or school and includes actionable tasks, person responsible, and a time line. The tasks should be specific and practical, and follow a series of sequential steps. The implementation process should help practitioners know when each step should be completed and understand the sequence as a whole.

The plan for each objective must have a reasonable expectation of leading to full implementation, and when it does not, the plan should be revised. In monitoring progress, the Leadership Team manages the completion of tasks for each objective and, when tasks are completed for an objective, the Leadership Team assesses the level of implementation. If the Leadership Team determines that the objective has been met, then the team addresses the questions listed earlier. If the Leadership Team determines that the plan has not resulted in a fully implemented objective, then the plan is revised and more tasks added. This is not simple work but "deep practice." This is how people learn best and how districts and schools are significantly improved.

To help the Leadership Team (and the district and school community) stay on track, sort through the research, and arrive at a clear understanding of effective professional practice, Indistar provides support through the following:

1. The coaching feature that enables someone who has expertise and is external to the district or school to follow the work of the Leadership Team, in real time, and to offer guidance.
2. Wise Ways briefs that provide a context for the indicator, research syntheses, examples, and references.
3. Indicators in Action tutorials with narrative and video demonstration of the indicators by administrators, teachers, and parents.

What Is Promising

A school-based Leadership Team typically drives school improvement. Scrutiny of student learning data informs the team's decisions and plans. An annual school improvement plan is the primary road map. The plan is created and followed for a year, then the cycle starts again. These plans begin by addressing specific subgroups of students and subject areas in which the annual assessment shows weakness. The goal is to improve the scores that are low. This approach to annual planning based on recent areas of deficiency has proved to be a feeble and ineffective means for achieving significant improvement.

Continuous improvement with indicators of effective practice follows a different path, with the Leadership Team's ongoing assessment, implementation, monitoring, and reexamination of practices as described through specific indicators. In addition to scrutiny of student learning data, the team analyzes the school staff members' professional practices that contribute to the student outcomes. Rather than focusing only on improvement where the last annual test showed weakness, continuous improvement examines professional practices schoolwide and seeks to elevate performance across the board, including the most recent areas of deficiency. Instead of creating a plan once a year, then following it, the team engages in a continuous improvement process that is always assessing current practice relative to indicators of effectiveness, planning immediate steps to full implementation, and monitoring progress. Periodically, a snapshot of the work creates a report that marks progress at that point in time, but the improvement cycle continues at pace and without interruption.

Planning and Assessment

The school team members must candidly prove to themselves that all the personnel for whom an indicator applies routinely demonstrate effective application of the indicator. The evidence must satisfy the meaning of the indicator and the high standard set by the team. Each indicator must be deconstructed in literal terms, so that the evidence shows clearly that the indicator is met. This requires not reams of documentation but access to specific data relative to the indicator and a succinct statement that the data conclusively show that the indicator is met.

The school team prioritizes the indicators to gain "quick wins", while also working over a longer time horizon ultimately to implement all indicators. As each indicator is assessed to determine the current level of implementation, it is also prioritized in terms of its importance and rated according to the difficulty of its achievement. This combination of priority and opportunity produces an index score that the team can take into account in planning improvement. Thus, indicators of relatively high priority that are also relatively easily achieved are tackled first, gaining quick wins that motivate the team to dig in and work toward the more difficult indicators.

A plan is constructed by setting forth a series of tasks that would logically lead to full implementation of the indicator (now called an "objective"). For each task, someone is assigned chief responsibility for seeing that it is carried out, and a target date is established for its completion.

The first task is to ask whether the people to whom the indicator applies are aware that this practice is expected of them. If not, then communicating the expectation might be a first task. A second task might deal with how the indicator is discussed with the people to whom the indicator applies (e.g., leaders, teachers, teams), so that they have a good understanding of the expectation. Some professional development may be needed. Then tasks would include methods for gathering the data necessary to know the status of implementation and to determine whether additional coaching or training is necessary.

When all the tasks leading to full implementation of an indicator (objective) are completed, the team reassesses the indicator. If the team's data show that the indicator has been achieved, the team provides its succinct evidence. If the data indicate that the tasks have been completed but the indicator was not achieved, the team adds tasks and continues its work toward full implementation.

At midcourse, a chosen indicator can be "reassessed." This is a continuous improvement process. If an indicator has been initially assessed as "fully implemented", the team may return to it at any time and change the assessment, so that it can plan its implementation. Once an indicator has been assessed as *not implemented* or *limited implementation*, the team can only change the assessment by completing the tasks (or deleting unnecessary tasks), then providing evidence of full implementation.

The Coach

In the methodology for a school improvement process that emphasizes effective practices and their indicators relative to SEL, support and guidance by a coach is advantageous for many schools. The coach may be engaged by the school or assigned by the district or state. Coaches are trained in the methodology of Indistar and operate with procedural and reporting expectations established by the state or district. The coach interfaces with a Leadership Team in many ways—meeting onsite for consultation, meeting via conference call or webinar, talking individually with the principal and other staff, and sending e-mails. But coaching comments embedded in the Indistar system provide a means for documenting key points of advice and congratulations—always with specific reference to the indicator and the team's work. The coaching comments allow the team members to respond with their own questions and clarifications, and the dialogue between the coach and the team is maintained. This provides a rich tracking of the coach's and the team members' thinking, and it is useful in future work and when a new coach or new team members may come on the scene. Also, the coach periodically conducts a more thorough review, using the Coach's Review feature and examining a variety of reports conveniently provided for him or her.

The coach's role in an indicator-based, continuous improvement process is always to build the capacity of the school team to function within a culture of candor, with the goals of accurately determining the level of implementation of effective practices, and striving toward universal and consistent practice. Where do student learning data come into play? Specific indicators address how individual teachers, teacher instructional teams, and the Leadership Team use real-time data in making decisions, designing instruction, reteaching, and both elevating expectations for students showing early mastery and providing support for students who lag behind. Truly, each student's progress is closely assessed at many points in time, and instruction is targeted to that student's needs and degree of mastery.

The coach serves the school best when helping the Leadership Team understand the meaning of each indicator, gather information necessary for an accurate assessment of current practice relative to the indicator, plan improvement, and monitor results until the team is assured that the practice is fully implemented across the school. The coach interacts with the team in a way that might be called "metacognitive guidance", which means "thinking out loud" to model for the team how to analyze current performance relative to an indicator and how to plan concrete steps leading to its full implementation. By thinking out loud, asking critical questions, and holding the team to a high level of candor, the coach embeds in the team the abilities and procedures for continuous improvement.

Examination of current practice provides the opportunity to show where practice is already strong, as well as where improvement is needed. Thus, recognizing excellence and deficiencies, the school team builds from strength while honing professional practice in leadership, team processes, instructional planning, classroom management, instructional delivery, and school community and family engagement. The emphasis is on what the adults do that makes high student achievement possible.

The first responsibility of the coach is to see that the Leadership Team meets regularly, with full participation by all members, and candidly addresses the indicators of effective practice. Second, the coach *coaches* the team to understand the indicators, to develop tasks leading to full implementation, and to describe adequately their evidence of full implementation.

Problems and Pitfalls

Like any improvement process, the Indistar method can fail most notably if school staff do not follow the step-by-step suggested planning, assessment, action steps, and periodic reassessment described generally and briefly in the previous sections.

Because Indistar was born out of the need to reform low-performing schools, it relies on sincere staff members who respond honestly to the indicators. If they give spurious and apparently favorable answers, they may cheat themselves and the students. It would be similar to a very sick patient who tells the doctor that all is well. In the case of schools, however, spurious answers corrupt and invalidate the Indistar results and make the system useless, and the risks include continued poor performance and the need for more drastic interventions. Hence, there is good reason for school staff members to take the Indistar system seriously in the several steps described here and, in more detail, in the computerized system itself. The coach is also essential in establishing a "culture of candor" by providing specific guidance and challenging halfhearted and spurious work.

Relying on self-assessment of current professional practices by a school's Leadership Team requires faith in the ability of school personnel, even in low-achieving schools, to examine their own work candidly and conscientiously, and methodically attend to its improvement. Unfortunately, school improvement processes have long been imposed on schools by external agencies, chiefly the U. S. Department of Education and state education agencies. Although these processes have been initiated with the admirable intention of improving learning outcomes for students, they have been couched in the regulatory compliance mechanisms of bureaucracies. As a result, school leaders and teachers have too often become passive and reactive, exerting minimal effort in meeting the demands of the external agencies. The improvement process outlined in this chapter places in the hands of school personnel the opportunity to apply their own talents and experience in charting the destiny of their institution (see also the chapter on organizational readiness by Wanless, Groark, & Hatfield, Chapter 24, this volume). It also places upon them considerable responsibility for engaging in the process with candor and diligence. Their accountability is chiefly to themselves and to the students they serve. Although this is where responsibility and accountability should reside in a professional community, it requires a shift in mindset from previous approaches.

The focus on effective practices, specific indicators, and convenient access to the underlying research and examples of implementation provides boundaries and structure for the work of the Leadership Team. The support and guidance of an external coach instills a healthy check on the quality of work and offers real-time advice in the daily work of improvement. Indistar facilitates electronic submission of reports to the district and state, reducing the time school personnel spend documenting compliance, and allowing more time for implementation of effective practice.

Summary and Conclusion

In this chapter we have described methods for distilling from research the most effective SEL practices, itemizing indicators that aid in understanding the level of current practice in a school, and setting plans for improvement. Indicators are employed in many fields as intermediate and specific measures of more general concepts, and they are highly promising in education. See, for example, the performance management literature from the field of business (e.g., Frear & Paustian-Underdahl, 2011).

Initially developed through funding from the U.S. Department of Education to ADI's CII, Indistar provides detailed assessments and the most likely paths of evidence-based reforms, particularly for schools in need of improvement. Now operating in more than 6,000 schools in 21 states, Indistar allows states to include indicators of effective SEL practice, developed with initial guidance of CASEL.

The central feature of Indistar is the indicator system derived from an edited book, summarizing research and extensive and varied experience in school reform (Walberg, 2007). The newly included SEL indicators are based on an objective, quantitative synthesis ("meta-analysis") of research on SEL effects (Durlak et al., 2011) and other work given in the references and described in the text.

Some states, school districts, and schools are now adopting SEL practices and even curriculum standards for students, and CASEL provides SEL principles and resources to plan and implement the best of both. Educators can benefit from the indicator-based process as included in Indistar to assess and improve their professional practices relative to SEL and other reforms. As states adopt the SEL indicators for inclusion in their Indistar systems, ADI will obtain field experience and evaluative data to report on the effectiveness of their use.

References

Bencivenga, A., & Elias, M. J. (2003). Leading schools of excellence in academics, character, and social–emotional development. *NASSP Bulletin, 87,* 60–72.

Berman, P., & McLaughlin, M. W. (1978). *Federal programs supporting educational change: Vol. VIII. Implementing and sustaining innovation* (R-1589/8-HEW). Santa Monica, CA: RAND Corporation. Retrieved June 17, 2011, from *www.rand.org/content/dam/rand/pubs/reports/2006/R1589.8.pdf.*

Cefai, C. (2008). *Promoting resilience in the classroom: A guide to developing pupils' emotional and cognitive skills.* London: Jessica Kingsley.

Collaborative for Academic, Social, and Emotional Learning (CASEL). (2003). *Safe and sound: An educational leader's guide to evidenced-based social and emotional learning programs.* Chicago: Author.

Collaborative for Academic, Social, and Emotional Learning (CASEL) & the UIC Research Group. (2011). Compendium of social and emotional assessment. Retrieved November 20, 2013, from *www.casel.org.*

Domitrovich, C. E., Bradshaw, C. P., Poduska, J. M., Hoagwood, K., Buckley, J. A., Olin, S., et al. (2008). Maximizing the implementation quality of evidence-based preventive interventions in schools: A conceptual framework. *Advances in School Mental Health Promotion, 1*(3), 6–28.

Durlak, J. A., & DuPre, E. P. (2008). Implementation matters: A review of research on the influence of implementation on program outcomes and the factors affecting implementation. *American Journal of Community Psychology, 41,* 327–350.

Durlak, J. A., Weissberg, R. P., Dymnicki, A. B., Taylor, R. D., & Schellinger, K. B. (2011). The impact of enhancing students' social and emotional learning: A meta-analysis of school-based universal interventions. *Child Development, 82*(1), 405–432.

Dusenbury, L., Brannigan, R., Falco, M., & Hansen, W. B. (2003). A review of research on fidelity of implementation: Implications for drug abuse prevention in school settings. *Health Education Research, 18*(2), 237–256.

Dwyer, K., Osher, D., & Warger, C. (1998). *Early warning, timely response: A guide to safe schools.* Washington, DC: U.S. Department of Education.

Ebener, P. A., Hunter, S. B., Imm, P., & Wandersman, A. (2007). *Getting To Outcomes: 10 steps for achieving results-based accountability.* Santa Monica, CA: RAND Corporation. Retrieved July 15, 2013, from *www.rand.org/pubs/technical_reports/tr101z2.*

Epstein, J. L. (2009). *School, family and community partnerships: Your handbook for action.* Los Angeles: Corwin Press.

Fixsen, D. L., Naoom, S. F., Blasé, K. A., Friedman, R. M., & Wallace, F. (2005). *Implementation research: A synthesis of the literature* (FMHI Publication No. 231). Tampa: University of South Florida, Louis de la Parte Florida Mental Health Institute, The National Implementation Research Network. Retrieved November 1, 2006, from *http://nirn.fmhi.usf.edu/resources/publications/monograph/pdf/monograph_full.pdf.*

Frear, K. A., & Paustian-Underdahl, S. C. (2011). From elusive to obvious: Improving performance management through specificity. *Industrial and Organizational Psychology, 4,* 198–200.

Haggerty, K., Elgin, J., & Woolley, A. (2011). *Social–emotional learning assessment measures for middle school youth.* Seattle: Raikes Foundation, University of Washington.

Herman, R., Dawson, P., Dee, T., Greene, J., Maynard, R., & Redding, S. (2008). *Turning around chronically low-performing schools: A practice guide.* Washington, DC: National Center for Education Evaluation and Regional Assistance, Institute of Education Sciences, U.S. Department of Education. Retrieved July 15, 2013, from *www.nsba.org/board-leadership/governance/policies.*

Kam, C., Greenberg, M. T., & Walls, C. T. (2003). Examining the role of implementation quality in school-based prevention using the PATHS curriculum. *Prevention Science, 4,* 55–63.

Larson, J. (2005). *Think first: Addressing aggressive behavior in secondary schools.* New York: Guilford Press.

Marzano, R., & Pickering, D. (2003). *Classroom management that works: Research-based strategies for every teacher.* Alexandria, VA: Association for Supervision and Curriculum Development.

Marzano, R. J. (2003) *What works in schools:*

Translating research into action. Alexandria, VA: Association for Supervision and Curriculum Development.

McPartland, J. M. (1994). Dropout prevention in theory and practice. In R. J. Rossi (Ed.), *Schools and students at risk: Context and framework for positive change* (pp. 255–276). New York: Teachers College Press.

Meyers, D. C., Durlak, J. A., & Wandersman, A. (2012). The Quality Implementation Framework: A synthesis of critical steps in the implementation process. *American Journal of Community Psychology, 50*, 462–480.

National Center on Safe Supportive Learning Environments. (2014). School climate survey compendia. Retrieved July 15, 2013, from *http://safesupportivelearning.ed.gov/topic-research/school-climate-measurement/school-climate-survey-compendium*.

Redding, S. (2006). *The mega system: Deciding, learning, connecting*. Lincoln, IL: Academic Development Institute. Retrieved July 15, 2013, from *www.adi.org*.

Redding, S., Murphy, M., & Sheley, P. (Eds.). (2011). *Handbook on family and community engagement*. Lincoln, IL: Academic Development Institute. Retrieved July 15, 2013, from *www.schoolcommunitynetwork.org/downloads/FACEHandbook.pdf*.

Ringwalt, C. L., Ennett, S., Johnson, R., Rohrbach, L. A., Simons-Rudolph, A., Vincus, A., et al. (2003). Factors associated with fidelity to substance use prevention curriculum guides in the nation's middle schools. *Health Education and Behavior, 30*, 375–391.

Social Development Research Group. (2011). *Social and emotional learning assessment measures for middle school youth*. Seattle: Raikes Foundation, University of Washington.

Stiggins, R. (2001). *Student-involved classroom assessment*. New York: Merrill/Prentice Hall.

Walberg, H. J. (Ed.). (2007). *Handbook on restructuring and substantial school improvement*. Charlotte, NC: Information Age.

Walberg, H. J. (2011). *Improving student learning: Action principles for families, schools, districts, and states*. Charlotte, NC: Information Age.

Zins, J. E., Weissberg, R. P., Wang, M. C., & Walberg, H. J. (2004). *Building academic success on social and emotional learning: What does the research say?* New York: Teachers College Press.

APPENDIX 25.1. School-Level Indicators of Effective Practice in the SEL Domain

Leadership

Effective Practice

The principal and Leadership Team promote, plan, and evaluate SEL.

Indicators of Effective Practice

1. The principal and school Leadership Team convey in written materials that promoting the SEL of all students is a school priority.
2. The principal and school Leadership Team have established a multiyear plan for implementing planned, ongoing, coordinated programming for SEL.
3. The school Leadership Team regularly looks at multiple measures (e.g., behavior data; aggregated classroom observation data; and school climate surveys of staff, students, and parents) and uses these data to make decisions about student SEL.
4. The principal acts to ensure that learning outcomes include SEL objectives.
5. The principal regularly monitors implementation of evidence-based SEL programs.
6. The principal celebrates individual, team, and school successes, especially related to student academic and SEL outcomes.

Professional Development

Effective Practice

The school provides professional development for staff on evidence-based approaches to promote SEL.

Indicators of Effective Practice

1. Professional development for the school staff includes social and emotional learning objectives, skills, strategies, and conditions for learning.
2. Professional development includes onsite coaching for teachers who implement classroom-based instruction for SEL.

Teaching and Learning

Effective Practice

Teachers and teacher teams plan, implement, and assess student mastery of SEL objectives.

Indicators of Effective Practice

1. The school has established a formal assessment system to track students' social–emotional skills development over time.
2. Instructional Teams use student data that shows current level of mastery of social–emotional objectives to plan social–emotional skills instruction.
3. All teachers are guided by a document that aligns social–emotional objectives, curriculum, instruction, and assessment.
4. Instructional Teams develop units of instruction that include SEL objectives at all grade levels.
5. Instructional Teams integrate strategies and materials to enhance SEL across academic areas of instruction (e.g., language arts, social studies, physical education, arts).
6. All teachers seek student input around their interests in topics as a way to increase motivation to learn.
7. All teachers use learning activities aligned with SEL objectives to meet the individualized learning needs of all students.
8. All teachers work collaboratively with students to develop and ensure classroom rules and procedures.
9. All teachers use misbehavior as an opportunity to reteach and reinforce previous social–emotional skills instruction.
10. All teachers model, teach, and reinforce social and emotional competencies.

Learning Environment

Effective Practice

The entire school community supports SEL through communication, education, and association of its members.

Indicators of Effective Practice

1. The school has a vision or mission statement that supports a learning environment that is emotionally safe and conducive to learning.
2. The principal promotes a sense of community, cooperation, and cohesion among teachers and staff to support the work of learning.
3. Staff interactions in all meetings (staff, problem solving, committees, planning, conferences, etc.) and in the instructional setting reflect a climate of trust, respect and

collaboration that is focused on norms and adult social and emotional competencies.

4. The school's discipline policy outlines developmentally appropriate consequences, endorses positive behavior management strategies, and guides teachers in using misbehavior as an opportunity to reinforce SEL concepts and skills.
5. The school's Compact outlines the responsibilities/expectations of teachers, parents, and students.
6. All staff members cultivate positive relations among students and teachers to promote student motivation and higher levels of engagement in academics and school life.
7. The student report card shows student progress toward meeting the SEL objectives.
8. Students are encouraged to apply their social and emotional skills in co-curricular activities.

PART IV

Toward Widespread Practice and Policy

CHAPTER 26

What Everyone Should Know About Implementation

Joseph A. Durlak

Authors of almost every chapter in this volume discuss implementation in one way or another, suggesting the need to devote special attention to this important topic. *Implementation* can be defined as "efforts designed to get evidence-based programs or practices of known dimensions into use via effective change strategies" (Damschroder & Hagedorn, 2011, p. 195). This definition seems straightforward. An evidence-based program has been shown to be effective elsewhere through careful evaluation; others find out about the program and want to use it in their setting, so they can obtain similarly positive results. Unfortunately, experience suggests that this translation from research to practice does not always go well because many programs are not implemented well enough in new settings to achieve their major goals. There can be many explanations for this. Sometimes, staff members are not sufficiently trained to execute the new program correctly; other times, they decide on their own to change the program substantially in structure or application from its original version; and at still other times, the new program may be unexpectedly shortened or even stopped entirely due to various administrative or practical issues. In other words, in many cases, the new program does not bear a close enough resemblance to the original version, so it is not surprising that poorer results are obtained.

These possible scenarios highlight an important aspect of Damschroder and Hagedorn's (2011) definition: Implementation occurs through the use of "effective change strategies." Effective implementation does not occur naturally or spontaneously but requires the use of systematic methods specifically designed to increase the odds of program success. To apply these methods, we need to understand what are the important elements or aspects of implementation, what steps should be taken to promote effective implementation, and what factors influence the implementation process for good or ill. These are the main issues I discuss in this chapter.

A Brief History of Implementation Research and Practice

Work on implementation can be traced back nearly 100 years due to its early focus on helping farmers learn and apply scientifically based agricultural practices (Rogers, 2003). However, implementation did not receive much attention in the social sciences until the late 1970s and early 1980s, when its importance was noted in the application of educational and psychosocial interventions for youth. There has been an exponential increase in implementation theory, research, and practice within the past 10–15 years, and the field has now developed into a full-fledged scientific undertaking due to the contributions from multiple disciplines.

Implementation is important for all types of organizations, programs, and populations. It is worthy of attention whether one is working with schools, mental health clinics, public health or health care organizations, businesses, governments, or social service agencies that are serving children, families, or adults. Moreover, implementation is important for both prevention and treatment. In summary, implementation is now receiving its due as an important area of theory, research, and practice that affects all types of interventions. The multidisciplinary research on implementation that has been conducted to date informs relevant research and practice on social and emotional learning (SEL) programs, which are the focus of this chapter.

In this chapter I present and briefly discuss 11 important findings about implementation, followed by brief discussion of several critical issues that need to be explored further and clarified in future research and practice. It is my hope that this method of presentation not only provides a user-friendly perspective on current research and practice on implementation relevant to SEL programming of all kinds but also offers suggestions for how to move the field forward. Several additional resources offer excellent review or commentary on various issues related to implementation (e.g., Bopp, Saunders, & Lattimore, 2013; Damschroder, Aron, Keith, Kirsh, Alexander, & Lowery, 2009; Domitrovich et al., 2008; Dusenbury, Brannigan, Hansen, Walsh, & Falco, 2005; Glasgow, Green, Taylor, & Stange, 2012; Humphrey, 2013; Johnson, Hays, Center, & Daley, 2004; Moore, Bumbarger, & Cooper, 2013; O'Donnell, 2008; Stirman et al., 2012).

Major Findings in Implementation Science

Quality Implementation Is the Sine Qua Non of Effective Programs

This is perhaps the most important of the established facts about implementation. There is now clear evidence that high-quality implementation (see below) is strongly associated with positive program outcomes (Durlak & DuPre, 2008). The converse is also true; low-quality implementation is usually associated with programs that have minimal or sometimes no positive effects. Moreover, quality implementation has strong practical consequences for schoolchildren as suggested by one review of over 200 SEL programs (Durlak, Weissberg, Dymnicki, Taylor, & Schellinger, 2011). When students involved in well-implemented SEL programs were compared to those in poorly implemented SEL programs, the former group demonstrated academic gains that were *twice* as high as those in the latter group. Furthermore, the levels of emotional distress and conduct problems noted in the former students were only half as large as those displayed by students in the latter group. School personnel need to understand they must invest in quality implementation in order to achieve better results. In summary, we should not think of programs by themselves as being effective; it is the *well-implemented* programs that are effective.

Monitoring Implementation Is an Essential Component of All Program Evaluations

Program outcomes cannot be interpreted appropriately without information regarding the level of implementation that was achieved. It is especially important in the face of negative results because a program that would otherwise be successful can produce poor results when it is poorly implemented. Even with positive program outcomes, measuring levels of implementation is important because these data provide information about what is needed to achieve a program effect and how the impact might be improved with even better implementation. Thus, monitoring implementation is vital for assessing a program's true value and can offer valuable guidance in terms of continual program improvement.

It Is Extremely Costly to Ignore Implementation

Another way to view the value of implementation is to consider the decision-making process commonly faced by virtually every school. Schools have limited resources and school personnel must make careful decisions about what programs to offer. Should they offer a new program or not, and, given alternatives among new programs, which one should they choose? These decisions should always be based not only on a program's potential impact but also in reference to the likelihood of achieving quality implementation. Schools experience serious short- and long-term costs if they do not conduct well-implemented programs.

The money, resources, and staff time spent on poorly implemented programs will be wasted because such programs are not likely to be successful. Furthermore, following poor results, school staff members are also likely to form erroneous beliefs, such as "SEL programs do not work", which limit their willingness to undertake related programs in the future.

Therefore, school personnel should not conduct an evidence-based SEL program unless they are committed to achieving quality implementation. Although quality implementation does not guarantee program success, without it, success is highly unlikely. In summary, a proper focus on implementation advances research, practice, and educational policy because it can lead to better decision making and better services for schoolchildren.

Implementation Is a Multidimensional Concept

Implementation of evidence-based programs or practices can be done a number of different ways. At least eight different components of implementation have been identified: fidelity, dosage, quality of program delivery, participant responsiveness, program differentiation, monitoring of control or comparison conditions, program reach, and adaptation (for definitions, see Durlak & DuPre, 2008). Each of these components combines to affect quality implementation. Although fidelity and dosage have been the most studied aspects, others also merit attention. For example, quality of program delivery refers not only to how well an initial lesson is presented but also to methods that promote the generalization and application of newly learned skills (Domitrovich, Gest, Jones, Gill, & DeRousie, 2010). "Participant responsiveness" (sometimes called "engagement") refers to how well a program stimulates the interest and holds the attention of participants. A program may look ideal on the drawing board, but if it does not effectively engage its audience, its impact will be diminished or nonexistent. Because of this, when a new SEL program is being considered, it is a good idea to solicit input from those who will be involved (i.e., teachers and students) to gain a good sense of how well the materials, activities, and goals of the program will effectively motivate and engage the target audience. This can be particularly important when the program is being offered to ethnically or culturally diverse students.

Implementation Exists along a Continuum

Implementation is not an all-or-nothing construct; rather, it exists in degrees along a continuum. For example, with respect to dosage, the continuum can range from 0% implementation (a new program is never begun) to 100% (indicating the entire program has been administered). Another way to view this continuum is in terms of *quality*, which can generally be defined as conducting the intervention along its multiple dimensions (dosage, quality, fidelity, etc.) at a level that provides the best chances that the program will be effective (i.e., that maximizes the benefits that can be attained by its participants). In other words, one can think of low, medium, and high levels of quality implementation. As noted earlier, levels of implementation can vary because teachers may decide to omit or change some parts of the intended program (i. e., make adaptations) when they are deliver it to their students.

Adaptations Are Common and May Improve Program Outcomes

Most new programs that are conducted in schools represent a blend of fidelity and adaptation. *Fidelity* refers to delivering the active ingredients of an intervention, that is, those elements that are crucial to producing intended effects. These active ingredients are what "power" the intervention and make it work. When new programs are tried, these ingredients (also sometimes called "core components") are what should be replicated. *Adaptations* refer to changes made in the original program. Adaptations are commonly made in schools because practitioners perceive that the change is necessary for the program to fit in relation to the school's capacity, resources, and operational features, or to meet the cultural values and life experiences of its staff and student body. Program features that are commonly modified include the exact timing and duration of program lessons; some of the specific activities, examples, language, or exercises in the lessons; and the pacing of the program, depending on student needs. *As long as the active ingredients of a program are retained*, it is acceptable to make adaptations such as these to suit the ecology of the school. In other words, any adaptation made to a program should be intentional. Program changes should not be undertaken merely because of personal preferences, and they should never undermine or interfere with the program's theoretical or empirically determined active ingredients (Moore et al., 2013).

In fact, some modifications may be necessary in order to gain the sufficient commitment and engagement of school staff to try the program in the first place because some aspects of the intended program may not fit with the school's culture and customary practices. Adaptations are not necessarily an alarming development because research suggests that well-planned adaptations can *improve* program impact (Durlak & DuPre, 2008). In addition, research clearly indicates that school staff members routinely adapt new programs in some fashion or another, with or without the guidance of program developers and researchers (Ringwalt et al., 2003). Finally, other research has clearly indicated for quite some time that flexible interventions (i.e., those that can adapted in some ways) are more likely to be widely disseminated and used by others (Rogers, 2003). In summary, to ensure the appropriate blend of fidelity and adaptation in new programs, it is important that those bringing the program into schools (funders, researchers, or original program developers) collaborate with staff in the host setting to determine an acceptable way to decide on the proper blend of fidelity and adaptation.

Effective Professional Development Services Are Essential for Quality Implementation

Just as quality implementation is the sine qua non of effective programs, good professional development services are the sine qua non of achieving quality implementation. Professional development services that comprise preprogram training plus ongoing technical assistance appear to be a requisite for implementing an evidence-based program or practice well. Fortunately, there are several available options for these kinds of services, although more are needed for truly widescale dissemination throughout our nation's schools (see *www.casel.org* and Durlak, 2013, for a partial listing of resources). School staff members cannot learn how to deliver a program effectively if they only participate in an informational workshop or simply read a training manual. They need the expertise of others who are familiar with the approach. Consultation with others helps school staff members learn things such as the core theory behind the intervention and its active ingredients, how to deliver the intervention appropriately in different situations, when repeating parts of the program is warranted, and what modifications are acceptable and perhaps necessary in fitting the intervention to a particular setting. The use of personal coaches (i.e., trained and experienced consultants) to help teachers and other school staff achieve quality implementation has been a growing feature of several successful professsional development efforts (Becker, Darney, Domitrovich, Keperling & Ialongo, 2013).

Multiple Factors Affect Implementation

Table 26.1 lists examples of 23 factors that research reviews have identified as influencing implementation (Domitrovich et al., 2008; Durlak & DuPre, 2008; Fixsen, Naoom, Blasé, Friedman, & Wallace, 2005; Greenhalgh et al., 2005). These factors are present at multiple ecological levels. For example, some occur at the societal or communitywide level (e.g., educational policies, political pressures, funding); others are characteristics of either the intervention (e.g., its complexity or flexibility) or the frontline providers who are to deliver the program

TABLE 26.1. Examples of Factors That Influence Quality of Implementation

1. Community-level factors
   a. Theory and research in the relevant area
   b. Political/administrator pressures
   c. Funding
   d. Educational policy and curriculum mandates

2. Characteristics of staff delivering the program
   a. Perceived need for the program
   b. Perceived program benefits
   c. Sense of self-efficacy or self-confidence
   d. Mastery of new skills

3. Features of the program to be offered
   a. Compatibility or fit with the host setting
   b. Flexibility or adaptability of the program

4. Features of the host school and its operating systems
   a. Positive work climate
   b. Organizational norms related to openness to change
   c. How well the program fits with usual school practices
   d. Shared vision regarding buy-in and commitment to the new program
   e. Shared decision making and supporting collaboration among stakeholders
   f. Working partnerships with other agencies
   g. Effective communication practices
   h. Effective formulation of workgroups and tasks
   i. Strong leadership
   j. A program champion advocating for the program
   k. Administrator support

5. Features of Professional Development services
   a. Quality of preprogram training
   b. Quality of ongoing technical assistance

Note. Based on Durlak and DuPre (2008).

(e.g., their openness to change and general attitudes about the program, their sense of self-efficacy, and their ability to master or blend new skills into their everyday duties and responsibilities). These factors can also be organizational elements, that is, parts of the systems or structures that are either created within the school that is hosting and delivering the program (e.g., leadership, climate, morale, or organizational capacity) or that are established to provide professional development services to members of the host organization (e.g., characteristics of training and ongoing technical assistance). The importance of professional development services has already been covered, and space does not permit discussion of all the other relevant factors. Some factors are mentioned in the next section when I describe the various steps of the implementation process.

Each ecological factor exists in degrees (rather than simply being present or absent) and can be viewed as either hindering *or* promoting quality implementation, depending on its features and amenability to change. For example, policies that support and encourage schools to choose evidenced-based programs are likely to lead to eventual improvements in school curricula. However, if those same educational policies do not support schools' attempts to secure sufficient professional development to achieve quality implementation, then positive changes in school services will be very slow to arrive, and they may not occur at all.

There Are at Least 14 Related Steps to Achieving Quality Implementation

Because implementation is so important to effective programs, it is imperative to understand what specific steps should be taken to achieve quality implementation. A research review that synthesized the available literature on what it takes to achieve quality implementation found that (1) there is considerable agreement among different authors from multiple disciplines and research areas about the existence of at least 14 critical steps, and (2) these steps may be divided into four sequential, or temporal, phases (Meyers, Durlak, & Wandersman, 2012). This synthesis of the important steps in implementation was called the quality implementation framework (QIF) and described the tasks that should be undertaken at each step. A major implication of this framework is that quality implementation involves a coordinated series of related plans and actions. In fact, one startling finding was that 10 of the 14 identified steps should be completed *before* implementation begins. Convergent validity for the QIF comes from the fact that its 14 steps target the ecological factors that affect implementation as determined by other independent research studies, as noted earlier.

In brief, the steps in the four stages of quality implementation can be illustrated by listing some of the questions that should be answered at each step. The first stage of implementation comprises eight steps and is largely guided by the results of different assessments designed to examine how well the planned intervention fits the school setting, and the school's readiness to host the intervention. For example, how well does the program respond to the needs of the staff and student body, and to its own mission and values? Are the staff members' expectations for what the program can accomplish realistic? To what extent does the school have sufficient capacity to deliver the program successfully (see Wanless et al., Chapter 24, this volume) Should the program be modified in any way, and if so, how should this be done without changing the program's active ingredients? Are the staff and school administrators genuinely supportive of the intervention? Will there be effective leadership at the school for this program? Can the school arrange for effective preprogram training?

The second stage comprises two steps related to creating the appropriate structure for implementation. Two important questions at this stage are (1) "Who will be members of the team whose responsibility is to monitor implementation?" and (2) "Can a realistic plan for implementation be created that specifies the duties and responsibilities of these team members?"

It is only after the first two stages and their corresponding steps are satisfactorily completed that the third stage of actual implementation begins. This stage involves providing ongoing technical assistance to frontline providers and developing mechanisms to collect information on implementation and offer supportive feedback on how well implementation is proceeding. These steps are important, so that the level of implementation can be quickly improved if necessary, and unanticipated obstacles or problems can be resolved. Therefore, some important questions to answer involve determining how implementation will be monitored, and how helpful feedback can be delivered periodically to various stakeholders about the progress of implementation.

The last stage in quality implementation comprises a single but important step related to improving future program applications. This step involves critical reflection and analysis of the program and its implementation. The central question is "What have we learned about conducting this program in this setting?" Supplemental and related issues involve consideration of factors that have affected program implementation both positively and negatively, and how the delivery of the program and its outcomes can be improved. Useful information on these matters requires open communication channels among all participants (e.g., those providing professional development services, school administrators, frontline providers, and, depending on the circumstances, funders, students, and their parents).

Some Qualifications

Experience suggests that the number and sequence of some of the 14 steps can be modified in certain situations. For example, some steps may have to be revisited (e.g., because of turnover among school administrators or leadership, or if commitment to the program diminishes), and others can be skipped in the presence of positive information (e.g., the school has obvious capacity and commitment, and has already carefully assessed its needs). Nevertheless the QIF offers useful guidance for future research and practice by describing the coordinated set of actions associated with achieving quality implementation and the planning that needs to occur to attain this end. Most notably, program implementation should not begin before several preliminary but necessary steps have been taken to increase the odds that implementation will be effective.

Quality Implementation Requires Collaboration among Multiple Stakeholders

Achieving quality implementation is the mutual responsibility of many groups, and each has a critical role to play. Some of these groups include state and federal agencies that mandate school practices and curricula; funders who finance new initiatives; and researchers, theorists, and program developers who are keen to produce the most effective and efficient programs. Others with important roles to play include school officials and administrators who must give school staff sufficient time and support to learn and practice new techniques through thoughtful professional development, and, of course, the frontline school staff members who must commit the necessary time and energy to delivering the program effectively. This latter group, in particular, can provide vital input into what is practical in each situation, such as what aspects of professional development are most helpful or unhelpful for them, and what modifications could be made in the program to improve its expected results. In summary, policy, theory, research, administration, and practice must come together to work synergistically in order to maximize program implementation.

The Same Factors That Influence Quality of Implementation Also Influence Sustainability

Sadly, sometimes even effective programs are discontinued after their trial period, and it is only recently that more attention has been given to sustaining SEL programs that work. The same factors mentioned previously in relation to quality implementation also affect whether a program will continue in a setting after its initial trial period is over. For example, if factors related to quality implementation are not favorable in the first place, such that the program is not a good fit for the school, sufficient buy-in and commitment is not obtained, or effective leadership is missing, then the implementation and impact of the program will be greatly diminished, and the motivation and required effort to continue the program are much less likely. Even if these factors remain positive (i.e., the staff members want to continue the program) subsequent events could interfere with program continuance. Several factors that deserve particular attention in order to increase the chances of sustaining programs include staff turnover, leadership, program costs, and new administrative mandates.

Staff turnover of both administrators and teachers can be high, depending on the situation, so as new staff members enter the school system, there is a need to orient them to the program and obtain their support. New teachers need to be trained to deliver the program, and this usually entails further financial costs for professional development. If turnover has affected those who provided strong program leadership (administrators and teachers), then the new personnel will have to be brought on board to support the program and provide the necessary leadership. Finally, schools may be pressured to respond to new mandates for curriculum changes that might interfere with the prior operations of the SEL program.

Therefore, it is important to anticipate potential problems and plan for program sustainability *at the outset*. In other words, taking the necessary steps toward quality implementation should include a discussion about what happens after the new program ends, and this discussion should be part of the *initial* collaboration with school staff. Whenever possible, initial discussions with involved stakeholders should involve obtaining their commitment to an empirical approach in educational programming by considering the results of both program implementation and program outcomes. These commitments should include finding ways to support a successful program using local budgets rather than depending on outside sources of financial support. Fortunately, sustaining the program often involves lower financial outlays than the initial program implementation because fewer new staff members need training and professional development, and the curriculum materials have already been purchased and are on hand. Planning for sustainability illustrates another instance of the importance of effective leadership. If the school or district leaders perceive new programs to be of value, they are much more likely to find the money to sustain them.

In summary, if stakeholders have committed to trying an evidence-based program, planning carefully to achieve quality implementation, evaluating the level of implementation obtained along with program outcomes, and then using the collected information to make further decisions, in effect, they have adopted a problem-solving approach using the scientific method. When considering the possible results of both the implementation process and program outcomes, there are usually four major options to consider: (1) continue the program as is because implementation was good and the program has achieved its primary objectives; (2) continue the program and try to improve it because although implementation was good, the program was only partially effective in achieving its goals; (3) continue the program but improve implementation as needed to provide an adequate test of the program's impact; and (4) discontinue the program because although implementation was good, the program was not at all effective, and search for another evidence-based program that suits the school's needs. Schools' adoption of this systematic approach would represent a radical departure and a decided improvement on current educational practices, which are rarely data-driven. The ultimate result is that more evidence-based programming would occur in schools, and ineffective programs would be replaced and eliminated.

In his survey of SEL programs that have been continued, stalled, or discontinued over time, Elias (2010) noted the importance of several factors associated with sustainability that have already been discussed (e.g., good initial training, ongoing technical assistance, and the importance of administrative leadership). He also emphasized two additional factors: (1) Teachers who emerge as positive role models for others can sustain the school's commitment and motivation, and (2) programs that are integrated and become part of the entire school and its daily practices, as opposed to being operational in only some classrooms, are more likely to continue.

Although our understanding of the issues related to quality implementation has increased substantially in the past few years, there are still several questions and issues for future exploration. Some of the major ones are discussed next.

What More Do We Need To Learn about Program Implementation?

Each of the following issues is an empirical question that seems best answered through carefully conducted research studies that combine the efforts of theorists, funders, administrators, researchers, and practitioners. Interventions must be studied under the real-world conditions that exist in various schools, and it should be remembered that school staff members are in the best place to offer essential feedback about what is practical and doable under different circumstances.

1. What are the thresholds for achieving quality implementation for different SEL programs? Implementation does not have to be perfect, but we do not know how imperfect it can be before SEL programs will not produce their intended goals. Research on the Life Skills Program indicated that a 60% level of implementation is associated with positive outcomes (Botvin, 2000), but the best implementation threshold is likely to differ across programs because of their varied target groups, contents, and objectives. A higher threshold might be required depending on the educational level of the students, their prior experiences, or current skills levels, for programs promoting different SEL skills, or for those interventions placing a higher priority on academic, personal, or social outcomes.

2. How can we design the most effective and efficient mechanisms to provide effective professional development services? Is it possible to individualize these services to take into account staff turnover and the individual needs of current staff with different learning styles and needs? How can technology be best used in delivering either or both initial training and ongoing technical assistance once the program is begun (e.g., through the Internet, using virtual reality classrooms, or mobile apps)?

3. How do the different aspects of implementation influence each other and program outcomes? For example, how do dimensions such as quality of delivery, fidelity, adaptation, and dosage interact? Would enhancing the quality of delivery of program components reduce the necessity of providing all program sessions (i.e., make it possible to reduce program dosage), or would enhanced delivery (or fidelity, or adaptation) increase program effects with more sessions?

4. How can we assess how the presence *and* levels of different ecological factors affect the process and final quality of implementation, and how do these different factors interact to influence implementation? For example, what are the best ways to assess a school's and its students' needs? What can

we do to obtain sufficient buy-in under unfavorable conditions (i.e., when political, fiscal, or administrative pressures create strong barriers toward moving forward)? Can the presence of an internal champion override an initial lack of full buy-in or commitment by constantly encouraging and motivating staff members? How can teachers overcome the lack of sufficient support from their key administrators? In determining program fit, *how much* fit, in terms of such factors as perceived need, staff buy-in, and the like, is necessary and sufficient to achieve quality implementation?

For example, in a study of Providing Alternative Thinking Strategies (PATHS), Kam, Greenberg, and Walls (2003) found that principal support was a crucial factor that interacted with the quality of program implementation to affect student outcomes. Only in those PATHS schools in which principal support was high did students demonstrate significant changes in their social competence and classroom behavior. Chaudoir, Dugan, and Barr's (2013) review of over 100 measures that have been used to assess the various ecological factors believed to affect implementation provides a perspective on how others have sought to measure different influences on implementation.

5. What are the active ingredients of evidence-based programs? There have been very few attempts to confirm empirically the influence of the presumed active ingredients of interventions. As a result, promotion of programs often is based on their *presumed* mechanisms of change by relying on either theory or logic models. It is essential that we discover the true active ingredients of different interventions in order to improve program implementation, efficiency, and effectiveness. Doing so would have strong future implications. Knowing an intervention's active ingredients would (a) influence how and in what ways programs could be adapted for different circumstances; (b) improve professional development services because it would pinpoint what skills school staff must have to conduct the program with quality; and (c) improve program efficiency and therefore make more programs attractive to others (e.g., some programs would be simpler to learn and briefer to conduct, which would reduce program costs by eliminating some program materials, some parts of professional development, and the time and effort expended by school staff in delivering the program).

6. How can we better articulate the various decisions and specific actions that should be taken to accomplish each step associated with quality implementation? Although the QIF described earlier provides an outline of the behavioral steps involved in reaching quality implementation, we need more specific information about how best to act to accomplish each step efficiently and most appropriately. Some research groups have developed practical approaches for various organizations whose application are likely to be very helpful in this regard (see, in this volume, Fagan, Hawkins, & Shapiro, Chapter 31, and Wright, Lamont, Wandersman, Osher, & Gordon, Chapter 33). What are the most efficient and valid ways to assess the various aspects of implementation? For example, levels of implementation tend to vary over time, so a single assessment is unlikely to provide a complete picture of attained implementation. However, it is unclear how often and in what ways implementation should be assessed. Dusenbury and colleagues (2005) provide a useful discussion of evaluating multiple components of the implementation of school-based programs using different assessment methods. Scientific progress requires accurate measurement of relevant constructs, so it is important to develop assessment tools and procedures that can evaluate the process and final results of implementation efforts. Moreover, it would be ideal if assessment tools were easy to use in everyday school practice.

The preceding issues are unlikely to lead to a single resolution but must be qualified by many circumstances, including the program's goals, contents, characteristics of a school and its student body, as well as the prevailing political and social environment. In general, the field will advance when the previously discussed issues are explored carefully in order to answer the following overarching question: How can various stakeholders work collaboratively to achieve quality implementation that is associated with what particular outcomes for which students?

Concluding Comments

At first glance, the challenges involved in achieving quality implementation may seem daunting. For example, the eight aspects of implementation, the 23 ecological factors affecting implementation, and the 14 steps involved in achieving quality implementation would seem to lead to an overwhelming number of possible permutations to consider and study. Furthermore, there is the need for multiple stakeholders, who typically do not collaborate well with each other, to learn how to work together to achieve the same end. In general, it seems that there is too much we do not know and too many obstacles to overcome.

Nevertheless, many schools have successfully implemented SEL programs. There has been tremendous progress within the science of implementation in the past few years, and there are several positive signs that this progress will continue. There are now journals exclusively devoted to implementation (i.e., *Implementation Science, www.implementationscience.com*) and several other outlets, such as those published by the American Psychological Association, that require data on implementation to be provided for publication. Policy, research, and practice are also beginning to be combined to support implementation. For example, governmental agencies in both the United State and the United Kingdom are now supporting special initiatives focused on implementation (Meyers et al., 2012), and an implementation training institute has been established in the United States (Proctor et al., 2013).

Things that are unknown or complicated do not deter progress in a scientific field; they actually serve as a catalyst for leaders' curiosity and creativity, and motivate others who are willing to take on challenges if something is important. Implementation is very important, and dedicated stakeholders can and will advance our understanding of what it takes to deliver SEL programs in ways that will bring maximum benefits to students.

References

Becker, K. D., Darney, D., Domitrovich, C. E., Keperling, J. P., & Ialongo, N. S. (2013). Supporting universal prevention programs: A two-phased coaching model. *Child Clinical and Family Psychology Review, 16*, 213–228.

Bopp, M., Saunders, R. P., & Lattimore. D. (2013). The tug-of-war: Fidelity versus adaptation throughout the Health Promotion Program life cycle. *Journal of Primary Prevention, 34*, 193–207.

Botvin, G. J. (2000). Preventing drug abuse in schools: Social and competence enhancement approaches targeting individual-level etiologic factors. *Addictive Behaviors, 25*, 887–897.

Chaudoir, S. R., Dugan, A. G., & Barr, C. H. (2013). Measuring factors affecting implementation of health innovations: A systematic review of structural, organizational, provider, patient, and innovation level measures. *Implementation Science, 8*, 22.

Damschroder, L. J., Aron, D. C., Keith, R. E., Kirsh, S. R., Alexander, J. A., & Lowery, J. C. (2009). Fostering implementation of health services research findings into practice: A consolidated framework for advancing implementation science. *Implementation Science, 4*, 50.

Damschroder, L. J., & Hagedorn, H. J. (2011). A guiding framework and approach for implementation research in substance use disorders treatment. *Psychology of Addictive Behaviors, 25*, 194–205.

Domitrovich, C. E., Bradshaw, C. P., Poduska, J. M., Hoagwood, K., Buckley, J. A. Olin, S., et al. (2008). Maximizing the implementation quality of evidence-based preventive interventions in schools: A conceptual framework. *Advances in School Based Mental Health Promotion, 1*, 6–28.

Domitrovich, C. E., Gest, S. D., Jones, D., Gill, S., & DeRousie, R. S. (2010). Implementation quality: Lessons learned in the context of the Head Start REDI trial. *Early Childhood Research Quarterly, 25*, 284–298.

Durlak, J. A. (2013). The importance of implementation for research, practice, and policy (Research brief for the Office of the Assistant Secretary for Planning and Evaluation, Office of Human Services Policy, U.S. Department of Health and Human Services). Retrieved September 10, 2013, from *http://aspe.hhs.gov/hsp/13/keyissuesforchildrenyouth/importanceofquality/rb_qualityimp.cfm.*

Durlak, J. A., & DuPre, E. P. (2008). Implementation matters: A review of research on the influence of implementation on program outcomes and the factors affecting implementation. *American Journal of Community Psychology, 41*, 327–350.

Durlak, J. A., Weissberg, R. P., Dymnicki, A. B.,

Taylor, R. D., & Schellinger, K. B. (2011). The impact of enhancing students' social and emotional learning: A meta-analysis of school-based universal interventions. *Child Development, 82*, 405–433.

Dusenbury, L., Brannigan, R., Hansen, W. B., Walsh, J., & Falco, M. (2005) Quality of implementation: Developing measures crucial to understanding the diffusion of preventive interventions. *Health Education: Research, Theory, and Practice 20*, 308–313.

Elias, M. (2010). Sustainability of social–emotional learning and related programs: Lessons from a field study. *International Journal of Emotional Education, 2*, 17–33.

Fixsen, D. L., Naoom, S. F., Blasé, K. A., Friedman, R. M., & Wallace, F. (2005). *Implementation research: A synthesis of the literature* (FMHI Publication No. 231). Tampa: University of South Florida, Louis de la Parte Florida Mental Health Institute, the National Implementation Research Network. Retrieved September 17, 2013, from *http://nirn.fpg.unc.edu/resources/implementation-research-synthesis-literature.*

Glasgow, R. E., Green, L. W., Taylor, M. V., & Stange, K. C. (2012). An evidence integration triangle for aligning science with policy and practice. *American Journal of Preventive Medicine, 42*, 646–654.

Greenhalgh, T., Robert, G., Macfarlane, F., Bate, P., Kyriakidou, O., & Peacock, R. (2005). *Diffusion of innovations in health service organizations: A systematic literature review.* Oxford, UK: Blackwell.

Humphrey, N. (2013). *Social and emotional learning: A critical appraisal.* Thousand Oaks, CA: Sage.

Johnson, K., Hays, C., Center, H., & Daley, C. (2004). Building capacity and sustainable prevention innovations: A sustainability planning model. *Evaluation and Program Planning, 27*, 135–149.

Kam, C. M., Greenberg, M. T., & Walls, C. T. (2003). Examining the role of implementation quality in school-based prevention using the PATHS curriculum. *Prevention Science, 4*, 55–63.

Meyers, D. C., Durlak, J. A., & Wandersman, A. (2012). The quality implementation framework: A synthesis of critical steps in the implementation process. *American Journal of Community Psychology, 50*, 462–480.

Moore, J. E., Bumbarger, B. K., & Cooper, B. R. (2013). Examining adaptations of evidence-based programs in natural contexts. *Journal of Primary Prevention, 34*,147–161.

O'Donnell, C. L. (2008). Defining, conceptualizing, and measuring fidelity of implementation and its relationship to outcomes in K–12 curriculum intervention research. *Review of Educational Research, 78*, 33–84.

Proctor, E. K., Landsverk, J. L., Baumann, A. A., Mittman, B. S., Aarons, G. A., Brownson, R. C., et al. (2013). The Implementation Research Institute: Training mental health implementation researchers in the United States. *Implementation Science, 8*, 105.

Ringwalt, C. L., Ennett, S., Johnson, R., Rohrbach, L. A., Simons-Rudolph, A., Vincus, A., et al. (2003). Factors associated with fidelity to substance use prevention curriculum guides in the nation's middle schools. *Health Education and Behavior, 30*, 375–391.

Rogers, E. M. (2003). *Diffusion of innovations* (5th ed.). New York: Free Press.

Stirman, S. W., Kimberly, J., Cook, N., Calloway, A., Castro, F., & Charns, M. (2012). The sustainability of new programs and innovations: A review of the empirical literature and recommendations for future research. *Implementation Science, 7*, 17.

CHAPTER 27

SEL and Preservice Teacher Education

Kimberly A. Schonert-Reichl, Jennifer L. Hanson-Peterson, and Shelley Hymel

How can we prepare teachers most effectively for the challenges of teaching? What are the courses and experiences that preservice teacher candidates need to equip them with the skills, dispositions, and knowledge necessary to promote the success of all of their students in diverse classrooms in the 21st century? A growing body of evidence has documented how students' academic and life successes, as well as their social–emotional well-being, are bolstered when attention is given to the social and emotional dimensions of teaching and learning (Durlak, Weissberg, Dymnicki, Taylor, & Schellinger, 2011). Consequently, understanding how preservice teacher education programs can best prepare teachers with the background knowledge necessary to succeed in the teaching profession has become a recent topic among educators, policymakers, and the public at large.

This chapter identifies the ways in which issues related to social and emotional learning (SEL)—including knowledge about students' social and emotional development, teachers' social and emotional competence, and how to create caring and supportive classroom environments that are well managed, participatory, and safe—are incorporated into preservice teacher education. We begin with a brief overview of teacher preparation in the United States and provide a rationale for the importance of including information on issues relevant to SEL in preservice teacher education programs. Then, we review the extant research on the degree to which this is currently occurring. We focus our discussion on recent research examining the nature and frequency with which coursework in teacher preparation programs focuses on topics related to the promotion of students' SEL and development. Given that much of what is incorporated into preservice teacher education is determined by state-level policy directives, we also report on our recent scan examining the extent to which dimensions relevant to SEL (e.g., implementation of SEL programs, teachers' social and emotional competence, the creation of classroom contexts that support students' social and emotional well-being) are incorporated into state-level teacher certification requirements. We conclude our chapter by offering some guidelines and recommendations for incorporating SEL into preservice teacher education and note some potential problems and pitfalls in doing so.

The Case for SEL in Preservice Teacher Education

In recent years, we have witnessed increased theoretical and empirical attention to the school-based promotion of students' social and emotional competence as educators, parents, and policymakers seek solutions to contemporary problems such as declining academic motivation and achievement (Eccles & Roeser, 2011), escalating dropout rates (Battin-Pearson et al., 2000), and increasing school bullying and aggression (Swearer, Espelage, Vaillancourt, & Hymel, 2010). Longitudinal research indicates that between ages 9 and 16, 37–39% of youth are diagnosed with at least one or more diagnosable psychiatric disorders (Jaffee, Harrington, Cohen, & Moffitt, 2005), with prevalence rates increasing to 40–50% by age 21 (e.g., Arseneault, Moffitt, Caspi, Taylor, & Silva, 2000). Lamentably, roughly 80% of children with social, emotional, and behavioral problems do not receive the services they need (U.S. Public Health Service, 2000), and all too often the services provided are neither appropriate nor evidence-based (U.S. Department of Health and Human Services, 1999). The Institute of Medicine's 2009 report on mental, emotional, and behavioral disorders of young people emphasized that prevention and the use of empirically supported interventions are essential strategies for reducing mental illness and promoting social and emotional health. Implicit in this trend is the assumption that educational interventions can be designed to foster students' strengths and resiliency.

Coupled with the need to train and prepare teachers adequately to promote their students' mental health, current theory and research suggest that a high-quality education should not just cultivate the intellectual skills of students; schools today also need to nurture the development of social and emotional competencies and positive human traits such as self-awareness, social awareness, self-management, relationship skills, and responsible decision making (Greenberg et al., 2003). SEL is the process of acquiring the competencies to recognize and manage emotions, develop caring and concern for others, establish positive relationships, make responsible decisions, and handle challenging situations effectively (Osher et al., 2008; Payton et al., 2000; Weissberg, Payton, O'Brien, & Munro, 2007). This attention to promoting students' SEL as a central aim of education is in accord with views espoused since the advent of public education, which stress that schooling should foster the development of skills such as empathy, collaboration, and conflict resolution in order "to prepare students to participate effectively as citizens in our constitutional democracy" (McClung, 2013, p. 38). Prior theory and evidence verify that these intrapersonal and interpersonal competencies can be taught and measured, that they promote developmental assets and reduce problem behaviors, and that they improve students' academic performance, citizenship, and health-related behaviors (e.g., Durlak et al., 2011). In particular, SEL skills can be fostered through nurturing and caring learning environments and experiences (Elias et al., 1997; Greenberg, 2010), with long-lasting effects (Hawkins, Kosterman, Catalano, Hill, & Abbott, 2008). Given that the very nature of school-based learning is relational, social and emotional skills create responsive, caring, and inclusive classrooms, and provide a foundation for building and sustaining learning relationships that promote academic success and responsible citizenship.

Importantly, teachers hold in high regard the role of SEL in their own teaching. For example, a nationally representative survey of more than 600 teachers (Bridgeland, Bruce, & Hariharan, 2013) indicated that most teachers, from preschool to high school, believe that social and emotional skills are teachable (95%), that promoting SEL will benefit students from both rich and poor backgrounds (97%), and will have positive effects on school attendance and graduation (80%), standardized test scores and overall academic performance (77%), college preparation (78%), workforce readiness (87%), and citizenship (87%). These same teachers also reported that in order to effectively implement and promote SEL, they need strong support from district and school leaders. Thus, although teachers are ready to promote SEL, there is a need for a systemic approach that supports implementation at the federal, state, district, and school levels. Results of a 2013 Gallup Poll indicate that sentiments of the general public echo those espoused by teachers (Bushaw & Lopez, 2013). Nevertheless, teachers report limited training and confidence in responding to student behavioral needs and, in turn, supporting students' SEL and development

(Reinke, Stormont, Herman, Puri, & Goel, 2011; Walter, Gouze, & Lim, 2006).

Research on teacher attrition provides some interesting insights into the value of understanding the ways in which social and emotional teaching and learning dimensions affect teachers. The evidence is now clear that teacher burnout and attrition is a major problem that poses a threat to efforts to improve teacher quality. According to a report from the National Commission on Teaching and America's Future (2007), teacher turnover costs the United States up to $7 billion a year, with the negative impact of teacher turnover being greatest at low-performing, high-poverty, high-minority schools. Stress and poor emotion management rank as the primary reasons why teachers become dissatisfied with the profession and leave their positions (Darling-Hammond, 2001). Another contributing factor is student behavior (Ferguson, Frost, & Hall, 2012). One study, for instance, indicated that of the 50% of teachers who leave the field permanently, almost 35% report reasons related to problems with student discipline (Ingersoll & Smith, 2003). Problems with student discipline, classroom management, and student mental health emerge at the beginning of teachers' careers, and first-year teachers feel unprepared to manage their classroom effectively and are unable to recognize common mental health problems such as anxiety (Koller & Bertel, 2006; Siebert, 2005). On a more positive note, data also suggest that when teachers receive training in the behavioral and emotional factors that impact teaching and learning in the classroom, they feel better equipped to propose and implement positive, active classroom management strategies that deter students' aggressive behaviors and promote a positive classroom learning climate (Alvarez, 2007). In order to understand the conditions under which the effective promotion of students' SEL and development can occur, institutional factors that may impact SEL promotion need to be addressed. Therefore, an important issue is to what extent preservice teacher education provides the necessary information, coursework, and/or experiences that prepare teachers to address dimensions relevant to SEL, including information on theories and research on the social and emotional development and the knowledge and skills necessary for creating classroom learning contexts that are well-managed and promote student mental health.

Preservice Teacher Preparation and SEL

Teacher Preparation in the United States

Preservice teacher preparation refers to the education and training provided to teacher candidates prior to entering the teaching profession. This education typically occurs within a college or university setting for which a set program of coursework and experiences is delineated by state-level requirements for teacher certification.[1] A full history and critical analysis of preservice teacher preparation is beyond the scope of this chapter, but readers interested in learning more about the current state of teacher education can find more information in Darling-Hammond (2010, 2013).

Currently, over 1,400 institutions of higher education prepare the majority of the nation's teachers (Greenberg, McKee, & Walsh, 2013). According to a report by the National Council on Teacher Quality (Greenberg, McKee, et al., 2013), approximately 200,000 teachers graduate each year from teacher preparation programs. Preservice teacher education programs vary considerably in terms of duration of training (e.g., 4-year bachelor's degree programs, or 1- or 2-year graduate programs), emphasis on subject content or pedagogy across particular school levels (e.g., elementary school, middle school, high school) and/or content area (middle school and/pre–high school teachers typically identify a subject area, such as Science, Math, Social Studies, etc.), length of practicum periods, and requirements for certification. Obtaining a degree in teacher education generally requires a minimum grade point average (GPA); completion of a bachelor's degree; knowledge about how social, institutional, and state policy affect the educational process; an understanding of how learning occurs and how to teach effectively; and successful completion of supervised field experiences (Zeichner & Paige, 2007). A certificate obtained in one country or state may not be recognized in another. Within the United States, state-to-state reciprocity is limited.

Research on the extent to which preservice teacher education includes direct information and/or training in SEL is in a nascent stage. However, findings from a few recent studies provide a glimpse into the extent to which factors that provide the foundation for promoting students' SEL in classrooms and schools are routinely included in teacher preparation. For example, knowledge about classroom management is essential for all teachers because the promotion of students' social and emotional competence is most effective when it occurs within a supportive, safe, caring, participatory, and well-managed learning environment that supports children's development and affords them opportunities for practicing SEL skills (Weissberg et al., 2007). The term "classroom management" refers to the ways in which teachers establish order, routine, and limits in their classrooms, deliver lessons, manage multiple transitions that occur between activities, and create an atmosphere of safety and support for students. Effective classroom management prevents the occurrence of disruptive or undesirable behaviors and increases engaged academic learning time in the classroom, which in turn leads to students' improved behavioral and academic performance. Issues including communication styles, high performance expectations, classroom structures and rules, school organizational climate, commitment to the academic success of all students, teacher social and emotional competence (Jennings & Greenberg, 2009), and openness to parental and community involvement are all important components of effective classroom management in general and SEL in particular. In the next section, we examine the extent to which SEL is currently incorporated into coursework in U.S. preservice teacher education programs.

Teacher Preparation and Knowledge about Child and Adolescent Development

One dimension that is considered central to effective, high-quality teaching and learning is teachers' knowledge and understanding of their students' social, emotional, and cognitive development (Comer & Maholmes, 1999; Daniels & Shumow, 2003; Darling-Hammond & Bransford, 2005; Sarason, 2001). More than a decade of research indicates that teachers who have knowledge about child and adolescent development are better able to design and carry out learning experiences in ways that support student social, emotional, and academic competence, and enhance student outcomes (Hamre & Pianta, 2006; Rimm-Kaufman & Hamre, 2010). Associations between successful social relationships in schools (i.e., student–teacher relationships and peer relationships) and positive social and academic outcomes have also been documented (Hamre & Pianta, 2001; Wentzel, 2003).

Recently, the National Institute of Child Health and Human Development (NICHD), the National Institute of Health (NIH), and the U.S. Department of Health and Human Services (USDHHS) (2007) and the National Council for Accreditation of Teacher Education (NCATE; 2010) collaborated in conducting two roundtable discussions on the critical relevance of child and adolescent development research for preservice teacher preparation, with input provided from a selected group of internationally renowned experts in teacher training and in child and adolescent development research. The reports that followed from these meetings (see NCATE, 2010; available at *www.ncate.org*) emphasized the importance of preservice teachers being knowledgeable about many issues related to SEL, including children's social and emotional development, teacher–student relationships, and the learning environment. The current status of child and adolescent development in teacher preparation programs was explored in a 33-item, online survey sent to unit heads at 595 NCATE-accredited institutions, both public and private, in 2005. Of the 283 responses received (48% response rate; 64% from public and 36% from private institutions), 90% indicated that they required teacher candidates to take at least one course in child–adolescent development, although several programs reported foregoing courses altogether because of state limitations on credit hours for preparation programs. The *application* of this knowledge to classroom practice may be more limited, however. Indeed, in the NCATE survey, the 20% of programs that did not themselves offer courses in development reported relying on psychology departments for such courses, where connections to the classroom are less likely. Furthermore, survey results indicated that for many of the texts used in courses, there was virtually no application of child–adolescent development to actual classroom practice, leaving instructors to create their own examples. Survey respondents underscored the potential benefits of a text that made more explicit connections between developmental research and its application.

With an ever-expanding knowledge base for the field of teacher education, it is the responsibility of both educators and preparation institutions to enrich and revise practices, programs, policies, and partnerships, and to determine critical foci. One conclusion that emerged from the NCATE (2010) report is that current efforts to incorporate coursework in the developmental sciences into teacher training are woefully inadequate. In order to advance the field of teacher education, they recommended that programs integrate academic study in the behavioral sciences with real opportunities to implement child and adolescent development best practices in classrooms and communities. Moreover, policymakers must consider the importance of child and adolescent development as they design new standards and assessments for evaluating student and teacher performance, particularly when evaluating low-performing schools, whose students are often in greater need of developmental supports to improve achievement.

Teacher Preparation and Student Social and Emotional Behavioral Problems, Mental Health, and Classroom Management

Recent educational research on the factors that promote students' social and behavioral competence and prevent negative outcomes, such as mental illness and aggression, has focused on the contributions of school context given evidence that empirically based school curricula can deter the onset of problem behaviors and emotional difficulties (Durlak et al., 2011; Sklad, Diekstra, De Ritter, & Ben, 2012; Weare & Nind, 2011). Teachers play a critical role in these initiatives by fostering positive student–teacher relationships and by creating supportive and caring classroom environments (Hamre & Pianta, 2005, 2006); there is evidence that teachers who effectively integrate SEL programs into their practice have students with more positive outcomes (Durlak et al., 2011). Less is known about the role of teachers in addressing student mental illness and social, emotional, and behavioral problems. Teachers are in a unique position to recognize significant adjustment problems in their students or to identify disruptive behaviors that are common in schools. However, the majority of teachers feel ill-prepared to address such issues (Walter et al., 2006), due to their lack of knowledge and skills in the area of student mental health and/or classroom management. Indeed, Koller, Osterlind, Paris, and Weston (2004) found that both experienced and first-year teachers reported that they did not receive adequate training in their teacher education programs to identify and manage the mental health concerns of their students. Similarly, in a national study of 2,335 educators, conducted by the Coalition for Psychology in Schools and Education (2006), teachers indicated that they did not receive adequate training on handling student behavior during preservice teaching, with the majority of teachers (especially first-year teachers) ranking classroom management as one of their top two professional development needs.

Analyses of educational curricula confirm that preservice teacher education programs are not adequately preparing teachers to deal with student social, emotional, and behavioral problems. State, Kern, Starosta, and Mukherjee (2011) collected and examined the content of syllabi in required educational courses of U.S. preservice teacher elementary preparation programs. They found that 42 of the 80 syllabi examined (53%) did not include *any* content related to students' social, emotional, and behavioral problems (SEB), and most of the other required courses provided very limited coverage. For example, relatively little class time was devoted to teaching student teachers how to identify student problems and/or how to promote SEL in students. With regard to course topics, among 38 syllabi, only eight (21%) focused on classroom management, six (16%) included information on the characteristics and identification of emotional and behavioral disorders, and only two (5%)

included information on children's social and emotional development.

With regard to the total amount of class time spent on the various SEB topics, State and colleagues (2011) estimated that an average of 168 minutes was spent in discussion of possibly useful interventions, whereas an average of 57 minutes was allocated to classroom management topics. For example, State and colleagues estimated that an average of *only 16 minutes* was spent discussing characteristics or identification of students with SEB problems, including psychiatric disorders, and an average of *only 7 minutes* of class time was spent on social–emotional development. Slightly less than 1 hour (mean = 57 minutes) was spent on classroom management. Overall, State and colleagues found that across all the required coursework, students received in the typical teacher education program, on average, only 6 hours and 50 minutes (range 1–1,331 minutes) were devoted to issues related to understanding, identifying, and managing students' problematic behaviors and promoting their social and emotional development. Obviously, the preparation of new teachers varies considerably on these topics. Some teachers receive no formal preparation at all, whereas others may receive quite a bit.

Expanding on State and colleagues' (2011) review, Vinnes, Keenan, and Green (2014) examined the extent to which university *graduate* teacher education programs included content related to four topics related to SEB—social development, emotional development, behavior management, and abuse/neglect. Analyzing course descriptions for all required classes in the top 50 graduate teacher education programs as designated by *U.S. News & World Report* (2012), they examined whether the inclusion of these topics varied as a function of program level (elementary vs. secondary training), type of university (public vs. private), or geographic location (Northeast, South, West, Midwest). Their final sample of 78 elementary and secondary education programs from 43 of the top 50 universities across the United States included those programs that posted publicly available online course descriptions.

Vinnes and colleagues (2014) found that over two-thirds of the 78 programs they reviewed required at least one course on the topics of social development, emotional development, behavior management, or abuse/neglect, although only one course included mention of abuse/neglect. Behavior management was the topic most frequently cited, although little more than half of the graduate teacher education programs reviewed (52.6%) included a course that specifically mentioned behavior, behavior management, or classroom management in its title or course description. Only one-fourth of the programs (26.9%) required a course on social development, one-fifth (20.5%) required two courses, and one program (1.3%) required three courses. Few programs required a course on emotional development (16.7%), although three programs (3.8%) required two classes on the topic. Inclusion of these topics did not differ across elementary and secondary programs or across public and private institutions. There were, however, significant regional differences, with fewer programs including social development located in the South, and behavior management more frequently addressed in programs located in the West. Vinnes and colleagues speculated that these differences might be due to variations in state legislation and policies related to school mental health service provision; teacher licensure requirements; and the value systems of schools, teachers, and school mental health service providers.

A recent report from the National Council on Teacher Quality (NCTQ; Greenberg, Putman & Walsh, 2013) echoed the relative inattention to classroom management in preservice education. Using course materials such as syllabi, textbooks, and student teaching observation/evaluation instruments, the NCTQ study examined classroom management-related professional coursework in 119 teacher preparation programs in 79 institutions of higher education in 33 states. Findings revealed that although 97% of the programs they reviewed included *some* mention of classroom management, instruction and practice in classroom management strategies were often scattered throughout the curriculum and did not draw from the latest scientific research identifying the most effective strategies. Moreover, there was relatively little attention given to providing preservice teachers with opportunities for translating knowledge of effective classroom management into practice during their student-teaching experience. Indeed, only one-third of the programs reviewed required the *practice* of classroom management skills as they were learned. Given the relative inattention to training and experience in classroom management in preservice teacher education, it is not surprising that a high percent of teachers report that student behavior is a significant impediment to their success in the classroom (Ingersoll & Smith, 2003).

In summary, the few studies to date that have examined the extent to which preservice teacher education programs include knowledge about dimensions relevant to SEL and its practical application consistently indicate that little attention is paid to equipping teachers with the knowledge and skills necessary for promoting their students' social and emotional competence and creating positive classroom environments that enhance student success (Jones & Bouffard, 2012). How can we influence preservice teacher education programs to expand their focus on SEL? Colleges and universities are directed by state and federal policy and certification requirements that mandate the topics and courses that must be included in teacher preparation programs for teachers to be licensed to teach. Accordingly, in the next section, we present findings from the Social–Emotional Learning in Teacher Education (SEL-Ted) project, a recent state-level scan of SEL of preservice teacher education K–12 certification requirements in the United States—a critical first step in ensuring that teachers are prepared for integrating SEL into educational practice.

SEL and State-Level Teacher Certification Requirements: The SEL-Ted Project

In the United States, there are requirements that teacher education programs must meet to be considered approved programs. The goal of these requirements is to ensure that high-quality training is provided to preservice teachers by providing benchmarks for the teacher education programs. These requirements usually include prescribed standards (statements that outline necessary teacher competencies) and coursework (a set of specific courses) that preservice teachers must complete successfully to receive a state-issued teaching certificate.

To investigate these requirements, we began by reviewing articles, reports, and government websites to understand the teacher certification process and identify the institutions responsible for prescribing teacher education program requirements in the United States. Each state, namely through a state department (e.g., Department of Education) or board (e.g., Board of Regents, State Board of Education), has the authority to develop its own teacher education program requirements. Some states mandate that teacher education programs be accredited by NCATE or the Teacher Education Accreditation Council (TEAC). The accreditation process for each of these nonprofit accrediting bodies involves reviewing teacher education programs to determine whether they meet the principles and standards established by these bodies. Some states do not mandate NCATE or TEAC accreditation but do use the NCATE professional standard as the foundation for their state standards.

Data Collection and Coding

Information was gathered for all 50 U.S. states and the District of Columbia on the prescribed standards and coursework requirements with which state-approved teacher education programs must comply. In the data collection process, the website of each state's department or board responsible for establishing the standards and coursework requirements was examined, and the documents that outlined these were located.

A coding guide was developed to analyze the teacher education program standards identified for the U.S. states, with definitions drawn from SEL theory and research by experts in the field (see Fleming & Bay, 2004; Jennings & Greenberg, 2009; Payton et al., 2000; Zins, Weissberg, Wang, & Walberg, 2004). The coding guide comprised three sections that addressed (1) Social and Emotional Competence (SEC) of Teachers (e.g., preservice teachers learn to foster their own SEL competencies, such as self-awareness, social awareness), (2) Social and Emotional Learning (SEL) of Students (e.g., preservice teachers learn to foster their students' SEL skills), and (3) the Learning Context (e.g., a focus on classroom, school, and community environments that promote students' SEL skills). The first two categories—SEC of Teachers and SEL of Students—were further divided into the five SEL dimensions outlined by the Collaborative for Academic, Social, and Emotional Learning (CASEL; 2013): (1) Self-Awareness, (2) Social Awareness, (3) Self-Management, (4) Relationship Skills, and (5) Responsible Decision Making. The latter category, the Learning Context, was further subdivided into four subcategories: (1) Classroom Context, (2) Supporting Schoolwide Coordination, (3) Developing School–Family Partnerships, and (4) Building School-Community Partnerships. These dimensions were designed to assess the extent to which preservice teachers learn to create an optimal environment in which SEL can be fostered and to collaborate with others beyond the classroom who can also enhance students' SEL skills.

When analyzing each standard, the unit of analysis was a meaningful unit, as opposed to the whole standard. However, the context of each standard was accounted for when performing the analysis. Take, for example, the following standard: "The pre-service teacher models effective verbal, nonverbal, and media communication techniques to foster active inquiry, collaboration, and supportive interaction in the classroom" (Missouri Department of Elementary and Secondary Education, 2006, p. 23). When coding this standard, rather than applying one code to the whole standard, it was split into four meaningful units: (1) "The pre-service teacher models effective verbal, nonverbal, and media communication techniques", (2) "to foster active inquiry", (3) "collaboration", and (4) "supportive interaction in the classroom" (p. 23). When coding each meaningful unit in this example, the research assistant considered whose SEL competencies were being exercised or fostered (e.g., the teacher or students) and via what means (e.g., the use of communication skills).

Trained research assistants reviewed the content of the gathered documents on the state standards for teacher education programs; SEL-related phrases in the standards were coded according to the coding guide, which used a qualitative approach to coding data (Creswell, 2007). Only standards that were "required", as opposed to "recommended", by the state were coded. Also, we distinguished between states that applied their standards to *all* preservice teachers and those that applied them to grade-level and subject-area-specific preservice teachers (e.g., preservice teachers specializing in elementary education, secondary language arts). We were most interested in finding and coding standards that applied to all preservice teachers in each state. Therefore, standards that applied to particular preservice teacher groups were considered only if there were no general standards that applied to all preservice teachers, or if the standards that applied to all preservice teachers did not meet at least one domain in the three SEL categories. In our review of the state standards, 90% of states had standards that applied to all preservice teachers, whereas only 10% only had standards that applied to grade-level and subject-area specific preservice teachers.

Interrater agreement and kappa statistics were used to assess the reliability of the coding system employed for the terms used to code the standards. Eight U.S. states were randomly selected, and two research assistants each coded those states' standards. Percent of interrater agreement and kappa statistics were as follows: 87.5% (kappa = .697) for SEC of Teacher, 95% (kappa = .722) for SEL of Student, and 100% (kappa = 1.000) for Learning Context.

Based on these codes, each state received a score for each of the three categories (i.e., SEC of Teacher, SEL of Student, and the Learning Context) based on the extent to which their teacher education standards/ requirements addressed the subcategories (e.g., Self-Awareness) of each category.[2]

Key Findings

In this section we present the key findings based on how many of the five SEL Competency of Teacher and Student domains, and the four Learning Context domains appeared in each state's standards.

Key finding 1: The promotion of the SEL competencies of teachers is given little

emphasis in state-level teacher education program standards. We found that *not one* state had standards that addressed all five core SEL Competency of Teacher domains. The vast majority of the states (71%) had standards that addressed between one and three of the five core SEL Competency of Teacher domains, whereas only 20% of states addressed four of the five core SEL Competency of Teacher domains. Furthermore, 10% of states had standards addressing SEL Competency of Teacher domains that were only applicable to preservice teachers in specific grade levels or subject areas, rather than all preservice teachers.

Of the five core SEL Competency of Teacher domains, the most commonly addressed in the standards were Responsible Decision Making (90% of states), Social Awareness (86% of states), and Relationship Skills (80% of states). In contrast, the most commonly absent SEL Competency of Teacher domains in the standards were Self Awareness (only 18% of states) and Self-Management (only 4% of states). In other words, very few states required preservice teachers to learn skills such as how to identify their feelings, strengths, and weaknesses, or how to control and appropriately express their feelings, manage stress, and monitor their progress toward achieving goals.

Below we provide examples of standards we found that fit each SEL Competency of Teacher domain:

- Self-Awareness—"Understand one's own . . . ethics and values" (Tennessee Department of Education, 2001, p. 1).
- Social Awareness—"A teacher must . . . understand developmental progressions of learners and ranges of individual variation within the physical, social, emotional, moral, and cognitive domains, be able to identify levels of readiness in learning, and understand how development in any one domain may affect performance in others" (Minnesota Department of Education, 2009, p. 3).
- Responsible Decision Making—"The ability to recognize and deal with dehumanizing biases, including, but not limited to, sexism, racism, prejudice, and discrimination, and an awareness of the impact such biases have on interpersonal relations" (Nebraska Department of Education, 2008, p. 14).
- Self-Management—"Teachers understand and utilize anger management . . . as appropriate in the classroom" (North Carolina State Board of Education, 2006, p. 2).
- Relationship Skills—"Ability to develop a positive relationship with every student" (Alabama State Board of Education, 2007, p. 260).

Key finding 2: Few state-level standards for teacher education programs have a comprehensive focus on promoting students' SEL competencies. One-third (33%) of states addressed all five SEL Competency of Student domains, 20% addressed four of the five domains, and 29% addressed between one and three of the five domains. Furthermore, 12% of states had standards addressing SEL Competency of Student domains that were only applicable to preservice teachers in specific grade levels or subject areas rather than all preservice teachers. SEL of Students was the only category that was not addressed at all by some of the states' standards, with 6% of states having standards that did not address any of the SEL Competency of Student domains.

Of the five core student competencies, the majority of states identified Responsible Decision Making (82%), Relationship Skills (78%), and Self-Management (73%) in their standards. Therefore, most states were concerned with preparing preservice teachers to enhance their students' abilities to make constructive and respectful choices; establish and maintain healthy relationships; and regulate their thoughts, emotions, and behaviors.

Less attention was given, however, to Self-Awareness (43%) and Social Awareness (51%) in the standards, indicating that fewer states were concerned with preparing preservice teachers to enhance their students' abilities to identify their feelings, strengths, and weaknesses, or take the perspective of and empathize with people from diverse backgrounds.

Below we provide examples of standards we found that fit each SEL student competency domain:

- Self-Awareness—" . . . uses assessment strategies to involve learners in self-assessment activities, to help them become aware of their learning behaviors, strengths, needs and progress" (Missouri Standards for Teacher Education Programs, cited in Missouri Department of Elementary and Secondary Education, 2006, p. 3).
- Social Awareness—"Teacher's instructional units . . . are designed to expose students to a variety of intellectual, social, and cultural perspectives" (South Carolina Department of Education, n.d., p. 5).
- Responsible Decision Making—"Create a values-oriented classroom environment that supports students' personal responsibility for their own learning and behaviors" (Maryland State Board of Education, 1994, p. 13).
- Self-Management—"The teacher uses an understanding of individual and group motivation and behavior to create a learning environment that encourages . . . self-motivation" (Commonwealth of Pennsylvania, 2000, p. 13).
- Relationship Skills—"Understands how to help students work cooperatively and productively in groups" (Illinois State Board of Education, 2001, p. 5).

Key finding 3: Almost every state's standards for teacher education programs require that teachers obtain knowledge of the Learning Context. The Learning Context was the most highly addressed category in the standards across the U.S. states. Specifically, 82% of states had comprehensive standards that addressed all four Learning Context domains; 6% addressed three of the four domains, and only 2% addressed one or two of the four domains. Moreover, 10% of states had standards addressing the Learning Context domains that were only applicable to preservice teachers in specific grade levels or subject areas, rather than all preservice teachers.

The majority of states included the four domains of the Learning Context in their standards: Schoolwide Coordination (90%), School–Community Partnerships (88%), School–Family Partnerships (86%), and Classroom Context (86%).

Below we provide examples of standards we found that fit each Learning Context domain:

- Classroom Context—"The competent teacher . . . understands principles of and strategies for effective classroom management" (Illinois State Board of Education, 2001, p. 5).
- Schoolwide Coordination—"The teacher fosters relationships with school colleagues . . . to support student learning and well-being" (South Dakota Department of Education, 2006).
- School–Family Partnerships—"Works actively to involve parents in their child's academic activities and performance, and communicates clearly with them" (Massachusetts Department of Elementary and Secondary Education, 2012).
- School–Community Partnerships—"The teacher values and utilizes the knowledge that all community members have something to contribute to the classroom to assist in the educational process" (New Mexico Public Education Department, 1998, p. 8).

Next Steps

For our next phase of the SEL-Ted project, we are coding the content of required coursework in over 300 public and private colleges of education across all 50 states and the District of Columbia via a stratified random sampling, using a framework that is similar to the one we used for coding of state-level certification requirements. Other aspects of our project will include interviews with Deans of Colleges of Education in the United States for their suggestions/reflections on how to integrate SEL into teacher preparation, as well as descriptions of exemplary preservice teacher education programs that are embedding SEL into teacher preparation. This work, coupled with our research on the state scan of SEL in state-level certification requirements, will provide a more comprehensive portrait of the extent to which SEL is being integrated into teacher preparation, allowing for informed decision making for advancing the science and practice of SEL in preservice teacher education.

Recommendations

Based on our review of the extant literature, we can offer seven recommendations to advance the field of SEL in relation to preservice teacher education.

1. State policymakers should redesign policies to ensure that teacher certification requires all educators to demonstrate their ability to apply contemporary knowledge of child and adolescent SEL and development to PreK–12 classroom practice. One example of this is currently unfolding in Massachusetts, where a group of educators and policymakers are working collaboratively to embed SEL into preservice teacher education (see *www.sel4mass.org*).
2. In accord with the recommendations of the NCATE (2010) report, more attention needs to be given to providing opportunities for teacher candidates to learn principles of child and adolescent social and emotional development by integrating developmental science principles throughout the teacher preparation curriculum.
3. Moreover, teacher candidates need to learn about the latest innovations and science in SEL and its practical application, with intentional and specific attention to all domains of SEL.
4. Preservice teacher education programs need to redesign their curricula so as to combine course content on SEL and practical application of SEL concepts into classroom teaching. This can be done through both supervised student teaching experiences and classroom-based video examples, role plays, and out-of-classroom mentorship.
5. A necessary prerequisite for incorporating domains of SEL into preservice education is having a cadre of teacher educators and classroom supervisors with the necessary SEL knowledge and skills. Thus, colleges and faculties of education need to hire new personnel with the required expertise and provide professional development for their current faculty in this area.
6. Relatedly, during their student teaching experience, teacher candidates need to be placed in classrooms with teachers who have expertise in the knowledge and implementation of SEL, so that teacher candidates can have firsthand experience in observing and then implementing SEL.
7. All teacher candidates should have supervised instruction in how to prepare their lesson plans to address their students' social and emotional, as well as academic, learning.

Potential Problems, Pitfalls, and Conclusions

Although we have delineated several recommendations to move SEL into preservice teacher education, there are also several potential problems and pitfalls that need to be mentioned. The first potential pitfall is ignoring the importance of promoting the SEL of educators (Jones, Bouffard, & Weissbourd, 2013). From our review, it is clear that little attention is given currently to the cultivation and promotion of preservice teachers' own social and emotional competence and well-being. This is problematic if we want to advance the science and practice SEL, particularly with regard to the effective implementation of SEL programs. Indeed, SEL programs are most likely to lead to positive outcomes for students when implemented with fidelity (Durlak et al., 2011). As recent evidence indicates, SEL programs are implemented poorly when teachers experience burnout (Ransford, Greenberg, Domitrovich, Small, & Jacobson, 2009), and when they do not "buy in" to SEL programming (Reyes, Brackett, Rivers, Elbertson, & Salovey, 2012). A second problem that may arise is the creation of courses that provide superficial knowledge about the social and emotional dimensions of teaching and learning, and exclude information about evidence-based SEL programs and practices, and their effective implementation. For example, upon reading the recommendations we have put forth regarding the importance of including SEL in preservice teacher education, a number of administrators and faculty members in teacher preparation programs may rush to create additional SEL courses that do not give adequate attention to providing experiences and opportunities for teacher candidates to *apply* SEL knowledge and skills in their student teaching. Indeed, poor-quality preparation of teachers will not advance the field. Finally, we must be cautious not to be shortsighted and rely only on good faith that preparing preservice teachers with SEL knowledge and experiences will lead to positive student outcomes. Indeed, we do not know how well the inclusion of SEL knowledge and practice in preservice teacher education translates to the promotion of student competencies in classrooms. Although we now have evidence demonstrating that quality teacher-led implementation of evidence-based SEL leads to positive student outcomes (Durlak et al., 2011), we do not yet know how well quality instruction in SEL during preservice teacher preparation leads to more positive outcomes for students.

New Initiatives in Teacher Preparation

Although the field has far to go, there are some emerging examples of teacher preparation programs that are now incorporating theory, research, and practical application of SEL into preservice education. For example, the faculty at San Jose State University in the Collaborative for Reaching and Teaching the Whole Child (*http://reachandteachthewholechild.org*) is committed to embedding the social–emotional dimension of teaching and learning into its teacher preparation program. Preservice courses that have been revised to embed the SEL lens include math and science methods and classroom management. Moreover, the faculty members at San Jose State not only focused on embedding SEL into coursework, but they also developed an observation protocol with an SEL lens for mentor teachers and university supervisors to use when observing preservice teachers during their student teaching.

In the Faculty of Education at the University of British Columbia in Canada, SEL has been explicitly integrated into a postbaccalaureate, 12-month teacher preparation program. Specifically, one of the nine options available to the approximately 400 elementary preservice teacher education students is the SEL Cohort (comprising approximately 36 students each year). Within this program, teacher candidates take the regular teacher education program with a special emphasis on SEL. Throughout all of their coursework, teacher candidates not only learn about current research and theory on SEL but are also provided with explicit training and opportunities for implementing SEL evidence-based programs and practices into classrooms during their student teaching practicum. There is even an "SEL Program" library in the Faculty of Education that includes a wide variety of SEL programs that teacher candidates can review and integrate into their coursework and student teaching. Practicum placements provide opportunities for teacher candidates to integrate SEL programs and practices into the classroom and curriculum. Moreover, in addition to explicit attention to SEL within this unique SEL Cohort, all teacher candidates, both elementary and secondary, are provided with specific coursework and active learning approaches for creating safe, caring, and participatory classroom and school environments (see *http://teach.educ.ubc.ca/bachelor-of-education-program/elementary*). Although promotion of SEL in preservice teacher education is, in our opinion, an important step, it is not without its challenges. Indeed, the addition of a course on creating safe, caring, and supportive learning contexts within an already demanding and intensive 1-year program has to be balanced by reductions in required coursework in other areas (e.g., child and adolescent development, specific curriculum areas). Thus, SEL must be recognized and promoted at the university and college level as a necessary part of teacher training efforts.

Concluding Comments

To create a world characterized by caring, cooperation, empathy, and compassion among all people, it is essential that educators, parents, community members, and policymakers work together to promote students' personal and social development, and embedding SEL into preservice teacher education is a step in the right direction. Indeed, it is critical that we make intentional efforts to devise the most effective educational practices that promote SEL both in teachers and their students. Such efforts must be based on strong conceptual models and sound research. The promotion of social and emotional competencies is fundamental to the mission of education (Jones et al., 2013).

Acknowledgment

We are grateful for the support of CASEL, which inspired and funded our State Scan of SEL in preservice teacher education certification requirements.

Notes

1. Although the majority of teachers receive their degrees from colleges or faculties of education in colleges or universities, a growing number of teachers receive their state teaching licensure via alternative certification routes. The National Association for Alternative Certification (*www.alt-teachercert.org*) indicated that about 30% of teachers in the United States receive their teacher certification through alternative routes, and this number continues to grow.

2. A subcategory was met if at least one of the multiple components in the category was addressed (e.g., if just "awareness of feelings" of teachers was addressed, but "constructive sense of self" of teachers is not, the Self-Awareness subcategory would nevertheless be considered met for the SEC of Teachers category).

References

Alabama State Board of Education. (2007). Rules of the Alabama State Board of Education: Chapter 290-3-3: Teacher Education: Professional Services. Retrieved April 4, 2012, from *http://coe.alasu.edu/ncate/documents/chapter%20290-3-3%20teacher%20education%20_adopted%208-6-07.pdf.*

Alvarez, H. K. (2007). The impact of teacher preparation on responses to student aggression in the classroom. *Teaching and Teacher Education, 23,* 1113–1126.

Arseneault, L., Moffitt, T. E., Caspi, A., Taylor, P. J., & Silva, P. A. (2000). Mental disorders and violence in a total birth cohort: Results from the Dunedin study. *Archives of General Psychiatry, 57,* 979–986.

Battin-Pearson, S., Newcomb, M. D., Abbott, R. D., Hill, K. G., Catalano, R. F., & Hawkins, J. D. (2000). Predictors of early high school dropout: A test of five theories. *Journal of Educational Psychology, 92,* 568–582.

Bridgeland, J., Bruce, M., & Hariharan, A. (2013). *The missing piece: A national survey on how social and emotional learning can empower children and transform schools.* Washington, DC: Civic Enterprises.

Bushaw, W. J., & Lopez, S. J. (2013, September). Which way do we go?: The 45th annual PDK/Gallup Poll of the public's attitudes toward the public schools. *Phi Delta Kappan, 95*(1), 8–25.

Coalition for Psychology in Schools and Education. (2006). *Report on the teacher needs survey.* Washington, DC: American Psychological Association.

Collaborative for Academic, Social, and Emotional Learning (CASEL). (2013). *2013 CASEL guide: Effective social and emotional learning programs—preschool and elementary school edition.* Chicago: Author.

Comer, J., & Maholmes, J. (1999). Creating schools of child development and education in the USA: Teacher preparation for urban schools. *Journal of Education for Teaching, 25,* 3–5.

Commonwealth of Pennsylvania. (2000). Chapter 354: Preparation of Professional Educators. Retrieved on April 6, 2012, from *www.pacode.com/secure/data/022/chapter354/022_0354.pdf.*

Creswell, J. W. (2007). *Qualitative inquiry and research design: Choosing among five traditions* (2nd ed.). Thousand Oaks, CA: Sage.

Daniels, D. H., & Shumow, L. (2003). Child development and classroom teaching: A review of the literature and implications for educating teachers. *Applied Developmental Psychology, 23,* 495–526.

Darling-Hammond, L. (2001). The challenge of staffing our schools. *Educational Leadership, 58,* 12–17.

Darling-Hammond, L. (2010). Teacher education and the American future. *Journal of Teacher Education, 61,* 35–47.

Darling-Hammond, L. (2013). *Powerful teacher education: Lessons from exemplary programs.* Hoboken, NJ: Wiley.

Darling-Hammond, L., & Bransford, J. (Eds.). (2005). *Preparing teachers for a changing world: What teachers should learn and be able to do.* San Francisco: Jossey-Bass.

Durlak, J. A., Weissberg, R. P., Dymnicki, A. B., Taylor, R. D., & Schellinger, K. B. (2011). Enhancing students' social and emotional development promotes success in school: Results of a meta-analysis. *Child Development, 82,* 474–501.

Eccles, J. S., & Roeser, R. W. (2011). School and community influences on human development. In M. H. Bornstein & M. E. Lamb (Eds.), *Developmental science: An advanced textbook* (6th ed., pp. 571–643). New York: Psychology Press.

Elias, M. J., Zins, J. E., Weissberg, R. P., Frey, K. S., Greenberg, M. T., Haynes, N. M., et al. (1997). *Promoting social and emotional learn-*

ing: *Guidelines for educators*. Alexandria, VA: Association for Supervision and Curriculum Development.

Ferguson, K., Frost, L., & Hall, D. (2012). Predicting teacher anxiety, depression, and job satisfaction. *Journal of Teaching and Learning, 8*, 27–42.

Fleming, J., & Bay, M. (2004). Social and emotional learning in teacher preparation standards. In J. E. Zins, R. P. Weissberg, M. C. Wang, & H. J. Walberg (Eds.), *Building school success through social and emotional learning: Implications for practice and research* (pp. 94–110). New York: Teachers College Press.

Greenberg, J., McKee, A., & Walsh, K. (2013). *Teacher prep review: A review of the nation's teacher preparation programs*. Washington, DC: National Council on Teacher Quality. Retrieved December 10, 2014, from *www.nctq.org/dmsstage/teacher_prep_review_2013_report*.

Greenberg, J., Putman, H., & Walsh, K. (2013). *Training our future teachers: Classroom management*. Washington, DC: National Council on Teacher Quality. Retrieved January 13, 2014, from *www.nctq.org/dmsview/future_teachers_classroom_management_nctq_report*.

Greenberg, M., Weissberg, R., O'Brien, M. U., Zins, J., Fredericks, L., Resnik, H., et al. (2003). Enhancing school-based prevention and youth development through coordinated social, emotional, and academic learning. *American Psychologist, 58*, 466–474.

Greenberg, M. T. (2010). School-based prevention: Current status and future challenges. *Effective Education, 2*, 27–52.

Hamre, B., & Pianta, R. C. (2001). Early teacher–child relationships and trajectory of school outcomes through eighth grade. *Child Development, 72*, 625–638.

Hamre, B. K., & Pianta, R. C. (2005). Can instructional and emotional support in the first grade classroom make a difference for children at risk of school failure? *Child Development, 76*, 949–967.

Hamre, B. K., & Pianta, R. C. (2006). Student–teacher relationships. In G. G. Bear & K. Minke (Eds.), *Children's needs III: Development, prevention, and intervention* (pp. 59–71). Bethesda, MD: National Association of School Psychologists.

Hawkins, J. D., Kosterman, R., Catalano, R. F., Hill, K. G., & Abbott, R. D. (2008). Effects of a social development intervention in childhood 15 years later. *Archives of Pediatric and Adolescent Medicine, 162*, 1133–1141.

Illinois State Board of Education. (2001). Content-area standards for educators. Retrieved on November 28, 2011, from *http://lrs.ed.uiuc.edu/students/gbequett/standards.pdf*.

Ingersoll, R. M., & Smith, T. M. (2003). The wrong solution to the teacher shortage. *Educational Leadership, 60*, 30–33.

Institute of Medicine. (2009). *Preventing mental, emotional, and behavioral disorders among young people: Progress and possibilities*. Washington, DC: National Academies Press.

Jaffee, S. R., Harrington, H., Cohen, P., & Moffitt, T. E. (2005). Cumulative prevalence of psychiatric disorder in youths. *Journal of the American Academy of Child and Adolescent Psychiatry, 44*, 406–407.

Jennings, P. A., & Greenberg, M. T. (2009). The prosocial classroom: Teacher social and emotional competence in relation to student and classroom outcomes. *Review of Educational Research, 79*, 491–525.

Jones, S. M., & Bouffard, S. M. (2012). Social and emotional learning in schools: From programs to strategies. *Society for Research on Child Development Social Policy Report, 25*(4), 1–22.

Jones, S. M., Bouffard, S. M., & Weissbourd, R. (2013). Educators' social and emotional skills vital to learning. *Phi Delta Kappan, 94*, 62–65.

Koller, J. R., & Bertel, J. M. (2006). Responding to today's mental health needs of children, families and schools: Revisiting the pre-service training and preparation of school-based personnel. *Education and Treatment of Children, 29*, 197–217.

Koller, J. R., Osterlind, S. J., Paris, K., & Weston, K. J. (2004). Differences between novice and expert teachers' undergraduate preparation and ratings of importance in the area of children's mental health. *International Journal of Mental Health Promotion, 6*, 40–45.

Maryland State Board of Education. (1994). *Essential dimensions of teaching*. Baltimore: Division of Certification and Accreditation Program Approval and Assessment Branch. Retrieved June 28, 2012, from *http://marylandpublicschools.org/nr/rdonlyres/2c7ffcc4-3f21-4b62-9406-311b06cdf2db/1500/edot1994.pdf*.

Massachusetts Department of Elementary and Secondary Education. (2012). 603 CMR 7.00 Regulations for Educator Licensure and Preparation Program Approval: 7.08: Professional Standards for Teachers. Retrieved April 4, 2012, from *www.doe.mass.edu/lawsregs/603cmr7.html?section=08*.

McClung, M. (2013). Repurposing education. *Phi Delta Kappan, 94*, 37–39.

Minnesota Department of Education. (2009). Minnesota Administrative Rules: 8710.2000 Standards of Effective Practice for Teachers.

Retrieved April 8, 2012, from *www.revisor.mn.gov/rules/?id=8710.2000.*

Missouri Department of Elementary and Secondary Education. (2006). Missouri standards for teacher education programs and benchmarks for preliminary teacher education programs. Retrieved April 28, 2012, from *www.dese.mo.gov/schoollaw/rulesregs/documents/mostep_10-06.pdf.*

National Commission on Teaching and America's Future. (2007). *The cost of teacher turnover in five school districts: A pilot study.* Washington, DC: Author. Retrieved June 1, 2007, from *www.nctaf.org/resources/demonstration_projects/turnover/documents/cttexecutivesummaryfinal.pdf.*

National Council for Accreditation of Teacher Education. (2010). The road less travelled: How the developmental sciences can prepare educators to improve student achievement: Policy recommendations. Retrieved September 1, 2011, from *www.ncate.org/public/researchreports/ncateinitiatives/increasingtheapplicationofdevelopmentalscienc/tabid/706/default.aspx.*

National Institute of Child Health and Human Development, National Institutes of Health (NIH), & U.S. Department of Health and Human Services (USDHHS). (2007). *Child and adolescent development research and teacher education: Evidence-based pedagogy, policy, and practice.* Washington, DC: U.S. Government Printing Office.

Nebraska Department of Education. (2008). Title 92, Chapter 20: Approval of Teacher Education Programs. Retrieved May 27, 2012, from *www.sos.ne.gov/rules-and-regs/regsearch/rules/education_dept_of/title-92/chapter-20.pdf.*

New Mexico Public Education Department. (1998). Title 6: Primary and Secondary Education: Chapter 61: School Personnel Specific Licensure Requirements for Instructors. Retrieved May 3, 2012, from *www.nmcpr.state.nm.us/nmac/parts/title06/06.061.0002.pdf.*

North Carolina State Board of Education. (2006). Specialty Standards. Retrieved June 28, 2012, from *www.dpi.state.nc.us/docs/ihe/materials/specialtystandards.pdf.*

Osher, D., Sprague, J., Weissberg, R. P., Axelrod, J., Keenan, S., Kendziora, K., et al. (2008). A comprehensive approach to promoting social, emotional, and academic growth in contemporary schools. In A. Thomas & J. Grimes (Eds.), *Best practices in school psychology V* (Vol. 4, pp. 1263–1278). Bethesda, MD: National Association of School Psychologists.

Payton, J. W., Graczyk, P., Wardlaw, D., Bloodworth, M., Tompsett, C., & Weissberg, R. P. (2000). Social and emotional learning: A framework of promoting mental health and reducing risk behavior in children and youth. *Journal of School Health, 70,* 179–185.

Ransford, C. R., Greenberg, M. T., Domitrovich, C. E., Small, M., & Jacobson, L. (2009). The role of teachers' psychological experiences and perceptions of curriculum supports on the implementation of a social and emotional learning curriculum. *School Psychology Review, 38,* 510–532.

Reinke, W. M., Stormont, M., Herman, K. C., Puri, R., & Goel, N. (2011) Supporting children's mental health in schools: Teacher perceptions of needs, roles, and barriers. *School Psychology Quarterly, 26,* 1–13.

Reyes, M. R., Brackett, M. A., Rivers, S. E., Elbertson, N. A., & Salovey, P. (2012). The interaction effects of program training, dosage, and implementation quality on targeted student outcomes for the RULER approach to social and emotional learning. *School Psychology Review, 41,* 82–99.

Rimm-Kaufman, S. E., & Hamre, B. K. (2010). The role of psychological and developmental science in efforts to improve teacher quality. *Teachers College Record, 112,* 2988–3023.

Sarason, S. (2001). *American psychology and the schools: A critique.* Washington, DC: Teachers College Press.

Siebert, C. J. (2005). Promoting preservice teachers' success in classroom management by leveraging a local union's resources: A professional development school initiative. *Education, 125,* 385–392.

Sklad, M., Diekstra, R., De Ritter, M., & Ben, J. (2012). Effectiveness of school-based universal social, emotional, and behavioural programs: Do they enhance students' development in the area of skill, behaviour, and adjustment? *Psychology in the Schools, 49,* 892–909.

South Carolina Department of Education. (n.d.). ADEPT Performance Standards for Classroom-Based Teachers. Retrieved June 28, 2012, from *www.ed.sc.gov/agency/programs-services/50/documents/adeptstandards.pdf.*

South Dakota Department of Education. (2006). South Dakota Legislature: Teacher Preparation Program Approval. Retrieved April 4, 2012, from *http://legis.state.sd.us/rules/displayrule.aspx?rule=24:53.*

State, T. M., Kern, L., Starosta, K. M., & Mukherjee, A. D. (2011). Elementary pre-service teacher preparation in the area of social, emotional, and behavioural problems. *School Mental Health, 3,* 13–23.

Swearer, S. M., Espelage, D. L., Vaillancourt, T., & Hymel, S. (2010). What can be done about school bullying?: Linking research to educational practice. *Educational Researcher, 39,* 38–47.

Tennessee Department of Education. (2001). *Ten-*

nessee Licensure Standards and Induction Guidelines. Nashville: Author. Retrieved April 6, 2012, from *www.tennessee.gov/education/lic/doc/accttchlicstds.pdf*.

U.S. Department of Health and Human Services (USDHHS). (1999). *Mental health: A report of the Surgeon General*. Washington, DC: U.S. Government Printing Office.

U.S. News & World Report. (2012). The Top 50, Best Education Schools. Retrieved June 1, 2013, from: *http://grad-schools.usnews.rankingsandreviews.com/best-graduate-schools/top-education-schools/edu-rankings*.

U.S. Public Health Service. (2000). *Report of the Surgeon's General's Conference on Children's Mental Health: A national action agenda*. Washington, DC: Department of Health and Human Services.

Vinnes, S., Keenan, J. K., & Green, J. G. (2014, October). *Pre-service training in social-emotional development and behavior management: A review of graduate teacher education programs*. Poster presented at the annual convention of the Northeastern Educational Research Association, Trumbull, CT.

Walter, H. J., Gouze, K., & Lim, K. G. (2006). Teachers' beliefs about mental health needs in inner city elementary schools. *Journal of the American Academy for Child and Adolescent Psychiatry, 45*, 61–68.

Weare, K., & Nind, M. (2011). Mental health promotion and problem prevention in schools: What does the evidence say? *Health Promotion International, 26*, i29–i69.

Weissberg, R. P., Payton, J. W., O'Brien, M. U., & Munro, S. (2007). Social and emotional learning. In F. C. Power, R. J. Nuzzi, D. Narvaez, D. K. Lapsley, & T. C. Hunt (Eds.), *Moral education: A handbook* (Vol. 2, pp. 417–418). Westport, CT: Greenwood Press.

Wentzel, K. R. (2003). Are effective teachers like good parents?: Teaching styles and student adjustment in early adolescence. *Child Development, 73*, 287–301.

Zeichner, L., & Paige, L. (2007). *The current status and possible future for "traditional" college and university-based teacher education programs in the U.S.* (Submission to the International Alliance of Leading Education Institutes). Madison: University of Wisconsin–Madison. Retrieved from *www.intalalliance.org*.

Zins, J. E., Weissberg, R. P., Wang, M. C., & Walberg, H. J. (Eds.). (2004), *Building academic success on social and emotional learning: What does the research say?* New York: Teachers College Press.

CHAPTER 28

Inserve Preparation for Educators

Patricia A. Jennings and Jennifer L. Frank

Teacher quality has become a top priority of our national agenda to improve student academic achievement and behavior because it is evident that teachers play a critical role in shaping students' formal learning context (Eccles & Roeser, 1999). To promote academic learning and prosocial behavior, teachers do much more than simply deliver curriculum content. They set the tone of the classroom by developing supportive and encouraging relationships with their students, designing lessons that build on students' strengths and abilities, establishing and implementing behavioral guidelines in ways that promote intrinsic motivation, coaching students through conflict situations, and encouraging cooperation among students. They also play an important role in the socialization of emotional competence among children and youth by providing important role models (Denham, Bassett & Wyatt, 2007).

Teachers must navigate the complexities of the social–emotional dynamics of their classroom in order to promote academic learning, juggling long-term, often mandated learning objectives with the immediate needs and capacities of individual students. The complexity of these dynamics increases as the level of diversity grows. Factors such as racial/ethnic diversity and economic, learning ability, and linguistic differences necessitate teachers' additional reflection and sensitivity to individual students' needs and resources. These factors intensify the difficulty of simultaneously addressing both social and emotional learning (SEL) and academic learning (Downer, Maier, & Jamil, 2011).

Shulman (2004), who has studied teacher professional development (PD) for over 30 years, stated:

> Classroom teaching . . . is perhaps the most complex, most challenging, and most demanding, subtle, nuanced, and frightening activity that our species has ever invented. In fact, when I compared the complexity of teaching with that much more highly rewarded profession, "doing medicine", I concluded that the only time medicine even approaches the complexity of an average day of classroom teaching is in an emergency room during a natural disaster. (p. 504)

Yet, compared to medical students, teachers receive only a fraction of training to prepare them for the reality of their chosen occupation. Furthermore, growing numbers of children come to school unprepared, many with disruptive behavior problems (Gilliam, 2005; U.S. Department of Health and Human Services, 2000). Disruptive behavior is a common problem in classrooms with high concentrations of economically disadvantaged students (Oliver & Reschly, 2007) and children with history of behavior problems demand more effort from their teachers (Hauts, Caspi, Pianta, Arseneault, & Moffitt, 2010). Furthermore, the advent of accountability linked to high-stakes testing may intensify teacher distress, especially among those who serve children at most risk of school failure (Darling-Hammond & Sykes, 2003).

This chapter explores issues related to how educators are prepared to manage these demands and to deliver SEL curriculum content and programming. We explain the ways in which teachers' social and emotional competence (SEC) influences student learning and review approaches to promote teacher SEC. This chapter addresses the role of teacher preparation and SEC in larger school reform efforts. Finally, we offer recommendations and guidelines for improving SEL PD and mention some potential problems and pitfalls.

Features of Effective PD

The current state of teacher PD is a critical issue that warrants review. In general, "high-quality PD" is defined as a sustained and coherent learning process that "systematically nourishes the growth of educators . . . through adult learner-centered, job embedded processes" focusing on helping educators attain the knowledge and skills required to promote student achievement (Speck & Knipe, 2005, pp. 3–4).

Historically, administrators have preferred the "one-shot" workshop approach to PD, in which training is provided by outside consultants or curriculum experts via a school's inservice days focused on a specific pedagogic or subject-area topic. However, this approach has been criticized because it lacks continuity and coherence, and fails to appreciate the challenges and complexity of teachers' work (Selman, 2003). Teachers need more time to assimilate, discuss, and practice new information and skills (Garet, Porter, Desimone, Birman, & Yoon, 2001).

A National Center for Education Statistics (NCES) study (Parsad, Lewis, & Farris, 2001) found that teachers typically spent a day or less in PD on any one content area and only 18% felt that the training was connected "to a great extent" to other school improvement activities. The proportion of teachers who felt their PD activity significantly improved their teaching ranged from only 12 to 27%. Although the federal No Child Left Behind Act of 2001 requires funded PD to include activities that "are not one-day or short-term workshops or conferences" (*www2.ed.gov/policy/elsec/leg/esea02/107-110.pdf*), there is little evidence that states and districts have the capacity to monitor this requirement effectively (Jaquith, Mindich, Ruth, & Darling-Hammond, 2011).

Although current PD practices do not always comply with best-practice standards, the features of effective PD are fairly well known. Over the past decade, there have been several highly influential studies documenting the characteristics of high-quality PD practices (Garet et al., 2001; Guskey, 2000, 2003; Parsad et al., 2001). The characteristics that influence the effectiveness of PD, however, are multiple and highly complex (Guskey, 2003). Using a national probability sample of 1,027 teachers, Garet and colleagues (2001) identified three core components of PD activities that have a significant positive effect on teachers' self-reported knowledge, skills, and changes in classroom instruction: (1) a focus on content knowledge, (2) opportunities for active learning, and (3) coherence with other, related professional activities. Garet and colleagues also identified three structural features that influence the effectiveness of PD via their influence on these core features. These structural design features include (1) the form of the PD event (e.g., workshop vs. ongoing reform activities), (2) duration of the PD (short, "one-shot" training vs. ongoing training and technical assistance), and (3) activities (lecture vs. opportunities for collective participation and collaboration among participants).

Combined, these factors provide insight into how teacher PD in SEL might be structured to achieve optimal impact. PD opportunities that are presented consistently over an extended period of time and involve active group participation and collaboration are superior to the typical "one-shot" workshop approach most teachers experience. Similarly, PD that helps deepen teachers' content knowledge of key SEL concepts and theories underlying SEL program practices, while also providing opportunities for teachers to actively apply this knowledge to real-life situations, is important for helping teachers generalize and transfer their new knowledge and skills to classroom settings. Finally, PD can play an important role in helping teachers understand how the goals of SEL programs fit within the broader context of other school, district, and statewide educational goals. Next, we review the features of PD currently offered to prepare teachers to implement evidence-based SEL programs.

Features of PD in Prominent SEL Programs

High-quality PD is a critical component of effective program implementation and intervention effectiveness (Weissberg & Greenberg, 1998). However, few teacher preparation programs provide training in social and emotional knowledge and skills relevant to effective delivery of SEL content (see Schonert-Reichl et al., Chapter 27, this volume). As a result, many teachers are not well prepared to deliver SEL curricular content, generalize SEL concepts to their classroom management efforts and interactions with students, and integrate SEL concepts into other curriculum areas need specialized PD.

The Collaborative for Academic, Social, and Emotional Learning (CASEL; 2012) has identified high-quality evidence-based K–5 SEL programs. To be recommended by CASEL, programs must offer PD to teachers before they implement the program. Although there are different kinds of approaches included in the guide that may require different skills, most SEL PD programs are designed to instruct teachers in the program's theory, principles, and strategies and to help them become familiar with required curricular activities, so that they can deliver the intervention with a high degree of fidelity. Once teachers begin to implement the program, CASEL recommends ongoing support to help them generalize and integrate the SEL concepts.

For this chapter, we closely examined nine CASEL Select programs that were also rated as high quality and as having availability of training and implementation materials by the Substance Abuse and Mental Health Services Administration's (SAMHSA) National Registry of Evidence-Based Programs and Practices (NREPP; see Table 28.1). We examined each program's ratings and the program websites, and reviewed research articles reporting on the results of studies to determine the efficacy of the programs and to learn how teachers were prepared to deliver each program for the purposes of the research.

Surprisingly, very little information regarding the details of the programs' PD was available from these sources. PD programs vary in terms of what is mandatory, recommended, or entirely optional. Most programs offer a 1- to 3-day introductory workshop to introduce teachers to the program's theory and the curriculum, and some offer ongoing coaching or consultation. However, programs' PD ranged in intensity from optional, online, self-directed instruction (Second Step) to required 1-year commitment to intensive PD, including a 4-day workshop plus ongoing consultation (Open Circle).

When measured against the standard best practices, Open Circle is an outstanding example of SEL PD. The 4-day intensive training involves introduction to the program curriculum, and interactive opportunities to practice facilitation skills and to learn ways to integrate lessons throughout the school day. The training includes regular coaching visits throughout the school year to help teachers implement the program. Furthermore, Open Circle was the only program surveyed that specifically addresses teachers' SEC through an optional Prosocial Educator Program. This additional service is delivered in three 2-hour workshops that introduce the connection between teachers' self-management and effective teaching. Participants learn to identify early signs of burnout and learn strategies for managing stress. Next we address specific issues related to implementation quality in SEL PD.

Issues Related to Implementation Quality

Programs that are implemented well are more likely to produce their intended results, and teachers are more likely to implement evidence-based programs with greater quality when they receive preimplementation training and ongoing technical assistance

TABLE 28.1. Elements of PD for Nine Evidence-Based SEL Programs

Program	PD hours	PD aims and activities
Caring School Community	Varies	Understand components of the CSC program, view and discuss classroom video, plan implementation, and learn the steps to successfully implement. Learn how to build an effective learning community in which students have a sense of belonging and connectedness to school.
I Can Problem Solve	3-day workshop	Learn problem-solving skills. Pre-problem-solving skills: identifying feelings and preferences, listening and paying attention, sequencing and timing and practice. Problem solving skills: alternative solution thinking, consequential thinking, means–end thinking, and practice dialogic skills.
Incredible Years	Optional 3-day workshop	Development of classroom management skills and proactive teaching strategies, building positive relationships with students, teaching social skills and problem solving in the classroom.
Michigan Model for Health	2-day workshop	Understand the program foundation and how to use the teacher manual. Become familiar with health content areas and materials. Learn how to apply skills-based instruction to health curriculum.
Open Circle	4-day Core Training plus ongoing consultation, yearlong commitment to PD required	Core Training: Strengthen teachers' social and emotional skills, improve their facilitation and classroom management skills and learn to teach the Open Circle curriculum. Prosocial Educator Program: Explores how enhancing educators' SEC can help increase their engagement in teaching, strengthen their relationships with students, and improve their stress management, all of which lead to improved student outcomes (additional three 2-hour workshops). The Relational Educator: Explores the links between adult relationships, effective teaching, and school climate (additional three 2-hour workshops).
PATHS	Optional but strongly encouraged 2-day workshop plus ongoing consultation, 2-year process of training and support	Understand the theory/model underlying the curriculum, basic developmental knowledge regarding emotions, emotional development, and brain organization; review the different units of the curriculum, video presentations of other teachers conducting PATHS lessons; observe live presentations of the lessons, small-group discussions, and active teacher role plays. Help teachers modify lessons to match their teaching style. Ongoing training designed to help teachers generalize concepts to everyday activities in the classroom and integrate concepts into regular curriculum.
Positive Action	1-day orientation training is optional, materials allow educators to train themselves	Assist new users in understanding the program vision and objectives. Establish cohesion and shared goals among members of a group of implementers. Provide PD and helpful tips for how to achieve the best results from the program.

(continued)

TABLE 28.1. *(continued)*

Program	PD hours	PD aims and activities
Second Step	Training is available online	An online Teaching Guide provides an orientation to all aspects of the program and includes video models of the program in action. Facilitators' Toolkit outlines a process for providing onsite PD and how to implement the program.
Too Good for Violence	Optional 2- to 3-day workshop, 10-session training manual	Curriculum Training: Introduction to the program research and rationale. Instruction in applying evidence-based best practices. Learn strategies for building resiliency. Teach life skills and prevention strategies. Practice delivering the Too Good program activities. Manual: A 10-session program designed to prepare teachers to deliver Too Good.

(TA) (Durlak & DuPre, 2008). However, questions remain as to how *much* training and what *type* of training and TA are required to achieve high implementation quality. Effectiveness studies have shown great variability in program implementation when programs are scaled up. Teachers often eliminate key points of the curriculum and/or program modules (Botvin, Baker, Dusenbury, Tortu, & Botvin, 1990) and are less likely to apply the interactive teaching methods, such as the small-group activities and role plays that are essential to program success (Ennett et al., 2003).

Teachers more successfully implement evidence-based programs when they have a positive attitude toward the program, are motivated to deliver the program with fidelity, and have strong self-efficacy to implement the program well (Durlak & DuPre, 2008; Gingiss, Gottlieb, & Brink, 1994). The teachers' professional background and other characteristics of the provider may also moderate program effects (Glasgow, Lichtenstein, & Marcus, 2003). For example, teachers with high levels of burnout and low levels of principal support are less likely to implement an SEL program with a high degree of quality and fidelity (Ransford, Greenberg, Domitrovich, Small, & Jacobson, 2009). Teachers who have an extraverted interpersonal style and authoritative teaching style, generally good teaching skills, and strong group leadership skills also tend to implement the program with higher levels of quality and fidelity (Gingiss et al., 1994; Sobol et al., 1989; Tobler, 2000; Young et al., 1990). However, few preimplementation PD programs aim to promote these skills and dispositions or prevent stress and burnout.

Problems with implementation quality may result from differences between the way researchers and educators conceptualize programs. Whereas prevention research defines programs as interventions, educators consider such programs to be curricula. Interventions are clinical approaches to behavior change. Clinicians are trained to understand the psychological theories and constructs that underlie an intervention's theory of change and recognize the need for strict adherence to an intervention delivery protocol. In contrast, curricula are the teaching, learning, and assessment materials developed for a given course of study. Teachers are trained in "pedagogy", that is, instructive strategies the teacher applies to promoting student learning. Teachers typically learn to adapt curricula to match their students' background knowledge, experience, and the learning context, as well as establish learning goals set by themselves and their students. Although the priority of intervention developers is that the program be delivered with high fidelity, the priority of teachers is to meet the individual educational needs of students, which may require modifications to the program. Furthermore, teachers must juggle a variety of demands on their instructional time, and they may place a lower priority on SEL curricula than on curricular areas in which students are required to demonstrate proficiency on standardized tests.

These contrasting concepts of intervention and curriculum and the conflicting priorities teachers manage may require additional collaboration between program developers and educators to find a balance between intervention fidelity and program adaptation (SAMHSA, 2002). Research is required to better understand which parts of any given evidence-based program are modifiable and which are core to the intervention's effects and should not be modified. Furthermore, SEL PD should address the issue of modifications and adaptations explicitly rather than dictate adherence to a perfect standard of implementation fidelity, which may contribute to teachers' resistance to deliver evidence-based programming.

Professional Knowledge Relevant for SEL Instruction

Although there is emerging consensus regarding the features of effective PD design (i.e., the how and why of PD), the actual content of PD programs are intimately tied to our assumptions regarding the professional knowledge educators must possess to engage in effective teaching. Within the field of curriculum design and pedagogy, Shulman's (1987) work has been central in helping to organize thinking around the basic domains of professional knowledge that teachers must possess to deliver a curriculum well.

Table 28.2 provides an overview of the domains of professional knowledge that Shulman identified as being essential to high-quality teaching. According to this model, teachers must possess general peda-

TABLE 28.2. Domains of Professional Knowledge Necessary for Effective Teaching

Domain	Overview	Relevance
General pedagogical knowledge	Broad principles and strategies related to teaching and classroom management that transcend subject matter.	Capacity to deliver and structure learning environments to maximize learning and engagement.
Knowledge of learners	Knowledge of the characteristics and backgrounds of learners.	Help engage students in learning and anticipate and plan for barriers to learning.
Knowledge of educational contexts	Knowledge of the operation of classroom groups, communities, and cultures.	Understanding of social dynamics and how to work with them to design effective learning environments.
Knowledge of educational outcomes	Understanding the goals, purposes, and ultimate applications of learning.	Help learners establish connections between learning and real-world outcomes.
Content knowledge	Understanding the content of the subject matter being taught.	How to effectively organize information, respond to content-specific questions, and engage in critical reflection; evaluation of curricular materials.
Curriculum knowledge	Understanding the operation of materials and tools designed for teaching a particular subject at a given grade level.	How to effectively utilize instructional materials and anticipate indications/contraindications for using a particular curriculum or set of program materials under specific circumstances.
Pedagogical content knowledge	Merging of content knowledge and pedagogy.	

Note. Based on Shulman's (1987) major categories of teacher knowledge.\

gogical knowledge, such as mastery of the principles of effective classroom management, in order to structure student learning environments effectively. However, teachers must also know their students and how their backgrounds, developmental status, and prior learning experiences can be used to engage them in learning. Such knowledge is also useful in forecasting potential misunderstandings or gaps in knowledge and development that may present a barrier to learning. Similarly, teachers' knowledge of the social dynamics of the educational environment and educational outcomes helps teachers design effective learning environments and helps to engage students in learning by making concrete links to real-world outcomes. Finally, teacher content knowledge and knowledge of the curriculum itself is critical to ensure that teachers have a solid understanding of the subject matter being taught and are able to effectively utilize and (if necessary) adapt or expand the curriculum to maximize student learning.

A major contribution of Shulman's work (1987) was to introduce the concept of *pedagogical content knowledge*, which is knowledge of how to teach most effectively within a given subject area. Specifically, pedagogical content knowledge is "blending of content and pedagogy into an understanding of how particular topics, problems, or issues are organized, represented, and adapted to the diverse interests and abilities of learners" (Shulman, 1987, p. 4). In many respects, mastery of pedagogical content knowledge is the ultimate goal and ideal outcome of PD program (see Table 28.2). As Shulman's model suggests, teaching is a complex activity that requires mastery of multiple domains of knowledge and knowledge application. We would argue that effective SEL PD should not only be structured to maximize implementation fidelity, but that the actual content of professional development programs should also help to build teacher knowledge and skills in each one of these domains.

However, as our earlier review suggests, the vast majority of SEL PD focuses on promoting teachers' content and curriculum knowledge—and how to implement SEL programs with fidelity—rather than engaging teachers in the type of sustained learning that is necessary to develop strong pedagogical content knowledge. We would argue that teachers must have *general pedagogical knowledge* relevant to SEL concepts and skills or they may inadvertently model behaviors that contradict SEL ideals. For example, if an SEL program teaches students to handle conflicts by applying problem-solving skills rather than rejecting others or being aggressive, but the teacher uses forms of rejection and verbal aggression to manage disruptive behavior, then his or her behavior may undermine SEL program efficacy. Therefore, authoritative and proactive strategies for classroom management may be an important component of SEL PD.

Knowledge of learners is critical to successful SEL program implementation, including applications to everyday events that occur in the classroom. Teachers must have a general understanding of social and emotional development and what competencies are developmentally appropriate for students at their grade level. They need to understand how risk and resilience factors may interfere with or promote social and emotional competencies, and how teachers' behaviors may support resilience or increase risk. For example, teachers should understand that children exposed to violence may have aggressive tendencies that are the result of misapprehension of peers' or adults' behavior as hostile. The "hostile attribution bias" is a tendency to expect that others will behave in hostile ways. Students who exhibit signs of this bias may require extra support from teachers to help them adjust to the school setting and to work through potential conflicts with peers (Crick & Dodge, 1996; Dodge & Price, 1994). This knowledge can be included in SEL PD, so that teachers may respond proactively to such problems rather than react without understanding how their reactions may exacerbate the problem.

To create learning environments that promote SEC, teachers need *knowledge of educational contexts*. For example, when teachers understand that peer reputations for social behavior and overall levels of peer acceptance predict students' future adaptation to school and to adult life (Gest, Sesma, Masten, & Tellegen, 2006), they may become more aware of their students' peer relationships and reputations, and may focus more attention on promoting positive relationships and discouraging negative ones.

Teachers need *knowledge of educational outcomes* and *pedagogical content* to apply social and emotional concepts effectively to promote SEL in their classroom. They need to understand how they may encourage prosocial behavior and to reinforce generalization of this learning outside of class. They need this understanding to weave SEL concepts into other curriculum areas. For example, problem-solving skills may be reinforced through connecting the concepts to literature that exemplifies these skills, or to resolving daily conflicts between students. Teachers must also understand that their behavior teaches SEL concepts and skills as much, if not more than the curriculum does, and that they must monitor their behavior to ensure that they are modeling the behaviors they aim to teach.

Teacher Dispositional Traits Relevant for SEL Instruction

As with all instruction, the dispositions of the individual teacher play an important role in shaping the instruction and learning environment in which SEL programs occur. For example, Alexander (1994) builds on the ideas presented by Shulman (1987) by distinguishing between observable pedagogical practices (e.g., content, curriculum-based knowledge) and teacher's implicit *ideas, values, and beliefs* that can also influence teaching in equally powerful ways (see Table 28.3). Alexander organizes this feature of pedagogy into three domains, which include ideas, values, and beliefs about *students, society*, and *knowledge* itself. Within the domain of SEL, these implicit beliefs may be more powerful than is the case with traditional content-based instruction. It is critical that effective SEL PD anticipate and challenge common implicit beliefs that may interfere with the delivery of SEL programs. For example if a teacher believes that talking about emotions in the classroom setting is inappropriate, it will be very difficult for him or her to deliver the curriculum effectively and model the naming of specific emotions. Furthermore, a teacher who endorses an autocratic approach to classroom management may dictate solutions to interpersonal problems rather than encourage students to learn problem-solving skills.

On a related note, Banks, Leach, and Moon (1999) introduced the theoretical concept of *personal constructs* as a necessary feature for understanding effective pedagogy and instruction. Personal constructs are defined as the "complex amalgam of past knowledge, experiences of learning, and personal view of what constitutes good teaching and belief in the purposes of the subject" (pp. 95–96). Teachers' *personal constructs* are formed as a result of their own personal experiences and help to drive not only ideas, values, and beliefs, as discussed by Alexander (1994), but also, to varying degrees, their own professional knowledge. Presumably, such personal constructs are continuously reassessed during a teacher's career, so both personal and professional experiences over time give shape to these constructs. These personal beliefs and the constructs discussed earlier are most influential in shaping the informal aspects of curriculum to which students are exposed. Even a teacher who implements a given SEL curriculum with high fidelity may

TABLE 28.3. Implicit Teacher Ideas, Values, and Beliefs as They Relate to SEL Pedagogy

Domain	Overview	Relevance
Beliefs about children	Beliefs about children's development, their needs, process of learning.	Presentation of ideas, curriculum delivery and coverage.
Beliefs about society	Beliefs about the needs of society in relation to education and needs of the individual to function in society.	Curriculum emphasis and coverage. Programming for generalization.
Beliefs about knowledge	Beliefs regarding children's way of knowing/understanding. Cultural influences on knowledge.	Anticipating and making thoughtful adaptations to accommodate differences due to developmental level, culture, and other relevant background characteristics.

undermine positive gains if societal or covert classroom curricula are not consistent with the ideas being taught. Next we address the less explicit dimensions of curriculum that may be most salient for SEL.

Dimensions of Curriculum Implementation Relevant for SEL Instruction

There is an emerging consensus regarding the features of an effective SEL curriculum. However, another weakness of the focus on promoting fidelity to this curriculum is that it fails to prepare teachers to recognize and proactively shape various aspects of the instructional environment necessary to support SEL goals. Within the field of education, there is increasing recognition that students' learning is not limited to just what they gain from the explicit curriculum, which includes the formal written set of text and materials to which students are exposed intentionally. Rather, students' learning and socialization are a function of this explicit curriculum in conjunction with what they learn from other, more implicit curricula (see Table 28.4). For example, Cortes (1981) discussed the *social curriculum*, which shapes what children learn through interactions with family, peer groups, neighborhoods, and various media outlets. Although not a formal written curriculum, the social curriculum is a powerful socialization force shaping children's assumptions about the social validity of SEL ideals.

Similarly, the organizational structure and operation of day-to-day school activities give shape to the "hidden" or "covert curriculum" through which children learn dynamics of social power and privilege (Longstreet & Shane, 1993). Observational learning, which occurs though watching adult-to-adult or adult-to-student interactions, is a powerful aspect of the hidden curriculum that provides instruction in a variety of SEL-relevant domains such as communication, self-management, relationship building, and conflict resolution (Bandura, 1985).

Finally, we would add the "null curriculum", which represents the totality of content that is not explicitly taught in school settings, as a final feature shaping student SEL in school settings. In many respects, what "is not taught" or discussed in school contexts sends as powerful a message to students as what *is* taught explicitly. For example, if issues germane to SEL, such as violence prevention and drug abuse prevention, are not a part of the regular curriculum, it indirectly sends a message that these issues are not

TABLE 28.4. Formal and Informal Curricula That Shape Student Learning

Curriculum type	Description	Relevance
Explicit curriculum	Formal written set of text and materials that guide learning and is intentionally delivered.	High-quality curriculum and materials are prerequisite for student learning. Teachers must be proficient in utilizing the curriculum.
Societal curriculum	Ongoing, informal, curriculum of family, peer groups, neighborhoods, mass media, and other socializing forces that "educate" us throughout our lives (Cortes, 1981).	Awareness of the societal curriculum students and teachers are exposed to is essential to understanding implicit beliefs, assumptions, and effective planning for generalization.
Hidden or covert curriculum	What children learn from the very nature and organizational design of the public school, as well as from the behaviors and attitudes of teachers and administrators (Longstreet & Shane, 1993).	Outside of direct instruction, observation of teacher behavior, school structures, and adult interactions provides a context for observational learning of SEL principles that can facilitate, or undermine, core instruction.
Null curriculum	Choices made regarding what is *not* taught.	What is not taught also communicates values to students.

important and are irrelevant to schooling. A power of SEL programs in general is that they make developmentally important topics part of the active curriculum and implicitly teach children the standards of acceptable behavior and performance. Considered together, although a teacher's dispositional traits are naturally tied to the quality of his or her instruction, they are particularly relevant for SEL because of their influence on the more informal dimensions of classroom curriculum.

The Importance of Adult SEC

We have examined the current status of SEL PD and how it might be improved by broadening the approach beyond content and curriculum knowledge, and adherence to program fidelity. The processes involved in effectively obtaining the knowledge and dispositions necessary to teach and model SEL ideals, as well as the understanding and recognition of opportunities to deliver the societal and hidden curricula, require from teachers a high degree of SEC. Now we consider the role that teachers' SEC plays in the successful implementation of SEL programming.

The Prosocial Classroom Model

The prosocial classroom model establishes teachers' SEC as an organizational framework that can be examined in relation to student and classroom outcomes (Jennings & Greenberg, 2009). According to this model, the teacher's well-being and SEC influence the classroom climate and student academic and behavioral outcomes. This effect is mediated by teacher–student relationships and quality of classroom management, and by effective SEL program implementation (see Figure 28.1). According to CASEL (2012), SEC comprises five dimensions: self-awareness, social awareness, responsible decision making, self-management, and relationship management. Although SEL programs apply these dimensions to child development, these dimensions may also be applied to adults. Jennings and Greenberg (2009) proposed that in order to teach children these competencies, teachers must demonstrate a degree of SEC. According to Jennings and Greenberg, teachers with SEC demonstrate high self-awareness: They recognize their emotions, emotional patterns, and tendencies, and can generate emotions such as joy and enthusiasm to motivate others' learning. They have an

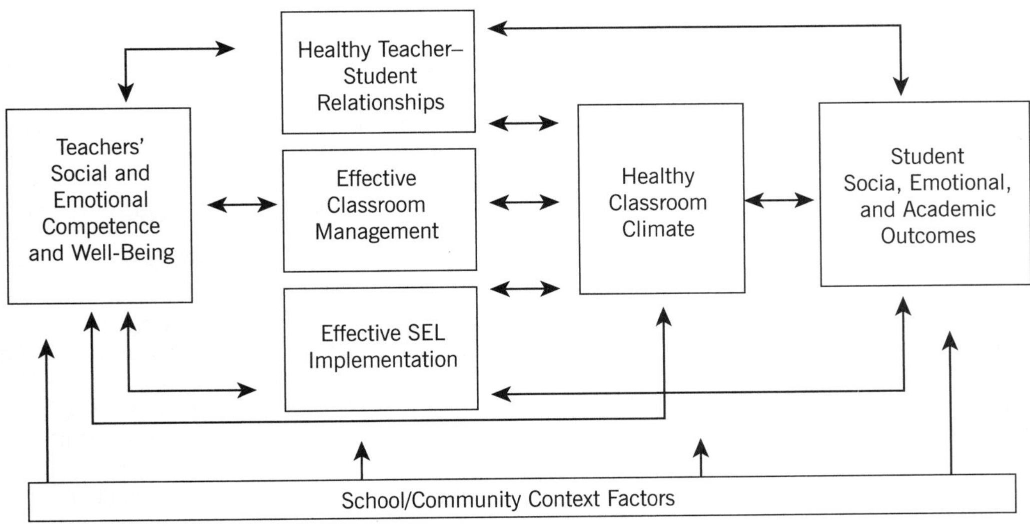

FIGURE 28.1. A model of teacher well-being and SEC, support, and classroom and student outcomes. From Jennings and Greenberg (2009). Copyright 2009 by Sage Publications, Inc. Reprinted by permission.

accurate understanding of their capabilities and understand their emotional strengths and weaknesses. Teachers with SEC also demonstrate high social awareness: They understand how their emotional reactions affect others. These teachers also recognize and understand others' emotions, and they build strong and supportive relationships through mutual understanding and cooperation. They negotiate solutions to conflict situations effectively and are culturally sensitive, understanding that others may have different perspectives than they do, which they take into consideration when interacting with students, parents, and colleagues.

High-SEC teachers display prosocial values. They respect their students and their students' families, and understand how their decisions may affect them. They also take responsibility for their actions and decisions. SEC teachers know how to regulate their emotions and their behavior, even when emotionally aroused by challenging situations. They manage their emotions in healthy ways that facilitate positive classroom outcomes without compromising their health. They set limits firmly but respectfully, yet they are comfortable with a level of ambiguity that comes from allowing students to figure things out for themselves.

SEC is associated with psychological well-being. When teachers experience mastery over social and emotional challenges, they feel more efficacious, and teaching becomes more enjoyable and rewarding (Goddard, Hoy, & Woolfolk Hoy, 2004). When they experience distress, their ability to provide emotional and instructional support to their students is impaired. Teachers' SEC and well-being are reflected in their classroom behavior and interactions with students, a primary mechanism through which socialization processes take place; teachers with higher levels of SEC provide higher levels of classroom organization and emotional and instructional support associated with a quality classroom climate (Hamre & Pianta, 2001).

Teacher Stress and SEC

High levels of stress impair SEC. Teachers report that having to cope with their negative emotional responses to student behaviors is a major stressor that impacts their performance (Carson, Weiss, & Templin, 2010; Montgomery & Rupp, 2005; Sutton & Wheatley, 2003). Students' misbehavior can provoke negative emotions such as frustration, anger, guilt, and sadness that can have a negative effect on teachers' instruction (Emmer & Stough, 2001). Experiencing frequent negative emotions may impair teachers' intrinsic motivation and self-efficacy (Kavanagh & Bower, 1985). Over time, constant distress can impair teachers' performance and may lead to burnout (Tsouloupas, Carson, Matthews, Grawitch, & Barber, 2010), deterioration in teacher performance, and increased student misbehavior (Osher et al., 2007). In contrast, teachers who regularly experience more positive emotions may be more resilient (Cohn, Brown, Fredrickson, & Conway, 2009; Gu & Day, 2007), intrinsically motivated, and better able to cope with the complex demands of teaching (Sutton & Wheatley, 2003). Teachers' enthusiasm is positively related to both students' motivation and their enjoyment of school (Frenzel, Goetz, Ludtke, Pekrun, & Sutton, 2009).

When teachers do not have the necessary resources to manage successfully the emotional challenges of teaching, students are less engaged (Marzano, Marzano, & Pickering, 2003). As the classroom climate deteriorates, it triggers a "burnout cascade" (Jennings & Greenberg, 2009). Increasing student misbehavior contributes to the deteriorating classroom climate, and the teacher becomes emotionally exhausted as she tries to manage it. Out of frustration, the teacher may become reactive and punitive, which may impair student motivation and contribute a cycle of classroom disruption (Osher et al., 2007).

Supporting teachers' stress management and SEC may be key to optimizing their classroom performance and ability to provide SEL to their students. Recently, several PD programs designed to promote teachers' SEC and address stress have been developed.

A growing number of interventions have been developed to apply a mindfulness-based approach to support teachers' SEC and promote prosocial student outcomes (Jennings, Roeser, & Lantieri, 2012; Roeser, Skinner, Beers, & Jennings, 2012). *Mindfulness* refers to a particular form of attention characterized by intentionally focusing on the present moment with a curious, nonjudgmental attitude (Kabat-Zinn, 1994). Mindfulness is conceptualized as both a way of paying attention and as the practice of paying attention in this way. Mindful awareness practices (MAPs) typically involve directing and maintaining attention on a specific target, such as the breath, but there are numerous other approaches (Vago & Silbersweig, 2012). Mindfulness-based interventions reduce stress and promote well-being among adults (see Eberth & Sedlmeier, 2012, for a recent meta-analysis). MAPs may also promote self-awareness and self-regulation—two important dimensions of SEC (Vago & Silbersweig, 2012).

Several PD programs that have evolved apply a mindfulness-based approach to supporting teachers' well-being and SEC (Flook, Goldberg, Pinger, Bonus & Davidson, 2013; Jennings, Frank, Snowberg, Coccia, & Greenberg, 2013; Jennings, Snowberg, Coccia, & Greenberg, 2011; Roeser et al., 2013; Simon, Harnett, Nagler, & Thomas, 2009). These programs aim to improve teachers' SEC and well-being by cultivating mindfulness-related skills and mindsets, the social and emotional climate of the classroom environment, the ways in which teachers interact with students (especially those whose behavior they find challenging), and teachers' efficacy in delivering the SEL curriculum more effectively. Research has just begun, and there is a need for well-designed clinical trials that assess teachers' health and mental health outcomes, as well as the quality of their teaching and the social and academic outcomes of their students. These data will provide the evidence required to determine whether such approaches should be included in comprehensive SEL PD.

Teacher SEC, SEL, and Education Reform

SEL is a critical component of school reform. Although academic success is important, we also want schools to "graduate responsible, caring, and emotionally intelligent students who are prepared to be lifelong learners, engaged citizens, and productive workers" (Zins, Walberg, & Weissberg, 2004, p. 33). A supportive social and emotional school climate creates the conditions for academic learning. Indeed, we now know that SEL programs can boost academic achievement (Durlak, Weissberg, Dymnicki, Taylor, & Schellinger, 2011). However, to scale-up SEL programming will require changes in policy that prioritize teacher education and support.

In general, both typical PD and SEL PD do not meet the standards for best practice. However, the typical "one-shot" workshop PD results from the fact that teacher PD is not very highly prioritized in most school districts. As a result, time constraints and a lack of resources continually reinforce the status quo. Operating within these limitations, SEL program developers have been required to fit their PD into the limited time frames that are usually available. Furthermore, given the extensive knowledge base and skills set that teachers need to implement SEL fully, it may be unrealistic to expect specific SEL programs to provide the comprehensive training that teachers require.

Given the complexity of the skills and knowledge required for teachers to deliver the SEL curriculum and model SEL ideals in their behavior, teachers need to have a broad understanding of social and emotional development and how it relates to academic learning. They also need opportunities to develop their own SEC, so that they have the necessary self-awareness and self-regulation to monitor their behavior to ensure they are modeling appropriate behavior. Finally, they need to learn how to manage the stress associated with teaching, so that they can maintain composure when they encounter socially and emotionally stressful situations. Next we provide guidelines and recommendations for ways policymakers and educators can make systematic changes in teacher education and PD that will prepare teachers to create and maintain classrooms that support SEL and deliver evidence-based programming effectively.

Guidelines and Recommendations

Considering the extensive knowledge base and skills set we described earlier, as a natural companion to studies and practicum in classroom management, teacher dispositions, and child development, SEL should be fully integrated into preservice teacher preparation at the undergraduate level. This learning and development can continue during the first few years of a teacher's career with the support of teacher induction and mentoring programs. Training in individual SEL programs can then be more easily integrated into later comprehensive PD systems that recognize both the broad knowledge base and skills set required, as well as the specifics of a particular program curriculum.

Graduate programs can also offer specializations in SEL. For example, the University of British Columbia (n.d.) offers a bachelor of arts degree and teaching certificate with a concentration in SEL and development (2013/14 UBC Teacher Education Viewbook). Graduates of these programs can become leaders in school-based initiatives to provide SEL-related PD and coaching to inservice teachers on a regular basis. In this way, schools can begin to build systematically the capacity to integrate an understanding of SEL at all levels of the school community. With strong school-level support and a solid knowledge and skills base in place, teachers will be much better prepared to deliver SEL programs effectively.

Finally, more research is required to understand better the preparation teachers need to create SEL-friendly classrooms and deliver SEL effectively. Research is required to examine how programs designed to help teachers manage stress and develop SEC may add value to SEL PD and implementation quality. Furthermore, research can help us understand how much and what type of PD is most helpful for SEL program scale up.

Potential Problems and Pitfalls

There are numerous potential problems and pitfalls involved in the reform of teacher education in general (Levine, 2006). Differences in opinion between educators and policymakers regarding basics such as what education is most effective in preparing teachers undermine successful teacher education reform. Finally, there is a dearth of high-quality research to provide guidance to teacher education reform efforts. The ideas presented earlier will be subject to these same challenges. Teacher preparation in the United States is conducted by a massive and diverse group of institutions of higher education. The teacher certification programs they offer are typically controlled by mandates from the states' departments of education. The recommendations described earlier will require not only changes in policy at the state level but also extensive cooperation and coordination between institutions that prepare teachers and those that deliver educational services. Teacher induction and mentoring programs will be required to make the transition from preservice to inservice training and the development of a seamless, coherent process. Furthermore, school leaders will need training to support the process. These reforms will require additional resources, and policymakers will need to articulate the importance of these changes to their tax-paying constituents. As is the case for many reform efforts, the high turnover in district and school leadership positions, as well as high teacher turnover, puts such efforts at risk of failure. Nevertheless, unless substantial changes are made in the ways we currently prepare teachers for their future roles, many teachers will not be favorably disposed or possess the necessary initial knowledge and skills set to appreciate fully and participate in SEL programming.

Summary and Conclusion

We have reviewed the features of effective teacher PD and the current state of SEL PD. We have explored professional knowledge and teacher dispositions that are relevant for SEL instruction, and how these and best practices in PD might be applied to improving SEL PD. We addressed the importance of teacher social and emotional development to effective classroom management, supportive teacher–student relationships, and effective SEL program implementation, and how these factors contribute to classroom climates that support prosocial behavior and academic success. We explored how teachers' stress and burnout may impair SEC and novel approaches to reducing stress and promoting SEC. Finally, we addressed how SEL PD may be expanded and integrated into preservice and inservice PD, and the potential problems and pitfalls of doing so.

Teacher effectiveness and professional improvement are coming to the forefront of school reform efforts. To improve school conditions and support teachers' care for their students and commitment to the profession, while improving students' academic and social–emotional growth, these critical issues demand greater attention from educational policymakers.

References

Alexander, R. (1994). Analysing practice. In J. Borune (Ed.), *Thinking through primary practice* (pp. 16–21). London: Routledge.

Bandura, A. (1985). *Social foundations of thought and action*. Englewood Cliffs, NJ: Prentice Hall.

Banks, F., Leach, J., & Moon, B. (1999). New understandings of teachers' pedagogic knowledge. In J. Leach & B. Moon (Eds.), *Learners and pedagogy* (pp. 89–110). London: Paul Chapman.

Botvin, G. J., Baker, E., Dusenbury, L., Tortu, S., & Botvin, E. M. (1990). Preventing adolescent drug abuse through a multimodal cognitive-behavioral approach: Results of a 3-year study. *Journal of Consulting and Clinical Psychology, 58*(4), 437–446.

Carson, R. L., Weiss, H. M., & Templin, T. J. (2010). Ecological momentary assessment: A research method for studying the daily lives of teachers. *International Journal of Research and Method in Education, 33*, 165–182.

Cohn, M. A., Brown, S. L., Fredrickson, B. L., Milkels, J. A., & Conway, A. M. (2009). Happiness unpacked: Positive emotions increase life satisfaction by building resilience. *Emotion, 9*(3), 361–368.

Collaborative for Academic, Social, and Emotional Learning (CASEL). (2012). *2013 CASEL guide: Effective social and emotional learning programs—Preschool and elementary school edition*. Chicago: Author.

Cortes, C. E. (1981). The societal curriculum: Implications for multiethnic educations. In J. A. Banks (Ed.), *Education in the 80s: Multiethnic education* (pp. 24–32). Washington, DC: National Education Association.

Crick, N. R., & Dodge, K. A. (1996). Social information-processing mechanisms in reactive and proactive aggression. *Child Development, 67*, 993–1002.

Darling-Hammond, L., & Sykes, G. (2003). Wanted: A national teacher supply policy for education: The right way to meet the "highly qualified teacher" challenge. *Education Policy Analysis Archives, 11*(33), 1–55.

Denham, S., Bassett, H. H., & Wyatt, T. (2007). The socialization of emotional competence. In J. E. Grusec & P. D. Hastings (Eds.), *The handbook of socialization: Theory and research* (pp. 614–637). New York: Guilford Press.

Dodge, K. A., & Price, J. M. (1994). On the relation between social information processing and socially competent behavior in early school-aged children. *Child Development, 65*, 1385–1397.

Downer, J. T., Maier, M., & Jamil, F. (2011). Implications of information processing theory for professional development of early educators. In R. Pianta, C. Howes, & B. Hamre (Eds.), *Effective professional development in early childhood education* (pp. 233–244). New York: Brookes.

Durlak, J. A., & DuPre, E. P. (2008). Implementation matters: Aa review of research on the influence of implementation on program outcomes and the factors affecting implementation. *American Journal of Community Psychology, 41*, 327–350.

Durlak, J. A., Weissberg, R. P., Dymnicki, A. B., Taylor, R. D., & Schellinger, K. B. (2011). The impact of enhancing students' social and emotional learning: A meta-analysis of school-based universal interventions. *Child Development, 82*, 405–432.

Eberth, J., & Sedlmeier, P. (2012). The effects of mindfulness meditation: A meta-analysis. *Mindfulness, 3*, 174–189.

Eccles, J. S., & Roeser, R. (1999). School and community influences on human development. In M. H. Bornstein & M. E. Lamb (Eds.), *Developmental psychology: An advanced textbook* (4th ed., pp. 503–554). Mahwah, NJ: Erlbaum.

Emmer, E. T., & Stough, L. M. (2001). Classroom management: A critical part of educational psychology, with implications for teacher education. *Educational Psychologist, 36*, 103–112.

Ennett, S. T., Ringwalt, C. L., Thorne, J., Rohrbach, L. A., Vincus, A., Simons-Rudolph, A., et al. (2003). A comparison of current practice in school-based substance use prevention programs with meta-analysis findings. *Prevention Science, 4*(1), 1–14.

Flook, L., Goldberg, S. B., Pinger, L., Bonus, K., & Davidson, R. J. (2013). Mindfulness for teachers: A pilot study to assess effects on stress, burnout, and teaching efficacy. *Mind, Brain, and Education, 7*(3), 182–195.

Frenzel, A. C., Goetz, T., Ludtke, O., Pekrun, R., & Sutton, R. E. (2009). Emotional transmission in the classroom: Exploring the relationship between teacher and student enjoyment. *Journal of Educational Psychology, 101*, 705–716.

Garet, M. S., Porter, A. C., Desimone, L., Birman, B. F., & Yoon, K. S. (2001). What makes professional development effective?: Results from a national sample of teachers. *American Educational Research Journal, 38*(4), 915–945.

Gest, S. D., Sesma, A., Masten, A., & Tellegen, A. (2006). Childhood peer reputation as a predictor of competence and symptoms 10 years later. *Journal of Abnormal Child Psychology, 34*, 509–526.

Gilliam, W. S. (2005). *Prekindergarteners left behind: Expulsion rates in state prekindergarten programs.* New York: Foundation for Child Development.

Gingiss, P. L., Gottlieb, N. H., & Brink, S. G. (1994). Increasing teacher receptivity toward use of tobacco prevention education programs. *Journal of Drug Education, 24*(2), 163–176.

Glasgow, R. E., Lichtenstein, E., & Marcus, A. C. (2003). Why don't we see more translation of health promotion research to practice?: Rethinking the efficacy-to-effectiveness transition. *American Journal of Public Health, 93*(8), 1261–1267.

Goddard, R. D., Hoy, W. K., & Woolfolk Hoy, A. (2004). Collective efficacy beliefs: Theoretical developments, empirical evidence, and future directions. *Educational Researcher, 33*, 3–13.

Gu, Q., & Day, C. (2007). Teachers' resilience: A necessary condition for effectiveness. *Teaching and Teacher Education, 23*, 1302–1316.

Guskey, T. (2000). *Evaluating PD.* Thousand Oaks, CA: Corwin Press.

Guskey, T. R. (2003). What makes PD effective? *Phi Deltan Kappan, 84*, 748–750.

Hamre, B., & Pianta, R. C. (2001). Early teacher–child relationships and trajectory of school outcomes through eighth grade. *Child Development, 72*, 625–638.

Hauts, R. M., Caspi, A., Pianta, R. C., Arseneault, L., & Moffitt, T. E. (2010). The challenging pupil in the classroom: The effect of the child on the teacher. *Psychological Science, 21*, 1802–1810.

Jaquith, A., Mindich, D., Ruth, C. W., & Darling-Hammond, L. (2011). Teacher professional learning in the U.S.: Case studies of state policies and strategies. *Education Digest, 77*(2), 33–39.

Jennings, P. A., Frank, J., Snowberg, K. E., Coccia, M. A., & Greenberg, M. T. (2013). Improving classroom learning environments by Cultivating Awareness and Resilience in Education (CARE): Results of a randomized controlled trial. *School Psychology Quarterly, 28*(4), 374–390.

Jennings, P. A., & Greenberg, M. T. (2009). The prosocial classroom: Teacher social and emotional competence in relation to student and classroom outcomes. *Review of Educational Research, 79*(1), 491–525.

Jennings, P. A., Roeser, R., & Lantieri, L. (2012). Supporting educational goals through cultivating mindfulness: Approaches for teachers and students. In A. Higgins-D'Alessandro, M. Corrigan, & P. M. Brown (Eds.), *The handbook of prosocial education* (pp. 371–397). New York: Rowman & Littlefield.

Jennings, P. A., Snowberg, K. E., Coccia, M. A., & Greenberg, M. T. (2011). Improving classroom learning environments by Cultivating Awareness and Resilience in Education (CARE): Results of two pilot studies. *Journal of Classroom Interactions, 46*, 27–48.

Kabat-Zinn, J. (1994). *Wherever you go, there you are: Mindfulness meditation in everyday life.* New York: Hyperion.

Kavanagh, D. J., & Bower, G. (1985). Mood and self-efficacy: Impact of joy and sadness on perceived capabilities. *Cognitive Therapy and Research, 9*, 507–525.

Levine, A. (2006). *Educating school teachers.* Washington, DC: Education Schools Project. Retrieved October, 22, 2013, from *www.edschools.org/pdf/educating_teachers_report.pdf.*

Longstreet, W. S., & Shane, H. G. (1993). *Curriculum for a new millennium.* Boston: Allyn & Bacon.

Marzano, R. J., Marzano, J. S., & Pickering, D. J. (2003). *Classroom management that works.* Alexandra, VA: Association for Supervision and Curriculum Development.

Montgomery, C., & Rupp, A. A. (2005). A meta-analysis for exploring the diverse causes and effects of stress in teachers. *Canadian Journal of Education, 28*, 458–486.

Oliver, R. M., & Reschly, D. J. (2007). *Effective classroom management: Teacher preparation and PD.* Washington, DC: National Comprehensive Center for Teacher Quality.

Osher, D., Sprague, J., Weissberg, R. P., Axelrod, J., Keenan, S., & Kendziora, K. T. (2007). A comprehensive approach to promoting social, emotional, and academic growth in contemporary schools. In A. Thomas & J. Grimes (Eds.), *Best practices in school psychology* (5th ed., Vol. 4, pp. 1263–1278). Bethesda, MD: National Association of School Psychologists.

Parsad, B., Lewis, L., & Farris, E. (2001). *Teacher Preparation and Professional Development: 2000* (NCES 2001–088). Washington, DC: U.S. Department of Education, National Center for Education Statistics.

Ransford, C. R., Greenberg, M. T., Domitrovich, C. E., Small, M., & Jacobson, L. (2009). The role of teachers' psychological experiences and perceptions of curriculum supports on the implementation of a social and emotional learning curriculum, *School Psychology Review 38*(4), 510–532.

Roeser, R. W., Schonert-Reichl, K. A., Jha, A., Cullen, M., Wallace, L., Wilensky, R., et al. (2013). Mindfulness training and reductions in teacher stress and burnout: Results from two randomized, waitlist-control field trials. *Journal of Educational Psychology. 105*(3), 787–804.

Roeser, R. W., Skinner, E., Beers, J., & Jennings, P. A. (2012). Mindfulness training and teachers' PD: An emerging area of research and practice. *Child Development Perspectives,* 6, 167–173.

Selman, R. L. (2003). *The promotion of social awareness: Powerful lessons from the partnership of developmental theory and classroom practice.* New York: Russell Sage Foundation.

Shulman, L. S. (1987). Knowledge and teaching: Foundations of the new reform. *Harvard Educational Review, 57,* 1–22.

Shulman, L. S. (2004). *The wisdom of practice: Essays on teaching, learning, and learning to teach.* San Francisco: Jossey-Bass.

Simon, A., Harnett, S., Nagler, E., & Thomas, L. (2009). *Research on the effect of the Inner Resilience Program on teacher and student wellness and classroom climate: Final report.* New York: Metis Associates.

Sobol, D. F., Dent, C. W., Gleason, L., Brannon, B. R., Johnson, C. A., & Flay, B. R. (1989). The integrity of smoking prevention curriculum delivery. *Health Education Research, 4, 59–67.*

Speck, M., & Knipe, C. (2005). *Why can't we get it right?: Designing high-quality PD for standards-based schools* (2nd ed.). Thousand Oaks, CA: Corwin Press.

Substance Abuse and Mental Health Services Administration (SAMHSA). (2002). Report to Congress on the prevention and treatment of co-occurring substance abuse disorders and mental disorders. Retrieved October, 22, 2013, from *www.samhsa.gov/reports/congress2002.*

Sutton, R. E., & Wheatley, K. E. (2003). Teachers' emotions and teaching: A review of the literature and directions for future research. *Educational Psychology Review, 15,* 327–358.

Tobler, N. S. (2000). Lessons learned. *Journal of Primary Prevention, 20*(4), 261–274.

Tortu, S., & Botvin, G. (1989). School-based smoking prevention: The teacher training process. *Preventive Medicine, 18*(2), 280–289.

Tsouloupas, C. N., Carson, R. L., Matthews, R., Grawitch, M. J., & Barber, L. K. (2010). Exploring the association between teachers' perceived student misbehaviour and emotional exhaustion: The importance of teacher efficacy beliefs and emotion regulation. *Educational Psychology, 30,* 173–189.

University of British Columbia. (n.d.). 2013/14 UBC Teacher Education Viewbook. Retrieved from *http://teach.educ.ubc.ca/201314-ubc-teacher-education-viewbook.*

U.S. Department of Health and Human Services. (2000). Report of the Surgeon's General's Conference on Children's Mental Health: A national action agenda. Retrieved October, 22, 2013, from *www.surgeongeneral.gov/topics/cmh/childreport.html.*

Vago, D. R., & Silbersweig, D. A. (2012). Self-awareness, self-regulation, and self-transcendence (S-ART): A framework for understanding the neurobiological mechanisms of mindfulness. *Frontiers in Human Neuroscience,* 6, 1–30.

Weissberg, R. P., & Greenberg, M. T. (1998). School and community competence-enhancement and prevention programs. In I. E. Siegel & K. A. Renninger (Eds.), *Handbook of child psychology: Vol. 4. Child psychology in practice* (5th ed., pp. 877–954). New York: Wiley.

Young, R. L., deMoor, C., Wilder, M. B., Gully, S., Hovell, M. F., & Elder, J. P. (1990). Correlates of health facilitator performance in a tobacco-use prevention program: Implications for recruitment. *Journal of School Health, 60*(9), 463–467.

Zins, J. E., Walberg, H. J., & Weissberg, R. P. (2004). Getting to the heart of school reform: Social and emotional learning for academic success. *NASP Communiqué, 33*(3), 33–35.

CHAPTER 29

Developing Socially, Emotionally, and Cognitively Competent School Leaders and Learning Communities

Janet Patti, Peter Senge, Claudia Madrazo, and Robin S. Stern

The School Leadership Landscape

Leadership is the second most influential school-level factor on student achievement, after teacher quality (Hallinger & Heck, 1998; Waters, Marzano & McNulty, 2004). Effective leadership inspires school transformation and instructional best practices that lead to student success (Leithwood, Louis, Anderson, & Wahlstrom, 2004). Principals positively shape school culture when they distribute leadership and build learning communities of self-directed professionals who assume responsibility for ongoing innovation in their teaching (Louis, Leithwood, Wahlstrom, & Anderson, 2010). School leaders have a great opportunity to impact student growth and achievement by shaping a culture that cultivates motivated, engaged, and effective teacher leaders.

Many additional factors, however, influence the success of a school, such as teacher quality, parent involvement, and human and fiscal resources. Furthermore, political agendas drive policies that impact our schools. Equity and access continue to be misunderstood and neglected because the center of the education conversation remains focused on competitiveness in the global marketplace. Accountability has become the nostrum to ensure that every child achieves school success and graduates career-ready, often neglecting how we can develop schools' capacities to achieve these desired results (West, Peck, & Reitzug, 2010). Academic achievement is the vehicle at the heart of this current crusade to reform education; however, we must be mindful of the development of students' character, cooperative spirit, and sense of purpose and responsibility—the capacities for life success. Without these important life skills, too many young people continue to fail in our systems: socially, emotionally, and academically.

A nation's belief about the purpose of school shapes the policies that drive curricula and instruction, but school leaders' beliefs and capabilities are central to shaping the culture that makes it happen. It is essential that we invest in high-quality leadership development to create and sustain school cultures that cultivate administrator and teacher leaders and school success (Patti, Holzer, Stern, & Brackett, 2012; Sparks, 2009). In this chapter, we introduce leadership development that is anchored in the five core competencies of social and emotional learning (SEL): self-awareness, social awareness, responsible decision making, self-management, and relationship skills (Weissberg & Cascarino, 2013). We describe how this type of social, emotional, and cognitive development can prepare school leaders at all levels to facilitate and sustain systemic change in schools. We provide a theoretical basis for this work and propose four core leadership skills: actionable self-reflection, facilitating and engaging in conversations, building generative relationships, and systems thinking. Finally, we offer guidelines and recommendations based on a promising model that builds the individual and collective capacity of all stakeholders to lead schools and sustain systemic change. We conclude the chapter by addressing some problems and pitfalls that may be encountered while pursuing this path of leadership development.

Current Trends in the Preparation of School Leaders

To date, no magic bullet has been found to attract and prepare the best and the brightest to become effective school leaders. Extensive field-based experiences supported by site-based mentoring or coaching continue to be among the most desirable approaches for aspiring leaders' development, but the costs to sustain such models limit their availability (Mitgang & Gill, 2012, p. 12). Furthermore, fewer people strive for the position of principal, with its heavy accountability markers tied to student achievement on standardized tests and expectations of school "turnaround", often within a year of stepping into the leadership shoes (Byrne-Jiménez & Orr, 2012).

As the role of school leaders in improving student learning has become paramount, so too has the importance of their development. School leaders must master a plethora of skills, from teaching and learning to management and community outreach. To accomplish effectively the wide gamut of tasks required, the school leader should encourage collaborative leadership structures that include teachers and staff (Leithwood & Mascall, 2008). Over two decades of research support the notion of shared leadership (Leithwood & Jantzi, 2000; Minckler, 2014; Senge, 1997). In order to truly share leadership, leaders build social capital; they motivate and develop potential leadership candidates from within their staff to be able and willing to take on responsibilities and assume leadership roles (Minckler, 2014). School leaders must be cognizant of this need when they hire staff members. Additionally, they must foster collaborative networks of people who contribute to all aspects of the mission of the school. Successful implementation of any reform, including collaborative leadership structures, is influenced by the perceptions of subgroup members who feel they have access to resources and expertise outside their own subgroup (Penuel, Fishman, Yamaguchi, & Gallagher, 2007). This bodes well for school leaders who have the skills to transform a school's culture into a community of continuous learners based on sharing resources through collegiality and trust. The traditional leader, who drives change from the top, often creates change-resistant organizations by failing to tap the leadership capacities of people at all levels within the organization (Leithwood & Mascall, 2008; Senge, 1996, 1997; Spillane & Diamond, 2007). Decades of research support the notion that transformational school leaders—leaders who motivate and enhance others' growth—are best positioned to create a culture that supports needed change (Minckler, in press). The link between transformational leadership and emotional intelligence is growing (Hackett & Hortman, 2008), but the research base on emotional intelligence and educational leadership is still in its nascent stages, with much of it based on individuals' self-reports. Cook (2006) examined the relationship among 143 elementary school principals' self-ratings on the Emotional Intelligence Appraisal, which measures four of the five SEL core competencies (self-awareness, social awareness, self-management, and relationship management) and a locally developed leadership improvement tool, which assesses leadership in nine areas: (1) leadership attributes, (2) visionary leadership, (3) community leadership, (4) instructional leadership, (5) data-driven improvement, (6) organization to improve student learning, (7) organization to improve staff efficacy, (8) cultural competence, and (9) education management. All of these, except for cultural competence and community leadership, were significantly related to principals' self-assessments of their emotional intelligence.

Hackett and Hortman (2008) explored the relationship among principals' emotional dispositions and leadership skills using the self-report version of the Emotional Competence Inventory–University edition (ECI-U) a measure of emotional intelligence competencies, and the Multifactor Leadership Questionnaire (MLQ), a measure of transformational leadership behaviors (Bass & Avolio, 2004). They found significant positive correlations between four of the five core competencies, particularly the social and relationship management competencies, with one or more of the five transformational leadership scales. Stone, Parker, and Wood (2005) also explored the relationship between emotional intelligence (EI) and aspects of school leadership. They wanted to identify specific emotional and social competencies required of principals and vice-principals that would lead to their success in meeting the demands and responsibilities of their jobs. Their sample comprised 464 principals and vice-principals from nine school boards in Ontario, Canada. The leaders who were designated as above average leaders by supervisors and staff scored higher in the four broad EI dimensions of intrapersonal and interpersonal relationships, adaptability, and stress management, and in overall EI than did those who were considered to be below average leaders.

Although development in leaders' EI is widely accepted as essential to effective performance in global business organizations (Prati, Douglas, Ferris, Ammeter, & Buckley, 2003), to educators, the concept of EI within leadership development is still new. Furthermore, although there are clear national standards for principals (Council of Chief State School Officers, 2008), and instructional leadership is essential, it is unclear which leadership skills, once mastered, separate the top performing principals from those who are mediocre or even deficient.

In this chapter, we propose that the development of social, emotional, and cognitive skills is the missing link in school leaders' preparation. These skills are neglected in leadership development today, despite their ability to transform teaching and learning through the human interactions between school leaders and others. We begin with a brief theoretical foundation to provide the reader with the context that supports this approach to leadership development.

Theoretical Foundation

Leadership development draws from theoretical foundations that include the Great Man theory, which defined the best and brightest leaders as those with inherent abilities, notions about the top-down leader of the early 1900s espoused by scientific management, and subsequent realizations that individual traits impact the leader's performance and that different situations require different leadership approaches (Bennis, 1959). Work by Wilkins and Ouchi (1983) was influential in stressing the importance that a leader should create a culture of trust and open communication with others, characterized by shared beliefs, values, and goals. Twenty-first century educational leadership theory continues to focus primarily on the leader as a change agent of needed reform in schools to improve instruction and raise student achievement (Hallinger & Heck, 2011). Simultaneously, there is a growing understanding that we cannot change the behavior of schools until we change the behaviors of the people who work in them. We believe that intensive change in school and in student learning will happen when school leaders develop their own social, emotional, and cognitive skills, and build professional capital through the transformation of teachers.

Our work in both preservice and inservice leadership development is informed by the evolution of leadership theory and anchored in four additional theoretical frameworks: adult learning, emotional and social intelligence (EISI), self-psychology, and systems thinking.

Adult Learning Theory

Adult learning theory reminds us that as we mature, our learning is enabled by (1) readiness in different moments of our lives, (2) internal sources of motivation, (3) willingness to be open to new learning and experiences, and (4) application through concrete, practical experiences. Adult learners can direct their own learning when provided with a trusting supportive environment in which they are able to take risks and are willing to be vulnerable, accept feedback, and try new ways of learning. Kegan's constructive development theory (Helsing, Howell, Kegan, & Lahey, 2008) reminds us that adults, like children, experience developmental stages ranging from more self-focused behaviors to more complex ways of locating self amid fields of forces and interactions, and placing personal desires in a larger, more service-oriented context. Having an understanding of these developmental stages can help school leaders gauge an approach to working with others to change behaviors and practices. Leading a school means recognizing that people and teams can be at different places in both experience and skills. In turn, this means that instead of one-size-fits-all professional development, effective interventions such as training, coaching, and mentoring must be calibrated for people and teams that are in very different developmental stages and have different needs and skills levels (Helsing et al., 2008).

Social and Emotional Intelligences

Thorndike first introduced the concept of a social intelligence as early as the 1920s (Thorndike & Stein, 1937). In recent years, this intelligence has taken on new meaning (Bass, 2002). Goleman, Boyatzis, and McKee (2013) promote the development of several competencies that are aligned with a leader's social intelligence: empathy, attunement, organizational awareness, developing others, inspiration, and teamwork. These competencies fall within the leader's social awareness and ability to manage relationships, both of which are critical to success.

EI "involves the ability to monitor one's own and others' emotions, to discriminate among them, and to use the information to guide one's thinking and actions" (Mayer & Salovey, 1993, p. 433). Unlike a fixed intelligence, EI continues to develop from childhood through adulthood. Self-awareness is foundational to our ability to manage our own behaviors and to develop productive relationships (Avolio & Gardner, 2005). The more self-aware we become, and the more we use the data our emotions provide us, the better decisions we can make (Brackett, Rivers, & Salovey, 2011). Our emotional abilities manifest behaviorally in our relationships with others; how we deal with feedback from our supervisors, peers, and those we supervise; and how we manage conflict and stress (Ashkanasy & Daus, 2005). Studies are in progress to further our understanding of the possible links between purposeful social and emotional competence training and effective school leadership.

Self Psychology

Self psychology, as an approach to psychological development, describes a lifelong pursuit of a "nuclear program" that makes use of a person's innate talents and skills (Kohut, 1984, p. 152) to realize his or her ambitions, mediated by his or her ideals. As a person develops throughout a lifetime and one or more careers, ambitions and ideals that evolve in turn demand that skills evolve as well. Meaningful growth relies on the individual's innate capacities and developed skills in the context of his or her unique integration of aspirations and values. Helping individuals to recognize their own values and aspirations builds self-efficacy and motivation toward actualizing a personal vision. The self psychology approach builds an empathic relationship with the person being developed; a "moment to moment attunement to unfolding experience, rather than content, facilitates a sense of being understood, which in turn promotes a deepening of self-reflection" (Warner, 2013, p. 69). This is essential in building the trust that leaders need to allow time for reflection.

Systems Thinking

Peter Senge (1996) broadened our understanding of the complexity of schools as a system of many interrelated parts. He referred to a school as a "learning organization", a collective that shares a common vision for the school and works together to achieve that end. Although we live in social systems, we generally have difficulty stepping back to see how these systems operate as a whole. Systems thinking implies "that the leader (1) examines his own assumptions and is prepared to shift these in pursuit of points of leverage to make improvements; (2) triangulates the data received by involving multiple points of view, collective thinking; and (3) recognizes that short-term fixes do not solve deep issues. It takes time to develop, apply, and measure the benefits of interventions" (online video clip; Senge, 2012). School leaders who espouse systems thinking *think systemically* about situations, events, and organizational culture and climate.

Each of the described theories provides a framework for the kind of leadership development that *is not* happening in the preparation of aspiring and veteran principals—that is, the development of the social, emotional, and cognitive skills that school leaders must include in adult professional development as they set a course to improve the social, emotional, and academic skills of young people. The four foundational core leadership skills described here are derived from the leadership literature, the SEL competence domains, and our experiences in the field of leadership in schools and organizations.

Core Leadership Skills

Moving theory into practice requires the application of skills that are visible in behavior—skills that transform self, others, and the organization. We liken them to the raw material from which the multitude of performance responsibilities and expectations can be accomplished (Waters et al., 2004). School leaders are expected to be able to (1) set a widely shared vision for learning; (2) develop a school culture and instructional program that isconducive to student learning and staff professional growth; (3) ensure effective management of the organization, operation, and resources for a safe, efficient and effective learning environment; (4) collaborate with faculty and community members, responding to diverse community interests and needs, and mobilizing community resources; (5) act with integrity, fairness, and in an ethical manner; and (6) understand, respond to, and influence the political, social, legal, and cultural context (Council of Chief State School Officers, 2008). To be able to meet these extensive expectations placed on them, school leaders need support in fostering actionable self-reflection, building generative relationships, enabling meaningful conversations, and thinking systemically. These skills, often regarded as the "soft skills", that lie at the core of our being—the way we think, the way we perceive and interact with others, the way we listen, and our ability to maneuver the daily challenges of the job with professionalism and grace—are foundational to adult performance and success (Brungardt, 2011). Research increasingly indicates that such affective and cognitive skills are essential in K–16 leadership for deeper learning to transpire. "Deeper learning is the process through which a person becomes capable of taking what was learned in one situation and applying it to new situations—in other words, learning for transfer" (Pellegrino & Hilton, 2013, p. 1).

These affective and cognitive skills also lie at the core of effective teamwork, an essential component of leadership (Druskat & Wolff, 2001). As we promote and support SEL instruction for young people, we cannot eliminate the need for adults to model these very same skills. The core leadership skills are inherent in the five core competencies of SEL: self-awareness, self-management, social awareness, relationship management, and responsible decision making. Our description of these core leadership skills follows.

Fostering Actionable Self-Reflection

The process of knowing oneself is complex, difficult to measure, and requires dedicated personal work in three aspects: (1) reflection on what matters—our deepest aspirations, (2) reflection on how we make sense of the events around us, and (3) reflection on our emotions. These three aspects of self-reflection become very important to the school leader when they become actionable; that is, when a leader uses the insight he or she has obtained from self-reflection to guide subsequent decision making and behaviors. One example of actionable self-reflection is the personal vision-based process that becomes the foundation for building shared, schoolwide visions (Kantabutra, 2005). Without the inspiration that is garnered from one's personal vision, it is very difficult to motivate others. The simple question "What do I and we truly want to create or achieve?" has great power if explored with discipline regularly. When the collective engages in a process to explore organizational vision, it is even more powerful.

Another dimension of actionable self-reflection is reflective practice with the mirror turned inward, on our mental models: the perceptions gained by one's personal experiences that may inhibit one's openness or ability to create needed change in self, others, or the organization . . . . Our perceptions are inescapably shaped by our life experience: our upbringing, culture of origin, and education and professional experience. We inevitably operate, based on our mental models—deep habits of thought and action we have built over a lifetime.

Finally, self-reflection can help us better facilitate our emotions and subsequent actions (Salovey & Mayer, 1990). As we become more aware of our emotional selves, develop our emotional vocabulary, understand the reasons for the emotions we feel, and express and regulate them appropriately, we become *more cognitively and emotionally intelligent*. Reflection without insight does not lead to changed behaviors (Grant, Franklin, & Langford, 2002). One might simply ruminate about the same thoughts repeatedly with no change, while others might use that reflection to make cognitive-behavioral choices. Unfortunately, the daily demands that are placed on the school principal leave little time for the kind of self-reflection that fosters insight and readiness for change. In a study conducted with 25 nationwide principals, Drago-Severson (2012) found that principals "yearn for regular ongoing opportunities to reflect with colleagues and fellow principals on the challenges of leadership" (p. 2). Yet only three of the 25 principals who participated in the study actually used reflection regularly. Other studies have supported the desire and need for reflection for renewal (Patti, Tobin, & Knoll, 2003). Professional development opportunities need to provide time for individual and collective renewal.

Building Generative Relationships

Effective school leaders' ability to build positive relationships with and among others has a great impact on the climate and culture of a school, a mediating variable to student achievement. But adult relationships must also be generative, so that adults working together create new and better ideas and solutions about teaching and learning. Generative relationships can occur when teachers participate in well-organized professional learning communities and/or inquiry groups, in which they explore student work, review professional literature, share successful practices, and seek ideas for improving challenge areas.

Effective school leaders foster a trusting environment that encourages and supports a climate for generative relationships to grow. The leader's ability to influence, inspire, and create trust impacts the quality of the adult relationships formed—how open they are, how well individuals communicate and coordinate their actions, how compassionate they are, and how they deal with conflict. Generative relationships require that each individual understand, express, and appropriately manage his or her own emotions in relationship with others. It is important to mention critical prerequisite skills for building generative relationships: the ability to be empathic, to actively listen, to hear others' perspectives, to be mindful, to read faces accurately, and to detect voice tones, to name a few (Goleman et al., 2013). A culture of empathy creates the safety in which generative relationships grow, and in which critical feedback can be given and received, differences are honored, and creativity flourishes.

Enabling and Facilitating Meaningful Conversations

Communication among staff members is often challenging given that teachers spend the majority of their day working directly with students, leaving minimal time for interaction with others. At best, weekly staff meetings address *business as usual*, rarely leaving time for meaningful conversations that can potentially move the organization forward. Meaningful conversations require dedicated time for sharing ideas and real listening; they encourage differing opinions and conflict that can lead to more productive solutions. First, in order to encourage these kinds of conversations, leaders need to address the delicate balance between providing information, discussion of pressing issues, and dialogues about teaching and learning. The flow of information back and forth between administrators and staff often requires pragmatic action for short-term gains, but members of the school community need time for reflective dialogue and inquiry about teaching and learning values, beliefs, and practices. These conversations can happen as a whole-group endeavor or work well in smaller learning communities led by teacher leaders who possess strong facilitation skills, a prerequisite for effective conversations. These conversations allow deeper learning to take place and contribute to longer-term solutions and needed change in individual practices (Pellegrino & Hilton, 2013).

Second, meaningful conversations require that leaders demonstrate effective conflict resolution strategies and that everyone in the school undergoes development in the same. Establishing teams to lead inquiry into school-based problem areas without skills development in how to agree to disagree effectively, mange conflict, and come to consensus as needed, will thwart desired results. Empowering staff members with the skills of conflict management is an essential prerequisite to any meaningful conversations. Stepping back and allowing the voices of teacher leaders to emerge will unite the community rather than create the potential to divide it.

Third, leaders need to understand their own conflict styles within different situations and with different constituencies. One way to do this is to use assessment (Thomas & Kilmann, 1978) as a reflective tool to investigate personal conflict styles and explore how they manifest in the workplace. Through reflection with a coach or with trusted colleagues, school leaders exchange stories, recognize that they are not alone, and set goals to improve challenging behaviors while relying upon strength behaviors (Patti et al., 2012).

Fourth, leaders need to participate in active learning, role plays, and simulations in which they enter into difficult conversations, practice reading verbal and nonverbal cues, and use language that opens up communication. Simple addition of assertive but nonoffensive language to a school leader's repertoire can be eye-opening for him or her. Effective supervision of others requires expert coaching skills that allow teachers to explore their own strengths and challenges with prompting and guiding, as necessary. Many school leaders use more offensive language that alienates the recipient and reduces the opportunity for effective resolution or change. "It is essential to learn how to have open and effective conversations when there is real conflict", says Tahoma superintendent Mike Maryanski. "If you cannot do this, you can forget about building a genuine learning culture" (Benson et al., 2012).

Thinking Systemically

Thinking systemically involves all of the aforementioned foundational skills and exemplifies the SEL competence of responsible decision making. School leaders adept at understanding the complexity and the interconnected relationships between the independent structures of their organization make decisions that consider the school as a whole. Every area of oversight, from effectively managing financial resources to ensuring student achievement, requires that school leaders see beyond immediate events and transcend the crisis-oriented leadership culture that afflicts many schools and school systems (Benson et al., 2012). With a comprehensive understanding of the system, they scan the school and perceive the needs of the stakeholders and structures—within the interrelated parts of the school's systems. With this skill, school leaders can identify gaps in the systemic structures of the school and build work cultures that encourage collaboration, risk taking, and disciplined reflection for improvement.

To prepare school leaders and their teams to think systemically, they need professional development that asks them to (1) engage in continual exercises that are aligned with their vision and (2) explore their mental models and systemically choose the best strategies for long-term change. This professional development employs three primary modalities: visual (constructing loops and diagrams of the interconnected events in the school); communicative (utilizing common vocabulary, skillful discussion, dialogue, inquiry and advocacy); and active learning (physical challenges, computer modeling, role play and simulations (Systems Thinking in Schools, Waters Foundation, 2014). The strategies acquired within each modality assist leaders with identifying the roots of systemic problems, the potential causes and effects of every aspect of a situation. Additionally, they are responsible decision makers as they consider possible ethical dilemmas and evaluate the wide range of perspectives of multiple stakeholders.

Using a multiple-case study design to investigate the use of evidence-based practice in systems thinking tools in two high schools in the southeastern United States, Kensler, Reames, Murray, and Patrick (2012) sought to determine whether school teams adept at using systems tools actually utilize these tools to dialogue about and measure team performance and outcomes. They found that although both schools had systems thinking abilities, only the school in which the principal participated in the professional development made full use of the tools. The results indicated that the school that intentionally utilized the systems thinking tools had 100% of team members fully engaged and committed to the improvement processes, while the school that did not utilize the targeted skills did not establish a culture of trust or develop into an effective community of practice. Systems thinking tools combine both cognitive and affective processes that develop all of the core social and emotional competencies, with a particular focus on responsible decision making.

We believe that the four skills (actionable self-reflection, generative relationship building, enabling and facilitating meaningful conversation, and thinking systemically) should be core elements of leadership development programs for school leaders. These essential skills, when developed, embody the five core competencies of SEL that we know contribute to establishing a climate and culture in which adults and young people can and do learn (Weissberg & Cascarino, 2013). The following section offers some guidelines and recommendations for leadership development based on the cultivation of these four key skills.

Guidelines and Recommendations for Leadership Development

In preservice education at both Hunter College of the City University of New York and the Summer Principals Academy at Teachers College, we have incorporated courses that address specific elements of the theory and core leadership skills discussed in this chapter (Patti et al., 2012). Our inservice development continues to integrate these elements through workshops, institutes, and coaching for school and district leaders and educational organizations. Recent development with school principals and superintendents provided by the Yale Center for Emotional Intelligence embeds this deeper learning that we have been discussing throughout the chapter. Similar efforts are unfolding in pockets around the globe, as we recognize the prerequisites for transformational learning. The guidelines and recommendations that follow are based on these experiences and the model of individual and collective development that we espouse. Although the guidelines are presented sequentially, the steps often occur in a more fluid manner based on the readiness level of the school leader and the complexity level of the school.

Guideline 1: Learning in a Safe Environment

Creating a safe climate is essential at the outset of any personal or collective change process. School leaders and their teams must learn in a safe ecology—one that encourages transparency, experiential learning, collegial inquiry, and self-directed learning. The motivation to experiment with new learning, especially new learning that may initially be outside of one's comfort zone, requires the use of the four core leadership skills addressed earlier in this chapter. Professional development opportunities must foster actionable self-reflection, enable and facilitate meaningful conversations, and build generative relationships and systematic thinking.

Emotional and psychological safety is built by creating a strong mission statement based on common values and norms of behavior by which the community lives. School leaders can facilitate exercises that will identify core values and community norms that become the foundation for the instructional work; some leaders invite an external facilitator to assist them with this process. Leithwood and Jantzi (2000) identify eight dimensions of transformational leadership that offer insight into characteristics of effective school leaders that contribute to an emotionally and psychologically safe learning environment: provides vision and/or inspiration, models behaviors, provides individualized support, provides intellectual stimulation, fosters commitment to group goals, encourages high performance expectations, provides contingent reward, and strongly encourages individual improvement. Furthermore, leaders create safe and purposeful spaces through countless small acts that demonstrate empathy and compassion, without losing sight of instructional expectations and goals.

Guideline 2: Building Personal and Shared Visions

Once a safe ecology exists, the next step is to create or expand both individual and collective visions. The vision directs the work to be done. It is what connects the reality of the present to the intentions for accomplishments in the future. Kantabutra (2005) conducted an extensive review exploring the relationship between vision and organizational performance, postulating that a strong vision should include brevity, future orientation, stability, challenge, abstractness, and ability to inspire. However, the ultimate power of a vision does not rest as much in the words that are crafted as in the commitment to a shared vision. There is a creative process set in motion by the gap between what we aspire to and what currently exists. This "creative tension" is the source of energy in the creative process. Creating a vision forces the capacity to tell the truth about what does or does not exist in the present, and what needs to be done to confront the gap. When working with school leaders, it is imperative to take them through a process of "envisioning." This can be accomplished in a number of ways with the assistance of a coach or facilitator, using a visualization process that may employ drawn or written reflections. Once the vision is created, it is compared to the current reality and the process of creating change takes place. This essential process for the leader and all members to experience thereby creates the possibility of a shared vision that is passionately embraced by all.

Guideline 3: Setting Goals Based on Vision

Visions need to be translated into specific goals that can be tracked and assessed in order to gauge progress and to self-correct. Just as we set goals to improve academic achievement, so too do we need to set individual and collective emotional and social behavioral goals, such as being able to hold difficult conversations without fear or disengagement, or regulating ourselves so as not to interrupt another speaker during a conversation. No matter what the goal is, each individual must attend to the social, emotional, and cognitive skills that may be impeding the accomplishment of personal and professional goals.

Just as with vision, effective goal setting encompasses the personal and the collective. In a school, for example, with a vision of integrating SEL into its culture, a collective goal might include training in conflict management or allowing for time to reflect and share thoughts and feelings on a given issue. Recently, two assistant principals spoke about their desire for goal-focused emotional development. One wanted to develop more compassion when she confronted feelings of frustration, especially when she worked hard and saw others not doing so. The other wanted to develop better self-control when she felt frustrated in certain situations. Both leaders decided to work on their compassion and empathy so they could see the person who was frustrating them in another light, then come up with strategies to deal with the person differently. Each came up with several specific cases in which they had the greatest need to be compassionate and crafted specific ways to respond compassionately so as to anchor their aspirations in concrete behaviors. Furthermore, by working together, they created a mutual support system motivated by common desire not to be overtaken when facing emotional challenges in their new leadership roles.

Guideline 4: Recognize and Use Social and Emotional Competencies

Leaders routinely face daily challenges that give them opportunities to apply social and emotional competencies that are otherwise neglected. For example, as principal Susan Ryan prepares to have a difficult conversation with a staff member who has been continuously late to school in the mornings, her self-talk reveals the skills related to recognizing and managing her emotions and expressing empathy to others that she consciously chooses to use:

> "I am really angry at Teacher *X*, so I need to take deep breaths before I begin and remind myself to breathe throughout the conversation. Teacher *X* has a hard time listening to feedback, and I don't want to get exasperated and let my emotions interfere with my ability to think clearly. [So I might say,] 'Teacher *X*, I appreciate having the opportunity to hear from you about the issues that you are facing that cause your lateness.' "

Susan's use of emotional skills arises from a combination of cognitive and affective skills that she consciously employs as a result of her self-reflective process. Sadly, school leaders are often the last people to receive honest feedback to help identify their social and emotional competencies, and their developmental edges. Leaders should seek out strategies that trigger emotional self and social awareness, such as journal writing, visualizations, tuning into one's self-talk, and taking formal assessments and having honest conversations with trusted colleagues (Patti, Stern, Martin, & Brackett, 2005) to provide helpful insight about individual interpersonal strengths and challenges in the social and emotional competencies.

Guideline 5: Coaching—A Tool for Reflective Process

Every school leader can benefit from a personal coach. It is during this coaching relationship that the school leader can reflect on his or her own strengths, challenges, and experiences, and develop insights and experiment with new ideas and behaviors. This is especially important when deeper change requires more than just new technical skills (Patti et al., 2012). The coach does not share his experiences; rather, the coach serves as a guide, a reflective mirror for the school leader to search for his or her *own* solutions and use that information to set goals for personal and professional change.

Research in the field of coaching psychology is still in its nascent stages (Grant & Cavanaugh, 2007), but a handful of empirical studies have begun to show the impact coaching has at the business and personal level, including increases in hope, well-being, self-efficacy, self-esteem, and improved interpersonal relationships (Grant, 2003; Spence & Grant, 2007). Furthermore, coaching anchored in compassion rather than compliance has a greater probability of promoting desired, sustainable change in attitudes and behaviors (Smith, Van Osten & Boyatzis, 2008). To date, there is little empirical research on coaching in the field of educational leadership. What exists touches on some aspects of development of coaching skills in principals for instructional improvement (Neumerski, 2013). Instructional coaching has traditionally supported teachers by focusing on knowledge transfer, modeling, skills practice, feedback (Knight, 2007), and novice educational leaders who require support on the job.

Effective coaching needs to take account of peoples' developmental stages, including some people who may not be ready for coaching. Often, those who seek out coaching support may already be operating from a more self-reflective level, as illustrated by the following principal's comments: "Relationships with the people you work with matter. [The training] enhanced the way I thought about people" (Maldonado Torres, 2012, p. 68). Interestingly enough, this principal's annual review process conducted a year after her coaching development, indicated, "This reflective school values professional development. . . . With insight and sensitivity, administration encourage and support teachers . . . to hone their skills as individuals and as a learning community" (p. 68). By contrast, less reflective and more self-protective school leaders may be less willing to open themselves up to such self-learning. For these individuals, other vehicles may be more productive, such as attending a series of social and emotional intelligence-based workshops or voluntarily participating in meetings.

Furthermore, strong peer networks among building leaders can make coaching more effective and lead to larger-scale systemwide impacts, as in the following case: A few years ago, a superintendent of a school district with 26,000 special education students in New York City invited her principals and their leadership teams to participate in a series of five leadership development coaching sessions to develop their social and emotional competencies. The coaching was voluntary, with no penalties attached for nonparticipation. Over the next 5 years, 25 of the 61 school principals participated in EI-based individual and team coaching, leading to many changes in behaviors and practices that enhanced their performance. With their coach, the principals created common goals to improve the schools' climate and students' academic, social, and emotional success. Through facilitated dialogue led by the coach, the school leaders talked about behaviors that were inhibiting and enhancing their common vision and their professional performance. They tuned into their emotional states to understand the cause of their emotions and to choose more appropriate behaviors in a variety of situations.

Eventually all of the participating principals and teams who were coached signed on to participate in schoolwide SEL. The individual and team coaching served as a catalyst for the principals to become invested in social and emotional development for every member of the school community.

Guideline 6: Practice and Reassess

All learning occurs over time, through ongoing processes of practice, feedback, reflection, and correction. The more demanding the new skills we are trying to build, the more time, patience, and ongoing practice is essential. More to the point, the intra- and interpersonal goals we establish often lead to taking steps that are uncomfortable for us, actions often attached to emotionally laden experiences with long personal histories. Through ongoing practice, we reframe and break old patterns; we begin to envision new ways of saying and doing things. We set up possibilities for learning new strategies and even elicit help from friends, family members, and life partners.

This process is not any different from the types of exercises that are typical of SEL programs with young people. Adults have had a longer period of time to get locked into unproductive behaviors, so more practice and reassessment is sometimes needed. Personal change is a transformational process during which a person may move from one developmental stage to another. This can be difficult, as a psychological shift has to occur within the person to be able to embrace the change. One example of this happened to a school leader with whom we had worked. She had previously been a teacher in the school that she now leads. The staff members who knew her as a colleague now had to accept her as principal. The principal was overly concerned about alienating any of her former colleagues. Revisiting our developmental stages momentarily, it is obvious that this principal's concern with maintaining her friendships and being liked (socialized stage of development) interfered with her ability to make needed decisions about teaching and learning. Whatever her vehicle for support, this principal had to recognize that as the leader of this school, the success of her students must come before her friendships with colleagues. These are the kinds of transformative changes to which we refer in our model that greatly impacts professional lives. They require school leaders to constantly use strategies to strengthen the five SEL competency domains both for themselves and all adults in the school.

Guideline 7: Build Resilient Peer Networks

In a truly collaborative peer community, the initiative and learning is *led by the peers themselves*. They come together to share instructional strategies that are effective, or to explore grade- or school-level academic data to determine where students need more help. Some may focus on resolving behavioral or climate issues, while others may actually conduct an inquiry lesson together to explore existing areas of academic concern. Effective peer learning communities are inclusive and empowered by the synergy of common passions, aspirations, and practical problems. There is a sense of belonging and trust that develops in these types of peer networks. This affiliation allows for individual risk taking and self-directed growth to occur.

School leaders benefit from participating in peer networks. Bengtson, Airola, Peer, and Davis (2012) conducted a study with 59 sitting principals who participated in the nationally recognized Arkansas Leadership Academy Master Principal Program. Using multiple methods, they explored the relationship between ongoing reflection within peer networks, increased reflective capacity of practitioners, and improvement in school performance. Narrative writings analyzed over 2 years of participation indicated higher scores in the principal's reflective practice. There was a correlation between these principal candidate's experience and improved performance of their schools.

Recently, such a network of principals was formed through their connection with New York City's Morningside Center, which brought together principals who were interested in deepening their understanding of SEL. Individual coaching was offered to them as part of this initiative. The majority of principals agreed to participate in the personal, professional coaching. When asked why they agreed to give their time to this intensive coaching process, one principal, responding for the group said, "It was a group decision. We are a network of about nine schools that have taken this on and are learning from one another [We see this as] a great opportunity to work on our emotional development as leaders" (J. Patti, personal communication, January 10, 2013). The positive group synergy clearly motivated these principals to continue their work together.

Another example of resilient peer networks can be seen in the promising program *Dia (*developing intelligence through art), a methodology created in Mexico, which has been used to train over 25,000 teachers and school leaders in more than 4,000 schools and 28 states throughout this country. The overarching aim is gradually to transform the traditional hierarchical, unilateral, instructional forms of teaching into a dialogic environment in which the teacher guides the process of thinking and learning collaboratively with the students. *Dia's* pedagogical framework transforms the learning space using visual art as a vehicle for developing the physical, mental, emotional, and social capacities of the individual and the community. Both adults and young people build a safe space to think, feel, share, and support one another as they individually and collectively make sense of a work of art. With equal focus on student and adult development, the aim is to increase the quality of education and develop 21st-century skills for teachers and students. Using this transformative pedagogy, *Dia* has created an extended learning community in which it is safe to take risks to learn new curriculum and pedagogical strategies. Today, *Dia* is regarded as an exemplar of best educational practices in Mexico. They have expanded their work to include a strong SEL component called SER that focuses on the four cluster competencies of emotional intelligence. *Dia* and *Ser* are becoming models for other countries of the power of extended peer learning networks in transforming pedagogy. We have much to learn from these efforts regarding institutionalization of best practices in adult transformation

Although these guidelines represent our collective experiences, and an emerging literature base, we would be remiss if we did not express the drawbacks that may be encountered in trying to pursue this path of leadership development. Furthermore, by no means are we recommending that the personal, professional development we describe in this chapter excludes other training opportunities that school leaders need in the "nuts and bolts" of everyday school leadership. Combined together, school leaders will be empowered to achieve success. Finally, the more knowledgeable we are of the possibilities and of the roadblocks we may encounter, the more success we will have in choosing impactful professional development.

Problems and Pitfalls

There are several reasons that school leaders might shy away from the professional development pedagogy described in this chapter. First and foremost, the reality of the pressures placed on educational leaders, particularly on school principals, to raise student achievement can cloud everything, and limit the willingness of principals to pursue this more reflective form of leadership development. Second, depending on the leadership style and developmental stages of school leaders, this type of development may be regarded as unnecessary, superficial, or even threatening to some. Third, school leaders who are *not* familiar with the research base in K–12 SEL may be less willing to explore this adult level of development. Strong, research-based SEL programs often include a certain amount of SEL skills development for school staff that can help to begin the adult development focus.

As with all effective professional development, this work requires more than an initial workshop or training. Regularly scheduled trainings and/or coaching and resilient peer networks will be needed to help with the transformational process. Although this kind of development is no more costly than many other learning opportunities, any intention to bring this work to the broader school community will require a time, space, and collaborative commitment by all school members. Finally, with little empirical research yet available in the educational field on what methods of leadership development are most effective, many may not see the value in making a long-term commitment to this process. More research must be conducted, so that successful practices can be identified and implemented more broadly. Finally, training providers must have an extensive knowledge of the field of SEL and adult professional development, as the two need to be intricately connected in creating a climate for learning in a culture that values the social, emotional, and cognitive development of children and the adults who teach them.

Conclusion

It is important to remember that we live in a time of profound change. Yet it is often easier to name the economic, social, and ecological crises we face than to deal with the emotions that block us from addressing them—the confusion, fear, anger, denial, and, ultimately, disengagement. We believe that many of the roots of these challenges lie in an education system that neither helps students understand the systemic causes of these problems nor develops the emotional maturity to face them productively. Shifting this paradigm starts with reframing professional development to focus on growing school leaders and resilient peer learning networks that can shape environments that nurture the cognitive, emotional, and social maturity students will need to be successful in their careers and as citizens.

References

Ashkanasy, N. M., & Daus, C. S. (2005). Rumors of the death of emotional intelligence in organizational behavior are vastly exaggerated. *Journal of Leadership Organizational Behavior, 11*(1), 441–452.

Avolio, B. J., & Gardner, W. L. (2005). Authentic leadership development: Getting to the root of positive forms of leadership. *Leadership Quarterly, 16*, 315–338.

Bass, B. M. (2002). Cognitive, social, and emotional intelligence of transformational leaders. In R. E. Riggio, S. E. Murphy, & F. J. Pirozzolol (Eds.), *Multiple intelligences and leadership* (pp. 105–118). Mahwah, NJ: Erlbaum.

Bass, B. M., & Avolio, B. J. (2004). *Multifactor Leadership Questionnaire: Manual and sampler set.* Menlo Park, CA: Mind Garden.

Bengtson, E., Airola, D., Peer, D., & Davis, D. (2012). Using peer learning support networks and reflective practice: The Arkansas Leadership Academy Master Principal Program. *International Journal of Educational Leadership Preparation, 7*(3), 1–17.

Bennis, W. G. (1959). Leadership theory and administrative behavior: The problem of authority. *Administrative Science Quarterly, 4*(3), 259–301.

Benson, T., Fullan, M., Kegan, R., Madrazo, C., Quinn, J., & Senge, P. (2012). Developmental stories: Lessons from systemic change for utilizing the new Common Core Standards for transforing education. Retreived January 15, 2014, from *www.schoolchange.net/groupspaces/nde/c21-learning/developmental.html.*

Brackett, M. A., Rivers, S. E., & Salovey, P. (2011). Emotional intelligence: Implications for personal, social, academic, and workplace success. *Social and Personality Psychology Compass, 5*, 88–103.

Brungardt, C. (2011). The intersection between soft skill development and leadership education. *Journal of Leadership Education, 10*(1), 1–22.

Byrne-Jiménez, M., & Orr, M. T. (2012). Thinking in three dimensions: Leadership for capacity building, sustainability, and succession. *Journal of Cases in Educational Leadership, 15*(3), 33–46.

Cook, C. R. (2006). *Effects of emotional intelligence on principals' leadership performance* (Order No. 3206272, Montana State University, Bozeman). *ProQuest Dissertations and Theses*, pp. 124–124. Retrieved January 15, 2014, from *http://search.proquest.com/docview/305276680?accountid=27495 (305276680).*

Council of Chief State School Officers. (2008). *Educational leadership policy standards: ISLLC 2008 as adopted by the National Policy Board for Educational Administration.* Retrieved January 15, 2014, from *www.ccsso.org/documents/2008/educational_leadership_policy_standards_2008.pdf.*

Drago-Severson, E. (2012). New opportunities for principal leadership: Shaping school climates for enhanced teacher development. *Teachers College Record, 114*(3), 1–44.

Druskat, V. U., & Wolff, S. B. (2001). Building the emotional intelligence of groups. *Harvard Business Review, 79*(3), 80–91.

Goleman, D., Boyatzis, R., & McKee, A. (2013). *Primal leadership: Unleashing the power of emotional intelligence.* Cambridge, MA: Harvard Business School Press.

Grant, A. (2003). Towards a psychology of coaching: The impact of coaching on metacognition, mental health, and goal attainment. *Social Behavior and Personality, 31*(3), 253–264.

Grant, A. M., & Cavanaugh, M. J. (2007). Evidence-based coaching: Flourishing or languishing? *Australian Psychologist, 42*(4), 239–254.

Grant, A. M., Franklin, J., & Langford, P. (2002). The Self-Reflection and Insight Scale: A new measure of private self-consciousness. *Social Behavior and Personality: An International Journal, 30*(8), 821–836.

Hackett, P. T., & Hortman, J. W. (2008). The relationship of emotional competencies to transformational leadership: Using a corporate model to assess the dispositions of educational leaders. *Journal of Educational Research and Policy Studies, 8*(1), 92–111.

Hallinger, P., & Heck, R. H. (1998). Exploring the principal's contribution to school effectiveness: 1980–1995. *School Effectiveness and School Improvement: An International Journal of Research, Policy and Practice, 9*(2), 157–191.

Hallinger, P., & Heck, R. H. (2011). Conceptual and methodological issues in studying school leadership effects as a reciprocal process. *School Effectiveness and School Improvement, 22*, 149–173.

Helsing, D., Howell, A., Kegan, R., & Lahey, L. (2008). Putting the "development" in professional development: Understanding and overturning a educational leaders' immunities to change. *Harvard Educational Review, 78*(3), 437–465.

Kantabutra, S. (2005). Improving public school performance through vision-based leadership. *Asia Pacific Education Review, 6*(2), 124–136.

Kensler, L. W., Reames, E., Murray, J., & Patrick, L. (2012). Systems thinking tools for improving evidence-based practice: A cross-case analysis of two high school leadership teams. *High School Journal, 95*(2), 32–53.

Knight, J. (2007). *Instructional coaching: A partnership approach to improving instruction.* Thousand Oaks, CA: Corwin Press.

Kohut, H. (1984). *How does analysis cure?* Chicago: University of Chicago Press.

Leithwood, K., & Jantzi, D. (2000). The effects of transformational leadership on organizational conditions and student engagement with school. *Journal of Educational Administration, 38*(2), 112–129.

Leithwood, K., Louis, K. S., Anderson, S., & Wahlstrom, K. (2004). *Review of research: How leadership influences student learning* (Report, Center for Applied Research and Educational Improvement, Ontario Institute for Studies in Education at the University of Toronto and University Minnesota Center for Applied Research and Educational Improvement). New York: Wallace Foundation.

Leithwood, K., & Mascall, B. (2008). Collective leadership effects on student achievement. *Educational Administration Quarterly, 44*(4), 529–561.

Louis, K., Leithwood, K. S., Wahlstrom, K. L., & Anderson, S. E. (2010). *Learning from leadership: Investigating the links to improved student learning* (Final report, Minneapolis: University of Minnesota, Toronto and Ontario: University of Toronto). New York: Wallace Foundation.

Maldonado Torres, M. (2012). *Emotional intelligence in principals and how it influences teacher–principal relationships* (Order No. 3517901, Fordham University). *ProQuest Doctoral Dissertations and Theses.* Retrieved January 15, 2014, from *http://search.proquest.com/docview/1033501376?accountid=27495.*

Mayer, J. D., & Salovey, P. (1993). The intelligence of emotional intelligence. *Intelligence, 17*(4), 433–442.

Minckler, C. H. (2014). School leadership that builds teacher social capital. *Educational Management Administration and Leadership, 42*(5), 657–679.

Mitgang, L., & Gill, J. (2012). The making of the principal: Five lessons in leadership training. Retrieved February 25, 2014, from *www.wallacefoundation.org/knowledge-center/school-leadership/effective-principal-leadership/documents/the-making-of-the-principal-five-lessons-in-leadership-training.pdf.*

Neumerski, C. M. (2013). Rethinking instructional leadership, a review: What do we know about principal, teacher, and coach instructional leadership, and where should we go from here? *Education Administration Quarterly, 49*(2), 310–347.

Patti, J., Holzer, A. A., Stern, R., & Brackett, M. A. (2012). Personal, professional coaching: Transforming professional development for teacher and administrative leaders. *Journal of Leadership Education, 11*(1), 263–275.

Patti, J., Stern, R., Martin, C., Brackett, M. A. (2005). *The STAR Factor emotional literacy coaching manual.* New York. Star Factor, LLC.

Patti, J., Tobin, K., & Knoll, M. (2003). In C. Patton & S. Strobl (Eds.), *School principal's strategies used to implement the Resolving Conflict Creatively Program (RCCP) in dispute resolution context: Cross-cultural and cross-disciplinary perspectives* (pp. 78–98) (Working Paper Series: Research Reports). New York: City University of New York, Dispute Resolution Consortium.

Pellegrino, J. W., & Hilton, M. L. (Eds.). (2013). *Education for life and work: Developing transferable knowledge and skills in the 21st century.* Washington, DC: National Academies Press.

Penuel, W. R., Fishman, B. J., Yamaguchi, R., & Gallagher, L. P. (2007). What makes professional development effective?: Strategies that foster curriculum implementation. *American Educational Research Journal, 44*(4), 921–958.

Prati, L. M., Douglas, C., Ferris, G. R., Ammeter, A. P., & Buckley, M. R. (2003). Emotional intelligence, leadership effectiveness, and team outcomes. *International Journal of Organizational Analysis, 11*(1), 21–40.

Salovey, P., & Mayer, J. D. (1990). Emotional intelligence. *Imagination, Cognition, and Personality, 9*(3), 185–211.

Senge, P. (1996). Leading learning organisations: The bold, the powerful, and the invisible. In F. Hesselbein, M. Goldsmith, & R. Beckhard (Eds.), *The leader of the future: New visions, strategies and practices for the next era* (pp. 41–58). San Francisco: Jossey-Bass.

Senge, P. M. (1997). Communities of leaders and learners. *Harvard Business Review, 75*(5), 30–32.

Senge, P. M. (2012, October). What is systems thinking?—Peter Senge explains systems thinking approach and principles [Online video clip]. Mutual Responsibility. Retrieved January 15, 2014, from *www.mutualresponsibility.org/science/what-is-systems-thinking-peter-senge-explains-systems-thinking-approach-and-principles.*

Smith, M. L., Van Osten, E. B., & Boyatzis, R. E. (2008). Coaching for sustained desired change. *Research in Organization Development and Change, 17*, 145–174.

Sparks, D. (2009). What I believe about leadership development. *Phi Delta Kappan, 90*, 514–517.

Spence, G. B., & Grant, A. M. (2007). Professional and peer life coaching and the enhancement of goal striving and well-being: An exploratory study. *Journal of Positive Psychology, 2*(3), 185–194.

Spillane, J., & Diamond, J. (2007). *Distributed leadership in practice.* New York: Teachers College Press.

Stone, H., Parker, J. D., & Wood, L. M. (2005). Report on the Ontario Principals' Council Leadership Study. Retrieved June 24, 2009, from *www.eiconsortium.org.*

Systems Thinking in Schools, Waters Foundation. (2014). *Systems Thinking strategies.* Pittsburgh, PA: Author. Retrieved July 22, 2014, from *http://watersfoundation.org/systems-thinking/systems-thinking-stragegies.*

Thomas, K. W., & Kilmann, R. H. (1978). Comparison of four instruments measuring conflict behavior. *Psychological Reports, 42*(3c), 1139–1145.

Thorndike, R. L., & Stein, S. (1937). An evaluation of the attempts to measure social intelligence. *Psychological Bulletin, 34*(5), 275–285.

Warner, A. (2013). Creativity and the self: A self-psychological approach to art and healing. *Clinical Social Work Journal, 41*(1), 68–76.

Waters, T., Marzano, R. J., & McNulty, B. (2004). McREL's balanced leadership framework: Developing the science of educational leadership. *ERS Spectrum, 22*, 1–14.

Weissberg, R. P., & Cascarino, J. (2013). Academic learning + social-emotional learning = national priority. *Phi Delta Kappan, 95*(2), 8–13.

West, D. L., Peck, C., & Reitzug, U. C. (2010). Limited control and relentless accountability: Examining historical changes in urban school principal pressure. *Journal of School Leadership, 20*(2), 238–266.

Wilkins, A. L., & Ouchi, W. G. (1983). Efficient cultures: Exploring the relationship between culture and organizational performance. *Administrative Science Quarterly, 28*(3), 468–481.

CHAPTER 30

SEL and Schoolwide Positive Behavioral Interventions and Supports

George G. Bear, Sara A. Whitcomb, Maurice J. Elias, and Jessica C. Blank

Throughout the history of American education, educators have been challenged with two primary aims related to school discipline and classroom management: (1) the short-term aim of managing and correcting student behavior and (2) the long-term aim of developing students' self-discipline (Bear, 2005). Unlike management and correction of behavior, which is largely adult-directed, "self-discipline" involves students inhibiting inappropriate behavior and exhibiting prosocial behavior under their own volition. This requires social, emotional, and behavioral competencies that underlie self-regulated behavior. Over the years, approaches to school discipline and classroom management have varied greatly in their emphases on these two aims, and in the strategies and techniques used to achieve them. This is as true today as in the past, as now seen in differences between three popular approaches to school discipline and prevention of behavior problems: (1) the zero-tolerance approach (see American Psychological Association Zero Tolerance Task Force, 2008), (2) the social and emotional learning (SEL) approach (Durlak, Weissberg, Dymnicki, Taylor, & Schellinger, 2011; Zins & Elias, 2006), and (3) the schoolwide positive behavioral interventions and supports (SWPBIS) approach (Sugai & Horner, 2009; Sugai et al., 2010).

The primary aim of the zero-tolerance approach is the short-term management of student behavior. Often framed in the context of school safety, students' behavior problems are to be corrected immediately, irrespective of circumstances involved, while relying primarily on punitive techniques. Removal of misbehaving students from the classroom or school is the most common, and controversial, technique employed in this approach. Sharing an emphasis on preventing behavior problems, and using positive rather than punitive techniques, the SEL and SWPBIS approaches stand in contrast to the zero-tolerance approach. However, as seen in this chapter, these two popular approaches also can stand in contrast to one another, with the two having a different primary aim and emphasizing different strategies and techniques to achieve it. As found in the zero-tolerance approach, the primary aim of the SWPBIS approach is the adult management of student behavior. In contrast, the primary aim of the SEL approach is the long-term development of social and emotional competence of self-discipline, so that students are inclined to govern themselves not only while in school but also upon leaving school. Consistent with the differing primary aims of the SEL and SWPBIS approaches, different strategies and techniques are emphasized in each, although few, if any, cannot be found to one degree or another in both approaches.

Given the popularity of the SEL and SWPBIS approaches, as well as their focus on differing yet perhaps equally important aims of school discipline, it is not uncommon that schools consider, or are challenged with, integrating the two. To best integrate the two approaches, it is necessary that educators understand the fundamental principles and practices driving each approach, so that they may see overlapping and complementary, and what might also be viewed as conflicting, features of these initiatives. This chapter is written primarily for those educators.

In this chapter we first give an overview of the SEL and SWPBIS approaches and describe their key features. Because the SEL approach is covered extensively throughout this volume, greater attention is directed to the SWPBIS approach. Next, we highlight strengths and limitations of the two approaches. We argue that the primary strengths of the SEL approach, which is developing self-discipline, and of the SWPBIS approach, which is managing student behavior, are largely complementary. As such, the primary strength of each approach addresses the primary weakness of the other (Osher, Bear, Sprague, & Doyle, 2010). Last, we discuss potential problems and pitfalls that schools are likely to encounter when integrating the two approaches, and how these might be surmounted.

The SEL Approach

Historically and theoretically, the SEL approach is rooted heavily in developmental psychology, and particularly constructivist learning theories (Piaget, 1932/1965; Vygotsky 1934/1987) and research on prevention and resilience (Greenberg, Domitrovich, & Bumbarger, 2001; Zins & Elias, 2006). It also draws from a range of theories related to human development and behavior, including, but not limited to, social cognitive theory, social problem solving, youth development, resilience, moral and prosocial development, emotional development, student engagement, authoritative discipline, and the ecology of human development. The SEL approach represents a comprehensive articulation of a system for developing SEL competencies that have long been recognized as important for personal growth and effective performance in school, family, workplace, and civic contexts (Elias et al., 1997). These include the five sets of SEL competencies elaborated elsewhere throughout this volume: (1) responsible decision making at school, home, and in the community; (2) self-management of emotions and behavior; (3) relationship skills, (4) social awareness, and (5) self-awareness. Included in these five sets of skills are a number of specific social cognitive and emotional skills and processes that research has shown to underlie self-discipline and prosocial behavior.

To properly understand SEL, one must think of it not only as a set of competencies but also the following:

- Systematic instruction and practice in SEL skills with explicit links to academics in a multiyear format with clear grade-by-grade articulation.
- Promotion of positive school culture and climate with unifying themes, such as respect, responsibility, fairness, and honesty.
- Developmentally appropriate instruction in specific, evidence-based health promotion and problem behavior prevention approaches.
- Services and systems that enhance students' coping skills and provide social support for handling transitions, crises, and conflicts.
- Systematic opportunities for positive, contributory service within and/or outside the school, as appropriate (Elias, Wang, Weissberg, Zins, & Walberg, 2002; Elias et al., 1997).

The richness and depth of SEL as a construct, linked to a wide range of prior research, is connected to the longitudinal and complex nature of interventions designed to develop the SEL skills noted earlier. Having a sustained and intensive impact on the context in which skills develop is essential. Relatedly, because of the constructivist nature of SEL theory, internal development of skills and mechanisms of self-discipline are seen as vital to long-term skills acquisition and generalization.

The SEL approach places great emphasis on achieving social, emotional, and behavioral competencies in contexts of supportive relationships. Research shows that warm and supportive relationships foster the development of SEL skills, as seen in the internalization of teachers' values (Hughes, 2012); they promote students' academic achievement (Danielsen, Wiium, Wilhelmsen, & Wold, 2010) and motivate students to act responsibly and prosocially (Wentzel, 2006). Positive teacher–student relationships are critical in the prevention and correction of behavior problems (Hamre, Pianta, Downer, & Mashburn, 2008), including bullying (Gregory et al., 2010). Research also strongly supports the role of peer relationships and classroom norms in preventing behavior problems and promoting academic achievement (Stearns, Dodge, & Nicholson, 2008; Thomas, Bierman, & the Conduct Problems Prevention Research Group, 2006). Finally, research supports the importance of building and maintaining supportive teacher–parent communication and relationships, with studies demonstrating that parents exert a great influence on their children's academic, social, and emotional development (Parke & Buriel, 2006).

As reviewed most extensively elsewhere in this volume (see Williford & Wolcott, Chapter 15, this volume), research indicates that SEL programs that include curriculum lessons targeting social–emotional competencies, and do so within a context of supportive relationships, are effective in achieving a wide range of valued academic, social, and emotional outcomes. Those outcomes include greater social and emotional skills, more positive attitudes toward self and others, more positive social behavior, fewer conduct problems, less emotional distress, and greater academic performance (Durlak et al., 2011).

The SWPBIS Approach

The recent popularity of the term "positive behavioral interventions and supports" (PBIS), including SWPBIS, can be directly linked to inclusion of PBIS in the amendments to the Individuals with Disabilities Education Improvement Act (IDEIA; 2004). IDEIA requires PBIS at the individual level, not the schoolwide level, for children with disabilities whose behavior impedes their learning or the learning of others [20 U.S.C. §1414(d)(3)(B)(i). The act also provides funding to states that is earmarked specifically for staff training and for technical assistance in implementing SWPBIS. The purpose of such funding is to prevent academic and behavioral problems, therefore reducing "the need to label children as disabled in order to address the learning and behavioral needs of such children" [20 U.S.C. § 145(a)(3)(B)(iii)(I)]. Despite the inclusion of the term PBIS, SWPBIS is not defined in IDEIA, or elsewhere in federal legislation. Likewise, as with the SEL approach, there is no single framework for SWPBIS (Knoff, 2008). Its developers have argued that SWPBIS is best viewed as simply positive behavior supports (PBS), as used with students with disabilities, applied to *all* students (Dunlap, Sailor, Horner, & Sugai, 2009). From this viewpoint, to understand SWPBIS one must first understand PBS and how it evolved into SWPBIS.

In brief, the term PBS was first introduced by Horner and colleagues (2009) to describe the "technology of nonaversive behavioral support" that they applied to individuals with severe disabilities, especially those adults exhibiting self-injurious, aggressive, and severely disruptive behaviors (Dunlap et al., 2009). The goal of PBS was to implement positive interventions and supports (i.e., PBIS) to increase adaptive behavior through the use of positive reinforcement instead of aversive forms of punishment such as electric shock, physical restraint, and exclusion. Those positive interventions and supports were guided by a functional behavioral assessment (FBA), which is viewed as an "essential foundation of PBS" (Dunlap et al., 2009, p. 8). Underlying FBA is the understanding that nearly all behaviors can be linked to two primary functions or purposes: obtaining desired events such as seeking attention and rewards or avoiding/escaping from aversive stimuli (Crone & Horner, 2003).

Because PBS was found to be effective in managing serious behavior problems of individuals with severe disabilities in institutions, it was then applied to students with emotional and behavioral disorders and young children with disabilities (Dunlap et al., 2009). The next step in PBS's progression to a schoolwide approach was guided by the developers' belief that techniques of PBS with individuals would be largely ineffective "if they were implemented in the context of chaotic classrooms and schools, where teachers were constantly addressing behavior problems of multiple students and where schoolwide or classroom-wide discipline was clearly absent" (p. 11). It was therefore in the context of disruptive schools and classrooms, and teachers lacking behavior management skills, that Horner, Sugai, and colleagues at the University of Oregon created SWPBIS (Dunlap et al., 2009; Sprague & Horner, 2006). In doing so, they applied FBA and general principles of applied behavior analysis (ABA) to a three-tier model of prevention, as commonly found in the literature on prevention and mental health (i.e., with Tier 1 focusing on the universal level; Tier 2 on the selected or secondary level; Tier 3 on the indicated or tertiary level).

Sugai and Horner (2009) emphasized that the theoretical and conceptual foundations of PBS and SWPBIS "are firmly linked to behavioral theory and applied behavior analysis" (p. 309). Similar to SEL, SWPBIS places great emphasis on system change, with the aim of preventing school problems and improving not only student behavior but also the "social culture" of the school. This emphasis is seen in the definition of SWPBIS in the 2010 Implementers' Blueprint and Self-Assessment (Sugai et al., 2010). Published by the Technical Assistance Center on Positive Behavioral Interventions and Supports, and funded by the U.S. Department of Education, Office of Special Education Programs, the blueprint is designed to guide schools in their implementation of SWPBIS. In the blueprint, SWPBIS is defined as "a framework or approach comprised of intervention practices and organizational systems for establishing the social culture, learning and teaching environment, and individual behavior supports needed to achieve academic and social success for all students" (p. 13). Similar to other popular definitions of SWPBIS (e.g., see Horner, Sugai, Todd, & Lewis-Palmer, 2005; Sugai & Horner, 2009), this definition is sufficiently broad and nonspecific to capture almost any program or model of school discipline and preventive mental health. Although the foundation of SWPBIS in ABA and PBS is lost in these definitions, the defining features of SWPBIS, delineated in the blueprint and commonly cited in the literature, clearly emphasize its theoretical foundation in ABA and PBS. Those features are summarized below.

Defining Features

Five defining features of SWPBIS are commonly cited in the literature (Horner et al., 2005; Sugai, Horner, & McIntosh, 2008; Sugai et al., 2010): *valued outcomes, ongoing collection and use of data for decision making, systems change, research-validated practices*, and *foundation in applied behavior analysis and biomedical sciences.*

Operationally Defined and Valued Outcomes

SWPBIS emphasizes that valued academic and behavioral outcomes are to be identified and targeted for intervention. Consistent with principles of ABA, outcomes are operationalized, measured, and routinely monitored to determine whether the use of SWPBIS practices positively affects students' behavior (George, Kincaid, & Pollard-Sage, 2009). Although office disciplinary referrals (ODRs) and suspension data are the most common outcomes measured (e.g., Bradshaw, Mitchell, & Leaf, 2010; Mass-Galloway, Panyan, Smith, & Wessendorf, 2008), other valued outcomes in studies of SWPBIS are school climate and academic achievement (e.g., Horner et al., 2009).

Ongoing Collection and Use of Data for Decision Making

ODR and suspension data are not only used to measure program effectiveness but also commonly collected and analyzed for formative decision making. These data are to be analyzed from the perspective of FBA (Crone & Horner, 2003; George et al., 2009). For example, if data show that a large number of ODRs come from fifth graders in math class, it might be hypothesized that those students are acting inappropriately to avoid what they find aversive (i.e., math) or to receive attention from peers or the teacher.

The decision might then be made to provide greater reinforcement of their on-task behavior and make math instruction and assignments more motivating.

Systems Change

Systems change (also often referred to as "supportive systems") is not new to schools (e.g., see Fullan, 2007), and the aspects of systems change in SWPBIS are shared by most other school reform initiatives. Those aspects include team-based selection and implementation of research-validated practices, data-based decision making, administrative and team leadership, staff commitment, communication and information systems, adequate personnel and time, and budgeted support. A major way in which the SWPBIS approach differs greatly from other systems change efforts, however, and reflecting the approach's behavioral perspective, is the recommended composition of the leadership team. To ensure that the evidence-based interventions are those associated with ABA and PBS, in the blueprint it is recommended that the leadership team include at least two individuals with expertise and experience in ABA.

Research-Validated Practices

The SWPBIS approach emphasizes implementation of "research-validated" practices (Sugai et al., 2010, p. 15) for preventing problem behavior and achieving valued outcomes. In SWPBIS, "research validated refers to studies that directly and systematically examine whether a functional relationship exists between the accurate implementation of a practice and important changes in the behavior or performance of the recipients of the practice" (p. 14). Four major research-validated practices, as described below, characterize SWPBIS schools.

1. *Clearly defined behavioral expectations.* Staff members are to develop three to five positively worded behavioral expectations that are clearly defined and related to specific observable behaviors in multiple locations throughout the school (e.g., cafeteria, hallway, and classroom; George et al., 2009). They often are presented in a matrix that specifies what behaviors students are expected to exhibit in each location of the building (e.g., to be respectful "walk quietly in the hallway").

2. *Direct teaching of behavioral expectations.* Staff members are to teach behavioral expectations to all students in a direct manner to ensure that they know school and classroom rules and develop social competencies (McIntosh, Filter, Bennett, Ryan, & Sugai, 2010). Rules and behavioral expectations, often delineated in a matrix, are taught throughout the school and in a manner similar to academic instruction; educators use a lesson plan that includes direct instruction, modeling, feedback and positive reinforcement, and role-playing examples of expected behavior (Sugai et al., 2010).

3. *Reinforcement of appropriate behavior.* Staff members are to acknowledge systematically, or positively reinforce, students for demonstrating behavior consistent with the school's behavioral expectations, particularly those expectations identified in the matrix developed by the school's SWPBIS team (Sugai et al., 2010). Various forms of positive reinforcement, such as tangible rewards (e.g., tokens, tickets), access to privileges or preferred activities, social recognition, and verbal praise, are to be used not only to teach new skills and to motivate students (George et al., 2009), but also to foster positive teacher-student relationships (McIntosh et al., 2010). Tokens and tickets also serve the purpose of prompting adults to reinforce targeted behaviors more frequently.

4. *A system for responding to inappropriate behavior.* Staff members are to develop a continuum of consequences that is aligned with the severity of inappropriate behavior. Educators are expected to use evidence-based behavioral techniques, including punishment (e.g., response cost, verbal reprimands), reteaching and practicing behavioral expectations. Minor behavior problems that should be managed by teachers in the classroom are distinguished from major problems that should be managed by administrators in the office.

Foundations in ABA and Biomedical Sciences

Application of principles of ABA are seen throughout each of previously described defining features (Dunlap et al., 2009; Sugai & Horner, 2009). In the blueprint, it is stated that SWPBIS also is grounded in "biomedical sciences." It is unclear, however, exactly what this term means as applied to SWPBIS and how it translates into educational practice, especially beyond principles of ABA. The authors simply state that there are five "major assumptions associated with adopting a behavioral and biomedical perspective" (Sugai et al., 2010, p. 15). Those assumptions are that behavior (1) can be taught, (2) is environmentally manipulable, (3) is lawful and predictable, (4) is affected by environmental factors, and (5) interacts with biophysical factors. Thus, biomedical science seems to be equated largely with ABA.

Major Strengths and Limitations of the SEL and SWPBIS Approaches

With any evaluation of strengths and weaknesses of the two approaches, it must be recognized that the substantial differences in programs *within* each approach may be as great as differences *between* the two approaches. As such, it is not always clear whether a program falls under the general umbrella of SEL, SWPBIS, or both, and why. This is especially true for many schools that embrace elements of both approaches. For SWPBIS, it is particularly difficult to identify its strengths and weaknesses when it is unclear whether the approach consists of the wide range of programs and practices referred to in some popular definitions of SWPBIS (e.g., Sugai & Horner, 2009; Sugai et al., 2010), or whether SWPBIS is the specific approach developed by Horner and Sugai that is wedded to ABA and PBS, and entails the previously described defining features and characteristics. If it is the former—anything that is effective in achieving outcomes valued by an individual school—then the approach adds little to the existing literature on school discipline, classroom management, and school reform. It also offers little with respect to guiding educational policy and practice, as considerable variance in programs and practices would be expected across schools. However, if SWPBIS is viewed as comprising the defining features and characteristics presented earlier, then its strengths and weaknesses can be identified, as we attempt to do below. A similar criticism, however, applies to the SEL approach. That is, SEL programs differ widely in their primary aims, as well as emphases on SEL strategies for achieving them. For example, multiple programs target specific areas of prevention, such as substance abuse and school violence; others target one or two specific SEL skills, such as empathy and social decision making; and still others target a wide range of SEL skills, including all five areas of SEL competency listed previously.

Commonalities and Strengths

In general, there are more commonalities and strengths than differences and weakness in the practices of SWPBIS and SEL. Both are school-based initiatives that are committed to increasing the social competencies of students while either explicitly or implicitly discouraging student problem behavior. Both value prevention over correction. Neither considers zero-tolerance or punishment-focused disciplinary policies particularly effective in creating safe and healthy schools, and both are committed to providing all students with critical life skills, a foundation on which academic success can be realized (Greenberg et al., 2003; Horner et al., 2005). Consistent with research on school reform (e.g., Fullan, 2007), both approaches recognize that successfully implementing any schoolwide program entails an ongoing process of systems change, which takes time. Both provide schools with valuable resources and supports for implementing their approach (see *www.casel.org* and *www.pbis.org*). For example, the Collaborative for Academic, Social, and Emotional Learning (CASEL; 2012) provides an extensive guide to support districts and schools as they plan to assess the social–emotional needs of their school population and the professional development needs of staff, selects an appropriate SEL program or approach, and monitors the implementation and effectiveness of the implemented program (Devaney, O'Brien, Resnick, Keister, & Weissberg, 2006). Likewise, the Technical Assistance Center on Positive Behavioral Interventions and Supports offers a large number of assessment and implementation tools and recommended practices.

Major Differences in Primary Aims and How to Achieve Them

Despite commonalities and strengths, the two approaches differ greatly in their primary aims, and the emphases on different strategies and techniques for achieving them. As noted previously, whereas the primary aim of the SEL approach is developing social and emotional competencies of self-discipline, the primary aim of the SEL approach is preventing and managing challenging behavior. The difference in these two primary aims, and strategies and techniques for achieving them, reflects each approach's theoretical framework. Any evaluation of the strengths and limitations of the two approaches must be in light of these major differences in primary aims.

Major Strength of SEL and Limitation of SWPBIS: Developing Cognitions, Emotions, and Behaviors of Self-Discipline

An essential element of SEL programming is developmentally appropriate and sequenced practices that include proactive instruction in SEL skills—skills that reflect how students think, feel, and act. The approach's focus on student behavior and on emotions and cognitions that underlie prosocial behavior and self-discipline differentiates it most greatly from the SWPBIS approach. Primary among the emotions and cognitions that research has shown to be linked to prosocial behavior and self-discipline are empathy, regulation of anger, moral reasoning, problem solving, and self-efficacy (Bear, 2012). Most SEL programs target those emotions and cognitions, and include structures designed to develop related skills and support their practice, maintenance, and generalization across time and settings (see CASEL, 2012, for reviews of programs, preschool through high school). For example, the *Responsive Classroom* approach includes practices such as daily morning meetings, student involvement in rule generation, use of positive teacher language, open-ended questioning, respectful listening, and problem-solving strategies that work to increase student self-efficacy, academic achievement, social skills, and positive relationships in school (Rimm-Kaufman & Chiu, 2007). The *Social Decision Making* approach has a specific set of prompts and cues that are used schoolwide to promote application of skills in varied contexts (Elias & Bruene, 2005). At a broader level, Durlak and colleagues (2011) suggest that the best SEL practices and programming are those that are sequenced, active, focused, and explicit (SAFE). Practices should include lesson content that is *systematic* and *sequenced. Active* practices are those that include role plays and other experiential activities. *Focused* programming includes adequate allotted instructional time, and *explicit* practices are those that focus on building and applying specific skills. Almost all evidence-based SEL programs have multiyear, nonrepeating lesson structures.

Ample research supports the SEL approach in achieving its primary aim and more. In the most comprehensive review of SEL interventions to date, which included a meta-analysis of 213 published studies of universal SEL interventions for children in preschool through 12th grade, Durlak and colleagues (2011) found that students in SEL programs had statistically significant and meaningful improvements in social–emotional skills, socially appropriate behavior, positive attitudes, and academic performance. Additionally, statistically significant decreases were found in conduct problems and emotional distress.

Whereas the development of SEL skills is a major strength of the SEL approach, it is a major weakness of the SWPBIS approach. Consistent with its ABA theoretical framework, little recognition is given to the importance of children's cognitions and emotions in behavior. Instead of targeting how children think and feel, the focus is on the use of teacher-centered behavioral practices to teach behavioral expectations and manage externally or control students' behavior. With its roots in behaviorism and ABA, SWPBIS assumes that environmental factors (i.e., educator practices) are primarily accountable for students' behavior problems; thus, educators are expected to change their practices more than students changing how they think, feel, and act.

Strength of SWPBIS and Limitation of SEL: Teacher-Directed Techniques for Managing Student Behavior

If one's aim is development of self-discipline, then SWPBIS's emphasis on teacher-directed techniques is a limitation of that approach, but this limitation mirrors its primary strength when one's aim is the management of student behavior. The opposite holds true for SEL: Its strength of developing self-discipline mirrors its limitation of teachers' managing student behavior. The SWPBIS approach provides a full range of evidence-based behavioral techniques, both preventive and corrective, for the effective short-term management of student behavior, and does so within a common framework for teachers and support staff. Behavioral techniques, particularly positive reinforcement, negative reinforcement, extinction, response cost punishment, and punishment involving aversives, are strongly supported by research as to their effectiveness in managing individual student behavior, especially in the short-term (Landrum & Kauffman, 2006). To one extent or another, all teachers, including those adhering to the SEL approach, use these behavioral techniques, typically in combination with other techniques (Bear, 2005; Brophy, 1996). They are common elements of nearly all models and approaches to schoolwide discipline, with research supporting their schoolwide application in preventing and correcting behavior problems (e.g., Embry, 2002; Gottfredson, Gottfredson, & Skroban, 1996). Nevertheless, behavioral techniques, and particularly the systematic use of positive reinforcement, receive much greater emphasis in SWPBIS than in the SEL approach. Positive reinforcement, using tangible rewards (e.g., tokens, tickets), access to privileges or preferred activities, social recognition, and verbal praise, is the cornerstone of the SWPBIS approach. It is systematically applied as a mechanism for recognizing positive behavior and "motivating students to use new skills" (George et al., 2009, p. 390). This systematic application of positive reinforcement, combined with active supervision, is designed not only to manage student behavior directly but also to increase indirectly the ratio of positive-to-negative interactions that staff members have with students, and therefore foster teacher–student relationships (McIntosh et al., 2010).

The effectiveness of the behavioral techniques in managing student behavior is well established in the SWPBIS approach, as seen in a large number of studies demonstrating reduced ODRs and suspensions (e.g., Bradshaw et al., 2010; Flannery, Fenning, Kato, & McIntosh, 2014; Mass-Galloway et al., 2008), and a randomized-control group study finding reduced bullying behaviors (Waasdorp, Bradshaw, & Leaf, 2012). That said, it is not clear that the systematic application of behavioral techniques as used in the research context of these studies is necessary for all students, or needed in the many classrooms and schools characterized by effective classroom management (Bear, 2013). Moreover, it remains to be determined whether those techniques lead to lasting change in student behavior or to a more positive school climate (other than as measured by ODRs; Bear, 2010; Osher et al., 2010). Research indicates that social skills taught using behavioral techniques seldom persist and often fail to generalize to other settings when instruction ends, and adults and consequences are no longer salient (Landrum & Kauffman, 2006).

The systematic application of behavioral techniques is most valuable when addressing the behavioral needs of students who fail to exhibit self-discipline, and especially those who are at risk of, or who currently exhibit, serious or chronic behavior problems (i.e., students needing support at Tiers 2 and 3). The SWPBIS approach provides greater guidance and wider range of evidence-based techniques than does the SEL approach for meeting the needs of those students. Direct teaching of behavioral expectations across settings (what behavior looks like in those settings), consistent application of consequences, use of a functional perspective of behavior (adjusting the antecedents and consequences to meet the function of the behavior to promote behavioral change), and establishment of a consistent message and structure in which students receive specific guidance from adults have been shown to be effective with students with behavioral problems and those who are not intrinsically motivated to engage in appropriate behaviors (Epstein, Atkins, Cullinan, Kutash, & Weaver, 2008).

Whereas most SEL programs include proactive instruction for students on how to handle negative emotions, how to engage empathically, and how to make healthy behavioral choices, few have built-in strategies and structures that guide teachers in deescalating major challenging behaviors or effective use of punishment (e.g., strategies to decrease negative behaviors). In this way, SEL programming might seem limiting, particularly for schools that are struggling to deal with large numbers of incidents of challenging behaviors.

A related strength of the SWPBIS approach is its emphasis on the ongoing collection and analyses of data to demonstrate that its targeted outcomes are attained, including the aim of managing student behavior. This is especially important when accountability data are highly valued. The routine gathering of not only multiple kinds of data on student behavior problems (e.g., office disciplinary referrals, suspensions) but also data on the school's strengths and needs, fidelity of implementation, and other student and school outcomes, enhances the ability of schools to target effectively areas of greatest need. Another advantage of collecting valid and multiple forms of data, as emphasized in SWPBIS, is that such data are often valuable in in persuading others (e.g., school boards and parents) that additional resources are needed. The kinds of data commonly used in the SWPBIS approach are discussed later in this chapter.

What Is Best for One's School: SEL, SWPBIS, or Both?

A school's choice between the two approaches might well depend on not only its primary aim, or aims, but also an assessment of the extent to which the two traditional aims of school discipline and classroom management are currently being achieved. That is, if student misbehavior is a major problem, and an environment exists that is not conducive to learning, including learning SEL competencies, then adoption of the SWPBIS approach would be a wise decision. Adding techniques commonly found in the SEL approach also would be wise not only to support short-term compliance but also to develop self-discipline in the long term. However, there would be little need to adopt the SWPBIS approach in schools implementing the SEL approach where few behavior problems are evident. There are many schools in which integrating *both* approaches would seem most appropriate, such as when both aims are highly valued and neither is being fully achieved. And there are schools that are given no choice—they are required, or mandated, to implement both approaches.

Integrating the two is most problematic, however, when SWPBIS and SEL are viewed as incompatible and separate rather than complementary. If viewed as polar opposites, if their underlying philosophies are understood too simplistically, or if evidence-based or promising practices stemming from either approach are avoided because of perceptions that they are either too complex or too limited, then the two approaches and the techniques and strategies inherent in each are likely to be perceived as incompatible. Under these circumstances, problems are likely to emerge, resulting in practices that are implemented ineffectively, incompletely, or not at all. In practice, where both exist, it is unlikely that one will be dropped, at least not in its entirety, and schools will likely find themselves working to accommodate both. For example, in Maryland and Illinois, where a large number of studies on the SWPBIS approach have been conducted (e.g., Bradshaw et al., 2010), schools are required to implement character education (Maryland) or SEL (Illinois). In a randomized controlled group study of SWPBIS in elementary schools in Maryland, Bradshaw and colleagues (2010) found that an average of 5.1 programs was being introduced in each school on "character education and /or development, social–emotional or social skills, bullying prevention, drug prevention (e.g., D.A.R.E. [Drug Abuse Resistance Education]), and conflict resolution and/or peer mediation" (p. 146).

Examples of potential strategies for integration of SWPBIS and SEL and common pitfalls that may occur with integration are highlighted in this section. We focus on four areas in which integration or pitfalls often occur when these approaches are implemented simultaneously. Specifically, we address (1) short-term and long-term aims of programming; (2) use of external rewards; (3) leadership structures for targeting behaviors, thoughts, and emotions; and (4) assessment and evaluation efforts.

Short-Term and Long-Term Aims

It may be useful to consider how schools and districts can use the most promising aspects of both SWPBIS and SEL to create a hybrid model of comprehensive and efficient service delivery that supports all children and values traditional aims of both school discipline and classroom management: managing student behavior in the short-term and developing self-discipline in the long-term. Such a combination of aims, and techniques and strategies for achieving them, would be consistent with an authoritative approach to child rearing (Baumrind, 2013) and school discipline (Bear, 2010; Brophy, 1996; Gregory et al., 2010). In authoritative discipline, both responsiveness (also often called *support*) and demandingness (also often called *structure*) are equally valued, and together are viewed as instrumental for effective discipline—in both the short and the long term. *Responsiveness* is best described as supportive and reciprocal relationships, and sensitivity to children's developmental needs, as emphasized in the SEL approach. *Demandingness* emphasizes clear behavioral expectations, rules, and accountability structures, as found in the SWPBIS approach. Whereas techniques of SWPBIS may be most effective for demandingness and achieving short-term goals, their ultimate success lies in having a connection to and articulation with the techniques of SEL that lead to internalized skill gains, including those of self-discipline. Thus, techniques associated with demandingness, whether positive or punitive, would be linked with responsiveness-focused techniques of SEL to achieve *both* short- and long-term goals. For example, if a SWPBIS schoolwide expectation is "respect others", and behavioral examples of respect or routines are defined by teachers (potentially with input from students) as "wait your turn to speak" and "listen", then providing children with explicit praise as they learn these rules is important to establish the behavior initially. However, the additional discussion of such rules (e.g., reasons why they are important other than the immediate consequences to oneself), and habitual practice and application of these behaviors, may serve to scaffold instruction and integration of important SEL competency building, such as relationship development and responsible decision making. Another example might be when a teacher institutes a behavioral consequence such as "time-out from reinforcement", in which a student is temporarily removed from a situation that appears to be reinforcing his or her challenging behavior. Linking this practice with follow-up teaching or reflecting on the behavior may help the child to try a different way to engage in the future. In these examples, the approach to SWPBIS teaching would be in sync with an SEL approach, and could ensure continuity and synergy of learning.

Use of External Rewards

In the SEL approach, adults are certainly expected to acknowledge and encourage the practice of SEL skills, but compared to the SWPBIS approach, there is much less emphasis in SEL on using tangible rewards, and especially to control student behavior externally. Given the often opposing perspectives on use of external rewards in SWPBIS and SEL, it might be helpful for professionals to reconceptualize this issue and think about using external rewards as a short-term bridge toward the longer-term development of SEL competencies, while also using them strategically (e.g., sparingly, only as needed, not in a contracted or social comparative manner, and while relying more on praise, privileges, and other forms of private and public recognition and feedback; Bear, 2010). The strategic use of external rewards, including tangible ones, may be completely appropriate, especially when problem behaviors are evident. Most aligned with an SEL orientation would be the use of classroom- or school-level rewards, with contingencies linked to cooperation and teamwork, and use of praise and rewards to reinforce not only desired behaviors but also the underlying cognitions and emotions.

A common pitfall often associated with SWPBIS, and particularly with an emphasis on teacher-centered practices, is the assumption that the systematic and frequent use of praise and rewards is sufficient for behavioral change—both short-term and long-term—and is easy to implement effectively. As noted in Brophy's (1981) extensive review of the research literature on praise and rewards, their effectiveness at the classroom level "has been seriously oversold" (p. 19). Implementing them strategically and wisely, especially classwide and schoolwide, is often a daunting task in light of the multiple demands on the teacher, and the effects on behavior are often minimal (Brophy, 1981). Their use also is inconsistent with the training of many general education teachers (Brownell, Ross, Colón, & McCallum, 2003), who learn that under certain conditions (e.g., used in a controlling manner and when social comparisons are highlighted; Deci, Koestner, & Ryan, 2001) rewards and even praise can be detrimental to students' intrinsic motivation. When thinking about reward systems that are "scaled up", such as in SWPBIS practices, getting teachers and staff members to implement rewards in a systematic and strategic manner is particularly challenging. When teachers are asked to change their current practices and to implement the "scaled-up" reward system, particularly when there is little evidence to indicate a need for change or that the new system will more effective than current practices, resistance should be expected, and rightfully so (Bear, 2013).

Whereas false promise of quick and lasting behavior change with the use of systematic reinforcement of specific behavioral expectations is a likely pitfall of the SWPBIS approach, a failure to appreciate the potential value of the strategic and wise use of praise and rewards in not only managing student behavior but also in developing self-discipline is a likely pitfall of the SEL approach. That is, following an overly rigid interpretation of a constructive approach, external rewards may be used too little, especially when new skills are being taught, when intrinsic motivation is lacking, and when desired behaviors are not exhibited. To be sure, the use of rewards and their potential harm to intrinsic motivation has been the subject of ongoing controversy and debate for several decades (see Cameron & Pierce, 1994; Deci et al., 2001). Such debate is likely to continue; however, it also is likely that the frequently voiced extremes in this debate (i.e., rewards are never harmful to intrinsic motivation, and rewards are almost always harmful) are equally wrong. Recent research suggests that when used in the context of an integrated SEL and SWPBIS approach, frequent use of praise and rewards is associated with greater extrinsic and intrinsic motivation for prosocial behavior (Blank, Bear, Mantz, & Farley-Ripple, 2014).

Leadership Structures

The SWPBIS and SEL literatures share consistent messages regarding the importance of building a school's capacity for sustainable and effective routines and practices. Both literatures suggest starting with a steering committee or leadership team (Devaney et al., 2006; Sugai et al., 2010). The representativeness of this group is particularly important, in that each member can serve as a liaison to various members of the school network (e.g., administrators, grade-level teacher teams, specialists, parents). Common pitfalls occur when there are too many teams facilitating too many initiatives, or when the team membership does not truly mirror the school community, such as when the number of special education and support staff on the team is not proportionate to the number of general education teachers in the school, or vice versa. When this occurs, resistance from the underrepresented members is likely.

A representative leadership team might develop a scope and sequence for a hybrid model of SWPBIS and SEL practices. For example, they might explicitly link each of the selected schoolwide behavioral expectations to particular SEL lessons from an adopted curriculum. With this road map, educators may have an easier time conceptualizing the overlaps between SWPBIS and SEL, and clearly and consistently communicating such overlaps to all students in their instructional delivery. Given the potential for competing practices and pitfalls, it is crucial that leadership committees guide the effort in clearly identifying developmentally appropriate, contextually fitting SEL and SWPBIS practices, and communicate the linkages between initiatives. If the goal is to create an atmosphere that includes both responsive relationships and demandingness, leadership committees and school professionals need to work from a relatively sophisticated understanding of the culture of reform in their particular school environment and the social–emotional needs of students.

Having an understanding of what innovations are already in place within a school is important for effective integration of new practices. For example, SWPBIS is based on a structured, tiered model of intervention that increases in intensity based on student need. Universal practices, focused on defining and teaching behavioral expectations to students across settings and acknowledging students for meeting such expectations, are typically enacted in a coordinated way among school staff members. If a school already has this coordinated structure in place, a natural extension of these practices would be formally to incorporate more student-centered strategies and techniques of SEL. SEL would extend students' understanding of the importance of core expectations (e.g., respect, kindness, responsibility), as well as help them to build skills that may be implicitly linked to expectations (e.g., conflict resolution, emotion regulation). In this way, practice of SEL skills may be more easily integrated across school settings and situations, and the frequent and systematic use of rewards (if needed) could be used strategically when new behaviors or routines are being taught and when students lack motivation to apply the skills. Such use of external rewards may not be necessary when students have consistent opportunities to reflect upon and internalize the links between behavioral expectations and social–emotional processes such as empathy, pride, and self-identity.

As a school moves through the implementation process, the leadership committee continues to serve as a data team that creates action plans based on regular analysis of assessments. Analysis of student outcome data may help to identify students in need of more intensive support, and analysis of implementation data helps to identify the extent to which practices are consistently being implemented schoolwide. The leadership committee could also use such data to plan staff professional development activities focused on the social–emotional instructional core originally defined by the school.

Assessment and Evaluation

Given that the leadership team facilitating SEL and SWPBIS must rely on accurate and efficient collection and management of data, a potential measurement pitfall that can occur is incomplete data collection. For example, schools may put intensive energy into the analysis of schoolwide office disciplinary data, while missing other important elements of behavioral change that have occurred as a result of either/both SWPBIS and SEL practices, and particularly those elements related to their long-term goals (e.g., increased prosocial behavior). On the other hand, schools may put energy into use of specific tools associated with perceptions of social and emotional behavior but have no system for collecting and analyzing data for decision making on a frequent, ongoing basis that can be easily used.

To avoid assessment pitfalls, it is critical that schools implementing SWPBIS and SEL use a comprehensive and multimethod approach in assessing needs (e.g., professional development, organizational support), fidelity of implementation, and program effectiveness. Readers are encouraged to refer to more in-depth analysis of SEL assessments elsewhere in this handbook. An example provided here includes the multimethod assessment approach used in Delaware's statewide school climate initiative, which integrates the SWPBIS and SEL approaches. Three different assessments are used to identify a school's strengths and weaknesses in four areas of comprehensive school discipline: developing self-discipline, preventing behavior problems, correcting behavior problems, and addressing the needs of students with serious and chronic behavior problems. The fifth key area assessed is staff development and program evaluation. As part of the three assessments, students, teachers/staff, and parents first complete the Delaware School Climate Survey (Bear, Gaskins, Blank, & Chen, 2011). Next, within the context of a professional learning community, school staff members complete and discuss a comprehensive strengths and needs assessment that consists of their ratings of 10 items linking each of the five previously mentioned areas. Finally, external evaluators complete a separate needs assessment in the same five areas based on interviews with teachers, staff, administrators, and students; school observations; and review of materials and policies (for the previously mentioned assessment tools, see *www.delawarepbs.org*). Upon their completion, schools are challenged to address identified barriers and obstacles in program implementation and to establish a school improvement plan. This plan might include strategies for minimizing barriers and maximizing effective and efficient program implementation.

In addition to gathering data that help staff members to understand stakeholders' perceptions of climate and the reach of service delivery, it may also be useful to consider universal measurement of individual student strengths and assets, and to screen for social and emotional deficits. Such added measurement may help schools to identify clearly which students are not responding to universal SEL–SWPBIS practices and may need more intensive, strengths-oriented interventions. In conjunction with analysis of climate and disciplinary data, universal social–emotional screening assessments allow professionals to compile information on all students' social–emotional behaviors within a school quickly and efficiently, which builds the capacity for more targeted intervention planning and progress monitoring.

Summary

In this chapter, we have compared the SEL and SWPBIS approaches, including a brief history of the SWPBIS approach and its defining features and characteristics. The primary strength and limitation of each approach was highlighted. We have argued that the foremost strength of each approach is the weakness of the other approach, particularly when one respects the two traditional aims of school discipline and classroom management—managing student behavior and developing self-discipline. The SWPBIS approach provides educators with evidence-based behavioral techniques, when needed, for managing student behavior. These teacher-centered techniques are often necessary when common student-centered techniques of SEL are insufficient for achieving this important short-term aim of school discipline. However, the SWPBIS approach largely neglects the long-term aim of developing self-discipline, especially emotions and cognitions related to self-discipline. In contrast, this is a strength, and primary focus, of the SEL approach, whereas managing student misbehavior is a relative weakness. Together, they provide a blend of demandingness (or structure) and responsiveness (or support) that defines authoritative discipline. Because many schools are now asked to implement the SWPBIS and SEL approaches, we have identified several major potential pitfalls that schools are likely to face with such integration and have offered suggestions for addressing them.

References

American Psychological Association Zero Tolerance Task Force. (2008). Are zero tolerance policies effective in the schools?: An evidentiary review and recommendations. *American Psychologist, 63*, 852–862.

Baumrind, D. (2013). Authoritative parenting revisited: History and current status. In R. E. Larzelere, A. S. Morris, & A. W. Harrist (Eds.), *Authoritative parenting: Synthesizing nurturance and discipline for optimal child development* (pp. 11–34). Washington, DC: American Psychological Association.

Bear, G. G. (with A. Cavalier & M. Manning). (2005). *Developing self-discipline and preventing and correcting misbehavior.* Boston: Allyn & Bacon.

Bear, G. G. (2010). *School discipline and self-discipline: A practical guide to promoting prosocial student behavior.* New York: Guilford Press.

Bear, G. G. (2012). Self-discipline as a protective asset. In S. Brock, P. Lazarus, & S. Jimerson (Eds.), *Best practices in crisis prevention and intervention in the schools* (2nd ed., pp. 27–54). Bethesda, MD: National Association of School Psychologists.

Bear, G. G. (2013). Teacher resistance to frequent rewards and praise: Lack of skill or a wise decision? *Journal of Educational and Psychological Consultation, 23*, 318–340.

Bear, G. G., Gaskins, C., Blank, J., & Chen, F. F. (2011). Delaware School Climate Survey—Student: Its factor structure, concurrent validity, and reliability. *Journal of School Psychology, 49*, 157–174.

Blank, J., Bear, G. G., Mantz, L., & Farley-Ripple, E. (2014). *Are the use of punishment, praise, and rewards in schools associated with more or less intrinsic motivation?* Manuscript submitted for publication.

Bradshaw, C. P., Mitchell, M. M., & Leaf, P. J. (2010). Examining the effects of schoolwide positive behavioral interventions and supports on student outcomes. *Journal of Positive Behavior Interventions, 12*, 133–148.

Brophy, J. E. (1981). Teacher praise: A functional analysis. *Review of Educational Research, 51*, 5–32.

Brophy, J. E. (1996). *Teaching problem students.* New York: Guilford Press.

Brownell, M. T., Ross, D. R., Colón, E. P., & McCallum, C. L. (2003). *Critical features of special education teacher preparation: A comparison with exemplary practices in general teacher education* (COPSSE Document No. RS-4). Gainesville: University of Florida, Center on Personnel Studies in Special Education.

Cameron, J., & Pierce, W. D. (1994). Reinforcement, reward, and intrinsic motivation: A meta-analysis. *Review of Educational Research, 64*, 363–423.

Collaborative for Academic, Social, and Emotional Learning (CASEL). (2012). *2013 CASEL guide: Effective social and emotional programs—Preschool and elementary edition.* Chicago: Author.

Crone, D. A., & Horner, R. H. (2003). *Building positive behavior support systems in schools: Functional behavioral assessment.* New York: Guilford Press.

Danielsen, A. G., Wiium, N., Wilhelmsen, B. U., & Wold, B. (2010). Perceived support provided by teachers and classmates and students' self-reported academic initiative. *Journal of School Psychology, 48*, 247–267.

Deci, E. L., Koestner, R., & Ryan, R. M. (2001). Extrinsic rewards and intrinsic motivation in education: Reconsidered once again. *Review of Educational Research, 71*(1), 1–27.

Devaney, E., O'Brien, M. U., Resnick, H., Keister, S., & Weissberg, R. P. (2006). *Sustainable schoolwide social and emotional learning (SEL).* Chicago: Collaborative for Academic, Social, and Emotional Learning.

Dunlap, G., Sailor, W., Horner, R. H., & Sugai, G. (2009). Overview and history of positive behavior support. In W. Sailor, G. Dunlap, G. Sugai, & R. Horner (Eds.), *Handbook of positive behavior support* (pp. 3–16). New York: Springer.

Durlak, J. A., Weissberg, R. P., Dymnicki, A. B., Taylor, R. D., & Schellinger, K. B. (2011). The impact of enhancing students' social and emotional learning: A meta-analysis of school-based universal interventions. *Child Development, 82*, 474–501.

Elias, M. J., & Bruene, L. (2005). *Social Decision Making/Social Problem Solving: A curriculum for academic, social, and emotional learning, grades 4–5.* Champaign, IL: Research Press.

Elias, M. J., Wang, M. C., Weissberg, R. P., Zins, J. E., & Walberg, H. J. (2002). The other side of the report card: Student success depends on more than test scores. *American School Board Journal, 189*(11), 28–30.

Elias, M. J., Zins, J. E., Weissberg, R. P., Frey, K. S., Greenberg, M. T., Haynes, N. M., et al. (1997). *Promoting social and emotional learning: Guidelines for educators.* Alexandria, VA: Association for Supervision and Curriculum Development.

Embry, D. D. (2002). The Good Behavior Game: A best practice candidate as a universal behavioral vaccine. *Clinical Child and Family Psychology Review, 5*, 273–297.

Epstein, M., Atkins, M., Cullinan, D., Kutash, K., & Weaver, R. (2008). *Reducing behavior problems in the elementary school classroom: A practice guide* (NCEE No. 2008-012). Washington, DC: National Center for Education Evaluation and Regional Assistance, Institute of Education Sciences, U.S. Department of Education. Retrieved January 8, 2013, from *http://ies.ed.gov/ncee/wwc/publications/practiceguides.*

Flannery, K. B., Fenning, P., Kato, M., McGrath, M. M., & McIntosh, K. (2014). Effects of school-wide positive behavioral interventions and supports and fidelity of implementation on problem behavior in high schools. *School Psychology Quarterly, 29*, 111–124.

Fullan, M. (2007). *The new meaning of educational change* (4th ed.). New York: Teachers College Press.

George, H. P., Kincaid, D., & Pollard-Sage, J. (2009). Primary-tier interventions and supports. In W. Sailor, G. Dunlap, G. Sugai, & R. H. Horner (Eds.), *Handbook of positive behavior support* (pp. 375–394). New York: Springer Science and Business Media.

Gottfredson, D. C., Gottfredson, G. D., & Skroban, S. (1996). A multimodel school-based prevention demonstration. *Journal of Adolescent Research, 11*, 97–115.

Greenberg, M. T., Domitrovich, C., & Bumbarger, B. (2001). The prevention of mental disorders in school-aged children: Current state of the field. *Prevention and Treatment, 4*, 1–62.

Greenberg, M. T., Weissberg, R. P., Utne-O'Brien, M. T., Zins, J. E., Fredericks, L., Resnik, H., et al. (2003). Enhancing school-based prevention and youth development through coordinated social, emotional, and academic learning. *American Psychologist, 58*, 466–474.

Gregory, A., Cornell, D., Fan, X., Sheras, P., Shih, T., & Huang, F. (2010). Authoritative school discipline: High school practices associated with lower student bullying and victimization. *Journal of Educational Psychology, 102*, 483–496.

Hamre, B. K., Pianta, R. C., Downer, J. T., & Mashburn, A. J. (2008). Teachers' perceptions of conflict with young students: Looking beyond problem behaviors. *Social Development, 17*, 115–136.

Horner, R. H., Sugai, G., Smolkowski, K., Eber, L., Nakasato, J., Todd, A. W., et al. (2009). A randomized, wait-list controlled effectiveness trial assessing school-wide positive behavior support in elementary schools. *Journal of Positive Behavior Interventions, 11*, 133–144.

Horner, R. H., Sugai, G., Todd, A. W., & Lewis-Palmer, T. (2005). Schoolwide behavior support. In L. M. Bambara & L. Kern (Eds.), *Individualized supports for students with problem behaviors: Designing positive behavior plans* (pp. 359–390). New York: Guilford Press.

Hughes, J. N. (2012). Teachers as managers of students' peer context. In A. M. Ryan & G. W. Ladd (Eds.), *Peer relationships and adjustment at school* (pp. 189–218). Charlotte, NC: Information Age.

Individuals with Disabilities Education Improvement Act, 20 U.S.C. § 1400 (2004).

Knoff, H. M. (2008). Best practices in implementing statewide positive behavioral support systems. In A. Thomas & J. Grimes (Eds.), *Best practices in school psychology* (5th ed., pp. 749–763). Bethesda, MD: National Association of School Psychologists.

Landrum, T. J., & Kauffman, J. M. (2006). Behavioral approaches to classroom management. In C. M. Evertson & C. S. Weinstein (Eds.), *Handbook of classroom management: Research, practice, and contemporary issues* (pp. 47–71). Mahwah, NJ: Erlbaum.

Mass-Galloway, R. L., Panyan, M. V., Smith, C. R., & Wessendorf, S. (2008). Systems change with school-wide positive behavior supports. *Journal of Positive Behavior Interventions, 10*, 129–135.

McIntosh, K., Filter, M. J., Bennett, J. L., Ryan, C., & Sugai, G. (2010). Principles of sustainable prevention: Designing scale-up of school-wide positive behavior support to promote durable systems. *Psychology in the Schools, 47*, 5–21.

Osher, D., Bear, G. G., Sprague, J. R., & Doyle, W. (2010). How can we improve school discipline? *Educational Researcher, 39*, 48–58.

Parke, R. D., & Buriel, R. (2006). Socialization in the family: Ethnic and ecological perspectives. In W. Damon & R. M. Learner (Series Ed.), & N. Eisenberg (Vol. Ed.), *Handbook of child psychology: Vol. 3. Social, emotional, and personality development* (6th ed., pp. 429–504). New York: Wiley.

Piaget, J. (1965). *The moral judgment of the child.* New York: Free Press (Original work published 1932)

Rimm-Kaufman, S. E., & Chiu, Y. I. (2007). Promoting social and academic competence in the classroom: An intervention study examining the contribution of Responsive Classroom. *Psychology in the Schools, 44*, 397–413.

Sprague, J. R., & Horner, R. H. (2006). Schoolwide positive behavioral supports. In S. R. Jimerson & M. J. Furlong (Eds.), *Handbook of school violence and school safety: From research to practice* (pp. 413–427). Mahwah, NJ: Erlbaum.

Stearns, E., Dodge, K. A., & Nicholson, M. (2008). Peer contextual influences on the growth of authority-acceptance problems in early elementary school. *Merrill–Palmer Quarterly, 54*, 208–231.

Sugai, G., & Horner, R. H. (2009). Defining and describing schoolwide positive behavior support. In W. Sailor, G. Dunlap, G. Sugai, & R. Horner (Eds.), *Handbook of positive behavior support* (pp. 307–326). New York: Springer.

Sugai, G., Horner, R. H., Algozzine, R., Barrett, S., Lewis, T., Anderson, C., et al. (2010). *School-wide positive behavior support: Implementers' blueprint and self-assessment.* Eugene: University of Oregon. Retrieved January 8, 2013, from *www.pbis.org.*

Sugai, G., Horner, R., & McIntosh, K. (2008). Best practices in developing a broad-scale system of school-wide positive behavior support. In A. Thomas & J. Grimes (Eds.), *Best practices in school psychology* (5th ed., pp. 765–779). Bethesda, MD: National Association of School Psychologists.

Thomas, D. E., Bierman, K. L., & the Conduct Problems Prevention Research Group. (2006). The impact of classroom aggression on the development of aggressive behavior problems in children. *Development and Psychopathology, 18*, 471–487.

Vygotsky, L. (1987). Thinking and speech. In L. S. Vygotsky, R. Rieber, & A. Carton (Eds.), *The collected words of L. S. Vygotsky: Vol. 1. Problems of general psychology* (pp. 37–285). New York: Plenum Press. (Original work published 1934)

Waasdorp, T. E., Bradshaw, C. P., & Leaf, P. J. (2012). The impact of schoowide positive behavioral interventions and support on bullying and peer rejection: A randomized controlled effectiveness trial. *Archives of Pediatrics and Adolescence Medicine, 166*, 149–156.

Wentzel, K. R. (2006). A social motivation perspective for classroom management. In C. M. Evertson & C. S. Weinstein (Eds.), *Handbook of classroom management: Research, practice, and contemporary issues* (pp. 619–643). Mahwah, NJ: Erlbaum.

Zins, J. E., & Elias, M. J. (2006). Social and emotional learning. In G. G. Bear & K. M. Minke (Eds.), *Children's needs III: Development, prevention, and intervention* (pp. 1–13). Bethesda, MD: National Association of School Psychologists.

CHAPTER 31

Taking SEL to Scale in Schools

The Role of Community Coalitions

Abigail A. Fagan, J. David Hawkins, and Valerie B. Shapiro

Several authors of chapters in this book (Durlak, Weissberg, Domitrovich, & Gullotta, Chapter 1; Jagers, Harris, & Skoog, Chapter 11; Rimm-Kaufman & Hulleman, Chapter 10; Williamson, Modecki, & Guerra, Chapter 12) and other research (e.g., Collaborative for Academic, Social, and Emotional Learning [CASEL], 2012; Durlak, Dymnicki, Taylor, Weissberg, & Schellinger, 2011; O'Connell, Boat, & Warner, 2009) have identified the existence of many high-quality, school-based social and emotional learning (SEL) programs that, when well implemented, enhance social–emotional competence; promote academic achievement; and prevent mental, emotional, and behavioral problems. Additional empirical research has supported these findings, linking social and emotional skills to better outcomes for youth, even among those living in adverse conditions. Such evidence indicates that schools have much to gain by implementing such curricula. However, research also reveals that effective SEL programs are not currently being used widely in schools (Gottfredson & Gottfredson, 2002; Ringwalt et al., 2011).

We discuss in this chapter how community coalitions can help increase the spread of SEL programs in classrooms, schools, and school districts. We identify some of the challenges likely to be faced when attempting to scale-up and increase dissemination of effective SEL programs, based on the experiences of 12 community coalitions implementing the Communities That Care (CTC) prevention system in the context of a randomized controlled evaluation of this system (for more details regarding this project, see Hawkins et al., 2008). In this multiyear project, while schools in some communities were initially reluctant to adopt SEL curricula, all communities eventually did so. As a result, over half of the middle school student population in these communities was provided with programming demonstrated to foster social and emotional competence and prevent the development of problem behaviors. We discuss how obstacles that typically hinder the adoption and implementation of SEL curricula were overcome when community coalitions using the CTC system partnered with school officials and personnel. Before reviewing the lessons we learned from this project, we begin with a description of CTC.

The CTC Prevention System

The CTC prevention system (Hawkins & Catalano, 1992) was developed to assist communities in incorporating scientific advances regarding the promotion of healthy youth development and prevention of youth problem behaviors (e.g., school dropout, teenage pregnancy, substance use, delinquency, and violence) into their everyday practices. The primary goal of CTC is to improve youth outcomes communitywide by increasing the use of programs and policies that have demonstrated effectiveness in reducing the risk factors associated with problem behaviors, increasing the protective factors associated with better outcomes, and achieving healthier youth development. Recognizing that widespread change will not be achieved through the efforts of one person, or even a small body of committed individuals, the CTC system relies on broad-based coalitions of community members to work together. Coalitions may include, for example, elected officials, law enforcement personnel, school administrators and staff, public health officials, faith leaders, youth, parents, and business representatives. The active involvement of community stakeholders, and increased skills, information, and resources that accompany this collaboration, should help to increase community consensus and buy-in for change efforts, minimize duplication of services, and result in more cost-effective services that are better implemented and more likely to be sustained (Hawkins, Catalano, & Arthur, 2002; Kania & Kramer, 2011; Stevenson & Mitchell, 2003; Wandersman & Florin, 2003).

The CTC system was developed to engage community members and foster their collective involvement in change efforts (i.e., enhancing their "collective impact"; see: Kania & Kramer, 2011). CTC is locally managed by a coalition of diverse community stakeholders, who, guided by data collected from school and community records and surveys of students in local schools, match community profiles with tested programs proven effective in controlled studies to produce better youth outcomes. The coalition oversees and monitors implementation of the new policies and programs in appropriate community organizations, including schools and health and human service organizations. CTC provides clear guidance to coalitions in the steps required to achieve change. Six structured training workshops are provided in order to identify, discuss, and practice the steps, processes, and actions (referred to as "benchmarks and milestones" in the CTC materials) that should be undertaken by coalitions to achieve change. Proactive technical assistance is offered throughout the process to assist coalition members.

Capitalizing on the natural appeal of coalitions, and the recognition that communities have different problems and will need different solutions to address them, CTC emphasizes that change efforts must be community specific and owned and operated by local community members (Hawkins et al., 2002; Hawkins, Van Horn, & Arthur, 2004). CTC does not stipulate that particular programs be implemented; rather, communities create unique action plans that address their particular needs using a variety of programming types and formats, including school, family, community, or individually focused interventions. In regards to the focus of this book, if significant proportions of local youth have reported deficits in social and emotional competencies, then coalitions may decide to select SEL programs to address these needs. Unlike the typical process used to adopt school programs (e.g., when decisions are made by a staff person or administrator), choices made by coalitions are based on group consensus of a diverse group of stakeholders, and new SEL curricula in schools are viewed as part of a communitywide change effort.

Although the CTC system does not mandate the use of school-based or SEL programs, the remainder of this chapter focuses on how CTC coalitions can help increase the spread of such curricula. We describe the barriers typically faced when adopting and implementing SEL and other school curricula, and strategies used by CTC coalitions when working with school partners to overcome these challenges. Our attention centers on not only decision-making processes related to the adoption of new programs but also issues related to implementation and sustainability of these interventions.

The Community Youth Development Study

Our findings are based on experiences of coalitions participating in the Community Youth Development Study (CYDS), a 10-year community randomized trial designed to test the efficacy of the CTC system in reducing adolescent risk factors, increasing protective factors, and decreasing problem behaviors (Hawkins et al., 2008). The project involved 24 small- to medium-size towns in seven states, ranging in size from 1,500 to 50,000 residents. These communities were randomly assigned in fall 2002 to implement the CTC prevention system (n = 12) or to provide prevention services as usual (n = 12). In the first 5 years of the project, the 12 intervention communities received training and technical assistance in the CTC system, funding for a full-time coalition staff member (the CTC coordinator), and up to $275,000 (across Years 2–5) to implement prevention programs targeting schools, families, and students in grades 5–9, the grade range that was the focus of the study.

Adoption of the CTC System in Intervention Communities

A process evaluation (Fagan, Hanson, Hawkins, & Arthur, 2009) indicated that all 12 intervention communities in this study fully implemented the CTC model. All intervention communities formed a prevention coalition in the first year of the study, and active coalitions were maintained over time. While a range of community stakeholders were represented on coalitions (including law enforcement, health and human service agencies, youth service groups, local or state government, business, religious groups, youth, and parents), school personnel tended to comprise the greatest proportion of all members in communities. In the first year of the research project, school representatives (superintendents, curriculum specialists, principals, vice-principals, prevention staff/counselors, teachers, and other staff members) made up 26% of the membership across communities (Fagan, Brooke-Weiss, Cady, & Hawkins, 2009).

Consistent with the CTC guidelines, local youth in all communities in grades 6, 8, 10, and 12 completed the CTC Youth Survey every 2 years during the study. This school-based survey provides valid and reliable self-reported measures of 30 risk and protective factors, as well as problem behaviors (Arthur, Hawkins, Pollard, Catalano, & Baglioni, 2002), and data from the survey were used to determine the foci of coalition efforts. In this study, coalition members reviewed trends in their local data to identify student-reported risk and protective factors that were consistently elevated or depressed over time. Coalitions then prioritized two to seven factors of concern, which they intended to target with prevention activities. To avoid duplication of services, coalition members also conducted a resource assessment of programs and policies already in place in their communities that addressed their priority areas.

In order to receive research funds, coalitions in this study had to select interventions that (1) addressed their community's prioritized risk and protective factors, and (2) had been tested in controlled trials and demonstrated to be effective for families or children in grades 5–9 in reducing risk factors, enhancing protective factors, and reducing behavior problems. During one of the CTC training workshops, coalition members reviewed information from the *CTC Prevention Strategies Guide* (*www.communitiesthatcare.net*), which provides short descriptions of 39 tested and effective programs for the study age group, including schoolwide interventions, school-based social and emotional learning curricula, tutoring, mentoring programs, after-school activities, parent training programs, and community-based interventions. Based on input from all coalition members, and taking into account program requirements, financial costs, human resources needed, and local social/political factors, coalitions selected programs that addressed their prioritized risk and protective factors and were considered feasible to implement. In Years 2–5 of the study, the new programs were implemented and monitored by coalition members to ensure they were being fully delivered (for a full description of implementation monitoring procedures used by coalitions, see Fagan, Hanson, Hawkins, & Arthur, 2008).

Adoption of School-Based Programs and SEL Curricula

CTC intervention communities all decided to adopt new school-based programs, including SEL programs, at some point during the first 5 years of this study. Their decisions to do so were influenced by the fact that (1) effective SEL programs were identified in the *CTC Prevention Strategies Guide*; (2) these programs were perceived to be relatively cost-effective, particularly when school staff members could teach them; and (3) the services could reach a large proportion of youth, especially if delivered in all the grades and schools in the community that served students in the age group targeted by the program. As shown in Table 31.1, five communities adopted school-based programs in Year 2 of the project, four communities adopted school-based programs in Year 3, one community did so in Year 4, and two communities adopted school programs in Year 5. Nine different school-based prevention programs were implemented across the 12 intervention communities during the study, and five sites implemented multiple school-based programs. As shown in Table 31.2, six of the nine programs used by CTC communities involved delivery of classroom-based curricula with SEL elements.

The adoption of new school-based programs in all 12 communities involved in this study is notable given prior research demonstrating that a large proportion of elementary, middle, and high schools in the United States are failing to implement effective school curricula (Gottfredson & Gottfredson, 2002; Hallfors & Godette, 2002; Ringwalt et al., 2011). For example, a national study of the diffusion of drug use prevention curricula (which may include SEL elements) indicated that only 47% of middle schools (Ringwalt et al., 2011) and 10% of high schools (Ringwalt et al., 2008) reported using programs that had been tested and shown to be effective. We think that the structured involvement of broad-based community coalitions contributed to this suc-

TABLE 31.1. School-Based Programs Implemented in the CYDS, by Community and Year

Community	Program(s) selected	Year(s) implemented
A	All Stars	Years 2–5
	Program Development Evaluation	Years 2–3
	Class Action	Year 5
T	Life Skills Training	Years 2–5
	Lions Quest Skills for Adolescence	Years 3–5
O	Lions Quest Skills for Adolescence	Years 2–5
C	Lions Quest Skills for Adolescence	Years 2–5
J	Life Skills Training	Years 2–5
I	Life Skills Training	Years 3–5
	Olweus Bullying Prevention	Years 3–5
N	Stay SMART	Year 3
	Life Skills Training	Years 4–5
H	Life Skills Training	Years 3–5
W	Project Alert	Years 3–5
	Project Towards No Drug Abuse	Year 5
Q	Olweus Bullying Prevention	Years 4–5
G	Project Towards No Drug Abuse	Year 5
X	Stay SMART	Year 5

Note. Year 1 of the study involved formation and training of CTC coalitions; program adoption and implementation occurred in Years 2–5.

TABLE 31.2. School-Based Programs Incorporating SEL Elements Implemented by CTC Communities

SEL elements	All Stars Core	Life Skills Training	Lions Quest Skills for Adolescence	Project Alert	Project Towards No Drug Abuse	Stay SMART
Identifying/managing emotions		✓	✓		✓	✓
Empathy/perspective taking			✓			
Goal setting	✓	✓	✓		✓	✓
Decision making	✓	✓	✓		✓	✓
Communication skills		✓	✓	✓	✓	✓
Conflict resolution		✓	✓			✓
Interpersonal problem solving		✓	✓	✓	✓	✓

cess. As noted by others (Mihalic, Fagan, Irwin, Ballard, & Elliott, 2004; Saul et al., 2008), the dissemination of evidence-based programs in schools is often hindered by a lack of information regarding what works, a lack of "champions" who will generate support for these curricula, competing beliefs about what should be taught in schools, and many structural barriers that impede incorporation of new innovations. As we describe in the next section, these challenges can be avoided or faced and overcome using the CTC system.

Strategies Used by CTC Coalitions to Foster Adoption and Dissemination of Effective SEL Programs

Providing Information about Effective SEL Programs

One of the first barriers to the adoption of school-based and/or SEL programming is the difficulty faced by school personnel in accessing scientific evidence regarding effective programming (Mihalic et al., 2004; Saul et al., 2008). Such information is often published in scientific journals that are inaccessible to school personnel, and these articles frequently describe methodological issues and procedures not easily understood by practitioners (Mihalic et al., 2004). While user-friendly materials and lists describing "best practice" and "model" programs are more readily available now than in the past (see, e.g., *www.bestevidence.org, http://ies.ed.gov/ncee/wwc*, and *www.colorado.edu/cspv/blueprints*), such lists often rely on differing criteria to establish effectiveness, and making sense of these data can still be difficult for school staff (Hallfors, Pankratz, & Hartman, 2007). Schools need assistance to obtain and comprehend information regarding tested and effective programs.

As previously described, the CTC prevention system provides coalitions with information about what works in the *CTC Prevention Strategies Guide*. Short summaries of effective programs and their implementation requirements are reviewed by coalition members during one of the CTC training workshops. School personnel participating in coalitions thus gain firsthand access to information about what works. In order to spread this information to school administrators and staff who did not participate in the CTC coalition or training, coalitions in this research trial held subsequent formal and informal meetings with school boards, principals, teachers, and other school personnel to describe effective program options. In some communities, coalition coordinators obtained copies of the new curricula and reviewed program content with teachers and administrators. One coalition coordinator and school principal visited a nearby town to observe delivery of a program under consideration (the Lions Quest Skills for Adolescence curriculum); following the visit, the principal decided to adopt the curriculum in his school.

Building Champions and Strong Supporters

Not all administrators were so easily convinced. In many communities, administrators voiced concerns about the burden (or waste) of using classroom time to teach curricula that were perceived to be peripheral to the core mission of the school. In our study communities, as in communities across the country, schools faced great pressure to improve academic outcomes and test scores, which often has resulted in the belief that the school has to focus exclusively on instructional programming that targets academic performance (Durlak et al., 2011; Elias, Butler-Bruene, Blum, & Schuyler, 2000; St. Pierre, 2001). These attitudes increase the difficulty of installing SEL programs.

In the CTC trial, coalitions realized they needed to create a "win–win" situation and demonstrate to school personnel that the adoption of SEL and other curricula would contribute to their central mission. To do so, some coalition coordinators obtained copies of state and local mandated learning requirements, then matched these objectives to program content to show how implementation of these curricula would help schools meet their academic needs. Another approach was to provide school administrators with research showing links between prevention programs and academic success. For example, there is evidence that schools whose students report less exposure to risk factors and more exposure to protective factors have higher standardized test scores and grades (Arthur, Brown, & Briney, 2006; Fleming et al., 2005). Coalition members emphasized that by implementing SEL curricula known to decrease risk and enhance protection, schools could improve students' academic performance. Other evidence suggests that, in regard to SEL programs, students with better problem-solving, emotional regulation, and decision-making skills are more likely to attend school regularly and have better academic achievement, and are less likely to engage in disruptive classroom behavior that can impede learning (Durlak et al., 2011; Greenberg, 2010). When community stakeholders share these findings with school personnel, they may help persuade them that the adoption of new programs is worth the investment. These messages can be particularly influential if delivered to school administrators by other key leaders in the community, which is facilitated by the broad participation of influential community stakeholders on the CTC coalition.

In all study communities, coalitions recognized the need to build "champions" who would advocate for the adoption of new programs. Strong support among key personnel must be present in order to ensure both the adoption and successful implementation of new programming (Miller & Shinn, 2005; Rohrbach, Grana, Sussman, & Valente, 2006). Such champions are needed both at the administrator level, from school superintendents and principals who have the authority to make programmatic decisions and allocate resources for their implementation, and from teachers and staff members who must be willing to teach new programs fully, with enthusiasm, and in a manner that elicits a positive response from students.

In the CTC study, all coalitions spent significant time building relationships and fostering support from school personnel. In some cases, coalition coordinators and/or other members had preexisting relationships that allowed immediate entrée to school staff. In other cases, relationships had to be built, usually through multiple conversations conducted during formal meetings and informal visits. The first step in the process was typically inviting key school representatives to join the CTC coalition, where they could learn more about effective prevention strategies and understand how school practices were connected to larger community goals. Our process evaluation indicated that schools that more quickly adopted new curricula tended to have more members on the CTC coalitions at the outset of the project (Fagan, Brooke-Weiss, et al., 2009). Direct training in the CTC model helped convince school representatives that adopting tested and effective programs to address elevated risk and depressed protective factors reported by students in their own community would benefit the school and the larger community, and that doing so would not compete with the need to improve students' academic achievement.

Coalitions were strategic in deciding whom to approach to participate on coalitions and whom to engage in conversations regarding new programming. They relied on their collective knowledge of the school to determine who was most open to change and innovation, who would best understand the benefits of new programs, and who was best able to influence the decision to adopt a new program. In some cases, communities decided that a "top-down" approach (i.e., engaging district or building administrators) was needed to leverage support for new programming, as decisions in their district had to be first endorsed by school executives. Coalition members then worked to build relationships with these administrators. "Bottom-up" approaches were also used. In these cases, coalitions recognized that the school administration was not likely to be receptive to new programming, particularly if it was introduced by someone who was not employed by the school district. Thus, the first step was to engage teachers, and once teacher support was gained, this staff person(s), rather than a coalition member, approached the administration to solicit approval for new programs.

A final strategy, used to generate support when full enthusiasm was lacking or systemic barriers to program adoption could not easily be overcome, was to pilot inschool programs. In two communities in our project, schools were averse to providing their own staff to teach new curricula, so the coalitions identified and funded a qualified instructor to deliver programs, with the hope that schools would eventually supply their own teachers. In another case, a community with seven elementary schools decided to initiate a new SEL program in the school with the most supportive principal, then invited teachers from all other schools to attend the initial program training workshop to become familiar with the program's content. The coalition also invited the school curriculum director to observe program lessons once implementation was under way in the early adopting school. In this manner, the coalition engendered further understanding of and support for the program and was able to implement it districtwide in the following year, with partial funding from the school district. As this example makes clear, "scaling up" SEL programs is often a process that must be nurtured over time.

Overcoming Structural and Organizational Barriers to Implementation

Even when schools are open to innovation and personnel perceive the benefits of SEL programming, there may still be structural or organizational barriers that impede the adoption of new curricula. When these situations arose in CTC communities, coalitions found it helpful to identify the particular issue that challenged program adoption and propose a mutually beneficial solution to it. In one community, for example, the coalition coordinator asked the superintendent specifically about his district's needs. Learning that his teachers needed individual time with low-performing students to improve their academic performance, the coalition decided to provide staff from outside the school to teach the new curriculum, which would allow classroom teachers time to meet with students.

In a few sites, coalitions found that other, noneffective or untested curricula were already in place, resulting in a lack of time in the school day to teach new curricula. Often, such curricula had been created by teachers and/or had strong local support, and school personnel were reluctant to discontinue their use. In these cases, coalition members worked with schools to determine whether current prevention efforts should be retained or dropped. Rather than criticize past choices, coalitions opted to compare and contrast the content and demonstrated benefits of the proposed program with current programming. In some cases, it was clear that content was not dramatically different between the two choices, but that new programs had been more carefully evaluated and demonstrated to be effective at improving student outcomes, whereas existing programs had not. Coalitions then reminded school officials of their common mission—to foster healthy and successful students—and challenged school personnel to invest their time and money in strategies that did work rather than those that were unproven. To address proactively the argument that new programs would be too costly to adopt, coalition members provided evidence that curricula that significantly reduce problem behaviors can save money in the long term; for example, by improving student graduation rates, preventing delinquency and crime, and reducing utilization of substance abuse and mental health services (Aos, Lieb, Mayfield, Miller, & Pennucci, 2004). They also had the advantage in this study of being able to provide some research funds to cover program startup costs.

Guidelines and Recommendations for Using Coalitions to Scale-Up SEL Programs

While there are many daunting challenges to overcome when attempting to install and scale-up new SEL programs in schools, the lessons learned from the evaluation of the CTC prevention system illustrate that community coalitions and school–community partnerships *can* help to increase the spread of effective SEL programs. Coalitions can draw upon preexisting relationships with school personnel that provide needed credibility and entrée to school administrators and staff when attempting to convince a school to adopt a new program. Even if success is not achieved immediately, locally based coalitions can take small steps, repeated over time, to bolster their credibility, demonstrate their interest in partnering with schools, and foster champions. By seeking adoption from within the community, coalitions engage in joint decision making and work with partners to achieve a common vision. Because these actions are not easy to undertake, we summarize in the next section some of the lessons we learned from our work and provide additional recommendations for fostering increased uptake of SEL programming.

Build a Coalition That Includes School Representatives and Other Community Members

Schools are all too often called upon to solve community youth problems, but they cannot do so alone. Fostering the healthy development of young people communitywide necessitates the active participation of stakeholders from all sectors of the community (Kania & Kramer, 2011). Thus, a foundation of the CTC system is the creation of diverse coalitions with representation from school personnel and all others who have a stake in improving the lives of youth. The creation of broad-based community coalitions is necessary to create a climate of shared communication, resources, accountability, and collaboration; that is, when diverse sectors of a community are involved in discussion and decisions regarding the mission, vision, and goals of the coalition, they are more likely to have a shared sense of accountability and collective responsibility for achieving targeted changes in behaviors (Kania & Kramer, 2011). Furthermore, their involvement allows each member or organization to understand how its particular goals are related to the larger mission. It is therefore important that coalitions communicate to school personnel how the implementation of SEL programs link to the larger community goals of fostering healthy youth development (Elias, Zins, Graczyk, & Weissberg, 2003). Doing so helps to integrate school efforts with community-based activities and create "win–win" situations.

It is important to note that the membership, operation, and potential to achieve success of the CTC coalition can be distinguished from that of school-level teams that are often created to help install or oversee the implementation of SEL curricula. Although such teams may also involve participation of community members, they are typically not as broad-based as CTC coalitions. The latter involve stakeholders from business, government, law enforcement, media, religious organizations, and advocacy groups, as well as health, education, and social service organizations in the community, parents, and youth, and are appointed to the CTC coalition by key community leaders (e.g., the mayor, police chief, and school superintendent). In the CTC model, decisions regarding policies and programs are made by this broad coalition of stakeholders. When SEL programs are called for and monitored by a large body of influential community members, and when these programs are viewed as part of a larger community effort to improve healthy youth development, the likelihood that they will be adopted, well implemented, and sustained is improved. SEL programs can potentially reach more students if initiated by community coalitions that include representatives from multiple schools, who all understand the need to implement services communitywide. School-based teams, in contrast, tend to focus on the needs of a particular school. Finally, CTC coalitions provide greater opportunities for resource sharing across agencies, such that schools do not necessarily have to cover all the costs associated with program materials and staff.

Get a "Foot in the Door" and Persist with Efforts to Engender Support for SEL Programs

Research has indicated that the adoption of SEL programs and other innovations is a process that must be fostered. Community agencies are often resistant to change and content with the "status quo" (Backer, 1995; Rogers, 1995), which, in the case of schools, often means reluctance to incorporate effective SEL programs into their core curricula (Durlak et al., 2011). Overcoming resistance to change requires persistent effort, demonstration of good faith, and continued negotiation and discussion. Coalitions may need to take small steps to "get a foot in the door", that is, to build credibility and trust with school personnel in the hope that they will eventually adopt a school-based program. If school personnel initially refuse to adopt SEL programming, coalitions may consider adopting community-based programs that foster academic, social, and emotional competencies, then communicate to school personnel how these extracurricular activities are helping students. For example, after-school tutoring programs can promote student academic learning and commitment to school, while parent training interventions can improve student–parent communication and family bonding. Coalitions may ask schools to help them recruit students and parents into these types of programs, or to provide space in which to conduct programming. In this manner, coalitions build trust and credibility with schools and engage school partners without asking them to sacrifice classroom time, personnel, or other resources. Furthermore, these activities demonstrate that the coalition is working along with schools to improve the healthy development of youth and their families, and that the school is not expected to do so alone.

At the same time, however, if the ultimate goal is to increase the uptake of SEL programs, coalitions must actively pursue this priority. Doing so will require persistent effort, engaging school personnel at all levels in multiple conversations, and repeated messaging so that both students and schools will benefit from adoption of SEL programming. In the CTC trial, all 12 communities eventually adopted new school-based programming, but in some cases, 3 years of negotiation were needed before this occurred.

Think Big but Start Small

In a similar vein, it is naive to believe that a school will move easily and rapidly through the stages of program adoption and implementation. More realistically, it is better to start small, piloting an SEL curriculum in one school or with one teacher (preferably one who is already supportive of the program), in order to become familiar with the program content and methods of delivery, identify implementation obstacles, and allow time for implementers to reach peak performance. Once initial challenges are faced and, we hope, overcome, a coalition can consider scaling up and spreading the new program to additional teachers, grades, and/or schools. Newly created champions can help engender support among new adopters and provide advice and solutions when delivery challenges are faced. By progressing slowly, the initiative is allowed time to grow, the school can adjust to new processes, and the foundation for larger, sustained efforts can be built. As Elias and colleagues (2003, p. 315) noted: "It is nice to think big, but in reality, small wins and baby steps provide the essential foundation on which later, larger, and enduring successes can rest."

School personnel should also be warned that SEL programs are not "magic bullets" that will result in immediate and large impacts on youth. Such programs tend to have relatively modest effects on children's social and emotional competence, and there are likely to be some delays before the full effects on outcomes are realized (Durlak et al., 2011). Yet high-quality implementation of these curricula with a large number of youth has the potential to produce communitywide changes that can then be celebrated and used to foster increased support for and dissemination of programming. In the CTC research trial, community coalitions ensured that school boards and the general public were regularly updated regarding program activities, the numbers of youth served by new programs, and evidence of effectiveness, and they publicly applauded school administrators and teachers for their efforts in promoting youth competencies. These efforts paid off. In some cases, school administrators and/or school boards approved the integration of the new program into the regular school programming and took over the costs of funding the program.

Potential Problems and Pitfalls

Some coalition-based change efforts have not resulted in successful school–community partnerships or desired improvements in children's well-being (Flewelling et al., 2005; Hallfors, Cho, Livert, & Kadushin, 2002; St. Pierre & Kaltreider, 2004). Significant challenges may arise when building and maintaining broad-based coalitions, and even strong coalitions may encounter obstacles when attempting to introduce, grow, and institutionalize new SEL programming into schools. In the final section of this chapter, we identify a few additional challenges that can impede the successful adoption of SEL curricula and offer solutions for overcoming these barriers.

Failure to Fully Engage the Community in Youth Development Efforts

Much research has noted the difficulties faced when attempting to engage community members in broad-based coalitions aimed at promoting healthy youth development (Feinberg, Chilenski, Greenberg, Spoth, & Redmond, 2007; Merzel & D'Afflitti, 2003; Stith et al., 2006). Even when coalition members share a concern or goal, it can be difficult to create and maintain a strong commitment to this cause, and moving the group from planning to action, which requires expenditure of resources and time, can be challenging. Most coalitions rely on volunteers who often participate during their personal time and may not always be available to attend meetings or to take necessary actions. It is also challenging to ensure cohesion and collaboration among coalition members who come from diverse backgrounds, and who may have different skills, needs, resources, and ideas about what is needed to achieve success. Membership turnover is likely to occur, which further complicates the ability to maintain focus, commitment, and support.

Because coalitions usually comprise volunteer members, it is important to employ dedicated staff members who can maintain functioning and ensure that tasks are achieved (Kania & Kramer, 2011). Communities should be prepared to set aside resources for at least one part-time or full-time paid staff member with a diverse skills set, including the ability to facilitate meetings, encourage collaboration, foster joint decision making, and delegate tasks. It will likely be difficult to find a community member who has this diverse skills set and to obtain sustainable funding for this position. However, in the CTC study, 2 years after study funding for the coordinator position had ended, seven of the intervention communities continued to support paid staff members using sources such as federal and state grants and local government funding (Gloppen, Arthur, Hawkins, & Shapiro, 2012). It can also be helpful to nominate a (volunteer) coalition chairperson, who can assist in facilitating meetings, promoting a sense of ownership for coalition activities among each member, providing meaningful opportunities for participation, keeping enthusiasm alive, and creating a climate of cohesion and joint decision making.

Personnel Turnover

Coalitions are likely to face turnover among the general membership, and instability may be even more common among school representatives. Some research has indicated that turnover rates are as high as 50% among new teachers, and that superintendents are employed an average of only 2 years in urban school districts (Elias et al., 2003). These figures suggest that coordinators should recruit multiple school representatives to participate in coalitions and that they refrain from identifying a single administrator or teacher as their only champion or agent of change. It is also important that once the decision to adopt the new SEL program is made, the coalition continues to work with school personnel to ensure that the curriculum is institutionalized in the school or school district. It is also likely that some of those charged with delivering SEL programs will leave. Thus, it is helpful to identify a program coordinator or, even better, an implementation team charged with overseeing implementation procedures and recruiting new implementers as needed (Elias et al., 2003).

Poor Implementation Quality

The decision to adopt a new program is only the first step in successfully implementing and scaling up SEL curricula. It is equally important to ensure that programs are fully implemented and delivered with fidelity, in accordance with the content, activities, and delivery methods specified by program creators. Evidence has shown that the quality of implementation of effective school-based programs suffers when these curricula are replicated in communities (Gottfredson & Gottfredson, 2002; Hallfors & Godette, 2002). School personnel often make changes to the core components of programs, for example, by shortening lessons, omitting key content or activities, or changing the mode of instruction outlined in the curriculum. Variation in teaching practices is often seen as desirable by school personnel, particularly when teachers make adjustments to curricula to respond to student strengths and needs or to better fit school cultures, practices, or leadership. However, it is also true that closer adherence to the core components of effective programs (i.e., strong implementation fidelity) is associated with more positive changes in student attitudes and behaviors (Durlak & DuPre, 2008; Fixsen, Naoom, Blase, Friedman, & Wallace, 2005).

In order to ensure high-quality implementation, it is important that all instructors charged with delivering SEL programs receive training from program developers to become familiar with the active ingredients responsible for program success (Fixsen et al., 2005). Such workshops typically allow time for demonstration and practice in teaching the curricula, which help instructors more quickly master the content. Because challenges are likely to arise in the classroom, it is also important for instructors to receive periodic booster trainings, if available from developers, and to have ongoing coaching or support from those familiar with the program. If the school has designated a program coordinator, he or she can act as a teacher/coach, especially if he or she has received training and is experienced in delivering the program.

Coalitions also have a role to play in ensuring high implementation quality of SEL curricula. In the CTC system, a workgroup of the coalition is charged with monitoring implementation practices of selected programs, identifying potential problems, and helping schools and other agencies take corrective actions to improve practices when challenges arise. In our research project, coalitions asked teachers to complete short surveys indicating the extent to which they taught each lesson, and community volunteers, as well as school personnel, observed lessons to assess implementation (Fagan et al., 2008). Coalitions then reviewed this information and worked with school personnel to provide feedback to teachers if problems were identified. Teachers were not always receptive to this assistance, especially during the startup phases of implementation, but their fears were alleviated when they realized that this information was not linked to job performance evaluations. Coalition members emphasized that monitoring and feedback was being used solely to improve the delivery of curricula in order to achieve the goal toward which the entire community was working: more positive outcomes for local youth. Furthermore, who would be allowed to observe lessons was decided in consultation with teachers and/ or school administrators in accordance with school policies.

Conclusion

Evidence indicates that high-quality SEL programming is available to communities, and that implementation of these programs can result in greater social and emotional competence, enhanced academic achievement, and more positive and healthy youth development. However, research also demonstrates that effective SEL curricula have not been widely adopted by schools. As we have outlined in this chapter, building community–school partnerships through the creation of broad-based coalitions is a promising strategy for increasing the dissemination and use of SEL programs.

Although this chapter has focused on the CTC model, other community-based coalition models also have evidence of effectiveness in installing and ensuring high-quality delivery of school programs, including SEL curricula. The PROmoting School–community–university Partnerships to Enhance Resilience (PROSPER) model, for example, explicitly focuses on building school–community partnerships to enhance the adoption of school SEL curricula. This strategy assumes that all youth will benefit from services that seek to strengthen individual competencies and parent–child interactions. Local university Cooperative Extension Service (CES) agents partner with school district personnel and other community members to select and oversee the implementation of school-based prevention curricula and workshops for parents (Spoth & Greenberg, 2005).

The Getting To Outcomes® (GTO®) model takes a somewhat broader approach, by providing services to coalitions and other organizations to help them plan for and deliver the implementation of a range of evidence-based services. This system could be used by schools to foster the adoption of SEL programming. In this case, administrators and teachers would be provided guidance in how to select the "right" SEL program (i.e., the program that best matches the needs, resources, and goals of the school), assess school and teacher capacities prior to implementation, carefully monitor the delivery of services, measure outcomes, and engage in quality assurance procedures as needed to ensure the effectiveness and sustainability of the program (Wandersman, Imm, Chinman, & Kaftarian, 2000; also see Wright, Lamont, Wandersman, Osher, & Gordon, Chapter 33, this volume).

Finally, organizations such as CASEL provide useful tools that help to increase the widespread delivery of SEL programming. In particular, the *2013 CASEL Guide* (CASEL, 2012) outlines SEL programs that have evidence of effectiveness for preschool and elementary students and provides user-friendly advice about how to ensure that new programs are integrated with existing services, well supported by school personnel, and carefully monitored to ensure success.

In our work with communities implementing the CTC prevention system, we have documented specific strategies that coalitions should consider when attempting to partner with schools to promote the adoption of SEL and other school-based programs. Ideally, these collaborations will be viewed as a win–win situation for all parties, as greater use of such programming helps schools achieve their core mission of improving students' academic performance, and helps coalitions to reach their goal of promoting communitywide youth development. In our project, while some schools were initially reluctant to devote instructional time to SEL curricula, all communities eventually did so. As a result, the 12 communities participating in this study reached over half their middle school student population, on average, with school-based programming demonstrated to reduce student risk, increase protection, including social and emotional competence, and prevent the development of problem behaviors (Fagan et al., 2008). These results are encouraging, and we hope that the lessons learned from this project will be used by other communities in order to foster more positive youth development nationwide.

Acknowledgments

This work was supported by research grants from the National Institute on Drug Abuse (No. R01 DA015183-03) with cofunding from the National Cancer Institute, the National Institute of Child Health and Human Development, the National Institute of Mental Health, the Center for Substance Abuse Prevention, and the National Institute on Alcohol Abuse and Alcoholism. The content of this chapter is solely the responsibility of the authors and does not necessarily represent the official views of the funding agencies.

We gratefully acknowledge the ongoing participation in the study and data collection efforts of the residents of the 24 communities described in this chapter.

References

Aos, S., Lieb, R., Mayfield, J., Miller, M., & Pennucci, A. (2004). *Benefits and costs of prevention and early intervention programs for youth.* Olympia: Washington State Institute for Public Policy.

Arthur, M. W., Brown, E. C., & Briney, J. S. (2006). *Multilevel examination of the relationships between risk/protective factors and academic test scores*. A report to the Washington State Office of the Superintendent of Public Instruction and the Washington State Division of Alcohol and Substance Abuse, Retrieved October 29, 2013, from *www1.dshs.wa.gov/pdf/dbhr/merrp-fats0706.pdf*.

Arthur, M. W., Hawkins, J. D., Pollard, J. A., Catalano, R. F., & Baglioni, A. J. (2002). Measuring risk and protective factors for substance use, delinquency, and other adolescent problem behaviors: The Communities That Care Youth Survey. *Evaluation Review, 26*, 575–601.

Backer, T. E. (1995). Assessing and enhancing readiness for change: Implications for technology transfer. In T. E. Backer, S. L. David, & G. Soucy (Eds.), *Reviewing the behavioral science knowledge base on technology transfer* (pp. 21–41). Rockville, MD: National Institute on Drug Abuse.

Collaborative for Academic, Social, and Emotional Learning (CASEL). (2012). *2013 CASEL guide: Effective social and emotional learning programs—Preschool and elementary school edition*. Chicago: Author.

Durlak, J. A., & DuPre, E. P. (2008). Implementation matters: A review of the research on the influence of implementation on program outcomes and the factors affecting implementation. *American Journal of Community Psychology, 41*, 327–350.

Durlak, J. A., Dymnicki, A. B., Taylor, R. D., Weissberg, R. P., & Schellinger, K. B. (2011). The impact of enhancing students' social and emotional learning: A meta-analysis of school-based universal interventions. *Child Development, 82*, 405–432.

Elias, M. J., Butler-Bruene, L., Blum, L., & Schuyler, T. (2000). Voices from the field: Identifying and overcoming roadblocks to carrying out programs in social and emotional learning/emotional intelligence. *Journal of Education and Psychological Consultation, 11*, 253–272.

Elias, M. J., Zins, J. E., Graczyk, P. A., & Weissberg, R. P. (2003). Implementation, sustainability, and scaling-up of social–emotional and academic innovations in public schools. *School Psychology Review, 32*, 303–319.

Fagan, A. A., Brooke-Weiss, B., Cady, R., & Hawkins, J. D. (2009). If at first you don't succeed . . . keep trying: Strategies to enhance coalition/school partnerships to implement school-based prevention programming. *Australian and New Zealand Journal of Criminology, 42*, 387–405.

Fagan, A. A., Hanson, K., Hawkins, J. D., & Arthur, M. W. (2008). Bridging science to practice: Achieving prevention program fidelity in the Community Youth Development Study. *American Journal of Community Psychology, 41*, 235–249.

Fagan, A. A., Hanson, K., Hawkins, J. D., & Arthur, M. W. (2009). Translational research in action: Implementation of the Communities That Care prevention system in 12 communities. *Journal of Community Psychology 37*, 809–829.

Feinberg, M., Chilenski, S. M., Greenberg, M. T., Spoth, R. L., & Redmond, C. (2007). Community and team member factors that influence the operations phase of local prevention teams: The PROSPER Project. *Prevention Science, 8*, 214–226.

Fixsen, D. L., Naoom, S. F., Blase, K. A., Friedman, R. M., & Wallace, F. (2005). *Implementation research: A synthesis of the literature* (FMHI Publication No. 231). Tampa: University of South Florida, Louis de la Parte Florida Mental Health Institute, the National Implementation Research Network.

Fleming, C. B., Haggerty, K. P., Catalano, R. F., Harachi, T. W., Mazza, J. J., & Gruman, D. H. (2005). Do social and behavioral characteristics targeted by preventive interventions predict standardized test scores and grades? *Journal of School Health, 75*, 342–249.

Flewelling, R. L., Austin, D., Hale, K., LaPlante, M., Liebig, M., Piasecki, L., et al. (2005). Implementing research-based substance abuse prevention in communities: Effects of a coalition-based prevention initiative in Vermont. *Journal of Community Psychology, 33*, 333–353.

Gloppen, K. M., Arthur, M. W., Hawkins, J. D., & Shapiro, V. B. (2012). Sustainability of the Communities That Care prevention system by coalitions participating in the Community Youth Development Study. *Journal of Adolescent Health, 51*, 259–264.

Gottfredson, D. C., & Gottfredson, G. D. (2002). Quality of school-based prevention programs: Results from a national survey. *Journal of Research in Crime and Delinquency, 39*, 3–35.

Greenberg, M. T. (2010). School-based prevention: Current status and future challenges. *Effective Education, 2*, 27–52.

Hallfors, D., Cho, H., Livert, D., & Kadushin, C. (2002). Fighting back against substance use: Are community coalitions winning? *American Journal of Preventive Medicine, 23*, 237–245.

Hallfors, D., & Godette, D. (2002). Will the "Principles of Effectiveness" improve prevention practice?: Early findings from a diffusion study. *Health Education Research, 17*, 461–470.

Hallfors, D., Pankratz, M., & Hartman, S. (2007). Does federal policy support the use of scientific evidence in school-based prevention programs? *Prevention Science, 8*, 75–81.

Hawkins, J. D., & Catalano, R. F. (1992). *Communities That Care: Action for drug abuse prevention.* San Francisco: Jossey-Bass.

Hawkins, J. D., Catalano, R. F., & Arthur, M. W. (2002). Promoting science-based prevention in communities. *Addictive Behaviors, 27,* 951–976.

Hawkins, J. D., Catalano, R. F., Arthur, M. W., Egan, E., Brown, E. C., Abbott, R. D., et al. (2008). Testing Communities That Care: Rationale and design of the Community Youth Development Study. *Prevention Science, 9,* 178–190.

Hawkins, J. D., Van Horn, M. L., & Arthur, M. W. (2004). Community variation in risk and protective factors and substance use outcomes. *Prevention Science, 5,* 213–220.

Kania, J., & Kramer, M. (2011). Collective impact. *Stanford Social Innovation Review, 9,* 36–41.

Merzel, C., & D'Afflitti, J. (2003). Reconsidering community-based health promotion: Promise, performance, and potential. *American Journal of Public Health, 93,* 557–574.

Mihalic, S., Fagan, A. A., Irwin, K., Ballard, D., & Elliott, D. (2004). *Blueprints for violence prevention.* Washington, DC: Office of Juvenile Justice and Delinquency Prevention.

Miller, R. L., & Shinn, M. (2005). Learning from communities: Overcoming difficulties in dissemination of prevention and promotion efforts. *American Journal of Community Psychology, 35,* 169–183.

O'Connell, M. E., Boat, T., & Warner, K. E. (Eds.). (2009). *Preventing mental, emotional, and behavioral disorders among young people: Progress and possibilities.* Washington, DC: National Academies Press.

Ringwalt, C., Hanley, S., Vincus, A. A., Ennett, S. T., Rohrbach, L. A., & Bowling, J. M. (2008). The prevalence of effective substance use prevention curricula in the nation's high schools. *Journal of Primary Prevention, 29,* 479–488.

Ringwalt, C., Vincus, A. A., Hanley, S., Ennett, S. T., Bowling, J. M., & Haws, S. (2011). The prevalence of evidence-based drug use prevention curricula in U.S. middle schools in 2008. *Prevention Science, 12,* 63–70.

Rogers, E. (1995). *Diffusion of innovations* (4th ed.). New York: Free Press.

Rohrbach, L. A., Grana, R., Sussman, S., & Valente, T. W. (2006). Type II translation: Transporting prevention interventions from research to real-world settings. *Evaluation and the Health Professions, 29,* 302–333.

Saul, J., Duffy, J., Noonan, R., Lubell, K., Wandersman, A., Flaspohler, P., et al. (2008). Bridging science and practice in violence prevention: Addressing ten key challenges. *American Journal of Community Psychology, 41,* 197–205.

Spoth, R. L., & Greenberg, M. T. (2005). Toward a comprehensive strategy for effective practitioner-scientist partnerships and larger-scale community health and well-being. *American Journal of Community Psychology, 35,* 107–126.

St. Pierre, T. L. (2001). Strategies for community/school collaborations to prevent youth substance use. *Journal of Primary Prevention, 21,* 381–398.

St. Pierre, T. L., & Kaltreider, D. L. (2004). Tales of refusal, adoption, and maintenance: Evidence-based substance abuse prevention via school-extension collaborations. *American Journal of Evaluation, 25,* 479–491.

Stevenson, J. F., & Mitchell, R. E. (2003). Community-level collaboration for substance abuse prevention. *Journal of Primary Prevention, 23,* 371–404.

Stith, S., Pruitt, I., Dees, J., Fronce, M., Green, N., Som, A., et al. (2006). Implementing community-based prevention programming: A review of the literature. *Journal of Primary Prevention, 27,* 599–617.

Wandersman, A., & Florin, P. (2003). Community intervention and effective prevention. *American Psychologist, 58,* 441–448.

Wandersman, A., Imm, P., Chinman, M., & Kaftarian, S. J. (2000). Getting To Outcomes: A results-based approach to accountability. *Evaluation and Program Planning, 23,* 389–395.

CHAPTER 32

Systemic Support for SEL in School Districts

Amy Kathryn Mart, Roger P. Weissberg, and Kimberly Kendziora

Social and emotional learning (SEL) can and should be a fundamental part of every child's education. Decades of rigorous study have identified programs and practices that promote SEL in educational settings, and these have been successfully implemented by many educators around the world (Humphrey, 2013; Merrell & Gueldner, 2010). There is also strong evidence that school-based SEL contributes to mental health, positive behavior, and academic success among children and adolescents (Durlak, Weissberg, Dymnicki, Taylor, & Schellinger, 2011; Sklad, Diekstra, De Ritter, Ben, & Gravesteijn, 2012; Weare & Nind, 2011). As the feasibility and benefits of school-based SEL become increasingly apparent, researchers, practitioners, and policymakers must begin to address a new set of questions: What can be done to ensure that all students receive a high-quality education that incorporates academic, social, and emotional learning? How can programs and practices that promote SEL endure and deepen over time? How do factors beyond the school building contribute to effective SEL?

In this chapter, we argue that the answers to these and other important questions depend on looking beyond schools and classrooms toward the larger systems that influence students' educational experiences. In particular, we focus on the importance of school districts and explore the potential benefits of collaborating with district leaders to embed support for SEL throughout district systems. We draw from literature on education reform and organizational change to conceptualize systemic support for SEL in school districts, and describe how district leaders can initiate changes that contribute to improvements in SEL for all students. We then describe current efforts by the Collaborative for Academic, Social, and Emotional Learning (CASEL) to apply and refine these ideas through collaboration with eight large school districts. Finally, we identify several issues for future exploration in practice and research. We hope that sharing these perspectives will (1) provide guidance for educational leaders and practitioners as they work to develop systemic support for students' social, emotional, and academic development, and (2) stimulate new lines of scholarly inquiry in this area.

Why School Districts?

At the most basic level, school-based SEL occurs as teachers interact with students every day, in every classroom. These most proximal influences have been a primary focus within the field of SEL, as researchers and practitioners have worked for decades to develop, refine, and disseminate classroom-based programs to improve students' social and emotional competence. More recently, implementation studies have demonstrated that the quality of SEL in classrooms is significantly influenced by characteristics of the schools context (Beets et al., 2008; Durlak & DuPre, 2008; Kam, Greenberg, & Walls, 2003). This broadening focus from classroom-based programs to schoolwide processes mirrors a broader trend in field of education, reflected in the expansion of comprehensive school reform models and school effectiveness research. Many interventions have aimed to embed support for SEL in the norms, routines, and structures of entire schools—some with great success (e.g., Devaney, O'Brien, Resnik, Keister, & Weissberg, 2006; Solomon, Battistich, Watson, Schaps, & Lewis, 2000).

However, scholars in the field of SEL, like their colleagues in many other areas of education, have noted that school districts are particularly influential in determining the success and sustainability of their efforts (Mart, Greenberg, Kriete, Schaps, & Weissberg, 2011). We build from this foundation to suggest that school- and classroom-level processes that influence SEL are themselves influenced by characteristics of the districts in which they are situated. This assertion is not merely a logical or theoretical extension of previous findings from the field of SEL; it is supported by decades of research on educational leadership and policy demonstrating that district-level factors influence educational quality and student outcomes (Spillane, 1996; Waters & Marzano, 2006).

Broadly defined, a *school district* is a geographically organized cluster of schools, overseen by a common administrative structure. In educational leadership and policy, the term "district" is often used to refer to the district central office and senior leadership as an institutional actor with the power to influence what occurs in its schools and classrooms (Rorrer, Skrla, & Scheurich, 2008). Until relatively recently, districts have often been treated as little more than gatekeepers for implementation of educational innovations or, at worst, sources of political and bureaucratic barriers. However, over the past 20 years, there has been increasing interest in district-led initiatives to ensure success for all students. Some have even suggested that school districts—particularly large urban districts—may be the ideal partner for promoting the spread of new educational programs and approaches (Supovitz, 2006).

Arguments for involving school districts in efforts to improve education are rooted in at least three rationales. First, district leaders control the resources that are required to implement and sustain new educational practices (McLaughin & Talbert, 2003; Spillane, 1996). Changes that are initiated at the school level can be difficult to implement fully and sustain without support from district administrators. Second, it is simply not feasible for researchers and program developers to intervene one school at a time. Collaboration with school districts offers access to a large number of schools and potential economies of scale that allow for widespread dissemination of effective programs and practices (Glennan, Bodilly, Galegher, & Kerr, 2004; Mart et al., 2011). Finally, the argument for district-led change can be rooted in a desire to ensure equity across schools. In most districts, the quality of education that students receive varies greatly from one school to the next, and districts have a responsibility to minimize these disparities proactively (Supovitz, 2006). When some schools struggle to implement effective programs and practices, district leaders have "a moral obligation to intervene in these schools on behalf of students, families, and the school community" (Fullan, Bertani, & Quinn, 2004, p. 8).

The literature on district-led improvement in education suggests that district-level changes can indeed improve the quality of educational practices and enhance student outcomes (Darling-Hammond et al., 2005; Elmore & Burney, 1997; O'Day, Bitter, & Gomez, 2011; Togneri & Anderson, 2003). A sizable literature on this topic includes descriptions of effective districts, case studies of districtwide change processes, and a variety of conceptual frameworks for understanding (1) how district-level factors influence student learning, and (2) how district leaders can create systemic changes to improve student outcomes. However, this literature focuses almost exclusively on the goal of improving scores on standardized academic achievement tests. Until now, there has been little guidance for district leaders who wish to pursue a reform agenda that is aimed at a more holistic set of outcomes (Elias, 2009; Levin, Datnow, & Carrier, 2012).

Meanwhile, spurred on by federal and state policy, leaders in thousands of school districts across the country are struggling to ensure that all students meet increasingly rigorous standards. The manner in which they execute this responsibility can either support or thwart schools' efforts to nurture social and emotional development. As evidence mounts that the promotion of social and emotional competencies is a promising approach to enhance academic learning (e.g., Durlak et al., 2011; Sklad et al., 2012), some district leaders are adopting a focus on SEL as part of their plans to improve outcomes for all students (Anderson & Rodway-Macri, 2009). In fact, this strategy will likely be endorsed in the reauthorization of the Elementary and Secondary Education Act, and it was supported in the recent call for submissions to the federal Race to the Top District competition (U.S. Department of Education, 2012). Having committed to support SEL, district leaders must face the challenge of changing practice in dozens—perhaps hundreds—of schools in ways that support social and emotional development as well as academic learning. Below, we offer research-based insights regarding how they might confront this challenge.

A Systemic Perspective on SEL

This chapter is grounded in a systemic perspective on SEL. Literally, the term "systemic" means having to do with systems, but it has been variously applied and defined in the literature on educational systems (Squire & Reigeluth, 2000). Our use of it here is intended to capture three fundamental ideas. First, *systemic* refers simply to large-scale interventions that are designed to influence all students within an educational system. In this regard, the term *systemic* has been applied to a wide range of federal, state, and local initiatives that aim to improve the quality of education in their respective jurisdictions (Smith & O'Day, 1990).

The word *systemic* is also used in psychology, education, and various other disciplines to denote application of Bronfenbrenner's (1979) ecological systems theory, which asserts that individual development is influenced by multiple nested and intersecting social systems. The individual interacts directly with a variety of *microsystems*, which form the primary context for development (e.g., family, classroom). *Mesosystems* represent the interactions between systems, such as the reciprocal relationship between schools and families. *Exosystems* are the larger political and institutional contexts in which these smaller systems are embedded, the influence of which is mostly mediated by microsystemic processes. All of these are encompassed by the larger *macrosystem* of beliefs, values, and ideologies that govern our society. This way of thinking has guided our work, as we recognize that students' development is influenced by classroom and school microsystems, which are themselves embedded within the district exosystem.

Finally, the term *systemic* applies to interventions that aim to transform the characteristics of social systems (e.g., organizations, communities) rather than merely changing the individuals within those systems (e.g., teachers, students). This definition resonates with what others have called "second-order change," "organizational change," "systemic reform," or "systems change." These terms are commonly used without clear definition, but when they are defined, authors have outlined a variety of frameworks for operationalizing systemic change (Foster-Fishman, Nowell, & Yang, 2007; Squire & Reigeluth, 2000; Tseng & Seidman, 2007). We draw from several such frameworks to define *systemic support* for SEL as the extent to which support for SEL is embedded in the *regulations*, *routines*, *resources*, and *culture* of an educational system.

Regulations are the formal rules and policies that can either encourage or deter educators from adopting practices that promote SEL. These can codify the district's commitment to SEL, remove barriers to implementation, and provide clarity around expectations for students and staff. *Routines* are the organizational structures and procedures that shape how work gets done. They include various aspects of the district bureaucracy, such as the departmental structure of the central office, the process for sharing information with schools, and patterns of communication among organizational units. The availability and allocation of *resources* throughout the district can also influence SEL in schools and classrooms. Financial, human (e.g., people, their knowledge, and skills), and social (e.g., the existence and quality of relationships among members) resources all influence what happens in schools and classrooms, as do the uses of time and space. Finally, *culture* refers to the norms, values, assumptions, and beliefs that are shared among members of the school community. Beliefs and assumptions about students' social and emotional development are of particular interest here, as are the norms that govern teachers' instructional practice (i.e., interactions with students in the classroom) and the professional interactions among adults throughout the district. Some elements of professional culture may pervade an entire district, whereas others may vary between schools, or even between subgroups within a school.

Each of the previous elements can be conceptualized at multiple ecological levels (e.g., classroom, school, district; see Table 32.1), and system elements interact within and across levels as they influence on individuals. For example, the hiring policies (regulations) in a district influence the availability of human resources at district, school, and classroom levels. Likewise, district policies (regulations) about the use of time (resources) can influence the frequency and quality collaboration among teachers (routines) and facilitate the development of shared understandings and norms for practice (culture).

In summary, systemic support for SEL refers to the extent to which educational systems are configured in ways that contribute to students' social and emotional development. Taking school districts as our primary level of analysis, we are interested in the ways that regulations, routines, resources, and culture in the district *exosystem* can be altered to strengthen school and classroom microsystems to support academic, social, and emotional learning for all students.

Building Systemic Support for SEL in School Districts

We have asserted that the regulations, routines, resources, and professional culture in school districts can influence processes in schools and classrooms, which, in turn, influence students' social, emotional, and academic development. Now, we turn to the challenging question of how district leaders can actively build systemic support for SEL.

TABLE 32.1. Examples of Systemic Support for SEL at the District, School, and Classroom Levels

System element	Examples		
	District	School	Classroom
Regulations	Fiscal policies allow schools to allocate sufficient funds to support SEL.	Nonpunitive discipline policies.	Behavioral expectations are clearly displayed and positively stated.
Routines	Induction process for new teachers includes training in SEL.	School leadership team regularly discusses SEL issues.	Students work in groups and pairs during their daily learning activities.
Resources	The district employs enough SEL specialists to support all schools.	The daily schedule allows sufficient time for teachers to teach social and emotional skills.	The teacher has access to high-quality instructional materials to teach social and emotional skills.
Culture	Interactions between district- and school-level personnel are characterized by respect and trust.	All staff in the school believe that social and emotional skills can and should be taught.	Strong peer norms support prosocial behavior and peaceful conflict resolution.

TABLE 32.2. Strategies to Build Systemic Support for SEL for all Students in School Districts

1. Assess resources and needs.
   a. Assess students' SEL.
   b. Identify and build from existing programs, practices, and policies.
   c. Focus on factors that will influence the change process.
2. Cultivate commitment to SEL.
   a. Develop a vision for SEL in the district.
   b. Communicate with stakeholders about SEL.
   c. Model social and emotional competence.
3. Build organizational support for SEL.
   a. Develop a long-term plan to for districtwide SEL.
   b. Align budgets and staffing to support SEL.
   c. Cultivate SEL-focused partnerships with schools.
4. Support instructional improvement.
   a. Establish learning standards for SEL.
   b. Adopt evidence-based programs and practices for SEL.
   c. Clarify links between SEL and other priority initiatives.
   d. Design systems for ongoing professional learning.
5. Create systems for continuous improvement.
   a. Monitor student outcomes.
   b. Monitor implementation.

We outline a set of research-based change strategies that include assessing needs and resources, building commitment for SEL, developing organizational support for SEL, supporting instructional improvement, and creating systems for continuous improvement (see Table 32.2).

Assess Resources and Needs

Successful, district-led change efforts grow out of identified needs and strategically build from existing resources (Togneri & Anderson, 2003). Therefore, we suggest that district leaders begin the process of building systemic support for SEL by looking broadly and deeply at what is already occurring in the district, with an eye toward three questions:

1. How are our students doing with regard to their social and emotional development?
2. What is the current status of programs, practices, and policies for SEL?
3. What factors are likely to influence the process of building systemic support for SEL in our district?

Assess Students' Social and Emotional Development

To begin, district leaders can analyze any available data that provide insight into the social and emotional development of students across the district. These may include student climate surveys, discipline referral rates, assessments of risk behavior, or even attendance data. Although these existing data sources can be quite informative, they are not a substitute for measures that focus specifically on students' social and emotional skills. Unless such measures are already part of the district's assessment system, new data collection may be necessary.

A thorough analysis of students' social and emotional development will likely reveal strengths and assets in the student population, and indicate some cause for concern about students' social and emotional well-being. When district leaders have the courage to take an honest look at how students are doing, they are often able to build a sense of urgency that energizes the change effort and builds commitment among local stakeholders (Chrispeels & Gonzalez, 2006; Mourshed, Chijoki, & Barber, 2010; Togneri & Anderson, 2003). Furthermore, these data provide a baseline from which to set goals, develop strategic plans, and monitor improvement.

Identify and Build from Current Programs, Practices, and Policies

The process of building systemic support for SEL typically does not start from scratch; rather, most districts already have a variety of programs that are intended to supports students' social and emotional development. Therefore, to avoid redundancy, fragmentation, and inefficiency, it is essential that district leaders take a comprehensive look at existing programs and practices before adopting new strategies to support SEL. A survey of schools will likely reveal a wide array of programs and practices that aim to enhance interpersonal and intrapersonal skills, build positive learning environments, and reduce behavior problems. These may include instructional programs that promote student engagement, persistence, and collaboration, along with discipline programs and school-based mental health services. Programs for college and career readiness, those that promote family and community engagement, and tiered intervention systems such as response to intervention (RTI) and positive behavioral interventions and supports (PBIS) may also have SEL components. A thorough inventory of programs and practices should document whether existing programs are reaching all students, whether they are coordinated to address a range of social and emotional competencies, and whether they have demonstrated evidence of effectiveness.

There is also great value in examining the extent to which the district's existing regulations and routines are aligned to support SEL. Is SEL reflected in the district's goals and long-term plans? Are there districtwide policies that encourage or discourage schools to promote SEL? Are there formal roles and responsibilities for SEL at the school and district level? To what extent is SEL embedded in systems for accountability and professional learning? Again, this inquiry process will likely reveal some existing sources of systemic support that can be leveraged to accelerate change, along with areas for future development.

Focus on Factors That Influence the Change Process

At the same time, district leaders can take stock of available financial, human, and social resources that are available to support SEL. Financial resources may include state and federal funds that can be allocated for social and emotional supports, contributions from local community partners, and funds from the district's own annual budget. Any district- and school-level staff with expertise in child development, psychology, prevention, and related fields may also be a valuable resource for advancing SEL in the district. Support from community stakeholders can be a valuable resource for SEL, and should be assessed at the outset (Rorrer et al., 2008). Are there community partners who can provide funds, expertise, or social advocacy that will support SEL in the district? Will the local teachers' union, school board, and other political partners stand behind the decision to support SEL? Are there community stakeholders who may be resistant to implementation of new programs and practices for SEL?

Finally, district leaders can use a variety of methods to assess the existing districtwide culture, as reflected in the attitudes, norms, and beliefs about SEL of personnel throughout the district. Beliefs about the value of SEL, teachers' role in promoting it, and student' capacity to learn social and emotional skills all have implications for the change process (Beets et al., 2008; Durlak & DuPre, 2008). These can be assessed formally (through surveys and interviews) or informally in conversations with key stakeholders.

Cultivate Commitment to SEL

A variety of factors may prompt district leaders to adopt SEL as a priority, but this alone will not lead to changes that promote SEL for all students. Commitment from practitioners and administrators throughout the district is essential for implementation of programs and practices that promote SEL (Durlak & DuPre, 2008). District leaders can build commitment by developing a compelling vision for SEL, communicating with stakeholders about SEL, and embodying the shared values that they hope to promote throughout the district (Fullan, 2007).

Develop a Vision for SEL

One of the primary functions of effective district leadership is to develop a compelling vision for high-quality education and engage as many people as possible in pursuing that vision (Chrispeels & Gonzalez, 2006; Darling-Hammond et al., 2005; Fullan, 2007; Rorrer et al., 2008; Stein & Coburn, 2007). Effective vision statements combine aspirations for student success with clarity about the kinds of educational experiences that should be provided so students can achieve this success (Togneri & Anderson, 2003). In districts that are pursuing improvements in SEL, a formal vision statement should convey the importance of social and emotional skills and positive learning environments. Such a vision can serve as a foundation for shifting the culture of the district and shaping practice in schools and classrooms (Chrispeels & Gonzalez, 2006; Jackson & Cobb, 2011). An important part of this process involves convening a representative group of stakeholders—including central office staff, teachers, school leaders, community members, and even students—to participate in creating a vision statement that incorporates academic, social, and emotional learning for all students. Ideally, this collaborative process instills a sense of ownership in participants and builds their commitment to making the vision a reality.

Communicate with Stakeholders about SEL

A well-crafted vision statement cannot shift the culture in a district until it becomes shared among the stakeholders throughout the district. Therefore, we suggest that district leaders implement a plan for communicating with a variety of audiences about what SEL is, why it is important, and how it can be promoted in schools and classrooms. Communication with families and community members can be accomplished through the district's website, press releases, newsletters, and a variety of other public venues. Ideally, district leaders work closely with district staff members who are responsible for overseeing communications and public relations to embed support for SEL throughout the district's overall communication plan. To foster commitment among local stakeholders effectively, these communications should build a rationale for SEL that connects to needs and concerns of the local community (Louis, Leithwood, Wahlstrom, & Anderson, 2010).

In addition to these public communication strategies, districts can employ various methods for internal communication with teachers, schools leaders, and other staff members. Brief information sessions can foster awareness of and commitment to SEL in the early stages of the change process. Over time, ongoing communications between the central office and schools can also serve as microinterventions, reiterating the importance of SEL, responding to concerns that arise in implementation, and inspiring educators to take action to support their students' social and emotional development (Hall & Hord, 2001). If they are clear and consistent, these internal communications can lead to the development of shared beliefs and norms that support SEL and guide day-to-day practice of educators throughout the district (Chrispeels & Gonzalez, 2006).

Model Social and Emotional Competence

In his landmark book on educational reform, Seymour Sarason (1990, p. 147) asserted that "to create and sustain for children the conditions for productive growth without those conditions existing for educators themselves is virtually impossible." He based this statement on research from psychotherapy, management, and other sectors, which suggests that the way people interact with those in their care (e.g., patients, subordinates, students) mirrors how they themselves are treated by their superiors. If one takes these ideas seriously, then a school district that supports SEL for all students must also be a place where all educators feel valued, connected, and supported. District leaders, from the superintendent on down, are well positioned to create such an environment by modeling caring, respectful behavior in all of their professional interactions. Leaders who "walk the talk" are also perceived as more authentic and trustworthy, and are therefore better able to inspire systemic change (Evans, 2001).

Build Organizational Support for SEL

District leaders have the power to catalyze systemic changes that support SEL by formally orienting the district organization toward promoting SEL alongside academic learning. That is, they can embed SEL in the district's policies and plans, and they can allocate resources accordingly (Honig, Copland, Rainey, Lorton, & Newton, 2010; Rorrer et al., 2008). This not only formalizes district leaders' commitment to SEL as a priority, but over time it can also contribute to the sustainability of new programs and practices (Elias, Zins, Graczyk, & Weissberg, 2003).

Develop a Long-Term Plan for Districtwide SEL

Once they have developed a vision for SEL, district leaders can work to develop specific, long-term plans that outline clear action steps to move the district toward improving SEL for all students (Togneri & Anderson, 2003). One might think of these plans as district-specific theories of action that build from the findings of needs and resource assessments to specify the precise strategies that district leaders believe will create systemic support for SEL (Connell & Klem, 2000). By formally drafting a long-term plan, district leaders make themselves accountable for ensuring that the vision for SEL is realized over time. This strategy may be particularly effective when plans to support SEL are part of a comprehensive strategy for improving education throughout the district. In either case, plans are most effective in guiding change when they include measureable goals and benchmarks that can be used to monitor progress over time.

Align Budgets and Staffing to Support SEL

Districts that achieve significant improvements in student outcomes do so, in part, by allocating time, funds, personnel, and other key resources in ways that are tightly aligned with their vision and long-term plans (McLaughlin & Talbert, 2003; Rorrer et al., 2008). In the case of SEL, funds must be allocated for program materials, professional development services, program evaluation release time for teachers and staff to participate in planning and professional learning, and any other strategies that are part of the district's plan to advance SEL. Temporary funds (from grants, donations) may be sufficient to support initial implementation of new programs and practices for SEL, but embedding funding for SEL in the district's annual budgeting process enhances sustainability and signals deeper commitment.

Although all stakeholders will take on some responsibility for students' social, emotional, and academic growth, there is a need for a few individuals to assume formal responsibility for advancing SEL in the district (Chrispeels & Gonzalez, 2006; Louis et al., 2010). Plans to build systemic support for SEL cannot progress unless qualified staff members are assigned to provide instructional leadership for SEL and oversee budgets, scheduling, and other administrative functions associated with SEL. This may require creating new positions that are exclusively dedicated to this work or to redefining existing positions. In either case, district leaders must make decisions about where supports for SEL will reside within the organizational structure of the central office, and how they will be linked to departments that oversee instruction, school leadership, professional development, and other essential functions. These decisions may seem inconsequential, but given the isolation that often exists between central office departments, it could mean the difference between SEL being tightly intertwined with academic learning, or relegated to a less prominent position in the district bureaucracy (Honig & Coburn, 2008).

Cultivate SEL-Focused Partnerships with Schools

A key organizational challenge for any districtwide change process is to bridge the gap between the central office and schools (Elmore & Burney, 1997; Honig, 2012; Stein & Coburn, 2007). District leaders can establish a vision, make strategic plans, and allocate resources accordingly, but school-level processes have a powerful influence on implementation of new programs and practice. Therefore, to promote changes that support SEL, district leaders and staff must partner with school leaders to build systemic support for SEL at the school level. Elsewhere, we describe a school-level theory of action that includes strategies analogous to those described here (CASEL, 2012). District leaders can work to ensure that schools implement these strategies, and do so in ways that are aligned with the districtwide vision and strategic plan.

District staff members who are responsible for building SEL-focused partnerships with schools should use a combination of strategies that include support, accountability, and relationship building (Burch & Spillane, 2004; Honig, 2012; Levin et al., 2012). We intentionally choose the word *partnership* here because previous research indicates that district staff members are much more successful at catalyzing deep changes in practice when they focus on building trusting relationships and shared understandings with school staff members while facilitating bidirectional communication between the central office and schools (Honig et al., 2010; Johnson & Chrispeels, 2010). When district staff members focus too heavily on holding schools accountable, they often prompt surface-level compliance and prevent deep engagement with the change process (Burch & Spillane, 2004). Although school leaders and staff members are unlikely to initiate changes without some measure of external accountability, mandates are ineffective in the absence of adequate resources and professional learning opportunities (Smylie & Perry, 1998).

Support Instructional Improvement

A consistent message in the literature on district-led educational reform is that in order to make a difference in student outcomes, district leaders must adopt a laser-like focus on improving the quality of instruction (Darling-Hammond et al., 2005; Honig et al., 2010; Rorrer et al., 2008; Togneri & Anderson, 2003). Therefore, we resonate with Dailey and colleagues' (2005, p. 3) statement that, in districts that succeed in improving outcomes for all students, "all leadership must become instructional leadership." To improve instruction in ways that support SEL, district leaders must devote their attention to embedding support for SEL in elements of the district system that are most directly tied to instruction. These include expectations for the *content* (i.e., what gets taught) and *methods* (i.e., how teachers teach) of instruction, along with processes for professional learning, assessment, and accountability (Jackson & Cobb, 2011).

Establish Learning Standards for SEL

Some of the earliest examples of systemic reform in education were based on adoption and implementation of learning standards (Smith & O'Day, 1990). Such standards define desired outcomes of instruction and provide clear guidance on what students should be learning in schools. They also create shared expectations for student learning among educators throughout the district, which can form the basis for clear communication and effective collaboration (Jackson & Cobb, 2011; Stein & Coburn, 2007).

In the past, most districts adopted learning standards that were based on those required by their respective state departments of education. State standards for early childhood education have a strong focus on SEL. In fact, all 50 states have preschool standards for SEL, and 45 states actually use the words *social* and *emotional* to characterize this domain of student learning standards (see Dusenbury et al., Chapter 35, this volume). In contrast, only three states (Illinois, Kansas, and Pennsylvania) have freestanding K–12 SEL standards; other states often integrate SEL with academic standards at the elementary, middle, and high school level (Dusenbury et al., Chapter 35, this volume; Dusenbury, Zadrazil, Mart, & Weissberg, 2011). Districts are now moving toward implementation of the Common Core State Standards, which creates opportunities for integration with SEL. We recommend that district leaders engage leaders and practitioners across the district to establish developmentally appropriate learning standards for SEL in preschool through grade 12. Beginning with exemplary SEL standards from other school systems, district leaders can lead a process similar to that used to adopt learning standards for other content areas. The resulting SEL standards not only clarify the goals of instruction for SEL, but they also are a concrete statement that every school in the district is responsible for ensuring that all students develop social and emotional competence (Dusenbury et al., Chapter 35, this volume).

Adopt Evidence-Based Programs and Practices for SEL

Learning standards provide the foundation for transforming instruction, but they do little to define *how* teachers should go about promoting students' mastery (Levin et al., 2012; Rorrer et al., 2008). Teachers need guidance on how to teach social and emotional skills and create positive learning environments, and they need instructional resources (e.g., lesson plans, visual aids) that support them in doing so effectively (Jackson & Cobb, 2011). This is the case in any content area, but it is particularly true for SEL. Whereas most teachers have some experience developing standards-based strategies for math, reading, and other content areas, they are unlikely to have experience developing and implementing universal strategies for promoting SEL (Schonert-Reichl, Hanson-Peterson, & Hymel, Chapter 27, this volume). For this reason, we encourage district leaders to develop a coherent curriculum for SEL that includes evidence-based programs and practices. These might include a series of lessons that explicitly teach social and emotional skills, general pedagogical practices that provide opportunities for SEL, and curricula that integrate social and emotional skills with academic content (CASEL, 2012).

Evidence-based programs and practices offer several advantages. First, as the name suggests, they have demonstrated evidence that, when implemented well, they produce good outcomes for students. Many programs are disseminated by organizations that can provide professional development and technical assistance to schools, which is a benefit for school districts as they build their own capacity to provide these services directly to schools. Evidence-based programs also help to ensure that teachers are not made to bear the full burden of developing their own lessons and materials for teaching SEL. Furthermore, in the same way that learning standards create clear understandings about *what* teachers should be teaching in the area of SEL, a packaged program offers a coherent response to the question of *how* teachers should go about promoting students' social and emotional competence. Here, again, this clarity can help to develop the shared understandings and common language that form the basis for collaboration, reflection, and improvement.

Districts may take various approaches to adopting evidence-based programs for SEL. Some studies of district-led reform suggest that district leaders should set expectations for student learning and allow each school to select programs and practices to meet the needs of their students (Levin et al., 2012). However, because school-based practitioners may not have the time to consider research evidence as they make decisions about program adoption, district leaders may be wise to provide some guidance in this area (Honig & Coburn, 2008). For example, district leaders may provide a list of approved programs from which schools can choose. An alternate approach is for district leaders to encourage adoption of the same evidence-based program for SEL across all schools throughout the district. Although this limits school-based autonomy, it may offer advantages in terms of efficiency, consistency across schools, and opportunities for collaboration among schools (Togneri & Anderson, 2003).

Clarify Links between SEL and Other Priority Initiatives

To change their practice in ways that promote academic, social, and emotional learning, teachers must make sense of many sometimes conflicting messages that are communicated through the myriad programs and policies they are asked to implement (Coburn, 2001). To provide coherent instructional leadership for SEL, district leaders must develop clear statements about how SEL aligns with existing initiatives that are aimed at teaching social and emotional skills and/or creating positive learning environments. Furthermore, they must be clear about how SEL diverges from or expands on other approaches with which practitioners are familiar. For each of the programs and practices identified during the process of assessing needs and resources, district leaders might ask:

1. "How does it relate to the district's overall strategy for SEL?"
2. "Should practitioners continue implementing it?"

The district's newly adopted SEL standards may provide a useful framework for clarifying how commonly used approaches contribute to developing students' social and emotional competence. For example, in districts that have adopted an RTI model for student support services, district leaders may need to clarify that schools are expected to adopt universal (Tier 1) interventions to support all students in mastering the SEL standards. In districts that have adopted PBIS as an approach to classroom management, it may be useful to clarify that this approach focuses on prescribing and enforcing expectations for behavior, whereas programs and practices for SEL focus on explicitly teaching social and emotional skills.

In addition to existing initiatives that are clearly linked to SEL, one can assume that virtually every district in the United States has already initiated one or more strategies aimed at improving instruction more generally (Louis et al., 2010). Instructional improvement efforts in many districts are currently driven by two prominent factors: the Common Core State Standards (CCSS) and associated assessments, and new systems for observing instruction to evaluate teacher quality, as called for by the federal Race to the Top program and in state waivers from No Child Left Behind requirements. District leaders can leverage these efforts to improve instruction in ways that simultaneously promote social and emotional development and academic learning.

CCSS presents a unique opportunity to do so because the kind of deep academic learning called for in these new standards will require instructional strategies that build positive learning environments and promote interpersonal and intrapersonal competence (National Research Council, 2012). These include pedagogies that give students an active role in the learning process and provide opportunities for collaboration and autonomy (Levin et al., 2012). Systems for teacher observation and evaluation not only influence administrative decisions about advancement and retention, but they also shape instructional guidance from school leaders, collaboration among colleagues, and teachers' thinking about what constitutes excellent practice (Honig et al., 2010; Jackson & Cobb, 2011).

Districts' approaches to teacher evaluation can either complement or undermine efforts to promote SEL, and we encourage district leaders to examine each element of their evaluation strategy through the lens of SEL. For example, they might ask whether their framework for teacher observation includes instructional practices that create positive learning environments and provide opportunities for students to develop and apply social and emotional skills. Many commonly used observation systems include these elements, but links to SEL may not always be readily apparent. By providing clear guidance to help teachers and instructional leaders make sense of these intersections, district leaders can begin building shared understandings of quality instruction that emphasize academic, social, and emotional learning.

Design Systems for Ongoing Professional Learning

Curriculum and standards provide a road map for instruction that promotes SEL, but their implementation depends on the knowledge, skills, and attitudes of teachers (Durlak & DuPre, 2008). Therefore, districts can only achieve widespread improvements in instruction when they provide ongoing opportunities that focus on systematically developing teachers' capacity to implement new forms of instruction (Elmore & Burney, 1997; Rorrer et al., 2008). To begin, teachers may benefit from a basic overview of SEL, its importance for student success, and the programs and practices that they are being asked to implement. However, effective professional development must go far beyond one-time informational workshops. Teachers' learning should be organized around the learning standards, curricula, and other documents that codify the district's vision for quality instruction, and teachers should have extended opportunities to engage with these documents (Jackson & Cobb, 2011; Learning Forward, 2011). Effective professional learning also requires ongoing coaching and opportunities for teachers to apply new instructional approaches, reflect on the experience, and receive feedback on their practice (Stein & Coburn, 2007). Teachers also need opportunities to collaborate with peers around authentic concerns that arise as they attempt to implement new forms of instruction for SEL (Hall & Hord, 2001; Learning Forward, 2011).

Effective professional learning systems must also ensure that school leaders are equipped to provide instructionally focused leadership for SEL. In fact, building strong instructional leadership at the school level is consistently noted as a core characteristic of successful district-led efforts to improve instruction, and the district reform literature includes many examples of effective districtwide improvement in which central office administrators take responsibility for building principals' capacity to lead reform

(Honig, 2012; Louis et al., 2010; McLaughlin & Talbert, 2003). Just like teachers, school leaders need professional development opportunities that build shared understanding of excellent practice, prompt reflection, and allow for collaboration with peers. Professional learning communities that bring together school leaders from multiple schools may be a particularly promising approach (Chrispeels & Gonzalez, 2006; Honig et al., 2010).

We have suggested that district leaders designate personnel to lead and support SEL. To facilitate improvements in instruction that support SEL, these individuals must have a thorough understanding of the core principles of the SEL, and they must also be skilled at building trusting, collaborative partnerships with school-level personnel (Burch & Spillane, 2004; Honig et al., 2010). Therefore, district leaders must provide professional learning opportunities for central office personnel, to ensure that they have the necessary knowledge, skills, and attitudes to lead and support new practices for SEL. Honig (2012) described how one district went to great lengths to develop the knowledge and skills of central office staff members, so that they could work directly with school principals to develop instructional leadership. Likewise, many districtwide reform efforts use central office staff as instructional coaches for teachers (Darling-Hammond et al., 2005). District leaders can examine their existing structures and resources for professional learning and explore whether these are truly adequate for improving instruction, and how they might be improved to support instruction for academic, social, and emotional learning.

Build Systems for Continuous Improvement

As a final strategy to build systemic support for SEL, we recommend that district leaders periodically assess the outcomes and processes specified in their strategic plans and use these data to inform their decisions (Honig & Coburn, 2008; Togneri & Anderson, 2003). This strategy can be thought of as an extension of the initial assessment of needs and resources, now tailored to focus on (1) monitoring desired outcomes and (2) implementation of new programs, practices, and policies. Although this process will necessarily vary according to each district's specific plans for existing assessment systems, we suggest that a few elements should be incorporated into all systems for continuously improving SEL.

Monitor Student Outcomes

First and foremost, because improving social and emotional competence for all students is the ultimate goal of all these efforts, districts must regularly assess students' development of social and emotional competence. These data can be used not only to assess the overall impact of the districtwide effort but also to inform decisions by school leaders, and they can be used by teachers to monitor individual student progress and plan instruction. Because the quality of the learning environment is so crucial for students' academic, social, and emotional development, we also recommend that districts regularly assess students' perceptions of school climate. Again, these data can inform decisions about support for SEL at multiple levels.

Monitor Implementation

In light of our focus on improving instruction, we urge district leaders regularly to take stock of the quality of instruction in the district as it pertains to both academic learning and SEL. Monitoring implementation of evidence-based programs and practices is of particular importance, particularly early in the change process. Ideally, these data can be used to provide teachers with feedback that will help improve their practice. Likewise, although all of the previously discussed data may be used to promote school accountability, they can be leveraged more effectively to provide support that is responsive to the needs of each school (McLaughlin & Talbert, 2003; Togneri & Anderson, 2003).

Effective districts use a variety of formal and informal feedback loops to understand the attitudes, experiences, and practices of leaders and educators throughout the district (Honig & Coburn, 2008). One can think of these as a means of monitoring implementation of the district's selected change strategies to inform effective decision making. For example, if the district has devoted considerable effort to encouraging adoption of a particular evidence-based program, yet people throughout the district report that they are not using it, this may be an indication that the current strategy for disseminating the program is ineffective. It may also signal barriers to implementation that warrant further exploration.

Future Directions, Recommendations, and Possible Pitfalls

In this chapter, we have introduced the concept of systemic support for SEL. We argue that school districts can play an essential role in ensuring that high-quality SEL is a reality for all students, and we propose a set of strategies for district leaders that we hypothesize will contribute to systemic changes that improve SEL for all students. Like all hypotheses, the previously discussed ideas are meant to be applied, tested, and refined. We have already undertaken our own efforts to do so, and we hope that many more practitioners, policymakers, and researchers will eventually join us in this pursuit. With that in mind, we now draw on lessons learned from our work to alert readers to a few potential pitfalls and propose an agenda for future research in this area.

The Collaborating Districts Initiative

In fall 2010, CASEL launched a multisite initiative to apply and refine our ideas about systemic support for SEL. Through collaboration with NoVo Foundation, the American Institutes for Research (AIR), and eight large school districts (Anchorage, Austin, Chicago, Cleveland, Nashville, Oakland, Sacramento, Washoe County), the Collaborating Districts Initiative (CDI) seeks to achieve two complementary goals. First, it is designed to build systemic support for SEL in each collaborating district, thereby improving social, emotional, and academic outcomes for students. Second, the CDI aims to develop a clearer understanding of how district leaders can effectively build systemic support for SEL, and how we and other external partners can assist them in doing so.

To build systemic support for SEL, CASEL supports leadership teams in each collaborating district by providing consultation, technical assistance, professional development, and tools to help them develop and implement long-term plans to make high-quality SEL a reality for all students. Furthermore, CASEL facilitates a cross-district learning community that allows district leaders to learn from one another and engage in collaborative problem solving. At the same time, NoVo Foundation provides yearly financial grants to each district that are used to support the development of systemic support for SEL. In turn, each district agrees to work closely with CASEL consultants to pursue the change strategies outlined earlier.

AIR's evaluation of the CDI serves both formative and summative purposes. It is designed to generate data that describe the change processes that unfold in each district in ways that can be used for continuous improvement by district leaders and CASEL consultants. The evaluation also explicitly tests the hypotheses: that implementation of these strategies will lead to systemic support for SEL at the district, school, and classroom level, which will in turn lead to improved outcomes for students. AIR's mixed-methods evaluation design combines district case studies and cross-case analysis with district level quasi-experiments and interrupted times series studies.

Early findings from the CDI evaluation show that key personnel in every district believe that their district will be able to integrate SEL successfully into instruction, and that doing so will improve the quality of learning, school climate, and social–emotional outcomes for students, including students who are currently at risk of dropout. The districts are doing well and making progress. Measures of district growth showed particularly large gains in SEL standards development and stakeholder commitment. The districts have all faced challenges, including staff readiness for change, budgetary and accountability pressures, and leadership change. Even so, district leaders' increasing sense of the need for and benefits of SEL, the support that CASEL has provided to districts leaders and SEL leads, and the districts' initial success with SEL professional development and implementation have created a momentum to overcome these challenges and sustain the project.

Potential Pitfalls and Possible Solutions

As in any change process, a handful of challenges have surfaced as district leaders and CASEL consultants collaborate to build systemic support for SEL. We explore four of these potential pitfalls below and briefly describe how districts have maintained their commitment to SEL in the face of these challenges.

Balancing Multiple Reforms

As noted earlier, most school districts are already pursuing a wide range of strategies to improve student performance. Many of our district partners have reported being overburdened with too many initiatives at once and suffering from "innovation fatigue." In this context, there is a danger that a districtwide initiative to promote SEL could divert attention from the district's other priorities, increase fragmentation, or compound feelings of confusion and exhaustion. Our collaborating districts have managed this problem in part by heeding our suggestion that they integrate SEL with other priority initiatives. In some cases, it seems that focusing on SEL may actually be an antidote to fragmentation, as districts have used SEL as a framework to organize and consolidate many related but previously disconnected efforts.

Leadership Turnover

In most of our collaborating districts, interest in pursuing SEL began with one person (often the superintendent or other senior leader) or a small group of people who fervently believe in the power of SEL to promote students' success. However, given that the average tenure for senior district leaders in large school districts is approximately 2 years, it is unlikely that they will remain in their positions long enough to implement a districtwide vision for SEL fully. In fact, each of our collaborative districts has experienced leadership turnover in the first 2 years of the CDI, but efforts to build systemic support for SEL have endured. This was possible because, in each district, leaders intentionally built distributed leadership for SEL by engaging other senior leaders, midlevel district staff, school personnel, and a variety of other stakeholders. Changes in district policy and culture can also ensure that support for SEL continues under any leadership.

Difficulty Reaching All Schools

As part of their strategic plans, each district must devise a strategy to ensure that SEL eventually reaches all schools. In most districts, it is not feasible to launch all strategies in all schools at the same time, so they develop plans to gradually expand over time. The dominant approach in our collaborating districts has been to begin with a few—often highly motivated—schools and over time gradually expand support to additional schools. However, the reality is that most reforms that begin in a few schools never fully spread, and schools that are not reached are often those in most need of support (Quint, Bloom, Black, Stephens, & Akey, 2005). On the other hand, it may be virtually impossible for districts to muster sufficient resources for all schools at once, and doing so may lead to support that is a mile wide and an inch deep. One potential solution to this problem, in light of limited resources at the central office, may be to promote cross-site collaboration between schools. In such a model, schools that are among the first to partner with the district can eventually be a resource for their colleagues in other schools. This approach has been successfully leveraged in a number of pervious districtwide reform efforts (Elmore & Burney, 1997; Fullan et al., 2004).

Need for Greater Capacity

Many of the strategies in our theory of action focus on embedding support for SEL in what the district is already doing. However, the proposition that district administrators should integrate SEL in existing systems for communication, instruction leadership, professional development, or continuous improvement assumes that districts already have reasonably effective systems for fulfilling these basic functions. In reality, however, many do not. In school districts where funding is scarce and the capacity for improvement is generally weak, we must leverage the process of building systemic support for SEL to develop the district's overall capacity to improve education for all students. This will require even stronger and more effective collaboration between the fields of SEL and education reform, and we are encouraged by possibilities that might emerge from this synergy.

Recommendations for Future Research

Efforts to understand and intervene in multilevel dynamic systems such as school districts call for sophisticated research methods. In the interest of promoting high-quality research on systemic support for SEL, we offer the following recommendations for future work in this area.

Research Design and Data Analysis

If one thinks in terms of multilevel statistical models, it becomes apparent that research in school districts can generate variables that pertain to at least four levels of analysis: individual, classroom, school, and district. This fact makes it challenging to articulate clear research questions, let alone feasible methods for answering them. In studying associations between variables, researchers must carefully articulate the level at which each variable is to be measured and analyzed (Shinn & Rapkin, 2000). If researchers wish to assess the impact of district-level interventions, then they must design evaluations that assign entire districts to control and experimental conditions. In cases where this is not feasible, such as the evaluation of our CDI, time series analyses can be used to monitor changes in each district over time. However, in the absence of a randomly assigned control group, one cannot confidently assert that such changes are attributable to the district-level intervention.

Reforming districtwide systems is a complex intervention with multiple components. Studies that capture the outcomes of such interventions are exciting, but they must also collect sufficient data to link district-level processes to student-level outcomes. To identify effective strategies and refine theories of systemic support for SEL, researchers must carefully document evidence of systemic change at the district, school, and classroom levels. The examples in Table 32.1 may serve as a starting point for considering potential sources of evidence for systemic change at the classroom, school, and district levels.

Measurement

When surveying educational leaders and practitioners about their current attitudes and practices with regard to SEL, researchers should take great care in clarifying respondents' understanding of various terms. For example, responses to the item "I feel confident implementing instruction for SEL," designed to assess efficacy, depends on the respondent's understanding of what it means to implement SEL instruction. Similar issues arise in assessing commitment, current practices, and other constructs. When such definitional issues exist, effective interventions may actually result in more negative responses over time because they clarify the meaning of constructs (e.g., instruction for SEL) and cause respondents to realize that their attitudes and practices are not consistent with these meanings (Shadish, Cook, & Campbell, 2002). These and other issues point to the continued need to refine and validate measures of individuals' commitment and expertise for SEL. Such work is currently under way as part of our evaluation of the CDI.

There is also a need for better measures of school- and classroom-level processes that may contribute to improvements in students' social and emotional learning. Most importantly, we urge researchers to focus on developing reliable, valid tools for assessing instructional practices that promote SEL. Because the impact of district-level interventions is ultimately mediated through changes in instruction, such measures are essential to furthering our understanding of the district's role in promoting SEL.

Focus on Problems of Practice

Finally, in addition to generating findings that drive educational practice and policy, researchers should allow their own work to be guided by needs and questions that emerge from administrators, teachers, and other staff members in relation to systemic support for SEL. For example, we have identified many gaps in districtwide instructional guidance systems for SEL that might be best addressed by feedback from those who implement SEL at the school level. For example, what do teachers need that they are not receiving? How might current support be modified or extended to be more effective? Frontline providers can play an important in crafting excellent research questions if researchers take the time and effort to solicit and discuss the former's input. Broadly speaking, there is a need—both here and in the broader literature on district-led reform—for more nuanced investigation of the conditions under which various reform strategies contribute to widespread improvements for students.

Concluding Comments

We began this chapter with the assertion that all students should have access to an excellent education that includes academic, social, and emotional learning. To make this vision a reality requires systemic support that goes beyond classroom-based programs and schoolwide activities. Lessons from the broader field of education reform clearly indicate that school districts play a critical role in ensuring quality education for all students. Our exploration of this topic has led us to conclude that district leaders can create the necessary conditions for widespread improvement SEL. They can do this by building commitment among stakeholders across the district, building districtwide infrastructure for SEL, and instructional improvements that promote SEL. To do so, they must build from existing needs and resources, regularly assess implementation and student outcomes, and use these data for planning and continuous improvement. External partners, including researchers, funders, and nonprofit organizations, can and should collaborate with district leaders to support this work. We hope that the ideas articulated in this chapter will serve as the basis for a host of new developments in research, practice, and policy that will advance district-level support for SEL.

References

Anderson, S., & Rodway-Macri, J. (2009). District administrator perspectives on student learning in an era of standards and accountability: A collective frame analysis. *Canadian Journal of Education, 32*(2), 192–221.

Beets, M. W., Flay, B. R., Vuchinich, S., Acock, A. C., Li, K. K., & Allred, C. (2008). School climate and teachers' beliefs and attitudes associated with implementation of the Positive Action Program: A diffusion of innovations model. *Prevention Science, 9*(4), 264–275.

Bronfenbrenner, U. (1979). *The ecology of human development: Experiments by nature and design.* Cambridge, MA: Harvard University Press.

Burch, P., & Spillane, J. (2004). *Leading from the middle: Mid-level district staff and instructional improvement.* Oakland, CA: Cross City Campaign for Urban School Reform.

Chrispeels, J. H., & Gonzalez, M. (2006). The challenge of systemic change in complex educational systems: A district model to scale up reform. In A. Harris & J. H. Chrispeels (Eds.), *Improving schools and educational systems: International perspectives* (pp. 241–273). New York: Routledge.

Collaborative for Academic, Social, and Emotional Learning (CASEL). (2012). *2013 CASEL guide: Effective social and emotional learning programs—Preschool and elementary edition.* Chicago: Author.

Coburn, C. E. (2001). Collective sense making about reading: How teachers mediate reading policy in their professional communities. *Educational Evaluation and Policy Analysis, 23*(2), 145–170.

Connell, J. P., & Klem, A. M. (2000). You can get there from here: Using a theory of change approach to plan urban education reform. *Journal of Educational and Psychological Consultation, 11*, 93–120.

Dailey, D., Fleischman, S., Gil, L., Holtzman, D., O'Day, J., & Vosmer, C. (2005). *Towards more effective school districts: A review of the knowledge base.* Washington, DC: American Institutes for Research.

Darling-Hammond, L., Hightower, A. M., Husbands, J. L., Lafors, J. R., Young, V. M., & Christopher, C. (2005). *Instructional leadership for systemic change: The story of San Diego's reform.* Lanham, MD: Scarecrow Education.

Devaney, E., O'Brien, M. U., Resnik, H., Keister, S., & Weissberg, R. P. (2006). *Sustainable schoolwide social and emotional learning: Implementation guide and toolkit.* Chicago: Collaborative for Academic, Social, and Emotional Learning.

Durlak, J. A., & DuPre, E. P. (2008). Implementation matters: A review of research on the influence of implementation on program outcomes and the factors affecting implementation. *American Journal of Community Psychology, 41*(3), 327–350.

Durlak, J. A., Weissberg, R. P., Dymnicki, A. B., Taylor, R. D., & Schellinger, K. B. (2011). The impact of enhancing students' social and emotional learning: A meta-analysis of school-based universal interventions. *Child Development, 82*(1), 405–432.

Dusenbury, L., Zadrazil, J., Mart, A., & Weissberg, R. P. (2011). *State learning standards to advance social and emotional learning.* Chicago: Collaborative for Academic, Social, and Emotional Learning.

Elias, M. J. (2009). Social–emotional and character development and academics as a dual focus of educational policy. *Educational Policy, 23*(6), 831–846.

Elias, M. J., Zins, J. E., Graczyk, P. A., & Weissberg, R. P. (2003). Implementation, sustainability, and scaling up of social–emotional and academic innovations in public schools. *School Psychology Review, 32*, 303–319.

Elmore, R., & Burney, D. (1997). *School variation and systemic instructional improvement in Community District 2, New York City.* Pittsburgh, PA: Learning Research and Development Center, University of Pittsburgh.

Evans, R. (2001). *The human side of change: Reform, resistance, and the real-life problems of innovation.* San Francisco: Jossey-Bass.

Foster-Fishman, P. G., Nowell, B., & Yang, H. (2007). Putting the system back into systems change: A framework for understanding and changing organizational and community systems. *American Journal of Community Psychology, 39*(3), 197–215.

Fullan, M. (2007). *The new meaning of educational change* (4th ed.). New York: Teachers College Press.

Fullan, M., Bertani, A., & Quinn, J. (2004). New lessons for districtwide reform. *Educational Leadership, 61*, 7–15.

Glennan, T. K., Bodilly, S. J., Galegher, J., & Kerr, K. (2004). *Expanding the reach of education reforms.* Santa Monica, CA: RAND Corporation.

Hall, G. E., & Hord, S. M. (2001). *Implementing change: Patterns, principles, and potholes.* New York: Allyn & Bacon.

Honig, M. I. (2012). District central office leadership as teaching: How central office administrators support principals' development as instructional leaders. *Educational Administration Quarterly, 48*(4), 733–774.

Honig, M. I., & Coburn, C. (2008). Evidence-based decision making in school district central offices toward a policy and research agenda. *Educational Policy, 22*(4), 578–608.

Honig, M. I., Copland, M. A., Rainey, L., Lorton, J. A., & Newton, M. (2010). *Central office transformation for district-wide teaching and learning improvement.* Seattle: Center for the Study of Teaching and Policy, University of Washington.

Humphrey, N. (2013). *Social and emotional learning: A critical appraisal.* London: Sage.

Jackson, K., & Cobb, P. (2011). Towards an empirically grounded theory of action for improving the quality of mathematics teaching at scale. *Mathematics Teacher Education and Development, 13*(1), 6–33.

Johnson, P. E., & Chrispeels, J. H. (2010). Linking the central office and its schools for reform. *Educational Administration Quarterly, 46*, 738–775.

Kam, C. M., Greenberg, M. T., & Walls, C. T. (2003). Examining the role of implementation quality in school-based prevention using the PATHS curriculum. *Prevention Science, 4*(1), 55–63.

Learning Forward. (2011). Standards for professional learning: Quick reference guide. Retrieved from *www.learningforward.org/docs/pdf/standardsreferenceguide.pdf.*

Levin, B., Datnow, A., & Carrier, N. (2012). *Changing school district practices.* Boston: Students at the Center.

Louis, K. S., Leithwood, K., Wahlstrom, K. L., & Anderson, S. E. (2010). *Investigating the links to improved student learning.* New York: Wallace Foundation.

Mart, A. K., Greenberg, M., Kriete, R., Schaps, E., & Weissberg, R. P. (2011, April). *Perspectives on scaling up social and emotional learning in school districts.* Paper presented at the annual meeting of the American Educational Research Association, New Orleans, LA.

McLaughlin, M., & Talbert, J. (2003). *Reforming districts: How districts support school reform.* Seattle: Center for the Study of Teaching and Policy, University of Washington.

Merrell, K. W., & Gueldner, B. A. (2010). *Social and emotional learning in the classroom: Promoting mental health and academic success.* New York: Guilford Press.

Mourshed, M., Chijoki, C., & Barber, M. (2010). *How the world's most improved school systems keep getting better.* New York: McKinsey & Company.

National Research Council. (2012). *Education for life and work: Developing transferable knowledge and skills in the 21st century.* Washington, DC: National Academies Press.

O'Day, J. A., Bitter, C. S., & Gomez, L. M. (2011). *Education reform in New York City: Ambitious change in the nation's most complex school system.* Cambridge, MA: Harvard Education Press.

Quint, J., Bloom, H. S., Black, A. R., Stephens, L., & Akey, T. M. (2005). *The challenge of scaling up educational reform: Findings and lessons from First Things First Final Report.* New York: Manpower Demonstration Research Corporation.

Rorrer, A. K., Skrla, L., & Scheurich, J. J. (2008). Districts as institutional actors in educational reform. *Educational Administration Quarterly, 44*(3), 307–357.

Sarason, S. B. (1990). *The predictable failure of educational reform: Can we change course before it's too late?* San Francisco: Jossey-Bass.

Shadish, W. R., Cook, T. D., & Campbell, D. T. (2002). *Experimental and quasi-experimental design for generalized causal inference.* Boston: Houghton Mifflin.

Shinn, M., & Rapkin, B. M. (2000). Cross-level research without cross-ups in community psychology. In J. Rappaport & E. Seidman (Eds.), *Handbook of community psychology* (pp. 309–330). New York: Kluwer Academic.

Sklad, M., Diekstra, R., De Ritter, M., Ben, J., & Gravesteijn, C. (2012). Effectiveness of school-based universal social, emotional, and behavioral programs: Do they enhance students' development in the area of skill, behavior, and adjustment? *Psychology in Schools 49*(9), 892–907.

Smith, M. S., & O'Day, J. (1990). Systemic school reform. *Journal of Education Policy, 5*(5), 233–267.

Smylie, M. A., & Perry, G. S. (1998). Restructuring schools for improving teaching. In A. Hargreaves, A. Lieberman, M. Fullan, & D. Hopkins (Eds.), *International handbook of educational change* (pp. 976–1005). Dordrecht, The Netherlands: Kluwer Academic.

Solomon, D., Battistich, V., Watson, M., Schaps, E., & Lewis, C. (2000). A six-district study of educational change: Direct and mediated effects of the Child Development Project. *Social Psychology of Education, 4,* 3–51.

Spillane, J. P. (1996). School districts matter: Local educational authorities and state instructional policy. *Educational Policy, 10*(1), 63–87.

Squire, K. D., & Reigeluth, C. M. (2000). The many faces of systemic change. *Educational Horizons, 78*(3), 143–152.

Stein, M., & Coburn, C. (2007). *Architectures for learning: A comparative case analysis of two urban school districts.* Seattle: Center for the Study of Teaching and Policy, University of Washington.

Supovitz, J. A. (2006). *The case for district-based reform: Leading, building and sustaining school improvement.* Cambridge, MA: Harvard Education Press.

Togneri, W., & Anderson, S. E. (2003). *Beyond islands of excellence: What districts can do to improve instruction and achievement in all schools: A leadership brief.* Alexandria, VA: Learning First Alliance.

Tseng, V., & Seidman, E. (2007). A systems framework for understanding social settings. *American Journal of Community Psychology, 39,* 217–228.

U.S. Department of Education. (2012). Applications for new awards; Race to the Top—District. Notice inviting applications. *Federal Register, 77, 49,* 654–677.

Waters, J. T., & Marzano, R. J. (2006). *School district leadership that works: The effect of superintendent leadership on student achievement.* Denver, CO: Midcontinent Research for Education and Learning.

Weare, K., & Nind, M. (2011). Mental health promotion and problem prevention in schools: What does the evidence say? *Health Promotion International, 26*(Suppl. 1), S29–S69.

CHAPTER 33

Accountability and SEL Programs

The Getting To Outcomes® Approach

Annie Wright, Andrea Lamont, Abraham Wandersman, David Osher, and Eric S. Gordon

Suppose you are a school superintendent. You have heard about social and emotional learning (SEL) programming and are considering whether to institute it in your schools. Like others around the country, you are trying to do more with less. You have competing priorities and limited resources. Programs designed to prevent bullying, substance abuse, dropout, and obesity are areas of concern, and academic achievement and high-stakes testing remain a paramount consideration. This is a common scenario in modern education systems: School leaders are regularly faced with competing priorities. Given multiple needs, how do school leaders decide which needs to prioritize, and how to address these needs? In this era of accountability, with an emphasis on evidence-based interventions and data-driven decision making, how do schools demonstrate the appropriateness of interventions that support academics and show effectiveness in ways that augment standardized tests?

In this chapter, we introduce the Getting To Outcomes®(GTO®) approach to support districts in bringing effective and evidence-based programs to individual schools. GTO[1] is a system of accountability that helps address key questions for school-based interventions, including "*What* are our schools needs and *what* are our goals?"; "*Which* program should we implement in our school, and *why*?"; "*How* will we know whether it worked?" (Wandersman, Imm, Chinman, & Kaftarian, 2000). GTO is a systematic process that can be used to support schools in selecting, implementing, and evaluating school-based programs that meet their individual needs and resources. As a flexible approach, GTO can be used across content areas (e.g., SEL; Common Core State Standards; 21st Century Learning Skills; science, technology engineering, and mathematics [STEM]; and technology integration, including 1:1 Computing; Wandersman & Hamm, 2014). In this chapter, we introduce how GTO thinking can be applied to SEL programs in school settings. We start with an overview of the GTO approach and note some key features that make GTO particularly useful for the implementation of evidence-based programs in schools, and illustrate how the GTO system can be integrated with the Theory of Action developed by the Collaborative for Academic, Social, and Emotional Learning [CASEL], (2012).

Then, we discuss how GTO thinking can specifically support schools in reaching desired SEL-related outcomes.

Each description of the GTO steps includes an example from the Cleveland, Ohio, Metropolitan School District to illustrate how the district's efforts can be viewed through a GTO perspective. This district was chosen because, although it did not explicitly use GTO, it went through each of the GTO steps in its efforts to improve outcomes. Among the value-added features of GTO that we address throughout this chapter are its intuitive, dynamic nature and practitioner-friendly language; the way it resonates with practitioners, evaluators, and quality improvement scientists; its comprehensiveness (10 steps); and its evidence base in quasi-experimental studies (e.g., Chinman et al., 2008; Chinman, Tremain, Imm, & Wandersman, 2010).

GTO: 10 Accountability Questions

GTO consists of 10 accountability questions, or "steps" (see Table 33.1) assessing needs and resources (GTO Step 1); setting goals and desired outcomes (GTO Step 2); selection of an evidence-based (or promising) program (GTO Step 3); assessing program fit (GTO Step 4); assessing organizational–community capacities forthe chosen best practice(s) (GTO Step 5); planning (GTO Step 6); implementation and process evaluation (GTO Step 7); outcome evaluation (GTO Step 8); continuous quality improvement (GTO Step 9); and sustainability (GTO Step 10). Empirical data demonstrate the effectiveness of GTO thinking in field settings (see, e.g., Chinman et al., 2008; Fisher, Imm, Chinman, & Wandersman, 2006; Imm, Chinman, & Wandersman, 2006; Lesesne et al., 2008).

TABLE 33.1. Relationship between GTO Steps and CASEL's Theory of Action

GTO 10 accountability questions	CASEL's theory of action for systemic SEL
1. *Needs and Resources:* What are the underlying needs and conditions in the community (district/school)?	Conduct an SEL-related resource and needs inventory.
2. *Goals:* What are the goals, target populations, and objectives (i.e., desired outcomes)?	
3. *Best Practices:* Which evidence-based models and best practice programs can be useful in reaching the goals?	Adopt evidence-based SEL programs.
4. *Fit:* What actions need to be taken so the selected program "fits" the community context?	Establish a shared SEL vision with all stakeholders.
5. *Capacities:* What organizational capacities are needed to implement the plan?	Provide ongoing professional development.
6. *Plan:* What is the plan for this program?	Develop an implementation plan.
7. *Implementation and Process Evaluation:* How will the quality of program implementation be monitored and assessed?	Integrate schoolwide policies and activities to foster the social, emotional, and academic learning of all students.
8. *Outcome Evaluation:* How well did the program work?	
9. *CQI:* How will continuous quality improvement strategies be incorporated?	Use data to improve practice.
10. *Sustain:* If the program is successful, how will it be sustained?	

In this chapter, we focus our examples on a district-level initiative; however, these accountability questions could also be applied to multiple levels of a school system. District staff members could address broad needs across multiple schools, perhaps adopting SEL programming in all schools. Individual schools could also answer the questions for their schools, classrooms, or certain populations (e.g., students with emotional disabilities; science, technology, engineering, and mathematics [STEM] teachers) within their school. The reader is encouraged to think broadly about how the accountability questions could be addressed at the level most relevant for his or her particular needs.

Empirical data support the use of GTO thinking in field settings. Chinman and colleagues (2008) tested the effectiveness of using GTO to improve prevention capacities and prevention programming outcomes of community coalitions in a 2-year longitudinal trial funded by the Centers for Disease Control and Prevention. Results indicated significant improvements in staff capacity and program performance in programs using GTO versus comparison programs. Greater exposure to GTO was associated with greater gains in prevention capacity. GTO has also been applied to other domains, including positive youth development (Fisher et al., 2006), preventing underage drinking (Imm et al., 2006), and teen pregnancy prevention (Lesesne et al., 2008).

Features of the GTO System of Accountability

There are features of the GTO approach that make it particularly relevant for school-based programming. First, GTO is a *process-oriented* way of achieving results, which means that it focuses on the ways that outcomes can be realistically achieved. This is particularly important in school systems with ongoing competing priorities, limited resources, multiple programs, and the need to show effectiveness. Second, GTO is a flexible approach that can be used with programs at any stage of their life cycle (e.g., at the beginning of a program or with a mature program). Third, GTO is designed to be customized to your setting. The aim is to achieve outcomes for *your* students, in *your* schools, and in *your* community, taking into account what you are already doing and what is already working.

GTO Is a Process-Oriented Approach

The traditional approach to evaluation typically focuses on summative evaluation (i.e., evaluators assess whether stated outcomes were achieved at the conclusion of an intervention). By itself, this approach has three notable limitations: (1) The end product message tends to be a simple dichotomous "It worked" or "It did not work", which does not provide sufficient data for improvement; (2) it does not increase the likelihood of reaching desired outcomes by encouraging midcourse corrections, if needed, during the implementation process; and (3) it is ill-suited to determine the reasons for a lack of outcomes. A failure to achieve desired outcomes could occur for multiple reasons, including problems with the program theory (e.g., "Does the model of the solution fit the model of the problem?"; "Is the theory of change for the program accurate?") or problems due to poor-quality implementation of the program (e.g., "Was the implementation of an effective program performed in a low-quality way?").

In contrast, GTO adopts an approach to program evaluation that views the summative evaluation as a necessary yet insufficient component for a full picture of program effectiveness. Outcome evaluation is one component of the broader GTO system of accountability, which uses evaluation data *throughout the life cycle of the program.* This approach provides information about programmatic effectiveness along the way, rather than waiting until the end of the program (when resources and time may have already been exhausted) to see whether the program worked.

A GTO-type approach is particularly important for implementing large-scale programs in school settings for a few key reasons. First, in public education settings, programs that fail to show desired outcomes are often quickly cast aside in favor of the next big idea. This cycling through interventions exhausts resources at multiple levels (e.g., fiscal capacities of the district are drained, school resources for training and supporting new initiatives are reduced, and teachers become overwhelmed with changing demands or skeptical about the utility of investing their efforts in another "flavor of the month"). By planning for accountability at the outset of a project, the GTO process helps schools advocate for sustained support for implementation, so that programs are not ended prematurely, before potential outcomes can be achieved and documented. Second, in the context of budget uncertainties, districts and schools must become skilled in justifying previous and future investments to potential funders. Here, GTO can be used to (1) prospectively justify program planning and/or (2) retrospectively evaluate programs that have been operating (e.g., fulfill requirements in grant applications or in justification for continuing funding). Finally, an overreliance on summative evaluation approaches, that is, simply determining *whether* stated outcomes were met, with less attention paid to *how* changes were made, means that schools and districts limit organizational learning. Schools or districts that focus only on *what* happened miss out on learning about *how* it happened, so that they can make it happen *better* in the future.

GTO Can Be Used at Any Stage of a Program's Life Cycle

Though movement through the GTO steps was written sequentially, starting with Step 1 and ending with Step 10, this logical sequence often does not accurately reflect the typical process of program adoption and implementation. Schools are in a constant process of programming a number of innovations and reforms simultaneously, and often are expected to implement a program or evaluate the effectiveness of a preexisting program without sufficient attention to earlier steps of the GTO sequence. GTO was designed to address these real-world demands.

GTO is like a "painter's palette", with users' application of (*painting with*) different steps (*colors*) of the process depending on their specific needs (see Figure 33.1). A common reality is that an evidence-based program is chosen, perhaps due to federal grant guidelines or by a state education office, and districts are instructed to implement the chosen program. Although data-informed decisions may have taken place at the state or federal level, it is often the case that this chain of command effectively

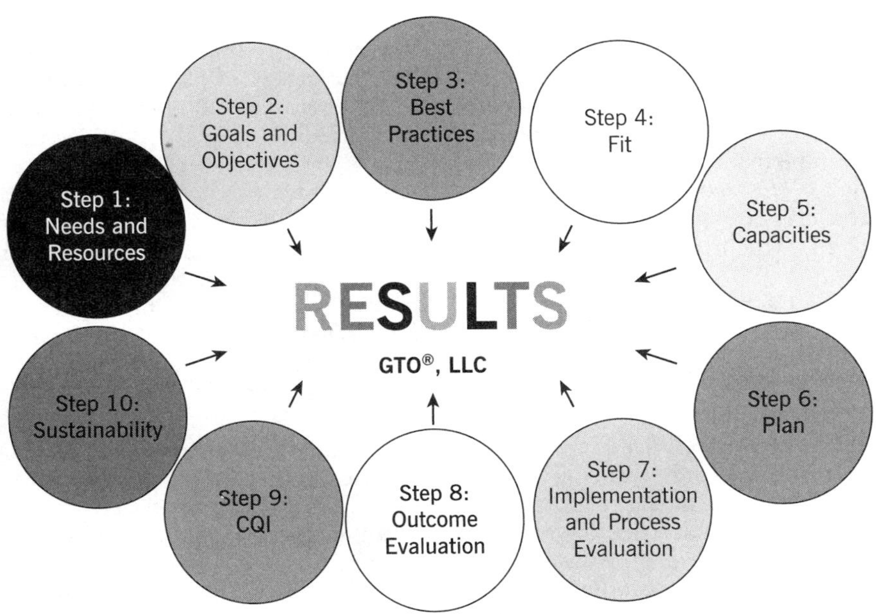

FIGURE 33.1. GTO as a painter's palette.

skips over a district or even school-specific needs assessment, determination of fit for the particular setting, and assessment of whether the school has the requisite capacity to implement the chosen program with fidelity to the program's model. In this situation, GTO may be effectively used by allowing schools to "jump" to Steps 6 through 10, choosing to focus on how they will plan for and monitor the implementation of the required program, what the setting-specific outcomes of the program will be, and how they can improve and sustain it in their own setting.

GTO Is Community and School Centered

The GTO approach addresses a limitation of the traditional research-to-practice model: that evidence-based programs are expected to generalize automatically across persons and settings of the target population (Wandersman et al., 2008). Often, there are substantial differences between program outcomes observed in a controlled research trial and outcomes observed when the same program is implemented in the "real world." The problem with the assumption of "generalizability" (that a program that worked under tight research circumstances should work anywhere) is that districts and schools differ from one another, and given competing priorities, diverse skills sets, and nuances of climate and culture in each setting, many schools are unable or unwilling to allocate the same level of resources and supervision to program implementation used during the efficacy trial. GTO recognizes that districts, schools, and classrooms are the real-world laboratory in which programs must be implemented.

Second, GTO acknowledges that no two schools or school districts are exactly the same. The GTO process advocates for individualized, yet accountable, solutions to adapting a program or practice to an individual district's or school's needs. Programs that are able to adapt the varying needs, resources, and attitudes of the school, while also maintaining adequate fidelity to program content and delivery features, are more likely to achieve outcomes (Osher, Dwyer, & Jackson, 2004). For example, some schools adopt the GTO process "in house", receiving brief training and technical assistance, whereas others may collaborate with outside evaluators or consultants to utilize the GTO system in their SEL initiative. GTO thinking helps school and district leaders and teams adopt evidence-based practices that suit their needs and fit within their broader school and district context, while simultaneously supporting schools and districts in using data to reach their desired outcomes.

GTO with SEL Programs

School systems in the 21st century bear the societal responsibility of fostering students' cognitive, social, emotional, and physical development. Because of schools' unique amount of access to youth over formative developmental years, they are often *the* delivery system for a wide range of services. An increasing body of research and practice indicates that academic outcomes improve when schools build student social and emotional competence, address their health needs, and build strong conditions for learning (Osher & Kendziora, 2010; Osher, Sprague, et al., 2008).

The Collaborative for Academic, Social, and Emotional Learning (CASEL) is leading some of the field's work in assessing SEL programs that simultaneously shape multiple student and teacher skills sets, spanning the full range of student academic, social, and emotional competencies (*www.casel.org*). CASEL (2012) has identified 18 programs for elementary school students that, when implemented well, are likely to address SEL needs in many schools. Positive outcomes include higher average student scores on standardized tests, better mental health outcomes, such as improved self-esteem and lower depression and anxiety, as well as increased engagement in school (Durlak, Weissberg, Dymnicki, Taylor, & Schellinger, 2011).

Below, we illustrate how GTO thinking can be applied to address SEL-specific needs. The questions inherent in the GTO accountability system overlap substantially with the CASEL (2012) theory of action, allowing the GTO process to be easily used as an additional resource by districts using or seeking to use CASEL resources (see Table 33.1).

GTO can be utilized at multiple levels of the school system (e.g., school districts, individual schools, individual classrooms/teachers, and individual students) to achieve SEL outcomes. In this chapter, we focus on applications at the district level. We show how one district selected, implemented, and utilized data to improve the implementation of evidence-based SEL programming as part of a comprehensive set of SEL and student support interventions aimed at building student and adult competencies, district capacity, and conditions for learning. We focus on one intervention, Providing Alternative Thinking Strategies (PATHS), which was Cleveland's first intentional effort at universal SEL, and which functioned as an anchor for other SEL programming. Cleveland implemented PATHS as part of a large holistic SEL program that eventually included preparation for the middle-grade curriculum Recognizing, Understanding, Labeling, Expressing, and Regulating (RULER) emotion effects (Rivers, Brackett, Reyes, Elbertson, & Salovey, 2012); implementation of SEL support in school "planning centers"; a safe haven for kids who need additional support; implementation of the Ripple Effects Whole Spectrum Intervention System (2009), an individualized SEL support tool; and implementation of school-based student support teams.

We chose Cleveland's PATHS program as an illustration because

1. One of us (D. O.) worked with the district's Chief Executive Officer (E. S. G.) in the planning and evaluation, and this firsthand experience provides important information about how each GTO step might work in your schools.
2. Cleveland faced the challenges of many urban, suburban, and rural districts, including funding changes, community buy-in, and the need to fit SEL programming into complex existing initiatives. The district collaborated with community stakeholders and external evaluators to develop creative and strategic plans for overcoming these challenges; we think this information will be valuable for other districts and schools grappling with similar issues.
3. It provides an example of how GTO steps can be used retrospectively. The GTO approach can be used *prospectively* to help a project or initiative be accountable and increase the probability of achieving results. Indeed, this was the original purpose of developing GTO. The use of the Cleveland example is a *retrospective* use of GTO for the purpose of illustrating what the GTO steps might look like in an SEL example. GTO was not formally applied either retrospectively nor prospectively in Cleveland. Nevertheless, application of the steps to the PATHS example will be useful to the reader to get a "real-life" example of how each GTO step could work for a complex SEL intervention.

Use of the GTO Accountability Process for Achieving SEL Outcomes in Schools

GTO Step 1: What are the underlying needs and conditions in your district (NEEDS AND RESOURCES)? Needs and resources assessments gather information about a district's most salient needs, as well as potential resources for addressing those needs. Comprehensive needs and resources assessments involve the identification of individual, school, and community strengths that may be able to address (or may already be addressing) identified needs. When framed as an assessment of existing resources and identified gaps in needed services, the needs assessment process itself can be seen as the first step to galvanizing community and school district support for an SEL program. An important part of the needs assessment process for school districts includes determining differences in school and student needs across the district; when it comes to choosing SEL programming, one size may not fit all.

Background of the Cleveland Example. Following a Fall 2007 school shooting that involved the death of the shooter, the Cleveland Metropolitan School District (the District) and the Mayor of Cleveland asked the American Institutes for Research (AIR) to conduct an analysis and make recommendations regarding what could be done in Cleveland's schools and by its mental health and other community agencies to improve the connectedness that students have to school, as well as their mental wellness and safety. The Chief Academic Officer (who led this District's work) and the Mayor wanted an actionable study that could drive change and assured AIR that the District would use the needs and resource assessment and evidenced-based recommendations to plan for and drive change. AIR conducted a study to look at systemic issues, and the strengths and needs as in different contexts. AIR provided 10 recommendations that could be implemented over a 5-year period (Osher, Poirer, et al., 2008). Cleveland subsequently asked AIR to help the district implement the recommendations and created a team, the Humanware Executive Team, which comprised student support staff members and teachers' union members, and reported to the Chief Academic Officer. AIR provided advice on principles of implementation and consultation to a number of stakeholders, including the Executive Team that oversaw planning and implementation of SEL programming, Community–School Task Forces, and the Chief Academic Officer.

GTO Step 1 is designed to ensure that the programs adopted by a district fit the needs of particular schools and are nonredundant with other existing programs. A first question, simply, is do our students need additional SEL programming *at all*? If district leadership—perhaps in collaboration with teachers, parents, and other community leaders—has determined that an SEL intervention is indeed warranted, a follow-up question involves a more detailed inquiry into what *specific* needs and resources exist. Described elsewhere in this handbook are specific strategies for assessing (1) students' skills sets related to the five domains of SEL and (2) teachers' pedagogical skills related specifically to SEL competencies. Ideally, a district will assess the needs and resources related to both students' and teachers' skills sets.

Cleveland Example. The Cleveland needs assessment recommended systemic classroom-based SEL instruction, a supportive school climate, coordinated mental health and health services, school–family–community partnerships, and after-school and community programming. AIR based these recommendations on a gap analysis and asset mapping that included a districtwide Conditions for Learning Survey (Osher & Kendziora, 2010). Survey data, case studies in randomly sampled schools, and focus groups conducted with randomly selected students, families, and teachers helped AIR identify (1) high levels of student need, (2) program allocation based on adult instead of student need, and (3) multiple interventions that were currently being implemented, often with insufficient monitoring, quality, and coordination. These included intervention-based assistance teams, a series of unaligned behavioral interventions, mental health services, and well-intended but uncoordinated and insufficiently evaluated community support programs.

Although a needs assessment specifically related to students' acquisition of SEL's five key skills might be most pertinent to a given school district's adoption of a SEL intervention, often program adoption does not follow this sequence. It is more likely that, just as in Cleveland, a number of ongoing innovations and related evaluations are taking place concurrently across a district, or that SEL programming itself might be one component of a larger intervention. Instead of being a problem, this allows needs assessments conducted for other purposes to be utilized in justifying whether an SEL intervention is needed. Given the underlying rationale that SEL competencies can improve academic achievement, even data demonstrating disparities in achievement indicators can be connected to the need for SEL intervention. In this instance, a district leadership team might ask: What data do we already have that point to the need for SEL programming in our schools?

GTO Step 2: What are the goals, target populations, and objectives (i.e., desired outcomes) (GOALS)? Step 2 builds on the information collected in the needs assessment in Step 1 and asks: What should change, for whom, and by when? This involves first *creating goals and objectives* (or desired outcomes) for each prioritized need identified in Step 1. Goals are broad statements of what the school would like to achieve in the long term. Objectives or desired outcomes are concrete statements about what will change as a result of the program. Clearly specified objectives indicate how the success of the program will be measured. The CASEL (2012) program guide provides an initial framework for charting what objectives/desired outcomes may be expected for your chosen program(s). Even if you do not choose a program from this list, your objectives and outcomes will likely have substantial overlap with the ones listed here.

In addition to identifying the changes that district leaders would like to see, this step involves clear specification of the *target population for services*. In a school, this may involve *all* students (e.g., universal prevention), specific schools within the district (e.g., feeder schools for a high school), specific grade levels within schools (e.g., all fifth-grade students), or specific types of students (e.g., special education or gifted students). Explicit attention to the population of interest *prior* to selecting an evidence-based practice (Step 3) is important for choosing an appropriate program.

Step 2 also involves clearly specifying the time line for expected change, and the ways in which change will be measured. Proactive explanation of the time line and measurement of change can be useful in selecting a program that fits your schools' or district's desired outcomes (e.g., selecting a program that would only reach desirable goals after multiple years of intervention would be insufficient for a school that needs immediate action). However, emerging evidence suggests how quickly SEL competencies may develop for different students in different programs, and some research suggests that some important changes can take place during a school year (CASEL, 2012).

Cleveland Example. Cleveland's needs were so great that the District chose to implement all 10 AIR recommendations. The recommendations were translated into four outcome areas: (1) Safe and Respectful Climate, (2) Challenge, (3) Student Support, and (4) SEL. Change in each of these areas was measured by teacher ratings of student social competence; attentiveness; aggression; measures of student attendance; behavior (reported as the average number of suspendable behavioral incidents per school), and removal from school (suspensions and expulsions). Tracking of these outcomes has been sustained in the district, and are now used for progress monitoring during the academic year, as well as for annual review and planning.

GTO Step 3: Which evidence-based models and best practices programs can be useful in reaching your district's goals and outcomes (BEST PRACTICES)? Once the need for SEL programming has been identified and prioritized by a district (Step1) and the target population, goals, and desired outcomes have been developed (Step 2), the next question in the GTO process is "What are the best practices for reaching each SEL-related objective?" If multiple objectives have been identified in Step 2, the question should be "What type of SEL program should be used for whom?" This step involves reviewing the empirical literature on effective evidence-based SEL programs and ensuring that the essential or core components of a proposed program are in place. The most thorough review of SEL programs is the *2013 CASEL Guide*. Another good source of program information is the What Works Clearinghouse (WWC) Intervention Reports organized under the Behavior Category, which includes many SEL programs (*http://ies.ed.gov/ncee/wwc*).

Cleveland Example. The district, led by the Humanware Executive Team, examined the data and the AIR analyse,s and decided that all schools could benefit from SEL programming, starting with elementary schools. Given financial resource limits and the long-term return on investment of intervening with students who would be in the district for many years, Cleveland decided to start in the elementary schools. The district planners also decided that due to student and faculty mobility, it made sense to adopt a single SEL program rather than have multiple programs in multiple schools, so that there would be a common SEL language and common protocols. The selection process was collaborative and focused on evidence. The Humanware Executive Team convened a task force of school and community stakeholders, including teachers, families, and agency leaders to develop selection criteria, identify a short list of programs for consideration, then make a selection. AIR provided criteria for selecting evidence-based practices (Chapter 6 of *Safe, Supportive, and Successful Schools Step by Step*; Osher et al., 2004) and Cleveland consulted with AIR and CASEL and utilized CASEL's earlier program review, *Safe and Sound: An Educational Leader's Guide to Evidence-Based SEL Programs*, (which has recently been updated by the *2013 CASEL Guide*), to develop a short list of programs to consider, including Second Step and PATHS.

GTO Step 4: What actions need to be taken so the selected program "fits" within your district (FIT)? In this GTO step, school districts are first expected to review the Step 3 program options in detail and select which program fits best within their school. It is likely that the review of evidence-based practices and practice-based evidence in Step 3 will result in a list of several viable SEL program options (as was the case in the Cleveland example). In Step 4, you determine which option is the *best fit* for your district or for particular schools (to select SEL programs, see CASEL, 2012). A common trap into which school districts fall is implementing programs because of their popularity or expected impact; yet systematically determining whether the program truly fits the setting is often overlooked and is essential. Just because a particular program has been effective elsewhere does not necessarily mean it will be equally successful in your setting.

Several resources exist for choosing a program that has the optimal fit with your setting. The *2013 CASEL Guide* describes a range of programs with slightly different features, and focuses on universal, teacher-taught programs. While all may focus on student SEL and skills that support academic achievement (i.e., the five core SEL competencies), the emphases may differ. Differences may be related to breadth or depth of learning, as well as the underlying pedagogies. Some may last a long time and be repeated annually as students progress through grade levels, while others may only be implemented for a year. SEL programs may also differ in how they integrate into the school: Some may be stand–alone programs, whereas others may be blended into broad curricula and implemented by classroom teachers.

Evidence-based programs may match the goals and characteristics of your setting extremely well but need some modifications of unessential elements to fit optimally. Making strategic adaptations to chosen programs wisely is an important part of Step 4 because some changes might dilute program effects and/or make the program harder to implement. For example, a chosen program may be intended to be taught 1 hour at a time over the course of 10 weeks, but given scheduling needs at your school, it would be preferable to teach the course for 30 minutes at a time over 20 weeks. There is much written on program adaptation (see Durlak & DuPre, 2008; Osher et al., 2004). We make two key recommendations here. First, districts should collaborate with program developers to ensure that program modifications do not exclude or dilute essential program components. Second, these adaptations should be monitored and documented regularly to ensure that the adaptation does not limit program effects.

The final component of GTO Step 4 stresses the importance of fit between the program mission and the broader values of the school context. The aim is to select a program that is both evidence based and culturally competent, both in terms of the cultures of the members of the school community and the culture of the school and district. Despite empirical evidence generated by researchers in highly controlled interventions, a given program may have reduced effects when implemented in different contexts. This may be partially related to a mismatch between the values and beliefs of the school (as well as the community within which the school is located) and the core components of the program. The salience of taking cultural context into consideration when selecting a program should not be underestimated. Assessing the fit increases buy-in to the program by ensuring that the program is aligned with the broader mission and values of the school.

Cleveland Example. To increase the likelihood that Cleveland's choice of an SEL program would fit within the district's context, the Humanware Executive Team factored in its own goals (e.g., impacts on academics, teacher support, and program success in a district like Cleveland) and conducted its own investigation. This investigation included identifying and speaking with personnel in other districts where the programs had been implemented successfully and interviewing practitioners in those communities. Once the list of possible

SEL programs to implement was reduced from six to two, the team invited the developers in for presentations, then selected PATHS based on its having been implemented successfully in similar contexts, its demonstrated impact on academics, their provision of external training (see Step 5, below), and the fact that it could be delivered as part on an integrated literacy instructional program (*www.channing-bete.com/paths*).

GTO Step 5: What organizational capacities are needed to implement the intervention (CAPACITY)? The focus of this step is the match between the capacities of your school to implement the requirements of a given program sufficiently. *Organizational capacity* refers to different types of resources an organization has to implement and sustain programs (see Wanless, Groark & Hatfield, Chapter 24, this volume). A mismatch between required program capacities and available school capacities could have a negative impact on program effects (Wandersman et al., 2000). Programs should be selected that match the existing capacities of the school or capacities that the school could realistically build prior to implementation. Districts and school personnel should also think about how to close the gap between needed capacities and existing ones. Organizational capacities are often categorized into five types: human, technical, fiscal, temporal, and physical.

1. *Human capacity.* Human capacity includes program staff (administrators and teachers) training, credentials, and experience. Building this type of capacity involves professional development and acquisition of the skills necessary to teach SEL effectively to a wide range of students. SEL programs that are more scripted (e.g., "manualized" and come with specific scope, sequence, instructions, and tools) may be an appropriate choice when teachers lack certain skills related to SEL interventions. On the other hand, if a set of teachers in a specific school or district have a high level of requisite skills for implementation, a less scripted program may be a better fit, allowing teachers to adapt materials more creatively to fit their students' needs and skills.

Cleveland Example. Cleveland personnel realized that neither their teachers, their principals, nor their supervisors had been trained in SEL, and they therefore lacked the necessary capacity to implement SEL programming on their own. They took this into account when selecting PATHS because its developer provided the level of external training and support that the Executive Team felt was necessary to support successful implementation. During its planning process and in consultation with the developer of PATHS, Cleveland personnel decided to also hire six PATHS coaches in order to increase teachers' capacity specifically to implement SEL programming.

2. *Technical capacity. Technical capacity* refers to the expertise needed to address all the aspects of program planning, implementation, and evaluation. At a school district level, capacity might include the knowledge and skills set of various implementation leaders and advocates to plan, implement, and evaluate an ongoing SEL program. Indeed, the ability to ask and to answer the 10 GTO questions themselves can be considered a form of technical capacity related to SEL initiatives.

Cleveland Example. Cleveland addressed issues of technical capacity by consulting with external organizations (AIR and CASEL) that provided coaching and support to the team responsible for overseeing the implementation of PATHS, as well as the other recommendations of the 2008 AIR Audit. This coaching helped senior leadership members who were directly responsible for ensuring the effective implementation of all components of the initiative: systemic, classroom-based SEL instruction and positive conditions for learning, coordinated mental health and health services, school–family–community partnerships, and links with effective after-school and community programming. However, the District later realized that it had failed to sufficiently train and support other key leaders, including the principals' supervisors and more senior leadership. This reinforced some separation of programming that existed in the District and caused the implementation of PATHS and related SEL programming to be considered a discrete program rather than a districtwide strategy. The District has subsequently broadened its training and support by accessing the support of AIR, CASEL, and the member districts of the Collaborating Districts Initiative.

3. *Fiscal capacity. Fiscal capacity* reflects the need to secure adequate funding to implement the program as planned, including securing appropriate staffing and materials to conduct programming effectively. Programs that are integrated into ongoing curricula may be more easily accommodated, while those requiring additional equipment, workbooks, and other print and/or electronic materials and specialized staff require more fiscal capacity.

Cleveland Example. Although the Executive Team had committed to hiring six PATHS coaches in order to ensure teachers' capacity to provide the PATHS curriculum, a sizable district budget deficit and unanticipated loss of grant income forced a midcourse change. Hiring of the coaches was delayed during the first year of implementation, and no coaches were hired the second year. This affected the breadth of teacher commitment and the breadth and quality of implementation (Kendziora & Osher, 2009). The Cleveland Teachers Union and the external consultants from AIR, PATHS, and CASEL worked together to develop a more cost-efficient approach to monitoring implementation and providing teacher support that did not depend on external coaches.

4. *Temporal capacity. Temporal capacity* involves providing enough time for an intervention to be implemented effectively. A common complaint from teachers is that they cannot possibly squeeze one more thing into their school day. Determining how the delivery of SEL programming can be integrated into the current school day and how adequate professional development and training to teachers will be provided is an important, yet often overlooked, aspect of program planning and implementation.

Cleveland Example. The 2008 AIR Audit recommendations were ambitious in terms of time and resources. Hence, implementation was phased in over 5 years, with infrastructure-building and evidenced-based SEL programs being identified in Year 1, implemented in Year 2, with SEL standards developed in Years 3–4. This timing was developed to moderate the burden of implementing too many things at once, as well as to build on the development of District capacity and commitment as the District trained staff, learned from experience, and used data to identify strengths, challenges, and continued needs.

5. *Physical capacity. Physical capacity* refers to the actual physical space needed for implementation. In overcrowded schools, the ability to set aside classroom or other gathering spaces necessary for SEL programming may prove challenging. However, integrating SEL work into the existing curriculum and therefore into the existing schedule and physical spaces can ameliorate this challenge.

Cleveland Example. In Cleveland, no extra space was required for the PATHS program per se. However, PATHS was an anchoring program for a broad set of school climate and culture interventions. A closely related program was the shift away from traditional inschool suspension rooms to the Planning Centers, which did require additional classroom space. The Planning Centers, which employed SEL strategies, were to be safe harbors instead of punitive inschool suspension settings for students. The Planning Centers allowed students to cool down, stop and think about alternative ways of handling problems, receive support from staff, utilize a computer based SEL program (Ripple Effects), and do their schoolwork.

GTO Step 6: What is the plan for implementing the selected program (PLAN)? The focus of Step 6 is on creating an implementation plan. Creating a specific and realistic plan for implementation increases the chances that the program will be implemented as intended and desired outcomes achieved. Quality plans involve creating a time line of anticipated program implementation tasks and activities. This increases the probability that program rollout proceeds in a sequenced and timely manner. A plan may have some additional helpful components, such as the following:

- What activities should be completed for successful program implementation?
- In what order should these activities be completed?

- Who is responsible for ensuring that each task is completed?
- When should each task be completed?
- How will we determine that the tasks are being completed with quality?

Cleveland Example. One of the key features of the Cleveland plan for the PATHS implementation (as well as implementation of the SEL Standards and the Planning Centers) was a detailed work plan that included provision of teacher time for training. The Humanware Executive Team met monthly to review progress on the work plan and used this data for continuous quality improvement. As the Executive Team reviewed the work plan, it quickly became evident that the plan failed to outline implementation plans and time lines in sufficient detail. Therefore, the Executive Team conducted a full-day workshop with the PATHS developers and technical assistance consultants to develop a second, more detailed implementation plan early in the first implementation year. This new, more detailed time line would enable the Executive Team to track early implementation efforts closely and provide personalized supports to schools in a more timely manner.

GTO Step 7: How will the quality of program implementation be monitored and assessed (IMPLEMENTATION AND PROCESS EVALUATION)? Step 7 is about implementation of the plan and process evaluation. It aims to ensure *quality* implementation (Meyers, Durlak, & Wandersman, 2012; Meyers, Katz, et al., 2012) of your chosen SEL program through careful monitoring of the plan that was developed in Step 6. Monitoring helps to ensure that programs are being implemented as planned and also identifies any areas in which mid-course corrections may be needed. Many evidence-based SEL programs that a school or district might wish to use also provide tools for monitoring teacher performance (CASEL, 2013). Even if you choose a different program, a review of these tools is an excellent starting place for determining how you will monitor SEL because the best ones encompass the questions posed earlier. *Ongoing monitoring* of implementation provides "real-time" feedback on progress toward goals and promotes quality of services, which in turn increases the probability of better outcomes and eventual impact for students.

Cleveland Example. Cleveland's Humanware Executive Team discovered that it is important to develop a plan that not only operationalizes all details but also monitors its execution. This monitoring includes monthly reviews of implementation data, and eliciting and acting on feedback from the PATHS consultants, teacher union representatives, and school principals. Monitoring has included both outputs (e.g., the number of teachers trained in PATHS) and measures (e.g., walkthrough observations of PATHS implementation). Here again, Cleveland's monitoring strategy took shape and improved over time as initial monitoring measures insufficiently or inaccurately captured implementation progress and additional and replacement measures were identified.

GTO Step 8: How well did the program work (OUTCOMES)? Step 8 addresses outcome evaluation and is the focus of traditional summative evaluation approaches. It answers the fundamental outcome evaluation question, "Did we reach our desired outcomes?" As previously noted, planning for the outcome evaluation in Step 8 of GTO starts early in the process (Step 2), when desired outcomes for programs are identified. The progression through the previous GTO steps is the core of the GTO logic: By effectively taking into consideration Steps 1–7, schools increase the likelihood of reaching desired outcomes and literally *getting to the outcomes* the District or school seeks. If the desired outcomes have been strategically written in Step 2 (what should change, by how much, for whom, and by when), then Step 8 is a relatively straightforward process of utilizing data to determine how much the target population changed during a specified time period. The *2013 CASEL Guide* provides some key outcomes associated with best-practice SEL programming (positive social behavior, fewer conduct problems, less emotional distress, and more academic success) that would likely fit the goals of your district established in Step 2.

Measuring change on each student domain, as well as additional domains that your district may choose to measure, will be best served by collecting data from multiple sources. School records are a good place to start because they provide data primarily on conduct problems and academic success. Student, teacher, and parent survey reports may be good ways to collect data on positive social behaviors and emotional distress. Many evidence-based SEL programs also provide tools for measuring student behavior (CASEL, 2012). A review of these tools as a starting place for completing Step 8 is recommended.

Cleveland Example. The PATHS program utilized in Cleveland has been evaluated in randomized controlled trials in grades PreK–5, and students have been followed for up to 3 years. Key outcomes have included improved academic performance, increased positive social behavior, and reduced conduct problems and emotional distress. The AIR evaluation found significant improvements for social competence and attention. However, PATHS did not have the impact on aggression that would otherwise have been anticipated by the empirical evidence of the PATHS program effects (Faria, Kendziora, Brown, & Osher, 2012; Osher, Poirer, Jarjoura, & Brown, 2013).

GTO Step 9: How will continuous quality improvement (CQI) strategies be incorporated? Step 9 links program evaluation to program improvement by ensuring that users assess available data received throughout the previous steps to plan and then implement program modifications. Often, schools and districts receive data about the previous school year's activities and outcomes during the summer months. This is an excellent time to review findings and engage in strategic CQI (Step 9). For example, a District at the end of the first year of an SEL intervention has received and carefully reviewed process data (Step 7) and outcome data (Step 8), and can utilize that data to make modifications by retracing steps Steps 1 through 6.

Cleveland Example. As evidenced in many of the earlier examples, the CQI process has been applied in Cleveland for 5 years. It has enabled the District to make many midcourse corrections, such as revising and clarifying the District's SEL goals and outcomes, redesigning the PATHS implementation when financial challenges emerged, reshaping technical support to provide increased coaching and capacity building for senior leaders, broadening SEL training to all senior leaders to better ensure institutional buy-in, and creating PATHS training videos and developing "train the trainers" to replace ongoing consultancy training.

In addition to using the CQI process of Step 9 to assess success of SEL program implementation, the logic inherent in this step can also be used to interpret outcomes. In the Cleveland example, the Humanware Executive Team and its school-based collaborators anticipated that student aggression would reduce as a result of PATHS implementation. However, the outcome evaluation did not show this change. This finding provides an opportunity to reapply GTO thinking. That is, it is appropriate to "back up" through the previous GTO questions and ask whether the failure to demonstrate expected decreases in student aggression could be answered by one of the preceding GTO steps.

1. *Step 1: Needs and Resources.* Was a specific need to reduce student aggression identified? Was enough specificity about the type of aggression (physical, emotional) or location of aggression (e.g., middle school boys) gathered?
2. *Step 2: Goals and Objectives.* What were the specific goals stated by the Humanware Executive Team related to student aggression? How much was student aggression targeted to change? Among which students? By when? Could the changes anticipated in the goals and objectives step have been overly ambitious?
3. *Step 3: Best Practices.* The Humanware Executive Team chose the PATHS curriculum for a number of good reasons (see Step 3), and indeed PATHS achieved most of the identified goals (see Step 8). Was student aggression a core component of PATHS? Is it possible that another SEL program with demonstrated effectiveness on student aggression could have been incorporated into the universal SEL programming?
4. *Step 4: Fit.* Was there already a program going on that could have caused a misfit with the PATHs components that were specifically targeted toward student aggression?

5. *Step 5: Capacities.* Changes in funding may have compromised teacher preparation and support for programming. Could this change in capacity help explain this outcome?
6. *Step 6: Plan.* When a more detailed plan for implementing PATHS was developed with the Executive Team, was the plan for implementing the core components of student aggression sufficiently addressed?
7. *Step 7: Implementation and Process Evaluation.* Were the components of PATHS that focus on student aggression implemented with quality? Were the process measures that monitored this implementation sufficient for measuring quality?

GTO Step 10: If the program is successful, how will it be sustained (SUSTAIN)? The final step of GTO relates to program sustainability. Sustainability is often equated with acquiring ongoing, consistent funding for programs, yet there are multiple elements that contribute to sustained program effectiveness over time. Sustainability is ultimately about the ability of a district to embed SEL programs into its ongoing, routine delivery of services so that it is not contingent on fluctuating allocation of resources. Sometimes referred to as *routinization* or *institutionalization*, this way of thinking about sustainability centers around the idea that new and demonstrably effective programs should become so integrated into the district or school that that delivery components of the program become "business as usual."

Cleveland Example. Sustainability of PATHS and all SEL programming in Cleveland has several key components. First, it has won District support for funding because it demonstrated effectiveness; that is, PATHS improved the conditions for learning for students in Cleveland just as it had proven to do so in previous effectiveness trials. Second, the District has implemented PATHS as part of a larger, more holistic SEL program; Cleveland has a districtwide SEL programming investment of which PATHS is an essential part. Third, PATHS and other SEL programs have been embedded into the District's Family and Community Engagement activities, so that parents, families, and community partners are increasingly using the same SEL strategies that the District uses and therefore rely on the continued District support of the strategy. Fourth, and finally, the District has included SEL in its strategic plan and district-level strategy measures. As a result of carefully using a process similar to GTO, Cleveland has successfully attracted the attention of national technical assistance networks (CASEL, Collaborating District Initiative, AIR, etc.) and both local and national funding networks (Cleveland Foundation, George Gund Foundation, Mt. Sinai Healthcare Foundation, the Abington Foundation, and the NoVo Foundation), which collectively assist the District both in sustaining and improving their SEL investments.

Summary

SEL is important for improving both school and community outcomes. Doing so requires more than identifying an evidenced based SEL program (or programs); it requires selecting the right evidence-based program(s) and implementing the program(s) in the right way(s). This involves finding programs and strategies that address local needs, align with the culture and capacity of the school and its staff, and have been demonstrated to achieve outcomes with similar students, staff, and schools in similar contexts. Moreover, once the right program is chosen, plans must be developed, implemented, and monitored to ensure that staff embrace and are able to implement the new program. This effective rollout depends on providing staff with the training and support to implement the new technologies, monitoring implementation and evaluating results, and using monitoring and evaluation data for continuous quality improvement. In this chapter, we have introduced the GTO approach, which is designed to address each of these needs.

A GTO approach to SEL implementation addresses the challenges that school systems face in an era of diminishing resources and increasing need to demonstrate accountability. While we have provided a SEL-specific example of how a district in Cleveland used GTO thinking in implementing the PATHS program, the GTO framework can be broadly applied to other areas (e.g., STEM, Common Core) across multiple settings. The GTO system demystifies accountability by laying out steps that are strategic and sequential, allowing districts to systematically document the need for programming, the quality with which programs are implemented, and their ultimate impact on students.

Note

1. Getting To Outcomes and GTO are registered trademarks of the University of South Carolina and the RAND Corporation.

References

Chinman, M. Hunter, S. B., Ebener, P., Paddock, S. M. Stillman, L., Imm, P., et al. (2008). The Getting To Outcomes demonstration and evaluation: An illustration of the prevention support system. *American Journal of Community Psychology, 41*, 206–224.

Chinman, M., Tremain, B., Imm, P., & Wandersman, A. (2010). Strengthening prevention performance using technology: An evaluation of interactive Getting To Outcomes®. *American Journal of Orthopsychiatry, 7*(4), 469–481.

Collaborative for Academic, Social, and Emotional Learning (CASEL). (2012). *2013 CASEL guide: Effective social and emotional learning programs—Preschool and elementary school edition*. Chicago: Author.

Durlak, J. A., & DuPre, E. P. (2008). Implementation matters: A review of research on the influence of implementation on program outcomes and the factors affecting implementation. *American Journal of Community Psychology, 41*, 327–350.

Durlak, J. A., Weissberg, R. P., Dymnicki, A. B., Taylor, R. D., & Schellinger, K. B. (2011). The impact of enhancing students' social and emotional learning: A meta-analysis of school-based universal interventions. *Child Development, 82*(1), 405–432.

Faria, A. M., Kendziora, K., Brown, L., & Osher, D. (2012). *PATHS implementation and outcome study in the Cleveland Metropolitan School District: Final report*. Washington, DC: American Institutes for Research.

Fisher, D., Imm, P., Chinman, M., & Wandersman, A. (2006). *Getting To Outcomes with developmental assets: Ten steps to measuring success in youth programs and communities*. Minneapolis, MN: Search Institute.

Imm, P., Chinman, M., & Wandersman, A. (2006). *Preventing underage drinking: Using the Strategic Prevention Framework and the Getting To Outcome model to achieve results*. Rockville, MD: Center for Substance Abuse Prevention.

Kendziora, K., & Osher, D. (2009). *Starting to turn schools around: The academic outcomes of the Safe Schools, Successful Students initiative*. Washington, DC: American Institutes for Research.

Lesesne, C. A., Lewis, K. M., White, C. W., Green, D., Duffy, J. L., & Wandersman, A. (2008). Promoting science-based approaches to teen pregnancy prevention: Proactively engaging the three systems of the Interactive Systems Framework. *American Journal of Community Psychology, 41*, 379–392.

Meyers, D. C., Durlak, J., & Wandersman, A. (2012). The quality implementation framework: A synthesis of critical steps in the implementation process. *American Journal of Community Psychology, 50*(3), 462–480.

Meyers, D. C., Katz, J., Chien, V., Wandersman, A., Scaccia, J. P., & Wright, A. (2012). Practical implementation science: Developing and piloting the quality implementation tool. *American Journal of Community Psychology, 50*(3), 481–496.

Osher, D., Dwyer, K., & Jackson, S. (2004). *Safe, supportive, and successful schools step by step*. Longmont, CO: Sopris West.

Osher, D., & Kendziora, K. (2010). Building conditions for learning and healthy adolescent development: Strategic approaches. In B. Doll, W. Pfohl, & J. Yoon (Eds.), *Handbook of youth prevention science* (pp. 121–140). New York: Routledge.

Osher, D., Poirier, J. A., Dwyer, K. P., Hicks, R., Brown, L. J., Lampron, S., et al. (2008). *Cleveland Metropolitan School District Humanware Audit: Findings and recommendations*. Washington, DC: American Institutes for Research.

Osher, D., Poirier, J., Jarjoura, R., & Brown, R. (2013). Avoid quick fixes: Lessons learned from a comprehensive districtwide approach to improve conditions for learning. In D. Losen (Ed.), *Closing the school discipline gap: Research to practice* (pp. 192–206). New York: Teachers College Press.

Osher, D., Sprague, J., Weissberg, R. P., Axelrod, J., Keenan, S., Kendziora, K., et al. (2008). A comprehensive approach to promoting social, emotional, and academic growth in contemporary schools. In A. Thomas & J. Grimes (Eds.), *Best practices in school psychology* (Vol. 4, pp. 1263–1278). Bethesda, MD: National Association of School Psychologists.

Ripple Effects Whole Spectrum Intervention System. (2009). *Software to positively change behav-*

ior. San Francisco: Author. Retrieved November 20, 2013, from *www.rippleeffects.com.*

Rivers, S. E., Brackett, M. A., Reyes, M. R., Elbertson, N. A., & Salovey, P. (2012). Improving the social and emotional climate of classrooms with emotional literacy skill building: A clustered randomized control trial of the RULER Approach. *Prevention Science, 14*(1), 77–87.

Wandersman, A., Duffy, J., Flaspohler, P., Noonan, R., Lubell, K., Stillman, L., et al. (2008). Bridging the gap between prevention research and practice: The Interactive Systems framework for dissemination and implementation. *American Journal of Community Psychology, 41*(3–4), 171–181.

Wandersman, A., & Hamm, D. (2014). Data-driven decision making and evidence based programs in schools: Expanding the vision, improving the practice. In M. Weist, N. Lever, C. Bradshaw, & J. Owens (Eds.), *Handbook of school mental health* (2nd ed., pp. 327–350). New York: Springer.

Wandersman, A., Imm, P., Chinman, M., & Kaftarian, S. (2000). Getting To Outcomes: A results-based approach to accountability. *Evaluation and Program Planning, 23*, 389–395.

CHAPTER 34

Current and Potential Uses of Technology to Enhance SEL

What's Now and What's Next?

Robin S. Stern, Tucker B. Harding, Allison A. Holzer, and Nicole A. Elbertson

By some estimates, more than 200 classroom-based social and emotional learning (SEL) programs are used in U.S. schools (Collaborative for Academic, Social, and Emotional Learning [CASEL], 2003). SEL encompasses a broad array of emotion skills, cognitions, and behaviors, organized as the five core competencies: self-awareness, social awareness, self-management, relationship skills, and responsible decision making (Zins & Elias, 2006). The growing field of SEL demonstrates that students can acquire these competencies through structured interventions, and that learning these competencies enhances their relationships, academics, and effectiveness at home, at school, and in life (Durlak, Weissberg, Dymnicki, Taylor, & Schellinger, 2011). In fact, students participating in SEL programs have shown increases in prosocial behavior, reductions in behavior problems, and improvements in academic performance (Durlak et al., 2011). Our intention in this chapter is to look at how SEL has incorporated and might envision incorporating various technologies to teach or enhance these five competencies. Research on outcomes of technology-enhanced SEL programming to date is sparse, yet the proliferation of new technologies invites us to explore potential ways they might support and enhance SEL competencies and educational programming. We start broadly by describing the state of research about technology in general education, and from there situate SEL into the larger educational landscape, looking at both research and practical application. We conclude by discussing the potential problems and pitfalls, as well as proposing recommendations for the research and application of technology in SEL. Our presentation of technology research and applications is not intended to be exhaustive; rather, we chose to highlight a representative sample of technologies with current use or future potential in SEL.

With gratitude and deep respect for Dr. Frank Moretti's contribution to elevating the conversation about digital technology and education, we dedicate this chapter to him. Sadly, Frank passed before he could see this chapter in print.

The Current State of Technology in Education

Researchers in the field of education have for decades been exploring and studying the use of various technologies for instructional purposes. A growing body of research has shown positive outcomes from using educational technology across a variety of subject areas in K–12 education. For example, a large-scale, second-order meta-analysis of 25 meta-analyses encompassing over 1,000 studies and 40 years of research on technology and classroom learning found that the use of technology in classrooms shows a moderately positive effect on student learning, as compared to technology-free traditional instruction (Tamim, Bernard, Borokhovski, Abrami, & Schmid, 2011). Another meta-analytic study by the U.S. Department of Education (USDE), Office of Educational Technology (2012) found evidence that hybrid models of instruction—those that combine online learning with traditional, face-to-face instruction—produce better test scores and grades than either wholly online or wholly face-to-face instruction alone, across courses and subjects. The types of technologies studied were diverse and included student-centered learning, learning through computer simulation, project-based learning with technology, video games, and collaborative learning.

A problem with many of the studies listed, however, is that although research has led to what are perceived to be positive results across pedagogical approaches and supportive technologies, most studies fall short of describing the specific aspects of various technologies, as well as the specific variables within their contexts of use, that seem to produce certain outcomes. We mention this problem of vagueness with technology research in education because it applies across educational domains. This poses a challenge to a nuanced understanding of how certain technologies might improve educational programming, within which SEL is of primary interest.

Though the level of detail we wish to have about specific technologies and their contribution to education is lacking, the increasing number of studies showing positive outcomes of incorporating technology into teaching should not be overlooked. The USDE has published a national education technology plan for better incorporation of educational technology into teaching and learning in public education (Office of Educational Technology, USDE, 2010). The plan calls for using prevalent technologies to enhance public education by improving student learning, scaling best practices, and using data for continuous improvement. The plan outlines a vision "to leverage the learning sciences and modern technology to create engaging, relevant, and personalized learning experiences for all learners that mirror students' daily lives and the reality of their futures" (Executive Summary; Office of Educational Technology, 2010, p. x). The plan also calls for "connected teaching" (p. xii), in which educators connect to "resources and expertise that improve their own instructional practices and guide them in becoming facilitators and collaborators in their students' increasingly self-directed learning" (p. 40). Educational institutions are incorporating technology into professional development via online courses, webinars, podcasts, and other technology with some promising findings in terms of increasing teacher media literacy and instructional efficacy (Barr & Bardige, 2012; King, 2002; Reich, Romer, & Barr, 2014). Given the push into educational technology being described by the USDE and the start of research on best practices of its use, our hope is that research will begin to shift toward more empirical testing that can help illuminate the features of specific technologies that improve learning. Furthermore, of central concern to this chapter, we look forward to more in-depth research into aspects of technology that can enhance the particular competencies of SEL. Yet, as we look at how the SEL field is beginning to incorporate a variety of technologies into programs, it is important to bear in mind that the evidence base supporting specific technologies in this effort is limited but promising, and requires more rigorously designed studies. Few studies investigating the specific aspects of technologies used in SEL have been done, and almost none have been carefully replicated to increase confidence in early findings.

A Brief History of Technology in Relation to Social and Emotional Variables

We are educating our children in a time when people are more connected to information and to each other than ever before. Eighty percent of teenagers in the United States use social networking sites; 93% of them have Facebook accounts; furthermore, U.S. students spend as much time using digital media as they do in the classroom (Rideout, Foehr, & Roberts, 2010). Important to remember is that Facebook, YouTube, Friendster, MySpace, and Twitter all originated between 2002 and 2009. At the same time, Daniel Goleman's book *Emotional Intelligence* (1995) was only a few years old, and the field that we now call SEL was just emerging. So, of course, the creators of these early social technologies were educated before SEL was as widespread as it is across schools today. By 2010, nearly half of U.S. Internet users had online social profiles; hundreds of millions accessed Facebook on their cell phones; and television viewing reached an all-time high (Arbitron, Inc. & Edison Research, 2010; Media Literacy Clearinghouse, 2010). These statistics about increased use of social technology have been accompanied by questions about whether being more connected through technology has possibly led to people being less connected to each other in other ways (Putnam, 2000; Putnam & Feldstein, 2004).

During the same time frame in history (1990–2000), the field of SEL developed alongside rapid growth of technology with leaders and educators in both SEL and technology discussing overlaps in concepts and applications. One of the first psychologists to write about the convergence of emotion and technology was Sherry Turkle, in her 1995 book *Life on the Screen: Identity in the Age of the Internet.* Turkle expounded on how people were developing new identities online. Her patients' struggles and triumphs made problematic the idea of self-awareness in the online world, and its impact on mental health and healing. That same year, scientists saw the nascency of emotional intelligence theory and research (Mayer & Salovey, 1997; Salovey & Mayer, 1990), and the popularization of the concept of emotional intelligence around the globe (Goleman, 1995). The field of SEL and its educational programs surfaced soon after (Weissberg, Gullotta, Hampton, Ryan, & Adams, 1997). In 2000, Rosalind Picard published her book, *Affective Computing*, basing its title on the term she had coined, to highlight the importance of emotion in human–computer interactions, to influence the design of such interfaces, and to create a vision for research on technology to sense, communicate, model, teach, and respond to human emotion. Higher education launched its interest in the intersection of technology and SEL competencies in the 90s. In 1996, Teachers College, Columbia University offered the first course on SEL competencies and digital technology. Just a year later, Teachers College held the first conference on the topic, and now, nearly two decades later, the conversation continues among educators, educational technologists, course designers, researchers, and psychologists around the world. In fact, in the late 1990s, one of the first technology platforms that specifically targeted SEL skills development for school communities, Project ExSEL, was launched. This interactive website, with a wide array of resources and games for students and teachers, was created in conjunction with a program bringing SEL into District 2 in New York City through the agency of school counselors. There are now a number of conferences, interdisciplinary research communities, and even departments at universities dedicated to understanding the relationships among technological innovation, social interactions, and emotion.

In response to the merging interplay of technology and SEL, some experts expressed skepticism about the potential for the Internet and social media to impact social and emotional development and well-being positively (Postman, 1993; Tiles, 1995). The perspective was that increasingly portable, omnipresent, and powerful communications technology was a large source of distraction and alienation. Now, 20 years later, some wonder whether social media have been stunting the emotional development of children (Gentile et al., 2004; Landhuis, Poulton, Welch, & Hancox, 2007; Zimmerman, Christakis, & Meltzoff, 2007). As Myers and Sadaghiani (2010) described in the introduction to their National Institutes of Health (NIH) study of millennialists in the workplace, popular media describe technologically savvy millennialists as being self-centered, lacking motivation, and acting in ways that are more disrespectful of or disloyal to supervisors and organizations than their generational counterparts. Millennialists are frequently categorized as digital natives, leaving some to wonder whether this has made them less attentive and more disconnected in face-to-face interactions. Nevertheless, attributing a causal relationship to technological progress and large-scale change in human social behavior is extraordinarily complicated, requiring great caution.

Counterbalancing the critical views of technology is a focus on the potential for positive impact on human development, and, specifically, SEL (Jones & Issroff, 2005). Thus, it seems the optimists' goals in a world of inevitable technological growth are to find solutions to the social and emotional problems that new technologies may create, to employ them to help solve existing social and emotional challenges, and to generate novel uses of them to enhance our social and emotional worlds in innovative ways. In these ways, technological advancement can be constructive instead of destructive, and its benefits can outweigh its detriments.

Leveraging Technology to Enhance SEL

Consistent with the USDE plan for educational technology integration that we mentioned earlier, it becomes incumbent on SEL leaders to identify how to leverage existing technologies, so many of which are social in nature, to enhance students' self-awareness, social awareness, self-management, relationship skills, and responsible decision making. In the pages that follow we discuss how some SEL programs have taken up this challenge. Many SEL organizations currently use technology to support program delivery, supplement professional development, and cultivate community, yet there is great potential to leverage technology further to enhance the five SEL core competencies. In this section we explore how the marriage between SEL and technology is currently unfolding and what it might look like in the future. In our efforts to understand the current landscape, we interviewed leadership personnel at the Committee for Children (Second Step), the Developmental Studies Center, Educators for Social Responsibility, Facing History and Ourselves, Open Circle, Responsive Classroom, Ripple Effects, and the Yale Center for Emotional Intelligence (RULER [Recognizing, Understanding, Labeling, Expressing, and Regulating Emotions]). Our primary objective in these interviews was to learn how leading organizations currently use (and envision using in the future) technology specifically to enhance SEL. What follows is a summary of our discoveries, outlined in Table 34.1 (Established, Emerging, and Future Technology to Enhance SEL). Our terms "established", "emerging", and "future" refer to the application of these technologies *within the field of SEL* specifically. During our interviews, we operationalized the term "established" to describe technologies mentioned by several (more than four) of the organizations. Technologies mentioned by only a few, or even just one, of the organizations were defined as "emerging." Finally, we compiled a list of "future" technologies that currently exist but do not have current applications, to our knowledge, within the field of SEL. In categorizing various types of technologies in this way, we hope to provide SEL organizations and program developers with a vision for how various technologies might be employed in the field of SEL in the years to come.

Established Technology to Enhance SEL

SEL organizations, knowing that teacher training/support, schoolwide coordination, integration with subject matter, and effective instructional strategies are key aspects to the successful implementation of SEL, approach teachers as agents of change (Elias, Zins, & Weissberg, 1997; Kress & Elias, 2006; Payton et al., 2000). In fact, in order for SEL programs to be identified as CASEL SELect, the program must offer "high-quality training and other implementation supports, including initial training and ongoing support to ensure sound implementation" (CASEL, 2012, p. 4). Therefore, it makes sense that many SEL organizations use teacher training as a point of entry to reach their goal of ultimately impacting students. Existing technologies, such as webinars, podcasts, online libraries, and discussion boards, support online training and resources for SEL programming by providing teachers with worldwide access to content, lesson plans, research, and skills-building strategies.

Several SEL programs, such as Second Step, RULER, Responsive Classroom, and

TABLE 34.1. Established, Emerging, and Future Technology to Enhance SEL

Established: Technology being used by > 4 interviewed organizations	Emerging: Technology being used by < 4 interviewed organizations	Future: Technology envisioned as future projects or directions
• Online supplementary trainings: o Webinars o Podcasts o Video conferencing (e.g., Skype, Hangout) • Online supplementary support materials: o Online libraries (i.e., PDF downloads, lesson plans) o Software support (DVD sets) o Online discussion forums o Blogs/microblogs o Social media	• Online professional development: o Certification/badging o Onsite/online hybrid o Synchronous–asynchronous • Online learning communities for teachers: o Mobile learning management systems or collaboration platforms o Remote video coaching o Video libraries or podcasts (showcasing best practices) o Digital teacher manuals • Online learning communities for students: o Mobile learning management systems or collaboration platforms o Video libraries or podcasts (showing SEL in action) o Student generated media • Adaptive learning technology • SEL-focused online games and mobile apps	• SEL-focused video games and mobile apps • Simulation centers (for teachers and students) o Avatars o Embodied agents o Multimodal sensors o Biofeedback • Current technologies with potential adaptation for SEL: o Social media sites o Texting o Digital media cartoons o Graphic novels

Open Circle, are moving supplementary trainings and support materials online to enhance communication between program users and to support sustainability. In fact, all of the organizations we interviewed use some combination of supplementary trainings, such as webinars, podcasts, and video conferencing, to provide elements of teacher professional development. Supplementary Web-based support materials, including online libraries, blogs, and discussion forums, extend access to research, curricula, lesson plans, teaching tips, and best practices to hundreds of thousands of teachers. For example, the Second Step website gives program users and families access to online training and extensive implementation support tools such as video libraries, implementation time lines and checklists, assessment tools, and electronic versions of sample homework. Furthermore, these groups track teacher engagement with their program materials using access keys linked to use of the site (J. Kandel, personal communication, November 26, 2013). Some organizations, such as Responsive Classroom and RULER, have been using webinars to provide ongoing training to their certified consultants, in addition to their professional development for teachers. These established uses of technology provide SEL organizations with opportunities to expand their reach and scale-up as they are able to communicate with and provide resources to a large number of program users quickly. For schools that have ready access to computers and the Internet, supplementary trainings and support materials online can provide low-cost (for user) pathways to keep teachers engaged as learners and to inform them about new SEL-related content. However, studies and evaluations of these technologies are necessary to determine whether they lead to more frequent use, more effective teacher instruction, or more effective student outcomes related to SEL programs.

Emerging Technology to Enhance SEL

Our interviews with leading SEL organizations revealed several categories of technologies that are being used or developed in less than four organizations, and sometimes in only one organization. Although some of these technologies have been used for many years within specific organizations (i.e., the use of adaptive learning technology [Ray, 2009] by Ripple Effects), we classify them as *emerging* with respect to wider use within the field of SEL. The categories of *emerging technology* we discuss in the next section include online professional development, online learning communities for teachers and students, adaptive learning technologies, and SEL-focused games and apps (see Table 34.1).

Online Professional Development

Beyond simple online resources for teachers, online professional development, complex in design and implementation, requires tech savvy content expertise and ongoing management. Courses, workshops, and seminars can be designed in a variety of ways that can blend in-person and online learning, synchronous and asynchronous activities, and even reward users with badges and certifications as participation milestones are achieved. An example of an organization using online professional development to teach SEL, particularly empathy, which falls under the core competency of "relationship skills", is Facing History and Ourselves (FHAO), which provides online, hybrid (both online and in-person), and face-to-face professional development generally delivered through an intensive seminar, followed by ongoing coaching and a wealth of online and actual resources that help teachers foster students' historical thinking skills, social and ethical reflection, and civic learning (Reich et al., 2015; Romer, 2011). This intervention integrates content and pedagogy intended to engage students with diverse backgrounds in an examination of racism, prejudice, and anti-Semitism, in order to promote the development of a more humane and informed citizenry. The goal of this professional development is to increase teachers' self-efficacy in creating student-centered classrooms and developing students' critical thinking and empathy. According to our interview with the organization, the online course strives to emulate this student-centered process that cultivates empathy skills. For instance, participants may enter an online space, where they can hear testimonials from Holocaust survivors or even tune into a live appearance with this type of speaker in a conference call in which they can converse with the speaker or other participants of the course (D. Chad, personal communication, November 21, 2013).

The CASEL SELect Second Step program created hybrid onsite and Web-based video training for middle school teachers, complete with all necessary materials and handouts that can be conducted in school in front of a live audience. Teachers watch the training video as if they are watching a live trainer, then stop at different points to have discussions and participate in small-group activities. This hybrid approach that blends the best of online professional development with the merits of live audience participation/collaboration allows them to scale their program and provide training that is easily accessible for all schools/districts (J. Kandel, personal communication, November 26, 2013).

The Developmental Studies Center provides SEL skills development to both teachers and students, embedded within math/literacy programs and as an explicit SEL program called Caring School Community. They have created an interactive, digital teacher manual that provides real-time (or "just-in-time") collaboration and professional development opportunities. For example, if a teacher wants to see an example of a particular instructional skill mentioned in a lesson plan, he or she can immediately access an information link or video using an iPad, mobile phone, or computer. Teachers can make notes about their lesson plans on the digital teacher manual, which can instantly be transferred to other teachers in their school using the same manual. This kind of instant access to information enhances collaboration among providers and has the potential to be used in similar ways with student populations (F. Snyder, personal communication, January 30, 2014).

Online Learning Communities

Online learning communities complement online courses by providing users with ongoing access to resources (i.e., video libraries) and opportunities to enhance self-awareness and practice other SEL skills like social awareness, relationship skills, and responsible decision-making, through reflection, feedback, and collaboration (i.e., collaboration platforms, video coaching). They provide users with an easily accessible way to engage in sustained learning on a particular topic and with a specific cohort or community (Luppicini, 2007). Moreover, they provide opportunities for educators across the world to engage in dialogue with one another, learning from diverse perspectives and experiences and cultivating empathy (Reich et al., 2015). There is a growing body of research describing the nature and impact of online communities on our social awareness and understanding of others. The term "online community" generally refers to people who meet and communicate in an online environment (Preece, Maloney-Krichmar, & Abras, 2003). An increasing number of people spend time in online communities to develop relationships and exchange emotional support (Rainie, Cornfield, & Horrigan, 2005) and more recently, to engage in educational experiences (Hollins-Alexander, 2013). Findings thus far suggest that among online communities, empathy occurs most often through textual communication (Dasgupta, 2006), primarily in various styles of posts, comments, and responses, rather than other forms of media, such as video or audio posts.

Some organizations focused on SEL have started developing these communities of learning for their certified consultants and/or program users. One example of such an organization is the Yale Center for Emotional Intelligence and its CASEL SELect program, The RULER approach to SEL (Rivers & Brackett, 2011). RULER uses a Web-based learning platform to create and support a community of educators who share their work, challenges, successes, and creative ideas. After educators receive initial in-person, intensive training, the online platform serves as a medium both for ongoing coaching support and for Yale researchers to monitor program fidelity of implementation. The platform also includes an online certification program for trainees, who move through the certification by attending coaching sessions in virtual meeting rooms, viewing instructional videos, uploading materials based on program implementation, journaling about their experiences with the program, and receiving feedback from Yale staff members. Teachers confronting various challenges can collaborate online with other teachers or with coaches to review student work, lesson plans, and videos of instructional practices.

Online communities also can provide platforms for remote video coaching and mobile collaboration. Open Circle, another CASEL SELect provider of evidence-based curricula and professional development for K–5 students–teachers, has historically focused on face-to-face training and coaching. Since 2012, they have started building in the option of online coaching to expand their geographic reach. Teachers using Open Circle film themselves teaching their lessons and review them, together with their coach, online using software such as Google Hangout with YouTube. Teachers have an opportunity to see themselves in action, watch their own emotional expressions and body language, hear their own tone of voice, and see their students' emotional reactions to them. Although this method of coaching has not yet been formally evaluated, the teachers self-report that alongside a coach, they are able to see strengths and weaknesses in themselves that they otherwise may not have seen, which helps them to become more emotionally literate and self-aware (N. Biro, personal communication, November 14, 2013).

Less common than online learning communities for teachers are online learning communities and collaboration platforms that include teachers and students. Only one of the organizations interviewed, FHAO, has developed and evaluated an online learning community that includes students in the online learning process and experience. The Digital Media Innovation Network was designed to help diverse educators around the world connect to share knowledge, resources, pilot materials, and strategies for how to incorporate new media into the teaching of FHAO curricula. During this project, teachers first engaged their own students with new media, then joined the other participating teachers and their students from diverse classrooms from across the world (United States, South Africa, China, Canada, and the United Kingdom) in a 1-week online community to share their online projects. The project had multiple learning goals for students: to provide new platforms for student expression and student-generated work; to enhance their media literacy; and to foster their appreciation of difference and their own agency. Teachers employed new media as knowledge and as culminating projects; students created and shared on a Ning platform their digital reports on topics ranging from teen pregnancy to voting rights to gang violence. To illustrate how this works, an urban student from the midwestern United States could watch and provide feedback on a video report created by a student in China, using the social media tools provided on the site. The FHAO evaluation team looked at student outcomes of this project by qualitatively analyzing and coding students' patterns of interaction during their online discussions and by collecting students' self-reports about their experiences. Although the evaluation was conducted internally, the evaluation team was separate from the educators working on the project. The evaluation results indicated that students increased their sense of agency and civic engagement while practicing tolerance for different cultures and points of view (Romer, 2011). The analyses suggested that the online platform helped students to engage in civic dialogue, experience diversity, and appreciate multiple perspectives from student peers all over the world at a much deeper and experiential level than simply studying the topics with their local peers.

Adaptive Learning Technology

Another type of technology that supports student SEL skills development directly is adaptive learning technology, in which computers adapt assignments and content based on students' learning styles, assessed through their responses. The most widely used, direct-to-learner SEL technology is the Ripple Effects Whole Spectrum Learning Intervention®, an adaptive (expert system), skills-building, and motivational counseling platform and library of content. In addition to systematic SEL skills building, it empowers students to address privately multidomain risk factors that may underlie presenting problems or emotional distress. Matching users' natural selection patterns to multidisciplinary domain expertise, the program provides the "set" of SEL strategies most correlated with effective approaches to each learner's case. Each of 700+ tutorials include at least nine instructional modes: case study, cognitive framing, behavioral instruction; peer modeling (video); assisted journaling, role-play opportunities, transfer training, and media analysis; and game-based assessment of content mastery (Ripple Effects, 2014). In addition, many have video true stories and interactive personal profiles. All content is illustrated and peer narrated. NIH and foundation-funded randomized controlled trials conducted by third parties in urban, suburban, and rural settings have demonstrated significant positive impacts on grades, retention in school after 1 year, suspension rates, empathy and problem-solving scores, and attitudes toward alcohol (De Long-Cotty, 2008; Perry, Bass, Ray, & Berg, 2008a, 2008b). An iPad-based app for early learners has recently been added to the suite.

SEL-Focused Online Games and Mobile Apps

Over the last couple of decades, online gaming and video gaming have been on the rise, and some developers have already established games and mobile apps that target SEL skills development. One example, The Empathy Games®, is an interactive teaching platform (available online and as a mobile app) that provides children with an opportunity to introspect and practice the skills of empathy in a fun and engaging way. When players enter the site, they begin a series of interactive games that lead them through an experiential process designed to reveal different aspects of the empathic attunement process. Integrating a variety of media, including video, images, audio, text, animation, and instant messaging, each game helps players become more aware of their personal self-state, as well as the inner experience of the other person. The games are designed to strengthen players' ability to put themselves into the other person's shoes. In essence, the games focus on increasing empathy skills, which can contribute to students' abilities to resolve conflict peacefully and respectfully. Another educational game that specifically aims to enhance SEL competencies, called IF, was developed out of a partnership between If You Can Company and educators and researchers from Nueva School, Yale, Stanford, and CASEL. This adventure video game teaches conflict resolution skills and stress reduction strategies such as breathing exercises. The game asks students to practice what they are learning in their lives. An IF app for adults allows parents, caregivers, and teachers of students to receive updates on what the children are learning, which includes discussion questions and activities to reinforce what the game is teaching. Games such as these create opportunities to increase access and exposure to effective educational programming for children everywhere. While some SEL-focused games and educational apps have existed for many years, many SEL organizations have yet to explore the tremendous potential of these learning tools.

Potential Technology to Enhance SEL in the Future

New technology emerges every day; yet many technologies that have been in use for years, or even decades, have yet to be explored in the context of SEL. In this next section, we discuss new technologies that have potential to enhance SEL in the *future*. The technology categories and specific applications mentioned here (and in Table 34.1) are by no means exhaustive, especially given the rapid pace of technology innovation across industries outside of education, from cinema to manufacturing. Nevertheless, our hope is that SEL program developers and users will find this overview helpful.

SEL-Focused Video Games and Mobile Apps

Although several SEL-focused games and apps currently exist as mentioned in *emerging technology*, we believe that there is great potential for further development of new games by SEL organizations and use of existing games within SEL programs and in schools. One example of an app that is in beta format, soon to be released to the public, is the Mood Meter, designed by HopeLab in collaboration with researchers at the Yale Center for Emotional Intelligence. This app helps users learn how to accurately recognize, label, understand, and manage their emotions by recording them on an emotion grid and tracking them over time. Users can see reports of their feelings over time to discover patterns, and the app provides recommendations on strategies to help manage different types of emotions. We envision many more games and apps like this one being developed in the future by SEL organizations in collaboration with game developers. In addition, as game developers become more aware of SEL through its increasing exposure, they might consider creating games that incorporate SEL competencies.

Simulation Centers: Avatars and Embodied Agents

Simulation centers that utilize avatars and embodied agents can provide opportunities for students to explore and develop core SEL competencies. Embodied agents are digital, visual representations of an interface, often taking a human form (Cassell, 2000). In the context of computers and the Internet, an *avatar* is defined as a graphical character that represents the user in another environment (Boberg, Piippo, & Ollila, 2008). An example of how technology can enhance students' understanding of others (social awareness) is through participatory role play conducted online through simulations in which embodied agents encourage emotional and cognitive engagement between the user and the online environment (Ong et al., 2011). Simulations offer opportunities to practice new scripts and behaviors in physically and emotionally safe online environments. One such example is Kognito Interactive, which creates role-playing training simulations and games related to behavioral health and well-being. Users learn effective communication skills for managing emotion-laden and difficult situations by practicing with animated, intelligent, and emotionally responsive embodied agents. Currently, a variety of Kognito products allow educators to learn how to support at-risk students or diverse student populations. Developers could create a series of interpersonal student simulations about a variety of challenging situations to teach SEL competencies such as relationship skills and social awareness. In the future, simulations of this kind have great promise for the social and emotional development of both adults and students. Some SEL organizations, such as the Developmental Studies Center (DSC), have already started developing simulation technology. DSC will be incorporating something called a "thoughtful discipline program" to support teachers with behavior challenges in the classroom. The simulation center provides teachers with a safe space to practice new scripts and behaviors, and get feedback on their communication and behavior modification style. This format allows teachers to learn from their mistakes without being in a vulnerable position in front of their colleagues; furthermore, this technology allows schools and districts to scale-up their professional development by providing teachers with quick access to this technology. Ultimately, DSC plans to develop similar types of virtual simulations for middle- and upper-grades schoolchildren to practice how they would handle challenging or emotion-laden situations.

The Trust Project, a collaboration between the Yale Center for Emotional Intelligence, Wright State University, and Firestorm software, creates a simulated environment that uses both avatars and embodied agents to teach social and emotional development for Army personnel. After a short, 5- to 10-minute training on how to navigate the simulation world, users create their avatars and meet their avatar teammates. They learn various SEL skills development tools used in the RULER approach to SEL (i.e., Mood Meter, Meta-Moment) guided by a computerized empathetic partner (or CEP). Once they have received the training, they have to perform a task within the virtual environment in which they can choose to listen to or ignore feedback from the CEP. While they are doing these tasks, multimodal sensors that measure skin conductance and track their eye movements (pupil dilation and initial fixation) measure their emotions and engagement (in the future, facial recognition software and electroencephalic [EEG] measurements will also be included). Eventually, this technology could be used to create software that responds to participants' emotional states in real time and gives congruent feedback. In a classroom, for example, the software could provide emotionally intelligent responses to students based on their facial expressions and physiological indicators (M. McCoy, personal communication, February 19, 2014).

Simulations like these can incorporate biofeedback technology to help users develop self-management skills. EmWave Desktop and Handheld Technology, developed in the last decade by a team of researchers at Rutgers University, provide students with computer-assisted learning supports to help them regulate emotion and obtain optimal performance and focus. The program provides biofeedback, auditory coaching, and a series of games that reinforces gradual progress toward optimal calm and focus. Through repeated practice, these methods help students learn, kinesthetically, how to regulate emotion and manage stress, leading to improved mental clarity and overall health. Studies on EmWave, some peer reviewed and others not, have demonstrated encouraging results in children with attention deficits (Goelitz & Lloyd, 2012; Lloyd, Brett, & Wesnes, 2010) and test anxiety (Bradley, McCraty, Atkinson, & Tomasino, 2010); we look forward to additional studies that clarify the specific role that EmWave contributes to these results. When bundled with simulations and other technologies such as Ripple Effects, students can learn in real time how their bodies respond to emotion-laden situations and practice self-regulation strategies.

Current Technologies with Potential Adaptation for SEL

In addition to video games, mobile apps, and simulation centers, several other, current technologies have potential adaptation uses for the field of SEL, including social media sites, texting, and digital media cartoons/graphic novels.

Social Media Sites. Although there are some potentially negative effects from the use of various social media sites, such as cyberbullying, these sites can also provide opportunities for ongoing social and emotional development. Victims of cyberbullying experience higher levels of depression and anxiety, poorer academic performance, and higher rates of suicidal thoughts and attempts (Bauman, Toomey, & Walker, 2013; Slonje & Smith, 2008). However, technology can create and preserve examples of damaging exchanges that occur; cyberbullying and harassment can be studied and reviewed; and discussion between parties and with teachers or other adults becomes possible. One example of how social media can be modified to help users deal with upsetting reactions is a current project by Facebook. Facebook is now collaborating with a team of psychologists and researchers at Yale University and the University of California at Berkeley to develop tools that can increase reporting of online abuse and encourage teens to communicate with one another safely and effectively. Originally, when users of Facebook experienced a problem with something that someone posted, the platform offered to "report" the post, then brought users to another screen with the option of either blocking the person or getting help from a trusted friend. With information gleaned from focus groups conducted by the Yale researchers, Facebook has added a series of screens that (1) ask users to select an option to describe their experience (e.g., "I just don't like it", "The post is mean or disrespectful", or "This is an example of threatening behavior"), (2) question how the post made them feel, (3) provide simple, effective guidance for less threatening versus more threatening posts, and (4) offer positive prepopulated messages based on the emotions users report, which they can edit and send to either the creator of the content or trusted adults or friends. The overarching goal of this project is to cultivate social awareness and responsible decision making in Facebook users and especially youth.

Texting. Texting is another technology being used by teens with potential for further exploration in SEL. One example of this is Crisis Text Line, a service that provides young people in any type of crisis access to free, 24/7, emotional support and information they need via text messaging. Essentially, a teen texts the Crisis Text Line, and a live, trained specialist receives the text and responds quickly with counseling and referrals through text message. SEL organizations might consider how texting could be used to share information with teens about effective social and emotional strategies, such as positive self-talk, and reframing of unpleasant emotions.

Digital Media Cartoons and Graphic Novels. Given the growing popularity of cartoons and graphic novels among teens today, these media translated online about SEL-specific content could have a positive impact. *The Transporters* (Baron-Cohen, Golan, Chapman, & Granader, 2009), a digital media cartoon series, teaches children how to read faces and emotions better. It was originally designed for children with autism but can be adapted to teach identification of feelings among a variety of young people. The content itself includes episodes showing basic emotions in context, interactive quizzes, and an instruction booklet for educators. The results of research on this project showed that the media helped teach children emotion recognition and the translation of this emotional awareness into real-life situations (Baron-Cohen et al., 2009). Certainly, digital media cartoon series, like this one, and online graphic novels can be targeted specifically to topics related to SEL for a wider student audience.

From video games to simulation centers and social media, a wide array of current technologies exist that have potential to support SEL professional development for teachers and programming for students.

Problems and Pitfalls

Although we have primarily focused on the new possibilities that technologies can offer the field of SEL, we cannot ignore the many challenges that need to be addressed. This following section provides the reader with some key problems and pitfalls within the current state of technology in SEL, most notably, that research on technology in SEL is very limited, technology can cause harm, and ethical concerns must be considered.

Research on Technology in SEL Is Very Limited

• Because of the momentum around technology in education, there is a tendency to assume rather than to confirm the advantages of using technology. For example, putting an SEL course online might not be the best way to conduct that course.

• SEL program research typically focuses on the effectiveness of the program overall (using a variety of criteria) and rarely includes empirical studies of the specific technology aspects used within the program and how they may (or may not) enhance the overall effectiveness of the program.

• Because many variables determine the outcome of an educational program, it is difficult to attribute cause-and-effect relationships between technologies and outcomes. The pitfall is the potential for attributing a falsely causal relationship between the technology used and a successful SEL outcome.

Technology Can Be Harmful

• Communications using technology without the nonverbal cues of face-to-face interactions, such as body language, tone of voice, facial expression, and other visual cues, can lead to miscommunication and misunderstanding, ultimately limiting and sometimes damaging social interactions. Some believe that technology may even weaken our skills in these areas by pulling us away from meaningful interpersonal exchanges.

• Social technologies permit the expression of potentially offensive or critical words that can be viewed by countless others and live in cyberspace for eternity. For example, bullying online is a repeat offense requiring just the click of a button; for such a simple action, the consequences for others can be life altering.

• Some studies have revealed that higher levels of self-disclosure exist in online spaces compared to face-to-face exchanges (Joinson, 2001); this may contribute to the growing trend in cyberbullying as personal information becomes fodder for hostility and public ridicule, which can remain potent long after its posting.

• Social technologies can promote unhealthy comparison, self-criticism, or devaluing, which can be more selectively avoided in offline interactions. For example, a person working through the breakup of a relationship and the associated feelings of loneliness can choose his or her offline interactions carefully, whereas being online can lead to continual updates and pictures that may make it difficult to be anything but self-critical about the situation.

Ethical Concerns Must Be Considered

• Using Web-based mobile technologies increasingly requires one to share personal information to various degrees. The decisions about where that information lives, who has access to it (and for how long), and who is making these decisions, is an ethical concern, particularly for educators who request student participation in these technology-driven programs. What responsibility do educators have, or might they have, to students whose information goes into cyberspace? This is particularly pertinent in SEL, where children are recording private thoughts and feelings online. Could these private moments accidentally be accessed and cause harm to the student in some way?

• Encouraging students to use certain social technologies requires their understanding and literacy about their online presence and reputation. The lines between private and public are blurring, and the ethical concern here is the degree to which teachers and parents are or should be responsible for this "literacy" of children, and when to shift that responsibility to students as they grow up.

• We must consider whose responsibility it is (e.g., parents, teachers, school leaders, game developers) to ensure developmentally appropriate exposure and involvement with technologies.

Recommendations and Guidelines

Though we cannot ignore the challenges that technology begets, we can focus on the potential that lies within technological development and its integration into the field of SEL. In this section, we provide recommendations and guidelines for schools committed to SEL, and SEL organizations and programs to consider. Specifically, we recommend how schools, application developers, and SEL organizations can (1) integrate research on technology into their SEL program evaluations, (2) look outside the field of SEL for inspiration, (3) form strategic partnerships, (4) develop more effective communication and delivery methods, and (5) address important ethical concerns.

Integrate Research on Technology

• Research and understand whether and how technology applications in SEL lead to more effective teacher professional development and instruction, and more effective student outcomes.

• Consider formal methods of educational technology creation to foster an iterative cycle of exploration, construction, and formative assessment. We recommend a method of development that allows for the study of technology and its use alongside established and empirical pedagogical theories and practices.

• Assess a range of positive and negative outcomes (e.g., attention problems, anxiety, stress management, self-efficacy, motivation) to understand what is likely or unlikely to be positively influenced by specific technologies and their applications.

• Conduct research on the best ways to disseminate different technologies effectively to various audiences.

• Evaluate blended learning: how technology impacts professional development and student learning. What is the most effective balance between online and offline learning in terms of successful training transference and sustainability, as well as student performance?

Look Outside of SEL for Inspiration

• Look at existing mobile technologies, video games, apps, and simulations that already teach skills that might be transferable to SEL programs.

• Look at technologies in development at universities or emerging companies that are beginning to test innovations in human–computer interactivity, such as robots, artificially intelligent agents, avatars, virtual realities, and simulated actors. These may have great potential for expanding teaching and learning of SEL across a variety of audiences.

• Continue to create and optimize emotion recognition software, computer games, and other technologies to help specialized populations with social and emotional deficits.

• Incorporate technologies such as Web and software resources, and online coaching and communities, into SEL skills training.

• Consider ways to incorporate SEL skills building into those systems that educators are already using as the framework for course delivery (learning management systems [LMS], such as Blackboard). The opportunity for skills building could exist alongside or be integrated within the formal academic curriculum.

• Ensure that game developers and curriculum designers have SEL experts as part of their groups prior to designing or building SEL into games or courses with technology.

Form Strategic Partnerships

• Align with organizations or educational institutions that already have wide distribution and online learning platforms (e.g., *amplify.com* and *greatschools.org*).

• Partner with technology centers and research institutions to evaluate technology in SEL programs and/or develop new technologies.

Develop More Effective Communication and Delivery Methods

• Develop more effective communication and delivery methods by getting parents and teachers on board with new mobile technologies.

• Offer more and varied courses on media literacy for students and for school staff.

• Use technology to promote SEL by educating various groups, such as the public, policymakers, educators, and researchers, about the value and application of SEL.

Address Important Ethical Concerns

• Monitor how technology is used and by what populations, and carefully evaluate any potentially negative, as well as positive, impacts it may have on students and adults.

- Increase awareness of cyberbullying and use technology platforms to create experiences that can foster a variety of means to prevent it and encourage more prosocial interactions and communities online.
- Encourage everyone, including researchers, educators, parents, and policymakers, to take up the challenge to educate themselves about the potential benefits and limitations of technologies as they are uncovered by evidence-based research and practice.

Concluding Comments

We look forward to a time when we can refer to a strong body of evidence showcasing the added value of technology in cultivating SEL competencies. Currently, state-of-the-art digital technologies are evolving so quickly that some approaches will likely be transformed or supplanted by the time this chapter goes to print. In the last few decades, scientists, psychologists, and educators have only scratched the surface of the many challenges and potential benefits of the marriage between technology and SEL. Far more than being just a medium for playing video games, sharing text messages, or passively watching hours of television, technology holds potential for active, interactive, creative, educational, and positive purposes, including social and emotional development. Despite some of the challenges cited in this chapter, we see tremendous potential and an abundance of hope for the future. It is both curious and exciting to ponder the possibilities that lie ahead for this unique partnership between digital innovation and SEL.

References

Arbitron, Inc. & Edison Research. (2010). The Infinite Dial 2010: Digital platforms and the future of radio. Retrieved January 15, 2014, from *www.edisonresearch.com/home/archives/2010/04/the_infinite_dial_2010_digital_platforms_and_the_future_of_r.php.*

Baron-Cohen, S., Golan, O., Chapman, E., & Granader, Y. (2009). Transported to a world of emotion. *McGill Journal of Medicine, 12*(2), 78.

Barr, D. J., & Bardige, B. (2012). Facing history and ourselves: A case study. In P. M. Brown, M. W. Corrigan, & A. Higgins-D'Alessandro (Eds.), *Handbook of prosocial education* (pp. 665–680). Lanham, MD: Rowman & Littlefield.

Bauman, S., Toomey, R. B., & Walker, J. L. (2013). Associations among bullying, cyberbullying, and suicide in high school students. *Journal of Adolescence, 36*, 341–350.

Boberg, M., Piippo, P., & Ollila, E. (2008, September). *Designing avatars.* Paper presented at the Proceedings of the 3rd International Conference on Digital Interactive Media in Entertainment and Arts, Athens, Greece.

Bradley, R. T., McCraty, R., Atkinson, M., & Tomasino, D. (2010). Emotion self-regulation, psychophysiological coherence, and test anxiety: Results from an experiment using electrophysiological measures. *Applied Psychophysiology and Biofeedback, 35*, 261–283.

Cassell, J. (2000). Nudge nudge wink wink: Elements of face-to-face conversation for embodied conversational agents. In J. Cassell, J. Sullivan, S. Prevost, & E. Churchill (Eds.), *Embodied conversational agents* (pp. 1–27). Cambridge, MA: MIT Press.

Collaborative for Academic, Social, and Emotional Learning (CASEL). (2003). *Safe and Sound: An educational leader's guide to evidence-based social emotional learning (SEL) programs.* Chicago: Author.

Collaborative for Academic, Social, and Emotional Learning (CASEL). (2012). *2013 CASEL guide: Effective social and emotional learning programs—Preschool and elementary school edition.* Chicago: Author.

Dasgupta, S. (Ed.). (2006). *Encyclopedia of virtual communities and technologies.* Hershey, PA: IGI Global.

De Long-Cotty, B. (2008). *Can computer-based training enhance adolescents' resilience?: Results of a randomized control trial.* Poster presented at the annual meeting of the Society for Prevention Research, Washington, DC.

Durlak, J. A., Weissberg, R. P., Dymnicki, A. B., Taylor, R. D., & Schellinger, K. B. (2011). The impact of enhancing students' social and emotional learning: A meta-analysis of school-based universal interventions. *Child Development, 82*, 405–432.

Elias, M. J., Zins, J. E., & Weissberg, R. P. (1997). *Promoting social and emotional learning: Guidelines for educators.* Alexandria, VA: Association for Supervision and Curriculum Development.

Gentile, D., Oberg, C., Sherwood, N. E., Story, M., Walsh, D. A., & Hogan, M. (2004). Well-child visits in the Video Age: Pediatricians and the American Academy of Pediatrics' Guidelines for Children's Media Use. *Pediatrics, 114*, 1235–1241.

Goelitz, J., & Lloyd, T. (2012) *Using EmWave technology for children with ADHD: An evidence-based intervention*. Boulder Creek, CA: Institute for HeartMath.

Goleman, D. (1995). *Emotional intelligence: Why it can matter more than IQ*. New York: Bantam Books.

Hollins-Alexander, S. (2013). *Online professional development through virtual learning communities*. Thousand Oaks, CA: Corwin Press.

Joinson, A. (2001.) Self-disclosure in computer-mediated communication: The role of self-awareness and visual anonymity. *European Journal of Social Psychology, 31*, 177–192.

Jones, A., & Issroff, K. (2005). Learning technologies: Affective and social issues in computer-supported collaborative learning. *Computers and Education, 44*(4), 395–408.

King, K. P. (2002). Identifying success in online teacher education and professional development. *Internet and Higher Education, 5*, 231–246.

Kress, J. S., & Elias, M. J. (2006). School-based social and emotional learning programs. In K. A. Renninger & I. E. Sigel (Eds.), *Handbook of child psychology* (Vol. 4, 6th ed., pp. 592–618). New York: Wiley.

Landhuis, C. E., Poulton, R., Welch, D., & Hancox, R. J. (2007). Does childhood television viewing lead to attention problems in adolescence?: Results from a prospective longitudinal study. *Pediatrics, 120*, 532–537.

Lloyd, T., Brett, D., & Wesnes, K. (2010). Coherence training improves cognitive functions and behavior in children with ADHD. *Alternative Therapies in Health and Medicine, 16*, 34–42.

Luppicini, R. (Ed.). (2007). *Online learning communities*. Greenwich, CT: Information Age.

Mayer, J. D., & Salovey, P. (1997). What is emotional intelligence? In P. Salovey & D. J. Sluyter (Eds.), *Emotional development and emotional intelligence: Educational implications* (pp. 3–34). New York: HarperCollins.

Media Literacy Clearinghouse. (2010). Media use statistics. Retrieved October 1, 2013, from *www.frankwbaker.com/mediause.htm*.

Myers, K. K., & Sadaghiani, K. (2010). Millennials in the workplace: A communication perspective on millennials' organizational relationships and performance. *Journal of Business Psychology, 25*, 225–238.

Office of Educational Technology, U.S. Department of Education. (2010). Transforming American education: Learning powered by technology. *National Education Technology Plan (NETP)*. Retrieved February 26, 2014, from *http://tech.ed.gov/netp*.

Ong, E. Y. L., Ang, R. P., Ho, J. C. M., Lim, J. C. Y., Goh, D. H., Lee, C. S., et al. (2011). Narcissism, extraversion and adolescents' self-presentation on Facebook. *Personality and Individual Differences, 50*, 180–185.

Payton, J. W., Wardlaw, D. M., Graczyk, P. A., Bloodworth, M. R., Tompsett, C. J., & Weissberg, R. P. (2000). Social and emotional learning: A framework for promoting mental health and reducing risk behaviors in children and youth. *Journal of School Health, 70*(5), 179–185.

Perry, S. M., Bass, K., Ray, A., & Berg, S. (2008a). Impact of Ripple Effects computer-based, social–emotional learning intervention on school outcomes among rural early adolescents. San Francisco: Ripple Effects. Retrieved on May 13, 2014, from *www.rippleeffects.com/research/pdfs/6secondary.pdf*.

Perry, S. M., Bass, K., Ray, A., & Berg, S. (2008b). Impact of social–emotional learning software on objective school outcomes among diverse adolescents: A summary analyses of six randomized controlled trials. Retrieved October 1, 2013, from *www.rippleeffects.com/research_/pdfs/summary8studies.pdf?*.

Picard, R. (2000). *Affective computing* (MIT Media Laboratory Perceptual Computing Section Technical Report No. 321). Cambridge, MA: MIT Press.

Postman, N. (1993). *Technopoly: The surrender of culture to technology*. New York: Vintage Books.

Preece, J., Maloney-Krichmar, D., & Abras, C. (2003). History of emergence of online communities. In K. Christensen & D. Levinson (Eds.), *Encyclopedia of community: From the village to the virtual world* (pp. 1023–1027). Great Barrington, MA: Berkshire Publishing Group.

Putnam, R. D. (2000). *Bowling alone: The collapse and revival of American community*. New York: Simon & Schuster.

Putnam, R. D., & Feldstein, L. (2004). *Better together: Reviving the American community*. New York: Simon & Schuster.

Rainie, H., Cornfield, M., & Horrigan, J. B. (2005). The Internet and Campaign 2004: Pew Internet & American Life Project. Retrieved January 15, 2014, from *www.pewinternet.org/2005/01/17/email-and-the-2004-campaign*

Ray, A. (2009). From multidisciplinary theory to multimedia SEL interventions: The conceptual underpinnings of *Ripple Effects Whole Spectrum Intervention System*. San Francisco: Ripple Effects. Retrieved May 13, 2014, from *www.rippleeffects.com/pdfs/theorybook.pdf*.

Reich, J., Romer, A., & Barr, D. (2015). Dialogue across difference: A case study of Facing History and Ourselves' Digital Media Innovation Network. In E. Middaugh & B. Kirshner (Eds.),

#youthaction: Becoming political in a digital age (pp. 127–145). Charlotte, NC: Information Age.

Rideout, V. J., Foehr, U. G., & Roberts, D. F. (2010). *Generation M2: Media in the lives of 8- to 18-year-olds.* Menlo Park, CA: Henry J. Kaiser Family Foundation.

Ripple Effects. (2014). [Screen shot illustration of *Whole Spectrum Intervention System*]. Retrieved February 1, 2014, from *www.rippleeffects.com/education/software/learnsys.html.*

Rivers, S. E., & Brackett, M. A. (2011). Achieving standards in the English Language Arts (and more) using the RULER approach to social and emotional learning. *Reading and Writing Quarterly, 27,* 75–100.

Romer, A. L. (2011). *How do new media and documentary film support Facing History teaching and learning?: Research on the Digital Media Innovation Network, 2010–2011.* Unpublished manuscripts. Brookline, MA: Facing History and Ourselves.

Salovey, P., & Mayer, J. D. (1990). Emotional intelligence. *Imagination, Cognition, and Personality, 9*(3), 185–211.

Slonje, R., & Smith, P. K. (2008). Cyberbullying: Another main type of bullying? *Scandinavian Journal of Psychology, 49,* 147–154.

Tamim, R. M., Bernard, R. M., Borokhovski, E., Abrami, P. C., & Schmid, R. F. (2011). What Forty years of research says about the impact of technology on learning: A second-order meta-analysis and validation study. *Review of Educational Research, 8,* 4–28.

Tiles, M. (1995). *Living in a technological culture: Human tools and human values.* New York: Routledge.

Turkle, S. (1995). *Life on the screen: Identity in the age of the Internet.* New York: Simon & Schuster.

U.S. Department of Education, Office of Educational Technology. (2012, January). *Understanding the implications of online learning for educational productivity.* Washington, DC: Center for Technology in Learning, SRI International.

Weissberg, R. P., Gullotta, T. P., Hampton, R. L., Ryan, R. A., & Adams, G. R. (Eds.). (1997). *Healthy children 2010: Enhancing children's wellness.* Thousand Oaks, CA: Sage.

Zimmerman, F. J., Christakis, D. A., & Meltzoff, A. N. (2007). Associations between media viewing and language development in children under age 2 years. *Journal of Pediatrics, 151,* 364–368.

Zins, J. E., & Elias, M. J. (2006). Social and emotional learning. In G. G. Bear & K. M. Minke (Eds.), *Children's needs III: Development, prevention, and intervention* (pp. 1–13). Bethesda, MD: National Association of School Psychologists.

CHAPTER 35

The Case for Preschool through High School State Learning Standards for SEL

Linda A. Dusenbury, Jessica Zadrazil Newman, Roger P. Weissberg, Paul Goren, Celene E. Domitrovich, and Amy Kathryn Mart

Our purpose in this chapter is to encourage the creation of high-quality preschool through high school educational standards for social and emotional learning (SEL) across the United States. To accomplish this, we (1) briefly review the research literature on learning standards generally in order to identify key components of high-quality standards, (2) provide a general assessment of where states are in the process of developing comprehensive well-articulated learning standards for SEL and, finally, (3) make recommendations to support development of high-quality SEL standards across the country.

Social and emotional competencies are the foundation for all learning, and the national conversation about learning standards increasingly focuses on the importance of student competencies related to SEL, as well as the need for learning standards to guide instruction that supports social and emotional development. For example, the recent National Research Council (NRC) report (2012, cited in Pellegrino & Hilton, 2012), *Education for Life and Work*, recommended development of learning standards to promote three sets of competencies that are essential for success in education and work: *intrapersonal*, *interpersonal*, and *cognitive skills*. The term *intrapersonal skills* refers to individual abilities needed to manage the self, including flexibility and initiative. The term *interpersonal skills* refers to abilities needed to interact effectively with others, such as social skills, collaboration, leadership, communication, and conflict resolution. Cognitive skills include responsible decision making and critical thinking.

The skills in the NRC framework align with social and emotional competencies included in the Head Start Child Development and Early Learning Framework (Head Start, 2010), which has helped to shape early learning guidelines and standards across the country. For example, in 2011, we reported that the Head Start Framework was cited in at least 48% of state early childhood standards (Dusenbury, Zadrazil, Mart, & Weissberg, 2011). Social–emotional development in the Head Start Framework includes four sets of competencies: *self-concept and self-efficacy*, *self-regulation*, *social relationships*, and *emotional and behavioral health*.

Both the NRC and the Head Start Framework skills align with the slightly more detailed framework developed by Collaborative for Academic, Social, and Emotional Learning (CASEL) collaborators. The CASEL (2012, p. 9) framework identifies five sets of SEL competencies:

> *self-awareness* (accurately recognizing one's feelings and thoughts and their influence on behaviors, accurately assessing one's strengths and limitations, and possessing a well-grounded sense of self-efficacy and optimism), *self-management* (regulating one's emotions, cognitions and behaviors, and setting and achieving personal and educational goals, persevering in addressing challenges), *social awareness* (taking the perspective of and empathizing with others, appreciating diversity, respecting others, and understanding social and ethical norms for behavior), *relationship skills* (establishing and maintaining healthy and rewarding relationships, communicating clearly, resisting inappropriate social pressure, negotiating conflict constructively, and seeking help when needed) and *responsible decision-making* (making constructive and respectful choices about personal behavior and social interactions based on consideration of ethical standards, safety concerns, social norms, the realistic evaluation of consequences of various actions, and the well-being of self and others).

Like the NRC framework and the Head Start Framework, the CASEL framework for SEL is grounded in theory and based on extensive research (e.g., Greenberg et al., 2003; Payton et al., 2000; Weissberg & Greenberg, 1998). Although all three frameworks are useful, the CASEL framework provides the most comprehensive articulation of the specific components of SEL and is the one we use as an organizing framework in this chapter.

The Importance of Learning Standards

Learning standards are statements about what students should know and be able to do as a result of educational instruction. As Chester Finn and Michael Petrelli write in their Foreword to the Thomas B. Fordham Report, *The State of State Standards—and The Common Core—in 2010* (Carmichael, Wilson, Porter-Magee, & Martino, 2010):

> Standards are the foundation upon which almost everything else rests—or should rest. They should guide state assessments and accountability systems; inform teacher preparation, licensure, and professional development; and give shape to curricula, textbooks, software programs, and more. Choose your metaphor: Standards are targets, or blueprints, or roadmaps. (p. 1)

Standards guide curriculum development and instruction by articulating specific goals and benchmarks for student learning within subject areas, grade by grade. They create uniformity and coherence in education by establishing and communicating priorities, and providing a common language and structure for instructions. When standards are taken seriously, they become the plan or blueprint for instruction, shaping and influencing what happens in the classroom. Standards tend to be taken more seriously when they are connected to assessment. In turn, this is likely to create demand and opportunities for high-quality professional development.

In the past two decades, learning standards have become the driving and organizing force in education, and are the cornerstone of the current educational reform movement (Finn, Julian, & Petrilli, 2006). By 1998, almost all states had developed learning standards for math and English language arts (ELA). Unfortunately, these standards were not uniform or standardized, and researchers and educational scholars noted that the quality of standards across the United States continued to be variable. Based on their important reviews of state learning standards, Finn and colleagues (2006) observed that learning standards were weak in many states because they were vague, overly focused on knowledge rather than skills, and not sufficiently rigorous.

The *State of the State Standards 2006* report by the Thomas B. Fordham Foundation presented several analyses linking high-quality standards in academic subject areas to student achievement measured on the National Assessment of Educational Progress (NAEP). The authors concluded:

> From 1998 to 2005, only seven states made statistically significant progress in the percentage of their students reaching proficiency in

> fourth-grade reading, and just six states made such progress for their poor or minority students. All of these states except for one received at least a "C" from Fordham for their English/Language Arts standards. That's not iron-clad proof that good standards boost achievement, but it seems to indicate that really bad standards make it much less likely. Still, lots of states received a "C" or higher from us but did not make progress on NAEP. So having decent standards could be considered "necessary but not sufficient." (Finn et al., 2006, p. 14)

Because academic learning depends on SEL, it is important for SEL be a part of learning standards. An extensive body of research, including a meta-analysis of 213 studies, has shown that academic outcomes are enhanced when education supports the development of SEL (Durlak, Weissberg, Dymnicki, Taylor, & Schellinger, 2011).

Across the country, states have the authority to develop their own learning standards, and school districts typically have some flexibility when adopting their local standards as long as they comply with the state's overall goals. In order to assist states and districts in the process of developing standards, various educational organizations have developed national model standards for different areas of the curriculum. To improve the quality of learning standards for math and ELA nationwide, states recently came together to develop the Common Core State Standards Initiative (2012). The Common Core State Standards (CCSS) were designed largely to replace participating states' own standards in math and ELA. This important effort to ensure high-quality instruction in ELA and math nationwide was coordinated by the Council for Chief State School Officers (CCSSO) and the National Governors Association (NGA) Center for Best Practices.

The CCSS are designed to present clear and consistent statements about what students should know and be able to do. Development of these standards was a response to observed variability in students' performance on high school "exit" tests across states, and concerns about global competitiveness. To respond to these concerns, the CCSS identified key skills that students need to succeed academically, and developed common goals and objectives for education across states that would prepare students to compete effectively in the global future. The CCSS also provided a common set of criteria for assessing students. The CCSS have been described as possibly "the most far-reaching experiment in American educational history" (Hacker & Dreifus, 2013).

Key features of the CCSS are their consistency and relevance to today's world. They are also grounded in evidence that includes a focus on skills development, and are developmentally and sequentially designed to prepare students for college and careers (Achieve, 2010a, 2010b). Sequence of instruction is important because research has shown that effective programs in SEL are developmentally appropriate and sequential, developing basic skills first, as the foundation for later, more advanced skills that are taught over time (Weissberg & Greenberg, 1998).

As of November 2014, 43 states, the District of Columbia, and four territories had adopted the CCSS. Because there is recognition of the unique characteristics and situation of each state, states have some flexibility in making the CCSS their own, and are permitted to incorporate up to 15% of their own standards into the Common Core. We discuss the relationship between the Common Core, and social and emotional competencies, in greater detail below, under our discussion of SEL.

Characteristics of High-Quality Standards

An important analysis of learning standards has been provided by Scott-Little, Kagan, and Frelow (2006) in their review of early childhood guidelines. Indeed, this review has helped shape preschool standards across the country. The work of these authors is instructive in understanding the key elements of effective standards in general. For example, Scott-Little and colleagues suggest that learning standards should be used to develop goals and benchmarks that are developmentally appropriate for children at different grade levels. They also stress that effective learning standards should be culturally and linguistically sensitive for diverse students and recommend that teachers be given guidelines on how to support development of each standard. Furthermore, they emphasize that standards documents should describe characteristics of the environment that can support child development, and include guidelines for creating a positive learning environment. Finally, they suggest that standards documents and companion resources should be available to support and ensure high-quality implementation of evidence-based programs, including high-quality professional development and assessment tools teachers can use to develop goals and support students in meaningful ways.

Similar recommendations from the National Association for the Education of Young Children (NAEYC, 2002) and the Alliance for Early Success (Tout, Halle, Daily, Albertson-Junkans, & Moodie, 2013) assert that early childhood education and standards should be informed by an understanding of child development, as well as the individual child, and the culture and context in which the child lives. NAEYC personnel have observed that effective teachers are intentional, and they set goals and provide experiences for children that are challenging and achievable. Drawing heavily on the findings and recommendations of Finn and colleagues (2006), Scott-Little and colleagues (2006), the NAEYC (2002), the Alliance for Early Success (Tout et al., 2013), and the CCSS, we summarize key features of high-quality SEL learning standards in Table 35.1.

In the next section we use the criteria summarized in Table 35.1 to assess where states are in their process of developing high-quality SEL standards. We begin with a review of preschool standards, then K–12 standards because preschool standards and K–12 standards tend to be developed independently and are managed by separate agencies within each state. We then conclude with recommendations for developing SEL standards that contain the key features of high-quality standards.

TABLE 35.1. Components of High-Quality SEL Standards

Freestanding SEL standards and documents supporting these standards should . . .
1. Be created for every grade level, preschool through high school.
2. Be integrated, as appropriate, into standards for other subject areas.
3. Provide simple, clear, and concise statements about what students should know and be able to do in each of the following areas: (a) self-awareness, (b) self-management, (c) social awareness, (d) relationship skills, and (e) responsible decision making.
4. Lead to goals and benchmarks that are developmentally appropriate for the age of children at different grades.
5. Be culturally sensitive, and linguistically relevant to diverse groups of students.
6. Include companion guidelines for how teachers and other adults can support development of each standard.
7. Describe characteristics of the environment that can support SEL, and include guidelines for creating a positive environment or climate to support SEL development.
8. Be available to support and ensure high-quality implementation, including evidence-based programs, high-quality professional development, and assessment tools that teachers can use to develop goals and support students in meaningful ways.

Note. These components of high-quality standards are based on findings and recommendations of Finn et al. (2006), Scott-Little et al. (2006), the NAEYC (2002), the Alliance for Early Success (Tout et al., 2013), and the CCSS Initiative (2012).

Assessment of State Learning Standards for SEL

Preschool Standards

Before discussing specific sources, it is important to note that different terminology is used across state and national documents (e.g., terms such as *guidelines, standards, foundations*, or *frameworks* have all been used). Although the terminology in different states has varied, we use the term *standards* to refer to broad statements and goals about what students should know and be able to do, and the terms *indicators* or *benchmarks* to refer to specific behaviors and skills one might expect to see at specific ages.

An extensive body of research has demonstrated the importance of high-quality preschool education to ensure school readiness (e.g., Barnett & Masse, 2007; Karoly & Bigelow, 2005; Schweinhart et al., 2005; Yoshikawa et al., 2013). In the past 10 years, in large part thanks to the example of the Head Start Framework, the efforts of organizations such as the NAEYC, the Early Learning and Development Standards website (see Early Learning Guidelines/Early Learning Development Standards [ELG/ELDS], 2013), and work by researchers (e.g., Scott-Little et al., 2006), states began developing learning standards for preschool.

In our most recent scan of state learning standards for SEL (Dusenbury et al., 2013), we found that, as of February 2013, 49 states had a free-standing set of preschool standards for SEL. Forty-five states (90%) actually used the words *social* and *emotional* in the title for what we would call their SEL domain. This was up from 40 states in the scan we completed 2 years earlier (Dusenbury et al., 2011)—a 10% increase. In 2013, the remaining five states used the words *social* and *personal*, or similar language in their title for this development domain.

In our 2013 scan, we found that preschool standards often contain many features of high-quality standards identified in Table 35.1. Specifically, we found that approximately 90% of states provided (1) student indicators for SEL, (2) guidance on how caregivers could support development for SEL, and/or (3) guidance for creating a positive learning environment. Furthermore, on average, nine out of 10 states provided guidelines on how to make instruction culturally relevant, and eight out of 10 provided guidelines on how to make instruction linguistically appropriate. Nevertheless, similar to the work of Scott-Little and colleagues (2006), there was wide variability in how states did each of these things. Ideally, one might hope to find specific statements about what teachers might do to address each specific standard. For example, one standard in the *Washington State Early Learning and Development Guidelines* is that children "cooperate with other children, share and take turns." Next to that statement, there is the suggestion for caregivers to "model fair ways to take turns and share." There was variability in not only how many but also how states provided guidelines for teachers for this and other topics (e.g., creating a positive learning environment, cultural and linguistic sensitivity). For example, states might provide a separate section in their document to address one or more of these topics, or they might include brief statements about the importance of one or more of these topics in general introductory material to the standards or in externally linked documents.

Similar to Scott-Little and colleagues (2006), in 2013, we found that there was also wide variability in the number and clarity of SEL standards each state provides, and in the range of age levels covered by preschool standard statements. For example, Alabama has a total of 16 standards statements in its social–emotional domain at the 4-year-old age level, while Alaska has 77 for 4-year-olds. Idaho has 113 for SEL that cover the age range from 36 to 60 months.

To illustrate the varied yet related ways states organize standards in the social and emotional domain, we present the structure of social and emotional development used by California (see California Department of Education, 2010) in Table 35.2. California organizes its social–emotional development frameworks for SEL into three broad strands: self, social interaction, and relationships. The California framework is presented in Table 35.2, as it would align with the CASEL SEL domains. It is interesting to note that the California framework focuses on four of the five domains of SEL in the CASEL framework. Indeed, it is fairly typical of states at the preschool level not to emphasize responsible decision making, perhaps because responsible decision making would be developmentally premature for preschoolers.

Overall, our scan of all 50 states in 2013 revealed that preschool standards have many strengths and serve as an excellent model for the development of well-articulated, comprehensive SEL standards for K–12. In the following section, we review K–12 standards for SEL.

Comprehensive Standards at the K–12 Level

In strong contrast to the fact that there now are freestanding preschool standards for SEL in all 50 states, it is still rare at the K–12 level to find comprehensive, freestanding standards for SEL. As of March 2013, we

TABLE 35.2. Example of How California Organizes SEL Standards at the Preschool Level

CASEL framework	Corresponding California Preschool Learning Foundations
Self-awareness	Self-awareness
Self-management	Self-regulation
Social awareness	Social and emotional understanding, empathy and caring
Relationship skills	Interactions with familiar adults, interactions with peers, group participation, cooperation and responsibility, attachments to parents, close relationships with teachers and caregivers, friendship
Responsible decision making	No clear corresponding standard

Note. Based on California Department of Education (2010).

found that states had taken four approaches to developing standards for SEL.

Freestanding, Comprehensive Standards for SEL

Illinois, Kansas, and Pennsylvania have adopted comprehensive sets of freestanding standards with developmental indicators for the entire K–12 range. (West Virginia also adopted SEL standards that contain developmental benchmarks in 2012.) Illinois was the first state to do so, in 2004, followed by Pennsylvania and Kansas in 2012. Pennsylvania adopted the same goals for K–12 SEL as Illinois, whereas Kansas adopted slightly different goals in the "Kansas Social, Emotional, and Character Development Model Standards." The SEL standards in each of these states are briefly described below.

Illinois SEL Standards. While K–12 standards for SEL were released in 2004 (see the Illinois State Board of Education, 2014c), in 2013 Illinois also released preschool standards that fully aligned SEL goals and standards at the preschool level with its K–12 SEL standards (see Illinois State Board of Education, 2013). The Illinois SEL standards include three major goals and 10 specific standards (See Table 35.3). The Illinois standards include between 90 and 149 performance descriptors for each goal at different developmental levels. For each developmental period, these performance descriptors provide examples of how students might demonstrate that they have achieved a standard, or how a teacher might

TABLE 35.3. Illinois Goals and Standards

Goal 1: Develop self-awareness and self-management skills to achieve school and life success.

A. Identify and manage one's emotions and behavior.
B. Recognize personal qualities and external supports.
C. Demonstrate skills related to achieving personal and academic goals.

Goal 2: Use social awareness and interpersonal skills to establish and maintain positive relationships.

A. Recognize the feelings and perspectives of others.
B. Recognize individual and group similarities and differences.
C. Use communication and social skills to interact effectively with others.
D. Demonstrate an ability to prevent, manage, and resolve interpersonal conflicts in constructive ways.

Goal 3: Demonstrate decision-making skills and responsible behaviors in personal, school, and community contexts.

A. Consider ethical, safety, and societal factors in making decisions.
B. Apply decision-making skills to deal responsibly with daily academic and social situations.
C. Contribute to the well-being of one's school and community.

Note. Based on Illinois State Board of Education (2014c).

know in practice whether a student knew or was able to do what the standard statement identified. For example, for Goal 3 (Demonstrate decision-making skills and responsible behaviors in personal, school, and community contexts), the Illinois SEL standards provide 114 performance descriptors across grades 1–5 (e.g., "Explain why hitting or yelling at somebody is hurtful and unfair"), and 111 performance descriptors across grades 6–12 (e.g., "Evaluate how ethical conduct might improve valued relationships").

In addition to the goals and standards descriptors, the Illinois SEL Standards website includes many of the additional features of high-quality standards. For example, the website also provides guidelines and principles for a comprehensive system of learning supports related to three tiers of intervention (i.e., universal approaches for all students, targeted early intervention for students at risk, and intensive individualized supports for specific populations in need), guidelines for involving families and improving conditions for learning (e.g., school leadership, climate and safety; see Illinois State Board of Education, 2014a, 2014b).

Pennsylvania Student Interpersonal Skills Standards. The Pennsylvania Student Interpersonal Skills Standards were adopted April 25, 2012 (see Pennsylvania Department of Education, 2012).

These standards are designed to promote the development of skills needed to navigate the challenges of the global world effectively. The Pennsylvania Standards for Student Interpersonal Skills are organized around four developmental periods (grades PreK–K, 1–5, 6–8, and 9–12). These standards are organized around the same three goals as the Illinois standards: (1) self-awareness and self-management; (2) establishing and maintaining relationships; and (3) decision making and responsible behavior.

Kansas Social, Emotional, and Character Development Model Standards. The Kansas Social, Emotional, and Character Development Model Standards (see Kansas State Department of Education, 2014b) acknowledge the influence of CASEL, the Illinois Standards, and the Anchorage SEL Standards. Like the Illinois and Pennsylvania standards, Kansas organizes its standards for Social, Emotional, and Character Development (SECD) under three broad goals, although the goals differ slightly and are in a different order than those in the Illinois and Pennsylvania standards. Specifically, the goals of the Kansas standards are (1) character development, which includes responsible decision making and problem solving, (2) personal development, which includes self-awareness and self-management; and (3) social development, which includes interpersonal skills. There are four developmental periods in the Kansas standards: grades K–2, 3–5, 6–8, and 9–12. Goal 1 (Character Development) focuses on ethics and good character, creating a caring community, mutual respect, and preventing cruelty and violence. Goal 1 also covers responsible decision making and problem solving, including understanding of multiple factors and goals in decision making, organizing time and managing responsibilities, playing a role in classroom management, and effective problem solving. Goal 2 (Personal Development) focuses on self-awareness and self-management across the four developmental periods. Goal 3 (Social Development) focuses on social awareness and interpersonal skills.

In addition to the SECD standards, the Kansas State Department of Education (2014a) also provides teacher instructional examples to support personal and social development.

Freestanding Standards in Other States. Three additional states have developed freestanding standards related to social and emotional development, but none of these has provided developmental benchmarks or indicators for students of different ages and each uses slightly different terminology to address SEL-related skills. Vermont's Vital Results standards address communication, reasoning and problem solving, personal development, and responsibility. Maine's Guiding Principles focus on skills such as communication and problem solving, and Missouri's Show-Me Standards emphasize gathering and analyzing information, effective communication, problem solving, and responsible decision making.

New York also deserves mention because it has many of the ancillary elements of high-quality standards (see New York State Department of Education, 2014b), although the state has not actually adopted learning standards statements for SEL. Nevertheless, the state's website provides a number of useful resources, including strategies for supporting social and emotional development (see New York State Department of Education, (2014a), principles of a supportive environment, and guidance on implementation.

States Aligning Social and Emotional Development with Early Elementary Education

Education experts believe that there should be alignment of early childhood education with K–12 education, so that learning is consistent and supported, year to year (Tout et al., 2013). A survey by Scott-Little, Lesko, Martella, and Millburn (2007) indicated that every state is working on aligning preschool and K–12 standards, although there were many different approaches to doing this. In addition to Illinois and Pennsylvania, which have already been discussed, Idaho and Washington have aligned their preschool standards for SEL from preschool into the early elementary grades.

Idaho's aligned standards extend from birth to grade 3, and are divided into eight developmental periods (see Idaho Early Learning eGuidelines, 2014). At each developmental period, there is a social domain (Goals 27 through 35) and an emotional domain (Goals 36 through 38). Consistent with the features of high-quality standards outlined in Table 35.1, the Idaho guidelines provide child indicator statements and caregiver strategies for each standard. The Washington State Early Learning and Development Guidelines span nine developmental periods from birth to grade 3 (see Washington State Department of Early Learning, 2014). Within each developmental period, the Social–Emotional Domain includes relevant standards in "About Me and My Family and Culture" and "Building Relationships." There is also relevant content on "Communicating" in Speaking and Listening.

The Idaho and Washington aligned standards are important because, as can be seen in Table 35.4, in addition to aligning all learning standards through third grade, they articulate standards that address at least four of the five SEL competencies. In terms of the fifth competency, as we discussed earlier, one reason it is uncommon

TABLE 35.4. Examples of Aligned Standards for SEL

CASEL framework	Idaho Early Learning eGuidelines	Washington State Early Learning and Development Guidelines
Self-awareness	Belief in personal abilities, being unique individuals	Self-concept
Self-management	Adapting to diverse settings, regulating feelings and impulses	Self-management, learning to learn
Social awareness	Respecting similarities and differences in people, awareness of behavior and its effects (including effects on others), sympathy and empathy, a sense of humor	Family and culture
Relationship skills	Interacting with adults, friendships with peers, positive negotiation skills, participating in group activities	Interactions with adults, interactions with peers, social behaviors, problem solving and conflict resolution, communicating
Responsible decision making	No clear corresponding standard	No clear corresponding standard

Note. Based on Idaho Early Learning eGuidelines (2014). and Washington State Department of Early Learning (2014).

to find responsible decision-making goals articulated in early childhood standards may be that responsible decision making becomes more appropriate developmentally later in childhood. Nevertheless, some activities related to responsible decision making probably are developmentally appropriate in younger children, such as participating in discussions of why rules are important and brainstorming alternatives to hitting—two examples found in the Illinois preschool standards for SEL. It may also be that some of the student indicators included under each of the standards in Idaho and Washington could actually be conceptualized as responsible decision making. In-depth analysis of state standards is needed to explore this possibility. Standards that are aligned from early childhood through early elementary grades have begun the process of articulating social and emotional standards and indicators through early elementary school. States with aligned standards can therefore serve as a model to other states on how to conduct this process.

Freestanding Focused Standards

A third approach to standards for SEL has been to develop freestanding standards that are relevant to SEL but are not comprehensive across the range of social and emotional competencies. For example, Washington (see State of Washington, 2005) and Kansas (see Kansas State Department of Education, 2014a) each have freestanding standards for the skills of Communication, which emphasize speaking and listening skills, as well as cooperation. (The Kansas Communication Standards are separate and apart from its standards for Character Development and SEL.) Tennessee (see Tennessee Department of Education, 2014) has freestanding standards in Service–Learning for grades 9–12, which include decision making and problem solving, goal setting, developing a plan of action, demonstrating a sense of purpose, and communication.

Integration of SEL into Other Sets of Learning Standards

Virtually all states have integrated at least some degree of social and emotional content into learning standards in other subject areas. However, often this content is not comprehensive across all five SEL domains and/or it is scattered and diffuse. Furthermore, the content may not be consistent across subject areas or grade levels, and development is not systematically and strategically supported. For example, New Jersey (see State of New Jersey, 2014) and West Virginia (see West Virginia Department of Education, 2014) base their academic learning standards on 21st Century Learning Standards, which integrate social and emotional development throughout, including problem solving, critical thinking, creativity, collaboration, and communication (Partnership for 21st Century Skills, 2013). 21st Century Learning skills recognize that in order to function in our increasingly complex world, students need skills related to critical thinking, problem solving, communication, and collaboration. They also need to be flexible, adaptable, able to learn independently, and respectful of people with different backgrounds. They need social skills and leadership skills, and to be highly responsible, productive, and accountable (Partnership for 21st Century Skills, 2011).

States often use sets of national model standards such as 21st Century Learning Skills to develop their own standards, and national model standards in different subject areas often contain elements of SEL. For example, as mentioned earlier, 45 states are in the process of adopting the CCSS in math and ELA, which contain standards on communication (especially speaking and listening), cooperation skills, and problem solving. Because of the importance of the Common Core, these standards are discussed in greater detail below. National model standards in social studies, which have been used by most states to develop state standards (National Council for Social Studies, 2002), help students recognize the influence of groups and emphasize responsible decision making and good citizenship. National model standards in science (National Research Council, 1996), used by 42 states, address problem solving.

National health education standards (Centers for Disease Control and Prevention, 1995), used by 42 states, aim to foster students' communication skills, decision-making skills, and goal-setting skills. As can be seen in Table 35.5, the National Health Education Standards are important because they overlap considerably with SEL. How-

TABLE 35.5. How National Model Health Education Standards Align with SEL Domains

CASEL SEL domain	Corresponding National Model Standards in Health
Self-awareness	No clear corresponding standard.
Self-management	Standard 6: Students will demonstrate the ability to use goal-setting skills to enhance health. Standard 7: Students will demonstrate the ability to practice health-enhancing behaviors and avoid or reduce health risks.
Social awareness	No clear corresponding standard.
Relationship skills	Standard 4: Students will demonstrate the ability to use interpersonal communication skills to enhance health and avoid or reduce health risks. Standard 8: Students will demonstrate the ability to advocate for personal, family, and community health.
Responsible decision making	Standard 2: Students will analyze the influence of family, peers, culture, media, technology, and other factors on health behaviors. Standard 5: Students will demonstrate the ability to use decision-making skills to enhance health.

Note. Based on Centers for Disease Control and Prevention (1995).

ever, health education standards are not sufficient as a blueprint for instruction in SEL, for several reasons. First, the national model health standards are not comprehensive across the SEL domains; they focus primarily and understandably on health behavior. Second, most students do not receive health education every year, from preschool through high school. Finally, time allocated for health education can be very limited, and there are often many other requirements for what is to be accomplished in health, including prevention of violence, drugs, and bullying. Because students may only have a few semesters of health, it is not sufficient to assume that health education will provide sufficient instruction in SEL.

At least seven states (Alabama, Kansas, Nevada, North Carolina, Oregon, Tennessee, and Wisconsin) have adopted the American School Counselor Association (ASCA; 2014) National Standards for Students, and these are fairly comprehensive in terms of SEL. For example, standards for career skills are highly relevant to the domain of self-awareness (e.g., "Students will understand the relationships between personal qualities, education, training, and the world of work"). Similarly, there is overlap between the ASCA Standards in Personal and Social Development and SEL (e.g., "Students will acquire the knowledge, attitudes, and interpersonal skills to help them understand and respect others and self" and "Students will make decisions, set goals, and take necessary actions to achieve goals"). However, ASCA standards are used primarily by guidance counselors and, like the National Model Health Education Standards, do not have sufficient influence on day-to-day instruction in education.

In conclusion, although integration into other sets of standards is one way of reinforcing SEL, our concern is that an exclusive reliance on this approach may not place sufficient emphasis on the broad application of social and emotional competencies to everyday interactions. Research has shown that regular practice is important to social and emotional development (e.g., Payton et al., 2000). When SEL standards are spread across other subject areas, they may not be emphasized, and regular practice may not occur. For these reasons, we recommend that states also adopt freestanding standards for SEL.

The Relationship between the Common Core State Standards and SEL

The vast majority of states have adopted and are beginning the process of implementing

TABLE 35.6. Examples of Overlap between SEL and the CCSS

CASEL competencies	Common Core Anchor Standard
Self-awareness	No clear corresponding standard
Self-management	Mathematical Practice: Make sense of problems and persevere in solving them. Habits of Mind: Demonstrate independence.
Social awareness	English Language Arts: Apply knowledge of language to understand how language functions in different contexts, to make effective choices for meaning and style, and to comprehend when reading or listening. Habits of Mind: Come to understand other perspectives and cultures.
Relationship skills	ELA Speaking and Listening: Prepare for and participate effectively in a range of conversations and collaborations with diverse partners, building on others' ideas and expressing one's own clearly and persuasively.
Responsible decision making	No clear corresponding standard

Note. Based on Common Core State Standards Initiative (2012).

CCSS. It is therefore important to consider how adoption of CCSS may alter the landscape of SEL standards in math and ELA in the future. In Table 35.6, we assess whether and how Common Core Anchor Standards for math and ELA, as well as Common Core Habits of Mind, overlap with the five SEL core competencies. Table 35.6 shows where SEL competencies appear to be implicit and foundational to the CCSS. For example, the CCSS assumes that students have self-management skills, such as being able to sit quietly and focus on a task, but these assumptions are not explicit. Nevertheless, for students to be capable of managing their feelings and impulses in order to sit quietly and pay attention, they must first be aware of their own feelings and impulses—that is, they must be self-aware in order to self-manage.

Recommendations for Developing High-Quality National Standards for SEL

This is a time of great opportunity for the development of high-quality, comprehensive standards for SEL from preschool to high school. Every state has freestanding standards for social and emotional development at the preschool level, but there is work to be done in aligning those standards with K–12 education. Furthermore, only three states have developed comprehensive, freestanding standards with developmental benchmarks for K–12 SEL. However, most states do integrate standards for SEL, at least to some degree, into learning standards for other subject areas, across the full range of grade levels. Although integration of SEL standards across learning areas is beneficial, we also believe it is important to develop freestanding, comprehensive standards in order to communicate SEL as a clear priority in education. Furthermore, because it may not be efficient for states to work in isolation to develop learning standards, we recommend that educational organizations and states create a partnership to develop national model standards for SEL. To support this effort, we provide recommendations on how these can be applied to develop voluntary national model standards for SEL.

Recommendation 1. Every state should have clear, comprehensive, freestanding preschool through high school SEL standards with age-appropriate benchmarks. Academic learning depends on SEL, and academic outcomes are enhanced when education is organized to also support the development of SEL. Research has shown that it is possible for regular classroom teachers to help their students develop social and emotional competencies through educational practice (Durlak et al., 2011). Learning standards can serve as a blueprint for providing explicit instruction to promote all five social and emotional competencies (Bond & Hauf, 2004; Devaney, O'Brien, Resnik, Keister, & Weissberg, 2006). SEL standards should include goals and benchmarks that articulate age-appropriate expectations for students at the different ages or grade spans. Because research has demonstrated that practice is an essential part of effective programming (Durlak et al., 2011), there should also be a plan for giving students extensive opportunities to practice new skills.

As a practical matter, SEL standard statements and benchmarks should be simple, clear, and of a reasonable number. Furthermore, they should focus on a single thing that students should know or be able to do. For example, rather than having one benchmark, such as "Students will be able to attend to a task and work collaboratively in a group", we recommend breaking these two ideas into two separate and specific statements to acknowledge that separate skills are necessary: for example, "Students should be able to attend to a task for at least ____ minutes" and "With support and assistance from teachers, students should be able to work collaboratively with their peers on assigned tasks for at least ____ minutes."

Recommendation 2. SEL standards should be culturally and linguistically appropriate. Effective SEL programming is relevant and appropriate to the cultural context of students (Bond & Hauf, 2004). Therefore, SEL standards should include guidelines to ensure that they are culturally and linguistically relevant. Ideally, each state would provide guidelines that honor the ethnic and cultural heritage of its students. Although many states recognize the importance of cultural and linguistic sensitivity, especially at the preschool level, we recommend that states provide specific guidance to support culturally and linguistically sensitive instruction with diverse student populations.

Recommendation 3. SEL standards should include guidelines on how to create a positive learning environment or climate. Research has shown that students need to be motivated and engaged if they are to learn and develop new skills (Greenberg et al., 2003; Payton et al., 2000; Zins, Bloodworth, Weissberg, & Walberg, 2004; Zins, Payton, Weissberg, & O'Brien, 2007). The literature on school climate and learning supports provides guidelines on what schools can do to create safe, nurturing environments (see, e.g., Adelman & Taylor, 2005; Garibaldi, Ruddy, Osher, & Kendziora, Chapter 23, this volume; National School Climate Center, 2014). Effective SEL programs build connections to school by creating caring, engaging classroom and school practices. As part of their SEL standards, states should provide specific guidelines on how to create positive learning environments that supports social and emotional development.

Recommendation 4. SEL standards should provide guidelines about teacher practices that support social and emotional development. All teachers may not intuitively know how to promote the development of social and emotional competencies. As many preschool standards already do, states should provide guidance on the specific practices teachers can use to support attainment of each standard. Ideally, the guidelines would be incorporated into teachers' professional development as well.

Recommendation 5. Standards should be linked to strategies to enhance implementation. Standards are not going to change everyday educational practices unless they are effectively implemented. Since SEL standards were introduced in Illinois in 2004, schools in that state have responded by developing plans, selecting evidence-based programs, and seeking out high-quality professional development for teachers. All 870 Illinois school districts now have policies to make SEL a part of their curriculum (Gordon, Ji, Mulhall, Shaw, & Weissberg, 2011). In contrast, because standards for SEL in Pennsylvania and Kansas were only recently adopted (in 2012), it is not yet clear how much they are being implemented. Particularly when standards are not directly tied to assessment, as is the case in all three states, it can be difficult to determine whether and how much standards are being used by teachers to shape instruction.

It is therefore important to develop effective strategies to support implementation of SEL standards. CASEL's Collaborating District Initiative (CDI) uses a Theory of Action (see CASEL, 2013b) that identifies critical factors in successful implementation. Specifically, the CDI Theory of Action suggests that successful implementation depends on effective leadership and a professional culture that supports instruction in SEL. The CDI identifies learning standards as one of the key components of successful instruction in SEL, along with SEL assessment, evidence-based practices and programs, and high-quality professional development. Thus, implementation of SEL standards will be enhanced in three important ways: (1) adoption of evidence-based programs, (2) use of SEL assessments that allow teachers to monitor student progress, and (3) high-quality professional development. Each of these is described below.

1. *Adoption of evidence-based SEL programs.* States often resist the idea of endorsing or recommending specific programs, but there are high-quality resources that can help schools identify evidence-based programs to support SEL. Research has identified numerous effective SEL programs and curricula (Durlak et al., 2011). The most relevant tool currently available to help schools identify and select evidence-based programs in SEL is the *2013 CASEL Guide* (CASEL, 2012). The CASEL Guide identifies 23 preschool and elementary school programs that successfully promote students' self-control, relationship building, and problem solving, among other social and emotional skills. The *2013 CASEL Guide*, the first review of its kind in nearly a decade, focuses on (1) universal school-based SEL programs intended for all students (not those targeting students with special needs or preexisting challenges) and (2) school-based programs that can be delivered by existing school personnel during the regular school day. CASEL is in the process of developing a guide to middle and high school SEL programs, as well. Until the CASEL guide to secondary programs is available, seven external search tools may be useful in identifying evidence-based tools that are relevant to SEL, although none of these focuses specifically on SEL, and users of these tools therefore need to review programs carefully to determine how thoroughly they address the SEL competencies:

- Blueprints for Violence Prevention—Model and Promising Programs (*www.colorado.edu/cspv/blueprints*)
- California Healthy Kids—Research Validated Programs (*www.californiahealthykids.org/rvalidated*)
- IES [Institute of Education Sciences] What Works Clearinghouse (*http://ies.ed.gov/ncee/wwc*)
- LINKS—Lifecourse Intervention to Nurture Kids Successfully (Child Trends) (*www.childtrends.org/links*)
- National Registry of Evidence-Based Programs and Practices (NREPP) (*www.nrepp.samhsa.gov/index.aspx*)
- OJJDP Model Programs Guide (Office of Juvenile Justice and Delinquency Prevention) (*www.ojjdp.gov/mpg*)
- Social Programs that Work (Coalition of Evidence-Based Policy) (*http://toptierevidence.org/wordpress*)

2. *SEL assessments.* Assessment is critical for measuring progress toward educational goals. In conjunction with SEL standards, states should recommend reliable and valid methods of assessments that teachers can easily use to monitor student progress toward achieving standards. There are resources available to help. Denham, Ji, and Hamre (2010) developed a compendium of assessment tools available to measure SEL; the compendium can be downloaded at *http://casel.org/publications/compendium-of-sel-assessment-tools.* Another important resource to help schools identify appropriate assessments for SEL is the Raikes Foundation Social–Emotional Learning Assessment Measures for Middle School Youth, which can be downloaded at *http://raikesfoundation.org/documents/seltools.pdf.* There continues to be a need for well-developed assessment tools that align with SEL standards (also see Denham, Chapter 19, this volume).

3. *Professional development for SEL.* Research has consistently and clearly demonstrated that students whose teachers imple-

ment a program with higher quality—as it is designed to be implemented—learn more and perform better on a variety of academic and behavioral outcomes than students whose teachers do not implement with high quality (Durlak et al., 2011). Training and ongoing support are critically important to ensure that teachers have a thorough understanding of standards and can implement evidence-based programs and practices effectively (see Schonert-Reichl, Hanson-Peterson, & Hymel, Chapter 27, this volume). Professional development equips teachers with the tools and resources they will need to support development of SEL. Ideally, each state should offer professional development specifically designed to support implementation of SEL standards.

Currently, there are several efforts under way to support high-quality professional development in SEL. At the national level there is proposed federal legislation (the Academic, Social, and Emotional Learning Act of 2013 [HR 1875], cited in CASEL, 2013a). If approved, this legislation would help to support education in SEL through high-quality professional development (the legislation can also be viewed at *http://casel.org/policy-advocacy/federal-policy*). CASEL's CDI project is also working with eight districts across the country to develop effective strategies for professional development (see CASEL, 2013b).

Conclusion

High-quality SEL standards (1) are freestanding; (2) are integrated, as appropriate, into standards for other subject areas; (3) provide simple, clear, and concise statements about what students should know and be able to do in each of the following areas: self-awareness, self-management, social awareness, relationship skills, and responsible decision making; (4) provide goals and benchmarks that are developmentally age-appropriate for children in different grades; (5) are culturally sensitive and linguistically relevant to diverse groups of students; (6) have accompanying guidelines for how teachers and other adults can support development of each standard; (7) are associated with corresponding guidelines for creating a positive environment to support development of SEL; and (8) identify companion resources to support and ensure high-quality implementation, including evidence-based SEL programs, SEL assessment tools, and high-quality professional development in SEL.

Developing comprehensive, quality preschool through high school standards for each of the SEL competencies in every state will be challenging. However, Illinois has already accomplished this task and can serve as a model for other states. Preschool standards can provide a good model for the development of SEL standards for later grades.

Acknowledgments

We are grateful for the support of the Buena Vista Foundation, which helped to inspire and launch this work. We also would like to thank NoVo Foundation, the Einhorn Foundation, and the 1440 Foundation for supporting and sustaining the CASEL State Scan, and for sharing our vision about the need for learning standards that can inform and improve education.

References

Achieve. (2010a). Achieving the Common Core: Understanding the K–12 Common Core State Standards in English Language Arts and Literacy in History/Social Studies, Science, and Technical Subjects. Retrieved August 6, 2013, from *www.achieve.org/files/achievingccss-elafinal.pdf.*

Achieve. (2010b). Achieving the Common Core: Understanding the K–12 Common Core State Standards in Mathematics. Retrieved August 6, 2013, from *www.achieve.org/files/achievingccss-mathfinal.pdf.*

Adelman, H., & Taylor, L. (2005). *The school leader's guide to student learning supports: New directions for addressing barriers to learning.* Thousand Oaks, CA: Corwin Press.

American School Counselor Association (ASCA). (2014). ASCA National Standards for Students. Retrieved January 30, 2014, from *http://ascamodel.timberlakepublishing.com/files/nationalstandards.pdf.*

Barnett, W. S., & Masse, L. N. (2007). Comparative benefit–cost analysis of the Abecedarian program and its policy implications. *Economics of Education Review, 26,* 113–125.

Bond, L. A., & Hauf, A. M. C. (2004). Taking stock and putting stock in primary prevention:

Characteristics of effective programs. *Journal of Primary Prevention, 24*, 199–221.

California Department of Education. (2010). California Preschool Curriculum Framework: Vol. 1. Retrieved January 2014, from *www.cde.ca.gov/sp/cd/re/documents/psframeworkkvol1.pdf.*

Carmichael, S. B., Wilson, W. S., Porter-Magee, K., & Martino, G. (2010). *The state of State Standards—and the Common Core—in 2010.* Washington, DC: Thomas B. Fordham Institute. Retrieved August 26, 2014, from *http://excellence.net/publications.*

Centers for Disease Control and Prevention. (1995). National Health Education Standards. Retrieved August 6, 2013, from *www.cdc.gov/healthyyouth/sher/standards/index.htm.*

Collaborative for Academic, Social, and Emotional Learning (CASEL). (2012). *The 2013 CASEL guide: Effective social and emotional learning programs—Preschool and elementary school edition.* Chicago: Author.

Collaborative for Academic, Social, and Emotional Learning (CASEL). (2013a). The Academic, Social, and Emotional Learning Act of 2013 (HR 1875). Retrieved January 26, 2014, from *http://casel.org/policy-advocacy/federal-policy.*

Collaborative for Academic, Social, and Emotional Learning (CASEL). (2013b). CASEL Collaborating District Initiative Fact Sheet. Retrieved January 30, 2014, from *http://static.squarespace.com/static/513f79f9e4b05ce7b70e9673/t/52aa8d55e4b0e46ab623a595/1386909013728/cdi-factsheet-20131212.pdf.*

Common Core State Standards Initiative. (2012). Implementing the Common Core State Standards. Retrieved August 1, 2013, from *www.corestandards.org/public-license.*

Denham, S. A., Ji, P., & Hamre, B. (2010). Compendium of preschool through elementary school social?emotional learning and associated assessment measures. Retrieved August 1, 2013, from *http://casel.org/wp-content/uploads/compendium_seltools.pdf.*

Devaney, E., O'Brien, M. U., Resnik, H., Keister, S., & Weissberg, R. P. (2006). *Sustainable schoolwide social and emotional learning: Implementation guide and toolkit.* Chicago: Collaborative for Academic, Social, and Emotional Learning .

Durlak, J. A., Weissberg, R. P., Dymnicki, A. B., Taylor, R. D., & Schellinger, K. B. (2011). The impact of enhancing students' social and emotional learning: A meta-analysis of school-based universal interventions. *Child Development, 82*, 405–432.

Dusenbury, L., Zadrazil, J., Domitrovich, C., Goren, P., & Cascarino, J. (2013). *Technical report on the State Scan Scorecard Project.* Chicago: Collaborative for Academic, Social, and Emotional Learning.

Dusenbury, L., Zadrazil, J., Mart, A., & Weissberg, R. P. (2011). *State scan of social and emotional learning standards, preschool through high school.* Chicago: Collaborative for Academic, Social, and Emotional Learning. Retrieved August 1, 2013, from *http://casel.org/publications/forum-brief-on-the-state-scan.*

Early Learning Guidelines/Early Learning Development Standards (ELG/ELDS). (2013). Early Learning Guidelines resource: Recommendations and issues for consideration when writing or revising Early Learning Guidelines. Retrieved August 1, 2013, from *www.earlylearningguidelines-standards.org.*

Finn, C. E., Jr., Julian, L., & Petrilli, M. J. (2006). *The state of state standards 2006.* Washington, DC: Thomas Fordham Institute. Retrieved August 26, 2014, from *www.edexcellence.net/publications/soss2006.html.*

Gordon, R., Ji, P., Mulhall, P., Shaw, B., & Weissberg, R. P. (2011). *Social and emotional learning for Illinois students: Policy, practice and progress—How Illinois SEL standards came to be and what the state has learned through putting them into practice.* Urbana, IL: Institute of Government and Public Affairs. Retrieved July 15, 2013, from *http://casel.org/wp-content/uploads/igpa-illinois-report-sel-chapter.pdf.*

Greenberg, M. T., Weissberg, R. P., O'Brien, M. U., Zins, J. E., Fredericks, L., Resnik, H., et al. (2003). Enhancing school-based prevention and youth development through coordinated social, emotional, and academic learning. *American Psychologist, 58*, 466–474.

Hacker, A., & Dreifus, C. (2013, June 8). Who's minding the schools? *New York Times*, p. SR1.

Head Start. (2010). The Head Start Child Development and Early Learning Framework promoting positive outcomes in early childhood programs serving children 3–5 years old. Retrieved August 1, 2013, from *http://eclkc.ohs.acf.hhs.gov/hslc/tta-system/teaching/eecd/assessment/child%20outcomes/hs_revised_child_outcomes_framework(rev-sept2011).pdf.*

Idaho Early Learning eGuidelines. (2014). Domain 3: Social/Emotional Development. Retrieved January 30, 2014, from *www.healthandwelfare.idaho.gov/portals/0/children/ieleguidelines/idaho_early_learning_eguidelines.htm.*

Illinois State Board of Education. (2013). Illinois Early Learning and Development Standards: For preschool—3 years old to kindergarten enrollment age. Retrieved January 30, 2014, from *www.isbe.net/earlychi/pdf/early_learning_standards.pdf.*

Illinois State Board of Education. (2014a). Comprehensive system of learning supports: Indicators of effective practice related to conditions for learning. Retrieved August 27, 2014, from *www.isbe.state.il.us/learningsupports/html/conditions.htm.*

Illinois State Board of Education. (2014b). Comprehensive system of learning supports: School climate. Retrieved August 27, 2014, from *www.isbe.state.il.us/learning supports/climate/default.htm.*

Illinois State Board of Education. (2014c). Standards for Social/Emotional Learning. Illinois Learning Standards: Social/Emotional Learning (SEL). Retrieved January 30, 2014, from *www.isbe.state.il.us/ils/social_emotional/standards.htm.*

Kansas State Department of Education. (2014a). Communication standards. Retrieved August 27, 2014, from *www.ksde.org/Default.aspx?tabid=482.*

Kansas State Department of Education. (2014b). Social, Emotional, and Character Development Standards and Learning Resources. Retrieved January 30, 2014, from *www.ksde.org/agency/divisionoflearningservices/careerstandardsandassessmentservices/contentaream-z/schoolcounseling/social,emotional,andcharacterdevelopment.aspx.*

Karoly, L. A., & Bigelow, J. H. (2005). *The economics of investing in universal preschool education in California.* Santa Monica, CA: RAND Corporation.

National Association for the Education of Young Children (NAEYC). (2002). *Early Learning Standards: Creating conditions for success* (A Joint Position Statement of the National Association for the Education of Young Children [NAEYC] and the National Association of Early Childhood Specialists in State Departments of Education [NAECS/SDE]. Retrieved August 1, 2013, from *www.naeyc.org/files/naeyc/file/positions/position_statement.pdf.*

National Council for Social Studies. (2002). National Standards for Social Studies Teachers. Retrieved December 20, 2013, from *http://downloads.ncss.org/ncssteacherstandardsvol1-rev2004.pdf.*

National Research Council. (1996). *National science education standards.* Washington, DC: National Academies Press.

National School Climate Center. (2014). School climate. Retrieved August 27, 2014, from *www.schoolclimate.org/climate.*

New York State Department of Education. (2014a). Educating the whole child engaging the whole school: Guidelines and resources for social and emotional development and learning (SEDL) in New York State. Retrieved February 6, 2014, from *www.p12.nysed.gov/sss/sedl/sedlguidelines.pdf.*

New York State Department of Education. (2014b). Social/emotional development and learning (SEDL). Retrieved February 6, 2014, from *www.p12.nysed.gov/sss/sedl.*

Partnership for 21st Century Skills. (2011). Framework for 21st century learning. Retrieved August 1, 2013, from *www.p21.org/storage/documents/1.__p21_framework_2-pager.pdf.*

Partnership for 21st Century Skills. (2013). 21st Century student outcomes and support systems. Retrieved August 1, 2013, from *www.p21.org/index.php.*

Payton, J. W., Graczyk, P. A., Wardlaw, D. M., Bloodworth, M., Tompsett, C. J., & Weissberg, R. P. (2000). Social and emotional learning: A framework for promoting mental health and reducing risk behavior in children and youth. *Journal of School Health, 70*, 179–185.

Pellegrino, J. W., & Hilton, M. L. (Eds.). (2012). *Education for life and work: Developing transferable knowledge and skills in the 21st century* (Committee on Defining Deeper Learning and 21st Century Skills, Board on Testing and Assessment and Board on Science Education, Division of Behavioral and Social Sciences and Education). Washington, DC: National Academies Press & National Research Council.

Pennsylvania Department of Education. (2012, April 25). Pennsylvania Standards for Student Interpersonal Skills: Grades PreK–12. Retrieved January 30, 2014, from *http://static.pdesas.org/content/documents/student_interpersonal_skills_standards.pdf.*

Schweinhart, L. J., Montie, J., Xiang, Z., Barnett, W. S., Belfield, C. R., & Nores, M. (2005). *Lifetime effects: The High/Scope Perry Preschool Study through age 40.* Ypsilanti, MI: High Scope Press.

Scott-Little, C., Kagan, S. L., & Frelow, V. S. (2006). Conceptualization of readiness and the content of early learning standards: The intersection of policy and research? *Early Childhood Research Quarterly 21*, 153–173.

Scott-Little, C., Lesko, J., Martella, J., & Millburn, P. (2007). Early learning standards: Results from a national survey to document trends in state-level policies and practices. *Early Childhood Research and Practice, 9.* Retrieved August 1, 2013, from *http://ecrp.uiuc.edu/v9n1/little.html.*

State of New Jersey. (2014). Department of Education 21st Century Life and Careers Standards Learning Progressions. Retrieved February 6,

2014, from *www.state.nj.us/education/cccs/progressions/9.*

State of Washington, Office of Superintendent of Public Instruction. (2005). Communication learning standards. Retrieved August 27, 2014, from *www.k12.wa.us/curriculuminstruct/communications/standards/default.aspx.*

Tennessee Department of Education. (2014). Service-learning standards. Retrieved August 27, 2014, from *www.state.tn.us/education/ci/service/doc/sl_grades_9-12.pdf.*

Tout, K., Halle, T., Daily, S., Albertson-Junkans, L., & Moodie, S. (2013). *The research base for a birth through age eight state policy framework.* Bethesda, MD: Child Trends.

Washington State Department of Early Learning. (2014). Washington State Early Learning and Development Guidelines Birth through 3rd Grade 2012. Retrieved January 30, 2014, from *www.del.wa.gov/publications/development/docs/guidelines.pdf.*

Weissberg, R. P., & Greenberg, M. T. (1998). School and community competence-enhancement and prevention programs. In W. Damon (Series Ed.), I. E. Sigel & K. A. Renninger (Vol. Eds.), *Handbook of child psychology: Vol 4. Child psychology in practice* (5th ed., pp. 877–954). New York: Wiley.

West Virginia Department of Education. (2014). Content Standards and Objectives Policies. Retrieved February 6, 2014, from *http://wvde.state.wv.us/policies/csos.html.*

Yoshikawa, H., Weiland, C., Brooks-Gunn, J., Burchinal, M. R., Espinosa, L., Gormley, L. T., et al. (2013). *Investing in our future: The evidence base on preschool education.* Ann Arbor, MI: Society for Research in Child Development. Retrieved October 26, 2013, from *http://fcd-us.org/sites/default/files/evidence%20base%20on%20preschool%20education%20final.pdf.*

Zins, J. E., Bloodworth, M. R., Weissberg, R. P., & Walberg, H. J. (2004). The scientific base linking emotional learning to student success and academic outcomes. In J. E. Zins, R. P. Weissberg, M. C. Wang, & H. J. Walberg (Eds.), *Building academic success on social and emotional learning: What does the research say?* (pp. 3–22). New York: Teachers College Press.

Zins, J. E., & Elias, M. J. (2006). Social and emotional learning. In G. G. Bear & K. M. Minke (Eds.), *Children's needs III: Development, prevention, and intervention* (pp. 1–13). Bethesda, MD: National Association of School Psychologists.

Zins, J., Payton, J. W., Weissberg, R. P., & O'Brien, M. U. (2007). Social and emotional learning and successful school performance. In G. Matthews, M. Zeidner, & R. D. Roberts (Eds.), *Emotional intelligence: Knowns and unknowns* (pp. 376–395). New York: Oxford University Press.

CHAPTER 36

Federal Policy Initiatives and Children's SEL

Martha Zaslow, Bonnie Mackintosh, Sarah Mancoll, and Sarah Mandell

Our purpose in this chapter is to describe federal policy initiatives that seek to foster children's social and emotional learning (SEL). We discuss several different federal policy "levers," including (1) social policy through Congressional legislative initiatives, (2) social policy through Executive Branch initiatives aimed at informing practice in schools and in other important settings for children (e.g., children's experiences during out-of-school time), and (3) science policy as manifested through the funding of research and setting standards for research.

A theme throughout this chapter is that federal policy initiatives using these three policy levers tend to focus narrowly on reducing problem behaviors and to do so in specific targeted populations. SEL programs certainly aim to reduce problem behaviors, and the evidence is clear that they are effective in addressing this goal. However, they also aim to strengthen positive social and emotional skills, and to do so universally, for all children in a school or early care and education program, extending such approaches through more intensive work with those showing deficits in social and emotional learning. This chapter points to some policy initiatives that do take the more encompassing approach of SEL programs, while identifying an overall tendency in federal policy initiatives to focus more narrowly on the reduction of problem behaviors in specific populations, and therefore on only one of a broader set of goals in SEL programs.

We begin this chapter by briefly recapitulating the distinctive features of SEL programs. Although other chapters in this book have provided similar introductions, a very brief summary is important here to make clear the distinction we will be following between federal policy initiatives that we do and do not see as focusing on the more encompassing and universal SEL approaches. We then turn to each of the three policy levers noted earlier, summarizing first the efforts clearly aimed at fostering more encompassing SEL approaches, and then providing examples of efforts focused more narrowly on reducing problem behaviors in specific populations. Although the more delimited and targeted approaches address an important subset of SEL skills, they are not anticipated to achieve the full set of benefits of the more encompassing approaches unless they complement universal and more broadly focused SEL programs. We conclude with a discussion of possible approaches to extending federal policy efforts focusing on SEL.

Distinctive Features of SEL Approaches

Central to this chapter is that SEL programs are proactive, focusing on the development of positive skills across the full spectrum of key social and emotional competencies, as well as the reduction of problem behaviors:

> Many programs related to children's social and emotional development focus on a single problem or issue such as preventing substance use. SEL, however, is an inclusive approach that covers the entire spectrum of social and emotional competencies that help children to be resilient and successful learners. (Collaborative for Academic, Social, and Emotional Learning, 2007)

Reviews of the research on social and emotional competencies have conceptualized and organized the SEL competencies in somewhat differing ways (see discussion of conceptualizations in Durlak, Weissberg, Domitrovich, & Gullotta, Chapter 1, this volume; Jones & Bouffard, 2012). However, one useful distinction is viewing SEL skills in terms of their primary focus on self, on others, or on decision making (which often involves both self and others) (Payton et al., 2000). Regarding self, competencies first involve self-awareness (recognition of one's own feelings and how they affect behavior, a sense of strengths and limitations), and then self-management (ability to regulate emotion, thought, and behavior effectively; e.g., controlling impulses, and setting and working toward goals). Regarding others, competencies again involve awareness (ability to understand and empathize with the perspectives of others, awareness of social and ethical norms), and then relating to others (forming and sustaining positive relationships with both adults and peers; using skills in listening, communication and cooperation effectively; managing conflict in constructive ways). Decision-making skills involve the ability to make constructive choices that take into account the consequences for self and others, ethical and social standards, and safety.

In considering federal policy, we also identify SEL approaches in light of the contexts in which they are implemented and the children they target. Many SEL programs are universal, targeting all children in a setting such as school, with the aim of fostering the skills noted earlier. Complementing universal approaches, more targeted efforts may then be addressed to those showing difficulties with SEL skills:

> The focus of most SEL programs is universal prevention and promotion, that is, preventing behavior problems by promoting social and emotional competence—rather than direct intervention. Smaller numbers of students may require moderate to intensive treatment that focuses on social–emotional competence, but SEL programming is intended to enhance the growth of all children, to help them develop healthy behaviors, and to prevent their engaging in maladaptive and unhealthy behaviors. (Zins & Elias, 2006, p. 2)

Jones and Bouffard (2012) indicate that there is much more widespread implementation and evaluation of SEL approaches in elementary school than in middle or high school, with a clear need to extend programming and research to older children and adolescents. They also note that it is interesting that programming and research to date start primarily in the elementary school grades, despite strong recognition of the need to support social and emotional development in the earliest years.

The review of effective SEL programs conducted by the Collaborative for Academic, Social, and Emotional Learning (CASEL; 2012) distinguishes among three distinct ways such programs are integrated into schools: (1) through a separate set of lesson plans and intentional instruction focusing on social and emotional skills; (2) through integration of goals for SEL into ongoing instruction in core academic subjects; and (3) through fostering positive teacher practices within classrooms throughout the day. These different approaches in applying SEL programming are important because as Jones and Bouffard (2012) caution, in some cases, students may be exposed to limited "dosages" of freestanding curricula (as little as half an hour a month). They also caution that SEL skills may not generalize fully unless they are monitored and supported in multiple settings, going beyond the classroom to include also hallways and transition times, recess, cafeteria, the bus, and bathroom. Jones and Bouffard hold that in order to affect school culture, SEL approaches need to permeate both instructional and noninstructional times in school settings.

A recent meta-analysis of the effectiveness of 213 studies of differing SEL programs implemented in schools found that, compared to controls, students who participated in SEL programs had significantly more positive attitudes about self and school, more positive social behaviors, lower levels of conduct problems and emotional distress. When SEL programs were implemented by school staff members, they also had higher levels of academic performance in terms of both grades and test scores. Program implementation also emerged as important in the meta-analysis: Effects of SEL programs were stronger when the programs were well implemented. Specifically, more effective programs were characterized by implementation of a sequenced set of activities that actively targeted a specific set of SEL skills (Durlak, Weissberg, Dymnicki, Taylor, & Schellinger, 2011).

In summary, this overview of the distinctive features of SEL approaches suggests that as we turn to consideration of federal policy, we should highlight those initiatives that focus on *proactive and preventive* programs, implemented *universally*, schoolwide, and that seek to foster the *full range of social and emotional skills* in all students. As we have noted, SEL approaches recommend complementing universal and broadly focused SEL programs with extensions specifically for those showing elevated levels of problem behavior. However, as will be seen, in many instances, programs for children with problem behaviors are being implemented and evaluated apart from a universally targeted and broadly focused SEL program in the same setting.

Legislative Branch Initiatives

Troubling and even tragic occurrences of bullying and violence in schools have provided the impetus for multiple legislative proposals focusing on these specific problems. Legislative proposals clearly focusing on SEL approaches and fulfilling the criteria noted earlier, seeking to foster positive social skills throughout the population of a school, while providing more intensive intervention for those already showing elevated problem behavior, have been less common than initiatives seeking only to diminish problem behaviors in targeted populations. Nevertheless, it is noteworthy that there has been some attention in Congress to the universal and more encompassing SEL approaches. In this section, we first describe the legislative initiatives that focus on universal SEL approaches aimed at the full set of key SEL outcomes (with the goal of both strengthening positive and reducing negative behaviors among all students, and providing more intensive components for those at risk). We then provide illustrative examples of the more frequently occurring targeted and problem-focused legislative initiatives.

Initiatives with Goals That Align with the Distinctive Features of SEL Programs

On July 7, 2011, H.R. 2437, the Academic, Social, and Emotional Learning Act of 2011, was introduced in the House of Representatives as part of efforts toward reauthorization of the Elementary and Secondary Education Act (ESEA), also known as No Child Left Behind (NCLB). The House Education and Workforce Committee had jurisdiction over H.R. 2437, and the bill had bipartisan sponsorship from within the committee, including sponsorship by both Judy Biggert (R–IL) and Dale Kildee (D–MI), both of whom completed their service in Congress in January 2013 (H.R. 2437—112th Congress: Academic, Social, and Emotional Learning Act of 2011, 2011).

The specific wording of the bill leaves no uncertainty about its focus on SEL approaches in schools. Indeed, the wording of the bill provides an illustration of the growing focus on evidence-based practices in legislative proposals, including a summary of research in the bill language. More specifically, the bill notes that

> Congress makes the following findings: (a) To succeed in school, students need to be engaged. They need to know how to maintain focus and effort in the face of setbacks, work effectively with others, and be good communicators and problem-solvers. (b) Social and emotional skills form a foundation for young people's success not just in school, but as healthy and caring adults, productive workers, and engaged citizens. (c) Not only can these skills be taught,

> they can be taught by regular classroom teachers in schools of every type to students of every background. (d) Academic outcomes resulting from social and emotional learning include greater motivation to learn and commitment to school, increased time devoted to schoolwork and mastery of subject matter, improved attendance, graduation rates, grades, and test scores. (e) These positive outcomes increase in students who are involved in social and emotional learning programming by an average of 11 percentile points over students who are not involved in such programming. (f) Social and emotional learning programming also results in reduced problem behavior, improved health outcomes, a lower rate of violent delinquency, and a lower rate of heavy alcohol use. (H.R. 2437—112th Congress: Academic, Social, and Emotional Learning Act of 2011, 2011)

This legislation proposed amending the ESEA by expanding the section on teacher and principal training to call for their preparation in practices supporting the social and emotional development of students on approaches with demonstrated effectiveness, such as through SEL programming shown to have positive effects. The bill went on to define SEL programs as those in which social and emotional skills are "taught, modeled, practiced, and applied so that students use them as part of their daily behavior" and where these skills help to prevent problems such as substance use, violence, and bullying and help to create "safe and caring learning environments that foster participation, engagement, and connection to learning and school" (H.R. 2437—112th Congress: Academic, Social, and Emotional Learning Act of 2011, 2011). Following introduction of the bill in July 2011, bipartisan support grew and the bill eventually had 22 cosponsors (14 Democrats, eight Republicans). However, the bill was referred to committee and did not proceed further.

Subsequent legislative proposals for ESEA reauthorization in 2011 and 2012 in the Senate and House made specific references to SEL. In October 2011, Senator Tom Harkin (D–IA and Chairman of the Health, Education, Labor and Pensions [HELP] Committee) announced that the committee had reached bipartisan agreement on a draft of ESEA reauthorization (S. 3578—112th Congress: Elementary and Secondary Education Reauthorization Act of 2011, 2011). The agreed-upon draft included the goal of fostering positive learning conditions in public schools and specifically listed developing social and emotional competencies as key activities for creating such conditions, for example, "helping staff and students to model positive social and emotional skills." In addition, in February 2012, House Education and Workforce Committee Chairman John Kline (R–MN) introduced the Student Success Act (H.R. 3989—112th Congress: Student Success Act of 2012, 2012). This legislation called for strengthening teacher understanding and skills in evidence-based strategies for improving student academic achievement, "including through addressing the social and emotional development needs of students."

After a period of intense focus, progress on reauthorization of ESEA in Congress slowed substantially after House and Senate committees came forward with widely differing proposals. Attention on ESEA has also shifted to Executive Branch activities. As we discuss further in the section of this chapter on Executive Branch initiatives, in September 2011, the Obama Administration released a plan to offer waivers from current requirements under ESEA, giving flexibility in the design of accountability and assessment systems for student achievement (U.S. Department of Education, 2013b). Much of the subsequent focus on ESEA reauthorization has been on the requirements for waivers under ESEA flexibility, and state approaches to implementation of the waivers.

However, in May 2013, Representative Tim Ryan (D–OH) reintroduced the Academic, Social, and Emotional Learning Act described earlier. At that time, H.R. 1875, the Academic, Social and Emotional Learning Act of 2013, was assigned to the House Education and the Workforce Committee, Subcommittee on Early Childhood, Elementary and Secondary Education, which had the discretion to send it on to the full House or Senate (H.R. 1875—113th Congress: Academic, Social, and Emotional Learning Act of 2013, 2013). However, no further action has been taken.

Beyond ESEA reauthorization, legislative initiatives in response to the tragedy in Newtown, Connecticut have also provided a context for proposals that reflect the combination in SEL approaches of universal supports for SEL and targeted approaches aimed at helping those with SEL deficits. In April 2013, the Senate agreed to add mental health amendments to gun control legislation. A mental health amendment offered by Senators Tom Harkin (D–IA) and Lamar Alexander (R–TN) included Title I, focusing on schoolwide prevention efforts involving positive behavioral interventions and supports, and encouraging school-based mental health partnerships; and Title II, focusing on suicide prevention, helping children recover from traumatic events, mental health awareness for teachers, and assessing barriers to integrating behavioral health and primary care. It must be acknowledged that this amendment called primarily for reauthorizing existing programs at the Departments of Health and Human Services and Education. However, the bipartisan support the amendment received in the Senate reflects an acknowledgment of the need to focus on mental health services for children, including preventive efforts aimed at supporting positive behaviors, as well as treatment approaches. Gun control legislation stalled in the Senate, and with it consideration of these specific proposals.

In the 113th Congress, a further legislative proposal directly related to SEL was introduced in the House on April 29, 2014, by Representative Susan Davis (D-CA). H.R. 4509, the Supporting Emotional Learning Act (H.R. 4509, 113th Congress: Supporting Emotional Learning Act, 2014), aimed to amend the Education Sciences Reform Act of 2002 by requiring research and teacher professional development on social and emotional learning. More specifically, under the bill the National Center for Education Research would be required to conduct research on social and emotional education, and the Commissioner for Education Research would be required to support research on social and emotional skills. The bill would require preparation for teachers on evidence-based teaching methods and assessment tools for social and emotional learning. It would also amend the Higher Education Act of 1965 by requiring highly qualified teachers to have the background needed to understand, use, and develop social and emotional learning programming. The bill gives a specific definition of social and emotional learning that clearly aligns with definitions provided in the research literature, including self-awareness and self-management skills, social awareness and relationship skills, and responsible decision making. On June 13, 2014, this bill was referred to the Subcommittee on Early Childhood, Elementary and Secondary Education of the House Education and the Workforce Committee. However, no further steps have been taken.

Those who have studied the linkages between research and policy argue that we often look only for the passage of legislation to signal that research has had an effect on policy. However another important way the influence of research is evident is through changing the foundational assumptions or conceptualizations on an important issue among policymakers (Tseng, 2012). An example of this more foundational function of research in policymaking is the greater acknowledgment by policymakers and the public of the importance of the early years for brain development and in laying the foundation for learning in elementary school. The inclusion of references to the research on SEL in multiple legislative proposals in Congress in recent years raises the possibility that there is growing awareness of the influence of this aspect of student functioning on academic achievement, student well-being and long-term development, and school climate. This understanding, in turn, may provide a foundational conceptualization for future specific legislative proposals.

If a foundational conceptualization of SEL as being important to student achievement and general well-being is to be shared and sustained, it will be important to continue to expose policymakers to the evidence for SEL as the research continues to grow. Efforts such as a Congressional briefing on SEL, held in September 2012, provide such opportunities. At this briefing, Representative Judy Biggert, then a Republican representative from Illinois, and Representative Tim Ryan (D–OH), underscored their sense of the importance of SEL in preparing children not just for school but also for later life. Roger Weissberg, the President and CEO of the Collaborative for Academic, Social, and Emotional Learning (CASEL; 2012), presented the recently released summary profiling effective SEL programs developed by the organization, and teachers from a school in Representative Biggert's district discussed their experiences in implementing one of the evidence-based programs, describing more collaborative classroom interactions that facilitated more effective teaching and learning strategies. Recurrent outreach to Congressional representatives and their staff members to update them about the most recent evidence on SEL will be important given that some Congressional offices with an interest in SEL, including that of Representative Biggert, have experienced turnover. Evidence on SEL will need to be introduced to new members of Congress and their staff members as well.

In summary, we have seen some legislative proposals with goals that align closely with the distinctive features of SEL programs. However, these proposals have thus far stalled. Further efforts could be directed at encouraging a more widespread foundational understanding of the evidence on SEL approaches in order to lay the groundwork for effective legislative proposals.

Initiatives with a Sole Focus on Problem Behavior in Targeted Populations

During the period discussed earlier, spanning 2011 through 2014, when several legislative proposals in the U.S. Congress made references to the importance of and evidence for SEL programs, a larger number of legislative proposals focused on problem behaviors that may be seen as reflecting deficits in social and emotional development. Specific legislative proposals were introduced to address bullying, to help school staff members address conflicts in schools, to provide mental health supports in schools, to address discrimination based on sexual orientation or gender identity, and to curb physical punishment. These, too, remained at the level of initial legislative proposals and were not passed into law, but the number of such bills suggests that there is a stronger focus in Congress on addressing problems in youth behavior than on working earlier, proactively, and universally to prevent problems and to promote positive social skills. Examples of legislative proposals taking a problem-focused approach from 2011 through 2014 include the following:

- On January 25, 2011, Representative Steven Cohen (D–TN) introduced the Restorative Justice in Schools Act of 2011. The proposed legislation would amend the ESEA to allow local educational agencies to use specific funds for professional development to train school staff in conflict resolution and restorative justice approaches (H.R. 415—112th Congress: Restorative Justice in Schools Act of 2011, 2011). On February 17, 2011, Representative Grace Napolitano (D–CA) introduced the Mental Health in Schools Act of 2011. This legislative proposal would amend the Public Health Service Act to authorize competitive grants to local school districts to help them fund services taking public mental health approaches in schools. Such services would include assistance to children who had experienced or witnessed violence, and access to school-based mental health programs (H.R. 751—112th Congress: Mental Health in Schools Act of 2011, 2011).
- On March 10, 2011, Representative Jared Polis in the House (D–CO), and Senator Al Franken in the Senate (D–MN) introduced the Student Non-Discrimination Act of 2011. The bill would prohibit public school students from being excluded from participating in, or being subject to discrimination under, any federally assisted educational program because of actual or perceived sexual orientation or gender identity (H.R. 998—112th Congress: Student Non-Discrimination Act of 2011, 2011).
- On September 22, 2011, Representative Carolyn McCarthy (D–NY) introduced the Ending Corporal Punishment in Schools Act of 2011. This bill would prohibit the Secretary of Education from providing education funding to any educational agency or institution that allowed school personnel to inflict corporal punishment on a student in order to modify undesirable behavior (H.R. 3027—112th Congress: Ending Corporal Punishment in Schools Act of 2011, 2011).
- On June 28, 2012, the House Judiciary Committee passed the Juvenile Accountability and Bullying Prevention and Intervention Act of 2012 (H.R. 6019—112th Congress: Juvenile Accountability Block Grant Reauthorization and the Bullying Prevention and Intervention Act of 2012, 2012). The bill's

provisions included reauthorization and expansion of grant programs to address the occurrence of bullying, including cyberbullying, and for gang prevention programs.

- In 2013, the Safe Schools Improvement Act was introduced in the House and Senate, calling for the Secretary of Education to provide an independent biennial evaluation of programs and policies to address bullying and harassment in schools, and requiring the Commissioner for Education Statistics to collect state data to determine the incidence and frequency of conduct prohibited by local education agencies (LEAs), which would be directed to establish policies to prevent and prohibit bullying, harassment and other conduct that is severe, persistent, and pervasive enough to limit a student's ability to participate in or benefit from school programs, or that creates a hostile and abusive educational environment. LEAs would be required to provide an annual notice of the conduct prohibited in their discipline policies, grievance procedures, and annual data on the incidence and frequency of such conduct at school and LEA levels (S. 403—113th Congress: Safe Schools Improvement Act of 2013, 2013).

In the 113th Congress (2013–2014), Representative George Miller (D-CA) introduced the Keeping All Students Safe Act (H.R. 1893, 113th Congress: Keeping All Students Safe Act, 2013). This legislative proposal would direct the Secretary of the Department of Education to set standards that would prohibit the use of physical restraint or seclusion in elementary and secondary schools as well as any behavioral intervention that could compromise students' health and safety. The bill also calls for awarding grants to states and local education agencies to establish and implement policies on these standards and to improve data collection and analysis on the use of physical restraint and seclusion. While focusing heavily on the issue of restraint and seclusion as problematic school practices, the bill also called for grants to states and local educational agencies for the implementation of positive behavior supports.

SEL programs have the dual goals of enhancing positive social behaviors *and* minimizing negative behaviors. Indeed, the meta-analysis examining the effects of SEL programs on the behavior of children and youth documents overall effects on aggressive behavior problems. It is recommended that SEL programs build in more intensive components for children at high risk of serious behavior problems (see, e.g., the work of the Conduct Problems Prevention Research Group, 2011, summarizing the results of the targeted and intensive Fast Track intervention complementing the universally implemented Promoting Alternative Thinking Strategies [PATHS] program). An important legislative development will be a greater focus on legislative proposals that aim both to strengthen positive and diminish problematic social behaviors among all students, and that provide additional, more intensive SEL opportunities for students at high risk.

Executive Branch Initiatives Focused on Practice

We turn now from legislative proposals in Congress to the activities of the Executive Branch in implementing specific laws or launching initiatives that fall within the broad authorization of a specific agency. We focus below on Executive Branch initiatives aimed at strengthening practice in educational and other key settings for children's development. As in the section on Legislative Branch initiatives, we distinguish between universal programs that target the full range of social and emotional skills, and those that focus more narrowly on children showing problem behaviors tied to deficits in social and emotional skills. We also discuss Executive Branch initiatives that target settings other than schools, the primary focus of SEL programs.

Initiatives with Goals That Align with Universal and Broadly Focused SEL Programs

As noted earlier, an important development pertaining to federal policy related to SEL is the shift from Legislative Branch activity to Executive Branch activity in the implementation of changes to ESEA. In the absence of agreement in Congress on how to proceed, and requirements of NCLB regarding progress toward achievement goals set for 2014, the Obama Administration decided to take action through state waivers, which were permitted under the legislation already in place. Those states awarded waivers have greater flexibility in addressing the existing goals of ESEA. For example, states with waivers are permitted to develop new annual measurable objectives when determining adequate yearly progress (AYP). At present, 43 states and the District of Columbia have been approved for waivers under the ESEA Flexibility initiative of the Obama Administration (U.S. Department of Education, Elementary and Secondary Education: ESEA Flexibility, 2014a).

In the present context, it is important to note that requirements for a state ESEA waiver include adhering to principles for turning around low-performing schools that encompass a focus on school climate and support for social and emotional skills in students. More specifically, the turnaround principles include "establishing a school environment that improves school safety and discipline and addressing other non-academic factors that impact student achievement, such as students' social, emotional, and health needs" (U.S. Department of Education, 2012a, p. 10). We see here a clear acceptance of the link between SEL and achievement. There have been several schoolwide SEL initiatives that could serve the purpose of overall school improvement as needed in turning around low-performing schools. We do note, however, that this assumption of a link between SEL and school achievement is referred to specifically for turning around low-performing schools and is not articulated as being foundational across all of the requirements for ESEA Flexibility.

Although the U.S. Department of Education indicated a priority for working with states on ESEA Flexibility, the Department does have the authority to grant waivers at the district level as well. In March 2013, a decision was made to give careful consideration to a waiver request from a consortium of eight California districts as part of the California Office to Reform Education (CORE). As the U.S. Department of Education (2013a) noted, these eight districts together serve 1.2 million students, which is more than most states. After review of the application from this consortium in August 2013, the U.S. Department of Education (2013b) approved the waiver.

The waiver proposal from the California districts focuses heavily on SEL and school climate, specifying that 40% of the School Quality Improvement goal will focus on these two areas (U.S. Department of Education, 2013c). The proposal notes that the participating districts "agree that monitoring and promoting students' non-cognitive skills is an indispensable factor in ensuring the preparation of college- and career-ready graduates. Including non-cognitive skills in the School Quality Improvement System is strongly supported by research. . . .The Participating LEAs [local education agencies] will examine the research and existing measures in the field to determine the best measures or indicators for use" (p. 94). Furthermore, "to create optimum conditions for student learning, the Participating LEAs acknowledge that school environment and student engagement must be continuously analyzed and nurtured to ensure safe and equitable learning experiences for all students" (p. 94).

It will be important to learn from the experiences of the CORE districts in identifying measures of SEL and school climate, in tracking these measures over time, and using the data as indicators of school improvement.

In addition to ESEA Flexibility, a further Executive Branch initiative whose focus aligns very closely with the distinctive features of SEL is a program jointly administered by the Departments of Education, Justice, and Health and Human Services called Safe Schools/Healthy Students (the website for this initiative is housed by the Substance Abuse and Mental Health Services Administration [SAMHSA] at *www.sshs.samhsa.gov*). It is noteworthy, particularly in the aftermath of the tragic school shootings in Newtown, Connecticut, that this initiative has its origins in school shootings in the late 1990s. Four-year grants are awarded to school districts to work in partnership with juvenile justice agencies and mental health providers on projects focusing on (1) safe school environments and violence prevention activities; (2) alcohol, tobacco, and other drug prevention activities; (3) student behavioral, social, and emotional supports;

(4) mental health services; and (5) early childhood SEL programs. Although grants are funded for periods of 4 years, in many instances, the collaborations initiated when applying for funding are sustained after the funding period has ended.

Grantees of the Safe Schools/Healthy Students initiative have access to programmatic training and technical assistance in the five priority areas. The primary technical assistance specialist assigned to each grantee is available in person or remotely to develop a technical assistance plan and to address needs as they emerge. Technical assistance specialists have both substantive expertise (e.g., in education, mental health, juvenile justice) and in effective program implementation. Training and technical assistance resources available to all grantees include a webinar series on supportive school discipline and presentations on topics such as strategies to support the social, emotional, and behavioral needs of students, and on positive school climate and academic excellence. This initiative clearly has not only an explicit SEL focus but also the proactive and preventive universal approach of SEL programs.

As a further example, in August 2012, the U.S. Department of Education's Office of Safe and Healthy Students organized a conference on Building and Sustaining Capacity to Improve Conditions for Learning. The meeting focused on multiple issues related to establishing positive school climate, including behavioral health, school safety, approaches to discipline and to address bullying and gender-based violence. Secretary of Education Arne Duncan focused his comments on links between school climate and student performance. The meeting was intended to provide input into the Department of Education's future efforts to address school climate. As noted by Jones and Bouffard (2012), changing school climate is a key goal of SEL programs.

While our focus in this section has been primarily on elementary and secondary schools, we would be remiss if we failed to note the strong focus on social and emotional skills, along with cognitive skills, in federal funding for early care and education, including Head Start (Advisory Committee on Head Start Research and Evaluation, 2012) and the recently awarded state Preschool Development Grants (U.S. Department of Education, 2014b).

Practice-Focused Initiatives That Align Less Closely with the Full Set of SEL Features

A number of critically important Executive Branch initiatives focus on social and emotional development; however, they do not fully align with the complete set of features of SEL approaches. These programs may be rooted in concern with specific problematic behaviors, may be implemented in settings other than schools, or may focus only on a delimited (though key) population. In discussing the lack of full alignment of these initiatives with SEL approaches, our intent is not to critique these extremely valuable initiatives. Rather, we ask whether introducing more elements of SEL approaches might extend these initiatives in important ways. Indeed, the number of Executive Branch initiatives with a strong focus on social and emotional *development* is worthy of recognition, without regard to the match or mismatch with the specific features of SEL approaches.

An example of a critically important initiative that makes reference to and draws upon but that does not fully align with the features of SEL programs is the *stopbullying.gov* website, a collaborative effort of the U.S. Department of Education and the U.S. Department of Health and Human Services (n.d.[b]; managed by the latter) that provides resources for youth, children, parents, educators, and community members to address bullying. The website includes information, presented in nontechnical language, to help target groups understand what bullying is, what cyberbullying is, who is affected by bullying, what can be undertaken to stop bullying, and how to get help in addressing bullying. The website makes available a series of podcasts on bullying, an analysis of state laws on bullying completed by the U.S. Department of Education, Office of Planning, Evaluation and Policy Development, Policy and Program Studies Service (2011), and profiles of anti-bullying programs. A helpline is made available for those who feel that they are in an urgent situation. Although focusing specifically on the narrow outcome area of bullying rather than the full range of social and emotional skills, the materials made available through the website do point to SEL approaches aimed at school climate as one approach to address bullying (see section on Prevention at School on *stopbullying.gov* website). Furthermore, school climate is broadly defined, including settings outside of the classroom. Indeed, a recent initiative made available through the website focuses on providing to school bus drivers the tools to address bullying (U.S. Department of Education & U.S. Department of Health and Human Services (n.d.[a]).

A very strong commitment to the positive social and emotional development of children and youth is apparent in the Information Memorandum made available on April 17, 2012, by the U.S. Department of Health and Human Services Administration on Children, Youth and Families (ACYF) on Promoting Social and Emotional Well-Being for Children and Youth Receiving Child Welfare Services (U.S. Department of Health and Human Services, Administration for Children and Families, 2012). The memorandum articulates the priority placed by ACYF on social and emotional well-being specifically for children in the child welfare system, seeks to encourage child welfare agencies to work toward improving these outcomes, and identifies specific policy steps that can assist in working toward this goal. The memorandum notes:

> While it is important to consider the overall well-being of children who have experienced abuse and neglect, a focus on the social and emotional aspects of well-being can significantly improve outcomes for these children while they are receiving child welfare services and after their cases have closed. . . .Research that has emerged in recent years has suggested that most of the adverse effects of maltreatment are concentrated in behavioral, social, and emotional domains. The problems that children develop in these areas have negative impacts that ripple across the lifespan, limiting children's chances to succeed in school, work, and relationships. Integrating these findings into policies, programs, and practices is the logical next step for child welfare systems to increase the sophistication of their approach to improving outcomes for children and their families. There is also an emerging body of evidence for interventions that address the behavioral, social, and emotional impacts of maltreatment.

The memorandum provides summaries of key research findings on the importance of addressing the social and emotional development of children in the child welfare system, and of intervention approaches to strengthen their development. It identifies strategies to align existing policies and requirements to focus on social and emotional development, including the goals of providing training for the staff in child welfare agencies in how to identify child social and emotional well-being issues, implementing trauma screenings and functional assessments on the impacts of exposure to maltreatment, scaling up evidence-based interventions, and scaling back and eliminating interventions that are not supported by evidence. Evidence-based SEL programs implemented in the schools that children in the child welfare system attend would be an appropriate approach to addressing their social and emotional well-being, particularly if complemented by more intensive SEL skills development for children at risk. It would be important to consider how more intensive SEL supports might be provided for children in the child welfare system without segregating or stigmatizing them. Perhaps the complementary and more intensive component could be provided with and through foster families or group homes.

Another Executive Branch initiative that includes a broad focus on social and emotional development, though not on SEL program approaches in particular, is the Maternal, Infant, and Early Childhood Home Visiting (MIECHV) program, which was authorized in 2010 as part of the Patient Protection and Affordable Care Act (Health Resources and Services Administration, 2013). The program, authorized and funded at $1.5 billion from 2010 through 2014 and then extended for an additional year, provides states with grants to plan, implement, and/or expand their home visiting services for families who live in at-risk communities. Although home visiting programs take different forms, they generally pair families that are expecting or have very young children with trained liaisons who meet with families in the home to address issues such as positive parenting practices, home safety, maternal and child health, and access to services. MIECHV requires that state grantees utilize evidence-based program models and/or promising program models and identifies a number of desired outcomes for the program, one of which is "improvements in child health and development, including the prevention of child injuries and maltreatment and improvements in cognitive, language, social–emotional, and physical developmental indicators" (Patient Protection and Affordable Care Act, 2010). Each state grantee has its own mix of vevidence-based and promising program model approaches. For example, Arizona uses the Nurse–Family Partnership, Healthy Families America, and Family Spirit models, whereas the Maine Families program uses the Parents as Teachers model.

Race to the Top (RTT) is another federal program that makes reference to the importance of social and emotional development without a particular focus on SEL programs. RTT, which has received $4.35 billion in funding since it was authorized as part of the American Recovery and Reinvestment Act of 2009, provides competitive funding for states around four areas of reform: (1) developing rigorous standards and better assessments; (2) adopting better data systems to provide educators and parents with information on student progress; (3) supporting teachers and administrators in becoming more effective; and (4) increasing emphasis and resources on the rigorous interventions needed to turn around the lowest performing schools (*www.whitehouse.gov/issues/education/k-12/race-to-the-top*) (RTT, n.d.). One of the priorities articulated in RTT is "Innovations for Improving Early Learning Outcomes." As stated in a Federal Register announcement calling for applications for RTT awards, "Of particular interest are proposals that support practices that (i) improve school readiness (including social, emotional, and cognitive); and (ii) improve the transition between preschool and kindergarten" (Overview Information; Race to the Top Fund; Notice Inviting Applications for New Awards for Fiscal year [FY] 2010, 2010, p. 19496).

We underscore the importance of each of the federal practice initiatives summarized in this section. Though they do not take the universal, school-based, proactive and preventive approach distinctive to SEL programs, they draw upon SEL approaches. Furthermore, there is clearly the potential to link with and make use of SEL approaches in these and multiple other federal initiatives seeking to address specific problems in social and emotional development, to address issues in key populations, or to work proactively with families at home rather than in a school setting. Indeed, Jones and Bouffard (2012), in their recommendations for policy responses to the evidence on SEL, call for establishing incentives for integrating SEL approaches into existing initiatives. They point specifically to this as a potential strategy for Title I education funding, Promise Neighborhoods, and the Supportive School Discipline Initiative. Such an approach would involve awarding additional points to grant proposals that incorporate plans to implement evidence-based SEL programs. A review of the federal practice-focused initiatives for which meaningful links with SEL programs could potentially exist would be a valuable contribution.

Interest in finding ways to link SEL approaches with existing federal practice-focused initiatives was apparent at a set of Executive Branch briefings on the research on SEL. These briefings were sponsored by the Society for Research in Child Development on the occasion of the publication of a special edition of the journal *Child Development*, which focused heavily on SEL research and included the meta-analysis on SEL programs described earlier (Durlak et al., 2011). A first briefing for staff at the U.S. Departments of Health and Human Services and Education, held on March 21, 2011, was called "Recent Research on Approaches to Improving Children's Social and Emotional Well-Being: Progress and Next Steps." At this briefing, Kenneth Dodge provided a presentation addressing the question "Why focus on the research on SEL?"; Roger Weissberg summarized the findings of the meta-analysis that he had coauthored with Durlak and others described earlier; Stephanie Jones provided the perspective of SEL research that extends downward in age to the early years of development; and Patrick Tolan discussed methodological and substantive next steps for this area of research and its application. A request was made to repeat the briefing for senior staff at the U.S. Department of Education, and a second briefing was held there on June 20, 2011. At both briefings, questions focused on how to use the growing body of research on SEL to inform federally funded programs at each agency. These two briefings further underscore the potential for introducing SEL approaches into existing federally funded programs.

Executive Branch Initiatives Focused on Research

It is important to consider the key role of the Executive Branch in not only funding specific practice-focused initiatives but also deciding on directions for research, funding research, and disseminating research findings. Multiple Executive Branch agencies have played important roles in funding research involving the evaluation of SEL programs. Furthermore, as the emphasis within the federal government on using evidence to inform policy has grown (see e.g., the memo from the Executive Office of the President, Office of Management and Budget, 2012, calling on heads of federal agencies to rely on evidence in proposing their budgets), federal agencies have also taken important steps to summarize the research identifying evidence-based practices. Research on SEL programs is featured on multiple federal websites whose goal is to share information on evidence-based programs in accessible formats.

The science policy function of Executive Branch agencies, including determining the directions for research, identifying methodological standards, and allocating funding for research, is clearly also important to consider in a discussion of the role of federal policy in SEL. Just as in other sections of this chapter, however, although we find a focus specifically on broad and encompassing SEL programs in Executive Branch funding and dissemination of research, we also find substantial allocation of funding for research that is limited to a focus on problem behaviors in high-risk populations. As we have noted, SEL programs do seek to diminish problem behaviors (and there is evidence that SEL approaches are effective in doing so). Broader SEL programs, in which the focus is both on strengthening positive behaviors and diminishing problem behaviors, and doing so universally throughout a student population, can build in further supports for those showing SEL deficits. Thus, research focusing only on problem behavior in a target population, while critically important, misses the breadth of SEL program goals and the range of students such programs seek to benefit.

In addition, basic research tends to seek to understand the predictors to and outcomes of social and emotional development. Although such research does not involve evaluations of SEL programs, it can inform the development of these programs. Thus, much federally funded research focuses on only one of the multiple goals of SEL programs (reducing problem behaviors) rather than on the full range of social and emotional skills, or attempts to extend understanding of the skills that SEL programs aim to strengthen rather than evaluate SEL programs per se. In this section, we provide examples of federal funding of research focusing on evaluations of SEL programs, then illustrations of research focusing only on reducing problem behavior (which we conceive to be an important but delimited component of SEL programs) and understanding children's social and emotional development more broadly (which we view as foundational to SEL programs).

Examples of Federal Funding Involving Evaluations of SEL Programs

The entries in the *2013 CASEL Guide* profiling evidence-based SEL programs often build on a body of research rather than a single study. Many of the studies supporting the inclusion of specific evidence-based programs included in the guide, in turn, were funded by the federal government. Out of a larger group of possible illustrations, we briefly summarize here two programs from the CASEL guide for which studies have recently been supported by the federal government.

As a first illustration, the 4Rs (Reading, Writing, Respect, and Resolution) intervention has been evaluated with funding from the Institute of Education Sciences of the U.S. Department of Education, in collaboration with the Centers for Disease Control and Prevention of the U.S. Department of Health and Human Services and the William T. Grant Foundation. The 4Rs intervention falls into the category of SEL programs in which content aimed at building children's positive social and emotional skills is embedded within the academic curriculum. Teachers in kindergarten through fifth grade throughout a school "use high-quality children's literature as a springboard for helping students gain skills and understanding in the areas of handling anger, listening, assertiveness, cooperation, negotiation, mediation, building community, celebrating differences, and countering bias" (Brown, Jones, LaRusso, & Aber, 2010, p. 156). Teachers receive both initial training and ongoing coaching in implementing the lessons of a literacy curriculum with content focusing on social and emotional skills. The evaluation of the 4Rs intervention involved 82 classrooms in 18 schools, with nine schools randomly assigned to the intervention and nine to the control group. Outcomes were assessed at both classroom and student levels (Social and Character Development Research Consortium, 2010.

As a second illustration, the Responsive Classroom program integrates specific practices throughout the day in classrooms and schools rather than relying on a separate curriculum. Practices include classrooms regularly having a morning meeting; helping students to create rules for the classroom; engaging in collaborative problem solving; teachers communicating in ways that support active engagement in learning and self-discipline, and responding to misbehavior in ways that help children understand the consequences of their actions and develop self-control; and students having choices in learning activities and following learning formats that involve guided discovery. A randomized controlled trial involving 24 schools and following students over 3 years was conducted with funding from the Institute of Education Sciences within the U.S. Department of Education (Rimm-Kaufman et al., 2012).

A review of recent research funding by federal agencies points to further studies that could be considered evaluations of SEL programs. For example, a randomized controlled trial of the Academic and Behavioral Competencies Program, funded by the Institute of Education Sciences, was implemented in urban elementary schools with children in grades 1–5, many of whom were from low socioeconomic backgrounds (Social and Character Development Research Consortium, 2010). This program aims to enhance students' social competencies and behavior through the use of schoolwide discipline strategies, social skills development, tutoring and mediation, and it also includes a parent component. The evaluation seeks to assess students' social and emotional competence and academic achievement, in addition to school climate and instructional practices (Social and Character Development Research Consortium, 2010).

Some program materials developed with funding from federal agencies help to strengthen the focus on older students that is somewhat lacking in current SEL programs and evaluations. For example, the School Materials for a Mental Health Friendly Classroom Training Package was piloted in high schools. This approach, with funding from the SAMHSA within the U.S. Department of Health and Human Services, aimed to promote a healthy learning environment through instructional practices that take individual learning styles into account and that foster a positive classroom climate (SAMHSA, Center for Mental Health Services, 2004).

In addition to funding SEL evaluations, federal agencies also disseminate the evidence from selected evaluations on multiple federal websites. These websites seek to distill the results of technical research publications and reports and present them in a consistent and accessible format, providing links to descriptions of the programs and research results. The websites also articulate standards for the evaluation research and note the extent to which specific studies meet the standards. Entries in the What Works Clearinghouse (*www.whatworks.ed.gov*) cited in the Institute of Education Sciences (n.d.), the National Registry of Evidence-Based Programs and Practices (*www.nrepp.samhsa.gov*) cited in SAMHSA (2013), and the Model Program Guide of the Office of Juvenile Justice and Delinquency Prevention (*www.ojjdp.gov/mpg*) cited in the Office of Juvenile Justice and Delinquency Prevention (n.d.) all aim to assist practitioners in identifying and implementing evidence-based programs, and include programs that are also listed in the *2013 CASEL Guide* (CASEL, 2012), depending on the specific goals of the website and its articulated standards of research evidence.

Federally Funded Research Focusing on Children with SEL Challenges

We have noted that SEL programs, which are universal and implemented schoolwide, can be followed by or complemented with more targeted treatment approaches to strengthen the skills of children with difficulty or delays in their social and emotional development. One set of studies funded by the federal government evaluates such approaches. Some of these targeted approaches work with parents and their children, whereas others work in the school setting. Although some are intended to complement universal SEL programs, others are freestanding. An important issue is whether these more targeted programs work better when layered on top of universal SEL approaches. Within this context, social acceptance of children at risk may be an especially important area of child outcomes for consideration.

The longitudinal experimental evaluation of the Fast Track program, funded by the National Institute of Mental Health, is an example of a targeted intervention that involves complementing a universal SEL program (in this instance, the PATHS intervention) with more intensive work with children identified in kindergarten as being at high risk for developing conduct disorders (Conduct Problems Research Group, 2011). Families randomly assigned to the intervention group receive home visits with both parent training and tutoring and social skills training for the children (grades 1–5). Continued intervention in grades 6–10 is provided for those children and families who continue to need it. Results of this longitudinal study show reductions in conduct disorders for children participating in the intervention group in follow-ups at 3 and 10 years (Conduct Problems Research Group, 2011).

As an example of a program that is school-based, the Institute of Education Sciences funded a randomized controlled trial evaluating the SCERTS curriculum for K–2 students with autism spectrum disorders. The SCERTS program seeks to increase children's engagement in social interactions and language use in various settings, while also addressing challenges in social communication and self-regulation (Institute of Education Sciences, 2011).

Basic Research Aimed at Understanding Social and Emotional Development

A clear priority has also been placed by the federal government on strengthening our general understanding of children's social and emotional development and on measuring development in this domain. Interagency consortia have worked together to fund projects aimed at improving the measurement of children's social and emotional development and including measures of children's social and emotional development in national surveys. As one example, in 2005, the *Eunice Kennedy Shriver* National Institute of Child Health and Human Development, the Administration for Children and Families (ACF) within the U.S. Department of Health and Human Services, and the Office of Special Education and Rehabilitation Services of the U.S. Department of Education funded a set of grants to develop measures of school readiness in an interagency consortium (Griffin, 2011). Two of the six funded projects in the Interagency Consortium on Measures focused on the development and testing of measures related to the social and emotional domain: a measure of executive function (Ursache, Blair, Willoughby, Tunvall, & Soliman, 2011) and an observational measure of young children's social and emotional functioning (Denham, Bassett, Kalb & Mincic, 2011). A current project seeks to inform the Federal Interagency Forum on Child and Family Statistics on indicators of early childhood social and emotional well-being. With the participation of more than 20 federal agencies, the Forum prepares and disseminates *America's Children*, a report of key indicators of child well-being (Federal Interagency Forum on Child and Family Statistics, 2013). This project is seeking input on whether and how to report on measures of children's social and emotional development as part of interagency efforts.

Federal funding of research on children's social and emotional development that falls outside the parameters we have noted for research focusing on SEL programs is nevertheless quite important to the work focusing directly on SEL. For example, such research can contribute stronger measures of social and emotional development for inclusion in studies of SEL programs. Basic research on the foundations and later outcomes of social and emotional development can help in informing the development of specific approaches within SEL programs. Evaluations of interventions for children with problems in social and emotional development are needed, so that evidence-based targeted approaches can complement the universal approaches used by SEL programs.

Conclusion

This chapter has identified three policy levers as relevant to the development and implementation of evidence-based SEL programs: federal legislative initiatives, practice-focused initiatives, and setting priorities and standards for research. For each of these policy levers, we have noted that there are efforts focusing on SEL programs that target positive social and emotional skills, as well as problem behaviors, in the full population of students in schools or programs, and that can be complemented with more intensive efforts addressed at students at risk; efforts focusing solely on reducing problem behaviors in those already at risk, approaches that while in keeping with the goals of SEL programs are more narrow in terms of outcomes and population targeted; and efforts focusing on issues related to children's social and emotional development more broadly that can inform the development of SEL programs. Although all three approaches are important, we have identified the need for further focus on universal SEL programs that aim to affect the full range of social and emotional skills.

We have noted that many legislative initiatives focus on addressing serious problems in social and emotional development once they have occurred rather than taking proactive and preventive approaches. It will be important for researchers to stress that SEL programs show effects in the specific areas that problem-focused legislative proposals are seeking to address. For example, SEL programs have been shown to have effects in diminishing aggressive behavior. Furthermore, when used in combination with universal SEL programming in a school, such approaches hold greater potential of affecting overall school climate.

There is already interest in linking SEL approaches with other existing, federally funded, practice-focused initiatives. Following up on recommendations made by Jones and Bouffard (2012), this chapter notes the need both to inform such efforts and create incentives for making such linkages. For example, a policy brief could identify very specifically how SEL approaches could be incorporated as components of ongoing federally funded initiatives. Such a brief could then give specific examples of how incentives for incorporating such approaches could be structured.

Finally, in strengthening federal funding for SEL programs and evaluations, it will be important to take into account the standards of evidence now being articulated by federal agencies for both funding and dissemination of evaluation research. As reliance on evidence-based practices is increasingly emphasized within the federal government, we are seeing growing emphasis on both the rigor of evaluations and the specificity with which the methodology of evaluations is summarized in reports and publications. Addressing these standards will be increasingly important for continuing to strengthen the evidence on SEL approaches that support children's academic achievement, as well as their social and emotional development.

References

Advisory Committee on Head Start Research and Evaluation. (2012). Final report. Retrieved December 12, 2014, from *www.acf.hhs.gov/sites/default/files/opre/eval_final.pdf.*

Brown, J. L., Jones, S. M., LaRusso, M. D., & Aber, J. L. (2010). Improving classroom quality: Teacher influences and experimental impacts of the 4Rs program. *Journal of Educational Psychology, 102,* 153–167.

Collaborative for Academic, Social, and Emotional Learning (CASEL). (2007). Background on social and emotional learning (SEL). Retrieved January 13, 2013, from *www.casel.org/publications/what-is-sel.*

Collaborative for Academic, Social, and Emotional Learning (CASEL). (2012). *2013 CASEL guide: Effective social and emotional learning programs—Preschool and elementary school edition*. Chicago: Author.

Conduct Problems Prevention Research Group. (2011). The effects of the Fast Track preventive intervention on the development of conduct disorder across childhood. *Child Development, 82*, 331–345.

Denham, S. A., Bassett, H. H., Kalb, S. C., & Mincic, M. S. (2011, March). *Observing preschoolers' social–emotional behavior: Structure, foundations, and prediction of early school success*. Poster presented at the biennial meeting of the Society for Research in Child Development, Montreal, Canada.

Durlak, J. A., Weissberg, R. P., Dymnicki, A. G., Taylor, R. D., & Schellinger, K. B. (2011). The impact of enhancing students' social and emotional learning: A meta-analysis of school-based universal interventions. *Child Development, 82*(1), 405–432.

Executive Office of the President, Office of Management and Budget. (2012, May 18). Memorandum to the Heads of Executive Departments and Agencies: Use of Evidence and Evaluation in the 2014 Budget. Retrieved December 8, 2013, from *www.whitehouse.gov/sites/default/files/omb/memoranda/2012/m-12-14.pdf*.

Federal Interagency Forum on Child and Family Statistics. (2013). *America's children: Key national indicators of well-being, 2013*. Washington, DC: U.S. Government Printing Office.

Griffin, J. (2011, March 31). *Developing the next generation of preschool outcome measures: The Interagency School Readiness Measurement Consortium*. Poster presented at the biennial meeting of the Society for Research in Child Development, Montreal, Canada.

Health Resources and Services Administration. (2013). Maternal, Infant, and Early Childhood Home Visiting Program. Retrieved December 8, 2013, from *www.mchb.hrsa.gov/programs/homevisiting*.

H.R. 415—112th Congress: Restorative Justice in Schools Act of 2011. (2011). Retrieved December 8, 2013, from *www.govtrack.us/congress/bills/112/hr415*.

H.R. 751—112th Congress: Mental Health in Schools Act of 2011. (2011). Retrieved December 8, 2013, *from www.govtrack.us/congress/bills/112/hr751*.

H.R. 998—112th Congress: Student Non-Discrimination Act of 2011. (2011). Retrieved December 8, 2013, from *www.govtrack.us/congress/bills/112/hr998*.

H.R. 1875—113th Congress: Academic, Social, and Emotional Learning Act of 2013. (2013). Retrieved December 8, 2013, from *www.govtrack.us/congress/bills/113/hr1875*.

H.R. 1893—the 113th Congress: Keeping All Students Safe Act of 2013. (2013). Retrieved December 17, 2014, from *www.congress.gov/bill/113th-congress/house-bill/1893*.

H.R. 2437—112th Congress: Academic, Social, and Emotional Learning Act of 2011. (2011). Retrieved December 8, 2013, from *www.govtrack.us/congress/bills/112/hr2437*.

H.R. 3027—112th Congress: Ending Corporal Punishment in Schools Act of 2011. (2011). Retrieved December 8, 2013, from *www.govtrack.us/congress/bills/112/hr3027*.

H.R. 3989—112th Congress: Student Success Act. (2012). Retrieved December 8, 2013, from *www.govtrack.us/congress/bills/112/hr3989*.

H.R. 4509—113th Congress: Supporting Emotional Learning Act. (2014). Retrieved December 17, 2014, from *www.congress.gov/bill/113th-congress/house-bill/4509*.

H.R. 6019—112th Congress: Juvenile Accountability Block Grant Reauthorization and the Bullying Prevention and Intervention Act of 2012. (2012). Retrieved December 8, 2013, from *www.govtrack.us/congress/bills/112/hr6019*.

Institute of Education Sciences. (2011). A randomized trial of the SCERTS curriculum for students with autism spectrum disorders in early elementary school classrooms. Retrieved December 8, 2013, from *http://ies.ed.gov/funding/grantsearch/details.asp?ID=978*.

Jones, S. M., & Bouffard, S. M. (2012). Social and emotional learning in schools: From programs to strategies. *Social Policy Report of the Society for Research in Child Development, 26*(4), 1–33.

Office of Juvenile Justice and Delinquency Prevention. (n.d.). Model Programs Guide. Retrieved December 8, 2013, from *www.ojjdp.gov/mpg*.

Patient Protection and Affordable Care Act. (2010). H.R. 3590, 111th Cong. Public Law No. 11-148, Section 2951 (enacted).

Payton, J. W., Graczyk, P. A., Wardlaw, D. M., Bloodworth, M., Tompsett, C. J., & Weissberg, R. P. (2000). Social and emotional learning: A framework for promoting mental health and reducing risk behavior in children and youth. *Journal of School Health, 70*, 179–185.

Race to the Top (RTT). (n.d.). Retrieved December 8, 2013, from *www.whitehouse.gov/issues/education/k-12/rade-to-the-top*.

Rimm-Kaufman, S. E., Larsen, R. A. A., Baroody, A. E., Curby, T. W., Ko, M., Thomas, J. B., et al. (2014). Efficacy of the Responsive Classroom approach: Results from a 3-year, longitudinal, randomized controlled trial. *American Educational Research Journal, 51*, 567–603.

S. 403—113th Congress: Safe Schools Improvement Act of 2013. (2013). Retrieved December 8, 2013, from *www.govtrack.us/congress/bills/113/s403*.

S. 3578—112th Congress: Elementary and Secondary Education Reauthorization Act of 2011. (2011). Retrieved December 8, 2013, *from www.govtrack.us/congress/bills/112/s3578.*

Social and Character Development Research Consortium. (2010). *Efficacy of schoolwide programs to promote social and character development and reduce problem behavior in elementary school children* (NCER 2011-2001). Washington, DC: National Center for Education Research, Institute of Education Sciences, U.S. Department of Education.

Substance Abuse and Mental Health Services Administration (SAMHSA). (2013). National Registry of Evidence-Based Programs and Practices. Retrieved December 8, 2013, from *www.nrepp.samhsa.gov.*

Substance Abuse and Mental Health Services Administration, Center for Mental Health Services. (2004). *Eliminating barriers for learning: Social and emotional factors that enhance secondary education* (SAMHSA Pub. No. P040478M). Rockville, MD: Center for Mental Health Services, Substance Abuse and Metnal Health Services Administration.

Tseng, V. (2012). The uses of research in policy and practice. *Social Policy Report of the Society for Research in Child Development, 26*(2), 1–23.

Ursache, A. M., Blair, C., Willoughby, M. T., Tunvall, F., & Soliman, M. N. (2011, March 31). *The measurement of executive function in young children.* Poster presented at the Society for Research in Child Development biennial meeting, Montreal, Canada.

U.S. Department of Education, Office of Planning, Evaluation and Policy Development, Policy and Program Studies Service. (2011). *Analysis of state bullying laws and policies.* Washington, DC: Author.

U.S. Department of Education. (2012, June 7). *ESEA flexibility policy document.* Retrieved December 8, 2013, from *www2.ed.gov/policy/elsec/guid/esea-flexibility/index.html.*

U.S. Department of Education. (2013a). Department of Education statement on request for flexibility from California's Core District Consortium. Retrieved December 8, 2013, from *www.ed.gov/news/press-releases/department-education-statement-request-flexibility-californias-core-district-con.*

U.S. Department of Education. (2013b). Obama Administration approves NCLB waiver request for California CORE districts. Retrieved December 8, 2013, from *www.ed.gov/news/press-releases/obama-administration-approves-nclb-waiver-request-california-core-districts.*

U.S. Department of Education. (2014a). Elementary and secondary education: ESEA flexibility. Retrieved December 17, 2014, from *www2.ed.gov/policy/elsec/guid/esea-flexibility/index.html*

U.S. Department of Education. (2014b). Preschool development grants. Retrieved December 17, 2014 from *www2.ed.gov/programs/preschooldevelopmentgrants/index.html.*

U.S. Department of Health and Human Services, Administration for Children and Families .(2012). Children's Bureau Information Memorandum 12-04. Retrieved December 8, 2013, from *www.acf.hhs.gov/programs/cb/resource/im1204.*

U.S. Department of Health and Human Services & U.S. Department of Education. (n.d.[a]). Prevention at school. Retrieved December 8, 2013, from *www.stopbullying.gov/prevention/at-school/index.html.*

U.S. Department of Health and Human Services & U.S. Department of Education. (n.d.[b]). StopBullying website. Retrieved December 8, 2013, from *www.stopbullying.gov.*

Zins, J. E., & Elias, M. J. (2006). Social and emotional learning. In G. G. Bear & K. M. Minke (Eds.), *Children's needs III: Developmental prevention and intervention* (pp. 1–14). Bethesda, MD: National Association of School Psychologists.

CHAPTER 37

International Perspectives on SEL

Catalina Torrente, Anjali Alimchandani, and J. Lawrence Aber

This chapter explores the educational status of social and emotional Learning (SEL) in select countries in Europe, Latin America, Asia, and sub-Saharan Africa, that is, how educational systems in these countries accommodate an SEL perspective. SEL can be conceptualized in at least three different ways: (1) as a human development process and field of study involving the acquisition of skills, knowledge, and attitudes; (2) as a set of specific programs; or (3) as a general educational approach, movement, or policy (Sherman, 2011). We focused on the latter of these three areas, namely, national educational movements and policies, to provide background information for discussions about opportunities for and challenges to the growth of SEL as a worldwide field of study or a specific set of programs.

Our point of departure was the Collaborative for Academic, Social, and Emotional Learning's (CASEL) overarching definition of social and emotional skills as *competencies and dispositions fundamental for school and life success.* These have been organized by CASEL into five domains: self-awareness (i.e., recognizing one's emotions, values, strengths, challenges); responsible decision making (i.e., making ethical constructive choices about personal and social behavior); relationship skills (i.e., forming positive relationships, working in teams, dealing effectively with conflict); social awareness (i.e., showing understanding and empathy for others); and self-management (managing emotions and behaviors to achieve one's goals). We conducted a Web-based search of national laws, policies, and educational programs targeting one or more of the five domains. Much like in the United States, international policies and programs that fit our criteria used a variety of terms, such as "education for mutual understanding", "peace education", "values education", "multicultural/intercultural education", "human rights education", "life skills", "citizenship, humanitarian or emotional education", "emotional intelligence", and "education for sustainable development." Even though the aims of some of those initiatives were sometimes narrower in scope compared to SEL, those initiatives shared SEL's call to expand the role of formal education beyond academics to target skills and dispositions included in CASEL's five domains. We used all of those variations as search terms. Most of the information used in this chapter came from Ministry of Education websites, but we also drew on the work of nongovernmental organizations (NGOs) promoting SEL principles and practices. Whereas most of our research concentrated on grey literature, we also conducted computer searches on PsycInfo to identify studies of national SEL programs that could point to relevant policy documents.

Several methodological constraints are to be noted at the outset. First, conducting an exhaustive review was not possible so we excluded some countries where important progress is being made in the field of SEL.[1] Instead, we included several Latin American, African, and Asian countries that are seldom given much attention. Second, our search was limited to data accessible in English, Spanish, or French (our shared language capacity). Third, our review focused on broad national movements and policies related to SEL instead of the impact of specific SEL programs. Thus, we did not attempt to review the level of success of different international initiatives. Last, we limited our search to school-based efforts even though SEL education takes place in other important settings. In spite of these limitations, we hope the chapter will spark interest in how countries around the world are making strides for the improvement of education, and encourage a more active exchange of ideas about SEL initiatives cross-nationally.

The chapter is organized as follows. We first provide an overview of cross-national policies, programs, and movements that have influenced work on the five SEL domains in numerous places of the world. Next, we review the status of SEL and similar movements in countries from four major regions: Europe, Latin America, sub-Saharan Africa, and Asia. We attempt to identify the main ideas framing educational policy in each country, and offer examples from policy documents and curricular reforms that reveal an interest in and progress toward SEL goals. To the extent possible, we list concrete skills, values, and behavioral dispositions that each country seeks to inculcate in its children, and draw parallels with CASEL's skills when appropriate. To conclude, we offer our thoughts about what this review has taught us and suggest future directions for SEL practice, research, and global dialogue.

Cross-National Influences

Five themes emerged repeatedly in analyzing international efforts. These consisted of citizenship education and four policies or globally driven programmatic efforts: the life skills framework and curriculum developed by the World Health Organization (WHO), the Universal Declaration of Human Rights, the Convention of the Rights of the Child (United Nations [UN], 1990), and the UN Millennium Development Goals (MDG).

Citizenship education, also referred to as civic, ethics, or moral education, was present in every region we investigated, although its connotation and overlap with SEL varied from country to country. According to the Iberoamerican States Organization (OEI, in Spanish: Organización de Estados Iberoamericanos, 2010, p. 108), as of 2010, there were at least three approaches to citizenship education, namely, education *for, through*, and *about* citizenship. Education *for* citizenship seeks to prepare students to be active and responsible members of society; it therefore underscores the acquisition of cognitive, communicative, and ethical *competencies*. Education *through* citizenship aims for students to learn civic values and behavioral dispositions as they experience them at school. Thus, school functioning is to be guided by the same principles that students are expected to learn, and school climate and teacher–student relationships are considered central. Last, education *about* citizenship centers on reflection and the development of moral judgment. In practice, drawing lines among these three approaches was not always possible because many endeavors combined these three aspects of education. Additionally, different discourses and purposes guided citizenship education in different places. In some countries, citizenship education had authoritarian and nationalistic undertones, while in others it was seen as central for the construction and continuity of democracy. Whereas Europe and Latin America commonly emphasized links with human rights, Asia and sub-Saharan Africa highlighted connections with a return to indigenous cultural and religious values. Other differences existed across countries, such as a strong focus on the importance of citizenship education in enhancing national economic productivity in some places, and the role of citizenship education in the prevention of aggression and violence in others. Differences aside, many citizenship education approaches shared SEL's goals to enhance students' social and emotional skills (e.g., four competencies targeted by the Colombian Program for Citizenship and Civic Education noted below). Therefore, this movement has the potential to serve as a platform for the development of educational initiatives aligned with the SEL agenda.

WHO's Life Skills framework and curriculum, and curricula inspired by WHO's work, were also present across all regions. In 1993, WHO's mental health division established a special unit on Skills for Life in education, which became instrumental in disseminating information and assisting countries and school systems in developing and implementing Life Skills programs (Diekstra, 2008). Their publication in 1993/94 aimed to provide a common terminology and guidelines for the design of Life Skills programs and materials. Under this framework, life skills were defined as teachable abilities that enable individuals to effectively deal with the demands of everyday life (WHO, 1994, p. 1). In the spirit of SEL perspectives, these skills were thought to have a value for overall physical, mental, and social well-being, instead of preventing a narrow set of problems. The following skills, grouped under five areas, were identified as essential: (1) decision making and problem solving, (2) creative and critical thinking, (3) effective communication and interpersonal relationship skills, (4) self-awareness and empathy, and (5) coping with emotions and stress (WHO, 1994, p. 3). With the exception of creative and critical thinking, these areas correspond with CASEL's dimensions. Even though WHO's Life Skills framework was present in every region reviewed, specific content focus varied by region and country. For example, we observed a strong emphasis on life skills for violence prevention and other public health phenomena in Asia, Africa, and Latin America, whereas countries in Europe highlighted emotional coping skills in an effort to address depression, aggression, and suicide.

The Universal Declaration of Human Rights, the Convention of the Rights of the Child, and the UN MDGs have also shaped an important number of school-based SEL initiatives in many countries. References to these frameworks usually went hand in hand with a discourse that viewed existing school systems as inadequate to prepare children and youth for the challenges of the 21st century, and the promotion of nonacademic skills—such as the ones fostered by SEL—as part of the solution.

To a lesser extent, but also noteworthy, the theoretical and empirical work of scholars from the Northern hemisphere emerged as an important influence in many countries. The contributions of Daniel Goleman on emotional intelligence, Howard Gardner's multiple intelligences, Albert Bandura's social learning theory, and Kohlberg's moral development, among others, found fertile ground in many places around the world. References to their work were found as part of the rationale and strategies on which national programs were built, especially in Europe and Latin America.

In addition to these overarching themes, other salient cross-national influences include the work of the UN bodies and several international NGOs. These organizations have collaborated with educational authorities in numerous countries to build educational programs focused on social and emotional development, with particular emphasis on conflict resolution, peace, and life skills. One of the largest programs of this nature is the UN International Children's Education Fund's (UNICEF) *Child-Friendly Schools* (CFS) program, an approach to education based on human rights that focuses on building schools that are safe, healthy, and protective, and that possess trained teachers, resources, and essential physical, emotional, and social conditions for learning. The model emphasizes gender equity, tolerance, respect, and personal empowerment, in addition to promoting positive civic engagement and critical thinking among students. At the time of our review, the program had been implemented in 95 countries across the globe (UNICEF, 2009). Another noteworthy example is *Healing Classrooms*, a model developed by the International Rescue Committee (IRC) to address the needs of children in postconflict and/or ongoing crisis situations. Healing Classrooms emphasizes teacher professional development and aims to create safe learning environments that nurture children's sense of belonging, self-worth, and sense of control, as well as positive relationships with teachers and peers (IRC, 2006). It is in the context of this set of cross-national influences on SEL policy that we now turn to cross-regional and country-specific emphases in SEL policy.

Regional Descriptions

Europe

Our review of European policy revealed an extremely diverse panorama in terms of the presence, progress, and origins of SEL and similar initiatives. The work of WHO was particularly salient, perhaps because mental illness (e.g., depression, aggressive behavior, suicide) was identified as a major health problem in high-income countries (Kimber, Sandell, & Bremberg, 2008). Fernández Berrocal (2008), for example, indicated that high incidence of psychological disorders stirred interest in promoting the psychological well-being of European citizens (see the European Commission's [2005] "Green Paper: Improving the Mental Health of the Population: Towards a Strategy on Mental Health for the European Union"). Even though only a few European countries had implemented Life Skills programs per se, mental illness prevention and health-promotion language were pervasive in European policy documents. In addition, European documents often referenced the UN Educational, Scientific and Cultural Organization's (UNESCO, 1996) "Learning: The Treasure Within", a report by the international commission on education for the 21st century. The report emphasized the idea that education and learning throughout life are privileged means of improving society. It contended that instead of solely focusing on the acquisition of factual knowledge, education should foster more harmonious forms of human development and interpersonal and intergroup relationships. Such an education effort should stand on four pillars, two of which are directly relevant to our discussion of SEL: learning to live together (i.e., developing an understanding of others and appreciation of interdependence and pluralism) and learning to be (i.e., the ability to act with autonomy, judgment, and personal responsibility) (UNESCO, 1996). In the following pages we describe findings from the United Kingdom, Sweden, Spain, Portugal, France, and Finland as six exemplars of similarities and differences across European nations.

United Kingdom

In the United Kingdom, a number of factors signaled burgeoning interest in children's social and emotional development (Clouder & Heys, 2008). These included recent changes in the organization of governmental institutions to better serve children and youth, shifts in the focus of education policies that increasingly revolve around educating the whole child (e.g., the Every Child Matters Agenda by the Department of Education and Skills, 2004), influential publications such as "Developing the Emotionally Literate School" (Weare, 2004) and "What Works in Developing Children's Emotional and Social Competence and Wellbeing" (Weare & Gray, 2003), and nationwide governmental initiatives such as SEAL (Social and Emotional Aspects of Learning; Downey & Williams, 2010). Given that England, Scotland, Wales, and Northern Ireland each have separate education systems and policies, our comments focus on England.

The British National Curriculum included Citizenship and Personal, Social, and Health Education (PSHE) among its primary subject matters at all educational levels. A wide array of skills, values, and dispositions were covered under this framework. In Key Stage 1 (5- to 7-year-olds), pupils were to be taught a variety of skills, including how to discern between right and wrong; recognize, name, and deal with feelings; set goals; understand, agree with and follow rules; take the perspective of others; participate in and contribute to the life of their class, school, and community; listen to others; identify and respect differences and similarities between people; and get help to deal with bullying. Examples were given as to how to promote those skills and dispositions throughout the curriculum. Moreover, "End of Key Stage Statements" (similar to SEL State Standards in the United States—see Illinois SEL standards at *www.isbe.net/ils/social_emotional/standards.htm*) were outlined to help teachers assess children's progress and levels of achievement (U.K. Department of Education, 2011). In spite of this level of specificity, Dunn (2012) contends that the PSHE approach to teaching social–emotional skills was inconsistent and lacked status before the introduction of SEAL. SEAL also faced an important number of practical challenges but had been implemented in about 90% of primary schools and 70% of secondary schools at the time of our review (Humphrey, Lendrum, & Wigelsworth, 2010).

Another noteworthy effort is a publication entitled "A Framework of Outcomes for Young People" (McNeil, Reeder, & Rich, 2012). This framework embraced a promotion approach and underscored the importance of social and emotional *capabilities* for both their own merit and their contribution to accomplishing other positive life outcomes, such as educational attainment and employability. Capabilities were defined as learnable "abilities to function in important ways, to create valuable outcomes, and to navigate choices and challenges" (p. 10). They were grouped in seven interrelated clusters: (1) management of feelings, (2) resilience and determination, (3) creativity, (4) relationships and leadership, (5) planning and problem solving, (6) confidence and agency, and (7) communication. Most of these capabilities overlap with those defined by CASEL. It is important to note that the authors provided a matrix of measurement tools, guidelines, and resources aimed at supporting evaluation and assessment efforts.

Two additional aspects of SEL in England are worth highlighting. First, *resilience*, or the ability to embrace challenges with optimism and to thrive in the face of adversity, emerged as a central theme in British educational policy. Resilience was conceived not only as a specific capability but also as one of the overarching goals of SEL education. Second, instead of assuming that one size fits all, British schools were given flexibility to decide and develop what and how to teach children. The rationale for this bottom-up approach was that less prescription enhances ownership, empowerment, and sustainability (Wigelsworth, Humphrey, & Lendrum, 2012). Thus, general guidelines were offered and schools were free to make adaptations to meet their students' specific needs. This approach complicates large-scale evaluation efforts, but it may also pay off in the form of programs that are perceived as more grounded, relevant, and suited to schools' realities.

Sweden

According to Dahlin (2008), around 1994, the Swedish government decided that schools should not only transmit knowledge but also support the development of a set of basic values. Hence, the national curriculum plan and related policy started placing more emphasis on the role of schools in children's upbringing. The 2008 curriculum included goals related to norms and values that overlap with citizenship and social and emotional education, including respecting all people; refusing to accept that others may be repressed or offensively treated; and developing empathy, a sense of community, solidarity, and democratic attitudes. However, Dahlin contended that there was little clarity about the meaning and practical significance of those values and goals, and that when implementation had been attempted, it had only been in the form of establishing general guidelines for teacher and student behaviors. As per Dahlin's account, programs for SEL in Sweden were often associated with bullying prevention and intervention; and there was no nationwide program even though several programs were used in schools and whole municipalities around the country (e.g., the Social and Emotional Training (SET) program—Kimber, 2012; Kimber et al., 2008).

More recently, Dunn (2012) argued that while Sweden does not implement nationwide programs, it aims to embed SEL into the school culture and curriculum. In line with this claim, the new curriculum for compulsory school (ages 7–16), preschool, and leisure-time stipulated that all school activities should be guided by democratic principles, and that students should develop ownership over their own learning process. A set of values, proclivities, and abilities that overlap with SEL's principles and domains were underscored; the set includes understanding and responsibility for others in the immediate group and for outsiders, empathy, compassion, appreciation of diversity, international solidarity, and critical thinking (Swedish National Agency for Education, in Swedish: *Skolverek*, 2006).

Spain

In Spain, the general law of education (Ministerio de la Presidencia, 2006) stated that education should foster a core set of values for democratic citizenship, responsibility, living well with others, solidarity, tolerance, respect, justice, and social cohesion. Children's social and emotional skills were highlighted and it was explicitly stated that teachers' responsibilities included attending to children's affective, social, and moral development (p. 17183). A survey of early childhood educators conducted in 2007, and again in 2009, found that teachers' advocated for curricular reforms nurturing children's social and emotional development, and revealed a critical stance toward curricula overemphasizing academic content (Sánchez Muliterno, 2009).

Arguably, along with the United Kingdom, Spain was one of the European countries where social and emotional education policy was more explicitly articulated. The theoretical frameworks forming the basis of this movement in Spain were very similar to those underlying the North American and British movements. As a matter of fact, early programs for social and emotional development in Spain were inspired by the work of British and North American psychologists such as Gardner, Salovey, Mayer, and Seligman. As in the United States, there was an explicit attempt to integrate interventions targeting problems with the same underlying causes, and that were thought to be preventable by developing a core set of skills. As in England, resilience was a predominant theme in Spanish policy documents.

One aspect to highlight from the Spanish case is its attention to training and support for teachers. The Institutes of Education Sciences (in Spanish: *Institutos de Ciencias de la Educación*)—based in every university—and the Teacher Centers (TCs)—the legal authorities with respect to education in each autonomous community—were tasked with channeling those efforts. Both had gradually included social and emotional education and emotional intelligence in their training programs (Fernández Berrocal, 2008). This is noteworthy because supports and training to introduce SEL into teachers' daily practices were lacking, or were not explicitly mentioned, in the majority of other countries reviewed.

Portugal

In the last few decades, specifically after the "Revolution of the Carnations" in 1974, Portugal has undergone myriad societal changes. According to Faria (2011), these rapid social transformations stirred up interest in transforming the education system. Attention to citizenship education and to personal and social development was evident in laws and policies governing the Portuguese education system. Article 47 of the Education Act of 1986 stated that in order to foster student development beyond academics, schools must operate democratically and include personal and social education (PSE) as part of their curricula (Faria, 2011). The Framework Law for Pre-School Education (Law No. 5/97) asserted that the general objectives of preschool education included encouraging children's personal and social development through the experience of democracy, with a view to education for citizenship (Vasconcelos, 1998).

In 1989, the Ministry of Education suggested four possible ways to carry out a PSE agenda: (1) distribution through the curriculum, (2) a noninstructional subject known as Project Area where students could develop interdisciplinary real-life projects, (3) 1 hour a week of instruction to foster personal and social development, and (4) extracurricular activities (Faria, 2011). In 1991, PSE was introduced nationally and pilot-tested in 19 schools along with the citizenship education program. According to Menezes (2003), official curricular guidelines were only defined in 1995 and actual implementation was minimal. Although PSE goals were present in schools' curricula, teachers and students seldom perceived PSE as an actual practice. Faria (2011) contended that after going nationwide in the 1990s, the development of the PSE program slowed down, possibly due to an increased focus on academic testing. In 2001, a decree was enacted that emphasized citizenship education instead of PSE. The main goal of this shift was to build national identity and develop civic awareness among students. More recently, the first few years of schooling have included various aspects that overlapped with SEL, such as moral education, emotional education, personal skills, and creativity. However, the focus in upper grades was on civic education, or the formal aspects of citizenship that relate to citizens' rights and duties, and Portugal's social and political transformations. Menezes underscored that while citizenship education may be a consensual goal in Portugal and other European countries, there is much progress to be made in agreeing on its meaning and practical implications.

France

In 2003, a process was undertaken in France to modify the laws and policies governing education. (Thélot, 2005). The process began with a national debate that included participants from different sectors of society and resulted in the publication of a decree in which the Ministry of National Education, Higher Education and Research (MENESR, in French: *Ministère Education Nationale Enseignement Supèrieur Recherche,* 2006) defined fundamental competencies that every student should master by the end of the compulsory education cycle, when students are about 16 years old. Such competencies were expected to enable students to exercise their citizenship, handle complex situations in school and life, understand the need to develop and protect the planet, continue learning throughout life, and appreciate the diversity of cultures and the universality of human rights. Specific abilities included the capacity to follow rules, communicate and work in teams, evaluate consequences, recognize and name emotions, be media-literate, and persevere. Educators were provided with tools to assess students' mastery at different levels. Unfortunately, our methodology did not permit ascertaining the extent to which those tools were actually used.

Finland

Social and emotional well-being has been a central concern in Finnish society. According to Kokkonen (2011), efforts for the improvement of students' social and emotional well-being sprang from different fronts and included the government's national curriculum, evidence-based interventions, and NGO programs (e.g., Kärnä et al., 2011, KiVa program). Below, we focus on governmental initiatives only.

The Finnish national curriculum emphasized psychological and social well-being as major responsibilities of the school community and included several sections focusing on "pupil welfare" and holistic growth. In addition to those general tenets, detailed learning objectives and specific content were provided as part of cross-curricular themes, such as "Growth as a Person" (Finnish National Board of Education, 2004). This particular theme overlapped substantially in content and goals with SEL, in that it addressed skills such as identification and regulation of emotions. There were also specific curriculum subjects, such as "health education", which aimed to improve children's cognitive, social, and emotion regulation and ethical skills (Kokkonen, 2011). Emphasis on students' agency and responsibility for their own learning process, and on promoting safe, encouraging, and communal learning environments stood out as particularly important for Finnish educators (Finnish National Board of Education, 2004).

Two noteworthy features of the Finnish case were the incorporation of social and emotional education principles across diverse subjects, including arts and crafts and physical education, and the importance of teacher autonomy. Finland has been one of the few countries across the globe where improving the motivation and job satisfaction of teachers is part of the rationale for enhancing children's social–emotional skills and well-being (Kokkonen, 2011).

Concluding Thoughts about Europe

It was difficult to find a common thread for SEL across European countries. Whereas in Spain, Finland, and England, initiatives addressing SEL were akin to those in North America, in Sweden, Portugal, and France they were more aligned with citizenship education and with rights-based perspectives. The most common feature among the European nations was heightened awareness about the need to address child and youth social and emotional development to promote their overall well-being and success. In this sense, the importance of social and emotional education was uncontestable. However, recognition of the crucial role of SEL was occasionally perceived to be at odds with movements advocating for a stronger focus on academic achievement. It was also accompanied by a cautious reminder about the paucity of empirical evidence for the European context and by calls for more rigorous domestic evaluation efforts. Building solid knowledge about what works and under what conditions should be a goal not only for European countries, but also for most countries around the globe.

Latin America

Several countries in Latin America have adopted an approach toward citizenship education that in many respects overlaps with the North American SEL movement. The main impetus for citizenship education in the region arose from the Convention of the Rights of the Child in the early 1990s and was fueled by turn of the millennium events such as the World Education Forum and the UN MDGs, among others. The resonance of this movement in Latin American societies stemmed from a diversity of factors that called for deep transformations of "traditional" education models and practices (OEI, 2010, p. 137). Motivating factors included a long history of social turmoil, growing concerns about persistent social problems (social exclusion, lack of trust in political and governmental institutions, school violence, etc.), and the recognition of new challenges, such as those emerging from the availability of new information and communication technologies.

In spite of being widespread, the extent to which citizenship education has been developed and implemented varied significantly from one Latin American country to the next. Here, we focus on those countries containing the most detailed information.

Mexico

In 2006 the Mexican Secretary of Public Education adopted an approach to foster competencies for civic and ethics education "following curricular tendencies from other Western countries" (García Cabrero & Conde Flores, 2011, p. 57). The Mexican Integral Program for Civic and Ethics Education (in Spanish: *Programa Integral de Formación Civica y Etica* [PIFCyE]) conceived children as responsible for, and active in, their own learning process. As such, it encouraged critical thinking, autonomous learning, the integration of students' previous experiences and knowledge in the construction of new learning, applying what is learned to new and challenging situations, and continuous learning throughout life (García Cabrero & Conde Flores, 2011, p. 61). As part of this program, Mexico selected eight competencies, inspired by Piaget's and Kohlberg's moral development theories, which formed the profile of the ideal Mexican student. These competencies included (1) self-knowledge and care; (2) self-regulation and responsible use of liberty; (3) respect and appreciation of diversity; (4) a sense of belonging to a community, a nation, and to humanity, (5) conflict resolution, (6) social and political participation; (7) a sense of justice and adherence to norms; and (8) an understanding and appreciation of democracy (Luna Elizarrarás, 2011, p. 116). Several of these overlap with the five domains defined by CASEL. Importantly, citizenship education was not an isolated subject, but an overall organizing framework for school functioning. It could take place in any subject and across all grades, and it was expected to infuse teaching practices, learning environments, and school–community connections (García Cabrero & Conde Flores, 2011, p. 64). As part of this effort, a strategy called the *democratization of schools*, inspired by Dewey's and Kohlberg's perspectives, was implemented to promote student participation in schools' decision-making, rule creation, and conflict resolution processes (Conde Flores, 2011, p. 84).

Colombia

In 2004, the Colombian government undertook a comprehensive reform of the education system that included the development of a program for citizenship and civic education (Jaramillo Franco, 2008). As in other Latin American countries, the initiative was initially inspired by the declaration of the rights of the child, but it also responded to the collective desire of Colombians to stop the violence that has afflicted the country for over 50 years. One of the pillars of the program was that democracy was seen as not only a form of government but also a way of life (Jaramillo Franco & Mesa, 2009). Therefore, it was developed with contributions from a diversity of actors and perspectives, and encouraged participatory processes across all levels of the education system, including the school and the classroom. Another central tenet of the program was an emphasis on *competencies* instead of knowledge (Jaramillo Franco, 2008, p. 27). "Citizenship competencies" were defined as the integration of basic knowledge, abilities, and dispositions that allow citizens to act constructively in a democratic society (Ministerio de Educación Nacional, 2004; Ruiz Silva & Chaux, 2005). The four targeted competencies were (1) *communicative* (i.e., expressing one's point of view, understanding other points of view, negotiating), (2) *cognitive* (i.e., perspective taking, critical thinking), (3) *emotional* (i.e., identifying, expressing, and managing emotions), and (4) *integrative* (i.e., the ability to apply all other competencies in public and private life) (Ruiz Silva & Chaux, 2005). Selection and definition of these competencies were informed by the work of Piaget and Kohlberg but transcended it by highlighting the interdependence between emotion and cognition (see Jaramillo Franco, 2008, p. 28). In addition, self-reflection was seen as a central strategy that allows individuals to become increasingly autonomous in making moral decisions that serve their own interests and those of others.

Colombia emphasized a commitment to assessment and evaluation. In 2003, developmentally anchored standards were defined that specified the minimum every student was expected to know, and assessments were developed to measure children's progress (Patti & Espinoza, 2007). Along with other countries in the region (i.e., Chile, Guatemala, Mexico, Paraguay, and Dominican Republic), and with support from the International Association for the Evaluation of Educational Achievement (IEA) and the BID (Banco Interamericano de Desarrollo), Colombia took part in the development of a system to promote and evaluate citizenship competencies in Latin America (see *www.colombiaparende.edu.co*).

Chile

Since 1990, the Chilean Ministry of Education has initiated a series of programs that seek to promote democratic citizenship and to make schools into places where children and youth can learn and practice the basic principles of democracy (see Alba Meraz, 2011, pp. 31–32; Conde Flores, 2011, p. 85). A report by the Citizenship Education Commission (in Spanish: *Comisión Formación Ciudadana*, 2004) acknowledged the need to instill in children a sense of belonging to a universal community, while underscoring the development of a national identity and belonging to local communities. In addition to the report, the Chilean curriculum took an integrative approach to citizenship education by establishing goals and content favoring the promotion of citizenship across different subjects and throughout all grades (Comisión Formación Ciudadana, 2004). The aim of the curriculum was to develop a general set of increasingly complex skills and attitudes, including children's ability and will to self-regulate their actions, autonomy, altruism, and solidarity, and respect for justice, human rights, and the common good (Alba Meraz, 2011). Pedagogical materials that emphasize a whole-school approach to citizenship education were developed to support teachers in blending the new contents into the academic curricula (see Ministerio de Educación República de Chile, 2004).

Brazil

In Brazil, moral education became a required subject during the military dictatorship from the mid-1960s to the 1980s, but during this period, it was mainly used as a means to indoctrinate the population and promote obedience. In 1996, the National Education Guidelines and Framework Law (in Portuguese: *Lei de Diretrizes e Bases de Educacao*) determined that moral education should no longer be a required subject, but in the same year, a curricular reform was established that encouraged schools to nurture ethics, pluralism, and health across different subjects (Araújo & Arantes, 2009). In 2003, in the spirit of the same law, the government launched the "Ethics and Citizenship Program: Constructing Values in School and Society." The program concentrated on four themes: (1) ethics, (2) democratic coexistence, (3) human rights, and (4) social inclusion (Araújo & Arantes, 2009). Among other skills, the program sought to nurture awareness of one's own feelings and the feelings of others, and commitment to community life and conflict resolution. These were to be acquired through deliberation, reflection, discussion, and by active engagement with the nearby community through the School Forum of Ethics and Citizenship. Similar to countries in the United Kingdom, individual schools were free to decide whether they wanted to implement the program, as well as to select the themes on which they wanted to focus.

Concluding Thoughts about Latin America

One of the defining features of the emerging citizenship movement in Latin America was an explicit acknowledgment that cognition, emotion, and action are necessarily intertwined. Several recent initiatives have gone beyond the acquisition of *factual knowledge* about values, democracy, or human rights to foster the processes by which individuals acquire the motivations, emotional dispositions, and skills needed to translate abstract principles into practice (Alba Meraz, 2011; Braslavsky, 2005; García Cabrero, 2011; Patti & Espinoza, 2007). Emotion self-regulation and moral emotions such as guilt and pride were also underscored because they were thought to organize and direct cognition and action, and to enable ethical and political behavior (García Cabrero, 2011, p. 50). Another common feature was an intended departure from citizenship education as a stand-alone subject. Instead, many initiatives aspired to transform whole-school cultures and learning environments by using citizenship as a holistic framework guiding multiple school activities (e.g., OEI, 2010, p. 110; Patti & Espinoza, 2007). Finally, there was a partial shift from civic education as an ideological tool for the promotion and maintenance of homogenizing nationalistic regimes, toward appreciation of multiculturalism, global interdependence, and intercultural dialogue (see Luna Elizarrarás, 2011, pp. 113, 115).

Sub-Saharan Africa

Although limited access to information posed constraints in data collection for all sections, this challenge was particularly acute in researching African nations. The relatively recent formation of nationhood in some African countries (within the last 50 years) likely played a role in the lack of literature regarding social–emotional educational policy (Swartz, 2010). However, many national governments were revamping remnants of colonial education systems and, in the process, were developing nationalized education policies that often integrated aspects of SEL. Despite the scarcity of information, we chose to include this section because community, social support, and social responsibilities—all of which overlap with SEL—have profound roots in the cultures of a number of African nations and were being integrated into formal education systems. This section is structured in the following manner. We first provide an overview of Africa-based philosophies of children's social and emotional development. Following this, we briefly summarize country-specific educational policies developed by ministries of education within sub-Saharan African countries.

African Philosophies Regarding Social and Emotional Development

There were two main findings relative to African perspectives on children's social and emotional development. The first concerned southern African philosophies of ideal education for youth. The second pointed to increasing criticism by African writers of westernization of education systems within the continent. In his analysis of child development as perceived through southern African contexts, Zimba (2002) highlighted particular indigenous values commonly seen in many communities. Reciprocity and kinship were viewed as critical values to be passed on to children, specifically, the idea that "I am because we are; and since we are, I am." The conception of "we" speaks to communal bonds that reach into the past to ancestors, as well as into the future to the unborn. Children were inculcated with the idea that their existence is inextricably linked with community; therefore, one cannot operate effectively in life without honoring the responsibilities associated with this kinship.

Venter (2004) further explicated these ideas through the lens of *Ubuntu,* which she described as a philosophy of life focused on humaneness. This philosophy dictated essential ideas and ethics to be taught to ensure that children are humble, virtuous, caring, generous, understanding, socially mature, and socially conscious. At its root, *Ubuntu* was a philosophy of communalism, altruism, and interdependence, which, according to Venter, shared some ideas with Buddhist conceptions of the holistic nature of individuals and communities comprised of interdependent spiritual, mental, biological, and psychological elements. Within this framework, individuals' happiness and success in life stemmed from living harmoniously with and supporting others.

The focus on integrating a criticism of the imposition of Western values within African educational systems was reflected in a number of other African writings on education. Specifically, two writers from Nigeria and Burundi, who focused largely on moral education, spoke to this criticism. In Burundi, Rwantabagu (2010) stated that the Western focus on cognitive outcomes of education had degraded traditional African education models by removing the emphasis on morals and ethical behavior. He advocated for a new curriculum developed in 2005 by the National Bureau for Catholic Education, which emphasized social responsibility, honesty, peace, respect, and positive citizenship. In Nigeria, Iheoma (1985) focused instead on the negative impact of Christian missionary work in schools across Africa. He stated that such work had made moral education synonymous with Western Christianity, which had erased the indigenous history of moral education within African philosophies of teaching. He also highlighted the detrimental impact of the materialism and individualism that accompany Western education and called for a return to teaching traditional communal and humanitarian ideas in African schools.

Summary of Country-Specific Findings: Botswana, Kenya, Namibia, Rwanda, and South Africa

We identified SEL principles integrated into education policy in Botswana, Kenya, Namibia, Rwanda, and South Africa. The greatest amount of information was available for South African education policies that sought to include SEL principles and practices. Over the last 10 years, the South African Ministry of Education developed a number of curriculum policies focused on life skills, personal expression, citizenship, cultural and religious understanding, respect, and conflict resolution. These subject areas fell under the heading of "life orientation" (LO) and were deemed an essential part of the national curriculum. The integration of LO into the curriculum aimed to honor the nation's commitment to outcomes-based education and was aligned with the constitutional mandate to build a society rooted in democratic values, social justice, and human rights, which maximized the potential of each individual. LO was to be implemented in a holistic manner that supported students in understanding the self in relation to other individuals and the larger society. The curriculum included goals aligned with SEL, such as learning to understand, recognize, manage, and express emotions in the self and others and developing empathy, self-confidence, and assertiveness (Ministry of Education, South Africa, 2002). Van Alphen (2013) noted that one of the main challenges faced by LO was that teachers were expected to decide how to present the new content. However, many South African teachers, lacking training on child-centered techniques, continued to rely on antiquated instructional methods that are not optimal for teaching LO.

The governmental educational policies of Botswana, Kenya, Namibia, and Rwanda reflected a strong emphasis on the social and emotional development of children, through their focus on integrating traditional communalist values into educational systems that may promote respect, tolerance, and conflict resolution (Ministry of Education, Namibia, 2006, 2008, 2009; Ministry of Education, Republic of Kenya, 2006; Ministry of Education, Republic of Rwanda, 2008; Ministry of Education and Skills Development, Botswana, n.d.). For example, the Namibian Ministry of Education (2006, 2009) developed a life skills curriculum for grades 5–7 and 11–12 that enforced a nationwide integration of life skills to promote holistic child development. These skills comprised social skills, social responsibility, cooperation, appreciation of traditional culture, citizenship, promotion of moral standards and gender equity, family and community participation, and emphasis on improving self-esteem and learning to learn. In addition, some of these governments cited a need to relinquish the hold of antiquated colonial education systems in order to develop educational models that prepared their students to live successfully as both national and global citizens (Swartz, 2010).

Concluding Thoughts about Sub-Saharan Africa

Two main factors motivated the integration of moral and/or values education into the school systems of the African countries we have reviewed. The first was recognition of the need to revamp existing education systems in order to adapt to an increasingly globally connected world and prepare students to be successful both in their native countries and as global citizens. The second was a desire to revive and integrate indigenous values and concepts into formal schooling to ensure that students maintain national connection and pride. Another common theme was a unique tension in the role of international bodies in transforming educational systems. Although many governments and local institutions were working with the UN and international NGOs in this process, criticisms were also emerging from these nations about the negative impact of Western influences on their youth and culture. Within this tension seemed to be a rejection of the idea that SEL concepts were new within Africa. Regardless of this conflict, our research indicated that some nations in Africa recognized and were making active efforts to ensure that social and emotional skills became a standardized part of national educational curricula.

Asia

Two primary organizing frameworks related to SEL were found in Asia: citizenship education and values education (Lee, Grossman, Kennedy, & Fairbrother, 2004). Both of these frameworks fit under the SEL umbrella through their focus on one or more skills or values overlapping with the five SEL domains identified by CASEL. The motivations and historical trajectories of these educational developments across different Asian nations varied greatly. However, common motivations to integrate citizenship and values education into school curricula included national economic growth, human rights advocacy, improvement in academic achievement, and promotion of national identity. A number of countries also claimed a long-standing culturally embedded commitment to both citizenship and values education. Lee and colleagues pointed to a few distinct commonalities that appear within the conceptualization of citizenship and moral training among many Asian countries. These include the ideas of harmony, spirituality, and self-cultivation or improvement that occur through collective realization. Lee and colleagues went on to explain that these three key factors outline a philosophical foundation that speaks to the importance of relationality—relationships of self with society, one's country, and the world. This relational stance was seen as fundamental to the nations' social, moral, and economic flourishing. The following section provides a brief overview of the specific findings in Thailand, Taiwan, Japan, India, and China.

Thailand

According to Pitiyanuwat and Sujiva (2000), the culture of Thailand places considerable emphasis on the integration of civics and values education, rooted in Buddhism, within formal schooling. They argue that the government's policy decisions to include civics education—also referred to as "character", "citizenship", or "moral education"—in schools stem from a belief that such instruction promotes economic success within a globalized world. However, they described a rich history of this approach to education within Thai history. For example, from 1932 to 1977, in addition to the Buddhist emphasis, the constitutional monarchy shaped the curriculum of civics education to focus heavily on responsibility toward country, community, family, and self. Since 1978, civics education has to some degree moved away from a Buddhist base focused primarily on identifying and eliminating causes of suffering for both self and others, to a more secular base focused on enhancing all aspects of physical and mental health and morality considered essential for good national and global citizenship. Such aspects include honesty, kindness, responsibility, reason, diligence, and fairness. In 1999, the Thai Ministry of Education released the National Education Act of B.E. 2542, which provided a set of national guidelines for education. In this policy, academic and nonacademic aspects of education were interwoven. Five main knowledge/skills areas were included: (1) awareness of Thai history, government, and democracy, and knowledge about self and the relationship between oneself and society; (2) knowledge of science and technology, including management, environmental conservation, and methods of environmentally sustainable living; (3) knowledge of religion, art, culture, sports, Thai wisdom, and the application of this wisdom; (4) knowledge of mathematics and language; and (5) knowledge of how to pursue a career and lead a "happy life" (Ministry of Education, Thailand, 1999). Some of the skills and knowledge in these areas loosely overlap with CASEL's five domains, particularly with self-awareness and social awareness, as they facilitate harmonic relationships between the self and others.

Taiwan

Civics education also appears prominently in Taiwanese culture. As with Thailand, the civics education curriculum has varied in accordance with political tides, particularly with the ongoing sensitive political relationship with the Mainland Chinese government. According to Meihui (2000), prior to 1980, civics education in Taiwan centered on uncritical Chinese patriotism, as well as traditional Chinese values and an emphasis on authoritarianism. The main goal of this approach was to promote a homogenous identity. Between 1980 and 2000, the focus of civics education shifted toward teaching young people the skills necessary to become productive, good, thoughtful citizens. In addition, the curriculum began to emphasize Taiwanese identity. Since 2000, Taiwanese education advocates have worked to build a more flexible, diverse, and decentralized system that fosters critical thinking and competence among students. In 2001, the Ministry of Education released a 9-year curriculum focused specifically on the integration of critical thinking and problem-solving skills in citizenship education. The term "critical thinking skills" was defined as the ability to understand and accept cultural differences, think and question in a systematic manner, and resolve conflict nonviolently (Yang & Chung, 2009). These touch on aspects of CASEL's responsible decision making, relationship skills, and social awareness. According to the Blueprint for Education, an education policy recently established by the Taiwanese Ministry of Education, educational systems in Taiwan aspire to establish a well-rounded and happy learning environment that cultivates high-quality citizens. Such individuals are expected to promote Taiwan's economic development, competitiveness, and quality of life. The concepts related to this policy include holistic education, life education, lifelong education, mastery learning, and a mentally and physically healthy environment (Ministry of Education, Republic of China (Taiwan), 2010).

Japan

According to Parmenter (2004), civics education in Japan reflects the emphasis on building responsible citizens that is seen in other Asian countries. Parmenter explained that moral education was observed in formal schooling in the 19th century. During the late 19th century, this education focused largely on nationalism and was used to support political agendas for war. After this time, civics education was banned until 1958. Current civics education centers on shaping thoughtful, caring, and independent citizens who maintain traditional Japanese culture and work toward global peace. The Basic Act of Education, created by the Ministry of Education, Culture, Sports, Science, and Technology in Japan (2006), articulated that the primary aim of education should focus on developing the whole personalities, minds, and bodies of its citizens in order to ensure a peaceful and democratic society. The educational objectives of this policy were to cultivate interest and passion in acquiring knowledge, while constructing a strong sense of morality, reason, and a healthy body; fostering creativity, independence, and an attitude that values labor; promoting justice, responsibility, equality, mutual respect, cooperation, and collaborative efforts; and encouraging respect for the lives of others and the environment. In its emphasis on concrete responsibilities of good citizens, such as peaceful resolution of conflict, social rights, and the interdependence of self and society, the Japanese attitude toward education resonates with the Confucian focus on responsibility. Parmenter highlighted that within current civics education, there is a heavy emphasis on the promotion of a homogenous Japanese identity, which may not be supported by all citizens. In an analysis of the challenges facing citizen education in Japan, Willis (2002) pointed to the efforts to integrate multiculturalism and respect for diversity within civics education programs. Specifically, Willis discussed the simultaneous rise of potentially conflicting tides: nationalism and fears of loss of Japanese identity in the wake of internationalization, and recognition of the growing diversity among Japanese people, and the need to increase national awareness and mutual understanding.

India

In India, recent efforts toward the promotion of social and emotional aspects of learning focus heavily on values education, particularly values related to the Indian government's characterization of traditional Indian cultural heritage. The 1992 National Policy on Education incorporated the teaching of cultural heritage into national curricula (Department of Secondary and Higher Education, Government of India, 2003). This included the history of India's freedom movement and civics training that is necessary to promote national identity and success, including concepts such as a common cultural identity, equality across gender and other social categories, democracy, secularism, promotion of the two-parent heteronormative family unit, and environmental protection. In addition, this national policy underscored the importance of integrating academic education with the teaching of Indian cultural tradition, as defined by the national government, in order to cultivate moral values that will unite Indians and counter superstition, fatalism, violence, and religious fanaticism. Arguably, the teaching of moral values can provide the basis for responsible decision making, harmonic relationships, and enhanced social awareness.

China

Historical trends in China have reflected a conflict between *yingshi jiaoyu*, or examination-oriented education, and *suzhi jiaoyu*, or quality/character education (Dello Iacovo, 2009). China has a long-standing tradition of rigorous examination-oriented education that can be traced to origins in imperial China over 1,000 years ago. Examination-oriented education utilizes rote memorization as its primary tool of implementation and has been criticized for a number of reasons, including an intense focus on testing, lack of integration of students' daily struggles and experiences into formal schooling, a teaching style that relies entirely on teacher talk, and an emphasis on cramming that fails to foster students' initiative and personal responsibility. Additional criticisms that arose in the 1990s focused largely on the neglect of holistic development of children within the narrow focus of examination-oriented education, along with increasing mental health concerns among Chinese students, including low levels of self-confidence, social skills, flexibility, and resilience (Dello-Iacovo, 2009). *Suzhi jiaoyu*, or quality education, emerged in an effort to address these criticisms by integrating moral and character education into national curricula. Quality education was linked to a nationalistic desire to produce citizens of "high quality", which is defined as well rounded, ethical, and patriotic (Dello-Iacovo, 2009). This idea was linked to long-standing Chinese traditions within martial arts and Confucian education that also emphasized similar values.

By embedding these concepts into traditional Chinese ideals and national historical narrative, quality education gained political ground and in 1999 was included as an individual component within the Chinese government's Action Plan for Invigorating Education in the 21st Century (Dello-

Iacovo, 2009). Over the years, it continued to grow and the government's recently released "Outline of China's National Plan for Medium and Long-Term Education Reform and Development (2010–2020)" also included holistic education as primary content area for national education curricula. According to Beijing Normal University Education Department faculty member Gu (2010), the plan's central guideline was a commitment to produce higher quality Chinese citizens through education to enable China to compete in a global economy and represent China well. The goals defined under this endeavor were to achieve universal education at higher academic levels; construct curricula that benefit all citizens; increase educational opportunity and lifelong learning; and build an educational system that promotes vitality, excellence, and vigor. This included an emphasis on the creation of healthy learning environments with well-trained and supported teachers. The primary themes, or content, emphasized within each of these goals focused on holistic development, increased notions of civic responsibility, enhanced capacity for innovation and exploration, increased problem-solving capacity and critical thinking, and enhanced moral development. Within the outline of these guidelines, "moral education" was defined as an emphasis on promoting socialist and nationalist ideals. In particular, the plan calls for an education that promotes socialist ideas of honor and disgrace, and encourages students to value unity, mutual assistance, honesty, trustworthiness, discipline, hard work, and a "plain" lifestyle, in addition to teaching notions of citizenship, equality, and social justice (People's Republic of China, Government, 2010).

Concluding Thoughts about Asia

Three common themes emerged among the Asian countries we reviewed. First, most countries in Asia interpreted social and emotional skills through the rubrics of citizenship and/or values education, and in tracking the historical development of educational systems, we observed a strong role of the state in shaping education to fit the political climate of the time. Second, as with Africa, several Asian nations referenced the need to revive and reintegrate traditional, indigenous value systems, often interwoven with aspects of SEL, into formal education systems in order to create strong national and global citizens. Third, many nations pointed to the importance of social and emotional skills in preparing young people to compete in the global economy and to represent their nations of origin well. In other words, the integration of SEL into schools was tied to both economic growth and promotion of a universal national identity.

Conclusions and Future Directions

Our attempt to provide a snapshot of the status of SEL around the globe was both a heartening and humbling experience. It was heartening because societies across the world are eager to improve and adapt their education systems to meet the challenges of our times, and creative methods and perspectives to develop positive values, dispositions, and nurture social competence are emerging in virtually every corner of the world. It was also humbling because summarizing the nature and progress of SEL and related initiatives worldwide comes at the price of oversimplification and keen awareness that we have only begun to scratch the surface. As a matter of fact, one of the clear-cut findings from our research is that there is ample diversity in terms of the approach, emphasis, and level of development in SEL and related initiatives across nations, and there is also rich within-country diversity that we did not get to characterize. Additionally, we were unable to review all countries in which excellent work is being conducted in the field of SEL. We hope that future reviews will incorporate information from countries that were not included in this chapter.

Despite the challenges and limitations of our review, we identified six important themes. First, we found plenty of evidence for an urge to transform "traditional" or "antiquated" education systems to meet the challenges of the new (21st) century. Globalization, cultural diversity, international cooperation and competition, violence in schools, and greater access to communication technologies were among the main opportunities and challenges faced—and considered central—by many contemporary societies and educators worldwide. Integration of SEL and similar approaches into formal schooling was often viewed as a viable strategy to meet some of those challenges, and to better prepare students to succeed and contribute to their communities in a rapidly changing world.

Second, citizenship education stood out as one of the most widespread and clearly articulated movements promoting the teaching and learning of fundamental skills for school, career, and life effectiveness. However, its rationale and operation differed considerably across countries. For example, many countries in sub-Saharan Africa and Asia cited nationalistic motivations for citizenship education. In particular, some governments emphasized the role of citizenship education in forming citizens who represent the country well in upholding national ideals and can also compete successfully in the global economy. In Latin America, in contrast, we often observed an explicit departure from nationalistic ideologies, and an emphasis on developing a sense of belonging to the global community. In some African and Asian countries, citizenship education overlapped substantially with values education and was rooted in the importance of maintaining and promoting ancient cultural heritage and values. This motivation stemmed from the premise that the teaching of moral and ethical values is a long-standing tradition within these countries and should be integrated into formal schooling to ensure cultural continuity among future generations. In other countries, citizenship education was built on a human rights perspective that underscored democratic principles and practices. Regardless of its underlying rationale in each country, we believe that citizenship education has the potential to serve as a natural stepping-stone for the articulation of initiatives nurturing a wide spectrum of social–emotional skills and dispositions.

Third, a common theme emerged in the emphasis on "learning to learn", along with a recognition of students' agency in the learning process. Students were increasingly seen as active learners instead of passive vessels of knowledge. Whereas this view may eventually transform the roles of teachers and students, it was in stark contrast with the dearth of concrete efforts to overhaul school and classroom cultures and climates. The few instances we found in our review made a compelling case for convergence between what children are taught in the classroom, how they are expected to behave, and what they learn by observing and participating in their surrounding environments. Also, the prevalence of new curricula and fresh perspectives on the role of students appears to be at odds with the relative lack of attention to teacher training and support. Lack of training in the context of high expectations and new challenges may increase teacher dissatisfaction and harm motivation and performance.

Fourth, the tension between academic learning and social and emotional development was a usual finding, as well as the resulting struggle in obtaining buy-in from educators who may see SEL programs as an additional burden. This tension was rooted in the long-held belief that the cognitive, emotional, and social aspects of development are independent from each other, and in the tendency for SEL programs to be introduced as add-on elements to enhance academic performance. Researchers should make it a priority to disseminate what we have learned as a field about the inherent interdependence between aspects of children's development that are often thought of as separate domains. Also, we contend that for SEL to be sustainable, it needs to become an integral part of the curriculum, seamlessly woven together with all subjects and other school activities. In addition, SEL efforts could be well served by discourses that highlight the merits of SEL in its own right, as reflected in several Asian and African countries, instead of presenting it as another strategy to raise test scores.

Over the last 20 years, SEL in the United States has become increasingly "evidence-based." It is founded on basic and applied research that informs the design and rigorous evaluation of programs and policies on children's academic, social, and emotional development. The fifth theme was how, in comparison to the United States, the role of basic and applied research in shaping educational policies for SEL seemed much less prominent in many regions of the world (with the exception of parts of Europe). Although many countries acknowledged the importance of evaluations, they were not being carried out, or were not accessible to us at the time of our review. There were, however, some cross-national measurement initiatives that represent extraordinary advances. These included the system to assess citizenship competencies in Latin America, and the Learning Metrics Task Force, which attempts to help countries and international organizations measure and enhance academic and SEL outcomes of youth worldwide (Learning Metrics Task Force, 2013). In cases where local resources are limited, cross-national assessments can be invaluable to inform policy decisions and should be strategically used for that end. However, programs developed in response to national policies should also be tested for efficacy and effectiveness in response to local needs before they are brought to scale, and we argue that this is particularly critical in countries with scant resources. In the absence of rigorous evaluation, low- and middle-income countries risk spending resources on programs with negligible or no impact.

Sixth, and perhaps most importantly, we noted that it is often difficult to determine whether national policies carry practical consequences. In many cases, it was not possible to discern whether SEL principles are only a set of aspirations and values, or whether there are any concrete, intentional, and explicit plans for the effective implementation of national initiatives. Across the board, we found that virtually every education system defines the values and skills they want to inculcate in their children. Such a step is a necessary but insufficient condition for SEL education to flourish and prosper. Explicit, high-quality implementation plans and learning goals, and standards and assessments need to be defined and appropriately executed if SEL is to become an essential aspect of a national agenda. More often than not, we were left with the sense that there may be a large gap between the claims and aspirations of governments and what is actually happening in schools, especially when no provisions are made to train and support teachers in carrying out new proposals.

Our review leaves us with a sense that although in many countries the climate was favorable for the development of SEL initiatives, much can be gained by increasing collaboration within and between countries. Whereas the diversity in approaches can be enriching, that potential can only be realized if lessons are shared in a systematic way. We hope that future work on SEL will be informed by the perspectives of the many people working in different parts of the world, as they are the true experts on the status of SEL and similar initiatives in their particular countries. We conclude our chapter with a few recommendations about action steps that can serve this goal.

Future Directions for the International Advancement of SEL

If we are right about our general conclusions—that there is global interest in transforming education systems to promote children's development beyond academic achievement; that the specific emphases are rarely (outside of the United States and parts of Europe) called "SEL" and most often framed as citizenship, values, and/or moral education; and that relatively few of these educational policy initiatives are founded on a strong foundation of evidence-based programs and practices that may be scaled—then we suggest several lines of activity to advance SEL internationally.

It is important to develop a common terminology and conceptual framework that captures various countries' efforts to promote competencies and dispositions fundamental to school and life success. We believe that there is no substitute for cross-national engagement among researchers, policymakers, and educators to develop terms, concepts, and theoretical frameworks that would enable global progress on SEL-like approaches within education. The Learning Metrics Task Force, convened by the UNESCO Institute for Statistics and the Center for Universal Education at the Brookings Institution, has specified "social–emotional" as one of seven critical domains of learning to be measured and monitored by the global community. We recommend that the task of developing a common language and framework be closely integrated with the global efforts to develop common metrics to measure and monitor progress.

We could not gauge the degree to which SEL-related policies truly penetrate school and classroom programs and practices. Beginning to map concrete initiatives at the country level is necessary to discern between rhetoric and reality. Additionally, with a few notable exceptions, there seem to be a dearth of rigorous evaluations of programs and practices to promote SEL, citizenship education, and the like, especially in Asia and the developing world. Consequently, we recommend that a clearinghouse for evidence-based initiatives across nations be developed and disseminated. The world would benefit from a "What Works Clearinghouse" or "Campbell Collaboration" type registry of rigorously evaluated programs and practices to advance SEL and citizenship education around the world. Mounting evidence on the positive impact of SEL initiatives might persuade national governments and international donor organizations that investments in SEL and citizenship education are culturally and economically sound.

Finally, there is a major advocacy agenda to develop and implement. Over the last two decades, and fueled in part by the MDGs, the world has made great progress in making primary school available to all children. Now, as the post-MDGs are being debated and developed, the global education community is making the transition from ensuring access for all to learning for all. A strategy for SEL would be to make SEL part of the "Learning for All" movement that is emerging.

Acknowledgments

We would like to express our gratitude to all those who made this chapter possible. We are very grateful to David Osher for providing valuable feedback on an earlier version of this chapter, and to Emily Jacobson for her diligent work on the literature review. We also want to thank the editors and all the colleagues who shared information about SEL work internationally, especially Kay Yu, Alicia Tallone, Birgitta Kimber, Julian Loaiza, Ivonne Sanchez, and Steve Leventhal.

Note

1. One such country is Australia. See *www.kidsmatter.edu.au* and *www.mindmatters.edu.au*, as well as Fundación Marcelino Botín (2008, 2010, 2011), which reports on approaches to social and emotional education occurring in many countries.

References

Alba Meraz, A. R. (2011). Ética y ciudadanía: Un panorama de las bases filosófico-políticas de la formación cívica y ética. In Secretaría de Educación Pública (Ed.), *La formación cívica y ética en la educación básica: Retos y posibilidades en el contexto de la sociedad globalizada* (pp. 23–37). Cuauhtémoc, México: Secretaría de Educación Pública.

Araújo, U., & Arantes, V. (2009). The ethics and citizenship program: A Brazilian experience in moral education. *Journal of Moral Education, 38*(4), 489–511.

Braslavsky, C. (2005). Diez factores para una educación de calidad para todos en el siglo XXI. In Proceedings from *XIX Semana Monográfica de la Educación. Educación de calidad para todos: Iniciativas Iberoamericanas* (pp. 11–27). Madrid, Spain: Fundación Santillana.

Clouder, C., & Heys, B. (2008). Aspects of social and emotional learning in the United Kingdom. In Fundación Marcelino Botín (Ed.), *Social and emotional education: An international analysis.* Santander, Spain: Author. Retrieved December 1, 2011, from *www.fundacionbotin.org/educacion_biblioteca-y-publicaciones.htm.*

Comisión Formación Ciudadana. (2004). *Informe comisión formación ciudadana.* Santiago, Chile: Dirección de Comunicaciones, Ministerio de Educación. Retrieved November 14, 2011, from *wwwfs.mineduc.cl/archivos//convivenciaescolar/doc/archivo_153.pdf.*

Conde Flores, S. (2011). El clima social del aula y de la escuela como escenarios para la formación en valores de la vida democrática y ética. In Secretaria de Educación Pública (Ed.), *La formación cívica y ética en la educación básica: Retos y posibilidades en el contexto de la sociedad globalizada* (pp. 83–94). Cuauhtémoc, México: Secretaría de Educación Pública.

Dahlin, B. (2008). Social and emotional education in Sweden: Two examples of good practice. In Fundación Marcelino Botín (Ed.), *Social and emotional education: An international analysis* (pp. 85–116). Santander, Spain: Author. Retrieved December 1, 2011, from *www.fundacionbotin.org/educacion_biblioteca-y-publicaciones.htm.*

Dello-Iacovo, B. (2009). Curriculum reform and quality education in China: An overview. *International Journal of Educational Development, 29*(3), 241–249.

Department of Education and Skills. (2004). Every child matters: Change for children. Retrieved November 8, 2011, from *www.education.gov.uk/publications/standard/publicationdetail/page1/dfes/1081/2004.*

Department of Secondary and Higher Education, Government of India. (2003). Scheme of financial assistance for strengthening education in human values. Retrieved November 1, 2011, from *http://mhrd.gov.in/sites/upload_files/mhrd/files/schttp://mhrd.gov.in/sites/upload_files/mhrd/files/scheme_ehv.pdfheme_ehv.pdf.*

Diekstra, R. F. W. (2008). Social and emotional education, or skills for life, in the Netherlands: A review of history, policies and practices. In Fundación Marcelino Botín (Ed.), *Social and emotional education: An international analysis* (pp. 119–149). Santander, Spain: Author. Retrieved December 1, 2011, from *www.fundacionbotin.org/educacion_biblioteca-y-publicaciones.htm.*

Downey, C., & Williams, C. (2010). Family SEAL—a home–school collaborative programme focusing on the development of children's social and emotional skills. *Advances in School Mental Health Promotion, 3*(1), 30–41.

Dunn, Z. (2012). *Investigating happiness lessons: The impact of social and emotional learning in American and Swedish schools.* Winston Churchill Memorial Trust Traveling Fellowship. Retrieved October 4, 2013, from *www.wcmt.org.uk/reports/1022_1.pdf.*

European Commission. (2005). Green paper: Improving the mental health of the population: Towards a strategy on mental health for the European Union. Retrieved January 9, 2012, from *http://ec.europa.eu/health/ph_determinants/life_style/mental/green_paper/mental_gp_en.pdf.*

Faria, L. (2011). Social and emotional education in Portugal: Perspectives and prospects. In Fundación Marcelino Botín (Ed.), *Social and emotional education: An international analysis* (pp. 33–65). Santander, Spain: Author. Retrieved November 14, 2012, from *www.fundacionbotin.org/educacion_biblioteca-y-publicaciones.htm.*

Fernández Berrocal, P. (2008). Social and emotional education in Spain. In Fundación Marcelino Botín (Ed.), *Social and emotional education: An international analysis* (pp. 153–187). Santander, Spain: Author. Retrieved December 1, 2011, from *www.fundacionbotin.org/educacion_biblioteca-y-publicaciones.htm.*

Finnish National Board of Education. (2004). National core curriculum for basic education 2004. Retrieved January 9, 2012, from *www.oph.fi/english/sources_of_information/core_curricula_and_qualification_requirements/basic_education.*

Fundación Marcelino Botín. (2008). *Social and emotional education: An international analysis.* Santander, Spain: Author. Retrieved December 1, 2011, from *www.fundacionbotin.org/educacion_biblioteca-y-publicaciones.htm.*

Fundación Marcelino Botín. (2010). *Social and emotional education: An international analysis.* Santander, Spain: Author. Retrieved December 1, 2011, from *www.fundacionbotin.org/educacion_biblioteca-y-publicaciones.htm.*

Fundación Marcelino Botín. (2011). *Social and emotional education: An international analysis.* Santander, Spain: Author. Retrieved November 14, 2012, from *www.fundacionbotin.org/educacion_biblioteca-y-publicaciones.htm.*

García Cabrero, B. (2011). El desarrollo de la persona moral. In Secretaria de Educación Pública (Ed.), *La formación cívica y ética en la educación básica: Retos y posibilidades en el contexto de la sociedad globalizada* (pp. 39–56). Cuauhtémoc, México: Secretaría de Educación Pública.

García Cabrero, B., & Conde Flores, S. (2011). El enfoque por competencias como sustento de los programas de formación cívica y ética: Implicaciones para la planeación e instrumentación de la práctica educativa y la evaluación de los aprendizajes. In Secretaría de Educación Pública (Ed.), *La formación cívica y ética en la educación básica: Retos y posibilidades en el contexto de la sociedad globalizada* (pp. 57–66). Cuauhtémoc, México: Secretaría de Educación Pública.

Gu, M. (2010). A blueprint for educational development in China: A review of "The national guidelines for medium-and long-term educational reform and development (2010–2020)." *Frontiers of Education in China, 5*(3), 291–309.

Humphrey, N., Lendrum, A., & Wigelsworth, M. (2010). Social and emotional aspects of learning (SEAL) programme in secondary schools: National evaluation. Retrieved February 17, 2012, from *www.education.gov.uk/publications/standard/publicationdetail/page1/dferr049.*

Iheoma, E. (1985). Moral education in Nigeria: Problems and prospects. *Journal of Moral Education, 14*(3), 183–193.

International Rescue Committee (IRC). (2006). *Creating healing classrooms: Guide for teachers and teacher educators.* New York: Author.

Jaramillo Franco, R. (2008). Educación cívica y ciudadana como respuesta a la violencia en Colombia. In G. I. Rodríguez Ávila (Ed.), *Formación de docentes para la educación en valores y ciudadanía: Tendencias y perspectivas* (pp 25–35). Bogotá, Colombia: Instituto para el Desarrollo y la Innovación Educativa IDIE—Formación de Docentes y Educadores.

Jaramillo Franco, R., & Mesa, J. A. (2009). Citizenship education as a response to Colombia's social and political context. *Journal of Moral Education, 38*(4), 467–487.

Kärnä, A., Voeten, M., Little, T. D., Poskiparta, E., Kaljonen, A., & Salmivalli, C. (2011). A large-scale evaluation of the KiVa Antibullying Program: Grades 4–6. *Child Development, 82*(1), 311–330.

Kimber, B. (2012). Social and emotional training in school: A contentious matter in Sweden. In J. A. O'Dea (Ed.), *Current issues and controversies in school and community and community health, sport and physical education* (pp. 35–44). New York: Nova Science.

Kimber, B., Sandell, R., & Bremberg, S. (2008). Social and emotional training in Swedish schools for the promotion of mental health: An effectiveness study of 5 years of intervention. *Health Education Research, 23*(6), 931–940.

Kokkonen, M. (2011). Multi-level promotion of social and emotional well-being in Finland. In Fundación Marcelino Botín (Ed.), *Social and emotional education: An international analysis*. Santander, Spain: Author. Retrieved November 14, 2012, from *www.fundacionbotin.org/educacion_biblioteca-y-publicaciones.htm*.

Learning Metrics Task Force. (2013). Toward universal learning: What every child should learn (Report No. 1, UNESCO Institute for Statistics and Center for Universal Education at Brookings). Retrieved March 10, 2013, from *www.brookings.edu/~/media/research/files/reports/2013/02/learning metrics/lmtfrpt-1towardunivrsllearning.pdf*.

Lee, W. O., Grossman, D. L., Kennedy, K. J., & Fairbrother, G. P. (Eds.). (2004). *Citizenship education in Asia and the Pacific: Concepts and issues*. Hong Kong: Comparative Education Research Centre, the University of Hong Kong/Kluwer Academic.

Luna Elizarrarás, M. E. (2011). De la formación con sentido nacional(ista) a la ciudadanía de la "aldea global." In Secretaria de Educación Pública (Ed.), *La formación cívica y ética en la educación básica: Retos y posibilidades en el contexto de la sociedad globalizada* (pp. 110–118). Cuauhtémoc, México: Secretaría de Educación Pública.

McNeil, B., Reeder, N., & Rich, J. (2012). A framework of outcomes for young people. Retrieved August 10, 2012, from *http://youngfoundation.org/publications/framework-of-outcomes-for-young-people*.

Meihui, L. (2000). Civics education in Taiwan: Values promoted in the civics curriculum. *Asia Pacific Journal of Education, 20*(1), 73–81.

Menezes, I. (2003). Civic education in Portugal: Curricular evolutions in basic education. Retrieved November 14, 2012, from *www.jsse.org/index.php/jsse/article/view/474*.

Ministère Education Nationale Enseignement Supèrieur Recherche (MENESR). (2006). Le socle commun des connaissances et des compétences: Décret du 11 juillet 2006. Retrieved November 12, 2011, from *http://cache.media.eduscol.education.fr/file/socle_commun/00/0/socle-commun-decret_162000.pdf*.

Ministerio de Educación Nacional. (2004). *Estándares básicos de competencias ciudadanas: Formar para la ciudadanía sí es posible: Lo que necesitamos saber y saber hacer* (Serie Guías, N. 6). Bogotá, Colombia: Author.

Ministerio de Educación Nacional República de Chile. (2004). Formación Ciudadana: Actividades de apoyo para el profesor: Historia y ciencias sociales (1o Básico a 4o Medio). Retrieved July 10, 2012, from *www.oei.es*.

Ministerio de la Presidencia. (2006). Ley Orgánica 2/2006, de 3 de mayo, de Educación. Retrieved October 10, 2012, from *www.boe.es/boe/dias/2006/05/04/pdfs/A17158-17207.pdf*.

Ministry of Education and Skills Development, Botswana. (n.d.). Revised junior secondary school syllabuses. Retrieved July 10, 2012, from *www.ibe.unesco.org/curricula/botswana/bs_ls_bs_2010_eng.pdf*.

Ministry of Education, Culture, Sports, Science, and Technology, Japan. (2006). Basic Act on Education (Act 120). Retrieved October 7, 2011, from *www.mext.go.jp/english/lawandplan/1303462.htm*.

Ministry of Education, Namibia. (2006). Upper primary phase: Life skills syllabus, grades 5–7. Retrieved July 10, 2012, from *www.nied.edu.na/publications/syllabusses/up folder/non pro subject folder/up life skills syllabus 08 oct 2007.pdf*.

Ministry of Education, Namibia. (2008). National curriculum for basic education. Retrieved July 10, 2012, from *www.nied.edu.na/images/national curriculum for basic education jan10.pdf*.

Ministry of Education, Namibia. (2009). Senior secondary phase: Life skills syllabus, grades 11 and 12. Retrieved July 10, 2012, from *www.nied.edu.na/publications/syllabusses/nssc folder/ordinary folder/syllabus folder/nssc life skills.pdf*.

Ministry of Education, Republic of China (Taiwan). (2010). An introduction to the ministry of education of R.O.C. Retrieved July 10, 2012, from *http://english.moe.gov.tw/ct.asp?xitem=263&ctnode=782&mp=1*.

Ministry of Education, Republic of Kenya. (2006). National early childhood development policy framework. Retrieved July 10, 2012, from *http://planipolis.iiep.unesco.org/upload/kenya/kenya-ecdpolicyframework.pdf*.

Ministry of Education, Republic of Rwanda.

(2008). Nine years basic education implementation: Fast Track strategies. Retrieved July 10, 2012, from *http://planipolis.iiep.unesco.org/upload/rwanda/rwanda_9_years_basic_education.pdf.*

Ministry of Education, South Africa. (2002). Revised national curriculum: Life orientation. Retrieved July 10, 2012, from *www.education.gov.za/linkclick.aspx?fileticket=tmpndabyske%3d&tabid=266&mid=72.*

Ministry of Education, Thailand. (1999). National education act of B.E. 2542 (1999). Retrieved March 10, 2012, from *www.moe.go.th/english/edu-act.htm#chapter 1.*

Organización de Estados Iberoamericanos (OEI). (2010). *2012 Metas educativas: La educación que queremos para la generación de los bicentenarios.* Madrid, Spain: Cudipal.

Parmenter, L. (2004). A solid foundation: Citizenship education in Japan. In W. O. Lee, D. L. Grossman, K. J. Kennedy, & G. P. Fairbrother (Eds.), *Citizenship education in Asia and the Pacific: Concepts and issues* (pp. 81–95). Hong Kong: Comparative Education Research Centre, the University of Hong Kong.

Patti, J., & Espinoza, A. C. (2007). Citizenship competencies in Colombia: Learning from policy and practice. *Conflict Resolution Quarterly, 25*(1), 109–125.

People's Republic of China, Government. (2010). Outline of China's national plan for medium and long-term education reform and development (2010–2020). Retrieved July 10, 2012, from *www.aei.gov.au/news/newsarchive/2010/documents/china_education_reform_pdf.*

Pitiyanuwat, S., & Sujiva, S. (2000). Civics and values education in Thailand: Documentary analysis. *Asia Pacific Journal of Education, 20*(1), 82–92.

Ruiz Silva, A., & Chaux, E. (2005). *La formación de competencias ciudadanas.* Bogota, Colombia: Ascofade.

Rwantabagu, H. (2010). Moral education in a post-conflict context: The case of Burundi. *Journal of Moral Education, 39*(3), 345–352.

Sánchez Muliterno, J. (2009). El estado de la Educación Infantil en España: La opinión de los maestros y educadores infantiles. *Participación Educativa, 12*, 56–73.

Sherman, R. (2011). Social and emotional learning action network white paper. Retrieved January 13, 2012, from *https://novofoundation.org/wp-content/uploads/2012/09/1-cgi-sel-action-network-white-paper.pdf.*

Swartz, S. (2010). The pain and the promise of moral education in sub-Saharan Africa. *Journal of Moral Education, 39*(3), 267–272.

Swedish National Agency for Education (in Swedish: *Skolverek*). (2006). *Curriculum for the compulsory school system, the pre-school class and the leisure-time centre Lpo 94.AB.* Ödeshög, Sweden: Danagårds Grafiska. Retrieved January 13, 2012, from *www.skolverket.se/om-skolverket/visa-enskild-publikation?_xurl_=http://www5.skolverket.se/wtpub/ws/skolbok/wpubext/trycksak/record?k=1070.*

Thélot, C. (2005). El debate nacional sobre la educación y la reforma en Francia. In *Proceedings from the XIX Semana Monográfica de la Educación: Educación de calidad para todos: Iniciativas Iberoamericanas* (pp. 67–79). Madrid, Spain: Fundación Santillana.

U.K. Department of Education. (2011). The school curriculum. Retrieved July 9, 2012, from *www.education.gov.uk/schools/teachingandlearning/curriculum.*

United Nations (UN). (1990). Convention on the rights of the child. Retrieved April 5, 2010, from *www.ohchr.org/en/professionalinterest/pages/crc.aspx.*

UN Educational, Scientific and Cultural Organization (UNESCO). (1996). *Learning: The treasure within.* Paris: Author.

UN International Children's Fund (UNICEF). (2009). *Child friendly schools programming: Global evaluation report.* New York: Author.

Van Alphen, P. (2013). La educación emocional y social en Sudáfrica: Los retos de la nación arco iris. In Fundación Marcelino Botín (Ed.), *Educación emocional y social: Análisis internacional* (pp. 209–256). Santander, Spain: Fundación Marcelino Botín. Retrieved November 6, 2013, from *www.fundacionbotin.org/analisis-internacional_plataforma-botin_educacion.htm.*

Vasconcelos, T. (1998). *Early childhood education in Portugal.* Lisbon, Portugal: Ministry of Education. Retrieved November 12, 2011, from *http://files.eric.ed.gov/fulltext/ed428885.pdf.*

Venter, E. (2004). The notion of Ubuntu and communalism in African educational discourse. *Studies in Philosophy and Education, 23*(2), 149–160.

Weare, K. (2004). *Developing the emotionally literate school.* London: Paul Chapman.

Weare, K., & Gray, G. (2003). *What works in developing children's emotional and social competence and wellbeing?* London: Department of Education and Skills.

Wigelsworth, M., Humphrey, N., & Lendrum, A. (2012). A national evaluation of the impact of the Secondary Social and Emotional Aspects of Learning (SEAL) programme. *Educational Psychology, 32*(2), 213–238.

Willis, D. B. (2002). Citizenship challenges for Japanese education for the 21st century: "Pure" or "multicultural"?: Multicultural citizenship education in Japan. *International Education Journal, 3*(5), 16–32.

World Health Organization (WHO). (1994). *Life Skills education for children and adolescents in schools: Introduction and guidelines to facilitate the development and implementation of Life Skills programmes.* Geneva, Switzerland: Author.

Yang, S. C., & Chung, T. Y. (2009). Experimental study of teaching critical thinking in civic education in Taiwanese junior high school. *British Journal of Educational Psychology, 79*(1), 29–55.

Zimba, R. F. (2002). Indigenous conceptions of childhood development and social realities in southern Africa. *Between Cultures and Biology: Perspectives on Ontogenetic Development,* 89–115.

AFTERWORD

Making SEL Work for All Children

James P. Comer

We began our child development process change model at the Yale Child Study Center in 1968. When we first disseminated it in 1985, the local facilitator asked me if I'd mind calling it the "Comer model." Because it focused heavily on promoting good relationships and included no curriculum or instructional program, many people believed it could not work. The approach was so contrary to traditional education's central emphasis on curriculum, instruction, and assessment that the facilitator wanted to point to a real-world example where a relationship development–based approach was working, especially for students and schools that had previously been underperformers. The name "Comer model" stuck, and the cluster of schools using the model was very successful.

Since that time, the move toward adopting a framework based in child development as well as social, emotional, *and* academic learning has been painfully and unnecessarily slow. I believe a major reason is that the speed of scientific and technological change, and its impact on the way we live, has far outpaced change in our educational thinking, structure, and work—resulting in a continued separation between home and school; a continued and more exclusive focus on academic learning at the expense of overall student development; continued inadequate attention to educator development and support; and a failed effort to promote useful student, staff, and community diversity and interactions.

The shortcomings of our system(s) of education were not so glaring until the last quarter century because of the availability of living-wage work without much education. And the culture of small-town and rural communities prepared most young people for school, work, and life, often despite poverty. As education and work opportunities became very closely tied together, the flaws in our preparatory or education systems at every level could not be denied. For the first time, the education enterprise was being asked to provide a good education to students who would have pulled out or been pushed out of schools in the past. The enterprise failed to adequately adjust.

Traditional thinking held that academic learning was based on the combination of individual ability and will and curriculum and instruction. And the measure of success for the student and the school was the test score. Students were on their own to get from test scores to success in life and making positive contributions to our democracy. This approach favored students who came from mainstream social networks and who usually received at home what they needed to succeed at school and in life, but it often doomed able nonmainstream students who didn't receive this support. Resultant developmental issues were often managed in ways that led to school behavior problems and sometimes to juvenile justice.

Strong evidence now shows that social, emotional, and academic learning is greatly influenced by good environment–brain interactions, by the mediators of these interactions, and by resultant child experiences. Schools that have created cultures that make this dynamic possible have demonstrated that, with the help of parents and educators, poor children and children of color can develop well and be academically successful and prepared for most life tasks. However, the blame game, political and economic opportunism, and harmful race–class–gender relationships, among other issues, have prevented our society from acting on what is almost common sense.

Given this situation, the publication of the *Handbook of Social and Emotional Learning* is of particular importance. To date, it has been possible to question the potential of growing but scattered successes in programs that were often difficult to sustain, making it difficult for a significant movement to get real and powerful traction. The contributors to this *Handbook* summarize substantial research evidence and practical experiences that demonstrate that an education approach based on what the biological and social sciences, public health, and effective models have taught us can be broadly effective, probably less costly, and more rewarding for students, parents, educators, and the public.

Most important, I was impressed, and a bit embarrassed, by the sophisticated discussions about informing policymakers and power brokers through influential contacts and networks, financing change, and other complex strategies that will be needed. I am a bit embarrassed because, when asked in 1968 how long I thought it would take to significantly improve schools serving poor children, I estimated 5 years. I knew about history and culture and even disagreement and conflict, but I had no idea how deeply entrenched and pervasive the forces maintaining the education status quo really were. This *Handbook* addresses these issues head-on and provides useful discussions about what to do about them.

The scope, structure, and processes laid out in these chapters are a long way from what some educators in the 1960s told me: "The parents should raise them, and we should teach them." It is now clear, as discussed in the *Handbook*, that providing a good education for all students will require "all hands on deck"—including parents, the entire school staff, those who lead educator preparatory programs, researchers, policymakers, power brokers, the public, and, most important, students themselves. Combining *all* hands on deck and all the knowledge we have learned together in a synchronous and synergistic way to support the busy lives of educators in highly interactive school systems, buildings, and classrooms—and using *all* community resources—is the next big challenge in a movement that must succeed. Good organization and management at district, building, and classroom levels are crucial to making everything that we put into education work, as the *Handbook*'s discussions of training, selection, and support of educators make very clear.

Finally, much of the education enterprise has historically treated athletics and the arts with ambivalence or disdain, even when they include a curriculum and a distinctive instructional approach. But these activities provide a great opportunity to promote social and emotional growth and overall development and learning. They also provide an opportunity for school and community interactions and help to promote some forms of diversity and respectful interactions among different groups. The behavior problems at a recent football game bring all three of these opportunities to mind.

A predominantly African American urban district played a predominantly white suburban district; both were once economically thriving industrial communities but were now equally distressed. The racial name-calling was open and ugly at the home field of the suburban team. The urban team promised revenge at their home game the next year. This was an important teaching and learning opportunity, but the responsible educators did not help these young people to consider the problems and gain responsible social and emotional capacities; they did not help to prepare them to live in an open and democratic society as adults. A productive follow-up response would have involved diverse members of the school staff, student body, and community helping the students to embrace responsible beliefs and conduct.

Real-world challenges like this are moving some leaders toward combining bottom-up and top-down approaches to policymaking, interventions, and research. This method entails a local initiative to bring together relevant community resources to plan and implement academic, social, emotional, and other developmentally focused programs and to carry out local research with a focus on preventing problems and promoting success, rather than on after-the-fact problem reduction and punishment.

Such an approach has a better chance of drawing from diverse experiences and perspectives, a skill very much needed in real-world practice and research. It can reduce the ill effects of "silo thinking" that prevents knowledge from flowing to and from the practice level, where it can be most useful and best observed. This approach can more quickly identify and require change of ineffective activities. And it makes it important to have a diversity of groups and perspectives among all the players at every level—policymakers, educators, researchers, community leaders, and families. To move beyond incremental gains, participatory research strategies involving multiple stakeholders may become more necessary.

Again, this *Handbook* reflects significant progress. But we still have a way to go to attain widespread acceptance of a combined development–academic focus in education. The effects of science and technology on how we live and what we must do to prepare students adequately are being felt ever more quickly. We do not have another 50 years to figure out how to bring all our students along, to make it possible for all to contribute constructively. Our challenge is to find a way to use the impressive findings that have been accumulated to date immediately—to make a big leap forward in the preparation of all students, particularly those that have been left behind. This *Handbook* suggests that we can.

AFTERWORD

The Future of SEL

Daniel Goleman

In the early 1990s, I joined a small group that met regularly to reimagine what a child's education should include. We envisioned an education of the whole child—not just the standard curriculum, but also attention to emotional and social skills. I was writing *Emotional Intelligence* at the time and saw the book as, in part, an argument for just such an education (Goleman, 1995).

Members of that group included several contributors to this volume: Timothy Shriver, Roger Weissberg, Mark Greenberg, and Maurice Elias. These four were already deeply involved in educational programs that became models for the field we were developing. They had come to these curricula via another route: as preventive interventions in youth crises such as school violence, dropouts, drug use, and bullying. A study of such programs, financed by the William T. Grant Foundation, had identified teaching social and emotional skills as the "active ingredients" in those programs that worked (Consortium on the School-based Promotion of Social Competence, 1992).

And so social and emotional learning, or SEL, was born. Its institutional entity, the Collaborative for Academic, Social, and Emotional Learning (CASEL), found its first home in the Yale Child Study Center, and then moved with its director, Roger Weissberg, to the University of Illinois at Chicago. As this volume attests, the SEL movement has been remarkably successful, growing from just a handful of pioneering programs to the robust field detailed here.

In considering SEL's future, a helpful conceptual distinction comes from the field of strategic thinking: exploitation versus exploration (March, 1991). In the exploitation strategy, an entity takes a product or process that works and tweaks it to make it better. The *Handbook of Social and Emotional Learning* documents just how well that strategy has benefited SEL.

While SEL has typically pertained to grades K–12, I am heartened to see that colleges, too, are introducing this approach. But I can suggest yet another education level to be cultivated with the same care: graduate schools. As Colleen S. Conley (Chapter 13, this volume) suggests, SEL in the form of mindfulness, cognitive-behavioral techniques, relaxation interventions, and social skills training has shown promise for college populations. I suspect a wider range of SEL methods borrowed from K–12 could be usefully deployed at the college level—and immediate benefits might be seen in decreased stress and anxiety, improved satisfaction, and better peer relationships. As some deans have told me, colleges are under pressure to prove their value-added benefits to students, and an SEL component could be a win–win for students and administrators alike.

As I write this, I have just returned from addressing the American Association of Medical Colleges, another group ripe for an SEL approach as an adjunct to medical training. Research reviews show that the SEL terrain—were it to be upgraded for medical students—covers competencies now required for every physician to qualify for the profession (Arora et al., 2010). The Accreditation Council for Graduate Medical Education specifies that training for physicians should include competence in creating a positive doctor–patient relationship, empathy, teamwork and communication skills, stress management, and leadership—all emergent abilities from the basics of SEL.

Beyond medicine, business schools are another graduate-level stratum ripe for an SEL upgrade. Businesses themselves have long studied the competencies that set their star performers apart from the average. Those "competence models" typically find that cognitive abilities are largely "threshold" capacities, which everyone must have at a given level to get into the field (Spencer & Spencer, 1993). But once in a business setting, the competencies that set top performers apart from average ones are mainly in the realm of SEL—and the higher one goes in an organization, the more pronounced the value of social and emotional skills.

Some business schools have already introduced the equivalent of SEL, at least in bits and pieces. One of the more comprehensive models was developed by Richard Boyatzis at the Weatherhead School of Management at Case Western University (Boyatzis, Stubbs, & Taylor, 2002). For almost two decades, he has had his graduate students and executive MBAs evaluated on the range of social and emotional competencies typical of models for business leaders, using an instrument in which people they trust and respect evaluate them anonymously on observable behaviors. Boyatzis then helps them use that data to choose and cultivate a social or emotional competence over the course of a semester and evaluates them again on the same measure. Evaluations by others at the students' subsequent workplaces show that these improvements can last as long as 7 years (Boyatzis & Saatcioglu, 2008).

Then, of course, there are schools of education. A good part of the learning in SEL takes the form of modeling: the teacher (and entire school staff, for that matter) ideally would model emotional and social competence for students. But that does not come naturally to all teachers; it can and should be included as part of their training to teach. SEL preparation will help them become more effective teachers.

Such are my thoughts on cultivating additional fields where SEL shows promise. Now I turn to exploration—where the field could go in the future. I foresee SEL growing tips in three areas: cultivating mindfulness, empathic concern, and systems learning.

In a Spanish Harlem second-grade class, I watched a session of "breathing buddies," part of the daily routine (Goleman, 2013). One by one, each child took a small stuffed animal from a cubby, found a place to lie down, and put the animal on his or her belly. Then the children watched the animals go up on their in-breath, counting 1-2-3-4-5, and down on their out-breath, to the same count.

This exercise, their teacher said, leaves them calm and focused for the rest of the day—a state sometimes hard to imagine given the tumultuous home lives typical of the housing project next to the school, where most of the second graders live.

Breathing buddies offers an age-appropriate training in attention—a new frontier I foresee for SEL. Beyond the emotional and social focus of the first phase of SEL, a natural extension would be into associated cognitive capacities, notably the one cultivated by exercises such as breathing buddies: cognitive control. This capacity to choose a single focus and ignore distracting thoughts and impulses is vital for a readiness to learn, and for associated abilities such as delaying gratification in pursuit of a goal.

As it happens, the same neural circuitry that becomes stronger with such attention training also functions to modulate distressing emotions and distracting impulses. As decades of research on this capacity have shown—think of Walter Mischel's famed "marshmallow test"—childhood cognitive control is itself a predictor of both academic performance and positive life outcomes (Mischel, 2014).

A longitudinal study of more than 1,000 children—followed up in their 30s—found that their level of cognitive control between the ages of 4 and 8 correlated more highly with adult financial success and health than did childhood IQ or family-of-origin socioeconomic status (Moffitt et al., 2010). The authors of that study note that children who happened to increase from low to high in cognitive control over those years accrued all the adult benefits of those who had always been better at it, and that this mental skill should be taught to all children. SEL seems the perfect vehicle for this training, most conveniently by adding mindfulness practice (Flook et al., 2010).

The second area for innovation in SEL has to do with social skill, particularly empathy. There are three kinds of empathy, each instantiated in different neural circuitry (Decety, 2010). Cognitive empathy—the basis for "theory of mind"—lets us understand another person's perspective and point of view and facilitates effective communication. The second variety, emotional empathy, helps us feel immediately what another person feels; this emotional bond builds rapport and facilitates positive interactions.

But it is the third variety that I foresee as a growing tip for SEL: empathic concern, or caring. This adds a needed implicit ethical dimension to empathy; cognitive empathy, after all, can be used by sociopaths to their advantage. But people with empathic concern are more motivated by kindness, and by the help they can give to others. This quality defines the best parents and spouses, workmates and bosses, and organizational and community citizens.

Recent studies suggest that the mammalian brain circuitry for caring, on which empathic concern depends, can be strengthened with the right training and that this, in fact, makes children kinder and more generous with others (Flook, Goldberg, Pinger, & Davidson, in press). Again, SEL could easily incorporate appropriate training in this area.

Finally, a third field in which SEL could grow—but this is perhaps the biggest stretch—is systems learning. In this pedagogy, children learn the elements of systems thinking from K–12, just as they learn social and emotional skills in SEL programs. They learn how to apply a "systems lens" to their relationships (e.g., analyzing in early grades why hurtful words lead to fights), to families and schools, and to the larger systems that regulate our lives.

One urgent argument for systems education, to my way of thinking, is the growing environmental crisis, a by-product of human systems such as transport, energy, industry, and commerce. That crisis will only grow more disastrous—possibly catastrophic—over the lifetime of today's children, and systems learning can give them a vital toolkit for imaginative solutions.

Here the SEL sector need not develop anything new. There has been a robust community of systems learning for more than a decade. I foresee folks in SEL partnering with those in systems education to integrate the two approaches, which I believe should make each of them stronger. Peter Senge and I have proposed exactly this approach as "the triple focus" in education (Goleman & Senge, 2014).

Two decades ago, the meetings of a small group sparked what has become the SEL movement. Perhaps today there is a small, dedicated group—or several of them—working to achieve some of the very targets I propose. As Margaret Mead is credited with saying, "Never doubt that a small group of thoughtful, committed citizens can change the world; indeed, it's the only thing that ever has."

References

Arora, S., Ashrafian, H., Davis, R., Athanasiou, T., Darzi, A., & Sevdalis. N. (2010). Emotional intelligence in medicine: A systematic review through the context of the ACGME competencies. *Medical Education, 44*, 749–764.

Boyatzis, R. E., & Saatcioglu, A. (2008). A 20-year view of trying to develop emotional, social, and cognitive intelligence competencies in graduate management education. *Journal of Management Development, 27*(1), 92–108.

Boyatzis, R. E., Stubbs, E. C., & Taylor, S. N. (2002). Learning cognitive and emotional competencies through graduate management education. *Academy of Management Learning & Education, 1*(2), 150–162.

Consortium on the School-based Promotion of Social Competence. [Elias, M. J., Weissberg, R.

P., Dodge, K. A., Hawkins, J. D., Jason, L. A., Kendall, P. C., et al.]. (1992). Drug and alcohol prevention curricula. In J. D. Hawkins, R. F. Catalano, & Associates (Eds.), *Communities that care: Action for drug abuse prevention* (pp. 129–148). San Francisco: Jossey-Bass.

Decety, J. (2010). The neurodevelopment of empathy in humans. *Developmental Neuroscience, 32*, 257–267.

Flook, L., Goldberg, S. B., Pinger, L., & Davidson, R. J. (in press). Promoting prosocial behavior and self-regulatory skills in preschool children through a mindfulness-based kindness curriculum. *Developmental Psychology.*

Flook, L., Smalley, S. L., Kitil, M. J., Galla, B. M., Kaiser-Greenland, S., Locke, J., et al. (2010). Effects of mindful awareness practices on executive functions in elementary school children. *Journal of Applied School Psychology, 26*, 70–95.

Goleman, D. (1995). *Emotional intelligence: Why it can matter more than IQ*. New York: Bantam Books.

Goleman, D. (2013). *Focus: The hidden driver of excellence.* New York: HarperCollins.

Goleman, D., & Senge, P. (2014). *The triple focus: A new approach to education.* Northampton, MA: More Than Sound.

March, J. (1991). Exploitation and exploration in organizational learning. *Organizational Science, 2*(1), 71–81.

Mischel, W. (2014). *The marshmallow test: Mastering self-control.* New York: Little, Brown.

Moffitt, T. E., Arseneault, L., Belsky, D., Dickson, N., Hancox, R. J., & Harrington, H. (2010). A gradient of childhood self-control predicts health, wealth, and public safety. *Proceedings of the National Academy of Sciences, 108*(7), 2693–2698.

Spencer, L. M., & Spencer, S. M. (1993). *Competence at work: Models for superior performance.* New York: Wiley.

Author Index

Subject Index

Page numbers followed by *f* indicate figure; *n*, note; and *t*, table